Frommer's

South America

4th Edition

by Shawn Blore, Alexandra de Vries,
Eliot Greenspan, Charlie O'Malley, Jisel Perilla,
Neil E. Schlecht & Kristina Schreck

WILEY

Wiley Publishing, Inc.

Wiley Publishing, Inc.

111 River St.
Hoboken, NJ 07030-5774

ISBN 978-0-470-23336-8

Editors: Matthew Brown and Marc Nadeau
Production Editor: Michael Brumitt
Cartographer: Roberta Stockwell
Photo Editor: Richard Fox
Production by Wiley Indianapolis Composition Services

Front cover photo: Boy with parrots in Cuzco, Peru
Back cover photo: Sea kayaking among glacial icebergs on Chile's Lago San Rafael

For information on our other products and services or to obtain technical support, please contact our Customer Care Department within the U.S. at 800/762-2974, outside the U.S. at 317/572-3993 or fax 317/572-4002.

Wiley also publishes its books in a variety of electronic formats. Some content that appears in print may not be available in electronic formats.

Manufactured in the United States of America

5   4   3   2

Contents

4   Argentina   75

by Charlie O'Malley

5   Bolivia   169

by Charlie O'Malley

6   Brazil   220

by Shawn Blore & Alexandra de Vries

7   Chile   359

by Kristina Schreck

8 Colombia   459

by Jisel Perilla

9 Ecuador   513

by Eliot Greenspan

10 Paraguay   595

by Charlie O'Malley

11 Peru   611

by Neil E. Schlecht

12 Uruguay   724

by Charlie O'Malley

13 Venezuela   742

by Eliot Greenspan

Index   807

List of Maps

About the Authors

A native of California, **Shawn Blore** (Brazil) has lived and worked in a half dozen countries and traveled in at least 50 more (but who's counting?). Long a resident of Vancouver, Shawn has for the past few years made his home in Rio de Janeiro. He is an award-winning magazine writer and the author of *Vancouver: Secrets of the City* and co-author of *Frommer's Brazil* and *Frommer's Portable Rio de Janeiro*.

Alexandra de Vries (Brazil) made her first journey to Brazil at the ripe old age of 1 month. (Alas, few of her food reviews from that trip survive.) In the years since, Alexandra has returned many times to travel, explore, and live in this amazing country. Alexandra co-writes *Frommer's Brazil* and *Frommer's Portable Rio de Janeiro* about her all-time favorite place to visit.

Eliot Greenspan (Ecuador, Venezuela) is a poet, journalist, and travel writer who took his backpack and typewriter the length of Mesoamerica before settling in Costa Rica in 1992. Since then, he has traveled almost ceaselessly around Latin America, writing articles and guidebooks to feed his travel habit. He feels particularly at home in the neotropics—in its rain and cloud forests, on its rivers, and under its seas. Eliot is the author of *Frommer's Ecuador, Frommer's Costa Rica* and *Frommer's Belize*.

Charlie O'Malley (Argentina, Bolivia, Paraguay, Uruguay) is a writer and wine enthusiast who can be found living in Mendoza, Argentina, when he's not traveling the rest of South America.

Jisel Perilla (Colombia) worked with a nonprofit microcredit organization in Medellín, Colombia, and has written about, lived in, and traveled throughout much of Latin America. She currently resides in the Washington, D.C., area and was at work on *Frommer's Panama* as this book went to press.

Neil E. Schlecht (Peru) first trekked to Machu Picchu in 1983 as a college student, spending his junior year abroad in Quito, Ecuador. The author of a dozen travel guides (including *Frommer's Peru* and *Spain For Dummies*), as well as articles on art and culture and art catalogue essays, and a photographer, he has lived for extensive periods in Brazil and Spain. He now resides in northwestern Connecticut.

Kristina Schreck (Chile) has traveled extensively throughout Latin America and has lived and worked in Argentina and Chile for 8 years. She is the former managing editor of *Adventure Journal* magazine and is co-author of the first edition of *Frommer's Chile & Easter Island.* Kristina currently resides in Santiago and the Andes, where she works year-round for Ski Portillo (and although she thinks it is the greatest ski resort in the world, to be fair, she asked an independent, impartial source to edit the Chile skiing coverage in this guide).

An Invitation to the Reader

In researching this book, we discovered many wonderful places—hotels, restaurants, shops, and more. We're sure you'll find others. Please tell us about them, so we can share the information with your fellow travelers in upcoming editions. If you were disappointed with a recommendation, we'd love to know that, too. Please write to:

Frommer's South America, 4th Edition
Wiley Publishing, Inc. • 111 River St. • Hoboken, NJ 07030-5774

An Additional Note

Please be advised that travel information is subject to change at any time—and this is especially true of prices. We therefore suggest that you write or call ahead for confirmation when making your travel plans. The authors, editors, and publisher cannot be held responsible for the experiences of readers while traveling. Your safety is important to us, however, so we encourage you to stay alert and be aware of your surroundings. Keep a close eye on cameras, purses, and wallets, all favorite targets of thieves and pickpockets.

Frommer's Star Ratings, Icons & Abbreviations

Every hotel, restaurant, and attraction listing in this guide has been ranked for quality, value, service, amenities, and special features using a **star-rating system.** In country, state, and regional guides, we also rate towns and regions to help you narrow down your choices and budget your time accordingly. Hotels and restaurants are rated on a scale of zero (recommended) to three stars (exceptional). Attractions, shopping, nightlife, towns, and regions are rated according to the following scale: zero stars (recommended), one star (highly recommended), two stars (very highly recommended), and three stars (must-see).

In addition to the star-rating system, we also use **seven feature icons** that point you to the great deals, in-the-know advice, and unique experiences that separate travelers from tourists. Throughout the book, look for:

Finds	Special finds—those places only insiders know about
Fun Fact	Fun facts—details that make travelers more informed and their trips more fun
Kids	Best bets for kids and advice for the whole family
Moments	Special moments—those experiences that memories are made of
Overrated	Places or experiences not worth your time or money
Tips	Insider tips—great ways to save time and money
Value	Great values—where to get the best deals

The following **abbreviations** are used for credit cards:

AE American Express	DISC Discover	V Visa
DC Diners Club	MC MasterCard	

Frommers.com

Now that you have this guidebook to help you plan a great trip, visit our website at **www. frommers.com** for additional travel information on more than 4,000 destinations. We update features regularly to give you instant access to the most current trip-planning information available. At Frommers.com, you'll find scoops on the best airfares, lodging rates, and car rental bargains. You can even book your travel online through our reliable travel booking partners. Other popular features include:

- Online updates of our most popular guidebooks
- Vacation sweepstakes and contest giveaways
- Newsletters highlighting the hottest travel trends
- Online travel message boards with featured travel discussions

What's New in South America

ARGENTINA

Argentina is currently experiencing a strong economic upswing after the disastrous 2001 economic crisis. Yet double-digit growth figures are complemented by double-digit inflation numbers, and the country is not the amazing bargain destination it used to be. However, it is still relatively cheap and one of the few countries where the dollar is still strong. Argentines are hoping their glamorous new president, Cristina Kirchner (wife of the previous president, Nestor Kirchner), will keep it all under control and Argentina will continue to experience a tourism boom. Crime remains a concern, particularly in big cities, so travelers should still take extra precautions when visiting. On another note, airfares for domestic flights have become prohibitively expensive and the national airline, Aerolíneas Argentinas, is plagued by strikes and delays. It is worth considering taking luxury overnight buses for parts of your itinerary.

BUENOS AIRES The Sofitel hotel chain has been delighting guests for several years now. Their latest venture in Puerto Madero, perfect for business travelers or families, is **Hotel Madero**, Rosario Vera Peñaloza 360, Dique 2 (© 11/5776-7777; www.hotelmadero.com).

MENDOZA WINE COUNTRY Mendoza's latest wine lodge, **Antucura**, Vista Flores (© 0261/425-5324; www.antucura.com), is set to become the region's top vineyard accommodation with splendid architecture and art. It is located in beautiful Valle de Uco.

THE NORTHWEST Long neglected by Argentines and foreigners alike, Salta and the Northwest is finally coming into its own. **Colomé** (© 03868/494-0444; www.bodegacolome.com) is an *estancia* that just so happens to make excellent wine and offers luxury accommodations.

BOLIVIA

Bolivian politics has taken a turn for the worse with its richer, eastern provinces attempting to break away and achieve autonomy. President Evo Morales has his hands full keeping the country together and there are frequent road blocks and strikes. Nevertheless, Bolivia remains a fascinating place, and its tumultuous state of affairs rarely affects visitors, especially if you choose to fly between cities. *Note:* United States citizens now require a special visa.

SALAR DE UYUNI Bolivia's salt plains are becoming the most talked about attraction in South America, and hard to beat for bizarre and magical landscapes. The journey itself is a serious undertaking. Contact **Mariana Tours,** Olaneta 101 A, Sucre (© 0104/6429-329; mtours@cotes.net.bo).

BRAZIL

New lodges in the Pantanal, new beaches in Bahia, new restaurants and samba clubs in Rio de Janeiro. And of course we are always on the lookout for wonderful places to eat or shop or drink or sleep.

RIO DE JANEIRO Where to Stay On everyone's lips for nearly 2 years, the new

Fasano hotel (℅ 021/3202-4000; www.fasano.com.br) has finally opened in Ipanema, the only hotel in the world designed top to bottom by renowned *enfant terrible* of the design world, Philippe Starck. Rooms, lobby, everything lives up to expectations. The rooftop pool deck is a thing of beauty.

Equally distinct, and quite a change from most of Rio de Janeiro's high-rise accommodations, the **Santa Teresa Cama e Café B&B network** (℅ 021/2224-5689 or 021/2221-7635; www.camaecafe.com.br) offers spectacular rooms in one of the city's most charming neighborhoods. The participating homes range from mock German castles to colonial homes to Art Deco mansions from the 1930s.

If you want to stay on a quaint hilltop and experience a higher standard of luxury, try **Mama Ruisa** (℅ 021/2242-1281), opened recently in a century-old hillside mansion. Beautifully decorated, each of the seven suites also features all the modern trimmings, such as wireless Internet, cable TV, and A/C.

Finally, one of the most venerable of Copacabana's hotels, the **Olinda Classic Othon** (℅ 021/2545-9091; www.hoteisothon.com.br), has gotten a much-needed makeover. The lobby has been transformed into an elegant salon with a restaurant and piano bar. In the rooms, the dark colonial furniture has been replaced by lighter woods, soothing pale colors, and stylish furniture.

RIO DE JANEIRO   Where to Dine Located on the second floor of the Modern Art Museum, the clean and modern interior of the **Laguiole** (℅ 021/2517-3129) restaurant matches the classic modern design of this Rio landmark building. The food is modern Brazilian, with a subtle touch of French, while the wine list is simply encyclopedic: over 600 labels and 8,000 bottles!

Up in the newly bustling hilltop 'hood of Santa Teresa, the new star on the block is **Espirito Santa** (℅ 021/2508-7095), which features excellent Brazilian food, with a strong flavoring from the Amazon.

Miam Miam (℅ 021/2244-0125) is a new hip eatery/lounge/bar, whimsically decorated with fabulous kitsch touches. The lounge is perfect to enjoy a cocktail and share some appetizers.

Steak lovers can take comfort in the advent of **Giuseppe Grill** (℅ 021/2249-3055), a worthwhile addition to the dining scene in Leblon. We were thoroughly impressed with the outstanding steak; the affordable wine list; the pleasant, modern room; and the attentive professional service.

Thomas Troisgros, the son of a famous French chef, opened **Bistrô 66** (℅ 021/2266-0838), offering a traditional take on French bistro food, at a fraction of what dad charges at his high-end French affair.

RIO DE JANEIRO   Nightlife For lovers of live music, the Lapa neighborhood continues strong, and now there's a "new Lapa" arriving on the scene. Just beyond the Praça Mauá, close to the port area, Gamboa features lovely 19th-century buildings, pretty squares, and a fascinating history (this is where slaves were brought upon arrival and according to many, the birth place of samba). A few visionary musical entrepreneurs have set up shop, including **Trapiche Gamboa** (℅ 021/2516-0868), a gorgeous three-story building from 1856 that has been transformed into a fabulous live venue playing, what else, samba. More recent newcomers include Rio's hottest new gay dance club, **The Week** (℅ 021/2253-1020), and **Sacadura** (℅ 021/2233-0378), a more upscale live music venue.

With **Botafogo's** revived nightlife scene it was only a matter of time before it would produce a decent live music venue, and the **Cinemathèque Jamclub** (© 021/2359-0216; www.jamclub.com.br) is all that. With only 150 seats, it remains small enough to feel intimate but big enough to draw some big names on the local music scene.

One of Rio's newest concert venues, the **Vivo Rio** (© 021/2272-2900), is located right next to the Museu de Arte Moderno on Rio's downtown waterfront.

SÃO PAULO Where to Stay Although not a Philippe Starck hotel like the one in Rio, the São Paulo **Fasano** (© 011/3896-4000) was the first hotel opened by the successful São Paulo restaurateur family. Using their many years of hospitality experience, the São Paulo Fasano has quickly become one of the top hotels in the city, located smack in the middle of São Paulo's most visitor-friendly Jardins neighborhood. If you prefer luxury over location, the **Sofitel São Paulo** (© 0800/703-7003 or 011/5574-1100) should be your first choice. The combination of French sophistication and Brazilian hospitality results in one fine luxury hotel.

SÃO PAULO Where to Dine One of São Paulo's hottest (or should we say coolest) dining lounges is **Skye** (© 011/3055-4702), at the Unique Hotel. The views of the São Paulo skyline are truly spectacular, and this modern lounge/restaurant serves up creative and innovative Brazilian cuisine.

SÃO PAULO What to See & Do The hottest new cultural attraction in Latin America's biggest city is, wait for it, the **Museum of the Portuguese Language** (© 011/3326-0775). Okay, I know what you're thinking, but it genuinely is very cool, even if your command of Portuguese is only limited. Set in a vast former train station, the museum takes full advantage of the space to offer displays that are creative, interesting, interactive, visually fabulous, and fun.

SALVADOR Where to Stay Finally Pelourinho has the boutique hotel it deserves; the **Convento do Carmo** (© 071/3327-8400) has the perfect location on the outside, and luxurious accommodations inside. The hotel's common areas—the round tiled pool and restaurant in the cloister, the lounge tucked into one of the arcades, the large library—are a delight.

Truly in the heart of Pelourinho, the new **Solar dos Deuses** (© 071/3320-3251) overlooks the square in front of the São Francisco church. All seven rooms are very elegantly furnished with period furniture and feature lovely high ceilings, hardwood floors, and large windows.

SALVADOR Where to Dine The trend in fine dining in Salvador continues out toward the harborfront, where the new **Amado** (© 071/3322-3520) offers ultimately cool waterfront dining—the room is vast and gorgeous, mixing wood and stone and glass with open views over the harbor and bay beyond. The cuisine takes traditional Bahian ingredients—mandioc and seafood, principally—and puts them to use in innovate ways, always with lovely presentation.

The other hot new area in Salvador is Rio Vermelho, home of the tiny hidden gem called **Dona Mariquita** (© 071/3334-6947). The food takes traditional Northeastern dishes and adds a twist or bit of spice. Even better, on Fridays there's live music.

NATAL Little more than a year old, the **Serhs Natal Grand** (© 084/4005-2000) is the newest and most luxurious of the top-end resorts strung along the oceanside Via Costeira. Rooms are fresh, bright, and modern, facing out over the sea. Recreational facilities at this Spanish run hotel are top notch. The entire front deck of the hotel is one sprawling wavy pool, dotted here and there with little Jacuzzi islands.

While in Natal, the ideal place to get a look and taste of Nordestino food—the cuisine of Brazil's dry, cattle-raising Northeast—is at **Mangai** (© **084/3206-3344**). Mangai offers a self-serve buffet—or better, a smorgasbord—featuring over 40 different Nordestino dishes.

THE PANTANAL   Wildlife viewing is always a matter of luck and patience, even in a place as rich as the Pantanal. Large predators such as jaguars are a particular challenge. But one of the best ways of improving your odds is to visit the **Jaguar Ecological Reserve** (© **065/3646-8557;** www.jaguarreserve.com), where an astonishing one in four guests sees one of these huge South American cats.

CHILE

The Chilean tourism industry is going strong. New deluxe lodging and high-end restaurants are opening with increasing frequency, satisfying luxury travelers and boosting the country's image abroad. The increase in interest in Chile as a travel destination, however, means that regions such as Torres del Paine National Park and San Pedro de Atacama are booking up well in advance—sometimes up to a year in advance for the travel period between November and March. Prices are on the rise, yet Chile is still a bargain for North American travelers when compared to Europe, and Argentina's inflation problem means that Chile is nearly on par, price-wise, with that country. In fact, most hotels with rates in U.S. dollars are less expensive than hotels of the same caliber in Argentina.

The bad news is that the reciprocity entry fee for first-time visitors from the United States has risen to US$132, but it's good for the life of the visitor's passport.

PLANNING YOUR TRIP   By Plane Lan Airlines has added new routes and increased service to Chile, and now offers direct service from L.A. and New York. Lan is also the only airline with service to

Chile that offers business class with flat beds, and all economy class seats come with individual in-flight entertainment.

Chile has overhauled its transportation system with a new bus system and ultra-modern highways. However, problems with bus service have pushed many commuters into the Metro system, which is now packed during rush hour from 7 to 10am and 5 to 7pm. Also, toll fares on highways have gone up sharply and can cost up to US$5 on weekends for popular routes such as Santiago–Viña del Mar.

SANTIAGO   Where to Stay   Santiago is now home to plenty of five-star hotels, including the only Ritz Carlton in Latin America. In late 2008, the W Hotel will also open the doors of its first South American property.

THE CENTRAL VALLEY   The hottest news coming from the Central Valley is Valparaíso. This emblematic city was formerly a day destination only, but new, gorgeous boutique hotels are popping up such as the **Casa Higueras** (© **32/249-7900;** www.hotelcasahigueras.cl), the **Zero Hotel** (© **32/211-3114;** www.zerohotel.com), and the **Hotel Manoir Atkinson** (© **32/ 235-1313;** www.hotelatkinson.cl). As well, the city is a now a foodie's destination, with plenty of gourmet restaurants, and its proximity to the Casablanca and San Antonio valleys makes it a perfect base for wine-tasting.

Chile's wine industry has seen unbelievable growth and an unprecedented improvement in quality over the past few years. By far the most exciting property—and one of Chile's best lodging experiences—is the Clos Apalta winery's **Apalta Casitas** (© **72/321803;** www.closapalta. cl). It's not cheap, but lodging includes meals and a bottle of their outstanding Clos Apalta wine.

THE DESERT NORTH   San Pedro de Atacama has evolved from a backpacker's haunt to a luxury lodging destination with the opening of the new **Hotel Awasi** (© **55/851460;** www.awasi.com). On the horizon will be Ski Portillo's new **Tierra Atacama Hotel** (www.tierraatacama.com), slated for opening in March 2008. This deluxe lodge will offer packages in conjunction with a ski holiday at Portillo.

PATAGONIA   Puerto Natales is becoming a destination in its own right now that a new road (with spectacular views of Torres del Paine) has opened. Leaving from town and arriving at the park's administration center is about a 1-hour drive. Many travelers are opting to lodge in town, visit the park by day, and also take part in other regional activities such as horseback riding or kayaking in the Eberhard Sound. Two new gorgeous design hotels have opened in Puerto Natales that are worth checking out: **Indigo Patagonia** (© **61/413609;** www.indigopatagonia.com) and **Hotel Remota** (© **61/414040;** www.remota.cl).

ECUADOR

The biggest news in Ecuador is the election of center-left President Rafael Correa in 2006. Although still early in his presidency, Correa is making waves. In April 2007, a public referendum passed overwhelmingly to allow Correa to call a Constituent Assembly to rewrite the national constitution.

QUITO   Old Town is starting to come alive with new hotel options and an increased sense of security. Both the **Patio Andaluz** (© **02/2280-830;** www.hotel patioandaluz.com) and **Plaza Grande** (© **02/2566-497;** www.plazagrandequito. com) are excellent upper-end hotels in the colonial core of the city.

On the dining front, I heartily recommend the hip and trendy **Zazu** (© **02/ 2543-559**), with its eclectic fusion fare and chic ambience.

For after-dark fun, head to **Club Gia** (© **02/2924-094**), the hottest and most happening new club in town.

OTAVALO & IMBABURA PROVINCE On the way to Otavalo, be sure to stop in at the new **Quitsato Mitad del Mundo Monument** (© **09/9701-133;** www. quitsato.org), the newest and most geographically accurate equatorial straddling attraction in the country. If you have a portable GPS, you can check for yourself.

EL ORIENTE   The riverboat *Manatee Jungle Explorer* (www.mamateeamazon explorer.com) has been certified by the Rainforest Alliance and *Conservacion y Desarrollo* (Conservation and Development) as a SmartVoyager vessel, making it the first tour operation in El Oriente to earn this green seal of approval.

CUENCA & THE SOUTHERN SIERRA   In downtown Cuenca, the new **Hotel El Dorado** (© **07/2831-390;** www.eldoradohotel.com.ec) is a unique and ultramodern addition to the hotel scene.

Following a dual fatality, rooftop riding on the famed **El Nariz del Diablo (The Devil's Nose)** train ride has been suspended. The train still runs regularly, but the thrilling and chilling chance to make the trip atop the train is currently prohibited. However, **Metropolitan Touring's Chiva Express** ✭ (© **02/2988-200;** www.chivaexpress.com), which also makes this run, still offers open-air rooftop seating for this trip.

GUAYAQUIL   The **Malecón del Estero Salado** is a new waterfront promenade, similar to the **Malecón 2000,** but located on the western end of Avenida 9 de Octubre along the narrow *Estero Salado* (Salt Water Estuary).

THE GALAPAGOS   UNESCO, which has declared the Galápagos Islands a World Heritage Site, announced in 2007 that the islands and their ecosystems are in danger of destruction. Although few formal measures have yet been adopted, the government of Ecuador has vowed to take steps to ensure that tourism is consistent with the archipelago's survival and sustainability as an ecological wonder.

One of the first measures adopted was to restrict scuba-diving activities. Scuba trips are still undertaken by many licensed operators, although some of the larger, general tour ships and boats have been prohibited from offering scuba trips for the time being. If you plan on doing any diving, be sure to check in advance if your boat can offer the service.

Metropolitan Touring (© 02/2988-200; www.metropolitan-touring.com) has begun taking reservations for the new 24-stateroom luxury yacht **La Pinta.**

PERU

Former President Alan García, who went into exile after a disastrous term (1985–90), was elected president for the second time in 2006. Another ex-president, Alberto Fujimori (who also had been living in exile and disgrace abroad), was extradited from Chile and promptly jailed in Peru. Fujimori is currently on trial for directing death squads to murder leftist guerrillas, making him the first president in Peruvian history to be tried for crimes committed during his administration.

Under García, Peru has enjoyed relative political and economic stability, in contrast to the tumultuous last years of the Toledo administration. The Peruvian economy has continued to expand, growing at a rate of 8.3% in 2007, and in December 2007, the U.S. and Peru signed a free-trade agreement.

A massive earthquake (7.9 on the Richter scale) struck a large coastal area south of Lima in September 2007, devastating the cities of Pisco, Ica, and parts of the Paracas National Reserve. The earthquake killed more than 500 people and left nearly 100,000 homeless. Though much of what travelers go to see was not affected, including the Nasca Lines, the region will take years to rebuild, a factor

travelers should keep in mind if they intend to travel to the area.

GETTING AROUND By Train The **Ferrocarril Central Andino** (© 01/361-2828; www.ferroviasperu.com.pe) is back up and running again from Lima to Huancayo in the Central Highlands. The scenic passenger train runs once a month between July and November (US$54–US$87/£27–£44 round-trip), leaving from the Estación de Desamparados in Lima.

LIMA Where to Stay Casa Andina inaugurated a new luxury flagship hotel—in what was Lima's original five-star hotel—in January 2008. The new **Private Collection Miraflores** (© 01/213-9700; www.casa-andina.com) is the chain's swankiest urban hotel yet. The new **Second Home Peru** (© 01/477-5021; www.secondhomeperu.com), an upscale B&B in Barranco, is also in an older building, but in this case it's very distinguished indeed; it's the home of the renowned Peruvian artist Victor Delfín.

LIMA Where to Dine Gastón Acurio, Peru's top celebrity chef, keeps on expanding; the informal cafe/bar/restaurant he opened with his wife Astrid, **T'anta** (© 01/421-9708), now has four branches, including one in Lima Centro (Pasaje Nicolás de Rivera del Viejo 142).

A favorite new restaurant in Barranco is the stylish **Chala** (© 01/252-8515), serving what it calls *costa fusión*, adding Mediterranean influences to Limeño standards.

CUSCO Where to Stay Casa Andina (© 084/232-610; www.casa-andina.com) opened one of its new, upscale "Private Collection" hotels in a historic building near Qoricancha—making that five hotels in the city, with another luxury version on the way, for the upstart Peruvian chain. **Casona les Pleiades** (© 084/506-430; www.casona-pleiades.com) is a new, cute and relaxed, French-owned boutique inn tucked in the San Blas neighborhood. **Niños Hotel** (© 084/231-424; www.ninoshotel.com), famous for its good works and great-value rooms, now has a country inn under its auspices: **Niños Hotel Hacienda,** in the town of Huasao, 30 minutes from Cusco (rates include transportation, lunch and dinner, and a tour of the local ruins).

CUSCO   Where to Dine   Don Esteban & Don Pancho (© 084/243-629), is a new and surprisingly chic and modern-looking restaurant serving Peruvian mountain and coastal favorites, as well as an entire host of pisco cocktails. The minichain also has a cafe and cafeteria in town—all going by the same name. **Greens** (Santa Catalina Angosta, 135; © 084/243-579), a longtime Cusco favorite, moved from its relaxed, bohemian-looking location in San Blas to a second-floor spot just off the Plaza de Armas. The new iteration is more refined, hushed, and elegant.

THE SACRED VALLEY OF THE INCAS   Where to Stay In Pisac, a genial small country inn owned by a New Yorker, **Hostal Paz y Luz** (© 084/203-204; www.pazyluzperu.com), is attracting folks looking to tap into the Sacred Valley's spiritualism, with Andean healing workshops and sacred plant ceremonies. Hoteliers continue to bet big on the Valle Sagrado, and more plans for new country-luxury hotels are in the works. The **Libertador Tambo del Inka,** Av. Ferrocarril s/n, Urubamba (© 084/201-126), is still undergoing a massive renovation; in 2009, it should become one of the valley's largest and most luxurious hotels. **Casa Andina Private Collection** (© 084/976-550; www.casa-andina.com) completed its onsite spa (if not the planned pool), and it is first rate all the way, with luxurious massage rooms, carved-stone Jacuzzis, and more.

THE SACRED VALLEY OF THE INCAS   Where to Dine Filling a niche in the Sacred Valley is the new chef-driven restaurant **El Huacatay** (© 084/201-790), in the heart of Urubamba. It's probably the most appealing restaurant in the Sacred Valley, where guests are much more accustomed to eating in their hotels.

Machu Picchu Prices continue to rise on PeruRail trains (and schedules continue to change), but none so much as the luxury **Hiram Bingham** train, which now costs an astounding US$588 (£294) round-trip. The climb to the peak Huayna Picchu, which offers astounding views of the ruins below, is now subject to new restrictive regulations. Only 400 people per day are permitted to make the climb; the path is open 7am to 1pm, and the first group of 200 must exit by 10am.

Machu Picchu was named one of the "New Seven Wonders of the World" in 2007. Sadly, though, Machu Picchu has made the notorious 2008 World Monuments Watch list of the 100 Most Endangered Sites in the World (the ruins were previously on the list but removed in 2002). According to the World Monuments Fund, "little has been done to address the impacts of tourism on the site or the resulting environmental degradation of the area." On a positive note, Yale University has agreed to return to Peru the lion's share of the artifacts collected by its archeologist Hiram Bingham, who is credited with discovering Machu Picchu in 1911. A new museum will be built in Cusco.

Hiking the Inca Trail The number of authorized agencies allowed to sell Inca Trail trekking packages has expanded exponentially, to at least 140, both in Cusco and beyond. The Camino del Inca, or Inca Trail to Machu Picchu, continues to climb in popularity and price; standard-class treks, the most common and economical service, start at about US$350

(£175) per person, including entrance fees (and premium group treks can cost as much as US$1,000/£500 per person). Several companies, including **Mountain Lodges of Peru** (© 084/236-069; www. mountainlodgesofperu.com), are now offering alternative and even luxury treks (in which hikers sleep not in campsites but comfortable lodges along the way) to Machu Picchu, avoiding the overcrowded Inca Trail.

PUNO & LAKE TITICACA Where to Stay Casa Andina (© 051/363-992; www.casa-andina.com) opened its new upscale **Private Collection Puno,** on the banks of Lake Titicaca. The hotel has its own train stop for folks coming in from Cusco.

AREQUIPA What to See & Do Like Machu Picchu, the great **Monasterio de Santa Catalina** also appeared on the 2008 World Monuments Watch list of Most Endangered Monuments; the convent is in danger of structural damage caused by pollution and earthquakes.

AREQUIPA Where to Stay Casa Andina, a chain on the move, added a new luxury hotel, **Private Collection Arequipa** (054/226-907; www.casa-andina. com), which occupies one of Arequipa's emblematic colonial buildings, the former Mint House, a national historic monument.

COLCA VALLEY Where to Stay The former Parador del Colca, owned by the luxury hotel chain Orient-Express, has completed its luxury transformation. With the 20 new super-luxe bungalows (each with private terrace and plunge pool) comes a new name: **Las Casitas del Colca** (© 01/610-8300; www.lascasitas delcolca.com). There's also a new spa and free-form swimming pool on the premises. The big changes mean that what was once a downright bargain is now targeting elites only: prices, which include all meals and activities, run US$1,000 (£500) double.

VENEZUELA

In December 2007, President Hugo Chávez suffered a prominent loss in a national referendum that would have created constitutional reforms allowing his perpetual reelection and cementing into law his increasingly sharp turn toward Cuban-style socialism. After more than 9 years in power, Chávez has experienced a marked decline in popularity at home.

Nonetheless, Chávez continues his fierce rhetoric and ongoing diplomatic sparring with the United States. He has also begun sparring with Colombia's president, Alvaro Uribe, to the point of accusing Colombia of "planning aggressions" against Venezuela.

PLANNING YOUR TRIP In January 2008, Venezuela officially changed its unit of currency from the **bolívar (Bs)** to the **bolívar fuerte (BsF).** The change simply involves chopping three decimal points off of the severely devalued bolívar. So BsF1 is equivalent to the old BS1,000. At press time, the official exchange rate was BsF2.15 to one U.S. dollar, and BsF4.37 to the British pound. However, the black-market exchange rate is radically different from the official rate. At press time, the unofficial exchange rate was approximately BsF4.50 to the dollar and BsF9.15 to the British Pound.

There is an airport departure tax of BsF38 (US$18/£8.60) combined with an airport tax of BsF94 (US$44/£21). One or both of these taxes are often included in the airline ticket price, so be sure to ask before paying twice.

CARACAS In the El Rodal district, **The Hotel** (© 0212/951-0268; www.the hotel.com.ve) is an ultramodern new boutique hotel, with all the amenities and technological bells and whistles you could ask for.

The popular *teleférico* (© 0800/ 28452) cable car to the top of Avila mountain has been taken over by the government. The gondola-style ride is now open Tuesday through Sunday from 10am to 8pm. The round-trip cost is BsF25 (US$12/ £5.70) for adults, BsF10 (US$4.65/£2.30) for children age 4 to 12.

LOS ROQUES NATIONAL PARK All visitors to Los Roques must pay a BsF38 (US$17/£8.65) one-time entrance fee for the national park, good for the duration of your stay.

Posada Albacora (© 0237/221-1305; posadalbacora@hotmail.com) is an intimate new lodging option, with cool, comfortable, and well-equipped rooms.

MERIDA, THE ANDES & LOS LLANOS The popular restaurant

L'Abadia has opened a sister establishment, **La Abadía del Angel** (© 0274/252-8013), on Calle 21 between Avenidas 5 and 6, with a similar menu and vibe.

CANAIMA, ANGEL FALLS & THE RIO CAURA The longstanding and deservedly popular **Jungle Rudy Campamento** (©/fax 0286/962-2359; www. junglerudy.com) is remodeling all its rooms, updating the furnishings and decor, and adding riverfront patios to several of the units.

In addition to all the longstanding options in Canaima, the folks at Cacao Expeditions have opened a new lodge on the banks of the Canaima lagoon. **Tapuy Lodge** (© 0212/977-1234; www.cacao travel.com) is a comfortable option, just off a pretty section of sandy beach.

1

The Best of South America

by Shawn Blore, Alexandra de Vries, Eliot Greenspan, Charlie O'Malley,
Jisel Perilla, Neil E. Schlecht & Kristina Schreck

Whether you're an archaeology buff, an outdoor adventurer, or a partyer in search of a good time, South America presents so many diverse travel options that it'll make your head spin. We'll help you plan a memorable trip, starting with our highly opinionated lists of the best experiences the continent has to offer.

1 The Most Unforgettable Travel Experiences

- **Visiting Iguazú (Iguaçu) Falls:** One of the world's most spectacular sights, Iguazú boasts more than 275 waterfalls fed by the Iguazú River, which can (and should) be visited from both the Argentine and the Brazilian (where it is spelled Iguaçu) sides. In addition to the falls, Iguazú encompasses a marvelous subtropical jungle with extensive flora and fauna. See "Puerto Iguazú & Iguazú Falls" in chapter 4 and "Iguaçu Falls" in chapter 6.

- **Traveling the Wine Roads of Mendoza:** Mendoza offers traditional and modernist wineries, set among vines that run into the snowcapped Andes. The wineries are free to visitors and easily accessible along leafy thoroughfares known as *los Caminos del Vino*. Over 100 wineries offer tours, but most are by appointment only. See "Mendoza" in chapter 4.

- **Everything Is Illuminated on Isla del Sol:** The brilliant birthplace of the Incas is also a dazzling place to visit. Every rock possesses a legend and the island is a laid-back and peaceful retreat with little infrastructure but lots of spirituality. See "Lake Titicaca" in chapter 5.

- **Celebrating Carnaval in Rio:** The biggest party in the world. Whether you dance it out on the streets, watch the thousands of participants in their elaborate costumes in the samba parade, or attend the fairy-tale Copacabana Palace ball, this is one event not to miss! See "Rio de Janeiro" in chapter 6.

- **Observing Red Macaws at Sunset:** The sunset over the red rock formations in the Chapada dos Guimarães north of Cuiabá in Brazil is a magical experience in itself. Even more special is the view of scarlet macaws working the thermals off the sheer cliffs in the warm glow of the setting sun. See "The Pantanal" in chapter 6.

- **Exploring the Madcap Streets of Valparaíso:** The ramshackle, sinuous streets of Valparaíso offer a walking tour unlike any other. Part of the fascination here is viewing the antique Victorian mansions and colorful tin houses that line terraced walkways winding around precipitous hills; yet also as worthwhile is spending the night here in one of the city's new boutique hotels and savoring the local cuisine at one of Valparaíso's gourmet restaurants. As well, Valparaíso's bars, which seem to have authored the word "bohemian," are what have brought this city notoriety. See "Around Santiago & the Central Valley" in chapter 7.

- **Sailing Past the Islands and Fiords of Southern Chile:** Quietly sailing through the lush beauty of Chile's southern fiords is an experience that all can afford. There are two breathtaking trajectories: a 3-day ride between Puerto Natales and Puerto Montt, and a 1- to 6-day ride to the spectacular Laguna San Rafael Glacier. Backpackers on a shoestring (as well as those who need spiffier accommodations) all have options. These pristine, remote fiords are often said to be more dramatic than those in Norway. Farther south, a small cruise line takes passengers through Tierra del Fuego and past remote glaciers, peaks, and sea-lion colonies, stopping at the end of the world in Puerto Williams. See "The Chilean Lake District" in chapter 7.

- **Visiting Colombia's Paradise on Earth:** The Eje Cafetero, with its plantain- and coffee-terraced slopes, verdant mountains, and quaint Spanish-style colonial, farm-houses remains one of the most traditional parts of the country. (Remember: Red pillars and shutters for Liberals, blue for Conservatives.) The lush vegetation, wild orchids, and perfect weather will make you think you're in some kind of earthly paradise. Here, you can lie back in a hammock and listen to the birds chirp, visit the hot springs of nearby Santa Rosa, or horseback ride through the endless coffee plantations—a world removed from the hectic Colombian cities. See "El Eje Cafetero" in chapter 8.

- **Watching Blue-Footed Boobies Dance for Love in the Galápagos:** Birds are usually shy, especially during mating season. But in the Galápagos Islands, where wild animals have no fear of humans, you can watch male blue-footed boobies spread their wings, lift their beaks, and dance wildly in a performance known as "sky pointing," all in hope of attracting a mate. If the female likes what she sees, she'll do the same. It's a scene right out of a *National Geographic* documentary. See "The Galápagos Islands" in chapter 9.

- **Floating on Lake Titicaca:** Lake Titicaca, the world's highest navigable body of water, straddles the border between Peru and Bolivia. To locals, it is a mysterious and sacred place. A 1-hour boat ride from Puno takes you to the Uros floating islands, where communities dwell upon soft patches of reeds. Visitors have a rare opportunity to experience the ancient cultures of two inhabited natural islands, Amantani and Taquile, by staying with a local family. You won't find any cars or electricity here, but there are remarkable local festivals. The views of the oceanlike lake, at more than 3,600m (11,800 ft.) above sea level, and the star-littered night sky alone are worth the trip. Even better, for those with a bit of adventure and extra time, are kayaking on Titicaca and spending the night on private Isla Suasi. See "Puno & Lake Titicaca" in chapter 11.

- **Gazing upon Machu Picchu:** However you get to it—whether you hike the fabled Inca Trail, hop aboard one of the prettiest train rides in South America, or zip in by helicopter—Machu Picchu more than lives up to its reputation as one of the most spectacular sites on earth. The ruins of the legendary "lost city of the Incas" sit majestically among the massive Andes, swathed in clouds. The ceremonial and agricultural center, never discovered or looted by the Spanish, dates from the mid-1400s but seems even more ancient. Exploring the site is a thrilling experience, especially at sunrise, when dramatic rays of light creep over the mountaintops. For classic postcard views, see the ruins from the Sun Gate or the top of Huayna Picchu. See "The Sacred Valley of the Incas" in chapter 11.

- **Visiting Punta del Este in Summer:** As Porteños (residents of Buenos Aires) will tell you, anyone who's anyone from Buenos Aires heads to Punta del Este for summer vacation. The glitzy Atlantic coast resort in Uruguay is packed with South America's jet set from December through February and offers inviting beaches and outstanding nightlife. See "Punta del Este" in chapter 12.

- **Enjoying the Splendor of Angel Falls:** From the boat ride through rapids in a dugout canoe, to the steep hike from the river's edge to the base of the falls, to a swim in the cool waters at the foot of this natural wonder and back again, this is an amazing experience, with spectacular views and scenery throughout. See "Canaima, Angel Falls & the Río Caura" in chapter 13.

- **Riding El Teleférico in Mérida, Venezuela:** The world's highest and longest cable car system will bring you to the summit of Pico Espejo at 4,765m (15,629 ft.). If you've ever wanted to get into thin air without the toil of actually climbing there, this is the way to go. Go early if you want the best views. But be careful: The effects of altitude can be felt, whether or not you actually climb. See "Mérida, the Andes & Los Llanos" in chapter 13.

2 The Best Small Towns & Villages

- **San Martín de los Andes,** Argentina: City planners in San Martín had the smart sense to do what Bariloche never thought of: limit building height to two stories and mandate continuity in the town's Alpine architecture. The result? Bariloche is crass whereas San Martín is class, and the town is a year-round playground to boot. The cornucopia of hotels, restaurants, and shops that line the streets are built of stout, cinnamon-colored tree trunks or are Swiss-style, gingerbread confections that all seem right at home in San Martín's blessed, pastoral setting. Relax, swim, bike, ski, raft, hunt, or fish—this small town has it all. See "The Argentine Lake District" in chapter 4.

- **Cafayate Wine Town,** Argentina: This small, sandy village in the Argentine Northwest is surrounded by multicolored mountain ranges and red rock desert. Vineyards punctuated by tall cactus sentinels stretch into the foothills. Home to the delicious white wine torrontes, Cafayate offers beautiful luxury wine lodges or more down-to-earth family-run hotels. See "Salta" in chapter 4.

- **The Isla del Sol,** Bolivia: There are actually several small villages on the Sun Island, but in total, only a few thousand people live here. There are no cars and barely any telephones. At rush hour, things get very chaotic: You may have to wait a few minutes while the locals herd their llamas from one end of the island to the other. Spend a day here, and you'll feel as if you have taken a trip back in time. See "Lake Titicaca" in chapter 5.

- **Porto de Galinhas,** Brazil: This village of three streets in a sea of white sand is the perfect spot to learn to surf. You'll never get cold, while steamed crab and fresh tropical juices between waves do wonders to keep you going. See "Recife & Olinda" in chapter 6.

- **Morro de São Paulo,** Brazil: Situated on a green lush island just a boat ride away from Salvador, this sleepy village offers some of the best laidback beach life on the northeast coast of Brazil. Car-free and stress-free, Morro de São Paulo offers the perfect mix of deserted beaches, watersports, and fun nightlife in an idyllic setting. See "A Side Trip from Salvador" in chapter 6.

- **San Pedro de Atacama,** Chile: Quaint, unhurried, and built of adobe brick, San Pedro de Atacama has drawn Santiaguinos and expatriates the world over to experience the mellow charm and New Age spirituality that waft through the dusty roads of this town. San Pedro hasn't grown much over the past 10 years—it has simply reinvented itself. Its location in the driest desert in the world makes for starry skies and breathtaking views of the weird and wonderful land formations that are just a stone's throw away. See "The Desert North" in chapter 7.

- **Pucón,** Chile: Not only was Pucón bestowed with a stunning location at the skirt of a smoking volcano and the shore of a glittering lake, it's also Chile's self-proclaimed adventure capital, offering so many outdoor activities that you could keep busy for a week. But if your idea of a vacation is plopping yourself down on a beach, Pucón also has plenty of low-key activities, and that is the real attraction here. You'll find everything you want and need without forfeiting small-town charm (that is, if you don't come with the Jan–Feb megacrowds).

Timber creates the downtown atmosphere, with plenty of wood-hewn restaurants, pubs, and crafts stores blending harmoniously with the forested surroundings. See "The Chilean Lake District" in chapter 7.

- **Villa de Leyva,** Colombia: You'd be hard pressed to find a place more picturesque than Villa de Leyva, one of the earliest towns founded by the Spanish. At 500 hundred years old, Villa de Leyva is nearly unspoiled by the ravishes of time. Offering green and white colonial-style churches, cobblestone plazas, delightful bed-and-breakfasts, a thriving arts community, and pristine countryside, it's no wonder Villa de Leyva has become the weekend getaway of choice for upscale Bogotanos. Villa de Leyva makes a great base for exploring the spectacular Boyacá countryside and participating in all sorts of adventure sports and eco-opportunities from repelling and kayaking, to nature walks through the nearby desert and waterfalls. See "A Side Trip from Bogotá: Villa de Leyva" in chapter 8.

- **Otavalo,** Ecuador: This small, indigenous town is famous for its artisans market. However, it also serves as a fabulous base for a wide range of adventures, activities, and side trips. Nearby attractions include Cuicocha Lake, Peguche Waterfall, Mojanda Lakes, and Condor Park See "Otavalo & Imbabura Province" in chapter 9.

- **Ollantaytambo,** Peru: One of the principal villages of the Sacred Valley of the Incas, Ollanta (as the locals call it) is a spectacularly beautiful place along the Urubamba River; the gorge is lined with agricultural terraces, and snowcapped peaks rise in the distance. The ruins of a formidable temple-fortress overlook the old town, a perfect grid of streets built by the

Incas, the only such layout remaining in Peru. See "The Sacred Valley of the Incas" in chapter 11.

- **Colca Valley Villages,** Peru: Chivay, on the edge of Colca Canyon, is the valley's main town, but it isn't much more than a laid-back market town with fantastic hot springs on its outskirts. Dotting the Colca Valley and its extraordinary agricultural terracing are 14 charming colonial villages dating to the 16th century, each marked by its handsomely decorated church. Yanque, Coporaque, Maca, and Lari are among the most attractive towns. Natives in the valley are descendants of the pre-Inca ethnic communities Collaguas and Cabanas, and they maintain the vibrant style of traditional dress, highlighted by fantastically embroidered and sequined hats. See chapter 11.

- **Colonia del Sacramento,** Uruguay: Just a short ferry trip from Buenos Aires, Colonia is Uruguay's best example of colonial life. The old city contains brilliant examples of colonial wealth and many of Uruguay's oldest structures. Dating from the 17th century, this beautifully preserved Portuguese settlement makes a perfect day trip. See "A Side Trip to Colonia del Sacramento" in chapter 12.

- **Mérida,** Venezuela: Nestled in a narrow valley between two immense spines of the great Andes Mountains, this lively college town is a great base for a wide range of adventure activities. Its narrow streets and colonial architecture also make it a great place to wander around and explore. See "Mérida, the Andes & Los Llanos" in chapter 13.

3 The Best Outdoor Adventures

- **Discovering Iguazú Falls by Raft:** This is a place where birds like the great dusky swift and brilliant morpho butterfly spread color through the thick forest canopy. You can easily arrange an outing into the forest once you arrive in Iguazú. See "Puerto Iguazú & Iguazú Falls" in chapter 4.

- **Raging down the Mendoza River:** Mendoza offers the best white-water rafting in Argentina, and during the summer months, when the snow melts in the Andes and fills the Mendoza River, rafters enjoy up to class IV and V rapids. Rafting is possible year-round, but the river is colder and calmer in winter months. See "Mendoza" in chapter 4.

- **Biking the Most Dangerous Road in Bolivia:** The 64km (40-mile) road that descends nearly 1,800m (6,000 ft.) from the barren high-plateau area of La Paz to the lush tropical area of Los Yungas is considered one of the most dangerous roads in the world. It's unpaved, narrow, and carved out of the edge of a cliff (without any guardrails). The road recently has become a popular mountain-biking challenge. The views are unbelievable, but don't stare at them too long—you have to keep an eye out for speeding trucks coming at you from the other direction. See "La Paz" in chapter 5.

- **Horseback Riding in the Pantanal:** The world's largest floodplain is best explored cowboy-style—on horseback. Spend some time quietly observing the many large bird species and every now and then take off on a fast gallop through the wetlands, startling alligators and snakes underfoot. See "The Pantanal" in chapter 6.

- **Hang Gliding in Rio:** Running off the edge of a platform with nothing between you and the ground 800m

(2,624 ft.) below requires a leap of faith, but once you do, the views of the rainforest and beaches are so enthralling that you almost forget about the ground until your toes touch down on the sand at São Conrado beach. See "Rio de Janeiro" in chapter 6.

- **Kayaking the Brazilian Amazon:** Perhaps the best way to really get in touch with the rainforest is by good old sea kayak. Drifting down an Amazon tributary, you have the time to observe the rainforest; to search the trees for toucans, macaws, and sloths; and to scout the water for anaconda and caiman. On daytime hikes, you explore and swim in rarely visited Amazon waterfalls. To truly make like a researcher, you can hoist yourself 60m (197 ft.) into the treetops and spend some time exploring the rainforest canopy. See "The Amazon: Manaus" in chapter 6.

- **Trekking in Torres del Paine:** This backpacking mecca just keeps growing in popularity, and it's no wonder. Torres del Paine is one of the most spectacular national parks in the world, with hundreds of kilometers of trails through ever-changing landscapes of jagged peaks and one-of-a-kind granite spires, undulating meadows, milky, turquoise lakes and rivers, and mammoth glaciers. The park has a well-organized system of *refugios* and campgrounds, but there are also several hotels, and visitors can access the park's major highlights on a day hike. See "Patagonia" in chapter 7.

- **Snorkeling in the Galápagos:** The sea lions in the Galápagos are a curious bunch. Once you put on a snorkeling mask and flippers, these guys will think you're one of the gang and swim right up to you. When you aren't playing with sea lions, you'll have the chance to see hammerhead sharks, penguins, sea turtles, and some of the most colorful fish in the world. See "The Galápagos Islands" in chapter 9.

- **Hiking the Inca Trail:** The legendary trail to Machu Picchu, the Camino del Inca, is one of the world's most rewarding eco-adventures. The arduous 42km (26-mile) trek leads across phenomenal Andes mountain passes and through some of the greatest natural and man-made attractions in Peru, including dozens of Inca ruins, dense cloud forest, and breathtaking mountain scenery. The trek has a superlative payoff: a sunset arrival at the glorious ruins of Machu Picchu, laid out at your feet. See "The Sacred Valley of the Incas" in chapter 11.

- **Exploring the Peruvian Amazon:** More than half of Peru is Amazon rainforest, and the country has some of the richest biodiversity on the planet. Cusco is the gateway to the southeastern jungle and two principal protected areas, **Tambopata National Reserve** and the **Manu Biosphere Reserve.** Manu is the least accessible and least explored jungle in Peru, with unparalleled opportunity for viewing wildlife and more than 1,000 species of birds, but it's not easy or cheap to get to. Iquitos leads to the accessible northern Amazon basin, with some of the top jungle lodges in the country. Eco-travelers can fish for piranhas and keep an eye out for pink dolphins, caiman, and tapirs. One of the best jungle experiences is viewing the dense forest from the heights of a rickety canopy walkway. See "The Southern Amazon: Manu & Tambopata" and "Iquitos & the Northern Amazon" in chapter 11.

- **Scuba Diving in Los Roques, Venezuela:** Los Roques offers much of the same coral, marine life, and crystal clear waters as the rest of the popular Caribbean dive destinations, but it's still virtually undiscovered. **Ecobuzos** (© **0237/221-1235;** www.ecobuzos.com) is the best dive operator on the archipelago. See "Los Roques National Park" in chapter 13.

- **One-Stop Adventure Travel from Mérida,** Venezuela: With a half-dozen or so peaks 4,500m (14,760 ft.) and above, raging rivers, and a couple of very competent adventure tour outfitters, you can go climbing,

trekking, mountain biking, white-water rafting, horseback riding, canyoneering, and even paragliding out of Mérida. You may need a couple of weeks to do it all, but both **Arassari Treks** (www.arassari.com) and **Natoura Adventure Tours** (www.natoura.com) can help you come up with an adventure package to fit your budget, skill level, and time frame. See "Mérida, the Andes & Los Llanos" in chapter 13.

4 The Most Intriguing Historical Sites

- **Manzana de las Luces,** Buenos Aires, Argentina: The Manzana de las Luces (Block of Lights) served as the intellectual center of the city in the 17th and 18th centuries. This land was granted in 1616 to the Jesuits, who built San Ignacio—the city's oldest church—still standing at the corner of Bolívar and Aslina streets. It's worth a visit to see the beautiful altar. See p. 97.

- **Teatro Colón,** Buenos Aires, Argentina: The majestic Teatro Colón, completed in 1908, combines a variety of European styles, from the Ionic and Corinthian capitals and French stained-glass pieces in the main entrance to the Italian marble staircase and exquisite French furniture, chandeliers, and vases in the Golden Hall. The Colón has hosted the world's most important opera singers. See p. 100.

- **Tiwanaku,** Bolivia: The Tiwanaku lived in Bolivia from 1600 B.C. to A.D. 1200. Visit the Tiwanaku archaeological site, which is about 2 hours from La Paz, and you'll see proof of some of the amazing feats of this pre-Columbian culture. The stone-carved Sun Gate could gauge the position of the sun. The technologically advanced irrigation system transformed this barren terrain into

viable farmland. The enormous and intricately designed stone-carved monoliths found here give testament to the amazing artistic talents of these people. Much here still remains a mystery, but when you walk around the site, it's exciting to imagine what life must have been like here for the Tiwanaku. See "La Paz" in chapter 5.

- **Potosí,** Bolivia: Once one of the richest cities in the world, and now one of the poorest, Potosí is a fascinating but tragic place. A silver mining town that once bankrolled the Spanish Empire, Potosí is a high-altitude relic featuring beautiful church architecture and primitive mining, both of which you can experience firsthand. See "A Side Trip to Potosí" in chapter 5.

- **Brasília,** Brazil: Built from scratch in a matter of years on the red soil of the dry cerrado, Brasília is an oasis of modernism in Brazil's interior. Marvel at the clean lines and functional forms and admire some of the best modern architecture in the world. See "Brasília" in chapter 6.

- **Pelourinho,** Brazil: The restored historical center of Salvador is a treasure trove of baroque churches, colorful colonial architecture, steep cobblestone streets, and large squares. See "Salvador" in chapter 6.

- **San Pedro de Atacama, Chiu Chiu,** and **Caspana,** Chile: The driest desert in the world has one perk: Everything deteriorates very, very slowly. This is good news for travelers in search of the architectural roots of Chile, where villages such as San Pedro, Chiu Chiu, and Caspana boast equally impressive examples of 17th-century colonial adobe buildings and the sun-baked ruins of the Atacama Indian culture; some sites date from 800 B.C. Highlights undoubtedly are the enchanting, crumbling San Francisco Church of Chiu Chiu and the labyrinthine streets of the indigenous fort Pukará de Lasana. See "The Desert North" in chapter 7.

- **Chiloé Island,** Chile: Chiloé's historical appeal is in large part derived from the fact that many citizens live much as they did 200 years ago, tilling fields with an ox and a plow, plying the coves with rickety wooden fishing skiffs, and hand-knitting sweaters to keep out the cold. Chiloé is home to a rare display of antique ecclesiastical architecture in the form of hundreds of 17th- and 18th-century wooden churches, two dozen of which were recently named a World Patrimony by UNESCO. See "The Chilean Lake District" in chapter 7.

* **Cartagena,** Colombia: Declared a UNESCO World Heritage site in 1984, the old-walled city of Cartagena is the greatest living outdoor museum dedicated to Spanish colonial history. A walk through one of Cartagena's narrow, cobblestone streets, complete with centuries-old Spanish mansions, flower-strewn balconies, and horse-drawn carriages showing tourists around town, might make you feel as if you've stepped onto the set of a colonial-era *telenovela*. Best of all, the finest attractions— the plazas, the fortress, and most of the churches—are free. See "Cartagena & the Atlantic Coast" in chapter 8.

- **Quito's Old Town,** Ecuador: When you walk around old Quito, you will feel as if you have stepped back in time. The oldest church here dates from 1535, and it's still magnificent. La Compañia de Jesús only dates from 1765, but it is one of the most impressive baroque structures in all of South America. It's rare to find a city with so many charming colonial-style buildings. When you wander through the streets, it really seems as if you are walking through an outdoor museum. See "Quito" in chapter 9.

- **The Nasca Lines,** Peru: One of South America's great enigmas are the ancient, baffling lines etched into the desert sands along Peru's southern coast. There are trapezoids and triangles, identifiable shapes of animal and plant figures, and more than 10,000 lines that can only really be seen from the air. Variously thought to be signs from the gods, agricultural and astronomical calendars, or even extraterrestrial airstrips, the Nasca Lines were constructed between 300 B.C. and A.D. 700. See "Lima" in chapter 11.

- **Cusco,** Peru: Cusco, the ancient Inca capital, is a living museum of Peruvian history, with Spanish colonial churches and mansions sitting atop perfectly constructed Inca walls of exquisitely carved granite blocks that fit together without mortar. In the hills above the city lie more terrific examples of Inca masonry: the zigzagged defensive walls of Sacsayhuamán and the smaller ruins of Q'enko, Puca Pucara, and Tambomachay. See "Cusco" in chapter 11.

- **Iglesia de San Francisco,** Caracas, Venezuela: This is the church where Simón Bolívar was proclaimed El

The Best of Sensuous South America

Your trip will not be complete until you indulge in at least one of the following uniquely South American experiences:

- **Get High in Bolivia:** With the world's highest capital city, highest commercial airport, and highest navigable lake, Bolivia's air is so thin, it will make your head spin. But Bolivia is also home to the infamous coca leaf, a perfectly legal, extremely nutritious source of energy and an antidote to altitude sickness. To learn the complete history of the coca leaf (and for free samples), stop in at the **Museo de la Coca** in La Paz. See p. 184.
- **Be the Girl (or Boy) from Ipanema:** Rio may have other beaches, but Ipanema is still the one with the best people-watching. Grab a spot, and food, drink, and eye-candy will come to you. See "Rio de Janeiro" in chapter 6.
- **Feel the Beat in Brazil:** At night the historic heart of Salvador comes alive with music. Most impressive of all are the Afro blocos, the all-percussion bands that create such an intense rhythm with their drums that it sends shivers down your spine. See "Salvador" in chapter 6.
- **Soak in Chilean Hot Springs:** The volatile Andes not only builds volcanoes; it also produces steaming mineralized water that spouts from fissures, many of which have been developed into hot springs, from rock pools to full-scale luxury resorts. Most hot springs seem to have been magically paired by nature with outdoor adventure spots, making for a thankful

Libertador in 1813, and the site of his massive funeral in 1842—the year his remains were brought back from Colombia some 12 years after his death. Begun in 1575, the church shows the architectural influences of various periods and styles, but retains much of its colonial-era charm. See p. 763.

5 The Best Museums

- **Museo Nacional de Bellas Artes,** Buenos Aires: This museum contains the world's largest collection of Argentine sculptures and paintings from the 19th and 20th centuries. It also houses European art dating from the pre-Renaissance period to the present day. The collections include notable pieces by Manet, Goya, El Greco, and Gauguin. See p. 99.
- **MALBA–Colección Costantini,** Buenos Aires: This stunning new private museum houses one of the most impressive collections of Latin American art anywhere. Temporary and permanent exhibitions showcase such names as Antonio Berni, Pedro Figari, Frida Kahlo, Candido Portinari, Diego Rivera, and Antonio Siguí. Many of the works confront social issues and explore questions of national identity. See p. 99.
- **Museu de Arte Sacra,** Salvador: When you walk into this small but splendid museum, what you hear is not the usual gloomy silence but the

way to end a day of activity. The Lake District is a noted "hot spot," especially around Pucón. See "The Chilean Lake District" in chapter 7.

- **Enjoy an Orgy of Sights, Sounds, and Smells in Ecuador:** The outdoor **artisans market in Otavalo** is an assault on your senses. The colors and textures of the intricate textiles mix with the sounds of musicians playing reed pipes, as you walk among the scents of herbs and flowers offered up for sale. See p. 556.

- **Feel the Wind Beneath the Condor's Wings in Peru:** Colca Canyon is the best place in South America to see giant Andean condors, majestic birds with wingspans of up to 3.5m (11 ft.). From a stunning lookout point nearly 1,200m (4,000 ft.) above the canyon river, you can watch as the condors appear, slowly circle, and gradually gain altitude with each pass, until they soar silently above your head and head off down the river. A truly spine-tingling spectacle, the flight of the big birds may make you feel quite small. See "Arequipa" in chapter 11.

- **Stroke a 3.6m (12-ft.) Anaconda in Venezuela:** There's no guarantee you'll wrangle an anaconda—many lodges frown on direct contact—but you can get awfully close. Try a stay at **Hato El Cedral** (© **0212/781-8995;** www.elcedral.com); sightings of the large anaconda here are common, particularly in the dry season. If you're lucky, you'll see a "mating ball," several males and one female entwined in a writhing ball of anaconda lust. See p. 799.

soft sweet sound of Handel. It's a small indication of the care curators have taken in assembling and displaying one of Brazil's best collections of Catholic art—reliquaries, processional crosses, and crucifixes of astonishing refinement. The artifacts are shown in a former monastery, a simple, beautiful building that counts itself as a work of art. See p. 280.

- **Museu de Arte Moderna,** Rio de Janeiro: It's impossible to miss the MAM. It's a long, large, rectangular building lofted off the ground by an arcade of concrete struts, giving the structure the appearance of an airplane wing. Inside are walls of solid plate glass that welcome in both city and sea. Displays present the best of contemporary art from Brazil and Latin America. See p. 244.

- **Museo Arqueológico Padre Le Paige,** San Pedro de Atacama: This little museum will come as an unexpected surprise for its wealth of indigenous artifacts, although the museum's famous mummies have been taken off display due to ethical questions. Still, considering that the Atacama Desert is the driest in the world, this climate has produced some of the best-preserved artifacts in Latin America, on view here. See p. 413.

- **Museo del Oro,** Bogotá: With over 20,000 pieces of gold, the Museo del Oro offers the largest collection of its kind in the world, providing a visual history of Colombia and Latin America from the pre-Columbian era to the Spanish conquest. Taking a guided tour of the museum is one of the best ways to learn about the indigenous groups that inhabited modern-day Colombia before the arrival of the Spaniards. Whatever you do, don't leave Bogotá without visiting the top-floor gold room, a dazzling display of 8,000 pieces of gold. See p. 479.

- **Fundación Guayasamín,** Quito: Oswaldo Guayasamín was Ecuador's greatest and most famous modern artist. His striking large paintings, murals, and sculptures had an impact on artists across Latin America and around the world. This extensive museum displays both his own work and pieces from his collection. Combined with the neighboring **Capilla del Hombre,** this is a must-see for any art lover or Latin American history buff. See p. 538.
- **Museo de la Nación,** Lima: Lima is the museum capital of Peru, and the National Museum traces the art and history of the earliest inhabitants to the Inca Empire, the last before colonization by the Spaniards. In well-organized, chronological exhibits, it covers the country's unique architecture (including scale models of most major ruins in Peru) as well as ceramics and textiles. See p. 636.

- **Monasterio de Santa Catalina** and **Museo Santuarios Andinos,** Arequipa: The Convent of Santa Catalina, founded in 1579, is the greatest religious monument in Peru. More than a convent, it's an extraordinary and evocative small village, with Spanish-style cobblestone streets, passageways, plazas, and cloisters, where more than 200 sequestered nuns once lived (only a handful remain). Down the street at the Museo Santuarios Andinos is a singular exhibit: Juanita, the Ice Maiden of Ampato. A 13- or 14-year-old girl sacrificed in the 1500s by Inca priests high on a volcano at 6,380m (20,926 ft.), "Juanita" was discovered in almost perfect condition in 1995. See p. 705 and p. 706.
- **Museo de Arte Contemporáneo de Sofía Imber,** Caracas: Occupying 13 rooms spread out through the labyrinthine architecture of Caracas's Parque Central, the permanent collection here features a small but high-quality collection of singular works by such modern masters as Picasso, Red Grooms, Henry Moore, Joan Miró, and Francis Bacon, as well as a good representation of the conceptual works of Venezuelan star Jesús Soto. See p. 763.

6 The Best Festivals & Celebrations

- **Carnaval,** Argentina, Brazil, and Uruguay: The week before the start of Lent, Mardi Gras is celebrated in many towns in Argentina, although to a much lesser extent than in neighboring Brazil. In addition to Rio's incredible party, Salvador puts the emphasis on participation: The action is out on the streets with the blocos, flatbed trucks with bands and sound systems leading people on a 3-day dance through the streets. Carnaval is celebrated throughout Uruguay with a passion topped only

by Brazil. Montevideo spares no neighborhood parades, dance parties, and intense Latin merrymaking. See chapters 4, 6, and 12.
- **Festival of the Virgen de la Candelaria,** Bolivia and Peru: The Virgen de la Candelaria is one of the most beloved religious icons in Bolivia. On February 2, parades and parties erupt in Copacabana in her honor. The festivities, which are some of the liveliest in Bolivia, combine a mixture of Catholic and ancient local influences. Puno, perhaps the epicenter of

Peruvian folklore, imbues its festivals with a unique vibrancy; their celebration of the Virgin is one of the greatest folk religious festivals in South America, with a 2-week explosion of music and dance, and some of the most fantastic costumes and masks seen anywhere. See "Lake Titicaca" in chapter 5 and "Puno & Lake Titicaca" in chapter 11.

- **New Year's Eve,** Brazil and Chile: Join up to a million revelers on Copacabana Beach for one of the largest celebrations in Brazil; fireworks, concerts, and the religious ceremonies of the Afro-Brazilian Candomblé make for an unforgettable New Year's Eve. In Chile, Valparaíso rings in the new year with a spectacular bang, setting off a fireworks display high above the city's shimmering bay for the throngs of visitors who blanket the hills. Pablo Neruda used to spend New Year's here, watching the exploding sky from his home high on a cliff. The yearly event is absolutely hectic, so come early and plan on staying late. See "Rio de Janeiro" in chapter 6 and "Around Santiago & the Central Valley" in chapter 7.

- **Inti Raymi,** Ecuador and Peru: June 24 to 29, the fiestas of San Pablo, San Juan, and Inti Raymi (a sun festival celebrating the summer solstice) all merge into one big holiday in the Otavalo area. For the entire week, local people celebrate with big barbecues, parades, traditional dances, and bonfires. In Peru, it takes over Cusco and transforms the Sacsayhuamán ruins overlooking the city into a majestic stage. See "Otavalo & Imbabura Province" in chapter 9 and "Cusco" in chapter 11.

- **Mendoza Wine Harvest Festival,** The first weekend of every March, Argentina's Malbec region celebrates the bumper harvest with wine, women, and song. Parades, concerts, and a carnival-like atmosphere culminate in a grand open-air spectacle of music, dance, and fireworks. See "Mendoza" in chapter 4.

7 The Best Hotels

- **Alvear Palace Hotel,** Buenos Aires (© **011/4808-2100**): Decorated in Empire- and Louis XV–style furnishings, this is the most exclusive hotel in Buenos Aires. Luxurious guest rooms and suites have chandelier lighting, feather beds, silk drapes, and beautiful marble bathrooms; service is sharp and professional. See p. 104.

- **Villa Huinid,** Bariloche, Argentine Lake District (© **02944/523523**): You won't have to rough it here— Villa Huinid's country-style cabins are luxurious enough to be considered small mansions, and there's a private beach and walking trail on the property. The surroundings offer fantastic views of Lake Nahuel Huapi and it's also not far from the lively nightlife of Bariloche. See p. 146.

- **El Hostal de su Merced,** Sucre (© **0104/6442-706**): Sucre is one of the most historic cities in Bolivia, so it makes sense to stay in a historic hotel. El Hostal de su Merced is housed in an elegant 300-year-old mansion. All the rooms have charming antiques, crystal chandeliers, and lace curtains. See p. 206.

- **Hotel Sofitel,** Rio de Janeiro (© **0800/241-232** or 021/2525-1232): Considered Rio's best hotel, the Sofitel combines old-world elegance and style with one of the city's best locations, across from the Copacabana Fort and steps from Ipanema. See p. 258.

- **Tropical Manaus Eco Resort** (☏ **0800/701-2670**): The Tropical Hotel in Manaus is without a doubt *the* hotel in town. Set in its own piece of rainforest on the banks of the Rio Negro, the hotel is built in an elegant colonial style. Rooms are spacious and the amenities are top-notch; archery lessons, a zoo, wakeboard lessons, a wave pool, a salon, and more await you in the middle of the Amazon. See p. 340.

- **Casa Higueras**, Valparaíso (☏ **32/249-7900**): Housed in an eggshell-white, elegant 1940's mansion that descends four floors on a slope of Cerro Alegre in Valparaíso, this hotel boasts one of the most culturally and architecturally interesting views in Chile. It is one of the country's few boutique hotels, and the combination of luxury lodging, an infinity pool and spa, umbrella-dotted terrace with a restaurant serving fine food, and a handsome, masculine design really earn kudos among travelers seeking something unique. See p. 399.

- **Hotel Awasi**, San Pedro (☏ **888/880-3219** in the U.S.): The intimate and stylish Awasi was one of the top hotels to open in all of Latin America in 2007, offering chic accommodations, out-of-the-ordinary excursions around San Pedro de Atacama, a spa, and fabulous cuisine. With just eight suites, the hotel encourages guests to get to know each other, and so it is not ideal for travelers seeking absolute anonymity, but suites—which come with indoor and outdoor showers—are large enough to escape to your own private paradise. The hotel, built of adobe and decorated with local art, is centered around an oasis-style pool and outdoor dining area and bar. See p. 416.

- **Hotel de la Opera**, Bogotá (☏ **1/336-2066**): A rarity among Bogotá's mostly modern, though uninspiring, lodging options, this is a truly charming hotel. Located in the heart of La Candelaria, Bogotá's historic and sentimental center, the de la Opera is a stunning restoration of two formerly dilapidated mansions once belonging to influential families. Old-world elegance blends effortlessly with modern-day amenities to make this Italian-style hotel the place to stay in Bogotá. Be sure to book in advance. See p. 484.

- **La Mirage Garden Hotel & Spa**, Otavalo (☏ **800/327-3573** in the U.S. and Canada, or 06/2915-237; www.mirage.com.ec): This luxurious hotel is one of Ecuador's finest. The manicured gardens make this place feel like a mini-Versailles, while the rooms are all palatial-style suites. Ancient Ecuadorian treatments are the specialty at the spa. See p. 560.

- **Royal Palm Hotel**, Santa Cruz, Galápagos (☏ **05/2527-409**; www.royalpalmgalapagos.com): This luxurious resort almost seems out of place in the remote and rustic Galápagos. The villas are truly sumptuous, each with a private Jacuzzi and an enormous bathroom with hardwood floors. Large windows open up to the lush tropical landscape and the awesome stretch of the Pacific in the distance. See p. 593.

- **Hotel Monasterio**, Cusco (☏ **084/241-777**): Carved out of a 16th-century monastery, itself built over the foundations of an Inca palace, this Orient Express hotel is the most dignified and historic place to stay in Peru. With its own gilded chapel and 18th-century Cusco School art collection, it's an attraction in its own right. Rooms are gracefully decorated with colonial touches, particularly the rooms off the serene first courtyard. See p. 661.

- **Machu Picchu Pueblo Hotel,** Aguas Calientes (© **800/442-5042** or **084/ 211-122** for reservations): It's not next to the ruins, but this rustic hotel is a compound of bungalows ensconced in lush tropical gardens and cloud forest, and it's the nicest place in Aguas Calientes. With lots of nature trails and guided activities, it's also great for naturalists. And after a day at Machu Picchu, the spring-fed pool is a great alternative to the thermal baths in town. Junior suites, with fireplaces and small terraces, are the most coveted rooms. See p. 687.
- **Belmont House,** Montevideo (© **2/ 600-0430**): A boutique hotel in Montevideo's peaceful Carrasco neighborhood, Belmont House offers its privileged guests intimacy and luxury close to the city and the beach. Small elegant spaces with carefully chosen antiques and wood furnishings give this the feeling of a private estate. See p. 732.
- **Conrad Resort & Casino,** Punta del Este (© **042/491-111**): This resort dominates social life in Punta del Este. Luxurious rooms have terraces overlooking the two main beaches, and there's a wealth of outdoor activities from tennis and golf to horseback riding and watersports. See p. 741.
- **Jungle Rudy Campamento,** Canaima (©/fax **0286/962-2359** in Canaima, or 0212/693-0618 in Caracas; www. junglerudy.com): The accommodations here are decidedly simple—no television, air-conditioning, or telephones. However, the setting, on the banks of the Río Carrao above Ucaima Falls, is spectacular. See p. 803.

8 The Best Local Dining Experiences

- **Grilled Meat in Argentina:** Widely considered the best *parrilla* (grill restaurant) in Buenos Aires, **Cabaña las Lilas** (© **011/4313-1336**) is always packed. The menu pays homage to Argentine beef cuts, which come exclusively from the restaurant's private *estancia* (ranch). The steaks are outstanding. See p. 111.
- *Salteñas* **in Bolivia:** In almost every town in Bolivia, the locals eat *salteñas* for breakfast. These delicious treats are made with either chicken or beef, spiced with onions and raisins, and all wrapped up in a doughy pastry shell. Most people buy them from vendors on the street. See chapter 5's "Tips on Dining" on p. 177.
- **Street Food in Brazil:** Whether you want prawns, chicken, tapioca pancakes, coconut sweets, or corn on the cob, it can all be purchased on the street for next to nothing. Indulge— don't be afraid to try some of the best snacks that Brazil has to offer. See chapter 6.
- **Prawns on Ilhabela:** Ilhabela has the most succulent, sweet, and juicy prawns in all of Brazil. Enjoy them grilled, sautéed, or stuffed with cheese—they're as good as they come. See "São Paulo" in chapter 6.
- **Fish in the Pantanal:** Anywhere in the Pantanal you can try the phenomenal bounty of the world's largest floodplain. Paçu, dourado, and pintado are just a few of the region's best catches. See "The Pantanal" in chapter 6.
- **The Mercado Central in Santiago:** The chaotic, colorful central fish-and-produce market of Santiago should not be missed by anyone, even if you are not particularly fond of seafood. But if you are, you'll want to relish one of the flavorful concoctions served at one of the market's simple restaurants. Hawklike waitresses guard the market's

passageways awaiting hungry diners and shouting "Hey, lady! Hey, sir! Eat here!"—but **Donde Augusto** is a good bet. See p. 376.

- *Bandeja Paisa* **in Medellín:** This tasty Antioquian dish of soup, rice, beans, avocado, salad, sausage, plantain, shredded beef, eggs, *arepa,* and *chicharrón* (pork rinds) will leave you stuffed for the rest of the day.

- **Fresh Fruit Drinks in Ecuador:** The tropical coastal climate in Ecuador is perfect for growing fruit. Almost every restaurant offers a wonderful selection of fresh local fruit, including pineapple, orange, passion fruit, coconut, blackberry, banana, and a variety of typical Ecuadorian fruits such as *guanábana* and *naranjilla.* My favorite is the **tamarillo (tree tomato),** which is often served as a breakfast drink. See chapter 9.

- *Ceviche* **in Peru:** Peruvian cuisine is one of the most distinguished in the Americas. Though cooking varies greatly from Andean to coastal and Amazonian climes, there are few things more satisfying than a classic Peruvian *ceviche:* raw fish and shellfish marinated in lime or lemon juice and hot chile peppers, served with raw onion, sweet potato, and toasted corn. It's wonderfully refreshing and spicy. (And if that's not adventurous enough for you, you can always try *cuy,* or guinea pig.) The perfect accompaniment is either *chicha morada,* a refreshment made from blue corn, or a pisco sour, a frothy cocktail of white grape brandy, egg whites, lemon juice, sugar, and bitters—akin to a margarita. See chapter 11.

- **Ice Cream at Heladería Coromoto,** Mérida (© **0274/252-3525**): This shop holds the Guinness world record for the most ice-cream flavors. Be adventurous and sample a scoop of smoked trout, garlic, beer, avocado, or squid ice cream. The count currently exceeds 850 flavors, with roughly 100 choices available on any night. See p. 796.

9 The Best Markets

- **San Telmo Antiques Market,** Buenos Aires: The Sunday market is as much a cultural event as a commercial event, as old-time tango and *milonga* dancers take to the streets with other performers. Here you will glimpse Buenos Aires much as it was at the beginning of the 20th century. See p. 95.

- **The Witch Doctors' Market,** La Paz: This is one of the most unusual markets in South America. The stalls are filled with llama fetuses and all sorts of good-luck charms. Locals come here to buy magic potions or small trinkets that will bring them wealth, health, or perhaps a good harvest. You'll be sure to find unique gifts here for all your friends at home. See p. 187.

- **Mercado Adolpho Lisboa,** Manaus: This is a beautiful iron-and-glass copy of Paris's now-demolished market hall in Les Halles. It's a great place to see fruits and fish fresh from the Amazon, but it's not for the squeamish. Vendors cut and clean the fish on the spot; some of the chopped-in-half catfish still wriggle. A short walk downstream, you can watch Amazon riverboats load up on supplies at the Feira do Produtor. See p. 338.

- **Ver-o-Peso Market,** Belém: The Ver-o-Peso is a vast waterside cornucopia featuring outrageously strange Amazon fish, hundreds of species of Amazon fruits found nowhere else, traditional medicine love potions, and just about anything else produced in the Amazon, all of it cheap, cheap, cheap. See p. 224.

- **Mercado Central,** Santiago: It would be a crime to visit Chile and not sample the rich variety of fish and shellfish available here, and this vibrant market is the best place to experience the country's love affair with its fruits of the sea. Nearly every edible (and seemingly inedible) creature is for sale, from sea urchins to the alien-looking and unfamiliar piure, among colorful bushels of fresh vegetables and some of the most aggressive salesmen this side of the Andes. See p. 376.

- **Feria Artesanal de Angelmó,** Puerto Montt: Stretching along several blocks of the Angelmó port area of Puerto Montt are rows and rows of stalls stocked with arts and crafts, clothing, and novelty items from the entire surrounding region, even Chiloé. This market is set up to buy, buy, buy! and it imparts little local color, but chances are you'll find yourself here before Temuco, which is more off the beaten path. Be sure to bargain for everything. See p. 439.

- **Otavalo,** Ecuador: Otavalo is probably one of the most famous markets in South America for good reason: You won't find run-of-the-mill tourist trinkets here. The local people are well known for their masterful craftsmanship—you can buy alpaca scarves, hand-woven bags, and a variety of other exquisite handmade goods. See "Otavalo & Imbabura Province" in chapter 9.

- **Pisac,** Peru: Thousands of tourists descend each Sunday morning on Pisac's liveliest handicrafts market, which takes over the central plaza and spills across adjoining streets. Many sellers, decked out in the dress typical of their villages, come from remote populations high in the mountains. Village officials lead processions around the square after Mass. Pisac is one of the best spots for colorful Andean textiles, including rugs, alpaca sweaters, and ponchos. Some travelers, though, like **Chinchero** (also in the Sacred Valley) even better; it's slightly more authentic, the artisans (in village dress) themselves sell their goods, and the setting is dramatic. See "The Sacred Valley of the Incas" in chapter 11.

- **Mercado del Puerto,** Montevideo: The Mercado del Puerto (Port Market) takes place afternoons and weekends, letting you sample the flavors of Uruguay, from small empanadas to enormous barbecued meats. Saturday is the best day to visit, when cultural activities accompany the market. See p. 732.

- **Hannsi Centro Artesanal,** El Hatillo (ⓒ **0212/963-7184;** www.hannsi. com.ve): This huge indoor bazaar has everything from indigenous masks to ceramic wares to woven baskets. The selection is broad and covers everything from trinkets to pieces of the finest craftsmanship. Most of the major indigenous groups of Venezuela are represented, including the Yanomami, Guajiro, Warao, Pemón, and Piaroa. See p. 765.

2

Introducing South America

by Shawn Blore, Alexandra de Vries, Eliot Greenspan, Charlie O'Malley,
Jisel Perilla, Neil E. Schlecht & Kristina Schreck

Many outsiders may think of South America as a third-world land of poverty and political instability. And historically, this hasn't been far from the truth. But South America is now beginning to come into its own, both politically and socially. The military dictatorships and guerrilla wars that plagued this region in the 1970s and 1980s are largely things of the past, and a new respect for traditional culture and indigenous people is beginning to ease social tensions—though there's still a long way to go. These social advances are great news for travelers, who are beginning to take notice. The increasing popularity of adventure, archaeological, and eco-tourism has brought waves of new visitors to South America, a trend that looks to continue.

1 South America Past & Present

It has been said that 57 million people were living in the Americas when Columbus landed here in 1492. The arrival of the Europeans in this isolated area of the world brought many problems for the local people. With their gunpowder and horses, the Europeans had a distinct military advantage and were able to destroy powerful empires. They also introduced foreign diseases, such as smallpox, measles, and typhus, which wiped out entire communities. But what a boon for the Spanish crown—explorers discovered precious "jewels" here, including corn, potatoes, chocolate, and, of course, gold and silver. Thus began the age of colonialism. Amazingly, 400 years after the Spanish conquest of South America, millions of indigenous people have managed to hold on to their pre-Columbian past. That's what makes South America so unique. Visitors can explore the ruins of old Inca palaces, hike along Inca trails, witness colorful local celebrations that honor the sun or Pachamama (Mother

Earth), and visit museums filled with amazing artifacts—gold chest plates, alpaca ponchos, tightly woven textiles, hand-carved silver figurines, wonderfully descriptive ceramic jugs—that give testament to the rich cultural heritage that existed here before the arrival of the Spanish.

ARGENTINA
A LOOK AT THE PAST

Several distinct indigenous groups populated the area now called Argentina well before the arrival of the Europeans. The Incas made inroads into the highlands of the northwest. Most other groups were nomadic hunters and fishers, such as those in the Chaco, the Tehuelche of Patagonia, and the Querandí and Puelche (Guennakin) of the pampas. Others (the Diaguitas of the northwest) developed stationary agriculture.

In 1535, Spain—having conquered Peru and being aware of Portugal's presence in Brazil—sent an expedition headed by Pedro de Mendoza to settle the country. Mendoza was initially successful in founding Santa María del Buen Aire, or Buenos Aires (1536), but lack of food proved fatal. Mendoza, discouraged by Indian attacks and mortally ill, sailed for Spain in 1537; he died on the way.

Northern Argentina (including Buenos Aires) was settled mainly by people traveling from the neighboring Spanish colonies of Chile and Peru and the settlement of Asunción in Paraguay. Little migration occurred directly from Spain; the area lacked the attractions of colonies such as Mexico and Peru, with their rich mines, a large supply of Indian slave labor, and easy accessibility. Nevertheless, early communities forged a society dependent on cattle and horses imported from Spain, as well as native crops such as corn and potatoes. Pervasive Roman Catholic missions played a strong role in the colonizing process. The Spanish presence grew over the following centuries, as Buenos Aires became a critical South American port.

The years 1806–07 saw the first stirrings of independence. Buenos Aires fought off two British attacks, in battles known as the Reconquista and the Defensa. Around this time, a civil war had distracted Spain from its colonial holdings, and many Argentine-born Europeans began to debate the idea of self-government in the Buenos Aires *cabildo* (a municipal council with minimal powers, established by colonial rulers). On July 9, 1816, Buenos Aires officially declared its independence from Spain, under the name United Provinces of the Río de la Plata. Several years of hard fighting followed before the Spanish were defeated in northern Argentina. But they remained a threat from their base in Peru until it was liberated by General José de San Martín (to this day a national hero) and Simón Bolívar from 1820 to 1824. Despite the drawing up of a national constitution, the territory that now constitutes modern Argentina was frequently disunited until 1860. The root cause of the trouble, the power struggle between Buenos Aires and the rest of the country, was not settled until 1880, and even after that it continued to cause dissatisfaction.

Conservative forces ruled for much of the late 19th and early 20th century, at one point deposing from power an elected opposition party president through military force. Despite the Conservatives' efforts to suppress new social and political groups—including a growing urban working class—their power began to erode. In 1943, the military overthrew Argentina's constitutional government in a coup led by then army colonel Juan Domingo Perón. Perón became president in a 1946 election and was reelected 6 years later. He is famous (although by no means universally applauded) for his populist governing style, which empowered and economically aided the working class. His wife, Eva Duarte de Perón (popularly known as Evita), herself a controversial historical figure, worked alongside her husband to strengthen the voice of Argentina's women. In 1955, the military deposed Perón, and the following years were marked by economic troubles (partly the result of Perón's expansive government spending) and social unrest, with a surge in terrorist activity by both the left and the right. While Perón was exiled in Spain, his power base in Argentina strengthened, allowing his return to the presidency in 1973. When he died in 1974, his third wife (and vice president), Isabel, replaced him.

The second Perónist era abruptly ended with a March 1976 coup that installed a military junta. The regime of Jorge Rafael Videla carried out a campaign to weed out anybody suspected of having Communist sympathies. Congress was closed, censorship imposed, and unions banned. Over the next 7 years, during this "Process of National Reorganization"—a period known as the Guerra Sucia (Dirty War)—the country witnessed a level of political violence that affects the Argentine psyche today: More than 10,000 intellectuals, artists, activists, and others were tortured or executed by the Argentine government. The mothers of these *desaparecidos* (the disappeared ones) began holding Thursday afternoon vigils in front of the Presidential Palace in Buenos Aires's Plaza de Mayo as a way to call international attention to the plight of the missing. Although the junta was overturned in 1983, the weekly protests continue to this day.

ARGENTINA TODAY

Public outrage over the military's human rights abuses, combined with Argentina's crushing defeat by the British in the 1982 Falkland Islands war, undermined the dictatorship's control of the country. An election in 1983 restored constitutional rule and brought Raúl Alfonsín of the Radical Civic Union to power. In 1989, political power shifted from the Radical Party to the Peronist Party (established by Juan Perón), the first democratic transition in 60 years. Carlos Saúl Ménem, a former governor of a province of little political significance, won the presidency by a surprising margin.

A strong leader, Ménem pursued an ambitious but controversial agenda with the privatization of state-run institutions as its centerpiece. Privatization of inefficient state firms reduced government debt by billions of dollars, and inflation was brought under control. After 10 years as president—and a constitutional amendment that allowed him to seek a second term—Ménem left office. Meanwhile, an alternative to the traditional Perónist and Radical parties, the center-left FREPASO political alliance, had emerged. Radicals and FREPASO formed an alliance for the October 1999 election, and their candidate defeated his Perónist competitor.

President Fernando de la Rua, not as charismatic as his predecessor, was forced to reckon with the recession the economy had suffered since 1998. In an effort to eliminate Argentina's ballooning deficit, de la Rua followed a strict regimen of government spending cuts and tax increases recommended by the International Monetary Fund. However, the tax increase crippled economic growth, and political infighting prevented de la Rua from implementing other needed reforms designed to stimulate the economy. With a heavy drop in production and steep rise in unemployment, an economic crisis loomed.

The meltdown arrived with a run on the peso in December 2001, when investors moved en masse to withdraw their money from Argentine banks. Government efforts to restrict the run by limiting depositor withdrawals fueled anger throughout society, and Argentines took to the streets in sometimes violent demonstrations. De la Rua resigned on December 20, as Argentina faced the worst economic crisis in its history. A series of interim governments did little to improve the situation, as Buenos Aires began to default on its international debts. On January 1, 2002, Peronist President Eduardo Duhalde unlocked the Argentine peso from the dollar, and the currency's value quickly tumbled.

Poverty and emigration followed. Under popular president Nestor Kirchner (known as "The Penguin" for his Patagonian roots), the situation improved. The weak peso caused an export boom; the country is now officially out of default and the economy is expanding. In October 2007, the phenomenally popular Kirchner mysteriously decided not to run for reelection (he could have easily won a second term) and handed the candidacy to his wife, Senator Cristina Fernández de

Kirchner. Her mix of glamour and intelligence completely wooed the electorate and she won by a large majority. With runaway inflation and an energy crisis, it remains to be seen if "Cristina" can keep Argentina on a steady course.

BOLIVIA
A LOOK AT THE PAST

Lake Titicaca, the birthplace of the Incas, is one of Bolivia's most sacred and historic sites. But the history of Bolivia begins thousands of years before the arrival of the Incas. The Tiwanaku culture, which eventually spread to the area from northern Argentina and Chile all the way up to southern Peru, was one of the most highly developed pre-Columbian civilizations. From 1600 B.C. to 100 B.C., the Tiwanaku made the important move of domesticating animals, which allowed them to become more productive farmers. From 100 B.C. to A.D. 900, the arts flourished in the Tiwanaku culture. But it wasn't until A.D. 900 to 1200 that the Tiwanaku became warriors and set out to dominate the area that is now Bolivia. A drought destroyed the heart of the Tiwanaku region in the 13th century, and when the Incas swooped down from Peru around 1450, the Tiwanaku had broken up into small Aymara-speaking communities. The Quechua-speaking Incas dominated the area until the arrival of the Spanish in 1525.

Bolivia proved to be the crown jewel of the Spanish empire. As early as 1545, silver was discovered in southern Bolivia. Over the next 200 years, Potosí, home of Cerro Rico (the "rich hill," which was the source of all the silver), became one of the largest and wealthiest cities in the world. Getting rich quickly was the name of the game for most European settlers in Bolivia. Other than the development of Potosí and transportation systems to deliver the silver to the rest of the world, much of Bolivia remained neglected.

Indigenous men were forced to work in the mines, often for no pay. This was only the beginning of a system of inequality and sharp class distinctions that to this day exist in Bolivia.

Not surprisingly, the first rumblings for independence arose in the area of Chuquisaca (present-day Sucre, which was then the administrative capital of Potosí). The first revolutionary uprising took place in Chuquisaca in 1809, but Bolivia did not win independence until August 6, 1825.

The age of the republic did not bring much glory to Bolivia. In the next 100-plus years, Bolivia lost its seacoast to Chile in the War of the Pacific (1879–83); in 1903, after a conflict with Brazil, Bolivia was forced to give up its access to the Acre River, which had become a valuable source of rubber; and in the Chaco War (1932–35), Bolivia surrendered the Chaco region, which was believed to be rich in oil, to Paraguay. The high price of silver in the late 19th century and the discovery of tin in the early 20th century kept Bolivia afloat.

After the Chaco War, which drained Bolivia's resources and caused great loss of life, the indigenous people began to distrust the elite ruling classes. In December 1943, the proworker National Revolutionary Movement (MNR) organized a revolt in protest of the abysmal working conditions and inflation. This was the beginning of the MNR's reign of power. In 1951, the MNR candidate, Víctor Paz Estenssoro, was elected president, but a military junta denied him power. In 1952, the MNR, with the help of peasants and miners, staged a successful revolution. The MNR managed to implement sweeping land reforms and nationalize the tin holdings of the wealthy. Under the reign of Estenssoro, the government also introduced universal suffrage and improved the educational system.

The MNR managed to hold on to power until a coup in 1964. For the next 20 years, Bolivia became a pawn in the Cold War between the United States and the Soviet Union. A series of military revolts brought power to both leftist and right-wing regimes. In 1971, Hugo Bánzer Suárez became president with the support of the MNR and instituted a pro-U.S. policy. In 1974, because of growing opposition, he set up an all-military government. He was forced to resign in 1978. In the coming years, a series of different leaders were unable to deal with the problems of high inflation, growing social unrest, increased drug trafficking, and the collapse of the tin market. Víctor Paz Estenssoro returned to power in 1985. He kept the military at bay and was able to create economic stability. Finally, in 1989, Jaime Paz Zamora, a moderate, left-leaning politician, was elected president; he worked to stamp out domestic terrorism, bringing a semblance of peace to the country. In 1993, a mining engineer, Gonzalo Sánchez de Lozada, was elected president. He worked successfully to reprivatize public business, an effort that actually helped the economy. In 1997, Hugo Bánzer Suárez returned to power. He worked with the United States to eradicate coca growing, with much opposition from local farm workers. The late 1990s marked another period of social unrest for Bolivia, with frequent strikes that paralyzed the nation.

BOLIVIA TODAY

President Gonzalo Sánchez de Lozada was elected president in 2002, but his cooperation with the United States in eradicating coca growing (and thus causing much unemployment) turned most of the country against him. When he signed a deal to export Bolivian gas to the United States and Mexico and transport it via Chile, he sparked a tinderbox of protest among the nation's indigenous people. In late 2003, the anger erupted in violent demonstrations in La Paz and El Alta, the neighboring city. Thousands of peasants flocked to the city from rural areas to participate in the revolt. The situation deteriorated quickly and more than 70 people were killed by the police. On October 17, 2003, more than a quarter of a million protesters rallied in La Paz's Plaza de San Francisco, near the Presidential Palace. Gonzalo Sánchez de Lozada stepped down and fled to Miami; Vice President Carlos Mesa was appointed president. Things returned to normal very quickly but again erupted in early 2005. The gas issue has polarized the nation, with the poorer indigenous people accusing the European elite of selling their country's valuable resources. In June 2005, Mesa was forced to resign and Supreme Court judge Eduardo Rodríguez was placed as head of an interim government. In December 2005, former coco farmer Evo Morales was declared Bolivia's first indigenous president. Feared by conservatives and pushed on by radicals, Morales has played a precarious balancing act. A new constitutional assembly has caused uproar in the eastern provinces, and nationalization of the country's gas reserves has scared off foreign investors. A declaration of autonomy by the eastern (richer) provinces has further polarized a society that some say is near a breaking point. It remains to be seen whether Morales can keep both sides happy and his country together.

BRAZIL
A LOOK AT THE PAST

At the time of the Europeans' arrival in 1500, there were between one million and eight million indigenous people in Brazil, speaking nearly 170 different languages. The Europeans were seeking paubrasil, a type of wood that could be processed to yield a rich red dye. Coastal Indians were induced to cut and sell timber in return for metal implements such as axes. It was an efficient system, so much so that within a little more than a generation, the trees—which had by then given their name to the country—were all but nonexistent.

But the Portuguese colony soon found a better source of income in sugar, the cash crop of the 16th century. Sugar cane grew excellently in the tropical climate of northeast Brazil. Turning that cane into sugar, however, was backbreaking work, and the Portuguese were critically short of labor. So the Portuguese began to import slaves from West Africa. Brazil was soon one leg on a lucrative maritime triangle: guns and supplies from Portugal to Africa, slaves from Africa to Brazil, sugar from Brazil back to Europe. Within a few decades, colonial cities such as Salvador and Olinda were fabulously rich.

Gold was soon uncovered in what would later be Minas Girais, while diamonds were found in the interior in Bahia. In addition to the miners, the other main beneficiary of the Minas gold rush was Rio de Janeiro, the major trans-shipment point for gold and supplies. In recognition of this, in 1762, the colonial capital was officially transferred to Rio. It would likely have remained little more than a backwater colonial capital had it not been for Napoléon. In 1807, having overrun most of western Europe, the French emperor set his sights on Portugal. Faced with the imminent conquest of Lisbon, Portuguese Prince Regent João (later King João VI) fled to his ships, opting to relocate himself and his entire court to Brazil. In 1808, the king and 15,000 of his nobles, knights, and courtiers arrived in the rather raw town of Rio. When the king returned to Portugal in 1821, Brazilians—among them the king's 23-year-old son, Pedro—were outraged at the prospect of being returned to the status of mere colony. In January 1822, Pedro announced he was remaining in Brazil. Initially, he planned on ruling as prince regent, but as the year wore on, it became clear that Lisbon was not interested in compromise, so on September 7, 1822, Pedro declared Brazil independent and himself Emperor Pedro I.

Brazil in this period was a deeply conservative country, with a few very wealthy plantation owners, a tiny professional class, and a great mass of slaves to cultivate sugar or Brazil's new cash crop, coffee. Though the antislavery movement was growing worldwide, Brazil's conservative landowning class was determined to hold on to its slaves at all costs. In the 1850s, under heavy pressure from Britain, Brazil finally moved to halt the importation of slaves from Africa, though slavery wasn't officially outlawed until 1888. Seeking a new source of labor, in 1857 Brazil opened itself up to immigration. Thousands poured in, mostly Germans and Italians, settling themselves in the hilly, temperate lands in the south of Brazil.

When reformist army officers and other liberals staged a coup in 1889, the 57-year rule of Pedro II (son of the first emperor) came to an end. The republic that took its place had many of the same ills of the old regime. Corruption was endemic, rebellions a regular occurrence. Finally, in 1930, reformist army officers staged a bloody coup. After several days of fighting, a military-backed regime took charge, putting an end to the Old Republic and ushering in the 15-year reign of the fascinating, maddening figure of Getúlio Vargas.

Vargas began his time in office as a populist, legalizing unions and investing in hundreds of projects designed to foster the industrial development of the country. When the workers nonetheless looked set to reject him in renewed elections, Vargas tore up the constitution and instituted a quasi-fascist dictatorship, complete with a propaganda ministry that celebrated every action of the glorious leader Getúlio. In the early 1940s, when the United States made it clear that Brazil had better cease its flirtation with Germany, Vargas dumped his fascist posturing, declared war on the Axis powers, and sent 20,000 Brazilian troops to take part in the invasion of Italy. When the troops came home at war's end, the contradiction between the fight for freedom abroad and the dictatorship at home proved too much even for Vargas's political skills. In 1945, the army removed Getúlio from power in a very quiet coup. In 1950, he returned, this time as the democratically elected president, but his reign was a disaster, and in 1954, he committed suicide.

In 1956, Juscelino Kubitschek (known as JK) took office, largely on the strength of a single bold promise: Within 4 years, he would transfer the capital from Rio de Janeiro to an entirely new city located somewhere in Brazil's vast interior. The site chosen in Brazil's high interior plateau (the *sertão*) was hundreds of miles from the nearest paved road, thousands from the nearest airport. Undaunted, JK assembled a team of Brazil's top modernist architects—among the best in the world at the time—and 4 years later, the new capital of Brasília was complete.

Democracy, unfortunately, did not fare well in the arid soil of the *sertão*. In 1964, the army took power in a coup, ushering in an ever more repressive military dictatorship that would last for another 20 years. For a time, no one complained much. Thanks to massive government investment, the economy boomed. São Paulo, which had been little more than a market town in the 1940s, exploded in size and population, surpassing Rio to become the heart of Brazil's new manufacturing economy. These were the days of the Brazilian "economic miracle."

In the early '70s, however, it became clear that much of the economic "miracle" had been financed on easy international loans, much of that invested in dubious development projects (roads that disappeared into the forest, nuclear power plants that never functioned) or channeled directly into the pockets of various well-connected generals. The international banks now wanted their money back, with interest. As discontent with the regime spread, the military reacted with ever-stronger repression.

The 1980s were perhaps Brazil's worst decade. Inflation ran rampant, while growth was next to nonexistent. Austerity measures imposed by the International Monetary Fund left governments with little money for basic infrastructure—much less social services—and in big cities such as Rio and São Paulo, *favelas* (shantytowns) spread while crime spiraled out of control.

In the midst of this mess, the army began a transition to democracy. In 1988, in the first direct presidential election in over 2 decades, Brazilians elected a good-looking millionaire named Fernando Collor de Mello. It proved to be a bad move, for Collor was soon found lining his pockets with government cash. The civilian government did prove capable of legally forcing him from office, however, paving the way in 1992 for the election of Fernando Henrique Cardoso.

Though an academic Marxist for much of his career, once in office FHC proved to be a cautious centrist. In his 8 years in office, he managed to reign in inflation, bring some stability to the Brazilian currency, and begin a modest extension of social services to Brazil's many poor.

The main opposition throughout this period was the Workers Party (PT), led by Luiz Inácio Lula da Silva, a charismatic trade unionist with a personal rags-to-riches story. Born into poverty in the Northeast, Lula, as he is usually known, left school to work as a shoeshine boy, got a job in a São Paulo factory, joined the metal workers' union, and began to get involved in politics. During the waning days of Brazil's dictatorship, he and others formed the Workers Party and only just lost Brazil's first democratic election in 1988. Lula persevered, however and, finally, in 2002, in his fourth attempt, was elected Brazilian president, the first democratically elected leftist to hold power in Brazil.

BRAZIL TODAY

Hopes for Lula's first term in office were enormous. Confounding expectations of financial markets and right-wing critics, Lula in office proved to be an economic moderate, continuing the tight-money policy of his predecessor. But to the disappointment of his supporters on the left, Lula also proved to be a poor and often absent administrator. Many of the hoped-for reforms—to the distribution of land, to access to education and healthcare, to environmental policy—were never enacted. As he approaches the end of his first term, his government has been plagued with scandal. Allegations of illegal campaign contributions and diversion of government funds has led to the resignation of a half-dozen of Lula's chief ministers.

In the cities, things have certainly improved. Governments have paid off the worst of the '80s debts and have funds available to spend on increased policing, better street lighting, and on extending services such as sewers, water, and schooling to urban slum dwellers. In the shantytowns of Rio and São Paulo, gangs remain stubbornly entrenched, but the major cities of Brazil are cleaner and safer than they've been in a generation. Though they're a few years yet from matching post-Guiliani Manhattan for safety, Brazil's cities are far and away superior when its comes to sheer joie de vivre.

CHILE
A LOOK AT THE PAST

Chile's history as a nation began rather inconspicuously on the banks of the Mapoche River on February 12, 1541, when the Spanish conquistador Pedro de Valdivia founded Santiago de la Nueva Extremadura. At the time, several distinct indigenous groups called Chile home, including the more advanced northern tribes (which had already been conquered by the Incas), the fierce Mapuche warriors of the central region, and the nomadic hunting and gathering tribes of Patagonia. In Spain's eyes, Chile did not hold much interest because of its lack of riches such as gold, and the country remained somewhat of a colonial backwater until the country's independence in 1818, which was led by Bernardo O'Higgins, the son of an Irish immigrant. Spain did, however, see to the development of a feudal landowning system whereby prominent Spaniards were issued a large tract of land and an *encomienda,* or a group of Indian slaves, that the landowner was charged with caring for and converting to Christianity. Thus rose Chile's traditional and nearly self-supporting hacienda, known as a *latifundio,* as well as a rigid class system that defined the population.

Chile experienced an economic boom in the early 20th century in the form of nitrate mining in the northern desert, a region that had been confiscated from Peru and Bolivia after the War of the Pacific in 1883. Mining is still a huge economic force, especially copper mining, and Chile's abundant natural resources have fostered industries in petroleum, timber, fishing, agriculture, tourism, and wine.

Chile enjoyed a politically democratic government until the onset of a vicious military dictatorship, led by General Augusto Pinochet, who took power from 1973 to 1990. In 1970, voters narrowly elected the controversial Dr. Salvador Allende as Chile's first socialist president. Allende vowed to improve the lives of Chile's poorer citizens by instituting a series of radical changes that might redistribute the nation's lopsided wealth. Although the first year showed promising signs, Allende's reforms ultimately sent the country spiraling into economic ruin. On September 11, 1973, military forces led by General Augusto Pinochet and supported by the U.S. government toppled Allende's government with a dramatic coup d'état, during which Allende took his own life. Upper-class Chileans celebrated the coup as an economic and political salvation, but nobody was prepared for the brutal repression that would haunt Chile for the next 17 years. Most disturbing were the series of tortures and "disappearances" of an estimated 3,000 of Pinochet's political adversaries, including activists, journalists, professors, and any other "subversive" threats. Thousands more fled the country.

Following a "yes" or "no" plebiscite in 1988, Chileans voted to end the dictatorship, and since that year, the country has put great effort into establishing a solid democracy. Today the country is considered the most politically stable in Latin America. Pinochet spent the next 2 decades living a cushy life until a banking scandal and judicial inquiries into human rights abuses forced him to spend his last years under house arrest until his death in 2006. Shortly before that, Chile elected its first female president Michelle Bachelet. The fact that Bachelet was tortured under Pinochet showed just how far the country had come.

Today the Chilean economy is one of the strongest in Latin America. It is rich in natural resources such as copper, forestry, salmon harvesting, and agriculture, and now tourism is becoming an economic heavyweight. In spite of one of the lowest rates of unemployment in Latin America and a relative lack of corruption, Chile still has far to go to solve social problems such as poverty, a well-defined class system, and inadequate education for the majority of its children.

CHILE TODAY

Today, the Chilean economy is considered one of the (if not *the*) strongest economies in Latin America. Chile still suffers from an unhealthy dose of classism; however, the country boasts a larger middle class than its neighbors Peru and Bolivia, with about 30% of the population living under the poverty level. Politically, in January 2006, Chile made history by electing Michelle Bachelet its first female president.

COLOMBIA
A LOOK AT THE PAST

Colombia has been inhabited for about 12,000 years. Unlike the Inca to the south and the Maya to the north, who developed vast civilizations, the dozens of indigenous groups that inhabited Colombia formed relatively small hunter-gatherer societies. The most notable of these societies were the Muisca, who inhabited the inner Andean region in and around what is today Bogotá, and the Tayronas, who inhabited the Atlantic Coast.

The Spaniards were able to pacify the indigenous peoples of Colombia fairly easily. Alonso de Ojeda was the first European to set foot in Colombia, in 1499, followed in 1525 by Rodrigo de Bastidas. On the northern coast, he founded Santa Marta, Colombia's oldest city. The important port city of Cartagena was begun in 1533 by Pedro de Heredia, a few years before Jiménez de Quesada founded the modern-day capital of Bogotá in 1538. Because Colombia never had a large number of indigenous peoples—and many of them were wiped out by disease after the arrival of the Spaniards—the slave trade began in the late 1500s. Millions of Africans arrived in Colombia via Cartagena, one of Latin America's most important slave-trading posts. For about the next 300 years, Spain ruled Colombia, which was then called the Presidencia del Nuevo Reino de

Granada, an area that included modern-day Colombia, Venezuela, and Panama.

Colombia's struggle for independence officially began in 1781 with the Revolución Comunera in the small town of El Socorro. Independence hero Simón Bolívar began his struggle against Spain in 1812, but didn't gain Colombia's independence until the final battle of Boyacá, on August 7, 1819. Thus, Bolívar became Colombia's first president.

Unfortunately, Colombia's independence didn't mean the end of bloodshed. In 1849, the formation of the Liberal and Conservative parties laid the foundation for the conflict that would—and still does—continue to haunt the country. Between 1849 and 1948, nearly half a million Colombians were killed in various insurrections pitting Liberals against Conservatives.

But it wasn't until 1948 that things really got ugly, with La Violencia, a violent time of upheaval that claimed the lives of another 500,000 Colombians in a decade. For several years, there was a period of relative peace, but in 1964, the Revolutionary Armed Forces of Colombia (FARC) was founded, pitting insurgent communists against the ruling elite. Although originally a political organization, the FARC, and later the National Liberation Army (ELN) and the M-19 guerilla groups, soon found their way into the Colombian cocaine trade, resulting in an even greater degree of violence and terrorism. Meanwhile, wealthy land owners, the military, and even government officials encouraged the organization of right-wing paramilitary units, armed groups whose aim was to fight the leftist guerilas. However, like the guerilas, the paramilitaries soon became involved in the drug trade, resulting in frequent, bloody battles between these two factions. Paramilitary power reached its pinnacle during the Pablo Escobar years (1980s and early 1990s), when Escobar and the

paramilitaries more or less controlled Colombia through frequent bombings, kid-nappings, and assassinations.

In 2002, conservative hard-liner Alvaro Uribe won the presidency, vowing to eliminate the guerillas and, through a peace accord, demobilize the paramilitaries.

COLOMBIA TODAY

True to his word, President Alvaro Uribe has restored much order in Colombia. In fact, an entire generation of Colombians is experiencing peace for the first time. Once holding the dubious title of being the most dangerous country in the world, President Uribe's government has reduced kidnapping and murder rates by more than 50%. Leftist guerillas have dramatically loosened their grip on Colombian politics and have been pushed out of the cities. (Two of the FARC's seven-member secretariat were killed in a single week in early 2008.) Once afraid to drive long distances because of kidnappings, Colombians are now taking to the road in record number as travel becomes safe again.

But it's not all good news: President Uribe's critics accuse him of government corruption and involvement with the paramilitaries. And if most Colombians seem to have accepted that Uribe has some paramilitary ties, the majority don't seem too bothered by this fact: Uribe's approval rating reached a record 84% in March 2008. Indeed, it's hard to think of another country so enamored of its president.

Like most of Latin America, Colombia continues to be a country divided by class. Despite attracting ever-more international investment, the gap between the rich and poor has never been greater. Forty percent of Colombians live in absolute poverty, many without life's basic necessities. A small minority of Colombians continue to control most of the country's wealth and resources.

ECUADOR
A LOOK AT THE PAST

Before the Spanish arrived in Ecuador in 1533, a group of diverse cultures lived in various areas throughout the country. Many of these cultures, including the Valdivia, Machalilla, and Chorrera, may not have left any written records, but the highly sophisticated pottery, beautifully designed artwork, and gold masks that have been unearthed in Ecuador prove that these cultures were highly developed. By the 16th century, the Incas had conquered the highland areas of the country of Ecuador. At its height, the Inca Empire encompassed an estimated 15 million people, belonging to roughly 100 ethnic or linguistic communities, and covered an area of over 6,000 sq. km (2,300 sq. miles), within which were more than 25,000km (15,500 miles) of roads. Cuenca, in southern Ecuador, was the second-most important city in the Inca Empire. In 1526, when the Inca leader Huayna Capac died, he divided the empire between his two sons. Huáscar gained control of Cusco and Peru, while Atahualpa inherited control of Cuenca and Ecuador. This split led to a bloody war, which weakened both sides. In part, because of this conflict, when the Spanish arrived in the mid–16th century, they had little trouble defeating the Incas.

Ecuador's indigenous cultures had a hard time under Spanish rule. Newly introduced diseases decimated the local population, and the Spanish system of *encomienda* (forced labor) broke the spirit and the health of the local people. Ecuador wasn't rich in natural resources and therefore wasn't of great value to the Spanish. In the 300 years before independence, Ecuador was alternately governed by the viceroyalty of Peru to the south and the viceroyalty of New Granada in Bogotá to the north.

Ecuador declared independence in 1820, but the independence forces weren't able to defeat the Spanish royalists until the Battle of Pichincha on May 24, 1822. At that time, Ecuador became a part of Gran Colombia, which consisted of Colombia and Venezuela. In 1830, Ecuador seceded from Gran Colombia and became its own republic. The rest of the 19th century was marked by political instability. Conflicts flared between the Conservatives, led by Gabriel García Moreno, and the Liberals, led by Eloy Alfaro. The Conservatives sided with the Catholic Church and Ecuadorians of privilege, while the Liberals fought for a secular government and social reforms.

At the end of the 19th century, Ecuador was getting rich off cocoa exports, and the economy was booming. Later in the early 20th century, when the demand for cocoa decreased, political unrest ensued. In 1925, the military seized power from the former procapitalist leaders. The 1930s were a time of uncertainty for Ecuador: From 1931 to 1940 a total of 14 different presidents spent time at the helm. In 1941, war erupted between Ecuador and Peru over land in the Amazon basin region. In an attempt to settle the dispute, Ecuador signed the Protocol of Rio de Janeiro in 1942 and surrendered much of the disputed land to Peru.

The post–World War II era was a time of prosperity for Ecuador. The country became one of the world's leaders in banana exports. From 1948 to 1960, there were three freely elected presidents who were all able to serve their full terms. In 1952, President José María Velasco implemented social reforms, including improvements in both the schools and the public highways. But in 1960, when Velasco was again elected president, he was faced with a failing economy, and he was unable to hold on to power. During the next 10 years, a series of military juntas controlled the country.

The economy rebounded in the 1970s. Ecuador became the second-largest oil-producing nation in South America, after Venezuela. The oil boom led to an increase in public spending and industrialization. But by the 1980s, when the oil bubble began to burst, the country was again faced with serious economic troubles, including inflation and an insurmountable international debt. In 1986, the price of oil collapsed, and in 1987, an earthquake partially destroyed one of Ecuador's major pipelines.

Rodrigo Borja came to power in 1988. In an attempt to alleviate his country's problems, he increased the price of oil while severely cutting back on public spending. But that wasn't enough—inflation soared, and civil unrest increased. In 1992, in a conciliatory move, the government ceded a large region of the rainforest to the indigenous people. In 1995, Ecuador again disputed its border with Peru in the Amazon area; it wasn't until 1998 that it finally settled with Peru and secured its access to the Amazon. The 3-year war proved to be a drain on the economy. In 1997, a national protest, with overwhelming support of all the Ecuadorian people, succeeded in ousting the corrupt President Abdalá Bucaram. The national congress appointed a new president and reformed the constitution. But again, low oil prices and the devastating effects of El Niño brought the economy to its knees.

ECUADOR TODAY

In recent years, the instability of Ecuador's executive branch has drawn international attention. Between 1996 and 2006, seven presidents attempted to govern the nation. They all failed to ameliorate the political volatility, either because of a hostile Congress, a military coup d'état, or sheer incompetence.

On July 12, 1998, the mayor of Quito, Jamil Mahuad, was elected president. His biggest success was negotiating a peace treaty with Peru over the country's borders in the Amazon, but he was unable to turn the economy around. His popularity reached a low point on January 9, 2000, when he announced his decision to eliminate the sucre, the national currency, and replace it with the U.S. dollar. On January 21, 2000, the military and police "failed" to quell chaotic nationwide protests. Mahuad was forced to resign, and his vice president, Gustavo Noboa, became president. Noboa continued on the course of dollarization, and in September 2000, the U.S. dollar became the country's official currency. This move helped to decrease the country's international debt, but it has never really been able to stem inflation.

In April 2005, President Lucio Gutiérrez was fired by Ecuador's congress for interfering with the Supreme Court. He was granted asylum in Colombia and Alfredo Palacio became president. In October 2005, Gutiérrez returned to Quito and was arrested upon his arrival.

In 2006, Ecuador went to the polls once more and elected Rafael Correa. The eighth president in 11 years, Correa is a center-left former economist who considers himself a personal friend of Venezuela's Hugo Chávez. He is making waves early on in his presidency, and in April 2007 he was rewarded with a victory in a public referendum allowing him to call a Constituent Assembly to rewrite the national constitution.

Despite the recent upswing in international petroleum prices, the gap between rich and poor remains wide. Estimates vary as to what percentage of the population lives below the poverty line, but most agree the rate is at least 40% and perhaps as high as 70%.

PARAGUAY
A LOOK AT THE PAST

Pre-Columbian Paraguay was a rich tribal patchwork with mostly Guarani settled in the south and a band of hunter-gatherers known as Aché inhabiting the subtropical areas that now border Brazil. The Chaco contained a diverse variety of people, known as Abipones, Tobas, Matacas, and Mbayás. Predominately peaceful people, they nevertheless often fought amongst themselves and resisted strongly any Spanish incursions. Indian hostility to foreign settlements continued into the 20th century.

Alejo Garcia was the first European to enter the area in 1524 from the Brazilian side. His discovery of silver in the Andes led to the naming of Río de la Plata (Silver River). Pedro Mendoza, fleeing Indian persecution in Buenos Aires, founded the first settlement at Asunción in 1527. He formed an alliance with the Guaraní and the 350 Spanish men assimilated into Guaraní culture, though eventually the Europeans became the dominant political and economic force.

The arrival of the Jesuits in the late 16th century lead to a huge social experiment, the remains of which can be seen today. The Jesuits had less success in the north where the non-Guarani tribes resisted strongly and launched raids on the settlements. The Jesuits were eventually expelled by the Spanish in 1767 and the crown lost interest in the Chaco when they realized it held neither gold nor silver or a transit route to Bolivia.

In fact the Spanish lost interest in the area completely and offered little resistance when independence was declared in 1811. Paraguay's first dictator thus emerged and Dr José Gaspar Rodríguez de Francia ruled the country with an iron fist and a strong touch of paranoia from 1814 to 1840. Such was his unpopularity that 30 years after his death, his enemies dug up his remains and threw them into the Río Paraguay.

Carlos Antonio López then lead the country for 20 years and ushered in a period of development, prosperity, and military might. This was all squandered by his son Francisco Solano López and his Irish mistress Eliza Lynch when they took power in 1862 and lead the country into a disastrous war with Brazil, Argentina, and Uruguay that became known as the War of the Triple Alliance. The result was a catastrophe for Paraguay, with a paranoid and bloodthirsty Solano López meeting his end in the northern jungle and the country decimated; half its population was lost to war, famine, and disease and 150,000 sq. km (58,500 sq. miles) of territory was lost forever.

A period of tumultuous politics followed with the opposing Colorado and Liberal parties engaging in a disordered tug of war for power right up to modern times. The economy slowly recovered with European and Argentine immigration. Agricultural was revived, sovereignty reestablished, and important reforms made.

Then the Chaco War erupted in 1932—a bloody squabble with Bolivia over the piece of Northern territory that many thought may hold oil—including Standard Oil and Shell Oil who were both accused of funding the opposing sides in return for exploration rights. In the end it proved a futile exercise and the area remains populated by isolated Indian tribes and self-sufficient Mennonite communities.

Colorado and Liberal rivalry continued, often taking on the characteristics of a full scale civil war. Then a military coup in 1954 ushered in the 35-year dictatorship of General Alfredo Stroessner. Brutal, corrupt, and repressive, it was not until another coup by General Andrés Rodríguez in 1989 and elections in 1991 that Paraguayans could eventually claim to have a "normal," fully fledged democracy.

Juan Carlos Wasmosy became Paraguay's first elected civilian president in 1993. The military menace remained, however, in the shape of General Lino

Oviedo. His threat of a coup landed him in jail, but he gained immediate release when his political ally Raúl Cubas won the 1998 election. The pardon caused public disgust followed by outrage at the assassination of critic and Vice President Luis María Argaña in 1999. Cubas and Oviedo eventually joined Stroessner in exile in Brazil and Luis Angel González Macchi assumed power. His initial popularity was soon tarnished with allegations of corruption, not helped by the fact that he drove a stolen BMW.

PARAGUAY TODAY

Economic mismanagement, inefficiency, and rampant corruption still dog Paraguayan politics. The Colorado party has remained the dominant political force but has at least maintained a semblance of democracy. General Lino Oviedo was finally jailed in 2004 for undermining the administration. Nicanor Duarte Frutos was elected president in 2003 and his promise of fighting corruption and reforming the political system are slowly bearing fruit, but with much resistance from vested interests. Duarte Frutos hopes to win re-election in 2008.

PERU
A LOOK AT THE PAST

Over the course of nearly 15 centuries, pre-Inca cultures settled along the Peruvian coast and highlands. By the 1st century B.C., during what is known as the Formative or Initial Period, Andean society had created sophisticated irrigation canals and produced its first textiles and decorative ceramics. Another important advance was labor specialization, aided in large part by the development of a hierarchical society.

Though Peru is likely to be forever synonymous with the Incas, who built the spectacular city of Machu Picchu high in the Andes, that society, in place when the Spanish conquistadors arrived at the end of the 15th century, was merely the last in a long line of pre-Columbian cultures. The Inca Empire (1200–1532) was short lived, but it remains the best documented of all Peruvian civilizations. The Incas' dominance was achieved through a formidable organization and highly developed economic system. They laid a vast network of roadways, nearly 30,000km (18,600 miles) total across the difficult territory of the Andes, connecting cities, farming communities, and religious sites. Their agricultural techniques were exceedingly skilled and efficient, and their stonemasonry remains unparalleled.

By the 1520s, the Spanish conquistadors had reached South America. Francisco Pizarro led an expedition along Peru's coast in 1528. Impressed with the riches of the Inca Empire, he returned to Spain and succeeded in raising money and recruiting men for a return expedition. In 1532, Pizarro made his return to Peru overland from Ecuador. After founding the first Spanish city in Peru, San Miguel de Piura, near the Ecuadorian border, he advanced upon the northern highland city of Cajamarca, an Inca stronghold. There, a small number of Spanish troops—about 180 men and 30 horses—captured the Inca emperor Atahualpa. The emperor promised to pay a king's ransom of gold and silver for his release, but the Spaniards, having received warning of an advancing Inca army, executed the emperor in 1533. It was a catastrophic blow to the Inca Empire.

Two years later, Pizarro founded the coastal city of Lima, which became capital of the new colony, the viceroyalty of Peru. The Spanish crown appointed Spanish-born viceroys the rulers of Peru, but Spaniards battled among themselves for control of Peru's riches, and the remaining Incas continued to battle the conquistadors. Pizarro was assassinated in 1541, and the indigenous insurrection ended with the beheading of Manco Inca, the last of the Inca leaders, in 1544. The

Inca Tupac Amaru led a rebellion in 1572, but he met the same fate. Over the next 2 centuries, Lima gained in power and prestige at the expense of the old Inca capital of Cusco and became the foremost colonial city of the Andean nations.

By the 19th century, grumbling over high taxes and burdensome Spanish controls grew in Peru. After liberating Chile and Argentina, José de San Martín set his sights north on Lima in 1821 and declared it an independent nation the same year. Simón Bolívar, the other hero of independence on the continent, came from the other direction. His successful campaigns in Venezuela and Colombia led him south to Ecuador and finally to Peru. Peru won its independence after crucial battles in late 1824.

After several military regimes, Peru finally returned to civilian rule in 1895. Landowning elites dominated this new "Aristocratic Republic." In 1941, the country went to war with Ecuador over a border dispute (just one of several long-running border conflicts). Though the 1942 Treaty of Rio de Janeiro granted the area north of the Marañón River to Peru, Ecuador would continue to claim the territory, part of the Amazon basin, until the end of the 20th century.

Peru's recent political history has been a turbulent mix of military dictatorships, coups d'état, and several disastrous civilian governments, engendering a near-continual cycle of instability. The country's hyperinflation, nationwide strikes, and two guerrilla movements—the Maoist Sendero Luminoso (Shining Path) and the Tupac Amaru Revolutionary Movement (MRTA)—produced violence and terror throughout the late 1980s and early 1990s. Meanwhile, Peru's role on the production end of the international cocaine trade grew exponentially.

With the economy in ruins and the government in chaos, Alberto Fujimori, the son of Japanese immigrants, became president in 1990. Fujimori promised to fix the ailing economy and root out terrorist guerrillas, and in 1992, his government succeeded in arresting key members of both the MRTA and the Shining Path (catapulting the president to unprecedented popularity). Fujimori's strong-arm tactics became suddenly authoritarian, however, shutting down Congress in 1992, suspending the constitution, and decreeing an emergency government (which he effectively ruled as dictator). Still Fujimori was reelected in 1995.

Most international observers denounced Peru's 2000 presidential election results, which were announced after Fujimori's controversial runoff with Alejandro Toledo, a newcomer from a poor Indian family. Public outcry forced Fujimori to call new elections, but he escaped into exile in Japan and resigned the presidency in late 2000 after a corruption scandal involving his shadowy intelligence chief, Vladimiro Montesinos. Toledo, a former shoeshine boy and son of an Andean sheep herder who went on to teach at Harvard and become a World Bank economist, won the election and became president in July 2001, formally accepting the post at Machu Picchu.

PERU TODAY

Peru remains a society dominated by elites. Toledo had labeled himself an "Indian rebel with a cause," alluding to his intent to recognize and his support for the nation's Native Andean populations, or *cholos*. Yet Toledo's once-hopeful program *Perú Posible* did not achieve the results Peruvians had hoped for. Toledo's government was mired in corruption and nepotism. Farmers and teachers on strike repeatedly paralyzed Peru, forcing Toledo to declare a national state of emergency. Toledo sadly limped to the end of his term in 2006.

The Peruvian economy has expanded steadily in the last decade. Former president Alan García—who had also fled Peru after a disastrous term in the

1980s—improbably returned from exile and won the presidency in 2006. A one-time populist, García has positioned himself as a centrist, seeking to put a clamp on inflation and pursuing free-market policies. Most notably, he pushed for a free trade agreement with the United States, a treaty that was ratified by the U.S. Congress in December 2007. The Peruvian economy recorded a growth rate of 8.3% in 2007, a 12-year high, and to date the García presidency has been largely stable and peaceful.

URUGUAY
A LOOK AT THE PAST

In 1516, a surprised Spanish sailor discovered the area of what would become Uruguay and was followed by Ferdinand Magellan, who in 1520 anchored outside present-day Montevideo. Despite the Spaniards' success in making the journey from home, they were less successful settling in the area, due to resistance from the Charrúa Indians who inhabited the land. Not until the early 17th century, as Spain competed with Portugal for South American territory, did Spanish colonization begin to take hold. Colonia del Sacramento was founded by the Portuguese in 1680. Not to be outdone, the Spanish responded by establishing Montevideo after the turn of the century.

Uruguay's history until the beginning of the 19th century was marked by colonial struggle for the Argentina-Brazil-Uruguay region. In 1811, José Gervasio Artigas initiated a revolt against Spain. The war lasted until 1828, when Uruguay earned its independence from Brazil, to which it had been annexed by the Portuguese. Argentine troops assisted the Uruguayan fighters in defeating the Brazilians, and Uruguay adopted its first constitution by 1830. Political instability dominated the rest of the century, as large numbers of immigrants arrived from Europe. By 1910, the population reached one million.

Uruguay experienced significant political, economic, and social progress under the two presidencies of José Batlle y Ordoñez, who in the early 20th century created what many considered a model social-welfare state. Life seemed to be getting better and better for Uruguayans, who achieved their first World Cup victory in 1930 and again in 1950. By the 1960s, however, Uruguay's charmed reputation as the "Switzerland of South America" was shattered by corruption, high unemployment, and runaway inflation. The instability of Uruguay's economy paved the way for military government, which seized control in 1973 and was responsible for the detention of more than 60,000 citizens during its time in power.

Civilians resumed control of the government in 1984, when Colorado Party leader Julio María Sanguinetti won the presidency. His tenure in office was focused on national reconciliation, the consolidation of democratic governance, and the stabilization of the economy. Violations under the military regime were controversially pardoned in order to promote reconciliation, and a general amnesty was given to military leaders charged with human rights abuses.

URUGUAY TODAY

The National Party's Luis Alberto Lacalle held the presidency from 1990 to 1995, during which time he reformed the economy in favor of trade liberalization and export promotion. He brought Uruguay into the Southern Cone Common Market (Mercosur) in 1991 and privatized inefficient state industries. Julio María Sanguinetti was reelected in 1995, continuing Uruguay's economic reforms and improving education, public safety, and the electoral system. The economy flagged at the end of the century, exacerbated by the Argentine economic meltdown in 2001. Tourism plummeted a staggering 90%. Currency devaluation followed, and with it a slow recovery. Uruguay's first socialist president, Tabaré Vázquez, took power in March 2005, ushering in a more stable and prosperous period. Uruguay's future looks to be brightening; the only blot is an environmental dispute with Argentina over two multi-billion-dollar paper mills that the Argentines say will pollute the River Plate. The argument has led to numerous border closures between both countries and looks set to continue for some time.

VENEZUELA
A LOOK AT THE PAST

The area we call Venezuela has been inhabited for more than 15,000 years. The earliest indigenous residents were predominantly nomadic; these peoples, descendents of the Carib, Arawak, and Chibcha tribes, left few traces and no major ruins. The most significant archaeological evidence left behind is some well preserved, although largely undeciphered, petroglyphs found in various sites around the country.

In 1498, on his third voyage, Christopher Columbus became the first European to set foot in Venezuela. One year later, Amerigo Vespucci and Alonso de Ojeda, leading another exploration to the New World, dubbed the land Venezuela, or "Little Venice," in honor of (or perhaps making fun of) the traditional indigenous stilt-houses along Lake Maracaibo, which called to mind the namesake city.

Lacking readily apparent gold and silver stores, Venezuela was never a major colonial concern for the Spanish crown. The first city still in existence to be founded was Cumaná, established in 1521. Caracas, the current capital, was founded in 1567. For centuries, the colony was governed from afar by Spanish seats in Peru, Colombia, and the Dominican Republic. The relative isolation and low level of development encouraged a certain amount of autonomy. Perhaps this is why Venezuela figured so prominently in the region's independence struggle.

Venezuela's struggle for independence from Spanish rule began in the early 19th century and took nearly 2 decades to consolidate. The principal figure in the fight was Simón Bolívar, El Libertador—a Venezuelan-born aristocrat considered the "Father of Venezuela" and the person most responsible for ending Spanish colonial rule throughout South America. Taking over in the wake of Francisco de Miranda's death, Bolívar led a series of long and bloody campaigns. In 1819, in the city of Angostura (currently Ciudad Bolívar), the rebel forces declared the independence of Gran Colombia, comprising the current states of Panama, Colombia, Ecuador, and Venezuela. Still, Royalist forces held on, and fighting continued for several more years, culminating in the decisive 1821 Battle of Carabobo. Nevertheless, both Bolívar's good fortune and the fledgling nation were short-lived. By 1830, El Libertador had died as a poor and pitiful figure, and Gran Colombia had dissolved into separate nation-states, including present-day Venezuela.

Over the next century or so, Venezuela was ruled by a series of strongman dictators, or *caudillos,* whose reigns were sometimes interspersed with periods of civil war and anarchy. One of the most infamous dictators was General Juan Vincente Gómez, who ruled from 1908 until his death in 1935. In addition to his cruelty and suppression of dissent, Gómez is best known for having presided over the first period of discovery and exploitation of Venezuela's massive oil reserves. Venezuela quickly became the world's number-one exporter of crude oil. However, there was little trickledown, and most of the wealth generated went to international oil companies and a small local elite.

By 1945, the opposition, led by Rómulo Betancourt, was able to take power and organize elections, granting universal voting rights to both men and women. In 1947, Rómulo Gallegos, the country's greatest novelist, became the first democratically elected president of Venezuela. However, the new democracy was fragile, and Gallegos was overthrown in a military coup within 8 months.

The subsequent military dictator, Colonel Marcos Pérez Jiménez, rivaled Gómez in brutality but will forever be remembered as the architect of modern Venezuela. Pérez Jiménez dedicated vast amounts of oil money to public works projects and modern buildings. In 1958, Pérez Jiménez himself was overthrown and a more stable democracy was instituted. Back in the spotlight, Rómulo Betancourt became the first democratically elected president to finish his term. For decades, Venezuela enjoyed a relatively peaceful period of democratic rule, with two principal parties amicably sharing power.

But Venezuela's almost sole dependence on oil revenues, modern ebbs and flows in international crude prices and production, and internal corruption and mismanagement all took their toll. In 1992, there were two unsuccessful coup attempts, one led by brash paratrooper Lieutenant Colonel Hugo Chávez Frías. Chávez spent several years in prison, but was not out for the count. In 1993, President Carlos Andrés Pérez was found guilty of embezzlement and misuse of public funds, was impeached, and spent more than 2 years under house arrest. More economic woe and political turmoil ensued, and in December 1998, Hugo Chávez, back in the spotlight, was elected president in a landslide.

VENEZUELA TODAY

Chávez's folksy populism and leftist rhetoric have given him a strong base of support among the poorer classes, although he has faced constant and fierce opposition from much of the political, business and academic classes, as well as an overwhelmingly hostile press. Soon after assuming power, Chávez orchestrated a series of maneuvers, including the dissolution of Congress and the drafting of a new constitution, which have granted him far-reaching powers.

Chávez's early years were marked by frequent public protests both in favor of and against his rule. Several of these protests turned violent, and fatal encounters between opposing sides were not uncommon. This turmoil caused massive capital and intellectual flight. In 2000, Chávez was reelected. However, in 2003, he was briefly ousted in an unsuccessful coup attempt. Soon after, the opposition called for a nationwide referendum on Chávez's rule, which Chávez won in 2004.

Bolstered by these electoral victories, and parallel victories of his party in the legislature, Chávez has been able to further his goals of leading a "Bolivarian revolution," which is an odd amalgam of Marx, Mao, Castro and Bolívar.

In 2007, Chávez's rhetoric and policies took a sharp socialist turn, closely following the Cuban model—even employing many of the same slogans and programs. Early results of this shift have included curbs on press freedom, a new national school curriculum, and increased antagonism toward the United States. However, in December 2007, Chávez suffered a significant setback, with the defeat of constitutional amendments that would have allowed him to be re-elected indefinitely. His current term ends in 2012.

Thanks to record-high oil prices, Venezuela is swimming in cash. This petro-dollar bonanza has filtered down some, and the country is enjoying high GDP. Still, critics claim that the benefits to the poor are far too few and often doled out according to political affiliation. Today, Venezuela remains fiercely divided, predominantly along class lines. Chávez's Bolivarian revolution remains a work in progress, and there are bound to be bumps in the road as it moves forward.

2 A South American Cultural Primer

It's estimated that 310 million people live in South America. The population is extremely diverse, and it would be difficult to generalize about the cultural makeup of the continent. But it is safe to say that of all the different people who live here, a large majority can trace their roots back to Spain, Portugal, Africa, or South America itself. Because of the Spanish and Portuguese influence, *mestizos* (people of both Amerindian and either Spanish or Portuguese ancestry) are also in the majority. From the late 19th century through 1930, the look of South Americans began to gradually change. Millions of Italians immigrated mainly to Brazil, Argentina, and Uruguay. Significant numbers of Germans, Poles, Syrians, Lebanese, and Japanese began to settle here as well.

THE CULTURAL MAKEUP OF SOUTH AMERICA
ARGENTINA

To understand how Argentina's European heritage impacts its South American identity, you must identify its distinct culture. Tango is the quintessential example: The sensual dance originated in the suspect corners of Buenos Aires's San Telmo neighborhood, was legitimized in the ballrooms of France, and was then reexported to Argentina to become this nation's great art form. Each journey you take, whether into a tango salon, an Argentine cafe, or a meat-only *parrilla,* will bring you closer to the country's true character.

But beyond the borders of Argentina's capital and largest city, you will find a land of vibrant extremes—from the Northwest's desert plateau to the flat grasslands of the pampas, from the rainforest jungle of Iguazú to the towering blue-white glaciers of Patagonia. The land's geographic diversity is reflected in its people; witness the contrast between the capital's largely immigrant population and the indigenous people of the northwest. Greater Buenos Aires, in which a third of Argentines live, is separated from the rest of Argentina both culturally and economically. Considerable suspicion exists between Porteños, as the people of Buenos Aires are called, and the rest of the Argentines. Residents of the fast-paced metropolis who consider themselves more European than South American share little in common with the indigenous people of the northwest, for example, who trace their roots to the Incas and take pride in a slower country life.

BOLIVIA

Bolivia has the highest percentage of indigenous people in all of South America. The country is twice as big as France, but its population is only 8.8 million (about the same as New York City's). And because of the country's rugged vastness, its indigenous groups have remained isolated and have been able to hold onto their traditions. In the rural highlands, lifestyles still revolve around agriculture and traditional weaving. It is also common to see people all over the country chewing coca leaves, a thousands-year-old tradition that is believed to give people energy. The customs of the indigenous people are in full flower not only in rural areas but in cities such as La Paz as well. In addition, Bolivians all over, particularly in rural highland areas, are known for their love of traditional music. It is a testament to the tenacity of Bolivian traditions that millions of Bolivians still speak Aymara, a language that predates not only the Spanish conquest of Bolivia but also the Inca conquest. Millions more speak Quechua, the language of the Incas. In fact, only half the population speaks Spanish as their first language. Of course, in the cities there are many *mestizos,* and most people speak Spanish.

Almost all Bolivians today are Roman Catholic, though traditional indigenous rituals are still practiced, even by devout Catholics. In the 18th and 19th centuries, a distinct "Mestizo Baroque" movement developed, where *mestizo* artists used indigenous techniques to create religious art. Even today, the mixture of the two influences is evident throughout Bolivian society. In Copacabana, where the Virgin of the Candelaria is one of the most revered Catholic symbols in all of South America, you can climb Calvario, the hill that looms over the cathedral, and receive blessings or have your coca leaves read by traditional Andean priests.

BRAZIL

Modern Brazil's diverse population is a melting pot of three main ethnic groups: the indigenous inhabitants of Brazil, the European settlers, and the descendants of black slaves from Africa. Within Brazil the blending of various cultures and ethnic groups varies from region to region. Rio de Janeiro's population is composed largely of people of mixed European and African heritage. In Salvador, more than any other area of Brazil, the people are mostly of African descent. Many of the freed slaves settled in this area, and the African influence is reflected in the food, religion, and music. In the Amazon, the cities are populated by migrants from other parts of Brazil, while the forest is predominantly populated by *caboclos* (a mixture of European and Indian ethnicities) and indigenous tribes, many of which maintain their traditional culture, dress, and lifestyle. European immigrants mostly settled the south of Brazil, with a few notable exceptions, such as the large Japanese and Middle Eastern communities of São Paulo.

Brazil remains the largest Roman Catholic country in the world, though Catholicism is perhaps stronger as a cultural influence than a religious force; many Brazilian Catholics see the inside of a church only once a year. Meanwhile, evangelical Protestant churches are growing fast, and African religious practices such as Candomblé remain important, particularly in northern cities such as Salvador.

Brazil is well known for its music. Local sounds encompass much more than samba and bossa nova, with Brazilian artists playing everything from rap, funk, jazz, and rock to regional rhythms such as the swinging afro-axé pop in Salvador and the fast maracatu in the Northeast. The cultural center of Brazil is São Paulo, and its rich theater and film scene is begrudgingly envied even by Cariocas (Rio residents). Rio remains the center of Brazil's sizable television industry.

CHILE

About 95% of Chile's population is mestizo, a mix of indigenous and European blood that includes Spanish, German (in the Lake District), and Croatian (in southern Patagonia). Other nationalities, such as Italian, Russian, and English, have contributed a smaller influence. Indigenous groups, such as the Aymara in the northern desert and the Mapuche in the Lake District, still exist in large numbers, although fewer than before the Spanish conquest. It is estimated that there are more than a half-million Mapuches, many of whom live on poverty-stricken *reducciones,* literally "reductions," where they continue to use their language and carry on their customs. In southern Chile and Tierra del Fuego, indigenous groups such as Alacalufe and Yagan have been diminished to only a few remaining representatives, and some, such as the Patagonian Ona, have been completely extinguished. One-third of Chile's 15 million residents live in the Santiago metropolis alone.

Until the late 1800s, the Roman Catholic Church exerted a heavy influence over all political, educational, and social spheres of society. Today, although more than 85% of the population claims faith in the Catholic religion, only a fraction attends Mass regularly. The church has lost much of its sway over government, but it still is the dominant influence when the government deals with issues such as abortion and divorce. It is estimated that less than 10% of Chileans are Protestants, mostly Anglican and Lutheran descendants of British and German immigrants, and fewer are Pentecostal. The remaining percentage belongs to tiny communities of Jewish, Mormon, and Muslim faiths.

Chile is a country whose rich cultural tapestry reflects its wide-ranging topography. From this range of cultures and landscapes have arisen some of Latin America's most prominent poets and writers, notably Nobel Prize winners Pablo Neruda and Gabriela Mistral, as well as contemporary writers Isabel Allende and José Donoso. Despite an artistically sterile period during the Pinochet regime, when any form of art deemed "suspicious" or "offensive" (meaning nothing beyond safe, traditional entertainment) was censored, modern art has begun to bloom, and even folkloric art and music are finding a fresh voice. Chile is also known for theater, and visitors to Santiago will find dozens of excellent productions to choose from. The national Chilean dance is the *cueca,* a courtship dance between couples that is said to imitate the mating ritual between chickens! The *cueca* is danced by couples who perform a one-two stomp while flitting and twirling a handkerchief.

COLOMBIA

Colombia's 45 million people live mostly on the high Andean triangle made up of Medellín, Bogotá, and Cali, as well as along the Caribbean Coast. Colombia is a country of incredible diversity: 58% of its citizens are *mestizo* (a mix of European and indigenous blood), 20% is of mostly European descent, and yet another 20% traces its ancestry to Africa. Moreover,

2% of the population is classified as indigenous, Arab, or "other."

About 90% of Colombians consider themselves Roman Catholic, although there is a growing Protestant and Evangelical movement, and numbers of Mormons, Seventh-Day Adventists and Pentecostals are on the rise. There is also a small but significant Jewish population, mostly in Bogotá, Medellín, and Barranquilla.

Colombia has a rich musical, artistic, and literary tradition. Some of the country's most well-known exports are Fernando Botero, one of the world's highest-paid artists; Nobel-prize-winning writer Gabriel García Márquez; Latin Grammy winners Shakira and Juanes; and actor John Leguizamo.

ECUADOR

About 25% of the Ecuadorian population is indigenous. There are 11 indigenous groups, each with its own language and customs. The largest is the Andean Quichua, over two million strong. Still, more than 65% of the population is considered *mestizo.* Just 3% of Ecuadorians are Afro-Ecuadorian, descendants of African slaves who were forced to work in the coastal areas. Caucasian, Asian, and Middle Eastern immigrants account for the remaining population. The population is about equally divided between the central highlands and the low-lying coastal region. Over the last few decades there has been a steady migration toward the cities, and today 60% of Ecuadorians reside in urban areas. El Oriente (the eastern, Amazon basin region of Ecuador) remains the least populated area in the entire country; only 3% of the population lives here.

In the highland areas, the local people have managed to hold on to their traditional culture. It's very common to see people still celebrating ancient holidays such as Inti Raymi—a festival welcoming the summer solstice. In Otavalo, in the northern highlands, the people still wear traditional clothing, and they have also kept their artisan traditions alive. The finest handicrafts in the country can be found here.

Because of the Amazon basin's isolated location, the locals here were able to escape domination by the Spanish and managed to maintain thousand-year-old rituals and customs. Some groups never had contact with "the outside world" until the 1960s and 1970s. Visitors to the Ecuadorian jungle who are taken to Amazonian villages will find that the people here live very much as their ancestors did thousands of years ago.

Much of the art you will see in Ecuador is folk art and crafts. When it comes to modern art, one name reigns supreme—Osvaldo Guayasamín. Renowned throughout Latin America and beyond, many of Guayasamín's most famous pieces are expressions of outrage at the military governments in South America in the 1970s.

A variety of musical traditions come together in Ecuador. The traditional music of the Andes features wind instruments such as the guaramo horn, the pifano and pinkullo flutes, and *rondador* (panpipes), supported by percussion. Its distinctive pentatonic scales give it a very haunting feel, and you are likely to hear familiar melodies if you happen upon any Adean bands, either playing in *peñas* (bars) or on public plazas.

PARAGUAY

Paraguay's population of 6.2 million is 95% mestizo—a mixture of Spanish and Guaraní Indian. Approximately 50% live in urban areas and many exist on subsistence farming. There are approximately 10,000 indigenous Indians living in the north of the country along with small communities of Mennonites. Some Japanese and Korean immigrants have settled in the south.

Despite the strong Guarani presence, Paraguayan culture has a strong European flavor, the legacy of Spanish colonial rule

and the Jesuit missions. This is most evident in traditional Paraguayan music where the harp is played using western compositions.

PERU

Peru's 27 million people are predominantly mestizo and Andean Indian, but there are also significant minority groups of Afro-Peruvians (descendants of African slaves, confined mainly to a coastal area south of Lima), immigrant Japanese and Chinese populations that are among the largest on the continent, and smaller groups of European immigrants, including Italians and Germans. Their religion is mainly Roman Catholic, though many people still practice pre-Columbian religious rituals inherited from the Incas.

Peru has, after Bolivia and Guatemala, the largest population, by percentage, of Amerindians in Latin America. Perhaps half the country lives in the *sierra,* or highlands, and most of these people, commonly called *campesinos* (peasants), live in either small villages or rural areas. Descendants of Peru's many Andean indigenous groups who live in remote rural areas continue to speak the native languages Quechua (made an official language in 1975) and Aymara or other Amerindian tongues, and for the most part they adhere to traditional regional dress. However, massive peasant migration to cities from rural highland villages has contributed to a dramatic weakening of indigenous traditions and culture across Peru.

Indigenous Amazonian tribes in Peru's jungle are dwindling in number—today, the population is less than two million. Still, many traditions and languages have yet to be extinguished, especially deep in the jungle—though most visitors are unlikely to come into contact with groups of unadulterated, non-Spanish-speaking native peoples.

Amerindian—Altiplano and Andina (highland)—music, is played on wind instruments such as bamboo panpipes and *quena* flutes, as well as *charangos* (small, bright-sounding, guitarlike instruments), among others. For many, this *música folklórica* is the very sound of Peru, but there are also significant strands of *música criolla* (based on a mix of European and African forms, played with guitar and *cajón,* a wooden box used as a percussion instrument), bouncy-sounding *huayno* rhythms played by *orquestas típicas,* and Afro-Peruvian music, adapted from music brought by African slaves.

Peru has one of the richest handicrafts traditions in the Americas. Many ancient traditions, such as the drop spindle (weaving done with a stick and spinning wooden wheel) are still employed in many regions. Terrific alpaca wool sweaters, ponchos, and shawls; tightly woven and brilliantly colored blankets and tapestries; and many other items of great quality are on display throughout Peru.

URUGUAY

There are 3.3 million Uruguayans, 93% of whom are of European descent. About 5% of the population is of African descent, and 1% is *mestizo.* The majority of Uruguayans are Roman Catholic. Most live in the capital or one of only 20 other significant towns. Uruguay enjoys high literacy, long life expectancy, and a relatively high standard of living. Despite Uruguay's economic troubles, this middle-income nation remains largely sheltered from the pervasive poverty and extreme socioeconomic differences characterizing much of Latin America.

Uruguay has a rich artistic and literary heritage. Among the country's notable artists are the sculptor José Belloni and the painter Joaquín Torres-García, founder of Uruguay's Constructivist movement. Top writers include José Enrique Rodó, a famed essayist; Mauricio Rosencof, a politically active playwright; and writer Eduardo Galeano.

VENEZUELA

Venezuela has a population of approximately 27 million people, some 80% of whom live in a narrow urban belt running along the Caribbean coast and slightly inland. Venezuela is a young country, with an estimated half the population under 20 and around 70% under 35. Almost 70% of the population is *mestizo.* Another 19% are considered white, and 10% are black. While indigenous peoples make up only about 1% of the population, their influence and presence are noticeable. Venezuela has more than 20 different indigenous tribes totaling some 200,000 people. The principal tribes are the Guajiro, found north of Maracaibo; the Pémon, Piaroa, Yekuana, and Yanomami, who live in the Amazon and Gran Sabana regions; and the Warao of the Orinoco Delta.

More than 90% of the population claims to be Roman Catholic, although church attendance is relatively low and Venezuelans are not considered the most devout of followers on the continent. There is a growing influx of U.S.-style Protestant denominational churches, as well as small Jewish and Muslim populations. The country's indigenous peoples were an early target of Catholic missionary fervor, although their traditional beliefs and faith do survive. One of the most interesting religious phenomena in the country is the cult of María Lionza, a unique syncretic sect that combines elements of Roman Catholicism, African voodoo, and indigenous rites.

Although Venezuela has its fair share of European-influenced colonial and religious art, its most important art, literature, and music are almost all modern. Jesús Soto is perhaps the country's most famous artist. A pioneer and leading figure of the kinetic art movement, Soto has major and prominent works in public spaces around Caracas. Novelist, essayist, and one-time president of Venezuela

Rómulo Gallegos is the defining literary figure in Venezuela. One important literary figure from the revolutionary era is Andrés Bello, a poet, journalist, historian, and close friend of Simón Bolívar. Venezuelans love to dance, and no one has been getting them up and moving longer and more consistently than Oscar D'León. Alternately known as El Rey (The King), El León (The Lion), and El Diablo (The Devil) of salsa, D'León has been recording and performing live for more than 32 years, and he shows no sign of slowing down.

3 Recommended Films & Reading

For a general primer on South America, Paul Theroux's *Old Patagonian Express: By Train Through the Americas* (Houghton Mifflin, 1997) provides a beautifully written account of his travels throughout the continent. Bruce Chatwin's *In Patagonia* (Penguin Classics, 2003) offers an alternate take on the Patagonia region covered in the Theroux work.

If you're interested in a scholarly read, pick up John Charles Chasteen's *Born in Blood and Fire: A Concise History of Latin America* (W.W. Norton & Company, 2000). The book only begins with the arrival of the Europeans in the Americas, but it gives a good overview of the diverse regions of Latin America.

If you'd like a visual overview of South America, *The Motorcycle Diaries* (MCA Home Video, February 2005), which chronicles a road trip taken by a young Che Guevara, is a good bet.

ARGENTINA   For a review of the country's history, try Nicolas Shumway's *The Invention of Argentina* (University of California Press, 1993). Argentine historians Jorge B. Rivera and José Gobello are instrumental in helping demystify modern Argentina. Their books are difficult to find in English; if you read Spanish, try Gobello's *Crónica General del Tango* (Editorial Fraterna, 1980). Jorgelina Corbatta offers the best account of Argentina's "dirty war" under the military dictatorship from 1976 to 1983 in *Narrativas de la Guerra Sucia en Argentina* (Ediciones Corregidor, 1999).

Jorge Luis Borges sits at the top of Argentine fiction writers; read *Collected Fictions* (Penguin, 1999) for an overview of his work. Manuel Puig's *Kiss of the Spider Woman* (Vintage, 1991) and Julio Cortázar's *The Winners* (New York Review Books, 1999) are good picks for more contemporary Argentine writing.

BOLIVIA   *The Fat Man from La Paz* (Seven Stories Press, 2000), edited by Rosario Santos, is a collection of contemporary short stories by Bolivian writers. The stories provide readers with a vivid picture of life in Bolivia.

Che Guevara spent his last days on the run in Bolivia. There are several books detailing his journey. One of the best accounts is the *Complete Bolivian Diaries of Che Guevara and Other Captured Documents* (Cooper Square Press, 2000) by Ernesto Guevara and Daniel James.

Herbert S. Klein's *Bolivia: The Evolution of a Multi-Ethnic Society* (Oxford University Press, 1992) does an excellent job of delving into the government, economics, and history of Bolivia. Klein also touches on art, architecture, and societal relations.

For more information about the sophisticated pre-Inca Tiwanaku culture, your best bet is Alan L. Kolata's *The Tiwanaku: Portrait of an Andean Civilization* (Blackwell Publishing, 1993).

BRAZIL   There is no single good general history covering Brazil from 1500 to the present. *Colonial Brazil*, edited by Leslie Bethell (Cambridge University

Press, 1983), is a scholarly but readable account of Brazil under the Portuguese, while Peter Flynn's *Brazil: A Political Analysis* covers political history from the birth of the first republic to the close of the second dictatorship. For a fascinating introduction to an entire range of topics in Brazil, pick up the excellent anthology *Travelers' Tales: Brazil,* edited by Annette Haddad and Scott Doggett (1997). *Tristes Tropiques* (Penguin, 1992) is a classic work of travel writing by the great French anthropologist Claude Lévi-Strauss.

Until he passed away in 2001, Bahian novelist Jorge Amado was considered a serious candidate for the Nobel Prize. His greatest novels revolve around the colorful characters of his beloved Bahia and include *Dona Flor and Her Two Husbands* (Avon, 1998) and *Gabriela, Clove and Cinnamon* (Bard Books, 1998). In a previous generation, Joaquim Maria Machado de Assis wrote fiercely ironic novels and short stories, many set in Rio towards the end of the 19th century. His works available in English include *The Epitaph of a Small Winner* (Noonday Press, 1990). Brazil's greatest social realist is Graciliano Ramos. His masterpiece *Barren Lives* (University of Texas Press, 1971) is considered to be one of Brazil's finest novels.

If you're interested in learning about Rio de Janiero's *favelas,* we recommend watching *City of God* (Miramax, June 2004).

CHILE A quick, comprehensive guide to all things Chilean, Susan Roraff and Laura Camacho's *Culture Shock! Chile* (Graphic Arts Center, 2002), explains Chilean etiquette and culture. For history and a look into the Pinochet legacy that came to define modern Chile, try the following books: *A History of Chile, 1808–1994* by Simon Collier and William F. Sater (Cambridge University Press, 1996); *A Nation of Enemies: Chile*

Under Pinochet by Pamela Constable and Arturo Valenzuela (W.W. Norton & Company, 1993); and *Chile: The Other September 11* by Ariel Dorfman et al. (Ocean Press, 2002).

Chile boasts two literary Nobel Prize winners, Gabriela Mistral and Pablo Neruda; however, most North Americans are probably most familiar with the Chilean export Isabel Allende, whose popular novels such as *Of Love and Shadows* (Bantam, 1998) and *House of the Spirits* (Bantam, 1989) have been made into major motion pictures.

COLOMBIA John Hemmings's *The Search for El Dorado* (Phoenix Press, 2001) gives readers insight into the history and conquest of Colombia by the Spanish. For a general overview of Colombia's economy, government, history, geography, destinations, people, and more, try *Colombia, a Country Study Guide,* by USA International Business Publications, which is updated yearly and aimed at businesspeople. To understand the political crisis and never-ending civil war in Colombia, try *Colombia: Fragmented Land, Divided Society* by Frank Safford and Marco Palacios (Oxford University Press, 2001); *The Making of Modern Colombia: A Nation in Spite of Itself* by David Bushnell, Georg Wilhelm, and Friedrich Hegel (University of California Press, 1993); or *Bandits, Peasants, and Politics: The Case of "La Violencia"* by Gonzalo Sánchez (University of Texas Press, 2001).

Colombia's—and all of South America's—premiere literary figure is Nobel Prize–winner Gabriel García Márquez, known for novels such as *Love in the Time of Cholera* (Penguin, 1994) and *One Hundred Years of Solitude* (Harperperennial Library, 1998), both of which are widely available. *Vivir para Contarla,* the first volume of his three-part autobiography, is now available in English as *Living to Tell the Tale* (Alfred A. Knopf, 2003).

Maria Full of Grace (HBO Home Video, December 2004) offers an engaging glimpse into Colombia's drug-running culture.

ECUADOR Ecuador and the Galápagos Islands have captured the imagination of many North American and British writers. Herman Melville's *Las Encantadas* (Fawcett Publications, 1967) is a collection of various pieces from the 19th century that provide descriptions of the islands themselves, the inhabitants, and the whalers who passed through the area. Kurt Vonnegut's *Galápagos* (Delta, 1999) is a hilarious story about human evolution. It starts off with a story about a small group of people who are shipwrecked and forever stuck on a small isolated island in the Galápagos. It then follows the evolution of these people for a million years into the future.

If you're interested in learning about how Charles Darwin formed his theory of evolution, you should pick up Darwin's *Voyage of the Beagle* (Penguin, 1989) or his *Origin of Species* (Grammercy, 1998). Michael H. Jackson's *Galápagos: A Natural History* (University of Calgary Press, 1994) is the best authority on the natural history of plants and animals in the Galápagos.

For a quick, simple, and concise history of Ecuador, try reading *In Focus Ecuador: A Guide to the People, Politics, and Culture* (Interlink Pub Group, 2000) by Wilma Roos and Omer Van Renterghem. Linda Newson's *Life and Death in Early Colonial Ecuador* (University of Oklahoma Press, 1995) looks at the native people living in Ecuador in the 16th century and discusses how they were affected by both the Inca and Spanish conquests.

PERU Perhaps the classic work on Inca history is *The Conquest of the Incas* by John Hemming (Harvest Books, 1973), a very readable narrative of the fall of a short-lived but uniquely accomplished empire.

Mario Vargas Llosa, Peru's most famous novelist and a perennial candidate for the Nobel Prize, was nearly elected the country's president back in 1990. *Aunt Julia and the Scriptwriter* (Penguin, 1995) is one of his most popular works; *The Real Life of Alejandro Mayta* (Noonday Press, 1998) is a dense meditation on Peruvian and South American revolutionary politics that blurs the lines between truth and fiction; and *Death in the Andes* (Penguin, 1997) is a deep penetration into the contemporary psyche and politics of Peru. Another side of the author is evident in the small erotic gem *In Praise of the Stepmother* (Penguin, 1991).

For a glimpse into Peru's recent political history, check out the documentary *The Fall of Fujimori* (Stardust Pictures, January 2006).

URUGUAY Lawrence Weschler reports on Uruguay's "dirty war" in *A Miracle, A Universe* (University of Chicago Press, 1998). Uruguayan journalist Eduardo Galeano examines the consequences of colonialism and imperialism in *Open Veins of Latin America* (Monthly Review Press, 1998).

Blood Pact & Other Stories (Curbstone Press, 1997) is one of the few collections of beloved writer Mario Benedetti available in English. A good place to start with José Enrique Rodó's essays is *Ariel* (University of Texas Press, 1988).

VENEZUELA Perhaps no piece of literature is as closely associated with Venezuela as Sir Arthur Conan Doyle's 1912 *The Lost World* (Doherty, Tom Associates, 1997), which is set in an area modeled after Venezuela's Amazonas region. *The Lost World* has spawned numerous imitators and literary offspring, and has served as the model for a host of films, including *Jurassic Park*.

Anyone with even the slightest interest in Venezuelan literature should start with Rómulo Gallegos's 1929 classic *Doña*

Bárbara (English translation by Robert Malloy; Smith Peter, 1990), a tale of love and struggle on the Venezuelan plains. Gallegos was a former president and is widely considered the country's principal literary light. Also of interest are Gabriel García Márquez's *The General in His Labyrinth* (Penguin, 1991), a fictional account of Simón Bolívar's dying days, and Isabel Allende's *Eva Luna* (Bantam, 1989), which is set in a town based on the Venezuelan city of Colonia Tovar.

For an excellent glimpse into one of the darker sides of present-day Venezuela—and Latin America, in general—try to see the recent film *Secuestro Express* (Miramax, 2005), which tells the story of an "express kidnapping" in downtown Caracas, within the context of the country's current political and social situation.

3

Planning Your Trip to South America

The country chapters in this guide provide specific information on traveling to and getting around individual South American countries. In this chapter, we provide you with general information that will help you plan your trip.

1 Entry Requirements

PASSPORTS

Allow plenty of time before your trip to apply for a passport; processing normally takes 3 weeks but can take longer during busy periods (especially spring). And keep in mind that if you need a passport in a hurry, you'll pay a higher processing fee.

For residents of Australia: You can pick up an application from your local post office or any branch of **Passports Australia,** but you must schedule an interview at the passport office to present your application materials. Call the **Australian Passport Information Service** at *©* **131-232,** or visit the government website at **www.passports.gov.au**.

For residents of Canada: Passport applications are available at travel agencies throughout Canada or from the central **Passport Office,** Department of Foreign Affairs and International Trade, Ottawa, ON K1A 0G3 (*©* **800/567-6868;** www.ppt.gc.ca).

For residents of Ireland: You can apply for a 10-year passport at the **Passport Office,** Setanta Centre, Molesworth Street, Dublin 2 (*©* **01/671-1633;** www.irlgov.ie/iveagh). Those under age 18 and over 65 must apply for a 3-year passport.

You can also apply at 1A South Mall, Cork (*©* **021/272-525**), or at most main post offices.

For residents of New Zealand: You can pick up a passport application at any **New Zealand Passports Office** or download it from their website. Contact the **Passports Office** at *©* **0800/225-050** in New Zealand or 04/474-8100, or log on to **www.passports.govt.nz**.

For residents of the United Kingdom: To pick up an application for a standard 10-year passport (5-year passport for children under 16), visit your nearest passport office, major post office, or travel agency, or contact the **United Kingdom Passport Service** at *©* **0870/521-0410,** or search its website at **www.ukpa.gov.uk**.

For residents of the United States: Whether you're applying in person or by mail, you can download passport applications from the U.S. Department of State website at **http://travel.state.gov**. To find your regional passport office, either check the U.S. Department of State website or call the **National Passport Information Center** toll-free number (*©* **877/487-2778**) for automated information.

CUSTOMS

For information about what you can bring with you upon entry, see the "Customs" or "Entry Requirements & Customs" section in individual country chapters.

WHAT YOU CAN BRING HOME

U.S. Citizens: Everyone older than 21 years of age may bring, free of duty, the following: (1) 1 liter of wine or hard liquor; (2) 200 cigarettes, 100 cigars (but not from Cuba), or 3 pounds of smoking tobacco; and (3) $100 worth of gifts. These exemptions are offered to travelers who spend at least 72 hours in the United States and who have not claimed them within the preceding 6 months. It is altogether forbidden to bring into the country foodstuffs (particularly fruit, cooked meats, and canned goods) and plants (vegetables, seeds, tropical plants, and the like). Foreign tourists may carry in or out up to $10,000 in U.S. or foreign currency with no formalities; larger sums must be declared to U.S. Customs on entering or leaving, which includes filing form CM 4790. For details regarding U.S. Customs and Border Protection, consult your nearest U.S. embassy or consulate, or **U.S.**

Customs (© 202/927-1770; www.customs.ustreas.gov).

Canadian Citizens: For a clear summary of Canadian rules, write for the booklet *I Declare,* issued by the **Canada Border Services Agency** (© 800/461-9999 in Canada, or 204/983-3500; **www.cbsa-asfc.gc.ca**).

U.K. Citizens: For information, contact **HM Customs & Excise** at © 0845/010-9000 (from outside the U.K., 020/8929-0152), or consult their website at **www.hmce.gov.uk**.

Australian Citizens: A helpful brochure, available from Australian consulates or Customs offices, is *Know Before You Go.* For more information, call the **Australian Customs Service** at © 1300/363-263, or log on to **www.customs.gov.au**.

New Zealand Citizens: Most questions are answered in a free pamphlet available at New Zealand consulates and Customs offices: *New Zealand Customs Guide for Travellers, Notice no. 4.* For more information, contact **New Zealand Customs,** The Customhouse, 17–21 Whitmore St., Box 2218, Wellington (© 04/473-6099 or 0800/428-786; **www.customs.govt.nz**).

2 When to Go

South America is a huge continent (it crosses both the Equator and the Tropic of Capricorn), and climatic conditions vary widely. In June, when it's freezing cold at the southern tip of Argentina, it's hot and humid in Venezuela. You can take into account, however, that more than 75% of the continent sits south of the Equator, which means that winter usually lasts from June through September and summer from December through March. In high-altitude cities, such as Quito, you can expect cool weather year-round; in the Amazon basin region—in the center of the continent, from Ecuador to Brazil—the weather is hot and humid year-round.

In general, the high season for travel in South America lasts from June through September, from mid-December through mid-January, and during Carnaval, which takes place the week before Ash Wednesday. The ski season in Chile and Argentina reaches its peak in July and August.

HOLIDAYS, CELEBRATIONS & EVENTS

Many of the holidays and festivals in South America correspond to Catholic and indigenous celebrations. (Sometimes they are a mixture of both.) The entire continent seems to turn into one big party zone during Carnaval, usually in February or March. During the solstices and equinoxes, many indigenous groups, which historically have worshipped the sun, organize traditional celebrations throughout South America.

SOUTH AMERICA CALENDAR OF EVENTS

February

Carnaval. Generally celebrated during the week before the start of Lent, the liveliest Carnaval festivities are held in Argentina, Uruguay, and, most famously, Brazil. In Salta, Argentina, citizens throw a large parade, which includes caricatures of public officials and "water bomb" fights. In Uruguay, Montevideo is the center for the main events, including parades, dance parties, and widespread debauchery. In Brazil, it's the party to end all parties— all life comes to a halt for 4 days of nonstop singing, dancing, drinking, and general over-the-top merrymaking. If you're going to Brazil, mark your calendar for February 21 to February 24, 2009, and February 13 to February 26, 2010.

Festival of the Virgen de la Candelaria. Lively festivities are held in honor of one of the most beloved religious symbols in Bolivia and Peru. In Copacabana, Bolivia, the home of the Virgin, the celebration includes parades and dancing in the street. In Puno, Peru, it's one of the largest and most colorful folk religious festivals in the Americas, with abundant music and dance troupes, many in fantastic costumes and masks. February 2.

Festival de la Canción (Festival of Song), Viña del Mar, Chile. This gala showcases Latin American and international performers during a 5-day festival of concerts held in the city's outdoor amphitheater. The spectacle draws thousands of visitors to an already packed Viña del Mar, so plan

your hotel reservations accordingly. Late February.

April

Festival Internacional de Teatro (Caracas International Theater Festival). This festival brings together scores of troupes and companies from around the world and across Venezuela for a 2-week celebration of the theater arts. Performances are held in a variety of theaters (and a plethora of languages) around Caracas, as well as in the streets and plazas. Begun nearly 30 years ago, this is the premiere theater festival in Latin America. For more information, contact the **Ateneo de Caracas** (© **0212/573-4400**). Early to mid-April.

Semana Santa, Uruguay. During Holy Week, Uruguay shuts down. In Montevideo and the smaller cities, you'll find gaucho-style barbecues all over the place. During this time, there are also parades, where you'll be able to hear local folk music. Wednesday through Friday before Easter.

June

Gaucho Parade, Salta, Argentina. The parade features music by folk artists and gauchos dressed in traditional red ponchos with black stripes, leather chaps, black boots, belts, and knives. June 16.

Septenario Festival (Corpus Christi), Cuenca, Ecuador. During this weeklong event, Cuenca is at its most festive. The streets around the main plaza are closed and a carnival atmosphere prevails with games, special food stalls, and nightly fireworks. Thousands of balloons are sent into the sky over the city on closing night. The exact date varies, but is usually mid-June.

Inti Raymi (Festival of the Sun). This Inca Festival of the Sun—the mother of all pre-Hispanic festivals—celebrates the winter solstice and honors the sun god with traditional pageantry, parades, and dances. In Argentina, celebrations take place in towns throughout the northwest on the night before the solstice (around June 20). In Peru, it draws thousands of visitors who fill Cusco's hotels; the principal event takes place on June 24 at the Sacsayhuamán ruins and includes the sacrifice of a pair of llamas. General celebrations continue for several days. In Ecuador, Inti Raymi merges with the fiestas of San Pablo and San Juan to create one big holiday from June 24 to 29 in the Otavalo area.

August

Feria de las Flores, Medellín, Colombia. Likely the largest flower festival in the World, Medellín's biggest annual celebration includes a long list of events such as the Cavalgata de Caballos (Horse Parade), Desfile de Carros Antiguos (Antique Car Parade), and—the most famous and well known—the Desfile de Silleteros, where young and old come out to show-off their hand made *silleteros,* or flower designs, in an hours-long parade. This festival is one of a kind and excitement rivals that of Carnaval in Barranquilla or Cartagena. First week of August.

Independence Day, Bolivia. To celebrate this holiday, Bolivians flock to Sucre, where the leaders of the Bolivian independence movement signed the declaration of independence in 1825. For several days before and several days afterward, there are colorful parades, fireworks, and all sorts of celebrations here. If you can't make it to Sucre, you'll find people partying throughout the country, especially in Copacabana. August 6.

September

Virgen del Valle, Isla de Margarita, Venezuela. The patron saint of sailors, fishermen, and all other seafarers is honored with street fairs and a colorful blessing of the fleet procession. September 8 to September 15.

Independence Day and **Armed Forces Day,** Chile. Chile's rich cultural heritage comes to life with plenty of drinking, dancing, rodeos, and military parades. This holiday can stretch into a 3- to 4-day weekend, and the best place to witness celebrations is in the Central Valley south of Santiago. September 18 and 19.

October

El Señor de los Milagros (Lord of the Miracles), Lima, Peru. Lasting nearly 24 hours and involving tens of thousands of participants, many of whom are dressed in purple, this procession celebrates a Christ image painted by an Angolan slave that survived the 1746 earthquake and has since become the most venerated image in the capital. October 18.

November

All Souls' Day and **Independence Day,** Cuenca, Ecuador. The city celebrates both the Day of the Dead and its independence day with parties, art shows, parades, dances in the streets, and food festivals. November 2 and 3.

December

Santuranticuy Festival, Cusco, Peru. Hundreds of artisans sell traditional carved Nativity figures and saints' images at one of the largest handicrafts fairs in Peru in Cusco's Plaza de Armas. December 24.

New Year's Eve, Rio de Janeiro, Brazil. The Copacabana beach is ground zero for an event that attracts more than one million people. The 9.6km (6 miles) of sand are jam-packed with New Year's revelers, and the entertainment never stops, with concerts and performances all night long leading up to the best fireworks display in the world. The evening is also an important one in the African Candomblé religion; it's the night to make an offering to the sea goddess Yemanjá. Candomblé followers, all dressed in white, offer small boats loaded with flowers, candles, mirrors, jewelry, and other pretty trinkets to the sea in a candlelit ceremony with music and dancing. The sight on the beach is truly spectacular. December 31.

3 Getting There

BY PLANE

Buenos Aires, Santiago, Lima, and São Paulo receive the greatest number of international flights to South America. If you're planning to explore the entire continent, you might consider starting off at one of these gateways and hooking up there for connecting flights to less-serviced destinations. See the individual country chapters for more detailed information.

FLYING FOR LESS: TIPS FOR GETTING THE BEST AIRFARE

- Passengers who can book their ticket either **long in advance or at the last minute,** or who **fly midweek** or **at less-trafficked hours** may pay a fraction of the full fare. If your schedule is flexible, say so, and ask if you can secure a cheaper fare by changing your flight plans.
- Search **the Internet** for cheap fares. The most popular online travel agencies are **Travelocity** (www.travelocity.co.uk); **Expedia** (www.expedia.co.uk and www.expedia.ca); and **Orbitz.** In the U.K., go to **Travelsupermarket** (© 0845/345-5708; www.travelsupermarket.com), a flight search engine that offers flight comparisons for the budget airlines whose seats often end up in bucket-shop sales. Other websites for booking airline tickets online include **Cheapflights.com, SmarterTravel.com, Priceline.com,** and **Opodo** (www.opodo.co.uk). Meta search sites (which find and then direct you to airline and hotel websites for booking) include **Sidestep.com** and **Kayak.com**—the latter includes fares for such budget carriers

as JetBlue and Spirit as well as the major airlines. **Site59.com** is a great source for last-minute flights and getaways. In addition, most **airlines** offer online-only fares that even their phone agents know nothing about. British travelers should check **Flights International** (© 0800/0187050; www.flights-international.com) for deals on flights all over the world.

- Keep an eye on local newspapers for **promotional specials** or **fare wars,** when airlines lower prices on their most popular routes.
- Try to book a ticket **in its country of origin.** If you're planning a one-way flight from Johannesburg to New York, a South Africa–based travel agent will probably have the lowest fares. For foreign travelers on multileg trips, book in the country of the first leg; for example, book New York–Chicago–Montreal–New York in the U.S.
- **Consolidators,** also known as bucket shops, are wholesale brokers in the airline-ticket game. Consolidators buy deeply discounted tickets ("distressed" inventories of unsold seats) from airlines and sell them to online ticket agencies, travel agents, tour operators, corporations, and, to a lesser degree, the general public. Consolidators advertise in Sunday newspaper travel sections (often in small ads with tiny type), both in the U.S. and the U.K. They can be great sources for cheap international tickets. On the down side, bucket shop tickets are often rigged with restrictions, such as stiff cancellation penalties (as high as

50%–75% of the ticket price). And keep in mind that most of what you see advertised is of limited availability. Several reliable consolidators are worldwide and available online. **STA Travel** (www.statravel.com) has been the world's leading consolidator for students since purchasing Council Travel, but their fares are competitive for travelers of all ages. **Flights.com** (© 800/TRAV-800; www.flights.com) has excellent fares worldwide, particularly to Europe. They also have "local" websites in 12 countries. **Fly-Cheap** (© 800/FLY-CHEAP; www.1800flycheap.com) has especially good fares to sunny destinations. **Air Tickets Direct** (© 800/778-3447; www.airticketsdirect.com) is based in Montreal books trips to places that U.S. travel agents won't touch, such as Cuba.

- Join **frequent-flier clubs.** Frequent-flier membership doesn't cost a cent, but it does entitle you to free tickets or upgrades when you amass the airline's required number of frequent-flier points. You don't even have to fly to earn points; **frequent-flier credit cards** can earn you thousands of miles for doing your everyday shopping. But keep in mind that award seats are limited, seats on popular routes are hard to snag, and more and more major airlines are cutting their expiration periods for mileage points—so check your airline's frequent-flier program so you don't lose your miles before you use them. *Inside tip:* Award seats are offered almost a year in advance, but seats also open up at the last minute, so if your travel plans are flexible, you may strike gold. To play the frequent-flier game to your best advantage, consult the community bulletin boards on **FlyerTalk** (www.flyertalk.com) or go to Randy Petersen's **Inside Flyer** (www.insideflyer.com). Petersen and friends review all the programs in detail and post regular updates on changes in policies and trends.

LONG-HAUL FLIGHTS: HOW TO STAY COMFORTABLE

- Your choice of airline and airplane will definitely affect your leg room. Find more details about U.S. airlines at **www.seatguru.com**. For international airlines, the research firm Skytrax has posted a list of average seat pitches at **www.airlinequality.com**.
- Emergency exit seats and bulkhead seats typically have the most legroom. Emergency exit seats are usually left unassigned until the day of a flight (to ensure that someone able-bodied fills the seats); it's worth getting to the ticket counter early to snag one of these spots for a long flight. Many passengers find that bulkhead seating (the row facing the wall at the front of the cabin) offers more legroom, but keep in mind that bulkhead seats have no storage space on the floor in front of you.
- To have two seats for yourself in a three-seat row, try for an aisle seat in a center section toward the back of coach. If you're traveling with a companion, book an aisle and a window seat. Middle seats are usually booked last, so chances are good you'll end up with three seats to yourselves. And in the event that a third passenger is assigned the middle seat, he or she will probably be more than happy to trade for a window or an aisle.
- Ask about entertainment options. Many airlines offer seatback video systems where you get to choose your movies or play video games—but only on some of their planes. (Boeing 777s are your best bet.)
- To sleep, avoid the last row of any section or the row in front of an

---

Tips Getting Through the Airport

- Arrive at the airport at least 1 hour before a domestic flight and 2 hours before an international flight. You can check the average wait times at your airport by going to the TSA **Security Checkpoint Wait Times** site (waittime.tsa.dhs.gov).
- Know what you can carry on and what you can't. For the latest updates on items you are prohibited to bring in carryon luggage or through the security checkpoint, go to **www.tsa.gov/travelers/airtravel**.
- Beat the ticket-counter lines by using the self-service electronic ticket kiosks at the airport or even printing out your boarding pass at home from the airline website. Using curbside check-in is also a smart way to avoid lines.
- Help speed up security before you're screened. Remove jackets, shoes, belt buckles, heavy jewelry, and watches and place them either in your carryon luggage or the security bins provided. In a security bin, place keys, coins, cellphones, and pagers, as well as liquids, gels, and aerosols (all 3.4 ounces or less and packed in a single 1-quart plastic bag).
- Use a TSA-approved lock for your checked luggage. Look for Travel Sentry certified locks at luggage or travel shops and Brookstone stores (or online at www.brookstone.com).

---

emergency exit, as these seats are the least likely to recline. Avoid seats near highly trafficked toilet areas. Avoid seats in the back of many jets—these can be narrower than those in the rest of coach. Or reserve a window seat so you can rest your head and avoid being bumped in the aisle.

- Get up, walk around, and stretch every 60 to 90 minutes to keep your blood flowing. This helps avoid **deep vein thrombosis,** or "economy-class syndrome."
- Drink water before, during, and after your flight to combat the lack of humidity in airplane cabins. Avoid alcohol, which will dehydrate you.
- If you're flying with kids, don't forget to carry on toys, books, pacifiers, and snacks and chewing gum to help them relieve ear pressure buildup during ascent and descent.

4 Money

At one time or another, inflation has been a thorn in the economies of every South American nation. Because of this, many South American hotels quote their rates in dollars, and in some South American countries, dollars are widely accepted. For specifics on currency and exchange rates, see the individual destination chapters.

ATMS

The easiest and best way to get cash away from home is from an ATM (automated teller machine), sometimes referred to as a "cash machine," or a "cashpoint." The **Cirrus** (© 800/424-7787; www.mastercard.com) and **PLUS** (© 800/843-7587; www.visa.com) networks span the globe. Go to your bank card's website to find

Regardless of where you're traveling in South America, the sun is always very strong, so be sure to bring **sunscreen** (including some for your lips), **sunglasses,** and a **wide-brimmed hat.** Showers can be a bit grimy, so you may want to consider throwing in an old pair of flip-flops.

If you're traveling in the Andes (parts of Venezuela, Ecuador, Peru, Bolivia, Chile, and western Argentina), be prepared for cold weather. **Layers** are the name of the game here. It can get hot during the day and very cold at night. We recommend a lightweight sweater or sweatshirt, a T-shirt, a fleece jacket, and a windbreaker. Many hotels don't have heat, so be sure to bring flannel or heavy pajamas. At night, you may need a hat and gloves.

Contrary to popular belief, it does get cold in Buenos Aires, Santiago, and Montevideo, especially from June through September. Be sure to bring a **jacket** with you if you're traveling in Argentina, Uruguay, and Chile.

The Tropic of Capricorn cuts its way through northern Chile, northern Argentina, and Paraguay, and through Brazil to São Paulo and Rio de Janeiro. The areas north of here and east of the Andes are considered tropical climates, and **lightweight clothing** is essential. In general, no one will be offended if you wear shorts or sleeveless tops in these areas. Because it can get chilly at night and it often rains, you should be sure to pack a light sweater and rain jacket. **Sport sandals,** such as Tevas, will also come in handy.

If you're heading to the Galápagos, waterproof sandals will be your best friends. During the cooler months from June through September, you should also consider bringing a **wet suit.** The snorkeling is great this time of year, but the water can be mighty frigid.

Most toiletries are available in all large cities. The exception is **tampons;** be sure to bring enough from home to last you through your trip. For some reason, the **toothpaste** in South America can be of poor quality, so bring your own from home. Except in the most rural areas, **film** and **batteries** are easy to find in South America. It can be difficult, however, to find common medicines in South America. We recommend packing a **mini–medicine kit,** just in case. Because food and waterborne illnesses are one of the most common ailments to affect travelers in this area, be sure to bring medicine to treat diarrhea and vomiting. Pain relievers (particularly acetaminophen or paracetamol and ibuprofen) and cold medication are also recommended. Taking multivitamins and vitamins such as super bromelain, which aids in the digestion of parasites, can also help you stay healthy. If you're traveling to the jungle or coastal area, mosquito repellent with DEET is imperative.

ATM locations at your destination. Be sure you know your daily withdrawal limit before you depart. *Note:* Many banks impose a fee every time you use a card at another bank's ATM, and that fee can be higher for international transactions (up to $5 or more) than for domestic ones (where they're rarely more than $2). In addition, the bank from which you withdraw cash may charge its own fee. For international withdrawal fees, ask your bank. *Tip:* Be aware that in some countries, including Argentina, ATMs may not allow you to withdraw more than $100 per transaction. Consult your bank before leaving on your trip.

Note: Banks that are members of the **Global ATM Alliance** charge no transaction fees for cash withdrawals at other Alliance member ATMs; these include Bank of America, Scotiabank (Canada, Caribbean, and Mexico), Barclays (U.K. and parts of Africa), and Deutsche Bank (Germany, Poland, Spain, and Italy), and BNP Paribas (France).

CREDIT CARDS

Credit cards are another safe way to carry money. They also provide a convenient record of all your expenses, and they generally offer relatively good exchange rates. You can withdraw cash advances from your credit cards at banks or ATMs but high fees make credit card cash advances a pricey way to get cash. Keep in mind that you'll pay interest from the moment of your withdrawal, even if you pay your monthly bills on time. Also, note that many banks now assess a 1 % to 3% "transaction fee" on **all** charges you incur abroad (whether you're using the local currency or your native currency).

TRAVELER'S CHECKS

You can buy traveler's checks at most banks. They are offered in denominations of $20, $50, $100, $500, and sometimes $1,000. Generally, you'll pay a service charge ranging from 1% to 4%.

The most popular traveler's checks are offered by **American Express** (© 800/ 807-6233 or © 800/221-7282 for card holders—this number accepts collect calls, offers service in several foreign languages, and exempts Amex gold and platinum cardholders from the 1% fee); **Visa** (© 800/732-1322)—AAA members can obtain Visa checks for a $9.95 fee (for checks up to $1,500) at most AAA offices or by calling © **866/339-3378;** and **MasterCard** (© 800/223-9920).

Be sure to keep a record of the traveler's checks serial numbers separate from your checks in the event that they are stolen or lost. You'll get a refund faster if you know the numbers.

American Express, Thomas Cook, Visa, and **MasterCard** offer **foreign currency traveler's checks,** useful if you're traveling to one country or to the Euro zone; they're accepted at locations where dollar checks may not be.

Another option is the new prepaid traveler's check cards, reloadable cards that work much like debit cards but aren't linked to your checking account. The **American Express Travelers Cheque Card,** for example, requires a minimum deposit, sets a maximum balance, and has a one-time issuance fee of $14.95. You can withdraw money from an ATM (for a fee of $2.50 per transaction, not including bank fees), and the funds can be purchased in dollars, euros, or pounds. If you lose the card, your available funds will be refunded within 24 hours.

5 Travel Insurance

The cost of travel insurance varies widely, depending on the destination, the cost and length of your trip, your age and health, and the type of trip you're taking, but expect to pay between 5% and 8% of the vacation itself. You can get estimates from various providers through **InsureMy Trip.com**. Enter your trip cost and dates,

your age, and other information, for prices from more than a dozen companies.

U.K. citizens and their families who make more than one trip abroad per year may find an annual travel insurance policy works out cheaper. Check **www.money supermarket.com**, which compares

> **Tips** **Medical Warning**
>
> The U.S. State Department's Office of Medical Services warns people suffering from the following ailments to exercise caution when traveling to high-altitude destinations such as La Paz, Lake Titicaca, Cusco, and Machu Picchu: **sickle cell anemia, heart disease** (for men 45 or over or women 55 or over who have two of the following risk factors: hypertension, diabetes, cigarette smoking, or elevated cholesterol), **lung disease,** and anyone with **asthma** and on the maximum dosage of medication for daily maintenance, or anyone who has been hospitalized for asthma within a year of their intended trip. It's best to talk with your doctor before planning a trip to a high-altitude destination in South America.

prices across a wide range of providers for single- and multitrip policies.

Most big travel agencies offer their own insurance and will probably try to sell you their package when you book a holiday. Think before you sign. **Britain's Consumers' Association** recommends that you insist on seeing the policy and reading the fine print before buying travel insurance. **The Association of British Insurers** (© 020/7600-3333; www.abi.org.uk) gives advice by phone and publishes *Holiday Insurance,* a free guide to policy provisions and prices. You might also shop around for better deals: Try **Columbus Direct** (© 0870/033-9988; www.columbusdirect.net).

TRIP-CANCELLATION INSURANCE

Trip-cancellation insurance will help retrieve your money if you have to back out of a trip or depart early, or if your travel supplier goes bankrupt. Trip cancellation traditionally covers such events as sickness, natural disasters, and Department of State advisories. The latest news in trip-cancellation insurance is the availability of **expanded hurricane coverage** and the **"any-reason"** cancellation coverage—which costs more but covers cancellations made for any reason. You won't get back 100% of your prepaid trip cost, but you'll be refunded a substantial portion. **TravelSafe** (© 888/885-7233;

www.travelsafe.com) offers both types of coverage. Expedia also offers any-reason cancellation coverage for its air-hotel packages.

For details, contact one of the following recommended insurers: **Access America** (© 866/807-3982; www.accessamerica.com); **Travel Guard International** (© 800/826-4919; www.travelguard.com); **Travel Insured International** (© 800/243-3174; www.travelinsured.com); and **Travelex Insurance Services** (© 888/457-4602; www.travelex-insurance.com).

MEDICAL INSURANCE

For travel overseas, most U.S. health plans (including Medicare and Medicaid) do not provide coverage, and the ones that do often require you to pay for services upfront and reimburse you only after you return home.

As a safety net, you may want to buy travel medical insurance, particularly if you're traveling to a remote or high-risk area where emergency evacuation might be necessary. If you require additional medical insurance, try **MEDEX Assistance** (© 410/453-6300; www.medexassist.com) or **Travel Assistance International** (© 800/821-2828; www.travelassistance.com; for general information on services, call the company's **Worldwide Assistance Services, Inc.,** at © 800/777-8710).

Canadians should check with their provincial health plan offices or call **Health Canada** (© 866/225-0709; www.hc-sc.gc.ca) to find out the extent of their coverage and what documentation and receipts they must take home in case they are treated overseas.

LOST-LUGGAGE INSURANCE

On international flights (including U.S. portions of international trips), baggage coverage is limited to approximately $9.07 per pound, up to approximately $635 per checked bag. If you plan to check items more valuable than what's covered by the standard liability, see if your homeowner's policy covers your valuables, get baggage insurance as part of your comprehensive travel-insurance package, or buy Travel Guard's "BagTrak" product.

If your luggage is lost, immediately file a lost-luggage claim at the airport, detailing the luggage contents. Most airlines require that you report delayed, damaged, or lost baggage within 4 hours of arrival. The airlines are required to deliver luggage, once found, directly to your house or destination free of charge.

6 Health

STAYING HEALTHY

For general information about health issues in South America, log on to the **Centers for Disease Control and Prevention**'s website at **www.cdc.gov/travel**. The CDC advises visitors to South America to protect themselves against hepatitis A and B. See "Health Concerns," in each destination chapter, for country-specific information.

GENERAL AVAILABILITY OF HEALTHCARE

Contact the **International Association for Medical Assistance to Travelers** (**IAMAT**; © 716/754-4883 or, in Canada, 416/652-0137; www.iamat.org) for tips on travel and health concerns in the countries you're visiting, and for lists of local, English-speaking doctors. The United States **Centers for Disease Control and Prevention** (© 800/311-3435; www.cdc.gov) provides up-to-date information on health hazards by region or country and offers tips on food safety. **Travel Health Online** (www.tripprep.com), sponsored by a consortium of travel medicine practitioners, may also offer helpful advice on traveling abroad. You can find listings of reliable medical clinics overseas at the **International Society of Travel Medicine** (www.istm.org).

WHAT TO DO IF YOU GET SICK AWAY FROM HOME

See in the "Fast Facts" section of the destination chapters for information on local hospitals and emergency phone numbers. For travel abroad, you may have to pay all medical costs upfront and be reimbursed later. Medicare and Medicaid do not provide coverage for medical costs outside the U.S. Before leaving home, find out what medical services your health insurance

---

Healthy Travels to You

The following government websites offer up-to-date health-related travel advice.

- **Australia:** www.dfat.gov.au/travel
- **Canada:** www.hc-sc.gc.ca/index_e.html
- **U.K.:** www.dh.gov.uk/en/Policyandguidance/Healthadvicefortravellers
- **U.S.:** www.cdc.gov/travel

Staying Safe

Millions of travelers visit South America without any problems. But as in any foreign destination, you should always keep your wits about you. Before you depart, check for travel advisories from the **U.S. Department of State** (www.travel.state.gov), the **Canadian Department of Foreign Affairs** (www.voyage.gc.ca), the **U.K. Foreign & Commonwealth Office** (www.fco.gov.uk/travel), and the **Australian Department of Foreign Affairs** (www.dfat.gov.au/consular/advice).

Once you're there, keep some common-sense safety advice in mind: Stay alert and be aware of your surroundings; don't walk down dark, deserted streets; and always keep an eye on your personal belongings. Theft at airports and bus stations is not unheard of, so be sure to put a lock on your luggage. See the destination chapters for information on country-specific safety concerns.

---

covers. To protect yourself, consider buying medical travel insurance (see "Medical Insurance," under "Travel Insurance," above).

Very few health insurance plans pay for medical evacuation back to the U.S. (which can cost $10,000 and up). A number of companies offer medical evacuation services anywhere in the world. If you're ever hospitalized more than 150 miles from home, **MedjetAssist** (© **800/527-7478;** www.medjetassistance.com) will pick you up and fly you to the hospital of your choice virtually anywhere in the world in a medically equipped and staffed aircraft 24 hours day, 7 days a week. Annual memberships are $225 individual, $350 family; you can also purchase short-term memberships.

U.K. nationals will need a **European Health Insurance Card (EHIC)** to receive free or reduced-costs health benefits during a visit to an European Economic Area (EEA) country (European Union countries plus Iceland, Liechtenstein and Norway) or Switzerland. The European Health Insurance Card replaces the E111 form, which is no longer valid. For advice, ask at your local post office or see **www.dh.gov.uk/travellers**.

If you suffer from a chronic illness, consult your doctor before your departure. Pack **prescription medications** in your carry-on luggage, and carry them in their original containers, with pharmacy labels—otherwise they won't make it through airport security. Carry the generic name of prescription medicines, in case a local pharmacist is unfamiliar with the brand name.

7 Specialized Travel Resources

TRAVELERS WITH DISABILITIES

Except for the most modern and upscale hotels in major cities, most buildings in South America are not well equipped for travelers with disabilities. Where elevators exist, they are often tiny. Many cities in South American streets are crowded and narrow. In the Andes, the high altitude and steep hills slow everyone down.

Nevertheless, a disability shouldn't stop anyone from traveling. There are more resources out there than ever before. Some of the best include **MossRehab** (© **800/CALL-MOSS;** www.mossresourcenet.org); the **American Foundation for the Blind** (AFB; © **800/232-5463;** www.afb.org); and **SATH** (**Society for Accessible Travel & Hospitality;**

© 212/447-7284; www.sath.org). **Air AmbulanceCard.com** is now partnered with SATH and allows you to preselect top-notch hospitals in case of an emergency.

Access-Able Travel Source (© 303/232-2979; www.access-able.com) offers a comprehensive database on travel agents from around the world with experience in accessible travel; destination-specific access information; and links to such resources as service animals, equipment rentals, and access guides.

Many travel agencies offer customized tours and itineraries for travelers with disabilities. Among them are **Flying Wheels Travel** (© 507/451-5005; www.flying wheelstravel.com) and **Accessible Journeys** (© 800/846-4537 or 610/521-0339; www.disabilitytravel.com).

Flying with Disability (www.flying-with-disability.org) is a comprehensive information source on airplane travel. **Avis Rent a Car** (© 888/879-4273) has an "Avis Access" program that offers services for customers with special travel needs. These include specially outfitted vehicles with swivel seats, spinner knobs, and hand controls; mobility scooter rentals; and accessible bus service. Be sure to reserve well in advance.

Also check out the quarterly magazine **Emerging Horizons** (www.emerging horizons.com), available by subscription ($16.95 year U.S.; $21.95 outside U.S).

The "Accessible Travel" link at **Mobility-Advisor.com** (www.mobility-advisor. com) offers a variety of travel resources to persons with disabilities.

British travelers should contact **Holiday Care** (© 0845-124-9971 in the U.K. only; www.holidaycare.org.uk) to access a wide range of travel information and resources for persons with disabilties and elderly people.

GAY & LESBIAN TRAVELERS

Most countries in South America are Catholic and conservative. However, in most large cities, there is a thriving underground gay community. To avoid offending local sensibilities or inviting possible verbal harassment in other parts of the continent, we recommend being discreet.

The International Gay and Lesbian Travel Association (IGLTA; © 800/448-8550 or 954/776-2626; www.iglta. org) is the trade association for the gay and lesbian travel industry, and offers an online directory of gay- and lesbian-friendly travel businesses and tour operators.

Many agencies offer tours and travel itineraries specifically for gay and lesbian travelers. **Above and Beyond Tours** (© 800/397-2681; www.abovebeyond tours.com) are Australia gay-tour specialists. San Francisco–based **Now, Voyager** (© 800/255-6951; www.nowvoyager. com) offers worldwide trips and cruises, and **Olivia** (© 800/631-6277; www. olivia.com) offers lesbian cruises and resort vacations.

Gay.com Travel (© 800/929-2268 or 415/644-8044; www.gay.com/travel or www.outandabout.com) is an excellent online successor to the popular *Out & About* print magazine. It provides regularly updated information about gay-owned, gay-oriented, and gay-friendly lodging, dining, sightseeing, nightlife, and shopping establishments in every important destination worldwide. British travelers should click on the "Travel" link at **www.uk.gay.com** for advice and gay-friendly trip ideas.

The Canadian website **GayTraveler** (gaytraveler.ca) offers ideas and advice for gay travel all over the world.

The following travel guides are available at many bookstores, or you can order them from any online bookseller: *Spartacus International Gay Guide, 35th Edition* (Bruno Gmünder Verlag; www.spartacus world.com/gayguide); *Odysseus: The International Gay Travel Planner, 17th Edition* (www.odyusa.com); and the *Damron* guides (www.damron.com), with separate, annual books for gay men and lesbians.

SENIOR TRAVEL

In most South American cultures, there is a deep respect for the elderly. Usually, if you ask for a senior discount, vendors will be happy to help you out. So don't be shy about asking for discounts, but always carry some kind of identification, such as a driver's license, that shows your date of birth. Also, mention the fact that you're a senior when you first make your travel reservations. All major airlines and many hotels offer discounts for seniors. In most cities, people over 60 qualify for reduced admission to theaters, museums, and other attractions, as well as discounted fares on public transportation.

Members of **AARP,** 601 E St. NW, Washington, DC 20049 (ⓒ **888/687-2277;** www.aarp.org), get discounts on hotels, airfares, and car rentals. AARP offers members a wide range of benefits, including *AARP: The Magazine* and a monthly newsletter. Anyone over 50 can join.

Many reliable agencies and organizations target the 50-plus market. **Elderhostel** (ⓒ **800/454-5768;** www.elderhostel.org) arranges worldwide study programs for those ages 55 and over. **ElderTreks** (ⓒ **800/741-7956** or 416/558-5000 outside North America; www.eldertreks.com) offers small-group tours to off-the-beaten-path or adventure-travel locations, restricted to travelers 50 and older.

Recommended publications offering travel resources and discounts for seniors include: the quarterly magazine *Travel 50 & Beyond* (www.travel50andbeyond.com) and the bestselling paperback *Unbelievably Good Deals and Great Adventures That You Absolutely Can't Get Unless You're Over 50 2005–2006, 16th Edition* (McGraw-Hill), by Joann Rattner Heilman.

FOR FAMILIES

Family values are very important in South America, so if you're traveling with your entire family, you can expect locals to welcome you with open arms. Children are treated with the utmost respect. When you take your kids out to eat, the staff will shower them with attention and make special provisions if your kiddies aren't up to eating exotic food. Rice, potatoes, and chicken are on almost every menu, so you won't have to worry about looking for a McDonald's.

South America is also great for children because the wildlife-watching opportunities are tremendous. Bring your kids to the jungle, and they will be eternally grateful to you for letting them get close to caimans and monkeys. In the Galápagos, swimming with sea lions will be an experience that your children will not soon forget. It's also a good idea to teach your children some South American history before your trip. They will be more willing to visit old cathedrals and museums if they understand the value of what they're seeing.

To locate accommodations, restaurants, and attractions that are particularly kid-friendly, refer to the "Kids" icon throughout this guide.

Recommended family travel websites include **Family Travel Forum** (www.familytravelforum.com), a comprehensive site that offers customized trip planning; **Family Travel Network** (www.familytravelnetwork.com), an online magazine providing travel tips; and **Travel WithYourKids.com** (www.travelwithyourkids.com), a comprehensive site written by parents for parents offering sound advice for long-distance and international travel with children.

FOR STUDENTS

The **International Student Travel Confederation** (ISTC; www.istc.org) was formed in 1949 to make travel around the world more affordable for students. Check out its website for comprehensive travel services information and details on how to get an **International Student Identity Card (ISIC),** which qualifies students for substantial savings on rail passes, plane tickets, entrance fees, and more. It also provides students with basic health and life insurance and a 24-hour helpline. The card is valid for a maximum of 18 months. You can apply for the card online or in person at **STA Travel** (© **800/ 781-4040** in North America; www.sta travel.com), the biggest student travel agency in the world; check out the website to locate STA Travel offices worldwide. If you're no longer a student but are still under 26, you can get an **International Youth Travel Card (IYTC)** from the same people, which entitles you to some discounts. **Travel CUTS** (© **800/ 592-2887;** www.travelcuts.com) offers similar services for both Canadians and U.S. residents. Irish students may prefer to turn to **USIT** (© **01/602-1904;** www. usit.ie), an Ireland-based specialist in student, youth, and independent travel.

FOR WOMEN

Besides the general safety advice offered in each country chapter, women traveling alone in South America should have few problems. Yes, in many cultures here, men have a very macho attitude, and women traveling alone can expect to get intense stares, catcalls, or even be followed for a few blocks by men asking for a date. But for the most part, these men are harmless. A simple *"Déjame en paz"* ("Leave me alone") will send the message that you're not interested.

There have been sporadic, unconfirmed reports of tour guides attacking single women travelers. It's always worth it to pay a few extra dollars to arrange a tour with a reputable travel agency. Talk to your fellow travelers and find out if they have had any problems. If you are attacked, contact the police immediately and notify your embassy. Safety specialists at your embassy will be able to assist you and hopefully work with the police to track down the assailant.

Check out the award-winning website **Journeywoman** (www.journeywoman. com), a "real life" women's travel-information network where you can sign up for a free e-mail newsletter and get advice on everything from etiquette and dress to safety. The travel guide *Safety and Security for Women Who Travel* by Sheila Swan and Peter Laufer (Travelers' Tales Guides), offering common-sense tips on safe travel, was updated in 2004.

8 Sustainable Tourism/Ecotourism

Each time you take a flight or drive a car CO_2 is released into the atmosphere. You can help neutralize this danger to our planet through "carbon offsetting"—paying someone to reduce your CO_2 emissions by the same amount you've added. Carbon offsets can be purchased in the U.S. from companies such as **Carbonfund.org** (www.carbonfund.org) and **TerraPass** (www.terrapass.org), and from **Climate Care** (www.climatecare.org) in the U.K.

Although one could argue that any vacation that includes an airplane flight can't be truly "green," you can go on holiday and still contribute positively to the environment. You can offset carbon emissions from your flight in other ways. Choose forward-looking companies that embrace responsible development practices, helping preserve destinations for the future by working alongside local people. An increasing number of sustainable tourism initiatives can help you plan a family trip and leave as small a "footprint" as possible on the places you visit.

Responsible Travel (www.responsible travel.com) contains a great source of sustainable travel ideas run by a spokesperson for responsible tourism in the travel industry. **Sustainable Travel International** (www.sustainabletravel international.org) promotes responsible tourism practices and issues an annual *Green Gear & Gift Guide.*

You can find eco-friendly travel tips, statistics, and touring companies and associations—listed by destination under "Travel Choice"—at the TIES website, **www.ecotourism.org**. Also check out **Conservation International** (www. conservation.org)—which, with *National Geographic Traveler,* annually presents **World Legacy Awards** (www.wlaward. org) to those travel tour operators, businesses, organizations, and places that have made a significant contribution to sustainable tourism. **Ecotravel.com** is part online magazine and part ecodirectory

that lets you search for touring companies in several categories (water-based, land-based, spiritually oriented, and so on).

In the U.K., **Tourism Concern** (www. tourismconcern.org.uk) works to reduce social and environmental problems connected to tourism and find ways of improving tourism so that local benefits are increased.

The **Association of British Travel Agents** (**ABTA;** www.abtamembers.org/ responsibletourism) acts as a focal point for the U.K. travel industry and is one of the leading groups spearheading responsible tourism.

The **Association of Independent Tour Operators** (**AITO;** www.aito.co.uk) is a group of interesting specialist operators leading the field in making holidays sustainable.

9 Planning Your Trip Online

SURFING FOR AIRFARES

The "big three" online travel agencies, **Expedia** (www.expedia.com), **Travelocity** (www.travelocity.com), and **Orbitz** (www.orbitz.com), sell most of the air tickets bought on the Internet. (Canadian travelers should try expedia.ca and Travelocity.ca; U.K. residents can go for expedia.co.uk and opodo.co.uk.) Each has different business deals with the airlines and may offer different fares on the same flights, so it's wise to shop around. Expedia and Travelocity will also send you **e-mail notification** when a cheap fare becomes available to your favorite destination. Of the smaller travel agency websites, **SideStep** (www.sidestep.com) has gotten the best reviews from Frommer's authors. It's a meta-search site that checks 140 sites at once for the best airfare, and then sends you directly to the appropriate site to make your purchase.

Also remember to check **airline websites;** you can often shave a few bucks

from a fare by booking directly through the airline and avoiding a travel agency's transaction fee. But you'll get these discounts only by booking online: Most airlines now offer online-only fares that even their phone agents know nothing about. For airlines that fly to and from your destination, see "Getting There," earlier.

Great **last-minute deals** are available through free weekly e-mail services provided directly by the airlines. Most of these are announced on Tuesday or Wednesday and must be purchased online. Most are only valid for travel that weekend, but some can be booked weeks or months in advance. Sign up for weekly e-mail alerts at airline websites.

SURFING FOR HOTELS & RENTAL CARS

Shopping online for hotels is generally done one of two ways: by booking through the hotel's own website or through an independent booking agency

Frommers.com: The Complete Travel Resource

Planning a trip or just returned? Head to **Frommers.com,** voted Best Travel Site by *PC Magazine.* We think you'll find our site indispensable before, during, and after your travels—with expert advice and tips; independent reviews of hotels, restaurants, attractions, and preferred shopping and nightlife venues; vacation giveaways; and an online booking tool. We publish the complete contents of over 135 travel guides in our **Destinations** section, covering over 4,000 places worldwide. Each weekday, we publish original articles that report on **Deals and News** via our free **Frommers.com Newsletters.** What's more, **Arthur Frommer** himself blogs five days a week, with cutting opinions about the state of travel in the modern world. We're betting you'll find our **Events** listings an invaluable resource; it's an up-to-the-minute roster of what's happening in cities everywhere—including concerts, festivals, lectures, and more. We've also added weekly **podcasts, interactive maps,** and hundreds of new images across the site. Finally, don't forget to visit our **Message Boards,** where you can join in conversations with thousands of fellow Frommer's travelers and post your trip report once you return.

(or a fare-service agency such as **Priceline;** www.priceline.com). These Internet hotel agencies have multiplied in mind-boggling numbers of late, competing for the business of millions of consumers surfing for accommodations around the world. This competitiveness can be a boon to consumers who have the patience and time to shop and compare the online sites for good deals—but shop they must, for prices can vary considerably from site to site. And keep in mind that hotels at the top of a site's listing may be there for no other reason than that they paid money to get the placement.

Of the "big three" sites, **Expedia** may be the top hotel-booking choice, thanks to its long list of special deals, "virtual tours," and photos of available rooms so you can see what you're paying for (a feature that helps counter the claims that the best rooms are often held back from bargain booking websites). Running a close second is **Travelocity,** which posts unvarnished customer reviews and ranks its properties according to the AAA rating system. Also reliable are **Hotels.com** and **Quikbook.** An excellent free program, **TravelAxe** (www.travelaxe.net), can help you search multiple hotel sites at once, even ones you may never have heard of.

10 Staying Connected

CELLPHONES

The three letters that define much of the world's wireless capabilities are **GSM** (Global System for Mobile Communications), a big, seamless network that makes for easy cross-border cellphone use throughout Europe and dozens of other countries worldwide. In the U.S., T-Mobile, AT&T Wireless, and Cingular use this quasi-universal system; in

Online Traveler's Toolbox

Veteran travelers usually carry some essential items to make their trips easier. Following is a selection of handy online tools to bookmark and use.

- **Airplane Food** (www.airlinemeals.net)
- **Airplane Seating** (www.seatguru.com and www.airlinequality.com)
- **Foreign Languages for Travelers** (www.travlang.com)
- **Maps** (www.mapquest.com)
- **Subway Navigator** (www.subwaynavigator.com)
- **Time and Date** (www.timeanddate.com)
- **Travel Warnings** (http://travel.state.gov, www.fco.gov.uk/travel, www.voyage.gc.ca, or www.dfat.gov.au/consular/advice)
- **Universal Currency Converter** (www.xe.com/ucc)
- **Visa ATM Locator** (www.visa.com), **MasterCard ATM Locator** (www.mastercard.com)
- **Weather** (www.intellicast.com and www.weather.com)

Canada, Microcell and some Rogers customers are GSM; and all Europeans and most Australians use GSM. GSM phones function with a removable plastic SIM card, encoded with your phone number and account information. If your cellphone is on a GSM system, and you have a world-capable multiband phone such as many Sony Ericsson, Motorola, or Samsung models, you can make and receive calls across civilized areas around much of the globe. Just call your wireless operator and ask for "international roaming" to be activated on your account. Unfortunately, per-minute charges can be high— usually $1 to $1.50 in Western Europe and up to $5 in such places as Russia and Indonesia.

For many, **renting** a phone is a good idea. While you can rent a phone from any number of overseas sites, including kiosks at airports and at car-rental agencies, we suggest renting the phone before you leave home. North Americans can rent one before leaving home from **InTouch USA** (✆ 800/872-7626; www.intouchglobal.com) or **RoadPost** (✆ 888/290-1606 or 905/272-5665; www.road

post.com). InTouch will also, for free, advise you on whether your existing phone will work overseas; simply call ✆ **703/222-7161** between 9am and 4pm EST, or go to **http://intouchglobal.com/travel.htm**.

Buying a phone can be economically attractive, as many nations have cheap prepaid phone systems. Once you arrive at your destination, stop by a local cellphone shop and get the cheapest package; you'll probably pay less than $100 for a phone and a starter calling card. Local calls may be as low as 10¢ per minute, and in many countries incoming calls are free.

VOICE OVER INERNET PROTOCOL (VOIP)

If you have Web access while traveling, you might consider a broadband-based telephone service (in technical terms, **Voice over Internet Protocol,** or VoIP), such as **Skype** (www.skype.com) or **Vonage** (www.vonage.com), which allows you to make free international calls if you use their services from your laptop or in a cybercafe. Check the sites for details.

INTERNET/E-MAIL
WITHOUT YOUR OWN COMPUTER

To find cybercafes in your destination check **www.cybercaptive.com** and **www.cybercafe.com**.

Most major airports have **Internet kiosks** that provide basic Web access for a per-minute fee that's usually higher than cybercafe prices. Check out such copy shops as **Kinko's** (FedEx Kinko's), which offers computer stations with fully loaded software (as well as Wi-Fi).

WITH YOUR OWN COMPUTER

More and more hotels, resorts, airports, cafes, and retailers are going **Wi-Fi** (wireless fidelity), becoming "hotspots" that offer free high-speed Wi-Fi access or charge a small fee for usage. Most laptops sold today have built-in wireless capability. To find public Wi-Fi hotspots at your destination, go to **www.jiwire.com**; its Hotspot Finder holds the world's largest directory of public wireless hotspots.

For dial-up access, most business-class hotels throughout the world offer dataports for laptop modems, and a few thousand hotels in Europe now offer free high-speed Internet access.

Wherever you go, bring a **connection kit** of the right power and phone adapters, a spare phone cord, and a spare Ethernet network cable—or find out whether your hotel supplies them to guests.

---

11 Escorted Tours, Package Deals & Special Interest Vacations

TOUR OPERATORS SPECIALIZING IN SOUTH AMERICA

Organizing a trip to South America can be a royal pain, especially if you don't speak Spanish or Portuguese. These tour companies have connections throughout the entire continent, and their staffs can make all of your travel arrangements for you. Here is a list of some of the best tour operators.

- **Abercrombie & Kent, Inc.** (© 800/554-7016; www.abercrombiekent.com) is the most upscale tour company arranging trips to South America. The company's tours will take you to the best parts of Patagonia, the Galápagos, Peru, Ecuador, Chile, and Argentina.

- **Kon-Tiki Tours & Travel** (© 877/566-8454; www.kontiki.org) is run by an American and Peruvian couple. The company specializes in trips throughout South America, including general highlights, and cultural and spiritual tours. You can choose from more than 30 different itineraries in Peru, Argentina, Bolivia, Brazil, Ecuador, and Chile. Prices include guides and airfare.

- **Ladatco Tours** (© 800/327-6162; www.ladatco.com) specializes in package tours to South and Central America. The company offers Carnaval specials, as well as air-only packages.

- **South American Expeditions** (© 800/884-7474; www.adventure sports.com/asap/travel/exped) offers adventure, cultural, off-the-beaten path, and women-only tours to Ecuador and Peru.

- **Tara Tours Inc.** (© 800/327-0080; www.taratours.com) is one of the most experienced agencies offering package tours to South America. Tours are personalized based on your interests; some of the specialties here include archaeology and spiritual journeys. In general, the company's package tours are great deals.

- **Condor Journeys and Adventures** (© 01700/841-318; www.condor journeys-adventures.com) is a British company that offers tour packages and active vacations throughout South America.

- **Journey Latin America** (℃ 020/ 8747-8315; www.journeylatinamer ica.co.uk) is one of the premier British travel agencies offering trips to South America. The company can arrange airfare and tour packages throughout the entire continent.
- **Adventure Associates Pty Ltd.** (℃ 02/9389-7466; www.adventure associates.com) is the best source in Australia for high-end package tours to South America and Antarctica.

SPECIAL INTEREST VACATIONS

Here's a list of companies offering educational and volunteer opportunities in South America:

- **AmeriSpan** (℃ 800/879-6640 or 215/751-1100; www.amerispan.com) helps students arrange programs that combine language study, travel, and volunteer opportunities throughout South America.

- **Amigos de las Américas** (℃ 800/ 231-7796 or 713/782-5290; www. amigoslink.org) is always looking for volunteers to promote public health, education, and community development in rural areas of Latin America.
- **Earthwatch Institute** (℃ 800/776-0188 or 978/461-0081; www.earth watch.org) supports sustainable conservation efforts of the earth's natural resources. The organization can always use volunteers for its research teams in South America.
- **Habitat for Humanity International** (℃ 229/924-6935, or check the website for local affiliates; www. habitat.org) needs volunteers to help build affordable housing in more than 79 countries in the world, including most countries in South America.
- **Spanish Abroad, Inc.** (℃ 888/722-7623 or 602/778-6791; www.spanish abroad.com) organizes intensive language-study programs throughout Latin America.

12 Getting Around

In general, the roads in South America are often in very poor condition. But there is an enormous network of bus lines, and if you have the time and patience, you can travel easily by bus from one country to another. Because car-rental agencies don't allow cars to be taken across international borders, it's very difficult to drive around the continent. There is also no reliable international train service. All in all, flying makes a lot of sense, especially if you're short on time.

See individual country chapters for complete details on getting around within each country.

BY PLANE

LAN offers the most comprehensive service in South America. Besides flying to most major cities in Chile and Peru, the airline also offers flights between Argentina, Brazil, Bolivia, Ecuador, Uruguay, and Venezuela. **Grupo Taca, Aerolíneas Argentinas,** and **Varig** also have several international routes.

If you plan on traveling between Chile, Argentina, Uruguay, and Brazil, you should consider buying a **Mercosur Air Pass.** The pass allows you to make two stopovers in each country, with a maximum of 10 stopovers. The pass is good for 7 to 30 days. Prices are based on mileage covered. You must buy the air pass outside of South America, and your initial flight must be on Aerolíneas Argentinas, American, Continental, Delta, LAN Chile, TAM, United, or Varig. For more information, contact

Globotur Travel at ℂ **800/998-5521** or visit **www.globotur.com**.

LAN Chile and American Airlines have joined forces to create the **Visit South America Airpass,** which allows you to travel between Argentina, Bolivia, Brazil, Colombia, Chile, Ecuador, Peru, Venezuela, and Uruguay. You must purchase a minimum of three flight segments, but you can only travel for 60 days or less. Again, fares are based on distance traveled. You must buy the pass in your home country. Contact **LAN** (ℂ **800/ 735-5526;** www.lan.com) or **American Airlines** (ℂ **800/433-7300;** www.aa. com) for more information.

BY BUS

It's possible to travel from Venezuela all the way to the tip of Argentina by bus. In fact, for most South Americans, buses are the main method of transportation. However, it's hard to find direct international routes. Usually, you take a bus to the border, where you must switch to a bus owned by a company in the country you have just entered. From there, you may have to take a bus to the largest nearby city, where you then can switch to a bus to your final destination. It's not the most efficient way to travel, but it's certainly cheap and a great way to see the countryside.

13 The Active Vacation Planner

Many outdoor activities can be arranged easily and cheaply upon arrival in South America. Local operators will have everything you need and can arrange guides and even companions. The nonprofit **South American Explorers** (www.samexplo.org) is a great resource if you're in Lima, Cusco, or Quito.

BIRD-WATCHING Over 3,100 species of birds either live or migrate through South America. Some of the rarest birds in the world live in and near the jungles of the Amazon rainforest. The jungle areas of Brazil, Peru, and Ecuador are among the best bird-watching spots in the world. The Galápagos Islands in Ecuador are also a birder's paradise— albatrosses; penguins; flightless cormorants; red-footed, blue-footed, and masked boobies; and the short-eared owl are just some of the rare birds that you'll see here. Peru's Manu Biosphere Reserve is also impressive: With more than 1,000 bird species recorded here, it has the highest concentration of birdlife on earth.

CLIMBING Many a mountaineer has traveled to South America to scale some

of the highest peaks in the world. The snowy peaks of Patagonia offer some of the most challenging climbs on the continent. But you don't have to head all way down south. In Ecuador, you can climb the glacier-covered Cotopaxi, which, at 5,804m (19,037 ft.), is the highest active volcano in the world.

DIVING The Galápagos Islands, off the coast of Ecuador, offer some of the most exciting diving in the world. You'll have the opportunity to see schools of hammerhead sharks as well as exotic underwater life. Serious divers should consider booking a special diving cruise around the islands. The Caribbean coast off of Venezuela is also a popular dive spot.

MOUNTAIN BIKING The 8,050km-long (5,000-mile) Andes mountain range offers some excellent mountain-biking opportunities. From Ecuador down to Patagonia, you'll find mountain-biking outfitters galore. But be careful: The roads are often poorly maintained. Some routes are narrow and open onto steep precipices. It's important to rent a high-quality bike that can deal with the conditions. The

South American Explorers Club advises bikers to use Kona, Trek, or Cannondale brand bikes. Cheaper bikes may not be able to survive the rough terrain.

RIVER RAFTING The Amazon is the world's second-longest river, and running it or one of its many tributaries is one of the great thrills in South America. The wildest parts run through Ecuador, Peru, and Brazil. And in central Chile, as the water rages down from the Andes to the Pacific, you'll find some of the wildest white-water rafting anywhere.

SKIING July and August are prime ski season in South America. The ski areas in Chile and southern Argentina are considered the Alps of South America. In Argentina, the glitterati head to Bariloche, while Chileans consider the ski resorts Valle Nevado (east of Santiago) and Portillo to be sacred ground.

SURFING It's been said that some of the longest breaks in the world exist off the coast of Peru. But small beach towns that cater to the surfing set dot the entire Pacific coast of South America. The Galápagos Islands have also begun to attract serious surfers to their windy shores. Not surprisingly, the Pacific can get quite cold—be sure to bring a wet suit. For warmer waters, surfers should head to the Caribbean coast of Venezuela. Henry Pitter National Park in Venezuela has become a hot spot.

SWIMMING, SNORKELING & OTHER WATERSPORTS The Atlantic coast of South America offers wonderful watersports opportunities. Punta del Este in Uruguay is one of the premier South American beach resorts. From December through March, the Argentine elite come here to sail, swim, water-ski, or just get close to the sea. The warm Caribbean waters off of Venezuela are also great for snorkeling, water-skiing, and windsurfing. The Pacific Coast isn't as enticing, but visitors to the Galápagos will find that the snorkeling there is out of this world.

4

Argentina

by Charlie O'Malley

Argentina is not just about tango and gauchos. The eighth-largest country in the world has 2.6 million km sq. (1 million miles sq.), meaning there's a lot of ground to cover, history to examine, and culture to experience. The diversity of countries that border Argentina—Uruguay, Brazil, Paraguay, Bolivia, and Chile—underscores its rich geography. The dazzling waterfalls and subtropical jungle of Iguazú contrast with the dry, polychromatic hills of Salta. The frigid scrublands of Patagonia are the opposite of the lush, green planes of the pampas. Like an ice-tipped spine, the Andes run south 5,500km (3,420 miles) to the end of the world, their foothills touching salt plains, tobacco fields, cactus hills, and bountiful vineyards. The people match the landscape and Argentina is a rattlebag of cultures and nationalities including Andean Incas, jungle-dwelling Indians, European immigrants, and Porteño Jews,

to mention just a few. Argentines are bold and joyful, though they also have a healthy dose of cynicism.

Argentina contains the most sophisticated city in South America, Buenos Aires. Here you'll find some of the best art and architecture on the planet and a treasure trove of restaurants, bars, and nightspots that would keep the most voracious hedonist occupied for a lifetime.

Argentina had a tumultuous 20th century. It started as one of the richest countries in the world and then underwent a rollercoaster of social upheavals and economic meltdowns, punctuated by Peronist populism and military manhunts. Its boom-and-bust cycle looked set to continue with a financial collapse that brought the country to its knees in 2001. It has since bounced back and devaluation has meant millions of visitors eager to enjoy a quality of life that few countries can boast.

1 The Regions in Brief

A short visit to Argentina creates the most tantalizing dilemmas: Buenos Aires is a must but so is Patagonia. Iguazú you have to see, but Mendoza sounds amazing. And what about Salta and the Lake District? One thing is for sure; you cannot see everything unless you have at least a month. Buenos Aires requires at least several days to appreciate. Iguazú from both the Argentine and Brazil sides requires at least 2 full days, though many people are happy to see just the Argentina side on a day trip from the capital. If you choose to head south, you can do it in a week, but you'd spend a good chunk of that time just getting down there. If you only have 2 weeks, split the country in two and save the other half for next time. Look upon it as a good excuse to come back.

BUENOS AIRES & THE PAMPAS Buenos Aires, a rich combination of South American energy and European sophistication, is a city of grand plazas and boulevards. Take time to wander its impressive museums and architectural sites, stroll along its fashionable waterfront, and immerse yourself in its dynamic culture and nightlife. A thick Argentine steak in a local *parrilla* (grill), a visit to a San Telmo antiques shop, a dance in a traditional tango salon—these are the small experiences that will connect you to the city's soul. One-third of Argentines live in greater Buenos Aires.

MENDOZA AND THE CENTRAL ANDES   Mendoza is a gorgeous oasis city of tree-lined avenues and elegant plazas. Open waterways carry melted snow from the ice tipped Andes in the background, feeding plains of dramatic vineyard country. The province is currently riding the wave of popularity: Argentine wine is experiencing global popularity and visitors are flocking here to visit beautiful wineries and try great regional cuisine. They are also coming to explore **Mount Aconcagua,** the tallest mountain outside the Himalayas, or raft on the famous Rio Mendoza.

MISIONES   This small province in the Mesopotamia enjoys a subtropical climate responsible for the region's flowing rivers and lush vegetation. The **Iguazú Falls** are created by the merger of the Iguazú and Paraná rivers at the border of Argentina, Brazil, and Paraguay. In this chapter, we explore Iguazú Falls, and I review lodging and dining on the Argentine side of the border. You can find similar information on the Brazilian part of the falls in chapter 6.

NORTHWEST   The Andes dominate the northwest, with ranges between 4,800m (15,744 ft.) and 6,900m (22,632 ft.). The two parallel mountain ranges are the Salto-Jujeña, cut by magnificent multicolored canyons called *quebradas.* This region is often compared with the Basin and Range regions of the southwestern United States, and can be visited from the historic towns of **Salta** and **Jujuy.** A must-see is the wine town of **Cafayate,** a sun-kissed village surrounded by vineyards and palatial wineries.

THE LAKE DISTRICT   Argentina's Lake District extends from Junín de los Andes south to Esquel—an Alpine-like region of snowy mountains, waterfalls, forests, and glacier-fed lakes. **San Martín de los Andes, Bariloche,** and **Villa La Angostura** are the chief destinations, but this isn't an area where you stay in one place. Driving tours, boating, skiing—you'll be on the move from the moment you set foot in the region.

PATAGONIA   Also known as the Magellanic Region or the Deep South, this dry, arid region at the southern end of the continent has recently soared in popularity. We discuss the Argentine part of Patagonia in this chapter, and the Chilean part of it in chapter 7.

Vast, open pampa, the colossal Northern and Southern ice fields, and hundreds of glaciers characterize Patagonia, as well as the jagged peaks of the Andes as they reach their terminus, emerald fiords, and wind, wind, wind. It's a long way but the journey pays off in the beauty and singularity of the region. **El Calafate** is a tourist-oriented village adjacent to the Perito Moreno Glacier. **El Chaltén** is a village of 200 residents whose numbers swell each summer with those who come to marvel at the towers of mounts Fitzroy, Cerro Torre, and Puntiagudo, for the singular nature of the granite spires that shoot up, torpedo-like, above huge tongues of ice that descend from the Southern Ice Field.

TIERRA DEL FUEGO   Even farther south than the Deep South, this archipelago at the southern tip of South America is, like Patagonia, shared by both Chile and Argentina. The main island, separated from the mainland by the Strait of Magellan, is a triangle with its base on the Beagle Channel. Tierra del Fuego's main town is **Ushuaia,** the southernmost city in the world. Many use the city as a jumping-off point for trips to Antarctica or sailing trips around Cape Horn.

2 The Best of Argentina in 2 Weeks

This country is so vast, it's wise to sacrifice some locations and not rush. Internal flights are the most convenient but increasingly expensive. Also Buenos Aires is the air transport hub, which means wherever you decide to go, it has to be through the capital, which can be annoying if traveling along the Andes. It is worth considering Argentina's long-distance buses for some of the journeys. Night buses are comfortable—indeed, luxurious—and what you lose in time you save on money plus hotel expenses. Car rentals should only be used for short distances because the regions between major destinations are often flat pampas or desert scrub and don't make for interesting scenery.

Days ❶–❷: Arrive in Buenos Aires ⌖

One of the greatest cities in the world demands your attention for at least 2 days. Put yourself in the lap of luxury at the **Alvear Palace Hotel** (p. 104), and explore the gothic elegance of **Recoleta Cemetery** (p. 96) and the grimy tangolopolis of **San Telmo.** Try to arrive on a weekend, as the city comes alive with antique markets, art fairs, and street performances. In the evening, catch a lavish tango show, or slum it at a neighborhood *milonga*.

Days ❸–❹: Iguazú Falls ⌖⌖⌖

Fly to **Iguazú** and peer into the abyss. Explore the clever system of walkways that take you so close you can almost touch the white, foaming torrent. Expect to get wet as you take a boat beneath the raging cascade that will drown your screams. Dry off in the nearby **Sheraton** (p. 121), and dine with a spectacular view. The following day, visit the Brazilian side, and do it all over again (don't forget that American and Canadian citizens require a visa to cross over) before returning to Buenos Aires by plane.

Days ❺–❻: Mendoza Wine Country ⌖⌖⌖

Catch a luxury night bus to the garden city of Mendoza. Spend the day among the tree-lined avenues, leafy plazas, and elegant parks. Enjoy a glass of Malbec on the sunny patio of the **Park Hyatt Mendoza** (p. 128) as you plot your wine tour for the following day.

Day ❼: Mount Aconcagua and the Andes

Take a day tour to the Andes. Follow the old Trans-Andean railway as it climbs through the stunning Uspallata valley and learn about its rich cultural and geographical history. At Aconcagua National Park, take a short hike to view the tallest mountain outside the Himalayas. Visit the picturesque Puente del Inca and enjoy a late lunch of kid goat in the mountain town of Uspallata.

Days ❽–❾: The Patagonian Glaciers

Go deep south to Patagonia and the town of El Calafate. Enjoy 2 days of all-inclusive pampering at **Los Notros** (p. 159), a luxury lodge with picture windows of the natural wonder that is Perito Moreno Glacier. Either sit back and enjoy the view, or go for guided ice walks and boat excursions to the wall of jagged blue ice. Watch out for the 10-ton chunks that fall into the water each day.

Days ❿–⓫: Fitzroy ⌖⌖

Hire a car and go north toward **El Chaltén,** enjoying the granite spires of the Fitzroy mountain range. Stop for a rustic lunch at **Patagonicus** (p. 162) before embarking on an overnight trek with **Fitz Roy Expediciones** (p. 160).

Itineraries in Argentina, Chile, Paraguay & Uruguay

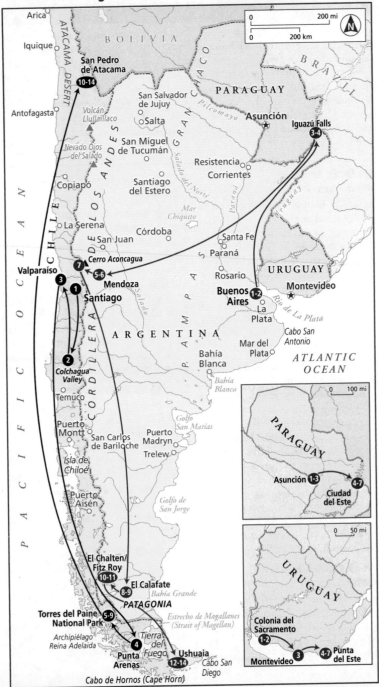

Days ⑫–⑭: The End of the World ❄
Fly to Ushuaia (there are flights from El Calafate Nov–Mar), the southernmost city in the world. Enjoy your final days in Argentina at **Las Hayas Resort** (p. 165).

Cruise the Beagle channel, where you can view sea lion and penguin colonies. Take a taxi and then a chair lift to the **Glacier Martial** (p. 164). On Day 14, fly back to Buenos Aires for your flight home.

3 Planning Your Trip to Argentina

VISITOR INFORMATION

IN THE U.S. The **Argentina Government Tourist Office** is located at 12 W. 56th St., New York, NY 10019 (© 212/603-0443; fax 212/315-5545); and 2655 Le Jeune Rd., Penthouse Suite F, Coral Gables, FL 33134 (© 305/442-1366; fax 305/441-7029).

IN CANADA Basic tourist information can be obtained from the **Consulate General of Argentina,** 2000 Peel St., Suite 600, Montreal, Quebec H3A 2W5 (© 514/842-6582; fax 514/842-5797; www.consargenmtl.com).

IN THE U.K. Contact the **Embassy of Argentina** in London (see "Entry Requirements," below) or consult **Argentina's Ministry of Tourism** website (see below).

ONLINE

- **www.embassyofargentina.us**: This site includes up-to-date travel information from the Argentine embassy in Washington, D.C.
- **www.sectur.gov.ar**: This Ministry of Tourism site has travel information for all of Argentina, including a virtual tour of the country's tourist regions, shopping tips, links to city tourist sites, and general travel facts.
- **www.mercotour.com**: This Spanish-language travel site focuses on adventure and ecological excursions, and includes information on outdoor activities in both Argentina and Chile.

ENTRY REQUIREMENTS

Citizens of the United States, Canada, the United Kingdom, Australia, New Zealand, and South Africa require a passport to enter the country. No visa is required for citizens of these countries for tourist stays of up to 90 days. For more information concerning longer stays, employment, or other types of visas, contact the embassies or consulates in your home country.

ARGENTINE EMBASSY LOCATIONS

In the U.S.: 1811 Q St. NW, Washington, DC 20009 (© 202/238-6400; www.embassyofargentina.us)

In Canada: Suite 910, Royal Bank Center, 90 Sparks St., Suite 910, Ottawa, ON K1P 5B4 (© 613/236-2351; fax 613/235-2659; www.argentina-canada.net)

In the U.K.: 65 Brooke St., London W1Y 4AH (© 020/7318-1300; fax 020/7318-1301; seruni@mrecic.gov.ar)

In Australia: John McEwen House, Level 2, 7 National Circuit, Barton, ACT 2600 (© 02/6273-9111; fax 02/6273-0500; www.argentina.org.au)

In New Zealand: Prime Finance Tower, Level 14, 142 Lambton Quay, Wellington (© 04/472-8330; fax 04/472-8331; www.arg.org.nz)

Telephone Dialing Info at a Glance

- **To place a call from your home country to Argentina,** dial the international access code (011 in the U.S., 0011 in Australia, 0170 in New Zealand, 00 in the U.K.) plus the country code (54), the city or region's area code, and the local number.
- **To make long-distance calls within Argentina,** dial a 0 before the city or region's area code. Note that tariffs are reduced from 10pm to 8am.
- **To place an international call from Argentina,** add 00 before the country code. Holders of **AT&T** credit cards can reach the money-saving USA Direct from Argentina by calling toll-free ℂ **0800/555-4288** from the north, or 0800/222-1288 from the south. Similar services are offered by **MCI** (ℂ **0800/555-1002**) and **Sprint** (ℂ **0800/555-1003** from the north, or 0800/222-1003 from the south).
- Dial **110** for **directory assistance** (most operators will speak English) and **000** to reach an **international operator.**

CUSTOMS

Travelers coming from countries not bordering Argentina are exempt from all taxes on traveling articles and new articles up to $300, and an additional $300 for goods purchased at Argentine duty-free shops.

MONEY

The official Argentine currency is the **peso,** made up of 100 **centavos.** Money is denominated in notes of 2, 5, 10, 20, 50, and 100 pesos and coins of 1 peso and 1, 5, 10, 25, and 50 centavos. Argentina ended its parity with the dollar in January 2002. At press time, the exchange rate was **3.17 pesos to the dollar** and **6.42 pesos to the British pound.** There are perpetual problems with getting small change throughout the country. *Tip:* To spot a fake note, hold the left hand number under a light. If it doesn't sparkle, you've been conned.

Since devaluation, Argentina has become a bargain for foreign visitors. Though prices have recovered significantly, especially hotel rates, visitors should still be amazed at the quality and value of goods and services. With a few exceptions, prices in this chapter are quoted in dollars, but realize that high inflation and volatile exchange rates will limit their accuracy.

CURRENCY EXCHANGE   U.S. dollars are widely accepted in Buenos Aires and can be used to pay taxis, hotels, restaurants, and stores. Do keep some pesos on hand because you might run into spots where you'll need them. U.S. dollars are less useful in rural areas (and places to exchange money less common), so plan ahead. You can convert your currency in hotels, at *casas de cambio* (money-exchange houses), at some banks, and at the Buenos Aires International Airport. Change American Express traveler's checks in Buenos Aires at **American Express,** Arenales 707 (ℂ **11/4130-3135**); it is difficult to change traveler's checks outside the capital. We recommend that you carry sufficient pesos (or purchase traveler's checks in pesos) when you venture into small-town Argentina.

ATMs   ATMs are easy to access in Buenos Aires and other urban areas, but don't bet on finding them off the beaten path. Typically, they are connected to **Cirrus** (© 800/424-7787) or **PLUS** (© 800/843-7587) networks. Many ATMs also accept Visa and MasterCard, less often American Express and Diners Club. Be aware that most ATMs allow only small withdrawals of as little as $100 (£50; this is a recent phenomenon which no banks seem to be able to explain or justify and is causing considerable frustration among travelers). Although the ATMs will allow several withdrawals in 1 day, it can still restrict your access to cash, and you get charged every time, sometimes up to $5 (£2.50). Consult your bank before leaving.

CREDIT CARDS   If you choose to use plastic, Visa, American Express, Master-Card, and Diners Club are the commonly accepted cards. However, **bargain-hunters take note:** Some establishments—especially smaller ones—don't like paying the fee to process your credit card and will give you a better price if you pay cash. Credit cards are accepted at most hotels and restaurants except the very cheapest ones. You cannot use credit cards in many taxis or at most attractions (museums, trams, and so on). To report a lost or stolen **MasterCard,** call © 0800/555-0507; for **Visa,** © 0800/666-0171; for **American Express,** call © 0810/555-2639.

WHEN TO GO

PEAK SEASON   The seasons in Argentina are the reverse of those in the Northern Hemisphere. Buenos Aires and the Lake District are ideal in fall (Mar–May) and spring (Sept–Nov), when temperatures are mild and crowds have yet to descend. The beaches and resort towns are packed with vacationing Argentines in summer (Dec–Mar), while Buenos Aires becomes somewhat deserted. (You decide whether that's a plus or a minus—hotel prices usually drop here in their summer.) Plan a trip to Patagonia and the southern Andes in their summer, when days are longer and warmer. Winter (June–Aug) is the best time to visit Iguazú and the Northwest, when the rains and heat have subsided; but spring (Aug–Oct) is also pleasant, as temperatures are mild and the crowds have cleared out. Mendoza is best visited from November to May, with the wine harvest season beginning in March.

CLIMATE   Except for a small tropical area in northern Argentina, the country lies in the temperate zone, characterized by cool, dry weather in the south, and warmer, humid air in the center. Accordingly, January and February are quite hot—often in the high 90s to more than 100°F (35°C–40°C)—while winter (about July–Oct) can be chilly.

PUBLIC HOLIDAYS   Public holidays are New Year's Day (Jan 1); Good Friday; Easter; Veterans' Day (Apr 2); Labor Day (May 1); First Argentine Government (May 25); Flag Day (June 20); Independence Day (July 9); Anniversary of the Death of General San Martín (Aug 17); Columbus Day (Oct 12); Feast of the Immaculate Conception (Dec 8); and Christmas (Dec 25). Note that many businesses are also closed on Christmas Eve (Dec 24).

HEALTH CONCERNS

Life in Argentina presents few health concerns. Argentina requires no vaccinations to enter the country, except for passengers coming from countries where cholera and yellow fever are endemic. Some people who have allergies (especially respiratory ones) can be affected by air pollution in the city and the high level of pollen during spring. Because motor vehicle crashes are a leading cause of injury among travelers, walk and drive defensively and always wear a seat belt.

Most visitors find that Argentine food and water is generally easy on the stomach. Water and ice are considered safe to drink in Buenos Aires. Be careful with food from street vendors, especially in dodgy neighborhoods of Buenos Aires and in cities outside the capital. Beef is a staple of the Argentine diet and an important export. The medical facilities and personnel in Buenos Aires and the other urban areas in Argentina are very professional and comparable to the U.S. standards. Argentina has a system of socialized medicine, where basic services are free. Private clinics are inexpensive by Western standards.

ALTITUDE SICKNESS   If you visit the Andes, ascend gradually to allow your body to adjust to the high altitude, thus avoiding altitude sickness. Altitude sickness, known as *soroche* or *puna,* is a temporary yet often debilitating affliction that affects about a quarter of travelers to the northern Altiplano, or the Andes, at 2,400m (8,000 ft.) and up. Nausea, fatigue, headaches, shortness of breath, and sleeplessness are the symptoms, which can last from 2 to 5 days. If you feel as though you've been affected, drink plenty of water, take aspirin or ibuprofen, and avoid alcohol and sleeping pills. To prevent altitude sickness, acclimatize your body by breaking the assent to higher regions into segments.

AUSTRAL SUN   The shrinking ozone layer in southern South America has caused an onset of health problems among its citizens, including increased incidents of skin cancer and cataracts. If you are planning to travel to Patagonia, keep in mind that on "red alert" days (typically Sept–Nov), it is possible to burn in *10 minutes.* If you plan to be outdoors, protect yourself with strong sun block, a long-sleeved shirt, a wide-brimmed hat, and sunglasses.

MALARIA & OTHER TROPICAL AILMENTS   The Centers for Disease Control and Prevention (www.cdc.gov) recommends that travelers to northwestern Argentina take malaria medication. Yet risk is very low and basic mosquito repellant should be sufficient. Cholera and dengue fever appear from time to time in the Northwest, but such tropical diseases do not seem to be a problem in the sultry climate of Iguazú.

GETTING THERE

Argentina's main international airport is **Ezeiza Ministro Pistarini** (EZE; ℂ **11/ 4480-0889**), located 34km (26 miles) outside Buenos Aires (allow 1 hr. to get to the city). You will be assessed a departure tax of approximately $20 (£10) upon leaving the country. For flights from Buenos Aires to Montevideo, Uruguay, the departure tax is $5 (£2.50). Passengers in transit and children under 2 are exempt from this tax. However, visitors are advised to verify the departure tax with their airline or travel agent, as the exact amount changes frequently. Be aware that any immediate domestic connection requires a 1-hour taxi ride to Buenos Aires internal airport **Aeroparque Jorge Newbery Airport** (ℂ **11/4514-1515**). This is hard to avoid except when traveling to Mendoza where flying via Santiago de Chile is more convenient as it does not require an airport change.

FROM THE U.S. & CANADA   Argentina's national airline, **Aerolíneas Argentinas** (ℂ 800/333-0276 in the U.S., 0810/222-86527 in Buenos Aires, or 1800/22-22-15 in Australia; www.aerolineas.com.ar), flies nonstop from Miami and New York's JFK. **American Airlines** (ℂ 800/433-7300 in the U.S., or 011/4318-1111 in Buenos Aires; www.aa.com) flies nonstop from Miami and Dallas–Fort Worth. **Copa Airlines** (ℂ 800/333-0425; www.copa.com) flies nonstop from Houston and New York (Newark). **Delta Airlines** (ℂ 800/241-4141 in the U.S., or 0800-666-0133;

www.delta.com) flies nonstop from Atlanta and Los Angeles. **LAN Chile** (© 866/
435-9526 in the U.S. and Canada, or 11/4378-2222 in Buenos Aires; www.lan.com)
flies nonstop from Los Angeles, Miami, and New York. **United Airlines** (© 800/241-
6522 in the U.S., or 0810/777-8648 in Buenos Aires; www.united.com) flies nonstop
from Miami; Washington, D.C. (Dulles Airport), Chicago; New York (La Guardia);
and Los Angeles. Approximate flight time from Miami to Buenos Aires is 9 hours. **Air
Canada** (© 888/247-2262 in Canada, or 11/4327-3640 in Buenos Aires; www.air
canada.ca) flies directly from Toronto to Buenos Aires.

FROM THE U.K. & EUROPE   **British Airways** (© 0845/773-3377 in the U.K.,
or 11/4320-6600 in Buenos Aires; www.britishairways.co.uk) flies nonstop from London Gatwick to Buenos Aires; approximate flight time is 13 hours. **Air France**
(© 800/423-7422 in Europe, or 11/4317-4700 in Buenos Aires; www.airfrance.com)
flies nonstop from Paris (Charles de Gaulle). **Iberia** (© 0845/601-2854 in the U.K.,
or 11/4131-1000 in Buenos Aires; www.iberia.com) connects through Madrid and
Barcelona. **Lufthansa** (© 0870/1288-737 in the U.K., or 11/4319-0600 in Buenos
Aires; www.lufthansa.com) flies nonstop from Frankfurt. **Aerolíneas Argentinas**
(© 0800/096-9747; www.aerolinas.com.ar) flies from Madrid, Barcelona, and Rome.
Alitalia (© 0810/777-2548; www.alitalia.com) operates flights from Rome.

FROM AUSTRALIA & NEW ZEALAND   **Aerolíneas Argentinas** (© 800/22-
22-15 in Australia; www.aerolineas.com.ar) flies from Sydney, with a stop in Auck-
land; approximate flight time from Sydney is 16 hours. **LAN** (© 300/36-14-00 in
Australia, or © 649/977-2233 in New Zealand; www.lan.com) and **Qantas** (© 13-
13-13 in Australia or 11/4514-4730 in Buenos Aires; www.quantas.com.au) now has
service from Sydney to Santiago with shared service continuing to Buenos Aires on
LAN Chile.

GETTING AROUND
BY PLANE

The easiest way to travel Argentina's vast distances is by air. **Aerolíneas Argentinas**
(© 0810/222-86527; www.aerolineas.com.ar) connects most cities and tourist destinations in Argentina, including Córdoba, Jujuy, Iguazú, Mendoza, and Salta. Its only
competitor, **LAN Argentina** (© 11/43782200; www.lan.com), serves Iguazú, Mendoza, and Bariloche, among others. By American standards, domestic flights within
Argentina are very expensive. Expect long delays with Aerolíneas Argentinas, which
has an 80% monopoly of the domestic market; the company is inefficient and guilty
of outrageous dual pricing, charging foreign travelers as much as 300% more than
locals.

In Buenos Aires, domestic flights and flights to Uruguay travel out of **Aeroparque
Jorge Newbery Airport** (© 11/4514-1515), 15 minutes from downtown. Inexpensive taxis and *remises* (private, unmetered taxis) cost about $20 (£10) to get you to and
from the city center. At both airports, only take officially sanctioned transportation
and do not accept transportation services from any private individuals. **Manuel
Tienda León** (© 11/4314-3636) is the most reliable transportation company, offering buses and *remises* to and from the airports (www.tiendaleon.com.ar).

BY BUS

Argentine buses are comfortable, safe, efficient, and surprisingly luxurious. They connect nearly every part of Argentina as well as bordering countries. In cases where two

classes of bus service are offered—*semicama* and *cama*—the latter offers wider seats, is very comfortable, and is only 10% more expensive. Some companies offer *cama ejecutivo*, which is basically a full horizontal bed and, again, only 10% more expensive than a *cama*. Most long-distance buses offer clean toilets, air-conditioning, TV entertainment, and dinner/bar service. Bus travel is much cheaper than air travel for similar routes, and for this reason, many people opt for a luxury night bus. My advice is to consider a night bus if you are on a budget and the journey is no more than 16 hours. Even committed air travelers are surprised at just how pleasant the night bus can be and it is a singular, South American cultural experience that the Argentines seem to have made an art of. One piece of advice: Take an extra sweater as some companies can be overly generous with the air-conditioning.

Among the major bus companies that operate out of Buenos Aires are **La Veloz del Norte** (© 11/4315-2482), serving destinations in the Northwest including Salta and Jujuy; **Singer** (© 11/4315-2653), serving Puerto Iguazú and Brazilian destinations; and **T. A. Chevallier** (© 11/4313-3297), serving Bariloche. **Andesmar** (© 11/4328-8240;** www.andesmar.com) is a first-class company that goes everywhere, including Santiago de Chile. They serve free wine and conduct on-the-road bingo sessions in case you get bored. Another recommended company is **CATA** (© 11/4311-5581; www.catainternacional.com), which operates between Argentina and Chile and thoughtfully serves a nightcap of whiskey before you drop off.

BY CAR

Argentine roads and highways are generally in good condition, with the exception of some rural areas. Most highways have been privatized and charge nominal tolls. In cities, Argentines drive exceedingly fast, and do not always obey traffic lights or lanes. When driving outside the city, remember that *autopista* means motorway or highway, and *paso* means mountain pass. Don't drive in rural areas at night, as cattle sometimes overtake the road to keep warm and are nearly impossible to see. Wear your seat belt; it's required by Argentine law, although few Argentines actually wear them. U.S. driver's licenses are valid in greater Buenos Aires, but you need an Argentine or international license to drive in most other parts of the country. A car that uses GNC (a hybrid fuel of gas and oil) is 50% cheaper than unleaded gas (known as NAFTA) but requires more frequent filling. ***Beware:*** In remoter areas many filling stations do not serve GNC so you must revert to NAFTA.

The **Automóvil Club Argentino (ACA),** Av. del Libertador 1850 (© 11/4802-6061), has working arrangements with International Automobile Clubs. The ACA offers numerous services, including roadside assistance, road maps, hotel and camping information, and discounts for various tourist activities.

CAR RENTALS   Many international car-rental companies operate in Argentina with offices at airports and in city centers. The major companies are **Hertz** (© 800/654-3131 in the U.S.; www.hertz.com), **Avis** (© 800/230-4898 in the U.S.; www.avis.com), **Dollar** (© 800/800-3665 in the U.S.; www.dollar.com), and **Thrifty** (© 800/847-4389 in the U.S.; www.thrifty.com); see "Buenos Aires," below, for locations in the capital. Car rental will cost about $70 (£35) per day for an intermediate-size vehicle, including unlimited miles and 21% tax (ask for any special promotions, especially on weekly rates). Check to see if your existing automobile insurance policy (or a credit card) covers insurance for car rentals; otherwise you should purchase full insurance that costs approximately $10 (£5) a day. Be aware that you cannot cross into neighboring countries in rental cars unless you acquire a special permit at the rental agency. **Avis** is the best company to do this with.

TIPS ON DINING

Argentines can't get enough beef. Indeed, the average citizen eats more than his or her own weight in meat each year. While exporting some of the finest beef in the world, they still manage to keep enough of this national treasure at home to please natives and visitors alike. Argentine meat is regarded as healthier and more free-range than its foreign counterparts. A huge sizzling steak is often item number one on many travelers' itineraries when they arrive here.

The Argentine social venue of choice is the *asado* (barbecue). Families and friends gather at someone's home and barbecue prime ribs, pork, chicken, sausages, sweetbreads, kidneys—the list goes on. You can enjoy this tradition while eating out; many restaurants are referred to interchangeably in Spanish as *parrillas* or *parrilladas,* with open-air grills and, occasionally, large spits twirling animal carcasses over a roaring fire. For the full experience, ask for the *parrillada mixta* (mixed grill), which includes many of the items mentioned above. And don't forget the *chimichurri* sauce—an exotic blend of chili and garlic—to season your meat. ***A note on steaks:*** You can order them *bien cocida* (well done), a *punto* (medium rare), or *jugoso* (rare, literally "juicy").

But vegetarians exhale: Argentina offers some great alternatives to the red-meat diet. One of the imprints Italians have left on Argentine culture is a plethora of pasta dishes, pizzas, and even *helados* (ice cream), reminiscent of Italian gelato. In addition, ethnic restaurants are springing up throughout Buenos Aires, stretching beyond traditional Spanish, Italian, and French venues to Japanese, Indian, Armenian, and Thai. Ethnic dishes come to life with fresh meats, seafood, and vegetables—the products of Argentina's diverse terrain. If you're just looking for a snack, try an empanada, a turnover pastry filled with minced meat, chicken, vegetables, or corn and varying a bit by region.

BEVERAGES

An immensely popular afternoon custom is the sharing of *mate,* a tea made from the *yerba mate* herb. In the late afternoon, Argentines pass a gourd filled with the tea around the table, each person sipping through a metal straw with a filter on the end. The drink is bitter, so you might opt to add some sugar. *Mate* is such an important part of daily life in Argentina that if people plan to be out of the house at teatime, they tote a thermos with them. A popular alcoholic drink is the Italian digestif Fernet, served with lashings of ice and cola.

Argentina boasts some spectacular wine-growing regions; the best known is Mendoza, but Salta, San Juan, and La Rioja also produce impressive vintages. Malbec is the best known Argentine red wine and is an engaging companion to any *parrillada mixta.* The Torrontes grape, a dry white wine, has won various international competitions as well. Other grapes to look out for: Tempranillo and Bonarda.

Tips Late-Night Dining

In Argentina, meal times are, on average, later than English-speaking travelers may be used to. Dinner frequently does not begin until after 9pm, and restaurants stay open until well past midnight.

TYPICAL ARGENTINE DISHES

Look for some of these favorites on your menu:

- *Bife de chorizo:* Similar to a New York strip steak, but twice as big. Thick and tender, usually served medium rare.
- *Bife de lomo:* Filet mignon, 7.5cm (3-in.) thick. Tender and lean.
- *Buseca:* Stew with sausages.
- *Locro criollo:* Beef stew with potatoes.
- *Milanesa:* Breaded meat filet, sometimes in a sandwich.
- *Panqueques:* Either dessert crepes filled with *dulce de leche* (caramel) and whipped cream, or salted crepes with vegetables.
- *Provoletta:* Charbroiled slices of provolone cheese served at a *parrilla.*

TIPS ON SHOPPING

Porteños (residents of Buenos Aires) consider their city a fashion capital. Buenos Aires boasts the same upscale stores you would find in New York or Paris. The big designer labels are in Recoleta and Belgrano and small, boutique designers in Palermo Viejo. Furs, wool, and leather goods are excellent quality across the country, while Buenos Aires is superb for antiques and vintage clothes. Keep your receipts for invoices over approximately $20 (£10) from stores participating in tax-free shopping; you should be able to get a refund of the 21% value-added tax (abbreviated IVA in Spanish) when you leave the country. Forms are available at the airport—desk 25 in Ezeiza. Get forms stamped and go through customs before collecting your refund upstairs. Opt for the cash refund, as credit card processing takes weeks. Technically they can ask to see goods, but this rarely happens since it is impractical—*except* at Aeroparque on flights to Uruguay. Be aware that credits over $170 (£85) require and authorization code from the store. Art items will often be stopped by customs unless accompanied by a special export permit provided by the vender and a certificate of authenticity by the artist. One possible way around the export permit is a letter from the artist saying the item is a gift.

FAST FACTS: Argentina

American Express Offices are located in Buenos Aires, Bariloche, Salta, San Martín, and Ushuaia. In Buenos Aires, the Amex office is at Arenales 707 (© 11/4312-1661). It's open Monday to Friday 9am to 5pm.

Business Hours Banks are open weekdays from 10am to 3pm. Shopping hours are weekdays 9am to 8pm and Saturday 9am to 1pm. Shopping centers are open daily from 10am to 8pm. Some stores close for lunch.

Electricity If you plan to bring a hair dryer, radio, travel iron, or any other small appliance, pack a transformer and a European-style adapter, since electricity in Argentina runs on 220 volts. Note that most laptops operate on both 110 and 220 volts. Luxury hotels usually provide transformers and adapters.

Embassies In Buenos Aires: **United States,** Av. Colombia 4300 (© 11/4774-5333); **Australia,** Villanueva 1400 (© 11/4777-6580); **Canada,** Tagle 2828 (© 11/4805-3032); **New Zealand,** Carlos Pellegrini 1427, 5th Floor (© 11/4328-0747); and the **United Kingdom,** Luis Agote 2412 (© 11/4803-6021).

Emergencies The following emergency numbers are valid throughout Argentina. For an ambulance, call ✆ **107;** in case of fire, call ✆ **100;** for police assistance, call ✆ **101.**

Hospitals The best hospitals in Buenos Aires are **British Hospital,** Perdriel 74 (✆ 11/4309-6400); **Sanatorio San Lucas,** Belgrano 369, San Isidro (✆ 11/4732-8888); and **Mater Dei,** San Martín de Tours 2952 (✆ 11/4809-5555). All have English-speaking doctors on staff.

Internet Access Cybercafes are on every corner in Buenos Aires and are found in other cities as well, so it won't be hard to stay connected while in Argentina. Access is reasonably priced (usually averaging 50¢/25p per hr.) and connections are reliably good. The bigger *cybers* are usually Skype, connected with hand phones attached to monitors. Wi-Fi is ubiquitous, especially in top hotels, cafes, and some city pedestrian streets.

Language Argentina's official language is Spanish, but it's easy to find English-speakers in major hotels, restaurants, and shops—particularly in the big cities. Many working-class Argentines speak little or no English, and it's even less common in rural areas.

Liquor Laws The official drinking age in Argentina is 18. Licensing laws are very liberal, though in some city districts stores cannot sell after 11pm.

Maps Reliable maps can be purchased at the offices of the **Automóvil Club Argentino,** Av. del Libertador 1850, Buenos Aires (✆ **11/4802-6061** or 11/4802-7071).

Newspapers & Magazines Major local papers are *Clarín* (independent), *Página* (center-left), and *La Nación* (conservative). The *Buenos Aires Herald* is the (quite good) local English newspaper. The *International Herald Tribune* is widely available at news kiosks around the country. Some hotels in Buenos Aires will deliver a *New York Times* headline news fax to your room. *Time Out Buenos Aires* is a city-listings magazine, and *Wine Republic* (www.wine-republic.com) is Mendoza's English-language publication.

Post Offices/Mail Post offices are generally open Monday through Friday from 8am to 6pm and Saturday from 8am to 1pm. Airmail postage for a letter weighing 7 ounces or less from Argentina to North America and Europe is $1. Mail takes on average between 10 and 14 days to get to the U.S. and Europe.

Restrooms Public facilities are generally very good; you can duck into hotel lobbies, restaurants, cafes, and shopping centers.

Safety Argentina is the safest country in South America after Uruguay. Nevertheless petty crime is widespread in Buenos Aires and growing elsewhere. Travelers should be especially alert to pickpockets and purse snatching on the streets and on buses and trains. Street crime is common in the suburbs of the capital and in Buenos Aires province. Avoid demonstrations, strikes, and other political gatherings. Always keep your belongings in sight while dining or drinking. Do not take taxis off the street in Buenos Aires; you should call for a radio-taxi or *remise* (private, unmetered taxi) instead—your hotel, restaurant, or bar will happily call for you.

Smoking Smoking used to be a pervasive aspect of Argentine society but now more and more provinces are banning it indoors, and people are taking heed. Where there are no restrictions, you can request a nonsmoking table in a restaurant, and you will usually be accommodated. There is never any smoking on buses or trains.

Taxes Argentina's value-added tax (IVA) is 21%. For tax-free shopping, see "Tips on Shopping," above.

Telephone & Fax Domestic and international calls are expensive in Argentina, especially from hotels (rates fall 10pm–8am). Direct dialing to North America and Europe is available from most phones.

Public phones take either phone cards (sold at kiosks on the street) or coins (less common). Local calls cost 20 centavos (about 6¢/3p) to start, and charge more the longer you talk. Telecentro offices—found everywhere in city centers—offer private phone booths where calls are paid when completed. Most hotels offer fax services, as do all Telecentro offices. For international calls, it is recommended you use phone cards such as Hablemas or Teletel. If you can follow the Spanish instructions, it means a 1-hour-and-40-minute call to the U.S. can cost as little as $3 (£1.50). Another good option is the many cyber cafes with Skype. See the "Telephone Dialing Info at a Glance" box on p. 80.

Time Zone Argentina does not adopt daylight saving time, so the country is 1 hour ahead of eastern standard time in the United States in summer and 2 hours ahead in winter.

Tipping A 10% tip is expected at cafes and restaurants. Give at least $1 (50p) to bellhops and porters, 5% to hairdressers, and leftover change to taxi drivers.

Water In Buenos Aires and along the Andes, the water is perfectly safe to drink; if you are traveling to more humid regions in the northeast, it's best to stick with bottled water for drinking.

4 Buenos Aires ★★

Enjoy a European city at a fraction of the price. Buenos Aires has it all—the glamour, the architecture, and the nightlife. Stroll through the neighborhoods of Recoleta or Palermo, full of buildings with neoclassical facades on broad tree-lined boulevards, and you'll start to understand why this place developed the reputation of being the Paris of South America. European immigrants to Buenos Aires, mostly from Spain and Italy, brought with them the warm ways of Mediterranean culture. Whiling away the night over a long meal is the norm, and locals pack into cafes, restaurants, and bars until the early morning hours.

You'll find a city of old historical cafes and restaurants competing with new ones opening up at a breakneck pace all over town, particularly in the trendy Palermo district. The city's post-crisis renaissance has lead to an incredible flourishing of all things Porteño, the word Buenos Aires locals use to describe both themselves and the culture of their city. Unable to import expensive foods from overseas anymore, Buenos Aires's restaurants are concentrating instead on cooking with Argentine staples such as Pampas grass-fed beef. What has developed is a spectacular array of Argentine-nouvelle cuisine of incredible quality. Chefs can't seem to produce it fast enough in the ever-expanding array of Buenos Aires's restaurants.

This new Argentine self-reliance and pride is not just limited to its restaurants. Importantly, the most Porteño thing of all, the tango, has also witnessed an explosive growth. Up until the peso crisis, Argentines worried that the dance would die out, but young Argentines and expats from all over the world who love the tango are making Buenos Aires the world's new hot city, the way Prague was at the end of the Cold War. The city is also home to an incomparable array of theaters and other traditional venues. Add to this the preparations for the city's bicentennial celebrations in 2010 and it means there is no better time to visit Buenos Aires, a city rich in cultural excitement.

ESSENTIALS
GETTING THERE
BY PLANE   See "Getting Around: By Plane," on p. 83.

BY BUS   The **Estación Terminal de Omnibus** (also known as Terminal Retiro), Av. Ramos Mejía 1680 (© **11/4310-0700**), located near Retiro train station, serves all long-distance buses. The terminal's official website, **www.tebasa.com.ar**, provides useful information on the buses serving the terminal and their destinations.

BY CAR   In Buenos Aires, travel by *subte* (subway), *remise*, or radio-taxi is easier and safer than driving yourself. Rush-hour traffic is chaotic, and parking is difficult. If you do rent a car, park it at your hotel or at a nearby garage and leave it there. You really don't need to have one in the city.

ORIENTATION
Although Buenos Aires is a huge city, the main tourist neighborhoods are concentrated in a small section near the Río de la Plata. The Microcentro, which extends from Plaza de Mayo to the south and Plaza San Martín to the north, and from Plaza del Congreso to the west and Puerto Madero to the east, forms the city center. San Telmo, La Boca, Puerto Madero, Recoleta, and Palermo surround the Microcentro. The city layout is fairly straightforward, where *avenidas* signify the broad avenues and *calles* smaller, one-way streets, while *diagonales* cut streets and avenues at 45-degree angles. Each city block extends about 100m (328 ft.), and building addresses indicate the distance on that street.

The **Microcentro** includes Plaza de Mayo (the political and historic center of Buenos Aires), Plaza San Martín, and Avenida 9 de Julio (the widest street in the world). Most commercial activity is focused here, as are the majority of hotels and restaurants. Next to the Microcentro, the riverfront area called **Puerto Madero** boasts excellent restaurants and nightlife as well as new commercial areas. Farther south, **La Boca, Monserrat,** and **San Telmo** are the historic neighborhoods where the first immigrants arrived and tango originated.

The city's most strikingly European neighborhood, **Recoleta,** offers fashionable restaurants, cafes, and evening entertainment amid rich French architecture. It's home to the Recoleta Cemetery, where key personalities, such as Evita, are buried. To the northwest is **Palermo,** actually made of several different and distinct neighborhoods. Palermo contains lots of parks, mansions, and gardens—making it perfect for a weekend picnic or evening outing. **Palermo Viejo,** further divided into **Palermo SoHo** and **Palermo Hollywood,** is full of funky bohemian boutiques and music bars, as well as the city's chicest restaurants.

Buenos Aires

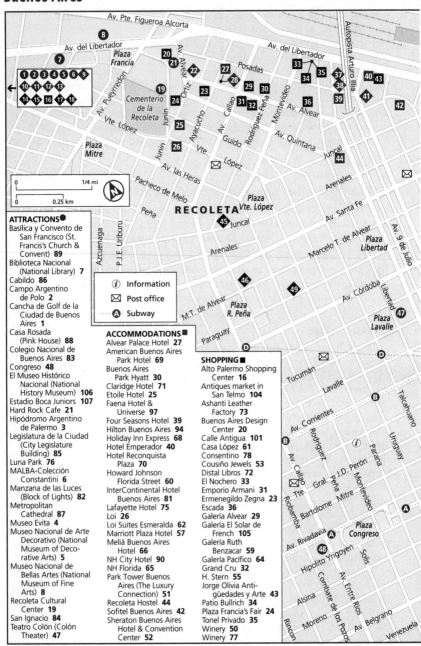

ATTRACTIONS ●

Basílica y Convento de San Francisco (St. Francis's Church & Convent) **89**
Biblioteca Nacional (National Library) **7**
Cabildo **86**
Campo Argentino de Polo **2**
Cancha de Golf de la Ciudad de Buenos Aires **1**
Casa Rosada (Pink House) **88**
Colegio Nacional de Buenos Aires **83**
Congreso **48**
El Museo Histórico Nacional (National History Museum) **106**
Estadio Boca Juniors **107**
Hard Rock Cafe **21**
Hipódromo Argentino de Palermo **3**
Legislatura de la Ciudad (City Legislature Building) **85**
Luna Park **76**
MALBA-Colección Constantini **6**
Manzana de las Luces (Block of Lights) **82**
Metropolitan Cathedral **87**
Museo Evita **4**
Museo Nacional de Arte Decorativo (National Museum of Decorative Arts) **5**
Museo Nacional de Bellas Artes (National Museum of Fine Arts) **8**
Recoleta Cultural Center **19**
San Ignacio **84**
Teatro Colón (Colón Theater) **47**

ⓘ Information
✉ Post office
Ⓐ Subway

ACCOMMODATIONS ■

Alvear Palace Hotel **27**
American Buenos Aires Park Hotel **69**
Buenos Aires Park Hyatt **30**
Claridge Hotel **71**
Etoile Hotel **25**
Faena Hotel & Universe **97**
Four Seasons Hotel **39**
Hilton Buenos Aires **94**
Holiday Inn Express **68**
Hotel Emperador **40**
Hotel Reconquista Plaza **70**
Howard Johnson Florida Street **60**
InterContinental Hotel Buenos Aires **81**
Lafayette Hotel **75**
Loi **26**
Loi Suites Esmeralda **62**
Marriott Plaza Hotel **57**
Meliá Buenos Aires Hotel **66**
NH City Hotel **90**
NH Florida **65**
Park Tower Buenos Aires (The Luxury Connection) **51**
Recoleta Hostel **44**
Sofitel Buenos Aires **42**
Sheraton Buenos Aires Hotel & Convention Center **52**

SHOPPING ■

Alto Palermo Shopping Center **16**
Antiques market in San Telmo **104**
Ashanti Leather Factory **73**
Buenos Aires Design Center **20**
Calle Antigua **101**
Casa López **61**
Consentino **78**
Cousiño Jewels **53**
Distal Libros **72**
El Nochero **33**
Emporio Armani **31**
Ermenegildo Zegna **23**
Escada **36**
Galería Alvear **29**
Galería El Solar de French **105**
Galería Ruth Benzacar **59**
Galería Pacífico **64**
Grand Cru **32**
H. Stern **55**
Jorge Olivia Antigüedades y Arte **43**
Patio Bullrich **34**
Plaza Francia's Fair **24**
Tonel Privado **35**
Winery **50**
Winery **77**

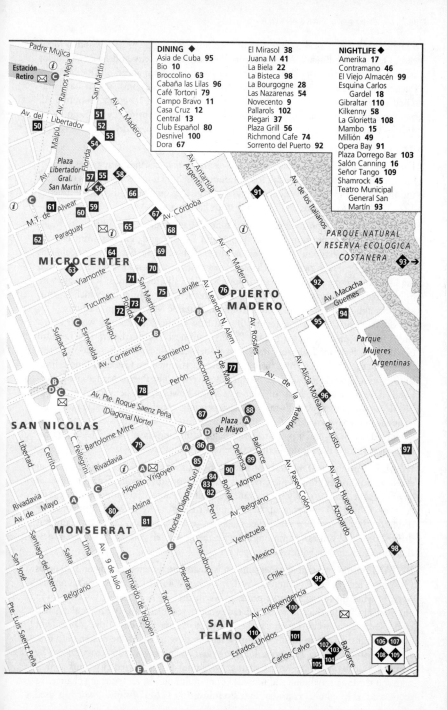

DINING ◆
Asia de Cuba **95**
Bio **10**
Broccolino **63**
Cabaña las Lilas **96**
Café Tortoni **79**
Campo Bravo **11**
Casa Cruz **12**
Central **13**
Club Español **80**
Desnivel **100**
Dora **67**

El Mirasol **38**
Juana M **41**
La Biela **22**
La Bisteca **98**
La Bourgogne **28**
Las Nazarenas **54**
Novecento **9**
Pallarols **102**
Piegari **37**
Plaza Grill **56**
Richmond Cafe **74**
Sorrento del Puerto **92**

NIGHTLIFE ◆
Amerika **17**
Contramano **46**
El Viejo Almacén **99**
Esquina Carlos
    Gardel **18**
Gibraltar **110**
Kilkenny **58**
La Glorietta **108**
Mambo **15**
Millión **49**
Opera Bay **91**
Plaza Dorrego Bar **103**
Salón Canning **16**
Señor Tango **109**
Shamrock **45**
Teatro Municipal
    General San
    Martín **93**

Estación Retiro

Padre Mujica
Av. Ramos Mejía
San Martín
Av. E. Madero
Av. del Libertador
Maipú
Florida
Plaza Libertador Gral. San Martín
M.T. de Alvear
Paraguay
Av. Antártida Argentina
Av. Córdoba
Av. E. Madero
Av. de los Italianos

PARQUE NATURAL Y RESERVA ECOLOGICA COSTANERA

MICROCENTER
Viamonte
Tucumán
San Martín
Lavalle
Florida
Maipú
Suipacha
Esmeralda
Av. Corrientes
Sarmiento
Perón
Reconquista
25 de Mayo
Av. Leandro N. Alem
Av. Rosales

PUERTO MADERO
Av. Macacha Guemes
Parque Mujeres Argentinas
Av. Alicia Moreau de Justo

Av. Pte. Roque Saenz Peña
(Diagonal Norte)

SAN NICOLAS
Libertad
Cerrito
C. Pellegrini
Bartolome Mitre
Rivadavia
Hipolito Yrigoyen
Alsina
Rivadavia
Av. de Mayo
Santiago del Estero
Salta
Lima
Av. 9 de Julio
Bernardo de Irigoyen

Plaza de Mayo
Defensa
Balcarce
Bolívar
Moreno
Perú
Av. Belgrano
Rocha (Diagonal Sur)
Av. Paseo Colón
Av. Ing. Huergo
Azopardo
Av. de la Rábida

MONSERRAT
San José
Belgrano
Pte. Luis Saenz Peña
Chacabuco
Piedras
Tacuari
Venezuela
Mexico
Chile
Av. Independencia

SAN TELMO
Estados Unidos
Carlos Calvo
Balcarce

STREET MAPS   Ask the front desk of your hotel for a copy of "The Golden Map" and "QuickGuide Buenos Aires" to help you navigate the city and locate its major attractions. Before leaving home, you can also get great maps ahead of time from the Buenos Aires–based company **De Dios** (www.dediosonline.com), which has laminated street maps and various themed maps, ranging from tango to shopping. All magazine kiosks sell a tiny invaluable booklet called *Guia T,* primarily for negotiating the city's myriad bus routes but also handy as a walking map guide.

GETTING AROUND

The Buenos Aires metro—called the *subte*—is the fastest, cheapest way to get around. Buses are also convenient, though less commonly used by tourists. Get maps of metro and bus lines from tourist offices and most hotels. (Ask for the "QuickGuide Buenos Aires.") All metro stations and most bus stops have maps.

BY METRO   Six *subte* lines connect commercial and tourist areas in the city Monday through Saturday from 5am to 11pm and Sunday and holidays from 8am to 11pm. This is an estimate, and the actual times will vary. The flat fare is 70 centavos (about 20¢/10p), with tickets purchased at machines or windows at every station. You can also buy a *subte* pass for 7 pesos (about $2/£1), valid for 10 trips. It's always wise to buy spare cards as they often demagnetize in the intense humidity which is common throughout the summer. Line A connects Plaza de Mayo to Primera Junta. This was the city's first line, it still retains the old turn-of-the-20th-century wooden cars, and it is like a moving museum. Line B runs from near Puerto Madero (Av. Leandro N. Alem) to Federico Lacroze. Line C travels between the city's train stations, Retiro and Constitución. Line D runs from Congreso de Tucumán to Catedral. Line E links Bolívar with Plaza de los Virreyes. Neither the Recoleta nor Puerto Madero neighborhoods have *subte* access. Most of Puerto Madero, however, can be reached via the L. N. Alem *subte*. (It's a 5- to 20-min. walk, depending on which dock you're going to.) Visit the website **www.subte.com.ar** for more information on the system, as well as downloadable maps and a point-to-point page estimating travel time. There is a now a new line H that runs from Avenida Caseros to Avenida Rivadavia.

BY BUS   Around 140 bus lines operate in Buenos Aires 24 hours a day and are an excellent way to get around the city. It is essential you buy a *Guia T* map booklet at any newspaper kiosk to truly take advantage of all the routes. The minimum fare is 80 centavos (25¢/10p) and goes up depending on the distance traveled. Pay your fare inside the bus at an electronic ticket machine, which accepts coins only. Many bus drivers, provided you can communicate with them, will tell you the fare for your destination and help you with where to get off.

BY TAXI   Fares are relatively inexpensive, with an initial meter reading of 2.90 pesos (91¢/£46) increasing 27 centavos (9¢/05p) every 200m (656 ft.) or each minute. Most of what the average tourist needs to see in the city is accessible for a $4-to-$5 (£1.90–£2.40) cab ride. *Remises* and radio-taxis are much safer than regular street taxis. Radio-taxis, when hailed on the street, can be recognized by the plastic light boxes that are usually on their rooftops. When heading to an off-the-beaten-path destination, or one along the miles-long *avenidas,* take note of the cross street. *Be warned:* Buenos Aires *taxistas* are sharks. Watch out for unwanted city tours as they take you the long way home and provide counterfeit notes when returning change. To request a taxi by phone, consider **Taxi Premium** (© **11/4374-6666**), which is used by the Four Seasons Hotel, or **Radio Taxi Blue** (© 11/4777-8888), contracted by the Alvear Palace Hotel.

BY CAR Driving in Buenos Aires is like warfare: Never mind the lane, disregard the light, and honk your way through traffic. It's far safer, and cheaper, to hire a *remise* or radio-taxi with the help of your hotel or travel agent. If you must drive, international car-rental companies rent vehicles at both airports. Most hotels offer parking for a small fee.

The main offices in Buenos Aires are **Hertz,** Paraguay 1122 (© 800/654-3131 in the U.S., or 11/4816-8001 in Buenos Aires); **Avis,** Cerrito 1527 (© 11/4300-8201); **Dollar,** Marcelo T. de Alvear 449 (© 11/4315-8800); and **Thrifty,** Av. Leandro N. Alem 699 (© 11/4315-0777). Expect to pay about $65 (£31) per day for an intermediate-size car, including unlimited miles and 21% tax. Add another $10 (£5) per day if you require insurance.

ON FOOT Buenos Aires is a walker's city. The Microcentro is small enough to navigate by foot, and you can connect to adjacent neighborhoods by catching a taxi or using the *subte.* If you have several days in Buenos Aires, it makes sense to slice your time into segments for walking tours—so spend a day in the Microcentro, for example; an evening in Puerto Madero; another day in La Boca and San Telmo; and another day in Recoleta and Palermo. Plazas, parks, and pedestrian walkways are omnipresent in the city center.

VISITOR INFORMATION

The central office of the **City Tourism Secretariat,** responsible for all visitor information on Buenos Aires, is located at Calle Balcarce 360 in Monserrat (© 11/4313-0187; www.bue.gov.ar), but this office is not open to the general public. Instead, you'll find several kiosks (with maps and hotel, restaurant, and attraction information) spread throughout various neighborhoods. These are found at J. M. Ortiz and Quintana in Recoleta, Puerto Madero, the central bus terminal, Calle Florida 100 (where it hits Diagonal Norte), and other locations in the city center. Most are open Monday through Friday from 10am to 5pm and on weekends, though some open and close later. In addition, individual associations have their own tourist centers providing a wealth of information, such as that for the Calle Florida Business Association in the shopping center Galerías Pacífico and where the pedestrianized shopping street Calle Florida ends at Plaza San Martín. There are branches at Ezeiza International Airport and Jorge Newbery Airport as well, which are open daily from 8am to 8pm.

The **Buenos Aires City Tourism office** also runs an information hot line (© 11/4313-0187), which is staffed from 7:30am to 6pm Monday to Saturday, and Sunday from 11am to 6pm. The city also provides free tours. Though the majority of these tours are in Spanish, a few are conducted in English. To find out more about the tours, call © 11/4114-5791 Monday to Friday from 10am to 4pm.

FAST FACTS It's easier to exchange money at the airport, your hotel, or an independent money-exchange house rather than at an Argentine bank. **American Express,** in a building next to Plaza San Martín at Arenales 707 (© 11/4312-1661), offers the best rates on its traveler's checks. It offers currency exchange for dollars only and is open Monday through Friday from 9am to 6pm. ATMs are plentiful in Buenos Aires. You can also have money wired to **Western Union,** Av. Córdoba 975 (© 0800/800-3030; www.westernunion.com).

For **police** assistance, call © **101;** in case of **fire,** © **100;** for an **ambulance,** © **107;** for an English-speaking hospital, call **Clínica Suisso Argentino** (© **11/4304-1081**).

You never have to venture more than a few blocks to find a **post office,** open Monday through Friday from 10am to 8pm and Saturday until 1pm. The main post office (Correo Central) is at Av. Sarmiento 151 (© **11/4311-5040**). Another postal alternative is **OCA,** a private company with branches throughout the city.

Unless you are calling from your hotel (which will be expensive), the easiest way to place calls is by going to a **locutorio,** a version of a public phone system, found on nearly every city block. Private booths allow you to place as many calls as you like, after which you pay an attendant. A running meter gives you an idea of what the call will cost and you can save on calls by using phone cards such as Teletel or Hablemas. Most locutorios also have fax and Internet capabilities with Skype.

WHAT TO SEE & DO

Buenos Aires is a wonderful city to explore and is fairly easy to navigate. The most impressive historical sites are located around Plaza de Mayo, although you will certainly experience Argentine history in neighborhoods such as La Boca and San Telmo, too. Don't miss a walk along the riverfront in Puerto Madero, or an afternoon among the plazas and cafes of Recoleta or Palermo. Numerous sidewalk cafes offer respite for weary feet, and there's good public transportation to carry you from neighborhood to neighborhood.

Your first stop should be one of the city tourism centers (see "Visitor Information," above) to pick up a guidebook, city map, and advice. You can also ask at your hotel for a copy of *The Golden Map* and *QuickGuide Buenos Aires* to help you navigate the city and locate its major attractions.

NEIGHBORHOODS TO EXPLORE
La Boca

La Boca, on the banks of the Río Riachuelo, developed originally as a trading center and shipyard. Drawn to the river's commercial potential, Italian immigrants moved in, giving the neighborhood the distinct flavor it maintains today.

At the center of La Boca lies the **Caminito,** a pedestrian walkway (and a famous tango song) that is both an outdoor museum and a marketplace. Surrounding the cobblestone street are shabby metal houses painted in dynamic shades of red, yellow, blue, and green, thanks to designer Benito Quinquela Martín. Today, many artists live or set up their studios in these multicolored sheet-metal houses. Along the Caminito, art and souvenir vendors work side by side with tango performers—this is one place you won't have to pay to see Argentina's great dance, but you will have to pay exorbitant prices for a beer or snack. Sculptures, murals, and engravings—some with political and social themes—line the street. This Caminito "Fine Arts Fair" is open daily from 10am to 6pm. I think the place has become too much of a tourist trap and has lost much of its authenticity, replaced by tacky vendors and bars that only want to fleece tourists. There are plans to revamp the area in time for the 2010 national bicentennial celebrations.

To catch an additional glimpse of La Boca's working-class spirit, walk 4 blocks to the corner of calles Del Valle Iberlucea and Brandsen. **Estadio de Boca Juniors**—the stadium for Buenos Aires's most popular *club de fútbol* (soccer club), the Boca Juniors—is here. Go on game day, when street parties and general debauchery take over the garbage-strewn area. Try not to dress like a tourist as this may attract unwanted attention. For information on *fútbol* games, see the *Buenos Aires Herald* sports section. Use caution in straying too far from the Caminito, however, as the less patrolled surrounding areas can be unsafe. ***Warning:*** Avoid La Boca altogether at night.

San Telmo

Buenos Aires's oldest neighborhood, San Telmo originally housed the city's elite. When yellow fever struck in the 1870s—aggravated by substandard conditions in the area—the aristocrats moved north. Poor immigrants soon filled the neighborhood, and the houses were converted to tenements, called *conventillos.* In 1970, the city passed regulations to restore some of San Telmo's architectural landmarks. With new life injected into it, the neighborhood has taken on a bohemian flair, attracting artists, dancers, and numerous antiques dealers 7 days a week. While the area maintains a generally rundown air about it, it is rapidly gentrifying.

After Plaza de Mayo, **Plaza Dorrego** is the oldest square in the city. Originally the site of a Bethlehemite monastery, the plaza is also where Argentines met to reconfirm their Declaration of Independence from Spain. On Sundays from 10am to 5pm, the city's best **antiques market** ✷✷✷ takes over the square. You can buy leather, silver, handicrafts, and other products here along with antiques, and tango dancers perform on the square. If you are in Buenos Aires on a Sunday, do not miss coming here as it is alive with people, music, and atmosphere.

San Telmo is full of tango salons, known as *milongas,* as well as show palaces; one of the most notable of the latter is **El Viejo Almacén** ✷ (at Independencia and Balcarce). During the day, you can appreciate the club as a landmark: An example of colonial architecture, it was built in 1798 and was a general store and hospital before its reincarnation as the quintessential Argentine tango club. Make sure to go back for a show at night (see "Buenos Aires After Dark," later in this chapter). If you get the urge for a beginner or refresher tango course while you're in San Telmo, look for signs advertising lessons in the windows of restaurants and clubs in this area.

Palermo

Palermo is a term used to define a considerable chunk of northern Buenos Aires, but it is composed of several distinct neighborhoods—**Palermo, Palermo Chico, Palermo Viejo,** which is further divided into **Palermo SoHo** and **Palermo Hollywood** and **Las Cañitas.**

Palermo is a neighborhood of parks filled with magnolias, pines, palms, and willows, where families picnic on weekends and couples stroll at sunset. You might want to think of this part as Palermo Nuevo when compared to Palermo Viejo, described below. Designed by French architect Charles Thays, the parks of Palermo take their inspiration from London's Hyde Park and Paris's Bois de Boulogne. The **Botanical Gardens** and the **Zoological Gardens** are both off **Plaza Italia.** Stone paths wind their way through the botanical gardens, and flora from throughout South America fills the garden, with over 8,000 plant species from around the world represented. Next door, the city zoo features an impressive diversity of animals. The eclectic and kitschy architecture housing the animals, some designed as exotic temples, is as delightful as the animals themselves. Peacocks and some of the other small animals are allowed to roam free, and feeding is allowed with special food for sale at kiosks, making it a great place for entertaining kids.

Palermo Chico is an exclusive neighborhood of elegant mansions off Avenida Alcorta, tucked behind the **MALBA** museum. Other than the museum and the beauty of the homes and a few embassy buildings, this small set of streets has little to interest the average tourist. Plus, there is no subway access to this neighborhood.

Palermo Viejo, once a run-down neighborhood full of warehouses, factories, and tiny decaying stucco homes few cared to live in as recently as 1990, has been transformed into the city's chicest destination. Once you walk through the area and begin to absorb its charms—cobblestone streets, enormous oak-tree canopies, and low-rise buildings giving a clear view to the open skies on a sunny day—you'll wonder why it had been forsaken for so many years. Palermo Viejo is further divided into **Palermo SoHo** to the south and **Palermo Hollywood** to the north, with railroad tracks and Avenida Juan B. Justo serving as the dividing line. The center of Palermo Hollywood is **Plaza Julio Cortázar,** better known by its informal name, **Plaza Serrano,** a small oval park at the intersection of calles Serrano and Honduras. Young people gather here late at night in impromptu singing and guitar sessions, sometimes fueled by drinks from the myriad funky bars and restaurants that surround the plaza. The neighborhood was named Palermo Hollywood because many Argentine film studios were initially attracted by its once-cheap rents and easy parking. Palermo SoHo is better known for boutiques owned by local designers, with some restaurants mixed in. Both areas were historically where Middle Eastern immigrants originally settled, and this presence is still apparent in the businesses, restaurants, and community centers that remain. **Las Cañitas** is a neighborhood adjacent to Palermo Viejo, famous for the polo grounds, and the restaurant-filled street Calle Baez.

Recoleta

The city's most exclusive neighborhood, La Recoleta wears a distinctly European face. Tree-lined avenues lead past fashionable restaurants, cafes, boutiques, and galleries, many housed in French-style buildings. Much of the activity takes place along the pedestrian walkway Roberto M. Ortiz, and in front of the Cultural Center and Recoleta Cemetery. This is a neighborhood of plazas and parks, a place where tourists and wealthy Argentines spend their leisure time outside. Weekends bring street performances, art exhibits, fairs, and sports.

The **Recoleta Cemetery** ✦✦✦, (© 11/4804-7040) open daily from 8am to 6pm, pays tribute to some of Argentina's historical figures and is a lasting place where the elite can show off their wealth. Once the garden of the adjoining church, the cemetery was created in 1822 and is the oldest in the city. You can spend hours wandering the grounds that cover 4 city blocks, adorned with works by local and international sculptors. More than 6,400 mausoleums form an architectural free-for-all, including Greek temples and pyramids. Some seem big enough to be small churches. The most popular site is the tomb of Eva "Evita" Perón, which is always heaped with flowers and letters from adoring fans. Many other rich or famous Argentines are buried here as well, including a number of Argentine presidents, various literary figures, and war heroes. As any Argentine will tell you, it's important to live in Recoleta while you're alive, but even more important to remain here in death. Guided English-language tours of the cemetery take place Tuesday and Thursday at 11am, weather permitting.

Adjacent to the cemetery, the **Centro Cultural Recoleta** ✦ (© 11/4803-1041) holds permanent and touring art exhibits along with theatrical and musical performances. Designed in the mid–18th century as a Franciscan convent, it was reincarnated as a poorhouse in 1858, and it served that function until becoming a cultural center in 1979. The first floor houses an interactive children's science museum where it is "forbidden not to touch." Next door, **Buenos Aires Design Center** features shops specializing in home decor; among the best is Puro Diseño Argentina.

Plaza de Mayo ✪

Juan de Garay founded the historic core of Buenos Aires, the Plaza de Mayo, in 1580. The plaza's prominent buildings create an architectural timeline: the Cabildo and the Metropolitan Cathedral are vestiges of the colonial period (18th and early 19th c.), while the seats of national and local government reflect the styles of the late 19th and early 20th century. In the center of the plaza, you'll find palm trees, fountains, and benches. Plaza de Mayo remains the political heart of the city, serving as a forum for protests. The mothers of the *desaparecidos,* victims of the military dictatorship's war against leftists, have demonstrated here since 1976. You can see them march every Thursday afternoon at 3:30pm.

The Argentine president goes to work every day at the **Casa Rosada (Pink House)** ✪✪✪. It is from a balcony of this mansion that Eva Perón addressed adoring crowds of Argentine workers. You can watch the changing of the guard in front of the palace every hour on the hour, and around back is a small museum (✆ 11/4344-3802) with information on the history of the building and the presidents of the nation who worked in it. It's open Monday through Friday from 10am to 6pm; admission is free.

The original structure of the **Metropolitan Cathedral** ✪✪ (✆ 11/4331-2845) was built in 1745; it was given a new facade, with carvings telling the story of Jacob and his son Joseph, and was designated a cathedral in 1836. Inside lies a mausoleum containing the remains of General José de San Martín, South American liberator regarded as the "Father of the Nation." (San Martín fought successfully for freedom in Argentina, Peru, and Chile.) The tomb of the unknown soldier of Argentine independence is also here.

The **Cabildo** ✪, Bolívar 65 (✆ 11/4334-1782), was the original seat of city government established by the Spaniards. Completed in 1751, the colonial building proved significant in the events leading up to Argentina's declaration of independence from Spain in May 1810. Parts of the Cabildo were demolished to create space for Avenida de Mayo and Diagonal Sur. The remainder of the building was restored in 1939 (the museum is open Tues–Fri 12:30–7pm and Sat–Sun 2–6pm; admission is $1).

A striking neoclassical facade covers the **Legislatura de la Ciudad (City Legislature Building),** at Calle Perú and Hipólito Irigoyen, which houses exhibitions in several of its recently restored halls. The building's watchtower has more than 30 bells. In front of the Legislatura, you'll see a bronze statue of Julio A. Roca, considered one of Argentina's greatest presidents. His legacy, however, also includes the murder of thousands of native Indians in the area surrounding Buenos Aires. For this reason, Argentina is a largely white society in comparison to other South American countries.

Farther down Calle Perú stands the enormous **Manzana de las Luces (Block of Lights)** ✪✪, Calle Perú 272, which served as the intellectual center of the city in the 17th and 18th centuries. This land was granted to the Jesuits in 1616, who then built **San Ignacio**—the city's oldest church—still standing at the corner of calles Bolívar and Alsina. San Ignacio has a beautiful altar carved in wood with baroque details. Also located here is the **Colegio Nacional de Buenos Aires;** Argentina's best-known intellectuals have gathered and studied at the National School, and the name "block of lights" recognizes the contributions of its graduates. Tours are usually led on Saturday and Sunday at 3 and 4:30pm and include a visit to the Jesuits' system of underground tunnels, which connected their churches to strategic spots in the city (admission is $2). The tunnels were also favorite hiding spots for the students when they wanted to get out of class. Over the years, paranoid dictators added to the tunnels, in the event they ever needed to escape a takeover of the nearby Casa Rosada. In addition to weekend tours, the Comisión Nacional de la Manzana de las Luces organizes a variety of cultural activities during the week, including folkloric dance lessons, open-air theater performances, art expositions, and music concerts. Call © **11/4331-9534** for information.

Puerto Madero

Puerto Madero became Buenos Aires's major gateway to trade with Europe when it was built in 1880. But by 1910, the city had already outgrown the port. The Puerto Nuevo (New Port) was established to the north to accommodate growing commercial activity, and Madero was abandoned for almost a century. Urban renewal saved the original port in the 1990s with the construction of a riverfront promenade, apartments, and offices. With so much new construction in the area, it can appear cold and antiseptic during the day, but at night, the area attracts a fashionable, wealthy crowd. It's lined with restaurants serving Argentine steaks and fresh seafood specialties, and there is a popular cinema showing Argentine and Hollywood films. Several luxury hotels have made their way into the district, but the lack of subway access means cabs are the most convenient way of getting to and from the area.

Plaza San Martín & Environs

Plaza San Martín 👁👁 is a beautiful park at the end of Calle Florida in the Retiro neighborhood. In summer months, Argentine businesspeople flock to the park on their lunch hour, loosening their ties, taking off some layers, and sunning for a while amid the plaza's flowering jacaranda. A monument to General José de San Martín towers over the scene. The San Martín Palace, one of the seats of the Argentine Ministry of Foreign Affairs, and the Marriott Plaza Hotel, one of the city's grande dames, face the square.

Calle Florida 👁👁👁 is the main pedestrian thoroughfare of Buenos Aires and a shopper's paradise. The busiest section, extending south from Plaza San Martín to Avenida Corrientes, is lined with boutiques, restaurants, and record stores. You'll find the upscale Galerías Pacífico fashion center here.

Avenida Corrientes 👁 is a living diary of Buenos Aires's cultural development. Until the 1930s, Avenida Corrientes was the favored hangout of tango legends. When the avenue was widened in the mid-1930s, it made its debut as the Argentine Broadway. Today, Corrientes, lined with cinemas and theaters, pulses with cultural and commercial activity day and night.

MUSEUMS

El Museo Histórico Nacional (National History Museum) 👁👁   Argentine history from the 16th through the 19th centuries comes to life in the former Lezama family home. The expansive Italian-style mansion houses 30 rooms with items saved from Jesuit missions, paintings illustrating clashes between the Spaniards and Indians, and relics from the War of Independence against Spain. The focal point of the museum's collection is artist Cándido López's series of captivating scenes of the war against Paraguay in the 1870s.

Calle Defensa 1600, in Parque Lezama. © **11/4307-1182.** Free admission. Feb–Dec Tues–Sun noon–6pm. Closed Jan. Metro: Constitución.

MALBA–Colección Costantini ★★★ The airy and luminescent Museo de Arte Latinoamericano de Buenos Aires (MALBA) houses the private art collection of Eduardo Costantini. One of the most impressive collections of Latin American art anywhere, its temporary and permanent exhibitions showcase such names as Antonio Berni, Pedro Figari, Frida Kahlo, Cândido Portinari, Diego Rivera, and Antonio Siguí. Many of the works confront social issues and explore questions of national identity. Even the benches are modern pieces of art. Latin films are shown Tuesday through Sunday at 2 and 10pm.

Av. Figueroa Alcorta 3415, at San Martín. © 11/4808-6500. www.malba.org.ar. Admission $4 (£2). Free admission Wed. Wed noon–9pm; Thurs–Mon noon–8pm. No Metro access.

Museo Evita ★★ It is almost impossible for non-Argentines to fathom that it took 50 years from the time of her death for Evita, the world's most famous Argentine, to finally get a museum. The Museo Evita opened on July 26, 2002, in a mansion where her charity, the Eva Perón Foundation, once housed single mothers and their children.

The Museo Evita's displays divide Evita's life into several parts, looking at her childhood, her arrival in Buenos Aires to become an actress, her ascension as Evita, first lady and unofficial saint to millions, and finally her death and legacy. You will be able to view her clothes, remarkably preserved by the military government, which took power after Perón's 1955 fall. Other artifacts of her life include her voting card, since it was Evita who gave Argentine women the right to vote. There are also toys and schoolbooks adorned with her image, given to children to indoctrinate them into the Peronist movement. Whether you hate, love, or are indifferent to Evita, this is a museum that no visitor to Argentina should miss.

Calle Lafinur 2988, at Gutiérrez. © 11/4807-9433. www.evitaperon.org. Admission $3.50 (£1.25) Tues–Sun 11am–7pm. Metro: Linea D Plaza Italia.

Museo Nacional de Arte Decorativo (National Museum of Decorative Arts) ★ French architect René Sergent, who designed some of the grandest mansions in Buenos Aires, also designed the mansion housing this museum. The building is itself a work of art, and it will give you an idea of the incredible mansions that once lined this avenue, overlooking the extensive Palermo park system. The building's 18th-century French design provides a classical setting for the diverse decorative styles represented within. Sculptures, paintings, and furnishings make up the collection, and themed shows rotate seasonally.

Av. del Libertador 1902, at Lucena. © 11/4801-8248. Admission $1 (50p). Mon–Fri 2–8pm; Sat–Sun 11am–7pm. No Metro access.

Museo Nacional de Bellas Artes (National Museum of Fine Arts) ★★ This building, which formerly pumped the city's water supply, metamorphosed into Buenos Aires's most important art museum in 1930. The museum contains the world's largest collection of Argentine sculptures and paintings from the 19th and 20th centuries. It also houses European art dating from the pre-Renaissance period to the present day. The collections include notable pieces by Renoir, Monet, Rodin, Toulouse-Lautrec, and van Gogh, as well as a surprisingly extensive collection of Picasso drawings.

Av. del Libertador 1473, at Agote. © 11/4803-0802. Free admission. Tues–Sun 12:30–7:30pm. No Metro access.

OTHER ATTRACTIONS

Among the city's other attractions is the **Café Tortoni,** long a meeting place for Porteño artists and intellectuals. For a full review, see p. 115, including information on the cafe's tango shows.

Basílica y Convento de San Francisco (San Francis's Church and Convent) ⚅

The San Roque parish to which this church belongs is one of the oldest in the city. A Jesuit architect designed the building in 1730, but a final reconstruction in the early 20th century added a German baroque facade, along with statues of St. Francis of Assisi, Dante, and Christopher Columbus. Inside, you'll find a tapestry by Argentine artist Horacio Butler along with an extensive library.

Calle Defensa and Alsina. © 11/4331-0625. Free admission. Hours vary. Metro: Plaza de Mayo.

Biblioteca Nacional (National Library) ⚅

Opened in 1992, this modern architectural oddity stands on the land of the former Presidential Residence in which Eva Perón died. (The building was demolished by the new government so that it would not become a holy site to Evita's millions of supporters after her death.) With its underground levels, the library's 13 floors can store up to five million volumes. Among its collection, the library stores 21 books printed by one of the earliest printing presses, dating from 1440 to 1500. Visit the reading room—occupying two stories at the top of the building—to enjoy an awe-inspiring view of Buenos Aires. The library also hosts special events in its exhibition hall and auditorium.

Calle Aguero 2502. © 11/4807-0885. Free admission. Mon–Fri 9am–9pm; Sat–Sun noon–8pm. No Metro access.

Congreso ⚅⚅

Opened on May 12, 1906, after nearly 9 years of work, and built in a Greco-Roman style with strong Parisian Beaux Arts influences, Congreso is the most imposing building in all of Buenos Aires. One of the main architects was Victor Meano, who was also involved in designing the Teatro Colón (below), but he was murdered—the result of a love triangle gone wrong—before completion of either building.

Tours take visitors through the fantastic chambers, which are adorned with bronzes, statues, German tile floors, Spanish woods, and French marbles, and lined with Corinthian columns. The horseshoe-shaped congressional chamber is the largest, with the senatorial chamber an almost identical copy but at one-fifth the size.

Entrance is usually through the Rivadavia side of the building, but it can switch to the Yrigoyen doors, so arrive early and announce to the guards that you are there for a visit. The tour guide will not be called down unless they know people are waiting. This is an incredible building and worth the confusion. Its beauty also speaks for itself, even if you have to take the Spanish tour and do not know a word of Spanish.

Entre Ríos and Callao, at Rivadavia. © 11/4370-7100 or 11/6310-7100, ext. 3725. Free guided tours in English Mon–Tues and Thurs–Fri 11am and 4pm; Spanish tours Mon–Tues and Thurs–Fri 11am, 4pm, and 5pm. Metro: Congreso.

Teatro Colón

Known across the world for its impeccable acoustics, the Colón has attracted the world's finest opera performers. Opera season in Buenos Aires runs from April to November. The Colón has its own philharmonic orchestra, ballet, and choir companies. The theater is currently closed for extensive renovations and its reopening has been constantly delayed, thus missing its 2008 100-year anniversary. As this book went to press, it appeared that Teatro Colón would be closed through 2009 and would reopen in time for Buenos Aires's bicentennial celebrations in 2010. Consult the website for more information.

Calle Libertad 621, at Tucumán. (C) **11/4378-7100.** www.teatrocolon.org.ar. Tickets $4–$30 (£2–£15). Metro: Tribunales.

SPECTATOR SPORTS & OUTDOOR ACTIVITIES

GOLF Argentina has more than 200 golf courses. Closest to downtown Buenos Aires is **Cancha de Golf de la Ciudad de Buenos Aires,** Av. Torquist 1426, at Olleros ((C) **11/4772-7261**), which is 10 minutes from downtown and boasts great scenery and a 71-par course. The **Jockey Club Argentino,** Av. Márquez 1700, San Isidro ((C) **11/4743-1001**), offers two courses (71 and 72 par).

HORSE RACING Over much of the 20th century, Argentina was famous for its thoroughbreds. It continues to send prize horses to competitions around the world, although you can watch some of the best right here in Buenos Aires. In the center of the city, you can see races at **Hipódromo Argentino de Palermo,** Av. del Libertador 4205, at Dorrego ((C) **11/4778-2839**), in Palermo, a track made in a classical design with several modern additions. The other big track is **Hipódromo San Isidro,** Av. Márquez 504 ((C) **11/4743-4010**), in the upscale northern suburb of the same name. Check the *Buenos Aires Herald* for schedule information.

POLO Argentina has won more international polo tournaments than any other country, and the **Argentine Open Championship,** held late November through early December, is the world's most important polo event. There are two seasons for polo: March through May and September through December, held at the **Campo Argentino de Polo,** Avenida del Libertador and Avenida Dorrego ((C) **11/4576-5600**). Tickets can be purchased at the gate for about $35 (£18) per person. This is one of the most important polo stadiums in the world, and visits by European royalty are not uncommon. Contact the **Asociación Argentina de Polo,** Hipólito Yrigoyen 636 ((C) **11/4331-4646** or 11/4342-8321), for information on polo schools and events.

SOCCER Any sense of national unity dissolves when Argentines watch their favorite clubs—River Plate, Boca Juniors, Racing Club, Independiente, and San Lorenzo—battle on Sunday in season, which runs from February until November. Catch a game at the **Estadio Boca Juniors,** Brandsen 805 ((C) **11/4362-2260**), in La Boca, followed by raucous street parties. Ticket prices start at $3 (£1.50) and can be purchased in advance or at the gate.

SHOPPING
BY NEIGHBORHOOD

MICROCENTRO Calle Florida, the pedestrian walking street in the Microcentro, is home to wall-to-wall shops from Plaza San Martín past Avenida Corrientes. The **Galerías Pacífico** mall is located at Calle Florida 750 and Avenida Córdoba ((C) **11/4319-5100**), with a magnificent dome and stunning frescoes. Over 180 shops are open Monday through Saturday from 10am to 9pm and Sunday from noon to 9pm, with tango shows held on Thursdays at 8pm. Food-court restaurants are open later. As you approach Plaza San Martín, you'll find a number of well-regarded shoe stores, jewelers, and shops selling leather goods.

RECOLETA Avenida Alvear is Argentina's response to the Champs-Elysées, and—without taking the comparison too far—it is indeed an elegant, Parisian-like strip of European boutiques and cafes. Start your walk from Plaza Francia and continue from Junín to Cerrito. Along Calle Quintana, French-style mansions share company with upscale shops. Nearby, **Patio Bullrich,** Av. del Libertador 750 (© **11/4814-7400**), is one of the city's best malls. Its 69 elegant shops are open daily from 10am to 9pm.

AVENIDA SANTA FE   Popular with local shoppers, Avenida Santa Fe offers a wide selection of clothing stores and more down-to-earth prices. You will also find bookstores, ice-cream shops, and cinemas. The **Alto Palermo Shopping Center,** Av. Santa Fe 3253 (© **11/5777-8000**), is another excellent shopping spot, with 155 stores open daily from 10am to 10pm. Food-court restaurants are open later.

SAN TELMO & LA BOCA   These neighborhoods offer antiques as well as arts and crafts celebrating tango. Street performers and artists are omnipresent. My opinion is that La Boca's souvenirs are overpriced. La Boca is considered dangerous at night, but rapidly gentrifying San Telmo is generally safer.

PALERMO VIEJO   The stalking ground of Borges is now awash with trendy bars and restaurants and a plethora of homegrown designer stores, offering everything from funky fashion to chic interior furnishings.

SHOPPING A TO Z

Most stores are open weekdays from 9am to 8pm and Saturday from 9am to midnight, with some stores closing for a few hours in the afternoon. Shopping centers are open daily from 10am to 10pm. You might find some shops open on Sunday along Avenida Santa Fe, but few will be open on Calle Florida.

Almost all shops in Buenos Aires accept credit cards. However, you will sometimes get a better price if you offer to pay with cash, and you won't be able to use credit cards at outdoor markets.

Antiques

Throughout the streets of San Telmo, you will find the city's best antiques shops; don't miss the antiques market that takes place all day Sunday at Plaza Dorrego (see "Markets," below). There are also a number of fine antiques stores along Avenida Alvear in Recoleta, including a collection of boutiques at **Galería Alvear,** Av. Alvear 1777. **Calle Antigua,** Calles Defensa 914 and Defensa 974, at Estados Unidos (© **11/4300-8782**), sells religious art, chandeliers, furniture, and other decorative objects. Credit cards are not accepted. **Galería El Solar de French,** Calle Defensa 1066, is a gallery with antiques shops and photography stores depicting the San Telmo of yesteryear. **Pallarols,** Calle Defensa 1015, San Telmo (© **11/4362-5438;** www.pallarols.com.ar), belongs to a family of the same name that makes and sells an exquisite collection of Argentine silver and other antiques.

Art

Galería Ruth Benzacar, Calle Florida 1000 (© **11/4313-8480**), is an avant-garde gallery, in a hidden underground space at the start of Calle Florida next to Plaza San Martín. **Jorge Oliva Antigüedades y Arte,** Suipacha 1409 at Arroyo, Space #11 (© **11/4390-4401**), offers an interesting art collection including local Argentine and some European artists as well as small antiques and decorative objects.

Cameras

Cosentino, Av. Roque Sáenz Peña 738 (© **11/4328-9120**), offers cameras, repairs, and high-quality developing services.

Fashion

Emporio Armani, Av. Alvear 1750 (© **11/4812-2880**), has suits, street clothing, and all kinds of accessories from the famous Italian retailer. The two-story building is one of the most beautiful on Alvear. **Ermenegildo Zegna,** Av. Alvear 1920 (© **11/4804-1908**), is a famous Italian chain that sells outstanding suits and jackets made of light, cool fabrics. **Escada,** Av. Alvear 1444 (© **11/4814-0292**), sells casual and elegant selections of women's clothing.

Jewelry

Cousiño Jewels, Av. San Martín 1225 (© **11/4312-2336** or 11/4313-8881), is located in the Sheraton hotel and features a brilliant collection of rhodochrosite, or Inca Rose, a beautiful form of milky-pink quartz. **H.Stern,** Marriott Plaza, Calle Florida 1005 (© **11/4318-3083**), or at the Sheraton Buenos Aires Hotel, Av. San Martín 1225 (© **11/4312-6762**), is an upscale Brazilian jeweler that sells an entire selection of South American stones, including emeralds and the unique imperial topaz.

Leather

Argentina is one of the world's best leather centers. If you're looking for high-quality, interestingly designed leather goods, especially women's shoes, accessories, and hand-bags, few places beat Buenos Aires. Many leather stores will also custom-make jackets and other items for interested customers. **Ashanti Leather Factory,** Calle Florida 585 (© **11/4394-1310**), offers a wide selection of leather goods. Ask for a tour of the basement factory. **Casa López,** Marcelo T. de Alvear 640 (© **11/4312-8911**), is widely considered one of the best *marroquinería* (leather-goods shop) in Buenos Aires. **El Nochero,** Posadas 1245, in the Patio Bullrich Mall (© **11/4815-3629**), is full of products made with first-rate Argentine leather and manufactured by local workers.

Markets

The **antiques market in San Telmo** ⚔, which takes place every Sunday from 10am to 5pm at Plaza Dorrego, is a vibrant, colorful experience. As street vendors sell their heirlooms, singers and dancers move amid the crowd to the music of tangos and *milongas.* Among the 270-plus vendor stands, you will find antique silversmith objects, porcelain, crystal, and other antiques. **Plaza Francia's Fair,** also known as the Recoleta Fair, is in front of the Recoleta Cemetery. You'll find ceramics, leather goods, and arts and crafts amid street musicians and performers. It's held Saturday and Sunday from 9am to 7pm.

Wine Shops

Stores selling Argentine wines abound, and three of the best are **Grand Cru,** Av. Alvear 1718; **Tonel Privado,** in the Patio Bullrich Shopping Mall; and **Winery,** which has branches at L. N. Alem 880 and Av. Del Libertador 500, both downtown.

WHERE TO STAY

Hotels here fill up in high season, so you should book ahead, even if it is only for your first night or two. Exponentially increasing amounts of tourists have made available hotel rooms a scarce commodity, and hotels are raising their rates accordingly. Still, bargains can be had on hotel rooms in Buenos Aires, especially in four-star properties located off the beaten path and in locally owned (rather than international) hotel chains in all categories. Another recent trend is upscale B&Bs and hostels in Palermo Viejo and San Telmo. Always try your luck and ask for a better rate. One trick is to use the Spanish version of a hotel's website when booking online.

As for choosing a location, it's a matter of deciding what is best for you and what you want out of your Buenos Aires vacation. For a more thorough discussion of neigh-borhoods, see the "Neighborhoods to Explore" section, earlier in the chapter.

PUERTO MADERO
Very Expensive
The Faena Hotel and Universe *(Overrated)*   Doubtless the most pompous hotel title I've ever came across, the Faena is actually a renovated grain silo once called El Porteño in Puerto Madero and is Buenos Aires's showcase design hotel. Although it's a Philippe Starck creation, the Faena is different from his usual barren, all-white environments. Where possible, original elements of the grain building are maintained. The rooms might best be described as midcentury classical–meets–modern, based on the white Empire-style furnishings encased in modern surroundings, with cut-glass mirrors reminiscent of colonial Mexico. An "Experience Manager" is on hand 24/7 to take care of your every need, but even so, service can be patchy. An outdoor pool is at the building's entrance but deck chairs are limited. I found the Faena all style and no substance, yet it's perfect for trendsetters and people watchers and accordingly it attracts a media-type clientele.

Martha Salotti 445 (at Av. Juana Manso), 1107 Buenos Aires. (C) **11/4010-9000.** Fax 11/4010-9001. www.faena hotelanduniverse.com. 83 units, including 14 suites; 20 apts of varying size, space, and price also available. From $550 (£275) double; from $770 (£385) suite. Rates include continental breakfast and airport transfer. AE, MC, V. Parking $17 (£8.50). No nearby Metro stations. **Amenities:** 3 restaurants; 3 bars; outdoor heated pool; large health club; spa w/extensive treatments; large sauna w/unique elements; business center w/secretarial services; 24-hr. room service; laundry service; dry cleaning. *In room:* A/C, home theater TV, high-speed Internet and Wi-Fi, minibar, hair dryer, large safe, individualized bath treatments.

Expensive
Hilton Buenos Aires *(★★)*   The Hilton is in Puerto Madero and lies within easy walking distance of some of the best restaurants in Buenos Aires yet feels somewhat isolated from the rest of the city. The strikingly contemporary hotel—a sleek silver block hoisted on stilts—features a seven-story atrium with more than 400 well-equipped guest rooms and an additional number of private residences. Spacious guest rooms offer multiple phone lines, walk-in closets, and bathrooms with separate showers and tubs. Next to the lobby, the **El Faro** restaurant serves California cuisine with a focus on seafood. The hotel has an impressive on-site pool and fitness center. Watch out for hefty late check-out penalty charges and the $20 (£10) Internet connection fee, which seems to me an unnecessary expense in these Web-surfing times.

Av. Macacha Güemes 351 (at Malecón Pierina Dealessi), 1106 Buenos Aires. (C) **800/445-8667** in the U.S., or 11/4891-0000. Fax 11/4891-0001. www.buenos.hilton.com. 418 units. From $259 (£130) double; from $509 (£255) suite. AE, DC, MC, V. 24-hr. parking $14 (£7). No nearby Metro stations. **Amenities:** Restaurant; bar; modern gym facility w/open-air pool deck and a service of light snacks and beverages; concierge; business center and secretarial services; 24-hr. room service; babysitting; laundry service; dry cleaning. *In room:* TV, high-speed Internet access, minibar, hair dryer, safe.

RECOLETA
Very Expensive
Alvear Palace Hotel *(★★★)*   Located in the center of the upscale Recoleta district, the Alvear Palace is the most exclusive hotel in Buenos Aires and one of the top hotels in the world. A gilded classical confection full of marble and bronze, the Alvear combines Empire and Louis XV–style furniture with exquisite French decorative arts. Recently renovated guest rooms combine luxurious comforts, such as chandeliers, Egyptian cotton linens, and silk drapes, with modern conveniences such as touch-screen telephones that control all in-room functions. All rooms come with personal butler service (they'll unpack and press any clothes you need), cellphones that can be

activated on demand, fresh flowers, fruit baskets, and daily newspaper delivery. Large marble bathrooms contain Hermès toiletries, and most have Jacuzzi tubs.

The formal hotel (no shorts or sandals in dining area, for example) provides sharp, professional service, and the excellent concierge staff goes to great lengths to accommodate guest requests. It is expensive, but the website offers discounts when occupancy is low. The Alvear Palace is home to one of the best restaurants in South America (**La Bourgogne;** p. 112). Even if you are not staying here, I recommend coming for their afternoon lunch buffet in their palm-court-style lobby restaurant, **L'Orangerie.**

Av. Alvear 1891 (at Ayacucho), 1129 Buenos Aires. (© 011/4808-2100. Fax 11/4804-0034. www.alvearpalace.com. 210 units, including 85 "palace" rooms and 125 suites. From $487 (£244) double; from $579 (£290) suite. Rates include luxurious buffet breakfast. AE, DC, MC, V. No Metro access. **Amenities:** 2 restaurants; bar; small health club; spa; concierge; elaborate business center; shopping arcade; 24-hr. room service; massage service; laundry service; dry cleaning; private butler service. *In room:* A/C, TV, free high-speed Internet access and Wi-Fi, minibar, hair dryer, safe.

Buenos Aires Park Hyatt 𝒜𝒜𝒜 The Hyatt is the latest in 5-star splendor to grace the Buenos Aires skyline. A main tower facing Posadas Street connects to the mansion Palacio Duhau via a garden, and below ground by an art-filled tunnel. This Hyatt has two lobbies, one in the new tower and another one in the Palace, accessed by a gorgeous double staircase that fronts the building. The side rooms and waiting areas that spill from it are magnificent. Rooms in the mansion exhibit the mix of modern and classical elements found throughout the hotel. Within the tower you'll find leather browns, charcoals, and silver-grays. Rooms are spacious, and suites come with extra bathrooms. Bathrooms in both buildings are enormous, containing a walk-in shower and a bathtub. In fact, the bathroom takes up 30% to 40% of each guest room. Within the spaces connecting the buildings underground, a wine-and-cheese bar stocks about 45 artisanal cheeses produced in Argentina, along with wine to enhance the selection. The spa and the adjacent health facilities are enormous.

Av. Alvear 1661 (at Montevideo), 1014 Buenos Aires. (© 11/5171-1234. Fax 11/5171-1235. http://buenosaires.park. hyatt.com/hyatt/hotels/index.jsp. 165 units, including 23 mansion units; 23 suites in both towers. $515 (£258) double; from $815 (£408) suite; from $2,200 (£1,100) select suites. AE, DC, MC, V. No Metro access. **Amenities:** 3 restaurants; lobby bar; heated indoor pool; exercise room; health club; sauna; concierge; multilingual business center; salon; room service; massage service; babysitting; laundry service; dry cleaning. *In room:* A/C, TV/VCR, high-speed Internet access, Wi-Fi, minibar, hair dryer, safe.

Four Seasons Hotel 𝒜𝒜𝒜 *Kids* A French-style garden and a pool separate two buildings—the 12-story "Park" tower and the Louis XIII–style "La Mansión." This is the only outdoor garden pool in all of Recoleta, creating a resortlike feeling in the middle of the city, though much of the pool is in shade until early afternoon. There's also a well-equipped health club on the premises offering spa treatments. The hotel's restaurant, **Galani,** serves excellent Mediterranean cuisine in a casual environment. Spacious guest rooms offer atypical amenities such as walk-in closets, wet and dry bars, stereo systems, and cellphones. Large marble bathrooms contain separate showers and water-jet bathtubs.

Posadas 1086–88 (at Av. 9 de Julio), 1011 Buenos Aires. (© 800/819-5053 in the U.S. and Canada, or 11/4321-1200. Fax 11/4321-1201. www.fourseasons.com. 165 units, including 49 suites (7 suites in La Mansión). $440 (£220) double; from $660 (£330) suite; $700–$6,000 (£350–£3,000) mansion suites. Prices do not include 21% tax. AE, DC, MC, V. Valet parking $10 (£5). No Metro access. **Amenities:** Restaurant; lobby bar; heated outdoor pool; health club; exercise room; large spa; sauna; concierge; multilingual business center; 24-hr. room service; massage service; babysitting; laundry service; dry cleaning. *In room:* A/C, TV/VCR, high-speed Internet access and Wi-Fi, minibar, hair dryer, safe.

Expensive

Hotel Emperador ✪✪ The theme here is Empire with a modern update; a bust of Julius Caesar overlooks the concierge desk. The lobby evokes a sense of the Old World. Behind the main restaurant, the lobby opens onto a large overgrown patio that has a gazebo and outdoor seating. The decor is attractive but could do with a revamp. All bathrooms are oversized, with cream and green marble. Suite bathrooms are even larger, with separated tub and shower stalls. Each room comes equipped with a large desk and high-speed Internet and Wi-Fi access, which will cost you about $10 (£5) a day. Check-in can be slow and check out even slower, so give yourself time. Also, in the high season the breakfast room can be uncomfortably crowded.

Av. del Libertador 420 (at Suipacha), 1001 Buenos Aires. ✆ 11/4131-4000. Fax 11/4131-3900. www.hotel-emperador. com.ar. 265 units, including 36 suites. $200 (£100) double; from $350 (£175) suite; $1,000 (£500) nuptial suite. Rates include buffet breakfast. AE, DC, MC, V. Valet parking $4 (£2). Metro: Retiro. **Amenities:** Restaurant; bar; small fitness center w/medium-size indoor heated pool and sauna; concierge; business center; 24-hr. room service; massage; babysitting; laundry service; dry cleaning; garden patio. *In room:* A/C, TV, high-speed Internet access and Wi-Fi, minibar, coffeemaker, hair dryer, safe.

Loi Suites ✪✪ Part of a small local hotel chain, the Loi Suites Recoleta is a contemporary hotel with spacious, functional rooms and excellent, personalized service. A palm-filled garden atrium and covered pool adjoin the lobby, which is bathed in various shades of white. Breakfast and afternoon tea are served in the "winter garden." Although the management uses the term "suites" rather loosely to describe rooms with microwaves, sinks, and small fridges, the hotel does in fact offer some traditional suites in addition to its more regular studio-style rooms. In-room Internet is free and there are also CD players. There's a less upscale **Loi Suites** at Marcelo T. de Alvear 842 (✆ **11/4131-6800**), which is particularly good for kids.

Vicente López 1955 (at Ayacucho), 1128 Buenos Aires. ✆ **11/5777-8950.** Fax 11/5777-8999. www.loisuites.com.ar. 112 units. From $302 (£151) double; from $453 (£227) suite. Rates include buffet breakfast. AE, DC, MC, V. Parking $12 (£6). No Metro access. **Amenities:** Restaurant; indoor pool; exercise room; sauna; small business center; limited room service; laundry service; dry cleaning. *In room:* A/C, TV, high-speed Internet access; CD player; minibar, fridge, hair dryer, safe.

Moderate

Etoile Hotel ✪ *Value* Located in the heart of Recoleta, the 14-story Etoile is an older hotel with a Turkish flair. It's not as luxurious as the city's other five-star hotels, but it's not as expensive either—making it a good value for Recoleta. The hotel labels itself a five-star but is really a high-quality four-star whose convention facilities allow it to retain a higher rating. Guest rooms are fairly large and are decorated with blue and neutral accents. Executive rooms have separate sitting areas and large, marble-lined bathrooms with whirlpool bathtubs. Rooms facing south offer balconies overlooking Plaza Francia, with a spectacular view of Recoleta Cemetery.

Roberto M. Ortiz 1835 (at Guido, overlooking Recoleta Cemetery), 1113 Buenos Aires. ✆ **11/4805-2626.** Fax 11/ 4805-3613. www.etoile.com.ar. 96 units. $158 (£79) double; from $170 (£85) suite. Rates include buffet breakfast. AE, DC, MC, V. Free parking. No Metro access. **Amenities:** Restaurant; rooftop health club w/indoor pool; exercise room; concierge; executive business services; limited room service; laundry service; dry cleaning. *In room:* A/C, TV, high-speed Internet access, minibar, hair dryer.

Inexpensive

The Recoleta Hostel ✪ *Finds* This is an inexpensive choice for young people who want to be in a beautiful neighborhood but can't ordinarily afford the prices. The rooms (bunk beds only) are simple, with bare floors and walls, beds, and a small wooden desk in the private rooms. Overall, the decor is rather reminiscent of a convent and facilities could be cleaner. Public areas have high ceilings, and there is an outdoor patio for guests' use. Bring your laptop for free Wi-Fi. One gripe: The $6 (£3) charge to leave luggage is something most other hostels and hotels would do for free.

Libertad 1216 (at Juncal), 1012 Buenos Aires. ℂ **11/4812-4419.** Fax 11/4815-6622. www.trhostel.com.ar. 76 bed spaces, including 4 in 2 bedrooms with attached bathroom. From $10 (£5) per bed; $32 (£16) private room with bathroom. Rates include continental breakfast. No credit cards. No Metro access. **Amenities:** Concierge; Internet center; Wi-Fi; lockers; TV room; laundry service; outdoor patio; shared kitchen. *In room:* Hair dryer.

MONSERRAT
Moderate
InterContinental Hotel Buenos Aires ✸✸✸ This luxurious tower hotel is decorated in the Argentine style of the 1930s. The marble lobby is colored in beige and apricot tones, heavy black and brass metal accents, and handsome carved-wood furniture and antiques inlaid with agates and other stones. The lobby's small **Café de las Luces** sometimes offers evening tango performances. The **Restaurante y Bar Mediterráneo** serves healthy, gourmet Mediterranean cuisine on an outdoor patio under a glassed-in trellis. Guest rooms continue the 1930s theme, with elegant black woodwork, comfortable king-size beds, marble-top nightstands, large desks, and black-and-white photographs of Buenos Aires. Some rooms need updating but all have nice touches such as fresh fruit and daily English-language newspapers. The staff is very helpful, if a little inconsistent in quality of service.

Moreno 809 (at Piedras), 1091 Buenos Aires. ℂ **11/4340-7100.** Fax 11/4340-7119. www.buenos-aires.interconti. com. 312 units. $224 (£112) double; from $475 (£236) suite. AE, DC, MC, V. Parking $10 (£5). Metro: Moreno. **Amenities:** Restaurant; wine bar; lobby bar; health club w/indoor pool; exercise room; sauna; concierge; business center; 24-hr. room service; massage service; laundry service; dry cleaning; executive floors; sun deck. *In room:* A/C, TV, dataport, minibar, hair dryer, safe.

NH City Hotel ✸✸ This hotel's jagged ziggurat exterior calls to mind buildings more associated with Jazz Age New York than with Argentina. Its lobby is a combination of Art Deco and Collegiate Gothic popular in that time period. It gives the place a hip and modern feel. Many of the rooms vary greatly in size and are on the dark side, with a masculine combination of simple materials in red and black. Others are brighter, with white walls and burnt-sienna offsets. All the bathrooms are spacious and luminous. Its location is very central (close to Plaza de Mayo) but the immediate environment (surrounded by government buildings) is somewhat dead at night. You might also try the **NH Florida,** at San Martín 839 (ℂ **11/4321-9850**).

Bolívar 160 (at Alsina), 1066 Buenos Aires. ℂ **11/4121-6464.** Fax 11/4121-6450. www.nh-hotels.com. 303 units, including 50 suites. From $211 (£106) double; from $303 (£152) suite. Generous buffet breakfast included in rates. AE, DC, MC, V. Parking $16 (£8). Metro: Bolívar or Plaza de Mayo. **Amenities:** 2 restaurants; bar; small gym facility w/open-air pool deck; spa; sauna; concierge; business center; 24-hr. room service; babysitting; laundry service; dry cleaning; executive floor; conference center. *In room:* TV, high-speed Internet access and Wi-Fi, minibar, hair dryer, large safe.

MICROCENTRO
Very Expensive
Marriott Plaza Hotel ✸✸ The historic Plaza was the grande dame of Buenos Aires for most of the 20th century, and the Marriott management has maintained much of its original splendor. The intimate lobby, decorated in Italian marble, crystal, and Persian carpets, is a virtual revolving door of Argentine politicians, foreign diplomats, and business executives. The veteran staff offers outstanding service, and the concierge will address needs ranging from executive business services to sightseeing

tours. Twenty-six rooms overlook Plaza San Martín, providing dreamlike views of the green canopy of trees in the spring and summer. The hotel's health club is one of the best in the city. Uniquely, guests whose rooms are not ready when they check in are provided access to a special lounge area in the health club where they can rest and shower. Four rooms are available for those with disabilities, but only two offer full access.

Calle Florida 1005 (overlooking Plaza San Martín), 1005 Buenos Aires. ⓒ **888/236-2427** in the U.S., or 11/4318-3000. Fax 11/4318-3008. www.marriott.com. 325 units. $228 (£114) double; from $268 (£134) suite. Rates include buffet breakfast. AE, DC, MC, V. Valet parking $20 (£10). Metro: San Martín. **Amenities:** 2 restaurants; cigar bar; excellent health club w/outdoor pool; exercise room; sauna; concierge; business center; salon; 24-hr. room service; massage service; laundry service; dry cleaning. *In room:* A/C, TV, minibar, coffeemaker, hair dryer, iron, safe.

Park Tower Buenos Aires (The Luxury Connection) 🏵🏵🏵

One of the most beautiful and expensive hotels in Buenos Aires, the Park Tower is connected to the Sheraton (see below) next door. The hotel combines traditional elegance with technological sophistication and offers impeccable service. Common areas as well as private rooms feature imported marble, Italian linens, lavish furniture, and impressive works of art. The lobby, with its floor-to-ceiling windows, potted palms, and Japanese wall screens, contributes to a sense that this is the Pacific Rim rather than South America. The rooms have stunning views of the city and the river. Guests also have access to 24-hour private butler service. The lobby lounge features piano music, a cigar bar, tea, cocktails, and special liquors.

Av. Leandro N. Alem 1193 (at Della Paolera), 1104 Buenos Aires. ⓒ **800/325-3589** in the U.S., or 11/4318-9100. Fax 11/4318-9150. www.luxurycollection.com/parktower. 181 units. From $220 (£110) double. AE, DC, MC, V. Valet parking $12 (£6). Metro: Retiro. **Amenities:** 3 restaurants; snack bar; piano bar; 2 pools; putting green; 2 lighted tennis courts; fitness center w/gym; wet and dry saunas; concierge; business center and secretarial services; limited room service; massage therapy; laundry service; dry cleaning. *In room:* A/C, TV/VCR, minibar, hair dryer, safe.

Sofitel Buenos Aires 🏵🏵

This classy French hotel near Plaza San Martín joins two seven-story buildings to a 20-story neoclassical tower dating from 1929, with a glass atrium lobby bringing them together. The lobby resembles an enormous gazebo, with six ficus trees, a giant iron-and-bronze chandelier, an Art Nouveau clock, and Botticcino and black San Gabriel marble filling the space. Adjacent to the lobby you will find an elegant French restaurant, **Le Sud,** and an early-20th-century style Buenos Aires cafe. The cozy library, with its grand fireplace and dark woods, offers guests an enchanting place to read outside their rooms. These rooms vary in size, mixing modern French decor with traditional Art Deco styles. The beautiful marble bathrooms have separate showers and bathtubs.

Arroyo 841/849, 1007 Buenos Aires. ⓒ **11/4909-1454.** Fax 11/4909-1452. www.sofitel.com. 144 units. From $290 (£145) double; from $390 (£195) suite. AE, DC, MC, V. **Amenities:** Restaurant and cafe; bar; indoor pool; fitness center; concierge; business center; room service; laundry service. *In room:* A/C, TV, dataport, minibar, hair dryer, safe.

Expensive

Claridge Hotel 🏵

The Claridge is living testimony to the once-close ties between England and Argentina. The grand entrance, with its imposing Ionic columns, mimics a London terrace apartment, and the lobby was renovated in a classical style with colored marbles. Guest rooms are spacious, spotless, tastefully decorated, and equipped with all the amenities expected of a five-star hotel. The restaurant's hunting-themed wood-paneled interior is a registered city landmark. Because it occasionally hosts conventions, the Claridge can become very busy. The rates at this hotel can go down significantly when rooms are booked via website promotions, pushing it into the moderate category.

Tucumán 535 (at San Martín), 1049 Buenos Aires. ℂ **11/4314-7700.** Fax 11/4314-8022. www.claridge.com.ar. 165 units. $325 (£163) double; from $490 (£245) suite. Rates include buffet breakfast. AE, DC, MC, V. Free valet parking. Metro: Florida. **Amenities:** Restaurant; bar; health club w/heated outdoor pool; exercise room; sauna; concierge; business center; 24-hr. room service; massage service; laundry service; dry cleaning. *In room:* A/C, TV, minibar, safe.

Meliá Buenos Aires Hotel 🌂🌂

Within easy walking distance of Plaza San Martín and Calle Florida, the Meliá offers spacious guest rooms, colored in soft earth tones, which feature overstuffed chairs, soundproof windows, and marble bathrooms. Large desks, two phone lines, and available cellphones make this a good choice for business travelers. Two rooms are available for the handicapped, with accessibility in the public spaces. Rooms in either the new building or old wing differ slightly in price, size, and layout, with more room and a slightly more modern decor in the newer area. The Meliá has a small Spanish restaurant and bar, and a 24-hour cafe.

Reconquista 945 (at Paraguay), 1003 Buenos Aires. ℂ **11/4891-3800.** Fax 11/4891-3834. www.solmelia.com. 209 units, including 22 suites. $160 (£80) double; from $230 (£115) suite. Rates include buffet breakfast. AE, DC, MC, V. Parking nearby at $7 (£3.50). Metro: San Martín. **Amenities:** Restaurant; bar; medium-sized heated indoor pool; exercise room; sauna; concierge; business services; 24-hr. room service; massage; babysitting; laundry service; dry cleaning. *In room:* A/C, TV, high-speed Internet access, minibar, coffeemaker, hair dryer, safe.

Sheraton Buenos Aires Hotel and Convention Center 🌂

The enormous Sheraton is situated in the heart of the business, shopping, and theater district and is an ideal location for business travelers and tour groups. Guest rooms are typical for a large American chain—they're well equipped, but lacking in charm. What the hotel lacks in intimacy, however, it makes up for in the wide range of services offered to guests, regardless of whether they're in town for business or tourism. It shares three restaurants with the neighboring Park Tower Buenos Aires (see above), and its "Neptune" pool and fitness center are among the best in the city. During conference time, the elevators can get overly busy and cause delays.

Av. San Martín 1225 (at Libertador), 1104 Buenos Aires. ℂ **11/4318-9000.** Fax 11/4318-9353. www.sheraton.com. 741 units. $290 (£145) double; from $360 (£180) suite. AE, DC, MC, V. Valet parking $15 (£7.50). Metro: Retiro. **Amenities:** 3 restaurants; snack bar; piano bar; 2 pools; putting green; 2 lighted tennis courts; fitness center w/gym; wet and dry saunas; concierge; activities desk; car-rental desk; business center; shopping arcade; salon; 24-hr. room service; massage therapy; babysitting; laundry service; dry cleaning. *In room:* A/C, TV, high-speed Internet access, minibar, hair dryer, safe.

Moderate

Amerian Buenos Aires Park Hotel 🌂🌂 *Finds*

One of the best four-star hotels in the city, this modern hotel (also known as the American Reconquista) is a good bet for tourists as well as for business travelers. The warm atrium lobby looks more like California than Argentina, and the highly qualified staff offers personalized service. Soundproof rooms are elegantly appointed with wood, marble, and granite, and all boast comfortable beds, chairs, and work areas. The suites, located on their own floor, come with whirlpool bathtubs. Many services are not directly provided by the hotel, such as massage and babysitting, but can be handled on request. The hotel is just blocks away from Calle Florida, Plaza San Martín, and the Teatro Colón.

Reconquista 699 (at Viamonte), 1003 Buenos Aires. ℂ **11/4317-5100.** Fax 11/4317-5101. www.amerian.com. 152 units, including 14 suites. $120 (£60) double; from $169 (£85) suite. Rates include buffet breakfast. AE, DC, MC, V. Parking $5 (£2.50). Metro: Florida. **Amenities:** Restaurant; pub; exercise room; sauna; concierge; business center; limited room service; laundry service; dry cleaning. *In room:* A/C, TV, minibar, coffeemaker (in suites only).

Holiday Inn Express 🌂

This hotel enjoys a convenient Microcentro location close to Puerto Madero and its restaurants and nightlife. Although it doesn't have room service, concierge, or bellhops, the hotel is friendly, modern, and inexpensive. Guest rooms have large, firm beds, ample desk space, and 27-inch cable TVs; half of the rooms boast river views. Coffee and tea are served 24 hours a day, and the buffet breakfast is excellent.

Av. Leandro N. Alem 770 (at Viamonte), 1057 Buenos Aires. (𝄞 11/4311-5200. Fax 11/4311-5757. www.holiday-inn. com. 116 units. From $140 (£70) double. Children under 18 stay free in parent's room. Rates include buffet breakfast. AE, DC, MC, V. Free parking. Metro: L. N. Alem. **Amenities:** Deli; exercise room; whirlpool; sauna; business center. *In room:* A/C, TV.

Hotel Reconquista Plaza 𝄞   Near busy Calle Florida, this hotel provides a good location and clean, modern amenities. The decor is harvest gold with dark wooden trims, and all rooms have enormous rounded windows overlooking the street. Suites are oversized rooms partially separated by a large wardrobe unit. A sleeper couch in this area provides extra bed space. Some suites have enormous terraces, with views overlooking the Microcentro. Double-glazing on the windows locks out noise, an important consideration in this area. Staff is exceptionally friendly and helpful. High-speed Internet access is available from all rooms for about $5 (£2.50) per day, and desks provide a workspace; large in-room safes provide space for a laptop. Access to a pool can be arranged.

Reconquista 602 (at Tucumán), 1003 Buenos Aires. (𝄞 11/4311-4600. Fax 11/4311-3302. www.reconquistaplaza. com.ar. 60 units, including 9 suites. From $213 (£107) double; from $330 (£165) suite. Rates include buffet breakfast. AE, MC, V. Parking $4 (£2). Metro: Florida. Cats allowed. **Amenities:** Restaurant; bar; small health club; sauna; concierge; business center; 24-hr. room service; laundry service. *In room:* A/C, TV, minibar, coffeemaker, hair dryer, large safe.

Howard Johnson Florida Street 𝄞𝄞 *Value*   This has a great location off Calle Florida near Plaza San Martín, with access through a shopping-and-restaurant gallery in the hotel's ground level. Guest rooms come equipped with king- or queen-size beds, sleeper chairs, large desks and dressers, and well-appointed bathrooms. Rooms are of an above-average size in this category. Each room has two phones, and local calls and Internet use are free—a rarity in Buenos Aires. There's a small, airy cafe and bar in the lobby, with additional food served in the gallery below. There is no pool or health club on premises, but access is offered free of charge to a nearby facility.

Calle Florida 944 (at Alvear), 1005 Buenos Aires. (𝄞 11/4891-9200. Fax 11/4891-9208. www.hojoar.com. 77 units. $200 (£100) double. Rates include buffet breakfast. AE, DC, MC, V. Metro: San Martín. **Amenities:** Restaurant; bar; business services; 24-hr. room service; laundry service; dry cleaning; conference center. *In room:* A/C, TV, high-speed Internet access, minibar, coffeemaker, hair dryer, iron, large safe.

Lafayette Hotel 𝄞 *Kids*   The Lafayette Hotel is good value for a mid-price-range hotel, with spacious rooms (some can accommodate an entire family) that are exceedingly clean and well maintained. Each has a desk and all rooms have Wi-Fi access. Street-side rooms are great for people-watching in the Microcentro, though you should expect some noise. Back rooms are quieter but offer no views. The location is ideal for Microcentro's Lavalle and Florida street shopping. The hotel is separated into two different elevator bays, so if staying with friends or family, request rooms in the same division of the hotel.

Reconquista 546 (at Viamonte), 1003 Buenos Aires. (𝄞 11/4393-9081. Fax 11/4322-1611. www.lafayettehotel.com.ar. 82 units, including 6 suites. From $135 (£68) double; from $200 (£100) suite. Rates include generous buffet breakfast. AE, DC, MC, V. Metro: Florida. **Amenities:** Restaurant; bar; concierge; small business center; limited room service; laundry service; dry cleaning. *In room:* A/C, TV, Wi-Fi, minibar, hair dryer, safe.

WHERE TO DINE

Buenos Aires offers world-class dining, with a variety of Argentine, Italian, and international restaurants. You've heard that Argentine beef is the best in the world; *parrillas* serving the choicest cuts are ubiquitous. Many kitchens have an Italian influence, and you'll find pasta on most menus. The city's most fashionable neighborhood for eating out is Palermo Viejo, where new restaurants are constantly opening—and closing. Additional top restaurants line the docks of Puerto Madero, with the majority focused on seafood. The Microcentro and Recoleta offer many outstanding restaurants and cafes as well. Cafe life is as sacred to Porteños as it is to Parisians.

Porteños eat breakfast until 10am, lunch between noon and 3:30pm, and dinner late—usually after 9pm. Many restaurants require reservations, particularly on weekends. Executive lunch menus are offered most places at noon, but dinner menus are usually a la carte. There is sometimes a small charge for bread and other items placed at the table. In restaurants that serve pasta, the pasta and its sauce are priced separately. Standard tipping is 10%, more for exceptional service. When paying by credit card, you will often be expected to leave the *propina* (tip) in cash, since many credit card receipts don't provide a place to include it. Many restaurants close between lunch and dinner, and are closed on Monday nights. Call ahead to make sure, as this can also change seasonally.

PUERTO MADERO
Expensive

Cabaña las Lilas ✯✯ ARGENTINE Widely considered the best *parrilla* in Buenos Aires, Cabaña las Lilas is always packed. The menu pays homage to Argentine beef, which comes from the restaurant's private *estancia* (ranch). The best cuts are the rib-eye, baby beef, and thin skirt steak. Order sautéed vegetables, grilled onions, or Provençal-style fries separately. Chicken and fish are also part of the offerings, and vegetarians don't have to stay at home, since there is a large selection of very fresh and crisp salads. Service is hurried but professional. This enormous spot offers indoor and outdoor seating, and in spite of its high price, it has a casual and informal vibe.

Alicia Moreau de Justo 516, at Villaflor in Dique 3. ✆ **11/4313-1336.** www.laslilas.com. Reservations recommended. Main courses $40–$60 (£20–£30). AE, DC, V. Daily noon–midnight. Metro: L. N. Alem.

Moderate

La Bisteca ✯✯ (*Value*) PARRILLA Puerto Madero's La Bisteca offers a wide range of choices. This is an all-you-can-eat establishment, locally called a *tenedor libre,* with a three-course lunch for about $21 (£11) and dinner ranging from about $15 to $25 (£7.50–£13). If you have come to Argentina to try the country's beef, make this a definite stopping point. The high-quality meat surprised me, especially considering the moderate price.

Av. Alicia Moreau de Justo 1890, at Peñaloza on Dique 1. ✆ **11/4514-4999.** AE, DC, MC, V. Daily noon–4pm and 8pm–1am. No Metro access.

Sorrento del Puerto ✯✯ ITALIAN The only two-story restaurant in Puerto Madero enjoys impressive views of the water from both floors. The sleek modern dining room boasts large windows, modern blue lighting, and tables and booths decorated with white linens and individual roses. People come here for two reasons: great pasta and even better seafood. The best seafood dishes include trout stuffed with crabmeat or sole with a Belle Marnier sauce. Sorrento has a second location in Recoleta at Posadas 1053 (✆ **11/4326-0532**).

Av. Alicia Moreau de Justo 410, at Guevara on Dique 4. ℂ 11/4319-8731. Reservations recommended. Main courses $25–$30 (£13–£15). AE, DC, MC, V. Mon–Fri noon–4pm and 8pm–1am; Sat 8pm–2am. Metro: L. N. Alem.

RECOLETA

Expensive

La Bourgogne ★★★ FRENCH   The only Relais Gourmand in Argentina, chef Jean Paul Bondoux serves the finest French and international food in the city. Decorated in a modern style, the formal dining room serves the city's top gourmands. To begin your meal, consider a warm foie gras scallop with honey wine sauce or perhaps the succulent *ravioli d'escargots*. Examples of the carefully prepared main courses include *chateaubriand béarnaise*, roasted salmon, veal steak, and lamb with parsley and garlic sauce.

Av. Alvear 1981, at Ayacucho (Alvear Palace Hotel). ℂ 11/4808-2100. www.alvearpalace.com. Reservations required. Jacket and tie required for men. Main courses $25–$40 (£13–£20). AE, DC, MC, V. Free valet parking. Mon–Fri noon–3pm; Mon–Sat 8pm–midnight. No Metro access.

Piegari ★★ ITALIAN   Piegari has two restaurants located across the street from each other (under a highway overpass, of all places); the more formal focuses on Italian dishes, while the other (Piegari Vitello e Dolce) is mainly a *parrilla*. Both are excellent, but visit the formal Piegari for outstanding Italian cuisine. Homemade spaghetti, six kinds of risotto, pan pizza, veal scallops, and black salmon ravioli are just a few of the mouthwatering choices.

Posadas 1042, at Av. 9 de Julio in La Recova, near the Four Seasons Hotel. ℂ 11/4326-9654. Reservations recommended. Main courses $26–$36 (£13–£18). AE, DC, MC, V. Daily noon–3:30pm and 7:30pm–1am. No Metro access.

Moderate

El Mirasol ★★ PARRILLA   One of the city's best *parrillas,* this restaurant serves thick cuts of fine Argentine beef. Its glassed dining area full of plants and trellises gives the impression of outdoor dining. A mammoth 2½-pound serving of tenderloin is a specialty. The best dessert is an enticing combination of meringue, ice cream, whipped cream, *dulce de leche,* walnuts, and hot chocolate sauce.

Posadas 1032, at Av. 9 de Julio in La Recova near the Four Seasons Hotel. ℂ 11/4326-7322. www.el-mirasol.com.ar. Reservations recommended. Main courses $11–$30 (£5.50–£15). AE, DC, MC, V. Daily noon–2am. No Metro access.

Inexpensive

Juana M ★★ (Value) PARRILLA   This amazing little *parrilla* is easily overlooked, but you shouldn't miss it. Located in the basement of an orphanage, this neoclassical building is one of the few saved from the highway demolition that created the nearby La Recova. This cavernous industrial-chic space is white and luminous by day. At night, when the space is lit only by candlelight, trendy young patrons flood in, chattering the night away. The menu is simple, high quality, and amazingly inexpensive.

Carlos Pellegrini 1535 (basement), at Libertador, across from the La Recova area. ℂ 11/4326-0462. Main courses $10–$12 (£5–£6). AE, MC, V. Daily noon–4pm and 8pm–12:30am. No Metro access.

La Biela ★★★ CAFE   Black-and-white photos of Argentine car racers decorate the huge dining room. Artists, politicians, and neighborhood executives (as well as a fair number of tourists) all frequent La Biela, which serves breakfast, informal lunch plates, ice cream, and crepes. The outdoor terrace sits beneath an enormous 19th-century gum tree, opposite the church of Nuestra Señora del Pinar and the adjoining Recoleta Cemetery. La Biela is a protected *bar notable.*

Av. Quintana 596, at Alvear. ℂ 11/4804-0449. www.labiela.com. Main courses $10–$15 (£5–£7.50). V. Daily 7am–3am. No Metro access.

Bars to Note

A *bar notable* is a special class of cafe or bar that protects the original interiors and atmosphere of historic Buenos Aires bars, which date from the late 1800s forward. A great deal of the bars are concentrated in the oldest areas of the city, such as San Telmo and La Boca.

PALERMO
Expensive
Casa Cruz ★★ *(Finds)* ITALIAN/INTERNATIONAL   With its enormous polished-brass doors and lack of a sign on the door, you almost feel like you are entering a nightclub, and inside, the dark modern interior maintains the theme. The impressive round bar leads into a spacious dining area full of polished woods and red upholstery. The menu here is eclectic and interesting. Rabbit, sea bass, Parma ham rolls, and other interesting and exotic ingredients go into the many flavorful dishes.

Uriarte 1658, at Honduras. ⓒ 11/4833-1112. www.casa-cruz.com. Reservations highly recommended. Main courses $15–$30 (£7.50–£15). AE, MC, V. Mon–Sat 8:30pm–3am, later Sat–Sun. No Metro access.

Moderate
De Olivas i Lustres ★★ MEDITERRANEAN   Located in Palermo Viejo, this magical restaurant is a Buenos Aires favorite. The small, rustic dining room displays antiques, olive jars, and wine bottles, and each candlelit table is individually decorated. The reasonably priced menu celebrates Mediterranean cuisine, with light soups, fresh fish, and sautéed vegetables as its focus. For about $20 (£10) each, you and your partner can share 15 such tapa-style dishes, brought out individually. The items are meant to contrast and surprise you as the night progresses.

Gorriti 3972, at Medrano. ⓒ 11/4867-3388. Reservations recommended. Main courses $6–$10 (£3–£5); fixed-price menu $20 (£10). AE, V. Mon–Sat 8:30pm–1:30am. Metro: Scalabrini Ortiz.

Novecento ★★★ INTERNATIONAL   Fashionable Porteños pack the New York–style bistro by 11pm, and waiters rush around with dishes such as salmon carpaccio and steak salad. The pastas and risotto are mouthwatering, but you may prefer a steak au poivre or a chicken brochette. Other wonderful choices include filet mignon, grilled Pacific salmon, and penne with wild mushrooms. Novecento has a sister restaurant in Soho.

Báez 199, at Arguibel. ⓒ 11/4778-1900. Reservations recommended. Main courses $8–$14 (£4–£7). AE, DC, MC, V. Daily noon–4pm and 8pm–2am; Sun brunch 8am–noon. Metro: Ministro Carranza.

Inexpensive
Bio ★★ *(Finds)* VEGETARIAN/MEDITERRANEAN   In a nation where meat reigns supreme, finding an organic vegetarian restaurant is a near impossibility. Bio is the exception. Their "meat" is made on the premises from wheat and then marinated to add more flavor. All the ingredients used at Bio are organic, and all are grown or produced strictly in Argentina. Piles of organic cheese line the counters. Quinoa, the ancient Incan grain, is also used in many of the dishes.

Humboldt 2199, at Guatemala. ⓒ 11/4774-3880. Main courses $7–$10 (£3.50–£5). Tues–Sun noon–3:30pm; daily 8pm–1am, often later Sat–Sun. Metro: Palermo is 4 blocks away.

Campo Bravo ★★ *(Value)* PARRILLA/ARGENTINE   This place serves as the virtual center of the Las Cañitas dining scene. It's relaxed during the day but insane at night.

Dining on the sidewalk here, you'll get a great view of the glamorous crowds who get dropped off by taxis to begin their night in this exciting neighborhood. The *parrilla* serves up basic Argentine cuisine, and its enormous slabs of meat are served on wooden boards. Expect long delays for an outside table on weekends. One good thing—they don't close between lunch and dinner, so early diners can enjoy a great meal here with no wait at all for a table.

Báez 292, at Arévalo. © **11/4514-5820.** Main courses $12–$15 (£6–£7.50). MC. Mon 6pm–4am; Tues–Sun 11:30am–2:30am (often later Sat–Sun, depending on crowds). Metro: Carranza.

MONSERRAT
Moderate
Club Español ✶✶ SPANISH   The Art Nouveau Spanish club boasts the most magnificent dining room in Buenos Aires. Despite the restaurant's architectural grandeur, the atmosphere is surprisingly relaxed and often celebratory; don't be surprised to find a table of champagne-clinking Argentines next to you. Tables have beautiful silver place settings, and tuxedo-clad waiters offer formal service. Although the menu is a tempting sample of Spanish cuisine, including the paella and Spanish omelets, the fish dishes are the chef's best.

Bernardo de Yrigoyen 180, at Alsina. © **11/4334-4876.** Reservations recommended. Main courses $10–$18 (£5–£9). AE, DC, MC, V. Daily noon–4pm and 8pm–midnight. Metro: Carlos Pelegrini.

MICROCENTRO
Expensive
Dora ✶✶ ARGENTINE/SEAFOOD   Nobody comes here for the decor. Dora has been open since the 1940s and run by the same family that opened it. The specialty at this expensive restaurant is fish, though a few beef, chicken, and pasta dishes are thrown in, too—almost as a second thought. The "Cazuela Dora" is the specialty—a casserole of fish, shellfish, shrimp, and just about everything else the sea offers thrown into one pot. Appetizers alone are expensive, from $10 to $24 (£5–£12), but some of the options are made with fresh seafood.

Reconquista 1076. © **11/4311-2891.** Main courses $18–$30 (£9–£15). V. Mon–Thurs 12:30pm–1am; Fri–Sat noon–2am. Metro: San Martín.

Plaza Grill ✶✶ INTERNATIONAL   For nearly a century, the Plaza Grill has dominated the city's power-lunch scene. The dining room is decorated with dark oak furniture, Indian fans from the British Empire, and Villeroy & Boch china place settings. Tables are well spaced, allowing for intimate conversations. Order a la carte from the international menu or off the *parrilla*—the steaks are perfect Argentine cuts. The restaurant's wine list spans seven countries, with the world's best Malbec coming from Mendoza.

Marriott Plaza Hotel, Calle Florida 1005, overlooking Plaza San Martín. © **11/4318-3070.** Reservations recommended. Main courses $14–$20 (£7–£10). AE, DC, MC, V. Daily noon–3pm and 7pm–midnight. Tea service from 5–7pm. Metro: San Martín.

Moderate
Broccolino ✶ ITALIAN   Taking its name from New York's Italian immigrant neighborhood—notice the Brooklyn memorabilia filling the walls—the restaurant has a distinctly New York feel. Three small dining rooms are decorated in quintessential red-and-white checkered tablecloths, and the smell of tomatoes, onions, and garlic fills the air. The restaurant is known for its spicy pizzas, fresh pastas, and, above all, its sauces (*salsas* in Spanish).

Esmeralda 776, at Córdoba. (€) **11/4322-7652.** Reservations recommended. Main courses $10–$15 (£5–£7.50). Daily noon–4pm and 7pm–11pm. Metro: Carlos Pelegrini.

Las Nazarenas ⚘ ARGENTINE   You only have two choices here: meat cuts grilled on the *parrilla* or cooked on a spit over the fire. Argentine presidents and foreign ministers have all made their way here. The two-level dining room is handsomely decorated with cases of Argentine wines and abundant plants. The food is excellent, and the service is unhurried, offering you plenty of time for a relaxing meal.

Reconquista 1132, at Leandro N. Alem. (€) **11/4312-5559.** Reservations recommended. Main courses $15–$30 (£7.50–£15). AE, DC, MC, V. Daily noon–1am. Metro: Plaza San Martín.

Richmond Cafe ⚘⚘ CAFE/ARGENTINE   The Richmond Cafe, a *bar notable,* is all that is left of the Richmond Hotel, an Argentine-British hybrid that opened in 1917 and once catered to the elite. The menu here is traditionally Argentine with a *confiteria* (cafe) section in the front. You'll find a mix of locals of all kinds here, from workers grabbing a quick bite to well-dressed seniors. The decor is that of a gentlemen's club, full of wood, brass, and red leather upholstery. Downstairs is a bar area full of billiard tables, and the restaurant offers hearty basics such as chicken, fish, and beef.

Calle Florida 468 at Corrientes. (€) **11/4322-1341** or 11/4322-1653. www.restaurant.com.ar/richmond. Main courses $12–$16 (£6–£8). AE, MC, V. Mon–Sat 7am–10pm. Metro: Florida.

Inexpensive
Café Tortoni ⚘⚘⚘ *(Moments* CAFE/ARGENTINE   This historic cafe has served as the artistic and intellectual capital of Buenos Aires since 1858. Wonderfully appointed in woods, stained glass, yellowing marble, and bronzes, the place tells more about its history by simply existing than any of the photos hanging on its walls could. This is the perfect spot for a coffee or a snack when walking along Avenida de Mayo. Stop by for one of the nightly tango shows (7:30 and 9:30pm), set in a cramped side gallery where the performers often walk through the crowd.

Av. de Mayo 825, at Esmeralda. (€) **11/4342-4328.** Main courses $4–$14 (£2–£7). AE, DC, MC, V. Mon–Thurs 7:30am–2am; Fri–Sat 8am–3am; Sun 9am–1am. Metro: Estación Piedras.

SAN TELMO
Moderate
Desnivel ⚘ PARRILLA   This place brings new meaning to the phrase greasy spoon, because everything in here seems to be greasy—from the slippery floor to the railings, glasses, and dishes. Even the walls, and the artwork on them, seem to bleed grease. This is one of San Telmo's best *parrillas,* and a flood of locals and tourists keep the place going.

Defensa 855, at Independencia. (€) **11/4300-9081.** Main courses $5–$10 (£2.50–£5). No credit cards. Daily noon–4:30pm and 7:30pm–1am. Metro: Independencia.

BUENOS AIRES AFTER DARK
From the Teatro Colón to dimly lit tango salons, Buenos Aires offers an exceptional variety of nightlife. Porteños eat late and play later, with theater performances starting around 9pm, bars and nightclubs opening around midnight, and no one showing up until after 1am. Thursday, Friday, and Saturday are the big going-out nights, with the bulk of activity in Recoleta, Palermo Viejo, and Costanera. Summer is quieter because most of the town flees to the coast.

　　Performing arts in Buenos Aires are centered on the highly regarded Teatro Colón, home to the National Opera, National Symphony, and National Ballet. In addition, there are nearly 40 professional theaters around town showing Broadway- and off-Broadway-style hits, Argentine plays, and music reviews. Buy tickets for most productions at the box office or through **Ticketron** (© 11/4321-9700) or **Ticketmaster** (© 11/4326-9903).

THE PERFORMING ARTS
Opera, Ballet & Classical Music

Luna Park   Once the home of international boxing matches, the Luna is the largest indoor stadium in Argentina, and as such, it hosts the biggest shows and concerts in Buenos Aires. Buchard 465, at Corriendes. © 11/4311-1990 or 11/4311-5100. Tickets $6 $30(£3–£15). Metro: L. N Alem.

Teatro Colón   Known across the world for its impeccable acoustics, the Colón has attracted the world's finest opera performers. Opera season in Buenos Aires runs from April to November. The Colón has its own philharmonic orchestra, ballet, and choir companies. The 2008 season should be particularly spectacular as it is the theater's centennial year, however delays in renovation (as we went to press, it was closed) mean it may not open until October 2008. Consult the website for more information. Calle Libertad 621, at Tucumán. © 11/4378-7100. www.teatrocolon.org.ar. Tickets $4–$30 (£2–£15). Metro: Tribunales.

Theaters & Exhibitions

Centro Cultural Recoleta (Recoleta Cultural Center) 🎭🎭   This cultural center is just one door over from the famous Recoleta Cemetery. It hosts Argentine and international art exhibits, experimental theater works, occasional music concerts, and an interactive science museum for children where they are encouraged to touch and play with the displays. Junín 1930, next door to the Recolta Cemetry. © 11/4803-1041. No Metro access.

Teatro Municipal General San Martín   This entertainment complex has three theaters offering drama, comedy, ballet, music, and children's plays. Its lobby often has special exhibitions of photography and art related to the theater and, on its own, is worth a special visit during the daytime. The lobby exhibitions are usually free. Corrientes 1530, at Paraná © 0800/333-5254. $6–$18 (£3–£9). Metro: Uruguay.

THE CLUB & MUSIC SCENE
Tango Dance Clubs & Show Palaces

In Buenos Aires, you can *watch* the tango or *dance* the tango. (Perhaps the former will lend inspiration to the latter.) You'll have many opportunities to see the dance during your visit: Tango dancers frequent the streets of La Boca and San Telmo, many high-end hotels offer tango shows in their lobbies and bars, and tango salons blanket the city. The most famous (besides Café Tortoni, p. 115) are in San Telmo and combine dinner and a show. Have a hotel driver or *remise* take you to San Telmo, La Boca, or Barracas at night, rather than taking the Metro or trying to walk.

Tango Palaces

El Viejo Almacén, Independencia and Balcarce (© 11/4307-6689), shows traditional Argentine-style tango. Sunday to Thursday shows are at 10pm; Friday and Saturday shows are at 9:30 and 11:45pm. **Esquina Carlos Gardel** 🎭🎭, Carlos Gardel 3200 (© 11/4876-6363), is perhaps the most elegant of the city's tango show palaces, held in a restaurant where Carlos Gardel used to dine with his friends. **Señor Tango,** Vieytes 1653 (© 11/4303-0212), is more akin to a Broadway production theater than to a traditional tango salon, but the dancers are fantastic and the owner, who clearly loves to perform, is a good singer.

Tango Clubs & Milongas

La Glorietta, Once de Septiembre and Echeverría (© **11/4674-1026**), offers tango in the open-air, although it can be slightly touristy. There is a show at 1am on Friday and Saturday. **Salón Canning,** Scalabrini Ortiz 1331 (© **11/4832-6753**), is among the most authentic of each of the city's *milongas.*

Other Dance Clubs

Dancing in Buenos Aires is not just about tango, with the majority of the younger population preferring salsa, *cumbia,* and European beats. The biggest nights out are Thursday, Friday, and Saturday. **Asia de Cuba** ★, P. Dealessi 750 (© **11/4894-1328** or 11/4894-1329; www.asiadecuba.com.ar), offers sophisticated drinking and dancing. Some of the entertainment, though, can be wild—of the women-dancing-in-cages variety. **Mambo,** Báez 243 (© **11/4778-0115;** www.mambobar.com.ar), does Latin shows and Latin dancing; they also offer Caribbean food from 8pm on. **Opera Bay,** Cecilia Grierson 225, at Dealessi in Dique 4 (no phone), is located, literally, on the water, on a pier jutting into Puerto Madero's harbor. It attracts an affluent and fashionable crowd, many over 40.

Gay & Lesbian Dance Clubs

Amerika, Gascón 1040 (© **11/4865-4416;** www.ameri-k.com.ar), is the city's most popular gay club, and even straight people are beginning to come here in droves for the great music. It's open Friday and Saturday only. **Contramano,** Rodríguez Peña 1082 (**11/4811-0494;** www.contramano.com), is popular with a mature crowd and was the first gay bar opened in Buenos Aires. **Glam,** Cabrera 3046 (© **11/4963-2521;** www. glambsascom.ar), is young and lively and increasingly popular.

THE BAR SCENE

Where to start? Where to go? B.A. is hopping with bar life, and below is just a small sample.

The Kilkenny, Marcelo T. de Alvear 399 (© **11/4312-7291**), is more like a rock house than an Irish pub and is packed with both locals and foreigners. **Plaza Dorrego Bar,** Calle Defensa 1098 (© **11/4361-0141**), has antique liquor bottles in cases along the walls, and anonymous writings engraved in the wood. **The Shamrock,** Rodríguez Peña 1220 (© **11/4812-3584**), is packed every night of the week, including Mondays. On weekends, the basement space opens up into a small disco, adding to the fun. **Gibraltar,** Peru 895 (© **11/4362-5310**), is a real pub, with draft beer that comes in pint glasses and food such as Thai curry. **Millión,** Parana 1048 (© **11/4815-9925**), is a lavish, renovated mansion attracting a beautiful crowd.

5 Puerto Iguazú & Iguazú Falls ★★★

1,330km (825 miles) NE of Buenos Aires

For the true sense of the oft-overused word "awesome," you must visit the breathtaking Iguazú Falls. Here, in a spectacular subtropical setting, you will find 14 miles (23km) of deafening waterfalls plummeting into a 230-foot (20m) giant gorge. A dazzling panorama of cascades whose power overwhelms the sounds of the surrounding jungle, declared a World Heritage Area by UNESCO in 1984, these 275 waterfalls were shaped by 120 million years of geological history and form one of Earth's most unforgettable sights. Iguazú Falls are shared by Argentina and Brazil and are easily accessible from nearby Paraguay. Excellent walking circuits on both the Argentine and

Brazilian sides allow visitors to peek over the tops of or stare at the faces of raging sheets of water, some with sprays so intense it seems as though geysers have erupted from below. Although a luxury hotel overlooking the falls exists in both the Argentine and Brazilian national parks, many visitors looking for less expensive accommodations stay in Puerto Iguazú in Argentina or in Foz do Iguaçu in Brazil.

Although Iguazú is best known for its waterfalls, the surrounding subtropical jungle is well worth including in your itinerary. Here, *cupay* trees (a South American hardwood) tower over the various layers of life that compete for light, and the national park is known to contain 200 species of trees, 448 species of birds, 71 kinds of mammals, 36 species of reptiles, 20 species of amphibians, and more than 250 kinds of butterflies. Spray from the waterfall keeps the humidity levels over 75%, leading to a tremendous growth of epiphytes (plants that grow on other plants without taking nutrients from their hosts). Iguazú's climate also provides for the flowering of plants year-round, lending brilliant color to the forest.

You can visit the waterfalls on your own, but you will most certainly need a tour operator to explore the jungle. Allow at least 1 full day to explore the waterfalls on the Argentine side, another to visit the Brazilian side, and perhaps half a day for a jungle tour (see chapter 6 for more details).

The sedate, ramshackle town of **Puerto Iguazú** is 18km (11 miles) from the park. Though hardly the most memorable place, it has a subdued charm, pretty vegetation, and friendly people—and is not yet ruined by the tourist trade. Accommodation options are improving all the time. If you want something more vibrant, expensive, and dangerous, go to the Brazilian town of Foz de Iguaçu on the other side (see the "Border Crossing" box).

ESSENTIALS
GETTING THERE
BY PLANE **Aerolíneas Argentinas** (✆ 0810/222-86527 or 3757/420-194) and **LAN Chile** (✆ 3757/424-296) offer up to five daily flights from Buenos Aires to **Aeropuerto Internacional Cataratas** (✆ 3757/422-013); the trip takes 1½ hours. Round-trip fares cost approximately $320 (£160), depending on whether any specials are on offer. Aerolíneas Argentinas occasionally offers flights to Iguazú out of Ezeiza international airport, usually on Saturday or Sunday. Catch a taxi (for about $15/£7.50) or one of the shuttle buses from the airport to town ($3/£1.50), a 20-minute drive.

BY BUS The fastest bus service from Buenos Aires is with **Vía Bariloche** (✆ 11/4315-4456 in Buenos Aires), which takes 18 hours and costs $50 to $70 (£25–£35) one-way, depending on the seat you choose. (The more expensive fare gets you a fully reclining *cama* seat.) Less pricey but longer (21 hr.) are **Expreso Singer** (✆ 11/4313-3927 in Buenos Aires) and **Expreso Tigre Iguazú** (✆ 11/4313-3915 in Buenos Aires), which both run for about $44 (£22) one-way.

GETTING AROUND
El Práctico local buses run every 45 minutes from 7am to 8pm between Puerto Iguazú and the national park, and cost less than $1 (50p). **Parada 10** (✆ 3757/421-527) provides 24-hour taxi service. You can rent a car at the airport, although this is much more a luxury than a necessity. Within both Puerto Iguazú and the national park, you can easily walk.

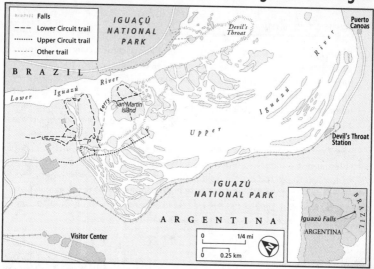

The Iguazú Falls Region

Map legend:
- Falls
- - - - Lower Circuit trail
- ····· Upper Circuit trail
- ······ Other trail

IGUAÇÚ NATIONAL PARK
BRAZIL
Lower Iguazú River
San Martín Island
Ferry
Devil's Throat
Puerto Canoas
Iguazú River
Upper
Devil's Throat Station
IGUAZÚ NATIONAL PARK
ARGENTINA
Visitor Center
0 — 1/4 mi
0 — 0.25 km

Iguazú Falls
ARGENTINA
BRAZIL

VISITOR INFORMATION

In Puerto Iguazú, obtain maps and park information from the **Parque Nacional** office at Victoria Aguirre 66 (𝄞 **3757/420-722**), Monday through Friday from 8am to 2pm. For information on the town, contact the **municipal tourist office,** at Victoria Aguirre and Brañas (𝄞 **3757/420-800**). It's open daily from 8am to 8pm. Visitor information is also available near the national park entrance (see below).

In Buenos Aires, get information about Iguazú from **Casa de la Provincia de Misiones,** Av. Santa Fe 989 (𝄞 **11/4322-0686**), Monday through Friday from 10am to 5pm.

VISITING THE NATIONAL PARK

Your first stop will likely be the **visitor center,** where you can get maps and information about the area's flora and fauna. New and environmentally friendly, the visitor center is located 1km (a half-mile) from the park entrance, next to the parking lot and footbridges for the waterfall circuits. Adjacent to the visitor center, you will find a restaurant, snack shops, and souvenir stores. A natural-gas train takes visitors to the path entrance for the Upper and Lower circuits and to the footbridge leading to the Devil's Throat (footpaths remain open for walkers, but the walk to Devil's Throat is about 3km/2 miles). The visitor center is staffed with a number of English-speaking guides, available for individual and private tours, so you may opt to see the falls on your own or with an experienced local guide. There is a $10 (£5) entrance fee for non-Argentines to enter the national park, which includes the train ride. The national park is open daily from 8am to 7pm in summer, and until 6pm in winter.

The two main paths to view the waterfalls are the **Circuito Superior (Upper Circuit)** 𝄇 and **Circuito Inferior (Lower Circuit)** 𝄇, both of which begin within walking distance of the visitor center. There's a small snack shop near the beginning of the trails. The Upper Circuit winds its way along the top of the canyon, allowing you to look down the falls and see the area's rich flora, including cacti, ferns, and orchids. The

Border Crossing

There is currently much confusion among American travelers concerning what their visa requirements are to enter the Brazilian side of the falls. They hear they are required to get a $120-dollar visa in advance, yet when they arrive, they find American citizens crossing the border freely and without hindrance. The fact is citizens from the United States, Canada, and Australia all must obtain a visa to enter Brazil, whether for 1 day or 90 days. On the ground, however, some local officials, hotel concierges, tourist agencies, and taxi companies ignore this rule to make an extra buck. But rules are rules, and it is illegal to enter a country without the proper papers. If you truly want to see the Brazilian side of Iguazú Falls, my advice is to get a visa.

This can be done at short notice in Puerto Iguazú. Visit the Brazilian Consulate, Av. Córdoba 264 (© **3757/421-348**), Monday to Friday 8am to 1pm. The process takes 2 hours and requires a passport photo.

Lower Circuit offers the best views, as magnificent waterfalls come hurtling down before you in walls of silvery spray. The waterfalls are clearly marked by signs along the way.

The best time to walk the Upper Circuit is early in the morning or late in the afternoon, and rainbows often appear near sunset. This 1km (.5-mile) path takes 1 to 2 hours, starting at the viewing tower and leading past **Dos Hermanos (Two Brothers), Bossetti, Chico (Small), Ramírez,** and **San Martín** (the park's widest) falls. You can come right to the edges of these falls and look over them as they tumble up to 60m (197 ft.) below. Along your walk, you can also look across to San Martín Island and the Brazilian side, and you'll pass a number of small streams and creeks.

The 1.8km (1-mile) Lower Circuit takes 2 hours to walk, leading you past **Lanusse** and **Alvar Núñez** falls, along the Lower Iguazú River past the raging **Dos Mosqueteros (Two Musketeers)** and **Tres Mosqueteros (Three Musketeers)** falls. The trail then winds its way toward **Ramírez, Chico,** and **Dos Hermanos** falls. Here, you'll find an inspiring view of the **Garganta del Diablo (Devil's Throat)** and **Bossetti** falls. From the Salto Bossetti, a small pathway leads down to a small pier where you can catch a free boat to **San Martín Island.**

Once on the island, climb the stairs and walk along clearly marked trails for remarkable views of the surrounding *cataratas*—to the left, you see Garganta del Diablo, **Saltos Brasileros (Brazilian Falls),** and **Ventana;** to the right, you overlook the mighty **Salto San Martín,** which sprays 30m (98 ft.) high after hitting the river below. This panoramic view looks out at dozens of falls forming an arch before you. San Martín Island also has a small, idyllic beach perfect for sunbathing and swimming.

Garganta del Diablo is the mother of all waterfalls in Iguazú, visible from vantage points in both the Brazilian and Argentine parks. Cross the walking bridge to the observation point, at the top of Diablo: The water is calm as it makes its way down the Iguazú River, although it begins to speed up as it approaches the gorge ahead. In front of you, Mother Nature has created a furious avalanche of water and spray that is the highest waterfall in Iguazú and one of the world's greatest natural spectacles. You might want to bring a raincoat—you *will* get wet.

TOUR OPERATORS

The main tour operator here is **Iguazú Jungle Explorer** (*C* 3757/421-696), located inside the national park and in the Sheraton International Iguazú. This company offers a Nautical Adventure ($16/£8) that visits the falls by inflatable raft, an Ecological Tour ($8/£4) that takes you to Devil's Throat and lets you paddle rubber boats along the Upper Iguazú Delta, and the Gran Aventura (Great Adventure) tour ($32/£16). This last tour begins with an 8km (5-mile) safari ride along the Yacoratia Path, the original dirt road that led through the forest and on to Buenos Aires. During the ride, you'll view the jungle's extensive flora and might glimpse some of the region's indigenous wildlife. You will be let off at Puerto Macuco, where you then hop in an inflatable boat with your tour group and navigate 6.5km (4 miles) along the lower Iguazú River, braving 1.6km (1 mile) of rapids as you approach the falls in Devil's Throat Canyon. After a thrilling and wet ride, the raft lets you off across from San Martín Island—you can then catch a free boat to the island, where there's a small beach for swimming and sunbathing as well as excellent hiking trails. You can combine the Ecological Tour and Great Adventure by buying a full-day Pasaporte Verde ($38/£19). Full-moon tours are also popular.

If you want to arrange a private tour for your specific interests, the best outfit is **Explorador Expediciones,** with offices in the Sheraton International Iguazú and in Puerto Iguazú at Puerto Moreno 217 (*C* 3757/421-632). The guides are experts on life in the Iguazú jungle. For other tours outside the national park (such as Che Guevara's childhood home or the Jesuit ruins of San Ignacio) try **Cataratas Turismo,** Tres Fronteras 301 (*C* 3757/420-970).

WHERE TO STAY

Peak season for hotels in Iguazú is January and February (summer holiday), July (winter break), Semana Santa (Holy Week, the week before Easter), and long weekends. On the Argentine side, the Sheraton International Iguazú is the only hotel inside the national park; the rest are in Puerto Iguazú, 18km (11 miles) away. Rates are often substantially discounted in the off season.

EXPENSIVE

Hotel Cataratas 🐾🐾   While not located next to the falls, Hotel Cataratas deserves consideration for its excellent service. None of the stuffiness you sometimes feel at luxury hotels is evident. Despite the hotel's unimpressive exterior, rooms are among the most modern and spacious in the area—especially the 30 "master rooms" that feature two double beds, handsome wood furniture, colorful artwork, large bathrooms with separate toilet rooms, in-room safes, and views of the pool or gardens. The hotel's many facilities make this a great choice for families.

Ruta 12, Km 4, 3370 Misiones. *C* 3757/421-100. Fax 3757/421-090. www.hotelcataratas.com.ar. 120 units. $170 (£85) double; from $250 (£125) suite. Rates include buffet breakfast. AE, DC, MC, V. **Amenities:** Restaurant; outdoor pool; tennis court; Jacuzzi; sauna; game room; concierge; secretarial services; room service; massage; laundry service. *In room:* A/C, TV, minibar, hair dryer, safe.

Sheraton Internacional Iguazú Resort 🐾🐾   The Sheraton enjoys a magnificent location inside the national park. Guests have little need to leave the resort, a self-contained paradise overlooking the falls. The hotel lies only steps from the Upper and Lower Circuit trails, and half of the guest rooms have direct views of the water (the others have splendid views of the jungle). The only drawback to the rooms is that they are fairly standard Sheraton decor. You can find better five-star accommodations outside the park, and the service here can be patchy, yet for the location this place is hard to beat. Book early as it's busy year-round.

Parque Nacional Iguazú, 3370 Misiones. ⓒ **0800/888-9180** local toll-free, or 3757/491-800. Fax 3757/491-848. www.sheraton.com. 180 units. $450 (£225) double with jungle view; $510 (£255) with view of waterfalls; from $650 (£325) suite. Rates include buffet breakfast. AE, DC, MC, V. **Amenities:** 2 restaurants; outdoor pool; 2 tennis courts; fitness center; concierge; car-rental desk; room service; laundry service; babysitting. *In room:* A/C, TV, minibar, hair dryer, safe.

MODERATE

Hotel Saint George ★ *(Finds)*   The Saint George features colorful, slightly dated rooms with single beds. The walls are not super thick, but everything is sparkling clean with well-lit bathrooms with toiletries. There is an inviting pool surrounded by lush vegetation and a commendable international restaurant that serves tasty fish from the local river. The breakfast buffet, however, is not the most memorable and needs improvement.

Av. Córdoba 148, 3370 Puerto Iguazú. ⓒ **3757/420-633.** Fax 3757/420-651. www.hotelsaintgeorge.com. 56 units. $75 (£38) double. Rates include buffet breakfast. AE, DC, MC, V. **Amenities:** Restaurant; bar; 2 pools (1 for children). *In room:* A/C, TV, hair dryer, minibar.

INEXPENSIVE

Hotel Lilian *(Value)*   Sometimes being on a budget does have its advantages, one of them being that you escape the tourist bubble and meet some real locals who are not in uniform. Hotel Lilian's big plus is a very helpful owner who will do her best to make sure your stay is as comfortable and rewarding as possible. This hotel has immaculate rooms surrounding a central courtyard. The bathrooms are of a decent size and more than adequate, but occasionally there is low water pressure.

Fray Luis Beltrán 183, 3370 Puerto Iguazú. ⓒ/fax **3757/420-968.** hotelliliana@yahoo.com.ar. 24 units. $40 (£20) double. Rates include breakfast. *In room:* A/C, TV.

Los Helechos *(Value)*   Family-run Los Helechos is a great bargain for those seeking comfortable, inexpensive accommodations in Puerto Iguazú. Located in the city center, this intimate hotel offers simple rooms, many of which surround a plant-filled courtyard. If you dislike humid nights, be sure to splurge for a room with air-conditioning (request it at the time of booking and be ready to cough up an additional $10/£5).

Paulino Amarante 76, 3370 Puerto Iguazú. ⓒ/fax 3757/420-338. 60 units. $45 (£23) double with A/C or TV; $35 (£18) without A/C and TV. AE, DC, MC, V. **Amenities:** Restaurant; bar; pool. *In room:* A/C, TV (in some rooms only).

WHERE TO DINE

Dining in Puerto Iguazú is casual and inexpensive, provided you're looking for a meal outside your hotel. Argentine steaks, seafood, and pasta are common on most menus. The Sheraton, inside the national park, has the area's best restaurant.

EXPENSIVE

Garganta del Diablo ★★ INTERNATIONAL   Located inside the national park at the Sheraton Internacional Iguazú, this restaurant serves excellent international and regional dishes. Open since the early 1980s, the restaurant is best known for its magnificent view of Devil's Throat. Enjoy a romantic table for two overlooking the falls, and consider ordering the grilled *suribí* (a mild fish from the river in front of you) or spider crab on couscous.

Parque Nacional Iguazú. ⓒ **3757/491-800.** Main courses $18–$30 (£9–£15). AE, DC, MC, V. Daily noon–3pm and 7–11pm.

INEXPENSIVE

El Charo *(Finds)* ARGENTINE   Renovations have altered this restaurant's previously ramshackle but cozy character. Now large and somewhat soulless, it still produces delicious food and is tremendously popular with both tourists and locals.

Av. Córdoba 106. *(C)* **3757/421-529.** Main courses $6–$10 (£3–£5). No credit cards. Daily 11am–1am.

La Rueda *(★) (Finds)* ARGENTINE   Nothing more than a small A-frame house with an outdoor patio, La Rueda is a delightful place to eat. Despite the casual atmosphere, tables have carefully prepared place settings, waiters are attentive and friendly, and the food—served in large portions—is very good. The diverse menu features pasta, steaks, and fish dishes.

Av. Córdoba 28. *(C)* **3757/422-531.** Main courses $6–$10 (£3–£5). No credit cards. Daily noon–4pm and 7pm–1am.

PUERTO IGUAZU AFTER DARK

Puerto Iguazú offers little in the way of nightlife, although the major hotels—including the Sheraton Internacional Iguazú and Hotel Cataratas—often have live music and other entertainment during peak seasons. Try **Café Central,** Av. Victoria Aguirre 320, a popular bar and restaurant with a small Casino; or **La Barranca,** Avenida Tres Fronteras and Costanera (*(C)* **3757/423-295**), a pub with live music every night. **Cuba Libre,** on Paraguay and Brazil, plays tropical beats until late.

6 Mendoza

710km (440 miles) NW of Buenos Aires; 721km (447 miles) SW of Córdoba

Snow-capped mountains tower over lush vineyards. Leafy lanes hide quaint rustic wineries and olive houses. Modern, high-tech temples to wine offer gourmet cuisine and luxury lodgings. World-class ski resorts compete with rafting camps for adrenaline junkies while Mount Aconcagua sits loftily in the background, the highest mountain outside the Himalayas and place of pilgrimage every year for thousands of ambitious mountain climbers. Yet ask locals what they like best about Mendoza, and they're likely to tell you *la tranquilidad*—the tranquillity of what must be Argentina's loveliest city. It's an artificial oasis receiving no more than 5 days of rain per year. A scarce commodity, water is celebrated in the trickling fountains of the city's many lovely plazas, in the shade of the dike-supported trees that line the boulevards, and in the tranquil nature of the residents who reap the benefits of the centuries-old roadside canal system. Give yourself time to linger in Mendoza's cafes, plazas, and many fantastic restaurants. This is a city that lives life outdoors, with many public places, cafes, and street-side restaurants that bustle from noon to night.

ESSENTIALS

GETTING THERE

BY PLANE   Mendoza's international airport, **Francisco Gabrielli** (also known as El Plumerillo; *(C)* **261/520-6000**), lies 8km (5 miles) north of town on Ruta 40. **Aerolíneas Argentinas** (*(C)* **0810/222-86527;** www.aerolineas.com.ar) offers seven daily arrivals from Buenos Aires. On Monday mornings, a flight departs from Ezeiza International Airport. **LAN** (*(C)* **0810/999-9526;** www.lan.com) flies to Mendoza from both Buenos Aires (two times a day) and from Santiago, Chile, once in the morning and once in the evening. If Mendoza is your first destination in Argentina it is much more convenient to fly in via Santiago as, unlike Buenos Aires, it requires no airport change.

BY BUS The **Terminal del Sol** (© 261/431-3001), or central bus station, lies just east of central Mendoza. Buses travel to Buenos Aires (12–14 hr.; $45/£23); Córdoba (12 hr.; $35/£18); Santiago, Chile (7 hr.; $19/£9.50); Las Leñas (7 hr.; $6/£3); and other cities throughout the region. **Chevallier** (© 261/431-0235), **Expreso Uspallata** (© 261/421-3309), and **Andesmar** (© 261/431-0585) are the main bus companies.

BY CAR The route from Buenos Aires is a long (10 hr.), easy, but boring drive on either the RN 7 or the RN 8. Mendoza is more easily reached by car from Santiago, Chile, along the RN 7, although the dramatic 250km (155-mile) trek through the Andes can be treacherous in winter, when chains are required and the border tunnel is often closed for several days. Give yourself 6 to 7 hours to make the journey from Santiago.

GETTING AROUND

You can easily explore central Mendoza on foot, although you will want to hire a driver or rent a car to visit the wine roads and tour the mountains. Taxis and *remises* (private, unmetered taxis) are inexpensive: Drivers cost no more than $10 (£5) per hour. Traditionally Mendoza is one of Argentina's safest cities, but it has experienced an increase in crime, especially bag snatching. For a *remise,* try **La Veloz Del Este** (© 261/423-9090) or **Mendocar** (© 261/423-6666). For a taxi, call **Radiotaxi** (© 261/430-3300).

If you do rent a car, parking is easy and inexpensive inside the city, with paid parking meters and private lots (called *playas*) clearly marked. Easy to navigate, the city spreads out in a clear grid pattern around Plaza Independencia. Outside the city, road signs are sometimes missing or misleading. The main highways are Highway 40, which runs north-south and will take you to Maipú and Luján de Cuyo; and Highway 7, which runs east-west and will take you to the Alta Montaña Route.

Both **Budget** (© 261/425-3114; www.budget.com) and **Hertz Annie Millet** (© 261/448-2327; www.hertz.com) rent cars at Mendoza's airport. Expect to pay about $55 (£28) per day for a compact car with insurance and 200km (124 miles) included. **AutoMendoza** (© 261/420-0022; www.automendoza.com), a locally run company, has flexible rates and will drop a car off wherever you need it. Rates start at $35 (£18) per day. You'll get a better deal if you pay in cash. Regular buses depart from various stops in town to the outlying wine areas, but the routes are unfathomable. El Troli, an old-fashioned tram, is fun and cheap, at 40¢ (20p) per ride. It's an easy way to get up to Parque San Martín and back, but exact change is required.

VISITOR INFORMATION

Mendoza's **Subsecretaría Provincial de Turismo,** Av. San Martín 1143 (© 261/420-2800), is open daily from 9am to 9pm. **Municipal tourist offices,** called Centros de Información, are located at Garibaldi near San Martín (© 261/423-8745; daily 8am–1pm), 9 de Julio 500 (© 261/420-1333; Mon–Fri 9am–9pm), and Las Heras 340 (© 261/429-6298; Mon–Fri 9am–1:30pm and 3–7:30pm). They provide city maps, hotel information, and brochures of tourist activities. You will find small visitor information booths at the airport and bus station as well. Information and permits for Aconcagua Provincial Park are available at the **Centro de Informes del Parques,** in Mendoza's Parque San Martín (© 261/420-5052). The office is only open during the climbing season, from December through March. During the rest of the year, you must contact the **Subsecretaría Provincial de Recursos Naturales** (© 261/425-2090). Permits to climb the summit cost $200 (£100), and you must go in person to obtain one.

Mendoza

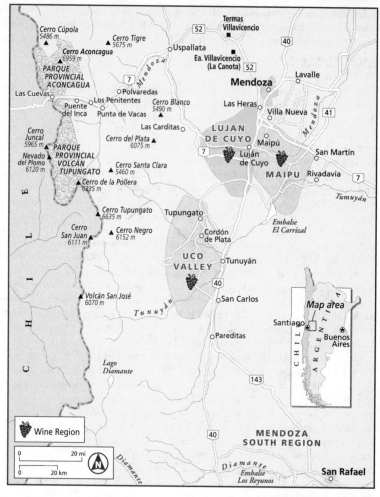

In addition, several websites offer useful tourist information: **www.turismo.mendoza. gov.ar**, **www.aconcagua.mendoza.gov.ar**, and **www.wine-republic.com** (the latter is also a free bimonthly publication, in English, available all around the city).

FAST FACTS   Two reliable exchange houses, both at the corner of San Martín and Catamarca, are **Maguitur** (✆ **261/425-1575**) and **Cambio Santiago** (✆ **261/420-0277**). They are open Monday through Friday from 8:30am to 1pm and from 5 to 8:30pm, and Saturday from 9:30am to 1pm. Major banks, with ATMs that have Cirrus and PLUS access, are located around the Plaza San Martín and along Avenida Sarmiento, including **Citibank** (Av. Sarmiento 20; ✆ **261/449-6519**).

For an **ambulance,** dial ✆ **107** or 261/424-8000; for **police,** dial ✆ **101** or 261/429-4444; in case of **fire,** dial ✆ **100. Hospital Central** (✆ **261/420-0600**) is near the bus station at Salta and Alem.

Internet access in most places costs a meager 1 or 2 pesos (30¢–65¢/15p–30p) per hour. The main post office, **Correo Argentino** (© 261/429-0848), is located at the corner of Avenida San Martín and Colón. It's open Monday to Friday from 8am to 8pm.

WHAT TO SEE & DO
IN TOWN

Plaza Independencia 🐾🐾 marks the city center, a beautiful square with pergolas, fountains, frequent artesian fairs, and cultural events. Following the 1861 earthquake, the new city was rebuilt around this area. Four additional plazas, San Martín, Chile, Italia, and España, are located 2 blocks off each corner of Independence Square. Surrounding the square you will find the Julio Quintanilla Theater, the National School, the Independencia Theater, the Provincial Legislature, and the small **Modern Art Museum** (© 261/425-7279; admission $1/50p). Adjacent to the "Alameda," a beautiful promenade under white poplars, **Museo Histórico General San Martín** 🐾, Remedios Escalada de San Martín 1843 (© 261/428-7947), pays homage to Argentina's beloved hero, who prepared his liberation campaigns from Mendoza. It's open Monday to Friday from 9:30am to 5pm and Saturday 10:30am to 1pm; admission costs $1 (50p). Another museum worth visiting is **Museo Fundacional** 🐾🐾, Videla Castillo between Beltrán and Alberdi (© 261/425-6927), located 3km (2 miles) from downtown. Chronicling the early history of Mendoza, it's a little short of real artifacts. It's open Tuesday through Saturday from 8am to 8pm, Sunday from 3 to 8pm; admission is $1 (50p). Something quirky to consider is **Museo de Motos Antiguas,** San Juan 646 (© 261/429-1469), a private collection of old motorbikes, including a Che Guevara replica. It's open Monday through Friday 8:30am to 12:30pm and 5 to 8:30pm; admission is $1.50 (75p).

Almost as big as the city itself, the wonderful **Parque General San Martín** 🐾🐾🐾 has 17km (11 miles) of idyllic pathways and 300 species of plants and trees. A tourist office, located near the park's main entrance at avenidas Emilio Civit and Bologne sur Mer, provides information on all park activities, which include boating, horseback riding (outside the park's perimeters), and hang gliding. A national science museum and zoo (daily 9am–6pm) are located inside the park, and you can also camp here. The best hike leads to the top of Cerro de la Gloria, which offers a panoramic view of the city and surrounding valley. Check out **Museo Moyano** (© 261/428-7666), the boat-shaped building at the end of the lake. Here you'll find fascinating exhibits such as giant condors and child mummies in a superb building that sorely needs renovating. The museum is open Tuesday to Friday 8am to 1pm and 2 to 7pm, Saturday and Sunday 3 to 7pm.

TOURING THE WINERIES

Mendoza offers some of the most stunning wine country in the world, vineyards dominated by a breathtaking backdrop of the snowcapped Andes. The wineries are very spread out but accessible along wine roads known locally as Los Caminos del Vino. These roads are as enticing as the wine itself, weaving and winding through tunnels of trees to vast dry valleys, punctuated by fruit orchards and olive groves. Some roads climb as high as 1,524m (5,000 ft.) in Valle de Uco while others lead to lower-level vineyards in Maipú. There are over 900 wineries surrounding Mendoza and numerous wine growing regions. The most important for visitors are Lujan de Cuyo, Valle de Uco, and Maipú. Different wine roads branch out through these and it is very easy to get lost. Three hundred wineries formally offer tours, but in reality less than 60 have an efficient set up to accept visitors, such as available guides and tasting rooms. The most and the best require prebooking at set times.

Lujan de Cuyo is known as La Primera Zone. It is the home of Malbec and where Argentina's most prestigious wineries—both old and knew—are located. It is situated 17km (11 miles) south of the city to the west of the Route 40 and hugging the wide dry Río Mendoza. Here you'll find Chacras de Coria, a beautiful leafy neighborhood where many of Mendoza's most luxurious wine lodges are located. There are a multitude of wineries to visit in Lujan and it is impossible to list them all; the following are my favorites. **Alta Vista,** Alzaga 3972 (© **261/496-4684;** admission $3/£1.50), is a masterful mix of old and new and produces excellent Malbec and Torrontes. **Achaval Ferrer,** Calle Cobos 2601 (© **261/488-1131;** admission $10/£5.00), is Argentina's star boutique winery, winning accolades around the world for some very fine blends. **Lagarde,** Ave. San Martín 1745 (© **261/498-0011;** free admission), has 120-year-old vines and a tiny champagne operation. **Tapiz,** RP15, Agrelo (© **261/490-0202;** free admission), gives a marvelous tank and barrel tasting and vineyard tour. **Ruca Malen,** RN7, Agrelo (© **261/425-7279;** free admission), does the best winery lunch in the Southern hemisphere. **Pulenta Estate,** Ruta 86 (© **261/420-0800;** free admission), is slick and modern and makes incredible wines. **Clos de Chacras,** Monte Libano, Chacras (© **261/496-1285;** admission $7/£3.50), is charming and quaint and within walking distance of Chacras plaza.

Valle de Uco is the new frontier in Argentine wine, a high-altitude wine region pushing against the Andes. It is 90 minutes south of Mendoza and definitely worth a visit for its seductive rural atmosphere and dramatic scenery. **O.Fournier,** Los Indios, La Consulta (© **261/451-088;** free admission), is a modernist masterpiece producing rich Tempranillos and exquisite lunches. **Salentein,** Tupungato (© **2622/423-550;** admission $3/£1.50), must be visited for its templelike cellar and ultramodern visitor center with art gallery. **Andeluna,** RP89, Gualtallary, Tupungato (© **261/429-9299;** admission free), has a marvelous old-world-style tasting room and premium wines. **Finca La Celia,** Av. De Circunvalación, San Carlos (© **261/413-4400;** admission free), is one of Mendoza's oldest wineries.

Maipú is the closest wine region to the city, 15 minutes away by taxi or bus. Popular for bike tours and large coach tours, it is a big region, with many wineries. The northern part is urban and ugly but the southern area is very beautiful. **Rutini,** Montecaseros 2625, Coquimbito (© **261/497-2013;** free admission), can be very touristy but has a fascinating wine museum. **Tempus Alba,** Perito Moreno 572 (© **261/481-3501;** free admission), is more intimate and modern with a beautiful roof terrace. **Carinae,** Videla Arande 2899, Cruz de Piedra (© **261/499-0470;** admission $3/£1.50), is small and charming, with the tour often conducted by the engaging French owners. **Zuccardi,** RP33 Km 7.5 (© **261/441-0000;** free admission), has excellent tours and delicious barbecue-style lunches amid the vines.

Organized wine tours vary greatly in quality, from run-of-the-mill urban tours with large groups and bad wines to more expensive, personalized excursions with gourmet lunches. **Ampora Wine Tours,** Sarmiento 647 (© **261/429-2931;** www.mendozawine tours.com), does quality day tours of all the regions. **Uncorking Argentina,** P. de la Reta 992 (© **261/155-103230;** www.uncorkingargentina.com), offers custom-made tours with small groups.

On the first weekend of every March, Mendoza celebrates the **Fiesta Nacional de la Vendimia (National Wine Harvest Festival).** This includes parades, concerts, folk dancing, and a final-night spectacular ending with the coronation of the festival's queen. For information on the festival events, the wineries, and Mendoza in general check out **www.wine-republic.com**, the Web's version of a free bimonthly magazine available around the city.

OUTDOOR ACTIVITIES

Turismo Uspallata, Las Heras 699 (© **261/438-1092;** www.turismouspallata.com), runs trips to rural *estancias* and sells bus transfers to all the surrounding areas, including San Rafael and Valle de Uco. **Cordon de Plata,** Las Heras 341, Mendoza (© **261/423-7423**), arranges single- or multiday hiking trips and a day of horseback riding in the Andes with an Argentine barbecue. **Argentina Rafting Expediciones,** P de la Reta 992 (© **261/429-6325;** www.argentinarafting.com), and **Ríos Andinos,** Ruta 7, Km 64, 5549 Potrerillos (© **261/431-6074**), offer rafting and trekking from their bases on Potrerillos.

SHOPPING

On Friday, Saturday, and Sunday, an outdoor **handicrafts market** takes place during the day on Plaza Independencia, as do smaller fairs in Plaza España and along Calle Mitre. Regional shops selling handicrafts, leather goods, gaucho paraphernalia, and *mate* tea gourds line Avenida Las Heras. For high-quality leather, visit **Alain de France,** Andrade 101 (© **261/428-5065**). More mainstream stores line Avenida San Martín, and Calle Arístides Villanueva is home to upscale fashion boutiques. The city's best shopping mall is **Palmares Open Mall,** on Ruta Panamericana 2650 in Godoy Cruz (© **261/413-9100**). Also outside the city but worth the visit is a huge emporium of South American handicrafts, **Ayllu,** Ruta Panamericana 8343 (© **261/496-1213;** www.aylluartepopular.com).

Most shops close from 1 to 5pm each day for siesta except in the malls. Some of the best wine boutiques in town include **Marcelinos,** Zapata and Benegas (© **261/429-3648**), **Sol y Vino,** Sarmiento 664 (© **261/425-6005**), and **MundoDivino,** Sarmiento 784 (© **261/425-6005**).

WHERE TO STAY

Mendoza has some interesting new hotels on the horizon, including three new five-star establishments, which should give the grande dame, the Park Hyatt, a run for its money. Keep an eye out for the new Sheraton, Diplomático, and Caesar chains, scheduled to open in 2008. Also popular are "apart-hotels," or suite-hotels. More than 30 hostels also dot downtown Mendoza.

Prices quoted below include the 21% tax and are for high season, which in Mendoza is January through March, July, and September through November. Hotel rates are often discounted 15% to 20% in the off season.

EXPENSIVE

The **Park Hyatt Mendoza** ✦✦✦, Chile 1124 (© **261/441-1234;** www.mendoza.park.hyatt.com), peers majestically over Plaza Independencia and serves as the cultural heart of Mendoza. Doubles start at $298 (£149), but check their website for a 10% discount. **El Portal Suites,** Necochea 661 (©/fax **261/438-2038;** www.elportalsuites.com.ar), has comfortable suites with a clean and modern style and is an especially good option for families. Rates start at $93 (£47). **Hotel NH Cordillera,** Av. España 1324 (© **261/441-6464;** www.nh-hotels.com), caters to business travelers and has four floors of crisp, compact rooms, half of which face Plaza San Martín.

Winery Lodges

A welcome phenomenon is the arrival of luxury winery lodgings in the nearby vineyards. The best is **Club Tapiz,** Ruta 60, Maipú (© **261/496-0131;** www.tapiz. com), a converted winery set amid 10 hectares (24 acres) of vineyards. **Finca Adalgisa,** Pueyrredon 2222, Chacras de Coria (© **261/496-0713;** www.finca adalgisa.com.ar), is an excellent choice, with vineyards and an old family *bodega.* **Baquero,** Perito Moreno, Maipú (© **261/496-0713**), is another authentic family winery with beautiful lodgings.

Doubles start at $150 (£75). **Park Suites Apart Hotel,** Mitre 753 (© **261/413-1000;** www.parksuites.com.ar), is a stylish hotel 2 blocks from Plaza Independencia. Single rooms are called "suites," and each room has hardwood floors, a kitchenette, firm mattresses, and a stereo system. Rates start at $85 (£43). **Hotel Argentino** ★★, Espejo 455 (© **261/405-6300;** www.argentino-hotel.com), overlooks the Plaza Independencia and is a very good value, with elegance and comfort starting at $94 (£47). **Posada de Rosas,** Martínez de Rosas 1641 (© **261/423-3629;** www.posadaderosas.com), is another attractive house with a gorgeous pool situated on a quiet residential street close to the park. Rooms start at $120 (£60). For a short-term luxury stay, try **Apartments Mendoza,** Leonidas Aguirre 175 (© **261/154-549357;** www.apartmentsmendoza. com). Rates start at $120 (£60).

MODERATE

Deptos Mendoza, Leandro N. Alem 41 (© **261/1541-94844;** www.deptosmendoza. com.ar), is a sleek new building of steel and brick that offers great value. The apartments are decorated with local art, with a focus on function and lighting. Rates start at $65 (£33). **Hotel Cervantes,** A M Amigorena 65 (© **261/520-0400;** www.hotel cervantesmza.com.ar), has been run by the Lopez family since 1945, and staff members are old-school hotel professionals. From the outside, the place is baroque and traditional with a lovely new garden out back and ample parking. Ask for a "special" room on the fourth floor for more space and style. Rates start at $65 (£33) for a double. **La Escondida Bed and Breakfast,** Julio A. Roca 344 (© **261/425-5202;** www.laescondida bb.com), is a family-run, friendly bed-and-breakfast in a pleasant and convenient neighborhood. All rooms have private bathrooms and a light and airy style, but some could do with updating. Insist on a room upstairs. Rooms start at $54 (£27).

INEXPENSIVE

Damajuana Hostel, Aristides Villanueva 282 (© **261/425-5858;** www.damajuana hostel.com.ar), is like a five-star resort at rock-bottom prices. This hostel is located in the heart of the happening Arístides district and has a huge pool, garden, and barbecue in the backyard. Bunk-bed rates start at $15 (£7.50). **Confluencia Hostel,** España 1512 (© **261/429-0430;** www.hostalconfluencia.com.ar), is one of those rare finds in Argentina, a hostel that doesn't pile them high like sardines. Confluencia has large, bright rooms for three, without a bunk bed in sight. Rooms start at $25 (£13).

WHERE TO DINE
EXPENSIVE

Francesco Ristorante ITALIAN   Francesco is the most elegant and classy Italian restaurant in town. The meat and homemade pasta dishes are equally excellent. The option of combining three stuffed pastas lets you try some of the highlights. Don't miss the tiramisu for dessert. Service is seriously professional here, including a doting sommelier. The outdoor garden is romantic and lovely, especially on a summer evening.

Chile 1268 (Espejo and Gutiérrez), Mendoza. © 261/429-7182. www.francescoristorante.com.ar. Reservations recommended. Main courses $10–$18 (£5–£9). AE, MC, V. Daily 7:30pm–1am.

MODERATE

Ana Bistro *(Moments* ARGENTINE   An attractive, roomy restaurant, Ana Bistro exudes modernity and style. Here you'll find armchairs and sofas spread across wooden platforms and a fragrant garden with a bamboo-covered patio. Dishes include delicious stir-fried chicken and trout *empanadas*. It's a great place for afternoon cocktails.

Av. Juan B. Justo 161. © 261/425-1818. Dinner reservations recommended. Main courses $7–$10 (£3.50–£5). AE, MC, V. Tues–Sun 11am–1am.

Azafrán *(Finds* INTERNATIONAL   The food here is imaginative, fresh, and eclectic. You may start with the house specialty—a platter of smoked meats and cheeses. For entrees, the rabbit ravioli in champagne sauce is delicate and unusual, and the vegetables and tofu baked in a puff pastry will please any vegetarian. The wood tables and vintage checkered floors give you a sense of dining in an old farmhouse.

Sarmiento 765 (Belgrano and Perú). © 261/429-4200. Reservations recommended. Main courses $7–$10 (£3.50–£5). AE, MC, V. Mon–Sat 11am–1am.

La Sal *(Finds* ARGENTINE   This classy restaurant offers a happy fusion of food and art, wine, and ambience. The menu changes every 3 months to take advantage of the seasons. Food includes smoked risotto and Thai chicken in coconut sauce, all served with live Spanish guitar in the background–a definite mood enhancer.

Belgrano 1096. © 261/420-4322. Main courses $7–$10 (£3.50–£5). AE, DC, MC, V. Tues–Sat 9pm–2am.

Mi Tierra ARGENTINE   This "thematic restaurant" is tucked inside an old townhouse, each room presenting the wines of a different local vineyard. The menu offers local specialties such as goat, young pork, wild boar, and rabbit. The pastas are excellent. For dessert, try the Chardonnay parfait.

Mitre 794 (Pueyrredón and General Lamadrid). © 261/425-0035. Reservations recommended. Main courses $9–$14 (£4.50–£7). AE, MC, V. Daily noon–3:30pm and 8:30pm–12:30am.

MENDOZA AFTER DARK

Mendoza nightlife has taken off in recent years with hundreds of the young and beautiful gathering on the bar street Aristides Villanueva any night of the week, especially in the summer, before heading to the super clubs in Chacras de Coria.

Start the night early at a local wine bar such as **The Vines of Mendoza,** Espejo 567 (© **261/438-1031**). The Park Hyatt Mendoza's **Bar Uvas,** Chile 1124 (© **261/441-1234**), offers a complete selection of Mendocino wines, a long list of cocktails, and live jazz and bossa nova groups playing most nights.

The city's best bars line Aristides Villanueva in the center of town. Try **Por Acá,** A. Villanueva 557 (no phone), for pizza and microbrewed beers; or **El Abasto,** A. Villanueva 308 (© **261/483-4232**), for good old rock 'n' roll. Nightclubs can be found on the principal avenue south to Godoy Cruz, 5 minutes by taxi. **Iskra,** San Martín 905 (© **261/15453-1038**), is popular and regularly jammed. **Geo,** San Martín Sur 576 (no phone), is another top disco in this area. Locals flock to **La Reserva,** Rivadavia 32 (© **261/420-3531**), on weekend nights for the drag show at midnight. The

Blah Blah Bar, Paseo Peatonal Alameda, Escalada 2301 Maipú (© **261/429-7253**), is great for a late-night drink. *Note:* In an effort to keep their wild offspring from staying out so late, the Mendoza powers-that-be have demanded clubs close their doors at 2:30am, though those inside can dance until dawn.

7 Salta ⊛

90km (56 miles) S of San Salvador de Jujuy; 1,497km (928 miles) N of Buenos Aires; 1,268km (786 miles) N of Mendoza

Cloistered nuns and gaucho waiters, gilded churches and mountain mummies: Salta province is a rich mix of all the things that make northwest Argentina so distinctive and truly South American. In this part of Argentina, the old meets the new—and the old wins. Time trips by at a more rhythmic pace, like the hoof-clopping music *chacareras* that pipes from every cafe and car. Salta city itself (population 500,000) is a sunny mix of colonial architecture, friendly, gracious people, colorful history, and indigenous pride. Conservative by nature, Salteños let their hair down during Carnaval, when thousands come out for a parade of floats celebrating the region's history; water balloons are also tossed from balconies with great aplomb. Ringed by green hills and blessed with a cooler, temperate climate, Salta city should be top of your list when visiting the area. (That is not to say it does not get hot; the high season here is actually the winter months Apr–Oct).

ESSENTIALS
GETTING THERE
I don't recommend making the long-distance drive to Argentina's northwest; it's safer and much easier to fly or take the bus.

BY PLANE   Flights land at **Martín Miguel De Guemes International Airport,** RN 51 (© **387/424-2904**), 8km (5¼ miles) from the city center. **Aerolíneas Argentinas** (© **0810/222-86527;** www.aerolineas.com.ar) and **Andes Lineas Aéreas** (© **0810/122-26337** or 387/416-2600) fly from Buenos Aires (some flights make a stop in Córdoba). Nonstop flights from Buenos Aires take 2 hours and cost between $155 (£78) and $255 (£128) each way, depending on the season and availability. A shuttle bus travels between the airport and town for about $3 (£1.50) one-way; a taxi into town will run about $6 (£3).

BY BUS   The **Terminal de Omnibus,** or central bus station, is at Avenida H. Yrigoyen and Abraham Cornejo (© **387/401-1143**). Buses arrive from Buenos Aires (18 hr.; $60/£30) and travel to San Salvador de Jujuy (2½ hr.; $4/£2) and other cities in the region. **Chevalier** (© **387/431-2819**), and **La Veloz del Norte** (© **387/431-7215**) are the main bus companies.

VISITOR INFORMATION
The tourism office, **Secretaría de Turismo de Salta,** Buenos Aires 93 (© **387/431-0950** or 387/431-0640; www.turismosalta.gov.ar), will provide you with maps and information on dining, lodging, and sightseeing in the region. It can also help you arrange individual or group tours. It's open every day from 9am to 9pm. In Buenos Aires, obtain information about Salta from the **Casa de Salta en Bs. As.,** Sáenz Pena 933 (© **011/4326-1314**). It's open Monday to Friday 10am to 6pm.

FAST FACTS   Exchange money at the airport, at **Dinar Exchange,** Mitre and España (© **387/432-2600;** Mon–Fri 9am–1:30pm and 5–8pm; Sat 10am–3pm) or at **Banco de La Nación,** Mitre and Belgrano (© **387/431-1909;** Mon–Fri 8:30am–2pm).

Dial ℂ 911 for **police,** ℂ 100 for **fire,** and ℂ 107 for an **ambulance.** For a hospital, **Saint Bernard Hospital,** Dr. M. Boedo 69 (ℂ **387/432-030**), is your best bet.

Arrange a tour of the region with **Saltur Turismo,** Caseros 485 (ℂ **387/421-2012**), or with **Incauca Turismo,** Mitre 274, Local 33 (ℂ **387/422-7568;** www.incauca turismo.com). The tourist office can also recommend English-speaking tour guides.

GETTING AROUND

Salta is small and easy to explore by foot, but be careful; drivers here are blind to pedestrians. The **Peatonal Florida** is Salta's pedestrian walking street—a smaller version of Calle Florida in Buenos Aires—where most of the city's shops are. The main sights are centered on **Plaza 9 de Julio,** where a monument to General Arenales stands in the center and a beautiful baroque cathedral stands at its edge. Built in 1858, the **Catedral** is considered Argentina's best-preserved colonial church. All the other attractions here, except the **Salta Tram** and the **Tren a las Nubes,** are within easy walking distance.

RENTING A CAR   Noa Rent a Car, Buenos Aires 1 Local 6 (ℂ **387/431-0740**), has subcompacts and four-wheel drives. **Hertz** is at Caseros 374 (ℂ **387/421-7553**) and at the airport (ℂ **387/424-0113**); prices range from $55 to $65 (£28–£33) per day.

WHAT TO SEE & DO

Most museums in northwest Argentina don't have formal admission fees; instead, they request small contributions, usually $1 (50p) or less. **El Cabildo,** Caseros 549 (ℂ **387/ 421-5340;** www.museonor.gov.ar), was first erected in 1582 and has 15 exhibition halls related to the Indian, colonial, and liberal periods of Salteño history. It opens Tuesday to Saturday 9:30am to 1pm and 3:30 to 8:30pm; Sunday it's open 9:30am to 1:30pm. **Iglesia San Francisco,** Córdoba and Caseros (no phone), is Salta's most prominent postcard image. The terra-cotta facade holds a bronze bell made from the cannons used in the War of Independence. It's open daily 8am to noon and 4 to 8pm.

Museo de Arqueología de Alta Montaña, Mitre 77 (ℂ **387/437-0499**), is a beautifully restored historic building and is dedicated to Andean culture and anthropology. On display are three amazingly preserved Andean mummies (over 500 years old) found in 1999. More than 100 other objects were found with the mummies—gold statues and other objects dating back to the Inca era. Admission is $10 (£5), and it's open Tuesday to Sunday 9am to 1pm and 4 to 9pm. **Museo Histórico José Evaristo**

Train to the Clouds 𐀃

This is one of the world's great railroad experiences—a breathtaking ride that climbs to 4,220m (13,842 ft.) without the help of cable tracks. The journey takes you 434km (269 miles) through tunnels, turns, and bridges, culminating in the stunning La Polvorilla viaduct. You will cross magnificent landscapes, making your way from the multicolored Lerma valley through the deep canyons and rugged peaks of the Quebrada del Toro and on to the desolate desert plateau of La Puña. The train operates April to November and departs Salta's General Belgrano Station. Tickets cost $90 (£45), not including lunch. For more information, contact the tourism office in Salta, **Secretaría de Turismo de Salta,** Buenos Aires 93 (ℂ **387/431-0950** or 387/431-0640; www.turismosalta.gov.ar).

Uriburu, Caseros 479 (© 387/428-174), is a simple adobe house, with a roof of reeds and curved tiles, exhibiting period furniture and costumes. It's open Tuesday to Saturday 9:30am to 1:30pm and 3:30 to 8:30pm. Admission is 30¢ (15p). **Museo Provincial de Bellas Artes de Salta,** Florida 20 (© 387/421-4714), houses a permanent collection of colonial art upstairs and religious and contemporary art downstairs. It's open Monday to Saturday 9am to 1pm and 4 to 8:30pm. Admission is 60¢ (30p). **San Bernardo Convent,** Caseros near Santa Fe, the oldest religious building in Salta, is a still-functioning Carmelite nunnery closed to the public. The entrance was carved from a carob tree by aborigines in 1762. **Teleférico,** H. Yrigoyen and San Martín (© 387/431-0641), is a cable car that has been in operation since 1987 and takes tourists to the top of San Bernardo Hill, 300m (984 ft.) over Salta. Admission is $3 (£1.50) adults, $2 (£1) children. It operates daily from 10am to 7:30pm.

OUTDOOR ACTIVITIES & TOUR OPERATORS

With gorges and canyons and volcanic peaks to negotiate, **trekking** is the most popular outdoor activity in the area. **Adventure Life Journeys** (1655 S. 3rd St. W., Missoula, MT 59801; © 800/344-6118 or 406/541-2677; www.adventure-life.com) offers 9-day treks through the region. Ecotourism is gaining popularity, with 1- to 4-day safaris and bird-watching expeditions organized by **Clark Expediciones** (Caseros 121, Salta; © 387/421-5390; www.clarkexpediciones.com.). The highlight is usually seeing the immense Andean Condor soaring over the mountains. Rafting, windsurfing, and other watersports are becoming popular in the Dique Cabra Corral, 70km (43 miles) south of Salta. For more information, contact **Salta Rafting** (Buenos Aires 88, Local 14; © 387/401-0301; info@saltarafting.com) or **Active Argentina** (Zuviria 982; © 387/431-1868).

SHOPPING

At the **Mercado Artesanal,** San Martín 2555 (no phone), you'll find authentic products from leather goods to candles made throughout Salta Province by local craftsmen and women. The price is controlled, too, so you don't have to worry about bargaining here. You'll also find beautiful jewelry and silver. The Mercado is open from 9am to 9pm daily

WHERE TO STAY
VERY EXPENSIVE
Alejandro Primero ★★★ *Value*   Salta's second five-star hotel beats the Sheraton (see below) for color and charm. Two gauchos greet you as you enter an 11-story glass-vaulted building of Andean chic. Carpets are adorned with miniature designs of *guanacos* (llamas), ostriches, and cacti. Corridors are enlivened with leather wall hangings, indigenous art, and the occasional ceramic pot. The rooms are spacious with panoramic views, and the double glazing ensures that the noisy downtown location does not intrude on your *tranquilidad.* Alejandro Primero offers all the luxury of a top hotel without losing the human touch.

Balcarce 252, Salta. © 387/400-0000. www.alejandro1hotel.com.ar. 167 units. $105–$140 (£53–£70) double; from $150 (£75) suite. Rates include buffet breakfast. AE, DC, MC, V. **Amenities:** Restaurant; bar; lounge; indoor pool; exercise room; sauna; business center with free Internet; meeting rooms; room service; laundry service; dry cleaning. *In room:* A/C, TV, minibar, hair dryer, safe.

Hotel Solar de la Plaza ★★★ *Finds*   This absolutely charming hotel used to be the residence of one of Salta's well-known families, Patron Costas. The four rooms in the older part of the building have been meticulously transformed into comfortable hotel rooms while retaining their old-world feel—hardwood floors, Jacuzzi tubs, and wrought-iron floor lamps. Service is gracious and refined, and the public areas are incredibly elegant, from the rooftop pool, with its adjoining sun deck, to the attractive restaurant serving regional specialties with a nouvelle twist.

Juan M. Leguizamon 669, 4400 Salta. ✆/fax 387/431-5111. www.reservassolardelaplaza.com.ar. 30 units. $145–$230 (£73–£115) double; $260 (£130) suite. Rates include continental breakfast and lunch. AE, DC, MC, V. **Amenities:** Restaurant; bar; lounge; small outdoor pool; exercise room; sauna; business center; limited room service. *In room:* A/C, TV, minibar, safe.

The Sheraton 🏵🏵 Salta's first five-star hotel lacks imagination but trumps on location. The design could be described as very "Sheratonesque"—bland but luxurious. A plain, cream-colored facade hangs over a dark lobby of stone walls, corduroy seating, and cobbled stones. Bright, terra-cotta hallways lead to anticlimactic rooms that are spacious but somewhat colorless and sterile. They nevertheless have all the creature comforts expected of a Sheraton. What really stands out is the view. The hotel is a U-shaped, seven-story building cut into the side of a hill overlooking the city (10-min. walk from the center). Every room offers an invigorating vista of the Andean *pre-cordillera* and the city's rooftops.

Av. Ejército del Norte 330, Salta. ✆ 387/432-3000. www.starwoodhotels.com. 145 units. $150–$215 (£75–£108) double; from $250 (£125) suite. Rates include buffet breakfast. AE, DC, MC, V. **Amenities:** Restaurant; bar; lounge; outdoor pool; exercise room; sauna; business center; meeting rooms; room service; laundry service; dry cleaning. *In room:* A/C, TV, minibar, hair dryer, safe.

EXPENSIVE

Casa Real Hotel 🏵🏵 *Value* Rooms here are very spacious and comfortable, with big picture windows (some overlooking the mountains), large-screen TVs, and firm, comfortable beds. Bathrooms are also large and very clean. The Casa Real boasts a decent-size exercise room and a good-size indoor pool, as well as an attractive restaurant and bar. The staff is friendly and can help in arranging transportation and tours.

Mitre 669, 4400 Salta. ✆ 387/421-5675. www.casarealsalta.com.ar. 83 units. $80–$100 (£40–£50) double; from $107 (£54) suite. Rates include buffet breakfast. AE, DC, MC, V. **Amenities:** Restaurant; bar; lounge; indoor pool; exercise room; sauna; business center with free Internet; meeting rooms; room service; laundry service; dry cleaning. *In room:* A/C, TV, minibar, hair dryer, safe.

Gran Hotel Presidente 🏵 This contemporary hotel has attractive guest rooms splashed in rose and apple green with sparkling white-tile bathrooms. The chic lobby features black and white marble with Art Deco furniture and leopard-skin upholstery. The pleasant international restaurant is located on the upstairs mezzanine, and there's a spa with a heated indoor pool, a sauna, a fitness room, and a solarium.

Av. de Belgrano 353, 4400 Salta. ✆/fax 387/431-2022. www.granhotelpresidente.com. 96 units. $110 (£55) double; $170 (£85) suite. Rates include buffet breakfast. AE, DC, MC, V. **Amenities:** Restaurant; small indoor pool; exercise room; sauna; meeting rooms; room service; laundry service; dry cleaning. *In room:* A/C, TV, minibar, hair dryer, safe.

MODERATE

Hotel Salta 🏵 *Moments* Opened in 1890, these are hardly the most modern accommodations you'll find, but the hotel's wood balconies and arabesque carvings, peaceful courtyard, refreshing pool, and beautiful dining room overlooking the plaza considerably increase its appeal. For $10 (£5) more, "A" rooms are larger than standard rooms and have bathtubs, as opposed to just showers. The friendly staff will arrange horseback riding, golf, and other outdoor activities upon request.

Buenos Aires 1, 4400 Salta. ©/fax **387/431-0740.** www.hotelsalta.com. 99 units. From $73 (£37) double; from $126 (£63) suite. Rates include buffet breakfast. AE, DC, MC, V. **Amenities:** Restaurant; bar; pool; sauna; small business center; meeting rooms; room service; massage; laundry service. *In room:* A/C, TV, minibar, safe.

INEXPENSIVE

Bloomers   Wacky rugs and arty lamps adorn the five rooms, along with luminous pouch seats and huge ceramic urns. One room has a regal ambience, with pink walls, an elegantly hung mosquito net, and silk cushions. The bathrooms are a decent size with colorful, mosaic-style tiling. Some rooms are bigger than others (ask for one out front) and only two have air conditioning. There is no pool, but there is a beautiful garden and a barbecue terrace. Small and quirky, Bloomers is a unique and charming place to stay in the city center.

Vicente López 129, 4400 Salta. ©/fax **387/422-7449.** www.bloomers-salta.com.ar. 5 units. From $65 (£33) double. Rates include breakfast. AE, DC, MC, V. **Amenities:** Kitchen, laundry service *In room:* A/C, TV.

Hotel del Antiguo Convento   The modern reception area opens onto three courtyards and a garden pool, all decorated with flowers and pots and flagstones. The surrounding rooms are midsize with air conditioning and TV. The bathrooms are small but sparkling clean and perfectly adequate. The gracious staff and central location make it a good choice for some quality accommodation.

Caseros 113, 4400 Salta. ©/fax **387/422-7267.** www.hoteldelconvento.com. 25 units. From $43 (£22) double. Rates include breakfast. AE, DC, MC, V. **Amenities:** Outdoor pool; laundry service. *In room:* A/C, TV.

Victoria Plaza   If your purpose in Salta is sightseeing rather than hotel appreciation, the Victoria Plaza should do just fine. Rooms are stark and simple but also clean, comfortable, and cheerfully maintained. The hotel has an excellent location next to the main plaza, the *cabildo* (town hall), and the cathedral. The cafeteria-like restaurant is open 24 hours, and the hotel offers free airport transfers.

Zuviría 16, 4400 Salta. ©/fax **387/431-8500.** 96 units. From $60 (£30) double. Rates include buffet breakfast. AE, DC, MC, V. **Amenities:** Tiny exercise room; sauna; meeting room; laundry service. *In room:* A/C, TV, fridge.

WHERE TO DINE

Northwest Argentina has its own cuisine influenced by indigenous cooking. *Locro* (a corn and bean soup), *humitas* (a sort of corn and goat-cheese soufflé), tamales (meat and potatoes in a ground corn shell), *empanadas* (a turnover filled with potatoes, meat, and vegetables), *lechón* (suckling pig), and *cabrito* (goat) occupy most menus. Traditional Argentine steaks and pasta dishes usually are available, too. In addition to the locations listed below, you might consider the **Mercado Central,** at Florida and San Martín, which has a number of inexpensive eateries serving regional food.

MODERATE

Café van Gogh CAFE   This cheeky cafe, surrounded by little white lights on the outside and decorated with van Gogh prints inside, serves pizzas, sandwiches, meats, hot dogs, and *empanadas*. Come evening, the cafe-turned-bar becomes the center of Salta nightlife, with live bands playing Wednesday through Saturday after midnight. Café van Gogh is also a popular spot for breakfast.

España 502. © **387/431-4659.** Main courses $6–$9 (£3–£4.50). AE, DC, MC, V. Daily 7am–2am.

El Solar del Convento ★★ ARGENTINE   This former Jesuit convent has long been an outstanding *parrilla* (grill) serving quality steaks and regional specialties such as *empanadas*, tamales, and *humitas*. The 10-page menu also includes beef brochettes, grilled salmon, chicken with mushrooms, and large, fresh salads. The atmosphere is festive and, even late on a Sunday night, you can expect the restaurant to be packed.

Caseros 444. 🕐 **387/439-3666**. Main courses $6–$9 (£3–£4.50). AE, DC, MC, V. Daily 11am–3pm and 8pm–midnight.

José Balcarce ⭐⭐⭐ *(finds)* INTERNATIONAL/REGIONAL   Andean cuisine with a modern flair is the specialty at Jose Balcance. Here's where you can try roasted llama meat served with Andean potatoes or quinoa. Or try llama medallions with prickly pear sauce. Local goat cheese is served drizzled over a "tower" of grilled aubergines and olive tapenade. The menu changes very often, and different world cuisines, in addition to the Andean, are featured occasionally. Order a well-chilled Torrontes white wine to round out your meal.

Mitre and Necochea. 🕐 **387/421-1628**. Reservations recommended. Main courses $6–$12 (£3–£6). AE, DC, MC, V. Mon–Thurs 9pm–midnight; Fri–Sat 9pm–1am.

Viejo Jack II *(Kids)* *(Value)* ARGENTINE   An inexpensive local *parrilla* frequented by locals, Viejo Jack II (Viejo Jack I is at Av. Virrey Toledo 145) serves succulent steaks and fresh pastas. Kids have access to a play area as well.

Av. Reyes Católicos 1465. 🕐 **387/439-2802**. Main courses $5–$10 (£2.50–£5). DC, MC, V. Daily 12:30–3:30pm and 8pm–1am.

A SIDE TRIP TO CACHI ⭐

Home of the Chicoanas Indians before the Spaniards arrived, Cachi is a tiny pueblo of about 5,000 people, interesting for its Indian ruins, colonial church, and archaeological museum. The Spanish colonial **church,** built in the 17th century and located next to the main plaza, has a floor and ceiling made from cactus wood. The **archaeological museum** is the most impressive museum of its kind in northwest Argentina, capturing the influence of the Incas and Spaniards on the region's indigenous people. Located next to the main plaza, the museum's courtyard is filled with Inca stone engravings and pre-Columbian artifacts. Wall rugs, ponchos, and ceramics are sold at the **Centro Artesanal,** next to the tourist office, on the main plaza (the people of Cachi are well respected for their weaving skills, and the ponchos they sell are beautiful). **La Paya,** 10km (6¼ miles) south of Cachi, and **Potrero de Payogasta,** 10km (6¼ miles) north of Cachi, hold the area's most important archaeological sites.

GETTING THERE   Cachi lies 157km (97 miles) west of Salta on RP 33. **Empresa Marcos Rueda** (🕐 **387/421-4447**) offers two buses daily from Salta; the trip takes 4 hours and costs $7 (£3.50).

VISITOR INFORMATION   You can pick up maps, excursion information, and tips on restaurants and hotels at the **Oficina de Turismo,** Avenida General Güemes (🕐 **3868/491902**), open Monday through Friday from 8am to 9pm, Saturday and Sunday 9am to 3pm and 5 to 9pm.

CAFAYATE ⭐⭐⭐

The wine town of Cafayate has distinct colors—pink dust, red hills, and olive green mountains. Corn-yellow sand gathers along the curbstones of this sun-kissed village, while donkeys graze on the central plaza; bicycles stand unlocked outside schools and the coffee-colored cathedral. Add to this pretty, palatial-style wineries, luxury lodges, excellent arts and crafts, and stunning vineyard country that produces the aromatic white torrontes, and you can see why this area is becoming known as the Tuscany of Argentina.

GETTING THERE   Cafayate lies 194km (120 miles) southwest of Salta on RN 68. **Empresa El Indio** (© 387/432-0846) offers two buses daily from Salta; the trip takes 3½ hours and costs about $8 (£4).

VISITOR INFORMATION   The **tourist office** (© 3868/421470) is located on the main plaza and provides maps, bus schedules, and lodging recommendations. Open hours are Monday through Saturday from 10am to 6pm.

WHAT TO SEE & DO

Wineries are becoming increasingly accessible to tourists, though many still have erratic hours. Most museums in this area are free or request a small donation, usually no more than $1 (50p). Often more interesting are the workshops producing handicrafts from the area.

Wineries

Bodegas Etchart, Finca la Rosa, RN 40 (© **3868/421-310;** www.bodegasetchart.com), is one of the region's most important vineyards, exporting its wine to more than 30 countries. Tours are offered Monday through Friday from 9am to 5pm and Saturday from 9am to noon. **Finca Las Nubes,** El Divisadero, Alto Valle (© **3868/422-129**), is a family-run winery a few kilometers up a dirt road from the center of town. Owners José and Mercedes Mounier will arrange for lunch to be served on their lovely terrace overlooking the vineyard (call ahead). **El Esteco,** RN40 at RP68 (© **3868/421-310**), offers guided tours in Spanish Monday through Thursday from 9am to 5pm and Friday from 9am to 4pm. **Vasija Secreta,** RN40 (© **3868/421-850**), is a large *bodega* with a small but interesting museum with wine-making equipment dating back to 1857. It's open Monday to Saturday 9am to 4pm. **El Porvenir,** Cordoba 32 (© **3868/422-007**), is an excellent, high quality winery with a beautiful tasting room located in town. **Yacochuya,** RN40 (© **3868/421-233;** www.yacochuya.com), is a boutique winery, owned by the Etchart family, 7km (4¼ miles) outside town. They offer visits by appointment only.

Museums & Workshops

Artesanías Víctor Cristófani, RN 40 at Arrollo Don Lelio (no phone), is a pottery workshop that provides an entertaining and fascinating tour. Owner Ana María wallops giant urns with a metal bar to demonstrate their strength. Huge clay ovens belch wood smoke while pots and urns and mud clay lie around in different stages of development. Visits are in the morning only. **Arte en Telar,** Colon 71 (no phone; rteentelar@hotmail. com), is a textile workshop that offers a fascinating look into the local tradition of hand weaving. It's open Monday to Saturday 10am to 2pm and 4 to 10pm. **Museo de Vitivinicultura,** RN 40 at Av. General Guemes (© **3868/421-125**), tells the story of grape-growing and wine-making in and around Cafayate. It's open Monday to Friday 10am to 1pm and 5 to 9pm. **Museo Regional y Arqueológico Rodolfo Bravo,** Colon 191 (© **3868/421-054**), displays indigenous ceramics, textiles, and metal objects discovered over a 66-year period by Rodolfo Bravo. The museum is open Monday to Friday 11am to 9pm. At weekends hours vary.

WHERE TO STAY

Cafayate has seen a surge in luxury accommodations, mostly of the wine-lodge variety. The town itself still lacks a high-end hotel, but many of the new lodges are within easy walking distance of the village.

Hostal Killa *(★★)*, Colon 47 (© **3868/422-254;** www.hostalkilla.com), has a long, rambling courtyard of whitewashed walls, giving it a bright Mediterranean feel. It is one of the most delightful places to stay in while touring the area, and owner Martha Chocobar is constantly at hand to help and give advice about where to go. Rooms start at $100 (£50), including breakfast. **Gran Real,** Av. General Guemes 128 (© **3868/ 421-231;** www.granrealcafayate.com.ar), is a modest hotel with quiet rooms and very simple furnishings. Some have pleasant mountain views. The hotel's saving grace is an attractive pool and barbecue area; rooms start at $35 (£18). **Villa Vicuña,** Belgrano 76 (© **3868/422-145;** www.villavicuna.com.ar), has 12 simple but well-appointed rooms in a building that is modern, but with some colonial touches (an arched entrance and street balcony, for example). Doubles start at $50 (£25).

WINE LODGES
Patios de Cafayate *(★★★)*, RN 40 at RP 68, part of El Esteco winery (© **3868/421- 747;** www.luxurycolection.com/cafayate), is Cafayate's most luxurious winery lodge. Flower-adorned courtyards lead to a palatial-style villa with fountains, vaulted corridors, and suitelike rooms. Walk down a jasmine walkway and you´re in the futuristic wine spa—a slate-gray cube of modernist indulgence. Rooms start at $300 (£150). **La Casa de la Bodega,** ST RP 68, Km 18 (© **3868/421-888;** www.lacasadelabodega. com.ar), is set in a desert of pink sand and cactus sentinels 18km (11 miles) outside Cafayate. It's on a twisting road that meanders through purple mountains that look like melted plasticine. The luxurious lodge itself is of sand-colored brick with lots of tile and wood, with eight rooms boasting Jacuzzis and hydromassage. Prices start at $100 (£50). **Viñas de Cafayate Wine Resort** *(★★)* (© **3868/422-272;** www.cafayate wineresort.com) is situated 3km (2 miles) outside the town in the mountain foothills, with a commanding view of the valley. The front facade of pillared arches leads to a large courtyard surrounded by 12 simple but spacious rooms. Doubles start at $75 (£38).

WHERE TO DINE
Machacha, Guemes 28 (© **3868/422-319;** daily 10am–3pm and 7pm–2am), is Cafayate's best gourmet restaurant, offering such exotic dishes as llama meat and duck. Platters of smoked cheese and cold meats compete with rabbit for your attention. Main courses range from $15 to $20 (£7.50–£10). **El Rancho,** Vicario Toscano 4 (© **3868/ 421-256;** daily noon–3:30pm and 9pm–1am), is the best restaurant on the main plaza. When locals go out to eat, they come here. The expansive dining room has an authentic bamboo roof, and the fans overhead keep things cool in the summer months. Main courses start at $4 to $7 (£2–£3.50). **La Carreta de Don Olegario,** Av. General Güemes 20 (© **3868/421004;** daily noon–3pm and 8–11pm), is popular with foreign visitors and serves up an authentic selection of regional dishes, including *cabritos.* Service is unhurried, so plan to enjoy a leisurely lunch or dinner if you come here. Main courses range from $3–$4 (£1.50–£2).

8 The Argentine Lake District *(★★★)*

The Lake District is Argentina's premier vacation destination, a ruggedly beautiful jewel characterized by snowcapped mountains, waterfalls, lush forest, the area's namesake lakes, and trout-filled crystalline rivers. The region stretches from north of Junín de los Andes to the south of Esquel, incorporating small villages, ranches, several spectacular national parks, and the thriving city of Bariloche. Visitors often liken the Lake District to Alpine Europe, as much for the landscape as for the clapboard architecture

The Lake District

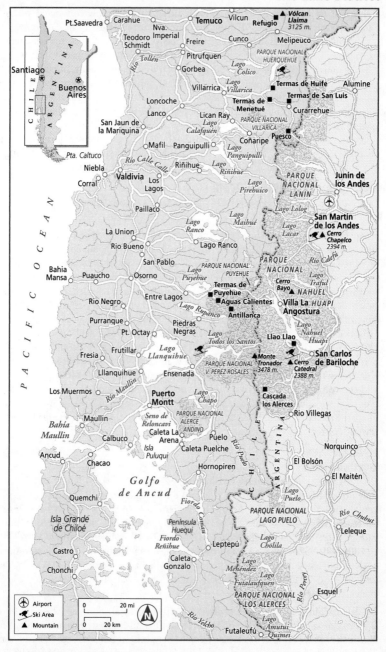

influenced by Swiss and German immigration. Although it is considered part of Patagonia, the Lake District has little in common with its southern neighbors.

The allure of the Lake District is that it offers year-round activities, from hiking to biking, fishing to hunting, sightseeing to sunbathing, summer boating to winter skiing. The region is also well known for its food—venison, wild boar, trout, smoked cheeses, wild mushrooms, sweet marmalades, chocolates, and more. Tourism is the principal economic force here, which means that prices soar as the swarming masses pour into this region from December to March and during the month of July. I highly recommend that you plan a trip during the off season, especially in November or April.

Many visitors include a trip to Chile's Lake District. (For more information, see chapter 7.) This can be done by boat aboard the popular "Lake Crossing," through Puerto Blest to Lago Todos los Santos near Ensenada, or by vehicle.

SAN CARLOS DE BARILOCHE

1,621km (1,005 miles) SW of Buenos Aires; 180km (112 miles) S of San Martín de los Andes

San Carlos de Bariloche sits in the center of Nahuel Huapi National Park and is fronted by an enormous lake of the same name. Bariloche offers many outdoor activities, sightseeing drives, boat trips, great restaurants, and shopping opportunities. The city itself embodies a strange juxtaposition: an urban city in the middle of beautiful wilderness. Unfortunately, Argentine migrants fleeing Buenos Aires, an ever-growing tourism industry, and 2 decades of unchecked development have left a cluttered mess in what once was an idyllic mountain town. Bits and pieces of the charming architecture influenced by German, Swiss, and English immigration are still in evidence, but visitors can be overwhelmed by the hodgepodge of ugly apartment buildings, dance clubs, and crowds that descend on this area, especially from mid-December until the end of February and during ski season in July. Yet drive 15 minutes outside town, and thick forests of pine, beech, and cypress will surround you, along with rippling lakes and snowcapped peaks that rival those found in Alpine Europe. If you're looking for a quiet destination, you'd be better off lodging in the town of Villa La Angostura or along the road to the Llao Llao Peninsula (see below). On the flip side, Bariloche offers a wealth of services.

ESSENTIALS
Getting There
BY PLANE　The **Aeropuerto Bariloche** (© **2944/426242**) is 13km (8 miles) from downtown. Buses to the city center line up outside the arrival area and a taxi to the center costs about $10 (£5). **Aerolíneas Argentinas,** Mitre 185 (© **2944/422548;** www.aerolineas.com.ar), runs at least three daily flights from Buenos Aires; in summer, it operates a daily flight from El Calafate as well. **LAN Argentina,** Mitre 534 (© **800/999-9526;** www.lan.com), runs two or three flights a day from Buenos Aires; LAN Chile schedules two weekly international flights to Santiago. **LADE,** Quaglia 238 no. 8 (© **2944/423562;** www.lade.com.ar), serves small destinations in the area such as Neuquen and Esquel.

BY BUS　The **Terminal de Omnibus** (© **2944/432860**) is at Av. 12 de Octubre 2400; a dozen companies serve most major destinations in Argentina and Chile. **Vía Bariloche** (© **2944/432444**) has eight daily arrivals from Buenos Aires (the trip lasts about 20 hr.) and one daily trip from Mar del Plata. **Andesmar** (© **2944/430211**) has service from Mendoza, Río Gallegos, and Neuquén, and service from Osorno,

ACCOMMODATIONS ■
Hostería La Pastorella **13**
Hostería Las Marianas **14**
Hotel Edelweiss **4**
Hotel Nahuel Huapi **8**
Hotel Panamericano **3**
Hotel Tres Reyes **6**
Perikos **12**
Villa Huinid **1**

DINING ◆
Casita Suiza **9**
Días de Zapata **11**
El Patacón **2**
Familia Weiss **10**
Jauja **7**
Kandahar **15**
Naan **16**

ATTRACTIONS ●
Museo de la Patagonia **5**

Valdivia, and Puerto Montt in Chile. In addition, there's a daily service from San Martín de los Andes via the scenic Siete Lagos (Seven Lakes) route (only during the summer); from Villa La Angostura, try **Ko-Ko** (© **2944/431135**).

BY CAR Motorists can reach Bariloche from San Martín via several picturesque routes. The 200km (124-mile) scenic **Siete Lagos route,** from San Martín de los Andes, follows *rutas* 234, 231, and the partially paved 237 (avoid this route when it's raining, as the dirt roads turn to mud). The 160km (99-mile) **Paso Córdoba** follows *rutas* 234, 63, and 237. The safest route for night driving or crummy weather, the **Collón Curá** runs 260km (161 miles) along *rutas* 234, 40, and the paved part of 237; the Collón Curá is the longest route, but it's entirely paved.

TRAVELING BY BOAT TO CHILE **Catedral Turismo** offers a spectacular **Cruce de Lagos** journey to the Lake District in Chile. It's a boat-and-bus combination that terminates in Lago Todos los Santos near Ensenada and Puerto Varas. If you're planning to visit Chile, it's a superb option that allows you to take in the beauty of the area. The trip costs $178 (£89) per person for the boat trip (including lunch), and an average of $135 (£68) double for an overnight at the Hotel Peulla. Book at any travel agency or from Catedral Turismo's offices in Bariloche at Moreno 238 (© **2944/ 425443;** www.crucedelagos.cl).

Getting Around

BY FOOT　When navigating the streets of Bariloche, be aware that two streets have similar names, though they are distinct routes: V.A. O'Connor runs parallel to the Costanera, and J. O'Connor bisects it. The city is compact enough to explore on foot.

BY CAR　Most savvy travelers rent a car to visit this area. You'll need wheels if you're staying outside the city center or planning to explore the scenic Circuito Chico. Most rental agencies have kiosks at the airport as well as a number of downtown offices: **Budget,** Mitre 106 (© 2944/422482); **AI Rent a Car,** Av. San Martín 127 (© 2944/ 436041); **Dollar,** Villegas 282 (© 2944/430333); **Hertz,** Quaglia 165 (© 2944/ 423457); **Bariloche Rent a Car,** Moreno 115 (© 2944/427638); and **Localiza,** V.A. O'Connor 602 (© 2944/435374). Rates are reasonable, starting at around $45 (£23) per day.

BY BUS　Bariloche's public bus system is cheap and efficient, whether you're heading to Cerro Catedral ski resort or exploring the lakeside route of Circuito Chico. Regular buses depart from calle San Martín, just in front of the national park headquarters, or from Moreno and Palacios. Rides cost less than $1 (50p).

Visitor Information

The **Secretaría de Turismo,** in the stone-and-wood Civic Center complex between calles Urquiza and Panzoni (© **2944/429850;** securismo@bariloche.com.ar), has general information and accommodations listings. They also operate an information stand in the bus terminal, open Monday through Friday from 8am to 9pm, and Saturday and Sunday from 9am to 9pm. For information about lodging and attractions surrounding Bariloche, try the **Secretaría de Turismo de Río Negro,** Av. 12 de Octubre 605, at the waterfront (© **2944/423188**); it's open Monday through Friday from 9am to 2pm. Good websites for all sorts of up-to-date travel information include **www.bariloche.org** and **www.interpatagonia.com.**

The **Club Andino Bariloche,** Av. 20 de Febrero 30 (© **2944/422266;** fax 2944/ 424579; www.clubandino.com.ar), provides excellent information about hiking, backpacking, and mountaineering in the area. They sell maps and provide treks, mountain ascents, and ice walks led by guides from the Club Andino, as well as rafting, photo safaris, and horseback rides; they are open daily from 9am to 1pm and 6 to 9pm during winter, daily from 8:30am to 3pm and 5 to 9pm during summer. For general information about **Nahuel Huapi National Park,** head to the park's headquarters across the street from the Civic Center (© **2944/423111**), open Monday through Friday from 8:30am to 12:30pm.

FAST FACTS　Most banks exchange currency, including **Banco de Galicia,** Moreno and Quaglia (© **2944/427125**), and **Banco Frances,** San Martín 332 (© **2944/ 430315**). Try also **Cambio Sudamérica,** Mitre 63 (© **2944/434555**).

For **emergencies,** dial **101.** For other matters, call © **2944/423434.** For medical assistance, your best bet is **Hospital Privado Regional,** 20 de Febrero 594 (© **2944/ 423074**).

Internet Access: Internet cafes are on just about every corner—and almost every hotel has Internet access, which is usually free for guests. There are two reliable Laundromats here: **Mileo,** at Villegas 145 (© **2944/422331**), and **Lavadero Huemul,** on Juramento 36 (© **2944/522067**). The central **post office** (no phone) is in the Civic Center, next to the tourist office.

WHAT TO SEE & DO IN & AROUND BARILOCHE

In Bariloche's **Civic Center,** you'll find the **Museo de la Patagonia Perito Moreno** (© **2944/422309**), open Tuesday through Friday from 10am to 12:30pm and 2 to 7pm, Saturday from 10am to 5pm. Admission is $1 (50p).

Tour Operators

A plethora of travel agencies offer everything under the sun along the streets of Bariloche. Most tours do not include lunch, and some charge extra for a bilingual guide. The best of the lot includes **Catedral Turismo,** Moreno 238 (© **2944/425443;** www.hotelpuertoblest.com.ar), and **Limay Travel,** V.A. O'Connor 710 (© **2944/420268;** www.limaytravel.com.ar). Both offer a wide variety of land excursions to El Bolsón, Cerro Tronador, and circuit sightseeing routes. **Huala Adventure Tourism,** San Martín 86 (© **2944/522438;** www.huala.com.ar), specializes in adventure sports such as white-water rafting, trekking, and horseback riding, as well as creative and fun multiday outings that combine activities.

Outdoor Activities

BIKING   Mountain-bike rental and information about bike trails and guided trips in Nahuel Huapi are available from **Bike Way,** V.A. O'Connor 867 (© **2944/424202**); **Bariloche Mountain Bike,** Gallardo 375 (© **2944/462397**); and **Dirty Bikes,** V. A. O'Connor 681 (© **2944/425616**).

FISHING   This region provides anglers with excellent fly-fishing on the Manso, Limay, Traful, and Machico rivers. Fisherman also troll on Lake Nahuel Huapi for introduced species such as brown trout, rainbow trout, and landlocked salmon. The fishing season opens in November and runs through April. You can pick up information and fishing licenses at the **Baruzzi Fly Shop,** Urquiza 250 (© **2944/424922**), or the office of the Parque Nacional Nahuel Huapi in the Civic Center. Bariloche is home to dozens of fly-fishing guides. Be sure to choose one who is fully licensed and provides lunch, transfers, and the appropriate gear. Recommended outfitters are **Martín Freedman** (© **2944/15-550-702;** www.flyfishingpatagonia.com) or the guides at **FlyMaster's** (© **2944/462101;** www.bariloche.com/flymasters). Costs generally run around $350 (£175) per day for up to two people. Trolling and spinning are also available. Tour agencies such as **Huala Adventure Tourism,** San Martín 86 (© **2944/522438;** www.huala.com.ar), offer half-day and full-day fly-casting and trolling excursions.

HIKING   The Nahuel Huapi National Park has a well-developed trail system for day hikes, multiday hikes, and loops that connect several backcountry *refugios,* some of which offer rustic lodging. The national park office in the Civic Center provides detailed maps and guides to the difficulty level of each trail. An excellent multilingual local hiking guide and naturalist is **Max Schoffel** (© **2944/15-669669;** www.patagoniatravelco.com). Another great source for information is the **Club Andino,** mentioned above.

HORSEBACK RIDING   Horseback rides in various areas of the park are offered by **Tom Wesley Viajes de Aventura,** Mitre 385 (© **2944/435040**), which also has a kid-friendly adventure camp. **Cumbres Patagonia,** Villegas 222 (© **2944/423283**), has trips to Fortín Chacabuco. For overnight or multiday horseback-riding trips, contact **Gatomancha** (© **2944/523009;** www.gatomancha.com).

MOUNTAINEERING   Experienced climbers, and those looking for a taste of the high peaks, have plenty of options in Bariloche, including the challenging 3-day climb of Mt. Tronador. Contact **AndesCross** (© **2944/467522;** www.andescross.com) for guiding services.

RAFTING   Various companies offer river rafting on the Río Manso in both Class III and Class IV sections, on either half-day or full-day trips. The average cost for a half-day is $35 to $45 (£18–£23); full-day is $65 to $75 (£33–£38). Easier floats down the Class I Río Limay are also available, for about $25 (£13) for a half-day. The two best local rafting companies are **Patagonia Rafting,** San Martín 86 (© **2944/522438**), and **Extremo Sur,** Morales 765 (© **2944/427301**).

SKIING & SNOWBOARDING   Bariloche's main winter draw is the ski resort at Cerro Catedral, perhaps South America's greatest ski hill. The scenery is stunning. The season usually runs from June through October, with mid-August the busiest time (when all Argentines have their 2-week winter holidays). Nonskiers can also enjoy the scene thanks to pedestrian lifts, open daily, that ferry passengers to the top. Every July or August, Catedral hosts the **National Snow Party,** with torchlight parades and other events. The bustling Villa Catedral is at the base of the resorts, with a jumble of shops, rental stores, and several lodging options. The nicest ski-in, ski-out hotel is **Pire-Hue Hotel and Resort** (© **2944/460040;** www.pire-hue.com.ar). **Sudbruck Hostería** has a handful of spacious rooms decorated with rustic cypress wood (© **2944/460156;** www.sudbruck.com). Rooms start at about $75 (£38) per night for a double. **Cabañas Antu Pukem** has cabins for six to eight guests; consult them directly for prices (© **2944/460035**).

WHERE TO STAY IN THE CITY CENTER

If you're looking for luxury, you'll find the most options along the main road outside town that runs parallel to the lake and leads to the Llao Llao Peninsula. The larger hotels in the city (such as the Panamericano, below) tend to cater to tour groups and aren't especially luxurious or service oriented, but their advantage is location. If you're planning to rent a car, then by all means stay outside the city.

Expensive

Hotel Edelweiss   With its reliable service and huge double bedrooms, this hotel is a solid choice in downtown Bariloche; just don't arrive expecting luxury. Double superiors were renovated in 2007 and come with two full-size beds, bay windows, and lake views, as do the suites. Standard doubles are smaller, with a single full-size bed or two twins and a view of a building in the back, but they are just as comfortable and $10 (£5) cheaper. The design is pleasant but very run-of-the-mill for a hotel that deems itself a five-star.

Av. San Martín 202, San Carlos de Bariloche. © **2944/445510.** Fax 2944/445520. www.edelweiss.com.ar. 100 units. $196 (£98) double superior; from $275 (£138) suite. Rates include buffet breakfast. AE, DC, MC, V. Valet parking. Amenities: 2 restaurants; bar; indoor pool; sauna; game room; room service. *In room:* TV, minibar, safe.

Hotel Panamericano *(Overrated)*   The massive Hotel Panamericano's deluxe rating is exaggerated. Rooms are spacious and comfortable, but the design needs a face-lift, and the interiors seem aged, tired, and boring. Lake views are available only above the fifth floor; in fact, the hotel rarely books rooms on the bottom floors unless they're hosting a convention. The back rooms face an ugly building, but they're cheaper. The junior suites are quite nice; they're actually a better deal than the regular suites. The hotel has another 100 or so rooms and a casino on the other side of the street, connected by an aerial walkway.

Av. San Martín 536, San Carlos de Bariloche. (℃/fax **2944/425846**. www.panamericanobariloche.com. 306 units. $200 (£100) double; $225 (£113) double with lake view; from $430 (£215) suite. Rates include buffet breakfast. AE, DC, MC, V. Valet parking. **Amenities:** 2 restaurants; bar; lounge; indoor pool; exercise room; sauna; room service; massage; laundry service; dry cleaning. *In room:* TV, dataport, minibar, coffeemaker, safe.

Moderate

Hostería Las Marianas 👭, 24 de Septiembre 218, (℃/fax **2944/439874;** www. hosterialasmarianas.com.ar), is a lovely, cozy inn just a few blocks from the Centro Cívico. It's a renovated, old Swiss-style mansion, and the beds have luxurious down comforters. Doubles start at $80 (£40). **Hotel Nahuel Huapi** 👭, Moreno 252 (℃/fax **2944/426146;** www.hotelnahuelhuapi.com.ar), is one of the better large hotels in downtown Bariloche. Standard rooms have wood floors and a crisp, clean decor, with off-white and green bedspreads and curtains. Doubles start at $130 (£65). **Hotel Tres Reyes,** Av. 12 de Octubre 135 (℃ **2944/426121;** fax 2944/424230; www.hoteltres reyes.com), has a stark, Scandinavian style that perhaps doesn't appeal to everyone. Nevertheless, the hotel has been superbly maintained, with architectural details such as wood ceilings and beechwood paneling, and the vast lounge area has dozens of chairs and a velvet couch to sink into while you gaze out over the lake. Rates range from $85 to $100 (£43–£50).

Inexpensive

Hostería La Pastorella, Belgrano 127 (℃ **2944/424656;** www.lapastorella.com.ar), is a cozy little place and was one of the first hotels in Bariloche, built in the 1930s. The rooms are a bit tired, but for the price and location, they're a good value. Try to get a room that looks over the garden. Room prices range from $66 to $106 (£33–£53). **Perikos,** Morales 555 (℃ **2944/522326;** www.overlandpatagonia.com), is the friend-liest hostel in town and is a great choice for any traveler on a budget. Perikos has 10 rooms ranging from $11 (£5.50) for a shared room to $38 (£19) for a private room, with breakfast included.

WHERE TO STAY THE ROAD TO THE LLAO LLAO PENINSULA
Very Expensive

Llao Llao Hotel & Resort 👭👭 *Kids*   The internationally renowned Llao Llao Hotel & Resort is one of the finest hotels in Latin America, as much for its magnifi-cent location as its sumptuous, elegant interiors and refined service. Situated on a grassy crest of the Llao Llao Peninsula, this is *the* place to spend the night if you're will-ing to splurge for a special evening. The lounge has glossy wood floors carpeted with incredibly long Oriental rugs, coffee-color wicker furniture, and soft lights.

A "winter garden" cafe looks out onto a large patio, the hotel's golf course, and Lake Nahuel Huapi beyond. Rooms are decorated in a rustic country design and have gleaming white bathrooms; they're nice, but the style is not as exceptional as one would expect from a hotel of this caliber. Myriad daily activities are included in the price of the rooms. The hotel's fine-dining restaurant, **Los Cesares,** is the best in the Bariloche area.

Av. Bustillo, Km 25. (℃ **2944/448530.** Fax 2944/445789. Reservations (in Buenos Aires): (℃ 11/4311-3434; fax 11/4314-4646. www.llaollao.com. 159 units. $340–$460 (£170–£230) double; $560–$2,230 (£280–£1,115) suite; $830–$1,500 (£415–£750) cottage. Rates include buffet breakfast. AE, DC, MC, V. **Amenities:** 2 restaurants; bar; lounge; small indoor heated pool; golf course; tennis courts; exercise room; fabulous spa; Jacuzzi; extensive water-sports equipment; children's center; video arcade; tour and car-rental desk; business center (with free Internet); shop-ping arcade; salon; room service; massage; babysitting; laundry service; dry cleaning. *In room:* A/C, TV, minibar, safe.

Cabanas

The southern shoreline of Nahuel Huapi Lake is dotted with cabin complexes for visitors. They're a nice way to be self-sufficient, prepare your own meals, and make yourself at home. Some can be very affordable, especially outside the high-season months of January and August. Bungalows and apart-hotels are similar options. Try the fun **El Bosque de los Elfos,** Avenida Bustillo, Km 5 (© **2944/442356;** www.bungalowsdeloselfos.com.ar), or **Cabañas Abril,** close to Playa Bonita at Aries 160 (© **2944/461070;** www.bariloche.com/abril). **Cabañas Arcadia,** at Av. Bustillo 5782 (© 2944/441817; www.arcadiapatagonia.com.ar), has five cabins built in the typical rustic wooden architecture of Bariloche.

Expensive

Villa Huinid ✿✿   The country-style luxurious cabins, suites, and the brand-new main building with three stories of lovely new rooms that make up the very modern Villa Huinid are top-notch choices for travelers looking for independent accommodations outside town. Facing the lake, just 2.5km (1½ miles) from the city center, the complex is backed by a thick forest with a walking trail. There are 12 cabins hand-crafted from knotty cypress, and a new hotel complex with 50 high-level rooms. Cabins have stone fireplaces, lovely decks with a full-size barbecue, and a handsome decor of floral wallpaper, plaid bedspreads, craftsy furniture, and other accents such as dried flowers and iron lamps. Also new is an acclaimed restaurant, called **Batistin,** and a large spa with a spectacular pool.

Av. Bustillo, Km 2.5. ©/fax 2944/5235234. www.villahuinid.com.ar. 62 units. $180–$245 (£90–£123) garden-view double; $220–$295 (£110–£148) lake-view double. Cabins sleeping 2–4 people $230–$360 (£115–£180). AE, DC, MC, V. **Amenities:** Restaurant; lounge; pool; gym; spa; games room; laundry service; business center. *In room:* TV, Wi-Fi, fridge, coffeemaker, safe.

WHERE TO DINE IN THE CITY CENTER

Bariloche is full of restaurants and cafes, especially on Avenida San Martín and the side streets leading to it. As with its accommodations, Bariloche's best restaurants are outside the city center. In addition to the restaurants listed below, the **Familia Weiss,** at the corner of Palacios and V. A. O'Connor (© **2944/435789;** daily 11:30am–1am) and the **Casita Suiza,** Quaglia 342 (© **2944/435963;** daily 8pm–midnight) are solid choices for lunch and dinner.

Expensive

Kandahar, 20 de Febrero 628 (© **2944/424702;** Mon–Sat 8pm–midnight), is one of the best restaurants in town. In this funky and colorful old house with cozy nooks, the food is creative and fresh. For main dishes, try homemade pastas such as gnocchi with olives, trout with spinach, rabbit with quince sauce, or peppered tenderloin. Main courses start at $15 (£7.50). **Naan,** Campichuelo 568 (© **2944/421785;** daily 8pm–midnight during the high season [Jan–Feb and July–Sep]; closed Mon during the rest of the year), is a revelation in Patagonia. Starters range from Italian and Middle Eastern dishes to Vietnamese and French specialties. Main courses, which include a lamb curry and a coconut chicken and prawns, costs between $15 and $20 (£7.50–£10).

Moderate

Jauja ✿✿, Elfleim 148 (© **2944/422952;** daily 11:30am–3pm and 7:30pm–midnight), is one of the best restaurants in the center of town, both for its extensive menu and woodsy atmosphere. You'll find just about everything on offer here, from regional to German-influenced dishes, including grilled or stewed venison, goulash with spaetzle, stuffed crepes, homemade pastas, barbecued meats, and trout served 15 different ways. Meals cost between $10 and $15 (£5–£7.50). **Días de Zapata,** Morales 362 (© **2944/423128;** daily noon–3:30pm and 7pm–midnight), is Bariloche's best Mexican restaurant and a nice change of pace from *parrillas.* You'll find the usual tacos, fajitas, and nachos on the menu, but you'll also find more uncommon Mexican dishes such as chicken *mole,* Veracruz conger eel, and spicy enchiladas. Happy hour is from 7 to 9pm. Main courses cost $10 to $15 (£5–£7.50).

Inexpensive

El Mundo, Mitre 759, (© **2944/423461;** daily noon–3pm and 8pm–midnight), serves up crispy pizza in more than 100 varieties, as well as *empanadas,* pastas, and salads. **Friends,** Corner of Mitre and Rolando (© **2944/423700;** daily 24 hr.), is worth a mention for the fact that it's always open, and it's popular among families with kids. The menu serves grilled meats and fish, crepes, sandwiches, soups, and salads.

WHERE TO DINE ON THE ROAD TO THE LLAO LLAO PENINSULA

El Patacón 🐷🐷 ARGENTINE/REGIONAL   This large restaurant is a 7km (4¼-mile) drive from the city center. The building is made of chipped stone inlaid with polished, knotty tree trunks and branches left in their natural shape. Start your meal with a platter of five provolone cheeses, served crispy warm off the grill. Follow it with venison ravioli or goulash, trout in a creamy leek sauce with puffy potatoes, wild boar in wine, or mustard chicken. The *parrilla* serves grilled meats and daily specials, and the *bodega* (wine cellar) offers an excellent selection of wines.

Av. Bustillo, Km 7. © **2944/442898.** Reservations recommended Sat–Sun. Main courses $20–$35 (£10–£18). AE, DC, MC, V. Daily noon–3pm and 8pm–midnight.

Il Gabbiano 🐷🐷 *Finds* ITALIAN   Located close to the Llao Llao, Il Gabbiano is a labor of love for its owners and the menu is authentic *Italiano.* Antipasti include bruschetti and salmon with grapefruit. Delicate homemade pastas are varied and fresh. Main entrees include *osso bucco,* rabbit with garlic and rosemary, and a simple trout with lemon. The wine cellar has more than 250 labels, including a good selection of European varieties, rare in Patagonia.

Av. Bustillo, Km 24.3. © **2944/448346.** Reservations highly recommended. Main courses $15–$25 (£8–£13). No credit cards. Wed–Mon 7:30pm–midnight.

BARILOCHE AFTER DARK

Open 24 hours a day, the lakefront wine bar **Trentis Lakebar,** J.M. de Rosas 435 (no phone), is a great place for a cocktail. Bariloche is home to a handful of clubs catering to the 16- to 30-year-old crowd. Try **Roket,** J.M. de Rosas 424 (© 2944/431940), or **Cerebro,** J.M. de Rosas 405 (© 2944/424965). Earlier in the evening, locals gather at **The Roxy,** San Martín 490 (© 2944/400451), for funky music and big-screen light shows. There are a number of local pubs, including **Wilkenny,** San Martín 435 (© 2944/424444), and **Pilgrim,** Palacios 167 (© 2944/421686). Microbrew pubs are also becoming popular in Bariloche. Downtown, try **Antares,** Elflein 47 (© 2944/431454). **Cervecería Blest,** Avenida Bustillo, Km 11.5 (© 2944/461026), is the oldest microbrewery in Argentina. Next door, **Berlina,** Avenida Bustillo, Km 11.75 (© 2944/523336), is hip and fresh.

SAN MARTIN DE LOS ANDES ★★

1,640km (1,017 miles) SW of Buenos Aires, 200km (124 miles) N of San Carlos de Bariloche

San Martín de los Andes, a charming mountain town of 35,000 inhabitants, is nestled on the tip of Lago Lácar between high peaks. The town is considered the tourism capital of the Neuquen province, a claim that's hard to negate, considering the copious arts-and-crafts shops, gear-rental shops, restaurants, and hotels that constitute much of downtown. The town is quieter than Bariloche and decidedly more picturesque, thanks to its timber-heavy architecture and Swiss Alpine influence. San Martín overflows with activities, including biking, hiking, boating, and skiing. The town is also very popular for hunting and fishing. The tourism infrastructure here is excellent, with every lodging option imaginable and plenty of great restaurants.

ESSENTIALS
Getting There
BY PLANE   **Aeropuerto Internacional Chapelco** (© 2972/428388) sits halfway between San Martín and Junín de los Andes and, therefore, serves both destinations. **Aerolíneas Argentinas/Austral,** Capitán Drury 876 (© 2972/427871), flies from Buenos Aires three times a week. A taxi to San Martín costs about $15 (£7.50); transfer services are also available at the airport for $24 (£12) per person. A taxi to Junín de los Andes costs $20 (£10); transfer services are $2 (£1) per person. **By Mich Rent a Car** and **Avis** both have auto rental kiosks at the airport.

BY BUS   The **Terminal de Omnibus** is at Villegas and Juez del Valle (© 2972/427044). **Vía Bariloche** (© 2972/422800) runs daily bus service to San Martín de los Andes from Buenos Aires (a 19-hr. trip). **Ko-Ko Chevalier** (© 2972/427422) also offers service to and from Buenos Aires, and serves Villa La Angostura and Bariloche by the paved or by the scenic Siete Lagos route. **Centenario** (© 2972/427294) has service to Chile and also offers daily service to Buenos Aires; Villarrica- and Pucón-bound buses leave Monday through Saturday, and those for Puerto Montt depart Tuesday through Thursday. **Albus** (© 2972/428100 or 2944/423552) has trips to Bariloche via the Siete Lagos route (about 3 hr.).

BY CAR   San Martín de los Andes can be reached from San Carlos de Bariloche following one of three routes: the popular 200km (124-mile) Siete Lagos route; the 160km (99-mile) Paso Córdoba route; and the longest, entirely paved 260km (161-mile) Collón Curá route. If driving at night, take the paved route.

Getting Around
San Martín is compact enough to explore by foot. For outlying excursions, tour companies can arrange transportation. **El Sol Rent a Car,** Av. San Martín 461 (© 2944/421870), will drop a car off in Junín de los Andes. **Hertz Rent a Car** is at Av. San Martín 831 (© 2972/430280), and **Nieves Rent-A-Car** is at Villegas 668 (© 2972/428684). Note that two main streets have similar names and can be confusing: Perito Moreno and Mariano Moreno.

Visitor Information
San Martín's excellent **Oficina de Turismo** (©/fax 2972/427347 and 2972/427695) offers comprehensive accommodations listings with prices and other tourism-related information. The office is open Monday to Sunday 8am to 8pm, at Rosas and Avenida San Martín, on the main plaza. The **Asociación Hotelero y Gastronomía,** San Martín 1234 (© 2972/427166), also offers lodging information, including photographs of

each establishment, though service is not as efficient as it is at the Oficina de Turismo. During the off-season, it's open daily from 9am to 1pm and 3 to 7pm; during high season, it's open daily from 9am to 10pm.

For information on Parque Nacional Lanín, drop by the park's information center, daily 9am to noon only, or visit **www.parquenacionallanin.gov.ar**. A website chock-full of valuable information is **www.smandes.gov.ar**.

WHAT TO SEE & DO

San Martín is a mountain town geared toward outdoor activities. If you're not up to a lot of physical activity, take a stroll down to the lake and kick back on the beach. Alternatively, rent a bike and take a slow pedal around town. Pack a picnic lunch and head to Hua Hum. **The Red Bus** (© 2972/421185) runs city tours on a double-decker bus that helps orient visitors and gives a glimpse into the town's history. Tours depart daily at 10:30am and 6:30pm from the Plaza San Martín. The tour costs $6 (£3).

Tour Operators & Travel Agencies

Both **Tiempo Patagónico,** Colonel Díaz 751 (©/fax **2972/427113;** www.tiempo patagonico.com), and **Pucará,** Av. San Martín 941 (© **2972/429357;** pucara@ smandes.com.ar), offer similar tours and prices, and also operate as travel agencies for booking plane tickets. Popular excursions include day trips to the village Quila Quina, via a sinuous road that offers dramatic views of Lago Lácar, and the hot springs Termas de Lahuenco. Try to do the gorgeous circuit trip to Volcán Lanín and Lago Huechulafquén. It shouldn't cost more than $17 (£8.50), not including lunch.

Outdoor Activities

BIKING   San Martín is well suited for biking, and shops offer directions and maps. Bike rentals are available at **Enduro Kawa & Bikes,** Belgrano 845 (© **2972/427093**); **HG Rodados,** Av. San Martín 1061 (© **2972/427345**); and **Mountain Snow Shop,** Av. San Martín 861 (© **2972/427728**).

BOATING   **Naviera Lácar & Nonthué** (© **2972/428427**), at the Costanera and main pier, offers year-round boat excursions on Lago Lácar. A full-day excursion to Hua Hum includes a short navigation through Lago Nonthué. Naviera also operates three daily ferry services to the beautiful beaches of Quila Quina (which are packed in the summer).

FISHING INFORMATION & LICENSES   **Jorge Cardillo Pesca,** General Roca 636 (© **2972/428372;** cardillo@smandes.com.ar), is a well-stocked fly-fishing shop that organizes day and overnight fishing expeditions to the Meliquina, Chimehuín, and Malleo rivers, among other areas. The other local fishing expert is **Alberto Cordero** (© **2972/421453;** www.ffandes.com), who will arrange fishing expeditions around the area. He speaks fluent English; for more information, visit his website. You can pick up a fishing guide at the **Oficina Guardafauna,** General Roca 849 (© **2972/427091**).

KAYAKING   The dozens of lakes near San Martín practically call out for kayakers. **Patagonia Traverse** (tel] **2972/15-609102;** www.patagoniatraverse.com) organizes half-day outings in touring or sea kayaks.

MOUNTAINEERING   The guides at **Lanín Expedition** (© **2972/429799;** www. laninexpediciones.com) have decades of experience and offer climbing and orientation courses and ascents of Volcán Lanín and Volcán Domuyo.

SKIING   The principal winter draw for San Martín de los Andes is **Cerro Chapelco,** one of the premier ski resorts in South America. Just 20km (12 miles) outside town,

Cerro Chapelco is known for its plentiful, varying terrain and great amenities. Although popular, the resort isn't as swamped with skiers as Bariloche is.

To drive to the resort from town, follow Route 234 south along Lago Lácar; it's paved except for the last 5km (3 miles). During the summer, the resort is open for hiking and sightseeing, with lift access. For more information, call © **2972/427460** or visit **www.sanmartindelosandes.com**.

TREKKING   The guides at **Patagonia Infinita** (© **2944/15-510988;** www. patagonia-infinita.com.ar) will take you deep into the Andes along dozens of excellent hiking trails.

WHERE TO STAY

San Martín has many, many *hosterías* and cabanas. And at last, there is a luxury option on the horizon, with the construction of the 80-room Loi Suites at the Chapelco Golf Resort. Rates almost double in most places from December 18 to March 1. For more information, go to **www.sanmartindelosandes.gov.ar**.

Expensive

Ten Rivers and Ten Lakes Lodge ★★ *Finds*   With undoubtedly the best view in all of San Martín, this tiny and cozy log-and-stone lodge is secluded and romantic. This boutique inn originally opened as a lodge for fly-fishers. They still have excellent fishing packages, but anyone is welcome to spend a few nights in the four rooms. Rooms are decorated with an understated luxury that will appeal to nature lovers, as will the absence of TVs. Big tubs, big beds, big windows, and still-unpretentious style characterize the interiors.

Cerro Díaz, Ruta de los Arrayanes. © **11/5917-7710/11.** www.tenriverstenlakes.com. 4 units. $220 (£110) double; $300 (£150) suite. AE, MC, V. **Amenities:** Restaurant; lounge and TV room.

Moderate

Hostería La Casa de Eugenia ★, Colonel Díaz 1186 (© **2972/427206;** www. lacasadeeugenia.com.ar), is a lovely old building with bright blue trim that now functions as a bed-and-breakfast. The charming living room with its large fireplace, piano, and colorful sofas leads to five bedrooms, named by color. Rooms range from $50 to $90 (£25–£45). **Hostería Monte Verde,** Rivadavia 1165 (© **2972/410129;** www. hosteriamonteverde.com.ar), is a simple and clean *hostería* and one of the newer inns in town. The lobby is sparsely furnished with a giant stone fireplace. Rooms are large and comfortable, with new beds and some rooms have Jacuzzi tubs and fireplaces. Rates range from $85 to $100 (£43–£50). **La Cheminée** ★, General Roca and Mariano Moreno (© **2972/427617;** fax 2972/427762; www.hosterialacheminee.com.ar), has warm, attentive service and snug accommodations, making it a top choice. New owners are toning down the Alpine Swiss design, emphasizing a new more neutral and modern look. Spacious rooms are carpeted and feature wood ceilings and a country design. Rates start at $90 (£45).

Inexpensive

Hostería del Chapelco, Almirante Brown 297 (© **2972/427610;** fax 2972/427097), has every kind of unit available including new hotel rooms and cabanas, and cheaper, older duplex and A-frame units. Although it sits on the lakeshore, the rooms do not benefit from the view, but a bright lobby takes advantage of the location with giant picture windows. Prices start at $28 (£14). **Residencial Italia,** Coronel Pérez 799 at Obeid (© **2972/427590**), is a little hotel run by a sweet, elderly woman and is simple and kept scrupulously clean. Rooms are modestly decorated in 1950s style. Downstairs rooms are slightly darker; I recommend booking the sunnier upstairs double or one of the two apartments. Doubles start at $35 (£18).

WHERE TO DINE

San Martín has several excellent restaurants. For sandwiches and quick meals, try **Peuma Café,** Av. San Martín 851 (© **2972/428289**); for afternoon tea and delicious cakes and pastries, try **Unser Traum,** General Roca 868 (© **2972/422319**).

Expensive

Avataras ⊕, Teniente Ramayón 765 (© **2972/427104;** daily 8:30pm–midnight), has exceptionally warm, friendly service, a kids' menu, and a marvelous variety of international dishes from Hungary to China to Egypt that make this restaurant an excellent, if slightly expensive, choice in San Martín. Main courses range from $11 to $19 (£5.50–£9.50). **La Tasca** ⊕, Mariano Moreno 866 (© **2972/428663;** daily noon–3:30pm and 7pm–1am), is a solid choice for its fresh, high-quality cuisine and extensive wine offerings. Regional specialties are the focus, such as venison flambéed in cognac and blueberries, saffron trout, and ravioli stuffed with wild boar. The cozy restaurant is festooned with hanging hams, bordered with racks of wine bottles, and warmed by a few potbellied iron stoves. Main courses start at $14 (£7).

Moderate

La Fondue de Betty ⊕, Villegas 586 (© **2972/422522;** daily 7pm–midnight), is a San Martín classic. Betty's friendly service and bubbling fondue pots make it an enchanting place for dinner, especially if you are with friends. A local favorite is *bagna cauda,* a Northern Italian fondue of anchovies, garlic, and cream, in which you dip vegetables. The menu also includes some nonfondue dishes. Main courses go from $8 to $13 (£4–£6.50). **La Reserva** ⊕, Belgrano 940 (© **2972/428734;** daily noon–3pm and 7:30pm–midnight), is one of the most romantic restaurants in Patagonia, with a stone fireplace, elegant cloth-covered tables, soothing music, and superb service. On the menu is grilled trout, tender venison with fresh berry sauce, or chicken breast stuffed with feta cheese and herbs. A main course should not cost more than $12 (£6).

Inexpensive

La Costa del Pueblo, Av. Costanera and Obeid (© **2972/429289;** daily 11am–1am), has a lake view and an extensive menu with everything from pastas to *parrilla.* The establishment ran as a cafe for 20 years until new owners expanded it to include a dozen more tables and a cozy fireside nook. Just don't come here in a rush; service can be really slow. Main courses range from $3 to $7 (£1.50–£3.50). **La Nonna Pizzería,** Capitán Drury 857 (© **2972/422223;** daily noon–3pm and 8pm–12:30am), offers specialty regional pizzas with trout, wild boar, and deer. Calzone fillings include chicken, mozzarella, and bell pepper. Pizzas start at $5 (£ 2.50). **Pura Vida,** Villegas 745 (© **2972/429302;** Mon–Sat for lunch and dinner) is San Martín's only vegetarian restaurant and also serves a few chicken and trout dishes (the curried chicken is excellent). Dishes start at $6 (£3).

SAN MARTIN AFTER DARK

With its nice outdoor patio and cool wood and stone interior, the **Dublin South Pub,** on the corner of Mariano Moreno and San Martín (© **2972/424938**), has a huge list of microbrewed beers and cocktails.

9 Patagonia & Tierra del Fuego ★★★

Few places in the world have captivated the imagination of explorers and travelers like Patagonia and Tierra del Fuego. It has been 4 centuries since the first Europeans sailed through on a boat captained by Ferdinand Magellan, and this vast, remote region is still, for the most part, unexplored.

A traveler can drive for days without seeing another soul on the vast Patagonian pampa. What seduces people to travel to Patagonia is the idea of the "remote"— indeed, the very notion of traveling to the end of the world. The people who live here (Chileans and Argentines, as well as some Welsh) are hardy survivors.

A harsh climate and Patagonia's geological curiosities have produced some of the most beautiful natural attractions in the world: the granite towers of Torres del Paine and Los Glaciares national parks (though the former is found across the Chilean border), the Southern and Northern ice fields with their colossal glaciers, and the flat pampa broken by multicolored bluffs.

EL CALAFATE ★★
222km (138 miles) S of El Chaltén; 2,727km (1,691 miles) SW of Buenos Aires

El Calafate is a tourist-oriented town that has seen phenomenal growth in the past 7 years. It's best known for being the base from which to see the spectacular Perito Moreno Glacier. The town hugs the shore of turquoise Lago Argentino, and this location, combined with the town's leafy streets, gives it the feel of an oasis in the desert Steppe. The town's population has grown from 5,000 in 1996 to 20,000 in 2006, and it's heavily dependent on its neighboring natural wonder, Perito Moreno Glacier, as well as the nine daily flights that arrive at the El Calafate International Airport packed with foreign and national tourists. Thousands of visitors come for the chance to stand face to face with this tremendous wall of ice, which is one of the few glaciers in the ice field that isn't retreating (scientists say it is "in balance," meaning it shrinks and grows constantly).

ESSENTIALS
Getting There
BY PLANE   El Calafate's **Aeropuerto Lago Argentino** (✆ **2902/491220**) is a modern complex that was built in 2000. It's already proving to be too small, though, for the increasing traffic. Service is from Argentine destinations only: **Aerolíneas Argentinas/Austral** (✆ **11/4340-3777** in Buenos Aires; www.aerolineas.com.ar) has daily flights from Buenos Aires and flights from Bariloche, Trelew, and Ushuaia several times a week. A daily 747 flight also arrives directly from Ezeiza International Airport in Buenos Aires during high season (all flights used to leave from Aeroparque, downtown, and you would have to change airports). Be sure to specify which airport you'd like to fly from. **LAN Argentina** (✆ **0810/999-9526;** www.lan.com) has recently opened up three flights per week from Buenos Aires, and it's planning to offer more in the future. **LADE** (**Líneas Areas del Estado;** ✆ **0810/810-5233;** www.lade. com.ar) has a weekly flight from Buenos Aires and weekly connection to Puerto Madryn, Ushuaia, and Bariloche.

It's "Chile" in Patagonia
For information on traveling on the Chilean side of Patagonia, see chapter 7.

Patagonia & Tierra del Fuego

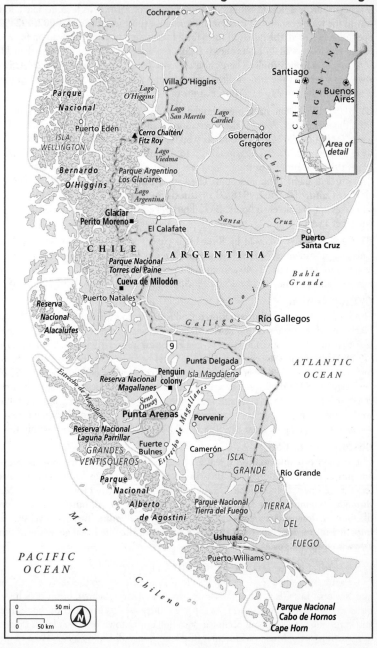

Cochrane

Villa O'Higgins

Lago O'Higgins

Parque Nacional

Puerto Edén

ISLA WELLINGTON

Lago San Martín

Lago Cardiel

Cerro Chaltén/ Fitz Roy

Gobernador Gregores

Bernardo O'Higgins

Lago Viedma

Parque Argentino Los Glaciares

Lago Argentina

Glaciar Perito Moreno

El Calafate

Chico

CHILE

ARGENTINA

Santa

Cruz

Puerto Santa Cruz

Parque Nacional Torres del Paine

Cueva de Milodón

Bahía Grande

Puerto Natales

Reserva Nacional Alacalufes

Coig

Gallegos

Río Gallegos

9

Punta Delgada

ATLANTIC OCEAN

Penguin colony

Isla Magdalena

Reserva Nacional Magallanes

Estrecho de Magallanes

Seno Otway

Porvenir

Punta Arenas

Reserva Nacional Laguna Parrillar

GRANDES VENTISQUEROS

Fuerte Bulnes

Camerón

ISLA

GRANDE

Río Grande

Parque Nacional

Alberto de Agostini

Parque Nacional Tierra del Fuego

DE

TIERRA

Mar

DEL

FUEGO

PACIFIC OCEAN

Ushuaia

Puerto Williams

Chileno

0   50 mi

0   50 km

Parque Nacional Cabo de Hornos

Cape Horn

Area of detail inset

Santiago

CHILE

ARGENTINA

Buenos Aires

Area of detail

153

The airport is 23km (14 miles) from the center of town, which seems like a long way in the wide openness of Patagonia. From the airport, **Aerobús** (© 2902/492492) operates a bus to all the hotels in town for $4 (£2); they can also pick you up for your return trip if you call 24 hours ahead. A taxi into town should cost no more than $10 (£5) for up to four people. There's also a Hertz Rental Car desk (© 2902/492525; www.hertz.com) at the airport. Please note that on the exit from this airport, all travelers are required to pay an airport exit tax of $18 (£9).

BY BUS   El Calafate has a bus terminal on Julio A. Roca, reached via the stairs up from the main street, Avenida del Libertador. To and from Puerto Natales, Chile, **Turismo Zaahj** (© 2902/491631) has six weekly trips leaving at 1pm. **Cootra** (© 2902/491144) leaves at 8am. The trip takes 5 to 6 hours, depending on how long it takes to get through border crossing procedures. To get to El Chaltén, three operators have departures at 6am, 1pm, and 6pm. The best is **Chaltén Travel** (© 2902/491833); also try **Caltur** (© 2902/491842) or **Interlagos Turismo** (© 2902/491179). The trip takes approximately 3 hours. Buy all bus tickets the day before, at least, to ensure you'll get a seat.

BY CAR   Ruta 5, followed by Ruta 11, is paved entirely from Río Gallegos to El Calafate. From Puerto Natales, cross through the border at Cerro Castillo, which will lead you to the famous RN 40 and up to the paved portion of Ruta 11. The drive from Puerto Natales is roughly 5 hours, not including time spent at the border checkpoint.

Getting Around

For information about transportation to and from Perito Moreno Glacier, see "Parque Nacional Los Glaciares & the Perito Moreno Glacier," later in this chapter. If you'd like to rent a car, you can do so at the **Europcar** office, Av. del Libertador 1741 (© 2902/493606; www.europcar.com.ar). Rates begin at $50 (£25) per day, including insurance and taxes. There's a brand-new **Hertz** rental car desk (© 2902/492525; www.hertz.com) at the airport as well. Most roads here are unpaved. Most of the town can be explored on foot, although many new hotels are either up a good-size hill or well out of town, so make sure your hotel offers a shuttle. Taxis in El Calafate are reasonably priced, ranging from $1.20 to $2.20 (60p–£1.10) for short trips within town.

Visitor Information

The city's **visitor information kiosk** is inside the bus terminal. They offer an ample amount of printed material and can assist in planning a trip to Perito Moreno Glacier; they're open daily October through April from 8am to 11pm, and daily May through September from 8am to 8pm (© 2902/491090). All other spots that look like information centers are travel agencies trying to sell tours. Two good websites for impartial information are **www.elcalafate.com.ar** or the municipal government's site at **www.elcalafate.gov.ar**.

WHAT TO SEE & DO IN EL CALAFATE

El Calafate is mostly a service town for visitors on their way to the glaciers (see "Parque Nacional Los Glaciares & the Perito Moreno Glacier," below), but it does have a pleasant main avenue for a stroll. As expected, there are lots of souvenirs, bookstores, and crafts shops to keep you occupied. Heading out of town on Avenida del Libertador, you'll pass the **Museo Municipal** (Calle G. Bonarelli s/n; © 2902/492799; free admission), open Monday through Friday from 10am to 9pm, with a collection of farming and ranching implements, Indian artifacts, and historical and ethnographical displays. It's worth a stop if you have the time. The **Los Glaciares National Park Headquarters,** Av. del Libertador 1302 (© **2902/491755**), has a good visitor information center and a lovely garden. If you are interested in bird-watching, you could take a short walk to the Bahía Redonda at the shore of Lago Argentino to view upland geese, black-necked swans, and flamingos.

ATTRACTIONS & EXCURSIONS AROUND EL CALAFATE

For information about visiting the glaciers and the national park, see "Parque Nacional Los Glaciares & the Perito Moreno Glacier," later in this chapter. Other typical excursions include the famous peaks of Cerro Torre and Mt. Fitzroy or visiting Chile's Torres del Paine National Park. For either of these, try **Patagonia Extrema,** Av. del Libertador 1341 (© **2902/492393**), or **AlwaysGlaciers** (© **11/5031-2869** in Buenos Aires).

HORSEBACK RIDING Try to avoid tours that depart directly from El Calafate. A company called **02902 Cerro Frías,** Av. del Libertador 1857 (© **2902/492808;** www.cerrofrias.com), offers half-day horseback riding trips in the wide-open plains of Patagonia that take you up to a gorgeous view point.

OFF-ROADING **Mil Outdoor Adventure,** Av. del Libertador 1029 (© **2902/491437**), takes you across rivers, over boulders, along ridges, and up to the El Calafate Balcony for a panoramic view. There are also fossils and rock mazes en route.

MOUNTAIN BIKING Explore the rolling hills and plains of the Patagonian Steppe. **Patagonia Bikes,** 9 de Julio 29 (© **2902/492767**), rents bikes and offers hour-long biking city tours and half- and full-day bike tours with private guides.

VISITING AN *ESTANCIA* An excellent day trip takes you to one of the several *estancias,* or ranches, that have opened their doors to the public. They typically run day activities and restaurant services, and some even offer lodging, should you opt to spend the night. They're a lovely way to experience the local history, immerse yourself in the wild landscapes, and experience Patagonia as authentically as possible. All of the following *estancias* offer meals, excursions such as horseback riding and trekking, and transportation from El Calafate. Close to town, **El Galpón del Glaciar** (© **2902/491793;** www.elgalpondelglaciar.com.ar) adds traditional *estancia* activities such as sheep-shearing. Perhaps the most exclusive ranch in the area is the **Estancia Helsingfors,** open from October to March, located on the shore of Lago Viedma about 150km (93 miles) from El Calafate. Helsingfors offers lodging, horseback riding, overflights, bird-watching, boat trips, and fine dining. For more information, contact their offices in Buenos Aires, Av Córdoba 827, 11A (©/fax **11/4315-1222;** www.helsingfors.com.ar). **Estancia Cristina** ★★ is situated at the end of the remote north arm of Lago Argentino. You take a spectacular 4-hour boat trip to get there, sailing past floating icebergs and the enormous Upsala Glacier. Contact their office in El Calafate at 9 de Julio 57, Local 10 (© **2902/491133;** www.estanciacristina.com).

The meticulously maintained **Estancia Alta Vista** (© **2902/491247;** altavista@cotecal.com.ar), 33km (20 miles) from El Calafate on the dirt road RP 15 near the beautiful area of Lago Roca, is open October through March and offers ranch activities and fishing. **Estancia Nibepo Aike** (© **2902/492797;** http://nibepoaike.com.ar) is picturesquely nestled on the southeast edge of the national park, about 60km (37 miles) from El Calafate. Closer to town, **Parque De La Bahía,** Padre Agostini and Av. Costaner (© **2902/496555**), has a nightly shearing show and in-depth presentation on all things wool- and sheep-related.

WHERE TO STAY

New hotels and *hosterías* are opening up every month in El Calafate. The bulk of them are 15-room inns in the outskirts of town. Really good value is hard to find here; most places capitalize on the short tourist season. Prices soar from December through February, making October to November and March to April the most economical time to visit.

Expensive

Design Suites, Calle 94 no. 190 (© **2902/494525,** or 11/5199-7465 for reservations in Buenos Aires; www.designsuites.com), overlooks the vast Lago Argentino and bills itself as *the* spot for style and design, popular with fashion-forward Europeans and Porteños. It is certainly creative, with eclectic art and furnishings and nature on display through the massive windows. In the evenings, it's a chic spot to watch the sunset and drink a martini. Doubles range from $145 to $235 (£73–£118) and suites $210 to $330 (£105–£165).

Esplendor de Calafate ⚘, Pte. Perón 1143 (© **2902/492454,** or 11/5217-5700 for reservations in Buenos Aires; www.esplendorcalafate.com), is similar to the Design Suites in its effort to be creative and modern, and it excels with a warm and cozy feeling. This former white elephant was transformed in 2006 into a sleek new multistory hotel with a unique earthy style and stunning windows. The suites, for around $59 (£29) more, are a real bargain: They have step-in rounded tubs, a living room, and plenty of windows. Doubles start at $292 (£146).

Hotel Kosten Aike, Gobernador Moyano 1243 (© **2902/492424** or 11/4811-1314 for reservations; fax 2902/491538; www.kostenaike.com.ar), is a downtown hotel that offers modern and attractive accommodations. It makes up for its lack of personal charm with its great location and dependability. Doubles range from $211 to $241 (£106–£121).

Moderate

El Faro del Calafate, Calle 405 no. 82 (© **2902/493899;** www.elfarocalafate.com.ar), is a comfortable and friendly midrange option. It is part of the new wave of small *hosterías* that have opened in the past few years on the outskirts of town. Decor is simple, with plain white walls and bedspreads, small TVs mounted in the corners, and very large bathrooms. A nice step up from a hostel, it offers plenty of space for you to relax in after a long day exploring Patagonia. Doubles start at $115 (£58). **Hostería Lupaza,** Calle 992 no. 19, Villa Parque Los Glaciares (© **2902/491110;** www.lupama.com.ar), is compact in size but big in heart. This charming new inn has towering windows and lovely wood architecture. The feeling inside is simple but rustic, with touches of wood and stone, and the spacious rooms upstairs have nice views. Doubles start at $150 (£75). **Kau Kaleshen,** Gobernador Gregores 1256 (© **2902/491188;** www.losglaciares.com/kaukaleshen), is a simple and charming inn with a central location. It's been around long enough to feel warm and authentic. Rooms are all located around the tranquil garden in back, and there is a lovely teahouse out front where breakfast is served, and where nonguests and guests alike can enjoy a $8 (£4) *té completo*—afternoon tea with homemade pastries.

Inexpensive

America del Sur Hostel, Puerto Deseado 151 (© **2902/493523;** www.americahostel.com.ar), is the best hostel in town with dorms starting at $10 (£5) per person and double rooms at $50 (£25). **Casa de Grillos,** Los Condores 1215, esq. Las Bandurrias

(© **2902/491160;** www.casadegrillos.com.ar), is the best bed-and-breakfast, with rooms starting at $55 (£28).

WHERE TO DINE

A number of cafes and espresso bars are along the main drag, Libertador, and its side streets. Try **Elba'r,** in the De los Pajaros plaza at 9 de Julio 57 (© **2902/493594**). Or the interesting **Borges & Alvarez Libro-Bar,** Av. del Libertador 1015 (© **2902/491464**), has a fantastic selection of books to peruse while you sip a *café con leche.* For a light snack, try **Almacenes Patagónicos,** at Av. del Libertador 1044 (© **2902/491042**).

Moderate

Casimiro Biguá 😊 *Moments* REGIONAL   This sleek wine bar and restaurant has quickly become the number-one hot spot in El Calafate. The chic and modern black-and-white decor, thick tablecloths, flickering candles on every table, and young and energetic waitstaff make this place a winner. You can sample one of the many wines while enjoying an appetizer platter of regional Patagonian specialties such as smoked trout, smoked wild boar, and a variety of cheeses.

Av. del Libertador 963. © 2902/492590. Reservations recommended. Main courses $8–$18 (£4–£9). AE, MC, V. Daily 10am–1am.

La Posta 😊😊 ARGENTINE   This has long been considered El Calafate's most upscale restaurant, serving great cuisine and choice wines in a formal, candlelit environment. The menu blends Argentine and international-flavored fare, such as filet mignon in a puff pastry with rosemary-roasted potatoes, king crab ravioli, almond trout, or curried crayfish. Desserts are superb.

Gobernador Moyano and Bustillo. © 2902/491144. Reservations recommended in high season. Main courses $8–$15 (£4–£7.50). AE, DC, MC, V. Daily 7pm–midnight.

Inexpensive

El Puesto, Gobernador Moyano and Av. 9 de Julio (© **2902/491620**), has 23 varieties of delicious pies that are dependably good. There are great pasta options as well. **La Cocina,** Av. del Libertador 1245 (© **2902/491758**), serves bistro-style food, including fresh pasta, such as raviolis and fettuccine, fresh trout, and meats prepared simply but well. **La Tablita,** Coronel Rosales 24 (© **2902/491065**), is all about meat, and it's one of the local favorites in town for its heaping platters and giant *parrilladas* (mixed grills) that come sizzling to your table on their own mini-barbecues.

EL CALAFATE AFTER DARK

In a rustic old building, **La Zaina,** Gob. Gregores 1057 (© **2902/496789**), is a cafe/bar rich with local atmosphere. The **Shackleton Lounge,** at del Libertador 3287 (© **2902/493516**), gets going a bit later, 3km (1¾ miles) down the road outside town. It has great sunsets, a long list of cocktails, semiregular evening slideshows, and lots of travelers in the crowd swapping tall tales.

PARQUE NACIONAL LOS GLACIARES & THE PERITO MORENO GLACIER 😊😊😊

The Los Glaciares National Park covers 600,000 hectares (1,482,000 acres) of rugged land that stretches vertically along the crest of the Andes and spills east into flat pampa. Most of Los Glaciares is inaccessible to visitors except for the park's two dramatic highlights: the granite needles, such as Fitzroy near El Chaltén (see "El Chaltén

& the Fitzroy Area," below), and this region's magnificent Perito Moreno Glacier. The park is also home to thundering rivers, blue lakes, and thick beech forest. Los Glaciares National Park was formed in 1937 as a means of protecting this unique wilderness, notable for its landscape carved and sculpted by ice-age and present-day glaciation.

If you don't get a chance to visit Glacier Grey in Torres del Paine, the Perito Moreno is a must-see. Few natural wonders in South America are as spectacular or as easily accessed as this glacier, and unlike the hundreds of glaciers that drain from the Southern Ice Field, the Perito Moreno is one of the few that is not receding.

What impresses visitors most is the sheer size of the Perito Moreno Glacier; it's a wall of jagged blue ice measuring 4,500m (14,760 ft.) across and soaring 60m (197 ft.) above the channel. From the parking lot on the Península Magallanes, a series of vista-point walkways descends, which take visitors to the glacier's face. It's truly an unforgettable, spellbinding experience. In 2007, a major infrastructure expansion project began at the Península Magallanes that will include refurbished boardwalk paths, a new restaurant, and a visitor center.

There are other magnificent glaciers in the national park; all are much harder to access than Perito Moreno but equally stunning. The Upsala Glacier is the largest in South America, and the Spegazzini Glacier has the largest snout of all the glaciers in the park. Onelli, Seco, and Agassiz are also gorgeous. All can be seen as part of the **All Glaciers Tour** organized by René Fernández Campbell, whose main office is at Av. del Libertador 867 (© **2902/492340**).

GETTING THERE & GETTING AROUND
At Km 49 (30 miles) from El Calafate, you'll pass through the park's entrance, where there's an information booth with erratic hours (no phone; www.calafate.com). The entrance fee is $10 (£5) per person.

BY CAR Following Avenida del Libertador west out of town, the route turns into a well-maintained road that is almost completely paved. From here, it's 80km (50 miles) to the glacier.

BY TAXI OR *REMISE* If you want to see the glacier at your own pace, hire a taxi or *remise*. The cost averages $100 (£50), although many taxi companies will negotiate a price. Be sure to agree on an estimated amount of time spent at the glacier, and remember that the park entrance fee of $10 (£5) per person is not included.

BY BUS **Cal-Tur** buses, Av. del Libertador 1080 (© **2902/491368**), leave downtown El Calafate twice a day (8am and 3pm, returning from the glacier at 1 and 8pm), allowing you to explore the glacier lookout area on your own. The bus ride costs a very reasonable $18 (£9), plus the $10 (£5) park entrance fee. Other buses leave on a similar schedule for similar prices from the bus terminal.

BY ORGANIZED TOUR Several companies offer transportation to and from the glacier, such as **Interlagos,** Av. del Libertador 1175 (© **2902/491179;** interlagos@cotecal.com.ar); and **TAQSA,** in the bus terminal (© **2902/491843**). For a more personalized tour (a private car with driver and a bilingual, licensed guide), contact **SurTurismo,** Av. del Libertador 1226 (© **2902/491266;** www.surturismo.com.ar).

OUTDOOR ACTIVITIES
You can see the Perito Moreno glacier close up on your own in a half-day's outing by taxi or bus. But several exciting activities in the Perito Moreno region afford a more

in-depth and thrilling experience. **"Minitrekking"** takes guests of all ages and abilities for a walk upon the glacier. More experienced, fit, and adventurous visitors can opt for the **Big Ice** ★★ option, which has a more technical approach. Both are organized exclusively by **Hielo y Aventura,** Av. del Libertador 935 (© **2902/492205;** www. hieloyaventura.com). **Solo Patagonia,** Av. del Libertador 963 (© **02902/491298;** www.solopatagonia.com.ar), offers visitors navigation trips through the Brazo Rico to the face of Perito Moreno, including treks to the base of Cerro Negro with a view of Glacier Negro. Both Solo Patagonia and **Upsala Explorer** ★, Av. 9 de Julio 69 (© **2902/491034**), offer a variety of combinations from Puerto Banderas to Los Glaciares National Park's largest and tallest glaciers—respectively the Upsala and Spegazzini.

LODGING NEAR THE GLACIER

Los Notros ★★★ *Moments*   Few hotels in Argentina boast as spectacular and breath-taking a view as Los Notros. This luxury lodge sits high on a slope looking out at Per-ito Moreno Glacier, and all common areas and rooms have been fitted with picture windows to let guests soak up the marvelous sight. Although the wood-hewn exteriors give the hotel the feel of a mountain lodge, the interior decor is contemporary. Inside the main building is a large, chic, and expansive restaurant. Guests at the Los Notros must opt for one of the multiday packages that include airport transfers, meals, box lunches for expeditions, guided trekking, boat excursions, and ice walks. The guides are great, but hotel service is a bit spotty, and the restaurant is definitely under-staffed. Note that prices jump substantially during Christmas, New Year's, and Easter week. The hotel prefers to sell its rooms to those buying their all-inclusive packages before releasing the rooms to those seeking just an overnight stay.

Main office in Buenos Aires: Arenales 1457, 7th floor. © 11/4814-3934. Fax 11/4815-7645. www.losnotros.com. 32 units. $967 (£484) per person for 2-night package Cascada bungalow; $1,145 (£573) per person for 2-night package in double superior; $1,543 (£772) per person for 2-night package in double premium. Rates include all meals and transfers. Room-only rates available by request, depending on availability. AE, DC, MC, V. **Amenities:** Restaurant; bar; lounge; tour desk; room service; laundry service. *In room:* Minibar.

EL CHALTEN & THE FITZROY AREA ★
222km (138 miles) N of El Calafate

El Chaltén is a tiny village of about 500 residents whose lifeblood, like El Calafate's, is the throng of visitors who come each summer. In the world of mountaineering, the sheer and ice-encrusted peaks of Mt. Fitzroy, Cerro Torre, and their neighbors are con-sidered some of the most formidable challenges in the world, and they draw hundreds of climbers here every year. El Chaltén is known as the "trekking capital of Argentina." Fitzroy's rugged beauty and great hiking opportunities have recently created somewhat of a boomtown. The town sits nestled in a circular rock outcrop at the base of Fitzroy, and it's fronted by the vast, dry Patagonian Steppe. It's a wild and windy setting, and the town has a ramshackle feel. Yet El Chaltén is preparing to step into the limelight: Completion of the pavement project on the road that links El Chaltén to El Calafate shortens the trip from 5 hours to just 2½ hours, coinciding with the opening of a new upscale hotel at Los Cerros. Populated by folk with a pioneering spirit, this rough-around-the-edges town has the feeling of a place on the fringe of modernity. The town's layout is somewhat haphazard, but there is a main drag, San Martín, where all the buses stop. Most hotels and restaurants don't have street numbers.

ESSENTIALS
Getting There
BY PLANE   All transportation to El Chaltén originates from El Calafate, which has daily plane service from Ushuaia and Buenos Aires. From El Calafate, you need to take a bus or rent a car; the trip takes from 2 to 2½ hours.

BY CAR   From El Calafate, take RN 11 west for 30km (19 miles) and turn left on RN 40 north. Turn again, heading northwest, on RP 23 to El Chaltén. The only place for a midtrip pit stop is the rustic Estancia La Leona, where you can grab a snack and a coffee.

BY BUS   Buses from El Calafate leave from the terminal, and each costs about $30 (£15) round-trip. **Chaltén Travel,** with offices in El Chaltén in the Albergue Rancho Grande on Avenida San Martín (© **2962/493005;** www.chaltentravel.com), leaves El Calafate daily at 8am and El Chaltén at 6pm. Chaltén Travel can arrange private tours and day trips to outlying destinations. **Caltur,** which leaves from El Chaltén's Hostería Fitzroy at Av. San Martín 520 (© **2962/491368;** www.caltur.com.ar), leaves El Calafate daily at 7:30am and leaves El Chaltén at 6pm.

Visitor Information
There is a $10 (£5) fee to enter the park. El Chaltén also has a well-organized visitor center at the town's entrance—the **Comisión de Fomento,** Perito Moreno and Avenida Güemes (© **2962/493011**), open daily from 8am to 8pm. In El Calafate, the **APN Intendencia** (park service) has its offices at Av. del Libertador 1302. Its visitor center is open daily from 9am to 3pm (© **2902/491005**).

There is neither a bank nor an ATM in El Chaltén and many inns, restaurants, and stores don't take credit cards.

OUTDOOR ACTIVITIES
Fitz Roy Expediciones ✸✸, Lionel Terray 212 (©/fax **2962/493017;** www.fitzroy expediciones.com.ar), offers a variety of trekking excursions. **Patagonia Mágica,** Fonrouge s/n (© **2962/493066**), rents mountain bikes and can help organize backcountry trips.

BOAT TRIPS   Similar to the Minitreks on the Perito Moreno Glacier, but with less than half the people, you can strap on some crampons and explore the nearby Viedma Glacier from El Chaltén. **Viedma Discovery** ✸ (© **2962/493110**) conducts such tours.

HORSEBACK RIDING   **Rodolfo Guerra,** Las Loicas 773 (© **2962/493020**), provides horseback rides and a horsepack service for carrying gear to campsites. Also try the El Relincho, Av. del Libertador s/n (© **2962/493007**).

HIKING & CAMPING   The best guides can be found at **Mountaineering Patagonia,** whose office is at E. Brenner 88 (© **2962/493915;** www.mountaineering patagonia.com). Also try Manuel Quiroga at **El Chaltén Mountain Guides** (no phone; www.ecmg.com.ar).

WHERE TO STAY
As the distances from El Calafate shrinks, thanks to highway pavement, El Chaltén is taking a swing upscale. Formerly a destination for backpackers and hostel-goers, it now affords interesting new lodging options.

Albergue Patagonia   Cozy and friendly, this is the smallest and best hostel in town. Service is caring and helpful, and the place fills up with mountain lovers. A total of 20 beds are spread among different rooms, none of which sleeps more than five. There is a big kitchen for guests to use.

San Martín s/n, El Chaltén. ℂ 2962/493019. 20 dorm beds, 3 private rooms. $60 (£30) double with shared bathroom, $30 (£15) dorm room with shared bathroom. No credit cards. **Amenities:** Kitchen; bike rentals; laundry room.

El Puma ⊛   A mainstay that has played host to many mountaineers over the years, El Puma offers comfortable accommodations and friendly service. Inside, warm beige walls and wooden beams interplay with brick, offset with soft cotton curtains and ironwork. Although the common areas have terra-cotta ceramic floors, all rooms are carpeted. The rooms are well designed and spacious; the lounge has a few chairs that face a roaring fire.

Lionel Terray 512, El Chaltén. ℂ/fax 2962/493095. www.hosteriaelpuma.com.ar. 12 units. $150 (£75) double. Rates include buffet breakfast and transfers from the bus stop. MC, V. Closed Apr–Oct. **Amenities:** Restaurant; bar; lunch catering; excursions; transfers; laundry services.

Hostería El Pilar ⊛   Seventeen kilometers (10 miles) from El Chaltén, Hostería El Pilar is yellow-walled and red-roofed and was once an *estancia;* now it's tastefully and artistically decorated without distracting you from the outdoors. The lounge has a few couches and a fireplace, and it's a comfy spot in which to hang out and read a book. Rooms are simple but attractive, with peach walls and comfortable beds. Superior rooms are all doubles and have bigger bathrooms.

Ruta Provincial 23, 17km (10 miles) from El Chaltén. ℂ/fax 2962/493002. 9 units. $120 (£58) double standard; $136 (£65) superior. No credit cards. Open Oct–Apr; rest of the year with a reservation. **Amenities:** Restaurant; bar; lounge.

Los Cerros Del Chaltén ⊛   Los Cerros inn is by far the most luxurious place in town. The common spaces have a new cottage feel, with comfy sofas and tall ceilings. The rooms, on either side of green hallways, are large and open to fabulous views stretching above the village and across the valley. There are no TVs or phones in the rooms. The restaurant is excellent, particularly the scrumptious baked goods. However, the all-inclusive nature of most packages keeps you from discovering the surprisingly fun and funky restaurants of El Chaltén.

San Martín s/n, El Chaltén. ℂ 2962/491185. www.loscerrosdelchalten.com. 44 units. 2-night packages $710–$811 (£355–£406) per person in double occupancy. All-inclusive packages include meals, transfers, and select excursions. Room and half-board-only options are also available. AE, MC, V. **Amenities:** Restaurant; lounge; small spa; excursions; gift shop; room service; laundry service; Internet point (in lobby); library; mini-cinema. *In room:* Hair dryer, safe, jetted tubs, no phone.

Nothafagus B and B ⊛ *(Value*   Owned and operated by a down-to-earth local couple, this B&B is bright, sunny, and well priced. There are seven simple and clean rooms. If you like the unpretentiousness of a hostel but want something more mature and quieter (although walls are a bit thin), this is a great choice. There is also a cozy reading room. A hearty breakfast is included.

Hensen s/n, El Chaltén. ℂ 2962/493087. www.elchalten.com/nothofagus. 7 units. $42 (£21) with shared bathroom; $76 (£38) with private bathroom. No credit cards. Open Oct–Apr; rest of the year with reservations only. **Amenities:** Laundry service; library.

WHERE TO DINE

During the winter, only one restaurant valiantly stays open: **La Casita,** Avenida del Libertador at Lionel Terray, in the pink building (ℂ 2966/493042). La Casita serves average, home-style fare, including sandwiches, meats, pastas, and stuffed crepes, along with absent-minded service; it accepts American Express, MasterCard, and Visa. Climbers gather during a stormy day at **Patagonicus,** Güemes at Andreas Madsen (© **2966/493025**), which serves mostly pizza and enormous salads in a woodsy dining area; no credit cards accepted. It's a good spot for an afternoon coffee. **Fuegia** ⚓, San Martín s/n (© **2966/493019**), has an eclectic, global menu including coconut chicken with cashews and excellent salads. There are also good vegetarian options. In a ramshackle old house loaded with character, **Ruca Mahuida,** at Lionel Terray 501 (© **2962/493018**), has the feel of an old alpine hut. The food is pure Patagonian, with stews, trout, and hearty pastas to fill you up after a day on the trail. Diners gather around a handful of tables, making this a great spot to meet new friends. Reservations are recommended. For a funky scene with cool music and creative food, head to **Estepa,** at the corner of Cerro Solo and Antonio Rojo (© **2962/493069**). The lamb in soft mint sauce, pizzas, and pumpkin sorrentinos are superb.

USHUAIA ⚓⚓
461km (286 miles) SW of Punta Arenas; 594km (368 miles) S of Río Gallegos

The windswept island of Tierra del Fuego has witnessed a rich history of shipwrecks, penal colonies, gold prospectors, and missionaries. Its capital, Ushuaia, is pinned snugly in a U-shaped cove facing the Beagle channel. It is a substantial metropolis of 70,000 people with colorful clapboard houses, rickety staircases, and corrugated roofs at impossible angles with a backdrop of beech trees and spirelike mountain summits. Not only is it the southern-most city in the world (Chilean Puerto Williams is actually lower but hardly qualifies as a city); it also has the distinction of being the only Argentine city on the other side of the Andes. What you find is a frontier town with lots of character and a surprisingly cosmopolitan feel. One hundred years ago the only people crazy enough to live here were convicts in chains. Indeed the city owes its existence to the prison as its inmates built its railway, hospital, and port. Now it attracts Argentines from all over the country who come for tax breaks and plentiful jobs. Visitors find lots to do, whether it is visit that same prison (now a fascinating museum), explore the many attractions of the Beagle channel, or use it as the last port of call before exploring Antarctica.

ESSENTIALS
Getting There
BY PLANE   The **International Airport Malvinas Argentinas** is located 5km (3 miles) from the city (© **2901/431232**). There is no bus service to town, but cab fares are only about $5 (£2.50). Always ask for a quote before accepting a ride. **Aerolíneas Argentinas/Austral** (© **0800/22286527** or 2901/437265; www.aerolineas.com.ar), operates eight or nine daily flights to Buenos Aires, one of which leaves from Ezeiza and stops in El Calafate. Average round fare is $450 (£225). Frequency increases from November to March, when there's also a daily flight from Río Gallegos and twice-weekly flights from Trelew. **LAN Chile** (© **0810/9999526** or 2901/424244) operates from Buenos Aires once a day, Monday, Wednesday, and Saturday. They also fly from Santiago de Chile. Tuesday and Thursday, **Aerovías DAP,** Deloqui 575, 4th floor (© **2901/ 431110;** www.aeroviasdap.cl), operates charter flights from Punta Arenas and over Cape Horn. It costs around $3,000 (£1,500) for a group of seven people (round trip), leaving whenever you want.

BY BUS   There is no bus station in the City. Buses usually stop at the port (Maipú and Fadul). The service from Punta Arenas, Chile, costs $35 (£18) and takes about 12 hours. **Tecni Austral** (© **2901/431408** in Ushuaia, or 61/613423 in Punta Arenas) ¶leaves Mondays, Wednesdays, and Fridays at 5:30am; tickets are sold in Ushuaia from the Tolkar office at Roca 157, and in Punta Arenas at Lautaro Navarro 975. **Tolkeyen,** San Martín 1267 (© **2901/437073;** ventas@tolkeyenpatagonia.com), works with the Chilean company Pacheco for trips to Punta Arenas, leaving on Monday, Wednesday, and Friday at 8am; it costs $60 (£30). To go to Río Grande, try **Lider LTD, Transporte Montiel,** or **Tecni Austral.** They offer eight daily departures, and the $12 (£6) trip takes around 4 hours.

BY BOAT   The company **Crucero Australis** (© **11/4325-8400;** www.australis.com) operates a cruise to Ushuaia from Punta Arenas, and vice versa, aboard its ship the M/V *Mare Australis.* If you have the time, this is a recommended journey for any age.

Getting Around

BY CAR   Everything in and around Ushuaia is easily accessible via bus or taxi or by using an inexpensive shuttle or tour service. Ushuaia's taxi drivers—seemingly the friendliest in Argentina—are fonts of information about the area. As there are a multitude of tourist excursions available (the best being by boat), renting a car is not necessary unless you want to explore the north of the island. Rentals, however, are very reasonable, from $55 to $65 (£28–£33) per day. *Note:* It's worth the extra cost for enhanced insurance as basic insurance requires you to pay up to $1,000 for initial damage in even a minor accident. **Avis,** Godoy 46, drops its prices for multiday rentals (© **2901/436665;** www.avis.com); **Cardos Rent A Car** is at Av. San Martín 845 (© **2901/436388**); **Dollar Rent A Car** is on Belgrano 58 (© **2901/437203;** www. dollar.com); and **Localiza Rent A Car** is on Sarmiento 81 (© **2901/437780**). Most of them rent 4×4 Jeeps with unlimited mileage. If you wish to cross into Chile at San Sebastián you will have to acquire a special permission document costing $50 (£25).

Visitor Information

The **Subsecretaría de Turismo** has two very helpful and well-stocked offices, one at San Martín 674 (© **2901/424550** or 0800/3331476; fax: 2901/432000) and the other in the tourism Pier, Maipú 505 (© **2901/437666;** fax 2901/430694; www.e-ushuaia. com). They also have a counter at the airport. From November to March, the offices are open daily from 8am to 10pm. The rest of the year they are open Monday through Friday from 8am to 9pm; Saturday, Sunday, and holidays from 9am to 8pm. The national park administration office can be found on Av. San Martín 1395 (© **2901/421315;** Mon–Fri 9am–3pm).

FAST FACTS   **Banco Patagonia,** Ave. San Martín and Godoy (© **2901/432080**), and **Banco Nación,** Av. San Martín 190 (© **2901/422086**), both exchange currency and have 24-hour ATMs. For laundry services, try **Los Tres Angeles,** Rosas 139, open Monday through Saturday from 9am to 8pm. **Andina,** Av. San Martín 638 (© **2901/ 423431**), is your best bet for a pharmacy.

Correo Argentino, at Ave. San Martín and Godoy (© **2901/421347**), is open Monday through Friday from 9am to 7pm, Saturday from 9am to 1pm; the private postal company **OCA** is at Maipú and Avenida 9 de Julio (© **2901/424729**), open Monday through Saturday from 9am to 6pm.

American Express travel and credit card services are provided by **All Patagonia,** Juana Fadul 48 (© **2901/433622**).

WHAT TO SEE & DO IN & AROUND TOWN

An in-town walk can be taken to the city park and **Punto Panorámico,** which takes visitors up to a lookout point with good views of the city and the channel. It can be reached at the southwest terminus of Avenida del Libertador and is free.

Glacier Martial/Aerosilla ⭐, Av. Luis Fernando Martial, is 7km (4¼ miles) from town. This is where you'll find a chairlift ($8/£4) that takes visitors to the small Glacier Martial. It's a long walk up the road, and no buses can take you there. Visitors usually hire a taxi for $6 (£3) and walk all the way back down. At the base of the chairlift, don't miss a stop at **La Cabaña** ⭐ (© 2901/424257), an excellent tea house.

Back in town the **Museo del Fin de Mundo,** Maipú 175 (© 2901/421863), has an assortment of Indian hunting tools and colonial maritime instruments as well as a natural history display of stuffed birds. There is also an excellent bookstore. Admission is $3 (£1.50) and it is open every day from 10am to 1pm and 3 to 7:30pm.

Museo Marítimo y Presidio de Ushuaia, Yaganes and Gobernador Paz (© 2901/437481), is sort of Ushuaia's Alcatraz, offering a fascinating look into prisoners and prison workers' lives during that time (early 20th century) through interpretive displays and artifacts, including the wool, striped prison uniforms that the prisoners were forced to wear. Admission is $3 (£1.50) and it is open every day from 9am to 8pm.

Outdoor Activities

BOATING   The best way to explore the Beagle channel is by boat, and numerous companies offer a variety of trips, usually in modern catamarans with excellent guides. Most companies visit the teeming penguin colony and pull the boats up to the shore where you can get very close and watch these marvelous animals. The most popular excursion is a half-day trip cruising the Beagle Channel to view sea lions, penguins, and more. You'll find a cluster of kiosks near the pier offering a variety of excursions. **Motonave Barracuda** (© 2901/437066) leaves twice daily for its 3-hour trip around the channel for $30 (£15) per person, visiting Isla de Lobos, Isla de Pájaros, and a lighthouse. **Motovelero Tres Marías,** (© 2901/436416) also leaves twice daily and sails to the same location. Cost is $75 (£38). **Pira Tur,** B. Yaganes Casa 127 (© 2901/15604646), offers walking tours onto the colony with controlled groups. **Motovelero Patagonia Adventure** (© 2901/15465842) has an 18-passenger maximum for its daily tours. **Ushuaia Boating,** Gob. Godoy 190 (© 2901/436193; www.ushuaia boating.com.ar), operates a small, speedy ferry service to Chilean Puerto Williams. It costs $350 (£175) round-trip.

FISHING   For a fishing license and information, go the **Club de Pesca y Caza** at Av. del Libertador 818 (no phone). The cost is about $10 (£5) per day for foreigners.

SKIING   Ushuaia's ski resort, **Cerro Castor** (© 2901/499302; www.cerrocastor. com), is surprisingly good, with more than 400 skiable hectares (988 acres), 15 runs, three quad chairs and one double, a lodge/restaurant, and a slope-side bar. The resort is open from June 15 to October 15. To get there, take the shuttle buses **Pasarela** (© 2901/433712) or **Bella Vista** (© 2901/443161); the fare is $9 (£4.50).

Tour Operators

All Patagonia Viajes y Turismo, Juana Fadul 48 (© 2901/433622; allpatagonia@all patagonia.com), is the local American Express travel representative and certainly one of the better agencies in town. It acts as a clearinghouse for everything. All Patagonia offers three glacier walks for those in physically good shape and impressive scenic flights over Tierra del Fuego ($70/£35) per person for 30 min.). They also arrange a bus and boat trip to Harberton and the penguin colony ($75/£38 per person), and they are one of the few agencies to operate afternoon tours of the National Park. **Canal Fun & Nature,** Rivadavia 82 (© **2901/437395;** www.canalfun.com), specializes in "unconventional tourism" and is a great company to choose if you want some hair-raising adventure. The company does 4×4 trips, kayaking, and nighttime beaver-watching, and they'll custom-build a trip for you.

PARQUE NACIONAL TIERRA DEL FUEGO ₲

Parque Nacional Tierra del Fuego was created in 1960 to protect a 63,000-hectare (155,610-acre) chunk of wilderness that includes mighty peaks, crystalline rivers, black-water swamps, and forests of *lenga,* or deciduous beech. Only 2,000 hectares (4,940 acres) are designated as recreation areas, part of which offer a chance to view the prolific dam building carried out by beavers introduced to Tierra del Fuego in the 1950s with disastrous consequences. Another surprising feature of the park is its rampant rabbit population. Chances are this park won't blow you away. Much of the landscape is identical to the thousands of kilometers of mountainous terrain in Patagonia, and there really isn't any special "thing" to see. Instead, it offers easy and medium day hikes, fresh air, boat rides, and bird-watching. Anglers can fish for trout in the park, but must first pick up a license at the **National Park Administration** office at Av. del Libertador 1395 (© **2901/421395;** Mon–Fri 9am–3pm), in Ushuaia. The Park Service issues maps at the park entrance showing the walking trails here, ranging from 300m (980 ft.) to 8km (5 miles); admission into the park is $5 (£2.50). Parque Nacional Tierra del Fuego is located 11km (7 miles) west of Ushuaia on Ruta Nacional 3. Camping in the park is free, and although there are no services, potable water is available. At the end of the road to Lago Roca, there is a snack bar/restaurant. All tour companies offer guided trips to the park, but if you just need transportation there, call these shuttle bus companies: **Pasarela** (© **2901/433712**) or **Bella Vista** (© **2901/443161**).

WHERE TO STAY

Accommodations are not cheap in Ushuaia, and quality is often not on a par with price. For all hotels, parking is free or street parking is plentiful.

Expensive

Cumbres del Martial ₲₲ *Finds* Cumbres del Martial must be the most romantic and charming hotel in Ushuaia. Situated at the entrance to the Martial Glaciar, the complex of pristine, immaculate wood cabins form a leafy view of the bay with the relaxing tinkle of a mountain stream in the background. Long, white Georgian windows illuminate spacious, well-upholstered luxury rooms. There are two larger cabins with chunky, log walls, stone floors and large Jacuzzis; but if you want charm and character and utter indulgence, I highly recommend the smaller cabins. This place is perfect for honeymooners, old romantics, and armchair tourists.

Luis Fernando 3560, Ushuaia. © 2901/424779. www.cumbresdelmartial.com.ar. 7 units. $170 (£85) double. Large cabins $280 (£140). AE, MC, V. **Amenities:** Teahouse; bar; spa. *In room:* TV.

Las Hayas Resort Hotel ₲₲ *Finds* Ushuaia's best hotel is located on the road to Glacier Martial, and sits nestled in a forest of beech, a location that gives sweeping views of the town and the Beagle Channel. The sumptuous lounge stretches the length of the building; here you'll find a clubby bar, formal restaurant, and fireside sitting area. The rooms are decorated with rich tapestries, upholstered walls, and bathrooms that are big and bright. The ultracomfortable beds with thick linens invite a good night's sleep. The hotel's gourmet restaurant is one of the best in Ushuaia.

Av. Luis Fernando Martial 1650, Ushuaia. (C) **2901/430710.** Fax 2901/430719. www.lashayas.com.ar. 93 units. $210–$250 (£110–£125) double; $275–$330 (£138–£165) junior suite; $290–$330 (£145–£165) junior suite superior; $360–$480 (£180–£240) deluxe suite. Rates include buffet breakfast. AE, DC, MC, V. **Amenities:** 2 restaurants; bar; lounge; indoor pool; exercise room; Jacuzzi; sauna; concierge; room service; massage; laundry service; dry cleaning. In room: TV, hair dryer, safe.

Tierra de Leyendas 😿😿   This delightful establishment has quickly gained a reputation as one of the best boutique hotels in Argentina, if not South America. A wooden mansion glows with warm, welcoming colors. The entire bottom floor is an open plan and is composed of a lounge room, restaurant, and reception area with huge windows overlooking the bay. A rust-colored sofa contrasts nicely with olive-green walls and a corn-yellow staircase. The five rooms are all named after a local fable. Ask for the *Los Yamanas* with its stunning view and incredibly relaxing, giant hot tub. The small restaurant is open to the public Monday to Saturday so if you do decide to stay elsewhere, take advantage and book a table. The hotel is located in the outskirts of the city in an upscale residential zone of rolling hills and huge mansions known as Río Pipo.

Calle Sin Nombre 2387, Ushuaia. (C) **2901/443565.** www.tierradeleyendas.com. 5 units. $130 (£65) double. AE, MC, V. **Amenities:** Restaurant; bar; room service. In room: TV/DVD, Jacuzzi.

Moderate

Hostal del Bosque Apart Hotel, Magallanes 709, ((C)/fax **2901/430777;** www.hostal delbosque.com.ar), gives guests a huge amount of space, including a separate living/dining area and a small kitchenette. The 40 guest rooms are spread out, much like a condominium complex. The exteriors and the decor are pretty bland, but very clean. Prices start at $120 (£60). **Hotel Lennox,** San Martín 776 ((C)/fax **2901/436430;** www.lennoxhotel.com), must be the hippest hotel in town, exuding style and modernity. In the lobby, modish sofas look out onto busy San Martín. The rooms are small but adequate and some of the sparkling bathrooms have a Jacuzzi. Be sure to ask for a room at the back facing the bay. Doubles start at $80 (£40). **Macondo,** Gobernador Paz 1410, ((C)/fax **2901/437576;** www.macondohouse.com), is a green-roofed boutique hotel with a young, bohemian feel, mixed with style and elegance. The common room is surrounded by wall-to-wall Georgian windows, a black stone floor, and colorful, cubed armchairs. The spacious bedrooms have a loft-house ambience with red roof beams and rafters. The seven rooms start at $102 (£51).

Inexpensive

Hostal Yaktemi, San Martín 626 ((C) **2901/437437;** www.yaktemihostal.com.ar), is a decent budget option, though lacking charm and character. Situated above some stores on San Martín, the hotel's wooden staircase leads to fair size rooms with basic furnishings. The toilets are adequate with shower and curtain rail. Centrally heated, the 13 rooms can get a little too warm and the bathrooms can be oppressively hot. Prices start at $70 (£35) for a double. **Galeazzi–Basily B&B,** Valdez 323, ((C) **2901/ 423213;** www.avesdelsur.com.ar.com), offers lodging in a family home and some well appointed cabins out back. The house rooms are small and basic and a little gloomy; the cabins are much more spacious with lots more light. The Galeazzi–Basily family all speak perfect English and are very engaging and helpful. The kitchen is accessible as is the living room sofa and TV and there is free Internet. Doubles start at $37 (£19).

WHERE TO DINE

A dozen *confiterías* and cafes can be found on Avenida del Libertador between Godoy and Rosas, all of which offer inexpensive sandwiches and quick meals of varying quality. Two of the best restaurants in town are at Las Hayas Resort Hotel and the Tierra de Leyendas lodge, mentioned above.

Chez Manu 𝄇 *(Finds)* SEAFOOD/FRENCH Chez Manu offers French-style cooking that uses fresh local ingredients. Dishes include black hake cooked with anise and herbs, or Fueguian lamb. Before taking your order, the owner/chef will describe the catch of the day, usually a cold-water fish from the bay such as Abejado or a Merlooza from Chile. The side dishes include a delicious eggplant ratatouille, made with extra-virgin olive oil and herbs of Provence.

Av. Luis Fernando Martial 2135. ℂ 2970/432253. Main courses $12–$18 (£6–£9). AE, MC, V. Daily noon–3pm and 8pm–midnight.

El Almacén de Ramos General COFFEEHOUSE This recently renovated, 100-year-old general store has an appealing, relaxing ambience. The principal room is large and atmospheric with shelves on either side and a long, low shop counter. What you find is a classic small-town emporium with old toys, fabrics, tools, and clothes all displayed from floor to ceiling. Situated in front of the port, the restaurant's menu offers cheese platters and generous king crab salads. Recommended is a very strong-smelling toasted brie sandwich. El Almacén makes for the perfect midmorning coffee stop while you tramp the wet streets of Ushuaia.

Maipú 749. ℂ 2901/424317. Main courses $9–$18 (£4.50–£9). AE, MC, V. Daily 9:30–12:30am.

Gustino 𝄇𝄇 *(Finds)* SEAFOOD/ARGENTINE Situated in the Albatros Hotel, this attractive, modern restaurant has all-glass walls overlooking the bay. The furnishings are clean cut and simple, with soft orange undertones and the occasional wood panel wall or rock pillar. The menu includes homemade lamb pâté and local lamb marinated in Syrah wine. The steaming starter of mussels is so tasty you want to chew on the shells. The highlight of the menu is lasagna made from pastry layers and smoked salmon. The salmon dish itself comes in a huge slab the size of a sirloin steak. The restaurant—open all day, every day—is also a good place to stop for a casual coffee or milkshake.

Maipú 505. ℂ 2901/430003. Main courses $14–$22 (£7–£11). AE, MC, V. Daily 8am–midnight.

Kapué Restaurant 𝄇 ARGENTINE Kapué is owned and operated by the friendly, gracious Vivian family. The menu is brief, but the offerings are delicious. Don't start your meal without ordering a sumptuous appetizer of king crab wrapped in a crepe and bathed in saffron sauce. Main courses include seafood, beef, and chicken; sample items include tenderloin beef in a plum sauce or a subtly flavored sea bass steamed in parchment paper.

Roca 470. ℂ 02901/422704. Reservations recommended on weekends. Main courses $12–$18 (£6–£9). AE, MC, V. Nov 15–Apr 15 daily noon–2pm and 6–11pm; rest of the year dinner only 7–11pm.

USHUAIA AFTER DARK

Nocturnal activities are somewhat sedate in this city. That is not to say it is completely dead, however, and some good bars can help you wash down that king crab dinner with some locally brewed beer. Two to try are **Dreamland,** 9 de Julio and Deloqui (ℂ **2901/421246**), and **Dublin Irish Pub,** 9 de Julio 168 (ℂ **2901/430744**). For something different, try **Kuar,** Ave. Perito Moreno 2232 (© **2901/437396**). With its cushioned mini-amphitheater facing a giant, shoreline view of the bay, Kuar is certainly the most avant-garde of Ushuaia's nightspots. The bar brews its own beer and the fermenting tanks can be spied through a glass panel beneath the dining room. It is located 2km (1¼ miles) east of the city center and opens Tuesday through Sunday from 5pm to 2am. **Saint Christopher,** Maipú 822 (© **2901/422423**), is a little more down-market and has a worn, roadhouse feel. Yet this is the place to come for a late-night drink and dance and it has a great central location right on the bay. There is usually a live band playing at weekends and it is full of young Argentines looking to live it up and sing along to some popular *rock nacional.*

5

Bolivia

by Charlie O'Malley

Bolivia will take your breath away—and not just because of its bracing altitude. It may have the highest capital city in the world, and the highest lake, but what really makes it so fascinating are the incredible range of habitats and the rich indigenous culture.

Bolivia is a vast, landlocked plateau of barren plains, lush jungle, and fertile highland valleys. It has the largest salt flats in the world, where the earth mirrors the sky and flamingos drink from crimson lakes. Elsewhere, daredevil roads and dinosaur footprints lead to gilded colonial cities and windswept mining towns. Here dynamite and coca leaf are sold, and you can trace the final, tragic steps of Che Guevara. You

can visit the birthplace of the Inca gods, dance with carnival devils, fish for piranha, or swim with jungle dolphins.

Bolivia's population is a teeming mass in petticoats and ponchos and jaunty bowler hats. Their country is the poorest in South America yet the richest in natural wealth. Their politics and history are tumultuous and tragic, but their culture has changed little in centuries. One might say that Bolivia is the most Andean of the Andean countries, the most South American in all of South America. *Tip:* For a map of suggested itineraries in Bolivia, please refer to the "Itineraries in Bolivia, Brazil, Colombia, Ecuador & Peru" map on p. 222.

1 The Regions in Brief

Bolivia sits practically in the middle of South America, sharing its borders with Peru, Chile, Argentina, Paraguay, and Brazil. Landlocked since losing access to a seacoast during the Pacific War (1879–84), Bolivia still maintains a navy to protect the sacred Lake Titicaca, which it shares with Peru. Much of Bolivia is defined by the Andes Mountains. The range is at its widest in Bolivia and consists of two parallel chains here, separated by the Altiplano (high plain), the most densely populated area of the country. As you move farther east, the Andes give way to the jungle and tropical landscapes.

Because Bolivia is so vast, it's difficult to get a good feeling for the country if you have only 1 week to spend here. But you will have enough time to see all the highlights of La Paz, take a day trip to Tiwanaku, visit Lake Titicaca, and view Inca ruins on Isla del Sol (Island of the Sun) and in Copacabana. If you have 2 weeks, you can also explore Sucre, tour the mines at Potosí, and relax in Santa Cruz. The more physically adventurous traveler might consider sea kayaking on Lake Titicaca, climbing Huayna Potosí, trekking around the Illampu circuit, or taking a 4-day journey through the salt flats and desert near Salar de Uyuni.

LA PAZ La Paz is the administrative capital of Bolivia. From here, you can easily travel to **Lake Titicaca,** which is considered to be the birthplace of the Incas. The impressive pre-Inca archaeological site, **Tiwanaku,** is also only 2 hours away. Drive 3 hours to the east, and you will descend into the tropical area known as **Los Yungas.**

SOUTHERN ALTIPLANO   This area made its mark on the world in the 16th, 17th, and 18th centuries, when **Potosí** was one of the great silver mining centers and consequently one of the wealthiest cities in the world. Today, highlights of the region include Potosí and **Sucre,** both of which are historical gems.

CENTRAL BOLIVIA   The area of central Bolivia extends from the pleasant town of **Cochabamba,** at the foothills of the Andes, all the way east to **Santa Cruz.** Cochabamba is one of the commercial centers of Bolivia, with several major industry headquarters here, including chicken farms, airlines, and shoe companies. Some of the most colorful markets in Bolivia take place in the rural areas outside the city. The dusty city of Santa Cruz is a good base to explore Amboró National Park, the Inca Ruins of Samaipata, Jesuit missions, and the town where Che Guevara made his last stand.

2 Best of Bolivia in 2 Weeks

Vertigo and claustrophobia are unwelcome conditions in a country where altitude is measured in gasps of air and your bus seat might be a stranger's lap. Fear of flying will disappear once you experience the kamikaze road network of potholes and deep ravines. Indeed, it's best to fly to get the most from your time here, but make sure you always reconfirm your confirmation.

Days ❶–❷: Arrive in La Paz 🕊
Soak up the atmosphere (and frequent rain showers) of a bustling market city lost in time. Mingle with the throngs of Indians in bowler hats and petticoats as you browse for something exotic at the witch doctors' market. Next, stop off at the Museo de la Coca and chew the infamous cud. Stay at the well-located **El Rey Palace Hotel** (p. 189), but dine at the Hotel Presidente; its restaurant, La Bella Vista, has a bird's-eye view of this chaotic city. The next day explore the historical Plaza Murillo and the fascinating textile exhibit at the **Museo Nacional de Etnografía y Folklore** (p. 184). Catch some live music and dance at a *peña* such as **Casa de Corregidor** (the House of Corrections; p. 191).

Day ❸: A Daredevil Mountain Ride 🕊🕊🕊
Bike down the most dangerous road in the world from La Paz to Coroico, or if that's too dramatic, just watch the beautiful scenery from the security of a tour bus (not much safer, in fact).

Day ❹: Tiwanaku
This pre-Inca city of monoliths and underground temples is a day trip from La Paz and well worth the journey.

Day ❺: Copacabana and Lake Titicaca
Take a taxi to the highest navigable lake in the world. Relax on Bolivia's only beach before visiting Copacabana Cathedral. Here you can see a colorful procession of new cars, trucks, and buses getting blessed with beer and holy water (Sat–Sun only). Lunch on fresh trout at La Orilla before taking a gentle hike to the Inca ruins of Asiento del Inca. Relax in a hammock at the artfully laid-back Hostal la Cupola.

Days ❻–❼: Empire of the Sun 🕊🕊🕊
Catch a ferry to Isla del Sol, the dazzling birthplace of the Inca gods, and stay 2 nights at Posada del Inca. Dip into the gentle rhythm of island life, exploring the many ruins and enjoying the spectacular sunsets.

Days ❽–❿: Cochabamba

Drag yourself from your island hideaway and take a taxi back to La Paz, where you can catch a plane to Cochabamba. Stay at the lovely **Hacienda de Kaluyo** (p. 212). When you tire of enjoying this splendid resort, take a taxi to see the biggest Jesus in the world, followed by a tour of a tin magnate's palace, Palacio Portales.

Days ⓫–⓭: Santa Cruz de la Sierra

Leave the Andes behind and descend into Bolivia's brand of brash *tropicalismo*. Stay

at the very comfortable **Hotel Los Tajibos** (p. 219), but get out and explore the city's hinterland of Inca ruins, Jesuit missions, and subtropical woodlands. Birdwatching in Amboro National Park is highly recommended.

Day ⓮: Return to La Paz

Enjoy your final day shopping for genuine handicrafts at bargain prices on Calle Sagárnaga. Have lunch at the colonialstyle **Surucachi** restaurant (p. 191) before catching a flight from La Paz airport.

3 Planning Your Trip to Bolivia

VISITOR INFORMATION

There are virtually no government-sponsored tourist offices outside Bolivia. The U.S.-based Embassy of Bolivia has a moderately useful website, **www.bolivia-usa.org**. For general travel information, you can also log onto **www.boliviaweb.com** or **www.bolivia biz.org**.

For more specific travel-related information, your best bet is to contact travel agencies that specialize in trips to Bolivia. Some of the best include:

- **Andean Summits,** Aranzaes 2974, Sopachi, La Paz (© **0102/2422-106;** fax 0102/2413-273; www.andeansummits.com). This Bolivia-based company specializes in active vacation packages, including sea-kayaking trips in Lake Titicaca and treks up Huayna Potosí.
- **Crillon Tours** ★★, 1450 S. Bayshore Dr., Suite 815, Miami, FL 33131 (© **888/ TITICACA** or 305/358-5353; www.titicaca.com). Based in Miami, this company has a huge infrastructure in Bolivia and is the owner of several fantastic hotels in the Lake Titicaca area.
- **Explore Bolivia, Inc.,** 2510 N. 47th St., Suite 207, Boulder, CO 80301 (© **877/ 708-8810** or 303/545-5728; www.explorebolivia.com). Specialists in kayaking, trekking, and mountain-climbing packages.
- **Rutahsa Adventures** (© **931/520-7047;** www.rutahsa.com) offers a 19-day journey that really takes you off the standard tourist trail, starting in Santa Cruz and including stops in Sucre, Potosí, La Paz, Copacabana, and Lake Titicaca, in addition to other towns. Prices start at $2,526 per person (£1,280).

IN BOLIVIA

Although the **Viceministerio de Turismo** has an office in La Paz (© **02/2358-213**), the staff doesn't speak English, and the only resources on hand are some promotional brochures. You're much better off heading to the visitor information office on Plaza del Estudiante, where you can buy regional maps; see "Visitor Information" in "La Paz," later in this chapter.

ENTRY REQUIREMENTS

A valid passport is required to enter and depart Bolivia. In 2007, the Bolivian government announced that all U.S. citizens are required to have a visa to enter the country.

Telephone Dialing Info at a Glance

- **To place a call from your home country to Bolivia,** dial the international access code (011 in the U.S. and Canada, 0011 in Australia, 0170 in New Zealand, 00 in the U.K.) plus the country code (591), plus the Bolivian area code minus the 010 (for example, La Paz 2, Santa Cruz 3, Cochabamba 4, Sucre 464, Potosí 262, Copacabana 2862), followed by the number. For example, a call from the United States to La Paz would be 011+591+2+0000+000.
- **To place a call within Bolivia,** you must use area codes if you're calling from one department (administrative district) to another. Note that for all calls within the country, area codes are preceded by 010 (for example, La Paz 0102, Santa Cruz 0103, Cochabamba 0104, Sucre 010464, Potosí 010262, Copacabana 0102862).
- **To place a direct international call from Bolivia,** dial the international access code (00), plus the country code of the place you are dialing, plus the area code and the local number.
- **To reach an international long-distance operator,** dial ℭ 35-67-00. Major long-distance company access codes are as follows: **AT&T** ℭ 0800-1111; **Bell Canada** ℭ 0800-0101; **British Telecom** ℭ 0800-0044; **MCI** ℭ 0800-2222; **Sprint** ℭ 0800-3333.

This must be applied for, before your journey, at the nearest Bolivian consulate. Visas are not required for stays of up to 30 days if you're a citizen of one of 44 designated countries, which include the United Kingdom, Canada, Australia, New Zealand, South Africa, France, Germany, and Switzerland. (Visit **www.bolivia-usa.org**, or check with your local embassy to determine whether you'll need a visa.) It's very easy to extend the tourist card for an additional 60 days by requesting one at an Oficina de Migración (Immigration Office). In La Paz, the office is located at Camacho 1433. It's open Monday through Friday from 9am to 12:30pm and 3 to 6pm; it's best to go late in the afternoon. For more information, call ℭ **0800/10-3007.**

BOLIVIAN EMBASSY & CONSULATE LOCATIONS

In the U.S.: 3014 Massachusetts Ave. NW, Washington, DC 20008 (ℭ **202/483-4410;** fax 202/328-3712; www.bolivia-usa.org)

In Canada: 130 Albert St., Suite 416, Ottawa, ON K1P 5G4 (ℭ **613/236-5730;** fax 613/236-8237)

In the U.K.: 106 Eaton Square, London SW1W 9AD (ℭ **020/7235-4248** or 020/7235-2257; fax 020/7235-1286; embolivia-londres@rree.gov.bo)

In Australia: The Consulate of the Republic of Bolivia is located at 74 Pitt St, Level 6, Sydney NSW 2000 (ℭ **02/9235-1858**)

CUSTOMS

Visitors to Bolivia are legally permitted to bring in up to $2,000 (£1,000) worth of items for personal use. If you bring in any new consumer goods with a value of more than $1,000 (£500), you must declare it at Customs.

There are very strict laws regarding removing national treasures. ***Beware:*** The Customs officials at the airports do search every person (for both drugs and national treasures) leaving the country.

MONEY

The Bolivian unit of currency is the **boliviano (Bs).** Besides coins with values of 1 and 2 bolivianos, all the currency is paper, in denominations of 2, 5, 10, 20, 50, and 100. It's very hard to make change, especially for a Bs100 note. If you are retrieving money from an ATM, be sure to request a denomination ending in 50. Restaurants seem to be the only places in the country capable of changing large bills.

Here's a general idea of what things cost in La Paz: A taxi within the center of town, Bs8 ($1/50p); a double room at a budget hotel with private bathroom, $15 to $30 (£7.50–£15); a double room at a moderate hotel with private bathroom, $40 to $65 (£20–£33); a double room at an expensive hotel, $100 to $200 (£50–£ 100); fresh juice on the street, Bs3 (38¢/19p); a 36-exposure roll of film, Bs30 ($3.70/£1.85); a three-course lunch for one at a cafe, Bs15 ($1.80/90p); a three-course dinner for one, Bs50 to Bs70 ($6.30–$8.80/£3.15–£4.40).

CURRENCY EXCHANGE & RATES   At press time, the boliviano was trading at a rate of **Bs7.94 to $1 (50p).** The boliviano has been relatively stable for the past few years. You should note, however, that Bolivia is the poorest country in South America, and it's hard to predict what will happen in the future.

When exchanging foreign currency in Bolivia, it's best to head to a *casa de cambio* (money-exchange house). Some banks will exchange American dollars and British pounds, but the lines are often long and the process can be chaotic. *Note:* U.S. dollars are widely accepted throughout Bolivia, especially at hotels and restaurants. **All hotel rates in this chapter, as well as some tours and airline fares, are quoted in U.S. dollars.**

ATMs   ATMs are ubiquitous in Bolivia, except in small towns such as Coroico, Sorata, and Copacabana. Major banks include **Banco Santa Cruz** and **Banco de Crédito;** there are **Citibank** branches in both La Paz and Santa Cruz. Most ATMs accept cards on the **Cirrus** (*©* **800/424-7787**) and **PLUS** (*©* **800/843-7587**) networks; however, they can't deal with PINs that are more than four digits. Before you go to Bolivia, make sure that your PIN fits the bill.

TRAVELER'S CHECKS   Citibank will exchange its own traveler's checks. But you can't change American Express traveler's checks at the American Express offices in Bolivia (sounds strange, but it's true). If you're traveling with traveler's checks, your best bet is to cash them at a *casa de cambio.* Most upscale hotels and restaurants in Bolivia will accept traveler's checks. For lost American Express traveler's checks, you must call collect to the United States at *©* **801/964-6665.**

CREDIT CARDS   MasterCard and Visa are accepted most everywhere in Bolivia. American Express is less common, but it's still widely accepted. To report a lost or stolen **MasterCard,** call *©* **0800-0172;** for **Visa,** call *©* **0800-0188;** for **American Express,** call *©* **800/327-1267** (via an AT&T operator).

WHEN TO GO

PEAK SEASON & CLIMATE   The peak season for travelers in Bolivia is mid-June through early September, but this is only because most travelers come here when it's summer in the Northern Hemisphere. Ironically, this is the coldest time of year in Bolivia. Fortunately, it's also the dry season.

In the high plateau areas of Bolivia—La Paz, Lake Titicaca, and Potosí—it's generally always cold. The weather is only mildly more pleasant in the off season. La Paz has an average daytime high of 57°F (14°C) and an average nighttime low of 34°F (1°C). Santa Cruz has a tropical climate, although it can get chilly from June through September. Cochabamba has a pleasant springlike climate year-round.

PUBLIC HOLIDAYS Each city in Bolivia celebrates its own independence day, which always seems to correspond with a local festival. La Paz's independence day is July 16. The entire world seems to converge on Sucre on August 6, Bolivia's official independence day. In small towns throughout the country, you'll find colorful indigenous festivals on or near the summer solstice (June 21). National holidays include: New Year's Day (Jan 1), Carnaval (dates vary), Good Friday, Labor Day (May 1), Corpus Christi (dates vary; usually in mid-June), Independence Day (Aug 6), All Saints' Day (Nov 1), and Christmas (Dec 25).

HEALTH CONCERNS

COMMON AILMENTS Travelers to Bolivia should be very careful about contracting **food-borne illnesses.** Always drink bottled water. Never drink beverages with ice, unless you are sure that the water for the ice has been previously boiled. Be very careful about eating food purchased from street vendors. I recommend taking a vitamin such as super bromelain, which helps aid in the digestion of parasites.

Because most of the popular tourist attractions in Bolivia are at an altitude of more than 2,500m (8,200 ft.), **altitude sickness** can be a serious problem. Common symptoms include headaches, nausea, sleeplessness, and a tendency to tire easily. The most common remedies include rest, abstaining from alcohol, drinking lots of bottled water, chewing coca leaves, or drinking coca tea. Coca leaves are readily available at street markets, and most restaurants offer some form of coca tea. To help alleviate the symptoms, you can also take the drug acetazolamide (Diamox); it's available by prescription only in the United States.

The **sun** can also be very dangerous in Bolivia, especially at high altitudes. Bring plenty of high-powered sunblock and a wide-brimmed hat. It gets very cold in cities such as La Paz and Potosí, but don't let this fool you into complacency—even when it's cold, the sun can inflict serious damage on your skin.

In general, the healthcare system in Bolivia is good enough to take care of mild illnesses. For a list of hospitals in La Paz, see "Hospitals" in "Fast Facts: Bolivia," below.

VACCINATIONS No vaccines are required, unless you're planning to visit the difficult-to-reach Pantanal in the far eastern end of Bolivia, in which case you'll need a yellow fever vaccination certificate. Additionally, the Centers for Disease Control and Prevention (CDC) recommend that visitors to Bolivia vaccinate themselves against hepatitis A. Fortunately, since mosquitoes can't live in high altitudes, malaria is not a risk in the high plateau region of Bolivia, but there have been cases reported in rural parts of the Beni area and Santa Cruz.

GETTING THERE
BY PLANE

At 3,900m (just under 13,000 ft.), La Paz's **El Alto Airport** (© **0102/2810-122**) is one of the highest commercial airports in the world. Large planes, such as 747s, cannot land at such a high altitude; even smaller planes have to make sure that they have a light load before touching down. For this reason, very few international flights fly directly into La Paz and instead land in Santa Cruz. All international passengers leaving by air from Bolivia must pay a $20 (£10) departure tax.

FROM NORTH AMERICA   American Airlines (© 800/100-229; 0102/2372010; www.aa.com) offers nonstop flights from the United States (via Miami) to La Paz. **Aerosur** (© 0102/2817-281; www.aerosur.com) offers nonstop flights from Miami to Santa Cruz, with connecting flights to La Paz. **Grupo Taca** (© 800/535-8780; www.grupotaca.com), which is a consortium of several South American carriers, offers flights from New York to La Paz, but you have to change planes both in San José, Costa Rica, and Lima, Peru. Currently, there are no direct flights from Canada to Bolivia. Canadian travelers must catch a connecting flight in Miami.

FROM THE U.K.   There are no direct flights from the United Kingdom to Bolivia. One good option is connect with **Aerosur** (© 0102/2817-881; www.aerosur.com) in Madrid and fly directly to Santa Cruz. You can fly **American Airlines** (© 020/8572-5555 in London, or 0102/2872-010 in La Paz; www.aa.com) direct from London to Miami, and then from Miami nonstop to La Paz. Alternatively, **Varig Airlines** (www.varig.com.br) offers direct flights from London to São Paulo, Brazil; from there, Varig offers a daily flight to Santa Cruz, continuing on to La Paz.

FROM AUSTRALIA   Get ready for a long, long flight. The easiest way to get to Bolivia from Australia is to hop on an **Aerolíneas Argentinas** (© 800/222-215; www.aerolineas.com.ar) flight from Sydney to Buenos Aires. From there, Aerolíneas Argentinas offers daily flights to Santa Cruz. Another route includes flying from Australia to Los Angeles to Miami and then on to La Paz. **Qantas** (© 13-13-13; www.qantas.com.au) offers flights from Australia to Los Angeles—but from there, you must switch to American Airlines to Miami and then Bolivia.

BY BUS

It is possible to travel by bus to Bolivia from Peru, Argentina, and Brazil. Usually, the bus routes end at the border, and you'll have to cross on your own and pick up another bus once you arrive in Bolivia. The most popular international route is from Puno, Peru, to Copacabana or La Paz. **Nuevo Continente,** Calle Sagárnaga 340 (between Illampu and Linares), La Paz (© 0102/2373-423), can arrange trips from both La Paz and Copacabana to Puno and beyond.

GETTING AROUND

Getting around Bolivia is often unpleasant. Only about 5% of all the roads in the country are paved. Flying is a much better option, though expect delays and always reconfirm your reservations.

BY PLANE

Traveling by plane is my preferred method of travel in Bolivia. Flights aren't too expensive ($55–$100/£28–£50) and tickets can be bought at short notice with no rise in price. Because the roads are so bad in Bolivia, it's really worthwhile to spend the extra money to fly. Additionally, if you take a plane instead of a bus, you will save at least 12 hours in travel time. Air travel has improved immensely, but it is imperative that you reconfirm your flight, or you might miss it (and the next departing flight might not leave for another 27 hr.!). After check-in make sure you pay the airport tax, known as *tasa*. Also, always hold onto your boarding card to prove luggage ownership at the other end.

Aero Sur, Av. 16 de Julio 1616, La Paz (© **0102/2312-244;** www.aerosur.com), is the largest airline in Bolivia (**LAB** disappeared after a drawn-out pilot strike in 2006). They now have a new fleet of planes and routes to every major city. I must warn you that these flights are not for the faint of heart. Delays are common and landings are harrowing as the thin air and short runways usually dictate a fast approach.

BY BUS

Traveling by bus in Bolivia has its charms, including economical bus fares and riding with the "real" Bolivians. (You may even have the opportunity to sit next to live chickens.) But overall, buses are horribly slow and uncomfortable and have a terrible safety record. Most buses don't have bathrooms, and bus drivers don't like to stop along their route—some 12-hour bus rides will only make two (!) bathroom stops during the entire journey. Buses are often crowded because most drivers will pick up anyone who needs a ride, regardless of how much space is left on the bus. Passengers sit on the floor, and then more passengers sit on their laps. Also, beware of strapping your bags to the top of buses since you might lose them along the way. Keep in mind, too, that 95% of the roads in Bolivia are unpaved, which means that 160km (100-mile) journeys can take more than 12 hours.

Overall, if you have a lot of time and not much money, the buses in Bolivia are perfectly adequate. If you're traveling on an overnight bus, I highly recommend splurging for the *bus cama* (buses where the seats recline enough to almost resemble a bed). *Bus camas* usually only cost Bs16 to Bs24 ($2–$3/£1–£1.50) more than the regular bus. Most bus companies offer very similar services. One of the most reputable companies is **Flota Copacabana** (© **0102/2281-596**). Note that in the rainy season from October through April, some roads may become impassable. Always have loose change to tip the baggage handler if storing your baggage below. With the better companies, you will receive a security ticket to retrieve your luggage later. It is always wise to sit on the right of the bus to keep an eye on luggage as people board and alight during the journey. Be prepared to pay a small bus terminal tax as you board.

BY CAR

In Bolivia, there are 49,311km (30,573 miles) of highway. Guess how many of those are paved? About 2,496km (1,548 miles). That's it. For the other 46,815km (29,025 miles), you're stuck on some of the bumpiest and most poorly maintained roads in the world. Additionally, there are no signs anywhere, so it's quite easy to get lost. If you decide to be adventurous and explore Bolivia by car, be sure to rent a 4×4. You'll definitely need it, especially in the rainy season (Oct–Apr), when most of the roads turn to mud.

Localiza Rent A Car (© 0800/2050; www.localiza.com) is one of the largest car-rental companies in the country. **International Rent A Car** has offices in La Paz (© 0107/1530-432), on Calle Federico Zuazo 1942, in Cochabamba (© 0107/1720-091), and in Santa Cruz (© 0103/3344-425). **Hertz** has offices in La Paz (© 0102/2772-929), Santa Cruz (© 0103/3336-010), and Cochabamba (© 0104/4450-081). The rate for 4×4 vehicles ranges from Bs350 to Bs650 ($45–$82/£23–£41) per day, including insurance. To rent a car in Bolivia, you must be at least 21 and have a valid driver's license and a passport.

TIPS ON ACCOMMODATIONS

Accommodations in Bolivia run the gamut in quality and expense. There are no world-renowned luxury hotels in Bolivia, but in both Santa Cruz and La Paz you will find some high-quality accommodations. Bolivia's specialty is historic hotels; in Sucre, you can stay in a 300-year-old mansion. Moderately priced hotels are usually spotless, with decent towels in the bathrooms. It's not uncommon to find hotels that only charge $5 (£2.50) a night—just don't expect anything other than a bed.

Most hotels, except for the very best ones, don't have heat. Some hotels have a limited number of space heaters *(estufas)*, but you must specifically request one. Otherwise, be sure to bring warm pajamas! Also note that most showers are heated by electric power. **All hotel prices are quoted in U.S. dollars.** Room availability is rarely an issue in Bolivia, except in Sucre on August 6, when rooms fill for Bolivia's independence day celebrations.

TIPS ON DINING

The food is good in Bolivia—it's just not terribly varied. The diet here is rich in meat, corn, and potatoes. For breakfast, it's common to eat *salteñas* (either chicken or beef, spiced with onions and raisins, and wrapped up in a doughy pastry shell). In most towns, you'll find vendors selling them on nearly every street corner. It's also very easy to buy freshly squeezed orange juice on the street. Most typical Bolivian restaurants offer similar menus with local specialties such as *ají de lengua* (cow's tongue in a chile sauce); *picante surtido,* which consists of *sajta* (chicken in a chile sauce) and *saice* (chopped meat in a chile sauce); and *silpancho* (a very thin breaded piece of veal with two fried eggs, onions, and tomatoes). *Chuño putti* (dehydrated potatoes mixed together with milk and cheese) is a popular side dish. Usually, these restaurants also offer more international fare such as filet mignon, pineapple chicken, pasta, and omelets. In La Paz, there are a good variety of ethnic restaurants including Japanese, Korean, French, German, and Italian. Outside La Paz, pizza and pasta are as international as it gets. To combat altitude sickness, many people drink *mate de coca,* which is tea made from coca leaves. *Tri-mate* tea, a combination of three herbal teas, is also a popular after-dinner drink. Fresh fruit is the most popular dessert. Flan (egg custard) is also available at many local restaurants.

TIPS ON SHOPPING

Handicrafts are the name of the game in Bolivia. The indigenous people have been creating beautiful hand-woven goods for thousands of years. In La Paz, Calle Sagárnaga is shopper's central. Here you'll have the opportunity to browse in thousands of stores selling handmade goods, including alpaca sweaters, hats, gloves, leather bags, and textile products. Besides handicrafts, you can also buy folksy good-luck charms, from llama fetuses to miniature homes (supposedly, if you buy something in miniature, you'll soon have the *real* thing). Local markets are also a great place to find unique gifts. The Sunday market in Tarabuco, about an hour outside Sucre, is considered one of the best in Bolivia.

Bargaining is not part of Bolivian culture—for the most part, prices are fixed. If you play your cards right, you may be able to shave a few dollars off the asking price, but in general, most salespeople won't drop their prices significantly. Fortunately, prices are already rock-bottom.

FAST FACTS: Bolivia

American Express There are two American Express travel offices in Bolivia, both run by Magri Turismo. Unfortunately, these are more travel agencies than American Express offices. Note that you can't exchange traveler's checks at either office. In La Paz, the office is located on Calle Capitán Ravelo 2101 (© **0102/2442-727**). In Santa Cruz, the office is located at the intersection of Calle Warnes and Calle Potosí (© **591/3334-5663**).

Business Hours In general, business hours are Monday through Friday from 9am to 12:30pm and from 2:30 to 6:30pm. In smaller towns, such as Sucre and Potosí, *everything* closes down from noon until 3pm. In La Paz and Santa Cruz, most banks are open from about 9am to 4pm. Some banks do close in the middle of the day, so it's best to take care of your banking needs early in the morning. Most banks, museums, and stores are open on Saturday from 10am to noon. Everything is closed on Sunday.

Drug Laws In Bolivia, it is legal to chew coca leaves and drink tea made from coca. (But note that it is illegal to bring these products into the U.S.) Cocaine, marijuana, and heroin are all highly illegal. Penalties are strongest for people caught selling drugs, but if you're caught buying or in possession, you're in for a lot of trouble.

Electricity The majority of outlets in Bolivia are 220 volts at 50 cycles. But in places such as La Paz and Potosí, it's common to see 110 volts at 50 cycles. To be on the safe side, always ask before plugging anything in.

Embassies & Consulates In La Paz: **United States,** Av. Arce 2780 (© 0102/2430-120); **Australia,** Av. Arce 2081, Edificio Montevideo (© 0102/2440-459); **Canada,** Calle Victor Sanjínez 2678, Edificio Barcelona, 2nd Floor (© 0102/2415-021); and the **United Kingdom,** Av. Arce 2708 (© 010/243-1377).

Emergencies Call © **110** for the police or © **118** for an ambulance.

Hospitals **Clínica Cemes,** Av. 6 De Agosto 2881 (© **0102/2430-360**), and **Clínica del Sur** (© **0102/278-4001** or 0102/278-4002), on Avenida Hernando Siles and the corner of Calle 7 in the Obrajes neighborhood, are the best hospitals in La Paz. These hospitals are also where you'll most likely find English-speaking doctors. For hospitals in other cities, see the "Fast Facts" for each individual city.

Internet Access Internet service is available almost everywhere in Bolivia, with the possible exception of Isla del Sol on Lake Titicaca. Connections in major cities cost Bs7 (90¢/45p) per hour. In more faraway places, such as Sorata and Copacabana, connections can cost up to Bs20 ($2.50/£1.25) an hour.

Language Spanish is the language most commonly used in business transactions. But indigenous languages, such as Quechua and Aymara, are also widely spoken throughout the country. It's best to come to Bolivia with a basic knowledge of Spanish. Outside of the most major tourist sights, it's hard to find someone who speaks English.

Liquor Laws The official drinking age in Bolivia is 18. At clubs you often need to show a picture ID for admittance.

Newspapers & Magazines La Razón (published in La Paz) is one of the most popular Spanish-language newspapers in Bolivia. El Nuevo Día (in Santa Cruz) and Los Tiempos (in Cochabamba) also provide local news for their respective regions. The Bolivian Times is a weekly English-language newspaper, available at newsstands throughout the country. If you're lucky, you may also find English copies of Time or Newsweek.

Police Throughout Bolivia, you can reach the police by dialing ✆ **110**. The tourist police can also help sort out your problems in non-emergency situations. In La Paz, call ✆ **0102/2225-016** and in Santa Cruz, ✆ **0103/3364-345**.

Post Offices/Mail Most post offices in Bolivia are open Monday through Friday from 8:30am to 8pm, Saturday from 8:30am to 6pm, and Sunday from 9am to noon. It costs Bs5 (63¢/33p) to mail a letter to the United States, Bs7 (88¢/44p) to Australia, and Bs6 (75¢/38) to Europe. From time to time, you can buy stamps at kiosks and newspaper stands. There are no public mailboxes, so you'll have to mail your letter from the post office.

Restrooms The condition of public facilities is surprisingly good in Bolivia. In museums, the toilets are relatively clean, but they never have toilet paper. Note that most buses don't have toilet facilities, and on long-distance bus rides, the driver may only stop once or twice in a 12-hour stretch. And when they do stop, the facilities are often horrendous—usually smelly, squat toilets. It's always useful to have a roll of toilet paper handy.

Safety La Paz and Santa Cruz are the most dangerous cities in Bolivia. You'll need to beware of camera snatchers and be careful in crowded areas and hold on tightly to your personal belongings. Watch out for thieves who try to stain your bags (usually with mustard or peanut butter); they offer to help clean you off while cleaning you out. Taxis in La Paz can also be dangerous; never get in an unmarked taxi. Legitimate cabs have bright signs on top that illuminate their telephone numbers. Before you get in, be sure to write down the cab's number. If ever in doubt, ask a restaurant or hotel to call you a taxi. Report all problems to the tourist police (see "Police," above.)

Telephone & Fax Most high-end hotels in La Paz, Santa Cruz, and Cochabamba offer international direct-dial and long-distance service and in-house fax transmission. But these calls tend to be quite expensive, as hotels often levy a surcharge, even if you're calling a toll-free access number.

Practically every single town in Bolivia has an **Entel** office (almost always located in the main plaza). From here, you can make local, long-distance, and international calls. It's actually much more economical to make your international calls from an Entel office than to use an international calling card. For example, for calls to the United States, AT&T, MCI, and Sprint all charge about Bs70 ($9/£4.50) for the first minute and Bs16 ($2/£1) for each additional minute, plus a 10% surcharge. Entel charges Bs5 to Bs10 (63¢–$1.25/32p–63p) per minute.

To make local calls from a public phone, you need a phone card. You can buy them at any Entel office or any kiosk on the street. The average local call costs about Bs2 (25¢/13p) for 3 minutes.

For tips on dialing, see "Telephone Dialing Info at a Glance," on p. 172.

Time Zone Bolivia is 4 hours behind GMT (Greenwich mean time), except during daylight saving time, when it is 5 hours behind.

Tipping Restaurants in Bolivia never add a service charge. It's expected that you will add a 10% to 15% gratuity to the total bill. Taxi drivers don't expect tips. It's common to tip hotel porters about Bs4 to Bs8 (50¢–$1/25p–50p) per bag.

Water Always drink bottled water in Bolivia. Most hotels provide bottled water in the bathrooms, and you can buy bottles of water on practically any street corner. Small bottles cost about Bs1 to Bs2 (13¢–25¢/7p–13p); large bottles cost just Bs3 (38¢/20p). Most restaurants use ice made from boiled water, but always ask to be sure.

4 La Paz ★★

The city of La Paz is nestled in a valley atop the Bolivian plateau, surrounded by snowy peaks and dominated by the white head of Illimani, the sacred mountain. The setting is sure to take your breath away (and if the setting doesn't, the 3,739m/12,264-ft. altitude will), but that's not what I love best about La Paz. The Paceños themselves, the city's inhabitants, are what make this place unforgettable. No other major South American city holds on to its past so firmly. Many of the women wear traditional clothing every day: colorful multilayered petticoats, fringed shawls, lace aprons, and (oddest of all) bowler hats, which look as if they came straight from a prewar London haberdashery. You'll see these women throughout the city—on the buses, in the churches, shopping, or perhaps setting up their own shops.

They probably won't be setting up shop inside, though—hardly anyone does in La Paz. The city is one giant street market. In stalls on the sidewalks or at street corners you can buy not only batteries and chewing gum, but also dice and leather dice-cups, socks, hats, sneakers, cameras, and telephones. In the Mercado Negro (Black Market) area of the city, computers, electric drills, bookcases, office supplies, and everything else you could think of are all displayed on the sidewalk. At the Mercado de los Brujos (Witch Doctors' Market), the discerning shopper can find the finest in good-luck statuettes and all the materials required for a proper offering to Pachamama, the Earth Mother, including baskets of dried llama fetuses. Perhaps *you* aren't in the market for such things, but just being in a place where people are is half the fun of La Paz.

ESSENTIALS
GETTING THERE
Getting to La Paz is not an easy feat. For information on arriving by plane or bus, see "Getting There" in "Planning Your Trip to Bolivia," earlier in this chapter.

El Alto Airport is 25 minutes from the center of La Paz. A **taxi** ride to the city center should cost about Bs50 ($6.30/£3.20). Most hotels will send a taxi to pick you up at the airport (when you arrive, a driver will be waiting for you with a welcome sign), but the taxi still costs about Bs55 ($7/£3.50). Alternatively, you can take a minibus into the center of town. **GoTransTur buses** wait outside the airport (behind the taxis) and leave every 4 minutes daily from 6:15am to 9pm. The minibuses go past Plaza San Francisco and up Avenida 16 de Julio (La Paz's main street) to Plaza Isabel La Católica. The ride costs only Bs5 (63¢/30p), but the buses usually fill up, and it's hard to squeeze into the tight seats if you have luggage.

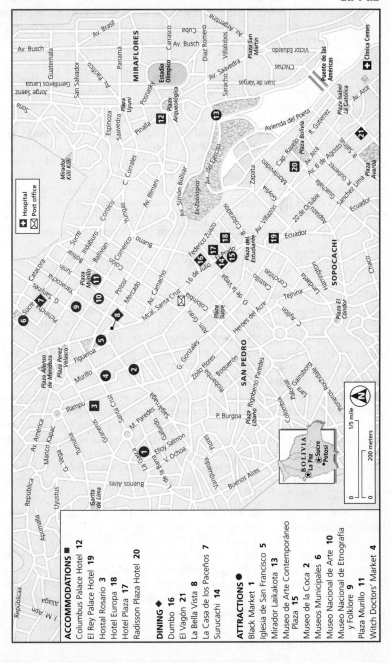

La Paz

Hospital
⊠ **Post office**

MIRAFLORES

SOPOCACHI

SAN PEDRO

0   1/5 mile
0   200 meters

BOLIVIA
★ Sucre
• Potosí
La Paz

If you're arriving by bus, the main bus terminal is located on Plaza Antofagasta at the intersection of Avenida Uruguay, a short taxi ride (about 4 min.; Bs8/$1/50p) from the heart of town. You'll easily find a taxi outside the terminal.

ORIENTATION

Historically, La Paz's main street—known interchangeably as El Prado, Avenida 16 de Julio, and Avenida Mariscal Santa Cruz—divided the city into two parts. The indigenous people lived to the south of this main area, the Spanish to the north. Before the age of cement, this main street was actually a river. It is still the lowest point of La Paz. So, if you're lost, just walk downhill and eventually you will arrive at El Prado. The old colonial divisions still linger: The Witch Doctors' Market, the Black Market, and most of the indigenous-run street stands are all still on the south side of El Prado, while the colonial buildings, main plaza, and government offices are all to the north. The area of town from Plaza San Francisco to Plaza del Estudiante is considered the heart of La Paz. Still considered quite central, the **Sopocachi** neighborhood extends south and east of Plaza del Estudiante. Along 20 de Octubre and Avenida 6 de Agosto, you'll find some of the trendier restaurants and bars in town. **Miraflores** borders Sopocachi to the north. This is mainly a residential area, but visitors do sometimes venture here to catch a soccer game at Estadio Hernando Siles or to admire the views of La Paz from the Mirador Laikakota.

GETTING AROUND

BY TAXI You will never be at a loss for a taxi in La Paz. Because unemployment is so high in Bolivia, many people have converted their cars into taxis. **But beware:** You'll hear sketchy stories about these rogue taxi drivers. The most reliable taxi companies display brightly lit signs with their telephone numbers on top of their taxis. Drivers don't use meters, but fares are generally fixed. Rides within the center of town or to the Sopocachi neighborhood should only cost Bs7 (88¢/44p).

BY *TRUFI* The streets of La Paz are clogged with *trufis* (minibuses), which are always packed with locals. The routes are convoluted and confusing, except in the center of town (from Plaza San Francisco to Plaza del Estudiante) where *trufis* travel down one street without making any turns. So, if you're in the center of town, and you're planning on going straight, flag down a *trufi*. There are no designated stops; drivers stop when they see prospective passengers. The fare is Bs2 (25¢/13p), payable to the driver at the end of your ride. To signal that you want to get off, simply shout, *"Bajo"* or *"Me quedo aquí."*

BY FOOT It's hard to walk anywhere at an altitude of 3,739m (12,264 ft.) without feeling winded. But it's especially hard to walk around La Paz, where it feels as if all the streets have a steep uphill climb. After you spend a few days acclimating to the altitude, walking gets a little easier. Still, on streets such as Calle Sagárnaga, where the number of street-side vendors is roughly equivalent to the number of pedestrians, trying to fight your way through the throngs of people can be quite a challenge. I recommend walking around the center of town; it's fascinating to see the local people on the streets. But if you have to go a long distance—from one side of the city to another— it's much easier on the feet and the body to take a taxi or *trufi*.

VISITOR INFORMATION

There are two very helpful government-run information offices in La Paz. The most centrally located office is at the end of El Prado (La Paz's main street) at Plaza del

Estudiante; you can buy excellent maps here. The other office is located just outside the main bus terminal. Both offices are open Monday through Friday from 9am to 6pm and Saturday from 10am to 12:30pm. Additionally, **Crillon Tours,** Av. Camacho 1233 (© **0102/2337-533,** or 305/358-5353 in the U.S.), is very helpful. The agents here can arrange city tours and trips throughout Bolivia.

FAST FACTS   To exchange traveler's checks or foreign currency, your best bet is to head to one of the *casas de cambio* on Avenida Camacho. Two of the best are **Cambios "America,"** Av. Camacho 1233 near the corner of Ayacucho, and the **Casa de Cambio,** Av. Camacho 1311 at the corner of Colón. In general, Avenida Camacho is the banking center of La Paz—you'll find all types of ATMs here, as well as most Bolivian banks. **Citibank** is nearby at Av. 16 de Julio 1434 (© **0800/10-2000**); they exchange Citibank traveler's checks for free.

In case of an **emergency,** call © 110 for the regular police. For the **tourist police,** call © 0102/2225-016. For an **ambulance,** call © 118 or © 0107/1268-502. If you need medical attention, the two best hospitals in La Paz are **Clínica Cemes,** Av. 6 De Agosto 2881 (© 0102/2430-360), and **Clínica del Sur,** at Avenida Hernando Siles and the corner of Calle 7 in the Obrajes neighborhood (© 0102/2784-001). **Farmacia Red Bolivia,** 16 de Julio 1473 (© 0102/2331-838), is probably the most centrally located 24-hour pharmacy in La Paz. If you need a delivery, try calling **Farmacia La Paz** at © 0102/2371-828.

There is no lack of Internet cafes in La Paz, especially on Avenida 16 de Julio. The average cost is Bs7 (88¢/44p) an hour. You'll find the fastest Internet connections at **WeBolivia,** Av. 16 de Julio 1764; **Punto Entel,** Av. 16 de Julio 1473; and **Pl@net,** Calle Sagárnaga 213 at the corner of Murillo.

The main **post office** is in a large building on the corner of Avenida Mariscal Santa Cruz and Oruro. The post office is open Monday through Friday from 8:30am to 8:30pm, Saturday from 8:30am to 6pm, and Sunday from 9am to noon.

Punto Entel is the main telephone provider in La Paz. There are two offices on El Prado: one at Mariscal Santa Cruz 1287, the other at Av. 15 de Julio 1473. You can make local, long-distance, and international calls from these offices. It costs about Bs8 ($1/50p) per minute to call the United States—a bargain compared to what most international companies charge. You can also buy phone cards here or at local kiosks to use the pay phones located throughout the city.

WHAT TO SEE & DO

Mirador Laikakota
From the lower points of La Paz, you may have noticed that, in the near distance, there is a large hill with a funky blue tower on top of it. This is the Mirador Laikakota, a good lookout point, offering a 360-degree view of La Paz. The Mirador isn't simply a *mirador* (view point)—it's also a very large children's park with rides, playgrounds, and food stands. To enjoy the best views, walk past all the playgrounds to the far end of the park. This is a good spot for a photo of the mighty snow-covered Illimani.

Av. del Ejército near the corner of Díaz Romero, Miraflores. Admission Bs7 (88¢/45p). Daily 8:30am–7pm.

Museo de Arte Contemporáneo Plaza ⚘⚘
The powerful art in this museum does an excellent job of conveying the issues that affect modern-day Bolivians. Notable permanent pieces include a collection of plaster sculptures by the museum's owner, Herman Plaza, called *Cuando los Hijos se Van (When the Kids Leave),* a very real

depiction of young people who are leaving Bolivia for the United States; and paintings by José Rodríguez-Sánchez who comes from Cochabamba, where the U.S.-directed program to eradicate coca growing in the region has wreaked havoc on the local people. The museum also houses the work of some well-known international artists Occasionally, there is a Spanish-speaking guide who can take you on a 30-minute tour of the museum.

Even if there were no art here, it still would be worth a visit to see the interior of the 126-year-old mansion that houses the museum. This building and the bus station are the only structures in Bolivia that were designed by Señor Eiffel, of Eiffel Tower fame.

Av. 16 de Julio 1698 (near Plaza del Estudiante). ℂ 0102/2335-905. Admission Bs15 ($1.90/95p). Daily 9am–9pm.

Museo de la Coca *(Moments*   This museum provides visitors with a true "only in Bolivia" experience. Coca leaves have been an important part of Bolivian culture for thousands of years, and this tiny museum is dedicated solely to the coca leaf and its history. You'll learn tons of interesting facts about the coca leaf's healing properties, its nutritional value, and how it's transformed into cocaine. However, the real highlight is learning the proper way to chew coca leaves. Apparently, you must chew the bitter leaves for several minutes on one side of your mouth; once you've mashed up the leaves, the museum's owner will give you a pasty but sweet coca substance to add to the mix. Goodbye, altitude sickness! Set aside about an hour for your visit here.

Linares 906 (near Calle Sagárnaga). ℂ 5912/2311-998. www.cocamuseum.com. Admission Bs8 ($1/50p). Daily 10am–7pm.

Museo Nacional de Arte   In the 17th and 18th centuries, Potosí may have been the mining center of the world. However, it was also a thriving cultural center and the home of some of the most famous colonial artists in the Americas. This museum is a treasure trove of colonial art, and it displays some of the most famous works of these artists. One of the most impressive is Gaspar Miguel de Berrio's two-paneled *Adoración de los Reyes y Adoración de los Pastores,* which is one of the few Bolivian colonial paintings with an African figure in it. There is an entire room dedicated to Melchor Pérez Holguín, who was actually a mestizo; if you look carefully at his work, you can see some indigenous influences. There are also several galleries dedicated to contemporary Bolivian art. The building dates from 1775. Plan on spending about an hour and a half here.

On the corner of Comercio and Socabaya (off Plaza Murillo). ℂ 0102/2408-600. www.mna.org.bo. Admission Bs10 ($1.25/65p). Tues–Sat 9:30am–12:30pm and 3–7pm; Sun 10am–1pm.

Museo Nacional de Etnografía y Folklore   This museum is dedicated to the rich local culture in Bolivia. There are exhibits dedicated to specific tribes, including the URKU, who live near Lake Titicaca, as well as art that relates to the Casa de la Moneda (the Royal Mint) in Potosí. The real star here, however, is the *Tres Milenios de Tejidos (3,000 Years of Textiles)* exhibit, a varied collection of richly colored ponchos, skirts, and blankets that women use to carry their children. When you see all of them together, you really begin to understand that these aren't simply ponchos, skirts, or blankets—rather, these are works of art and self-expression. Plan on spending about 45 minutes here.

Ingavi 916 (at the corner of Genaro Sanjinés). ℂ 591/22408-640. www.musef.org.bo. Free admission. Mon–Sat 9am–12:30pm and 3–7pm; Sun 9am–12:30pm.

Museos Municipales   The Museos Municipales is actually a collection of four museums all located on the beautiful Spanish-style Calle Jaén. One ticket—purchased from the Museo Costumbrista Juan de Vargas (see below)—will allow you to gain access to all of them. Visiting four museums sounds like a lot, but they are all small, and it only takes about an hour to see everything. *Note:* There are very few explanations in English at the museums, and the ones in Spanish aren't especially descriptive.

If you only have time (or patience) for one museum, I recommend visiting the **Museo de Metales Preciosos** ✸, Calle Jaén 777, where you'll see interesting gold and silver belts, necklaces, bowls, crowns, and bracelets from both the Inca and Tiwanaku cultures, as well as a Tiwanaku monolith. The courtyard here is also quite interesting: If you look closely at the ground, you can see the remains of sheep bones, which the Spanish used as home decorations during the colonial era.

The **Museo Costumbrista Juan de Vargas,** Calle Jaén on the corner of Calle Sucre, specializes in the early-20th-century history of La Paz. Some amazing photographs are on display, as well as old pianos and phonographs and many modern figurines depicting all styles of life and clothing in La Paz.

The **Museo del Litoral Boliviano,** Calle Jaén 789, is the least interesting of the bunch. It's tiny, and it houses relics from the Pacific War (1879–84), when Bolivia lost its access to the sea. On display are portraits of Bolivian generals, uniforms, guns, gun cases, and information about Ignacia Zeballos (one of the founders of the Red Cross, who was from Santa Cruz, Bolivia).

The **Museo Casa de Murillo,** Calle Jaén 790, is a beautiful old mansion dating from the 18th century. Inside, you will find baroque-style carved-wood furniture, including intricate picture frames. The house itself is also historically significant—the home of General Murillo, a prominent player in Bolivia's independence movement, is where the revolutionary leaders drew up Bolivia's declaration of independence.

Calle Jaén (near Calle Sucre). ② **591/22280-553**. Admission Bs4 (50¢/25p) adults, free for students and seniors over 65. Tues–Fri 9:30am–12:30pm and 3–7:30pm.

Plaza Murillo   Plaza Murillo is the historical center of La Paz. During colonial times, Plaza Murillo was on the Spanish side of the Prado, and it became the center of the action because it was the main water source in town. In its glory days, the plaza was surrounded by eucalyptus trees and a statue of Neptune. In 1900, the plaza was officially named Plaza Murillo after General Murillo, one of the heroes of the Bolivian independence movement.

On one side of the plaza, you'll find the neoclassical **cathedral,** which took 152 years to build (1835–1987). The towers are the newest part—they were constructed for the arrival of Pope John Paul II in 1989. If you want to visit the inside of the cathedral, it's open Monday to Friday from 3:30 to 7pm and in the mornings on Saturday and Sunday.

Next to the cathedral is the colonial **Government Palace,** also known as the Palacio Quemado (burned palace). Originally La Paz's City Hall and now the office of Bolivia's president, the building has been burned eight times. Every Thursday at 9am, you can take 15-minute guided tours in Spanish. Outside the Government Palace, you will probably notice guards in red uniforms. During the Pacific War (1879–84), when Bolivia lost its sea coast to Chile, the soldiers wore red uniforms. Today, these uniforms send the message that Chile must return that land to Bolivia.

Across from the palace is the **Congress** building, which has a long history: It was a convent, a jail, and a university before a 1904 renovation to house Bolivia's congress.

Standing opposite the cathedral and the Government Palace is the 1911 **Grand Hotel París,** the first movie house in Bolivia.

To get here from El Prado, walk 3 blocks on Calle Ayacucho or Calle Socabaya.

Iglesia de San Francisco ✪ The intricately stone-carved facade of the San Francisco church is one the finest examples of baroque-mestizo architecture in the Americas. Look closely and you'll see a wealth of indigenous symbols—from masked figures to snakes, dragons, and tropical birds. The cornerstone for the original San Francisco church was placed in this spot in 1548, 1 year before the founding of La Paz. The church standing here today is not the original; it was completed in 1784. Once inside, the baroque influence seems to disappear. The small cedar altars with gold-leaf designs are much more typical of the neoclassical era.

Plaza San Francisco, at the north end of Av. Mariscal Santa Cruz. Free admission. Mon–Sat 4–6pm.

SPORTS & OUTDOOR ACTIVITIES

Bolivia is a haven for outdoor enthusiasts. It's nice to spend a few days in La Paz, but the surrounding mountains are truly spectacular and mighty enticing. Nearby you have the opportunity to climb some of the highest peaks in the world, bike down one of the most dangerous roads in the world, golf in one of the highest courses in the world, or ski down one of the highest slopes in the world.

CLIMBING, HIKING & TREKKING If you're serious about climbing, you should check out **Club Andino** on Calle México 1638 (© **0102/2312-875** or 0102/2324-682; Mon–Fri 9:30am–12:30pm and 3–7pm). The staff here can help arrange treks and climbs as well as recommend the best outfitters and guides. They can also help organize a trip to an acclimatizing center or a ski outing to **Chacaltaya** (see "Skiing," below). But you don't have to be a skier to enjoy Chacaltaya: You can hike from the ski lift to the glacier. At 5,240m (17,187 ft.), the air is thin, but the views are what's really breathtaking. Hiking trips to Chacaltaya cost Bs80 ($10/£5), including transportation and admission.

Bolivian Journeys ✪, Sagárnaga 363 between Linares and Illampu (© **0102/2357-848;** www.bolivianjourneys.org), is one of the most experienced climbing and hiking outfitters and organizes trips up the 5,990m (19,647-ft.) **Huayna Potosí.**

FUTBOL (SOCCER) Four teams play year-round at **Estadio Hernando Siles** in Miraflores. There are games most every week on Tuesday, Wednesday, and Sunday. You can buy tickets on game day at the stadium. Prices range from Bs10 to Bs25 ($1.25–$3.15/65p–£1.60). To get here, just hop on any *trufi* with a sign marked ESTA-DIO in the front window, or take a taxi.

GOLF The 18-hole, 6,900-yard **Mallasilla La Paz Golf Club** (© **0102/2745-462**), located about 15 minutes outside of La Paz, is considered to be one of the highest golf clubs in the world. Greens fees are Bs550 ($69/£35) per person plus Bs80 ($10/£5) for equipment and Bs80 ($10/£5) for a caddie. **Crillon Tours,** Av. Camacho 1233 (© **0102/2337-533,** or 305/358-5353 in the U.S.), can arrange golf packages.

MOUNTAIN BIKING **Gravity Assisted Mountain Biking** ✪✪, Av. 16 de Julio 1490 (© **0102/2313-849;** www.gravitybolivia.com), is by far the best biking outfitter in Bolivia. They specialize in the 64km (40-mile) descent from La Paz to Coroico along the most dangerous road in the world. The road is narrow, unpaved, crowded with trucks, and carved out of a cliff. *Be careful:* In 2001, a woman died here when her brakes snapped. Make sure your bike is in good condition. Gravity Assisted Mountain Biking also arranges rides to Sorata and the Zongo Valley.

SKIING   From January through May, you can ski on the glacier at Chacaltaya, one of the highest ski slopes in the world. **Club Andino,** Calle México 1638 (© **0102/2312-875**), is in charge of arranging ski outings. Transportation costs Bs80 ($10/£5) per person, equipment rental is Bs80 ($10/£5), and you have to pay Bs55 ($7/£3.55) for the lift ticket. Dress warmly (although at this altitude the sun is brutal) and make sure that you have acclimated to the altitude—there's not much air at 5,156m (16,912 ft.).

SHOPPING

At times, it feels as though La Paz is one big shopping center. The streets teem with vendors peddling everything you can imagine. The city is a mecca for handmade arts-and-crafts products. **Calle Sagárnaga** is shopper's central, with thousands of stores all packed to the gills with local handicrafts. In general, most of the quality is mediocre, but the variety and uniqueness of the goods sold here is mighty impressive. Some of the more popular items include alpaca sweaters (usually about Bs62–Bs77/$7.80–$9.70/£3.90–£4.85 each), hand-woven shoulder bags, leather bags, wool hats, textiles and gloves. **ComArt,** Calle Linares 958, is the only association of organized workers in La Paz. When you buy something here, your money goes directly to the workers, not the shopkeepers. If you're trying to find some differences between all the stores in the area, here's a tip: Both **Millma,** Calle Sagárnaga 225, and **Artesanía Sorata,** Calle Sagárnaga 311 and Calle Linares 862, sell some of the best quality alpaca sweaters in town. On the other side of town, you'll find beautiful silver jewelry at **Kuka Pradel,** Av. 6 de Agosto 2190.

Note that Bolivian vendors are not seasoned negotiators—they may drop the price by a dollar or two, but for the most part, prices are firm.

THE WITCH DOCTORS' MARKET ★★   Venture off of Calle Sagárnaga onto Calle Linares and you'll find yourself in the appropriately named Witch Doctors' Market. Here, you can buy a ghoulish variety of charms, spices, and magic potions to help cast a positive spell on your future. Llama fetuses are one of the most popular items for sale here. If you're looking for luck, here's a list to help you decode the meaning of all the amulets on display: Frogs are said to bring good fortune; turtles are the symbol of long life; owls bring knowledge; snakes are a sign of progression (or moving in the right direction); koa—a dried plant made with molasses—is supposed to help your harvest; and pumas will help you achieve victory over your enemy.

THE BLACK MARKET   Need a computer, a toilet bowl, tools, or a stereo? You'll find them all at the Black Market. Apparently, everything here is smuggled in from Chile. It's widely known that the merchandise is not always totally legit, but these days, even police officers do their shopping here. You'll find some incredible bargains. Even if you can't fit a toilet bowl in your suitcase, it's still a hoot to wander the crowded streets and watch as the locals wheel and deal. The Black Market is a few blocks uphill from the heart of Sagárnaga, past Max Paredes; you'll find a lot of action around Calle La Gasca and Eloy Salmón.

WHERE TO STAY
EXPENSIVE
Hotel Europa ★★★   Located on a quiet street just off the Prado, the Hotel Europa is an island of calm in this city of chaos. It is undoubtedly the best hotel in La Paz and

resembles more an upscale business-style American hotel than anything from the old continent as its name implies. The large, cream-colored rooms have fancy green and white carpets, built-in desks, and fresh plants. Mattresses are firm and all beds come with luxurious down comforters. The spacious bathrooms have white tiles and marble sinks. The Hotel Europa is the only hotel in Bolivia to have "floor heating" and a state-of-the-art air-circulation system. The suites are all full apartments with kitchenettes; some even have Jacuzzis. Opened in 1998, it is still relatively new by Bolivian standards but could definitely do with a makeover. The staff are very friendly and helpful but service can be patchy and there seems to be a perpetual shortage of slippers. Expect your first shot of coca tea when you arrive.

Calle Tiwanaku 64 (between El Prado and F. Zuazo), La Paz. ✆ 0102/2315-656. Fax 0102/2315-656. www.summit hotels.com. 110 units. $105–$165 (£53–£83) double; $200–$355 (£100–£178) suite. AE, MC, V. **Amenities:** 2 restaurants; bar; largest indoor pool in La Paz; really tiny exercise room; sauna; concierge; small business center; salon; room service; massage; babysitting; same-day laundry service; dry cleaning; nonsmoking rooms; executive floor. *In room:* A/C, TV, dataport, minibar, hair dryer, safe; fax and kitchenette in suites.

Hotel Plaza ⟨ᴋ⟩   Hotel Plaza has an airy, expansive lobby with colorful modern art. The not-so-bright rooms with dark carpets and aging satiny bedspreads were undergoing renovations at press time, so be sure to ask for a remodeled room. All rooms are spacious and those on the seventh floor and above come with wonderful views of the city and mountains. You can open the windows here, a rarity in high-rise hotels. The marble bathrooms are small but clean, with big mirrors. There's a formal restaurant on the top floor with amazing views, and an informal coffee shop (adjacent to the lobby) that serves an excellent buffet lunch. The Plaza has the best hotel gym in La Paz, but the pool area is not very attractive. Rooms can be cold and the staff could be more helpful. Also hot water could be hotter and more plentiful. All in all, this is a good value if you score a good rate, but if you're paying full price, choose instead Hotel Europa (see above).

Paseo del Prado, La Paz. ✆ 0102/2378-311. Fax 0102/2378-318. www.plazabolivia.com.bo. 147 units. $119–$150 (£60–£75) double; $220 (£110) suite. Rates include breakfast. AE, MC, V. **Amenities:** 2 restaurants; bar; small indoor pool; large exercise room; Jacuzzi; sauna; concierge; business center; room service; laundry service; dry cleaning; nonsmoking rooms; executive floor. *In room:* A/C, TV, minibar, hair dryer.

Radisson Plaza Hotel ⟨ᴋᴋ⟩   You can expect all the amenities of an exclusive business hotel here, but compared to modern, sexy Hotel Europa (see above), it feels more like a comfortable old shoe. The lobby looks fantastic but the rooms are disappointing. The Radisson's rooms do have enough space for two double beds, a large dresser, and two chairs, but its decor is very dated and there are perpetual problems with temperature control—either too cold or too stuffy. Huge picture windows used to offer great views of the city but unfortunately a high-rise went up right in front and ruined it for many. The sleek **Aransaya Restaurant,** which has outstanding views, looks like it was airlifted here from New York City and is undoubtedly the hotel's best asset. This is also one of the only hotels in La Paz that offers a free airport shuttle. Be sure to ask for the "Super Saver" rates that sometimes shave almost 30% off the regular prices, or check the website for deals.

Av. Arce 2177 (corner of F. Guachalla), La Paz. ✆ 800/333-3333 in the U.S., or 0102/2441-111. Fax 0102/2440-402. www.radisson.com/lapazbo. 246 units. $80–$180 (£40–£90) double; $200–$290 (£100–£145) suite. Rates include breakfast. AE, MC, V. **Amenities:** 2 restaurants; bar; small indoor pool; exercise room; Jacuzzi; sauna; activities desk; large business center; room service; massage; babysitting; laundry service; dry cleaning; nonsmoking rooms; executive floor. *In room:* A/C, TV, minibar, hair dryer, safe.

MODERATE

El Rey Palace Hotel ✯ *Value*   The dark wood paneling, uniformed porters, and black leather sofas give this quality hotel an old-fashioned feel. Yet all the rooms are large and comfortable and have bright red carpeting with dark wood furniture. The doubles have two king-size beds, a large dressing table, and a small table with two chairs. The higher floors have good views of the city, but the lower floors are quite dark. Note that the elevator stops at the seventh floor. The El Rey has a great location—it's only about 2 blocks from the action of the Prado, but it's on a quiet street that feels millions of miles away. If you're staying longer than a month, the daily rate goes down to $56 (£28) for a room for two people.

Av. 20 de Octubre 1947, La Paz. ✆ 0102/2418-541. Fax 0102/2367-759. www.hotel-rey-palace-bolivia.com. 60 units. $80 (£40) double; $85 (£43) junior suite; $95–$105 (£48–£53) suite. Rates include buffet breakfast. AE, MC, V. **Amenities:** Restaurant; bar; small business center; room service; laundry service; dry cleaning. *In room:* TV, dataport, minibar, hair dryer, safe.

INEXPENSIVE

Columbus Palace Hotel *Finds*   There are not many hotels in Bolivia that give you a choice of seven types of pillows, including "Rock" for those who like something firm to rest their heads on. You'll get that at the Columbus, which used to be the new kid on the block, but like most hotels in La Paz is now in need of a revamp. The rooms are small but the beds are comfortable and decor cheery. The shiny, tiled bathrooms are also small but very clean. All the rooms have large, double-paned windows, which offer nice views. Unfortunately, service here can be nonexistent. The hotel's main disadvantage is its 15-minute walk from the center, but a taxi only costs about Bs8 ($1/50p), and rooms here are much less expensive than similar hotels in the city center.

Av. Illimani 1990 (at the corner of Plaza del Estadio), La Paz. ✆ 0102/2242-444. Fax 0102/2245-367. www.hotel-columbus.com. 33 units (shower only). $36 (£18) double; $45 (£23) triple; $45 (£23) suite. Rates include buffet breakfast. AE, MC, V. **Amenities:** Restaurant; dance club; room service; in-room massage; babysitting; laundry service; dry cleaning. *In room:* TV, minibar.

Hostal Rosario ✯   Hostal Rosario is a converted colonial mansion with two peaceful colonial-style courtyards. The rooms are small but cozy in a charming way, with parquet floors and bright Andean-style bedspreads. The bathrooms aren't big, either, but they do have bright, spotless tiles. The owners are constantly making improvements, so although the hotel is old, it feels new. If you're traveling in a group, request the suite, which has great views and sleeps up to six people. The hotel is close to the Witch Doctors' Market and all the handicrafts stores on Calle Sagárnaga. Be aware that the rooms out front can be noisy at night if it is Carnaval time. There is an excellent upscale restaurant and tour agency on the premises, which is highly recommended.

Av. Illampu 704 (between Graneros and Santa Cruz), La Paz. ✆ 0102/2451-658. Fax 0102/2451-991. www.hotelrosario.com. 45 units (3 with shared bathroom, most with shower only). $39–$43 (£20–£22) double; $57 (£29) triple; $78 (£39) suite. Rates include continental breakfast. AE, MC, V. **Amenities:** Restaurant; bar; tour desk; room service; laundry service. *In room:* TV, dataport, safe.

WHERE TO DINE
MODERATE

El Vagón/El Vagón del Sur ✯✯ BOLIVIAN   If you're looking for typical, high-quality Bolivian food that's not simply grilled meat, El Vagón should be your first choice. These two restaurants are a father/son team. The father runs the restaurant in the downtown area of La Paz; the son is the manager of El Vagón del Sur in the ritzy

Zona Sur (a 15-min., Bs30/$3.70/£1.85 taxi ride from the center of La Paz). El Vagón feels a bit older and dowdier than El Vagón del Sur. For some atmosphere, try to sit in the back room near the fireplace. In contrast, the Zona Sur location looks as if it could be in California, with nice wood floors, stone walls, folksy art, hand-painted chairs, and colorful tablecloths. In the warmer months (Nov–Mar), there's a huge garden for outdoor dining. Order the *picante surtido* (tongue, chicken, and chopped meat all in a spicy red-chile sauce), served with *chuño putti*. You can also order more conventional dishes such as *pejerrey* (fresh kingfish from Lake Titicaca). All dishes come with a complimentary chicken empanada (nice touch!).

El Vagón: Pedro Salazar 382 (near Plaza Avaroa and 20 de Octubre). ℂ 0102/2432-477. Main courses Bs39–Bs70 ($5–$9/£2.50–£4.50). MC, V. Mon–Fri noon–3pm and 7–10pm; Sun noon–3pm. El Vagón del Sur: Av. Julio C. Patiño 1295 (corner of Calle 19; Calacoto, Zona Sur). ℂ 0102/2793-700. Main courses Bs39–Bs70 ($5–$9/£2.50–£4.55). MC, V. Tues–Sat noon–3pm and 7–11pm; Sun noon–3pm.

La Bella Vista ★★★ *(Moments* BOLIVIAN/INTERNATIONAL   The aliens have landed! Right here in La Paz on top of the Hotel Presidente. No one knows what happened to the aliens themselves, but they left behind their spaceship, which has been converted into an excellent restaurant with spectacular views of the city. This restaurant—hands down the best in the city—really feels like something from outer space, with an unbeatable 360-degree view of La Paz at night. The food is out of this world as well. If you like fish, you must order the grilled trout—I have never eaten a more succulent piece of fish. The *parrilla mixta* (assorted cuts of grilled meat for two people) is also excellent. The menu also includes homemade pasta, lamb kabobs, grilled chicken, and seafood.

In the Hotel Presidente, Calle Potosí 920 (at the corner of Genaro Sanjinés). ℂ 0102/2406-666. Reservations recommended Thurs–Fri. Main courses Bs45–Bs117 ($5.70–$15/£2.90–£7.50). AE, MC, V. Daily 11am–3pm and 7–11pm.

INEXPENSIVE

Dumbo *(Kids* BOLIVIAN/ICE CREAM   Located right in the middle of the Prado, Dumbo is one of the most popular places in La Paz for a light snack. The specialties here are ice cream and pastries. Some of my favorites are the Milk Shake Hawaii (pineapple, strawberries, strawberry ice cream, and milk) and the California (orange juice, vanilla ice cream, creme chantilly, and orange slices). But Dumbo is also great for full meals: There's a nice selection of sandwiches, and you can also sample Bolivian specialties here, such as *lomito a la paila* (filet served in a bowl of soup with potatoes and an egg). The restaurant is very cheerful, with colorful walls, waterfalls, fresh plants, and an enclosed patio in the back.

Prado 1523 (between Bueno and Campero). ℂ 0102/2313-331. Ice cream dishes Bs17–Bs19 ($2.15–$2.40/£1.10–£1.20); sandwiches Bs7–Bs20 (88¢–$2.50/45p–£1.25); main courses Bs27–Bs30 ($3.40–$3.75/£1.70–£1.90). MC, V. Daily 7am–11pm.

La Casa de los Paceños BOLIVIAN   This charming restaurant is housed on the second floor of an old colonial building, and it doesn't look as if much has changed in this dining room since colonial times. Traditional Bolivian food is the specialty here. For example, you can order *ají de lengua* (cow's tongue in a chile sauce) or, if you're feeling adventurous, *picante surtido,* which consists of *sajta* (chicken in a chile sauce), *saice* (chopped meat in a chile sauce), *ranga* (cow's stomach), *fritanga* (pork), and *charquekán.* More timid eaters should opt for the *pollo dorado* (chicken grilled in olive oil). If you're looking for Bolivian food in a livelier atmosphere, you should head to the newer La Casa de los Paceños in the Zona Sur (Av. Fuerza Naval 275, between 18th and 19th sts; © 0102/2794-629), where there is outdoor seating and live music on the weekends. A taxi from the center should cost no more than Bs30 ($3.80/£1.90).

Av. Sucre 856 (between Genaro Sanjinés and Pichincha). © 0102/2280-955. Main courses Bs22–Bs33 ($2.80–$4.15/£1.40–£2.10). AE, MC, V. Tues–Fri 11:30am–4pm and 6–10pm; Sat–Sun 11:30am–4pm.

Surucachi (Finds) BOLIVIAN   You may have noticed that between 12:30 and 2:30pm, the streets of La Paz become mighty quiet. That's probably because everyone and his mother is eating lunch here at Surucachi. The food is pure Bolivian—*milanesas* (fried chicken or veal cutlets), *pejerrey* (kingfish from Lake Titicaca), and *picante mixto* (tongue, chicken, and chopped meat all in a spicy chile sauce). The *almuerzo del día* (lunch special), which includes a salad, soup, a main course, and dessert, is only Bs20 ($2.50/£1.25). Add a colonial building with fancy gold-leaf moldings and huge picture windows to the mix, and you've got yourself the most popular lunch spot in town.

Av. 16 de Julio 1598. No phone. Lunch special Bs20 ($2.50/£1.25); a la carte main courses Bs25–Bs40 ($3.15–$5/£1.60–£2.90). No credit cards. Daily 9am–10pm.

LA PAZ AFTER DARK

Once the sun sets in La Paz, the temperature drops dramatically. Instead of going home (often to unheated apartments), many locals seek the warmth of bars and pubs. The nightlife scene in La Paz can hardly compare to New York or even Buenos Aires, but there are some funky places in the heart of the city where you can relax and kick back with a few drinks. *Peñas,* bars with live music, provide a place for visitors to experience traditional folk music and dance, although they tend to be very touristy. *Note:* Most bars (except in hotels) are open only Wednesday through Saturday.

BARS & PUBS   The best hotel bar in La Paz is at the **Radisson** (p. 188); they have a very popular happy hour nightly from 6:30 to 8:30pm offering two-for-one drinks, and it's popular with expatriates and tourists alike. One of the most popular British-style watering holes in the city is **Mongo's** ★★, Hermanos Manchego 2444 (near the corner of Pedro Salazar, half a block up from Av. 6 de Agosto). It has a cozy feel and a wood-burning fireplace. Get here early, as the place fills up late at night; the food here is also surprisingly good. Another good expat bar is **The Britannia** (© 0102/2793-070) on Avenida Ballivián between calle 15 and 16, Calacoto. **Coyote Bar,** Av. 20 de Octubre 2228 (corner of Pasaje Medinacelli), is smaller and less popular than Mongo's. **Malegría,** Calle Goitia 155 (a few steps from the Plaza del Estudiante), is very popular on Thursday nights for its Afro-Bolivian band; the lively music sometimes gets people dancing on the bar.

DANCE CLUBS   El Loro en Su Salsa (© 0102/2342-787), down from 6 de Agosto on Rosendo Gutiérrez, is one of the best dance clubs in La Paz; salsa is the specialty here. Also popular are **Forum,** Sanjinés 2908, with eclectic music but strict dress code and Bs40 ($5/£2.50) cover charge, and **Noa Noa** on Calle Conchitas between 20 de Octubre and Heroes del Arce. In general, the cover charge for clubs in La Paz is about Bs10 ($1.25/65p).

PEÑAS & LIVE MUSIC   These days, it's hard to find an authentic *peña* that caters to locals. Fortunately, for the most part, you'll hear authentic Andean music and watch folk dancers wearing unique but traditional costumes. **Restaurant Peña Marka Tambo,** Calle Jaén 710 near the corner of Indaburo, puts on a good show Thursday through Saturday nights. The cover is Bs25 ($3.15/£1.60). The show starts at 9:30pm. **Casa de Corregidor** (© 0102/2363-633), Calle Murillo 1040, is a similar venue—typical Bolivian food and music but feels a bit more laid-back than Marka Tambo. **Boca y Sapo,** Indaburo 654 (corner of Jaén), attracts locals as well as tourists; there's no dinner here, only live music, which makes it feel a bit more authentic.

Equinoccio, Sánchez Lima 2191 between Aspiazu and Guachalla, is one of the best venues for live music; the club manages to book some great local bands. For live jazz, try **Thelonious Jazz Bar,** Av. 20 de Octubre 2172. A lot of the bands that play here are from the United States.

SIDE TRIPS FROM LA PAZ
TIWANAKU ⊛

A visit to Tiwanaku will take you back in time to an impressive city built by an extremely technologically advanced pre-Inca society. The Tiwanaku culture is believed to have lasted for 28 centuries, from 1600 B.C. to A.D. 1200. In this time, they created some of the most impressive stone monoliths in the world, developed a sophisticated irrigation system, and gained an advanced understanding of astronomy and the workings of the sun. Their territory spread from northern Argentina and Chile through Bolivia to the south of Peru. These people never came into contact with the Incas. By the time the Incas made it to Peru, a 100-year drought had ravaged the Titicaca area. The Tiwanaku people had long ago left the region in small groups and moved to different areas in the Altiplano or valleys.

Stop in at the museum before you visit the site. The Incas and the Spaniards destroyed the site while searching for gold and silver and even the most respected archaeologists disagree on the meanings of the monoliths and the sun gate. But when you actually see these impressive structures firsthand, you can't help but stand in awe and wonderment of the amazing achievements of this pre-Columbian society. You gain a deep insight into the daily life and rituals of the people who inhabited this area for thousands of years. Highlights of the site include the **Semi-Underground Temple** ⊛, the **Kalassaya** ⊛, and the **Akapana (pyramid).** The museum and the archaeological site are open daily from 9am to 4:30pm. Admission is Bs15 ($1.90/95p).

GETTING THERE Tiwanaku is located 1½ hours outside La Paz. I strongly recommend coming here on a guided tour. **Diana Tours,** Sagárnaga 326 (℅ **0102/2350-252**), organizes English-speaking tours to Tiwanaku for only Bs70 ($8.80/£4.50), not including the Bs15 ($1.90/95p) site admission fee. **Crillon Tours,** Av. Camacho 1233 (℅ **0102/2337-533**), also arranges tours to the area. If you prefer to visit on your own, **Trans Tours Tiwanaku,** Calle José Aliaga, operates buses that stop at Tiwanaku. The buses leave from the Cementerio District every half-hour from 8am to 4:30pm. The ride costs Bs7 (90¢/45p).

THE BEST OF LOS YUNGAS: COROICO

Coroico makes a popular side trip for visitors to La Paz, but you'll probably remember the journey better than the destination. The road to Coroico narrows to one unpaved lane twisting down through the mountains. To one side is the mountain, to the other, a sheer drop of often hundreds of feet to the lush valley below. There will be times when the passage is tight and your vehicle is only an inch or two from the edge; there will be other times when you round a blind curve and your driver, confronted by oncoming traffic, has to slam on the brakes.

When the ride is over and your heart rate has returned to normal, you may be surprised at the tranquility of Coroico. The views of the surrounding hills are lovely, the nearby hiking trails are picturesque, the bars and restaurants in town are pleasant, and there are some worthwhile excursions; but there's really nothing here to take your breath away. Nonetheless, Coroico makes a wonderful contrast to La Paz. Here in this tropical town, you'll find fruit orchards, twittering birds, coca fields, endless greenery, oxygen-rich air, warm weather, and friendly locals. The climate here seems to put everyone in a better mood.

The town of Coroico itself isn't anything special, but it's a lot of fun to explore the lush, colorful surrounding area. You can take a half-day tour of **Tocaña** ⭐, a small Afro-Bolivian community located about 7km (4⅓ miles) downhill from Coroico. It feels as if not much has changed over the past few hundred years in this farming village, where the locals survive mainly by growing coca. Also nearby are the **Vagante River Springs.** Here you can swim under a waterfall and in beautiful pools of water. **Vagantes Ecoaventuras,** located at the kiosk in the Coroico main plaza, provides guides (not always English-speaking) and jeeps to Tocaña and Vagante River Springs. Note that the jeeps are open and the roads aren't paved, so you will get extremely dirty.

It's surprising that in a town like Coroico, which is set high up in the mountains, there aren't many **hiking trails.** Perhaps this is because most of the land in the area is farmland. The most popular hike is the 6km (3¾-mile) trek to the waterfalls *(las cascadas)*. It's not really a hike, but more of a long walk on a dusty road. The waterfalls are pleasant, but you can't swim in them, and to be honest, I'm not sure they are worth the long walk. However, the mountains and the valleys on the road are breathtaking. For more information about this and other walks in the area, contact the tourist information office on Coroico's main plaza.

In the dry season, the rivers in the Coroico area become low and unsuitable for **rafting.** However, in January through March, the Coroico River runs wild. River levels range from Class III to Class V. **Vagantes Ecoaventuras** (at the kiosk in Coroico's main plaza, on the corner of Heroes del Chaco) organizes rafting and kayaking tours in the area.

GETTING THERE   Buses for Coroico leave La Paz on a frequent schedule from the Villa Fátima neighborhood, which is about 15 minutes by taxi from the center of La Paz. (It costs about Bs9/$1.15/60p.) Most of the bus companies are located on Calle Yanacachi. One of the best is **Yungueña** (© 0102/2213-513; call ahead for the schedule); the ride costs Bs15 ($1.90/95p) each way. I recommend leaving around 10am—this way, you'll arrive in Coroico for lunch and then have the rest of the afternoon to walk around town or hang out by a pool. Buses depart less frequently in the afternoon (the last one leaves at about 4pm), but it's much nicer to travel during daylight and enjoy the view. *Tip:* Try to get a seat on the left side of the bus for the best views.

For information about **trekking** or **biking** to Coroico, see "Sports & Outdoor Activities," earlier in this section.

5 Lake Titicaca ⭐⭐⭐

Copacabana: 151km (94 miles) NW of La Paz; 8km (5 miles) N of Kasani (the border of Peru)

Still, serene, spiritual, this vast lake of blinding light and calm water is the birthplace of one of the greatest empires in history. At Lake Titicaca the children of the Sun stepped forth from the sacred rock that still stands near the northwest tip of the Isla del Sol (the Sun Island) and the Incas began.

The rugged, snow-covered peaks of the Cordillera Real loom over the shores of the lake, but its waters are calm and relaxing to the eye. They're disturbed only by the operators of a few tour boats, launches, and hydrofoils, and by local fishermen searching for trout, often in wooden sailboats or rowboats. Even the most primitive of these vessels are relative newcomers. The swaying reeds on the water's shore provided the material for the first boats on Lake Titicaca, and today there are still a few craftsmen who remember how to make boats from reeds, as their ancestors did.

Besides the lake itself, and the Isla del Sol within it, the highlight of the region is the picturesque lakeshore town of Copacabana, allegedly established by the Inca Tupac Yupanqui. Copacabana has a number of small but important Inca ruins, but all of them are overshadowed by the town's main attraction, the Virgin of Copacabana. Pilgrims travel from all over South America for the Virgin's blessing. If you're here on a Sunday, you'll notice above all the car and truck drivers, who come to have their vehicles blessed by one of the local priests in a ceremony that involves lots of garlands, the shaking and spraying of fizzy drinks, and, of course, a small donation to the church. Nobody seems to mind paying.

ESSENTIALS
GETTING THERE

BY BUS Buses from La Paz to Copacabana leave from the Cementerio District, not from the main terminal; it costs about Bs15 ($1.90/95p) to get here by taxi from the center of La Paz. **Trans "6 de Junio,"** Plaza Tupac Katari no. 55 (© **0102/2455-258**), is one of the most reliable bus companies. A one-way ticket costs Bs15 ($1.90/95p); buses depart at 9:30 and 10:30am; noon; and 2:30, 5, 6, 7:30, and 8:30pm. The ride takes 3 hours, including a 3-minute ferry ride (Bs2/25¢/15p) across the Straits of Tiquina. Here, you must disembark from the bus and take a ferry across to the other side. The bus is carried over on a separate boat.

BY GUIDED TOUR **Crillon Tours,** Av. Camacho 1233 (© **0102/2337-533** or 305/358-5353 in the U.S.; www.titicaca.com), specializes in tours to the Lake Titicaca area. The company owns two of the best hotels in the area—Inca Utama Hotel & Spa in Huatajata and La Posada del Inca hotel on the Sun Island—and is the only company that operates hydrofoils on the lake. Because of a business deal meant to protect local businesses, you can't stay at these hotels or use the hydrofoil if you're traveling independently. Crillon's tours are really the best way to see the area; they include excellent English-speaking guides and all transportation.

GETTING AROUND

Copacabana, the largest city in the Lake Titicaca area, is where you'll find the best hotels and travel agencies, as well as some Inca ruins and the famous statue of the Virgen de Copacabana. From here, you can easily take a day trip to the Isla del Sol. **Huatajata** isn't much of a town—its only attraction is Inca Utama Hotel & Spa—but it's only 1½ hours by car from La Paz. So instead of traveling 3 hours to Copacabana, you can spend the night here, and then hop on the hydrofoil for a quick jaunt over to the Sun Island. The hydrofoil also makes stops in Copacabana.

The only way to go from Copacabana or Huatajata to the Sun Island is by **boat.** From Huatajata, you can also take a hydrofoil to Copacabana or the Sun Island; contact **Crillon Tours** (© **0102/2337-533** or 305/358-5353 in the U.S.; www.titicaca. com) for more information. From Copacabana, nonhydrofoil boats leave around 8:15am and arrive at the Sun Island at 10:30am. The boat returns to pick you up at 4pm. If you want to walk from one side of the island to the other, the ride costs Bs30 ($3.75/£1.90); if you want the boat to take you around the island, the whole trip will

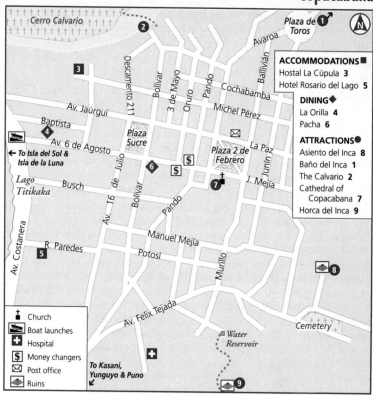

Copacabana

ACCOMMODATIONS ■
Hostal La Cúpula **3**
Hotel Rosario del Lago **5**

DINING ◆
La Orilla **4**
Pacha **6**

ATTRACTIONS ●
Asiento del Inca **8**
Baño del Inca **1**
The Calvario **2**
Cathedral of
  Copacabana **7**
Horca del Inca **9**

† Church
🛶 Boat launches
➕ Hospital
$ Money changers
✉ Post office
🗺 Ruins

set you back Bs35 ($4.40/£2.20). If you plan on spending the night on the Isla del Sol, you can catch a boat back to Copacabana at 10:30am. Both **Grace Tours,** Av. 6 de Agosto 200 (☎ **0102/862-2160**), and **Titicaca Tours,** located at the dock at the end of Avenida 6 de Agosto (☎ **0102/862-2060**), are recommended tour agencies.

Transturin (☎ **0102/242-2222;** www.turismobolivia.com) on Avenida 6 de Agosto, about half a block up from the beach, organizes cruises to the Isla del Sol and to Puno on the Peruvian side of the lake. Day trips to both the Sun Island and Puno cost Bs480 ($60/£30). You can also sleep on the boat; overnight trips to the Sun Island cost Bs600 ($75/£38) per person.

VISITOR INFORMATION

The main tourist office is located on Plaza 2 de Febrero at the corner of Ballivián and La Paz in Copacabana. The office doesn't have a phone, the hours of operation are sporadic, there are no maps available, and, in general, the staff is of limited help.

FAST FACTS: COPACABANA   There are several **banks** on Avenida 6 de Agosto; note that none of them exchange traveler's checks or have ATMs. You'll find a **pharmacy** on Plaza Tito Yupanqui right across from the Entel office behind the basilica. The **post office** is located on La Paz near the corner of Ballivián. You can take care of all your **laundry** needs at Hostal Sucre, Murillo 228 near the corner of José P. Mejía.

For Internet cafes, try **ALF@Net,** Av. 6 de Agosto 100, at the corner of Avenida 10 de Julio, and **Alcadi,** beside the post office in front of the cathedral. Rates are about Bs20 ($2.50/£1.25) per hour.

WHAT TO SEE & DO
IN COPACABANA

Copacabana was an important religious site way before the Spanish realized that the world was round. Lake Titicaca is believed to be the birthplace of the Incas, and for many years, this city was one of the holiest of the Inca Empire. These days, pilgrims come from far and wide to visit the Cathedral of Copacabana to pay homage to the Virgin of Copacabana (also known as the Queen of Bolivia and the Virgin of Candelaria), who has supposedly bestowed many miracles upon her true believers. She is the most venerated virgin in all of Bolivia. In addition to visiting the most important Catholic icon in Bolivia, you can also explore some important Inca ruins.

THE CATHEDRAL OF COPACABANA In 1580, the Virgin of Copacabana appeared in a dream to Tito Yupanqui. He was so taken by this vision that he set out to Potosí (then one of the most important art centers in the world) to learn to sculpt. With his new skill, he hand-carved the Virgin from the wood of a maguey cactus. He then carried her, by foot, from Potosí to Copacabana (a journey of more than 640km/400 miles), where she was placed in an adobe chapel in 1583. Immediately afterwards, the crops of those who doubted her power were mysteriously destroyed. The Spanish, smitten with the Virgin, completed this Moorish-style cathedral for her in 1617. The Virgin stands in a majestic mechanical altar. On weekends, the priests rotate the Virgin so that she faces the main chapel; on weekdays, when there are fewer pilgrims here, they spin her around so that she looks over a smaller chapel on the other side. The silver ship at the bottom of the altar represents the moon, while the gold statue above the Virgin's head is believed to symbolize the power of the sun. Believers have bestowed millions of dollars worth of gifts upon the Virgin. In 1879, the government of Bolivia sold some of her jewelry to finance the War of the Pacific against Chile. The cathedral is open daily from 11am to noon and from 2 to 6pm; admission is free.

THE CALVARIO In the 1950s the Stations of the Cross were built on a hill overlooking the lake. The strenuous uphill walk takes more than 30 minutes, but the views of the lake are worth the effort. At the very bottom of the stairs, there is a man who can divine your future by dropping lead into a boiling pot of water. About halfway up, you will find native priests burning candles and working with coca leaves. If you're so inclined, this is a good place to stop and learn about the ancient rituals of fortune telling. For the trip down, there are two options: You can return the way you came up, or you can take a rocky path that will lead you to the shores of the lake. Note that the winding path can get steep and narrow—it's best to descend it only if you're wearing a good pair of hiking shoes.

INCA RUINS Within Copacabana, there are three interesting archaeological sites. They are open Tuesday through Sunday from 9am to noon and from 2 to 5pm; admission to all three costs Bs10 ($1.25/65p).

The **Asiento del Inca (Seat of the Inca)** ✸✸ is my favorite of the three sites. No one knows the actual purpose of the stone carvings here, but some archaeologists speculate that this may have been a meeting point for Inca priests. The carvings are called Asiento del Inca because the huge indentations in the rocks resemble thrones. The rock carvings span different levels and what appear to be different rooms, and the "seats" don't all face the same direction. It's fun to sit on one of the thronelike rocks and dream about what may have happened here. To get here, walk from Plaza 2 de Febrero along Calle Murillo for 4 blocks until you reach the road to La Paz, where you should take a left. Walk 3 blocks uphill to the cemetery. The Asiento del Inca is about 90m (300 ft.) from the cemetery, in what looks to be a small farm.

A bit farther outside of town is the **Horca del Inca,** a three-rock structure that resembles a gallows (hence the name). In actuality, it's believed that the Incas used these rocks as a tool to observe the sun and stars. If you happen to be here during one of the equinoxes, you can actually observe the sun as it reflects off the boulders. Unfortunately, the Spanish destroyed much of the site because they thought gold might be hidden inside some of the rocks. Of course, they found nothing. To get here, walk straight on Calle Murillo from the plaza until the road ends; here, you will see a rocky hill. About halfway up the hill, you'll find the Horca del Inca. The walk up to the actual site is steep and the terrain is rough. You should only head up here if you have good walking shoes and lots of energy. Young boys hanging around the area will offer to show you the way to the site for about Bs8 ($1/50p). I recommend taking them up on their offer, because the climb is tricky.

At the **Baño del Inca,** about 30 minutes outside town, you'll find a small museum dedicated to some archaeological finds in the area. Behind the museum, there's a pretty little spring, which is said to have mystical powers. Baño del Inca is a nice peaceful spot outside of the city—great for a romantic picnic. To get here, start at Plaza 2 de Febrero and walk straight down Ballivián to Plaza de Toros. From Plaza de Toros, walk straight for about 20 minutes, until you see a green house. Take a right here and walk uphill for about 10 minutes. The Baño del Inca is on the right-hand side across from a church. There is no sign, but it's right behind a small farm.

ISLA DEL SOL ✦✦✦ & ISLA DE LA LUNA

Welcome to the birthplace of the Incas. The **Isla del Sol,** measuring only 9km (5½ miles) long by 6km (3¾ miles) wide, is one of the most spectacular places in all of Bolivia. On the north end are Challapampa and some fascinating Inca ruins. Yumani, on the south end, is the largest town on the island and also the site of the Inca steps.

Most tour operators run a day trip from Copacabana to the Sun Island, with a quick stop at the Isla de la Luna (Moon Island). You'll leave Copacabana at 8:15am and arrive at Challapampa around 10:30am. Here you pay a Bs15 ($1.90/95p) entry fee, and a Spanish-speaking guide will show you around Chinkana (see "Challapamba," below, for more information). If you're feeling ambitious, you can walk from here all the way to the Fuente del Inca on the southern end of the island. I highly recommend this long and hilly hike. Along the way, you'll come across wild llamas, herds of sheep, and some of the most breathtaking vistas in the world. But keep in mind that the hike is difficult and more than 4 hours long, so you won't have time to sit and eat a proper lunch. If you have a hard time walking, you might not make it to the other side in time for the last boat to Copacabana at 4pm.

If you don't want to walk, the boat will then drop you off for a quick stop at the **Isla de la Luna.** During the time of the Incas, this island was used to house "chosen" women. The island was similar to a convent. The women here wove garments by hand with alpaca wool and performed special ceremonies dedicated to the sun. Unfortunately, most of the structures here have been destroyed. From the 1930s to the 1960s, this island became a political prison. In the 1960s, when some archaeologists got wind of what had become of the island, the prisoners were ordered to rebuild the main palace, which has 35 rooms around a courtyard. This is historically significant because the Aymara culture—not the Incas—used constructions with courtyards, thus proving that the Moon Island was used by pre-Inca cultures. However, most of the remaining doors are trapezoidal shaped, which is very typical of the Incas. As you first walk onto the island, keep an eye out for the polished stones. These stones are similar to what you'd find in Machu Picchu, and they allow you to understand how the Incas used hinges to hold rocks together.

Note: When your boat driver forces you to choose between visiting the Moon Island and walking across the Sun Island, I recommend opting for the walk on the Sun Island. You won't miss much if you don't stop off at the Moon Island, and the setting of the sun on Sun Island is much more spectacular.

CHALLAPAMPA ★★   A visit to Challapampa will be the highlight of your visit to the Sun Island. Here, you will find the ruins of **Chinkana (labyrinth).** It's a huge stone complex full of mazes, believed to be a seminary for Inca priests. The construction is actually a bit sloppy, which is very uncharacteristic of the Incas; some archaeologists theorize that the Incas must have been in a rush when they built it. A natural spring here runs under the island and appears again in a sacred stone fountain in Yumani (see below). On the path back to the town of Challapampa, about 100m (328 ft.) from Chinkana, you will pass by the **sacred rock,** carved in the shape of a puma. As you continue along this path toward Challapampa, look down: You will soon see two very large footprints, said to have been created when the sun dropped down to earth to give birth to Manco Capac and Mama Ocllo, the Adam and Eve of the Incas.

YUMANI/INCA STEPS   If you arrive by boat to Yumani, you will have to walk up 206 steps to reach the main part of the town here. These steps are original Inca constructions, and they lead up to a sacred stone fountain with three separate springs, which are said to be a fountain of youth.

PILKOKAYNA   There is a half-mile path from the top of the Inca Steps down to Pilkokayna (which literally means "where birds sleep"). This 14-room structure may have been used as a fortress to guard the Virgins of the Sun who were living nearby on the Moon Island. From here, you have a very clear view of the Moon Island. The structure does have trapezoidal doors, which means that it was used by the Incas. However, some archaeologists speculate that the buildings here date back to the Classic Age of the Tiwanaku period (A.D. 100–900). One of the most impressive features is the remains of the original stone roof.

IN HUATAJATA

The **Andean Roots Cultural Complex,** connected to Crillon Tours' Inca Utama Hotel & Spa, is the only attraction in Huatajata. Essentially, it's the "Williamsburg" of Lake Titicaca. The complex consists of an Andean Eco Village, the Altiplano Museum, and the Kallawaya Museum. The **Andean Eco Village** recreates an historic Andean village, with buildings and farms typical of this area. It's an attempt to preserve local cultures and traditions. The people here are working exactly the same way their ancestors did—taking care of llamas and vicuñas, growing guinea pigs, storing corn, cooking traditional food, and weaving alpaca shawls. In the Andean Village, there is also a full-size reproduction of the reed boat, the *RA II,* used by Thor Heyerdahl to cross the Atlantic and designed by the local Limachi brothers, who work here building new reed boats. The **Altiplano Museum** is a small museum with exhibits

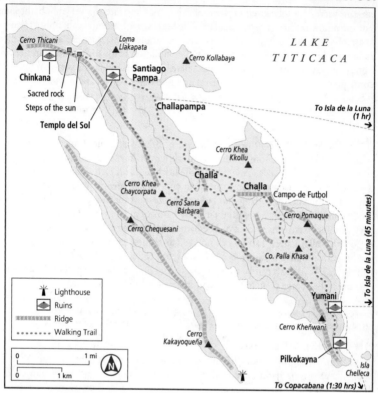

about the history of Bolivia, with emphasis on the Tiwanaku and Inca cultures. The **Kallawaya Museum** 🐸🐸 is one of the most interesting museums in Bolivia. At the beginning of the museum, you will learn about the healing powers of local herbs, plants, fruits, and vegetables. When you reach the end, you will enter a small brick room, brightened only by the warm glow of candles. Here a Kallawaya natural medicine doctor will bless you and, with the help of some coca leaves, tell you about your future. Finally, there is an observatory here (with the second-most powerful telescope in Bolivia), where you can learn about all the constellations in the Southern Hemisphere.

WHERE TO STAY
IN COPACABANA
Hostal La Cúpula *Finds* There's something to be said for artists who open hotels. The owner of La Cúpula is a sculptor, and the beautiful garden areas here are filled with delightful pieces of his work. The guest room walls are covered with modern art, and some even have lofts, so you really feel as though you're staying in an artist's studio. Some of the rooms have views of the lake, while others look out onto the surrounding mountainside. They are all bright with big windows and funky bamboo furniture. The Honeymoon Suite is probably the quirkiest hotel room in all of Bolivia: Accessed through the ceiling, it has a large cupola, views of the lake, a hammock, and

its own veranda. Only seven of the rooms here have private shower-only bathrooms, but the public facilities are immaculate. The hotel is a 10-minute walk uphill from the heart of Copacabana, but it's not much of a problem. After eating at the excellent restaurant (or cooking your own meal in the public kitchen), you can relax in the cozy library or play one of many board games here. It can be cold in the winter months, so come prepared. Each room has a heater and hot-water bottles are provided.

Calle Michel Pérez 1–3, Copacabana. ℰ 0102/862-2029. www.hotelcupula.com. 17 units (7 with private bathroom, shower only). $14–$32 (£7–£16) double; $20–$28 (£10–£14) triple. MC, V. **Amenities:** Restaurant. *In room:* No phone.

Hotel Rosario del Lago ⟨★⟩   The design of this lakeside hotel blends in perfectly with its surroundings. From the outside, the bright yellow stucco building looks like an old Spanish colonial–style castle. Inside, the brick tiles and earthy tones envelop you in a soothing way. In every room, there is a cozy sitting area with large bay windows, where you can curl up with a good book and gaze out over the shores of Lake Titicaca. The rooms aren't fancy, but with their shiny hardwood floors and dark-red bedspreads, they certainly have tons of charm. The bathrooms are small, but the rooms are so cute, it doesn't really matter. Families should try to request the suite—it feels like a small apartment, complete with two bedrooms, a refrigerator, and a separate living room and dining area. If you're sensitive to noise, make sure that your room is toward the back of the hotel; the rooms close to the reception area tend to be quite loud.

Rigoberto Paredes and Av. Costanera, Copacabana. ℰ 0102/862-2141. Fax 0102/862-2140. www.hotelrosario. com/lago. 32 units (shower only). $43–$48 (£22–£25) double; $58–$63 (£29–£32) triple. Rates include breakfast. AE, MC, V. **Amenities:** Restaurant; game room; room service; laundry service; travel agency. *In room:* TV, safe.

ON THE ISLA DEL SOL

Most of the accommodations on the Sun Island are, to put it kindly, rustic. Very few rooms have private bathrooms, and it's almost impossible to find a hot shower here. But once all the day-trippers leave, you will have the island to yourself. I think it's worth it to stay here just to feel the magic of the island.

There is one exception to the rule, however: Crillon Tours' **La Posada del Inca** ⟨★★⟩ is probably one of the best hotels in all of Bolivia. By Sun Island standards, it's luxurious—all rooms come with private bathrooms, hot showers, and electric blankets (a nice touch on those freezing nights). The Spanish-style adobe hotel feels like an old farm. The rooms are cute, with handmade bamboo beds and Andean area rugs. Overall, the hotel is unbelievably charming. To book a room, you must reserve in advance with **Crillon Tours,** Av. Camacho 1233, La Paz (ℰ **0102/2337-533** or 305/358-5353 in the U.S.; www.titicaca.com).

WHERE TO DINE

Copacabana is the culinary capital of Lake Titicaca. Almost every restaurant here specializes in preparing trout fresh from the lake. The best restaurants are on Avenida 6 de Agosto. They all have pretty much the same menu, which consists of trout, pasta, and pizza. But **La Orilla** (on Av. 6 de Agosto, about 20m/66 ft. from the beach) has a terrace that overlooks the lake. In the evening, the lights go dim, and the dining room feels like a romantic hideaway. The trout curry is highly recommended. Other excellent options include a vegetable stir-fry, fajitas, and the spring roll. On the weekends, live bands sometimes perform here. Another good restaurant for trout is **Pacha,** Bolívar and Avenida 6 de Agosto (ℰ **0102/8622-497**). An excellent coffee stop with

English breakfasts and fruit juices is **Café Bistrot,** Avenida Costanera and Tito Yupan-qui (© **0102/8622-497** or 71518310).

On the Sun Island, there are a few small restaurants. None have names or addresses, but they all have similar menus, including fresh trout and grilled chicken. Your best bet is to ask your hotel for a recommendation.

LAKE TITICACA AFTER DARK

Don't expect to find a wild nightlife scene anywhere near Lake Titicaca. In Copaca-bana, **Sol y Luna,** Av. 16 de Julio 3, is one of the hippest places in town. Live bands sometimes play here, but it's more of a laid-back place, where you can kick back with a few drinks while playing some of their board games, or choose something to read from their book exchange. If you stay at **Inca Utama Hotel & Spa,** 86 Carretera Asfaltada in Huatajata, you can enjoy a live folk music show after dinner in the main restaurant. And, since the hotel is in possession of the second-most powerful telescope in Bolivia (a gift from NASA), this is a great place for stargazing.

6 Sucre ★★

701km (435 miles) SE of La Paz; 366km (227 miles) SE of Cochabamba; 612km (379 miles) SW of Santa Cruz; 162km (100 miles) NE of Potosí

During Bolivia's glory days, when Sucre—or, as it was known then, Chuquisaca—existed solely for the purpose of administering the silver mines in nearby Potosí, the wealthy locals here would often brag, "My mines are in Potosí, but I live in Chuquisaca." For those who could afford it, it made sense to live 162km (100 miles) down the road from Potosí in the relative lowlands (2,706m/8,876 ft.) of Sucre, which is blessed with a mild climate and a much cheerier disposition. Gradually, Sucre became a city of understated prestige. It's been called the Paris of South America because the wealth here attracted some of the finest arts and culture from all over the world. It's also been known as the Athens of South America because it's home to the continent's second-oldest and most prestigious university, San Francisco Xavier University, which dates to 1624 and has educated presidents of Argentina, Paraguay, Chile, Uruguay, and, of course, Bolivia. (Today, out of a total pop. of about 200,000, over 30,000 are students, many of them studying medicine or law.)

For a city like Sucre, money, prestige, and knowledge weren't enough. It also had to have a place in the history books. In 1825, some of the most important South American revolutionaries converged upon the city and signed the country's declaration of independence. Sucre then became the capital of the new republic.

These days, Sucre is the capital of Bolivia in name only—both the executive and leg-islative branches of the government left long ago for La Paz. The silver in nearby Potosí has pretty much run out, and the high culture has returned to Paris. Nevertheless, the city remains one of the most colorful and interesting places in Bolivia. Visitors can sit in the room where the Bolivian declaration of independence was signed, tour churches and museums that still have impressive collections of colonial art, and view the dinosaur tracks that archaeologists recently discovered right in Sucre's backyard.

ESSENTIALS
GETTING THERE
BY PLANE   Aero Sur (© **0103/3364-446** in Santa Cruz, or 0104/6462-141 in Sucre; www.aerosur.com) offers daily flights to Sucre from La Paz, Cochabamba, and Santa Cruz. One-way tickets cost about Bs550 ($70/£35) each. All planes arrive at the

Juana Azurduy de Padilla Airport, which is only a few miles outside town. Taxis from the airport to the center of town cost Bs25 ($3.15/£1.60). Airport tax on departure is Bs10 ($1.30/65p).

BY BUS The Sucre bus terminal is about 1.5km (1 mile) northeast of the center of town at the corner of Alfredo Ostria Gutiérrez and Bustillos. See "Getting Around: By Bus" in "Planning Your Trip to Bolivia," earlier in this chapter, for bus company information. The 14-hour ride from La Paz costs Bs70 ($8.75/£4.40) for a normal bus, Bs90 ($11/£5.50) for a *bus cama* (bus with seats that fold out to almost become a bed). Buses from Cochabamba take about 12 hours and cost Bs30 ($3.75/£1.90) for a normal bus, Bs50 ($6.25/£3.10) for a *bus cama*. Buses from Santa Cruz take 12 hours and cost Bs60 ($7.50/£3.75) for a normal bus, Bs80 ($10/£5) for a *bus cama*. Buses from Potosí leave in the morning, midafternoon, and early evening (around 5pm). The 2½- to 3-hour ride costs Bs20 ($2.50/£1.25).

BY TAXI You can take a taxi from Potosí to Sucre for Bs150 ($19/£9.50) for four people. I recommend using **Expreso Infinito** (© 0104/6422-277).

GETTING AROUND

Most of the banks, travel agencies, hotels, and attractions in Sucre are within easy walking distance of Plaza 25 de Mayo, the commercial heart of the city. If you want to get a bit off of the beaten path, the best option is to take a taxi. It's easy to hail one right off the street, but your hotel can also call one for you.

VISITOR INFORMATION

The main tourist office is located on Estudiantes 35. There aren't any maps available here, but the staff is knowledgeable and helpful. The office is open daily from 8:30am to 12:30pm and 2:30 to 6:30pm. The very friendly staff at **Candelaria Tours** ⊀⊀, off the central square at Audiencia 1 (© 0104/6461-661; www.candelariatours.com), can also answer any questions you may have about the sights in the city or nearby attractions (including Potosí).

FAST FACTS You can exchange money and traveler's checks at **Cambios "El Arca,"** on España 134, or **Casa de Cambio Ambar,** on Ravelo 7 at the corner of Arce. You'll find ATMs on Calle España and all around the main Plaza. **Hospital Santa Bárbara,** Destacamento 111 at the corner of Arenales (© 0104/6460-133), and **Hospital Gastroenterológico,** Avenida Colón between El Villar and Japón (© 0104/6454-700), are the two best hospitals in Sucre. The **post office** is located on Junín and the corner of Ayacucho. You can take care of all your laundry needs at **LaveRap,** Calle Bolívar 617 between Olañeta and Azurday. It's one of the few Laundromats in all of Bolivia that is open on Sundays (only until 1pm). You'll find Internet cafes on all the side streets that lead off the plaza.

WHAT TO SEE & DO
MUSEUMS

Museo Casa de la Libertad ⊀ The United States has Liberty Hall in Philadelphia; Bolivia has the equivalent in Museo Casa de la Libertad. On August 6, 1825, the freedom fighters of Bolivia assembled here to declare independence from Spain. You can visit the exact room where the liberators met. Now known as the Salón de la Independencia, it's filled with portraits of the great liberators and baroque-style wood chairs painted in gold leaf. The portrait here of Simón Bolívar is believed to be the most lifelike reproduction of the great independence hero.

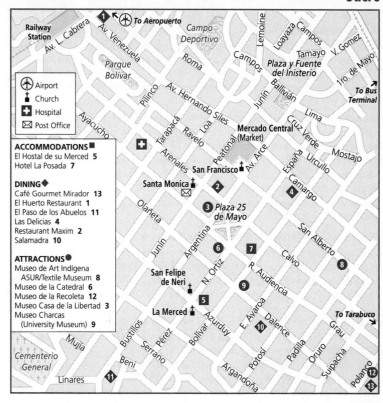

Railway Station

To Aeropuerto

Campo Deportivo

Parque Bolívar

Av. L. Cabrera · Av. Venezuela · Roma

Lemoine · Loayaza · Campos · V. Gomez

Tamayo

Plaza y Fuente del Inisterio

1ro. de Mayo.

To Bus Terminal

✈ Airport
✝ Church
✚ Hospital
✉ Post Office

ACCOMMODATIONS ■
El Hostal de su Merced **5**
Hotel La Posada **7**

DINING ◆
Café Gourmet Mirador **13**
El Huerto Restaurant **1**
El Paso de los Abuelos **11**
Las Delicias **4**
Restaurant Maxim **2**
Salamadra **10**

ATTRACTIONS ●
Museo de Art Indígena
 ASUR/Textile Museum **8**
Museo de la Catedral **6**
Museo de la Recoleta **12**
Museo Casa de la Libertad **3**
Museo Charcas
 (University Museum) **9**

Ayacucho · Pilinco · Av. Hernando Siles · Junín · Ballivián · Lima · Cruz Verde · Mostajo

Tarapacá · Ravelo · Loa · Peatonal · Av. Arce · España · Urcullo · Camargo

Mercado Central (Market)

Arenales · San Francisco ✝ · Santa Monica ✝ ✉ · **2**

Olañeta · **3** Plaza 25 de Mayo

San Alberto

Junín · Argentina · N. Ortiz · **6** · **7** · Calvo · **8**

San Felipe de Neri ✝ · R. Audiencia · **9**

5 · La Merced ✝ · Azurduy · E. Ayaroa · Dalence · Grau

To Tarabuco

10

Bustillos · Serrano · Perez · Bolívar · Potosi · Padilla · Oruro · Suipacha · Polano

Cementerio General

Mujia · Beni · Linares · **11** · Argandoña · **12** · **13**

The museum complex was originally part of a Jesuit university that dates from 1624 (one of the oldest in Bolivia). In addition to the Salón de la Independencia, there are several galleries here dedicated to the history of Bolivia. Items on display include the first Argentine flag (the Bolivians refuse to return it to Argentina, saying "We are all the same"), a copy of the Bolivian declaration of independence, and paintings of the city of Sucre in the independence era. There's also a room dedicated to Mariscal Sucre, the first president of Bolivia. Plan on spending about 45 minutes here.

Plaza 25 de Mayo 25. ℂ **0104/6454-200.** Admission Bs10 ($1.25/60p). Tues–Sat 9–11:15am; Sun 9am–2pm.

Museo Charcas (University Museum Colonial & Anthropological) This museum, which is housed in a 17th-century mansion, consists of three different mini-museums: colonial art, an ethnography and folk collection, and modern art. Overall, the museum provides a comprehensive look at the wide breadth of art forms—both indigenous and European—in Bolivia.

In the Colonial Museum, most of the art dates from the 16th and 17th centuries. The museum houses paintings by the half-indigenous Melchor Pérez Holguín, including his most famous work, *San Juan de Dios,* which has an almost perfect depiction of human hands. You'll also find a collection of beautiful antique furniture on display. In the Ethnographic and Folkloric Museum, you can learn about local rituals and view a

---

⌒Moments **Take a Walk**

Be sure to set aside some time to stroll around Sucre's main Plaza 25 de Mayo. This is the largest and most beautiful square in all of Bolivia, ringed with palm and jacaranda trees.

---

collection of mummified bodies that provide insight on local death rituals. Also on display is a good collection of pottery from the Yampara culture. Its pottery is some of the most beautiful and technically advanced of all pre-Columbian cultures—you can see tears on the faces and evidence of ponchos. The pieces in the Modern Art Gallery reflect contemporary Bolivian artists' focus on poverty and the back-breaking labor involved in working in the mines. Set aside at least 1½ hours to visit the entire collection.

Bolívar 698 (near the corner of Olañeta). ✆ 0104/6453-285. Admission Bs10 ($1.25/60p). Mon–Sat 8:30am–noon and 2:30–6pm.

Museo de Arte Indígena ASUR/Textile Museum ✸✸ ASUR is an acronym for Anthropologists of the Andean South, who are trying to recover the lost artesian techniques of the local population. This museum does an excellent job of displaying some magnificent pieces of art, mainly in the form of textiles that provide a real insight into these local cultures. For example, the Inca culture had three commandments: Don't be a thief, don't be a liar, and don't be lazy. Apparently, the indigenous people would create big intricate textiles as proof that they weren't being lazy. In the collection from the Tarabuco culture, the artists would only weave images of what they knew—people plowing the land, dancers, and horses.

In addition to viewing textiles, you can also see artists hard at work using ancient techniques of weaving, washing, and spinning the wool. It's amazing to witness the intense work that goes into creating these unique forms of art. There is also a wonderful gift shop here that supports local communities. Plan on spending at least 2 hours here.

San Alberto 413 (near the corner of Potosí). ✆ 0104/6453-841. Admission Bs16 ($2/£1). Mon–Fri 8.30am–noon and 2:30–6pm; Sat 9:30am–noon. Closed Sat Oct–May.

Museo de la Catedral ✸✸ The Museo de la Catedral houses an excellent collection of colonial art and silver religious relics, but the **Chapel of the Virgin of Guadalupe** ✸✸ is the star of the show here (and will probably be the highlight of your visit to Sucre). Fray Diego de Ocaña painted the original *Virgen de Guadalupe* in 1601. Today, you can see some remains of this oil painting and the canvas, but mostly it has been destroyed by the thousands of pounds of jewelry that the faithful have offered the Virgin over the past 400 years. The weight of the jewels (and 40,000 emeralds can certainly do a lot of damage) have torn the canvas to bits. All that survive are her face, her hands, and the face of the baby—the rest is pure gemstones. In addition to the Chapel of the Virgin, you can also visit the cathedral, which dates from 1559 but is purely neoclassical. After the independence from Spain in 1825, the liberators tried to erase all colonial influences from the churches in the area. Instead of seeing the elaborate baroque designs from the colonial period, you'll find that this cathedral is very simple and understated.

Calle Nicolás Ortiz 61 (around the corner from Plaza 25 de Mayo). ✆ 0104/6452-257. Admission Bs15 ($1.90/95p). Mon–Fri 10am–noon and 3–5pm; Sat 10am–noon.

Museo de la Recoleta ✪✪ *(Moments)* This museum is housed in a convent that dates from the year 1600. Inside, you will find an excellent collection of colonial art and a courtyard that offers an incredible bird's-eye view of Sucre. Plus, you'll get a glimpse of what it must have been like to live and work here in the 17th century. For example, you can visit a re-created priest's room, very basic accommodations with only one blanket and a whip (used for self-flagellation). The **Courtyard of the Orange Trees** ✪✪ is the most impressive part of the museum, featuring an orange tree that is said to be more than 1,000 years old. Before the Spanish arrived, the indigenous people used this tree as a totem pole. The museum also houses works by colonial painter Melchor Pérez de Holguín, pieces from the Cusqueña school, and an interesting painting of Jesus with an exaggerated flagellation scene, said to justify all the abuse being committed at that time. As you walk around the museum, you may notice that the walls are crooked. This is intentional—it protects the building from the destructive powers of earthquakes. It'll take you an hour to visit the museum and spend a little time enjoying the beautiful courtyard.

Polano 162 (right in front of Plaza Anzures). Admission Bs10 ($1.25/60p). Mon–Fri 9:30–11:30am and 2:30–4:30pm; Sat 3–4:30pm.

AN ATTRACTION OUTSIDE OF TOWN
Cal Orck'o (Dinosaur Tracks) ✪✪ *(Moments)* This is definitely one of the most unique attractions in Bolivia. At first glance, the dinosaur tracks look like simple holes in rocks. But after your eyes adjust, you'll start to see distinct patterns of movement. All of sudden, it's very easy to envision dinosaurs slopping through the mud, trying to escape from their enemies, and searching for water. It is believed that the rocks in the area date back some 68 million years—well before the Andes were formed. Supposedly, there was a lake here surrounded by a forest. Dinosaurs trudged through the mud in the forest toward the lake in search of water. Before the footprints had a chance to disappear (about a 2-week time period), they would be covered by sediment, which settled over the mud and preserved the prints. The bilingual guides will be able to tell you their theories about which dinosaurs were doing what when they walked through this area 68 million years ago. I recommend taking the Dino-Truck to get here—you'll ride in the back of a pickup through the outskirts of Sucre and along roads with beautiful vistas. If you choose to take a taxi, it will cost you about Bs24 ($3/£1.50). The tour lasts about 1½ hours.

About 20 min. outside Sucre on the road to Cochabamba. ✆ 0104/6451-863. Take the Dino-Truck, which leaves daily from the Cathedral on Plaza 25 de Mayo at 9:30am, noon, and 2:30pm. Dino-Truck and admission is Bs30 ($3.75/£1.90). Admission without transportation is Bs20 ($2.50/£1.25). Guided tours daily 10 and 11:30am and 12:30, 2, and 3pm.

SHOPPING
Sucre and the surrounding area are famous for handicrafts. If you happen to be in town on a Sunday and you're looking for handicrafts, you should head to the market in **Tarabuco** ✪ (about 56km/35 miles from Sucre). Here, you will find thousands of different textiles, hats, gloves, bags, and other hand-woven goodies. The market is one of the best in Bolivia. On Sunday mornings, buses leave from Sucre for Tarabuco from 7 to 9am at the corner of Avenida de la Américas and Manco Capac. The 1½-hour ride costs Bs15 ($1.90/95p) each way. **Candelaria Tours** ✪✪, right off the central square at Audiencia 1 (✆ 0104/6461-661; www.candelariatours.com), also organizes day trips to the market and the surrounding area.

The gift shop at the **Museo de Arte Indígena ASUR/Textile Museum,** on San Alberto 413 (near the corner of Potosí), offers the best selection of textiles and hand-made crafts in Sucre. **Artesanías Sucre,** Calle Olañeta 42 at Plazuela Zudáñez, and **Artesanías Tesoros del Inca,** Calle Camargo 514, also sell local handicrafts. You will find everything under the sun at the unique **Central Market** on the corner of Junín and Ravelo. I recommend heading up to the second floor to try the local *tojorí* drink for breakfast. The drink consists of boiled corn, cinnamon, and sugar. Because of its high protein content, it's called "the cornflakes of the Andes."

Para Ti *(★★* on Arenales (about a third of a block in from the plaza) sells delicious handmade chocolate.

WHERE TO STAY
El Hostal de Su Merced *★★★ Finds*   Once you have stayed at this hotel, you can rest assured that you have slept in the best small hotel in Bolivia. The hotel is housed in a magnificent converted mansion from the 18th century. It's not luxurious, but what it lacks in luxury, it makes up for in charm and character. All the rooms are unique, with thick white adobe walls and antique furniture (some is original to this house). Room no. 7 is a junior suite with a separate sitting area with large antique chairs and a hand-embroidered ottoman, hand-carved wooden doors, lace curtains, a brass bed, and the aura of true elegance. All the rooms have similar personal touches—including crystal chandeliers, brick floors, adorable basket-weave bins, sloped ceilings, and antiques galore. If you plan on staying here for a while, try room no. 16. It's very private, and it has its own quiet patio. The beautiful rooftop terrace has awesome views of the Cathedral; it's a lovely place to lounge in the sun.

Calle Azurduy 16 (between N. Ortiz and Bolívar), Sucre. Ⓒ 0104/6442-706. Fax 0104/6912-078. www.boliviaweb. com/companies/sumerced. 16 units. $45 (£23) double; $60 (£30) triple; $60 (£30) junior suite. Rates include breakfast. AE, MC, V. **Amenities:** Restaurant; room service; laundry service; dry cleaning. *In room:* TV, minibar in junior suites.

Hotel La Posada *★★ Value*   If you can't stay at the Hostal de su Merced, this hotel is an excellent second choice, especially if you're looking for the best bargain in Sucre. Opened in 2003 in a renovated old house, La Posada's rooms overlook a lovely court-yard with mature trees and colorful plants; they all have tile floors, colorful blue-and-yellow bedspreads, and wrought-iron lamps. Rooms on the second floor have wood-beamed ceilings and are slightly more spacious than those on the ground floor. Bathrooms are nicely tiled and sparkling, if a bit small. The Posada's restaurant is excellent, serving a daily three-course menu for lunch and dinner priced at Bs20 ($2.50/£1.25); in warm weather, you can dine outside under elegant parasols. If you're looking for the best deal in town with a healthy dose of charm, then this is it.

Calle Audiencia 92, Sucre. Ⓒ 0104/6460-101. Fax 0104/6913-427. www.laposadahostal.com. 9 units. $50 (£25) double; $90 (£45) suite. Rates include breakfast. MC, V. **Amenities:** Charming restaurant; room service. *In room:* TV.

WHERE TO DINE
You will dine really well in Sucre; this city has tons of interesting and delicious eateries. In addition to the restaurants listed below, here are some other good choices: The most delicious *salteñas* in town can be found at **El Paso de los Abuelos,** Bustillo 216 (Ⓒ **0104/6455-173**); they're open daily from 8am to 1pm. The newest and hippest cafe/restaurant is **Salamadra,** Calle Avaroa 510 (Ⓒ **0104/6913-433**), where the crème de la crème of Sucre's residents gather for lunch, dinner, and coffee and snacks. For a much simpler but exquisite local experience, visit **Las Delicias** *★*, Estudiantes

50 (© **0104/6442-502**). Here, owner (and baker) Dorly Fernández de Toro serves her amazing pastries; some are very unusual but delicious, such as the *sonso,* made from mashed yucas. There's also a good selection of yummy empanadas and *humitas* (a Bolivian version of the tamale). Las Delicias is open only Tuesday through Saturday from 4 to 8pm; come early as this place fills up fast.

The best place for lunch with a terrific view is the **Café Gourmet Mirador,** Plaza Anzures, across from the Recoleta (© **0104/6440-299**). You'll dine outside under lovely bamboo umbrellas with Sucre stretched at your feet; the specialty here is crepes. They're open daily until 6pm.

El Huerto Restaurant ★ *Moments* BOLIVIAN   In Spanish, *el huerto* means "the orchard," and that's exactly where you'll feel like you are when you dine outside in the lovely garden area of this popular lunch spot. Your fellow diners will probably be some of Sucre's biggest bigwigs, who come here for the relaxed atmosphere and excellent food. This is a great place to try some of Sucre's local specialties, such as *chorizos chuquisaqueños especiales* (a spicy pork sausage). You can also order more international fare, including filet mignon, pineapple chicken, and omelets. For dessert, I highly recommend the homemade ice cream.

Ladislao Cabrera 86 (it's a bit outside of town, so take a taxi). © 0104/6451-538. Main courses Bs39 ($5/£2.50). V. Daily noon–3pm; Thurs–Sat noon–9pm.

Restaurant Maxim ★ BOLIVIAN/FRENCH   This restaurant feels very formal in a European way. The walls are covered with fancy lace French-style wallpaper, crystal chandeliers hang from the ceiling, and the tablecloths have hand-embroidered paisley designs. The waiters wear white tuxes and cater to your every need. Although the ambience is unique, the food here has its own special flair. For an appetizer, you can order the tasty *ceviche de pejerrey* (raw kingfish marinated in a tangy lemon juice and served in an oyster shell). The *pollo Maxim* (chicken filled with ham and cheese) is one of the house specialties. In addition, you can order local dishes such as *chorizos chuquisaqueños* (pork sausage) and *picante mixto.* In a nod to French cooking, almost all of the dishes come bathed in a cream sauce, except for the *chuletas de cerdo glaseados* (pork chops in a red-wine sauce with a touch of sugar).

Arenales 19 (half-block from the main plaza; on the 2nd floor). © 0104/6451-798. Reservations recommended on weekends. Main courses Bs25–Bs40 ($3.25–$5.20/£1.60–£2.60). MC, V. Mon–Sat 7–11pm.

SUCRE AFTER DARK

Because Sucre is crawling with young university students, there are tons of charming bars near Plaza 25 de Mayo, especially on Calle N. Ortiz leading away from the square. I recommend the **Joy Ride Café & Bar,** Calle N. Ortiz 14 (© **0104/6425-544;** www.joyridebol.com), owned by a Dutch guy and serving good beer and excellent light meals. This is where many gringos spend the evening and sign up for one of their biking or hiking tours. Next door, **Picadilly** is another popular bar that also serves Indonesian food. If you fancy *mojitos* with a Bolivian twist—coca leaf—go to **Locots,** Bolivar 465 (© **6915958**). Another good bar with both locals and foreigners is **Kultur Café Berlin,** Calle Avaroa 326 (© **6424521**). If you're looking to dance, try **Mitos** (no phone), Calle Francisco Cerro at the corner of Calle Loyaza; and **Tío Lalo** (no phone), Calle San Alberto 680. Note that most everything is eerily quiet during the week; the above bars and clubs, with the exception of Joy Ride, are open only Wednesday through Saturday.

A SIDE TRIP TO SALAR DE UYUNI

Salar de Uyuni is quickly becoming one of Bolivia's star attractions. This eerie land-scape is the largest salt lake in the world. To see the area, you have to travel on a guided tour that usually lasts for 4 days and 3 nights. There are no roads in these parts, so all the agencies use almost-antique Toyota Land Cruisers to transport you through the desert. The trip can be rough, especially on your bottom. But the desert landscape, with its volcanoes in the background and bizarre rock formations, is truly surreal. Some of the highlights of the trip include a stop at the salt lake itself; the oddly shaped **Isla del Pescado,** which is covered with cactuses; and the **Laguna Colorado,** with its red algae that attracts flamingoes. My favorite stop on the tour is the **Sol de la Mañana,** where you can see geysers, fumaroles, and mud boiling in the earth. It's called Sol de la Mañana because it's best seen early in the morning. At the **Laguna Verde** (in the farthest southwest corner of Bolivia), be sure to hold on tightly to your hat, because the wind here is vicious. The emerald green Laguna Verde sits right below the Lincancabur Volcano (5,835m/19,139 ft.) and makes for a fantastic photograph.

I only recommend this trip for people who are ready to rough it. The accommoda-tions along the way are very basic (simple dorm-style rooms and rustic outhouses). Bring tons of warm clothing and a thick sleeping bag, because the temperature can drop below zero Celsius (32°F), and there's no heat.

The town of Uyuni is located at the lake's edge. The best hotel is **Los Girasoles** (© **0102/6933-323;** www.girasoleshotel.com). Located at Calle Santa Cruz 155, the hotel boasts simple, clean rooms with private bathrooms, heating, and 24-hour hot water. Doubles cost $25 (£13) including breakfast. Another hotel to try is **Magia de Uyuni** (© **0102/6932-541**), located on Avenida Colón between Sucre and Camacho. You'll pay $22 (£11) per night for a double with bathroom, including breakfast and electric heat.

GETTING THERE   The easiest way to get to Uyuni is to take a **bus** from Potosí. Buses leave daily at 11:30, 11:45am, and 6:30pm from the small bus terminal on Avenida Universitaria at the intersection of Sevilla. (They leave Uyuni for Potosí at 10am and 7pm.) The 5-hour ride costs Bs25 ($3.15/£1.60).

If you want a **guided tour,** it's not easy to find a reputable company. I suggest con-tacting **Mariana Tours,** Olaneta 101 A, Sucre; (© **0104/6429-329;** mtours@cotes. net.bo); ask to speak to the manager, Rodrigo Garron, and he'll arrange the highest quality trip for you. Their tours are tailor-made to fit your needs and leave from either Sucre or Potosí. Another well-known operator is **Andes Salt Expeditions,** 3 Alonso de Ibanez, Potosí (© **0102/6225-175;** www.andes-salt-uyuni.com.bo).

7 Cochabamba

385km (239 miles) SE of La Paz; 473km (293 miles) W of Santa Cruz; 366km (227 miles) NW of Sucre

Cochabambinos are famous for their love of the good life. Their sun-bleached city is set-tled in a dusty hollow at the very center of Bolivia. The quiet plazas invite you to linger and the year-round springlike climate encourages you to stroll along the quaint streets. Overlooking all this is the largest statue of Christ in the world, the 33m (108-ft.) Cristo de la Concordia. There's something very welcoming about Cochabamba: There may not be much to see and do in the city itself except eat and drink to your heart's con-tent, but Cochabamba is a great place to relax and get to know the people of Bolivia.

Or you can travel to the small towns in the nearby valleys and visit some of the most colorful local markets in the country.

ESSENTIALS

GETTING THERE

BY PLANE   Aero Sur (© **0103/3364-446** in Santa Cruz, or 0104/400-912 in Cochabamba; www.aerosur.com) offers daily flights to Cochabamba from La Paz, Santa Cruz, and Sucre. One-way tickets cost about Bs470 ($60/£30) each. All planes arrive at the very modern Aeropuerto Internacional Jorge Wilstermann. Taxis from the airport to the center of town cost about Bs24 ($3/£1.50).

BY BUS   The Cochabamba bus terminal, Avenida Ayacucho and Avenida Aroma, is probably the nicest bus station in all of Bolivia. Buses from La Paz arrive almost every half-hour. The 8-hour journey costs Bs35 ($4.40/£2.20) for a regular bus, Bs50 ($6.25/£3.10) for a *bus cama.* Buses from Santa Cruz take 11 hours and cost Bs35 ($4.40/£2.20) for a normal bus, Bs60 ($7.50/£3.75) for a *bus cama.* Buses from Sucre take 11 hours and cost Bs30 ($3.75/£1.90) for a normal bus, Bs50 ($6.25/£3.10) for a *bus cama.* See "Getting Around: By Bus" in "Planning Your Trip to Bolivia," earlier in this chapter, for bus company information.

GETTING AROUND

Cochabamba is an extremely walkable city. For the most part, the city is compact. The streets Ayacucho and Las Heroínas are the center of Cochabamba. From Ayacucho the streets are labeled north and south. From Las Heroínas, the streets are numbered east to west. The best restaurants and hotels are located in the upscale residential neighborhood known as Recoleta; it's best to take a taxi, which only costs about Bs8 ($1/50p) from the center of town. To reach the statue of Christ, you can walk east 15 minutes from the center of town, or take a taxi for about Bs20 ($2.50/£1.25) round-trip. *Trufis* are available throughout the city for Bs1.50 (20¢/10p); numbers are clearly marked on the front of the vans.

VISITOR INFORMATION

The tourist information office is on General Acha and Calle Bautista; it's open Monday through Friday from 8:30am to 4:30pm. But unless you speak Spanish and have a very specific question, the tourist office is virtually useless.

   Ranabol Expeditions, Av. Ayacucho 112 (© **0104/4583-039;** www.aventura bolivia.com), can help you find your bearings with their organized city tours and trips to the valley, Tunari, and the Chapare area. They have trips ranging from 1 to 20 days with experienced guides, camping equipment, and sleeping bags. If you're looking for an English-speaking tour guide, I highly recommend **Tim Johnson;** contact him at tim@bolivia.com.

FAST FACTS   To change traveler's checks or exchange money, you should head to the travel agency **Exprintbol S.R.L,** Plaza 14 de Septiembre 242 (© **0104/4255-834**). **Hospital Belga** (© **0104/4251-579**), on Antezana between Paxxieri and Venezuela, is the best hospital in town. Pharmacies abound in Cochabamba. **Farmacia Boliviana** on 14 de Septiembre E-0202 was the first pharmacy in Cochabamba; **Farmacia San Mateo** on Las Heroínas E-0323 (between España and 25 de Mayo) is a bit more modern. The **post office** is on the corner of Las Heroínas and Ayacucho; the entrance is on Ayacucho. The best **Internet cafe** is **Black Cat Internet,** which is located on General Acha, just half a block off the Plaza de 14 Septiembre. **Entelnet** on the Prado, Av. Ballivián 539 adjacent to Plaza Colón, is also reliable for Internet use.

WHAT TO SEE & DO

In addition to the sights listed below, you can also visit the **Capilla Cristo de las Lágrimas de San Pedro,** a chapel where there is a sculpture of Christ that allegedly cries tears of human blood every Good Friday. The tears have been tested in an Australian lab, and they are indeed of human blood. There are pictures of what this particular sculpture looked like when it was new (much less blood). The chapel, located on the corner of Belzu and Las Heroínas, is open Monday and Wednesday through Saturday from 3 to 6pm.

The new **Casona Santiváñez,** at 158 Calle Santiváñez, is also worth a stop if you're downtown. An old house, restored in 2001 by the municipality of Cochabamba, it is now a cultural center. It's home to the **Museo de Fotografía Antigua,** which has some interesting old photographs of the city. There's also a room devoted to writers, the **Museo de Escritores,** with letters and photos from Latin American writers. The salons upstairs are worth a peek if they're open (official city functions are held here); they are grand with old colonial furniture. Admission is free and the center is open Monday through Friday from 9am to noon and 2:30 to 6pm.

Centro Simón I Patiño/Palacio Portales

A visit to the Palacio Portales is a must for anyone interested in seeing how the upper, upper crust of Bolivia lived in the early 20th century. Ironically, the tin baron Simón Patiño never lived here—he suffered a heart attack during its construction, and his heart condition prevented his return to his native country. In fact, Charles de Gaulle is the only person who has ever spent the night in the house. What a pity, because this mansion is a real beaut.

Patiño was originally from the Cochabamba area, but he discovered an enormous tin deposit near the mining town of Oruro. By the turn of the 20th century, he controlled 10% of the world's tin. He commissioned a French architect to design and build the house from 1915 to 1927 while he was living in Europe. You enter the house through a round, neoclassical entrance. Inside, your guide will take you to several different rooms, which speak of the opulence of that time period. The walls are covered with silk wallpaper; crystal chandeliers from Venice hang from the rafters; and green-and-white marble fireplaces were built to keep the house warm. Each room has its own unique floor design. Thanks to the dry climate of Cochabamba, everything here has been impeccably preserved. Today, the house is used as a cultural center. After the tour, you can walk through the beautiful Japanese gardens or visit the Contemporary Art Center (Mon–Fri 3–9pm; admission is 3Bs/40¢/20p). Plan on spending about an hour here.

Av. Potosí 1450 (near the intersection of Av. Portales). Admission Bs10 ($1.25/60p). Tours in English Mon–Fri at 5:30pm and Sat at 11am. Take *trufi* no. 10 north from the corner of San Martín and Bolívar.

Cristo de la Concordia 🎯 *Moments*

This steel-and-cement sculpture is believed to be the largest statue of Christ in the world. Because Christ died when he was 33 years old, it measures 33m (108 ft.). I recommend riding the cable car to the top, but if you're feeling energetic, you can climb the 2,000 litter-strewn steps. However you reach the summit, you will be rewarded with lovely views of the area. Christ faces the lower valley area of Cochabamba. From here, you can see Tunari—at 4,800m (15,744 ft.), these are the highest twin peaks in the area. The Cristo Redentor (Christ the Redeemer) statue in Rio de Janeiro is the model for Cristo de la Concordia, but the locals like to think that this one is more loving—the face has more human features and, unlike its counterpart in Rio, its hands seem to be in a welcoming embrace. There is an outdoor Mass here every Sunday morning. Set aside at least 2 hours for your visit, and do *not* go late at night

Located at the far eastern end of Av. Las Heroínas. Cable car fare Bs3 (40¢/20p) each way. Tues–Sat 10am–7pm; Sun 9am–8pm.

HISTORIC CHURCHES & PLAZAS

Cochabamba was founded in 1574. By walking around the city's plazas and visiting the historic churches, you can travel back in time and feel what it must have been like to live here hundreds of years ago. In **Plaza San Sebastián,** you can see one of the first houses ever built in Cochabamba. Nearby is the first railroad station built in Bolivia. **Plaza 14 de Septiembre** is the historic heart of Cochabamba. September 14 is known as Cochabamba Day, when Cochabamba formally became a city. The plaza dates from 1571, and it is most remarkable because it has preserved its colonial archways on all four sides. (Very few plazas in South America can boast that the buildings on all four sides are original.) On this plaza, you can visit the **cathedral,** which was the first church of Cochabamba. It still has its original baroque facade, and there's a good collection of colonial art inside. Nearby on Ayacucho and Santiváñez is **Santo Domingo,** which is one of my favorite churches. It's very simple inside (unlike the cathedral), which gives it a majestic air. The wooden doors are from 1612.

SHOPPING

MARKETS   Cochabamba and the surrounding area are famous for their colorful markets. If you happen to be in town on a Wednesday or Saturday, you must stop in at **La Cancha,** Avenida San Martín between Tarata and Pulacayo, a huge market where you can find handicrafts, fresh produce, herbs, and just about anything else you could ever want.

In the valleys outside Cochabamba, there are also several towns that have authentic markets. **Caixa Tours,** Esteban Arze S-0563 (© **0104/4250-937**), organizes day trips to these market towns. **Tarata,** in the Upper Valley, is a lovely historic village about 1 hour from Cochabamba; market day is Thursday. The market in **Punata** (about 1½ hr. from Cochabamba) is considered to be one of the best and biggest in Bolivia. It's also one of the least touristy. On Sunday, you should head to **Cliza** for a taste of real Bolivian cooking. One of the specialties here is baked pigeon. Minibuses to these towns leave from the corner of Avenida Barrientos and Avenida 6 de Agosto; the trip costs Bs5 (65¢/35p).

HANDICRAFTS   Shopping at the local markets can be a chaotic experience. If you're looking for something more tranquil, you should stop by **Vicuñita Handicrafts,** on Av. Rafael Pabón 777 (© **0104/4255-615**). Here you can shop for leather goods, tapestries, bags, and ceramic figurines (all handmade!) in the comfort of a private, uncrowded warehouse. For alpaca sweaters, I recommend **Amerindia** on Calle España 264.

WHERE TO STAY

Anteus Apart Hotel *Value*   This is Cochabamba's best value: An attractive budget hotel located in the upscale Recoleta residential neighborhood. A rather plain three-story building overlooks a nice garden in the back and the eastern range of the Andes in the distance. Rooms are bright and cheerful with large windows and simple, modern furnishings. The smallish bathrooms are nicely tiled and come with shower only. The 10 apartments come with a fully equipped kitchen and separate living area, and at $35 (£18) they are a great bargain. Also, free transportation is offered from and to the airport. You can walk from here to several good cafes, restaurants, bars, and a huge grocery store.

Av. Potosí 1365, Cochabamba. ℂ 0104/4245-067. Fax 0104/4320-166. www.hotelanteus.com. 24 units (shower only). $30 (£15) double; $40 (£20) triple; $50 (£25) quad; $35 (£18) apt for 2; $50 (£25) apt for 3. Additional person $10 (£5). MC, V. **Amenities:** Restaurant; laundry service. *In room:* TV.

Hotel Aranjuez ⋆⋆ *(Finds)*   This is the most atmospheric hotel in town. Ignore the peeling paint outside—inside you'll find an elegant lobby of black sofas and wooden floors that lead to a charming courtyard with fountain. It is a rambling family mansion of open fireplaces, gold-gilded mirrors, and hidden nooks and crannies. On top there is a beautiful rooftop terrace. The rooms are worn but have nice details such as arched door frames and walk-in wardrobes. Hugo Chávez and his entourage regularly take it over whenever there's a summit in town. The hotel is family run with extremely helpful staff. It is located on a quiet residential street in the Recoleta area.

Av. Buenos Aires E-0563 Cochabamba. ℂ 0104/4240-158. www.aranjuezhotel.com. 30 units. $69 (£35) double. MC, V. **Amenities:** Restaurant; small pool; laundry service. *In room:* TV.

Portales Hotel ⋆   Portales Hotel is genteel and gracious, if a little neglected. It's located in Cochabamba's ritziest residential neighborhood, Recoleta, surrounded by the city's most popular restaurants and bars. Almost all the rooms look out onto the sunny and lush pool area. They are all comfortable and spacious with dark-wood tones and very clean, but somewhat dated, carpets. The sparkling, tiled bathrooms are large, with their own bidets. Don't expect much luxury here, though: The rooms are more like what you'd find in a roadside motel in the U.S.—functional but not elegant. The suites have separate sitting areas with a table and two chairs. The bathrooms in the suites are enormous and wood-paneled—they feel like locker rooms in an exclusive club. One complaint: The exercise room, sauna, and Jacuzzi are pretty run down and in desperate need of renovation; I suggest paying the Bs20 ($2.50/£1.25) admission to enjoy the facilities of a nearby health club; the friendly staff will happily give you directions.

Av. Pando 1271, Cochabamba. ℂ 0800-6868 or 0104/4285-444. Fax 0104/4242-071. 106 units. $95 (£48) double; $170 (£85) suite. Rates include buffet breakfast. AE, MC, V. **Amenities:** 2 restaurants; bar; outdoor pool w/beautiful landscaping; squash court; really tiny exercise room; Jacuzzi; sauna; small business center; salon; room service; massage; same-day laundry service; dry cleaning. *In room:* A/C, TV, minibar, hair dryer, safe.

A HOTEL OUTSIDE TOWN

Hacienda De Kaluyo Resort ⋆⋆⋆ *(Finds)*   For the ultimate escape, stay 30 minutes outside town at the most interesting resort in all of Bolivia. A grand private driveway leads to a beautiful hacienda built next to a 19th-century chapel (where weddings are frequently held). The vistas are beautiful, the swimming pool is incredibly serene, and the outdoor restaurant overlooks the endless fields leading down to a large lake. Rooms are in a two-story building, separate from the pool and restaurant area, so guests won't be disturbed when events are in progress. Every piece of furniture in the rooms was designed and built in Bolivia—from the lovely wooden beds to the delicate wrought-iron lamps and ceramic sconces. The bathrooms are spacious and sparkling. There are also two large cabins with their own private garages and kitchenettes; these cabins are very cozy and rustic with wood-beam ceilings and exposed brick. There are hiking trails all around the property, a lovely open-air gym, a soccer field, and a basketball court. If you ask the friendly owners, they will arrange a water-skiing excursion for you; mountain bikes are also available.

Camino La Angostura (at the intersection of the old hwy. to Santa Cruz), Tarata. ℂ **0104/4576-593**. Fax 0104/4451-662. www.kaluyo.com. 17 units. $60 (£30) double; $120 (£60) cabin for 4 people. Rates include breakfast. AE, MC, V. **Amenities:** 2 restaurants; bar; lounge; beautiful outdoor pool w/magnificent vistas; tennis court; outdoor exercise room; limited watersports equipment rental; game room; laundry service. *In room:* TV, kitchenette in cabins.

WHERE TO DINE

Salteñería "Los Castores" ⚶, on Av. Ballivián 790 at the corner of Oruro (ℂ **0104/4259-585**), specializes in *salteñas*. There's no menu here; you can only order *salteñas de pollo* (chicken) or *salteñas de carne* (meat). They cost Bs3.50 (45¢/25p) each, and they are out of this world. You can do as the Bolivians do and eat breakfast here, but the place is open until 2pm.

Casa de Campo ⚶ *(Finds)* BOLIVIAN   Cochabamba's best Bolivian restaurant is enormous. On weekends the place is filled to the brim with locals enjoying traditional cuisine. It's an unassuming place but the food is divine. Come here to sample real Cochabamban dishes such as the *chanka de pollo* (chicken soup with beans) or the spicy *pique lobo* soup. If you're feeling adventurous, try one of the local sausages— chorizo or *chuleta*. For the main course, there are several stews; the most popular is the *picante de pollo* (a bit spicy with a locally grown green pepper). If you're in the mood for meat, the "lapping" is excellent. It's a very thin (although sometimes not very tender) steak, grilled and served with broad beans, tomatoes, and sliced onion. (It seems to be a big mystery to everyone why it's called lapping.) This place really gets busy after 9pm on Friday and Saturday when there's a long wait for tables, so arrive early.

Av. Uyuni 618. ℂ **0104/4243-937**. Main courses Bs24–Bs35 ($3–$4.40/£1.50–£2.20). MC, V. Daily noon–midnight (till 1am Fri–Sat).

La Cantonata ITALIAN   This is one of the most romantic restaurants in town, with fancy tablecloths, formal place settings, and flickering candles. You can also relax by the cozy fireplace and gaze through the huge picture windows. For a few hours, you might forget that you're in Bolivia; it's easy to imagine that you're in your local Italian restaurant. All the pasta, except the spaghetti, is homemade. Choices include ravioli Bolognese and *pasta al pesto*. Besides pasta, there is a good selection of meat and fish, including several different types of steak. I recommend the *surubí alla Cantonata* (an Amazonian fish with oysters, white wine, and lemon sauce). The pizza here is also quite good.

Calle Mayor Rocha 409 (corner of España). ℂ **0104/4259-222**. Main courses Bs31–Bs84 ($3.90–$11/£1.95–£5.50). AE, MC, V. Daily noon–2:30pm and 6:30–11:30pm.

COCHABAMBA AFTER DARK

Cochabamba is a university town with more than 27,000 students. On Friday and Saturday nights, this town is hopping. Most of the trendy bars and cafes are clustered around Avenida España between Colombia and Ecuador. One of the most happening is **Metrópolis** on the corner of España and Ecuador. In Recoleta, there are several bars and nightclubs on Avenida Uyuni, close to La Estancia restaurant. Also, locals come out in droves on the weekends to sip beer and watch the action on the Prado—there are tons of cafes and places on Avenida Ballivián (Paseo el Prado).

A SIDE TRIP TO POTOSI

You might find it hard to believe that bleak, wet and windy Potosí was once one of the richest cities in the world. It's been said that enough silver was pulled from the bowels of nearby Cerro Rico to build a bridge from Potosí all the way to Madrid—and enough people died inside the mines to build a bridge of bones all the way back.

Nowadays, visitors can still see the two disparate sides of the city. Seven thousand workers still eke out a living from a mine where millions died. You can take tours there that will bring you face to face with these miners and the dreary conditions in which they work. In contrast you can then tour the sights that evoke the city's former glory.

Potosí is not a heartwarming place. At more than 3,900m (12,792 ft.), it's one of the highest cities in the world. Even when the sun is shining bright, there is always a bitter chill in the air. It's painful to visit the mines and learn about the past exploitation of these workers, but it's also fascinating to see the remains of a place that was once the home of some of the wealthiest people in the world.

GETTING THERE   The Potosí bus station is on the edge of town at the end of Avenida Universitaria (near the intersection of Av. Sevilla). Buses from Santa Cruz go through Cochabamba or Sucre. The 3-hour ride from Cochabamba costs Bs30 ($3.75/£1.90). Buses depart from Sucre in the morning, midafternoon, and early evening (around 5pm). The 2½- to 3-hour ride costs Bs15 ($1.90/95p). Buses depart from Uyuni at 10am and 7pm. The 5-hour ride costs Bs25 ($3.15/£1.60). You can also take a taxi from Sucre for Bs150 ($19/£9.50) for four people. Contact **Expreso Infinito** (© 0104/6422-277).

WHAT TO SEE & DO   The main tourist office is located in a kiosk on Plaza 6 de Agosto. No maps are available here, but the staff is knowledgeable and helpful. I recommend making a quick stop at the **Museo Sacro Jerusalén,** on Avenida Camacho at the corner of Avenida del Maestro. The church here dates from 1708. To really understand the history of Potosí, you have to visit **Casa Nacional de la Moneda,** Calle Ayacucho between Quijarro and Bustillos (© 0102/6223-986), once the biggest building in the Americas. This former Spanish royal mint it is now dedicated to Bolivian weapons, modern art, minerals, and archaeology. **Convento Museo Santa Teresa,** Calle Santa Teresa 15 and Calle Ayacucho (© 0102/6223-847), was a working convent from 1691 through 1976 (nowadays, the sisters live next door). Here, the nuns were separated from their callers by a dark screened wall. They weren't allowed to touch or see their guests; they could only exchange words. You can visit the impressive church and countless galleries full of colonial art, antiques, Murano glass, and hand-painted porcelain dishes.

VISITING THE MINES   The history of Potosí is inextricably linked to Cerro Rico. Taking a tour of the mines will open your eyes to a different side of Potosí, to the world of the people who actually work here. Let me warn you beforehand that it's not a pretty picture. Not much has changed here over the past few hundred years. Fortunately, the miners now work in cooperatives, and they do earn a percentage of what they find. The average salary here is equivalent to about $100 (£50) a month.

You will see workers igniting dynamite to open new areas, shoveling rocks, and carrying heavy loads, all in one of the most abysmal work environments that you could ever imagine. These miners often spend 24-hr. stretches in utter darkness, with cigarettes, soda, and coca leaves as their only form of sustenance. There are no proper stairways with handrails and the paths are narrow and very steep; and there is mud everywhere, which makes walking treacherous. Expect to get dirty. I would recommend that anyone with heart or breathing problems or claustrophobia skip the trip to the mines.

There are several companies in Potosí that offer mine tours. The best ones use guides who are former miners. Overall, however, the quality of the tours is horrendous: The equipment (hard hats, waterproof clothing, gloves, boots, lamps, surgical masks) is often in poor condition, and the guides can be unreliable. **Koala Tours,** Ayacucho 5 in front of Casa de la Moneda (© **0102/6222-092**), is one of the more reputable companies. Tours leave Monday through Saturday, but it's best to go on a weekday because the mines are quiet on the weekends. The 5-hr. tour costs Bs80 ($10/£5) per person; a percentage of the profits is donated to the cooperatives working in the mines.

WHERE TO STAY   Most visitors come to Potosí on a day trip from Sucre or Cochamaba; accommodations here are nothing special and many don't have heat (it gets real cold at night). **Hotel Cima Argentum,** Av. Villazon 239 (© **0102/6229-538;** fax 0102/6122-603; www.hca-potosi.com), is situated about 6 blocks from the center of town, but it's worth the walk. Rooms are modern with colorful bedspreads, dark clean carpets, and wood furniture. **Hostal Colonial,** Calle Hoyos 8 (© **0102/6224-809;** fax 0102/6227-146; hcolonial_potosi@hotmail.com), is one of the best hotels in Potosí, but don't expect anything extraordinary. It's one of the few places in town with heat. **Hostal Cerro Rico Velasco,** Calle Ramos 123 (© **0102/6223-539**), offers modern and clean rooms, though the staff is surly and not very helpful.

8 Santa Cruz de la Sierra

858km (532 miles) SE of La Paz; 473km (293 miles) E of Cochabamba; 612km (379 miles) NE of Sucre

Santa Cruz (also known as Santa Cruz de la Sierra) is undergoing a renaissance. Often dismissed as the brash oil capital of Bolivia, the city is asserting itself and increasingly attracting visitors. Traditionally it was a major railroad hub with oil refining as its main industry. People came to Santa Cruz to make money and to escape their past. Here SUVs outnumber *trufis.* The flat roads here seem terribly out of place in a country of mountains and peaks. Compared to the cold nights and thin air so characteristic of the high plateau area, the tropical heat and humidity might feel a bit oppressive. Surprisingly for a new city, its streets are lined with low pillared buildings and tiled roofs. A visionary mayor has cleaned up the center and made the plaza one of the prettiest in Bolivia. Tourists are finally coming to Santa Cruz, using it as a base to explore a wealth of attractions—Inca ruins, historic Jesuit missions, and a unique national park, all only a few hours away from this booming metropolis.

ESSENTIALS
GETTING THERE
BY PLANE   **Aero Sur** (© **0103/3364-446** in Santa Cruz; www.aerosur.com) offers daily flights to Santa Cruz from La Paz, Cochabamba, and Sucre. One-way tickets cost between Bs470 and Bs870 ($60–$110/£30–£55) each. Additionally, both **Aero Sur** and **American Airlines** (© **0102/237-2010**) use Santa Cruz as their main hub for international flights to Miami and Madrid, so it may well be your first city when arriving to Bolivia.

All planes arrive at the very modern Viru Viru Airport, which is about 16km (10 miles) outside town. Taxis from the airport to the center of town cost between Bs50 and

Bs60 ($6.25–$7.50/£3.10–£3.75). There's also an airport bus, which leaves the airport about every 20 minutes and drops passengers off at the bus terminal and in the nearby neighborhoods. The ride costs Bs8 ($1/50p).

BY BUS The Santa Cruz bus terminal on Avenida Cañoto and Avenida Irala is a truly mad scene. Thousands of people crowd the station at all times of the day, and there's no central information office, so you have to figure out on your own where the bus you want is leaving from. Plus, not all the buses leave from the terminal—many buses depart from offices across the street from the terminal. Many bus companies have offices outside the terminal on Avenida Irala. Buses from La Paz usually arrive in the morning. The 14-hour journey costs Bs120 ($15/£7.50). Buses from Cochabamba take 10 hours and cost Bs50 ($6.25/£3.10) for a normal bus, Bs80 ($10/£5) for a *bus cama*. Buses from Sucre take a grueling 12 hours and cost Bs60 ($7.50/£3.75) for a normal bus, Bs80 ($10/£5) for a *bus cama*. See "Getting Around: By Bus" in "Planning Your Trip to Bolivia," earlier in this chapter.

GETTING AROUND

A map of Santa Cruz resembles a large pizza. It is a circular city, with each neighborhood known as a "ring" *(anillo)*. The first ring is the first circle around the city; as you move farther from the center, you reach the second and third *anillos*. Santa Cruz is quickly becoming a prime example of urban sprawl. The center of the city is getting smaller, while the outskirts of town keep moving farther and farther away. Taxis are, by far, the easiest way to get around. From the center of town to the hotels and restaurants in the nearby suburbs, a taxi should cost Bs15 to Bs23 ($2–$3/£1–£1.50). Plaza 24 de Septiembre is the commercial heart of Santa Cruz; from here, you can walk to all the banks, travel agencies, and centrally located hotels. For car rental try **A. Barrons Renta Car,** Av. Alemana 50 (© 0103/342-0160; www.rentacarbolivia.com). They also have offices in Cochabamba and Tarija.

VISITOR INFORMATION

You'll find **Tourist Information** on the north side of the main plaza (© 0103/334-6776), housed in a beautiful neocolonial building. It's open daily until 8pm. Beside the Cathedral there is a brand new exhibition center called **Manzana 1,** housing a gallery and exhibition center. An open-top city bus leaves from here on 3-hour tours of the city. For information about this and nearby attractions (the Jesuit missions, the Inca ruins of Samaipata, and Amboró National Park), your best bet is to contact **Rosario Tours** ✦ (© 0103/3369-656; www.rosariotours.com), Arenales 193 between Beni and Murillo. Another excellent tour operator is Dutch-owned **Ruta Verde** (© 0103/339-6470; www.rutaverdebolivia.com). They offer a good variety of tours including trips to the Jesuit missions, Amboro National Park, and the town where Che Guevara made his last stand.

FAST FACTS **Magri Turismo** (© 0103/345-663; www.magri-amexpress.com.bo), Calle Warnes and the corner of Potosí, is the American Express representative in Santa Cruz. Unfortunately, you can't change traveler's checks here. If you need to change traveler's checks or exchange money, you should head to **Cambio Alemán Transatlántico,** on Calle 24 de Septiembre in the main plaza. There is also a **Citibank** on Avenida Mons Rivero at the corner of Asunción. **Hospital Universitario Japonés** (© 0103/462-032), on Avenida Japón in the *tercer anillo* (third ring), is the best hospital in town. In an emergency, call © 0103/462-031. If you need a **pharmacy,** try

Farmacia Gutiérrez at 21 de Mayo 26; for deliveries, call ℂ **0103/361-777.** Also nearby is **Farmacia Santa María,** on the corner of 21 de Mayo and Junín. The **post office** is located at Junín 150 between Plaza 24 de Septiembre and 21 de Mayo. You can take care of all your **laundry** needs at **Lavandería España** on Calle España 160. The best **Internet cafe** is **Full Internet,** Ayacucho 208, on the corner of Velasco; the entrance is on the second floor, so look for the stairs on Ayacucho.

WHAT TO SEE & DO

The city's main attraction is the recently restored central plaza. Brass bands play beneath palm trees and there are frequent street events. As traffic is cut off at both ends the square is a tranquil retreat from what is a chaotic city. The **Museo Etnofolklórico Municipal,** located in Parque Arenal, has an interesting display of tools, baskets, and musical instruments used by indigenous groups of Bolivia. The museum is open Monday through Friday from 8:30am to noon and 2:30 to 6:30pm; admission is Bs5 (65¢/35p). Right next door, you can explore **Parque Arenal,** where you can rent paddleboats for Bs8 ($1/50p) per half-hour. The **cathedral** on Plaza 24 de Septiembre houses a small religious museum that is open on Tuesday and Thursday from 10am to noon and 4 to 6pm and on Sunday from 10am to noon and 6 to 8pm. The **Museo de Historia y Archivo Regional de Santa Cruz de la Sierra,** Junín 151, offers a host of exhibits ranging from ceramics to photography; it's open Monday to Friday from 8am to noon and 3 to 6:30pm. Admission is free. **Casa de Cultura Franco Aleman,** 24 de Septiembre 36 (ℂ **0103/333-3392;** www.ccfrancoaleman.org), is a beautifully restored colonial building facing the main plaza. It houses an exhibition room, small cinema, and theater.

SAMAIPATA

Samaipata is a charming mountain town located about 2 hours southwest of Santa Cruz. The main attraction here is the Inca ruins known as **El Fuerte.** The ruins are a huge mysterious complex, much of it unexcavated. From what remains, it's hard to envision the site's former glory. The most impressive structure is the **Chinkana** ✦, also known as the labyrinth. It consists mainly of a hole that was originally 30m (9 ft.) deep. From the top of El Fuerte, you have great views of the surrounding mountains and perfect sightlines of other Inca sites. Most scientists believe that the Incas built these villages in a pattern. At this site, you will also see what are believed to be amphitheaters and temples for religious ceremonies. The site is open daily from 9am to 5pm, and admission is Bs20 ($2.50/£1.25).

GETTING THERE   To understand Samaipata and the ruins of El Fuerte, you really need an experienced guide. **Rosario Tours** ✦, Arenales 193 between Beni and Murillo (ℂ **0103/369-977;** www.rosariotours.com), organizes day trips here with English-speaking guides. **Michael Blendinger Nature Tours** (ℂ **0103/9446-227;** www.discoveringbolivia.com) also arranges trips to El Fuerte and nature hikes through the area. His office is in Samaipata, but he can arrange transportation from Santa Cruz. You can also arrange your own private taxi to Samaipata by contacting **Expreso Samaipata** (ℂ **0102/2335-067**). In Santa Cruz, the taxis leave from the Residencial Señor de Los Milagros on Avenida Omar Chávez Ortiz.

AMBORO NATIONAL PARK

Amboró, one of the most pristine national parks in all of Bolivia, is only 3 hours west of Santa Cruz. The park covers more than 600,000 hectares (1.5 million acres) and encompasses four different biodiversity zones, including a part of the Amazon basin, subtropical forests, temperate woodlands, and the cool mountainous terrain of the Andes. More than 700 species of birds have been seen in the area. Some of the rarer species include the red-fronted macaw, Bolivian recurvebill, and rufous-faced antpitta. You'll also have the opportunity to see monkeys here. There are some fantastic hiking trails that will take you to caves and waterfalls.

GETTING THERE   The roads to Amboró can be rough. I highly recommend taking a trip here with a guided tour. **Rosario Tours** ✶ Arenales 193 between Beni and Murillo (**𝒞 0103/369-977;** www.rosariotours.com), organizes overnight bird-watching trips. **Michael Blendinger Nature Tours** (**𝒞 0103/9446-227;** www.discovering bolivia.com) also arranges excursions into the park, as does **Ruta Verde** (**𝒞 0103/ 339-6470;** www.rutaverdebolivia.com).

THE JESUIT MISSIONS ✶

In the late 16th century, the Jesuits set out to the hinterlands of Bolivia and developed thriving cultural and religious centers for the local people. Victims of their own success they were expelled from South America in 1773. Today, you can visit some of these missions, which have been amazingly preserved and restored. **San Javier** and **Concepción** are the two closest and most accessible missions from Santa Cruz. The 5-hour drive to San Javier is a sight itself: Along the way, you'll pass through Mennonite communities and see the landscape change from lush green farmland to tropical shrubbery. The road is paved, but it can be a bit rough.

San Javier was founded in 1691 and at its height included about 3,000 people. The remarkable church was constructed entirely of local wood. The ornate woodcarvings painted with local dyes are quite spectacular; the gold-colored interior is just as impressive.

The road to Concepción from San Javier is mostly unpaved. You will find a similarly ornate wood church (with a silver altar), cloisters, and a historic main plaza. In the workshops adjacent to the church, you can observe local artisans restoring statues and creating new ones. These two missions are the most impressive of the six Jesuit missions in the Santa Cruz area and the most accessible.

GETTING THERE   It's extremely difficult to arrange public transportation to the Jesuit missions. Your best bet is to arrange a trip through a travel agency. I recommend using **Rosario Tours** ✶, Arenales 193 between Beni and Murillo (**𝒞 0103/369-977;** www.rosariotours.com). The trip includes an English-speaking guide, transportation, and all meals. The price varies depending on how many people are on the trip. **Magri Turismo,** Calle Warnes and the corner of Potosí (**𝒞 0103/345-663;** www.magri-express.com), also organizes excursions to the missions.

SHOPPING IN SANTA CRUZ

Because Santa Cruz is one of the largest and wealthiest cities in Bolivia, you'll find many trendy boutiques and international retailers here. If you're looking for unique gifts typical of the area, you should buy jewelry or handicrafts. For jewelry, I recommend **Joyería Andrea,** at Junín 177. This store specializes in a stone called the Bolivian, a mix of amethyst and citrine. For high-quality handicrafts, your best option is **ARTECAMPO,** at Mons Salvatierra 407 (near the corner of Vallegrande). This beautiful store is an association of artists from the countryside—all the money you spend here will go directly to them.

WHERE TO STAY

If you're in town for the International Trade Fair (held annually in late Sept), you won't find a better place than **Buganvillas** ✦, Av. Roca Coronado 901 (℗ **0103/551-212;** www.hotelbuganvillas.com). The hotel complex is located right next to the convention center (although it is about a 15-min. ride from the center of the city). The beautiful rooms actually are all fully equipped apartments. The complex has three pools, a spa, several restaurants, and a minimart. Rates range from $97 (£49) for a one-bedroom apartment to $187 (£94) for a five-bedroom apartment.

If you're looking for budget accommodations, I recommend **La Siesta Hotel,** Calle Vallegrande 17, near the corner of Ayacucho (℗ **0103/3330-146;** lasiesta@infonet. com.bo). The rooms aren't fancy ($35/£18 for a double), but they have cable TV and air-conditioning. Plus, when it gets hot here, you can relax by the pool.

Gran Hotel Santa Cruz ✦, Calle René Moreno 269 (℗ **0103/3348-811;** www. granhotelsantacruz.com), is the best hotel downtown. Double rooms run from $97 to $107 (£49–£54), and suites are $117 to $127 (£59–£64). The best hotel in all of Santa Cruz, however, is **Hotel Los Tajibos** ✦✦, Av. San Martín 455 (℗ **0103/3421-000**), which is a 10-minute taxi ride from the center of town. If you stay here, you can walk to the many bars and restaurants on Avenida San Martín and take advantage of its lush pool area and first-rate restaurants. Rooms run from $120 to $140 (£60–£70) for doubles, $200 (£100) for suites.

WHERE TO DINE

If you need a break while wandering downtown, stop in at the **Victory Café,** in the Galería Pasco Viejo at Junín and 21 de Mayo (℗ **0103/3322-935**). There's a great big terrace on the second floor where locals gather for coffee, drinks, and light meals. It's the most happening place near the main plaza; it's open Monday through Saturday from 9am to 2am.

For truly authentic Bolivian cuisine, definitely visit **Casa del Camba** ✦✦✦, Av. Cristóbal de Mendoza 539 (℗ **0103/427-864**), which boasts nightly entertainment by local singers and dancers, in addition to a beautiful alfresco dining area. It's open daily from noon to 4pm and 6pm to 2am. If you like steak, don't miss **Parrilla Don Miguel** ✦, Av. Viedma 586 (℗ **0103/3321-823**), which is the best place in town for anything grilled. It's open daily 11:30am to 3pm and 6:30pm to 1am.

SANTA CRUZ AFTER DARK

The **Irish Pub,** on Calle 24 de Septiembre right on the main plaza, is a popular watering hole for foreigners. **Avenida San Martín,** in the second ring, is lined with outdoor cafes, bars, and pubs. **Automanía,** on Calle Comercial El Chuubi, and **La Ronería** (right next door) are two of the most happening places in town. Salsa dancers should seek out **El Loro en Su Salsa,** at Warnes 280. For something more central try **Café 24,** Calle René Moreno and Sucre (℗ **0103/330-4228**). This relaxing daytime cafe near the central square comes alive at night with bands and young clientele.

6

Brazil

by Shawn Blore & Alexandra de Vries

There's a joke Brazilians like to tell: During the creation of the world, one of the archangels peering over God's shoulder at the work in progress couldn't help noticing that one country had been especially favored. "You've given everything to Brazil," he said. "It has the longest beaches, the largest river, the biggest forest, the best soil. The weather's always warm and sunny. There are no floods or hurricanes, no natural disasters at all. Don't you think that's a little unfair?" "Ah," God replied, "but just wait until you see the people I'm putting there."

One hundred percent accuracy rarely comes with a punch line, but there is a large grain of truth in that joke. Brazil, as a nation, is unusually blessed, especially if you're a visitor. There are 8,050km (5,000 miles) of coastline, some of it packed with cafes and partygoers, some of it blissfully empty. For adventurers and wildlife-watchers, there are rainforests and wetlands teeming with all manner of exotic critters. For those who thrive on cities and civic architecture, Brazil has some of the oldest in the New World— and some of the newest in the whole world. For foodies, there are restaurants to match the loftiest standards, and regional cuisine that's as yet unavailable in New York. For those who like music, Brazil could be a lifetime study. And for those who like their music loud and outdoors, preferably with cold beer to boot, there's Carnaval (and New Year's Eve, not to mention almost any night of the week in Salvador).

In recent years, Brazil has been devoting extra time and resources to its tourism infrastructure. New hotels and inns have gone up throughout the country. Many cities have brand-new airports. Yet despite the modern Western appearance of the place, no one could ever accuse Brazilians of making a religion of efficiency. When it comes to getting things done, Brazilians much prefer to get along.

Harmony can mean literally staying in key when you sing along at a street party, or it can mean spending all of Sunday watching soccer, or taking off weekends and some afternoons for quality time with your buddies at the beach. It can mean devoting countless hours of effort to a single night's party. Mostly, harmony seems to require never taking anything all that seriously. At this, Brazilians excel.

1 The Regions in Brief

Brazil's 170 million citizens inhabit the fifth-largest country in the world, a nation about 10% larger than the continental United States. The **Amazon** dominates the northern third of the county—a vast tropical rainforest with the river at its heart. The country's central interior is dominated by the *planalto,* a high dry plateau covered in *cerrado,* a type of dry scrub forest reminiscent of California chaparral. The chief city in this region is the planned federal capital Brasília. West of the *planalto* but south of the Amazon rainforest you find the **Pantanal,** a wetland the size of France that is one of best places to see wildlife in the whole of South America. Brazil's **Northeast** is a land apart. Running roughly from São Luis to Salvador, the coast is dominated by midsize cities and sugar cane, the culture strongly Afro-Brazilian, while on the very dry interior plateau those Nordestinos who haven't yet fled to the cities eke out a bare living on the land. Brazil's two chief cities, **Rio de Janeiro** and **São Paulo,** stand within a few hundred miles of each other close to the country's south coast. São Paulo is the larger and more important of the two, but Rio, the former capital and *cidade maravilhosa* (marvelous city), is by far the more interesting. The small southern tip of the country is inhabited largely by descendants of European immigrants. It's the most densely settled and best-organized part of Brazil. The area boasts the astonishing natural wonder of **Iguaçu Falls,** for many visitors a must-see. The island of Santa Catarina, also known as **Florianópolis,** boasts over 40 beaches and is the favorite summer destination in the south.

RIO DE JANEIRO   Few cities are as striking. The city folds itself into the narrow bits of land between tropical beaches and mountains that leap to 750m (2,460-ft.) heights (one of these is crowned by the city's landmark statue of Jesus Christ). The city offers much in the way of sightseeing, from nature to sunbathing to museums and historic neighborhoods. The culture, perhaps best expressed in music and nightlife, is just as appealing. Samba is alive and well, augmented by many vibrant newer forms of distinctly Brazilian music. The event of the year is Carnaval, the biggest party in the world. And believe me when I say that Cariocas—as Rio residents are known—know how to throw a party.

SAO PAULO   Some 25 million people live in and around São Paulo, the largest city not only in Brazil, but in all of South America. São Paulo is Brazil's New York City. It's the melting pot that attracts the best and brightest to make their fortune. The city overflows with restaurants, including the best fine dining in Brazil. São Paulo has emerged as the cultural capital of Brazil, rich with art galleries and strong in new theater. And it's the best place in Brazil to shop.

THE NORTHEAST   Even in a country with such strong regional distinctions, Brazil's Northeast (Nordeste) stands apart. Roughly speaking, the Nordeste encompasses the area from Salvador to São Luis, including cities such as Recife, Natal, and Fortaleza. Everything Nordeste is different: the food richer, the cities more historic, the beaches longer and whiter, the music more vibrant, and the politics more Byzantine, as well as traditionally more corrupt. This was the first part of Brazil to be settled, the area where sugar cane and slavery dominated economy and society for more than 3 centuries. The downturn in the sugar economy left the area a backwater, and only with the recent advent of tourism have Nordeste fortunes really begun to pick up. For visitors, the Northeast offers a year-round tropical climate with long white sandy beaches, historic cities, and a vibrant Afro-Brazilian culture, which is reflected in the cuisine, the festivals and, especially, the music and dance. Olinda is a quiet colonial gem of a city, while Salvador's 16th-century colonial core has been transformed into a permanent musical stage.

THE AMAZON   The largest rainforest in the world is so vast that it defies easy description: All of Western Europe would fit comfortably with room to spare beneath its leafy canopy. Thanks in large part to media coverage of the many threats to this

Itineraries in Bolivia, Brazil, Colombia, Ecuador & Peru

region, interest in eco-tourism and visits to the Amazon have skyrocketed. The main staging ground for trips to the Brazilian Amazon is the city of Manaus, located where the Rio Negro joins the Rio Solimões to form the Amazon. Manaus itself is surprisingly modern. Moderately interesting in itself, its real interest is as the starting point for expeditions into the rainforest. Options include everything from day trips on the Amazon to multiday trips to virgin rainforest where one can catch sight of countless unique plants and animals. In contrast to Manaus, the city of Belém, located at the mouth of the Amazon, is an old and settled city, with a historic downtown and the incredible Ver-o-Peso market, where produce from the Amazon is bought and sold. Close to Belem, in the mouth of the Amazon river, is Marajó, an island larger than Switzerland, dotted with buffalo ranches and rich with birdlife.

THE CENTER WEST   Brazil's center west is a broad flat plain, dotted here and there with craggy highlands, and populated chiefly by ranchers, cowhands, and increasingly by large commercial farms. It was in the midst of this vast and not especially intriguing region that nearly 50 years ago Brazil erected its striking Modernist capital, Brasília. While the capital may be the region's man-made wonder, the natural wonder is the Pantanal. A wetland the size of France, the Pantanal has traditionally been overlooked in favor of the Amazon, but that's changing as people become increasingly aware of the incredible wildlife-viewing opportunities the area offers. More than 600 bird species, anacondas, jaguars, caiman, giant otters, and anteaters are just some of the animals found in the wetlands. As this area lacks the dense foliage of the Amazon, the animals are much easier to spot.

THE SOUTH   The southern part of Brazil, made up of the states of Paraná, Santa Catarina, and Rio Grande do Sul, boasts a temperate climate and good soil, attributes that long attracted large numbers of European immigrants. It's a settled, well-organized region. The prime beach destination in the south is Florianópolis, a large island that boasts over 40 beaches, clean waters, and excellent restaurants and nightlife. The Iguaçu Falls, a UNESCO World Heritage Site, are located on the border of Brazil, Argentina, and Paraguay. These spectacular falls are made up of 275 falls that cascade from 72m (236 ft.) down a 2.5km-wide (1½ mile) precipice in a fabulous jungle setting.

2 The Best of Brazil in 2 Weeks

In 2 weeks, you can get a good taste of Brazil at a pace that won't leave you with post-holiday stress disorder. The route below takes you to Rio de Janeiro and the historic city of Salvador. You then have the option of spending time in the Amazon or on a beautiful Bahian beach. The Amazon is fascinating, but it requires both money and travel time. This route includes Iguaçu Falls, and a brief taste of the urban sophistication that is São Paulo.

Days ❶–❸: Rio de Janeiro ★★★
To get into the Brazilian spirit, start off your trip in **Rio de Janeiro.** After getting settled in your hotel, head for the beach. Enjoy the scene, tan a bit (but don't overdo it), and watch the sunset from **Arpoador.** You'll be tired from the flight, so take it easy with a good dinner in one

of the top restaurants of **Ipanema** or **Leblon.** On Day 2, get out and see the mountains. Take a tram up to the **Corcovado,** or take a jeep tour up through **Tijuca Forest.** Stop by Cinelandia in Rio's Centro in the afternoon. That night, discover the late-night Carioca lifestyle. Have dinner 'round 11pm, and then catch some samba, played live in **Lapa.** You'll be sleeping late the next day, so spend some more time at the beach, or take a trolley up to explore the hillside neighborhood of **Santa Teresa.** All this should acclimatize you to the Brazilian way before you set off to explore the rest of the country.

Days ❹–❻: Salvador ✦✦✦

Early on Day 4, catch a flight for **Salvador.** This is the city where the country's African roots are strongest. Stay in one of the lovely *pousadas* in **Pelourinho.** Wander through Pelourinho's 17th-century streets. In the evening, try some Bahian cuisine, and then go out and enjoy the music in Pelourinho after dark. Next day, take the boat tour of the **Bay of All Saints,** or head out to the church of **Bomfin.** On your third day, dig deeper into this city's treasures at a leisurely pace; tour the lovely **Museu de Arte Sacre** or see the lighthouse and beaches of **Barra.**

Days ❼–⓫: The Amazon ✦✦✦

Catch an early flight to **Manaus.** It's time to experience a bit of the largest standing rainforest on earth, the Amazon. On your first day you should have time to see the highlights of Manaus, including the famous **Opera House.** The next morning, set off early for a jungle lodge—or

better yet, if you have more time, go kayaking through the forest with **Amazon Mystery Tours** (p. 346). Choose a smaller lodge farther from the city. Don't go to the Ariau. Although the area around Manaus is hardly unexplored, a few days will allow you to experience the fauna and flora of a tropical rainforest. Enjoy the trees, the monkeys, the caiman, and the bright pink dolphins.

Day ⓬: Transit

It's going to take a day of taxis, boats, and airplanes to get you to your next destination, Iguaçu.

Days ⓭–⓮: Iguaçu Falls ✦✦✦

A final must-see—one of the most awe-inspiring natural wonders of the world—**Iguaçu Falls.** The early flight from Salvador should get you to Iguaçu before 2pm. Store your stuff and go see the falls. Stick to the Brazilian side today. Don't forget to take the **Macuco Boat Safari** (p. 356). Unforgettable. The next day, go explore the falls from the Argentinean side. You can catch an early flight to São Paulo and spend the next day exploring, or you can dawdle by the hotel pool in Iguaçu or go see the **Bird Park** (p. 356), before catching a later flight to São Paulo and connecting to your evening flight home.

3 Planning Your Trip to Brazil

VISITOR INFORMATION

Travelers planning their trip to Brazil can browse the site of the Brazilian national tourism agency **Embratur** at **www.embratur.gov.br**. The Brazilian Embassy in the United Kingdom has an outstanding website with links to all the state and many city tourism websites at **www.brazil.org.uk**. Visitors to Rio de Janeiro can get in touch with the city's tourist agency **Riotur** at ⓒ 212/375-0801 or **www.riodejaneiro-turismo. com.br**. Other useful websites include the following:

- **www.brazilnuts.com**: For information on packages and tours of Brazil.
- **www.naturesafaris.com.br**: A commercial site with a good, basic natural history of the Amazon.
- **www.emtursa.ba.gov.br**: Salvador's good official tourism agency.
- **www.infobrasilia.com.br**: For great info on Brasília's architecture and design.
- **www.iguassu.com.br**: Iguaçu's very good official site.

Telephone Dialing Info at a Glance

Brazilian phone companies are going from seven-digit dialing to eight-digit dialing. In São Paulo both seven- and eight-digit numbers are used and many cities haven't started the switchover yet. Telephone numbers are up-to-date as of press time, but if you encounter difficulty getting through to a number, check with the hotel staff for any recent changes. In some cities, new numbers just require adding one digit; in other cities, entire prefixes are being changed.

- **To place a call from your home country to Brazil,** dial the international access code (011 in the U.S. and Canada, 0011 in Australia, 0170 in New Zealand, 00 in the U.K.), plus the country code (55), plus the Brazilian area code minus the first 0, followed by the number. For example, a call from the United States to Rio would be 011+55+21+0000+0000.

- **To place a long-distance call within Brazil,** you must use the access code of a *prestadora* (service provider). Any phone can be used to access any provider; however, the only code that works in all of Brazil—and as a visitor, the only one you need to remember—is the one for Embratel, which is 21. For example, to call Salvador from Rio, dial 021+071+000+0000. Note that for all calls within the country, area codes are preceded by 0.

- **To place a direct international call from Brazil,** dial the access code (021), plus the country code of the place you're calling, plus the area code and the local number.

- **To reach an international operator,** dial ✆ 000-111. Major long distance company access codes are as follows: **AT&T,** ✆ 0800-890-0288; **Canada Direct,** ✆ 0800-890-0014; **MCI,** ✆ 0800-890-0012; and **Sprint,** ✆ 0800-888-8000.

IN BRAZIL

Within Brazil, you'll have to rely on each city's tourist office, varying in quality from the extremely helpful ones in Rio, Salvador, Recife, and Manaus to the more indifferent one in São Paulo. There is no helpful **Embratur** office in Brazil to provide assistance to the traveler in need of Brazil-wide information; its website (www.embratur. gov.br) is your best bet. For more detailed planning information, contact **Brazil Nuts** (✆ **800/553-9959;** www.brazilnuts.com). The staff possesses a vast amount of knowledge about the country and its attractions. Its website is a fount of information; it can answer any questions you may have about Brazil.

Tip: Good countrywide or regional maps are almost nonexistent in Brazil. It's best to bring a good map with you.

ENTRY REQUIREMENTS

Nationals of the United States, Canada, and Australia require a visa to visit Brazil. British nationals and holders of an E.U. passport do not require a visa, but do need a passport valid for at least 6 months and a return ticket. A number of visa types are available; cost, processing time, and documentation requirements vary. American citizens pay $100 for a standard single-entry tourist visa that is valid for 90 days; count on at least 2 weeks of processing time. For Canadians, a similar visa costs C$72 and takes about the same processing time. Visas for Australians cost A$90 plus local handling fees; visas take about 2 weeks to process.

Upon arrival in Brazil, visitors will receive a 90-day entry stamp in their passport and a stamped entry card. Hang on to the card for dear life, as losing it will result in a major hassle and a possible fine when you leave. If necessary, the visa can be renewed once for another 90 days. Visa renewals are obtained through the local Polícia Federal. In Rio de Janeiro, the office is located at Av. Venezuela 2, Centro, just behind Praça Mauá (© 021/2291-2142). In São Paulo, the office is located at Av. Prestes Maia 700, Centro (© 011/223-7177, ext. 231). Hours for both offices are daily from 10am to 4pm. This is best done in large cities where the staff has experience with tourists.

Brazil requires children under 18 traveling alone, with one parent, or with a third party to present written, notarized authorization by the absent parent(s) or legal guardian granting permission to travel alone, with one parent, or with a third party. Additionally, the authorization must be authenticated by the Brazilian embassy or consulate and translated into Portuguese. For more details, contact your embassy or consulate.

BRAZILIAN EMBASSY LOCATIONS

In the U.S.: 3006 Massachusetts Ave. NW, Washington, DC 20008 (© **202/238-2700;** fax 202/238-2827; www.brasilemb.org)

In Canada: 450 Wilbroad St., Ottawa, ON K1N 6M8 (© **613/237-1090;** fax 613/237-6144; www.brasembottawa.org)

In the U.K.: 32 Green St., London W1K 7AT (© **020/7399-9000;** fax 020/7399-9100; www.brazil.org.uk)

In Australia: 19 Forster Crescent, Yarralumla, ACT 2600 (© **02/6273-2372;** fax 02/6273-2375; www.brazil.org.au)

In New Zealand: 10 Brandon St., Level 9, Wellington 6001 (© **04/473-3516;** fax 04/473-3517; www.brazil.org.nz)

CUSTOMS

As a visitor, you are unlikely to be scrutinized very closely upon arrival; Customs officers are too busy nabbing returning Brazilians loaded down with consumer goods far in excess of their duty-free limit. However, there are random checks, and your luggage may be thoroughly inspected. Visitors are allowed to bring a reasonable amount of personal belongings, including electronics such as a camera and a laptop.

Other countries normally force you to do your duty-free shopping before arrival, and they only allow you to bring in a single measly bottle of liquor, a box of cigarettes, and a few bottles of perfume. In Brazil, you're allowed to spend up to US$500 in the duty-free shop *upon arrival,* and it's completely up to you whether you blow the

---

Tips Photo ID

You are required to carry ID in Brazil, and it is sometimes requested when entering office buildings or even tourist sites. We recommend bringing an alternative picture ID, such as a driver's license or student ID, to use instead of carrying your passport with you at all times.

money on cases of Johnny Walker or gallons of aftershave. In the airport, just follow the signs after immigration but before going through Customs. Prices in these duty-free shops are much cheaper than you'll find in the rest of Brazil. Note that the generous import allowance counts *only* for goods purchased in the Brazilian duty-free shop upon arrival.

MONEY

The Brazilian unit of currency is the **real** (R$), pronounced "hey-*al*" (plural reais, pronounced "hey-*eyes*"), which is made up of 100 centavos. The real comes in bills of 1, 5, 10, 50, and 100, and coins of R$1 and 1, 5, 10, 25, and 50 centavos. There seems to be a chronic lack of small bills in Brazil, particularly in the Northeast. Try paying for a R$4 item with a R$10 bill, and you may have to wait a half-hour while the vendor moans about the horror of making change and then runs around begging other shopkeepers to help him break a R$10 bill. Buses, street vendors, and taxi drivers also usually carry little or no change, so hoard those ones and fives!

Here's a general idea of what things cost in Rio: a taxi ride from downtown Rio to Copacabana, R$25 (US$13/£7.25); a ride from Rio's airport to an Ipanema hotel, R$65 (US$33/£18); a double room at a budget hotel in high season, R$160 (US$80/£43); a double room in a moderate hotel, R$150 to R$250 (US$75–US$125/£40–£67); a double room in an expensive hotel, R$350 to R$600 (US$175–US$300/£95–£162); a Coca-Cola, mineral water, or can of beer from a street vendor, R$2 to R$3.50 (US$1–US$1.75/55p–95p); lunch for one at a moderate restaurant, R$8 to R$12 (US$4–US$6/£2.15– £3.25); dinner for one in a moderate restaurant, R$12 to R$20 (US$6–US$10/£3.25– £5.40); and a roll of film costs R$12 to R$15 (US$6–US$7.50/ £3.25–£4).

CURRENCY EXCHANGE & RATES   The ongoing fall of the U.S. dollar, in some cases, has made it difficult to get accurate rates. Up until 2004, many businesses based their rates on the U.S dollar. With the dollar's fall, some businesses have lowered their **real** prices to keep a steady dollar price, others have increased the real rate, still others have switched over to accounting in euros. For U.S travelers, it means that Brazil has gotten a little bit more expensive. When prices are listed in U.S. dollars only, it's because these companies quote their prices directly in dollars. If in doubt, ask. And though it's a bad idea to carry large wads of cash, it can be helpful to bring a small amount of U.S. cash ($10s or $20s only, no $100s) as an emergency supply in case that ATM is broken or your credit card isn't working. Even in the smallest towns people will know the exchange rate, and someone will be happy to take the U.S. dollars off your hands. Throughout this chapter, we give the prices in reais, U.S. dollars, and British pounds; as of press time, the exchange rate was R$2 to US$1 and R$3.70 to £1.

Banks usually provide a slightly better exchange rate but have limited hours of operation for currency exchange (usually 11am–2pm), and the wait can be long. *Casas de cambio* (money-exchange houses) are often more efficient and have better hours of

---

Tips Currency Exchange Receipts

When exchanging money, whether it is cash or traveler's checks, always keep the receipt. You will need it in case you want to change back any unused reais at the end of your trip.

operation, but the rates may be less favorable. The best rates are available through ATMs and credit cards (bring your PIN).

ATMs   Brazil's financial infrastructure is very sophisticated and ATMs are everywhere in Brazil, even in the smallest towns. The only trick is finding one that works with your card. **Cirrus** (② **800/424-7787;** www.mastercard.com) and **PLUS** (② **800/843-7587;** www.visa.com) are the two most popular networks; call or check online for ATM locations. Be sure your PIN is four digits, and find out your daily withdrawal limit before you depart.

The vast majority of travelers find they are able to use the HSBC, Citibank, Bradesco, and Banco do Brasil ATMs bearing a PLUS/Visa logo. However, it's not a bad idea to bring two different cards to increase your access options. (Small towns normally have only one ATM, accepting PLUS/Visa or Cirrus/MasterCard, but not both.) When in doubt, check with your bank to find out which Brazilian bank networks are compatible with your card. Finally, make sure that during New Year's and Carnaval you get enough cash ahead of time, as machines often run out of money by the end of the holidays.

TRAVELER'S CHECKS   Traveler's checks don't work well in Brazil. Most shops won't accept them, hotels give a miserable exchange rate, and many banks won't cash your traveler's checks unless you have an account at that branch of that bank. Others, such as Bank Boston, will only cash a minimum of US$500 (£256). The Banco do Brasil is the only bank that will cash them with minimum hassle (expect to spend at least 20–30 min.) but charges a flat rate of US$20 (£10) for the pleasure. Only American Express will cash their own checks for free, but they have only a few offices in major centers such as Rio, Salvador, and São Paulo.

CREDIT CARDS   The best exchange rates can be obtained through credit cards, which are accepted at most shops, hotels, and restaurants. Just keep in mind that you are sometimes able to negotiate a better discount on a room or in a store if you pay cash. The most commonly accepted cards are Visa and MasterCard. American Express and Diners Club are also frequently accepted. It's a good idea to have at least two cards as some stores and restaurants accept only one card (usually Visa). Discover is rarely (if ever) accepted in Brazil.

If you need to report a lost or stolen credit card or have any questions, you can contact the agencies anywhere in Brazil at the following numbers: **American Express,** ② **0800/785-050; MasterCard** and **Visa,** ② **0800/784-456;** and **Diners Club** ② **0800/784-444.**

WHEN TO GO

PEAK SEASON   High season in Brazil lasts from the week before Christmas until Carnaval (which falls sometime in Feb or early Mar, depending on the year). Flights and accommodations are more expensive and more likely to be full during this period. Book well ahead of time for accommodations during New Year's and Carnaval. This is the most fun time to travel—towns and resorts are bustling as many Brazilians take their summer vacations, the weather's warm, and New Year's and Carnaval are fabulously entertaining. If you want to spend New Year's in Brazil, it's best to arrive after Christmas. The 25th is really a family affair, and most restaurants and shops will be closed.

Other busy times of year include Easter week and the months of July, when schools and universities take their winter break, and August, when most Europeans visit during the summer vacation. This is probably the worst time of year to travel; prices go

Heads Up: Beware of Dengue Fever in Brazil

Brazil occasionally experiences outbreaks of dengue fever, a malaria-like illness transmitted by mosquitoes. Most cases are reported in the state of Rio de Janeiro, with additional outbreaks in São Paulo as well.

There is no vaccine for dengue fever; symptoms can be treated with bed rest, fluids, and medications such as acetaminophen (Tylenol) to reduce fever, but aspirin should be avoided. The most important precaution a traveler can take is to avoid mosquito bites when visiting a dengue-prone area. Try to remain in well-screened or air-conditioned areas; use mosquito repellents (preferably those containing DEET) on skin and clothing; use aerosol insecticides indoors; and sleep with bed nets. For the most up-to-date information on the status of dengue fever in Brazil, consult the Centers for Disease Control and Prevention website (www.cdc.gov) before departing.

---

up significantly, and except for in the north and parts of the Northeast, the weather can be iffy and downright chilly anywhere south of Rio de Janeiro. If you want to take advantage of the best deals and still have good weather, consider visiting Brazil in October or November. The spring weather means warm days in São Paulo, Iguaçu, and Rio, and tropical heat everywhere else; in the Amazon and the Pantanal you'll be there just before the wet season starts. As an added bonus, in Rio you'll be able to attend some of the samba school rehearsals as they get ready for Carnaval (yes, they start 4 months early). Another good period for a visit is after Carnaval (early to mid-Mar, depending on the dates) through May, when you can take advantage of low-season prices, particularly in hotels, while still enjoying good weather.

CLIMATE   As Brazil lies in the Southern Hemisphere, its seasons are the exact opposite of what Northern Hemisphere residents are used to: **summer is December through March and winter June through September.** Within the country the climate varies considerably from region to region. In most of Brazil, the summers are very hot. Temperatures can rise to 110°F (43°C) with high humidity. The **Northeast** (from Salvador north) is warm year-round, often with a pleasant breeze coming off the ocean. Temperatures hover between the low 80s to mid-90s (upper 20s to mid-30s Celsius). The winter months (June–July) are slightly wetter, but even then the amount of rain is limited—a quick shower that cools things down briefly before giving way to more sunshine. As befits a rainforest, the **Amazon** is also hot and humid year-round, with temperatures hovering around the mid-90s to low-100s (mid- to high 30s Celsius). The dry season lasts from June to December and is often called "summer" by the locals as it is hot and sunny. The wet season typically runs from December to May and is referred to as "winter." The **Pantanal** is very hot in the rainy season, with temperatures climbing over the 100°F mark (low 40s Celsius). Most of the rain falls December through March. The driest time of the year is May through October. **Rio** has very hot and humid summers—100°F (38°C) and 98% humidity are not uncommon. Rio winters are quite mild, with nighttime temperatures dropping as low as 66°F (19°C), and daytime temperatures climbing to the pleasant and sunny mid-80s (30°C). **São Paulo** has a similar climate to Rio's, hot in the summer and mild in winter. As São Paulo sits atop a plateau at approximately 700m (2,300 ft.) of elevation it can sometimes get downright chilly, with daytime lows June through September sometimes reaching 54°F (12°C). **South of São Paulo,** things get even colder in the winter. In Florianopolis, many restaurants and even some hotels and pousadas shut down for the winter season. Also, in the mountain resort of **Petrópolis** and the historic towns of **Ouro Prêto** and **Tiradentes,** it often gets cold enough to see your breath (41°F/5°C) in the fall and winter, and Brazilians travel here to experience winter.

PUBLIC HOLIDAYS   The following holidays are observed in Brazil: New Year's Day (Jan 1); Carnaval (Feb 2–Feb 5, 2008, Feb 21–24, 2009, Feb 13–16, 2010); Easter (Mar 21, 2008, and Apr 10, 2009); Tiradentes Day (Apr 21); Labor Day (May 1); Corpus Christi (May 22, 2008, and June 7, 2009); Independence Day (Sept 7); Our Lady of Apparition (Oct 12); All Souls Day (Nov 2); Proclamation of the Republic (Nov 15); and Christmas Day (Dec 25). On these days banks, schools, and government institutions will be closed, and some stores may be closed as well.

HEALTH CONCERNS

COMMON AILMENTS   The main concerns for visitors are yellow fever, malaria, and dengue fever. **Yellow fever,** which is transmitted by mosquitoes, is endemic in most of Brazil's interior and occasionally makes forays into the hinterland of São Paulo and Minas Gerais. Also transmitted by mosquitoes is **malaria.** Mostly travelers to the Amazon are at risk; however, lodges around Manaus have not experienced any problems with malaria. Ask for your doctor's specific recommendations on malaria prophylaxes, as the guidelines change regularly.

Another mosquito-borne disease that is widespread in Brazil, particularly on the coast around Rio and São Paulo, is **dengue fever.** First-time sufferers will experience severe flulike symptoms (fever, joint pain, and headache) that can last up to 10 days. Unlike yellow fever and malaria, dengue has no vaccine or prophylaxis—the best prevention is to avoid mosquito bites.

Other tropical diseases, such as cholera or Chagas' disease, are only found in very remote areas. For those planning to explore beyond the beaten track, please obtain more detailed advice from a travel clinic before heading out.

VACCINATIONS   It's always a good idea before going on a trip to check your vaccinations and get booster shots for tetanus and polio, if necessary. Children 3 months to 6 years may be required to show proof of polio vaccination. The one vaccination that is definitely required for Brazil is **yellow fever.** If you're traveling to the Amazon, the Pantanal, Brasília, or even Minas Gerais, you may come in contact with it. Get an international certificate of vaccination, as Brazilian authorities sometimes require proof of vaccination for people going to or coming from an effected area. Travelers who have been to Colombia, Bolivia, Ecuador, French Guyana, Peru, or Venezuela within 90 days before arriving in Brazil are also required to show proof of yellow fever vaccination. Please keep in mind that the vaccine takes 10 days to take effect. If you're traveling to the Amazon or the Pantanal, a **malaria** prophylaxis (usually pills that you take daily) may be recommended as well. Consult your doctor and the Centers for Disease Control and Prevention (CDC) website (www.cdc.gov/travel/tropsam.htm) prior to traveling, as advisories change regularly.

HEALTH PRECAUTIONS   Brazil's standards for hygiene and public health are generally high. If you do wind up with traveler's tummy or some other ailment, Brazilian pharmacies are a wonder. Each has a licensed pharmacist who is trained to deal with small medical emergencies and—better yet—fully authorized to give prescriptions. The service is free, and medication is fairly inexpensive. If you're taking medication that may need replacement while in Brazil, ask your doctor to write out the generic name, as many drugs are sold under different brand names in Brazil. Many drugs available by prescription only in the United States and Canada are available over the counter in Brazil.

According to recent U.N. statistics, Brazil ranks third in the world for the total number of people with HIV infections. Be careful and be safe—always insist on using a condom. Though condoms are readily available in Brazilian pharmacies, it's best to bring your own, as North American and European brands are more reliable. To purchase condoms in Brazil ask for *camisinha* (literally "small shirt").

GETTING THERE
BY PLANE

Rio de Janeiro's **Antonio Carlos Jobim Airport** (© **0800/999-099** or 021/3398-5050) and São Paulo's **Guarulhos Airport** (© **011/6445-2945**) are the two major gateways to Brazil and are served by most international airlines.

Up until 2006, **Varig** (© **800/Go-VARIG;** www.varig.com) was the Brazilian airline with the most international connections to North America, Europe, Asia, and the rest of South America. However, after going through a major crisis and hovering on the edge of bankruptcy, Varig—though it survived—had to give up most of its international routes. **TAM** (© **888/2FLY-TAM;** www.tam.com.br) has picked up some of Varig's slack and has added more international flights to Europe and in the U.S. to Miami and New York. Relative new-comer, low budget carrier **Gol** (www.voegol.com.br) has also done well in the Varig shake-up and now offers a number of South American destinations (Argentina, Chili, Peru and Bolivia); a good alternative for those traveling within South America.

From North America   U.S. airlines that fly to Brazil include **United** (© **800/241-6522;** www.ual.com), with nonstop flights from Miami to Rio and São Paulo; **American** (© **800/433-7300;** www.aa.com), which serves Rio and São Paulo from New York and Miami; and **Continental** (© **800/231-0856;** www.continental.com), which offers nonstop flights from Houston and New York. **Delta** (© **800/241-4141;** www.delta.com) offers direct flights from its Atlanta hub to Rio and São Paulo. Canadian travelers can book with **Air Canada,** offering nonstop Toronto–São Paulo service (© **888/247-2262;** www.aircanada.ca).

From the U.K.   British Airways (© **0845/702-0212;** www.british-airways.com) offers several nonstop flights to Rio and São Paulo. Travelers from Europe can also choose from an array of nonstop flights to Rio and/or São Paulo; **Alitalia, Lufthansa, Air France, Iberia, Tap,** and **KLM** offer daily (or almost daily) service.

From Australia & New Zealand   Travelers from Australia can fly **Qantas** (© **13-13-13** in Australia, or 0800/0014-0014 in New Zealand; www.qantas.com) and connect with its partner, **British Airways,** in London, or fly to Los Angeles and transfer to a **Varig** flight.

BY PACKAGE TOUR

Many travel agencies offer package tours to Brazil, but few have the knowledge to effectively customize your trip or make interesting recommendations. To book a package with Brazil travel experts, contact **Brazil Nuts** (© **800/553-9959** or 914/593-0266; www.brazilnuts.com). The owners and staff are indeed nuts about Brazil and possess a vast amount of knowledge about the country and its attractions. Depending on your needs, you can book just a flight and hotels or you can add one or more group excursions to more inaccessible places such as the Amazon. Its website is a fount of information, and its staff can answer any questions you may have about Brazil.

Another excellent Internet-based company is **South America Travel** (formerly 4StarBrazil), PO Box 11552, Washington, DC 20008; © **800/747-4540;** www.south americatravel.com). Similar to Brazil Nuts, South America Travel offers packages customizable to whatever level you're comfortable with. The company has recently added on a number of other South American travel destinations, making it easy to put together your own customized package. The company has local offices in Rio, Lima, and Buenos Aires.

A good travel agency to book your ticket through is **Santini Tours,** 6575 Shattuck Ave., Oakland, CA 94609 (© **800/769-9669** or 510/652-8600; www.santours.com). The owner and many of the travel agents are Brazilian and can give you many useful suggestions on air-pass routings and answer any questions you have about your itinerary.

GETTING AROUND
BY PLANE
Though there are highways and buses, the sheer vastness of Brazil (and the absence of rail travel) makes flying the only viable option for those who want to visit a variety of cities and regions. Over the last few years, fares have come down significantly, making air travel the most affordable and fastest option for exploring the country.

If you are doing a lot of air travel you may want to check into purchasing an air pass with **TAM** (© **0800/123-100** in Brazil; www.tam.com.br). It offers four segments for US$479 (£245) if you arrive on an international Tam flight (otherwise the pass costs US$560/£287]), with the option of a fifth leg for another US$120 (£62). The pass is valid for 21 days. Check TAM's special English-language site for more details on the air pass, **www.tamairlines.com**. If you're traveling to only one or two destinations within Brazil, it can be cheaper to skip the air pass and buy a separate ticket. You can check the prices with TAM or **Gol** (© **0300/789-2121** in Brazil; www.voegol.com.br). This airlines has modeled itself after American discount carriers such as Southwest and JetBlue, offering no-frills flights to most domestic destinations and now also to Argentina, Chile, Bolivia and Peru.

BY BUS
Bus travel in Brazil is very efficient and affordable—the only problem is that it's a long way between destinations. To see the country by bus, you will need a lot of time, especially in the west and northwest, where roads are precarious. The 644km (400-mile) journey from Campo Grande to Cuiabá, the two gateway cities into the Pantanal, takes about 11 hours on the bus. Still, for shorter distances and for the occasional long haul, Brazilian buses are excellent; all buses are nonsmoking, and on many popular routes, travelers can opt for a deluxe coach with air-conditioning and *leito,* reclinable seats. See individual city sections in this chapter for more information about bus travel. Many local travel agencies will have schedule information and may sell tickets. You can also contact the bus station *(rodoviária)* directly.

BY CAR
Car rentals are expensive in Brazil, and the distances are huge. For example, from Recife to Brasília is a distance of 2,121km (1,400 miles), while from Salvador to Rio, it's an 1,800km (1,100-mile) drive. Within Brazilian cities, renting a car is only for

the bold and the foolish: Drivers are aggressive, rules are loosely observed, and parking is a competitive sport. Still, there are occasions—a side trip to the mountain resorts of Rio, for example, or a drive to the Chapada dos Guimarães outside of Cuiabá—when renting a car does make sense. Each company normally has a national rate, and only rarely are there local discounts or special offers. For a tiny car (a Fiat Palio or Gol) with air-conditioning, you can typically expect to pay around R$110 (US$55/£30) per day with unlimited mileage. Add to that another R$30 (US$15/£8) per day for comprehensive insurance. Gasoline costs R$2.60 (US$1.30/70p) per liter, about US$4.50/£2.45 per gallon. Officially you need an international driver's license, but we have never encountered any problems having a U.S., Canadian, or European license.

TIPS ON ACCOMMODATIONS

Brazil offers a wide range of accommodations. In the large cities, there are modern high-rise hotels as well as apartment hotels (known in Brazil as apart-hotels). The apart-hotels are often a better deal than regular hotel rooms, offering both cheaper rates and more space; the drawback is that you often don't get the pool and restaurants and other amenities of a hotel. Outside of the large cities, you will often find *pousadas,* essentially the equivalent of a bed-and-breakfast or small inn.

Accommodations prices fluctuate widely. The rates posted at the front desk—the rack rate or *tarifa balcão*—are just a guideline. Outside of the high season and weekends, you can almost always negotiate significant (20%–30%) discounts. Notable exceptions are Brasília and São Paulo, where business dies during high season and weekends, and rooms are heavily discounted. Hotel charges for children are all over the map. Most hotels allow children under 6 to stay for free in their parent's room, but for children over 6, the rates can vary from a 10% surcharge to a full adult supplement rate. Please note that these rates and policies are always negotiable. *Tip:* Always check the quotes you have obtained from a hotel with a travel agency, such as Brazil Nuts or 4Star, as many hotels will give their best rates to travel agents and stick it to individual travelers or those who book via the Internet. The Copacabana Palace quoted us a price of US$220 to US$450 (£113–£230) for a room, while Brazil Nuts can sell you that same room for US$150 (£77)!

Unlike North American hotel rooms, Brazilian hotel rooms have neither coffeemakers nor iron and ironing board as standard features. On the other hand, except for some five-star hotels, a generous breakfast is always included.

Accommodations taxes range from nothing to 15%, varying from city to city and hotel to hotel. Always check in advance what taxes will be added to your final bill.

TIPS ON DINING

Brazilians love to eat out. There is no shortage of eateries, from beach vendors selling grilled cheese and sweets, to lunch-bars serving pastries and cold beers, to fine French cuisine complete with the elegance and pretensions of Paris. Lunch is traditionally a full hot meal, but these days you can also find North American–style sandwiches and salads as a lighter alternative. Dinner is eaten late; most restaurants don't get busy until 9 or 10pm and will often serve dinner until 1 or 2am. In Rio and São Paulo, the restaurant scene is very cosmopolitan: excellent Japanese restaurants, fabulous Italian eateries, traditional Portuguese and Spanish food, as well as popular restaurants that serve Brazilian food—rice, black beans, *farofa* (manioc flour), and steak.

Brazilian cuisine comes in many regional varieties, but the one truly national dish is *feijoada,* a black-bean stew that originated with African slaves who used leftovers to make a tasty meal. Traditionally served on Saturday, the beans are spiced with garlic, onions, and bay leaves and left to stew for hours with a hodgepodge of meats that may include sausage, beef, dried meat, and bits of pork. Accompanied by rice, *farofa,* slices of orange, and stir-fried cabbage, it's a meal in itself.

Brazil's most distinguished regional cuisine is found in coastal Bahia, a region with very strong African influences. Bahia's most famous dish is the *moqueca,* a rich stew made with fresh fish or seafood, coconut milk, lime juice, cilantro, and spicy *malagueta* peppers and flavored with the red oil from a dendê palm. In the Amazon and the Pantanal, local cuisine makes the best of the large variety of freshwater fish and local fruits and vegetables. The fish is delicious—firm white meat that tastes best plainly grilled with salt and herbs or sometimes served in a spicy stew. In the south and southwest of Brazil, the cuisine is more European, and meat is always present on the menu. *Churrascarias,* or Brazilian steakhouses, are everywhere. Often, *churrascarias* operate on a *rodízio* (all-you-can-eat) system. Waiters scurry from grill to tables bearing giant skewers of beautifully roasted beef or chicken or pork or sausage, from which they slice off a few succulent slices onto your plate. The parade of meat continues until you throw your hands up and cry, "Enough!"

Almost everyone has heard of Brazil's most famous cocktail, the *caipirinha* (made with limes, sugar, and *cachaça*), but even Brazilians can't live on booze alone. It makes sense in a tropical country to have lots of cold drinks, often made with tropical fruits. Freshly made juices *(suco)* or milkshakes *(vitaminas)* can be ordered at snack bars and restaurants. Tastier than regular cola drinks is Brazil's very own Guaraná, a sparkling ginger ale–like drink made with Amazonian guaraná berries. Wine lovers may want to experiment with some Brazilian wines but will probably be better off choosing a more reliable Argentine or Chilean varietal; Brazil's wine industry is small and still developing. Beer is drunk the way it is meant to be in a hot country: ice cold and light. Remember that *cerveja* refers to beer served in a can or bottle and *chopp* means draft beer.

Saying that Brazilians have a sweet tooth is like saying that Italians have been known to eat pasta. Most Brazilian desserts are just a few ingredients shy of pure sugar. Most traditional sweets are just variations on the combination of sugar, egg yolks, and coconut. *Cocada,* the little clusters of coconut you see everywhere, are nothing more than grated coconut with white or burnt sugar; *quindim,* something between a pudding and a pie, is made with coconut, an incredible number of egg yolks (at least 10 per tiny serving!), and sugar; and *manjar,* a soft pudding often served with plum sauce, combines sugar, coconut milk, and milk. My personal favorite is *babá de moça,* made of coconut milk, egg yolks, and sugar syrup. The name translates as "girl drool."

TIPS ON SHOPPING

Brazil offers excellent shopping opportunities, particularly for precious stones; leather goods such as shoes, belts, purses, and wallets; and Brazilian music and musical instruments. Clothing is also very affordable and often of good quality. Rio and São Paulo are the best cities for buying fashionable clothes and shoes. If you plan on visiting Petrópolis, do so early in your trip and stock up on inexpensive clothes. Styles follow the opposite seasonal calendar, so those visiting Brazil during the Northern Hemisphere winter can stock up on an excellent summer wardrobe. Sizes follow the European numbering system (36, 38, 40, and so on) or are marked P (*pequeno,* small), M (*medio,* medium), and G (*grande,* large).

Expect to haggle with street vendors. Even in stores, you can ask for a discount when buying more than one item or when paying cash. Shops will often advertise prices *"a vista"*—this means cash purchases only, and they can be 10% to 20% cheaper than paying by credit card.

Each region has its own crafts traditions. In the Amazon and Pantanal, good buys include Indian carvings and hammocks. The Northeast is particularly well known for its lovely linen and woodcarvings. Throughout Brazil, there are plenty of opportunities to shop for semiprecious stones, although the largest collections can be found in Rio and São Paulo jewelry stores.

FAST FACTS: Brazil

Addresses Large buildings or attractions such as museums, palaces, or churches often don't have a street number and are listed as s/n (*sem numero*—"without a number"). This is also often the case in small towns with just a few streets. In most cases, what you are looking for is pretty obvious and hard to miss. Other address notes to pay attention to: *sala* (room or office), *loja* (shop), *sobre loja* (first floor), and *subsolo* (basement).

Business Hours Stores are usually open from 9am to 7pm weekdays, 9am to 2pm on Saturdays. Most places close on Sundays. Small stores may close for lunch. Shopping centers are open Monday through Saturday from 10am to 8pm most places, though in Rio de Janeiro and São Paulo they often stay open until 10pm. On Sundays, many malls open the food court and movie theaters all day, but mall shops will only open from 2 to 8pm. Banks are open Monday through Friday either from 10am to 4pm or from 9am to 3pm.

Credit Cards If you need to report a lost or stolen credit card or have any questions, you can contact the agencies anywhere in Brazil with the following numbers: American Express, © 0800/785-050; MasterCard, © 0800/891-3294; Visa, © 0800-891-3680; and Diners Club, © 0800/784-444.

Electricity Brazil's electric current varies from 100 to 240 volts, and from 50 to 60Hz; even within one city there can be variations, and power surges are not uncommon. For laptops or battery chargers, bring an adaptor that can handle the full range of voltage. Most hotels do a good job of labeling their outlets, but when in doubt, check before plugging in! Brazilian plugs usually have three prongs: two round and one flat. Adapters for converting North American plugs are cheap (R$3/US$1.50/80p) and widely available.

Embassies & Consulates All embassies are located in Brasília, the capital. Australia, Canada, the United States, and Great Britain have consulates in both Rio and São Paulo. New Zealand has a consulate in São Paulo.

In Brasília: **Australia**, SES, Quadra 801, Conjunto K, lote 7 (© 061/3226-3111); **Canada**, SES Av. das Nações Quadra 803, lote 16 (© 061/3424-5400); **United States**, SES Av. das Nações Quadra 801, lote 03 (© 061/3312-7000); **United Kingdom**, SES Av. das Nações Quadra 801, lote 8 (© 061/3329-2300); and **New Zealand**, SHIS QI 09, conj. 16, casa 01 (© 061/3248-9900).

In Rio de Janeiro: **Australia**, Av. Presidente Wilson 231, Suite 23, Centro (© 021/3824-4624); **Canada,** Av. Atlântica 1130, 5th floor, Copacabana

(📞 021/2543-3004); **United States,** Av. Presidente Wilson 147, Centro (📞 021/3823-2000); and **United Kingdom,** Praia do Flamengo 284, Flamengo (📞 021/2555-9600).

In São Paulo: **Australia,** Alameda Ministro Rocha Azevedo 456, Jardim Paulista (📞 011/3085 6247); **Canada,** Av. das Nações Unidas 12901, 16th floor (📞 011/5509-4321); **United States,** Rua Henri Dunant 500, Chácara Santo Antonio (📞 011/5186-7000); **United Kingdom,** Rua Ferreira de Araujo 741 (📞 011/3094-2700); and **New Zealand,** Al. Campinas 579, 15th floor, Cerqueira Cesar (📞 011/3148-0616).

Emergency Numbers For police dial 📞 **190;** for ambulance or fire department dial 📞 **193;** for fire dial 📞 **193.**

Internet Access Web access is widespread in Brazil; even in the smallest of towns we found at least one Internet cafe. Rates are usually US$2 to US$6 (£1–£3) per hour.

Language The language of Brazil is Portuguese. If you speak Spanish you will certainly have an easier time picking up words and phrases. In the large cities you will find people in the tourism industry who speak good English, but in smaller towns and resorts English is very limited. If you are picking up language books or tapes, make sure they are Brazilian Portuguese and not Portuguese from Portugal: big difference! A good pocket-size phrase book is *Say It in Portuguese* (Brazilian usage) by Prista, Mickle, and Costa; or try *Conversational Brazilian Portuguese* by Cortina.

Liquor Laws Officially Brazil's drinking laws only allow those over 18 years to drink, but this is rarely enforced. Beer, wine, and liquor can be bought any day of the week from grocery stores and delis. Beer is widely sold through street vendors, bakeries, and refreshment stands.

Mail Mail from Brazil is quick and efficient. Post offices *(correios)* are found everywhere, readily identifiable by the blue-and-yellow sign. A postcard or letter to Europe or North America costs R$1.60 (US80¢/40p). Parcels can be sent through FedEx or regular mail (express or common; a small parcel—up to 2.5kg/5½ lb.—costs about R$45 [US$23/£12] by common mail and takes about a week or two).

Maps Good maps aren't Brazil's strong suit. Your best bet for city maps is the *Guia Quatro Rodas—mapas das capitais;* this pocketsize book, for sale at all newsstands (R$15/US$7.50/£4), has indexed maps of all state capitals, including São Paulo, Rio, Salvador, Manaus, Brasília, and Recife. Unfortunately, it does not include any highways. The best highway map is sold with the *Guia Quatro Rodas Brasil* (for sale on newsstands for R$35/US$18/£9.50), a Brazilian guidebook.

Newspapers & Magazines There are no English newspapers or magazines in Brazil. Foreign papers and magazines are only easily found in Rio and São Paulo. The most popular Brazilian newspapers are *O Globo* and *Jornal do Brasil,* published out of Rio, and *Folha de São Paulo,* the leading business paper published in São Paulo. The most popular current affairs magazine (the equivalent of *Newsweek*) is *Veja,* published weekly. In Rio and São Paulo, *Veja* magazine always includes an entertainment insert that provides a detailed listing of nightlife, restaurants, and events.

Restrooms Restrooms in Brazil can be marked in a few different ways. Usually you will see *mulher* or an M for women and *homem* or an H for men. Sometimes it will read *damas* or D for ladies and *cavalheiros* or C for gentlemen. It's not a bad idea to carry some toilet paper with you as in many public restrooms, the toilet attendant doles out sheets only grudgingly.

Safety Sometime in the 1980s Brazil began developing a world reputation for violence and crime. Some of this was pure sensationalism, but there was a good measure of truth as well. Fortunately in the early '90s things began to turn around. Governments began putting money back into basic services, starting with policing. Though still not perfect by any means, Rio, São Paulo, and Brazil's other big cities have bounced back to the point where they're as safe as most large international cities. Statistically, of course, Rio and other big Brazilian cities still have very high crime rates. Most of that crime, however, takes place in the favelas and shantytowns of the far-off industrial outskirts. Avoid wandering in or near the hillside favelas. At night use taxis instead of public transportation, and stick to well-lit and well-traveled streets. Don't flash jewelry or wads of cash. And beware of pickpockets. Outside of the main cities, Brazil remains quite safe.

Taxes There are no taxes added to goods purchased in Brazil. Restaurants and hotels normally add a 10% service tax.

Time Zones Brazil has three time zones. The coast, including Rio de Janeiro, Salvador, and as far inland as São Paulo and Brasília, is in one time zone. The ranching states of Mato Grosso and Mato Grosso do Sul, the Pantanal, and the Amazon around Manaus are in the second time zone, 1 hour behind Rio. The third time zone includes the state of Acre and the western part of the Amazon, 2 hours behind Rio. The time difference between cities in Brazil and North America varies by up to 2 hours over the course of the year as clocks spring forward and fall back for daylight saving time. From approximately March to September, Rio de Janeiro is in the same time zone as New York City. From October to February, Rio is at least 1 and often 2 hours ahead of New York (for example, noon in New York City is 2pm in Rio).

Telephones Public phones in Brazil can be found everywhere and are called *orelhões.* To use these phones you need a phone card, for sale at all newsstands. Ask for a *cartão telefonico.* Dialing a local number is straightforward; just dial the number without the area code. However, for long-distance dialing, telephone numbers are normally listed with a three-digit prefix, followed by the area code, followed by the seven- or eight-digit number (for example, 0XX-21-0000-0000). The two digits that fill in the XX are the number of the appropriate service provider (in Portuguese this is called the *prestadora*). Any phone can be used to access any service provider. In some cities there may be a choice of two or three providers. The only code that works in all of Brazil (and the only *prestadora* code you need to remember) is the one for *Embratel*—21 (which also happens to be the area code of Rio). So, if you were dialing long distance to a number in Rio, you would dial 0-21 (selecting Embratel as your provider), 21 (Rio's area code), and 0000-0000 (the number). Dialing long distance to a number in São Paulo, you'd dial 0-21-11-0000-0000.

To phone internationally, you dial 00 + 21 + the country code + area code + phone number. International collect calls can be requested by dialing ℂ **000-111,** or automatically by dialing 90 + 21 + country code + area code + phone number. Major long-distance company access codes are as follows: AT&T, ℂ **0800/890-0288;** MCI, ℂ **0800/890-0012;** Sprint, ℂ **0800/888-8000;** and Canada Direct, ℂ **0800/890-0014.**

Tipping A 10% service charge is automatically included on most restaurant and hotel bills, and you are not expected to tip on top of this amount. If service has been particularly bad you can request to have the 10% removed from your bill. Taxi drivers do not get tipped; just round up the amount to facilitate change. Hairdressers and beauticians usually receive a 10% tip. Bellboys get tipped R$1 to R$2 (US50¢–US$1/25p–50p) per bag. Room service usually includes the 10% service charge on the bill.

Water The tap water in Brazil is increasingly safe to drink. However, as a result of the treatment process, it still doesn't taste great. To be on the safe side, drink bottled or filtered water (most Brazilians do). All brands are reliable; ask for *agua sem gas* for still water and *agua com gas* for carbonated water. However, you can certainly shower, brush your teeth, or rinse an apple with tap water.

4 Rio de Janeiro

ESSENTIALS

Say "Rio" and mental images explode: the glittering skimpy costumes of Carnaval; the statue of Christ, arms outspread on the mountaintop; the beach at Ipanema or Copacabana, crowded with women in miniscule bikinis; the rocky height of the Sugar Loaf; or the persistent rhythm of the samba.

Fortunately in Rio there's much more beyond and behind the glitter: historic neighborhoods, compelling architecture, wildlife and nature, dining (fine and not so fine), nightspots, bookshops, cafes, museums, and enclaves of rich and poor. In Rio, the more you explore, the more there is.

Stunning as the physical setting is—mountains tumbling down to sandy beaches, and then the sea—Rio was not always the *cidade maravilhosa* it would become. The town grew up as a shipping center for gold and supplies during Brazil's 18th-century gold rush. In recognition of the city's growing commercial importance, the capital was transferred from Salvador to Rio in 1762, though the city remained a dusty colonial backwater.

In 1808, Portuguese's Prince Regent Dom João (later King João VI) fled Lisbon ahead of Napoleon's armies and moved his court and capital to Rio. Accustomed to the style of European capitals, the prince and the 12,000 nobles who accompanied him began to transform Rio into a city of ornate palaces and landscaped parks. High culture in this new imperial city arrived in the form of a new library, an academy of arts and sciences, and the many glittering balls held by the imported elite. King João's son, Pedro, liked Rio so much that when the king returned to Lisbon, Pedro stayed on and declared Brazil independent.

Now the capital of a country larger and richer than many in Europe, Rio grew at a phenomenal pace; by the late 1800s it was one of the largest cities in the world. Many of the newcomers came from Europe, but a sizable portion were Brazilians of African descent who brought with them the musical traditions of Africa and the Brazilian Northeast.

A new "low culture" of distinctly Brazilian music began to develop in the city's poorer neighborhoods. The high point of the year for both high and low cultures was the celebration of Carnaval. In palace ballrooms, the elite held elaborate costume balls. In the streets, poorer residents would stage their own all-night parades. Not until the 1920s did the two celebrations begin to merge. It became, if not respectable, at least possible for elite and middle-class Brazilians to be seen at on-street Carnaval parades. At about the same time, the first road was punched through to Copacabana, and Cariocas (as Rio residents are called) flocked to the new community by the beach.

In the years following World War II, São Paulo took over as Brazil's industrial leader; the federal capital was moved inland to Brasília in the early 1960s. By the 1980s, violence and crime plagued the country, and Rio was perceived as the sort of place where walking down the street was openly asking for a mugging. For a time Cariocas feared for the future of their city—needlessly, it turned out. In the early 1990s, governments began pouring money back into basic services; cops were stationed on city streets, on public beaches, and anywhere else there seemed to be a problem. Public and private owners began renovating the many heritage buildings in the city's colonial core. Rio's youth rediscovered samba, returning to renovated clubs in the old bohemian enclave of Lapa. Now a city of some seven million and growing, Rio remains the country's media capital, an important finance center, and Brazil's key tourist destination.

GETTING THERE

BY PLANE   Antonio Carlos Jobim Airport, often called Galeão (✆ 021/3398-4527), is where all international flights and most domestic flights arrive. Regular taxis can be hailed outside the airport; a ride to Copacabana should cost about R$45 (US$19/£9.75) in average traffic. The most comfortable ones are the radio taxis, usually with air-conditioning, that allow you to prepay the fee to your destination. They are usually a little bit more expensive but give you peace of mind. Buy prepaid vouchers at the **Transcoopass** desk in the arrivals hall (✆ 021/2560-4888; all major credit cards accepted). Rates range from R$58 (US$29/£16) to Flamengo, and R$60 to R$70 (US$30–US$35/£16–£19) to the beach hotels of Copacabana and Ipanema. **Realtur/Reitur Turismo** (✆ 0800/240-850) runs an airport bus to the tourist areas along the beaches. From 5:30am to 11pm, a bus departs every 30 minutes and takes about 1 hour to make the full trip; the ride costs R$6 (US$3/£1.60) per person.

Rio's second airport, **Santos Dumont** (✆ 021/3814-7070), is located downtown and is used by Gol, Varig, and Tam for the Rio–São Paulo shuttles. The Realtur bus from Galeão stops here on its way to and from the Zona Sul. A taxi ride to Ipanema will cost about R$30 (US$15/£8) or a prepaid voucher can be purchased in the arrivals hall at the **Transcoopass.**

BY BUS   All long-distance buses arrive at the **Rodoviária Novo Rio,** Av. Francisco Bicalho 1, Santo Cristo (✆ 021/3213-1800; www.novorio.com.br), 5 minutes from downtown in the old port section of the city. It's not a good idea to walk from the station with all your belongings. Prepaid taxi vouchers are available at the booth next to

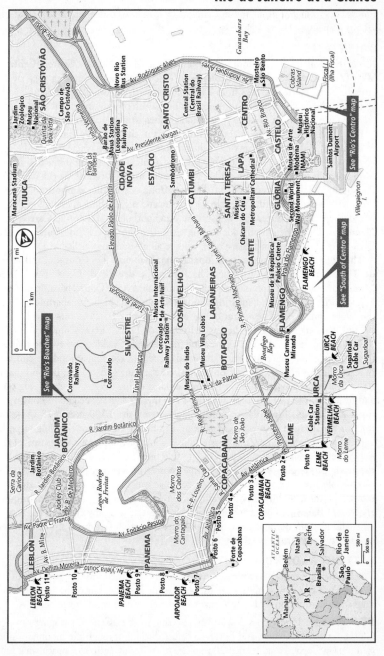

241

the taxi stand; a ride from the bus station to Ipanema costs about R$35 (US$15/ £9.50) prepaid.

ORIENTATION

Rio is traditionally divided into four zones: **North (Zona Norte), Center (Centro), West (Zona Oeste)** and **South (Zona Sul).** One of the least interesting areas of the city, the Zona Norte stretches from a few blocks north of Avenida Presidente Vargas all the way to the city limits. This region is a dull swath of port, industrial suburb, and *favela.* It is not the sort of place you should wander around unaccompanied.

Rio's Centro neighborhood contains most of the city's notable churches, squares, monuments, and museums, as well as the modern office towers where Rio's white-collar elite earn their daily bread. Roughly speaking, Centro stretches from the **São Bento Monastery** in the north to the seaside **Monument to the Dead of World War II** in the south, and from **Praça XV** on the waterfront east to the **Sambódromo** (near Praça XI). Just to the south of Centro lies the fun and slightly bohemian hilltop neighborhood of **Santa Teresa,** as well as the neighborhoods of **Glória, Catete,** and **Flamengo.** Other neighborhoods in this section of the city include **Botafogo** and **Urca** (nestled beneath the Sugar Loaf). They're all pleasant and walkable.

The Zona Sul neighborhoods of **Copacabana, Ipanema, São Conrado,** and **Barra de Tijuca** face the open Atlantic. The first to be developed, Copacabana's wide expanse of beach still impresses locals and visitors alike. Like Copacabana, Ipanema is a modern neighborhood, consisting almost exclusively of high-rise apartments from the 1960s and 1970s. The area at the far end of Ipanema beach is known as Leblon. Behind Ipanema is a lagoon, the Lagoa Rodrigo de Freitas; known simply as Lagoa, this body of water is circled by a pleasant 8.5km (5-mile) walking and cycling trail. At the far end of Ipanema and Leblon, the road carries on, winding around the cliff face to reach the tiny enclave of São Conrado, where the hang gliders land. Beyond that is Barra de Tijuca (usually called just Barra), an area of big streets, big malls, big cars, and little intrinsic interest. Backstopping all of these Zona Sul neighborhoods is the massive **Tijuca National Park.** Mostly mountainous, the 3,300-hectare (8,151-acre) forest is cut through with excellent walking and hiking trails, many leading to peaks with fabulous views. The Zona Oeste houses some of the poorest and some of the richest neighborhoods of the city. On one side there's Cidade de Deus—featured in the movie *City of God*—a huge low-income housing project built in the 1960s to relocate people from downtown slums out to what was then the far edge of the city. Nowadays, those with money are voluntarily relocating to the seaside condominium enclaves in **Barra da Tijuca** and **Recreio.** Most visitors will only ever visit the restaurants and malls in Barra or drive through Recreio to reach **Grumari,** a pristine beach on the city's outskirts.

GETTING AROUND

The Rio neighborhoods in which visitors spend most of their time are very easy to get around. You can almost always see the mountains or the ocean or both; with landmarks like that, it's pretty hard to stray too far from where you want to go.

BY SUBWAY Line 1 goes downtown, covering most of Centro, swinging through Glória, Catete, Flamengo, and Botafogo before ducking through the mountain to its terminus in Copacabana. It takes 20 minutes to go from Centro to Copacabana. Line 2 starts in downtown and is useful for going to the Maracanã stadium and the Quinta da Boa Vista (National Museum). The system is very safe, and it operates daily 6am to 11pm. A single ride costs R$2.40 (US$1.20/65p). Multiple tickets are available, but there's no volume discount.

BY BUS   Rio's buses follow direct pathways, always sticking to the main streets. On the Centro-Copacabana route alone, there are more than 30 different buses. The route number and final destination are displayed in big letters on the front of the bus. Smaller signs displayed inside the front window and posted on the side of the bus list the intermediate stops. *Tip:* If you're going from Ipanema or Copacabana all the way to Centro (or vice versa), look for a bus that says VIA ATERRO in its smaller window sign. These buses get on the waterfront boulevard in Botafogo and don't stop again until they reach downtown.

Have your bus money ready—R$2 to R$4 (US$1/55p–US$2/£1)—as you will go through a turnstile right away. There are no transfers. Buses are quite safe during the day; later in the evening (after 8pm), it's better to take a taxi.

BY TAXI   Regular taxis can be hailed anywhere on the street or at the many taxi stands around the city. Radio taxis are about 20% more expensive and can be contacted by phone; try **Coopertramo** (© 021/2560-2022) or **Transcoopass** (© 021/2560-4888). Radio taxis have air-conditioning and are supposedly more reliable, but we've never had a problem with regular taxis.

BY FERRY   Rio's ferries are operated by **Barcas SA** (© 021/2533-7524) and depart from Praça XV downtown. The service to Niterói runs 24 hours a day, with hourly service between midnight and 5am. The cheapest ferry costs R$2 (US$1/55p) and takes about 25 minutes to cross.

BY CAR   Driving in Rio is not for the meek of soul or weak of heart. Traffic is hectic, street patterns are confusing, and drivers are just a few shades shy of courteous. Things get even trickier later at night, when drivers start to regard red lights as optional. Be careful when approaching intersections.

At Antônio Carlos Jobim International Airport, there are **Hertz** (© 021/3398-4421), **Interlocadora** (© 021/3398-3181), and **Unidas** (© 021/3398-3452). At Santos Dumont Airport, there are **Hertz** (© 021/2262-0612), **Interlocadora** (© 021/2240-0754), and **Unidas** (© 021/2240-6715). In Copacabana, there are **Hertz,** Av. Princesa Isabel 500 (© 021/2275-7440), and **Localiza Rent a Car,** Av. Princesa Isabel 150 (© 021/2275-3340). Rates start at R$100 (US$50/£27) per day for a compact car with air-conditioning. Insurance adds R$30 (US$15/£8) per day.

VISITOR INFORMATION

Riotur (© 021/2217-7575; www.riodejaneiro-turismo.com.br) operates a number of offices and kiosks around town. There are information booths at Galeão airport (© 021/3398-2245), located in the international arrivals hall of Terminal 1 and open daily 6am to noon, and at Terminal 2, open daily 6am to noon and 5 to 11pm. There's also a booth in the domestic arrivals hall, open from 6am to noon and 5 to 11pm. Another Riotur kiosk is in the arrivals area of the Novo Rio Rodoviária bus station, open from 8am to 8pm (© 021/2263-4857). The main Riotur information center is located at Av. Princesa Isabel 183, Copacabana (© 021/2541-7522). Open Monday through Friday from 9am to 6pm, this office has the largest selection of brochures and information. This office also operates an information phone line, **Alô Rio,** at © 021/2542-8080 with an English-speaking staff; it's available Monday through Friday from 9am to 6pm.

FAST FACTS **Banco do Brasil** has branches at Rua Joana Angelica, Ipanema (© **021/2522-1442**); Av. N.S. de Copacabana 594, Copacabana (© **021/2548-8992**); and at the international airport, Terminal 1, third floor (© **021/3398-3652**); all have 24-hour ATMs. For currency exchange, try **Bank Boston,** Av. Rio Branco 110, Centro (© **021/2508-2700**); **Citibank,** Rua da Assambleia 100, Centro (© **021/2291-1232**); and **Imatur,** Rua Visconde de Pirajá 281, Loja A, Ipanema (© **021/2219-4205**).

In an emergency, call the **police** at © **190;** for the **fire brigade** or an **ambulance,** call © **193.** You can also try the **tourist police** at Av. Afranio de Melo Franco 159, Leblon (© **021/3399-7170**). If you need a **doctor,** call **Medtur,** Av. N. S. de Copacabana, Copacabana (© **021/2235-3339**). The city's best **hospital** is **Copa D'or,** Rua Figueiredo de Magalhães 875, Copacabana (© **021/2545-3600**).

Should you require any further vaccinations, contact the **Health Office,** Rua Mexico 128, Centro (© **021/2240-3568**); vaccinations are given Monday through Friday from 10 to 11am and 2 to 3pm.

You will find **post offices** all over town; look for the yellow-and-blue signs that read CORREIOS. Three main locations are Rua Primeiro de Março 64, Centro (© **021/2503-8331**); Av. N. S. de Copacabana 540, Copacabana (© **021/2503-8398**); and Rua Visconde de Pirajá 452, Ipanema (© **021/2563-8568**). These branches are open Monday through Friday from 10am to 4pm.

WHAT TO SEE & DO
THE TOP ATTRACTIONS
Centro

Ilha Fiscal ⭐⭐   This blue-green ceramic castle in the bay off Praça XV looks like the dwelling place of a princess, but in fact, it was built as the headquarters of the Customs service. When construction was finished in 1889, the normally reclusive Emperor Dom Pedro II decided to have a grand ball on Ilha Fiscal. Arriving by boat, Dom Pedro stumbled on the stone steps of the quay but recovered and quipped, "The monarch may have slipped, but the monarchy remains in place." Six days later, the empire collapsed. Visitors to the island get to see some of this history, notably a large oil painting entitled *The Last Ball of the Monarchy,* and you can see the building itself, which is a gorgeous piece of work. The tour lasts about 2½ hours.

Av. Alfredo Agache s/n. Centro (behind Praça XV). © 021/2104-6992. Admission R$8 (US$4/£2) adults, R$4 (US$2/£1) children 12 and under. Guided tours only. Departures Thurs–Sun. Boat tours depart at 1:15 and 3:15pm; visits to the Ilha Fiscal depart at 1, 2:30, and 4pm. Closed statutory holidays. Call to confirm hours at © 021/2233-9165. Bus: 119 or 415 (Praça XV).

Museu de Arte Moderna (MAM) ⭐⭐   Located in the waterfront Flamengo Park, the MAM is a long rectangular building lofted off the ground by an arcade of concrete struts. Like the arches of a Gothic cathedral, the concrete struts do all the load-bearing work, allowing for walls of solid-plate glass that welcome in city and sea and provide a vast display area free of obstructions. The MAM presents the best of what's happening in Brazil and Latin America and hosts traveling international exhibits. As with all modern art museums, some stuff is obscure to the point of utter boredom, while some is quite remarkably clever. Signage is in both English and Portuguese. Allow an hour to 90 minutes to view the entire museum.

Av. Infante Dom Henrique 85, Parque do Flamengo (Aterro), Centro. © 021/2240-4944. www.mamrio.com.br. Admission R$5 (US$2.50/£1.35) adults, R$2 (US$1/50p) students and seniors, free for children 12 and under. Tues–Fri noon–6pm; Sat–Sun noon–7pm. Metrô: Cinelândia. Bus: 472 or 125 (get off at Avenida Beira Mar by the museum's footbridge).

Rio's Centro

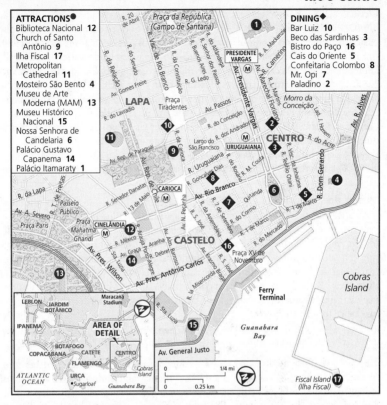

ATTRACTIONS●
Biblioteca Nacional **12**
Church of Santo
  Antônio **9**
Ilha Fiscal **17**
Metropolitan
  Cathedral **11**
Mosteiro São Bento **4**
Museu de Arte
  Moderna (MAM) **13**
Museu Histórico
  Nacional **15**
Nossa Senhora de
  Candelaria **6**
Palácio Gustavo
  Capanema **14**
Palácio Itamaraty **1**

DINING◆
Bar Luiz **10**
Beco das Sardinhas **3**
Bistro do Paço **16**
Cais do Oriente **5**
Confeitaria Colombo **8**
Mr. Opi **7**
Paladino **2**

Museu Histórico Nacional ⟨★★⟩   This is the place for anyone looking for a good overview of Brazilian history, from Cabral's arrival in 1500 to the events of the present day. Exhibits on themes such as "Early Exploration" and "Coffee Plantations" are illustrated with abundant maps and artifacts. Even better, much of the Portuguese signage comes with English translation. Allow 2 hours to see it all.

Praça Marechal Âncora s/n. ℭ 021/2550-9224. www.museuhistoriconacional.com.br. Admission R$6 (US$3/£1.60) adults, R$3 (US$1.50/£1) seniors and children 12 and under. Tues–Fri 10am–5:30pm; Sat–Sun 2–6pm. Bus: 119 or 415 (10-min. walk from the Praça XV).

Santa Teresa

Museu Chácara do Céu ⟨★★⟩   A wealthy man with eclectic tastes, Raymundo Castro Maya had this mansion built in the hills of Santa Teresa, and then filled with all manner of paintings and pottery and sculpture. The house itself is a charmer, a stylish melding of hillside and structure that evokes Frank Lloyd Wright's work in the American West. The views from the garden are fabulous. Castro Mayo seems to have had three main interests: European painters, including Monet, Matisse, Picasso, and Dalí; Brazilian art, particularly 19th-century landscapes; and Chinese pottery. Also worth perusing are the maps and paintings, particularly those of Rio in its early years.

Rua Murtinho Nobre 93, Santa Teresa. ℭ 021/2507-1932. www.museuscastromaya.com.br. Admission R$3 (US$1.50/£1) adults, free for children under 12. Free admission Wed. Wed–Mon noon–5pm. Tram: Curvelo.

Catete

Museu da República/Palácio do Catete ⚅⚅   Located in a gorgeous baroque palace that served as the official residence of Brazilian presidents from 1897 to 1960, this museum tries very hard to engage visitors in the history and politics of the Brazilian republic. The best exhibit is the three-room hagiography of President Getúlio Vargas. It's a curious treatment for this museum, given that in 1930, Vargas launched the coup that brought the first republic to an end. Still, they do a fabulous job, creating a multimedia sensory experience of Getúlio's life and times. In the final room, in a softly backlit glass case, lies the pearl-handled 32-caliber Colt that Getúlio used to blast a hole in his heart in 1954. Allow an hour to 90 minutes.

Rua do Catete 153, Catete. ⓒ 021/2558-6350. www.museudarepublica.org.br. Admission R$6 (US$3/£1.60) adults, free for seniors and children 11 and under. Free on Wed and Sun. Tues–Fri noon–5pm; Sat–Sun 2–6pm. Metrô: Catete.

Botafogo & Urca

Museu do Indio ⚅⚅ *Kids*   The Indian Museum's exhibits are some of the most innovative and artistic we have come across in a Brazilian museum, including striking wall-size photos adorned with colored feathers, and a display of kids' toys where the objects dangle from the ceiling at various heights. The symbolism of the hunt is portrayed in a dark room with just a ray of light casting an eerie glow on spears and animal skulls. There is no English signage, but the exhibits are so vivid, they speak for themselves. For kids, there is a gallery with body paint and stamps so they can practice adorning themselves as warriors or hunters. It's a great spot for children and an easy place to spend 2 hours.

Rua das Palmeiras 55, Botafogo. ⓒ 021/2286-8899. www.museudoindio.org.br. R$3 (US$1.50/£1) all ages (children in strollers are free), free on Sun. Tues–Fri 9am–5:30pm; Sat–Sun 1–5pm. Metrô: Botafogo.

Sugar Loaf (Pão de Açúcar) ⚅⚅⚅   Along with samba, beaches, and beautiful people, the Sugar Loaf remains one of the original and enduring Rio attractions. When you stand on its peak, the entire *cidade maravilhosa* (marvelous city) lays at your feet—it's a truly beautiful sight. The cable car leaves every half-hour from 8am to 10pm, more frequently if there are enough people waiting. The ascent takes two phases: the first from the ground station in Urca to the 220m (722-ft.) Morro de Urca, the second up to the 396m (1,300-ft.) Sugar Loaf itself. Trams are timed, so it's next to impossible to make both trips without spending transition time on the halfway stop. The Morro offers excellent views, as well as a cafe, a snack bar, a restaurant, souvenir stands, and a children's play area.

Av. Pasteur 520, Urca. ⓒ 021/2546-8400. www.bondinho.com.br. Admission R$35 (US$18/£9.50) adults, R$18 (US$9/£5) children 6–12, free for children under 6. Daily 8am–9pm. Last ride up at 8pm. Metrô: Botofogo, and then catch the integração bus marked Urca.

Lagoa

Jardim Botânico ⚅   A photograph of the botanical gardens' stately imperial palms graces nearly every tour brochure of Rio. The reality is a pretty and calm refuge with lots of interesting plants. The 141-hectare (348-acre) gardens have 6,000 species of tropical plants and trees in their collection. The gardens make no effort to explain the collection so you're pretty much on your own. Plant lovers will love the bromeliad and orchid greenhouses. Our personal favorite is a greenhouse full of pitcher plants and Venus flytraps. There's a cafe and a small bookshop onsite.

Rua Jardim Botânico 1008. ⓒ 021/3874-1808. www.jbrj.gov.br. Admission R$4 (US$2/£1) adults, free for children 7 and under. Daily 8am–5pm. Bus: 170 (from Centro), 571 (from Glória-Botafogo), or 572 (from Zona Sul)

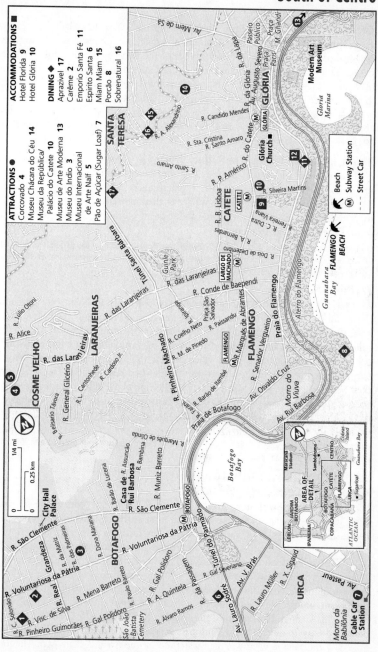

Cosme Velho

Corcovado 🎭🎭🎭   The price is a bit steep but then so is the rail line, its narrow gauge winding upwards past hillside shacks and tangled rainforest creepers, up to the very feet of Christ. The *Cristo Redentor* (Christ the Redeemer) is a stylish Art Deco statue, standing 30m (98 ft.) tall on the top of Corcovado Mountain, 710m (2,330 ft.) above sea level. The view from his toes is definitely worth the money—it's enough to give you feelings of omniscience. Allow about 2 hours round-trip.

(Train Station) Rua Cosme Velho 512, Cosme Velho. ⓒ 021/2558-1329. www.corcovado.com.br. Admission R$36 (US$18/£10) adults, R$18 (US$9/£5) children 6–12, free for children 5 and under. Trains going up depart every 30 min. from 8:30am–6:30pm daily. Last train down 7:30pm. Bus: 422, 583, or 584 to Cosme Velho.

Museu Internacional de Arte Naïf do Brasil 🎭🎭   Don't miss the Museu de Arte Naïf, located just a few hundred yards from the Corcovado train station. Sometimes known as "primitive" or "ingénue" art, its practitioners paint from the heart, portraying the daily life of common folks. Whatever they may lack in technical skill, they more than make up for with cheerful and expressive drawing and a vibrant use of color. Expect to spend 45 minutes.

Rua do Cosme Velho 561, Cosme Velho. ⓒ 021/2205-8612. www.museunaif.com.br. R$6 (US$3/£1.50) adults, R$3 (US$1.50/£1) children (your Corcovado train ticket gives you 50% discount at the museum). Tues–Fri 10am–6pm; Sat–Sun noon–6pm. Bus: 422, 583, or 584 to Cosme Velho.

Farther Afield

Museu de Arte Contemporânea–Niterói 🎭🎭   Oscar Niemeyer's spaceship design for Niterói's new contemporary art museum has done for this bedroom city what Gehry's Guggenheim did for Bilbao: put it on the map (at least in Brazil). As a gallery, however, the museum has drawbacks. Circular buildings are inherently difficult to make functional, on top of which the finishing on the inside seems extraordinarily cheap, as if most of the budget was spent on architectural fees. The curators do their best, bringing in a constantly changing selection of the best of Brazilian contemporary art. Even so, you can't help thinking that the best piece of work on display is the building itself. Allow about an hour.

Mirante de Boa Viagem s/n, Niterói. ⓒ 021/2620-2400. www.macniteroi.com.br. Admission R$4 (US$2/£1), free for children 7 and under. Tues–Sun 10am–6pm. From Praça XV, take the ferry to Niterói, and then take a short taxi ride along Niterói's waterfront and up the hill to the museum.

ARCHITECTURAL HIGHLIGHTS
Historic Buildings & Monuments

For a city so blessed with mountains and ocean and historical roots several centuries deep, Rio's movers and shakers have suffered from a striking sense of inferiority. As a result, since the early 1900s, various well-meaning Cariocas have taken turns ripping out, blowing up, filling in, and generally reconfiguring huge swaths of their city in order to make Rio look more like Paris or Los Angeles or, lately, Miami Beach.

Armed with the slogan "Rio Civilizes Itself!" and a deep envy of what Baron Haussman had done in Paris, engineer-mayor Pereiro Passos set to work in 1903 ripping a large swath through Rio's Centro district to create the first of the city's grand boulevards, the Avenida Central. Now renamed the **Avenida Rio Branco,** the 32m-wide (105-ft.) boulevard runs from Praça Mauá south past the grand neoclassical Igreja de Nossa Senhora da Candelária to what was then waterfront at the Avenida Beira Mar. The four-story Parisian structures that once lined the street are now found only on the **Praça Floriano,** referred to by most Cariocas by the name of its subway stop, Cinelândia.

Rio's Beaches

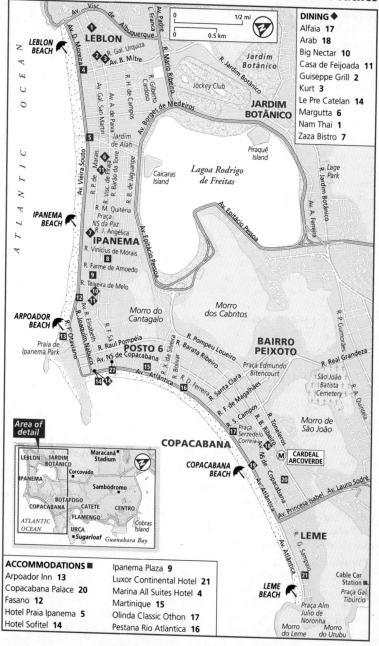

Anchored at the north end by the extravagant beaux arts Theatro Municipal, and flanked by the equally ornate Museu de Belas Artes and neoclassical Biblioteca Nacional, the *praça* beautifully emulates the proportions, the monumentality, and the glorious detail of a classic Parisian square.

The next stage in urban reform came in 1922, when the 400-year-old hilltop castle south of Praça XV was blown up, the hill leveled, and construction begun on a series of government office towers inspired by the modernist movement. The first of these—now known as the **Palácio Gustavo Capanema** (Rua da Imprensa 16)—listed among its architects nearly all the greats of Brazilian architecture, including Lucio Costa, Oscar Niemeyer, and Roberto Burle Marx, with painter Candido Portinari. International architects sat up and took note; other less avant-garde government departments commissioned architects with different ideologies, resulting in the War of the Styles that raged through the remainder of the 1930s. The resulting enclave of office towers, known as **Castelo,** lies on a patch centered on the Avenida Presidente Antonio Carlos. Chiefly of interest to architectural buffs, it should be toured only during office hours.

When it came to razing the city, Passos had nothing on Brazilian dictator Getúlio Vargas. In 1940, on Vargas's personal order, a monster 12-lane boulevard, the Avenida Presidente Vargas, was cut through the city fabric from the beautiful Nossa Senhora da Candelária church through the Campo de Santana Park to the northern edges of downtown. Anchoring this new mega-boulevard was the **Central Station,** a graceful modern building with a 132m (433-ft.) clock tower that still stands overlooking the city. Vargas's plan called for the entire 4km (2½-mile) street to be lined with identical 22-story office blocks. Only a few were ever built; they can be seen on the block crossed by Rua Uruguaiana.

The next great reconfiguration of Rio came 2 years after the federal capital fled inland to Brasília. City designers scooped away the huge high hill—Morro Santo Antônio—that once dominated the Largo Carioca, and dumped the earth on the beach from Lapa to Flamengo to create a vast new waterfront park. On the raw spot where the hill once stood arose the innovative cone-shaped **Metropolitan Cathedral,** and at the intersection of the new avenidas República do Chile and República do Paraguai, a trio of towering skyscrapers were built, the most interesting of which is the "hanging gardens" headquarters of Brazil's state oil company **Petrobras.** On the waterfront park—officially called **Parque do Flamengo** but most often referred to as Aterro, the Portuguese word for landfill—designers created new gardens and pathways, a new beach, and a pair of modernist monuments: the **Modern Art Museum** and the impressive **Monument to the Dead of World War II.** Not incidentally, the park also bears two wide and fast roadways connecting Centro with the fashionable neighborhoods in the Zona Sul.

Churches & Temples

Rio is awash with churches, with about 20 in Centro alone. The most impressive traditional church in Rio is **Nossa Senhora da Candelária** ⊛, set on a traffic island of its own at the head of Avenida Presidente Vargas (© **021/2233-2324**). It's open Monday through Friday from 7:30am to 4pm, Saturday and Sunday from 7:30am to noon. Also impressive, if not quite worth the hype or the long trek, is the **Mosteiro São Bento,** located on a hill on the far north corner of downtown (access is via an elevator located in Rua Dom Gerardo 40; © **021/2291-7122**). The main church itself is a shining example of the Golden Church, the high baroque practice of plastering every inch of a church's richly carved interior in gold leaf. It's open daily from 8 to 11am and 2:30 to 6pm. Newly reopened, the **Igreja da Ordem Terceira de São Francisco da Penitência** ✺, Largo da Carioca 5 (✆ **021/2262-0197**), is set on a hilltop overlooking Largo Carioca. It and the next-door **Church of Santo Antônio** (✆ **021/2262-0129**) form part of the large Franciscan complex in the city center. The São Francisco church is simply outstanding: Interior surfaces are filled with golden carvings and hung with censers of heavy ornate silver. You can pay a visit Wednesday through Friday from 11am to 4pm. Last and most innovative of Rio's significant churches is the **Catedral Metropolitana** ✺✺, Av. República de Chile 245 (✆ **021/2240-2869**). The form is ultimately modern, and the feeling is soaring High Gothic. It's open daily from 7am to 6pm.

BEACHES, PARKS & PLAZAS
Beaches

The older bay beaches such as **Botafogo** and **Flamengo** are now unfortunately quite polluted. They're fine and picturesque places for an afternoon stroll, but a poor spot if your heart is set on swimming. The first of the ocean beaches to see development back in the 1920s, **Copacabana** ✺✺ remains one of the favorites. The wide and beautifully landscaped Avenida Atlântica is a great place for a stroll. **Ipanema beach** ✺✺ was famous among Brazilians even before Tom Jobim wrote his famous song about the tall and tan and lovely girl he saw and sighed over. Stretching nearly 3km (2 miles) from the foot of the Pedra Dois Irmãos to the Ponta Arpoador, Ipanema is a carnival. Watch volleyball or *footvollei* (like volleyball but no hands allowed), beach soccer, hand shuttle, surfing, and wake boarding. Forgot your bikini? Wait but a moment, and one will come by for sale, along with towels, hats, shades, peanuts, beer, cookies, suntan lotion, Styrofoam airplanes, sticks of grilled shrimp, and coconuts. Off on its own, surrounded by mountains, **São Conrado** beach offers some fine scenery and a (relative) sense of isolation. Its other main claim to fame is as a landing strip for all the hang gliders who leap from nearby peaks.

Parks & Gardens

On the waterfront near Centro is **Flamengo Park,** a good place to stroll in the late afternoon if you're looking for a nice view of the Sugar Loaf. The city's most impressive park, the **Parque Nacional Da Tijuca (Tijuca National Park)** is a wonder. At 3,300 hectares (8,151 acres), it's the biggest urban forest in the world, and one of the last remnants of Atlantic rainforest on Brazil's southern coast. It's a great place to go for a hike (see "Sports & Outdoor Activities," below), splash in a waterfall, or admire the view.

Squares & Plazas

Tucked away just a few hundred meters uphill along Rua Cosme Velho from the Corcovado train station is one of Rio's prettiest squares, the **Largo de Boticario** ✺✺, named for the druggist Luis da Silva Souto who settled there in 1831. It's a gem of a spot, with five gaily painted colonial houses encircling a fountain in the middle of a flagstone square. If you're going to the Corcovado anyway, it's well worth the 5-minute detour.

Perhaps the city's prettiest square (next to Cinelândia) is the **Largo do Machado** in the Catete neighborhood. Perfectly proportioned, the square is dominated by the **Igreja Matriz de Nossa Senhora da Glória,** a strange but rather elegant combination of traditional Greek temple and a three-story bell tower. As an added bonus, there are a number of Parisian-style sidewalk cafes on the square's northern flank.

SPORTS & OUTDOOR ACTIVITIES

GOLF   One of the city's best courses (18 holes) is the elegant **Gávea Golf Club,** Estrada da Gávea 800, São Conrado (© 021/3332-4141). However, the club—like virtually every golf course in Brazil—is private. The Copacabana Palace Hotel and the Sheraton Rio Hotel are a few of the hotels that have an arrangement allowing their guests to tee off. If you are a golf fiend, check first with your hotel of choice for privileges.

HANG GLIDING   If you want to do some hang gliding, contact **Just Fly Rio** (© 021/2268-0565 or 021/9985-7540; www.justfly.lookscool.com). Flight instructor Paulo Celani has soared in tandem with hundreds of people ages 5 to 85. There are no special skills necessary, aside from a willingness to run off a ramp into the open sky. It's well worth the R$160 (US$80/£43) per flight, with pickup and drop-off included.

HIKING   Rio Hiking (© 021/9721-0594; www.riohiking.com.br) offers guided hiking trips to most of Rio's peaks. The 4-hour Sugarloaf trip, which includes a short stretch of rock climbing, costs R$120 (US$60/£32). The 6-hour Pedra da Gávea hike offers terrific views, a waterfall in the middle, and an ocean dip at the end. Cost is R$150 (US$75/£40). Less strenuous is the Tijuca Forest tour, which involves a tour of the forest, stops at a waterfall and a couple of lookouts, and a 2-hour hike to Pico de Tijuca. Cost is R$170 (US$85/£46), with the option of returning via the fascinating hilltop neighborhood of Santa Teresa.

SURFING   Rio has a number of good spots to catch the waves. The surfing beach closest to the main part of Rio is **Arpoador beach** in Ipanema. Waves are between 1m and 3m (3–10 ft.). **São Conrado beach** is off and on—sometimes there are good 1.8m (6-ft.) waves; sometimes it's dead. Out in Barra de Tijuca, the main surf beach is **Barra-Meio,** a half-mile stretch in the middle of the beach (around Av. Sernambetiba 3100). Waves average around 1.8m (6 ft.). Continue down that same beach another 8km (5 miles) and you come to **Macumba-Pontal,** a beach with waves of up to 3m (10 ft.).

If you need a board, **Hot Coast,** Galeria River, Rua Francisco Otaviano 67, Loja 12, Ipanema (© 021/2287-9388), rents short boards, fun boards, and long boards for R$40 (US$20/£11) a day. You need to book ahead if you want a board on Saturday or Sunday. If you're looking for **lessons** there's a surf school conveniently located in Ipanema. The **Escolinha de Surf Paulo Dolabella** (© 021/2259-2320) is in front of the Caesar Park Hotel. The regular lessons are Tuesday and Thursday from 8am to 10am and 3pm to 5pm, but you can also arrange for a lesson on the weekends or other days. Drop-in rates are R$30 (US$15/£8) per hour, including the equipment. If you've brought your board and just need transportation, there's a **surf bus** that departs the Largo do Machado (the square by the Metrô stop of the same name) daily at 6am and 2pm, going along Copacabana, Arpoador, São Conrado, and Barra de Tijuca before returning (check www.surfbus.com.br for details).

SHOPPING

Shoppers will be in heaven in Rio. Browse the crafts markets in Ipanema or Copacabana for souvenirs, or check out the small shops in downtown's pedestrian streets.

Upscale shoppers will love the Rio Sul mall and the fancy boutiques in Rio's tony Ipanema.

ARTS & CRAFTS   **Brasil & Cia,** Rua Maria Quitéria 27, Ipanema (✆ 021/2267-4603; bus no. 472) specializes in high-end Brazilian arts and crafts made from wood, ceramics, paper, and fibers. **Pé de Boi,** Rua Ipiranga 55, Laranjeiras (✆ 021/2285-4395; bus no. 584), goes beyond Brazilian handicrafts and sells works from popular Peruvian, Ecuadorian, and Guatemalan artists. **Trilhos Urbanos,** Rua Almirantes Alexandrino 402, Santa Teresa (✆ 021/2242-3632; tram stop: Largo dos Guimarães), is a great little store that sells a variety of Brazilian artwork, as well as photographs and posters.

BEACHWEAR & SURF SHOPS   **Bum Bum,** Rua Vinicius de Morais 130, Ipanema (✆ 021/2521-1229), is the best store to shop for the infamous Rio bikini. Collections vary constantly, but one thing never changes—the smaller, the better. Known for its original designs and prints, **Blue Man,** Visconde de Pirajá 351, Loja 108, Ipanema (✆ 021/2247-4905), is one of the beachwear trendsetters. **Galeria River,** Rua Francisco Otaviano 67, Ipanema (✆ 021/2267-9943), is not just one shop but a mini-mall with at least a dozen sports and outdoor stores that sell surf gear as well as other sporting goods, and accessories such as clothing and sunglasses.

BOOKS   **Livraria da Travessa** invites browsing sessions of several hours or more with its great collection of English-language books, including all the usual pocketsize books, plus children's books and guidebooks. There are two locations, one at Av. Rio Branco 44, Centro (✆ 021/2242-9294), and another at Rua Visconde de Pirajá 462A, Ipanema (✆ 021/2521-7734). For an excellent selection of foreign magazines and newspapers, check out **Letras e Expressões,** Rua Visconde de Pirajá 276, Ipanema (✆ 021/2521-6110), or in Leblon at Av. Ataulfo de Paiva 1292 (✆ 021/2511-5085).

CLOTHING FOR MEN   Rio's the perfect place to add to your summer wardrobe, especially if you like a bit of color. **Toulon,** Rua Visconde de Pirajá 135, Ipanema (✆ 021/2247-8716), is an excellent spot to pick up some smart casual wear: good-quality jeans, khakis, colorful long-sleeved cotton dress shirts, and T-shirts at reasonable prices. If you're shopping for some shirts or informal jackets, check out **Sandpiper,** Rua Santa Clara 75, Copacabana (✆ 021/2236-7652).

CLOTHING FOR WOMEN   Carioca women like to dress up, and even though most of their ensembles may seem a tad too colorful for North American tastes, adding a few pieces to your wardrobe is bound to spice things up. **Folic,** N.S. de Copacabana 690, Copacabana (✆ 021/2548-4021), sells sophisticated and elegant clothes that fit beautifully. For young and trendy pieces, check out **XPTO,** Rua Gonçalves Dias 55, Centro (✆ 021/2252-3100), a popular store with Rio's 18- to 30-year-olds. The collection includes lots of dresses made out of excellent-quality cotton. Many of the pretty skirts come with matching tops that can be bought separately or mixed and matched with other styles.

JEWELRY   The best-known name in Brazil for gems, jewelry, and souvenirs made with semiprecious and precious stones is **Amsterdam Sauer,** Rua Visconde de Pirajá 484, Ipanema (✆ 0800/266-092 or 021/2512-9878). The store offers a wide range of jewelry and loose gemstones such as emeralds, aquamarines, imperial topaz (mined only in Brazil), tourmalines, citrines, and Brazilian opal.

MALLS & SHOPPING CENTERS   One of the most popular malls in the city, **Rio Sul,** Rua Lauro Muller 116, Botafogo (© 021/2545-7200), has more than 450 stores, a movie theater, and an excellent food court. For serious shoppers, **Barra Shopping** will have everything you need. The largest mall in Latin America, with close to 600 stores, the disadvantage is its distance from the rest of Rio; it's located at Av. das Americas 4666, Barra da Tijuca (© 021/2431-9922). **Botafogo Praia Shopping,** Praia de Botafogo 400, Botafogo (© 021/2559-9559), has an excellent selection of clothing stores such as Dimpus, Folic, Corpo and Alma, Exchange, Old Factory, and Madame MS.

MUSIC   Music buffs will think they have died and gone to heaven at **Modern Sound,** Rua Barata Ribeiro 502, Copacabana (© 021/2548-5005). This store houses an amazing collection of music. In the evenings, the store is often used as a small concert venue.

CARNAVAL

Carnaval—what a party! Thousands of people—many of them of limited means or just plain poor—spend hundreds of hours preparing for the Samba School Parade that culminates this 4-day celebration. Originally, Carnaval marked the last few days of fun before Lent, the 40-day period of fasting and penitence preceding Holy Saturday and Easter. The religious aspect of the celebration faded some time ago, but Carnaval's date is still determined by the ecclesiastical calendar. If you're not able to attend Carnaval itself, the **rehearsals**—which usually start in mid-September or early October—are an absolute must, the closest thing you'll experience to the event itself. In the 2 weeks leading up to the big event, you'll begin to see the **blocos.** These are community groups—usually associated with a particular neighborhood or sometimes with a bar—who go around the neighborhood, playing music and singing and dancing through the streets. Carnaval finally kicks off the Friday before Ash Wednesday with an explosion of lavish *bailes* (balls). Then there is the pièce de résistance, the **Samba School Parade,** an event that the samba schools plan and sweat over for an entire year. Starting Sunday and continuing Monday night, the 14 top-ranked samba schools show their stuff in the Sambódromo, a mile-long concrete parade ground built in the center of Rio especially for this annual event.

WATCHING THE SAMBA PARADE

One of Carnaval's unique events, the Samba School Parade is an all-night feast of color and sound. Tens of thousands of costumed dancers, thousands of percussionists, and hundreds of gorgeous performers atop dozens of floats all move in choreographed harmony to the nonstop rhythm of samba. Over the course of 2 nights, 14 teams compete for the honor of putting on the best show ever.

Well before the parade starts, the grounds surrounding the Sambódromo are transformed into Carnaval central. A main stage hosts a variety of acts and performances and hundreds of vendors set up shop with food and drinks. This *terreirão do samba* **(samba land)** is open the weekend before Carnaval, Friday through Tuesday during Carnaval, and again the Saturday after for the Parade of Champions. Contact **Riotur** (© 021/2217-7575) for more detailed programming information.

It is next to impossible to buy tickets directly from Liesa, the **Liga das Escolas de Samba** (© 021/2253-7676; www.liesa.com.br). The tickets go on sale a few months before carnival and always sell out in 20 minutes. The few tourist tickets that remain, Liesa sells at an extraordinary markup. Most tourists are left buying from scalpers or travel agencies. Reputable travel agencies include **Blumar** (© 021/2142-9300;

> ## *Tips* Participating in the Parade
>
> If you think watching the parade from up close sounds pretty amazing, imagine being in it. To parade (*desfilar* in Portuguese), you need to commit to a school and buy a costume. Many schools now have websites with pictures of their costumes (search for *"fantasia"*). To contact a school directly, see the websites and phone numbers below, under "Rehearsals." Prices range from about R$500 to R$900 (US$250–US$450/£135–£243). A number of agencies in Rio will organize it all for you, at a markup of 25% to 50%. **Blumar** (© 021/2511-3636) can organize the entire event for you for R$900 (US$450/£243). For other organizations, contact **Alô Rio** at © 021/2542-8080.

www.blumar.com.br) and **BIT** (© **021/2256-5657;** www.bitourism.com), both of which sell good tickets at reasonable rates, but both of which often sell out early. If you've got your heart set on seeing the parade, buy your tickets by October or at the latest November preceding the year you want to go.

The parade starts at 9pm, but unless you want to stake out a particular spot, you may as well take your time arriving, as the event will continue nonstop until about 6am.

REHEARSALS

Every Saturday from September until Carnaval, each samba school holds a general samba rehearsal *(ensaio)* at its home base. The band and key people come out and practice their theme song over and over to perfection. People dance for hours, taking a break now and then for snacks and beer. Both Mangueira and Salgueiro are located no more than a R$25 (US$13/£7) cab ride from Copacabana. Plan to arrive anytime after 11pm. When you are ready to leave, there'll be lots of taxis around. The events are well attended and very safe; just don't go wandering off into an unfamiliar neighborhood. To find out more about rehearsals or participating in the parade, contact the **Liga das Escolas de Samba** at © **021/2253-7676,** or check out **www.liesa.com.br**. You can also contact the schools directly: The easiest ones to get to are **Mangueira** (Rio's favorite school and close to downtown), Rua Visconde de Niterói 1072, Mangueira (© **021/3872-6786;** www.mangueira.com.br); **Salgueiro,** Rua Silva Telles 104, Andaraí (© **021/2238-5564;** www.salgueiro.com.br); and **Rocinha,** Rua Bertha Lutz 80, São Conrado (© **021/3205-3303;** www.academicosdarocinha.com.br). If you can't find anyone who speaks English, contact **Alô Rio** for assistance at © **021/2542-8080.**

BLOCOS

Don't miss the blocos, neighborhood groups of musicians and merrymakers who parade through the streets in the days and nights before and during Carnaval. Everyone is welcome, and you don't need a costume, just comfortable clothes and shoes. Riotur publishes an excellent brochure called *Bandas, Blocos and Ensaios,* available through **Alô Rio** (© **021/2542-8080**), or pick one up at Av. Princesa Isabel 183, Copacabana. In the list of blocos below, the days of the week refer specifically to the days of Carnaval unless otherwise stated.

Saturday morning, **Cordão do Bola Preta** meets in front of the Bola Preta Club, on the corner of Rua Treze de Maio and Rua Evaristo da Veiga just across from the Theatro Municipal in Cinelândia. Though this is not a gay group, men often dress in drag. Lots of musicians join in the **Bloco do Bip Bip,** the first and last bloco to parade. The first time begins at the stroke of midnight on Friday and the last time at 9:30pm on Tuesday evening, with Ash Wednesday looming just a few hours away. They meet at Bar Bip Bip, Rua Almirante Gonçalves 50 (close to the Luxor Regente Hotel). The biggest bloco of all is the **Banda de Ipanema,** counting up to 10,000 followers in its throng. The group meets on the two Saturdays preceding Carnaval as well as on Saturday during Carnaval at 3pm, starting at the Praça General Osorio. You'll see quite a few costumes at this parade, although not as many as at the **Banda da Carmen Miranda,** the prime gay parade. This bloco is an absolute blast, with outlandish costumes, extravagant drag queens, great music, and even some floats. It takes place on the Sunday before Carnaval, gathering at 4pm on the corner of Avenida Visconde de Pirajá and Rua Joana Angelica. The only bloco so far with a website, **Simpatia é Quase Amor** has close to 10,000 followers who all dress in the group's lilac-and-yellow shirts. The shirt is for sale at the meeting place, Praça General Osorio, starting at 3pm on the Saturday before Carnaval and the Sunday during Carnaval. Check out **www.sitesbrasil.com/simpatia** to see some wonderful pictures of the crowds.

BAILES

More formal than the blocos, the samba *bailes* are where you go to see and be seen. Contact **Âlo Rio** (© 021/2542-8080) for details and ticket information. The popular Copacabana nightclub **Le Boy** in Copacabana (p. 270) organizes a differently themed ball every night during Carnaval, Friday through Tuesday. These balls are gay-friendly but by no means gay-only. Call © **021/2240-3338** for details and ticket information. The prime gay event—and one of Rio's most famous balls—is the Tuesday night **Gala Gay** at the Scala nightclub, Av. Afranio de Melo Franco 296, Leblon (© **021/2239-4448**). TV stations vie for position by the red carpet to interview illustrious or notorious arrivals; wild and colorful costumes are a must. The grand slam of all Carnaval balls is the Saturday night extravaganza at the Copacabana Palace Hotel, the **Baile do Copa.** The hotel plays host to the crème de la crème of Rio's (and Brazil's) high society, dressed in tuxedos and elegant costumes. Tickets start at US$250 (£128) per person and sell out quickly. Call © **021/2548-7070** for more details.

WHERE TO STAY

The only neighborhood to avoid staying in is downtown Rio. Hotels always list the rack rates on a sign behind the desk, but you can usually expect to pay 50% to 80% of this amount, depending on the season, the staff person, and your bargaining skills. Always negotiate. Be sure to ask about taxes that will be added to your bill. Most hotels charge a 10% service tax, a 5% city tax, and if they are a member of the Rio Convention and Visitor's bureau, a tourist tax of US$1 to US$3 (50p–£1.55) per day.

A substantial breakfast *(café de manha)* is included at most Brazilian hotels. In recent years, a few of the more expensive hotels have taken to charging for *café de manha;* if this is the case, it's noted in the rate information below.

IPANEMA/LEBLON
Very Expensive
Fasano 👁👁👁 The famous *enfant terrible* of the design world, Phillippe Starck is known for his chairs and hotel lobbies and other high-end hotel bits the world over; this was his first ever opportunity to design a complete hotel. From lobby lounge and restaurant to rooftop pool deck, the hotel displays Starck's sense for space and materials. The rooftop pool, in particular, is a thing of beauty, a low square pond of chiseled

white marble with an infinite edge that seems to flow out the parapet and join with sand and sea. Inside, rooms feature the same design sense and the quality of everything in all rooms—bedding, bathroom products, bathrobes—is all top notch. And if you can't afford the room rate, it's still worth coming in for a fancy cocktail in the lobby lounge or big white restaurant bar, to admire the high design and watch the beautiful people at play.

Av. Vieira Souto 88, Ipanema, Rio de Janeiro, 22420-000 RJ. © 021/3202-4000. Fax 021/3202-4010. www.fasano. com.br. 91 units. R$945 (US$470/£255) superior double; R$1,440 (US$720/£389) deluxe ocean view; R$2,500 (US$1,225/£675) ocean view suite. Extra bed R$150 (US$75/£40). Children 12 and under stay free in parent's room. Inquire about seasonal discounts. AE, DC, MC, V. Free valet parking. Bus: 415. **Amenities:** Restaurant; bar; rooftop pool; small spa; well-equipped fitness center; sauna; concierge; business center; room service; massage; babysitting; laundry; dry cleaning; nonsmoking floors. In room: A/C, TV, dataport, minibar, hair dryer, safe.

Marina All Suites Hotel ★★★ Finds

Design, with a capital D. The Marina All Suites is the brainchild of a consortium of local architects and decorators who bought, gutted, and redecorated all the rooms, in the process reducing the original layout of six rooms per floor to a very spacious three. All are so precociously modern they positively squeak, with original pieces of art and a style unique to each unit. The two-bedroom Suite Diamante must be the most beautiful suite in Rio. The "basic" suites (*basic* being an understatement) are studio apartments. The design suites have a separate bedroom. All feature an American kitchen (microwave, fridge, and wet bar), ample desk space and sitting areas, spacious bathrooms, and luxurious furnishings, making this truly one of Rio's most outstanding hotels.

Av. Delfim Moreira 696, Leblon, Rio de Janeiro, 22441-000 RJ. © 021/2172-1100. Fax 021/2294-1644. www.marina allsuites.com.br. 38 units (some with showers only). R$700–R$930 (US$350–US$465/£189–£251) basic suite; R$980–R$1,200 (US$490–US$600/£265–£324) design suite; R$1,900 (US$950/£513) Suite Diamante. AE, DC, MC, V. Free parking. Bus: 474. **Amenities:** Restaurant; pool; excellent gym; sauna; game room; concierge; business center; room service; massage; babysitting; laundry service. In room: A/C, TV, dataport, kitchen, minibar, fridge, microwave, toaster and coffeemaker, hair dryer, electronic safe.

Expensive

Hotel Praia Ipanema ★★★

Straddling the border between Ipanema and Leblon, the Praia Ipanema offers luxury beachfront accommodations at a less than luxury price. All 105 units offer balconies and ocean views, a full one in the case of the 55 deluxe rooms and a partial (from the side) view for the 46 superior rooms (which, it should be noted, are actually larger than the deluxe rooms). The best rooms begin at the 10th floor and carry upwards, as the views of sand and sea get ever more spectacular. Three-day weekend specials (Fri–Sun) often include drinks, lunch or dinner, and a late check-out for the same price as 2 regular nights.

Av. Vieira Souto 706, Ipanema, Rio de Janeiro, 22420-000 RJ. © 021/2540-4949. Fax: 021/2239-6889. www.praia ipanema.com. 105 units. R$500 (US$250/£135) superior double; R$595 (US$298/£161) deluxe view double. AE, DC, MC, V. No parking. Bus: 474 or 404. **Amenities:** Restaurant; 2 bars; rooftop outdoor pool; small gym; tour desk; business center; room service; laundry service and dry cleaning; beach service. In room: A/C, TV/VCR, dataport, minibar, fridge, hair dryer, safe.

Ipanema Plaza ★★★

The Ipanema Plaza is located just 1 block from Ipanema beach. The hotel's modern and sleek design looks fabulous and the attention to detail carries over into the rooms. Furnished in beige tones and cherry wood, the rooms are quite spacious, particularly the deluxe rooms. A number of them come with a large balcony, and all double beds are king size; twin beds are much larger than the average Brazilian single bed. The hotel is close to Rio's upscale gay neighborhood, and has a reputation for being very gay-friendly.

Rua Farme de Amoedo 34, Ipanema, Rio de Janeiro, 22420-020 RJ. © **021/3687-2000**. Fax: 021/3687-2001. www. ipanemaplazahotel.com. 135 units. R$400 (US$200/£108) superior double; R$490 (US$245/£132) deluxe double; R$610 (US$305/£165) Ipanema floor double. Extra person 25%. Children under 10 stay free in parent's room. AE, DC, MC, V. Bus: 474 or 404. **Amenities:** Restaurant; bar; rooftop outdoor pool; small gym; tour desk; business center; room service; laundry service and dry cleaning; beach service. *In room:* A/C, TV/VCR/DVD, dataport, minibar, hair dryer, safe.

Moderate

Arpoador Inn 🏖 *Value*   The only budget-priced oceanfront hotel in Ipanema, the Arpoador Inn has a privileged location on a quiet stretch of beach popular with the surf crowd, and just around the corner from Copacabana. Even better, the beach in front of the hotel is closed to cars and therefore pleasantly quiet. The deluxe rooms all face the ocean. Their furniture is a little dated but the rooms are bright and spotless. Obtaining these does require booking ahead; if they're full, the superior rooms, which look out over the street behind the beach, make an acceptable alternative. The only rooms to avoid are the standard ones, which are very small, dark, and look into an interior wall.

Rua Francisco Otaviano 177, Ipanema, Rio de Janeiro, 22080-040 RJ. © **021/2523-0060**. Fax 021/2511-5094. www. arpoadorinn.com.br. 50 units (showers only). R$170 (US$85/£46) double; R$220 (US$110/£59) street-view superior double; R$350 (US$175/£95) deluxe ocean view. Extra person R$90 (US$45/£24). Children 6 and under stay free in parent's room. AE, DC, MC, V. No parking. Bus: 474. **Amenities:** Restaurant; room service; laundry. *In room:* A/C, TV, fridge, safe.

COPACABANA

Very Expensive

The Copacabana Palace 🏖🏖   The spot where beachfront luxury in Rio all began, the Copacabana Palace is the place to splurge. Even today, the 82-year-old Palace still maintains its Jazz Age charm. Taking full advantage, however, requires approaching things with Gatsbyesque confidence. Take, for example, the superior rooms and Avenida suites. Or rather, don't take them. Though slightly cheaper, they offer not a drop of ocean view. To get value for money at the Palace, it's really a case of go big or go home, and there's nothing bigger than the penthouse suites. Elegant and tastefully decorated, these spacious one-bedroom suites have their own private veranda overlooking Copacabana beach. Just as stylish and almost as spacious are the poolside suites, which also feature a partial ocean view. Note that the rates listed here are rack rates. Check the website or contact a travel agency for discounts.

Av. Atlântica 1702, Copacabana, Rio de Janeiro, 22021-001 RJ. © **0800/211-533** or 021/2548-7070. Fax 021/2235-7330. www.copacabanapalace.orient-express.com. 226 units. R$1,010 (US$510/£273) deluxe city view double; R$1,380 (US$690/£373) deluxe ocean view double; R$1,830 (US$915/£494) junior suite double; 1-bedroom suite R$2480 (US$1240/£670). Seasonal discounts available, special weekend packages, 2 nights for the price of 1, including breakfast and Sat Feijoada lunch. Extra person about 25%. Children 12 and under stay free in parent's room. AE, DC, MC, V. Free parking. Metrô: Arcoverde. **Amenities:** 2 restaurants; bar; large outdoor pool; rooftop tennis courts; health club; Jacuzzi; sauna; concierge; tour desk; car rental; business center; salon; room service; massage; babysitting; laundry; dry cleaning; executive-level rooms. *In room:* A/C, TV, dataport, kitchen, minibar, hair dryer, safe.

Hotel Sofitel 🏖🏖🏖   Located on the edge of Copacabana directly opposite the Copacabana Fort, this flagship of the French Sofitel chain offers elegant accommodations and superb service to match. All rooms have balconies, soundproof windows, and electronic safes big enough to hold a laptop. Superior rooms are elegantly decorated but lack an ocean view. Deluxe rooms differ only in offering a guaranteed full ocean view. The Imperial Club rooms come with perks such as personalized stationery and business cards, international newspapers, and access to the outstanding lounge with a well-stocked multilingual library. For sunbathing, there's a complementary beach service on Copacabana beach itself, or else a choice of two swimming pools, one to catch the morning sun and the other for the afternoon rays. Breakfast not included.

Av. Atlântica 4240, Copacabana, Rio de Janeiro, 22070-002 RJ. ⓒ **0800/241-232** or 021/2525-1232. Fax 021/2525-1200. www.accorhotels.com.br. 388 units. R$468 (US$234/£126) superior double; R$675 (US$338/£182) deluxe double; R$900 (US$450/£243) junior suite double. Children 12 and under stay free in parent's room. AE, DC, MC, V. Free parking. Bus: 474. **Amenities:** 2 restaurants (see Le Pré-Catelan under "Where to Dine," later in this chapter); bar; 2 pools; health club; sauna; concierge; tour desk; car rental; business center; shopping arcade; room service; massage; babysitting; laundry; dry cleaning; nonsmoking rooms and floors; executive-level rooms. *In room:* A/C, TV, dataport, minibar, fridge, hair dryer, safe.

Expensive

Pestana Rio Atlantica ✶✶✶
Always one of the nicest hotels on the Avenida Atlantica, the Pestana looks brand-new, thanks to a recent overhaul. The best rooms in the house, without doubt, are the Oceanica suites. These large rooms offer ocean views, large balconies, and come elegantly furnished with dark wooden furniture and splashes of yellow and beige. The standard and superior rooms are more plainly furnished and have a side view. Standard rooms look out over the buildings adjacent to the hotel. Superior rooms (on the 10th floor or higher) have a partial ocean view. Breakfast is not included, but can be purchased for R$33 (US$14/£7.15).

Av. Atlântica 2964, Copacabana, Rio de Janeiro, 22070-000 RJ. ⓒ **021/2548-6332.** Fax 021/2255-6410. www.pestana.com. 216 units. R$432 (US$216/£117) double; R$478 (US$239/£129) superior double; R$730–R$1070 (US$365–US$535/£197–£289) suite oceanica. Children 10 and under stay free in parent's room. AE, DC, MC, V. Free valet parking. Metrô: Arcoverde. **Amenities:** Restaurant; bar; outdoor pool; health club; Jacuzzi; sauna; concierge; tour desk; business center; room service; massage; babysitting; laundry; dry cleaning; nonsmoking rooms; rooms for people w/limited mobility. *In room:* A/C, TV, dataport, minibar, hair dryer, safe.

Moderate

Luxor Continental Hotel ✶✶✶ *(Finds)*
Located in a quiet residential neighborhood just off Copacabana, the Luxor offers outstanding value. Rates seldom top R$240 (US$120/£65), and those who book on the Internet can reserve a room for as little as R$160 (US$80/£43). For that you get services that are worthy of a deluxe hotel: room service and business center, high-speed Internet, large fitness room, and a rooftop pool. The rooms themselves are comfortable albeit a tad on the plain side with a double bed or twins with a small table and chairs and counter. The Luxor is set 1 block from Leme Beach, which is really the continuation of Copacabana beach. To make the most of the view, reserve a room on the 16th floor or up, facing the ocean. Nonsmokers will be happy to know that the entire hotel is nonsmoking.

Rua Gustavo Sampaio 320, Leme, Rio de Janeiro, 22010-010 RJ. ⓒ **021/2546-1070.** Fax 021/2541-1946. www.luxorhoteis.com.br. 275 units (showers only). R$218 (US$109/£59) standard double; R$240 (US$120/£65) superior double; R$272 (US$136/£73) deluxe double. Extra person 25% extra. Children 12 and under stay free in parent's room. AE, DC, MC, V. No parking. Bus: 472. **Amenities:** Restaurant; bar; outdoor pool; health club; sauna; concierge; 24-hr. business center; room service; laundry; nonsmoking hotel; rooms for those w/limited mobility. *In room:* A/C, TV, dataport, minibar, hair dryer, safe.

Olinda Classic Othon ✶✶ *(Value)*
A lovely heritage building, the Olinda has finally gotten a much-needed makeover. The lobby has been transformed into an elegant salon with a restaurant and piano bar. All the common spaces have Wi-Fi Internet access. Elevators have been upgraded to the 21st century and all the rooms have been renovated. Rooms now feature a modern phone system, electronic keys, a flatscreen TV, and broadband Internet service. The superior rooms, which face the back of the building, are a bit smaller and have twin beds or a queen-size bed. The much nicer

Santa Teresa Bed & Breakfast Network 𝒜𝒜

Quite a change from most of Rio de Janeiro's high-rise accommodations, the Santa Teresa Cama e Café B&B Network (© **021/2224-5689** or 021/2221-7635; www.camaecafe.com.br) offers spectacular rooms in one of the city's most charming neighborhoods. The participating homes are often beautiful, ranging from century-old mansions to Art Deco villas to spacious apartments with fab views, and prices range from R$90 to R$180 (US$45–US$90/£24–£49), depending on the luxuriousness of your digs. But for as little as R$120 (US$60/£32) you can book yourself into a fabulous house with great views, swimming pool, and garden. The drawback to Santa Teresa is it's relative isolation. In the evening, you need to rely on taxis to get around. However, in the daytime you can grab a bus and be at the Metrô or downtown in 20 minutes. Santa Teresa in itself is worth a day or two of exploration. It's a perfect retreat, away from the beach.

---

deluxe oceanview rooms have a king-size bed. Some rooms also have a balcony. The spacious suites are worth the upgrade; these all face the ocean and have a veranda and a separate sitting room.

Av. Atlântica 2230, Copacabana, 22041-001 RJ. ©/fax **021/2545-9091**. www.hoteis-othon.com.br. 102 units (showers only). R$205 (US$102/£55) double standard; R$285 (US$142/£77) double deluxe; R$330 (US$165/£89) double suite. Extra person add 40%. Children 10 and under stay free in parent's room. AE, DC, MC, V. No parking. Metrô: Arcoverde. **Amenities:** Restaurant; bar; room service; laundry. *In room:* A/C, TV, minibar, safe.

Inexpensive

Martinique 𝒜 *Value*   The Martinique is the newest budget option of the Windsor chain. The best rooms are the superior ones that look out over the street. The ones closest to the corner (rooms that end in 13, such as 413) even have a partial ocean view. The standard rooms look out over the back lots of the adjacent buildings. However, all are pleasantly furnished in bright colors and have comfortable beds. Nice details at this price level include the hair dryer, make-up mirror, electronic safe and high-speed Internet in each room. The hotel even has a rooftop pool and sun deck, but with the beach only 90m (300 ft.) away you'd have to be pretty lazy not to make it out the door.

Rua Sá Ferreira 30, Copacabana, Rio de Janeiro, 22071-100 RJ. © **021/2195-5200**. Fax 021/2195-5222. www.windsor hoteis.com. 117 units. R$190–R$220 (US$95–US$110/£51–£59) double. Extra person 25%. Children 10 and under stay free in parent's room. AE, DC, MC, V. Bus: 415. **Amenities:** Restaurant; rooftop pool; cardio equipment; concierge; room service; nonsmoking floors; laundry. *In room:* A/C, TV, high-speed Internet access, minibar, hair dryer, safe.

FLAMENGO, CATETE & GLORIA

Expensive

Hotel Florida 𝒜𝒜 *Finds*   A gem of a hotel, the Florida is popular with business travelers from São Paulo who know a good deal when they see one: On top of a reasonable room rate, the Florida offers free parking, free local calls, and free Internet access. The standard rooms overlook the rear or the side of the building and come with showers only. Both the superior and deluxe rooms offer views and have bathrooms with whirlpool tubs. The nicest rooms are those overlooking the lush gardens of the Palácio do Catete, Brazil's former presidential palace. The deluxe rooms are the most spacious, with a large entrance hall, king-size bed, sitting area, and desk. The hotel offers excellent discounts on weekends when its regular business travelers stay home.

Rua Ferreira Viana 81, Flamengo, Rio de Janeiro, 22210-040 RJ. (C) **021/2195-6800**. Fax 021/2285-5777. www. windsorhoteis.com. 312 units. R$250 (US$125/£67) standard double; R$275 (US$137/£74) superior double; R$320 (US$160/£86) deluxe double. Extra person add 25%. Children 10 and under stay free in parent's room. AE, DC, MC, V. Free parking. Metrô: Catete. **Amenities:** Restaurant; bar; outdoor rooftop pool; weight room; sauna; concierge; tour desk; business center; room service; laundry; dry cleaning; nonsmoking floors. *In room:* A/C, TV, dataport, minibar, fridge, hair dryer, safe.

Hotel Glória ★★ The Grande Dame of Rio hotels, the Glória was built in 1922 (a year before the Copacabana Palace) to provide luxury accommodation for dignitaries attending Brazil's centennial celebrations. An annex was added in the '70s in the same style, making the 630-room Glória one of Rio's largest hotels. If you can, reserve a deluxe room—the views of the bay and the Sugar Loaf are well worth it. A little bit smaller than the deluxe rooms, the pleasant superior and standard rooms offer garden views. All the rooms in the annex have been completely renovated and look great, though they are not overly large. But no matter which room you get, you can indulge in the outstanding amenities: lovely gardens; the best sun deck in the city with views of the bay, marina, and Sugar Loaf; two large heated swimming pools; and an outstanding fitness center.

Rua do Russel 632, Glória, Rio de Janeiro, 22210 RJ. (C) **0800/213-077** or 021/2555-7272. Fax 021/2555-7283. www. hotelgloriario.com.br. 630 units (standard rooms in annex have showers only). Standard rooms R$285–R$360 (US$142–US$180/£77–£97) double; superior and deluxe rooms R$320–R$460 (US$160–US$234/£86–£124) double. Extra person R$80 (US$40/£22). Children 10 and under stay free in parent's room. AE, DC, MC, V. Metrô: Glória. **Amenities:** 4 restaurants; bar; 2 outdoor heated pools; health club; sauna; concierge; tour desk; car rental; business center; salon; room service; massage; babysitting; laundry; dry cleaning; nonsmoking floors. *In room:* A/C, TV, dataport, minibar, fridge, hair dryer, safe.

WHERE TO DINE
CENTRO
Expensive
Confeitaria Colombo ★★★ BRAZILIAN/DESSERTS This stunning ornate tearoom hasn't changed much since it opened in 1894. Two large deli counters flanking both sides of the entrance serve up sweet and savory snacks with coffee. The remainder of the ground floor is taken up by the elegant tearoom, where a variety of teas, sandwiches, salads, and sweets are served on fine china beneath a 1920s stained-glass window. The upstairs room is reserved for full lunches—on Saturday, the *feijoada* is worth the trip downtown.

Rua Gonçalves Dias 32, Centro. (C) 021/2232-2300. www.confeitariacolombo.com.br. Tearoom snacks and lunches R$10–R$25 (US$5–US$13/£2.70-£6.75); buffet lunch or Sat Feijoada buffet R$45 (US$23/£12) including dessert. Tea service R$8–R$20 (US$4–US$10/£2–£5.40). AE, DC, MC, V. Mon–Fri 8:30am–7pm; Sat 9am–5pm. Metrô: Carioca.

Laguiole ★★★ BRAZILIAN On the second floor of the Modern Art Museum, the Laguiole restaurant fits in with its surroundings. The long, rectangular dining lounge is clean and modern, with clean metallic finishings. The food is modern and Brazilian, with a subtle touch of French. Some of our favorites include the large grilled prawns with mango chutney, or duck breast with wild cherries. Fish lovers will enjoy the sole filet, served on a bed of spinach with a carrot soufflé. As for choosing some wine to go with lunch, you may want to ask for help from sommelier—the wine list is one of the largest in the country, over 600 labels and 8,000 bottles!

Inside the MAM, Av. Infante D. Henrique 80, Aterro do Flamengo. © 021/2517-3129. Main courses R$36–R$50 (US$18–US$25/£10–£14). DC, MC, V. Mon–Fri noon–5pm. Taxi recommended.

Moderate

Bistro do Paço 🐟 *Finds* BRAZILIAN   The perfect spot to escape the heat and noise in downtown Rio. Inside this little oasis in the historic Paço Imperial, the thick white-washed walls keep out the bustle while you recharge your batteries in the cool shade of the inner courtyard. The restaurant serves mostly bistro fare as well as a daily lunch special that will set you back R$15 to R$23 (US$6.25–US$9.50/£3.20–£4.90) for a plate of roast beef with a side order of pasta, spinach crepes with a ricotta-and-mush-room stuffing, or a chicken filet with apple sauce and sautéed vegetables. Desserts are strictly European: Austrian *linzertortes*, German fruit strudels, and Black Forest choco-late cakes, all of which go so well with a Brazilian *cafezinho*.

Praça XV 48 (inside the Paço Imperial), Centro. © 021/2262-3613. Main courses R$15–R$26 (US$7.50–US$13/ £4–£7); sandwiches and quiches R$8–R$16 (US$4–US$8/£2–£4.25). AE, DC, MC, V. Mon–Fri 10am–8pm; Sat–Sun noon–7pm. Bus: 119 or 415.

Mr Ôpi 🐟🐟 KILO   One of the better kilo restaurants, Mr Ôpi indulges both the calorie conscious and the gluttons. The special light cuisine dishes are marked and list ingredients and calories; the rest of us can feast on the excellent choices of pasta, cheeses and antipasto, in addition to the meat and fish served fresh from the grill. On Fridays, the buffet always includes *feijoada*.

Rua da Quitanda 51, Centro. © 021/2507-3859. Per kilo R$34 (US$17/£9). DC, MC, V. Lunch Mon–Fri 11am–4:30pm. Bus: 119 or 415 to Praça XV.

Inexpensive

Paladino BRAZILIAN   Is it a liquor store? Is it a deli? Or is it, as the crowds seem to indicate, a bustling lunch bar with some of the best draft beer in town? Does it mat-ter? Probably not. What matters is that the beer is clear and cold, the atmosphere is that of Rio in the Belle Epoque, and the sandwiches and snack plates are delicious. *Pratinhos,* as the latter are known in Portuguese, cost next to nothing—R$4 to R$8 (US$2–US$4/£1–£2.15)—and come loaded with sardines (whatever you do, order the sardines!) or olives, cheese, or great heaping stacks of smoked sausage.

Rua Uruguaiana 226, Centro. © 021/2263-2094. Reservations not accepted. Sandwiches and side dishes R$4– R$15 (US$2–US$7.50/£1–£4). No credit cards. Mon–Fri 7am–8:30pm; Sat 8am–noon. Metrô: Uruguaiana.

SANTA TERESA

Expensive

Aprazível 🐟🐟🐟 *Finds* BRAZILIAN   Part of Aprazível's charm is the house itself. The restaurant takes up several rooms and spills over into the garden. And then there is the view of downtown Rio and the Bay of Guanabara. The kitchen serves up a variety of Brazilian cuisine, with an emphasis on tropical flavors. Interesting starters include fresh grilled palm hearts (very different from the canned varieties) and the pumpkin-cream soup with prawns, tart apple, and cream. A popular main course is the *peixe tropical,* grilled fish in an orange sauce, served with coconut rice and baked bananas. Desserts are best savored slowly. Our favorites were the *Morango do amor* (strawberries flambéed in orange juice and Cointreau) and the *Folia de Ouro Preto* (grilled pineapple served with lime zest and coconut ice cream and a dash of Limoncello lemon liquor).

Rua Aprazível 62, Santa Teresa. © 021/3852-4935. www.aprazivel.com.br. Reservations recommended. Main courses R$38–R$55 (US$19–US$28/£10–£15). AE, MC, V. Thurs 8pm–midnight; Fri–Sat noon–midnight; Sun 1–6pm. Taxi recommended.

Espirito Santa ⭐⭐ BRAZILIAN   One of the newcomers in Santa Teresa, Espirito Santa seems to have found the perfect formula for success: a cute restaurant, a great patio looking out over Santa Teresa and excellent Brazilian food. A very popular starter is the Tambaqui "ribs," breaded pieces of *tambaqui* (a popular Amazonian fish) served with a pesto made from the jambu herb. Main courses include a variety of fish and seafood dishes as well as meat dishes. The seafood *bobó,* a stew with coconut milk and spices, is excellent and great for sharing. For a lighter meal opt for the grilled fish with a cashew crust, served on a bed of grilled fresh palm heart. Meat lovers should try the *bacuri* steak, grilled fillet mignon served with a bacuri (Amazonian fruit) sauce and mashed sweet potatoes. Equally exotic is the grilled duck filet, served with an *açai* sauce. For desert, there's warm gateau filled with guava cream and cheese.

Rua Almirante Alexandrino 264, Santa Teresa. ✆ **021/2508-7095.** Main courses R$28–R$44 (US$14–US$22/ £7.50–£12). AE, DC, MC, V. D. Mon, Wed, and Sun noon–7pm; Thurs–Sat noon–midnight. Bus: 214, or take the tram, getting off just before the Largo dos Guimarães.

Moderate

Sobrenatural ⭐⭐ SEAFOOD/BRAZILIAN   Sobrenatural is one of the more popular restaurants in Santa Teresa. The menu offers a variety of seafood options, but the house specialty is really the *moqueca.* Just pick what kind of fish you want, and it will come served in a piping hot stew with coconut milk, palm oil, shrimp sauce (optional), rice, and *pirão* (a polenta-like paste made with mandioc flour and broth and spices). Portions are generous; *moquecas* serve two people, the seafood spaghetti feeds up to three. *Note:* This open, breezy restaurant is great in summer but is best avoided on windy and rainy days.

Rua Almirante Alexandrino 432, Santa Teresa. ✆ **021/2224-1003.** Main courses R$46–R$58 (US$23–US$29/ £13–£16) for 2. AE, DC, MC, V. Daily noon–midnight. Bus: 214, or take the tram, getting off at the Largo dos Guimarães.

FLAMENGO, GLORIA & CATETE
Expensive

Emporio Santa Fé ⭐⭐ BRAZILIAN/PASTA   This lovely two-story restaurant overlooking the Aterro do Flamengo is one of the best restaurants in Flamengo. The ground floor has a small wine bar and a few tables, but you really want to head upstairs and, if possible, grab one of the window tables in the elegant L-shaped dining room. The chef's forte is pasta; all dishes are made fresh and combine some creative flavors. We loved the ravioli with prawns in a leek sauce with mushrooms as well as the *tortele tricolor,* pasta rounds stuffed with smoked ricotta, figs, and Parma ham. Steak lovers have plenty to choose from, including filet mignon medallions with grilled brie and potatoes, or grilled tournedos in a balsamic jus, served with rice and fungi mushrooms. The wine list has over 400 options, covering most of the world's regions; many are reasonably priced under R$70/US$35/£19.

Praia do Flamengo 2, Flamengo. ✆ **021/2245-6274.** Reservations accepted. Main courses R$32–R$58 (US$16– US$29/£9–£16). AE, DC, MC, V. Sun–Thurs noon–midnight; Fri–Sat noon–2am. Bus: Any bus to Praia do Flamengo.

Porcão ⭐⭐ BRAZILIAN/STEAK   A mass carnivorous orgy, Porcão is where you go to gorge yourself on some of the best beef in the world and, in this case, served up with some of the best views in the world. Porcão operates on the *rodízio* system: It's one all-you-can-eat price (dessert and drinks are extra), and once you sit down, waiters come bearing all manner of meats (steak cuts, roast cuts, filet mignon, chicken breast, chicken hearts, sausages, and much more), which they slice to perfection on your plate. Also included is a buffet with dozens of antipasto items, hot and cold seafood dishes, and at least 15 different kinds of salad and cheese. No doggie bags allowed.

Avenida Infante Dom Henrique s/n, Parque do Flamengo. ℂ **021/2554-8535**. Reservations accepted. R$68 (US$34/£18) per person all-you-can-eat meat and buffet. 50% discount for children 6–9, free for children under 6. AE, DC, MC, V. Daily 11:30am–1am. Taxi recommended.

BOTAFOGO
Very Expensive
Carême 𝕽𝕽𝕽 *Finds* BRAZILIAN   These days you are more likely to see chef Flavia Quaresma on TV than at her own restaurant. Ever since she opened her cozy Botafogo bistro, Flavia has turned into a food sensation. The menu is deliberately kept small in order to give dishes the attention they deserve. On our most recent visit, we started off with a cold salad of smoked salmon on a crisp *galette* of sweet potatoes, and for a hot appetizer, we ordered the potato-and-porcini soup with lentils and bacon. The pastas and risottos can be ordered in a small version as an appetizer or in a larger version as an entree. The menu usually offers a fish of the day as well and one or two meat options, such as the grilled rack of lamb served on a bed of polenta with a cocoa-and-pepper sauce. Those who just want to leave their menu choices in the hands of Flavia or one of her capable staff can order the five-course tasting menu and let themselves be surprised. The wine list is conservative with a small selection of well-chosen merlots, cabernet sauvignons, and Chilean chardonnays.

Rua Visconde de Caravelas 113, Botafogo. ℂ **021/2537-2274**. Reservations required. R$48–R$58 (US$24–US$29/ £12–£15). AE, DC, MC, V. Tues–Sat 8pm–close (usually around 1am). Bus: 176 or 178.

Expensive
Miam Miam 𝕽𝕽 CONTEMPORARY   Funky is hard to find in Rio de Janeiro, so Miam Miam has found the perfect niche to fill. This funky and hip eatery/lounge/bar is whimsically decorated with fabulous kitsch touches, without trying too hard. The result is a cozy room divided into a lounge area with comfortable couches and love seats and a somewhat more staid dining room. The lounge area is really the place to be, perfect for enjoying a cocktail and sharing some appetizers. The menu offers a range of high end pub food: salads, sandwiches, pastas, risotto and a few main courses such as a grilled tuna in a peppercorn crust or a steak with baked potato. If you are planning to eat a full meal, you may want to opt for one of the Formica tables, but make sure you grab that spot on the couch for dessert and an after-dinner drink.

Rua General Góes Monteiro 34, Botafogo. ℂ **021/2244-0125**. Main courses R$21–R$37 (US$8.75–US$16/ £4.25–£8). Tues–Fri noon–3pm and 7:30pm–midnight; Sat 8pm–1:30am. Bus: 472.

COPACABANA & LEME
Very Expensive
Le Pré-Catelan 𝕽𝕽𝕽 FRENCH   Ever since French chef Roland Villard took over the kitchen in 1998, it's been raining awards at Le Pré-Catelan. Updated every 2 weeks, the menu offers a selection of appetizers, main courses, and a dessert for R$140 (US$70/£38), a steal considering the quality of the ingredients, the preparation, and the service. Some of the best dishes we've tried so far include a rigatone stuffed with quail, foie gras, and wild mushrooms; the duck breast with a red-wine sauce and orange-perfumed polenta; and the veal medallions served with a tart sauce of cherry-like *jabuticaba* fruit. All dishes are beautifully presented.

Hotel Sofitel, Av. Atlântica 4240, Copacabana. ℂ 021/2525-1232. Reservations required. Dress is business casual. Main courses R$44–R$68 (US$22–US$34/£12–£18). AE, DC, MC, V. Mon–Wed 7:30–11:30pm; Thurs–Sat 7:30pm–midnight. Bus: 415.

Moderate

Alfaia ★★ (Finds) PORTUGUESE   This lovely neighborhood restaurant has been serving up great Portuguese food for 15 years. The house specialties are the dishes made with *bacalhau* (salted cod fish). Start off with the perfectly deep-fried *bolinhos de bacalhau* (cod fish dumplings). The most popular main course is the *bacalhau à Bras,* oven-baked cod fish served with potatoes, scrambled egg, onion, and olives. The cod dishes also come in half portions. We found that with appetizers and dessert the half dish was plenty for two people. The wine list includes some excellent Portuguese whites and reds. For dessert try the *pastel de nata,* a flaky pastry stuffed with creamy custard.

Rua Inhangá 30, Copacabana. ℂ 021/2236-1222. Main courses R$46–R$85 (US$23–US$43/£12–£23) for 2. AE, DC, MC, V. Mon–Sat noon–midnight; Sun noon–11pm. Metrô: Cardeal Arcoverde.

Arab ★★★ MIDDLE EASTERN   Arab not only has a terrific waterfront patio, it also serves delicious Middle Eastern cuisine. For lunch, the kitchen puts on an excellent kilo buffet, great for trying a variety of dishes. In the evenings, dishes are a la carte. Our favorites include the tray of *mezzes* (appetizer plates). Perfect for sharing, these plates come with enough munchies for three or four people and include hummus, baba ghanouj, savory pastries with ground beef or lamb, and other finger food. For a main course, try the lamb dishes such as the *fakhas kharouf* (lamb stew in red wine served with saffron rice and toasted almonds). Desserts are dangerously rich, featuring sweet pastries made with sugar, rosewater, and almonds or pistachios.

Av. Atlântica 1936, Copacabana. ℂ 021/2235-6698. Main courses R$25–R$42 (US$13–US$21/£6.75–£11). A, DC, MC, V. Mon 5pm–1am; Tues–Sun 8am–1am. Metrô: Cardeal Arcoverde.

IPANEMA
Very Expensive

Margutta ★★★ ITALIAN   Margutta's forte is simple food done well—no convoluted sauces, long lists of ingredients, or fancy fusion. The result is a simple and elegant cuisine that brings out the best in all ingredients. We started off with deliciously sautéed mushrooms, followed by the *farfalle al gamberi e zafferano,* or bow-tie pasta with prawns in creamy saffron sauce. For our entrée, we tried the signature dish, the *Pesce alla Neroni* (oven-roasted fish with fine herbs and a side of roasted potatoes and tomatoes). The restaurant itself is lovely: cozy and intimately lit and pleasantly decorated with linen and fresh flowers.

Av. Henrique Dumont 62, Ipanema. ℂ 021/2259-3718. Reservations recommended. R$28–R$68 (US$14–US$34/£7.50–£18). AE, DC, MC. Mon–Fri 6pm–1am; Sat and holidays noon–1am; Sun noon–midnight. Bus: 415.

Expensive

Zazá Bistrô Tropical ★★ BRAZILIAN/FUSION   Zazá, Rio's funkiest eatery, fuses South American cuisine with Oriental flavors. Everything about Zazá is fun, from the playful and eclectic decorations to the unique and excellent dishes. The menu offers plenty of choices. Appetizers include a deliciously grilled squid salad served on a bed of greens with an orange vinaigrette and mango chutney, or an order of mini-*acarajés* served with tomato chutney instead of the usual hot-pepper sauce. Main courses also mix up the flavors. Try the *namorado* fish filet served with a purée of banana and palm heart, or a prawn ravioli served with grilled salmon in a saffron sauce. For vegetarians, there is always a daily special, made with seasonal produce and interesting spices.

Rua Joana Angelica 40, Ipanema. ⓒ 021/2247-9101. R$28–R$42 (US$14–US$21/£7.50–£11). AE, DC, MC, V. Sun–Thurs 7:30pm–1am; Fri–Sat 7:30pm–1:30am. Bus: 415.

Moderate

Casa da Feijoada ⭑ BRAZILIAN   The Casa da Feijoada allows you to experience Brazil's national dish with all the trimmings any day of the week. To get off to a good start try the *caldo de feijão* (bean soup), washed down with a *batida de limão* (lime cocktail). Now you are ready to bring on the actual bean stew, served in a clay pot with whatever meat you've a hankering for, be it sausage, bacon, *carne seca* (dried meat, highly recommended), pork loin, and other more obscure cuts. Side dishes include white rice, stir-fried cabbage, *farofa* (roasted manioc flour), and orange slices. If you add some *malagueta* pepper sauce, make sure you have another lime cocktail standing by.

Rua Prudente de Moraes 10, Ipanema. ⓒ 021/2523-4994. R$21–R$38 (US$8.75–US$16/£4.50–£8.20) main course; feijoada meal R$49 (US$25/£13) per person, including appetizers, dessert, and drinks. AE, DC, MC, V. Daily noon–11pm. Bus: 415.

Inexpensive

Big Nectar ⓥⱥˡᵘᵉ QUICK BITES   The menu in this standing-room-only spot lists just over 25 different kinds of fruit juice. In addition to the standards such as *maracujá* (passion fruit), *abacaxi* (pineapple), and *caju* (cashew fruit), there's *carambola* (star fruit), *goiaba* (guava), *jáca* (jack fruit), and *açerola* (red juice from the tiny *açerola* fruit). You can mix flavors—try *laranja com açerola* (orange juice with *açerola*), *maracujá* with mango, pineapple with guava, or cashew with *açerola*.

Teixeira de Melo 34A, Ipanema. No phone. Everything under R$12 (US$6/£3.25). No credit cards. Daily 7am–midnight. Bus: 404 or 474.

LEBLON

Expensive

Giuseppe Grill ⭑⭑ STEAK   This newcomer in Leblon seems to have it all: outstanding steak, an affordable wine list, a pleasant modern dining lounge and excellent and attentive service. The house specialty is beef, no doubt about it. You can choose from grilled beef or slowly roasted beef on a charcoal grill. Both options include excellent cuts such as prime rib, Argentinean chorizo steak, filet mignon, rump steak as well as beef ribs, pork, and chicken. Each main course comes with a side-dish; you can choose from a variety of salads, rice and potatoes served fried, roasted, baked, or sautéed. And then oddly enough, the restaurant also serves up a selection of outstanding fresh seafood. Have a look at the catch of the day and ask for the waiter's recommendation. We went with the octopus, grilled to perfection and served tossed with arugula as a warm salad, and were thoroughly impressed.

Ave. Bartolomeu Mitre 370, Leblon. ⓒ 021/2249-3055. Main courses R$36–R$58 (US$18–US$29/£10–£16). AE, DC, MC, V. Mon–Thurs noon–4pm and 7pm–midnight; Fri–Sat noon–1am; Sun noon–11pm. Bus: 415.

Nam Thai ⭑⭑ THAI   The best Thai restaurant in Rio is also the only Thai restaurant in Rio. Fortunately, the food is quite good and serves up all the classic Thai dishes and a few selections from other Asian countries, including dim sum appetizers, Vietnamese pho soup, and a Malaysian mild curry. We recommend starting off with one of the Thai soups, either the Tom Kha Kai, a rich coconut broth with chicken and lemon grass, or the clear and spicy shrimp soup, Tom Yum Kung. Main courses include a variety of Thai curries, either green or red and your choice of beef, prawn,

Rio's Avenida Gourmet

We could probably fill half the Rio section with reviews of restaurants on the **Rua Dias Ferreira**. This windy street on the far edge of Leblon has become a one-stop-shop for gourmands. For vegetarians, there's not one but two restaurants. There's the excellent kilo restaurant, **O Celeiro** (Rua Dias Ferreira 199; ✆ 021/2274-7843). You pay by the weight, so help yourself to the delicious buffet to try a variety of salads and grab a spot on the large patio. And there's the new kid on the block, **Quitanda Vegetal** (Rua Dias Ferreira 135; ✆ 021/2249-2301), which sells health food and a variety of vegetarian and light cuisine dishes. To enjoy a stylish afternoon tea, head over to **Eliane Carvalho** (Rua Dias Ferreira 242; ✆ 021/2540-5438). This gorgeous gift shop/tea room serves a wonderful tea with all the trimmings. Those who prefer to linger over their food can try **Doce Delicia** (Rua Dias Ferreira 48; ✆ 021/2249-2970), which serves grilled chicken, steak, or fish and your choice of two side dishes. For pasta there's **Quadrucci,** (Rua Dias Ferreira 233; ✆ 021/2512-4551), which is open for lunch and dinner and has a great patio. For fine dining there are a number of options, mostly open in the evenings only. **Zuka** (Rua Dias Ferreira 233; ✆ 021/3205-7154) offers creative seafood dishes such as the crab in filo pastry or the grilled tuna in a cashew-nut crust. Across the street you'll find **Carlota** (Rua Dias Ferreira 64; ✆ 021/2540-6821), chosen by *Condé Nast Traveller* as one of the 50 most exciting restaurants in the world. Chef Carlota's dishes are fresh and creative, although people have complained that the portions are small. Farther down is the city's sushi hot spot, **Sushi Leblon** (Rua Dias Ferreira 256; ✆ 021/2512-7830).

chicken or duck. Other dishes worth trying include the pad Thai rice noodle or the fried rice noodle with squid, broccoli and fresh basil. Fish lovers will enjoy one of the steamed fish dishes, delicately flavored with lemon grass or ginger and garlic.

Rua Rainha Guilhermina 95, Leblon. ✆ 021/2259-2962. www.namthai.com.br. Main courses R$22–R$48 (US$11–US$24/£6–£13). AE, DC, MC, V. Mon 7pm–1am; Tues–Fri noon–5pm and 7pm–1am; Sat noon–1am; Sun noon–11pm. Bus: 415.

Inexpensive

KURT *(Value* DESSERT   A mainstay of Leblon, German pastry maker Kurt passed away a few years ago, but his legacy (and treats) live on. Now in the hands of Kurt's grandsons, this tiny shop in Leblon remains one of the best places in town to go for an *apfel strude,* pecan pie, or apricot cake.

Rua General Urquiza 117 (corner of Rua Ataulfo de Paiva), Leblon. ✆ 021/2294-0599. Everything under R$15 (US$7.50/£4). No credit cards. Mon–Fri 8am–7pm; Sat 8am–5pm. Bus: 415.

JARDIM BOTÂNICO
Expensive

Quadrifoglio ✶✶✶ ITALIAN   Chef and owner Silvia Bianchi proves that you don't need fancy gimmicks to run a good restaurant. No frilly, prissy cuisine; Silvia's food is rich and hearty. Memorable dishes include the *mignonette al Gorgonzola* (steak in a creamy Gorgonzola sauce, served with fresh pasta) and the *agnello al rosmarino* (a succulently grilled filet of lamb with fresh rosemary and a side of pumpkin gnocchi). Those who like veal will love the tender veal on a bed of orange risotto. True, this is not exactly light cuisine, but the dishes are worth a calorie splurge. And speaking of splurging, one of the best desserts we have come across recently was the *profumi mediterranei*—roasted fresh fig served with a scoop of lavender ice cream and topped with toasted almonds and some *crème anglaise*.

Rua J.J. Seabra 19, Jardim Botânico, ℂ 021/2294-1433. Reservations recommended. Main courses R$34–R$58 (US$17–US$29/£9–£16). AE, DC, MC, V. Mon–Fri noon–4pm and 7:30pm–1am; Sat 7:30–1am; Sun noon–5pm. Bus: 572 (from Leblon or Copacabana) or 170 (from downtown).

Moderate

Couve Flor 🍴 KILO   The mother of all kilo restaurants, Couve Flor is where it all started in the mid-'80s. Even now that the system has been widely adopted, Couve Flor still goes the extra mile. The menu is truly astonishing with at least 40 dishes to choose from and includes elaborate and interesting choices such as rabbit stew, fish *moqueca*, fresh pasta, at least 20 different kinds of salads, and grilled meats. In the evenings, Couve Flor also serves a selection of pizzas from a wood-burning oven, and the weekend lunch buffet is legendary, with even more dishes and a choice of 15 desserts.

Rua Pacheco Leão 724, Jardim Botânico. ℂ 021/2239-2191. www.couveflor.com.br. Main courses R$15–R$30 (US$6.25–US$13/£3–£6.50). AE, DC, MC, V. Mon–Fri noon–5pm and 7–11pm; Sat noon–11pm; Sun 11:30am–9pm. Bus: 572 (from Leblon or Copacabana) or 170 (from downtown).

RIO AFTER DARK

There's a lot to do in Rio, whether you want live music, samba school rehearsals, modern clubs, or seaside patios. Everything starts early and continues late. For updated listings, check the Friday edition of *O Globo* or *Jornal do Brasil* newspapers. Under *musica* or *show*, you will find the listings for live music; listings under *pista* refer to events at nightclubs or discos. *Couvert* is the cover charge and *consumação* states the drink minimum; it's quite common to see two rates, one for women *(mulher)* and one for men *(homem)*. The days of the week are given in abbreviations: *seg* or *2a* (Mon), *ter* or *3a* (Tues), *qua* or *4a* (Wed), *qui* or *5a* (Thurs), *sex* or *6a* (Fri), *sab* (Sat), and *dom* (Sun).

In most clubs, you can expect to pay a cover charge or drink minimum. In most venues, you are handed a card upon entry to record all of your purchases. The bill is then settled when you leave. A 10% service charge will be included, and a tip beyond that is not required. Hang on to your card for dear life—if you lose it you'll be charged an astronomical fee.

PERFORMING ARTS

The elegant Parisian-style **Theatro Municipal,** Praça Marechal Floriano s/n, Centro (ℂ 021/2299-1633; www.theatromunicipal.rj.gov.br), stages everything from opera to ballet to symphony concerts. Ticket prices range from R$15 to R$70 (US$7.50–US$35/£4–£19) for most performances.

Located in downtown Rio, the small **Teatro Rival,** Rua Alvaro Alvim 33, Centro (ℂ 021/2240-4469; www.rivalbr.com.br), does an outstanding job of booking local and popular national acts, mostly of MPB *(musica popular brasileira)*. Ticket prices are quite reasonable—usually R$10 to R$60 (US$5–US$30/£3–£16)—so give it a shot. You may be looking at the next Marisa Monte or one of Brazil's many talented performers who haven't yet made it big internationally.

CLUBS & LIVE MUSIC

GAFIEIRAS   The traditional ballroom dance halls known as *gafieiras* are a legacy of the elegant days of old, when couples would dress for the occasion and everyone knew the steps. Most folks don't show up in suits or ball gowns anymore, but couples still dance with elegance, and the tunes are unmistakably Brazilian: samba and *pagode*, a bit of rumba or fox-trot, and nowadays, lots of *forró*. One popular *gafieira* is the **Elite,** Rua Frei Caneca 4, Centro (℘ **021/2232-3217**). Even if you can't dance, it's worth having a drink and watching in awe and admiration as some of the older folks strut their stuff; it's open Friday after 7pm, Saturday after 10pm, and Sunday after 6pm. **Gafieira Estudantina,** Praça Tiradentes 79, Centro (℘ **021/2507-8067**), is another mainstay on the Carioca ballroom scene. A 10-piece band plays every weekend. It's open on Friday and Saturday from 11pm.

LIVE MUSIC   It's old and tattered and the sightlines aren't terrific, but the **Canecão,** Av. Venceslau Brás 215, Botafogo (℘ **021/2543-1241**), has tradition. Everyone who's anyone in Brazilian music has played this aging 3,000-person auditorium. Downtown, the **Centro Cultural Carioca,** Rua do Teatro, Centro (℘ **021/2242-9642;** www.centroculturalcarioca.com.br; Metrô: Cinelândia), is housed in a restored 1920s historic building and provides a fabulous venue for local musicians and big names who specialize in samba, MPB, *choro*, and *gafieira*. There are no shows on Sundays usually. **Carioca da Gema,** Rua Mem de Sá 79, Lapa (℘ **021/2221-0043**), is a fine little restaurant, but music is really the chief thing on order. On Friday and Saturday nights, the place is packed. The show normally kicks off about 8pm, but space is very limited, so come early.

DANCE CLUBS   Located right next to the planetarium, **00** (pronounced *zero-zero*), Rua Padre Leonel France 240, Gávea (℘ **021/2259-8675**), has a fabulous outdoor deck; perfect for those warm summer evenings. Inside, there's a restaurant, a small bar, and dance floor. One of the most happening dance clubs in Rio, **Baronneti,** Rua Barão da Torre 354, Ipanema (℘ **021/2522-1460**), attracts a well-to-do and attractive crowd in their 20s to 40s. The classy upscale club offers two floors of fabulous dance music to dance the night away, plenty of couches and a chill-out space. **Fosfobox,** Rua Siqueira Campos 143, basement, Copacabana (℘ **021/2548-7498**), is Copacabana's trendy *club du jour*—or rather *du nuit*. Located in a small basement off Rua Siqueira Campos, the club only has room for about 150, who hear discs spun by a variety of DJs.

BARS & PUBS

BOTEQUINS   *Botequins* are to Rio what pubs are to London and cafes are to Paris: the spot where locals traditionally gather, whether it be for end-of-day drinks or impassioned late-night philosophizing. Tucked away in an alley just off the Praça XV, the **Arco do Teles** looks like a movie set of old Rio with colonial two-story walk-ups set on narrow cobblestone streets lined with restaurants and cafes. (From the Praça XV, facing the bay, you will see the arch that marks the entrance to the alley on your left.) Prime time is after work hours, especially on Thursday and Friday nights, when office workers flock here to grab a few cold beers and catch some music.

Unanimously voted the best *botequim* in town, **Bracarense,** Rua Jose Linhares 85, Leblon (℘ **021/2294-3549**), serves up a perfectly chilled beer and delicious munchies. Another acclaimed *botequim*, **Bip Bip,** Rua Almirante Gonçalves 50, Copacabana (℘ **021/2267-9696**), owes its fame to an outstanding musical program.

Tuesday and Sunday nights are the best evenings to catch some great samba or *pagode*. One of the trendier *botequins,* **Jobi,** Av. Ataulfo de Paiva 1166, Leblon (© **021/2274-0547**), is busy every day of the week, but on Friday and Saturday, a good lineup is guaranteed.

OTHER BARS & PUBS   A field trip to the **Academia da Cachaça,** Rua Conde de Bernadote 26, Loja G, Leblon (© **021/2239-1542**), puts the concept of advanced education in a whole new light. It is here that 40 members of the Cachaça Academy meet to dispute, discuss, and sample the finer points of the fiery white-cane liquor that is Brazil's national drink. **Bar do Adão,** Rua Dona Mariana 81, Botafogo (© **021/2535-4572**) serves up some of the best *pasteis* in town. Made out of light fluffy dough, the *pasteis* come in an amazing variety of fillings, are quickly deep-fried and arrive piping hot at your table. The 60 different flavors include brie and apricot, gorgonzola and sundried tomato, prawns and cream cheese, shiitake mushrooms and more. By day a mild-mannered (and quite fun) fruit-and-vegetable market, the **Mercado Cobal,** Cobal de Humaitá, Rua Voluntarios da Patria 446, Botafogo, transforms itself at night into a huge outdoor bar scene with seven or eight different restaurants and *chopperias* melding into one large bustling patio. On a hot summer night there is nothing better than spending an evening with a blonde *(loura),* redhead *(ruiva),* or brunette *(morena)*—home brews, that is. **Devassa,** Rua General San Martin 1241, Leblon (© **021/2540-6087**), a casual bistro, is the perfect neighborhood cafe and serves draft beer from its own microbrewery.

GAY & LESBIAN NIGHTLIFE

Rio's gay community is fairly small and, despite Rio's reputation for sexual hedonism, fairly restrained. As lasciviously as heterosexual couples may behave in public, open displays of affection between same-sex couples are still not accepted in Brazil. To find out what's hot and happening, pick up the latest edition of the *Gay Guide Brazil,* a small booklet available at some of the clubs and bookstores in Ipanema, or check out **http://riogayguide.com** and **www.gay-rio.com**. The Brazilian term for gay-friendly is *GLS,* which stands for gay, lesbian, and sympathizers.

A great afternoon meeting spot is **Bar Bofetada,** Rua Farme de Amoeda 87 (© **021/2227-6992**). Located just a few blocks from Ipanema's prime gay beach, this *botequim* is perfect for a beer, a snack, and to flirt with local guys.

Set in a lovely small gallery stunningly decorated with a changing display of work by local artists, the **Galeria Café** at Rua Teixeira de Melo 31E, Ipanema (© **021/2523-8250;** www.galeriacafe.com.br.; bus no. 415), packs a gorgeous collection of men, shoulder to shoulder, bicep to bicep, into its combo art space, dance club, and bar. Those who can't fit—and there are many—just hang out in front. Also popular is **Dama de Ferro (the Iron Lady),** Rua Vinicius de Moraes 288, Ipanema (© **021/2247-2330;** www.damadeferro.com.br). Dama is the it spot at the moment, popular with gays and straights (although it's definitely gay); a high tolerance for electronic music is a must. **Le Boy,** Rua Raul Pompeia 102, Copacabana (© **021/2513-4993;** www.leboy.com.br; bus no. 415), is the largest and best-known gay club in Rio. It's glamorous, funky, and extremely spacious with a soaring four-story ceiling hovering somewhere above the dance floor. All for equal opportunity, Le Boy's owner recently inaugurated **La Girl** next door, Rua Raul Pompeia 102 (© **021/2247-8342;** www.lagirl.com.br), Rio's first truly upscale nightclub for gay women, with excellent DJs and go-go girl shows. **The Week,** Rua Sacadura Cabral 154, Saude (© **021/2253-1020;** www.theweek.com.br), is the new hottest gay dance club in town. This huge mega–dance club can hold 2,000 people and is packed every Saturday night. Famous national and international guest DJs and go-go boys keep the crowd going. It opens Saturdays at midnight and is often open for events on Fridays and Wednesdays; check listings.

SIDE TRIPS FROM RIO

On weekends and holidays, many Cariocas direct their tires northward to the beach resorts dotting the warm Atlantic coast. First and most famous of these is the town of **Búzios,** set on the tip of a long peninsula jutting out into the clear blue Atlantic. Heading up and inland, you find the summer refuge of an earlier generation, the mountain resort **Petrópolis,** the former summer capital of Emperor Pedro II. Just an hour or so from Rio, this green and graceful refuge offers good strolling and some great museums.

BÚZIOS

It's anyone's guess how small or sleepy the fishing town of Búzios truly was when French starlet Brigitte Bardot stumbled onto its sandy beaches in 1964, but it's certain that in the years since, the little town used the publicity to turn itself into Rio's premier beach resort. Much of that charm is due to the sheer beauty of the surroundings; the number of beaches close to town makes it easy to experience all the wonderful permutations of Brazilian beach culture.

Essentials

GETTING THERE   **Malizia Tours,** in Búzios (© **022/2623-1226** or 022/2623-2622; malizia@mar.com.br), offers transfer to/from Rio by van and taxi. Cost in a 15-person air-conditioned minibus is R$50 (US$25/£14) per person one-way. Pickup can be at your hotel or from the airport. **Auto Viação 1001** (© **0300/313-1001;** www.autoviacao1001.com.br) has departures seven times a day from Rio's main bus station (**Novo Rio Rodoviaria,** Av. Francisco Bicalho 1, Santo Cristo; © **021/3849-5001**). Cost of the 3-hour trip is R$20 (US$10/£5.40). In Búzios, buses arrive at the Búzios bus station on Estrada da Usina at the corner of Rua Manoel de Carvalho (© **022/2623-2050**), a 10-minute walk from the center of town.

VISITOR INFORMATION   The **Búzios Tourism Secretariat** (© **0800/24-999** or 022/2623-2099) has an information kiosk on the downtown Praça Santos Dumont 111; it's open daily from 9am to 10pm. Two good websites for information about Búzios are **www.buziosonline.com.br** and **www.buziosturismo.com**.

What to See & Do in Búzios

The charm of Búzios lies largely in its beaches, the 20 stretches of sand large and small within a few miles of the old town. Thanks to the irregular topography of this rugged little peninsula, each beach is set off from the other and has developed its own beach personality. Farthest from the old town is **Manguinhos** beach. Sheltered from the heavy surf, this gentle beach is where many learn to sail and windsurf. Closer to town is **Ferradura,** or Horseshoe, beach; this beach offers calm, crystal-clear waters, making it the perfect place for a long, lazy afternoon's snorkel. Back on the calm inland side of the peninsula, **João Fernandes** and the pocket-size **João Fernandinho** beaches are happening places lined with beachside cafes.

On **Ferradura** beach, **Happy Surf** (© **022/2623-3389**) rents **sailboards, lasers** (a type of one-person sailboat), **Hobie Cats,** and **kayaks.** Happy Surf also gives **courses.** A 6-hour beginner's **sailboard** course costs R$150 (US$75/£40). Lasers rent for R$35

(US$18/£9.50) per half-hour, R$45 (US$23/£12) with instructor. Hobie Cats rent for R$25 (US$13/£7) per half-hour, R$40 (US$20/£11) with instructor. Kayaks rentals start at R$5 (US$2.50/£1.35) per half-hour. Rental equipment is also available at **João Fernandes Beach: kayak rental,** R$5 (US$2.50/£1.35) for 30 minutes; **mask and snorkel package,** R$12 (US$6/£3.25) per hour; and **sailboard,** R$30 (US$15/£8) per hour.

Schooner trips are a great way to spend a day in Búzios. Onboard, you trundle along in the sunshine, eating complimentary fresh fruit and drinking free *caipirinhas* (or mineral water). At any of the beaches, you're free to get off, hang out, and swim for a bit. One company is **Malizia Tour** (© 022/2623-1226), but just walk along Rua das Pedras anywhere near the pier and you're guaranteed to be approached by a schooner tout. Depending on the season and time of day, expect to pay from R$30 to R$50 (US$15–US$25/£8–£14) for a half-day cruise.

The islands just off Búzios are—along with Angra dos Reis and Arraial do Cabo—some of the best diving spots within a 1-day drive of Rio. Coral formations are fairly basic, but there are lots of parrotfish and, often, sea turtles (green and hawksbill) and stingrays of considerable size. Visibility ranges from 10 to 15m (33–49 ft.). A good dive shop in town is **Casa Mar,** Rua das Pedras 242 (© 022/2623-2441; www. casamar.com.br). It offers a full range of services including cylinder refill and courses all the way from basic to nitrox. For a certified diver, a two-dive excursion costs R$150 (US$75/£40), including all the equipment.

For more active pursuits in the surrounding region, contact **Canoar,** Travessa Oscar Lopez 63, Loja 02 (© 022/2623-2551). This company runs **nature treks, rappelling trips,** and **rafting expeditions** in the Serramar region, about 30 minutes inland from Búzios. Rates vary from R$30 (US$15/£8) for a 2-hour hike, to R$60 (US$30/£16) for rappelling or rafting. Minimum age is 12.

Where to Stay in Búzios

Búzios is well known for its *pousadas,* similar to a North American bed-and-breakfast. However, you will not find too many at bargain prices. By avoiding high season (Dec–Mar and July) and weekends throughout the year, you should be able to get a discount.

Colonna Park Hotel 🏖🏖, Praia de João Fernandes, Armação dos Búzios (© 022/2623-2245; www.colonna.com.br), offers a superb setting, straddling the hill between the beaches of João Fernandes and João Fernandinho. Rooms in this sprawling Mediterranean-style mansion are spacious and simply, yet elegantly, furnished in cool tones of white and blue. If you're in the mood for a splurge, try suite 20; it comes with Jacuzzi tub and a large deck with a view of both beaches. In high season, a double without a view costs R$480 (US$240/£130), a double with a view costs R$520 (US$260/£140), and a suite will run you R$570 (US$285/£154). Tucked away on Orla Bardot, **Pousada Byblos** 🏖🏖, Morro do Humaitá 8, Praia da Armação (© 022/2623-1162), is just a 5-minute walk from busy Rua das Pedras. The best rooms are the oceanview rooms with a balcony (the top two floors). The top floor of the Pousada Byblos boasts a fabulous rooftop deck with a small swimming pool and a lounge. Rooms start at R$288 (US$144/£78) in low season and R$396 (US$198/£107) in high season.

A good, relatively inexpensive option in town, **Búzios Internacional Apart Hotel,** Estrada da Usina Velha 99 (©/fax 022/2537-3876; www.buziosbeach.com.br), is located just a few blocks from Rua das Pedras. Units are all self-contained flats equipped with a living room with foldout couch, a kitchen, and either one or two bedrooms. All units come with balconies and hammocks looking out over a central garden. In the low season, the price is the same whether you're one person or four (or six in the two-bedroom units). In high season, rates are (US$120/£65) for 2, R$300 (US$150/£81) for 4; in low season, they're R$200 (US$100/£54) for 2, R$250 (US$125/£67) for 4.

Where to Dine in Búzios

Sawasdee, Av. José Bento Ribeiro Dantas 500, Praia da Armação (© **022/2623-4644**), is the perfect spot to indulge that craving for some satay skewers with spicy peanut sauce or a steaming bowl of Tom Kha Gai, the fragrant coconut soup with lemon grass and coconut. For a main course try the prawns and fresh pineapple in Thai curry or the prawns with shitake mushrooms in oyster sauce. Spiciness has been toned down significantly for Brazilian customers, so if you like it hot, tell the kitchen to spice it up.

Buzin, Rua Manoel Turibe de Farias 273 (© **022/2633-7051**), is one of the better kilo restaurants in town, offering a large buffet of excellent salads, antipasto, and vegetables. The grill serves up a variety of cuts of steak, grilled to your preference. Of course, being right by the sea the restaurant also includes a daily selection of fresh seafood and fish in its offerings.

At **Estancia Don Juan,** Rua das Pedras 178 (© **022/2623-2169**), the menu includes only meat: *linguiça* (smoked sausage) and numerous exquisite beef cuts such as picanha, entrecôte, and *olho de bife* (rib-eye). Dine on a lovely flowered patio or in a multilevel hacienda dripping with atmosphere (R$40–R$120/US$20–US$60/£11–£32).

Búzios After Dark

If you're on a mission for a night out, Rua das Pedras is the place to crawl. This 1.2km (¾-mile) street boasts pubs, bars, dance clubs, and restaurants open on weekends until 3 or 4am. If you prefer your entertainment live, there's **Patio Havana**, which features a nightly selection of jazz, blues, and MPB (Musica Popular Brasileira). Should you get bored of the band, you can wander out to the ocean-side patio and enjoy the nighttime view. To dance till you drop, there's no better place than **Privilege.** But remember, don't bother showing up until 1 or 2am. Two popular Rio bars have set up shop in Buzios recently; both **Devassa** and **Conversa Fiada** serve up good beer and excellent pub food.

PETRÓPOLIS

Petrópolis is one of Rio de Janeiro's premier mountain resorts, located 850m (2,788 ft.) above sea level. Only an hour from Rio, it seems light years away from the traffic-jammed streets, concrete high-rises, and beaches. Emperor Dom Pedro II founded the city of Petrópolis in 1843 and built the summer palace (now the Imperial Museum) on a piece of land acquired by his father.

Nowadays, Petrópolis is a favorite weekend getaway for Cariocas—in the summer to escape from the hot and humid climate in Rio; in the fall and winter for a chance to experience "really cold" weather, wear winter clothes, eat fondue, and sit by the fireplace. Exploring Petrópolis can easily be done as a day trip from Rio using public transit. The historic part of the city, centered on the Museu Imperial and the cathedral and more or less bounded by Avenida Barão Rio Branco and Rua Imperador, contains the majority of the monuments and museums. Please note that most museums, historic buildings and shops are closed on Mondays.

Essentials

GETTING THERE   **Unica/Facil** (© 021/2263-8792) offers daily service from Rio to Petrôpolis. The trip takes a little more than an hour. Buses leave Monday through Friday every 15 minutes from 5:15am to midnight; on Saturday and Sunday, buses depart until approximately 10pm. Tickets cost R$14 (US$7/£4). Buses depart from the main bus station in Rio, **Novo Rio Rodoviaria,** Av. Francisco Bicalho 1, Santo Cristo (© 021/2291-5151). Buses arrive at the new bus station in Petrópolis on the outskirts of the city. A short taxi ride will take you to all the attractions.

VISITOR INFORMATION   **Petrotur**'s main office is at Av. Koeler 245 Centro (© 024/2243-9300). Kiosks are located at Rua do Imperador (by the obelisk) and Casa do Barão de Mauá; both are open Monday through Sunday from 9am to 5pm. The English version of the excellent "Petrôpolis Imperial Sightseeing" brochure comes with a map, visitor information, and opening hours for each of the attractions.

What to See & Do in Petrópolis

The historic heart of Petrôpolis can be easily explored on foot. Following the directions below will take you to most points of interest.

Starting on the corners of Avenida Ipiranga and Tiradentes, the first thing you see is the **Catedral São Pedro de Alcantara,** a neo-Gothic church named for both the patron saint of the empire and Emperor Dom Pedro II himself. Construction began in 1876, but the celebratory first Mass wasn't held until 1925. Just inside the main doors to the right is the Imperial Chapel containing the remains of Emperor Dom Pedro II, Empress Dona Teresa, and their daughter Princesa Isabel and her husband, whose name no one remembers. Continuing along the Avenida Koeler as it follows the tree-lined canal, it's a 5-minute walk to the beautiful **Praça da Liberdade.** The bridge in front of this square offers the best view of the cathedral and the canal. Just behind the Praça da Liberdade is the **Casa de Santos Dumont,** Rua do Encanto 22, Petrôpolis (© 024/2231-3011). Dumont was Brazil's most famous aviator and, in 1906, the first in the world to take off and land under his own power (unlike the Wright brothers, who were catapulted on their first flight at Kitty Hawk). From here, follow Avenida Roberto Silveira, and then turn right on Rua Alfredo Pachá to the **Palácio de Cristal,** Rua Alfredo Pachá s/n (© 024/2237-7953). Ordered by Princesa Isabel and built in France, the structure was inaugurated in 1894 as an agricultural exhibition hall. Nowadays, the palace is used for cultural events and exhibits. Crossing the bridge to Avenida Piabanha, you come to the **Casa Barão de Mauá,** Praça da Confluencia s/n (© 024/2231-2121), which was built in 1854 in neoclassic style by the industrial baron who constructed Brazil's first railway.

Continue by taking Rua 13 de Maio—right across the street from the Casa Barão de Mauá—toward the cathedral and then turning left on Avenida Ipiranga at the intersection just before the cathedral. Along this street are a number of interesting buildings as well as some gorgeous mansions and villas. Standing on the right side of the street, at no. 346, is the 1816 **Igreja Luterana,** the oldest church in Petrópolis (open for visitation only during Sun morning service at 10am). A bit farther along the Avenida Ipiranga, at no. 716, is the lovely **Casa de Petrópolis** (© 024/2246-0996), a museum, cultural center, restaurant, and garden. Guided tours of this beautifully preserved house will take you through numerous salons lavishly decorated with satin curtains and wallpaper, gold-leaf chandeliers, and ornate and beautiful furniture. From here, it's a simple matter to retrace your steps to the cathedral and the **Museu**

Imperial, Rua da Imperatriz 220 (© **024/2237-8000**). Built by Dom Pedro II in 1845 as his summer palace, the much-loved Museu Imperial is now Petrópolis's premier museum. The self-guided visits take you through numerous ground-floor salons decorated with period furniture, household items, and lovely paintings and drawings depicting the life and landscapes of 19th-century Rio. Best of all is Brazil's equivalent to Britain's crown jewels: Dom Pedro II's crown, weighing almost 4 pounds, is encrusted with 639 diamonds and 77 pearls. After you get your historic fix, make sure you stroll down the **Rua Teresa** (it runs parallel to the main street). The center of Rio's garment industry, this windy street is packed with hundreds of clothing stores selling inexpensive fashion and accessories.

Where to Dine in Petrópolis

Petrópolis offers a range of dining opportunities, from schnitzel to sushi to *churrasco*. Check opening times carefully, as a number of restaurants are closed Monday through Wednesday or Monday through Thursday.

Tucked away in the left corner of the gardens surrounding the museum, the **Museu Imperial Tearoom,** Rua da Imperatriz 220 (© **024/2237-8000**), is the perfect place for tea or lunch. Full tea service is available, including cakes, pies, croissants, madeleines, toast, jam, cold cuts, and pâté. For lunch, the restaurant also serves a variety of quiches, omelets, soups, and sandwiches, as well as pastas. A traditional-looking *churrascaria* with wood panels and booths, **Majoricá,** Rua do Imperador 754 (© **024/2242-2498**), is a local favorite when it comes to a good steak. Most dishes serve two people. For a nice Italian meal, try **Luigi,** Praça Rui Barbosa 185, Centro (© **024/2246-0279**). The large menu lists pasta and sauce separately allowing guests to mix and match. There are also a variety of stuffed pastas such as cannelloni, ravioli, and lasagna, and an outstanding salad buffet.

5 São Paulo

429km (266 miles) SW of Rio de Janeiro

The largest metropolis in South America and, with 17 million people, the third-largest city in the world, São Paulo was but an obscure market town until the 1850s, when it became one of the largest coffee exporters in the world. When slavery was abolished in Brazil in 1888, coffee growers began encouraging immigration. Italians, Japanese, Eastern Europeans, Spanish, Portuguese, and Germans all made their way to São Paulo; to this day, São Paulo is the most culturally diverse city in Brazil.

Prospective visitors often shy away from Brazil's big city, which is a shame. Visitors to São Paulo get all the benefits of a sophisticated, cosmopolitan city—they can eat at the finest restaurants in Brazil, shop at boutiques that even New York doesn't have, browse high-end art galleries, check out top-name Brazilian bands most any night of the week, and take advantage of one of Brazil's most dynamic nightlife scenes to party until the wee-est of hours.

Best of all, time in São Paulo provides a chance to get to know that subspecies of Brazilian known as the Paulista. Paulistas are proud of their work ethic and their "un-Brazilian" efficiency. They dominate Brazilian politics. They run Brazilian business. Dining out is an almost religious observance. And in São Paulo, the music and nightlife never end. However, if your time is truly limited, Iguaçu Falls, Salvador, or even Manaus will provide a more exotic Brazilian travel experience.

ESSENTIALS
GETTING THERE
BY PLANE   All international flights arrive at **Guarulhos International Airport** (*℡* **011/6445-2945**), a 45-minute drive northeast of the city. Prepaid taxi fares from Guarulhos to anywhere in São Paulo are available with **Taxi Guarucoop** (*℡* **011/6440-7070**). Some sample fares include Congonhas Airport R$84 (US$42/£23), São Paulo Centro R$66 (US$33/£18), and Jardims and Avenida Paulista R$74 (US$36/£20). São Paulo's domestic airport, **Congonhas** (*℡* **011/5090-9000**), is only a 15- to 20-minute taxi ride from Jardims or Avenida Paulista. R$28 to R$38 (US$14–US$19/£7.50–£10). The **Airport Service** (*℡* **011/6445-2505**) also operates shuttle buses between Congonhas Airport, Praça da República, Avenida Paulista (stopping at major hotels along the street), and the Rodoviária Tietê (bus station). Cost is R$24 (US$12/£6.50), and each route takes approximately 50 minutes (longer in rush hour). Buses depart about every half-hour from 6am to 11pm, and then hourly overnight.

BY BUS   There are four bus terminals *(rodoviaria)*. All are connected to the Metrô system. **Barra Funda,** near the Barra Funda Metrô, serves buses to the interior of São Paulo, northern Paraná, and Mato Grosso. **Bresser,** next to the Bresser Metrô, provides buses to Minas Gerais. **Jabaquara,** next to the Jabaquara Metrô, provides transportation to Santos and the south coast. The **Rodoviaria Tietê** (for buses to Rio and connections to Paraguay, Uruguay, and Argentina) is by far the largest and most important bus station, located on the Tietê Metrô stop. Buses depart from here to Rio, and most major Brazilian cities, as well as international destinations. The general information number is *℡* **011/3235-0322.**

ORIENTATION
The old heart of the city stands around **Praça da Sé.** São Paulo's original main street, **Rua Direita,** leads through a maze of downtown streets to a viaduct crossing over a busy freeway into the "newer" section of the old town, centered on leafy green **Praça República.** Together, the newer and older halves of the inner city are known as **Centro.**

Immediately west of Centro is one of São Paulo's original upscale suburbs, **Higienópolis.** Though long since swallowed up in the city, Higienópolis remains a green and leafy enclave with some good restaurants and the city's Museu Arte Brasileira (Museum of Brazilian Art).

Due south of Centro is **Liberdade,** said to have the largest Japanese population of any city outside Japan. Southwest of Centro lies **Bela Vista,** more often referred to as **Bixiga,** São Paulo's Little Italy. Bela Vista butts up against São Paulo's proudest street, the **Avenida Paulista.** Set on a ridge above surrounding neighborhoods, the Avenida Paulista was long ago given up to rank upon rank of skyscrapers, the headquarters of the city's powerful banking and financial interests. On the adjacent side streets, there are numerous hotels catering to business travelers. Halfway along the street is São Paulo's top-notch Museum of Art, the MASP.

Extending southwest from Avenida Paulista is a series of upscale neighborhoods named *jardims,* or gardens. Though each area has a particular name—Jardim Paulista, Jardim America, Cerqueira César, Jardim Europa—Paulistas tend to refer to them simply as **Jardins.** There are few attractions, per se, in the Jardins, but they do offer some terrific restaurants and the best shopping in São Paulo, notably where Rua Augusta is intersected by Alameda Lorena and Rua Oscar Freire.

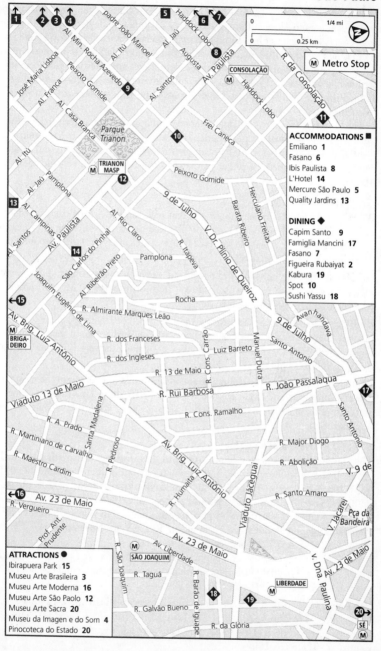

São Paulo

Metro Stop Ⓜ

ACCOMMODATIONS ■
Emiliano **1**
Fasano **6**
Ibis Paulista **8**
L'Hotel **14**
Mercure São Paulo **5**
Quality Jardins **13**

DINING ◆
Capim Santo **9**
Famiglia Mancini **17**
Fasano **7**
Figueira Rubaiyat **2**
Kabura **19**
Spot **10**
Sushi Yassu **18**

ATTRACTIONS ●
Ibirapuera Park **15**
Museu Arte Brasileira **3**
Museu Arte Moderna **16**
Museu Arte São Paolo **12**
Museu Arte Sacra **20**
Museu da Imagem e do Som **4**
Pinocoteca do Estado **20**

From here, Rua Augusta continues its run straight through the Jardins, changing names as it goes to Avenida Europa and finally Avenida Cidade Jardim. At this point, it intersects with another broad and important street, Avenida Brigadeiro Faria Lima. Less fashionable than Rua Augusta, Avenida Brigadeiro Faria Lima is home to a number of big, American-style shopping malls. Continuing northwest, it leads to another Jardim-like area called **Pinheiros,** while going the opposite direction leads first to **Itaim Bibi** and then to a fun and slightly funky area of restaurants and clubs called **Vila Olimpia.**

The last key element to São Paulo is not a neighborhood but a green space—Ibirapuera Park. Located immediately south of the Jardins, Ibirapuera is to São Paulo what Central Park is to New York. It's a place for strolling, lazy sun-tanning, and outdoor concerts and it's home to a couple of the city's top cultural facilities, including the Modern Art Museum.

GETTING AROUND

BY FOOT   Many of the neighborhoods that make up the city are compact enough to be easily explored on foot. During the day, the city is very safe; the only areas to avoid at night are the quiet side streets of Centro, particularly the streets around Praça da Sé, Bixiga, and Luz station.

BY SUBWAY   The north-south line and the east-west line run from 5am to midnight. The line under Avenida Paulista runs from 6am to 10pm. Metrô tickets cost R$2.30 (US$1.15/60p) for a single ride.

BY BUS   São Paulo buses are plentiful and frequent. The large sign on the top of the bus mentions the final stop or neighborhood, while a smaller sign in the window and on the side of the bus will mention a few key stops along the way. Buses cost R$2.30 (US$1.15/60p).

BY TAXI   **Rádio Táxi Vermelho e Branco** (Red and White) is one of the most reliable taxi companies and can be reached at ✆ 011/3146-4000. Taxis can also be hailed anywhere on the street, and taxi stands *(pontos de taxi)* are found at many major squares and main streets.

VISITOR INFORMATION

The city tourism information booths (**Central de Informações Turisticas,** or **CIT**) can be found downtown at Praça da República in front of Rua 7 de Abril (✆ 011/3231-2922; daily 9am–6pm), and at Avenida Paulista in front of Trianon Park (✆ 011/251-0970; Mon–Fri 9am–6pm and Sat–Sun 10am–4pm). CIT booths in terminals 1 and 2 of Guarulhos Airport are open daily from 7am to 7pm. The **SET** (State Information Booths) can be found at **Rua XV de Novembro** 347, Centro (✆ 011/3231-1445), open daily from 9am to 6pm.

For sale on the newsstands is a publication called *Este Mês São Paulo* (or *São Paulo This Month*), a bilingual tourist guide. It has some maps, listings, and contact information, and it costs R$5 (US$2.50/£1.35).

FAST FACTS   To exchange currency, go to **Banco do Brasil** at Av. Paulista 2163, Centro (✆ 011/3066-9322); Rua São João 32, Centro (✆ 011/3234-1646); or Guarulhos Airport (✆ 011/6445-2223). There's also a **Citibank** at Av. Paulista 1111, Centro (✆ 011/5576-1000).

In an emergency, call the **police** at ✆ 190 or the **fire brigade** or an **ambulance** at ✆ 193. You can also contact the **tourist police** at Avenida São Luis (1 block from

Praça da República), Centro (℃ **011/3214-0209**), or Rua São Bento 380, 5th Floor, Centro (℃ **011/3107-5642**).

For **medical attention,** go to **Albert Einstein Hospital,** Av. Albert Einstein 627, Morumbi (℃ **011/3747-0307**), or **Hospital das Clinicas,** 255 Av. Doutor Eneias de Carvalho Aguiar s/n (℃ **011/3069-6000**). If you need a **dentist,** contact **Dr. Marcelo Erlich,** Rua Sergipe 401, Suite 403, Higienópolis (℃ **011/3214-1332** or 011/9935-8666; open 24 hr.; English is spoken).

Two good places for **Internet access** are **Centro Cultural FNAC,** Praça dos Omaguás s/n, Pinheiros (℃ **011/4501-3000**), open daily from 10am to 10pm; and just off Avenida Paulista at the corner of Pamplona, **Monkey,** Alameda Santos 1217 (℃ **011/3253-8627**), open daily 9am to 6am, R$4 (US$2/£1) per hour.

A note about telephone numbers: Many phone numbers in São Paulo either have changed in the past 3 years or will change soon. If you are not able to get through to a number, especially if it's a seven-digit number, it has likely been changed recently. Ask the front desk of your hotel to verify the number for you, or if your Portuguese is up to snuff, call the **automated directory assistance service** at ℃ **800/771-5104.**

WHAT TO SEE & DO
THE TOP ATTRACTIONS

Ibirapuera Park 𝕽𝕽   Often called São Paulo's beach, Ibirapuera Park attracts more than 200,000 visitors on an average weekend. You can wander the paths beside pleasant lagoons or in the Japanese garden; or you can jog the exercise track or rent a bicycle (R$5/US$2.50/£1.35 per hour). On Sunday morning, there's always a free outdoor concert in the park's Praça da Paz. Just nearby, there's the excellent **Museu Afro Brasil** (see below) and the **OCA Auditorium,** a flying saucer–shaped building that often hosts traveling art exhibits.

Administration. ℃ **011/5045-5177.** Free admission. Daily 5am–midnight. Metrô: Brigadeiro, and then take bus 5100 or 5131.

Monument to Latin America 𝕽𝕽   Designed by famed Brazilian architect Oscar Niemeyer, the monument is, well, *so* Niemeyer—shy of a visit to Brasília, it's the best place to see Brazilian modernism in all its pure concrete austerity. The South American Parliament and Art gallery are likely to be of the most interest to visitors unimpressed by architecture. The art gallery hosts changing fine-art exhibits, while the hall is the permanent home to a fun and fascinating display of folk art from across Latin America.

Av. Auro Soares de Moura Andrade 664, Barra Funda (next to the Barra Funda Metrô stop). ℃ **011/3823-4600.** www.memorial.org.br. Free admission. Tues–Sun 9am–6pm. Metrô: Barra Funda.

Museu Afro Brasil 𝕽𝕽   Brazil has the largest black population outside of Africa, so it's curious that only in the past decade or so has black or Afro consciousness really begun to take root. This new museum—one of the most popular cultural institutions to open in São Paulo in recent years—is dedicated to showing the cultural achievements of Africans and their descendents enslaved in Brazil. If you think you might be letting yourself in for a hectoring, guilt-inducing lecture, think again. The museum is a celebration of the art and accomplishments of the African Diaspora. Displays show short biographies of writers or painters or politicians who were black, including lots of their artwork and artifacts. Displays are gorgeous—particularly the art and photography—and the museum has wonderful natural light. Allow an hour.

Parque do Ibirapuera. ℂ 011/5579-0593. Free admission. Tues–Sun 10am–6pm. (Hours and admission charges subject to change due to funding.) Metrô: Brigadeiro, and then bus: 5100 or 5131.

Museu Arte Brasileira/FAAP 🎔🎔　Don't let the name fool you. What this majestic and slightly pompous building (think Mussolini monumental) in quiet Higienópolis plays host to is not Brazilian art, but an ever-changing parade of grand international exhibits—2 years ago it was Egypt, currently it's Napóleon. The museum also claims to house a number of the Brazilian greats—Portinari, Di Cavalcanti, and others—but they're never actually on display. (You may also see the museum referred to as FAAP, which is the acronym for the cultural institute where it's located.)

Rua Alagoas 903, Higienópolis. ℂ 011/3662-7200. www.faap.br/museu. Admission varies from free to R$15 (US$7.50/£4) depending on exhibit. Tues–Fri 10am–8pm; Sat–Sun 1–5pm. Bus: 137T.

Museu Arte São Paulo (MASP) 🎔🎔　Part of the MASP experience is the building itself. The main display space is a single long box raised two stories off the ground on bright red concrete pilings. The idea was to create a broad courtyard with a view of the Anhangabaú Valley. Inside, the museum is somewhat of a disappointment. It does contain an excellent selection of Western art, from 14th-century Italian religious imagery to Picasso's early-20th-century works, but with the exception of one room dedicated to Candido Portinari, Brazilian art is entirely absent. The Western art collection is worth a visit, but if Brazilian art is what you want, go to the Pinacoteca instead (p. 281).

Av. Paulista 1578, Cerqueira César. ℂ 011/3251-5644. www.masp.art.br. Admission R$15 (US$7.50/£4) adults, free for seniors and children 10 and under. Tues–Sun 11am–6pm. Metrô: Trianon-MASP.

Museu de Arte Moderna (MAM) 🎔　Small but intriguing, the MAM in Ibirapuera Park has two galleries that it devotes to ever-changing exhibits of modern work, be it in the form of painting, sculpture, video, textile, or some other medium. At any one time, each of the main building's two spacious and well-lit galleries are given over to a particular artist. Check the website for upcoming exhibits. Surrounding the museum is a **sculpture garden** featuring 28 works by different Brazilian artists. Allow 45 minutes.

Parque do Ibirapuera, Gate 3. ℂ 011/5085-1300. www.mam.org.br. Admission R$5.50 (US$2.75/£1.75) adults, free for seniors 60 and over and children 10 and under. Free admission Sun. Tues–Sun 10am–6pm. Metrô: Brigadeiro, and then bus 5100 or 5131.

Museu de Arte Sacra 🎔🎔　"Sacred Art" refers to objects—chalices, crosses, statues, paintings, sculptures—created to adorn churches or for use in Catholic service. The Mosteiro da Luz provides the perfect solemn and serene setting to view these works; choral music echoes through the stone corridors, and light from the cloister casts a warm glow on the collection. The collection also displays beautifully carved and hand-painted oratories. Portuguese and English texts explain the origins and name of each piece. Expect to spend about an hour here. Outside, in the garden, is the Presepio, a miniature village composed of more than 1,600 pieces depicting life in an 18th-century Neapolitan village; admission is included with the ticket to the Museu de Arte Sacra.

Av. Tiradentes 676, Luz. ℂ 011/3326-1373. http://artesacra.sarasa.com.br. Admission R$4 (US$2/£1) adults, free for seniors and children 5 and under. Tues–Sun 11am–7pm. Metrô: Luz or Tirandentes.

Museu da Lingua Portuguesa 🎔🎔　The Museum of the Portuguese Language is creative, interesting, interactive, visually fabulous, and fun. Unfortunately there's no

English signage, but anybody with a basic understanding of Portuguese, or an interest in the language, will enjoy the experience.

The most magnificent display tells the history of the Portuguese language, as it developed from Latin, only much later to be influenced by Arabic, eventually by African and Indian words, and later by French and English. On the right side, a giant time line and several interactive displays impart a myriad of interesting facts; on the left, a giant 100m-long (328 ft.) screen runs the full length of this former train station, showing images and clips relating to unique Portuguese words associated with cultural events such as Carnaval, religion, soccer, and music. Allow 2 hours.

Praça Luz s/n, Administration. © 011/3326-0775. www.museudalinguaportuguesa.org.br. R$4/US$2/£1. Tues–Sun 10am–6pm. Metrô: Estação Luz.

Museu do Ipiranga or Museu Paulista ✦   Located at the birthplace of Brazilian independence—it was here, in 1822, that Dom Pedro I declared Brazil's independence from Portugal—the museum is a grand neoclassical building with perfectly manicured Versailles-like gardens out front and a "wilder" botanical garden out back. The collection houses some real gems of Brazilian art. There are also a number of photo exhibits showing the development of 19th-century São Paulo. The remainder of the exhibit consists of period furniture, a collection of 19th-century horse-drawn fire trucks, household objects, and clothing. Unfortunately, there are no English signs. The park and gardens behind the museum are pleasant and packed with Paulistas on weekends. Expect to spend an hour in the museum.

Praça da Independencia s/n, Ipiranga. © 011/6165-8000. www.mp.usp.br. Admission R$2 (US85¢/£50) adults and children over 6, free for children 6 and under. Tues–Sun 9am–5pm. Closed statutory holidays. Bus: 4506 Jardim Celeste.

Pinacoteca do Estado ✦✦✦   The Pinacoteca offers one of the best-curated Brazilian art collections in the city. The museum does an excellent job of displaying some of the best Brazilian artists from the 19th and 20th centuries, from the landscapes of Antonio Parreiras and João da Costa to still-life painters such as Georgina de Albuquerque and João Batista Pagini. The 20th-century work starts to break free of European influence and includes some interesting examples of expressive Brazilian pieces, colorful and bursting with energy. In addition to paintings, the Pinacoteca collection contains sculpture including a lovely statue by Raphael Galvez entitled *O Brasileiro,* as well as works by Alfredo Ceschiatti, the artist who designed many of the sculptures in Brasília. Allow 2 hours.

Praça da Luz 2, Luz. © 011/3229-9844. www.pinacoteca.sp.gov.br. Admission R$5 (US$2.50/£1.25) adults, R$2 (US$1/50p) students, free for children 10 and under. Tues–Sun 10am–6pm. Guided tours leave at 10, 11:30am, 1, and 2:30pm. Metrô: Luz.

SHOPPING

Paulistas say that if you can't buy it in São Paulo, you can't buy it in Brazil. They're probably right. Even city-proud Cariocas begrudgingly admit that São Paulo's shopping scene is superior to theirs.

The city has a number of shopping areas, all unique and interesting to explore. **Jardins,** the upscale neighborhood just southwest of downtown, is well known for its high-end fashion boutiques. The main shopping streets in this neighborhood are Rua Augusta, the parallel Rua Haddock Lobo, and their cross streets Rua Oscar Freire and Alameda Lorena. On any given weekday during office hours, the many pedestrian streets of Centro—in particular **Rua Direita, Rua São Bento, Rua 25 de Março,** and

Rua 24 de Maio—are one long outdoor fair, featuring every item you'd care to name, all of them cheap.

Then there are the malls: In São Paulo, the mall has been elevated to an elegant, upscale, and refined shopping experience. The best-known malls are **Morumbi Shopping,** Av. Roque Petroni Junior 1089, Brooklin; **Iguatemi Shopping,** Av. Brigadeiro Faria Lima 2232, Jardim Paulistano; and **Patio Higienópolis,** Av. Higienópolis 615. All are located in upscale neighborhoods close to the city center. More downscale is the **Shopping Paulista,** Rua Treze de Maio 1947, Paraiso, close to the city center.

ART GALLERIES   It's hard to miss **Britto**'s colorful and bold pop-art style, Rua Oscar Freire 562 (© **011/3062-7350**). The store sells original and limited edition prints of Britto's work, as well as accessories such as mugs and mouse pads decorated with his work. **Galeria Fortes Vilaça,** Rua Fradique Coutinho 500, Vila Madalena (© **011/3032-7066**), represents over 20 Brazilian and international artists who work in Brazil. Exhibits range from paintings to installation art, sculpture, and mixed media. One of the older contemporary art galleries in town, **Galeria Luisa Strina,** Rua Bela Sintra 1533 (© **011/3081-9492**), now showcases work from a number of young national and international artists. This gallery usually has interesting exhibits of artwork done in various media: paintings, bronze pieces, glass, or photo art.

BOOKS   The **Centro Cultural FNAC,** Av. Pedroso de Moraes 858 (© **011/3097-0022**), boasts many floors of books, but it also has a coffee shop, cybercafe, and large music and video department. The foreign language section is extensive, and the guidebook and map section offers a good selection for travelers. **Haddock Lobo Books and Magazines,** Rua Haddock 1503 (© **011/3082-9449**), open daily until midnight, has an excellent selection of international magazines.

MARKETS   Located to the north of Praça da Sé, the fruit-and-vegetable market **Mercado Central,** Rua da Cantareira 306, is an imposing neo-Gothic hall built in 1933, with huge stained-glass windows. It's open Monday through Saturday from 5am to 4pm. Every Sunday from 10am to 5pm, there's an **antiques fair** in the open space beneath the MASP building on Avenida Paulista. Dealers are registered, and the quality of the wares is often good. On Sunday on the **Praça da Liberdade** (next to the Liberdade Metrô stop), São Paulo's Japanese residents celebrate their heritage with an outdoor market featuring an excellent and inexpensive selection of Japanese cuisine.

MUSIC   Casa Amadeus, Av. Ipiranga 1129, Centro (© **011/228-0098**), sells a great selection of Brazilian sheet music and a variety of Brazilian musical instruments. **Saraiva,** Shopping Morumbi, Av. Roque Petroni Junior 1089, Brooklin (© **0800/177-600**), sells books and magazines as well as CDs. The CD collection is quite large, though it's limited to commercially successful artists.

WHERE TO STAY

São Paulo attracts business travelers Monday through Friday, and then sits empty from Friday afternoon to Monday morning. Prices drop by as much as 50% if you can time your visit to this city on a weekend.

AVENIDA PAULISTA
Very Expensive
L'Hotel 𝕮𝕮𝕮   Just off the Avenida Paulista, L'Hotel is one of São Paulo's most elegant boutique hotels. The plain modern facade does not do justice to the chic interior. L'Hotel's interior is warm and welcoming, and with only 80 rooms, the service is

attentive and friendly. Rooms are luxuriously furnished with elegant antique furniture, a queen- or king-size bed with top-quality linen, and a pleasant well-lit work space. Bathrooms feature bathtubs and lovely marble finishings. The suites feature a separate sitting room with a comfortable couch and armchair, a stereo, and cordless phone. There's a small but well-designed fitness center, small heated indoor pool, and a business center.

Alameda Campinas 266, Jardim Paulista, 01404-000 SP. ✆ **0800/13-0080** or 011/2183-0500. Fax 011/2183-0505. www.lhotel.com.br. 80 units. R$825 (US$412/£223) double; R$1,200 (US$600/£324) double suites. Children 12 and under stay free in parent's room. Extra person 25%. AE, DC, MC, V. Free valet parking. Metrô: MASP. **Amenities:** Restaurant; bar; small indoor pool; fitness center; business center; 24-hr. room service; laundry; dry cleaning; nonsmoking floors. *In room:* A/C, TV, dataport, minibar, hair dryer, electronic safe.

Expensive
Quality Jardins ☆
The Quality Jardins offers some of the best affordable accommodations just off the Avenida Paulista. Rooms are a cross between a studio and a regular hotel room, featuring a desk and TV on a swivel in order to separate the sitting area from the sleeping area. The furnishings are modern and pleasant with light colors, blond wood, and comfortable lighting. Women travelers can reserve a room on the women-only floor. The hotel has a good-size fitness room with saunas and a pool.

Alameda Campinas 540, São Paulo, 01404-000 SP. ✆ **0800/555-855** or 011/2182-0400. Fax: 011/2182-0401. www.atlanticahotels.com.br. 220 units (showers only). R$185–R$210 (US$92–US$105/£50–£57) superior double; R$215–R$245 (US$107–US$122/£58–£66) deluxe double; R$245–R$310 (US$122–US$155/£66–£84) premium double. Extra person add R$30 (US$15/£8). Children 5 and under stay free in parent's room. AE, DC, MC, V. Free parking. Metrô: Trianon-MASP. **Amenities:** Restaurant; pool; health club; sauna; concierge; business center; room service; laundry; nonsmoking floors. *In room:* A/C, TV, dataport, minibar, hair dryer, safe.

Moderate
Ibis Avenida Paulista ⓥalue
The Accor group's budget Ibis brand offers predictable but quality accommodations in the heart of the business district. All 236 rooms are standard (more than half of them nonsmoking), identically furnished with good firm double or twin beds, a desk, and a nice, hot shower. Breakfast is not included but can be ordered at the restaurant for R$9 (US$4.50/£2.50). The rates listed below are the online rates.

Av. Paulista 2355, Cerqueira Cesar, 01420-002 SP. ✆ **011/3523-3000.** Fax 011/3523-3030. www.accorhotels.com.br. 236 units. R$129 (US$65/£35) double. Children 12 and under stay free in parent's room. AE, DC, MC, V. Free parking. Metrô: Consolação. **Amenities:** Restaurant; limited room service; laundry; nonsmoking floor; rooms for those w/limited mobility. *In room:* A/C, TV, dataport, minibar, safe.

JARDINS
Very Expensive
Emiliano ☆☆☆
The Emiliano is five-star treatment all the way, from the welcome massage to the minibar stocked according to your preference to the personalized selection of pillows, carefully fluffed and placed on your Egyptian cotton sheets. The Emiliano offers two types of rooms: deluxe studios and suites. The studios (really just a large room) are marginally cheaper, but is this really the time to skimp? The prime rooms are the fabulous, spacious suites. These come decorated with designer furniture and feature original artwork and the latest home entertainment electronics. The bed is king-size and the bathroom is a minispa in itself; toiletries are customized to your skin type and you can sit back and relax in the claw-foot tub, maybe watch a little TV, or contemplate life on your heated toilet seat.

Rua Oscar Freire 384, Cerqueira César, 01426-000 SP. © 011/3069-4369. Fax 011/3068-4398. www.emiliano. com.br. 57 units. R$800 (US$400/£216) double room; R$1,400 (US$700/£378) double suite. Special packages are available. Please check the website. Extra person add 30%. Children 10 and under stay free in parent's room. AE, DC, MC, V. Free parking. **Amenities:** Restaurant; upscale lobby bar; small exercise room; outstanding spa; concierge; business center; salon; 24-hr. room service; massage; babysitting service; laundry; dry cleaning; nonsmoking floors. *In room:* A/C, TV, dataport, minibar, hair dryer, safe.

Fasano 👑👑👑   The Fasano family, successful São Paulo restaurateurs, decided several years ago to apply their hospitality experience to the hotel industry and in 2003 opened this luxury boutique hotel. Elegantly decorated, the hotel combines 1930s period furniture with modern design elements. All 50 rooms and 10 suites are beautifully appointed with sober, modern furniture, hardwood floors, Persian rugs, Venetian blinds and feature a king size bed with 500-thread Egyptian cotton sheets and goose down pillows. Of course in terms of food, guests are in excellent hands here. The hotel's signature restaurant, Fasano, is one of the top Italian restaurants in South America, and breakfast and room service are prepared by the chef of the Nonno Ruggero, the hotel's upscale *trattoria*.

Rua Vitório Fasano 88, Cerqueira César, 01426-000 SP. © 011/3896-4000. Fax 011/3896-4155. www.fasano. com.br. 57 units. R$800 (US$400/£216) superior double room; R$990 (US$495/£243) deluxe double room; R$1,400 (US$700/£378) double suite. Extra person add 30%. Children 6 and under stay free in parent's room. AE, DC, MC, V. Free parking. **Amenities:** 2 restaurants; upscale jazz bar; small exercise room; small spa; concierge; business center; salon; 24-hr. room service; massage; babysitting service; laundry; dry cleaning; nonsmoking floors. *In room:* A/C, TV, dataport, minibar, hair dryer, safe.

Expensive

Mercure São Paulo Jardins 👑   A pleasant modern hotel, everything is crisp and clean, the decoration Scandinavian modern with blond wood, simple design, and lots of light shining in everywhere. Rooms are spacious with king-size beds (a rarity in Brazil), a couple of small sitting chairs, a maple-wood desk with desk lamp, and phone and power jacks for laptops. Bathrooms have nice fixtures but are functionally compact. More than half the hotel rooms are nonsmoking. The leisure area is small, offering only an indoor pool and sauna, but the Mercure's location is excellent, only a hop and a skip to the Avenida Paulista and a 15-minute walk downhill to the best shopping and dining in Jardins.

Alameda Itu 1151, Cerqueira César, 01421-001 SP. © 0800/703-7000 or 011/3089-7555. Fax 011/3089-7550. www.accorhotels.com.br. 126 units (showers only). R$260 (US$130/£70) double Mon–Fri; R$168 (US$84/£45) double Sat–Sun. No triple rooms are available. Children 10 and under stay free in parent's room. AE, DC, MC, V. Free parking. Metrô: Consolação. **Amenities:** Restaurant; laptop-friendly bar; small pool; 24-hr. room service; laundry; dry cleaning; nonsmoking floors. *In room:* A/C, TV, dataport, minibar, hair dryer, safe.

Moderate

Quality Imperial Hall 👑👑   The Quality Imperial Hall sits in the heart of São Paulo's toniest neighborhood, surrounded by restaurants, designer boutiques, and trendy shops. The building is new and the 190 rooms are modern and pleasantly furnished. Built with the business traveler in mind, the hotel offers firm beds, large closets, a small kitchen, in-room high-speed Internet, and a large desk with easy access to lots of plugs. The Master Rooms on the 13th to 19th floors feature balconies and a few perks such as bathrobes and clock radios. There's also a floor exclusively for women travelers.

Rua da Consolação 3555, Jardins, São Paulo, 01416-001 SP. © 011/2137-4555. Fax 011/2137-4560. www.atlantica hotels.com.br. 190 units. R$215 (US$107/£58) double; R$285 (US$142/£77). Extra person add 25%. Children 6 and under stay free in parent's room. AE, DC, MC, V. Free parking. **Amenities:** Restaurant; rooftop pool; small weight room; sauna; spa; business center; 24-hr. room service; laundry; nonsmoking rooms; women-only floor. *In room:* A/C, TV, dataport, kitchen, safe.

Transamerica Opera ✦ *Value*   The bargain of the century in the heart of the city's best neighborhood. The Opera offers spacious flats, featuring a separate sitting room with comfy couch and TV and small dinette table, plus a good-size work desk with lamp and lots of plugs, plus a bedroom with firm queen bed and vast closets and full length mirror, plus a kitchenette with stove and fridge, all for less than many hotels charge for just a bed. True, the furnishings are a tad dated, but on the positive side, step out the door and you're in the heart of the Jardins shopping district. Rooms on the 11th floor and above have high-speed Internet now; the rest should have it soon.

Alameda Lorena 1748, Cerqueira César, 04003-010 SP. ✆ **011/3062-2666.** Fax 011/3062-2662. www.transamerica flats.com.br. 96 units. R$205 (US$102/£55) double. Discounts available Sat–Sun. Children 10 and under stay free in parent's room. AE, DC, MC, V. Free parking. Metrô: Consolação. **Amenities:** Restaurant; bar; room service; small pool; small gym; sauna; laundry; nonsmoking floors. *In room:* A/C, TV, high-speed Internet access, kitchenette, minibar, safe.

WHERE TO DINE

São Paulo is the gourmet capital of Brazil. It's the city with the money to attract the country's best chefs. Plus, with no beaches or mountains to play on, Paulistas like to eat out for amusement. People go out around 9 or 10pm at the earliest. Most restaurants don't accept reservations; if you don't want to wait for a table, it's better to arrive unfashionably early, around 8pm.

CENTRO
Moderate
Famiglia Mancini ✦✦ ITALIAN   A São Paulo tradition, you can find a line-up at the Famiglia Mancini almost every night of the week. Start your meal off at the antipasto buffet, where you can choose from a sizable spread of olives, cold cuts, marinated vegetables, cheeses, quail eggs, and salads. With that on your plate you'll have the energy to tackle the enormous pasta menu. There's every kind of pasta you could dream of, and more than 30 different sauces to match. There are also stuffed pastas such as cannellonis, raviolis, and lasagna. Portions are huge; they serve at least two people, often three. Desserts are uninspiring, but most people are too stuffed to contemplate eating more.

Rua Avanhandava 81, Centro. ✆ **011/3256-4320.** Reservations not accepted. Main courses R$34–R$68 (US$17–US$34/£9–18) for 2. AE, DC, MC, V. Sun–Wed 11:30am–1am; Thurs 11:30am–2am; Fri–Sat 11:30am–3am. Metrô: Anhagabau.

AVENIDA PAULISTA
Very Expensive
Antiquarius ✦✦✦ PORTUGUESE   Antiquarius offers the perfect elegant setting to savor Portuguese cuisine served up with style and tradition. The menu offers dishes that are hard to find outside Portugal such as the *cataplana de peixes e frutos do mar,* a rich stew of seafood and fish, with bacon and sausage thrown in for seasoning, all served in a traditional pot resembling a wok with a lid. Another traditional seafood favorite is *açorda*—crab, shrimp, and mussels baked together in a clay dish, with an egg on top of the food for decoration. Then there's the cod *(bacalhau),* which has been a staple of Portuguese cooking since long before Columbus set sail. The wine list leans to higher-end reds, with a large selection drawn almost exclusively from Portugal and France.

Alameda Lorena 1884, Jardim Paulista. ✆ **011/3064-8686.** Main courses R$62–R$110 (US$31–US$55/£17–£30). DC, MC, V. Mon 7pm–1am; Tues–Fri noon–3pm and 7pm–1am; Sat noon–2am; Sun noon–6pm. Metrô: Trianon-MASP.

Expensive

Spot ✿ BRAZILIAN   Ten years old and still trendy, Spot seems to be the exception to the rule that all things trendy soon melt into air. The daytime crowd consists of mostly well-dressed businesspeople, however, it's the evening crowd that keeps Spot buzzing when musicians, designers, models, and other trendy types crowd into this glass-enclosed downtown cocoon to flirt, schmooze, and preen. The food is nice but not outstanding. There are pasta dishes, salads (try the Spot Salad—lettuce, Gorgonzola, dried pears, and nuts), grilled salmon, and tuna with vegetables. It may just be that Spot's owners have created a perpetual motion machine: The young and beautiful flock to see the young and beautiful, who flock to see the young and beautiful, and so on.

Rua Min. Rocha Azevedo 72, Cerqueira Cesar. ✆ 011/3283-0946. Reservations accepted only until 9pm. Main courses R$28–R$46 (US$14–US$23/£7.50–£13). AE, DC, MC, V. Mon–Fri noon–3pm and 8pm–1am; Sat–Sun 1–4:30pm and 8pm–1am. Metrô: Trianon-MASP.

Moderate

Mestiço ✿✿ *Value* THAI/BAHIAN   Mestiço is run by a woman from Bahia and her partner from Thailand—each brings her own culinary traditions to bear in the cuisine. Traditional Thai noodle salads sit side by side on the menu with *acarajé,* a Bahian fast food made with beans and shrimp and served with hot sauce. The salads are outstanding; the Malibu comes stuffed with tuna, carrots, rucula, lettuce, and mango in a balsamic-honey dressing, while the Cubana boasts squid, palm hearts, grilled banana, and an intriguing variety of lettuces. For more substantial meals there's Thai dishes such as chicken with shiitake mushrooms in ginger sauce, and grilled prawns with roasted peanuts in a sweet-and-sour sauce. Service is friendly, and the prices are very reasonable. Alas, we're not the only ones to have discovered this restaurant; on weekends the wait can be at least an hour.

Rua Fernando de Albuquerque 277, Consolação. ✆ 011/3256-3165. www.mestico.com.br. Reservations accepted. R$20–R$45 (US$8.40–US$19/£4.30–£9.75). AE, DC, MC, V. Sun–Thurs noon–midnight; Fri–Sat noon–2am. Metrô: Consolação.

LIBERDADE

Expensive

Sushi Yassu ✿✿ JAPANESE   Long a standard-bearer in Liberdade, the second-generation owners are now trying to make the menu a little less standard by introducing some new and different dishes to the Paulista palette. Customers can try the grilled white tuna or anchovy, in salt or with a sweetened soy sauce, or a steaming bowl of udon noodle soup in a rich broth with seafood or tempura vegetables. There is of course a large variety of sushi and sashimi dishes, as well as the stir-fried teppanyaki and yakisoba noodles with meat and vegetables. Expect a bit of a wait on Sunday afternoons when this restaurant makes a popular lunch destination for those visiting the Liberdade street market.

Rua Tomas Gonzaga 98, Liberdade. ✆ 011/3209-6622. Main courses R$16–R$36 (US$8–US$18/£4.30–£10). AE, DC, MC, V. Tues–Fri 11:30am–3pm and 6–11:30pm; Sat noon–4pm and 6pm–midnight; Sun noon–10pm. Metrô: Liberdade.

Moderate

Kabura JAPANESE   Kabura offers late-night dining in the heart of São Paulo's little Japan. The restaurant serves up the usual Japanese faves—sushi, sashimi, *donburi,* and tempura—all at a reasonable price. The food is fresh, and the portions are generous. For an interesting cold appetizer try the sashimi made from Brazilian top picanha beef. An excellent hot appetizer is the plate with six breaded and crunchy deep-fried oysters.

Rua Galvão Bueno 54, Liberdade, Sao Paulo. ℭ 011/3277-2918. Reservations accepted. R$18–R$39 (US$9–US$20/ £5–£11). No credit cards. Mon–Sat 7pm–2am. Metrô: Liberdade.

JARDINS & ITAIM BIBI
Very Expensive

Fasano ᚛᚛᚛ ITALIAN   Considered the best Italian restaurant in the country, Rogerio Fasano doesn't seem the least bit intimidated about living up to this expectation. It helps to have a beautiful restaurant. Located in the Fasano hotel, the dining room combines black marble and dark furniture with exquisite lighting to create an intimate and warm ambience. The mainstays of the menu are dishes from northern Italy, more specifically Lombardy, from where the Fasanos originally hailed. However, over the last few years, chef Salvatore Loi has been diversifying the menu with dishes from other Italian regions. Start off with a traditional tomato soup with prawns and Italian bread or try the antipasto. Pasta courses include favorites such as the delicate pumpkin tortelli, a hearty duck ravioli in orange sauce or try one of the risotto's with Tuscan sausage and white beans or with marinated tuna. For mains, the menu offers excellent meat and seafood options. Choose from classic veal cutlets, roasted lamb, filetto alla Rossini with foie gras and truffles or perhaps a lighter choice, the grilled tuna steak with Sicilian lemon. Diners can also opt for the 5-course tasting menu and let Chef Salvatore take them on a gastronomic journey around Italy.

Rua Vittorio Fasano 88, Cerqueira Cesar. ℭ 011/3062-4000. Main courses R$98–R$160 (US$49–US$80/£27–£43); 5-course tasting menu R$240 (US$120/£65). AE, DC, MC, V. Mon–Sat 7:30pm–1am. Bus: 206E.

Expensive

Capim Santo ᚛᚛ BRAZILIAN   Modeled after the Capim Santo restaurant in Bahia, the São Paulo version is set in a lovely garden with lush mango trees and plenty of outside tables. The specialty is seafood. Try the *robalo* fish with a crust of cashew nuts and a side of *vatapá* shrimp stew, or the perfectly tender grilled tuna. Another delicious dish is the stew of prawns in coconut milk served in a hollowed-out pumpkin. Desserts include some favorites with a tropical twist, such as the guava crème brûlée or the tarte tartin with banana.

Rua Ministro Rocha Azevedo 471, Cerqueira César. ℭ 011/3068-8486. www.restaurantecapimsanto.com.br. Main courses R$26–R$49 (US$13–US$25/£7–£13). AE. Tues–Sat noon–3pm and 7pm–midnight; Sun 12:30–4:30pm. Metrô: MASP.

Figueira Rubaiyat ᚛᚛᚛ BRAZILIAN/STEAK   Surely the most beautiful restaurant in the city, Figueira ("fig tree") Rubaiyat is built around a magnificent old fig tree. Seating can either be "outside" in the gazebo around the tree or in the beautiful restaurant. The menu specializes in a la carte meats; most of the beef, chicken, and other meats served at Rubaiyat are home-grown at the owners' *fazenda* (cattle ranch), ensuring that the quality is always top-notch. Fish dishes include paella, cod fish, and grilled seafood.

Rua Haddock Lobo 1738, Cerqueira Cesar. ℭ 011/3063-3888. Main courses R$44–R$89 (US$22–US$40/£12–£24). V. Mon–Fri noon–3:30pm and 7pm–midnight; Sat–Sun noon–12:30am. Bus: 206E.

VILA MADALENA
Expensive

Kabuki ᚛᚛ JAPANESE   Romantic and rustic-chic are adjectives not usually associated with Japanese restaurants, but Kabuki is an exception. The candle-lit dining room is furnished with lovely dark wood and the exposed brick walls are adorned with tasteful artwork. However, the menu is all Japanese. There's a large menu of cold and hot appetizers such as sautéed shitake or shimeji mushrooms, deep-fried prawn, and an assortment of grilled skewers with meat, seafood, or vegetables. Main courses include a variety of sushi and sashimi combos, tempuras, yakisoba noodles, and grilled meats. Interesting desserts include the flambéed mango and banana or tempura ice cream, a wonderful sensation of a hot, crunchy crust and a soft, cold, creamy center.

Rua Girassol 384, Vila Madalena. ℂ 011/3814-5131. Reservations accepted. Dinner R$22–R$70 (US$11–US$35/£6–£19). AE, DC, MC, V. Mon 7–11pm; Tues–Sun noon–3pm. Metrô: Vila Madalena.

Moderate

Santa Gula 𝐴𝐴 *Finds* ITALIAN   Following the fairy-tale lane with lush tropical plants, banana trees, and flickering candlelight leads you to Santa Gula's dining room. Handmade furniture and rustic decorations give the restaurant the feel of a simple Tuscan villa. The kitchen serves up a mix of Italian and Brazilian flavors—think risotto with palmheart or pasta stuffed with *carne seca* (a flavorful dried meat) and pumpkin purée. Equally intriguing is the duck with red-wine sauce and a pineapple risotto. For dessert, don't pass up on the *charlotte de cupuaçu*—lady fingers soaked in *cupuaçu* fruit mousse and slathered in chocolate sauce.

Rua Fidalga 340, Vila Madalena. ℂ 011/3812-7815. Reservations recommended. Dinner R$26–R$40 (US$13–US$20/£7–£11). AE, DC, MC, V. Mon 8pm–midnight; Tues–Thurs noon–3pm and 8pm–1am; Fri–Sat noon–4pm and 8pm–2am; Sun noon–5pm. Metrô: Vila Madalena.

SÃO PAULO AFTER DARK

Most Paulistas won't even set foot in a club until midnight. Most places will stay open until at least 4am, and on weekends as late (or early) as 6am. For those looking to catch the big names in popular Brazilian music, São Paulo gets more of the stars, performing more often, than any other city in Brazil.

THE PERFORMING ARTS

São Paulo's classical music scene is excellent, and the theater scene is positively thriving. The vast majority of high-culture performances take place at just two halls: the **Theatro Municipal,** Praça Ramos de Azevedo s/n (ℂ 011/3223-8698), and the **Sala São Paulo,** Praça Julio Prestes s/n (ℂ 011/3337-5414).

MUSIC & DANCE CLUBS

Many bars and clubs charge a drink minimum instead of, or sometimes in addition to, a cover charge. Patrons receive a little card or slip of paper upon arrival. All your expenses are recorded on the card and tallied up when you leave. Lose the card and you get charged a ridiculously steep fee.

LIVE MUSIC   Exclusively dedicated to Brazilian music, **Tom Brasil,** Rua Olimpiadas 66, Vila Olimpia (ℂ 011/3044-5665), was recently voted as best MPB venue in São Paulo. In the land of samba, *forró,* and *axé,* **Bourbon Street,** Rua dos Chanes 127, Moema (ℂ 011/5561-1643), also puts some blues and jazz on the menu. **Grazie a Dio!,** Rua Girassol 67, Vila Madalena (ℂ 011/3031-6568), is also one of the few places where you see some live music every day of the week. Bands vary from night to night. Expect anything from pop to samba-rock to salsa or merengue.

DANCE CLUBS   Even in the land of Samba, Latin rhythms are stealing the show. **Azucar,** Rua Mario Feraz 423, Itaim Bibi (ℂ 011/3078-3130), the latest hit on São Paulo's club scene, plays lots of salsa, merengue, and other Latin beats to get the crowd going. **D-Edge,** Alameda Olga 170, Barra Funda (✆ **011/3667-8334**), is São Paulo's newest, hottest dance club and features wall-long flashing monster woofers, Saturday Night Fever flashing disco floor and some of the hottest heaviest funk beats this side of Birmingham. **Love Club,** Rua Pequetita 189, Vila Olimpia (✆ **011/3044-1613**), offers a lotta love indeed for lovers of electronic music. Brazilian and international celebrity DJs make regular appearances here and spin techno and house.

BARS & PUBS

LOUNGES   Located on the 41st and 42nd floors of the Edificio Italia, **Terraço Italia,** Av. Ipiranga 344, Centro (✆ **011/3257-6566**), provides a prime view of São Paulo. Time your arrival just before sunset so you can see the city lights come on over the rim of your evening cocktail. São Paulo's most upscale club, **Lotus,** Av. Nações Unidas 12551, second floor of the São Paulo World Trade Center (✆ **011/3043-7130**), is a modern and sleek lap of luxury geared to attract the city's high rollers. The rich and beautiful have been flocking here en masse, so take advantage of the exchange rate and your exotic foreign accent and head on down. The *lounge du jour,* **Skye,** Av. Brigadeiro Luis Antonio 4700, Jardim Paulista (✆ **011/3055-4702**), is on the top floor of the Hotel Unique. A DJ plays great background music (not quite dance club loud) and the party extends to the pool deck. The view of the Avenida Paulista skyscrapers is quite something and best observed while sipping a sweet martini.

BARS   Voted best singles bar in the city, **Tipuana,** Rua Fiandeiras 555, Vila Olimpia (✆ **011/3848-9067**), is the place for a close encounter with those Paulistas. In the evening, DJs spice up the beat. Also in Vila Olimpia, **MonteCristo** (Rua Jesuino Cardoso 194, corner of Atilio Innocenti; ✆ **011/3846-7483**), doesn't charge a cover, and as a result is often packed with patrons spilling out onto the sidewalks. Farther down at Atilio Innocenti 780 is the **Buena Vista Club** (✆ **012/3045-5245**). Despite the Cuban-sounding name, the music is mostly Brazilian from Wednesday to Saturday. **Bar Favela,** Prof. Atilio Innocenti 419 (✆ **011/3848-6988**), is anything but downscale. This hip bar attracts a happening crowd that come to see and be seen. Over in Vila Madalena, **Bossa Nueva,** Rua Wisard 138 (✆ **011/3814-4164**), offers a pleasant casual atmosphere, with small tables downstairs awash in mellow music. Just a few blocks over, **Fidel,** Rua Girassol 398 (✆ **011/3812-4225**), is an intimate bar decorated with black-and-white photos of the revolution and lots of cigar paraphernalia. The music is a blend of Latin, bossa nova, and Brazilian.

GAY & LESBIAN NIGHTLIFE

A little low-key bar in Jardins, the **Director's Gourmet,** Rua Alameda Franca 1552, Cerqueira Cesar (✆ **011/3064-7958**) attracts a mellow crowd of mostly men. A DJ spins some tunes to add to the atmosphere, but this is by no means a dance club. **Lust Club,** Av. Nove de Julho 225, Centro (✆ **011/3167-6664**), is definitely for those who prefer large clubs. Brand new in 2005, this huge club has a capacity of 3,000 people and plays some of the best techno in town. Although the house is gay-friendly at all times, the night to see and be seen is Saturday. On the ground floor of a commercial building, the **Vermont Itaim,** Rua Pedroso Alvarenga 1192, Itaim Bibi (✆ **011/3071-1320**), is one of the relatively few GLS bars outside the Jardins. There's live music most nights—MPB on Wednesdays, danceable pop Thursday though Saturdays. The boys predominate through the week and on Saturday, but Sundays the girls take over with a nine-woman samba band.

6 Brasília

1,140km (707 miles) NW of Rio de Janeiro, 1,015km (629 miles) N of São Paulo, 1,415km (877 miles) SW of Salvador

There are other planned cities in the world—Washington, D.C., Chandigarh, Canberra—but none have the daring and sheer vision of Brasília. In the 1950s, a country that had shucked off a failed monarchy, a corrupt republic, and a police-state dictatorship decided to make a clean break from the past by creating a brand-new space for politics. The style they chose was Modernism. Brazil was blessed with some of the foremost practitioners in the world. The city plan was done by Lucio Costa. The buildings were designed by Oscar Niemeyer.

The site, on Brazil's high interior plateau, was nothing but *cerrado*—short scrubby forest, stretching thousands of miles in every direction. It was nearly 400 miles from the nearest paved road, over 75 miles from the nearest railroad, 120 miles from the nearest airport.

Groundbreaking began in 1957 and by April 21, 1960, there was enough of a city for a grand inauguration. In place of a grid, there were but two great intersecting streets, one straight, one curved. Viewed from on high, the city looked bold and monumental—like an airplane in flight, or an arrow shooting forward into the future.

Over the years, Brasília has been a source of controversy. Urbanists were beginning to doubt the rationality of rationalist Modern planning. Cities, it was being discovered, were vital, growing, entities, whose true complexity could perhaps never be encompassed in a single master plan. For visitors, the attractions here are purely architectural. Brazil's best designers, architects, and artists were commissioned to create the monuments and buildings and make them beautiful. A visit to Brasília is a chance to see and judge their success.

ESSENTIALS
GETTING THERE

Brasília's **Aeroporto Internacional** (© **061/3364-9000**) is located about 10km (6 miles) west of the Eixo Monumental. **TAM, Varig,** and **Gol** fly here from Rio and São Paulo. Taxis from the airport to the hotel zones cost about R$35 (US$18/£9.50). Long-distance buses arrive at Brasília's bus station at the far western point of the Eixo Monumental (© **061/3363-2281**). A taxi ride from the station costs approximately R$20 (US$10/£5.40) to the main hotel section.

ORIENTATION

What makes Brasília unique besides its architecture is its layout. The city consists of two main axes: The Eixo Monumental runs dead straight from east to west, and the Eixo Rodoviário runs from north to south, curving as it goes. Seen from above, the city resembles an airplane or an arrow notched into a partially bent bow. Where the two axes intersect is the city's central bus station, the Rodoviária.

All the city's residential areas are in one of the two perfectly symmetrical wings, the *Asa Norte* or *N* (north wing) and the *Asa Sul* or *S* (south wing), on the Eixo Rodoviário. All of the city's important government buildings are located on the eastern end of the Eixo Monumental. All of the city's hotels are located in two hotel districts near the Rodoviária. All the city's offices, shopping malls, theaters, and hospitals are all located in their own little designated clusters.

Brasília

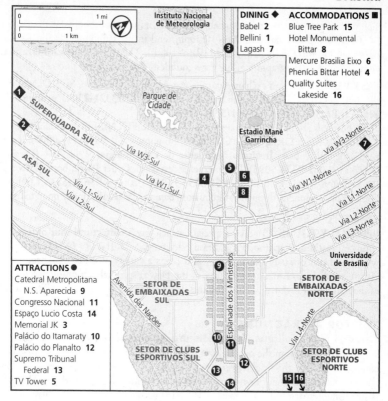

DINING ◆
Babel **2**
Bellini **1**
Lagash **7**

ACCOMMODATIONS ■
Blue Tree Park **15**
Hotel Monumental
 Bittar **8**
Mercure Brasília Eixo **6**
Phenícia Bittar Hotel **4**
Quality Suites
 Lakeside **16**

ATTRACTIONS ●
Catedral Metropolitana
 N.S. Aparecida **9**
Congresso Nacional **11**
Espaço Lucio Costa **14**
Memorial JK **3**
Palácio do Itamaraty **10**
Palácio do Planalto **12**
Supremo Tribunal
 Federal **13**
TV Tower **5**

GETTING AROUND

All city buses go through the Rodoviária, where the Eixo Monumental and Eixo Rodoviário intersect. It's also where you transfer from an east-west bus to a north-south one. Most of the city's attractions, malls, and hotels are within walking distance of the Rodoviária.

BY BUS Buses run from the tip of the south wing to the tip of the north wing, along roads W1 and W3 on the west side of the Eixo Rodoviário and on roads L1 and L3 on the east side of the Eixo Rodoviário. To travel across town, all you need to do is catch a bus traveling to the opposite part of the city; for example, from Asa Sul, catch a bus that says Asa Norte, or vice versa.

On the Eixo Monumental, you can catch buses labeled PLANO PILOTO CIRCULAR, which circle up and down this main boulevard. Many buses will go via the Rodoviária, which is right in the center of town. These will get you pretty close to the main monuments, hotels, and malls along the Eixo Monumental. Bus tickets are R$1.80 (US90¢/ 50p).

BY TAXI Taxis are plentiful. From the center of town to the tip of the Asa Sul costs approximately R$25 (US$13/£7). To contact a taxi, call **Brasília** (© **061/3344-1000**) or **Rádio Táxi** (© **061/3325-3030**).

VISITOR INFORMATION

The official government tourist agency **Setur** has information booths at the airport (© **061/3033-9488;** daily 7:30am–10:30pm) and in the Conjunto Nacional shopping mall (© **061/3326-7387;** daily 10am–10pm). The website **www.infobrasilia. com.br** has short biographies of the city's founders, and some great photos.

FAST FACTS   You can exchange currency at **Air Brazil Turismo,** SHS Quadra 01, Bloco A, Loja 33/4, Gallery of the National Hotel (© **061/3321-2304**), or **Banco do Brasil** at Brasília Airport (© **061/3365-1183**).

All hospitals are in the Hospital section (SHLS and SHLN). For medical attention, try **Hospital Santa Lucia,** SHLS, Quadra 76, Conjunto C (© **061/3445-0000**). If you need a dentist, contact **Instituto Brasiliense de Odontologia,** SQLS 406, Bloco A, Loja 35 (© **061/3244-5095**). For Internet access check **Cyber Point,** bottom floor of the Conjunto Nacional mall (© **061/3036-1495**); charging R$6 (US$3/£1.60) per hour, it's open Monday through Saturday from 8am to 10pm and Sunday noon to 6pm.

WHAT TO SEE & DO

SPECIALTY TOURS   To take a specialized half-day **architectural tour** of the city, contact **Prestheza Turismo,** Patio Brasil Shopping, Sala 917 (© **061/3226-6224;** www.prestheza.com.br). The company also offers a variety of other tours, such as a visit to the Vale do Amanhecer (Valley of the Dawn) spiritual community or to one of the national or regional parks in the area. Half day tours start at R$80 (US$40/£22) per person.

THE TOP ATTRACTIONS

Catedral Metropolitana Nossa Senhora Aparecida ✦✦✦   The cathedral is surprisingly small from the outside, but once you descend through the walkway, you emerge in perhaps the brightest and most spacious church you have ever seen. The floors and walls are made of white marble, with an expanse of glass overhead. The altar is surprisingly sparse, all white marble decorated with a plain image of Christ on the cross. Sculptor Alfredo Ceschiatti designed the statues of the four apostles in front of the cathedral, as well as the angels suspended from the ceiling inside. You'll spot his name on other sculptures around Brasília, such as the figure of Justice in front of the Federal Supreme Court.

Esplanada dos Ministerios. © 061/3224-4073. Daily 8am–5pm. Mass Mon–Fri 6:15pm; Tues–Fri 12:15pm; Sat 5pm; Sun 8:30am, 10:30am, and 6pm. No touring of the cathedral during Mass. No shorts of any kind. Bus: Rodoviaria (short walk to the cathedral) or the Plano Piloto Circular.

Memorial JK ✦   This remarkably shaped monument was built in 1980 by Niemeyer to honor the founder of Brasília, Juscelino Kubitschek. Inside on the second floor, the former president's remains rest beneath a skylight in a granite tomb, his only epitaph an inscription on the coffin reading O FUNDADOR. Aside from this slightly spooky scene, the memorial contains a lot of JK's junk that no one could ever care about (JK's ribbons and medals, JK's suits and tie clips) and, upstairs, some fairly interesting stuff about Brasília, including photographs of the city under construction and copies of the designs that didn't get chosen.

Eixo Monumental Oeste. © 061/3225-9451. Admission R$4 (US$2/£1). Tues–Sun 9am–6pm. Bus: Plano Piloto Circular.

Palácio do Itamaraty ✦✦✦   One of the most beautiful Modernist structures ever created (designed by Niemeyer with landscaping by Burle Marx and detailing by

Milton Ramos), the Palácio do Itamaraty now serves as a ceremonial reception hall for the Department of Foreign Affairs. The interior is a match for the outside, so it's worth taking the tour. The ultramodern structure—mostly open space inside—is decorated with rich antique furnishings of Persian carpets, hand-carved jacaranda-wood furniture, and 18th- and 19th-century paintings. Somehow it really works.

Esplanada dos Ministerios. (☎ 061/3411-8051. Free admission. Mon–Fri 2–4:30pm; Sat–Sun 10am–3:30pm. Guided tours only, call to confirm; no shorts or tank tops allowed. Bus: Plano Piloto Circular.

TV Tower ★★★ *Value*   The best view in town and it's free! Just take the elevator up to the 72m-high (236-ft.) lookout, and Brasília is laid out at your feet. You'll get the best perspective of the Eixo Monumental with the ministry buildings lining the boulevard like dominos waiting to be knocked over. If Brasília has one of its fiery red sunsets, it's worth heading back to the tower to take in the view. You can skip the gem museum without qualms.

Eixo Monumental (close to the bus station and malls). (☎ 061/3321-7944. Free admission. Tues–Sun 9am–6pm; Mon 2–6pm. Bus: Rodoviaria.

ARCHITECTURAL HIGHLIGHTS

The important buildings in Brasília were all designed by architect Oscar Niemeyer. The strength of this Brazilian ubermodernist has always been form; his structures are often brilliant. His weaknesses have always been detailing, materials, and landscaping. Fortunately, Niemeyer was teamed up with Brazil's best landscape designer, Roberto Burle Marx; detailing and materials-focused architects such as Milton Ramos; and talented sculptors and artists such as Alfredo Ceschiatti. Every building also had to conform to the overall plan of Lucio Costa. The result is a collection of buildings that has rightly been called the highest expression of architectural modernism on earth. Niemeyer's works are scattered far and wide throughout the city, but the best of the best are on the eastern portion of the Eixo Monumental, from the Rodoviário to the Praça dos Tres Poderes on the far side of the Congresso Nacional. To take a specialized architectural tour of the city, contact **Bluepoint,** SEPN, Q. 509, Third Floor (☎ **061/3274-0033;** www.bluepoint.com.br).

PRAÇA DOS TRES PODERES

Behind the Congress building, the Praça dos Tres Poderes is immediately identifiable by the huge Brazilian flag flapping 99m (330 ft.) above the wide, hot, open space below. The plaza is named for the three branches of government that surround it: the judiciary branch in the **Supremo Tribunal Federal,** the executive branch in the presidential **Palácio do Planalto,** and the legislative branch in the **Congresso Nacional.** The last one is Brasília's best-known photo image: the shot of the two towers on the Planalto, flanked by the two "bowls," one face up and one face down. It is quite beautiful in an abstract way, contrasting with the red dirt and blue sky. A must for Brazilian visitors, but of marginal interest to foreigners, the Congresso Nacional is open to the public for guided tours or a short visit; no shorts or tank tops allowed. The *praça* itself is pure Niemeyer, a vast expanse of pure white stone, with nowhere to hide from the blazing Brasília sun. Don't visit on a hot afternoon—you'll fry. Near the front of the square, there's a long, white marble box about the size and shape of a semitrailer, but cantilevered one floor off the ground. This is the **Museu de Cidade,** open Tuesday through Sunday from 9am to 6pm. Inside, it's a bare marble room with eight inscriptions on each long wall telling the story of Brasília. No maps, no photos, just words. However, it is cool, and they provide a pamphlet with English translations.

Next to it, sunk below the square, is the **Espaço Lucio Costa.** Brasília owes its shape and design to Lucio Costa, an urban planner and architect. This space contains a full-scale model of the city, but it has very little on Costa's life and career. On the back wall, there are some photos of the city under construction and, best of all, reproduced and enlarged photostats of Costa's original submission.

SHOPPING

There are two big shopping areas on either side of the bus station, one in the Setor Commercial Norte (SCN), and the other in the Setor Commercial Sul (SCS). In the residential parts of town, the main streets inside the Super Quadras also have some shops, but these are geared more to the daily needs of neighborhood residents and are not interesting for browsing. Built in 1971, the **Conjunto Nacional,** Asa Norte, SCN (© 061/3316-9733), was the first mall in Brasília. Stores include two large drugstores, the Pão de Açúcar supermarket, and a post office (Mon–Sat 9am–10pm). The large Siciliano bookstore has a CD department, Internet access, and a good variety of English magazines. Just past the Setor Hoteleiro Norte (North Hotel Sector), **Brasília Shopping,** Asa Norte, SCN QD 5, Lote 2 (© **061/3328-5259**), has a number of movie theaters and trendy clothing boutiques as well as a very popular bar, Frei Caneca (p. 297). **Feira de Artesanato da Torre de Televisão,** a large crafts fair, takes place every weekend underneath the TV Tower. Many of the stalls sell crafts from the Northeast and the interior made from leather, semiprecious stones, dried flowers, and ceramics. It's open Saturday and Sunday from 8am to 6pm.

WHERE TO STAY

All hotels are located in either the two hotel sections close to the monuments or at the lakeside just outside the monument area. The two sections close to the monuments are the SHN (Setor Hoteleiro Norte) and the SHS (Setor Hoteleiro Sul). Both areas are within a 5-minute walk of each other and of the city's two shopping sectors. Most hotel guests in Brasília are politicians and businesspeople in town for meetings and government business on weekdays; on weekends, beds are mostly empty, allowing visitors to get great deals. *Note:* Many monuments are open Saturday and Sunday and closed on Monday. The exception to the Hotel Sector rule are these two hotels situated on the shores of the lovely man-made lake surrounding the city.

LAKESIDE
Expensive
Blue Tree Park ⭐⭐⭐   The Blue Tree Park sits at the edge of the artificial lake created to surround the city. You're a 15-minute taxi ride from the sights and the ministry buildings, which can make it a bit inconvenient if you have meetings to attend, but the pool deck and lake views make it worthwhile if you have leisure time to spend. Rooms feature sophisticated modern decor, with firm queen beds and top-quality linen, plus good-size work desk with an adjustable/reclinable desk chair. Even better are the amenities—the pool deck overlooking the lake, the tennis courts, spa, sauna, and exercise room. The hotel restaurant, **Herbs,** features funky "Jetsons" furnishings and innovative cuisine.

Setor de Hoteis e Turismo Norte, Trecho 1, Lt. 1-B, Bl. C (Lago Norte), Brasília, 70800-200 DF. © 0800/150-500 or 061/3424-7000. Fax 061/3424-7001. www.bluetree.com.br. 394 units. R$320 (US$160/£86) standard double; R$375 (US$188/£101) superior double. Off-season rates 40% discount. AE, DC, MC, V. Free parking. **Amenities:** Restaurants; bar; outdoor pool; tennis courts; gym; spa; sauna; concierge; tour desk; car rental; business center; salon; room service; massage; laundry service; nonsmoking rooms. *In room:* A/C, TV, dataport, minibar, fridge, hair dryer, safe.

Moderate

Quality Suites Lakeside ⚸⚸ *Value* Of Brasília's two lakeside hotels, the Quality is undoubtedly the better value. Like the Blue Tree, the Quality nestles by the shores of a man-made lake, but the Quality makes even better use of its location, including not just a lakeside pool deck, but a marina where you can rent boats and jet skis. There are also tennis courts and a soccer field, and a good-quality gym. Rooms are comfortable but not luxurious, featuring a firm queen bed plus good-size desk with its own desk lamps, and clean and functional bathrooms.

Setor de Hoteis e Turismo Norte, Trecho 1, Lt. 1-B, Bl. C (Lago Norte), Brasília, 70800-200 DF. ✆ **061/3035-1100.** Fax 0613035-2144. www.atlanticahotels.com.br. 177 units. R$185 (US$93/£50) standard double; R$230 (US$115/£62) superior double. Off-season 20% discount. AE, DC, MC, V. Free parking. **Amenities:** 2 restaurants; bar; outdoor pool; tennis courts; gym; spa; sauna; marina w/boat and jet ski rental; concierge; tour desk; car rental; business center; salon; room service; massage; laundry service; nonsmoking rooms. *In room:* A/C, TV, dataport, safe, minibar, fridge, hair dryer.

SETOR HOTELEIRO SUL
Expensive

Mercure Brasília Eixo ⚸⚸⚸ This 5-year old hotel offers comfortable and pleasant accommodation in the heart of the hotel sector. The decorations are modern and bright and the spacious rooms feature a king-size bed, kitchen, 29-inch TV and views of the city. The hotel also offers a swimming pool and sauna. Time your visit during Saturday and Sunday, and the rate drops by more than 50% and includes breakfast. On weekdays, there is an additional charge of R$18 (US$9/£5) per person for breakfast.

SHN, Q. 5, Bl. G, Brasília, 70710-300 DF. ✆ **061/3424-2000.** Fax 061/3424-2001. www.mercure.com.br. 358 units. Superior double R$380 (US$190/£103); deluxe double R$400 (US$200/£108). Sat–Sun and off-season superior double R$130 (US$65/£35); deluxe double R$170 (US$85/£46). AE, DC, MC, V. Free parking. **Amenities:** 2 restaurants; bar; pool; sauna; concierge; tour desk; business center; limited room service; laundry service; dry cleaning; nonsmoking rooms. *In room:* A/C, TV, dataport, kitchen, minibar, fridge, hair dryer.

Moderate

Hotel Phenicia Bittar ⚸ One of the smaller hotels in the Setor Sul, the Phenicia recently renovated its floors and rooms as part of a transformation into a boutique hotel. The renovated rooms have either lovely hardwood floors or new carpets, double or twin beds, light-wood furniture, a sitting area, and brand-new beds. The renovated suites are particularly nice. They feature a living room with a dining table, large desk, and a spacious bedroom with a second desk, furnished with stylish furniture. A third bed can easily be added for those with children.

SHS, Q. 5, Bl. J, Brasília, DF 70322-810. ✆ **0800/707-5858** or 061/3321-4342. Fax 061/3225-1406. www.hoteisbittar.com.br. 130 units (showers only). R$165 (US$83/£45) double. Discount 30% Sat–Sun and off-season. AE, DC, MC, V. Free parking. **Amenities:** Restaurant; tour desk; car rental.

SETOR HOTELEIRO NORTE
Moderate

Hotel Monumental Bittar ⚸ The low-rise Monumental looks unassuming, but it's actually a pleasant, moderately priced hotel. A recent spruce-up by the Bittar chain has meant new bedding and drapery. Rooms have either wall-to-wall carpeting or wood floors. The latter is far more comfortable. Rooms with double beds are better than those with two twins; they have larger desks and closets and are larger overall. Avoid the east-facing ones which face the main street. A few rooms are adapted for travelers with disabilities.

SHN, Q. 3, Bl. B, Brasília, 70710-300 DF. ℭ 0800/707-5858 or 061/3328-4144. www.hoteisbittar.com.br. 111 units (showers only). R$140 (US$70/£38) double; R$100 (US$50/£27) Sat–Sun and off-season. R$30 (US$15/£8) extra person. AE, DC, MC, V. Free parking. **Amenities:** Restaurant; bar; tour desk; car rental; business center; salon; room service; laundry service; dry cleaning; nonsmoking rooms. *In room:* A/C, TV, dataport, minibar, fridge.

WHERE TO DINE

Brasília has some outstanding restaurants; politicians and businesspeople like to eat well. The restaurants are more sophisticated than they are elsewhere in Brazil.

EXPENSIVE

Babel ✦ FUSION   Fusion has finally found its way to Brasília. Babel mixes ingredients from eastern and western schools of cooking to intriguing and delicious effect. Think duck filet with shitake couscous, or lightly breaded shrimp in tamarind sauce with red-pepper risotto. The wine list features selections from Argentina, Australia, and California.

SCLS 215, Bl. A, Loja 37. ℭ 061/3345-6042. Main courses R$25–R$60 (US$13–US$30/£7–£16). MC, V. Mon–Sat 7–11:30pm. Bus: W3 Asa Sul.

Belini ✦ *Finds* ITALIAN   This gourmet complex encompasses a deli, food store, restaurant, cafe, and cooking school. It's a great place to grab an espresso and some sweets, or buy some fresh bread and cold cuts for an impromptu picnic. The casual outdoor patio serves sandwiches (the pastrami, mortadella, and brie is good) for R$6 to R$10 (US$3–US$5/£1.60–£2.70). For a more formal occasion, the restaurant upstairs serves fine Italian dishes such as lamb filet with mint sauce and risotto, or large prawns in an apple-and-ginger sauce. The restaurants also serves breakfast and afternoon tea.

SCLS 113, Bl. D, Loja 36. ℭ 061/3345-0777. www.belini-gastronomia.com.br. Main courses R$9–R$40 (US$4.50–US$20/£2.50–£11). MC, V. Restaurant Tue–Sat noon–3pm and 7pm–midnight; Sun noon–4pm. Bakery daily 7am–11pm. Bus: W3 Asa Sul.

Lagash ✦✦ MIDDLE EASTERN   The best Middle Eastern food in Brasília. (Okay, there's not a lot of competition, but the quality here is excellent.) Appetizers include baba ghanouj, made with eggplant and tahini; hummus; or roasted *merguez* (lamb sausage). The most popular entree is the Moroccan lamb—tender pieces of boneless lamb cooked with nuts, scallions, onions, and rice. The wine list is heavy on the Italian and French reds to accompany the hearty and spicy dishes.

SCLN 308, Bl. B, Loja 11. ℭ 061/3273-0098. R$20–R$60 (US$10–US$30/£5.40–£16). AE, DC, MC, V. Mon–Sat noon–4pm and 7pm–midnight; Sun noon–6pm. Bus: W3 Asa Norte.

ELSEWHERE

Alice ✦✦✦ FRENCH   Alice serves her meals in a lovely large room bedecked with mirrors with a view out into the garden of this private home in Brasília's swank mansion district. Chefs in the open kitchen prepare regional French cuisine, with dishes such as boar with red-wine sauce, or free-range chicken with spices and couscous. Wine list features some fine French vintages, as well as the usual suspects from Argentina and Chile. Note that there is no sign outside. Make sure your taxi driver knows where he is going before you set out.

SHI Norte Ql. 11, Cj. 9 Casa 17 (Lago Norte). ℭ 061/3368-1099. Reservations required. Main courses R$25–R$60 (US$13–US$30/£6.75–£16). AE, D, MC, V. Fri–Sat 8pm–2am. No public transit.

Patu Anu ✦✦✦ BRAZILIAN   The ultimate experience in Brazilian dining. Located opposite the presidential palace (Palacío de Alvarado) but on the far side of the lake, the restaurant features an outdoor deck with stunning views and a sumptuous indoor dining room. Chefs here take traditional local ingredients and traditional Brazilian recipes, and tweak them slightly to bring them up to the level of haute cuisine. Appetizers include delicacies such as skewers of capybara, boar, lamb, and baby buffalo with a spicy chocolate sauce, while mains include fresh sole roasted in banana leaf with mango chutney and coconut-milk rice, or prawns flambéed in ginger liqueur with fresh fruit risotto.

Setor de Mansões de Lago Norte, Trecho 12, Cj. 1 Casa 7 (Lago Sul). © 061/3369-2788. www.patuanu.com.br. Reservations required. Main courses R$38–R$65 (US$19–US$33/£10–£18). D, MC, V. Tues–Sat 8:30pm–2am; Sun 1:30pm–6pm. No public transit.

BRASILIA AFTER DARK

Designed by Oscar Niemeyer, the **Teatro Nacional,** Setor Cultural Norte (© **061/ 3325-6240**), resembles the dark base of a pyramid. However, the dark reflective glass conceals a bright interior lobby with landscaping by Burle Marx. Most classical concerts, dance, and theater performances in Brasília take place here. For program information, stop by the box office, which is open daily from noon to 8pm.

The **Armazém do Bras,** CLN 107, Bloco B, Loja 49, Asa Norte (© **061/3340-7317**), has a great patio and gets quite hopping at night. The antipasto buffet (available Sat–Wed only) allows you to load up on your favorite selection of goodies (R$36/US$18/£10 per kilo). The beer list offers an unusual variety of imported beers. **Frei Caneca,** Brasília Shopping, SCN (© **061/3327-9467**), is a popular hangout for the 28- to 40-year-old crowd. The club has a large spacious covered patio, dance floor, and bar. In the mood for a nice cold beer and a lively crowd? Head to **Bar Brasília,** 506 Sul, Bl. A, Loja 15 (© **061/3443-4323**). The bar is inspired on the classic Rio botiquim and decorated with lovely antique wooden furnishings that predate all of the buildings that surround this bar. For a mellow night out away from the teenage crowds, check out **Othello Piano Bar,** CLN 107, Bl. D, Loja 25 (© **061/3272-2066**). This is the place to come for some MPB, samba, or *choro.*

7 Salvador

1,726km (1,070 miles) NE of Rio de Janeiro, 2,052km (1,272 miles) NE of São Paulo

Salvador is an easy place to enjoy. The sun shines almost year-round, and beneath the surface beauty of beaches and the island-studded Baía de Todos os Santos (Bay of All Saints), there's a deep and powerful culture that bubbles up in things such as the rich cuisine and the infectious rhythms of Bahian music.

Discovered by Italian navigator Amerigo Vespucci—the first European to set eyes on the Baía de Todos os Santos—the wealth of the new colony was not in silver or gold, but something almost as lucrative: sugar. Sugar cane thrived in the heat and rich soil of the Northeast. As plantations grew the Portuguese planters found themselves starved for labor, and so plunged headfirst into the slave trade. By the mid–19th century, close to five million slaves had been taken from Africa to Brazil.

The wealth earned by that trade is evident in the grand mansions and golden churches in Pelourinho. The legacy of the slave trade is also reflected in the population. Modern Salvador is a city of two million, and approximately 80% of its people are of Afro-Brazilian descent.

This heritage has had an enormous influence on Salvador's culture, food, religion, and especially its music. The last 20 years has seen the resurrection of Salvador's

Pelourinho neighborhood. Derelict until as recently as the '80s, Pelourinho has been painstakingly brought back to its former glory.

Beyond Salvador, a trip to Bahia is a chance to stock up on two of Brazil's greatest nonexportable products—sand and sunshine. Beaches come blessed by sunshine, lapped by a warm southern ocean, and infused with a laid-back spirit that is uniquely Bahian.

And then there's Carnaval. With over a million people out dancing through the city's streets, Salvador may soon claim to hold the biggest street party in the world.

ESSENTIALS
GETTING THERE
BY PLANE   Salvador's international airport, **Aeroporto Deputado Luis Eduardo Magalhães** (© 071/3204-1010), is 32km (20 miles) from downtown. The airport is serviced by **Varig, TAM,** and **Gol.** To reach your hotel, **Coometas** taxi (© 071/3244-4500) offers prepaid fares: The trip to **Pelourinho** costs R$75 (US$38/£20), to **Ondina** R$65 (US$33/£18), and to the northern beaches (such as **Itapuã**), R$35 (US$18/£9.50). Regular taxis are cheaper; on the meter a taxi from the airport to Pelourinho costs around R$60 (US$30/£16). If you do not have too much luggage, an inexpensive bus runs along the coast from the airport to Pelourinho; its final stop is Praça da Sé on the edge of Pelourinho. The bus runs daily from 7am to 8pm and costs R$6 (US$3/£1.60)

BY BUS   Buses arrive at the **Terminal Rodoviária de Salvador Armando Viana de Castro,** Av. Antonio Carlos Magalhães 4362, Pituba (© 071/3460-8300). Regular city buses to Pelourinho are marked PRAÇA DA SE. For the coast, look for buses marked VIA ORLA or with the destinations of the specific neighborhoods such as Ondina. Ticket prices range from R$1.80 (US90¢/50p), for a regular city bus, to R$4 to R$6 (US$2–US$3/£1–£1.60), for an air-conditioned express bus.

GETTING AROUND
Pelourinho, the historic old downtown, sits on a cliff overlooking the Bay of All Saints. This area is also sometimes called the Cidade Alta (the upper city). At the foot of the cliff lies **Comércio,** a modern area of commercial office towers. This area is also sometimes known as the Cidade Baixa (the lower city). The upper and lower cities are connected via a cliffside elevator, the Lacerda. Except to visit a large crafts market called the Mercado Modelo, there's little reason to visit Comércio.

The **Avenida Sete de Setembro** starts on the southern edge of Pelourinho. At its beginning, Avenida Sete de Setembro has many small shops. A little farther south, as it enters **Vitória,** it becomes more residential. Below that, the street drops down to the coast and continues by the ocean until it reaches the area around the lighthouse, or Farol de Barra. Known as **Barra,** this neighborhood has a number of good restaurants and hotels.

As it rounds the point, Avenida Sete de Setembro becomes **Avenida Oceanica** (also called Av. Presidente Vargas) and continues past a number of good hotels in the oceanside neighborhood of **Ondina.** From here out, neighborhoods (and road name changes) come thick and fast: **Vermelho, Amaralina, Pituba, Pituaçu, Piatã, Itapuã,** all the way to **Stella Maris** adjacent to the airport. There are pleasant beaches all along this stretch.

BY FOOT   Pelourinho is a stroller's dream; the narrow streets and cobblestone alleys open onto large squares with baroque churches. The lower part of the city, Cidade Baixa around the Mercado Modelo, is less safe at night.

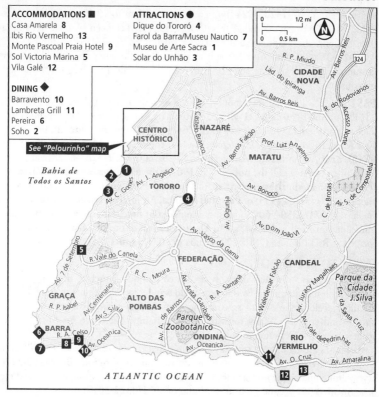

Salvador

ACCOMMODATIONS ■
Casa Amarela **8**
Ibis Rio Vermelho **13**
Monte Pascoal Praia Hotel **9**
Sol Victoria Marina **5**
Vila Galé **12**

ATTRACTIONS ●
Dique do Tororó **4**
Farol da Barra/Museu Nautico **7**
Museu de Arte Sacra **1**
Solar do Unhão **3**

DINING ◆
Barravento **10**
Lambreta Grill **11**
Pereira **6**
Soho **2**

BY BUS   Buses are marked by name instead of number; the main buses for travelers going from any of the beach neighborhoods to downtown are marked PRAÇA DA SE for Pelourinho or COMERCIO for the lower city. To travel to the city's main bus station, take a bus marked IGUATEMI. When going from downtown to the beaches, take a bus marked VIA ORLA and make sure that the bus's final destination lies beyond the beach neighborhood you want to reach. Along the coast, you have the option of taking a regular bus for R$1.80 (US90¢/50p) or an air-conditioned bus, called a *frescão* (fresh one) for R$4 to R$6 (US$2–US$3/£1–£1.60).

BY TAXI   For a radio taxi, contact **Teletaxi** (© 071/3341-9988) or **LigueTaxi** (© 071/3357-7777). You usually pay a surcharge of R$3 to R$5 (US$1.50–US$2.50/80p–£1.35), but these taxis have air-conditioning and can be ordered ahead of time.

VISITOR INFORMATION
Bahiatursa, the state's tourist information service, has booths and kiosks throughout the city. The staff is friendly, although as of press time they had no useful brochures and pamphlets because the new state government was going to redo all of the materials. However, they should be able to help you with general information. There are Bahiatursa booths at the following locations: **Salvador International Airport** in the

arrivals hall (℃ **071/3204-1244**), open daily from 7am to 10:30pm; **Mercado Modelo,** Praça Cayru 250, Cidade Baixa (℃ **071/3241-0242**), open Monday to Saturday 9am to 6pm; and **Pelourinho,** Rua das Laranjeiras 12 (℃ **071/3321-2463** or 071/ 3321-2133), open daily from 8:30am to 10pm. Both the city of Salvador site (www. emtursa.ba.gov.br) and the state of Bahia site (www.bahiatursa.ba.gov.br) are quite informative.

FAST FACTS   To exchange money, go to **Banco do Brasil** at Praça Padre Anchieta 11, Pelourinho (℃ **071/3321-9334**), or Rua Miguel Bournier 4, Barra Avenida, parallel to the Avenida Oceanica (℃ **071/3264-5099**). There are **Citibank** branches at Rua Miguel Calmon 555, Comércio, close to the Mercado Modelo (℃ **071/3241-4745**), or at Av. Almirante Marques Leão 71, Barra (℃ **071/3264-6728**).

In an emergency, call the **police** at ℃ **190,** or the **fire brigade** or an **ambulance** at ℃ **193.** For **medical attention,** go to **Hospital Portugues,** Av. Princesa Isabel 2, Barra (℃ **071/3203-5555**) or **Hospital Aliança,** Av. Juracy Magalhães 2096, Rio Vermelho (℃ **071/3350-5600**). You can also ask your hotel for a referral to the nearest clinic. If you need a **dentist,** go to **Dentist Prontodonto,** a 24-hour dental clinic located at Rua Piauí 143, Sala 202, Pituba (℃ **071/3240-1784**).

WHAT TO SEE & DO

Pelourinho boasts a wealth of richly decorated baroque churches, tiny squares, and fine old colonial mansions. By day, you could wander its cobblestone streets for hours. At night, Pelourinho's small squares and larger *praças* come alive with bands and singers and concerts. Many tourists attend, certainly, but so do an equal or even greater number of Salvadorans.

Salvador's attractions are so easily accessible that it's not really necessary to take an organized city tour, but if you want to do so, contact **Tatur** (℃ **071/3450-7216;** www.tatur.com.br); for Pelourinho, you can book a tour guide through **Singtur,** Praça Jose Anchieta 12, Second Floor, Pelourinho (℃ **071/3322-1017**).

THE TOP ATTRACTIONS
Pelourinho 𝕬𝕬𝕬

In 1985, the historic core of colonial Salvador was rightly designated a World Heritage Site by the United Nations. You could spend years getting to know the history of the churches, squares, and colorful colonial mansions in this old part of the city. What follows is but a brief introduction.

The place to start a tour of Pelourinho is the main square, called the Terreiro de Jesus. Dominating the west end of the square is the 17th-century **Catedral Basilica.** Flanking the cathedral is the neoclassical Antiga Faculdade de Medicina, now home to the excellent Afro-Brazilian Museum. Facing the cathedral at the far end of the square is the **Igreja de Ordem Terceiro de São Domingos de Gusmão.** Built between 1713 and 1734, this baroque church suffered through an 1870s renovation that destroyed most of its fine interior painting and tile work.

On the south side of the church is a wide cobblestone street with a tall cross in the middle; this is the Praça Anchieta. The saint on the cross is São Francisco de Xavier, patron saint of Salvador. At the far end of this little *praça* stand two of the most impressive churches in the city. The large two-towered one on the right is the **Igreja de São Francisco,** the central element in the surrounding **Convento de São Francisco.** The richest church in all of Brazil, it was built in 1708 by the sugar barons of Salvador to let folks know that their colony had *arrived.* More than 100 kilograms

Pelourinho

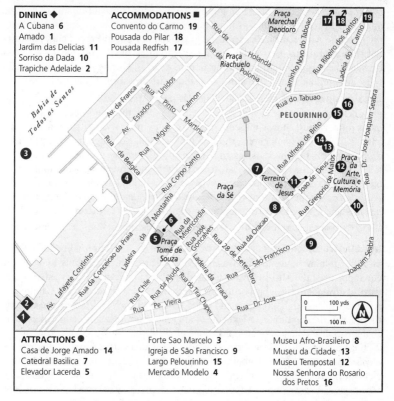

DINING ◆
A Cubana **6**
Amado **1**
Jardim das Delicias **11**
Sorriso da Dada **10**
Trapiche Adelaide **2**

ACCOMMODATIONS ■
Convento do Carmo **19**
Pousada do Pilar **18**
Pousada Redfish **17**

ATTRACTIONS ●
Casa de Jorge Amado **14**
Catedral Basilica **7**
Elevador Lacerda **5**

Forte Sao Marcelo **3**
Igreja de São Francisco **9**
Largo Pelourinho **15**
Mercado Modelo **4**

Museu Afro-Brasileiro **8**
Museu da Cidade **13**
Museu Tempostal **12**
Nossa Senhora do Rosario dos Pretos **16**

(220 lbs.) of gold are slathered over every available knob and curlicue in the richly carved interior of this high baroque church. The result could hardly be called beautiful, but it's impressive. Next to it is the **Igreja de Ordem Terceira de São Francisco,** immediately recognizable by its ornately carved sandstone facade.

Back at the Terreiro de Jesus, the two streets on either side of the Church of São Pedro—Rua João de Deus and Rua Alfredo de Brito—both run downhill to the **Largo Pelourinho.** This small, steeply sloping triangular square gets its name from the whipping post that used to stand at its top end. This was where slaves and criminals were flogged. The smaller building at the top of the square—now the **Casa de Jorge Amado**—used to serve as the city's slave market. Looking downhill, on the right-hand side of the largo, you'll find the blue-and-creamy yellow **Nossa Senhora do Rosário dos Pretos.** Literally translated as "Our Lady of the Rosary of the Blacks," this high baroque structure was erected over the course of the 18th century by slaves. Today, much of the congregation is still of African descent; new paintings inside show the Passion of Christ with an all-black Holy Family, and drums have largely taken the place of the organ in church services.

At the lowest point of the Largo Pelourinho, a narrow street leads steeply uphill to a trio of old baroque churches: the **Igreja de Carmo, Igreja de Ordem Terceiro de Carmo,** and **Igreja do Santissimo Santo do Passo.** Only the Ordem Terceiro is open, and the views over the city are only okay. Retrace your steps and explore one of the other delights of Pelourinho, its hidden interior courtyards. There are four of them: the **Praça de Arte, Cultura e Memoria; Praça Tereza Batista; Praça Pedro Arcanjo;** and **Praça Quincas Berro d'Agua.** Their entrances branch off the little streets between the Largo Pelourinho and the Terreiro de Jesus. During the day, they contain cafes, artisan booths, and museums. At night, nearly every one features a band.

Casa de Jorge Amado *Overrated*   Though Jorge Amado was long one of Brazils' most beloved writers (he died in 2001 at the age of 93), there's not really much to see in his former house, now a museum dedicated to his memory. The ground-floor cafe has a collage of his book covers, showing the wide range of languages into which his dozens of works have been translated. On the upper floors, the text-heavy exhibits that tell the story of Amado's life are written exclusively in Portuguese. Better to just read one of his books. His most popular works are all set in Bahia. *Dona Flor and Her Two Husbands* is set in Pelourinho, and *Gabriela, Clove and Cinnamon* (my personal favorite) and *Tieta do Agreste* take place in provincial towns farther south.

Largo do Pelourinho 51, Pelourinho. ℂ 071/3321-0122. Free admission. Mon–Sat 10am–6pm. Bus: Praça da Sé.

Museu Afro-Brasileiro/Faculdade de Medicina ℛ   This fine old building (built in 1808) is now home to the Museu Afro-Brasileiro, which attempts to show the development of the Afro-Brazilian culture that arose as African slaves settled in Brazil. Particularly good is the large portion of the exhibit space dedicated to the Candomblé religion, explaining the meaning and characteristics of each god *(orixá)* and the role they play in the community. Make sure to ask for one of the English-language binders at the entrance—they contain translations of all of the displays. In the back room, 27 huge carved wood panels—the work of noted Bahian artist Carybé—portray the *orixás* and the animal and symbol that goes with each. The museum staff can also provide information on Candomblé celebrations. Allow 30 to 45 minutes.

Antiga Faculdade de Medicina, Terreiro de Jesus s/n, Pelourinho (just to the right of the basilica). ℂ 071/3321-2013. Admission R$5 (US$2.50/£1.35). Mon–Fri 9am–6pm and Sat–Sun 10am–5pm. Bus: Praça da Sé.

Museu de Arte Sacra ℛℛℛ   This small but splendid museum displays one of Brazil's best collections of Catholic art. The artifacts are shown in the former Convent of Saint Teresa of Avila, a simple, beautiful building that itself counts as an artwork. The collection includes oil paintings, oratorios (a cabinet containing a crucifix), metal work, and lots of wooden statues of saints. In general the cabinetry is better than the carving: the jacaranda-wood oratorios are things of beauty, while the wooden saints seemed to have kept the same look of stunned piety through more than 2 centuries. If you're pressed for time, head for the two rooms of silver at the back. Allow 1½ hours.

Rua do Sodré 276. ℂ 071/3243-6310. www.mas.ufba.br. Admission R$5 (US$2.50/£1.35) adults, R$3 (US$1.50/80p) students with valid ID, free for children under 7. Mon–Fri 11:30am–5:30pm. Located just south of Pelourinho. From Praça de Sé, walk 10 min. south on Av. Carlos Gomes, turn right and walk downhill on Ladeira Santa Teresa for 45m (150 ft.). Bus: Praça de Sé.

Cidade Baixa

Forte São Marcelo ℛ   After years of admiring this perfectly round fort at the entrance of the lower city from a distance, it is now open for visitation. Originally built in 1650 and modified to its current configuration in 1812, it's pretty cool to be able to set foot in the fort and have a look around, but it is not worth more than a 30-minute visit. For those who want to stretch their visit, a good restaurant called Buccaneros is inside the ramparts. Boats ferry visitors from shore regularly, leaving from inside the Centro Nautico (across from the Mercado Modelo, where also the catamarans to Morro de São Paulo leave from). If you are eating at the restaurant, you are not required to pay the museum fee. Please inform the ticket office.

Access from the Terminal Maritimo da Bahia (across from the Mercado Modelo), Cidade Baixa. (C) **071/3495-8359**. www.fortesaomarcelo.com.br. R$10 (US$5/£2.70), R$5 (US$2.50/£1.35) children 7 and older, children under 7 are free. Tues–Sun 9am–6pm. Bus: Comércio.

Mercado Modelo 🦀 There's no sense in pretending you're not a tourist in the Mercado Modelo. If you're here, you are. Still, it's a fun place to wander around. This former Customs building houses just about everything Bahia has to offer in terms of arts and crafts and souvenirs. There are musical instruments (drums, whistles, tambourines, and berimbaus), woodworks of all sorts of *orixás*, fine linen tablecloths, thick cotton hammocks, a wide collection of *arte naïf*, jewelry, and much more.

Praça Cayru, Comércio (just across from the elevator). (C) **071/3243-6543**. Mon–Sat 8am–7pm; Sun 8am–noon. Bus: Comércio.

Solar do Unhão 🦀🦀 An old sugar mill, the Solar consists of a number of beautifully preserved heritage buildings centered on a lovely stone courtyard that dates back to the 18th century. Half the fun is just to wander around and explore the various buildings set on the waterfront (the views are fabulous). The main building houses a small modern art museum; you'll find some works of Portinari and Di Cavalcanti amongst the works on display. The restaurant, where a nightly folklore show is hosted, is located on the lower level of the main building. Taking the path to the right of the main building will take you out above the rocks to the sculpture garden, with works by Caribé and Mario Cravo. The rest of the small collection is housed in a side building behind the sculpture garden. Expect to spend 1 to 2 hours.

Ave do Contorno 8, Cidade Baixa. (C) **071/3329-0660**. Free admission. Tues–Sun 1–7pm. It is best to take a taxi from the Mercado Modelo or Pelourinho.

Barra

Museu Nautico da Bahia, Farol da Barra & Forte de Santo Antônio 🦀 This lighthouse, fort, and museum are mostly worth a visit for the views over the Bay of All Saints. Erected in 1534, the Forte de Santo Antônio was the first and most important Portuguese fortress protecting Salvador. The lighthouse was added in 1698 on the orders of the Portuguese king, who was rather annoyed by the sinking of one of his treasure galleons. The museum inside the lighthouse contains a small collection of maps and charts, navigational instruments, and a number of archaeological finds from shipwrecks that the lighthouse obviously didn't prevent. The cafe on the fort's upper ramparts is one of the prime sunset spots of the city.

Farol da Barra, Praia da Barra s/n, Barra. (C) **071/3264-3296**. Admission R$6 (US$3/£1.60). Mon 8:30–noon; Tues–Sun 9am–7pm museum; 9am–10pm cafe. Bus: Barra or Via Orla.

Bonfim

Nosso Senhor do Bonfim 🦀🦀 This is not the prettiest church in Salvador by any means, but it's likely the one in which faith still beats the strongest. You'll be swamped on arrival by kids selling *fitas*, the colorful ribbons that people tie around their wrist for good luck. Step inside and you'll likely be distracted from the tall barrel vault and blue wall tiles by the fervor of the people offering up their prayers. To really see the extent of their devotion, go to the Room of Miracles at the back where people request

Candomblé

Candomblé is practiced throughout Brazil, but its roots are deepest in Salvador. In its original form, it was brought to Brazil by slaves from West Africa, who believed in a pantheon of gods and goddesses (orixás) who embodied various forces of nature, such as wind, ocean, and fire. A believer who is prepared and trained can become possessed by a certain orixá. In Catholic Brazil, the practice of Candomblé was prohibited; Brazilian slaves were converted to Catholicism. But by translating each of their gods into an equivalent saint, Candomblé followers found they could continue their native worship under the very noses of their priests and masters.

The actual ceremonies are both fun and fascinating; there's lots of chanting and drumming plus wonderful foods and perfumes, all used in order to please the orixás and encourage them to come and possess those present. Many terreiros (areas of worship) in Salvador accept visitors, provided they follow a few basic rules: no revealing clothing (white clothing is preferred) and no video- or picture-taking. Real terreiros will not quote an admission fee but would definitely appreciate a donation.

To attend a Candomblé session, get in touch with **Tatur Turismo** (© 071/ 3450-7216; www.tatur.com.br) before your arrival to find out on which dates ceremonies take place, or check with **Federação Baiana de Culto Afro Brasileiro,** Rua Alfredo de Brito 39, 2nd Floor, Pelourinho (© 071/3321- 1444). Another good resource is the **Afro-Brazilian Museum,** Terreiro de Jesus s/n, Pelourinho (© 071/321-0383). Some terreiros that accept visitors are **Menininha do Gantois,** Alto do Gantois 23, Federação (© 071/3331- 9231; service led by Mãe Carmen); and **Casa Branca,** Av. Vasco da Gama 463, Vasco da Gama (close to Rio Vermelho; © 071/3334-2900), the oldest terreiro in the city, dating from 1836.

or give thanks for miracles by donating valuable or important objects. Definitely eye-catching are the numerous hanging body parts—models made of wood, plastic, and even gold.

Largo do Bonfim. © 071/3312-0196. Free admission. Tues–Sun 6:30am–noon and 2–6pm. Located about 8km (5 miles)—or a R$18 (US$9/£5) taxi ride—north of Pelourinho on the Bonfim Peninsula. Bus: Catch a Bonfim bus at Praça de Sé or at the bottom of the Elevator Lacerda in Comércio.

OUTDOOR ACTIVITIES

BEACHES & PARKS With more than 48km (30 miles) of beaches within the city limits, finding a beach is much less trouble than deciding on which one to go to. The beaches on the bay side of town (**Boa Viagem** and **Monte Serrat**) are not recommended for bathing. **Barra** is the closest clean beach area to downtown, and its protected waters are great for swimming. Just around the bend is **Praia de Ondina,** the first of the true ocean beaches. It's popular with the many visitors who stay in the Ondina hotels. **Praia de Amarelina** is as much known for its food stalls as for the excellent surf and windsurf conditions; the strong seas make it less ideal for swimming. The **Jardim de Alah** is more park than beach, but its palm trees, grass, and small calm beach make for pleasant strolling. Some 5km (3 miles) up the road, **Praia dos Artistas** is highly recommended for swimmers and has waves gentle enough for children. **Praia de Piatã** has that tropical paradise look with lots of palm trees and kiosks offering cold drinks and perfect seafood snacks. One of the prettier beaches, **Itapuã** has inspired many a song. Fishermen still bring their rafts in at the end of the day. The most recently trendy beaches are the ones farthest from downtown; **Praia de Stella Maris** and **Flamengo** are where the young and beautiful gather on the weekends. The buses from downtown that are marked VIA ORLA will follow the coastal road connecting all the beaches until their final destination. Sit on the right-hand side, check it out, and get off when you see the beach you like.

Parque Metropolitano do Abaeté, located just a short walk from Itapuã beach, is famous for the huge blackwater lagoon surrounded by dazzling-white sand dunes. From Pituaçu beach, you can access **Parque Metropolitano de Pituaçu,** a 425-hectare (1,050-acre) reserve of Atlantic rainforest. This park has 18km (11 miles) of cycling trails (plus bikes for rent). A pleasant park close to downtown, the real attraction of **Dique do Tororó Park** is the set of 6m-tall (20-ft.) sculptures of eight *orixás* in the middle of the lake. In the evening, these are beautifully illuminated.

CAPOEIRA   There is no better place than Salvador to see capoeira. There are two good schools in Pelourinho where you can either watch or learn this most Bahian of sports. **Mestre Bimba**'s academy, located on the Rua das Laranjeiras 1, Pelourinho (© 071/3492-3197; www.capoeiramestrebimba.com.br), is the best known and set up to receive foreign students of all levels of experience, even those who want to try it for the first time. The academy offers 1-hour lessons for R$15 (US$7.50/£4) per person, no experience required.

Another popular school is the **Associação Brasileira de Capoeira Angola,** Rua Gregorio de Matos 38, Pelourinho (© 071/3321-3087). Drop-in lessons are held Monday to Friday from 8 to 10am and Monday and Wednesday from 12:30 to 2pm. Each class costs R$20 (US$10/£5.40) or you can purchase a package of six lessons for R$75 (US$38/£20).

DIVING   The bay around Salvador has some interesting dive spots, including reefs and ship wrecks. The prices are pretty competitive; expect to pay around R$160 (US$80/£43) for a dive trip, including full equipment rental. Contact **Dive Bahia,** Av. Sete de Setembro 3809, Barra (© 071/3264-3820; www.divebahia.com.br), for more information.

GOLF   The **Sofitel Hotel** has a golf course that is open to the general public. The 18-hole course is located in Itapuã and subject to availability, as guests have preferred tee times. Greens fees are R$65 (US$33/£18) for 9 holes and R$120 (US$60/£32) to play the full 18-hole course. Contact the Sofitel at © 071/3374-8500 or the golf club directly at © 071/3374-9296.

SHOPPING

Salvador offers some of the best crafts in all of Brazil. The best buys include crafts made out of wood, ceramics, or leather; musical instruments; and CDs of *axé* music. Pelourinho's many gift shops sell wooden berimbaus, miniature terra-cotta figurines, woodcarvings of *orixás,* white-lace tablecloths and blouses, colorful *arte naïf* paintings, and much more. Remember to bargain.

Pricey but unique pieces can be bought at the many galleries in Pelourinho. **Galeria 13,** Rua Santa Isabel 13 (© 071/3242-7783), has a large exhibit space with regular showings of work by local artists. **Galeria de Arte Bel Borba,** Rua Luis Viana 14 (© 071/3243-9370), specializes in the sculptures and paintings by Bel Borba; his work is colorful and fresh. For top-of-the-line names check out **Oxum Casa de Arte,** Rua Gregorio de Matos 18 (© 071/3321-0617). The large collection of art includes work by Mario Cravo and Carybé, who did the large wood panels of the *orixás* in the Afro-Brazilian museum.

Instituto de Artesanato Visconde de Mauá, Rua Gregorio de Matos s/n, Pelourinho (© 071/321-5638), was founded by the government to promote and support regional artists and offers a huge collection of Bahian arts and crafts. It's open Monday and Wednesday through Friday from 8am to 7pm, Tuesday from 8am to 6pm, and Saturday and Sunday from 10am to 4pm.

GIFTS & SOUVENIRS For a different kind of souvenir, try **Lembranças da Fé,** Rua João de Deus 24, Pelourinho (© 071/3321-0006), which specializes in religious articles. **Projeto Axé,** Rua das Laranjeiras 9 (© 071/3321-7869), is a nonprofit organization that sells great skirts, shorts, kangas, and other clothing to raise funds to support projects for street children. The big problem with buying souvenirs at **Delicias Bahia,** Rua Inacio Accioli 9, Pelourinho (© 071/3241-0775), is that they may not last until you get home. The shop has a large selection of coconut sweets, chocolates, jams, candied fruit, and more than 100 different kinds of fruit or spice liquors.

MUSIC To pick up the latest *axé* or Afro-reggae tunes, stop in at **Aurisom,** Praça da Sé, Pelourinho (© 071/3322-6893). The compilation CDs of *axé* music that come out every summer give you the best of a whole crop of Bahian artists. This store also has a fabulous selection of LPs of old Brazilian music.

SHOPPING MALLS Closest to the historic center is the **Shopping Barra,** Av. Centenario 2992, Barra (© 071/3339-8222), just a few blocks from the Farol da Barra. Next to the bus station is one of the larger malls, **Shopping Iguatemi,** Av. Tancredo Neves 148, Pituba (© 071/3350-5060); to get here, take a bus marked RODOVIARIA.

CARNAVAL

Carnaval is Salvador's biggest party of the year. More than 1½ million people join in. In contrast to Rio's more spectator-oriented celebration, in Salvador, the accent is on participation. The beat of choice is *axé;* the action is out on the streets with the blocos.

In Salvador, blocos started out as flatbed trucks with bands and sound systems leading people on an extended dance through the streets. As the number of participants has grown, Salvador blocos have evolved into more highly organized affairs. All now follow set routes, and many have corporate sponsorship. Your dancing-through-the-streets-of-Salvador experience now comes with a better sound system, security guards, and a support vehicle with washrooms and first-aid attendants. Unavoidably, it also now comes with a price tag.

The revelers that follow a bloco must buy a T-shirt *(abadá)* to identify themselves. In return, they get to sing and dance behind the music truck in a large cordoned-off area, staffed by security guards who keep troublemakers out. If you follow the entire route, you can expect to be on your feet for at least 6 hours. Most blocos parade 3 days in a row, and your *abadá* gives you the right to come on all 3 days. It is also possible to purchase an *abadá* for just 1 day.

Tip: Do not bring any valuables with you, and dress casually. For blocos, just wear your *abadá,* shorts, and running shoes; otherwise, shorts and a tank top will do just fine.

BLOCOS & REHEARSALS

The blocos parade Friday through Tuesday, some for 3 days, others for 4 days. Order and start times vary, so pick up an updated calendar just before Carnaval at one of the Bahiatursa offices. See below to help you decide which blocos you want to see. To purchase an *abadá,* you can contact the bloco directly or contact **Central do Carnaval** (✆ **071/3372-6000;** www.centraldocarnaval.com.br); they represent at least a dozen of the most popular blocos. You'll pay R$400 to R$900 (US$200–US$450/ £108–£243 for 2 or 3 days. The Central can also sell you an *abadá* for a day if you don't want to commit to the entire 3 days or want to try different blocos. The most convenient location of the Central do Carnaval is in the heart of Pelourinho, Rua Gregorio de Matos 13 (corner of the Rua Laranjeiras), ✆ **071/3321-9365.**

One of the most popular blocos, **Beijo,** parades on Sunday, Monday, and Tuesday. The lead singer, Gil, is a popular Bahian artist. **Camaleão** parades Sunday through Tuesday. Carlinhos Brown was the lead artist for a few years; now, Chiclete com Banana has taken on that role. **Cerveja & Cia** is owned by the producer of Salvador's biggest musical sensation, Ivete Sangalo, so it only makes sense that she is the star attraction of this bloco that parades Thursday through Saturday. One of the most traditional Afro blocos, **Ilê Aiyê** only lets people of African descent parade, but everyone is welcome to watch. The drums are phenomenal. The group parades on Saturday, Sunday, and Tuesday.

A small number of blocos meet regularly in the months leading up to Carnaval. The most popular group is **Olodum,** which meets on Tuesday night at the Praça Teresa Batista s/n, Pelourinho (✆ **071/3321-3208**). Tickets are R$25 (US$13/£6.75). On Sunday, Olodum holds a free rehearsal starting at 6pm at Largo do Pelô.

WHERE TO STAY

In days of yore, Salvador's top quality hotels were all located close to the beach, a 15- to 30-minute drive from historic Pelourinho. In recent years, in response to the ever-increasing number of foreign visitors, a number of pousadas have opened up on the edge of Pelourinho, most of them located in restored historic buildings. Visitors now have a much greater range of options, though the central dilemma remains: you have to decide between staying in something old in Pelourinho or something new on the coast, at 20-minute drive from downtown. Salvador's peak season ranges from mid-December to early March, and maxes out during Carnaval. Most Carnaval packages start at R$1,500 (US$750/£405) and can go up to R$4,000 (US$2,000/£1,080). Even at these prices, rooms go fast. In the off-season (Apr–June and Aug–Nov), hotels give as much as a 50% discount.

PELOURINHO

There are numerous advantages to staying in Pelourinho—you get to stay in restored 18th-century buildings, and you're minutes from the bustle and fun of the old city.

Very Expensive

Convento do Carmo ★★★ Finally Pelourinho has the boutique hotel it deserves, housed in an original, carefully restored 17th-century convent. All rooms come with a large comfy queen bed fitted out with softest of linens and piled high with a cornucopia of pillows. Bathrooms—converted monks cells, still with massive walls and thick wooden shutters—feature delightful rainfall showers, l'Occitane beauty products, plus a frosted window looking onto the cloister, where at night the fountain gushes quietly. The hotel's common areas—the round tiled pool and restaurant in the cloister, the lounge tucked into one of the arcades, the large library—are a delight; at night, subtle lighting is used to show off the convent to lovely effect.

Rua do Carmo 1, Centro Histórico, Salvador, 40030-170 BA. ©/fax **071/3327-8400**. www.pousadas.pt. 79 units. R$470 (US$235/£127) double; R$600 (US$300/£162) luxury double. Extra person add R$50 (US$25/£14). Children 9 and under stay free in parent's room. AE, DC, MC, V. Free parking. Bus: Praça de Sé. **Amenities:** Restaurant; bar; outdoor pool; small health club; library; spa; concierge; tour desk; car rental; business center; 24-hr. room service; massage; laundry; nonsmoking rooms. *In room:* A/C, TV, dataport, minibar, hair dryer, safe.

Expensive

Pousada Redfish ★★   The Redfish is located in a gorgeous renovated colonial home and managed to keep the features that provide that old colonial feeling, including spacious rooms with high ceilings and tall windows. Standard rooms feature two queen-size beds with new firm mattresses, high ceilings, plus spacious bathrooms and a small balcony; avoid the two "garden" standard rooms that are just outside the breakfast area. The luxury rooms have a vast king-size bed plus a second single bed, leather arm chair, armoire, vaulted ceiling, plus a large veranda with fresh ocean breezes and a view of the city. A ground floor gallery features the owner's artwork.

Ladeira do Boqueirão 1, Centro Histórico, Salvador, 40030-170 BA. ©/fax **071/3243-8473**. www.hotelredfish.com. 8 units. R$240 (US$120/£65) standard double; R$300 (US$150/£81) luxury double. Extra person add R$50 (US$25/£14). Children 6 and under stay free in parent's room. MC, V. Parking unavailable. Bus: Praça de Sé. **Amenities:** Laundry. *In room:* A/C, minibar, safe.

Moderate

Pousada do Pilar ★★   Pilar's beautiful heritage building has been gutted and renovated, giving rooms a modern feel and bringing them fully up to modern standards. All 12 rooms are huge and come with all the modern facilities such as A/C, nice en suite bathrooms, and good lighting. Seven of the rooms have verandas and face out over the port and the ocean. The remaining five rooms have small balconies (standing room only) and look out over the street. A wonderful breakfast with regional cakes and foods is served on the rooftop patio overlooking Salvador's waterfront.

Rua Direita de Santo Antônio 24, Centro Histórico, Salvador, 40301-280 BA. © **071/3241-2033**. Fax 071/3241-3844. www.pousadadopilar.com. 12 units. City view R$230 (US$115/£62); ocean view and veranda R$270 (US$135/£73). Children 5 and under stay free in parent's room. Extra bed R$60 (US$30/£16). AE, DC, MC, V. Bus: Praça de Sé. **Amenities:** Laundry. *In room:* A/C, TV, minibar, safe.

BARRA

If you opt not to stay downtown, Barra offers sea and sun and a good bit of fun in neighborhood restaurants and cafes, in easy striking distance of Pelourinho.

Expensive

Monte Pascoal Praia Hotel ★★ *Value*   Fabulously located across from Barra beach and recently completely renovated, the Monte Pascoal Praia offers great value. All rooms come with a king-size bed or two double beds—great for families traveling with young children. Every room has a balcony and at least a partial view of the ocean. The one room that has been fully adapted for travelers with disabilities has wide doorways, handrails, an adapted toilet, and a chair for use in the shower.

Av. Oceanica 591, Barra, Salvador, 40170-010 BA. © **071/2103-4000**. Fax 071/3245-4436. www.montepascoal. com.br. 80 units. R$200–R$250 (US$100–US$125/£54–£68) double standard; R$220–R$300 (US$110–R$150/£59–£81) double ocean view. Extra person R$60 (US$30/£16). Seasonal discounts available. Children under 6 stay free in parent's room. AE, DC, MC, V. Parking R$12 (US$6/£3.35) per day. **Amenities:** Restaurant; bar; outdoor pool;

fitness room; sauna; game room; small business center (computer, Internet, fax, and printing) with 24-hr. access; salon; 24-hr. room service; laundry service. *In room:* A/C, TV, dataport, minibar, hair dryer, safe.

Moderate

Casa Amarela ★ *Value*   You can't miss the yellow house (the Casa Amarela) on Barra beach. It is also called Hospederia de la Habana, but when you arrive at the bright canary yellow house you can see why that name never caught on. This pleasant and comfortable inn offers one of the best deals along the Salvador waterfront. All 13 rooms have views of the bay, private bathrooms, and are clean and simply furnished. An excellent breakfast is included in the price. The Casa Amarela is right on the major carnival parade route, so book early if you plan to be here to celebrate Salvador's largest event of the year.

Av. Oceânica 84, Barra, Salvador, 40170-010 BA. © 071/3237-5105. www.hospederiadelahabana.com.br. 13 units. R$110 (US$55/£30) double. Children under 6 stay free in parent's room. No credit cards. Street parking. **Amenities:** Bar; laundry service; Internet access. *In room:* A/C, TV.

RIO VERMELHO

Rio Vermelho is an oceanside neighborhood that begins around the bend from Barra and Ondina on the open Atlantic coast. A number of good hotels are located right on the waterfront.

Very Expensive

Pestana Bahia ★★★   Set on an outcrop overlooking Rio Vermelho, the Pestana's privileged location guarantees all 430 units an ocean view. The rooms on the 2nd through the 17th floors are superior; the ones on the 18th to the 22nd floors are deluxe. The difference is really in the small details; the deluxe rooms have bathtubs, 29-inch TVs, and a couch. Other than that the rooms are identical, very spacious with modern and funky decorations. The outdoor pool and sundeck overlook the beach; the Pestana's beach service includes towels, chairs, umbrellas, and drinks.

Rua Fonte do Boi, Rio Vermelho, Salvador, 41940-360 BA. © 071/3453-8005. Fax 071/3453-8066. www.pestana hotels.com.br. 430 units. R$295 (US$148/£80) superior double; R$375 (US$188/£101) deluxe double. Extra person add 30%. Children 12 and under stay free in parent's room. AE, DC, MC, V. Free parking. Bus: Rio Vermelho. **Amenities:** 3 restaurants; bar; large outdoor pool; small health club; concierge; tour desk; car rental; business center; salon; 24-hr. room service; massage; laundry; nonsmoking floors. *In room:* A/C, TV, dataport, minibar, safe.

Inexpensive

Ibis Rio Vermelho ★   The brand-new Ibis provides inexpensive accommodations without giving up much comfort. The no-frills brand of the Accor group (same owners as the Mercure next door) specializes in clean and plain rooms with the quality basics such as a nice firm bed with good linen, a desk or worktable, and a clean and hot shower. The rates are low because the hotel doesn't charge you for a lot of fancy services that aren't always used by guests, such as dry cleaning, gift shop, business center, buffet breakfast, or valet parking. You even have the possibility of getting an ocean view at bargain rates; there is no price difference between the rooms that look towards the ocean, so request one when you reserve or check in. Breakfast is an additional R$8 (US$3.35/£1.70).

Rua Fonte do Boi 215, Rio Vermelho, Salvador, 41940-360 BA. © 071/3330-8300. Fax 071/3330-8301. www.accor hotels.com.br. 252 units. R$119 (US$60/£32) double. Extra person add 30%. Children 12 and under stay free in parent's room. AE, DC, MC, V. Bus: Rio Vermelho. **Amenities:** Restaurant; bar; tour desk; limited room service; laundry; nonsmoking floors. *In room:* A/C, TV, dataport, minibar, safe.

WHERE TO DINE
PELOURINHO
Expensive

Sorriso da Dadá *Overrated* BAHIAN   Brazilians and foreigners come from far and wide to taste Chef Sorriso da Dadá's food, journalists write articles about her, and gourmet magazines rave about her cozy restaurant. And after coming here year after year, we were a bit disappointed this last time. There is nothing wrong with the food, thankfully. However, the restaurant was looking a bit rundown and the service was inattentive. Considering the prices she charges—typically 25% more than other restaurants—we were disappointed. It could just be that she has been too busy expanding her food empire, opening new restaurants, and writing books. However, the lack of attention shows, and that's too bad.

Rua Frei Vicente 5, Pelourinho. (C) 071/3321-9642. Main courses R$36–R$68 (US$18–US$34/£10–£18) for 2. AE, DC, MC, V. Daily 11am–midnight. Bus: Praça da Sé.

Moderate

Jardim das Delicias *Finds* BRAZILIAN/CAFE   Tucked away inside an antiques store on the ground floor of a colonial house in Pelourinho, this lovely courtyard restaurant is the perfect getaway from the bustle and crowding of Pelourinho. The restaurant serves a full Bahian menu, including *moquecas, bobô de camarão,* and even foods from the interior such as beans with smoked meat and sausage. In the evenings, there is live music. However, the Jardim is also very nice for just a drink (the *caipirinha,* made with cashew fruit, is delicious) or a coffee and some sweets.

Rua João de Deus 12, Pelourinho. (C) 071/3321-1449. Main courses R$20–R$50 (US$10–US$25/£5.40–£14); the more expensive dishes serve 2. Sweets and desserts are all under R$10 (US$5/£2.70). AE, DC, MC, V. Daily noon–midnight. Bus: Praça da Sé.

Inexpensive

A Cubana *Finds* DESSERT   It's only right that a city with an abundance of tropical fruits and a year-round warm climate would have great ice cream. One of the oldest *sorveterias* (ice-cream parlors) in town, A Cubana can be found in the heart of Pelourinho. Try the unusual fruit flavors such as *jáca* (jack fruit) or *cupuaçu,* a fruit only found in the Northeast and Amazon.

Rua Alfredo de Brito 12, Pelourinho. **Note:** There is also an A Cubana store right next to the upper exit of the Lacerda elevator. (C) 071/3321-6162. Everything under R$12 (US$6/£3.25). No credit cards. Daily 8am–10pm. Bus: Praça da Sé.

COMERCIO
Located at the foot of a cliff directly below Pelourinho, the business and marina district of Comércio is fine for wandering in the daytime during office hours, but come evening, we recommend taking a taxi.

Very Expensive

Amado *Finds Finds* CONTEMPORARY   Ultimately cool waterfront dining—the room is vast and gorgeous, mixing wood and stone and glass with open views over the waterside deck and the harbor and bay beyond. The cuisine takes traditional Bahian ingredients—mandioc and seafood principally—and puts them to use in innovate ways, always with lovely presentation. For starters we had *lambretas* (a local shellfish) in white wine, *rolinhos de camarão* (little shrimp rolls) and a salad of octopus and sweet potato. For mains, we tried the giant squid stuffed with shrimp and leek in a Provencal sauce, the shrimp in a gorgonzola and pistachio sauce, and a broiled *badejo* fillet

Bahian Food Glossary

Unique in its overwhelming African influences, Bahian cuisine comes with its own ingredients and terminology. Here's a list of the most common dishes and ingredients:

- **Acarajé:** The dough is made with mashed beans and then deep-fried in dendê oil and stuffed with a shrimp sauce, hot peppers, and an onion-tomato vinaigrette.
- **Bobó de camarão:** A stew made with shrimp, cassava paste, onion, tomato, cilantro, coconut milk, and dendê oil.
- **Dendê oil:** A staple ingredient, this oil comes from the dendê palm tree and has a distinct red color. The oil has a strong nutlike flavor; it tastes much like walnut or sesame oil.
- **Ensopado:** A lighter version of a *moqueca*, made without dendê oil.
- **Moqueca:** Bahia's most popular dish, the ingredients include any kind of seafood stewed with coconut milk, lime juice, cilantro, onion, and tomato.
- **Vatapá:** A stew made with fish, onion, tomato, cilantro, lime juice, dried shrimp, ground cashew nuts, peanuts, ginger, and coconut milk. The sauce is thickened with bread.

in a crust of cashews with an okra tapenade, and banana purée on the side. For those not into fish, the menu boasts an equally intriguing array of chicken and beef creations. Service is young, pretty, and efficient.

Av. do Contorno 660, Comercio. © 071/3322-3520. www.amadobahia.com.br. Reservations recommended on weekends and in high season. Main courses R$30–R$46 (US$15–US$23/£8–£12). AE, DC, MC, V. Mon–Sat noon–3pm and 7pm–midnight; Sun noon–4pm. Taking a taxi is recommended. Even though it's not too far from the Mercado Modelo, the street is dark and very quiet at night.

Trapiche Adelaide ✸✸✸ ITALIAN/FRENCH Dining at Trapiche Adelaide is a visual experience. The restaurant sits on pilings over the water and features floor-to-ceiling windows looking out over the bay. The menu has a definite Italian/French twist with dishes such as the grilled *robalo* fish with herbs in an extra virgin olive oil or the grilled sole with fresh asparagus and orange-basil sauce. However, there is a tropical influence as well; worth trying are the prawns with mustard-and-pineapple sauce or the *carne seca* (sun-dried meat) with pumpkin purée served with crisp cassava. Desserts are tempting too. Try the green-apple pie with cashew nuts and ice cream, or the caramelized mango, banana, and apple in a puff pastry.

Praça do Tupinambás 2, Av. Contorno, Comércio. © 071/3326-2211. www.trapicheadelaide.com.br. Reservations required on weekends, recommended in high season. Main courses R$38–R$60 (US$19–US$30/£10–£16). AE, DC, MC, V. Mon–Thurs noon–4pm and 7pm–1am; Fri–Sat and holidays noon–1am; Sun noon–4pm. No shorts or tank tops allowed at night. Taking a taxi is recommended. Even though it's not too far from the Mercado Modelo, the street is dark and very quiet at night.

Expensive

SOHO ✸✸✸ JAPANESE Soteropolitanos (as residents of Salvador are called) seem to have taken to sushi like fish to water. Located inside the Bahia Marina, it's worth waiting for an outside table. The large menu offers most of the usual Japanese suspects but what earns this restaurant an above-average rating are intriguing local dishes such as the *shake lounge* (salmon sashimi with orange sauce, lime and balsamic vinegar) or the *uramaki shake* (salmon with green onion and sesame seeds). Also worth trying are the *marina maki* (a salmon and prawn roll flambéed in *cachaça*) and the *kyo* (a lightly grilled tuna and nira in a thick soya sauce). The *gunkon especial* (warm grilled mushrooms rolled in a slice of salmon) was so good we ordered it three times.

Av. do Contorno s/n, inside the Bahia Marina, Comércio. (C) 071/3322-4554. Reservations recommended. Main courses R$18–R$36 (US$9–US$18/£5–£10). AE, DC, MC, V. Mon 7pm–midnight; Tues–Sun noon–3pm and 7pm–midnight. Taking a taxi is recommended. Even though it is not too far from the Mercado Modelo, the street is dark and very quiet at night.

BARRA

This beach neighborhood is a popular dining destination for locals getting together with friends; with the many hotels concentrated in this area, it's always a lively spot in the evening.

Expensive

Pereira (★★ INTERNATIONAL   This beautiful faux-rustic modern restaurant with exposed brick and expansive glass walls opens up to a lovely patio overlooking the ocean and seawall in Barra. In addition to the typical Brazilian snacks such as deep-fried cod or prawn dumplings (*bolinho de bacalhau* and *pastel de camarão*), you'll find bruschetta with ham and goat cheese or grilled squid in teriyaki sauce. Main courses range from pastas and risottos to grilled seafood and steak. The restaurant has a large wine list with a number of affordable Portuguese, French and Italian wines in the R$40–R$90 (US$20–US$45/£11–£24) range.

Av. Sete de Setembro 3959, Porto da Barra. (C) 071/3264-6464. Main courses R$32–R$48 (US$16–US$24/ £8.50–£13). AE, DC, MC, V. Mon–Wed 6pm–midnight; Thurs–Sun noon–3pm and 6pm–midnight. Bus: Barra or via Orla.

Moderate

Barravento (★ BAHIAN   Underneath a large sail-shaped roof, Barravento offers alfresco dining on a beach patio overlooking all of the beach as far as the Farol da Barra. The menu includes a large selection of typical Bahian dishes such as *moquecas*, *marriscadas* (seafood stews), and grilled fish. One dish that every Baiano will recommend is the *moqueca de siri mole* (soft-shell crab). If you're not in the mood for a full meal, Barravento serves a variety of appetizers such as *casquinha de siri* (spiced crabmeat) and fish pastries; the view is complimentary.

Av. Getulio Vargas 814 (aka Av. Oceanica), Barra. (C) 071/3247-2577. Main courses R$18–R$38 (US$9–US$19/ £5–£10); all dishes for 2. DC, MC, V. Daily noon–midnight (if busy, open later on weekends and in high season). Bus: Barra or via Orla.

RIO VERMELHO

Over the last few years, Rio Vermelho has grown into a bustling, lively restaurant destination. You will find several excellent options and most are centered around the main square, **Praça Brigadeiro Farias Rocha,** so you can stroll around and see what strikes your fancy. One restaurant that you are less likely to stumble across is the **Lambreta Grill,** Rua Alexandre Gusmão 70 ((C) 071/3335-0107; Mon–Sat 6pm–2am). Japanese chef Fukino runs one of the most popular yet laid back seafood restaurants in town. Try the lambretas (small oysters) grilled with a variety of toppings or the seafood specials. Our favorite dish is the seafood symphony—a piping hot steel griddle is brought to your table, piled high with juicy and tender morsels of squid, prawns, mussels, and octopus, served with a side of potatoes and hearts of palm. *Note:* This small street can be hard to find. It runs uphill off the main waterfront street beyond a popular bar called Ex-tudo (give that as a reference to your taxi driver).

SALVADOR AFTER DARK

Salvador's nightlife is one of the most vibrant in all of Brazil. Pelourinho explodes at night with music and people and activity, what Brazilians call *movimento.*

THE PERFORMING ARTS

Home to the Bahian Symphony Orchestra and the Balé (ballet) de Castro Alves, **Teatro Castro Alves,** Praça Dois de Julho s/n, Campo Grande (© **071/3339-8000**), is your best bet for catching some fine-arts performances. One of the best places to see contemporary bands is at the **Teatro Sesi Rio Vermelho,** Rua Borges dos Reis 9, Rio Vermelho (© **071/3334-0668**). Housed in a renovated heritage building, it specializes in local and Brazilian acts. Music varies from jazz to blues to MPB and even pop.

LIVE MUSIC & DANCE CLUBS

In the evenings, Pelourinho often comes alive with music. Two of the most popular venues for concerts are the **Praça Quincas Berro D'Agua** and the **Largo Pedro Archanjo.** Check with the Bahiatursa office in Pelourinho or look in the newspaper for information on events (programming has become a bit spottier, alas, since a new state government cut back on cultural funding).

LIVE MUSIC   Every Friday and Saturday the three bars ringing Pelourinho's **Praça do Reggae,** Ladeiro do Pelourinho, by the Nossa Senhora do Rosário dos Pretos church, bring in a band that plays on their common front yard. One of the best-known groups in Salvador, Olodum performs every Tuesday night at the Praça Teresa Batista (© **071/3322-1396**), starting at 8pm.

DANCE CLUBS   Salvador's upscale Lótus, Rua Marques de Leão 46, Barra (© **071/3264-6787**), is where you are most likely to rub shoulders with Brazilian celebrities such as Ivete Sangalo. Of course they will most likely be in the VIP area on the second floor, but the lounge and dance floor are not too shabby either. Music ranges from hip-hop (also called "Black music" in Brazil) to pop and dance. **Boomerangue,** Rua da Paciência 307, Rio Vermelho (© **071/3334-6640**), is Salvador's hottest live music venue, at least for now. This two-story club (decorated with boomerangs, hence the name) often features two different bands or may feature one band and a DJ. Open Friday and Saturday only; doors open at 10pm, but don't bother to get there before midnight.

BARS & PUBS

A prime sunset spot, **Bar da Ponta,** Praça dos Tupinambas 2, Avenida Contorno (© **071/3326-2211**), is tucked away on the waterfront next to the Trapiche Adelaide restaurant and offers sweeping views of the Bay of All Saints. So what if you and every other tourist in town are at **Cantina da Lua,** Praça Quinze de Novembro 2, Terreiro de Jesus, Pelourinho (© **071/3322-4041**). It happens to be one of the loveliest and largest patios on the Praça Terreiro de Jesus. A great casual bar for after the sun has set is the **Bahia Café** (© **071/3328-1332**), Quartel dos Aflitos s/n (entrance is towards the end of the square at the view point). The view is spectacular—the large open bar overlooks the bay and there are plenty of seats on the large sprawling patio. There is live music on Tuesdays (acoustic guitar and voice) and Thursdays (reggae).

GAY & LESBIAN NIGHTLIFE

A great resource for gay travelers is the **Grupo Gay da Bahia,** Rua Frei Vicente 24, Pelourinho (© 071/3321-1848; www.ggb.org.br). The group has information on tourism and recreational opportunities in Salvador as well as on local social issues and community activism.

The dance club at **Queens Clube,** Rua Teodoro Sampaio 160, just behind the Biblioteca Nacional (© 071/328-6220), is open Friday and Saturday midnight to 6am. Also popular, **Off Club,** Rua Dias d'Avilla 33, Barra (© 071/267-6215; www.off club.com.br) attracts a mixed crowd of both male and female clubbers; it's open Thursday through Sunday. **Espaço Originally,** Rua Marques de Queluz 43, Pituaçu (© 071/3497-0002), is open only on Sundays from 5pm to 2am, and very popular with women. There are usually two local bands each night, and occasionally shows will include famous Brazilian artists.

A SIDE TRIP FROM SALVADOR
MORRO DE SÃO PAULO

To really get away from it all (as if the rest of Bahia wasn't relaxed enough) consider the ultimate beach holiday in Morro de São Paulo. Located on an island only accessible by boat or plane, this small beachside village is blissfully isolated—no cars, no motorcycles, no traffic lights or city noise, and definitely no McDonald's. The island itself is lush and green and the beaches vary from busy and fun to quiet or almost deserted.

Essentials

GETTING THERE   By Catamaran   The most direct route to Morro de São Paulo is via the catamaran departing from downtown Salvador; the Terminal Maritimo do Mercado Modelo is just across the street from the Mercado Modelo. There are several daily departures: 8:30am, Lancha Ilhabela (© 071/9118-2393 or 9132-8262); 1:30pm, Catamarã Farol do Morro (© 071/3319-4570); and at 9am and 2pm, Catamarã Biotur (© 071/3641-3327). Each costs R$50 (US$25/£14) and takes about 2 hours. The boats return from Morro de São Paulo at 9am (Farol do Morro), 11:30am (Biotur), and 2pm (Ilhabela). Note that the sea can get rough, and voyagers on this boat often get seasick.

BY PLANE   The quickest way to get to Morro de São Paulo is to fly. Both **Addey** (© 071/3377-1993) and **Aerostar** (© 071/3377-4406) offers at least three flights a day, more on weekends and in high season; one-way fare is R$198 (US$99/£53), and flying time is 30 minutes. Flights depart and arrive at Salvador's international airport, making for convenient connections with onward flights.

VISITOR INFORMATION   The **CIT** (Central de Informações Turisticas), Praça Aureliano Lima s/n (© 075/3483-1083), can assist you with accommodations and transportation as well as to book excursions. It also has a number of Internet terminals and doubles as the post office. An excellent website on the area is **www.morrode saopaulo.com.br**.

What to See & Do in Morro de São Paulo

The main attraction of Morro de São Paulo is the beach, or better, the beaches. Each has a unique flavor. **First beach** is mostly residential. **Second beach** has lots of pousadas and people; this is where you'll find vendors, watersports, and restaurants. **Third beach** is quite narrow; at high tide it almost disappears. It is much more quiet, perfect for a stroll. **Fourth beach** is the (almost) deserted tropical island beach; wide, white sand, palm trees, and a few small restaurants. The town itself consists of just a few streets and the main square. During the day it's pretty quiet, as most people hang out at the beach. Around dinner time a craft market starts up and the main square fills with restaurants packed with diners.

More active pursuits include boating, horseback riding, and hiking. There are a number of interesting local excursions. See below for more information.

Outdoor Activities

Marlins, Rua da Prainha s/n (© 075/3652-1242), the island's main tour operator, offers a number of trips. The most popular is the **8-hour boat trip** around the island with plenty of stops for swimming or snorkeling. Another great boat tour goes out to **Ilha de Boibepa** (a small island off the main island). Tours cost R$50 (US$25/£14) per person, lunch not included. More active trips include **hikes** to waterfalls or a **walk** along the cliffs and beach to Gamboa R$20 to R$30 (US$10–US$15/£5.40–£8 per person).

Another operator that offers a number of interesting activities is **Quarta Praia Sul,** Rua da Prainha 75 (along the trail that connects second and first beach; © 075/3652-1284; www.quartapraiasul.com.br). The focus of this young company is to show visitors more of a nature experience. One of the more interesting walking tours is the Trilha do Mar (Ocean Trail), which takes hikers through the three main ecosystems of the region: the Atlantic rainforest, the mangroves, and the beach. Guides point out flora and fauna and explain how the ecosystems function. Cost is R$25 (US$13/£7). Other tours include horseback riding, various hikes, and boat tours. This tour operator also offers excellent, inexpensive accommodations packages at the Anima Hotel (see review below under "Where to Stay in Morro de São Paulo").

Where to Stay in Morro de São Paulo

Morro de São Paulo is not a luxury destination; although there are many lovely *pousadas,* most tend to be small, simple, and casual. Amenities are minimal.

Located in the heart of the village overlooking the main square, **Pousada o Casarão** 🏨🏨, Praça Aureliano Lima s/n (© 075/3483-1022; www.ocasarao.net), offers pleasant rooms in the main heritage building, but what you can't see from the street is the lush back garden with nine bungalows set against the sloping hillside. Each is decorated in a different style—Indonesian, Japanese, Indian, African—with rich furnishings and artwork. Double rooms and bungalows range from R$130 to R$210 (US$65–US$105/£35–£57).

For a little more peace and quiet, try **Vila Guaiamú** 🏨, Terceira Praia (© 075/3483-1035; www.vilaguaiamu.com.br). This lovely *pousada* consists of 24 cabins set amongst the lush green gardens. All are simply furnished and come in standard or deluxe, the only difference being the air-conditioning and TV in the deluxe rooms. The *pousada* is located halfway down Terceira Praia, about a 20-minute walk from the village. It's closed May and June. High-season rates are R$210 (US$105/£57) for a double with air-conditioning and TV.

The lovely **Anima Hotel,** Quarta Praia (© 075-3652-2077; www.animahotel.com), sits in splendid isolation on the outer reaches of fourth beach. Accommodation is in self-contained bungalows. Some face the sea, others hide back in the coconut groves. All feature comfortable queen beds with top-quality linen, big windows, high ceilings, rattan chairs for relaxing, and hammocks on the balconies for relaxing even more. All the bungalows are exquisitely decorated with local artwork and crafts. High-season rates range from R$260 to R$310 (US$130–US$155/£65–£75) double.

Where to Dine in Morro de São Paulo

For a small village in the middle of nowhere, Morro de São Paulo has a surprising number of excellent restaurants. The main street in the village, Broadway, is literally lined with eateries. Although most are open for lunch, in the evening things really get hopping. **Restaurante e Pizzaria Bianco e Nero** (© 075/3652-1097) sells some of the world's best pizza, hot out of the wood-burning oven. It also offers a number of excellent seafood, grilled meat and chicken, and pasta dishes; it's closed Monday. Almost across from the pizzeria is **Sabor da Terra** (© 075/3652-1156), famous for its generous portions of outstanding *moquecas* and *bobó de camarão* (prawn stew). Meat eaters can order the *picanha na chapa,* tender steak served at your own table grill. The tables on the veranda (if you can snag one) offer great views of the main street. One of the prettiest viewpoints in town is that of **O Casarão** (© 075/3652-1022), overlooking the main square. The menu offers a number of excellent fish and seafood dishes (portions serve two people) including *moquecas* and grilled fish. Closed Sunday. All the restaurants mentioned above accept Visa.

8 Recife & Olinda

2,392km (1,483 miles) NE of Rio de Janeiro, 2,716km (1,684 miles) NE of São Paulo, 842km (522 miles) NE of Salvador

Olinda and Recife stand within sight of each other on Brazil's northeast coast, the one city on a hilltop, the other in a river mouth, the one founded by the Portuguese, the other by the Dutch.

Recife is the second-largest city in Brazil's Northeast, and aside from a small but pretty historical core, it's not really worth a visit.

Then there's Olinda. Founded by the Portuguese in 1530 on a steep hill overlooking the harbor, Olinda grew rich and proud on sugar exports. The Dutch, keen to move in on the sugar business, took the Pernambico capital, Olinda, in 1630. With the exception of a few churches, the city was utterly destroyed. In need of a capital of their own, the Dutch set to work draining and diking the islands at the mouth of the harbor and built the city of Mauritstad. When the Dutch were expelled in 1654, the Portuguese rebuilt Olinda, but the center of the region had shifted. The former Dutch city of Mauritstad was renamed Recife, after the long coral reefs that menace the harbor. By the 19th century, Recife had far outgrown Olinda, still in its largely pristine 17th-century condition.

Restoration work began on Olinda in the 1970s. In 1982, its lovingly preserved historic core was declared a UNESCO World Heritage Site. Unlike Salvador's Pelourinho, however, Olinda feels very much lived in. Walk its streets and you'll come across kids playing soccer on a patch of hard-packed dirt and women carrying groceries. The city is hilly but distances are short, and with so much to capture your attention, it's a joy to explore.

ESSENTIALS

GETTING THERE

BY PLANE Recife's **Aeroporto Internacional dos Guararapes,** Praça Ministro Salgado Filho s/n, Boa Viagem (© 081/3464-4188), is located 11km (7 miles) south of the city center and just a few miles from the beachside hotels in Boa Viagem. A taxi

Recife

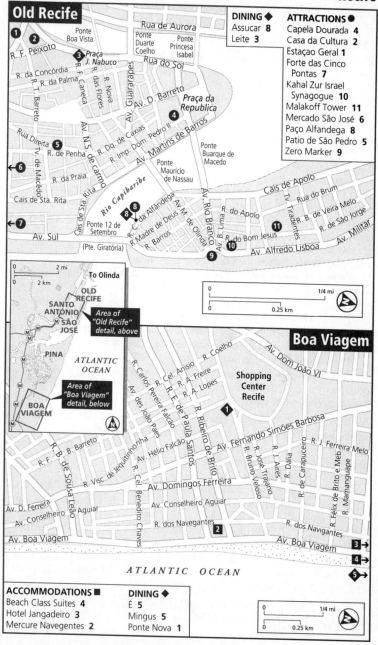

Old Recife

DINING ◆
Assucar **8**
Leite **3**

ATTRACTIONS ●
Capela Dourada **4**
Casa da Cultura **2**
Estaçao Geral **1**
Forte das Cinco Pontas **7**
Kahal Zur Israel Synagogue **10**
Malakoff Tower **11**
Mercado São José **6**
Paço Alfandega **8**
Patio de São Pedro **5**
Zero Marker **9**

Rua de Aurora
Ponte Boa Vista
Pónte Duarte Coelho
Ponte Princesa Isabel
R. F. Peixoto
Praça J. Nabuco
Rua do Sol
R. da Concórdia
R. da Palma
Av. D. Barreto
Praça da Republica
R. T. Barreto
R. Nova das Flores
R. Caneca
Av. Guararapes
Rua Direita
R. N.S. de carmo
R. Dq. de Caxias
R. Imp. Dom. Pedro II
Av. Martins de Barros
Ponte Buarque de Macedo
R. de Penha
Tv. de Macedo
R. da Praia
Ponte Maurício de Nassau
Cais de Sta. Rita
Rio Capibaribe
Cais de Apolo
Cais de Sta. Rita
R. da Alfândega
Av. Rio Branco
R. do Apolo
Tv. Tiradentes
Rua do Brum
R. B. de Veira Melo
R. de São Jorge
Ponte 12 de Setembro
R. Madre de Deus
Av. M. de Olinda
R. B. Lima
R. do Bom Jesus
Av. Militar
Av. Sul
(Pte. Giratória)
R. Barros
Av. Alfredo Lisboa

Inset map

0 — 2 mi
0 — 2 km
To Olinda
OLD RECIFE
SANTO ANTÔNIO
SÃO JOSÉ
Area of "Old Recife" detail, above
PINA
ATLANTIC OCEAN
Area of "Boa Viagem" detail, below
BOA VIAGEM

0 — 1/4 mi
0 — 0.25 km

Boa Viagem

Av. Dom João VI
R. Coelho
R. Cel. Anísio
R. A. Freire
R. A. Lopes
Shopping Center Recife
R. Carlos Pereira Falcão
Av. des João Paes
R. E. de Paula Santos
Av. Fernando Simões Barbosa
R. Ribeiro de Brito
R. José Trajano
R. J. Aires
R. Dália
R. de Carapuceiro
R. J. Ferreira Melo
R. Bruno Veloso
R. Félix de Brito e Meb
R. Marhanguape
R. F. B. Barreto
Av. Hélio Falcão
Av. Domingos Ferreira
R. Visc. de Jequitinhonha
R. B. de Sousa Leão
R. Cel. Benedito Chaves
Av. Conselheiro Aguiar
R. dos Navegantes
R. dos Navegantes
Av. D. Ferreira
Av. Conselheiro Leão Aguiar
Av. Boa Viagem
Av. Boa Viagem

ATLANTIC OCEAN

0 — 1/4 mi
0 — 0.25 km

ACCOMMODATIONS ■
Beach Class Suites **4**
Hotel Jangadeiro **3**
Mercure Navegentes **2**

DINING ◆
É **5**
Mingus **5**
Ponte Nova **1**

to Boa Viagem costs R$14 to R$22 (US$7–US$11/£3.75–£6) and to Olinda, R$45 to R$60 (US$23–US$30/£12–£16). You'll find a queue for **Taxi Coopseta Aeroporto** (⊘ **081/3464-4153**) on the arrivals level.

BY BUS   Buses arrive at Recife's **Terminal Integrado de Passageiros** (**TIP,** pronounced *tchee-pee*), Rodovia BR232, Km 15, Curado (⊘ **081/3452-1999**), located 15km (9 miles) west of downtown. A Metrô connects the bus station to downtown Recife's final station Estação Central. All interstate buses arrive at this terminal. *Note:* Buses to Olinda leave from downtown and Boa Viagem, not from this station.

GETTING AROUND

Downtown Recife consists of two main areas: **Bairro do Recife** (often called Recife Velho, or Old Recife) and **Santo Antônio.** Recife Velho is the oldest part of the city. Ongoing renovations are reviving and revitalizing this area. On the key street, **Rua da Bom Jesus,** the restored colonial warehouses are now home to bars and cafes, and at night, there's often free live music on the street. Three bridges connect Old Recife with **Santo Antônio.** This is the home of many of Recife's most interesting sights, as well as one of its main commercial areas. The principal street in Santo Antônio is **Avenida Dantas Barreto,** a wide boulevard that runs down the spine of the island. Buses to and from downtown leave from this street, either from Praça da Independencia, where Dantas Barreto meets Rua Primeiro de Março, or from farther up opposite Nossa Senhora do Carmo Basilica.

The main beach and residential area of Recife starts just south of downtown. The first stretch, where Avenida Boa Viagem begins, is called **Pina.** The area around **Polo Pina** is a popular nightlife spot. Farther along the beach, the neighborhood changes its name to **Boa Viagem,** the city's main hotel area and beyond that **Piedade.**

Olinda lies 6km (4 miles) north of downtown, a hilltop redoubt now almost swallowed by Recife's suburban sprawl. Regular buses make the trip in about 30 minutes. Buses arrive at the Praça do Carmo bus station. The town is small enough that in a day's wandering you'll see everything.

BY BUS   Most travelers stay either in Boa Viagem or Olinda. From Boa Viagem, regular buses run along Avenida Domingos Ferreira into downtown. The trip takes about 20 minutes. Those marked CONDE DA BOA VISTA will loop through Boa Vista and into Santo Antônio, stopping at Praça da Independencia. Once you're downtown, all sights are easily accessible by foot.

From Boa Viagem, two regular buses travel directly to and from Olinda's Praça do Carmo bus station: Setubal-Principe or Setubal-Conde da Boa Vista. The trip takes about 50 minutes.

From Olinda, all buses depart from the bus station on Praça do Carmo. Buses marked RIO DOCE go to Santo Antônio, stopping on Avenida N. S. do Carmo. Buses marked JARDIM ATLANTICO also go to Santo Antônio but stop in front of the post office on Rua Siqueira Campos. The trip takes about 30 minutes. All buses cost R$2.30 (US$1.30/60p).

BY TAXI   **Coopseta Aeroporto** (⊘ **081/3464-4153**) specializes in airport service. Both **Ligue-Taxi** (⊘ **081/3428-6830**) and **Tele-Taxi** (⊘ **081/3429-4242**) can be booked ahead of time.

BY METRÔ   There's a Metrô in Recife, but it's not very useful to tourists. The stations are too far from Boa Viagem to walk, and by the time you've taken a bus to the station to take the Metrô downtown, you might as well just take the bus the entire way into town.

VISITOR INFORMATION

Recife's airport has a **tourist information booth** at the arrivals level that's open daily from 8am to 6pm (© **081/3462-4960**). The best information booth is at Praça Boa Viagem, open daily from 8am to 8pm (© **081/3463-3621**). The staff is helpful and will provide an excellent free map of Recife.

In Olinda, the tourist information office is located near the Largo do Amparo on Rua do Bonsucesso 183 (© **081/3439-9434**), open daily from 9am to 6pm. There is also a kiosk at the Praça do Carmo, where buses from Recife arrive.

FAST FACTS To exchange currency, try **Banco do Brasil,** Rua Barão De Souza Leão 440, Boa Viagem (© **081/3462-3777**); in Olinda, Av. Getúlio Vargas 1470, Bairro Novo (© **081/3439-1344**). **Monaco Cambio,** Praça Joaquim Nabuco 19, Santo Antônio (© **081/3424-3727**); or **Colmeia Cambio,** Rua dos Navegantes 783, Boa Viagem (© **081/3465-3822**).

In an emergency, contact the **tourist police,** Praça Min. Salgado Filho s/n (© **081/ 3326-9603**). For medical attention, go to **Centro Hospitalar Albert Sabin,** Rua Senador Jose Henrique 141, Ilha do Leite (© **081/3421-5411**) For nonurgent cases, ask your hotel for a referral to the nearest walk-in clinic.

WHAT TO SEE & DO

The attraction of both Olinda and Recife lies not so much in particular sights as in the urban fabric. Particularly in Olinda, while any one church wouldn't merit a special trip, the ensemble of all that 300- to 400-year-old architecture makes for a memorable stroll.

BUS TOURS **Luck Viagens** (© **081/3464-4800;** www.luckviagens.com.br) offers a range of bus tours. There's a 4-hour city tour that shows the highlights of Recife and Olinda (R$30/US$15/£8). There is also a full-day tour to Itamaracá island (R$75/ US$38/£28), where the Dutch built Fort Orange in 1631, as well as day trips to Porto de Galinhas for the best beaches and snorkeling in the area (R$65/US$33/£18).

The way to truly explore Olinda is by hitting the cobblestones and setting off on foot. Buses from Recife will drop you off at the Praça do Carmo, dominated by the lovely **N. S. do Carmo Church** 𝕏. The large leafy square on the front side of the church is known as **Praça da Abolição (Abolition Square)** because of the statue of Princess Isabel, who was responsible for abolishing slavery in 1888. Follow Avenida da Liberdade and you'll pass by the 1590 **Church of São Pedro Apostolo** before turning right and walking up the steep **Ladeira da Sé** to the **Igreja da Sé** 𝕏. The square in front of the Igreja da Sé provides the best view in town. You see the red-tiled roofs and church towers of Olinda, and thick stands of tropical trees set against the sparkling blue ocean below. Farther south, you get great views of Recife's skyline all the way to Boa Viagem.

The very steep **Ladeira da Misericordia** leads down towards the **Rua do Amparo** 𝕏𝕏. This is one of Olinda's prettiest streets, featuring small, brightly colored colonial houses packed with galleries, restaurants, and shops. The **Largo do Amparo** 𝕏 has the feel of a little Mexican square. On the square itself, **N. S. do Amparo** (built in 1613) features two bell towers on the outside, and some nice tiles and gold work inside. Farther up the hillside, **N. S. do Rosário dos Pretos** and **São João Batista** aren't worth hoofing it up the hill.

Leaving the square and following Rua Amparo until it becomes **Rua Treze de Maio,** you come to the **Mamulengo Puppet Museum** (⽊), which is open Tuesday through Friday from 9am to 5pm, Saturday through Monday from 11am to 5pm; admission is free. The small three-floor museum assembles puppets used in northeastern folk drama. The guide explains the puppets and then lets you play with them. Some have hidden levers that cause them to stick out their tongues—and other ruder appendages.

Farther down, the Rua São Bento leads to the **Mosteiro de São Bento,** which is unfortunately now closed. From the monastery, Rua XV de Novembro leads down to the **Largo do Varadouro;** the large crafts market **Mercado Eufrasio Barbosa** is worth a visit. Those returning to Recife can take a bus from this square instead of returning to the Praça do Carmo.

RECIFE

The place to start a tour of Recife is at the **Zero Marker** in the heart of Old Recife. In the center of this open round plaza, there's a small disc, the point from which all distances in Pernambuco are measured. Gaze out toward the ocean from here, and about 98m (321 ft.) offshore, you'll see the long low reef from which the city draws its name.

A block back from the Zero Marker is the **Rua do Bom Jesus.** The street and this entire island are the oldest part of Recife, founded by the Dutch. Taking the Avenida Rio Branco across the bridge will lead you to **Santo Antônio,** called Mauritspolis under Dutch rule, after the founder Maurits van Nassau. The large green neoclassical square almost at the foot of the bridge was once van Nassau's private estate, but it is now the **Praça da República.** This pretty park, with a fountain circled by Imperial Palms and Roman statuary, is enclosed on three sides by grand *beaux-arts* buildings: the **Palácio da Justiça,** the **Palácio do Campo das Princesas,** and the **Teatro Santa Isabel.**

Behind the Palácio da Justiça at Rua do Imperador Dom Pedro II 206, you pass by the **Capela Dourada (Golden Chapel).** Aptly named, its altar is a two-story arch of jacaranda and cedar, all covered in gold leaf. Christ hangs on a golden cross with gold and silver rays shining out behind his head.

Crossing Primeiro do Marco and sneaking south through the fun maze of narrow streets (parallel to but not on Av. Dantas Barreto), you will come—provided you find **Rua do Fogo** on the far side of Avenida N. S. do Carmo—to the **Pátio de São Pedro.** This broad cobblestone square is enclosed by dozens of small restored shops, all gaily painted in bright pinks, blues, and greens.

Crossing Avenida Dantas Barreto from here, you come to the **N. S. de Carmo Basilica,** currently closed for repairs, and some blocks beyond that, the **Casa da Cultura** and the **Estação Geral,** Recife's former train station. In the other direction, a maze of fun and narrow streets leads to the **Mercado São Jose.**

Casa Da Cultura (⽊)   This former jail was built in the shape of a cross, with a center hall and four hallways to allow the guards to stand in one spot and keep an eye on all four wings. The building has been hardly modified at all since its prison days; the cells, still with their original numbers, are now occupied by souvenir shops. The best time to visit is on Friday afternoon when there are concerts after 4pm. On Sunday, only a few stalls open.

Rua Floriano Peixoto, Santo Antônio. (℡) 081/3224-2850. Mon–Sat 9am–7pm; Sun 10am–5pm.

Olinda

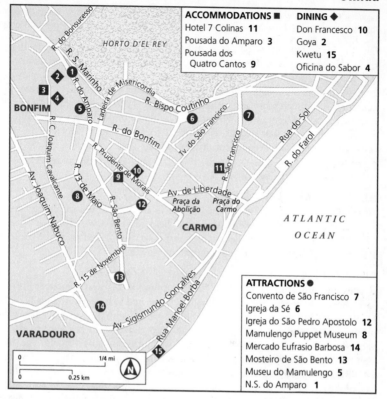

ACCOMMODATIONS ■
Hotel 7 Colinas **11**
Pousada do Amparo **3**
Pousada dos
  Quatro Cantos **9**

DINING ◆
Don Francesco **10**
Goya **2**
Kwetu **15**
Oficina do Sabor **4**

HORTO D'EL REY

R. do Bonsucesso
R. S. Marinho
R. do Amparo
Ladeira de Misericordia
R. Bispo Coutinho
R. do Bonfim
Tv. do São Francisco
R. São Francisco
Rua do Sol
R. do Farol
R. C. Joaquim Cavalcante
R. Prudente de Morais
Av. Joaquim Nabuco
R. 13 de Maio
R. São Bento
Av. de Liberdade
Praça da Abolição
Praça do Carmo
R. 15 de Novembro
Av. Sigismundo Gonçalves
Rua Manoel Borba

BONFIM

CARMO

ATLANTIC OCEAN

VARADOURO

0 ————— 1/4 mi
0 ————— 0.25 km

ATTRACTIONS ●
Convento de São Francisco **7**
Igreja da Sé **6**
Igreja do São Pedro Apostolo **12**
Mamulengo Puppet Museum **8**
Mercado Eufrasio Barbosa **14**
Mosteiro de São Bento **13**
Museu do Mamulengo **5**
N.S. do Amparo **1**

Centro Cultural Judaico de Pernambuco/Kahal Zur Israel Synagogue ⟡⟡

This reconstructed synagogue is built on the foundations of the original Kahal Zur Israel Synagogue, built in the 1640s when Recife was ruled by religiously tolerant Holland. In the late 1990s, traces of the old synagogue were discovered in the form of a *mikve,* or ritual bath. The reconstructed building is not a replica of the original but more a monument that honors the Jewish community in Recife. The museum tells the history of Jews in Recife. On the ground floor you can see the remains of the 17th-century temple. The second floor houses the actual synagogue; and if you aren't familiar with Jewish traditions, a guide will show you around. Expect to spend an hour.

Rua do Bom Jesus 197, Bairro do Recife. ⟡ 081/3224-2128. Tues–Fri 9am–5pm; Sun 3–7pm. R$4 (US$2/£1). Bus: Conde de Boa Vista.

Forte das Cinco Pontas/City Museum ⟡⟡

This 1677 fort has been wonderfully restored; unfortunately, the city has crept out, leaving the once-seaside fort outflanked by a freeway. The city museum, which takes up two wings, is extremely well done. Two air-conditioned rooms are devoted entirely to the Dutch period, and there's a wealth of maps and drawings of this early colony. Other rooms show the development of Recife over time; as late as the 1950s, Boa Viagem had nothing but a few lonely beach cottages.

Largo dos Cinco Pontas, Bairro de São José. $\mathcal{C}$ **081/3224-8492.** Admission R$3 (US$1.50/80p) adults, R$1.50 (US75¢/40p) students and seniors, free for children 7 and under. Mon–Fri 9am–6pm; Sat–Sun 1–5pm. Bus: São Jose.

Oficina Cerâmica Francisco Brennand 𝒦𝒦 Although somewhat off the beaten track, this ceramics workshop/museum is more than worth the price of admission. The lifelong work of ceramic artist Francisco Brennand is on display at this sprawling estate/workshop. Although famous for some notorious giant phallic sculptures, his collection is so much more and includes thousands of sculptures, tiles and pieces of ceramic art, as well as drawings. His work is beautifully displayed in several buildings as well as various outdoor settings. The Burle Marx garden was designed by the landscape artist himself and decorated with Brennand statues.

Propriedade Santos Cosme e Damião s/n, Várzea. $\mathcal{C}$ **81/3271-2466.** www.brennand.com.br. Admission R$4 (US$2/£1). Mon–Fri 8am–5pm. Taxi recommended.

OUTDOOR ACTIVITIES
Wreck divers will be in heaven; at least 15 wrecks are diveable and within easy reach. For excursions contact **Projeto Mar,** Rua Bernardino Pessoa 410, Boa Viagem ($\mathcal{C}$ **081/3326-0162;** www.projetomar.com.br). Two dives including all the gear cost R$130 (US$65/£35); a nondiving companion pays R$30 (US$15/£8).

SHOPPING
Recife's downtown neighborhood of **Santo Antônio** boasts a large number of small local shops. The streets around the Patio São Pedro, and in between Avenida N. S. do Carmo and Rua Primeiro de Março, are all jam-packed with little shops. Some of the alleys are so narrow that they resemble Asian street markets. The best time to explore these streets is weekdays during office hours, when it is busy and bustling. The most beautiful mall is the **Shopping Paço Alfandega,** Cais da Alfandega 35, Recife Antigo, ($\mathcal{C}$ **081/3419-7500**). Housed in the restored 18th-century Customs building, this is one of the city's prime shopping and entertainment destinations.

Olinda's historic downtown also offers prime shopping. You will find many galleries and interesting shops once you start to explore the winding streets. Two markets sell a good variety of local handicrafts. **Mercado Eufrasio Barbosa** (or Mercado Varadouro) is located in the former customs house at Sigismundo Gonçalves s/n ($\mathcal{C}$ **081/3439-1415**), and it's open Monday through Saturday from 9am to 6pm. Up the hill close to the Praça João Alfredo is another arts-and-crafts market, the **Mercado Ribeira,** Bernardo Vieira de Melo s/n ($\mathcal{C}$ **081/3439-1660;** daily 9am–6pm). The merchants specialize in religious arts, paintings, woodcarvings, and regional crafts.

WHERE TO STAY
RECIFE
Recife's main hotel neighborhood is Boa Viagem beach, the closest you can get to downtown while still being in a safe neighborhood on a clean beach.

Expensive
Beach Class Suites 𝒦𝒦𝒦 The only bright light in Boa Viagem, this brand-new tower with bright and spacious rooms offers the best accommodation in town, at a lower rate than some of the five-star properties. All rooms are decorated with modern furniture, predominantly white with some splashes of colorful art. A number of the rooms have balconies; some also have small kitchens with microwaves and coffeemakers. A nice feature is the women-only floor, ideal for women traveling alone. In-room

amenities include free broadband Internet. The hotel also has a fitness center and outdoor pool overlooking the beach. Internet rates offer as much as 50% savings over the rack rate.

Av. Boa Viagem 1906, Boa Viagem, Recife, 51011-000 PE. (C) **0800/55-5855** or 081/2121-2626. www.atlantica hotels.com.br. 145 units (showers only). R$390 (US$195/£105) double, Internet special R$170–R$230 (US$85–US$115/£46–£62). Extra person in room add 25%. Children 7 and under stay free in parent's room. AE, DC, MC, V. Free parking. Bus: Boa Viagem. **Amenities:** Restaurant; bar; outdoor pool; sauna; exercise room; room service; business center; laundry; nonsmoking rooms. *In room:* A/C, TV, dataport, minibar, hair dryer, safe.

Blue Tree Towers 🌟 *(Kids)*   This excellent modern hotel is located south of Boa Viagem in Piedade, the adjacent beach neighborhood. All 180 rooms have an ocean view and a private balcony. To seriously splurge, book on of the duplex suites with private swimming pool and sauna. In the low season (Sept to mid-Dec and Mar–June) these can be had for as little as R$335 (US$167/£90). The hotel is right on the beach and offers excellent services such as chairs, umbrellas, towels, and refreshments. Families traveling with children will also appreciate the fabulous swimming pool and sundeck, with ocean view, of course!

Av. Bernardo Vieira de Melo 550, Praia da Piedade, Recife, 54310-001 PE. (C) **0800/15-0505** or 081/3468-1255. Fax: 081/3468-2466. www.bluetree.com.br. 180 units (showers only). R$160–R$240 (US$80–US$120/£43–£65) double; R$335–R$500 (US$167–US$250/£90–£135) suite. Extra person in room add 25%. Children 12 and under stay free in parent's room. AE, DC, MC, V. Paid parking (R$10/US$5/£2.70). Bus: Piedade. **Amenities:** Restaurant; bar; large pool; children's pool; fitness center; sauna; tour desk; car rental; room service; laundry; nonsmoking rooms. *In room:* A/C, TV, dataport, minibar, fridge, hair dryer, safe.

Recife Palace Hotel 🌟🌟🌟   Size does matter. Recife's top hotel, the Recife Palace offers a prime location across the street from Boa Viagem beach, and the largest rooms in all of Recife. The amenities of a five-star hotel don't hurt. Recent renovations have left rooms looking fabulous: fresh and modern with pleasant lighting, blond wood, and soft-toned colors. Each room has a bathtub and a partial view (superior room) or full view (deluxe room) of the ocean, but again, it's the spaciousness that most impresses: ample closet space and a desk large enough for two people to work side by side.

Av. Boa Viagem 4070, Recife, 51012-000 PE. (C) **0800/702-8383** or 081/4009-2500. Fax 081/3465-2525. www. lucsimhoteis.com.br. 295 units. R$260–R$350 (US$130–US$175/£70–£95) superior double; R$310–R$400 (US$155–US$200/£84–£108) deluxe double; R$475–R$600 (US$238–US$300/£128–£162) suite. Check Internet for off-season discounts. Children under 12 stay free in parent's room; over 12 are charged 25% of room rate. AE, MC, V. Bus: Boa Viagem. **Amenities:** 2 restaurants; dance club; bar; pool; gym; sauna; tour desk; concierge; car rental; business center; salon; room service; babysitting; dry cleaning; laundry; rooms for those with limited mobility. *In room:* A/C, TV, dataport, minibar, fridge, hair dryer, safe.

Moderate

Hotel Jangadeiro 🌟🌟 *(Value)*   Overlooking Boa Viagem beach, Hotel Jangadeiro offers the best value for money in this upscale neighborhood. This small pleasant hotel has been recently renovated and the rooms are spacious and bright. It's worth paying a little bit extra for the oceanview rooms; all come with balconies and offer stunning views of Boa Viagem beach. The standard rooms look out onto the neighboring buildings, or have a partial ocean view but lack the balcony. Bathrooms come with showers only but are spotless and modern.

Av. Boa Viagem 3114, Boa Viagem, Recife, 51020-001 PE. (C) **081/3465-3544.** Fax 081/3466-5786. www.jangadeiro hotel.com.br. 93 units (showers only). R$110–R$190 (US$55–US$95/£30–£51) standard double; R$200–R$280 (US$100–US$140/£54–£76) oceanview double. Significant discounts in the low season. Children under 8 stay free in parent's room; over 8 are charged 25% of room rate. AE, MC, V. Free parking. **Amenities:** Restaurant; small rooftop pool; room service; laundry service. *In room:* A/C, TV, dataport, minibar, fridge.

OLINDA

Olinda offers some of the nicest accommodations for those who appreciate small bed-and-breakfasts or inns at a fraction of the cost in Recife.

Expensive

Hotel 7 Colinas ★★★ (Kids) Set on the grounds of a former sugar plantation, the hotel has the best leisure area of any hotel in the region. Rooms are divided over a few low-rise buildings and all come with verandas that overlook the garden. Rustic room interiors feature tile floors and dark-wood furniture. Even the smaller standard rooms are still very pleasant. The hotel's large outdoor pool is set in the lovely garden and perfect for kids.

Ladeira de São Francisco 307, Olinda 53020-170 PE. ℭ/fax **081/3439-6055.** www.hotel7colinas.com.br. 45 units (showers only). R$230–R$270 (US$115–US$73/£62–£73) standard double; R$260–R$360 (US$130–US$180/£70–£97) deluxe double. Extra person add about 25%. Children 5 and under stay free in parent's room; children 6–12 pay 15% of room rate. AE, MC, V. Free parking. Bus: Rio Doce. **Amenities:** Restaurant; large outdoor pool; children's pool; laundry. In room: A/C, TV, minibar, safe.

Pousada do Amparo ★★★ The most charming place to stay in all of greater Recife is this concatenation of two 200-year-old colonial buildings in the heart of historic Olinda. Views down the hillside from the sumptuous back garden and pool deck are fabulous. Rooms come in several configurations; most are quite spacious, and several have verandas. All are furnished with a combination of antiques and modern artwork. The three rooms that face directly onto the street are a bit noisy and are better avoided. The best room is the Alto da Sé, on the top floor; it has its own small balcony with a fabulous view and a hammock.

Rua do Amparo 199, Olinda, 53020-170 PE. ℭ **081/3439-1749.** Fax 081/3419-6889. www.pousadadoamparo.com.br. 18 units (showers only). R$240 (US$120/£65) standard double; R$360–R$460 (US$180–US$230/£97–£124) deluxe double. Extra person add about 25%. Children 10 and under stay free in parent's room. V. Street parking. Bus: Rio Doce. **Amenities:** Restaurant; small pool; children's pool; sauna; car rental; laundry. In room: A/C, TV, minibar, safe.

Moderate

Pousada dos Quatro Cantos ★ A lovely large colonial building, this *pousada* takes up the entire block, hence the name (*quatro cantos* means "four corners"). The best rooms are the three deluxe rooms that offer a view of the pool or the city. Also very nice are the newly upgraded deluxe superior rooms that have jetted tubs. The best room is the Veranda Suite, a spacious chamber overlooking the garden. Avoid the two ground-floor rooms; these lack air-conditioning and bathrooms, and are next to the lobby. An annex across the garden contains five more rooms, which are comfortable but lack character.

Rua Prudente de Morais 441, Carmo, Olinda PE. ℭ **081/3429-0220.** www.pousada4cantos.com.br. 17 units (showers only). Annex room double (no bathroom, no A/C, fan only) R$95 (US$47/£26); standard room double R$140 (US$70/£38); deluxe and deluxe superior double R$190–R$250 (US$95–US$113/£51–£68). Seasonal discounts up to 20%. Extra bed add 25%. Children 5 and under stay free in parent's room. MC, V. Street parking. Bus: Boa Viagem. **Amenities:** Small outdoor pool; car rental; laundry. In room: A/C, TV, fridge.

WHERE TO DINE

RECIFE

Assucár REGIONAL We don't often recommend restaurants in shopping malls but then Paço Alfândega is not just any mall. The kitchen serves up modern, regional cuisine with plenty of seafood, grilled fish, and steak dishes. For desert, Assucár serves a table of sweets—*a mesa de doces*—for only R$10 (US$4.15/£2.10) per person. The best part of dinner, however, is the panoramic view over the Capibaribe River. It's worth waiting at the bar to get a window table.

Cais da Alfandega 35, Recife Antigo (top floor of the mall). *©* **081/3419-7582.** Reservations recommended on Fri–Sat evenings. Main course R$24–R$39 (US$12–US$19/£6.50–£11). AE, D, MC, V. Mon–Tues noon–10pm; Wed–Sat noon–midnight, Sun noon–6:30 pm.

É *ஃஃ* CONTEMPORARY   Recife's best restaurant of the year takes you on a culinary tour of some interesting cuisines with touches of Vietnam, Thailand, Japan, Italy and France. Some interesting dishes you will find on the menu include *Fillet Ban Chá* (grilled beef medallions served on pasta with a Dijon, miso, and green tea sauce) and the Thai prawns (deep-fried and served with a sweet-and-sour honey sauce). Try the *Filet do Chef,* a beef medallion served with slices of foie gras and a fig compote on pasta, or the *Filet ao pâté de foie,* grilled beef with a foie gras pâté and port sauce, served with a cheese petit gâteau and sweet potato. The kitchen is open late, until 1:30am.

Rua do Atlântico 147, Boa Viagem. *©* **081/3325-9323.** www.egastronomia.com.br. Reservations recommended Sat–Sun. R$36–R$52 (US$18–US$26/£10–£14). AE, DC, MC. Tues–Sat 8pm–1:30 am. Bus: Boa Viagem.

Leite *ஃ* INTERNATIONAL   One of the oldest restaurants in all Brazil, Leite is an oasis of old-world elegance with fine linen and china. The menu includes a variety of meat dishes such as steak au poivre and, of course, seafood; the *sinfonia maritima* is a delicious sauté with lobster, fish, oysters, and prawns.

Praça Joaquim Nabuco 147, Santo Antônio. *©* **081/3224-7977.** R$26–R$45 (US$13–US$23/£7–£11). DC, MC, V. Sun–Fri 11:30am–4pm.

Mingus *ஃஃ* CONTEMPORARY   Mingus, named in honor of jazz bassist and composer Charles Mingus, is beautifully decorated with photos and musical instruments. However, it is the harmony in the kitchen that has people raving about this place. Mingus serves up excellent contemporary cuisine; try the grilled lamb with shiitake mushrooms and baby potatoes, or the grilled partridge with linguine au poivre. Seafood lovers will also be pleased with dishes such as the grilled fish in cashew crust with leek risotto or the salmon with a ham and melon risotto. Desserts are deliciously decadent and worth lingering over . . . especially the warm apple compote with a cashew crust and vanilla ice cream or the warm chocolate biscuit with nuts and chocolate mousse topped with rich crème anglaise and red fruit.

Rua do Atlântico 102, Boa Viagem. *©* **081/3465-4000.** www.mingus.com.br. Reservations recommended in the evening. R$29–R$48 (US$15–US$24/£8–£13). DC, MC, V. Sun–Mon noon–3:30pm; Tues–Sat noon–3:30pm and 7pm–midnight. Bus: Boa Viagem.

Ponte Nova *ஃஃ* CONTEMPORARY   Only a year after opening, this restaurant has already made the top 10 list for the city. The food is modern and interesting. Mains include *camurim,* a grilled fish marinated in lemon grass and herbs. The chef's baby, however, is the lamb, which is marinated for 4 hours in rosemary and honey before being grilled and served with an apricot risotto. For dessert don't miss the rich strawberry cappuccino—strawberries topped with vanilla ice cream and a layer of mascarpone, and finished with a crumble.

Rua Bruno Veloso 528. Boa Viagem. *©* **081/3327-7226.** Reservations recommended in the evening. R$23–R$38 (US$12–US$19/£6–£10). AE, DC, MC, V. Mon–Sat 7:30pm–midnight and Fri noon–4pm. Taxi recommended.

OLINDA

Expensive

Kwetu ⭐⭐⭐ *(finds)* FRENCH   Located in a lovely house by the water, Kwetu offers an intimate indoor setting or alfresco dining in the garden looking out over the ocean. To start off, order one of the fresh salads such as the Breton, with greens, cheese, and seafood, or the *coquille* with fish and prawns in white wine au gratin. Kwetu is probably one of the few places in Recife where you can order rabbit stew, the *lapin a Catalana,* with white wine, tomatoes, herbs, and red peppers. Also worthwhile is the *frango archiduc,* chicken with fresh mushrooms, parsley, and lime. For dessert there's the *trés* French *Dame Blanche,* a large glass of vanilla ice cream with hot chocolate sauce.

Rua Manoel Borba 338, just behind the Praça do Jacaré, Olinda. ② 081/3439-8867. R$26–R$38 (US$13–US$19/£7–£10). DC, MC, V. Mon and Wed–Thurs 6pm–midnight; Fri–Sat noon–4pm and 6:30pm–midnight; Sun noon–9pm. Taxi recommended.

Moderate

Don Francisco ⭐⭐⭐ *(finds)* ITALIAN   Owner and chef Francesco Caretta and his wife, Norma, serve up some of the best Italian food in town. Many of the herbs and vegetables come from their organic garden. For starters there is the homemade minestrone soup, a rich and satisfying blend of 20 vegetables. The pastas are made from scratch by Francesco and served with simple sauces such as the organic pesto, fungi mushrooms, Gorgonzola, or tomato with basil and ricotta. All desserts, except for the ice cream, are made by chef Francesco. He is particularly proud of the tiramisu, made with fresh mascarpone, and the apple pie with cinnamon ice cream. It's impossible to resist when he insists.

Rua Prudente de Moraes 358, Olinda. ② 081/3429-3852. R$15–R$26 (US$7.50–US$13/£4–£7). V. Mon–Fri noon–3pm and 7–11pm; Sat 7pm–midnight.

Goya ⭐⭐ BRAZILIAN/SEAFOOD   Although there are a variety of outstanding restaurants on the Rua do Amparo, Goya seems to take the regional cuisine one inventive step further. The menu showcases the best seafood in combination with tropical fruits and regional ingredients. One of the most creative dishes is the *Lagosta ao Goya,* pieces of lobster flambéed in *cachaça* and served with pineapple and mashed *macaxeira* (manioc). The atmosphere is bustling and pleasant, and the service is knowledgeable and friendly.

Rua do Amparo 157, Olinda. ② 081/3439-4875. Reservations accepted. Main courses R$18–R$36 (US$9–US$18/£5–£10). AE, DC, MC, V. Mon noon–5pm and 6pm–midnight; Wed–Sat 6pm–midnight and Sun noon–5pm. Bus: Rio Doce.

Oficina do Sabor ⭐⭐⭐ BRAZILIAN   You can expect the Oficina to be busy—this restaurant's well-deserved reputation has spread far beyond Olinda. The most popular dishes are the *jerimums,* a local variety of pumpkin. The best-seller is the *Jerimum recheado com camarão ao maracuja* (pumpkin filled with prawn and passion fruit sauce). Inside, the Oficina is a beautifully decorated space in a lovely restored building—but that's just icing on the pumpkin. The patio offers gorgeous views of Olinda.

Rua do Amparo 335, Olinda. ② 081/3429-3331. www.oficinadosabor.com.br. Reservations recommended for weekends. R$34–R$60 (US$17–US$30/£9–£16), most dishes serve 2. AE, DC, MC, V. Tues–Fri noon–4pm and 6pm–midnight; Sat noon–1am; Sun noon–5pm.

RECIFE & OLINDA AFTER DARK

Recife's historic downtown has undergone a complete face-lift, becoming a cultural and entertainment district. Activities center around the **Rua do Bom Jesus;** lined with at least 15 bars and restaurants, this is one of the best places in town Thursday through Saturday and Sunday afternoons.

One of Old Recife's nicest bars is the **Arsenal do Chopp,** Praça Artur Oscar 59, at the corner of Rua do Bom Jesus (© **081/3224-6259**). Most tables are spread out over the sidewalk; for a quiet spot grab a table inside. Recife's hottest dance club is **Cuba do Capibaribe,** Shopping Paço Alfandega, Recife Antigo (© **081/3419-7502;** www. cubadocapibaribe.com.br). This Cuba-inspired bar serves up a great *mojito* accompanied by the sound of live Latin and salsa music from Thursday to Saturday.

Another great venue downtown is the **Patio de São Pedro.** Beautifully restored, this square now hosts a variety of free outdoor music events. On Tuesdays, locals gather for the Terça Negra, an event with *afoxé* music. On Saturdays, a younger crowd gathers to dance to *maracatu, mangue beat,* and other regional tunes. Events start at 7 or 8pm.

In Boa Viagem a favorite nightspot is **Biruta Bar,** Rua Bem-te-Vi, Pina (© **081/ 3326-5151;** www.birutabar.com.br). The bar features a large veranda looking out over the ocean, making it the perfect setting for a special date. On Thursdays, Biruta presents blues bands and on Fridays there's *forró.* The best night for dancing at **Boratcho,** Av. Herculano Bandeira 513 (inside Galeria Joana d'Arc; © **081/3327-1168**) is Thursday when DJs play a variety of music, including samba-rock and regional rhythms. **Boteco,** Av. Boa Viagem 1660, Boa Viagem (© **081/3325-1428**), is a popular destination almost any night of the week. Serving the best beer in town, the bar is often packed with locals stopping by for an ice-cold *chopp.* Open daily.

Olinda is not known for its nightlife; most folks settle for wine and conversation over a late-night supper. Brand new is the **Casa Maloca,** Rua Amparo 183 (© **081/ 3429-7811**), an antiques stores with a restaurant and at the very back the lovely **Bar Olindita.** Guests can sit at a long bar or funky tables scattered about the room. The best spots are on the patio, looking out towards Recife.

A SIDE TRIP TO PORTO DE GALINHAS

Porto de Galinhas is one of the nicest beach destinations in the Northeast. There are no high-rise buildings, just small *pousadas* and a few low-rise hotels. The town of Porto de Galinhas boasts perhaps four streets, enough for a dozen restaurants, a bank, some surf shops, and a beachside bar or two. **Cupe beach** stretches 4km (2½ miles) north from town; it's wide and warm, punctuated at either end by small coral reefs full of fish. Around the point in the other direction, **Maracaípi beach** is the place for surfers; the beach regularly hosts national and international surfing competitions.

ESSENTIALS

GETTING THERE   Only 69km (43 miles) from Recife by car, you can take BR 101 south until it connects with the PE 60. Stay on the PE 60 until the turnoff for the PE 38 that leads to Porto de Galinhas; destinations and exits are well marked.

BY BUS   Buses to Porto de Galinhas leave daily from 6:30am to 6:30pm every hour on the half-hour from the Avenida Dantas Barreto bus terminal in downtown Recife (across from N.S. do Carmo). Tickets are R$6 (US$3/£1.60) and the drive takes about 2 hours. A number of these buses go through Boa Viagem, and all stop at the airport on the way.

BY TAXI   A taxi from Recife airport or downtown will cost from R$80 to R$120 (US$40–US$60/£21–£34) for up to four people and luggage, depending on your bargaining skills. Don't go on the meter, but agree on a price beforehand. Many hotels and *pousadas* can book a taxi service for you at a reasonable rate.

VISITOR INFORMATION The **tourist office** is at Rua da Esperança 188 (© **081/3552-1480;** www.portodegalinhas.com.br). Hours are Monday through Friday from 9am to 5pm, Saturday and Sunday from 9am to 3pm.

WHAT TO SEE & DO IN PORTO DE GALINHAS

The main attraction at Porto de Galinhas is the beach, whether you swim, surf, snorkel, or snooze. If that gets dull, the options include nature hikes, trips to nearby islands, or dive trips to reefs offshore.

The best way to see the local beaches is to head out in a buggy. The most popular tour is the Ponta-a-Ponta, which takes you to four different beaches from the northern end of Porto de Galinhas to the southern end. A full-day trip costs R$110 (US$55/£30), leaving from your hotel or from Avenida Beira Mar at the main square. Contact the buggy drivers at (© **081/9192-0280**). You can fit four in a buggy, but you'll likely have more fun with just two or three so that one person doesn't have to sit in the boring passenger seat.

The specialist in soft adventure in town is the firm **Pé no Mangue,** Rua da Esperança 101, first floor (© **081/3552-1935** or 081/9211-1450; www.penomangue.com. br), run by a congenial pair of young São Paulo refugees. They have a wide range of outings, all under R$50 (US$25/£14), including guide and transfer. Options include guided **nature hikes** through Atlantic rainforest or low-lying mangrove forest, a 2-hour **kayak tour, horseback rides,** and various **boat trips,** ranging from a 3-hour *jangada* trip to the less-visited coral reefs off Maracaípi to 4- and 6-hour trips to offshore islands and beaches.

WHERE TO STAY IN PORTO DE GALINHAS

Accommodations are mostly in small family-run *pousadas* and a few larger cabana-style hotels. Prices are affordable and the quality of the accommodations is high.

Located 5km (3 miles) from the village, **Tabapitanga** ✺✺✺, Praia Pontal do Cupe (© **081/3552-13211;** www.tabapitanga.com.br), offers gorgeous accommodations on the beach. Rooms are in one- or two-story chalets. All rooms are spacious and decorated with unique, colorful artwork. Furnishings are luxurious; the rooms have king-size beds, large flatscreen TVs, and big bathrooms. Each room also comes with a veranda or deck with patio furniture and a hammock. A fabulous breakfast is included. In high season, rooms range from R$300 to R$450 (US$150–US$225/£81–£122).

A little closer to town is the **Tabajuba** ✺✺, Av. Beira Mar s/n (© **081/3552-1049;** www.tabajuba.com.br). Specializing in romantic getaways for young couples, the *pousada* is colorful and playfully decorated in a rustic, tropical-beach-house style and set right on the beach. Children under 12 are not allowed. It's a 30-minute stroll to the center of Porto de Galinhas—very romantic on a starlit night. The best rooms are those on the second floor, which have a small balcony and more of a sea view. The entire facility is nonsmoking. Rooms cost R$260 (US$130/£70) for a double in high season.

Pousada Canto do Porto ✺✺, Av. Beira Mar s/n (© **081/3552-2165**), is a great option for those who want to stay close to the village without being smack in the middle of things. Only a 5-minute walk from the main square, the *pousada* is set right on the beach and has 14 rooms. The affordable master suites have a partial ocean view and a veranda. The only rooms to avoid are the small standard ones. These are set back behind the *pousada* in an annex and have no verandas or views. High-season rates range from R$140 to R$230 (US$70–US$115/£38–£62).

WHERE TO DINE IN PORTO DE GALINHAS

One of the best restaurants in the region, **Beijupirá,** Via Porto de Galinhas s/n (© **081/3552-2354**), is also one of the loveliest. Set in a garden aglow with hundreds of candles and lanterns, Beijupirá's cute and whimsical decorations offer plenty of eye candy. The menu offers seafood cooked up with interesting spice mixes and a blend of sweet and savory dishes.

One of the best views of the Porto de Galinhas beach is from the patio of **Peixe na Telha,** Av. Beira Mar s/n (© **081/3552-1590**), an excellent seafood restaurant open all day. It's a great spot to grab some appetizers and a beer.

9 Natal

2,680km (1,661 miles) NE of Rio de Janeiro, 2,981km (1,848 miles) NE of São Paulo, 1,111km (689 miles) NE of Salvador

Natal has been overlooked for much of its history, noticed only when someone else tried to take it away. The Portuguese founded a town on the banks of the Potengi River only to drive out the French, who tried to establish a base from which to raid Portuguese shipping. The laying of the fort's foundation was celebrated with a mass on December 25, 1599, and so the city was named *Natal* (the Portuguese word for Christmas). Natal's real glory days wouldn't come until World War II, when Americans used Natal as an air and communications base. The closest point in the Americas to Africa, the city became known as the "Trampoline of Victory." These days, the big boom is in tourism. Natal today is a sprawling, modern place, a city little history and less culture, for which it compensates with beautiful waterfront views, endless sunshine, lots of beaches for surfing and tanning, and dunes—glorious dunes, hundreds of feet high and spilling down to within inches of the seashore.

ESSENTIALS

GETTING THERE

BY PLANE   TAM (toll-free © **0800/570-5700** or 084/4002-5700); **Gol** (© **0300/ 115-2121**); and **Varig** (© **084/4003-7000**) offer daily flights from all major cities in Brazil. All flights arrive at **Aeroporto Augusto Severo,** Rua Eduardo Gomes s/n (© **084/3643-1000**), about 15km (9¼ miles) from downtown. Taxis from the airport are about R$30 (US$15/£8) to Ponta Negra and R$35 (US$18/£9.50) to Praia dos Artistas, close to downtown. City buses marked VIA COSTEIRA stop in Ponta Negra before continuing to downtown.

BY BUS   Long-distance buses arrive at the **Rodoviaria,** Av. Cap. Mor Gouveia 1237, Cidade Esperança (© **084/3232-7310**), about 5km (3 miles) from downtown and Ponta Negra beach.

GETTING AROUND

A small downtown aside, Natal is a postwar creation; it resembles the modern, sprawling cities of the southwestern United States. The original city was founded on a peninsula between the Potengi River and the Atlantic Ocean. Just off the tip of the peninsula, where ocean and river meet, the original **Forte de Reis Magos** still stands, a forgotten bit of the 17th century, now dwarfed by a brand new suspension bridge over the Potengi. Where the fort's causeway touches the mainland the 21st century begins—a modern oceanside boulevard that under various names runs from here south through the length of the city and out into the dunes beyond. About 3km (1¾ miles) south of the fort the street is called **Avenida Presidente Café Filho,** and the surrounding neighborhood is **Praia dos Artistas.** From here the road climbs a bit, becoming **Avenida Governo Silvio Pedroso,** and then **Via Costeira,** which runs for some 9km (5½ miles) between the ocean and a vast nature preserve called **Parque das Dunas.** There are a number of five-star resort hotels nestled in between the parkway and the ocean. Where the park ends, the road swings away from the beach a bit and becomes **Avenida Engenheiro Roberto Freire,** the backbone of the city's best beach neighborhood, **Ponta Negra.** The beach itself has no traffic at all along this stretch, just a pedestrian walkway and seawall, punctuated by beachside kiosks, or *barracas.* About two-thirds of the way along the lovely 3km (1¾-mile) beach, Av. Roberto Freire drops downhill to the waterfront and becomes **Av. Erivan França,** a beachside boulevard lined with pubs and restaurants that runs all the way to **Morro do Careca (Bald Mountain),** the 117m (390-ft.) sand dune that overlooks the beach.

Going the other direction from the Forte dos Reis Magos, along the banks of the **Rio Potengi,** you pass under the new suspension bridge that now leads across the river to **Genipabu.** The road then climbs and enters **Centro,** also called the **Cidade Alta,** the commercial heart of Natal.

North of Natal, the dunes and beaches begin as soon as you cross the river. This area is called the **Litoral Norte** (north coast). The first settlement in the Literal Norte is the quiet village of **Genipabu,** about 25km (16 miles) north of downtown Natal. Once a fishing village, Genipabu now caters to tourists who come to swim at the beach and buggy and climb through the huge surrounding dunes.

South of Ponta Negra there's a long stretch of beaches known as the **Litoral Sul** (south coast), with something for everyone. **Búzios** beach is excellent for snorkelers, while **Barra de Tabatinga** is a surfer's hotspot. Capping off the string of south coast beaches is **Praia da Pipa,** a gorgeous stretch of sand and a destination in its own right.

BY TAXI You can hail a taxi anywhere. To reserve one, phone **Disk Taxi Natal** (© 084/3223-7388) or **CoopTax** (© 0800/84-2255). A taxi from Ponta Negra to downtown will cost about R$25 to R$30 (US$13–US$15/£7–£8).

BY CAR Localiza (© 0800/979-2000 or 084/3643-1557), **Avis** (© 0800/725-2847 or 084/3644-2503), **Unidas** (© 0800/121-121 or 084/3643-1222), and **Hertz** (© 084/3087-1428) all offer rentals.

VISITOR INFORMATION

Natal's **airport** has a tourist information center (© 084/3643-1811) in the arrivals hall, open daily from 9am to 5pm. The **main tourist information center** is in Natal's Centro de Turismo, Rua Aderbal de Figueiredo 980, Petrópolis (© 084/3211-6149). See "Shopping," below for more details

FAST FACTS To exchange money, try **Banco do Brasil,** Banco do Brasil, Av. Rio Branco 510, Cidade Alta (© 084/3216-4500), which also has a 24-hour ATM; in Ponta Negra, **Banco do Brasil,** Rua Dr. Ernani Hugo Gomes 2700 (© 084/3219-4443), next to the Praia Shopping.

For medical attention, to go **Monsenhor Walfredo Gurgel,** the largest hospital in Rio Grande do Norte state; it's located at Avenida Salgado Filho s/n, Tirol (© 084/3232-7501).

For Internet access, visit **Sobre Ondas** restaurant, Rua Erivan Franca, Beiramar, Ponta Negra (*C* **084/3219-4222**), which has an Internet cafe with four terminals. Cost for 1 hour is R$5 (US$2.50/£1.50).

WHAT TO SEE & DO

Natal is a small city with a limited number of historical attractions. If you've already been or will go to Salvador or Olinda, the man-made bits of Natal will seem a little empty. That's fine; odds are you're here for the beach or to see those famous dunes.

TOP EXCURSIONS FROM NATAL

Buggy Expeditions 🐾🐾🐾 Untouched dunes, beaches, and lagoons stretch away north and south of Natal for hundreds of kilometers. The best way to see them in all their glory is to rent a dune buggy with a driver and head out to explore. Prices average around R$150 (US$75/£40) for a full day for up to four people.

The classic north-coast day trip crosses the Potengi River and proceeds up to **Genipabu,** where you have the chance to ride camels or slide down the dunes on a sand board (see "Outdoor Activities," below). From there you float your buggy across another small stream on a tiny raft and carry on up the beach to **Jucumã,** where you can try your bum at *aerobunda* (see "Outdoor Activities," below). From there, it's another 35km (22 miles) of sand until you get to **Maracajaú,** a magic spot where at low tide you can snorkel in the natural pools in the offshore coral reef. (Buggy tours normally time the tour so that you arrive at low tide.). At the end of the day, the driver will take you to Genipabu to see the sun set over the dunes.

An excellent *bugreiro* who speaks English is **Kadmo Donato** of **Buggy & Cia** (*C* **084/9982-3162** or 084/9416-2222; www.buggyecia.com.br). There is also **Buggy Tour** (*C* **084/3086-2258**) and, in Genipabu, **Villa do Sol** (*C* **084/3225-2132**).

Snorkeling the Pools at Maracajaú 🐾🐾 The coast north of Natal is hemmed with shallow coral reefs that make for perfect snorkeling. Nowhere are they more impressive than in Maracajaú, about 1 hour north of Natal. You need to time your arrival with low tide to get the most out of your snorkeling. From the beach a boat takes you about 7km (4¼ miles) offshore to a moored diving platform. At low tide the honeycomb of reefs forms natural pools rich in tropical fish and other marine life. As the maximum depth is about 4.8m (16 ft.), these pools can be easily explored with just a mask and snorkel. Expect to spend at least 2 hours.

Maracajaú Diver, Praia de Maracajaú. *C* **084/3261-6200** or 084/9983-4264 (cellphone). www.maracajaudiver.com. br. Snorkeling costs R$55 (US$27/£15) for adults, R$35 (US$17/£9.50) for children 6–12, free for children under 5.

OUTDOOR ACTIVITIES

AEROBUNDA JACUM At Lagoa Jacumã, Litoral Norte, Km 35, there's a dune about 60m (200 ft.) high. At its foot is a big lake. At the top of the dune someone has hammered in three telephone poles to make a scaffold, and then attached a thick rope from there to another peg on the far side of the lake. To execute the *aerobunda,* you slide your butt into a sling hanging from a pulley attached to the line. The attendant then lets go. You scream down towards the lake, gathering speed and momentum. Splash! Huge fun. Cost is R$3 (US$1.50/80p) per ride, and it's open daily from 8am to 5:30pm. For more information call *C* **084/3228-2402.**

JANGADA **RIDING** A *jangada* is a narrow raft made of balsa wood (nowadays augmented with Styrofoam) and equipped with just one triangular sail. Taking a *jangada* is a quiet, gentle way to get out to the small offshore reefs. You'll find them along Genipabu beach. Cost is R$10 (US$5/£2.50) per person for an hour or so.

SAND BOARDING Sand boarding is worth doing as long as you believe that no sport is too stupid to be tried at least once. As snowboarders, we felt obligated. If you're interested, look for the entrepreneurs at the south end of Genipabu beach; cost is R$5 (US$2.50/£1.50) per trip (less, if you bargain).

SURFING The beach at Ponta Negra is a great place to learn to surf. Marcelo Alves of **Sem Limites** surf school is a great instructor (✆ **084/9418-4030** cellphone). One-on-one instruction will get you up in no time. Lessons cost R$20 (US$10/£5.50) per hour. The school is about halfway along Ponta Negra beach.

ORGANIZED TOURS

The Natal-to-fortaleza buggy Adventure ⊛⊛⊛ On this 800km (500-mile) adventure trip from Natal north along the beach to Fortaleza, you'll visit 85 beaches and countless dunes, some of them massive monsters seemingly transplanted from the Sahara. You'll pass through petrified forests and pocket deserts, and float your buggy across dozens of little estuaries on rafts, and visit little fishing towns that rarely if ever see tourists. **Buggy & Cia,** Rua Belo Monte 213 (✆ **084/9982-3162;** www.buggy ecia.com.br) specializes in this trip. The expedition takes 4 days, usually starting from Natal. Cost is R$2,500 (US$1,250/£675) total for two people, including accommodations and breakfast plus buggy and driver. The owner, Kadmo Donato, speaks English. Note that with Buggy & Cia, a driver does most or all of the driving. The only company that does allow guests to drive is the Paris-based firm **Brésil Aventure** (www. bresil-aventure.com). However, Bresil Aventure's trips from Natal to Fortaleza take 2 weeks, and their guides speak only French.

ECOTOURS **Cariri Ecotours** (✆ **084/3206-4949;** www.caririecotours.com.br) offers single and multiday 4×4 trips south to Praia da Pipa and north to Maracajaú. The one-day "eco-trip" to Praia de Pipa includes a guided walk through the Atlantic rainforest and dolphin spotting at Enseada do Madeiro.

HEADING INLAND

The hot, dry interior of the Northeast hides some places of outstanding natural beauty: Based in Natal, **Cariri Ecotours** (✆ **084/3206-4949;** www.caririecotours. com.br) offers a 4-day, 3-night Valley of the Dinosaurs package that strikes inland for the far west of Paraiba state to explore the dinosaur tracks left in the bottom of a great shallow lake over 120 million years ago. The tour then swings towards the Cariri region, to the vast and magic rock formations at **Lajedo do Pai Mateus** and **Saca de Lã.** The expedition finishes up at one of Brazil's most significant archaeological sites, a stone wall inscribed with the symbols and artwork of a now vanished prehistoric people. Cost per person for groups of two to four people is R$2,400 (US$1,200/ £648) by Fiat Duplo, R$2,955 (US$1,477/£798) by Land Rover. Most meals are included.

PRAIA DA PIPA

Located 80km (50 miles) south of Natal by road (or a mere 55km/34 miles if you go by beach buggy), **Praia da Pipa** is one of the most picturesque beaches in all Brazil's northeast. The village of Pipa is known for its night-time activity, and for the cafes and restaurants lining its cobblestone streets. Down on the long crescent beach there are natural pools and reefs for snorkeling. Traveling south from Pipa one finds a string of beaches—**Praia do Amor, Praia do Moleque**—snuggling at the foot of tall coastal cliffs.

Pipa does not lack for places to stay. **Toca de Coruja** (Av. Baía dos Golfinhos 464; ℂ 084/3246-2226; www.tocadacoruja.com.br) is an *Roteiro de Charme* property that features luxurious self-contained chalets with private outdoor Jacuzzis, all in a large private garden; **Sombra e Agua Fresca** (Rua Praia do Amor 1000, ℂ 084/3246-2258; www.sombraeaguafresca.com.br) is located on the clifftop overlooking the bay, offering large, comfortable rooms and two pools with terrific views.

Excellent restaurants in Pipa include the seafood oriented **Cruzeiro do Pescador** (Rua da Gameleira s/n; ℂ 084/3246-2262; daily 7–11:30pm) and for more varied fare, **Agua na Boca** (Av. Baia dos Golfinhos 687; ℂ 084/3246-2641; Mon–Sat 6pm–midnight).

SHOPPING

At the **Centro de Turismo,** Rua Aderbal de Figueiredo 980, Petrópolis (ℂ 084/3211-6149), features some 40 crafts shops, an art gallery, and a coffee shop, all housed in the cells of the former state prison. The market is open daily from 9am to 7pm. The **tourist information booth** at the entrance is open daily from 9am to 5pm.

Recently opened in Ponta Negra, the **Shopping do Artesanato Potiguar** (Av. Engenheiro Roberto Freire 8000; ℂ 084/3215-9781) features more than 180 shops packed with souvenirs and local handicrafts.

WHERE TO STAY
PONTA NEGRA

Ponta Negra is the most popular beach within the city limits. It's wide, clean and busy, with good waves for surfing. A pleasant waterfront walkway runs along the beach past a number of beachside restaurants and *barracas.* Downtown Natal is a 15-minute cab ride or a 30- to 40-minute trip by city bus.

Very Expensive

Manary Praia Hotel 🐾🐾🐾   A small hotel with not a hair out of place. Done up like a Spanish hacienda, with old dark-beam, red-tile roofs, and large cool flagstones on the floor, the Manary is a member of the Roteiro de Charme association of select inns and *pousadas.* The location is premium, with a large deck—and two pools, including a children's pool—facing out over sea. In the rooms, the mattresses, linen, and furniture are all top-notch. All rooms come with balconies and views of the ocean.

Rua Francisco Gurgel 9067, Praia de Ponta Negra, Natal 59090-050 RN. ℂ/fax **084/3204-2900**. www.manary. com.br. 24 units. High season Nov–Feb and July R$550–R$875 (US$275–US$438/£148–£236) double; off-season R$450–R$725 (US$225–US$363/£121–£196) double. Extra person add 25%. Children 6 and under stay free in parent's room. AE, DC, MC, V. Free parking. Bus: Ponta Negra. **Amenities:** Restaurant; bar; 2 pools; game room; tour desk; business center; room service; laundry. *In room:* A/C, TV, dataport, minibar, hair dryer, safe.

Expensive

Visual Praia Hotel 🐾🐾   It will be tough to find a nicer spot at this price with such a fabulous location. Right on the seawall in Ponta Negra, the Visual Praia Hotel provides direct access to the lovely beach just below. Rooms are all very comfortable and beautifully furnished with blond wood and marble desktops. Breakfast is served on the patio overlooking the beach.

Rua Francisco Gurgel 9184, Praia Ponta Negra, Natal, 59090-050 RN. ℂ **084/646-4646**. www.visualpraiahotel. com.br. 86 units (showers only). High season R$275–R$325 (US$92–US$108/£46–£54) double; extra person R$45

($15/£8) extra. 30% discount in low season. Children up to 5 stay free in parents' room. AE, DC, MC, V. Free parking. Bus: Ponta Negra. **Amenities:** Restaurant, bar; large pool; children's playground; laundry service. *In room:* A/C, TV, minibar, fridge, safe.

VIA COSTEIRA

The Via Costeira parkway looks like a lovely place for a hotel (and it is) but there are a couple of drawbacks. Though you get outstanding views and unmatched isolation, there's almost always a strong shore breeze, the ocean is rougher, and there is nothing within walking distance, so you're looking at a cab ride any time you want to leave the hotel.

Serhs Natal Grand ★★★   Little more than a year old, the Natal Grand is the newest and most luxurious of the top-end resorts strung along the oceanside Via Costeira. Rooms are fresh, bright and modern, all with tile floors, clean bright bathrooms and balconies facing out over the sea. Superior rooms feature firm double beds and small writing desks. Family rooms feature two double beds, but no extra space, making them a little squished. Junior suites are more spacious, with separate sitting rooms and fold-out couches, making them a good option for those traveling with kids. A couple looking to splurge should opt for a Senior or even an Executive Suite, both of which feature outdoor terraces with Jacuzzis built for two. Recreational facilities are top-notch. The entire front deck of the hotel is one sprawling wavy pool, dotted here and there with little Jacuzzi islands.

Av. Via Costeira 6045, Praia de Ponta Negra, Natal 59090-001 RN. ⓒ 084/4005-2000. Fax 084/4005-2001. Toll-free 0800-702-2411. www.serhsnatalgrandhotel.com. 396 units. R$495–R$647 (US$248–US$324/£134–£175) double; R$800–R$1,000 (US$400–US$500/£216–£270) suite. Extra person add 25%. Children 6 and under stay free in parent's room. Off-season discounts (20%) Sept–Oct and Mar–May. AE, DC, MC, V. Free parking. Bus: Via Costeira. **Amenities:** 4 restaurants; 3 bars; 4 large outdoor pools; children's pool; sports center with weight room, volleyball, basketball, soccer courts; Japanese spa; sauna; 3 Jacuzzis; children's game room; business center; room service; laundry; 10 wheelchair accessible rooms. *In room:* A/C, plasma TV, Internet, minibar, hair dryer, safe.

WHERE TO DINE
ELSEWHERE

Mangai ★★ Value REGIONAL   The ideal place to get a look and taste of *Nordestino* food, the cuisine of Brazil's dry, cattle-raising Northeast. Mangai offers a self-serve buffet—or better, a smorgasbord—featuring over 40 different Nordestino dishes, some of them traditional favorites, other wonderful inventions made using traditional local ingredients such as *carne-de-sol* (sun-dried beef), *macaxeira* (sweet manioc root), *farofa* (ground, roasted manioc root), beans, and rice. The *carne-de-sol na nata* (butter-sautéed sun-dried beef) is a house specialty. Mangai is truly best for a long leisurely lunch.

Av. Almintos Barros 3300 (on the inland road between Ponta Negra and downtown, about halfway between the 2) ⓒ 084/3206-3344. www.mangai.com.br. Reservations not accepted. Main courses R$10–R$25 (US$5–US$13/ £3–£7). V. Wed–Sun 7am–10pm. Bus: Centro.

VIA COSTEIRA

Tábua de Carne ★ Value BRAZILIAN   Perched on a clifftop overlooking the beach on the Via Costeria, Tabua offers carnivorous dining at its lip-smacking best. The menu now includes such treats as lamb and pork chops and even fish (though if you're in the mood for seafood you really should go elsewhere) as well as the traditional favorites of *carne de sol* (salted sun-dried beef, a specialty of northeastern Brazil) and chicken and good old Brazilian *picanha* (sirloin steak). For the decision-shy, there's the Tábua, a wood platter containing picanha, sausage, chicken, and *carne de sol*. There's a second location in Ponta Negra, also with Wi-Fi, though it's on a viewless stretch of Av. Engeneiro Roberto Freire 3241 (© **084/3642-1236**).

Av. Senador Dinarte Mariz 229 © **084/3202-5838**. www.tabuadecarne.com.br. Main courses R$18–R$32 (US$9–US$16/£5–£9) for 2. AE, DC, MC, V. Daily 11:30am–11pm. Bus: Via Costeira.

PONTA NEGRA

Camarões BRAZILIAN/SEAFOOD   With a name that means "prawns," it's not hard to guess the house specialty. Papa Jerimum prawns are served in a pumpkin, while Champagne prawns are sautéed with butter in a champagne/apple sauce. The tiny creatures are also featured in sauces such as the *Espaguete de Camarão,* sautéed prawns in a creamy cognac sauce with basil served on spaghetti. Portions are generous enough to serve two.

Av. Eng. Roberto Freire 2610, Ponta Negra. © **084/3219-2424**. www.camaroes.com.br. R$26–R$58 (US$13–US$29/£7–£16) for 2. AE, DC, MC, V. Mon–Sat 11:30am–3:30pm and 6:30pm–midnight; Sun 11:30am–5pm. Free parking. Bus: Ponta Negra.

Camarões Potiguar BRAZILIAN/SEAFOOD   Like its parent, this new hatchling of the long-established Camarões restaurant features a menu heavy on prawns and seafood, but while the mothership is more international, here the emphasis is on local ingredients such as pumpkin, coconut, and cashews and traditional Brazilian recipes. The architecture of this smaller space matches the new locally flavored menu—charmingly rustic, with flashes of sophistication.

Av. Eng. Roberto Freire 2610, Ponta Negra. © **084/3219-2424**. www.camaroes.com.br. R$26–R$58 (US$13–US$29/£7–£16) for 2. AE, DC, MC, V. Mon–Sat 11:30am–3:30pm and 6:30pm–midnight; Sun 11:30am–5pm. Free parking. Bus: Ponta Negra.

Manary ★★ SEAFOOD/REGIONAL   The best place in Natal for seafood, the Manary offers top-notch ingredients, good service, and a lovely setting—an outdoor patio overlooking the seawall and beach of Ponta Negra. The most tempting menu item is the *misto fritti di mare*—a platter of grilled lobster, shrimp, octopus, mussels, fish, and grilled vegetables. The wine list is short, but well-chosen.

Rua Francisco Gurgel 9067, Praia de Ponta Negra. ©/fax **084/219-2900**. www.manary.com.br. Main courses R$24–R$44 (US$12–US$22/£7–£12). AE, DC, MC, V. Daily 10am–11pm. Bus: Via Costeira.

NATAL AFTER DARK
CLUBS & BARS

Natal's nightlife scene centers on **Alto de Ponta Negra,** located on the heights on the inland side of the busy Avenida Roberto Freire (around the corner of Av. Roberto Freire with Rua Dr. Manoel. A.B. de Araújo).

ALTO DE PONTA NEGRA

If you're in the mood for a snack before or instead of partying, **Casa de Taipa** (Rua Dr. Manoel A.B de Araújo 130A; © **084/3219-5798**) offers tapioca pancakes with over 40 different types of filling, not to mention coffee and homemade ice cream. It's open daily 5pm to midnight. One of the best spots for dancing in Alto de Ponta Negra, the **Salsa Bar** (Rua Manoel A.B. de Araújo 174; © **084/3236-2573;** 7pm–2am) is packed with tourists and locals showing off their Latin moves. The **Taverna Pub,** Rua Manoel A.B. de Araújo 174 (© **084/3236-3696;** www.tavernapub.com.br), may be low and dark and sweaty and cramped, but it's also the most popular spot in Alto Ponta Negra. Open daily from 11pm to 4am, it charges a cover of R$15 (US$7.50/£4).

VIA COSTEIRA

Cervejaria Via Costeira   A big sprawling barn of a place, with tasty brews on tap and a credible cold-cut buffet and pub-food kind of restaurant. Open daily 6pm to 1am. Via Costeira 4197A. ℂ **084/3202-1089.**

DOWNTOWN

Forró com Turista   If those feet of yours want to dance forró, but you don't quite know the steps, come to this traditional forró party, held every Thursday night in the old prison courtyard of the Centro de Turismo. There are numerous instructors (both male and female) to take you in hand and show you how it's done. Open Thursday 10pm to 2am. Rua Aderbal Figueiredo 980, Petrópolis (Centro de Turismo). ℂ **084/3211-6218.** www.forrocomturista.com.br. Cover R$15 (US$6.25/£3.05).

10 The Amazon: Manaus

Manaus: 3,281km (2,034 miles) NW of Rio de Janeiro, 3,156km (1,957 miles) NW of São Paulo

On the surface, Manaus looks a lot like other Brazilian cities. The old downtown is shabby and bustling. Along the shoreline in the upscale Ponta Negra area you'll find the same beachside high-rises, the same kiosks, and the same wide streets. But stop for a moment and contemplate: You're in the middle of nowhere with 1,000 miles of forest in every direction.

The largest city in the Amazon, Manaus's 1.6 million people live on the shores of the Rio Negro, just upstream from where it joins the Rio Solimões to become the Amazon. Though first settled in the 1600s, there's a frontier feel to the place.

Near the end of the 19th century, when the Amazon was the world's only rubber supplier, there was a 30-year boom in rubber and Manaus got rich indeed. Some of the city's finest buildings date back to this time, among them the Customs house and the famous Teatro Amazonas. The boom ended around 1910, some years after an enterprising Brit stole some Amazon rubber seeds and planted them in new plantations in Malaya (modern-day Malaysia).

These days, foreigners come to learn about the rainforest. Manaus is the main departure point for trips into the Amazon. We've reviewed numerous options for exploring the forest, from comfortable lodges to luxury cruises to simple expeditions by kayak.

ESSENTIALS

GETTING THERE

BY PLANE   Manaus's international airport **Eduardo Gomes,** Avenida Santos Dumont (ℂ **092/3652-1212**), is located 16km (10 miles) south of downtown. The airport is serviced by **Varig, Gol,** and **TAM** airlines. A taxi to Manaus Centro will cost about R$45 (US$25/£12). You also have the option of taking a **regular city bus,** no. 306 to Centro, for R$1.80 (US90¢/50p). Guests of the Tropical can take the **Fontur shuttle,** for R$15 (US$7.50/£4) per person.

BY BOAT   Boats dock at the **Hidroviaria do Amazonas (Riverboat Terminal;** ℂ **092/3621-4359**), Rua Marquês de Santa Cruz 25. Boats arrive or depart from here several times a week for downriver destinations, such as Belém at the mouth of the Amazon, and upriver destinations, such as Porto Velho in the state of Rondônia. From here, it is a short walk or taxi ride to the downtown hotels. From the terminal it's a

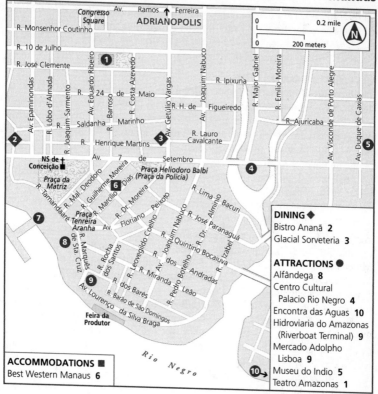

Manaus map showing streets, attractions, dining, and accommodations.

DINING ◆
Bistro Ananã **2**
Glacial Sorveteria **3**

ATTRACTIONS ●
Alfândega **8**
Centro Cultural
  Palacio Rio Negro **4**
Encontra das Aguas **10**
Hidroviaria do Amazonas
  (Riverboat Terminal) **9**
Mercado Adolpho
  Lisboa **9**
Museu do Indio **5**
Teatro Amazonas **1**

ACCOMMODATIONS ■
Best Western Manaus **6**

short walk or taxi ride, R$10 to R$15 (US$5–US$7.50/£2.70–£4), to the downtown hotels. To the Hotel Tropical it's a 20-minute taxi ride R$50 (US$25/£14).

GETTING AROUND

In downtown Manaus, all activity gravitates toward the waterfront on the Rio Negro. The main attractions for visitors are concentrated in a 20-block radius around the port and are easily accessible on foot. The downtown bus terminal is directly in front of the port. To the east of the terminal are a number of narrow parallel streets, centered on **Rua Guilherme Moreira,** that form Manaus's main downtown shopping district. The busy east-west **Avenida Sete de Setembro** marks the end of the oldest section of downtown. The only real site of interest north of here is the Teatro Amazonas, 4 blocks north on Rua Barroso. **Ponta Negra** beach, about 18km (11 miles) from downtown, is one of the more upscale neighborhoods where the beachfront has become a popular nightlife and entertainment area.

BY BUS From the Ponta Negra beach and the Hotel Tropical to downtown, take bus no. 120; the ride will take about 35 to 40 minutes and costs R$1.80 (US90¢/50p). Once downtown, all attractions are within walking distance.

BY TAXI Taxis can be hailed on the street or reserved by phone for a specific time. Contact **Coopertaxi** at © **092/3652-1544.** In town, call **Tele-Rádio Táxi** at

(C) **092/3633-3211.** In Ponta Negra, call **Ponta Negra Rádio Táxi** at (C) **092/3656-6121.** Taxis to and from the Hotel Tropical operate on a fixed price—currently R$50 (US$25/£14)—and don't run the meter. If you negotiate you can often knock R$10 (US$5/£2.70) off the price, but make sure you bargain before getting in the cab.

VISITOR INFORMATION

The city tourist information agency, **Manaustur,** Av. Sete de Setembro 157 ((C) **092/3622-4986**), is open Monday through Friday 9am to 6pm, but it's inconveniently in a run-down part of the port. Stop in at the airport instead. The tourism information desk at the airport is open from 7am to 11pm and located in the arrivals hall ((C) **092/3652-1120**). They can provide city maps, brochures, hotel information, and telephone numbers of tour operators.

Equally useful, the State of Amazonas tourism agency, **AmazonasTur,** has an info center at Rua Saldanha Marinho 321 (near the Opera House; (C) **092/3233-1928; www.amazonastur.am.gov.br**), that's open Monday through Friday from 9am to 6pm. There are also free public bathrooms here.

FAST FACTS   An **American Express** office is located at Praça Adalberto Valle 17 ((C) **092/3622-2577**). To exchange currency, try **Banco do Brasil,** Rua Guilherme Moreira 315, Centro ((C) **092/3621-5000**); **Cortês Câmbio,** Av. Sete de Setembro 1199, Centro ((C) **092/3622 4222**); or **Amazonas Shopping** ((C) **092/3642-2525**).

For medical attention, go to **Pronto Socorro e Hospital dos Acidentados,** Av. Joaquim Nabuco 1755, Centro ((C) **092/3663-2200**). If you need a dentist, contact Sos Dentista, Rua 24 de Maio 220 (Rio Negro Center), Room 710, Centro (C) **092/9982-1133**).

The **Tropical Hotel** has an **Internet cafe** open daily from 9am to 10pm; charge is R$18 (US$9/£5) per hour. In Centro, try **Amazon Cyber Café,** Av. Getulio Vargas 626 ((C) **092/3232-9068**), open Monday through Friday 9am to 11pm, Saturday from 10am to 8pm, and Sunday from 1 to 8pm (R$4/US$2/£1 per hour).

WHAT TO SEE & DO IN MANAUS
THE TOP ATTRACTIONS

Encontro das Aguas   The Meeting of the Waters is certainly a remarkable sight. The dark slow water of the Rio Negro meets the faster muddy brown water of the Rio Solimões, and because of differences in velocity, temperature, and salinity, the two rivers don't immediately blend but carry on side-by-side for miles. It's a classic Manaus day trip. If you're booked at a lodge downstream of Manaus, you'll pass through the Meeting of the Waters on the way there and back. If you haven't, there are day trips, most of which unfortunately include a trip to the detestable **Lago Janauary Ecological Park.** Located about an hour from Manaus, the Lago Janauary features some elevated boardwalks weaving through the trees and giant floating Vitoria Regia lily pads. It's reasonably pretty, but generations of tourists have spoiled the place. *Note:* In the dry season (approximately Aug–Dec), the trip through the Lago becomes impossible and tour operators will take you to the **Ilha da Terra Nova** instead to see the rubber trees and cocoa plantations.

All Manaus agencies offer day tours for about R$100 (US$50/£27). Try Viverde (C) 092/3248-9988.

Mercado Adolpho Lisboa (★)   The Adolpho Lisboa is a beautiful iron-and-glass copy of the now demolished market hall in Les Halles, Paris. It's a great place to see some of the local fish, fruits, and vegetables. All the fish vendors are kept in one area;

the variety of fish is overwhelming. Not for the squeamish, the vendors cut and clean the fish on the spot; though chopped in half, some of the larger catfish still wriggle. In case you want to heal thyself, stop in at one of the herb stalls. Who needs a pharmacy when the cures for diabetes, kidney failure, obesity, heart problems, and headache are all laid out in dried bunches of leaves?

Rua dos Barés 46, Centro. ✆ 092/233-0469. Mon–Sat 6am–6pm; Sun 6am–noon.

Museu do Indio   Spread out over six rooms, this museum presents the culture and social structure of the peoples of the Upper Rio Negro. Artifacts and clothing give an overview of their hunting and fishing traditions, as well as showing the spiritual rituals of a funeral and healing ceremony. The displays contain photos, drawings, a large number of artifacts, and occasionally models and replicas. All descriptions are in Portuguese, English, and German. Allow 1 hour.

Rua Duque de Caxias 356, Centro. ✆ 092/3635-1922. Admission R$5 (US$2.5/£1.35) Mon–Fri 8:30–11:30am and 2–4:30pm; Sat 8:30–11:30am.

Teatro Amazonas 🖈🖈   This is one tourist "must-see" that is actually worth seeing. This remarkable landmark was erected in the midst of the Amazon jungle in 1896 at the peak of the rubber boom. The tour shows off the lobby of marble and inlaid tropical hardwoods, the fine concert hall, and the romantic mural in the upstairs ballroom. Even better is to see a concert (see "Manaus After Dark," below). For the moment, the theater's official website unfortunately has no programming information.

Praça São Sebastião. ✆ 092/3622-1880. www.teatroamazonas.com.br. Guided 30-min. tours in English and Portuguese, departs every 30 min. R$6 (US$3/£1.60). Mon–Sat 9am–noon and 2–4pm.

SHOPPING

Downtown Manaus is one big shopping area: Vendors hawk their wares, stalls clog up the sidewalks and squares, and the streets are jam-packed with little stores. The main shopping streets run behind the **Praça Tenreiro Aranha, Rua Marcilio Dias, Rua Guilherme Moreira,** and **Rua Marechal Deodoro.** The streets around the market at **Rua dos Barés** sell more household goods and hammocks. The church square, **Praça da Matriz,** has a large market during weekdays, selling everything from clothing to hair accessories and bags. The city's largest mall is **Shopping Amazonas,** Av. Djalma Batista 482, Parque 10 (✆ 092/3642-3555). It's open Monday through Saturday from 10am to 10pm. Take bus no. 203, 209, or 214 from Praça da Matriz, Centro.

Feira de Artesanato, the crafts market located on the Praça Tenreiro Aranha s/n, Centro, sells a wide variety of Indian crafts. There is usually a large selection of necklaces, bracelets, woodcarvings, T-shirts, baskets, and handbags. Go early in the day for a better selection.

WHERE TO STAY IN MANAUS
CENTRO
Expensive
Best Western Manaus 🖈   Located within walking distance of all the main sites, this hotel is convenient for those who are only in town for a night before heading into the forest. The hotel is similar to North American Best Westerns. The rooms have recently been upgraded. Make sure to request a room in the new wing, which end in 12 through 18 (such as 312 through 318). All come with tile floors and new furnishings and have bright, modern colors. The old rooms have dated furniture and tatty carpets, and feel much smaller because of the dark furnishings.

Rua Marcilio Dias 217, Centro, Manaus, 69005-270 AM. (✆) **0800/761-5001** or 092/3622-2844. www.bestwestern. com.br. 102 units (showers only). R$280 (US$140/£76) standard; R$310 (US$155/£84) suite double. You can usually negotiate a 30% discount on these rates. Extra bed R$45–R$75 (US$23–US$38/£12–£20). Children under 6 stay free in parent's room. AE, DC, MC, V. Free parking. **Amenities:** Restaurant; bar; tour desk; room service; laundry service; nonsmoking floor. *In room:* A/C, TV, dataport, minibar, fridge.

PONTA NEGRA

Nineteen kilometers (12 miles) from downtown, Ponta Negra beach is a popular nightlife district on the bank of the Rio Negro. Access to Manaus is quick by bus or taxi, and the hotels have a regular shuttle as well; all excursions and tours include hotel pickup, and many boat tours depart from the dock of the Hotel Tropical.

Very Expensive

Tropical Manaus Business 🐦🐦🐦　Located right on the shore of the Rio Negro, the Tropical Manaus Business is the newest addition to the Tropical complex. Whereas the *old* Tropical oozes elegance and conjures up visions of explorers ready to take off on a jungle adventure, the new Tropical is all business. Bright and sleek, the hotel offers modern and spacious rooms with king-size beds, high-speed Internet, efficient A/C and phone system, 21st-century plumbing, electronic safes, no funny smells, and fabulous views of the Rio Negro. As perks, the hotel offers a free shuttle service to the airport and downtown and free 24-hour access to the business center. The hotel has a large outdoor pool and sundeck overlooking the Rio Negro and a state-of-the-art fitness center. Guests may also use all facilities of the Tropical Eco Resort.

Av. Coronel Teixeira 1320, Ponta Negra, Manaus, 69037-000 AM. (✆) **0800/701-2670** or 092/2123-3000. Fax 092/ 2123-3021. www.tropicalhotel.com.br. 184 units. R$425 (US$213/£115) double; R$497 (US$249/£134) suite. Inquire about discounts for Varig ticket-holders and Amex cardholders. Extra person add 25%. Children 10 and under stay free in parent's room. AE, DC, MC, V. Bus: 120. **Amenities:** Restaurant; 2 bars; large outdoor pool; health club; sauna; concierge; tour desk; car rental; business center; room service; laundry; dry cleaning; nonsmoking rooms and floors. *In room:* A/C, TV, dataport, minibar, hair dryer, safe.

Tropical Manaus Eco Resort 🐦🐦🐦　After the Copacabana Palace, this is the most famous hotel in Brazil. Built on the shores of the Rio Negro, within its own little patch of rainforest, the Tropical is a destination in itself. Outside there's a zoo, children's play area, archery range (lessons complimentary), a jogging trail, beach volleyball and soccer fields, horseback riding, and the list goes on. The large pool complex includes a wave pool. Inside, the original wing of the hotel is referred to as *ala colonial,* in contrast to the more modern *ala moderna.* Where you stay is more a matter of preference than quality. The colonial rooms have more character, with beautiful dark-wood furniture and hardwood floors, but they can also be a bit musty. The more modern wing is pleasantly furnished with carpets and contemporary decor in light colors. All rooms are a good size with high ceilings and large windows, and the bathrooms are spacious and modern, with showers and bathtubs. The rates below are the Internet rates. A travel agent can probably do better.

Av. Coronel Teixeira 1320, Ponta Negra, Manaus, 69029-120 AM. (✆) **0800/701-2670** or 092/3659-5000. Fax 092/ 3658-5026. www.tropicalhotel.com.br. 601 units. Standard or superior double R$365–R$400 (US$183–US$200/£99– £108); deluxe double R$510 (US$255/£138); junior suite double R$930 (US$465/£251). There is often a 10%–30% discount on these rates. Extra person add 25%. Children 10 and under stay free in parent's room. AE, DC, MC, V. Bus: 120. **Amenities:** 3 restaurants; 2 bars; dance club; large pool complex; tennis courts; health club; spa; sauna; watersports rental; children's program; game room; concierge; tour desk; car rental; business center; shopping arcade; salon; room service; massage; babysitting; laundry; dry cleaning; nonsmoking rooms and floors. *In room:* A/C, TV, dataport, minibar, fridge, hair dryer, safe.

ELSEWHERE

Mango Guest House ⓖ   The Mango is a nice small guesthouse, unfortunately located in a boring walled-off suburb about halfway between downtown and Ponta Negra. Rooms are simple, small, and pleasant, with tile floors, firm single or double beds, and clean, functional bathrooms with super-hot showers. All rooms have a small terrace that looks out on a grassy courtyard and small pool. The guesthouse has several nice lounges and sitting rooms and free Internet access. The Mango is perfect for those who just need to spend a night in Manaus. All tours pick up and drop off here, and the guesthouse will happily store your excess luggage while you are off in the rainforest.

Rua Flavio Espirito Santo 1, Kissia II, 69040-250 AM. ⓒ 092/3656-6033. Fax 092/3656-6101. www.naturesafaris. com.br. 14 units. R$150 (US$75/£41) double. Extra person add 25%. Credit cards only when booking online or via travel agency: AE, DC, MC, V. No credit cards accepted at the guesthouse. No public transit. **Amenities:** Restaurant; outdoor pool; free shared Internet terminal. *In room:* A/C, fridge.

Mercure Apartments Manaus ⓖ   Where the business travelers stay in Manaus. Located in Adrianópolis—fast becoming the city's restaurant hot spot—this new member of the well-respected Mercure chain offers comfortable clean rooms with tile floors and a single queen or two twin beds, plus a small functional work desk with plug ins for laptops and high-speed Internet. The hotel is only 4 years old, so everything has a new feel, and as with all Mercure properties the service is brisk and efficient.

Avenida da Recife 1000, Adrianópolis, 69040-250 AM. ⓒ **092/2101-1100.** Fax 092/2101-1101. www.accorhotels. com.br. 109 units. R$350 (US$175/£95) double. Extra person add 25%. AE, DC, MC, V. Bus: 118. **Amenities:** Restaurant; bar; rooftop pool; fitness center; Jacuzzi; laundry; room service. *In room:* A/C, TV, high-speed Internet access, minibar, fridge.

WHERE TO DINE

Manaus is not known for fine dining. Most restaurants are pretty casual affairs. You will probably have the best local cuisine on the boat trips or at the jungle lodges. If you do have a night or two in town, try these spots.

ADRIANÓPOLIS

In the past year or so, the upscale neighborhood of Adrianópolis has emerged as Manaus' culinary hot spot, with a number of fine restaurants in a relatively concentrated area. In addition to the Village (one of the city's best, see below), there's top quality (and top dollar) Portuguese cuisine at **Casa do Bacalhau** (Rua Paraíba 1587-A; ⓒ **092/ 3642-1723**). For local—and more affordable—Amazonian dishes there's **Choupana** (Av. Recife 790; ⓒ **092/3635-3878;** Wed–Sat 11am–3pmand 6:30–11pm, Sun noon–4pm). Even cheaper, and arguably more fun, is **Açaí e Companhia** (Rua Acre; ⓒ 092/3653-3637; daily noon–midnight), a kind of outdoor kiosk that specializes in local fish dishes such as jambu and tambaqui. On Friday and Saturday evening there's live music.

Village BRAZILIAN   One of the city's best restaurants, the Village is a dining destination for the city's elite. The menu covers a vast range, with seafood and fish dishes, risottos and pastas, meat and chicken lamb all on offer. The chef's approach has a slight Italian tinge, while the use of Brazilian ingredients (such as catupiry cheese with Bahian prawns) gives the dishes their local flavor. The wine list is likely the most extensive in Manaus.

Rua Recife 948, Adrianópolis. ⓒ **092/3234-3296.** www.villagerestaurante.com.br. Main courses R$24–R$48 (US$12–US$24/£6.50–£13). AE, DC, MC, V. Mon–Sat noon–3pm and 6pm–midnight.

Amazonian Cuisine

Amazonian cuisine uses lots of ingredients available only locally. The star attraction is fish. It's worth visiting the market in Manaus just to see what some of these creatures look like. Make sure you try the *tucunaré*, one of the prime fishes with meat so tasty it's best served plainly grilled. *Pirarucú* is known as the cod of the Amazon. *Tambaqui* and *paçu* also have delicious firm flesh that works well in stews and broths.

Tacacá is a delicious local soup made with the yellow *tucupí* cassava, *murupí* peppers, garlic, onion, and dried shrimp. You'll often find it for sale on the streets, traditionally served in a gourd. All Amazon dishes are usually served with some cassava, a drier version of the *farofa* you find in Rio and São Paulo.

The region is also very rich in fruits, many of which are found only in the Amazon. The citruslike *bacuri* has soft spongelike skin and white flesh; like Christmas mandarins, you can't have just one. The *cupuaçu* is a large round fruit, like a small pale coconut but with an odd taste of sweet and sour. It's usually served in desserts and juices. *Tucumã* is a small and hard fruit similar to an unripe peach. Locals eat slices of it on bread. *Açaí* is a popular fruit, but it can't be eaten raw; the berries are first soaked and then squashed to obtain the juice. You will find it in juices and ice cream. Some people also eat the dark purple pulp with a bit of sugar and manioc *(açaí na tijela)*.

CENTRO

Bistrô Ananã BRAZILIAN   This charming little bistro prepares dishes with Amazonian ingredients that you won't find anywhere else. The signature dish is rack of tambaqui (fish) ribs in a chutney of tucupi, with Bahian risotto and a *farofa* (manioc flour) of local bananas.

Travessa Padre Ghisland, 38, Centro (near the Colégio Dom Bosco). ℰ **092/3234-0056.** Main courses R$24–R$48 (US$12–US$24//£6.50–£13). AE, MC, V. Wed–Sat 7:30pm–midnight.

Glacial Sorveteria DESSERT   One of the best ways to try many of the exotic fruits of the Amazon is in the form of ice cream. Some suggested flavors are *cupuaçu, açaí, jaca, bacaba,* and *graviola.* Grab a couple of flavors and taste away. There is another shop in Ponta Negra (ℰ **092/3658-3980**).

Av. Getulio Vargas 161, Centro. ℰ **092/3233-4172.** www.glacial.com.br. R$4.50–R$9 (US$2.25–US$4.50/ £1.20–£2.50). No credit cards. Mon–Thurs 8am–11pm; Fri–Sun 8am–11:30pm.

MANAUS AFTER DARK

Better than just touring the **Teatro Amazonas,** Praça São Sebastião s/n, Centro (ℰ **092/3622-2420;** www.teatroamazonas.com.br), is actually sitting back in the plush chairs and taking in a performance. The theater has a resident philharmonic orchestra, choir, and dance group who perform regularly.

In downtown Manaus, the best spot for an evening drink is **Bar do Armando,** Rua 10 de Julho 593 (ℰ **092/3232-1195**). Located on the square in front of the Opera House, this venerable drinking spot is the nighttime home of Manaus's artists, intellectuals, journalists, and other ne'er-do-wells.

The city's best nightlife spot is out near the Tropical Hotel at **Ponta Negra Beach.** People stroll up and down the wide boulevard, there are regular concerts and events at the amphitheater, and a number of bars have live entertainment in the evening. Most places open at 5 or 6pm Monday to Friday and stay open until at least 1 or 2am. On Saturday and Sunday, many venues open at 11am and stay open until 3 or 4am. Inside the Tropical Hotel, the disco **Studio Tropical Night** (© 092/3659-5000) has DJs Thursday through Saturday.

Two popular gay bars can be found in Centro: **Enigma's Bar,** Rua Silva Ramos 1054, Centro (© 092/3234-7985), open Thursday through Sunday, offers live music and DJs. **Turbo Seven,** Rua Vivaldo Lima 33, Centro (© 092/3232-6793), features drag shows and go-go boys; it's only open on Saturday and Sunday, from 11pm onwards.

THE AMAZON

There are many ways of exploring the Amazon. What suits you best depends on how much time you have and how comfortable you want to be. Most people choose to stay at a lodge within a few hours by boat from Manaus. Lodges vary in luxury and size, but the programs offered are pretty similar. Another comfortable way of seeing the Amazon is by boat. The vessel serves as your home base, and you take excursions in canoes up the smaller channels. Specialized operators offer expedition-style trips where the emphasis is on truly experiencing the rainforest. You don't need to be in top shape for these; you just have to be able to hike or paddle a boat, and be willing to forego amenities such as minibars and hot showers for a more hands-on jungle experience. One excellent adventure outfitter is **Amazon Mystery Tours** (see "Deeper into the Amazon: Expeditions," below).

LODGES

You can contact lodges directly or contact a tour operator who can assist you in choosing the right package. One of your best options is to contact the experts at **Brazil Nuts** (© 800/553-9959; www.brazilnuts.com). In Manaus, contact **Viverde,** Rua dos Cardeiros 26 (© 092/3248-9988). They have an excellent English-language website (www.viverde.com.br) with detailed information on both tours and the Amazon in general. Another reputable agency is **South America Travel** (© 800/747-4540; www. southamerica.travel). **Note:** All prices are per person and include transportation, all meals, and basic excursions. Airport transfer is usually included in the price, but always check. The policies for children vary per lodge and per season; depending on occupancy you may have bargaining power. Most lodges offer up to a 50% discount for children 12 and under; ask when making reservations. All rates are given in U.S. dollars only; most lodges will accept foreign currencies.

Lodges Close to Manaus

Amazon Ecopark Lodge ✪✪   The Amazon Ecopark is one of the better lodges close to Manaus, as long as you arrive with the right expectations. The lodge itself is about a 2-hour boat trip from Manaus and sits on a private reserve. The *igarapé* (small tidal inlet) is of exclusive use to the lodge, which gives it a secluded feel. In the dry season, several beaches are right across from the lodge and the vegetation is lush and beautiful. The lodge also has some natural pools for swimming, particularly nice for people who are never quite comfortable swimming in the dark waters of the Rio Negro. Most of the excursions take place in close proximity to the lodge and are done in unmotorized canoes. Paddling into the flooded forest, you'll be able to get a good sense of the sights and sounds of the jungle. All packages include airport transfers, all meals (the food is fabulous), deluxe accommodations, and well-trained guides who speak excellent English.

Reservations office in Rio. ☎ 021/2547-7742 or ☎/fax 021/2256-8083. www.amazonecopark.com.br. 64 units (showers only). 3-day packages start at US$395 per person, 4-day packages US$475 per person (both these packages include a tour to the Meeting of the Waters). Children 6–12 pay 25% of rate, 13–16 pay 50% of rate. AE, DC, MC, V. **Amenities:** Restaurant; bar; pool. *In room:* A/C, fan, no phone.

Amazon Village Lodge ⚘

The Amazon Village is a well-run operation with its own small rainforest reserve, now alas being seriously encroached upon by ever-growing cattle operations and the beginnings of urban sprawl from the city. It's too bad, because the Amazon Village is a class act—owners treat guides well and do a good job presenting the rainforest. If at all possible, chose something farther from the city, but if you do for some reason have to be close, this would be a good option. The lodge buildings are attractively designed with local wood in the native *maloca* style, while rooms are small and clean with private toilets and showers. There is no hot water, and electricity is limited to the evening hours. There's the usual package of excursions. The lodge doesn't have a swimming pool, but you can swim in the river.

Rua Ramos Ferreira 1189, sala 403, Manaus, AM 69010-120. ☎ 092/3633-1444. Fax 092/3633-3217. www.amazon-village.com.br. 45 units (showers only). 3-day packages start at US$540 per person. AE, DC, MC, V. **Amenities:** Restaurant; bar.

Tiwa Amazonas Ecoresort

The Tiwa fills an odd ecological niche, neither jungle lodge nor city hotel. It sits directly opposite the Tropical, on the far bank of the Rio Negro. Access is via fast motor launch; the trip takes about 20 minutes, and boats go back and forth every other hour. Each of the sizable rooms takes up half a log cabin, which are set in a circle around a small pond. The hotel pool is lovely. Theoretically, the Tiwa could serve as an alternative to the Tropical—a luxury resort, just a little farther from the city. But what the Tiwa is selling itself as is a jungle lodge, with 2- and 3-day packages and the usual outings including caiman spotting and treetop walking. But the Tiwa is just simply too close to the city for that. If you don't have time to go to a jungle lodge, and just want a teensy-tiny taste of the Amazon, the Tiwa may be an option. Otherwise, go elsewhere.

Caixa Postal 2575, Manaus, AM 69005-970. ☎ 092/9995-7892. www.tiwa.com.br. 52 units (showers only). 1-night, 2-day packages US$380 double; each additional day approximately an extra US$275 double. Policy for children negotiable. AE, DC, MC, V. **Amenities:** Restaurant; bar; outdoor pool; beach; Hobie Cat rentals. *In room:* A/C, fridge, minibar, no phone.

Lodges Farther from Manaus

Amazonat ⚘⚘

If you like space to move around, you will love the Amazonat, set on its own 900-hectare (2,223-acre) reserve of *terra firme* 160km (1,000 miles) east of Manaus. Amazonat is surrounded by extensive walking trails that you can roam at will. Though the lodge is not on a river, there is a lake with a beach for swimming and an orchid park with over 1,000 specimens to see and sniff and wonder at. The 3-day package includes a number of guided walks and a river trip on the Urubu for birdwatching, as well as plenty of time to explore on your own. The lodge itself is set in beautiful jungle gardens and the chalets are more than comfortable.

Caixa Postal 1273, Manaus, AM 69006-970. ☎ 092/3328-1183 (hotel), or ☎/fax 092/3652-1359 (reservations office). www.amazonat.com.br. 18 units (showers only). 4-day packages start at US$400 per person, 5-day packages US$645 per person. Children 6–12 pay 25% of rate, 13–16 pay 50% of rate. AE, DC, MC, V. **Amenities:** Restaurant; bar; pool. *In room:* Fan, minibar, no phone.

Amazon Eco Lodge ★★   Located just a few kilometers from the Juma Lodge (see below), the Amazon Eco Lodge has the same excellent forest surroundings, and the same long trip from Manaus. The package of outings at both lodges is also essentially the same. The one thing the Eco Lodge has over the Juma is it's fleet of small canoes, always at the ready should a guest feel like going off for a paddle. The Eco Lodge floats on the lake, on top of huge log rafts, which is really quite charming. It's also a great place for river swimming. The disadvantage is that accommodations are in fairly small rooms, built in wings with wooden walls; it can get noisy. Also, toilets and showers are shared, in a shower block near the center of the raft complex. Prices at the Juma and Eco Lodge are comparable, but for the money Juma provides better value.

Rua Flavio Espirito Santo 1, Kissia II, Manaus AM 69040-250. © 092/3656-6033. Fax 092/3656-6101. www.nature safaris.com.br. 18 units (common bathrooms and showers). 4-day, 3-night packages. US$599 per person. Policy for children negotiable. AE, DC, MC, V. **Amenities:** Restaurant; bar; outdoor pool; beach; Hobie Cat rentals. *In room:* A/C, fridge, minibar, no phone.

Ariaú Jungle Towers *(Overrated*   Avoid this place. Just don't go. The Ariaú is all that is wrong with Amazon "eco-tourism"; it is the Disneyland Ford Factory of jungle lodges. Marketing photos of treehouses and boardwalks may suggest a Swiss Family Robinson adventure, but what the Ariaú delivers is mass-market tourism, with hundreds of guests getting trundled each day along a set tourist route that has already been trodden—literally—tens of thousands of times. Repetition is a factor at any lodge, but the Ariaú has a serious problem of scale—there are over 300 units in place—combined with a management fixation on minimum expense and maximum profit. Excursions are the usual, but at the Ariaú group size runs up to 25. Trips are always in motorized canoes, equipped with noisy, fume-spewing two-stroke *rabete* motors.

Rua Leonardo Malcher 699, Manaus, AM 69010-040. © 092/3232-4160. Fax 092/3233-5615. www.ariautowers.com. 300 units (showers only, cold water). 3-day packages start at US$450, 4-day packages US$550. Prices are negotiable; suites can be had for as little as US$200 per package when occupancy is low. AE, DC, MC, V. **Amenities:** Restaurant; bar; TV room; pool; gym; spa; laundry service; Internet room (intermittent connection). *In room:* A/C, fridge, no phone.

Flotel Piranha ★★   The Flotel is unique among all the lodges in that it floats on *varzea*, flooded forest in the richer "white water" of the Solimões river system. White-water systems flow through younger, richer soils, and are thus richer in dissolved nutrients. Forests in the upland areas of white-water rivers have bigger, taller trees (though don't expect the trees close to the lodge to be huge—trees of the flooded forest, on both white and black rivers, don't grow to enormous sizes, simply due to the stress of getting covered for 4 months of the year in water). White-water rivers support richer, denser populations of aquatic life—more fish, and consequently more birds. The catch to all this, of course, is that the base of the food chain is also more abundant; white-water rivers are much richer in insect life, including mosquitoes.

In truth, the mosquitoes aren't that bad and certainly nowhere nearly as bad as they are, for example, in the hardwood forests of the eastern U.S. or Canada. The lodge has good screens on the rooms and dining areas. The benefit is you get to see and hear constant splashes from jumping fish, and see more and larger birdlife, particularly wading birds.

Rua Flavio Espirito Santo 1, Kissia II, Manaus AM 69040-250. © 092/3656-6033. Fax 092/3656-6101. www.nature safaris.com.br. 20 units (showers only). 4-day, 3-night packages. US$590 per person. Policy for children negotiable. AE, DC, MC, V. **Amenities:** Restaurant; bar; swimming platform. *In room:* A/C, no phone.

Juma Lodge ★★   One of the best of the lodges in the area, the Juma gets jungle points for its small size and its distance from Manaus. Rooms are all in comfortable small cabins built on stilts. The best rooms are the charming self-contained doubles (rooms 9, 10, and 11) with a view out over the lake. From your veranda, you can often see dolphins and caiman. Cabins are connected to the dining hall by elevated board-walks. The Juma is located in the middle of a sizable private nature reserve, so the for-est surroundings are quite well preserved. The lodge offers the standard excursions.

Lago do Juma (no mailing address). ℭ 092/3245-1177 (lodge) or 092/3232-2707 (reservations office). www.juma lodge.com.br. 11 units (showers only). 3-day, 2-night packages start at US$590 per person, 4-day packages. US$708 per person. Children 6–12 pay 50% of rate. AE, MC, V. **Amenities:** Restaurant; bar. *In room:* Fan, fridge, no phone.

BOAT TRIPS

On a boat-tour package, the experience is similar to that of a lodge; there are excur-sions on the small side channels, a sunset and sunrise tour, caiman spotting, piranha fishing, and a visit to a *caboclo* (river peasant) settlement. The difference is that in the time you're not on an excursion, you're moving on the river. There is always something to see, even if it's just the vastness of the river itself.

Viverde, Rua dos Cardeiros 26, Manaus (ℭ/fax **092/3248-9988;** www.viverde. com.br), can arrange boat voyages or charters. Their website has photos and descrip-tions of the better Manaus-based touring boats.

Amazon Clipper Cruises (ℭ **092/3656-1246;** www.amazonclipper.com.br) has three old-style Amazon riverboats—the *Amazon Angler, Selly Clipper,* and *Selly Clip-per II*—which make regular 3- and 4-day trips departing from the Hotel Tropical. The boats have cabins with bunk beds and private bathrooms, and in the evening the cab-ins have air-conditioning. The 3-day tour stays on the Solimões River; the 4-day tour goes up the Rio Negro. Both tours include a visit to Janauary Park and the Meeting of the Waters. The price for the 3-day Solimões tour is US$420, and the 4-day Rio Negro tour costs US$580. Children age 11 and younger receive a 50% discount.

Swallows and Amazons ℛ   Swallows and Amazons is run by New Englander Mark Aitchison and his Brazilian wife, Tania. The company's core trip is a 7-day pack-age that spends a day in Manaus and then sets off up the Rio Negro to explore the ter-ritory around the Anavilhanas Archipelago. Transportation is on company-owned traditional wooden riverboats, while exploration is done either on foot or by canoes. Accommodation is either on the riverboat or in a comfortable but basic lodge near the Anavilhanas Archipelago. Maximum group size on any trip is eight. Cost for any of the trips is about US$140 (£72) per day if you book directly. These trips run year-round; check the website for timing and availability.

Rua Quintino Bocaiuva 189, 2nd Floor, Manaus, AM 69005–110. ℭ 0923/3622-1246. www.swallowsandamazons tours.com.

DEEPER INTO THE AMAZON: EXPEDITIONS

Amazon Mystery Tours ℛℛℛ *Value* If you want to really explore the jungle, this is the company to go with. Amazon Mystery has the skills and experience to bring you deep into the rainforest, make your time there safe, fun, and informative, and then get you back to town again. The company's core adventure is kayak descents of Amazon tributary rivers upstream of Manaus. A typical day includes a few hours of paddling, followed by a delicious lunch of fresh fish, followed by a hike to a waterfall or hidden cavern that few have ever seen. At night, you head out with a spotlight to search for caiman or other jungle creatures. The camping is very comfortable, the food is excel-lent (always important), and the company knows to bring along the little extras, such as folding chairs, that make camping civilized. You sleep in hammocks. At present,

Amazon Mystery has 6- and 7-day descents of the Rio Urubu, 4- and 5-day descents along Rio Tupanâ, and 8- and 10-day descents on the Rio Jatapu. On many trips there's also tree climbing, where you hoist yourself 60m or 70m (197 ft.–230 ft.) up into the rainforest canopy the way researchers do. This is truly magical.

Av. Djalma Batista 385, sala 103, Manaus. 𝒞 092/3633-7844. Fax 092/3233-2780. www.amazon-outdoor.com. Prices average US$150–US$200 (£77–£103) per person per day, which includes all airport transfers, accommodations in Manaus, equipment, drinks (alcoholic and non), meals, guides, and excursions.

11 The Pantanal

Cuiabá: 1,978km (1,226 miles) NW of Rio de Janeiro, 1,608km (997 miles) NW of São Paulo Campo Grande: 1,414km (877 miles) NW of Rio de Janeiro, 992km (615 miles) NW of São Paulo

The best place in South America to see wildlife is not the Amazon but the Pantanal, a France-size wetland on the far western edge of Brazil that is bursting with animals—capybaras, caimans, jaguars, anacondas, giant otters, colorful Hyacinth macaws, kites, hawks, and flocks of storks and herons. The largest flood plain in the world, the Pantanal's rhythm is governed by the rivers. In the wet season, from November through April, the rivers fill up and flood to cover a vast alluvial plain for months. Millions of birds are attracted to this aquatic paradise, and mammals take refuge on the remaining few mounds of dry land. As the water drains, from May onwards, the land dries up, and the situation slowly reverses: Animals are attracted to the few remaining water pools. Fish get trapped in these pools, and birds and mammals alike gather for water and food as they wait for the rains to start.

Thanks to this yearly cycle, the land cannot be farmed intensively. Most farms use the land for cattle grazing in the dry season only, moving the cattle when the fields flood. Few roads of any kind exist in the Pantanal; the best way to explore the area is to make like the locals and head out on horseback. Many of the cattle *fazendas* (ranches) in the area have been slowly converting over to tourism. Staying at one of these lodges is your best option for exploring the area.

Tip: If you only have a limited time to spend in the Pantanal, we recommend seeing the North Pantanal; allow for at least 3 days at a lodge, and 4 days is ideal. We highly recommend Araras Eco Lodge (p. 348); accommodations are basic, but the territory is fabulous and the guides are excellent.

CUIABA & THE NORTH PANTANAL

Cuiabá is a modern town with little in the way of attractions. All lodges will pick up guests at the airport and whisk them out to the Pantanal without the need to spend any time in the city.

GETTING THERE & VISITOR INFORMATION

Cuiabá's airport, **Aeroporto Marechal Rondon,** is located 6km (4 miles) south of the city center in the adjacent municipality of Varzea Grande. The airport is serviced by **Varig, Gol,** and **TAM** airlines. A taxi to downtown will cost about R$25 (US$13/£7). The only buses to Centro are regular city buses and are not recommended for travelers with luggage. *Note:* If you have booked a tour to a Pantanal lodge, make sure the operator has your flight information to arrange for pickup.

BY BUS Cuiabá's efficient bus terminal, **Engenheiro de Sá** (𝒞 065/3621-1040), is on Av. Marechal Deodoro s/n in Alvorada, just north of the city center. Buses to Campo Grande, gateway to the south Pantanal, depart daily at 7am and 8 and

9:30pm, and take approximately 10 hours. The overnight buses have comfortable reclining chairs. Contact **Motta** (© **065/3621-2514;** www.motta.com.br). The fare is R$60 (US$30/£16).

TOUR OPERATORS IN THE NORTH PANTANAL

One of the best tour operators is **Pantanal Explorer,** Av. Governador Ponce de Arruda 670, Varzea Grande (© **065/3682-2800;** fax 065/3682-1260; www.araraslodge.com. br). Stays in the Pantanal are at the excellent Araras Eco Lodge. In addition, the company offers trips to the Chapada dos Guimarães, boat trips in the Pantanal, as well as eco-tours to the Mato Grosso part of the Amazon rainforest. Another well-known tour operator is **Anaconda Turismo,** Rua Marechal Deodoro 2142, Goiabeiras (© **065/ 3028-5990;** www.anacondapantanal.com.br). This operator works with a large number of *fazendas* and *pousadas* and can customize a package according to your interests. It also operates in the Chapada dos Guimarães (see "A Side Trip to Chapada dos Guimarães," below). If you want to reserve your Pantanal package before arriving in Brazil, you can contact **Brazil Nuts** (© **800/553-9959** or 914/593-0266; www. brazilnuts.com) or **4StarBrazil** (© **866/464-7827;** www.4starbrazil.com).

Most packages—including transportation, English-speaking guides, accommodations, and meals—cost around R$300 (US$150/£81) per day per person, depending on the time of year and number of people in your party.

THE TRANSPANTANEIRA

Despite the name, this gravel road stops dead at Porto Jofre, 143km (89 miles) from where it began, and at least that far from the far edge of the Pantanal. Had it been completed, it would likely have destroyed the Pantanal by totally skewing the ecosystem's drainage pattern, but in its unfinished state, it has become one of the great wildlife-viewing areas in the world. The ditches on either side of the roadbed have become favorite feeding grounds for kingfishers, egrets, jabiru storks, and more than four varieties of hawks and three different kinds of kites. Beneath the many rickety bridges are small rivers or pools where *jacaré* (caiman) gather by the hundreds. Spend but a day on the Transpantaneira, and you'll see more wildlife than you'd see in a week in the Amazon.

To reach the Transpantaneira, take highway BR-163 west from Cuiabá. After about 18km (11 miles), turn southwest on highway MT-060 and follow it for 75km (46 miles) to the small town of Poconé. Follow the signs through the small downtown to the beginning of the Transpantaneira on the far side of town.

LODGES IN THE NORTH PANTANAL

Araras Eco Lodge 🐦🐦   Araras Lodge is likely the best spot for exploring the north Pantanal. The location by the Transpantaneira is excellent, and lodge owner Andre Thuronyi has done extensive work to improve the local wildlife habitat. With only 14 rooms, the lodge is pleasantly small and rustic. No fancy rooms or amenities are available, but each guest room comes with a private bathroom and a hammock on the veranda. The guides are usually good quality. Activities include hikes along a rustic boardwalk through the flooded fields to the lodge's lookout tower. Other excursions include boat or canoe trips on a small local river known for large hawks and giant river otters (we saw both). On drives along the Transpantaneira, even in a 3-hour time span, you'll lose track of the number of birds you'll see. Horse lovers will be in heaven riding through the flooded fields. If you know how to ride, the guides are happy to let

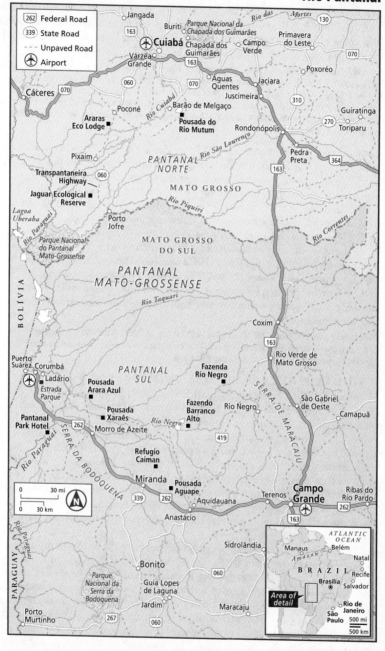

The Pantanal

Legend:
- 262 Federal Road
- 339 State Road
- - - - Unpaved Road
- ✈ Airport

Jangada
Buriti
Parque Nacional da Chapada dos Guimarães
Rio das Mortes
130
163
Cuiabá ✈
Chapada dos Guimarães
Campo Verde
Primavera do Leste
070
Várzea Grande
163
070
Cáceres
070
060
Aguas Quentes
070
Jaciara
Poxoréo
Poconé
Rio Cuiabá
Barão de Melgaço
Juscimeira
310
Pousada do Rio Mutum
Rondonópolis
Guiratinga
270
Toriparu
Araras Eco Lodge
Pixaim
PANTANAL NORTE
Rio São Lourenço
Pedra Preta
364
Transpantaneira Highway
060
MATO GROSSO
163
Jaguar Ecological Reserve
Rio Piquiri
Lagoa Uberaba
Rio Paraguai
Porto Jofre
MATO GROSSO DO SUL
Rio Correntes
Parque Nacional do Pantanal Mato-Grossense
PANTANAL MATO-GROSSENSE
Rio Taquari
BOLÍVIA
Coxim
163
Rio Verde de Mato Grosso
Puerto Suárez
Corumbá ✈
Ladârio
PANTANAL SUL
Fazenda Rio Negro
Estrada Parque
Pousada Arara Azul
SERRA DE MARACAJU
São Gabriel de Oeste
Camapuã
Pantanal Park Hotel
262
Pousada Xaraês
Morro de Azeite
Rio Negro
Fazendo Barranco Alto
Rio Negro
Rio Paraguai
SERRA DA BODOQUENA
419
Refugio Caiman
Miranda
Pousada Aguape
Terenos
Campo Grande ✈
Ribas do Rio Pardo
0   30 mi
0   30 km
339
262
Aquidauana
163
262
Anastácio
PARAGUAY
Rio Paraguai
Sidrolândia
Bonito
060
Parque Nacional da Serra da Bodoquena
Guia Lopes de Laguna
Jardim
Maracaju
Porto Murtinho
267
060

Inset map:
ATLANTIC OCEAN
Manaus
Belém
Amazon
Natal
BRAZIL
Recife
Brasília
Salvador
Area of detail
São Paulo
Rio de Janeiro
500 mi
500 km

you have some fun and gallop through the fields, startling caiman and snakes underfoot. The food is delicious and plentiful, often including excellent local fish. Araras Eco Lodge offers a package deal with a 3-night stay at the lodge and a 1-night stay in the Chapada dos Guimarães for some good hiking and swimming.

Transpantaneira Hwy. Reservation office: Av. Governador Ponce de Arruda 670, Varzea Grande, MT. © **065/3682-2800.** Fax 065/3682-1260. www.araraslodge.com.br. 19 units (showers only). R$980 (US$490/£265) per person for a 3-day, 2-night package; R$2,484 (US$1,242/£671) 6-day package (including the Chapada Guimarães), including airport pickup and drop-off plus all meals and guided activities. Extra person add about 25%. Children 10 and under stay free in parent's room. AE, DC, MC, V. Free parking. **Amenities:** Restaurant; bar; outdoor pool; laundry. *In room:* A/C, no phone.

Jagaur Ecological Reserve ★★ Wildlife viewing is always a matter of luck and patience, particularly when it comes to large predators such as jaguars. But one of the best ways of improving your odds is to visit this lodge—the centerpiece of a private ecological reserve—where an astonishing one in four guests sees one of these huge South American cats. It's a very long way (110km/68 miles) down the bumpy Transpantaneira, and the accommodations are expensive and only basic, but for a view of that big cat it may be worth it. For the 75% of guests who do not see jaguars, there is still the usual vast array of caiman and colorful birds, so rare in the rest of the world, so common in the Pantanal. Note that it's probably best to book your stay here through **Open Door Tours** (© **067/3321-8303;** www.opendoortur.com.br). The JER has been in operation for a number of years, and while operations in the field run smoothly, their booking operations have been a little on the amateur side. Better to deal with professionals.

Transpantaneira Km 110, Poconé, MT. © **065/3646-8557** (office) or 067/9919-5518 (lodge). www.jaguarreserve.com. 9 units (showers only). R$1,290 (US$645/£348) 4-day 3-night package per person, meals and transfers included. Free parking. **Amenities:** Wildlife-viewing. *In room:* No phone.

A SIDE TRIP TO CHAPADA DOS GUIMARÃES

In appearance, the Chapada dos Guimarães has much in common with the desert buttes of Arizona or Utah—weird, wonderful formations of bright red rock, and long beautiful canyons. Vegetation is dry and scrubby, except where the many river channels flow; then you get waterfalls streaming down into basins lush with tropical vegetation. The Chapada is a quiet, laid-back place with a slight counterculture feel and is the most convenient base from which to set off exploring. Hiking nearby is excellent; trails are clear even if—as ever in Brazil—they're completely without markers or signage. Most trails end at either a viewpoint, a waterfall, or a natural pool (sometimes all three!). Wildlife is not up to the standard set by the Pantanal, but in the Chapada you do have the opportunity of seeing the gorgeous red macaw, oftentimes playing in the thermals by a cliff side.

The best time to visit is May through September, when the weather is dry and sunshine almost guaranteed. The heavy rains in the summer (Dec–Apr) can make some of the trails treacherous and the dirt roads inaccessible. The best hikes include **Cachoeira Veu de Noiva,** the tallest waterfall in the park; **Mirante da Geodesia,** a fabulous lookout over the lowlands below the Chapada, with Cuiabá in the distance; **Cidade de Pedra (City of Stone),** which is named after the eroded formations that appear to form structures and look like ruins of buildings; and **Morro São Jerônimo,** the highest point in the Chapada. Morro São Jerônimo can be reached by a 4-hour hike; bring lots of water and sunscreen, as you will be exposed to the hot sun for most of the way.

If you're staying overnight, there are a couple of good options. **Solar do Inglês** (★, Rua Cipriano Curvo 142, Centro (✆ **065/3301-1389;** www.chapadadosguimaraes. com.br/solardoingles), is a simple *pousada* right in town. It offers eight nicely furnished rooms, plus a nice pool and a garden. The main advantage of staying at this hotel is that you can walk to the restaurants and shops. Rooms cost R$190 (US$95/£51) for a double, including breakfast and afternoon tea. A bit out of town, the **Pousada Penhasco** (★, Rodovia Penhasco (2.5km/1½ miles from the center of town), Boa Clima (✆ **065/3624-1000;** www.penhasco.com.br), boasts a great location, on the edge of a cliff with a view out over the flatland below all the way to Cuiabá. Rooms are in small cabins spread out over the property. Inside, the cabins are simple, but spacious and pleasant. The Inn's leisure area includes a beautifully landscaped outdoor pool area. Rooms cost R$219 (US$110/£59) double.

To stuff yourself silly on a variety of regional dishes, head to **O Mestrinho,** Rua Quinco Caldas 119, Centro (✆ **065/9957-2113**). Dishes include chicken and beef stews, beans, *farofa,* and grilled fish. It's open daily from 11am to 5pm. Perched on the edge of the plateau and overlooking the plains below the Chapada is **Morro dos Ventos** (★, Chacara Morro dos Ventos via Estrada do Mirante (✆ **065/3301-1030**). The menu offers regional home cooking. Dishes are huge and serve at least three people. A good choice is chicken stew with okra served in a heavy cast-iron pot with generous side dishes of beans, salad, *farofa,* and rice. It's open daily from 9am to 6pm.

GETTING THERE   The Chapada is 72km (45 miles) north of Cuiabá. By car, follow the MT 251 to the park and the town of Chapada. Direct buses leave from Cuiabá's *rodoviária,* R$8 (US$4/£2). **Viação Rubi** (✆ **065/3624-9044**) has daily departures at 9am, 10:30am, 2pm, and 6:30pm.

The tourist office will have you believe that you could easily spend a week here, but we figure 2 days is plenty. An excellent local tour operator, **Ecoturismo Cultural,** Praça Dom Wunibaldo 464 (✆ **065/3301-1393;** www.chapadadosguimaraes.com.br), arranges day trips with guides and transportation and can assist with accommodations. The tour operators listed under "Tour Operators in the North Pantanal," above also provide day trips or overnight packages to the Chapada, in combination with a visit to the Pantanal.

CAMPO GRANDE & THE SOUTH PANTANAL

Campo Grande is a fairly new town; established at the end of the 19th century, it is an important transportation hub for the region. The Pantanal in Mato Grosso do Sul is a little less wild, a little more given over to cattle ranching, and significantly harder to access.

GETTING THERE

BY PLANE   **TAM, Varig,** and **Gol** service Campo Grande from Rio and São Paulo. Campo Grande's airport is 7km (4¼ miles) west of downtown on Avenida Duque de Caxias (✆ **067/368-6093**). A taxi from the airport to the center of town should cost about R$25 (US$13/£7).

BY BUS   The bus station in Campo Grande is at Rua Dom Aquino and Rua Joaquim Nabuco (✆ **067/3321-8797**). Buses connect Campo Grande to Cuiabá (approximately 10 hr.), Bonito (5 hr.), and Corumbá (7 hr.).

VISITOR INFORMATION

There is a **tourist information booth** at the **airport** (© **0800-647-6050** or 067/3363-3116 and the **main bus terminal** (© **067/3382-2350**). Both are open 9am to 6pm Monday through Saturday, but neither offer English-speaking staff. However, they can offer a few maps of the city, and some information on the Pantanal, Bonito, and other sights of interest.

TOUR OPERATORS IN THE SOUTH PANTANAL (CAMPO GRANDE)

Located in Campo Grande, **Open Door** has some excellent packages for the Pantanal, for Bonito, and for combinations of the two. If you're just interested in the **Pantanal,** a **4-day/3-night** package tour at a Pantanal lodge including all meals and activities, with transfer from and to Campo Grande airport, starts at R$1,398 (US$699/£378). Trips to **Bonito** include admission to a few of the most popular activities, such as a visit to the blue lake cave and snorkeling on the Rio Sucuri. A **2-night/3-day Bonito** trip starts at R$812 (US$406/£219), including accommodations and transfers from and to Campo Grande. The longer **6-day, 5-night combo tours,** with a 3-night stay in the Pantanal and a 2-night stay in Bonito, including all transfers, start at R$2,460 (US$1,230/£665) per person. Contact Open Door at Rua Barão do Rio Branco, Campo Grande 314 (© **067/3321-8303;** www.opendoortur.com.br).

LODGES IN THE SOUTH PANTANAL

Fazenda Barranco Alto 🌟🌟   This south Pantanal farm lies on the Rio Negro, in a region known for its landscape of small salt lakes (called *salinas*) and freshwater ponds, as well as its large populations of animals and birds. The owner has counted 407 bird species so far; hyacinth macaws are common, as are trogons, jacamars, toucans, raptors, and many other species. The best time to visit is from March to October. For migrant birds the best months are July to October. All tours are accompanied by either the owner, Lucas Leuzinger (who has a masters in biology), or his wife, Marina (who has a master's in agronomy), together with local Pantanal guides. The farm guesthouse has a triple and three double rooms, all simply but comfortably furnished with firm double or single beds. All rooms have a private veranda. There are never more than nine guests on the farm. The best way to reach the fazenda is by private plane from Campo Grande. The pilot charges R$1,500 (US$750/£405), which covers the flight in *and* out. The plane can fit three passengers, provided they bring limited luggage. In the dry season (Mar–Oct) you can also come in by 4×4. The 6-hour drive costs R$900 (US$450/£243) (again, in and out) with room for four to five people.

Caixa postal 109, Aquidauana, 79200-000 MS. © **067/9986-0373.** www.fazendabarrancoalto.com.br. 4 units (showers only). R$340 (US$170/£92) per person per night, including all meals, drinks (including beer), guides, and activities. Owner recommends staying 4 days, but there is no minimum. Children 5 and under are free; ages 6–13 pay 50% of adult rate. AE, MC, V. **Amenities:** Internet; laundry. *In room:* A/C, hammock, no phone.

Refugio Caiman 🌟🌟 *Kids*   The most luxurious lodge in the Pantanal, the Refugio Caiman is set on a huge cattle ranch outside the town of Miranda, about 250km (155 miles) from Campo Grande. The land is not as rugged as in the North Pantanal but the *refugio* is still every bit the working cattle ranch. Activities here are very safe and "soft adventure"—perfect for families with young children. Avid horseback riders should avoid this place; there is no trotting or galloping allowed (ever!), no matter how good your riding skills. Excursions are geared to those who lack the fitness level for longer hikes or expeditions. Fortunately, even with the somewhat stronger human imprint, the population of wildlife is still quite stunning. Huge jabiru storks, flocks of roseate spoonbills, egrets of all shapes and sizes, caiman, and capybaras can all be seen within steps of the lodge. Hyacinth macaws are frequently spotted. The food is outstanding and the accommodations, in an old hacienda with a new central pool, are positively luxurious. Listed below are the rack rates; contact travel operators for less expensive packages. Transportation from Cuiabá is not included. The lodge can arrange this for R$110 (US$46) per person, one-way. When booking a package the transfers can be included.

Reservations: Avenida Brigadeiro Faria Lima 3015, cj. 161,Itaim Bibi São Paulo. (*) 011/3706-1800. Lodge (*) 067/3242-1450. www.caiman.com.br. 25 units (showers only). R$395 (US$197) per person per night, including all meals, guides, activities, and insurance. Children 2 and under stay free in parent's room; children 3–10 pay 50% adult rate; children over 10 pay full adult rate. AE, DC, MC, V. Free parking. **Amenities:** Restaurant; bar; outdoor pool; game room; laundry. *In room:* A/C, no phone.

12 Iguaçu Falls

1,421km (881 miles) SW of Rio de Janeiro, 1,019km (632 miles) SW of São Paulo

There are but three great waterfalls in the world, and curiously they all seem to fall on borders: Niagara Falls, on the border between the United States and Canada; Victoria Falls, between Zimbabwe and Zambia; and Iguaçu Falls, which form the border between Brazil and Argentina.

I've seen all three, and Iguaçu is without doubt the most beautiful. The water pours down over not one but some 275 different cataracts, spread over a precipice some 5km (3 miles) wide and 81m (266 ft.) high. The fine mist tossed up by all that falling water precipitates down and creates a microclimate of lush rainforest, filled with tropical birds and an abundant population of glorious tropical butterflies.

Aside from the falls, there's not a lot to see in Iguaçu. Beyond the immediate zone of the falls, the national park is closed to visitors. The zodiac trips upstream towards the falls are highly recommended. There are also rubber-raft trips through the rapids downstream, as well as an extraordinary 50m (164-ft.) rappel from the top of the gorge all the way down to the edge of the Iguaçu River.

With a Brazilian airpass, Iguaçu makes a perfect 2-day stopover. Those without a pass should consider whether the falls—glorious though they may be—are worth the 1,000km (620-mile) trip from Rio or São Paulo.

ESSENTIALS
GETTING THERE
BY PLANE   The **Aeroporto Internacional Foz do Iguaçu** (*(*) 045/3521-4200*) is on BR-469 halfway between downtown and the national park. The 13km (8-mile) taxi ride to downtown Iguaçu costs about R$30 to R$40 (US$15–US$20/£8–£11). Many of Iguaçu's hotels are on the highway into town, making taxi fare considerably less.

BY BUS   Long-distance buses arrive at the **Terminal Rodoviária,** Av. Costa e Silva s/n (*(*) 045/3522-2590*). The station is 4km (2½ miles) northeast of downtown. For buses to and from Rio de Janeiro or São Paulo, contact **Pluma** at *(*) 045/3522-2515.* Pluma also has buses to Buenos Aires.

GETTING AROUND
Foz do Iguaçu (normally just called Iguaçu) is a small modern city of 250,000 people. To the south of the city lies the Iguaçu River and beyond it, Argentina. The falls are

a 27km (17-mile) drive southeast from downtown on the Avenida das Cataratas (Hwy. BR-469). There are quite a few good hotels and some other attractions and restaurants along this road. About 6km (4 miles) from downtown, there's a turnoff for the Ponte Tancredo Neves, which crosses into Argentina. The city's downtown is small and easy to navigate, but except for some decent shopping, it offers few attractions.

BY BUS   City buses begin and end their routes at Avenida Juscelino Kubitschek (Av. J. K.) at the corner of Avenida República Argentina. Falls buses are marked CATARATAS (fare is R$2/US$1/50p) or PARQUE NACIONAL (fare is R$1/US50¢/25p). They run every 20 minutes until 6:40pm. The trip to the park gate and visitor center takes 45 minutes. From the park gate, a free shuttle (departing every 20 min.) will take you the rest of the way to the falls.

BY TAXI   There are taxi *pontos* (stands) throughout the city or you can flag a taxi on the street. A trip across town costs around R$15 (US$7.50/£4). A taxi from the center of town to the park gates costs R$40 (US$20/£11). Hiring a taxi to take you to the Argentinean Falls and wait while you see them then bring you back costs about R$180 (US$90/£49). **Coopertaxi** (© **0800/524-6464** or 045/3529-8821) has cabs available 24/7.

VISITOR INFORMATION

Iguaçu's tourist bureau employs excellent English-speaking attendants who have up-to-date and accurate information at their fingertips. They also give out free maps of the city. The main **tourist information center** is at Praça Getulio Vargas (Av. JK and Rua Rio Branco; © **045/3521-1455;** www.fozdoiguacu.pr.gov.br; Mon–Fri 9am–5pm). There are also tourist information booths at the airport and bus station or you can call the Iguaçu tourist information service **Teletur** (© **0800/451-516** toll-free within Brazil). The service operates daily from 7am to 11pm.

FAST FACTS   To exchange currency or use the ATM, go to Banco do Brasil, Av. Brasil 1377 (© **045/3521-2525**). The HSBC branch is nearby at Av. Brasil 1151 (© **045/3523-1166**).

For medical attention, go to **Hospital Internacional,** Av. Brasil 1637 (© **045/ 3523-1404**). If you have a dental emergency, contact the **Clinica Odontologica** at © **045/3523-5965;** it's open 24 hours a day.

WHAT TO SEE & DO
THE FALLS THEMSELVES
Parque Nacional do Iguaçu (Brazilian Falls) 𝒜𝒜𝒜   The Brazilian Falls now boast a newly renovated visitor center and a new restaurant—Porto Canoas—above the falls. A new observation deck is also complete. The **visitor center** is where you buy your entry tickets and where you board a shuttle bus and set off down the parkway for the falls. The bus will stop at the **Macuco Safari center** (from where rafting and zodiac trips depart, but do that after you've seen the falls), the pink **Tropical das Cataratas Hotel,** and then at **Porto Canoas** restaurant before heading back to the visitor center. The Tropical is the place to get off. A small viewpoint at the foot of the hotel lawn is where you get your first magic view of the falls. From here, the pathway zigzags down the side of the gorge and trundles along the cliff face, providing views across the narrow gorge at water cascading down in a hundred different places. There are 275 separate waterfalls, with an average drop of 60m (197 ft.). While you walk, you'll see colorful butterflies fluttering about the trail and grumbling *coati* (a larger

Foz do Iguaçu

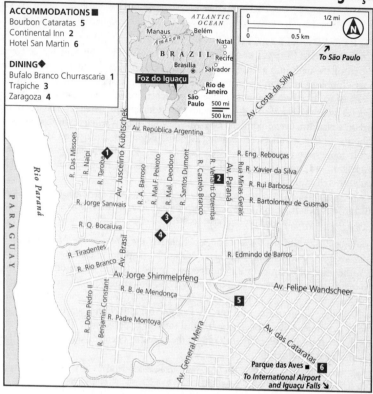

ACCOMMODATIONS ■
Bourbon Cataratas **5**
Continental Inn **2**
Hotel San Martin **6**

DINING ◆
Bufalo Branco Churrascaria **1**
Trapiche **3**
Zaragoza **4**

relative of the raccoon) begging for food. At the end of the trail there is an elevated walkway leading out *in front* of one of the falls. The wind and spray coming off the falls are deeply exhilarating and guaranteed to have you soaked in seconds.(You can buy a plastic coat from the souvenir stand for R$5/US$2.50/£1.35.) Allow at least a half-day.

Rodovia dos Cataratas, Km 18. ☎ 045/3572-2261. www.cataratasdoiguacu.com.br. Admission R$20 (US$10/£5.40) adults, R$5 (US$2.50/£1.35) children 2–6, includes transportation inside the park. Parking R$8 (US$4/£2.15). Daily 9am–5pm (summer until 6pm). Bus: Cataratas or Parque Nacional.

Parque Nacional Iguazú (Argentinean Falls)   For complete listing coverage on the Argentine Falls, including boat tours, please see p. 117.

Av. Victoria Aguirre 66, Puerto Iguazú, 3370 Misiones, Argentina. ☎ 03757/420-722. www.iguazuargentina.com. R$40 (US$20/£11) adults, R$20 (US$10/£5.40) children ages 6–11, free for under 6. Oct 1–Mar 31 daily 7:30am–6:30pm; Apr 1–Sept 30 daily 8am–6pm. *Getting There:* From Foz do Iguaçu take the PORTO IGUAZÚ bus from downtown. Customs formalities at the border are minimal. Stay on the bus, tell the customs officer who boards that you're going to the Parque Nacional and—for citizens of the U.S., U.K., Canada, and Australia—you'll be waved through without even a stamp in your passport. The bus then goes to the main bus station in Puerto Iguazú. Go to stall no. 5, where a bus departs every hour from 7:40am–7:40pm for the 20-min. trip to the park. Including connections, total trip time from Brazil will be at least an hour. The bus from Brazil to Argentina costs R$3 (US$1.50/80p), and the bus from Puerto Iguazú to the falls costs R$5 (US$2.50/£1.35). A taxi to or from the Argentine side costs about R$80 (US$40/£22) each way. *Getting Back:* The bus from Parque Nacional to the Puerto Iguazú bus station departs hourly from 8am–8pm. Once back at the bus station, go to stall no. 1 and catch the bus marked FOZ DO IGUAÇU back to Brazil.

OTHER TOP ATTRACTIONS

Canion Iguaçu (Rappel and Climbing Park) ★★   This company has converted a part of the park into a delightful adult playground. Very popular is the *arvorismo* (tree-climbing) trail, an obstacle course made out of ropes, wires, and platforms attached to the trees. The more challenging higher obstacles will take you at least 25 feet up into the trees. If that doesn't make your stomach flip there's the 120 feet of rappel off a platform overlooking the falls. Maybe your thing is going up instead of down? The park offers a variety of climbing options. Beginners can try the artificial wall, while more experienced climbers can explore over 33 different routes on the basalt rock face. And, last but not least, the company runs daily rafting trips over a 4km (2½-mile) stretch of the river.

Parque Nacional do Iguaçu. ✆ 045/3529-6040. www.campodedesafios.com.br. Rappel R$70 (US$35/£19). Rafting R$80 (US$40/£22). Tree climbing R$80 (US$40/£22) for higher part, R$40 (US$20/£11) for lower part only. Climbing R$50 (US$25/£14). Daily 9am–5:30pm. Bus: Parque Nacional or Cataratas.

Macuco Boat Safari ★★★   Niagara Falls has the *Maid of the Mist.* Iguaçu has *Macuco.* I know which one I'd choose. *Macuco* participants pile aboard 25-foot zodiacs, the guide fires up twin 225-horsepower outboards, and you're off up the river, bouncing over wave trains, breaking eddy lines, powering your way up the surging current until the boat's in the gorge, advancing slowly towards one of the (smaller) falls. As the boat nears, the mist gets thicker, the roar louder, the passengers wetter and more and more thrilled (or terrified), until the zodiac peels away, slides downstream, and hides in an eddy till everyone's caught their breath. Then you do it all again. Allow 1 hour for the entire trip.

Parque Nacional do Iguaçu. ✆ 045/3523-6475. www.macucosafari.com.br. R$150 (US$75/£41) per person, children 7–12 half-price. Mon 1–5:30pm; Tues–Sun and holidays 8am–5:30pm. Bus: Parque Nacional or Cataratas.

Parque das Aves ★★   Set in 4.8 hectares (12 acres) of lush subtropical rainforest, the Bird Park offers the best bird-watching in Iguaçu. A large number of birds are in huge walk-through aviaries, some 24m (79 ft.) tall and at least 60m (200 ft.) long, allowing visitors to watch the birds interact as they go about their daily routines. Highlights include the toucans and multicolored tanagers as well as a Pantanal aviary with roseate spoonbills, herons, and egrets. Signage is in English. The best time to visit is early in the day when the birds are most active. Allow 2 hours.

Rodovia das Cataratas, Km 17, 300m (984 ft.) before the national park entrance. ✆ 045/3529-8282. www.parquedasaves.com.br. R$20 (US$10/£5.40), free for children under 9. Daily 8:30am–5:30pm. Bus: Parque Nacional or Cataratas.

SHOPPING

Iguaçu's Centro is a popular shopping district. Most shops are concentrated around the Avenida Brasil, Rua Barbosa, Rua Almirante Barroso, and Quintino Bocaiuva. You'll find excellent leather goods such as jackets and purses. The one and only souvenir shop worth visiting is **Tres Fronteiras,** BR 469 Rodovia das Cataratas, Km 11, just before the turnoff for Argentina (✆ **045/3523-1167;** www.tresfronteiras.com.br). Tres Fronteiras sells crafts and souvenirs from all of Brazil. The deli sells a selection of Brazilian wines, coffees, sweets, and delicious handmade chocolates from Rio Grande do Sul. The shop is open daily from 9am to 8pm.

WHERE TO STAY
CENTRO
Continental Inn ★★ *Finds*   Recently renovated, the Continental Inn is a real gem. The comfortable regular rooms feature firm twin or double beds, modern Art Deco–ish decor, good desk space, and showers with lots of high-pressure hot water. The suites are outstanding: Regular suites feature a separate sitting area, firm queen bed, and a large round bathtub, while the top-quality master suites have hardwood floors, king-size bed, fancy linens, a large desk, separate sitting area, walk-in closet, and a bathroom with Jacuzzi tub and a view over the city. Rooms for travelers with disabilities are available.

Av. Paranà 1089, Foz do Iguaçu, 85852-000 PR. ✆ 0800/707-2400 or 045/3523-5000. www.continentalinn.com.br. 113 units (102 with showers only). R$200 (US$100/£54) double; R$250–R$285 (US$125–US$143/£68–£77) suite; R$350 (US$175/£95) master suite. In low season 20% discount. Children under 5 stay free in parent's room; 5 and over R$30 (US$15/£8) extra. AE, DC, MC, V. Free parking. **Amenities:** Restaurant; large pool; exercise room; sauna; game room w/video arcade; business center; room service; laundry. *In room:* A/C, TV, dataport, minibar, fridge, hair dryer, safe.

ON THE PARK ROAD
Bourbon Cataratas ★★★ *Kids*   The real draw of the Bourbon is its leisure space. True, all the rooms are beautifully appointed. In the original wing, the standard rooms look out over the front of the hotel, while the superior rooms have a veranda and look over the pool. The new wing houses the master suites—really just a room, but with newer furnishings and huge windows providing lovely views. Out back, there's a 2km (1.25-mile) trail through orchards and lovely gardens; keep an eye out for toucans, parakeets, and colorful butterflies in the aviary. The vast pool complex includes three large pools, one especially for children. In high season, activity leaders organize all-day children's activities.

Rodovia das Cataratas, Km 2.5, Foz do Iguaçu, 85853-000 PR. ✆ 0800/451-010 or 045/3521-3900. www.bourbon. com.br. 311 units. R$415–R$540 (US$208–US$270/£112–£146) superior or master double. Extra person R$140 (US$70/£38). AE, DC, MC, V. Free parking. Bus: Parque Nacional or Cataratas. **Amenities:** 3 restaurants; huge pool complex (2 outdoor pools, 1 small indoor pool); outdoor lighted tennis courts; sauna (dry and steam); children's programs; game room; concierge; tour desk; car rental; business center; shopping arcade; salon; room service; massage; laundry service; nonsmoking rooms. *In room:* A/C, TV, dataport, minibar, fridge, hair dryer, safe.

San Martin ★ *Kids*   Also located on the park road, the San Martin is near the park entrance, close to the bird park. Although the accommodations are slightly dated, the rooms are clean and pleasantly furnished and the rates are very affordable. Most of the superior rooms have been renovated and now feature hardwood floors and elegant, modern furnishings. Families will appreciate the two-bedroom suits that come with two double and two single beds. Also great for kids are the hotel's park-like grounds with several play areas, a soccer field, a swimming pool and gardens.

Rodovia das Cataratas, Km 17, Foz do Iguaçu, 85853-000 PR. ✆ 0800/645-0045 or 045/3521-8088. www.hotel sanmartin.com.br. 135 units. R$165 (US$85/£46]) standard double; R$200 (US$100/£54) superior double; R$325 (US$162–£88) family superior, sleeps 4–6 people. Extra person R$60 (US$30/£16). AE, DC, MC, V. Free parking. Bus: Parque Nacional or Cataratas. **Amenities:** Restaurant; swimming pool; tennis court; sauna; children's play area; game room; tour desk; business center; 24-hour room service; laundry service; nonsmoking rooms. *In room:* A/C, TV, minibar, safe.

WHERE TO DINE
In town the best *churrascaria* is **Búfalo Branco,** Rua Rebouças 530, Foz do Iguaçu (✆ 045/3523-9744). Certainly not touristy like the Rafain, the restaurant offers a

good selection of cold dishes, salad, dessert, and of course *churrasco.* In addition to the succulent, well-prepared cuts of beef, the waiters also serve up grilled fish such as suru-bim. As an alternative to beef, **Zaragoza,** Rua Quintino Bocaiúva 882 (© **045/3574-3084;** www.restaurantezaragoza.com.br), offers excellent seafood with a strong Spanish flavor. The menu is particularly strong on prawns, lobster, and local fish served grilled or broiled. On Sunday, people come from far and wide to savor the paella for lunch. Another good seafood alternative is the **Trapiche,** Rua Marechal Deodoro 1087, (©**045/3527-3951**). The large menu includes everything from grilled fish such as tilapia, salmon, and trout to Bahian seafood stews such as moqueca, bobó, and caldeirada (with crab, shrimp, and octopus).

7

Chile

by Kristina Schreck

Sandwiched between the Andes and the Pacific Ocean, Chile's lengthy, serpentine shape at first glance seems preposterous: Nearly 4,830m (3,000 miles) of land stretches from Peru to Cape Horn (about the same distance as New York to Los Angeles), but the average width is just 185m (115 miles). Chile is a geographical extravaganza, encompassing such a breathtaking array of landscapes and temperate zones that it is difficult not to fall back on the old travel cliché "a country of contrasts"; but that is indeed what Chile is, and it is precisely what makes this South American country so unique. The north is home to the earth's driest desert, the Atacama; the Central Valley has a Mediterranean-like climate and a burgeoning wine and agricultural industry; farther south lie the volcanoes and forests of the Lake District; and at the very end are the vast plains, glaciers, and granite cathedrals of Patagonia. Chile also claims Easter and Robinson Crusoe islands in the Pacific Ocean, as well as a slice of Antarctica.

Chile provides travelers with the widest variety of adventure-travel activities in South America. The hundreds of rivers that descend from the Andes draw anglers from around the world for the phenomenal fly-fishing opportunities here, not to mention some of the planet's wildest white-water rafting. Snowy peaks and volcanoes provide excellent terrain for skiing and mountain climbing. The northern desert's eerie land formations and high-altitude salt flats are as easily explored by 4×4 as by mountain bike. The country's prize gem, the national park Torres del Paine, offers hiking, climbing and backpacking. And there are kayak trips through remote sounds and slogs through exuberant rainforest. There are plenty of low-key activities here as well, such as cruises through emerald fjords, soaks in hot springs, or just kicking back on a golden beach.

Best of all, Chile's strong economy and modern infrastructure promise high-quality amenities and services. Chile also boasts a solid reputation as the safest country in Latin America, and corruption is rare. It is also one of the most economically prosperous in Latin America, envied by its neighbors on all sides.

1 The Regions in Brief

Chile's enormous length makes traveling by air the fastest way to get around if you are planning to pack several destinations into one trip. The country has frequent air service and efficient transfers to get you from point A to B. If you have only a week to spare, you won't be able to visit more than two regions of the country. Visitors with 7 to 10 days who plan to visit Patagonia or a remote lodge with a long transfer time should be able to squeeze in a night or two in Santiago and maybe a quick day visit to the coast or the wine country, but little else. You may consider skipping more remote destinations to sample two widely different regions in Chile—for example, spend several days in the Atacama Desert, and then enjoy a few days in the Lake District. This would allow time for a day trip to the coast from Santiago. You might also consider a weeklong loop through the adjacent lake districts of both Chile and Argentina. (For information on Argentina's Lake District, see chapter 4.) Travelers with 2 to 3 weeks will have the freedom and the time to pick and choose destinations at will.

NORTHERN CHILE   This region claims the world's driest desert, a pastel-colored "wasteland" set below a chain of volcanoes and high-altitude salt flats. The sun-baked region is flecked with oases such as **San Pedro de Atacama,** an adobe-built pueblo typical of the region, as well as plentiful and well-preserved Indian ruin sites. The arid climate and the geological forces at work in this region have produced far-out land formations and superlatives such as the highest geyser field in the world.

SANTIAGO & CENTRAL CHILE   The central region of Chile, including Santiago and its environs, features a mild, Mediterranean climate. This is Chile's breadbasket, with fertile valleys and rolling fields that harvest a large share of the country's fruit and vegetables; it is also Chile's wine-producing region. Santiago's proximity to ski resorts, beach resorts, and the idyllic countryside, with its campestral and ranching traditions and colonial estates, offer plenty for the traveler to see and do.

LAKE DISTRICT   Few destinations in the world rival the lush scenery of Chile's Lake District. This region is packed with a chain of conical, snowcapped volcanoes, glacier-scoured valleys, several national parks, thick groves of native forest, hot springs, jagged peaks, and, of course, many shimmering lakes. Temperatures during the summer are normally warm and pleasant, but winter is characterized by overcast days and drizzling rain. It's an outdoor lover and adventure seeker's paradise, especially in **Pucón** and **Puerto Varas.**

PATAGONIA   Also known as the Magellanic Region, this part of the southern end of the continent has soared in popularity over the past 10 years, drawing visitors from all over the world to places such as **Torres del Paine National Park.** Patagonia is characterized by vast, open pampa, the colossal Northern and Southern ice fields and the glaciers that descend from them, the rugged peaks of the Andes as they reach their terminus, a myriad of fjords and sounds that wind around thousands of uninhabited islands, and wind, wind, wind. Getting here is an adventure—it usually takes 24 hours if you're coming directly from the United States or Europe. But the long journey pays off in the beauty and singularity of the region.

2 The Best of Chile in 2 Weeks

This itinerary will take you from the windswept pampas and granite peaks of Patagonia, to the fertile valleys and the golden coast of central Chile, to the pastel-washed moonscape of the northern desert. Visitors with an eye toward relaxation might consider exchanging Patagonia for a Lake District destination such as Pucón, which has hot springs, a lakeshore for swimming and kicking back, and shopping, in addition to adventure sports. Travelers with less time will need to drop a destination all together, due to the country's enormous length and travel times. *Tip:* For a map of suggested itineraries in Chile, please refer to the Itineraries in Argentina, Chile, Paraguay, and Uruguay map on p. 78.

Day ❶: Arrive & Tour Santiago 🖈🖈

Santiago, Chile's capital and home to nearly half the country's population, is not as culturally rich or exciting as Buenos Aires or Rio—however, there are plenty of top attractions to fill 1 day, including climbing **Cerro San Cristobal** for sweeping views of the city spread before the Andes, visiting the **historic downtown** and the **Pre-Columbian Museum,** taking a tour of famed poet **Pablo Neruda's house,** and dining on the country's famed seafood in the **Mercado Central.** See section 4, "Santiago."

Day ❷: Sip Chile's Best Export—Wine 🖈🖈

Santiago's perk is its proximity to a bounty of activities, including wineries, skiing, and hundreds of miles of golden coastline. It is possible to combine both wine tasting and a visit to the coast, by stopping early for a tasting in the Casablanca Valley on your way out to Valparaíso or Viña del Mar. However, a better trip is a full-day visit to the **Colchagua Valley,** Chile's answer to Napa Valley, located 2 hours south of Santiago. You'll have time to visit three internationally acclaimed wineries and feast on a traditional, country-style Chilean lunch. See section 5, "Around Santiago & the Central Valley."

Day ❸: Head West 🖈🖈

Spend the day exploring historical **Valparaíso,** Chile's storied bohemian port town and most singular city. Lose yourself wandering the city's madcap streets and marveling at colorful antique homes that cling to the hillsides. Some of the region's best restaurants are here, so come hungry, and whatever you do, don't forget your camera. If you have time, head to the resort town **Viña del Mar** for a stroll or a little beach time. Return to Santiago, or spend the night at an oceanfront hotel in Viña or a cozy B&B in Valparaíso. See section 5.

Day ❹: Fly to Punta Arenas, Patagonia 🖈🖈

Catch an early flight to **Punta Arenas,** and spend the day touring the city, including the Alice-in-Wonderland city cemetery, the port on the Strait of Magellan, and the **Palacio de Sara Braun museum.** Be sure to plan for a 5pm visit to a **penguin rookery** to watch the amusing birds waddle out to sea. In the evening, dine on the region's specialty, king crab. See section 8, "Patagonia."

Days ❺–❾: Torres del Paine National Park 🖈🖈🖈

Head early from Punta Arenas to Torres del Paine, Chile's breathtakingly beautiful national park. Spend the following days hiking, horseback riding, or touring the park by van. Hotels, such as Explora and Hostería Grey, offer all-inclusive packages that include lodging, meals, and day tours with bilingual guides. Or plan to backpack the "W" trail, sleeping in tents or in comfortable *refugios* (shelters). Either way, don't miss **Glacier Grey** and, if you can hack it, the 6-hour **Towers Hike** to the granite spires that give the park its name. Your final day is mostly spent driving back to Punta Arenas for a late afternoon flight to Santiago. Spend the night in Santiago. See p. 454.

Days ❿–⓮: Fly High to the Enigmatic Northern Desert 🖈🖈🖈

Spend the morning relaxing, or head to **Patio Bellavista** to buy gifts for friends and family (or yourself!). Take an afternoon flight to Calama, and then the 1-hour shuttle to **San Pedro de Atacama.** Spend the late afternoon lazily strolling the dirt streets of this charming village, and visit one of the best pre-Colombian museums in South America. Book a nighttime astronomy tour; these are the some of the clearest skies in the world. During the next few days, hike or bike to

Atacaman Indian ruins; visit the Salt Lake and take a dip; 4×4 to a lofty, turquoise Altiplanic lake; view the world's highest geyser field at sunrise; and finish the day with a soak in a hot spring. Book a flight back to the Santiago airport that allows for enough time for catching your international flight home. See section 6, "The Desert North."

3 Planning Your Trip to Chile

VISITOR INFORMATION

You'll find a municipal tourism office in nearly every city and a **Sernatur (National Tourism Board)** office in major cities (www.sernatur.cl). The quality of service and availability of printed matter, such as maps and brochures, varies from office to office. Visitors are usually better off planning ahead via Internet research, booking a tour, or seeking the assistance of a hotel concierge than relying on the advice of a Sernatur clerk. **Turismo Chile,** which promotes tourism outside of Chile, has a U.S.-based office with a toll-free number; and they will mail information (© **866/YESCHILE;** www.turismochile.travel).

ENTRY REQUIREMENTS

Citizens of the United States, Canada, the United Kingdom, and Australia need only a valid passport to enter Chile. Visitors from New Zealand must apply for a tourist visa. Chile charges a **reciprocity fee** upon entry to citizens of the following countries: $100 for the U.S., $56 for Australians, and $132 for Canadians. Visitors from the U.K. and New Zealand do not pay a fee. Note that this fee is good for the life of a traveler's passport and is charged when entering through the **Santiago airport only.** Travelers crossing over land do not pay this fee. Before entering Chile, you'll need to fill out a tourist card that allows visitors to stay for 90 days. **Do not lose this card,** as you will need to present it to Customs when leaving the country. Also, many hotels waive Chile's 19% sales tax applied to rooms when guests show this card and pay with U.S. dollars. The easiest (and free) way to renew your 90-day stay is to cross the border and return. For $100, tourist cards can be renewed for another 90 days at the **Extranjería,** Agustinas 1235, Second Floor, in Santiago (© **2/550-2400**), open Monday to Friday 8:30am to 3:30pm (be prepared for excruciatingly long lines), or at any Gobernación Provincial office in the provinces. The extension must be applied for 1 month before the visa's expiration date. Bring the original card, your passport, and photocopies of the two.

Contact the Chilean consulate closest to you for information about children under 18 traveling alone, with one parent, or with a third party, as departure Customs may demand written authorization by the absent parent(s) or legal guardian granting permission.

LOST DOCUMENTS

Report lost tourist cards at the nearest police station or, in Santiago, at the **Policía Internacional,** Departamento Fronteras, General Borgoña 1052 (© **2/565-7863**), open Monday to Friday 9am to 5pm. If you lose your passport, contact your embassy for a replacement. It is imperative that you carry a **photocopy of your passport** with you and another form of ID to facilitate the process.

CHILEAN EMBASSY LOCATIONS

In the U.S.: 1732 Massachusetts Ave. NW, Washington, DC 20036 (© **202/785-1746;** fax 202/887-5579; www.chile-usa.org)

Telephone Dialing Info at a Glance

Kiosks and convenience stores sell phone cards with individual instructions on long-distance dialing, and phone booths at telephone centers will provide instructions on dialing according to the carrier they use. Otherwise, long-distance calls must be prefixed by a carrier's three-digit number—Telefónica (188), Entel (123), BellSouth (181), and Chilesat (171) being the most widely used. Visitors may rent **cellular phones** at the Santiago airport from the Entel desk near baggage claim.

- **To place a call from your home country to Chile,** dial the international access code (011 in the U.S. and Canada, 0011 in Australia, 0170 in New Zealand, 00 in the U.K.) plus the country code (56), plus the Chilean area code, followed by the number. For example, a call from the United States to Santiago would be 011+56+2+000+0000. Cellphone numbers begin with a 9, 8, or 7. When dialing from outside Chile, dial the prefix 569 before the number; or from a land line within Chile dial 09 and then the number.

- **To place a call within Chile,** dial a carrier prefix, then the area code, and then the number. (To place a collect call, dial a prefix, and then 182 for an operator.)

- **To place a direct international call from Chile,** dial a carrier prefix followed by 0, and then the country code of the destination you are calling, plus the area code and the local number.

In Canada: 1413-50 O'Connor St., Ottawa, ON K1P 6L2 (© **613/235-4402;** fax 613/235-1176; www.chile.ca)

In the U.K.: 12 Devonshire St., London W1G 7DS (© **020/7580-6392;** fax 020/7436-5204; www.echileuk.demon.co.uk)

In Australia: 10 Culgoa Circuit, O'Malley, ACT 2600 (© **02/6286-2430;** fax 02/6286-1289; www.embachile-australia.com)

In New Zealand: 19 Bolton St., Wellington (© **04/471-6270;** fax 04/472-5324; www.embchile.co.nz)

CUSTOMS

Any travel-related merchandise brought into Chile, such as personal effects or clothing, is not taxed. Visitors entering Chile may also bring in no more than 400 cigarettes, 500 grams of pipe tobacco, or 50 cigars, and 2.5 liters of alcoholic beverages per adult.

MONEY

The unit of currency in Chile is the **peso.** The value of the peso has held steady at around 535 pesos to the dollar, which is the rate used for prices listed in this book. Bills come in denominations of 1,000, 2,000, 5,000, 10,000, and 20,000 pesos. There are currently six coins in circulation, in denominations of 1, 5, 10, 50, 100, and 500 pesos; however, it's unusual to be issued 1 peso or even 5. In slang, Chileans commonly call 1,000 pesos a *luca*.

Chile levies a steep 19% **sales tax,** called IVA (Impuesto al Valor Agregado), on all goods and services. Foreigners are exempt from the IVA tax when paying in U.S. dollars for hotel rooms and vacation packages; however, you might find this is not the case with low-budget hotels and hostels. Do a little math when offered a price in dollars, as the peso rate might be cheaper due to a proprietor's improper or inflated exchange rate.

Traveler's checks seem like an anachronism these days, given that 24-hour ATMs are ubiquitous and offer the best exchange rate. A Chilean ATM is known as a "Redbanc," which is advertised on a maroon-and-white sticker. Redbancs are compatible with a variety of networks, including Cirrus, PLUS, Visa, and MasterCard. Chilean banks do not charge a fee to use their ATMs, but your own institution might charge you for foreign purchases or withdrawals, so check before you go. You'll find ATMs in banks, grocery stores, gas stations, and pharmacies.

If you feel safer carrying a few traveler's checks just in case, **American Express** (© **800/221-7282**) offers denominations of $20, $50, $100, and $500, with a service charge of between 1% and 4% (unless you are a platinum or gold member). Traveler's checks, dollars, and euros can be exchanged at a *casa de cambio* (money-exchange house) for a small charge; *casas de cambio* are generally open Monday through Friday from 9am to 6pm (closed 1–3pm for lunch), and Saturday until 1pm.

Visa, MasterCard, and American Express are widely accepted throughout Chile, and Diner's Club isn't far behind. Many Chilean businesses are charged 2% service fee and will pass that cost on to you, so expect cheaper deals with cash.

WHEN TO GO

PEAK SEASON High season for Chilean, Brazilian, and Argentine vacationers is during the summer from December 15 to the end of February, as well as the 2 middle weeks of July and Holy Week (Semana Santa), the week preceding Easter Sunday. These dates coincide with school vacations. Everybody, it seems, takes their vacation during these dates, and consequently the teeming masses seen in popular destinations such as Pucón or Viña del Mar during this time can be overwhelming. In spite of the fact that hotels double their prices during peak season, reservations sell out quickly, so book far in advance or come between late September and early December or March and mid-May. This "midseason" sees cheaper rates, pleasant weather, and uncrowded views. As well, the Desert North is scorching hot from November to February, and Patagonia typically experiences the strongest wind and its most capricious weather during the same period.

CLIMATE Chile's thin, drawn-out territory stretches over 38 degrees of latitude, encompassing every climate found in the world, except tropical. In many areas there are microclimates, pockets of localized weather that can completely alter the vegetation and landscape of a small area.

The northern region of Chile is so dry that some desert areas have never recorded rain. Summer temperatures from early December to late February in this region can top 100°F (38°C), and then drop dramatically at night to 30°F (–1°C). Winter days, from mid-June to late August, are crisp but sunny and pleasant, but as soon as the sun drops, it gets bitterly cold. Along the coast, the weather is mild and dry, ranging from 60°F to 90°F (16°C–32°C) during the summer.

The Santiago and Central Valley region features a Mediterranean climate, with rain during the winter only and temperatures that range from 32°F to 55°F (0°C–13°C) in the winter, and 60°F to 95°F (16°C–35°C) during the summer. Farther south, the Lake District and the Carretera Austral are home to sopping wet winters, and overcast days and rain are not uncommon during the summer, especially in the regions around Valdivia and Puerto Montt.

The Magellanic Region presents unpredictable weather patterns, especially during the summer, with extraordinary windstorms that can reach upwards of 120kmph (75 mph), and occasional rain. The windiest months are mid-December to late February, but it can blow any time between October and April. Winters are calm, with irregular snowfall and temperatures that can dip to 5°F (–15°C).

PUBLIC HOLIDAYS   Chile's national holidays are New Year's Day (Jan 1); Good Friday (late Mar or Apr); Labor Day (May 1); Remembrance of the War of the Pacific Victory (May 21); Corpus Christi (late May or early June); St. Peter & St. Paul Day (June 26); Asunción de la Virgen (Aug 15); Independence Day and Armed Forces Day, the major holiday of the year (Sept 18–19); Indigenous Day (Oct 12); All Saint's Day (Nov 1); Feast of the Immaculate Conception (Dec 8); and Christmas (Dec 25).

Virtually every business in Chile shuts on public holidays, as is the case with national and local elections (from midnight to midnight). Alcohol is not sold on election days.

HEALTH CONCERNS

Chile poses few health risks to travelers, and no special vaccinations are required. In fact, there are no poisonous plants or animals in Chile, either. Nevertheless, standard wisdom says that travelers should get tetanus and hepatitis boosters.

Few visitors to Chile experience anything other than run-of-the-mill traveler's stomach in reaction to unfamiliar foods and any microorganisms in them. Chile's tap water is clean and generally safe to drink, though not particularly tasty. Bottled water is widely available throughout Chile. *Warning:* Do not, under any circumstances, drink tap water while in San Pedro de Atacama. It contains trace amounts of arsenic.

Altitude sickness, known as *soroche* or *puna,* is a temporary yet often debilitating affliction that affects about a quarter of travelers to the northern Altiplano, or the Andes at 2,400m (7,872 ft.) and up. Nausea, fatigue, headaches, shortness of breath, sleeplessness, and feeling "out of it" are the symptoms, which can last from 1 to 5 days. If affected, drink plenty of water, take aspirin or ibuprofen, and avoid alcohol and sleeping pills; or prevent the condition by breaking the climb to higher regions into segments.

The thin ozone layer in the Patagonia and Tierra del Fuego is not to be taken lightly. During "red alert" days (typically Sept–Nov), fair-skinned visitors can burn within *10 minutes.* Protect yourself with sunblock, a long-sleeved shirt, a wide-brimmed hat, and sunglasses.

GETTING THERE
BY PLANE
Santiago's **Comodoro Arturo Merino Benítez Airport** is the international arrival point for Chile (www.aeropuertosantiago.cl).

BY CRUISE SHIP
South America is the hot new cruise destination, and most companies now offer some version of the loop around the Cape Horn. Journeys typically span 11 to 15 days and

sail from Buenos Aires to Valparaíso, Chile, or vice versa, sometimes embarking in Florida or continuing on to the Panama Canal after Chile or Peru. Stops include Montevideo; Uruguay; and Chile's Puerto Montt, Puerto Chacabuco, and Punta Arenas; and Argentina's Ushuaia, Puerto Madryn, and occasionally the Falkland Islands. It is a pity that cruisers get to spend so little time ashore; however, sailing through the southern region's fjords and around the Cape is truly remarkable. The following companies are best bets for sailing voyages; check for itineraries and prices: **Celebrity Cruises** (© 800/647-2251; www.celebrity.com), **Crystal Cruises** (© 800/804-1500;** www.crystalcruises.com), **Holland America** (© 877-SAIL HAL; www.holland america.com), **Princess Cruises** (© 800/PRINCESS; www.princesscruises.com), **Radisson Seven Seas** (© 877/505-5370; www.rssc.com), and **Silversea** (© 877/760-9052; www.silversea.com).

GETTING AROUND
BY PLANE
Travelers, especially those short on time, must fly if planning to visit several destinations. **LAN Airlines** (© 866/435-9526 in the U.S., or 600/526-2000 in Chile; www. lan.com) is the leader of the pack in terms of destinations, frequency, and quality of service. LAN serves Arica, Iquique, Calama, Antofagasta, Concepción, Temuco, Valdivia, Osorno, Pucón (Dec–Feb only), Puerto Montt, Coyhaique (Balmaceda), and Punta Arenas. **Sky Airlines** (© 600/600-2828; www.skyairline.cl) is another Chilean domestic carrier, with daily flights to all major destinations. The Spanish-owned **Aerolineas del Sur** (© 800/710-300) offers daily economical Santiago—Punta Arenas flights, and they fly to Puerto Montt, Calama, Antofagasta, and Iquique.

BY BUS
Chile has an efficient and inexpensive bus system, with three classes of service. Standard buses go by the name *clásico* or *pullman* (no relation to the giant bus company Pullman); an *ejecutivo* or *semicama* offers lots of legroom, and seats that recline; and the *salón cama* is fitted with seats that fold out into beds. Travelers seeking economical transportation to the Lake District should consider a night bus on a *salón cama*. Short-haul coach rides to destinations such as Viña del Mar leave dozens of times a day; nevertheless it is a good idea to buy a round-trip ticket in advance during holidays and on weekends.

BY CAR
You won't need a vehicle for Santiago, but rentals do provide freedom to wander along the coast or sightsee in the Lake District. To make a reservation from the United States, call **Alamo** (© 800/GO-ALAMO; www.alamo.com), **Avis** (© 800/230-4898; www.avis.com), **Budget** (© 800/527-0700; www.budget.com), **Dollar** (© 800/800-4000; www.dollar.com), or **Hertz** (© 800/654-3001; www.hertz.com). If renting once you're already in Chile, don't overlook a few of the local car-rental agencies for cheaper prices; you'll find their booths at major airports. Rental agencies at the Santiago airport now charge a small fee (around $5/£2.55) for the Costanera Norte, a toll charged automatically to the vehicle when passing through the express tunnel from downtown to Las Condes, and Ruta 5 through the Santiago vicinity.

Save yourself a lot of frustration and avoid driving in Santiago if possible. Drivers here are aggressive, especially bus drivers, and it can be maddening to find your way around the labyrinth of one-way streets. Chile recently inaugurated the new four-lane Panamericana Highway, which charges tolls either at the on-ramp or on the highway itself. Expect to pay between 75¢ and $5.50 (40p–£2.25) at a tollbooth. Car-rental agencies provide emergency road service. Be sure to obtain a 24-hour number before leaving with your rental vehicle.

BY FERRY

Travelers concentrating on the Lake District and Patagonia regions might consider the 3-day journey aboard **Navimag,** a passenger and cargo ferry that sails between Puerto Montt and Puerto Natales, introducing visitors to the remote, virgin fjordland that makes up the southern third of Chile. It is not a luxury liner, but some berths provide enough standard comfort for finicky travelers. **Transmarchilay** has cargo ferries (for vehicles) that link Puerto Montt and Chiloé with the Carretera Austral. The upscale **Skorpios** has 4- and 7-day cruises from Puerto Montt or Puerto Chacabuco, stopping at Chiloé before or after visiting the Laguna San Rafael Glacier. Skorpios has a new service from Puerto Natales that sails to the only advancing glacier, Pío XI. **Andina del Sud** offers a land-and-lake crossing from Lago Todos los Santos in Vicente Pérez Rosales National Park near Puerto Varas, to a connection with the company Cruce de Lagos for the final leg to Bariloche, Argentina. **Terra Australis** offers memorable one-way and round-trip cruises from Punta Arenas to Ushuaia. See individual regional listings for more information.

TIPS ON ACCOMMODATIONS

It is imperative that travelers consider Chile's high season when considering accommodations, as prices soar and reservations are hard to come by without advance planning (See "When to Go" above). Chile's hotel rates, even for American chains, are substantially lower than hotels of equivalent quality in the U.S. Comfy, midrange hotels and cabañas are plentiful—you can often find a terrific little place for $50 to $80 (£26–£41) that is as good as an "expensive" hotel. The prices listed in this book are **rack rates,** but most hotels offer cheaper rates and promotional deals through their websites. *Hotel tip:* Don't be shy about negotiating a discount during the off-season, as some hotel owners are willing to pass a travel agent's 10% to 20% commission on to you in the form of a discount. Hotels might charge a "midseason" rate during November and March. **Price ranges listed in hotel write-ups reflect low to high season.**

Price categories in this guide are listed according to **Very Expensive,** $125 (£64) and up; **Expensive,** $80 to $124 (£41–£64); **Moderate,** $40 to $79 (£21–£41); and **Inexpensive,** under $39 (£20). Prices shown reflect double occupancy; ask for details about a "single" rate, as single rooms are often small and come with a twin-size bed.

TIPS ON DINING

Chilean gastronomy is coming into its own, but for the most part you will not return from your trip raving about the country's cuisine. The focal point of Chilean *cocina de autor* (nouveau and fusion cuisine) is in Santiago; however, many restaurants in tourist-oriented destinations and most major hotels employ talented chefs and a long list of high-caliber wines. When ordering lunch, ask whether the restaurant has a *menú del día* or *menú ejecutivo,* a fixed-price lunch for $5 to $10 (£2.55–£5.10) that typically includes an appetizer, main course, beverage or wine, coffee, and dessert. The lunch *menú* is normally a cheaper and fresher alternative to anything listed on the *carta* (menu). What beef is to Argentina, seafood is to Chile, and Chileans eat it all, from sole to sea urchin to conger eel.

TIPS ON SHOPPING

Bargaining for goods is accepted at stalls in central markets that sell arts and crafts and regional goods, but it is not a common practice. Chileans love to window shop, and therefore malls heave with shoppers on weekends. The diverse regions of Chile produce their own specialties. The **Lake District** produces silver Mapuche Indian–influenced jewelry, smoked meats and seafood, cheeses and sweet goodies such as marzipan and German cakes. **Chiloé** is known for its colorful woolen sweaters and scarves. The **Central Valley** specializes in wool ponchos and other Chilean cowboy gear, lapis lazuli jewelry (mostly Santiago), wine, and ceramic pottery (in Pomaire). One-stop shopping (a little of everything from Chile) is best at Los Dominicos or the Fería Santa Lucía in Santiago, or the markets in Chillán and Puerto Montt. Last-minute shoppers can pick up just about any curio, CD, book, or label of wine at the airport.

FAST FACTS: Chile

American Express The American Express office is at Av. Isidora Goyenechea 3621, Piso 10 (② 2/350-6855). It's open Monday through Friday from 9am to 2pm and 3:30 to 5pm. The 24-hour customer service number in the U.S. is ② 800/545-1171, although you will be charged for the call.

Business Hours Banks are open Monday to Friday from 9am to 2pm and are closed on Saturday and Sunday. Many commercial offices close for a long lunch hour, which can vary from business to business. Generally, hours are Monday through Friday from 10am to 7pm, closing for lunch around 1 or 1:30pm and reopening at 2:30 or 3pm.

Doctors Many doctors, especially in Santiago, speak basic English; for a list of English-speaking doctors, call your embassy.

Drug Laws Possession and use of drugs and narcotics are subject to heavy fines and jail terms.

Electricity Chile's electricity standard is 220 volts/50Hz. Electrical sockets have two openings for tubular pins, not flat prongs; adapters are available from most travel stores.

Embassies/Consulates The only U.S. representative in Chile is the **U.S. Embassy** in Santiago, located at Av. Andrés Bello 2800 (② 2/232-2600; www.usembassy.cl). The **Canadian Embassy** is at Nuevo Tajamar 481, 12th Floor (② 2/362-9660; www.dfait-maeci.gc.ca/chile). The **British Embassy** can be found at El Bosque Norte 0125 (② 2/370-4100; www.britemb.cl). The **Australian Embassy** is at Isidora Goyenechea 3621 (② 2/550-3500; www.chile.embassy.gov.au). The **New Zealand Embassy** is at Av. Golf 99, no. 703 (② 2/290-9800; www.nzembassy.com/chile).

Emergencies You'll want to contact the staff if something happens to you in your hotel. Otherwise, for a police emergency, call ② 133. For fire, call ② 132. To call an ambulance, dial ② 131.

Hospitals *Clínicas* and private hospitals are always better than a town's general hospital. The cost of medicine and treatment can be expensive, but most hospitals and pharmacies accept credit cards. Many doctors, especially in Santiago, speak basic English; for a list of English-speaking doctors and medical special-ists in Santiago, call your embassy. The best hospitals in Santiago are **Clínica Las Condes** at Lo Fontecilla 441 (© **2/210-4000**) and **Clínica Alemana** at Vitacura 5951 (© **2/212-9700**).

Internet Access   No matter where you are in Chile, you should find an Internet station, either in a cafe or at telephone centers Telefónica or Entel. Most hotels, even hostels, have their own Internet service, and some even have wireless service. If they don't, the hotel staff can point out where to find one. Expect to pay $2 to $4 (£1–£2.05) per hour.

Language   Spanish is the official language of Chile. Many Chileans in the tourism industry and in major cities speak basic English, but don't count on it. Try to learn even a dozen basic Spanish phrases before arriving; *Frommer's Spanish Phrasefinder & Dictionary* will facilitate your trip tremendously.

Liquor Laws   The legal drinking age in Chile is 18. Alcohol is sold every day of the year, except during elections.

Police   Police officers wear olive-green uniforms and are referred to as *cara-bineros,* or colloquially as *pacos.* Dial © **133** for an emergency. Police officers in Chile are not corrupt and will not accept bribes on any occasion.

Safety   Santiago is probably the safest major city in South America. Serious vio-lent crime is not unheard of, but it's not common either. Visitors should take measures against being pickpocketed, especially in crowded areas, and they should not leave valuables in a parked vehicle due to frequent break-ins.

Telephone   For more information, see "Telephone Dialing Info at a Glance," earlier in this chapter. The country code for Chile is **56.** A local phone call requires 100 pesos (US20¢/10p); phone cards sold in kiosks offer better rates.

Time   Chile is 4 hours behind Greenwich mean time (GMT) from the first Sun-day in October until the second Sunday in March; the country is 6 hours behind during the rest of the year.

Tipping   Diners leave a 10% tip in restaurants. In hotels, tipping is left to the guest's discretion. Don't tip taxi drivers.

4 Santiago

Santiago, one of South America's most sophisticated cities, is a thriving metropolis that's home to five million people, or nearly a third of Chile's entire population. Though it ranks third behind Miami and Sao Paulo for Latin American business travel, it is one of Chile's least popular tourist destinations, given the amount of trav-elers who use Santiago only as a jumping-off point to locations such as Patagonia or the Lake District. You won't find the rich, vibrant culture that defines such cities as Rio de Janeiro or Buenos Aires, or a wealth of things to do and see either. But that said, as the city booms economically and memories of the stifling Pinochet dictator-ship fade, Santiago is reinventing itself, and the arts, nightlife, and restaurant scene have improved considerably as of late. As well, no other Latin American city has the proximity that Santiago has to such a diverse array of day attractions, including winer-ies, ski resorts, and beaches.

Santiago also boasts a one-of-a-kind location sprawled below some of the highest peaks of the Andes range, providing a breathtaking city backdrop when the air is clear and the peaks are dusted with snow. Unfortunately, smog and dust particles in the air often shroud the view, especially during the winter months. From December to late February, when *Santiaguinos* abandon the city for summer vacation and the city is blessed with breezier days, the smog abates substantially. These are the most pleasant months to tour Santiago.

Architecturally, Santiago's city planners have shown indifference to continuity of design during the last century. Rather than look within for a style of their own, Chileans have instead copied the architecture of other continents: first Europe and now the U.S. Earthquakes and neglect eradicated most of Santiago's colonial-era buildings decades ago, and what 19-century architecture remains is in danger of demolition to make way for yet another glitzy skyscraper or one of the ubiquitous and monotonous apartment buildings so popular with residents here.

ESSENTIALS

GETTING THERE

BY PLANE   Santiago's **Comodoro Arturo Merino Benítez Airport** (© 2/690-1900; www.aeropuertosantiago.cl) is served by LAN, Sky Airline and Air Comet (formerly Aerolíneas del Sur), and most major international carriers. Within the customs area is a **currency-exchange** kiosk. Men in olive jumpsuits at the arrival and the outdoor-departure curb work as airport bellhops, and they will assist you with your luggage for a $1 or $2 (50p–£1) tip.

Depending on traffic, your Santiago destination, and how you get there, the city can be reached in 20 to 45 minutes. Most hotels offer a private car or van pickup free of charge or for about $25 (£13). A **taxi** to Santiago costs around $20 and $26. *Tip:* Buy a taxi ride at the official counter to the right of the customs exit door to avoid getting ripped off. **TransVip** (© 2/677-3000) and **Tur Transfer** (© 2/677-3600) that charge, per person, $9 for downtown Santiago and $11 to Las Condes. The drawback with this service is that you may stop at several other destinations before arriving at your own. The blue bus **Centropuerto** leaves every 10 minutes from 6am to 10:30pm and drops passengers at Los Héroes Metro station on the main avenue Alameda. **Tur Bus** leaves every 30 minutes from 6:30am to 9pm, dropping passengers off at Terminal Alameda at the Univ. de Santiago Metro station. The cost is $2.50 (£1.25).

BY BUS   There are three principal **bus stations** in Santiago. The station for international arrivals and departures to and from destinations in southern Chile is **Terminal Buses Estación Central,** formerly known as the Terminal Santiago and not to be confused with the actual Estación Central train station and Metro stop; it's located at Alameda 3850 (© 2/376-1755; Metro: Universidad de Santiago). The **Terminal Alameda** next door at Alameda 3750 is the terminal for the Pullman and Tur Bus companies, two well-respected, high-quality services. For departures to northern and central Chile, you'll go to **Terminal San Borja,** Alameda 3250 (© 2/776-0645; Metro: Estación Central). The smaller **Terminal Los Héroes,** Tucapel Jiménez 21 (© 2/423-9530; Metro: Los Héroes), has service to a variety of destinations in both northern and southern Chile.

ORIENTATION

Santiago incorporates 32 *comunas,* or neighborhoods, although most visitors will find they spend their time in just a few. **Downtown,** or *el centro,* is the financial, political, and historic center of Santiago, although many businesses have now relocated to **Providencia, Las Condes,** and the tiny area that separates the two, **El Golf** (also known as El Bosque). These neighborhoods are clean and modern, especially when compared to older, scruffier downtown. **Vitacura,** separated from Las Condes by Avenida Kennedy, is home to Santiago's tony boutiques and several top restaurants. Santiago is bisected by the Río Mapocho; on the northern side rises Cerro San Cristóbal, a forested park and recreation area. Below this park is the artists' neighborhood **Bellavista,** with dozens of bars and restaurants.

GETTING AROUND

Santiago is beset with traffic congestion during the day, making the Metro the fastest way to get around, especially from 4 to 7pm.

BY METRO   Santiago's subway system, called the "Metro," is clean and efficient, however with the overhaul of the city's transportation system, more commuters are crowding the Metro, and peak hours (7–10am and 5–8pm) can be packed; www.metro santiago.cl). Line 1 runs from Las Condes to downtown, following Avenida Alameda. This line will take you to most major attractions. Line 2 runs from Cal y Canto (near the Mercado Central) to Lo Ovalle (near the Palacio Cousiño). Lines 4 and 4a are residential lines connecting Avenida Alameda with La Reina. Line 5 runs from La Florida to Baquedano. There are two fares: 85¢ from 7 to 9am and 6 to 8pm; 70¢ from 6 to 7am, 9am to 6pm, and 8 to 11pm.

BY BUS   The Santiago bus system has undergone an overhaul, replacing old yellow buses with new gleaming white-and-green "TransSantiago" coaches, which you cannot ride without a "BIP" transit card. However, it is nearly impossible for a foreigner (or even a local) to find a BIP kiosk to buy one. In other words, city buses, or *micros,* are out of the question for travelers.

BY TAXI   Taxis are reasonably priced and plentiful. They are identifiable by their black exterior and yellow roof; there's also a light in the corner of the windshield that displays a taxi's availability. Always check to see that the meter is in plain view, to avoid rip-offs. Drivers do not expect tips. Do not confuse taxis with *colectivos,* which are similar in appearance but without the yellow roof—these are local, shared taxis with fixed routes that are too confusing to visitors to recommend taking one.

BY RENTAL CAR   Do not rent a vehicle if staying within metropolitan Santiago, but consider doing so if you are an independent traveler seeking to visit the coast or wine country. Santiago's slick new Costanera Norte (an express transit tunnel that runs from La Dehesa and Las Condes to the Panamericana Highway and the airport) has entrances and exits along the River Mapocho, but finding one can be confusing (www.costaneranorte.cl). The city's new "TAG" system (an automatic toll charged electronically to the vehicle) is included in the rental price. Downtown Santiago, and the entire length of Avenida Alameda/Avenida Providencia are not recommended for timid drivers. Buses and other drivers steadfastly refuse to let other vehicles merge into their lane, so be prepared early to turn or exit a highway. Also, do not drive inside the yellow bus lanes unless preparing to turn.

CAR RENTALS   At the airport you'll find most international rental agencies, such as **Alamo** (© 2/690-1370; www.alamochile.com), **Avis** (© 2/690-1382; www.avis chile.cl), **Budget** (© 2/690-1233; www.budget.cl), **Dollar** (© 2/202-5510; www. dollar.cl), and **Hertz** (© 2/601-0977; www.hertz.com); and local agency **Rosselot**

(© 800/201298; www.rosselot.cl). All agencies have downtown or Providencia offices. Generally, Rosselot and Dollar are lower in cost.

PARKING   Most hotels offer parking on their own property or in a nearby lot. Downtown street parking is virtually impossible except for Sundays. In Providencia, along Avenida Providencia, there is a series of underground lots. Commercial and downtown streets are manned by meter maids. Chile is also home to the parking *cuidador,* where unofficial "caretakers" stake out individual blocks and "watch" your car for you. They are everywhere, even at grocery store lots, and they expect a small tip, about 100 to 200 pesos (US20¢–US40¢/10p–20p), when you leave. *Cuidadores* in busy commercial areas are very aggressive. *Tip:* Never leave valuable items in your vehicle when parking on the street due to frequent break-ins that occur throughout Santiago.

ON FOOT   Santiago is not laid out on a perfect grid system; however, the neighborhoods most visitors stick to run along the length of the Mapocho River. Always carry a map with you. Saturday afternoons and Sundays are quieter days to explore neighborhoods such as downtown. Pedestrians should be alert at all times and never stand too close to sidewalk curbs due to buses that roar by dangerously close to sidewalks. Drivers do not always give the right of way to pedestrians, so cross streets quickly and carefully.

VISITOR INFORMATION

The **National Tourism Service (Sernatur)** office is at Av. Providencia 1550 (© **600/ SERNATUR;** www.sernatur.cl; Metro: Manuel Montt), open Monday through Friday from 9am to 5:45pm, Saturday from 9am to 2pm. Sernatur also has an information desk on the departure level of the airport open daily from 9am to 5pm (no phone). There's also an **Oficina de Turismo** downtown, inside the Casa Colorada at Merced 860 (© **2/632-7783**), with information about downtown Santiago attractions only. The **Yellow Pages** has detailed maps of the entire city of Santiago, or you can pick up a pocket guide to the city, called **"Map City"** (www.mapcity.com), sold at newsstands and kiosks for $8 (£4.10).

FAST FACTS   **Banks** are open from 9am to 2pm, closed on Saturday and Sunday. ATMs are referred to as "RedBancs" and can be identified by a RedBanc maroon-and-white logo sticker. Currency-exchange offices, called *casa de cambios,* are open from 9am to 7pm Monday to Friday, and 9am to 3pm Saturdays. On Sundays, currency can be exchanged at hotels or at an exchange house at Parque Arauco or Alto Las Condes malls. Exchange offices downtown are clustered at Paseo Huérfanos and Agustinas; in Providencia, at Avenida Pedro de Valdivia and Avenida Providencia.

For a **police emergency,** call © **133.** For **fire,** call © **132.** To call an **ambulance,** dial © **131.** If you need medical attention, the American Embassy can provide a list of English-speaking medical specialists in Santiago. The best hospitals in Santiago are private: **Clínica Las Condes,** Lo Fontecilla 441 (© **2/210-4000**), **Clínica Alemana,** Vitacura 5951 (© **2/210-1111**), and **Clínica Indisa Santa María** (© **2/362-5555**).

Every hotel has a computer with Internet connection for its guests, and many hotels now offer free Wi-Fi in guest rooms or public areas. Hours for phone centers and cafes are typically 9am to 10pm.

The main **post office** is on the Plaza de Armas (Mon–Fri 8:30am–7pm; Sat 8:30am–1pm). Branches are at Moneda 1155 in downtown and Av. 11 de Septiembre 2239. **FedEx** is at Av. Providencia 1951 and in the Dimacofi center at Moneda 792 (© **2-361-6000**).

WHAT TO SEE & DO

Even if you have just 1 day in Santiago, you should be able to pack in a sizable amount of the city's top attractions. It's a push, but nearly all attractions lie within a short walk or taxi ride from each other, which makes it easy to pick and choose according to your interests.

DOWNTOWN HISTORIC & CIVIC ATTRACTIONS

Begin your tour of Santiago at the historic heart of the city, the **Plaza de Armas** ★★★, which can be reached by taking the Metro to Estación Plaza de Armas. Chile's founder, Pedro de Valdivia, laid plans for the plaza in 1541 as the civic nucleus of the country and its importance was such that all distances to other parts of Chile were, and still are, measured from here. Take a seat and soak in the ambience of shoeshiners, religious fanatics, local artists, kissing couples, old men crouched over chessboards, and other colorful characters milling about.

Catedral Metropolitana & Museo de Arte Sagrado ★★   Santiago's grand cathedral spans a city block and is the fifth cathedral to have been erected at this site due to earthquake damage. The cathedral was also the subject of intrigue in 2005 when renovations unearthed the lost body of Diego Portales, the principal ideologist for the Chilean Constitution of 1833. The cathedral, designed by the Italian architect Joaquin Toesca in a neoclassical-baroque style, took nearly 30 years to complete, finishing in 1780. Of most interest here are the hushed, cavernous cathedral interiors, with columns that soar high to arched ceilings, and an ornate alter made of marble, bronze, and lapis lazuli, and brought from Munich in 1912. The cathedral is currently undergoing a renovation that has taken far longer than planned; with any luck it will be completed by the publication of this book.

Paseo Ahumada, on the west side of the plaza. No phone. Free admission. Mon–Sat 9am–7pm; Sun 9am–noon. Metro: Plaza de Armas.

Palacio de la Real Audiencia/Museo Histórico Nacional ★★   This excellent museum is a must-see for history buffs and travelers seeking insight to Chile's past, from the Conquest to present day, in a size and scope that doesn't feel overwhelming. The museum is housed in the elegant, lemon-colored Palacio de la Real, where Chile held its first congress following independence. The museum winds around a central courtyard, beginning with the Conquest, and finishing with a photo montage depicting modern political turmoil and literary and artistic accomplishment in Chile. Along the way, visitors can view weapons, agricultural tools, traditional costumes, household appliances, oil paintings depicting early Chile, and reproductions of home life during the 18th and 19th centuries. There are, unfortunately, no tours in English, and all interpretative information is in Spanish; however, most displays are self-explanatory. Plan to spend 30 minutes to 1 hour here.

Plaza de Armas 951. ℭ 2/411-7010. Admission $1.25 (63p) adults, 60¢ (30p) children under 18; free Sun and holidays. Tues–Sun 10am–5:30pm. Metro: Plaza de Armas.

Casa Colorada & Museo de Santiago ★ *Overrated*   Widely regarded as the best-preserved colonial structure in Santiago, the Casa Colorada, or Red House, was built between 1769 and 1779 as a residence for the first president of Chile, Mateo de Toro y Zambrano. Today, the Casa Colorada operates as the Santiago Museum, depicting the urban history of the city until the 19th century. The tiny museum, on the whole, is somewhat amateurish, seemingly directed at kids more than adults. A **visitor center** with information about downtown Santiago is also located in the Casa Colorada.

Merced 860. ℂ **2/633-0723**. Admission 70¢ (35p). Tues–Fri 10am–6pm; Sat 10am–5pm; Sun 11am–2pm. Metro: Plaza de Armas.

Museo Chileno de Arte Precolombino ✦✦✦   Heading back on Merced and past the plaza to Bandera, you'll find the notable Chilean Museum of pre-Colombian Art, housed in the elegant 1807 ex-Royal Customs House. This is one of the better museums in Chile, both for its collection of pre-Columbian artifacts and its inviting design. There are more than 1,500 objects on display here, including textiles, metals, paintings, figurines, and ceramics spread throughout seven exhibition rooms. The collection is encompassing but not as extensive as, say, the Anthropological Museum of Mexico, but the exhibition does offer a vivid exhibition of indigenous life and culture before the arrival of the Spanish. There's also a well-stocked bookstore that sells music, videos, and reproductions of Indian art, textiles, and jewelry. Docents offer tours in English at 1 and 5pm Tuesday through Friday and at 10am and 2pm Saturday, but visitors must call ahead for a reservation.

Bandera 361. ℂ **2/688-7348**. www.precolombino.cl. Admission $4 (£2.05) adults, free for students; free for everyone Sun and holidays. Tues–Sun 10am–6pm. Metro: Plaza de Armas.

PLAZA CONSTITUCION & THE COMMERCE CENTER

The Plaza Constitución, located between Agustinas, Morandé, Moneda, and Teatinos streets, is an expansive plaza used primarily as a pedestrian crossway and a venue for protests. It's also where you'll find the infamous **Palacio de la Moneda** ✦✦, the Government Palace and site of the September 11, 1973, coup d'état led by Augusto Pinochet to oust the socialist president Salvador Allende. The building, the largest erected by the Spanish government during the 18th century, was the focus of much criticism for being too ostentatious, but today it is considered one of the finest examples of neoclassical architecture in Latin America. Visitors are allowed to enter the courtyard and walk around after showing guards their passport. If you're lucky, you might catch the **changing of the guard** ✦✦, when dozens of *carabineros* (police) march in step to the Chilean anthem in front of the palace, every other day at 10am.

One block east from the plaza at Moneda and Bandera is the **Bolsa de Comercio** ✦✦ (ℂ **2/399-3000**; www.bolsadesantiago.cl), Santiago's stock market exchange, housed in an elegant, dome-roofed 1917 building and set amid some of downtown's more charming streets. Inside the Bolsa, traders group around La Rueda (The Wheel), a circular railing where they conduct hectic transactions—few people know that you can observe the action Monday to Friday 9am to 5pm.

Centro Cultural Palacio La Moneda ✦✦   Chile's newest attraction opened with great fanfare, but quickly fell victim to budget cuts and a lack of funds to keep noteworthy exhibitions coming in. This could change soon, so do not miss a quick visit here. The center is located underground before the Palacio (Citizen's Plaza) and can be accessed by walking down a ramp at either Teatinos or Morandé streets. The space is architecturally a sensational example of urban-contemporary design and focuses on revolving exhibitions of Latin American modern and historical art and photography. There is also a center displaying *artesanía,* or arts and crafts, textiles, clothing, and jewelry. The center also has an art-house cinema, library, educational center, and a sleek cafe. Check their website for upcoming exhibitions and events, and plan to spend about 30 minutes here.

Plaza de la Ciudadanía (underground). ℂ **2/355-6500**. www.ccplm.cl. Admission $1.15 (58p) adults, 60¢ (30p) students and seniors, kids under 5 free, Sun free for all. Tues–Sun 10am–9pm. Metro: La Moneda.

ATTRACTIONS OFF THE ALAMEDA

Barrio París-Londres ✿✿   This incongruous neighborhood is just a few blocks in diameter and was built between the 1920s and '30s on the old gardens of the Monastery of San Francisco. The neighborhood oozes charm—it looks as if a chunk of Paris's Latin Quarter was airlifted and dropped down in the middle of downtown Santiago. The cobblestone streets of this neighborhood end at tacky, mismatched buildings on the neighborhood's outskirts.

The streets between Prat and Santa Rosa, walking south of Alameda O'Higgins. Metro: Univ. de Chile.

Calle Dieciocho & Palacio Cousiño ✿ *Overrated*   During the turn of the 20th century and before Santiago's elite packed it up and moved away from the downtown hubbub, Calle Dieciocho ranked as the city's toniest neighborhood. The tourism board touts Calle Dieciocho as a step back in time, but neglect has taken its toll, and the only site really worth visiting here is the **Palacio Cousiño Macul,** once the home of Chile's grandest entrepreneurial dynasties, the Goyenechea-Cousiño family. When finished in 1878, the palace dazzled society with its opulence: lavish parquet floors, Bohemian crystal chandeliers, Italian hand-painted ceramics, and French tapestries. A visit here not only provides an opportunity to view how Santiago's elite lived during the late 1800s, it also offers a chance to admire the most exquisite European craftsmanship available during that time. To get here, take a taxi or the Metro to Estación Toesca (turn left when leaving the station). Take a 10-minute detour around the corner (east on San Ignacio) to Parque Almagro, a scruffy park that nevertheless affords a view of the little-known, almost Gaudiesque **Basílica del Santísimo Sacramento,** constructed between 1919 and 1931 and modeled after the Sacre Coeur in Montmartre, Paris.

Dieciocho 438. ✆ 2/698-5063. Admission $4 (£2.05) adults, $1.60 (80p) children under 12. Bilingual tours given Tues–Fri 10am–12:30pm and 2:30–4pm; Sat–Sun 10am–12:30pm. Metro: Toesca.

Iglesia, Convento, y Museo de San Francisco ✿✿   The Church of San Francisco is the oldest standing building in Santiago, and although this landmark has been renovated over the years, the main structure has miraculously survived three devastating earthquakes. The highlights are the museum and the convent, the latter with an idyllic patio planted with flora brought from destinations as near as the south of Chile and as far away as the Canary Islands. The garden, with its bubbling fountain and cooing white doves, is so peaceful, you'll find it hard to believe you're in downtown Santiago. The museum boasts 54 paintings depicting the life and death of San Francisco, one of the largest and best-conserved displays of 17th-century art in South America.

Londres and Alameda. ✆ 2/639-8737. Admission to convent and museum $2 (£1) adults. Tues–Sat 10am–1pm and 3–6pm; Sun and holidays 10am–2pm. Metro: Santa Lucía.

CERRO SANTA LUCIA

Materializing as if out of nowhere on the edge of the city's downtown limits, the **Cerro Santa Lucía** ✿✿✿ is a lavishly landscaped hilltop park and one of the more delightful attractions in Santiago. Native Mapuche Indians called this hill Huelén (Pain) until conqueror Pedro de Valdivia seized the property and planted the Spanish flag in 1570, thereby founding Santiago. In the late 1800s, Governor Benjamin Vicuña envisioned the hill as a recreation area and transformed Santa Lucía into an extravagant labyrinth of gardens, fountains, and flagstone promenades that gently spiral up to a 360-degree view of the city. The park is open daily, September through March, from 9am to 8pm, and April through August from 9am to 7pm; admission is free, though you'll be asked to sign a guest registry. The **Centro de Exposición de Arte** has indigenous crafts, clothing, and jewelry for sale, but you'll find better deals across the avenue at the **Centro Artesanal de Santa Lucía,** with handicrafts, T-shirts, and more.

PARQUE FORESTAL & PLAZA MULATO GIL DE CASTRO

Santiago's burgeoning arts and cafe scene centers around the tiny **Plaza Mulato Gil de Castro** ☞☞, located at José Victorino Lastarria and Rosal streets. The fine examples of early 1900s architecture at the plaza and many of the dozen streets that surround it provide visitors with a romantic step back into old Santiago. From Thursday to Sunday, antiques and book dealers line the plaza, but the highlights here are the **Museo de Artes Visuales (MAVI)** ☞☞☞ and the **Museo Antropología (MAS)** ☞☞ (© 2/638-3502; www.mavi.cl; Tues–Sun 10:30am–6:30pm; $2/£1 adults, $1/50p students, Sun free). Many of Chile's most promising contemporary artists exhibit their work at MAVI. The newly renovated MAS offers archeological displays of artifacts produced by indigenous peoples throughout the length of Chile. The collection at MAS is extensive, but the museum is small and takes no more than 10 minutes to peruse. If you're short on time, skip the pre-Colombian museum and visit this one in tandem with the arts museum.

Parque Forestal is a slender, century-old park that skirts the perimeter of the Mapocho River from the Metro station Baquedano to the park's terminus at the Mapocho station. Lofty trees, soft grass, and park benches provide a restful stop for the weary traveler, and you can visit the nearby **Museo Nacional de Bellas Artes** ☞☞, José Miguel de la Barra and Ismael Valdés Vergara (© 2/633-0655; www.mnba.cl; Tues–Sun 10am–6:50pm). The Museo de Bellas Artes (Fine Arts Museum) is housed in a regal, neoclassical and Art Nouveau–style edifice built in 1910 to commemorate Chile's centennial. The museum's permanent collection showcases Chilean art from the colonial period to the 20th century only; international art expositions take place as temporary exhibits.

Mercado Central ☞☞☞ *Kids*   It's the quintessential tourist stop, but the colorful, chaotic Mercado Central is nevertheless a highlight for visitors to Santiago. Chile's economy depends on the exportation of natural products such as fruits, vegetables, and seafood, and the market here displays everything the country has to offer. Lively and staffed by pushy fishmongers who quickly and nimbly gut and fillet while you watch, the market displays every kind of fish and shellfish available along the Chilean coast. Depending on your perspective, the barking fishmongers and waitresses who harangue you to choose *their* zucchini, *their* sea bass, *their* restaurant can be entertaining or somewhat annoying. Either way, don't miss it, especially for the market's lofty, steel structure that was prefabricated in England and assembled here in 1868.

Vergara and Av. 21 de Mayo. No phone. Sun–Thurs 6am–4pm; Fri 5:30am–5pm; Sat 5am–5pm. Metro: Cal y Canto.

BARRIO BELLAVISTA & PARQUE METROPOLITANO (CERRO SAN CRISTOBAL)

The **Parque Metropolitano** ☞☞☞ is a 730-hectare (1,803-acre) park and recreation area with swimming pools, walking trails, a botanical garden, a zoo, picnic grounds, restaurants, and children's play areas. The park is divided into two sectors, Cumbre and Tupahue, both of which are accessed by car, cable car, funicular, or foot. On a clear day, the sweeping views of the city render this attraction as the best in the city, but it can be disappointing on a particularly smoggy day. To get here, head to the Plaza Caupolican at the end of Calle Pío Nono, where you'll encounter a 1925 **funicular** that lifts visitors up to a lookout point, open Monday from 1 to 6pm, and Tuesday through Sunday from 10am to 6:30pm; tickets cost $3 (£1.55) adults, $1.50 (75p) children ages 3 to 13. The lookout point is watched over by a 22m-high (72-ft.) statue of the **Virgen de la Inmaculada Concepción.** Along the way, the funicular stops at the **Jardín Zoológico** (© 2/777-6666) ♠♠, open Tuesday through Sunday from 10am to 6pm; tickets cost $4 (£2.05) adults, $2 (£1) children ages 3 to 13. This surprisingly diverse zoo features more than 200 species of mammals, reptiles, and birds, including native condors, pumas, and guanacos. Below the statue is the *teleférico* (cable car) that connects the two sections of the park, open Monday 1:30 to 5:30pm, Tuesday through Sunday from 11:30am to 5:30pm. Tickets cost $2.25 (£1.15) adults, $1 (50p) children; ticket combinations with the funicular cost $4 (£2.05) adults, $2 (£1) children. The *teleférico* is a lot of fun, especially for kids, but it can be a roasting oven in the summertime heat. Admission for vehicles is $2 (£1). It's also possible to take a taxi up, but you'll need to pay the park entrance fee as well as the fare. The Parque Metropolitano's hours are daily from 8:30am to 9pm, cars until 10pm.

Below the Cerro San Cristobál sits the bohemian neighborhood **Bellavista** ♠♠♠. One of the more interesting neighborhoods in the city, its streets are lined with trees and colorful antique homes, many of which have been converted into restaurants and studios for artists and musicians. It's a pleasant place for an afternoon stroll; in the evening, Bellavista pulses to the beat of music pouring from its many nightclubs and bars.

You might begin your visit with a trip to Bellavista's prime attraction, **La Chascona** ♠♠♠ (Fernando Márquez de la Plata 0192; © 2/777-8741). Located a block east of the Plaza Caupolican (entrance point to the Parque Metropolitano), this is one of three homes once owned by Chile's most famous literary artist, the Nobel Prize–winning poet Pablo Neruda. As with Neruda's other two homes, La Chascona is packed with quirky collections of antiques and whimsical curios collected during his travels. The home is headquarters for the Fundación Pablo Neruda, which provides guided tours. Admission is $5 (£2.55) for adults for the Spanish tour, $6 (£3.10) for the English tour; and it's open Tuesday through Sunday from 10am to 6pm. Call to make a reservation, or just show up and wait in the cafe until a guide frees up.

ESPECIALLY FOR KIDS

The Parque Metropolitano Zoo, the Mercado Central, and the aerial tram at Cerro San Cristobal described above are all kid-friendly. The spacious **Parque Bernardo O'Higgins** was recently relandscaped and is frequented by blue-collar Santiaguinos who come to fly kites and barbecue on the weekends. The prime kid attraction here is **Fantasilandia,** a modern amusement park (© 2/476-8600; www.fantasilandia.cl); admission is $13 adults and $7.50 children. It's open April through November, Saturday, Sunday, and holidays only, from noon to 8pm; December through March Tuesday through Sunday from noon to 8pm. It's the largest amusement park in Chile, with four stomach-churning roller coasters, a toboggan ride, and haunted house. The **Museo Interactivo Mirador (MIM)** ♠♠♠ and the **Santiago Aquarium** ♠♠ are neighbors within an 11-hectare (27 acre) park in the La Granja barrio. Inaugurated in 2000, MIM dedicates itself to providing children with an introduction to the world of science and technology. The ultramodern museum has more than 300 exhibits, mostly interactive displays that cover the range of paleontology, computer animation, robotics, and 3D cinema. You could spend nearly a full day here if you choose to check out the aquarium and its frolicking sea lion show. Buy a combo ticket for both if you have enough time. It's located fairly far from the city center; to get here, take the Metro Line 5 to the Mirador stop or take a taxi (two entrances: Sebastopol 90 and Punta Arenas 6711; ⓒ **2/280-7800;** www.mim.cl; $6/£3.10 adults, $4/£2.05 children; combo ticket with aquarium, $9/£4.60 adults, $7/£3.60 children).

The **Parque Quinta Normal,** located at 502 Av. Matucana is also home to several museums ideally suited for kids. The **Museo Nacional de Historia Natural** ⓕ (ⓒ **2/ 680-4615;** www.mnhn.cl; admission is $1.60/80p adults, $1/50p students Tues–Sat 10am–5:30pm, Sun and holidays noon–5:30pm; Sun and holidays from Sept–Mar 11am–6:30pm) displays native flora and fauna, and anthropological exhibits, and has a new interactive area and fresh new design. The **Artequín Museum** ⓕⓕ at Av. Portales 3530 (ⓒ **2/682-5367;** www.artequin.cl; admission is $1.60/80p adults, $1/50p students, free on Sun; Tues–Sat 9am–5pm, and Sat, Sun, and holidays from 11am– 6pm.) The museum is housed in a cast-iron building accented with a kaleidoscope of colorful glass; it was built for the Chilean exhibition at the 1889 Parisian centenary of the French Revolution, and then shipped here. The museum strives to introduce visitors to the art world through 120 reproductions of well-known works by artists from Picasso to Monet. A popular museum with kids is the **Museo de Ciencia y Tecnología** ⓕ (ⓒ **2/681-6022;** www.museodeciencia.cl; admission $1.60/80p adults, $1.25/65p students), with engaging, hands-on displays, and the **Museo Ferroviario** (ⓒ **2/681-4627**) with exhibits that include 14 steam engines and railway carriages; both are open Tuesday through Friday from 10am to 6pm and Saturday and Sunday from 11am to 6pm. To get to the park, take a cab or the Metro to Estación Quinta Normal.

ORGANIZED TOURS

Major hotels work with quality tour operators and can recommend a tour even at the last minute; however, you'd be better off planning ahead and reserving a tour with an operator who can show you the more interesting side of Santiago, or who is more attuned to foreign guests' desires or needs (i.e., a guide who is truly bilingual).

Santiago Adventures offers a variety of set and custom-planned city tours and visits to attractions around the greater Central Valley region, including wine tours (ⓒ **2/ 244-2750;** www.santiagoadventures.com). **Santiago Culinary Tours,** operated by American expat Liz Caskey, kicks off with a walking tour through a typical farmers' market, or the "Vega"—the city's central food market—to purchase ingredients for lunch, held at Liz's apartment in Parque Forestal; she also offers wine tours paired with gastronomy to the outer regions of Santiago. For more information and a price quote, contact ⓒ **2/226-6939** or 9/821-9230 (www.lizcaskey.com). **Slow Travel** focuses on wine, food, and nature, with journeys to neighboring wine and food regions outside of Santiago, and culinary tours within the city (ⓒ **2/207-5372;** www.slowtravel.cl).

SPECTATOR SPORTS & RECREATION

HORSE RACING Two racetracks hold events on either Saturday or Sunday throughout the year: the recommended **Club Hípico** at Blanco Encalada 2540 (ⓒ **2/ 683-9600**) and the **Hipódromo Chile** at Avenida Vivaceta in Independencia (ⓒ **2/270- 9200**).

SWIMMING Your best bet for swimming are the public pools **Tupahue** and **Antilén,** atop Cerro San Cristóbal (ⓒ **2/777-6666;** both Nov 15–Mar 15 Tues–Sun 10am–7pm; both $10/£5.15 adults, $7/£3.60 children). You'll need a cab to Antilén, or you can walk northeast past the Camino Real to get here, about a 10-minute walk.

FUTBOL (SOCCER)   Top games are held at three stadiums: **Estadio Monumental,** Avenida Grecia and Marathón; **Universidad de Chile,** Camp de Deportes 565 (both are in the Ñuñoa neighborhood); and **Universidad Católica,** Andrés Bello 2782, in Providencia. The most popular teams, Colo Colo, Universidad Católica, and Universidad Chile, play at these stadiums. Check the sports pages of any local newspaper for game schedules.

SHOPPING

Santiago is home to two American-style megamalls: **Parque Arauco,** Av. Kennedy 5413 (Mon–Sat 10am–9pm, Sun and holidays 11am–9pm), and **Alto Las Condes,** Av. Kennedy 9001 (Mon–Sun 10am–10pm). Public transportation is difficult, so take a cab.

The brand-new and beautifully designed **Patio Bellavista** (between Constitución and Pío Nono sts., a half-block from Dardignac; ℭ 2/777-4766; www.patiobellavista. cl) is a collection of shops hawking high-quality arts and crafts, jewelry, woolens, and woodwork, and centered around a cobblestone patio with a couple of cafes and outstanding restaurants. Patio Bellavista is open Wednesday through Sunday from 10am to 9pm, and Thursday though Saturday from 10am to 10pm. Farther away, but just as fun to visit, is **Los Domínicos** (Av. Apoquindo 9085; no phone), open Tuesday through Sunday and holidays from 10:30am to 7pm. Los Domínicos is a folksy, mock colonial village with shops selling hand-knit sweaters, lapis lazuli, arts and crafts, antiques (expensive), and Chilean traditional wear such as ponchos.

Santiago's version of Rodeo Drive is Ave. Alonso de Cordoba in the Vitacura neighborhood, with upscale stores and brands such as Louis Vuitton. Supermarkets offer a wide selection of more traditional wines at cheaper prices than specialty shops. For those hard-to-get wines you won't find back in the U.S., try **El Mundo del Vino** at Av. Isidora Goyenechea 2931 (ℭ **2/584-1172;** www.elmundodelvino.cl), open Monday through Wednesday 10:30am to 8:30pm, Thursday through Saturday 10am to 9pm, and Sunday 11am to 6pm. El Mundo del Vino has an extensive selection and knowledgeable staff, but my pick for wine stores is undoubtedly **La Vinoteca** (ℭ **2/ 334-1987**), located at Avenida Isidora Goyenechea 3520, and open Monday through Friday from 10am to 9pm, Saturday 10am to 8pm. La Vinoteca's sales team really know their stuff, and the shop specializes in boutique and hard-to-find wines. Also, La Vinoteca has a shop in the airport; if you buy a case here, they'll wrap it up so you can check it like luggage.

WHERE TO STAY

Where you stay in Santiago will likely shape your opinion of the city. The cheapest accommodations are located in the downtown area, *el centro*. This neighborhood is congested and older, yet it is close to the lovely Parque Forestal/Lastarria neighborhood. City sights are concentrated in or near *el centro*, yet a Metro or taxi ride transports visitors staying in Providencia or Las Condes here quickly. Parking is free unless otherwise indicated in the review. High season is generally October through March, yet many hotels offer cheaper deals in January and February.

DOWNTOWN SANTIAGO
Expensive
Hotel Plaza San Francisco ★★   The Hotel Plaza is downtown's best bet for upscale accommodation, and it recently underwent an extensive renovation. The hotel

Downtown Santiago

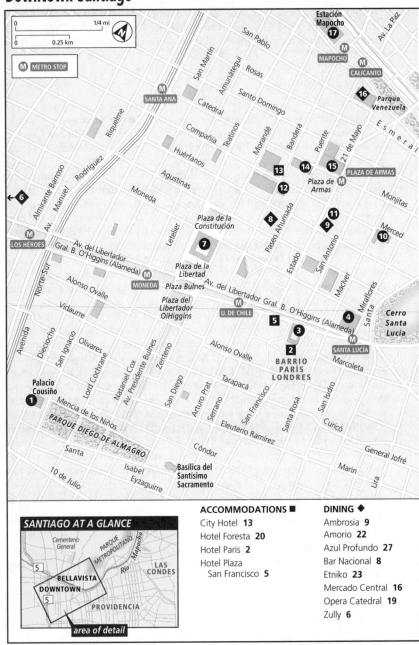

METRO STOP Ⓜ

1/4 mi
0.25 km

Av. La Paz
San Pablo
Estación Mapocho **17**
Ⓜ MAPOCHO
Ⓜ CALICANTO
San Martín
Amunátegui
Rosas
Santo Domingo
Catedral
Ⓜ SANTA ANA
Riquelme
Compañía
Teatinos
Huérfanos
Morandé
Bandera
Puente
21 de Mayo
Parque Venezuela **16**
Esmeralda
Agustinas
Moneda
Almirante Barroso
Av. Manuel Rodríguez
Leteiler
Plaza de la Constitución
13 **14** **15** PLAZA DE ARMAS
12
Plaza de Armas Ⓜ
Monjitas
Merced
8 **11** **10**
9
Paseo Ahumada
San Antonio
Machver
Estado
6 ←
Ⓜ LOS HÉROES
Av. del Libertador Gral. B. O'Higgins (Alameda)
Norte-Sur
Alonso Ovalle
Vidaurre
Plaza de la Libertad
Ⓜ MONEDA
Plaza Bulnes
Plaza del Libertador OiHiggins
Av. del Libertador Gral. B. O'Higgins (Alameda)
Ⓜ U. DE CHILE
5
3
2
4
Ⓜ SANTA LUCÍA
Miraflores
Santa
Cerro Santa Lucía
Marcoleta
Alonso Ovalle
BARRIO PARÍS LONDRES
Avenda
Dieciocho
San Ignacio
Olivares
Lord Cochrane
Nataniel Cox
Av. Presidente Bulnes
Zenteno
San Diego
Arturo Prat
Serrano
Tarapacá
San Francisco
Santa Rosa
San Isidro
Curicó
Palacio Cousiño **1**
Mencia de los Niños
PARQUE DIEGO DE ALMAGRO
Santa
10 de Julio
Isabel
Eyzaguirre
Córdor
Eleuterio Ramírez
Basílica del Santísimo Sacramento
Marin
General Jofré
Lira

SANTIAGO AT A GLANCE

Cementerio General
PARQUE METROPOLITANO
Río Mapocho
LAS CONDES
5
BELLAVISTA
DOWNTOWN
5
PROVIDENCIA
area of detail

ACCOMMODATIONS ■
City Hotel **13**
Hotel Foresta **20**
Hotel París **2**
Hotel Plaza San Francisco **5**

DINING ◆
Ambrosia **9**
Amorio **22**
Azul Profundo **27**
Bar Nacional **8**
Etniko **23**
Mercado Central **16**
Opera Catedral **19**
Zully **6**

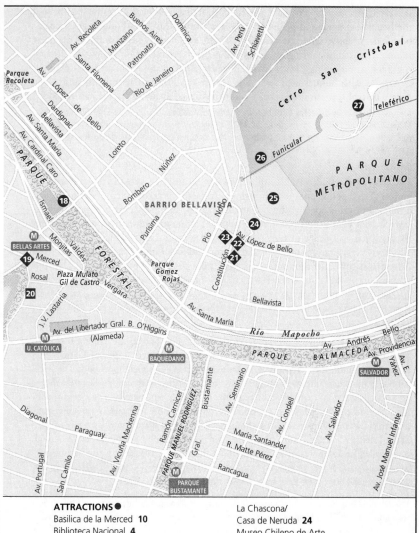

ATTRACTIONS ●

is located on bustling Avenue Alameda, with its frenzied pace of traffic, but behind the hotel lie the tranquil pedestrian streets of the Barrio Paris–Londres microneighborhood. Attentive service is a trademark here, as is meticulous cleaning of the guest rooms. The traditional English décor, using richly colored fabric wallpaper, Oriental rugs, and wood ceilings, lends an executive-travel air to the hotel, and accordingly it is popular with businessmen, who also choose the Plaza for its full amenities. The hotel's **Bristol Restaurant** has been honored with many awards in the past decade.

Alameda 816. ℂ 2/639-3832. Fax 2/639-7826. www.plazasanfrancisco.cl. 155 units. $139–$149 (£71–£76) double; $220–$250 (£113–£128) executive suite. AE, DC, MC, V. Metro: Univ. de Chile. **Amenities:** Restaurant; bar; indoor pool; gym; whirlpool; concierge; business center; wine shop; room service; massage; laundry service; art gallery. *In room:* A/C, TV, minibar, safe, stereo.

Moderate

City Hotel ℛ   Built in 1938, the City Hotel features a Gotham City–like exterior and Art Deco period antiques throughout its guest rooms, polished wood floors, and a manual elevator operated by the hotel's bellhop. The rooms are very spartan, and beds are not firm and of just average quality. Bathrooms are spacious and clean, but fixtures such as toilets and sinks look like they're from the hotel's inauguration year. The hotel's restaurant oozes old-world charm, and its location a half-block from Plaza de Armas is convenient for sightseeing. The front desk staff borders on gruff, but this is common in old Chilean hotels in this price range.

Compañía 1063. ℂ 2/695-4526. Fax 2/695-6775. www.cityhotel.cl. 72 units. $60 (£31) double. AE, DC, MC, V. Metro: Plaza de Armas. **Amenities:** Restaurant; bar; limited room service; laundry service. *In room:* TV.

Inexpensive

Hotel Foresta ℛℛ 𝘝𝘢𝘭𝘶𝘦   One of Santiago's quirkier hotels, the Foresta boasts an ideal downtown location across the street from the forested slopes of Cerro Santa Lucia, and within the Parque Forestal cafe-cum-artist microneighborhood. The hotel is housed in a charming, well-maintained stone building, and though the guest rooms are clean, each room features an eclectic mix of dated (some would say tacky) furnishings. Nevertheless, this hotel is a good value, with a friendly staff and an on-site restaurant that has panoramic views of the park. Always ask for a room that faces Cerro Santa Lucia as interior rooms are depressingly dark. Double rooms are large enough to be called junior suites, with an additional sitting area. Breakfast is not included.

Victoria Subercaseaux 353. ℂ 2/639-6261 or 2/639-4862. Fax 2/632-2996. 35 units. $36 (£18) double. AE, DC, MC, V. Parking available. Metro: Santa Lucía. **Amenities:** Restaurant; bar. *In room:* TV, minibar.

Hotel París ℛ 𝘝𝘢𝘭𝘶𝘦   There's nothing luxurious about this budget hotel, but it is a step above most. The Hotel París is old and atmospheric, a mansion-turned-hotel with rooms of differing sizes and lots of winding stairs; some rooms feature Oriental rugs and mahogany molding. There's a newer annex (worth the extra $8/£4.10 per night), but you really need to be a backpacker to not mind the simplicity and worn-out look of the rooms in the older annex. When booking, ask for a room with a terrace because they are the same price. Continental breakfast costs $3 (£1.55).

París 813. ℂ 2/664-0921. Fax 2/639-4037. carbott@latinmail.com. 40 units. $40 (£21) double new wing; $32 (£16) double old room. AE, DC, MC, V. Parking across the street $3–$5 (£1.55–£2.55) per day. Metro: Univ. de Chile. **Amenities:** Cafe; laundry service. *In room:* TV (in some rooms).

PROVIDENCIA
Very Expensive

Sheraton Santiago ℛℛ   With its crystal chandeliers and marble floors, the Sheraton Santiago is all about glamour, whereas the Park Plaza is low-key elegance. There

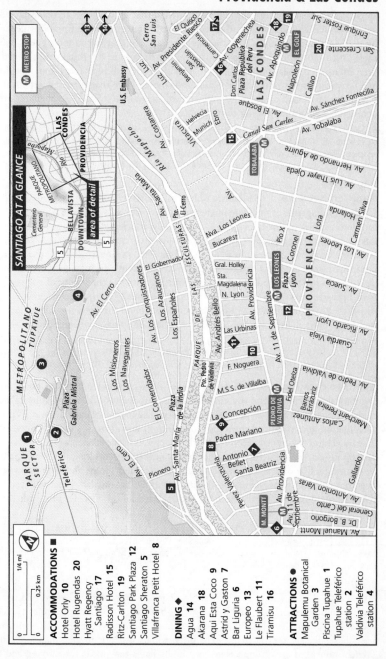

SANTIAGO AT A GLANCE

M METRO STOP

ACCOMMODATIONS ■
Hotel Orly **10**
Hotel Rugendas **20**
Hyatt Regency Santiago **17**
Radisson Hotel **15**
Ritz-Carlton **19**
Santiago Park Plaza **12**
Santiago Sheraton **5**
Villafranca Petit Hotel **8**

DINING ◆
Agua **14**
Akarana **18**
Aqui Esta Coco **9**
Astrid y Gaston **7**
Bar Liguria **6**
Europeo **13**
Le Flaubert **11**
Tiramisu **16**

ATTRACTIONS ●
Mapulemu Botanical Garden **3**
Piscina Tupahue **1**
Tupahue Teleférico station **2**
Valdivia Teleférico station **4**

are actually two hotels here, the old Sheraton, and the San Cristóbal Tower with conference centers and luxury executive rooms. The Sheraton is cut off from Providencia by the Río Mapocho and a busy thoroughfare, and for that reason most guests take cabs, as it is about a 15-minute walk to the Metro station. Anything over the 10th floor offers spectacular views. The "old" Sheraton offers comfortable rooms, yet the San Cristóbal Tower offers luxury accommodations. Note that their restaurants are pricey; better to grab a cab and dine in Providencia or Bellavista. The Sheraton can occasionally sell out to visiting conventioneers.

Av. Santa María 1742. ⓒ 2/233-5000. Fax 2/234-1066. www.sheraton.cl. 379 units. $225–$280 (£113–£141) double standard. AE, DC, MC, V. Metro: Pedro de Valdivia. **Amenities:** 3 restaurants; bar; outdoor and indoor pools; tennis courts; whirlpool; sauna; concierge; travel agency; rental car agency; business center; shopping gallery; salon and barber; massage; babysitting; laundry service. *In room:* A/C, TV, minibar, hair dryer, safe, stereo.

Expensive

Radisson Hotel ⓕⓕ   The Radisson Hotel is housed within the glitzy World Trade Center building, one of the more interesting, avant-garde skyscrapers in Santiago. The location is very convenient for tourists and business travelers alike because it is close to Las Condes–district businesses and the El Bosque restaurant row, as well as a few good bars. Best of all, the guest rooms were freshly renovated in January 2007, with a smart, contemporary decor that updated what used to be seriously frumpy guest rooms and gave them what they needed: a synergistic pairing with the modernity of the hotel's glass high-rise exterior. Get a room that faces the Andes (seventh floor and up). At night, the towering ultramodern buildings that surround the hotel provide glittering nighttime views. The health club and pool on the rooftop have panoramic views.

Av. Vitacura 2610. ⓒ 800/333-3333 in the U.S., or 2/203-6000 in Santiago. www.radisson.cl. 159 units. $159 (£80) double. AE, DC, MC, V. Metro: Tobalaba. **Amenities:** Restaurant; 2 bars; indoor pool; whirlpool; sauna; concierge; travel agency; business center; salon; babysitting; laundry service; wine shop. *In room:* A/C, TV, minibar, hair dryer, safe.

Santiago Park Plaza Hotel ⓕⓕ   The Park Plaza calls itself a boutique hotel, but the uniformed bellhops and traditional decor (not to mention 104 rooms) make it a midsize hotel known for its personalized service. The hotel's salient feature is its perfect location on a tree-lined street just 1 block from Providencia's shops and services. The hotel has a traditional decor, with Oriental rugs, brocade fabrics, wingback chairs, and wood-paneled walls. Although the hotel is kept spotlessly clean, the hotel's claim of luxury guest rooms is a push, and many of the guest rooms and bathrooms are beginning to show wear and tear. One gets the feeling that the Park Plaza will need to renovate sometime within the next year. Still, their rooftop pool is a nice perk, and you simply can't beat the location.

Ricardo Lyon 207. ⓒ 2/372-4000. Fax 2/233-6668. www.parkplaza.cl. 104 units. $126 (£65) standard double; $259 (£133) suite. Parking available. Metro: Los Leones. **Amenities:** Restaurant; bar; indoor rooftop pool; gym; sauna; city tours and transfers to tennis and golf courts; business center; room service; babysitting; laundry service; Internet. *In room:* A/C, TV, minibar, hair dryer, safe, Wi-Fi.

Moderate

Hotel Orly ⓕⓕⓕ *(Finds)*   This irresistible boutique hotel is my favorite midrange lodging option in Santiago, and it is close to absolutely everything. The price is nice too: at least a third less than other Santiago hotels of the same caliber, with attentive, friendly service at no extra charge. The Orly is housed in a renovated mansion with French-influenced architecture. The cozy lobby has a few nooks for relaxing and a small, glass-roofed patio; there's also a bar and a dining area where the staff serves a hearty buffet breakfast. The interiors are a restful white and decorated with country manor furnishings. Room sizes vary; doubles come with two twins or a full-size bed and are of average size; a few singles are decidedly not for the claustrophobic.

Av. Pedro de Valdivia 027. © 2/231-8947. Fax 2/334-4403. www.hotelorly.cl. 28 units. $95–$105 (£49–£54) double; $30–$140 (£15–£70) junior suite. AE, DC, MC, V. Metro: Pedro de Valdivia. **Amenities:** Cafe; bar; room service; laundry service; tours. *In room:* A/C, TV, minibar, hair dryer, safe.

Vilafranca Petit Hotel ★★★ *Finds*   One of Santiago's only B&B-style hotels, the Vilafranca is housed in a superbly refurbished old mansion and provides travelers with a more personalized lodging option brimming with character and coziness, at a price that's reasonable. As with any B&B, the feeling that you're bunking in an old home is clearly evident, yet the interiors are bestowed with a French Provençal design, and lovely old antique armoires and nightstands, fresh white linens, and walls painted in soothing tones of ecru and decorated with dried sprigs of flowers and simple sketch art. And what a value—for such a pretty hotel, it is hard to believe that a double costs just $70 (£36) a night, but then many rooms are very small. Common areas include a living room with overstuffed sofas, and a cobblestone patio fringed in greenery.

Perez Valenzuela 1650. © 2/232-1413. www.vilafranca.cl. 8 units. $70 (£36) double with a double bed. AE, DC, MC, V. Metro: Manuel Montt. **Amenities:** Cafe. *In room:* A/C (some rooms), TV, high-speed Internet, Wi-Fi, hair dryer, safe.

LAS CONDES
Very Expensive
Grand Hyatt Regency Santiago ★★★   The Grand Hyatt is a 24-story atrium tower with two adjacent wings and four glass elevators that whisk guests up to their split-level rooms and terraced suites. Inside it feels as spacious as an airport hanger, but it exudes a sense of glamour lacking in so many high-end hotels. What sets this hotel apart is the flawless service provided by the staff, amply spacious guest rooms with views of the Andes (rooms with an eastern orientation from the 10th floor up), a palm-and-fern-fringed pool and the best gym/spa of any hotel in Santiago. Guests in suites enjoy their own 16th-floor private lounge for lingering over breakfast and soaking up the spectacular view. On the down side, you'll always need to take a taxi because the location at the head of a crazy traffic loop makes it difficult and too far away to walk anywhere from here. Cheaper deals can be found when booking on their website.

Av. Kennedy 4601. © 2/950-1234. Fax 2/950-3155. www.hyatt.cl. 310 units, 26 suites. $389 (£199) Grand Deluxe (double); $370 (£190) Grand Suite. AE, DC, MC, V. **Amenities:** 3 restaurants; bar; outdoor pool; tennis courts; gym; whirlpool; sauna; concierge; American Airlines office; Hertz car-rental office; business center; shopping arcade; salon; 24-hr. room service; massage; babysitting; laundry service; solarium; valet service. *In room:* A/C, TV, dataport, minibar, hair dryer, safe.

Ritz-Carlton Santiago ★★★   Expect to be pampered here. Though the exterior of the new Ritz-Carlton is remarkably plain, it is one of Santiago's finest hotels. Not only are the interiors luxurious in the Ritz-Carlton fashion, the hotel has a fabulous rooftop health center with a glass-dome ceiling that provides a sweeping view of the city and the Andes. The Ritz is located near restaurants and the thriving economic hub of Santiago, making this a more convenient choice than the Hyatt. But what really stands out here is the gracious, attentive service. The hotel's lobby, which has a two-story rotunda and floors made of imported marble, leads to the hotel lounge and a plush wine bar "345." In the spotless guest rooms, the beds are heavenly comfortable. I recommend that guests head to the hotel's high patio at sunset to soak in the breathtaking view of the Andes. Note that the Ritz in Santiago is more economically priced than many of their other hotels, and they offer special packages on their website.

El Alcalde 15. (C) **800/241-3333** from the U.S., or 2/470-8500. Fax 2/470-8501. www.ritzcarlton.com. 205 units. $269–$349 (£138–£179) Quality Room; $319–$379 (£164–£194) Deluxe Room; $329–$409 (£169–£210) Club Room. AE, DC, MC, V. Metro: El Golf. **Amenities:** 3 restaurants; bar; indoor rooftop pool; gym; whirlpool; sauna; concierge; car rental; business center; salon; room service; massage; babysitting; laundry service; valet service. *In room:* A/C, TV, minibar, hair dryer, safe.

Expensive

Hotel Rugendas 🌟   The Hotel Rugendas is a high-quality choice in Las Condes for its location near El Bosque restaurants and services; it's on a leafy residential street several blocks from busy Avenida Apoquindo. During the week, businessmen are the hotel's primary clients, meaning the price drops on weekends, so ask for promotions when booking a Friday or Saturday stay. The Tuscan-style hotel recently converted its 10th floor into guest rooms; these rooms are newer and the same price, however all guest rooms are cozy and neatly maintained. Junior suites are small but worth the extra money. For views, book anything on the seventh floor up and ask for a room oriented toward the Andes.

Callao 3123. (C) **2/370-5700.** Fax 2/246-6570. www.hotelrugendas.cl. 51 units. $130–$150 (£67–£77) double. AE, DC, MC, V. Metro: El Golf. **Amenities:** Restaurant; bar; gym; sauna; business center; laundry service. *In room:* A/C, TV, minibar, hair dryer, safe.

WHERE TO DINE

Santiago's gastronomic scene has undergone a culinary revolution during the past decade with an influx of ethnic restaurants and trendy eateries serving fusion-style, creative cuisine commonly known as *cocina de autor.* Many restaurants are clustered along several streets in neighborhoods such as Bellavista, and along the streets Av. El Bosque and Isabel Goyenechea—visitors might find it more adventurous to stroll around these neighborhoods until something takes their fancy. Don't forget that most major hotels, notably the Hyatt, the Ritz, and the Hotel Plaza San Francisco, have outstanding restaurants.

DOWNTOWN

Most downtown eateries are open for lunch only and closed on Sunday. The only exception is the Lastarria Street/Plaza Mulato Gil de Castro neighborhood (located on the other side of Cerro St. Lucia), at the following restaurants: **La Pérgola de la Plaza** (© **2/639-3604;** Mon–Fri 11am–midnight, Sat 11am–2am, Sun 11am–4pm), a bistro with a slightly expensive fixed-price lunch menu and outdoor seating; **"R"** (© **2/664-9844;** Mon–Sat 12:30–4:30pm and 7:30pm–1:30am), a cozy spot for wine and conversation, although the food is overpriced and could be a lot tastier; and the newest cafe, **Mosqueto Café** (corner of Villavicencio and Lastarría; © **2/639-1627;** daily 8:30am–10pm); serves coffee, cakes, and sandwiches in a gorgeous, meticulously restored antique building.

Expensive

Zully 🌟🌟 *Finds* INTERNATIONAL   Chic, yet true to the utterly charming, historical neighborhood in which it is located, Zully is the new restaurant of the moment—and a fun place to dine. The American-owned restaurant covers four floors of a lovingly restored old mansion and boasts a wine-tasting cellar, an interior patio, and trendily decorated dining rooms. I've had many memorable meals here, but other times the quality has been just so-so (especially considering the price). No matter, you won't be sorry you taxied over when you lay eyes on this architectural gem. It's best to take a taxi here at night; during the day you can take the Metro to the stop República, walk out the north exit and head east 1½ blocks to Calle Concha y Toro, and turn left.

Concha y Toro 34. ℂ **2/696-3990.** Reservations recommended for dinner. Main courses $16–$21 (£8.20–£11). AE, DC, MC, V. Mon–Fri 1–4pm and 8pm–1am; Sat 8pm–2am (when the last guest leaves; either slightly earlier or later). Metro: República.

Moderate

Ambrosía ✿✿ INTERNATIONAL   Tucked behind the Casa Colorado Museum (enter the museum and cross the patio to get here), Ambrosía is a chic little eatery and quiet haven from the boisterous downtown street outside. The menu features an eclectic offering of Peruvian, French, and Italian dishes, each prepared blending creative flavors and elements for a decidedly eclectic menu. Examples include panko-breaded shrimp in peanut sauce, beef tenderloin with candied carrots, and sea bass with port sauce and shiitake mushrooms. With its patio dining, this restaurant is ideal for summer days. Service is friendly, too, and attentive in a way common with family businesses.

Merced 838. ℂ **2/697-2023.** www.ambrosia.cl. Main courses $7–$12 (£3.60–£6.15). AE, DC, MC, V. Mon–Fri 9am–6pm. Metro: Plaza de Armas.

Bar Nacional ✿ CHILEAN   These two traditional restaurants have been a hit with downtown workers for more than 50 years, serving honest Chilean food in a diner-like atmosphere. On Calle Bandera and Paseo Huérfanos, both are relatively identical. This is where to try Chilean favorites such as empanadas, *cazuela* (a hearty chicken soup), *pastel de choclo* (a meat-and-corn casserole), and the cholesterol-boosting *lomo a lo pobre* (steak and fries topped with sautéed onions and a fried egg).

Bar Nacional 1 at Huérfanos 1151; ℂ **2/696-5986.** Bar Nacional 2 at Bandera 371; ℂ **2/695-3368.** Main courses $7–$11 (£3.60–£5.65); sandwiches $3–$4 (£1.55–£2.05). AE, DC, MC, V. Mon–Fri 7:30am–11pm; Sat 7:30am–4pm. Metro: Plaza de Armas.

Opera & Catedral ✿✿✿ CONTEMPORARY FRENCH/CHILEAN   Just what was missing from the Santiago dining/drinking scene wasn't fully obvious until these two eateries opened in 2006. Both have a sleek look that would fit in nicely in New York, and accordingly, both are wildly popular with the young glitterati of Santiago, the arts scene, and discerning customers who enjoy a little more sophistication in their dining experience. Opera is a polished, fine-dining establishment, with exposed brick walls and white linen tablecloths. Upstairs at inexpensive Catedral, the look is minimalist, with gun-battle-gray walls, wicker chairs, and a couple of leather couches, and there is also a outdoor terrace for summer evenings. Cathedral serves modern takes on Chilean classics, with a few Asian-influenced dishes, gourmet sandwiches, and a very tasty *crudo,* or steak tartare.

Both located at the corner of Merced and José Miguel de la Barra. ℂ **2/664-3048.** www.operacatedral.cl. Reservations required at Opera; reservations not accepted at Catedral. AE, DC, MC, V. **Opera:** Main courses $15–$21 (£7.55–£11). Mon–Fri 1–3:15pm and 8–10:30pm; Sat 8–10:30pm. **Catedral:** Main courses $5–$11 (£2.50–£5.55). Mon–Wed 12:30pm–2am; Thurs–Sat 12:30pm–5am. Metro: Bellas Artes.

BELLAVISTA & PROVIDENCIA
Expensive

Amorío ✿✿ CONTEMPORARY CHILEAN   Breathing new life into a staid Bellavista dining scene, Amorío is the restaurant of the moment and part of the Mori Cultural Center that, along with a theater and art cinema, is housed inside a beautifully recycled old mansion that sat unused for far too long. The dining area is one of the most chic ambiences in Santiago: think retro-style hibiscus-flower wallpaper, exposed brick walls, refurbished Louis XIV chairs, parquet floors and lots of soft halogen lighting. The first floor is more formal, with a full menu, and the second is more casual and offers a tapas menu and cocktails. The food strives for "new" cuisine that is finding its way onto Santiago menus, and it is inconsistent but on average decent. Try the *asado de tiro estofado,* a tender stewed beef, and save room for dessert.

Constitución 181. *©* **2/777-1454.** Main courses $7–$13 (£3.60–£6.65). AE, DC, MC, V. Tues–Fri 1–4pm and 8pm–midnight; Sat 8pm–midnight; Sun 1–4pm. Metro: Baquedano.

Aquí Está Coco *©©* SEAFOOD   This eclectic restaurant not only serves some of the city's freshest seafood, it's also a fun place to dine. Housed in a 140-year-old home, the restaurant is owned by one charismatic Jorge "Coco" Pacheco, who gave the place its name: "Here's Coco." The ambience is kitschy, but it's the fish that brings them back every time. Every kind of seafood is available, including hake, swordfish, cod, sea bass, tuna, and shellfish, and a host of tantalizing seafood appetizers such as crab cakes or broiled scallops in a barnacle sauce. I recommend the trout stuffed with king crab and lobster béchamel sauce. Attentive service and a menu in English are reasons you'll see many gringos here, but Chileans love Aquí Está Coco, too. Note that the restaurant has a good selection of meat dishes for those not fond of seafood.

La Concepción 236. *©* **2/235-8649.** www.aquiestacoco.cl. Main courses $13–$20 (£6.65–£10). AE, DC, MC, V. Mon–Sat 1–3pm and 8–11pm. Metro: Pedro de Valdivia.

Astrid y Gastón *©©©* INTERNATIONAL   If you're looking to blow your budget, this is your place. Gaston, his wife Astrid, and his kitchen staff have created a wonderfully provocative menu filled with delicious flavor combinations using luxurious ingredients in unexpected ways. Think cuisine influenced by Peru, Spain, France, and Japan, and you'll have an idea of the exciting dishes that await your taste buds. The ambience is brightly lit, elegant, and better for a meal among friends than a romantic date. The service at Astrid y Gastón is flawless, with a sommelier and one of the city's most interesting and varied wine lists. Try the fresh goose liver, or my favorite, king crab ravioli. Dessert orders must be placed early so that the kitchen staff can make each one from scratch.

Antonio Bellet 201. *©* **2/650-9125.** Reservations required. Main courses $15–$20 (£7.70–£10). AE, DC, MC, V. Mon–Fri 1–3pm and 8pm–midnight; Sat 8pm–midnight. Metro: Pedro de Valdivia.

Moderate

Etniko *©©* ASIAN   Etniko is one of Santiago's hippest restaurants, serving Asian-influenced cuisine to the modern beat of house music played by resident DJs. The place is trendy and sophisticated, and frequented by Santiago's stylish yuppies and expats. The menu offers a diverse selection, but the mainstay is the 16 varieties of sushi. Also on offer are Japanese tempura and Chinese and Vietnamese stir-fries. The bar is a lively, fun place for a cocktail, and there is an extensive wine and champagne menu. Don't expect the place to fill until 9 or 10pm.

Constitución 172. *©* **2/732-0119.** Main courses $7–$14 (£3.60–£7.20). AE, DC, MC, V. Reservations recommended. Daily noon–4pm and 8pm–midnight (until 2am Fri–Sat).

Le Flaubert *©©* *Finds* FRENCH/CHILEAN   Le Flaubert is a petit French/Chilean bistro whose understated elegance and romantic, Provençal-style ambience makes the ideal place for a date or intimate meal among friends. The plant-filled outdoor dining area in the back patio is soothing and cool on a hot day, and the waitstaff is mindful without being overbearing. Le Flaubert offers five appetizers and as many main dishes presented on a chalkboard, with delicious fare such as duck confit, crab casserole, and a recommended sea bass with a shrimp and avocado sauce. This is one of the only restaurants in Providencia that is open on Sunday; they have a takeout service and will deliver for free if you're within 2 blocks of the restaurant.

Orrego Luco 125. (✆) 2/231-9424. www.leflaubert.cl. Main courses $10–$15 (£5.10–£7.70). AE, DC, MC, V. Mon 12:30–4:30pm and 7:30–11:30pm; Tues–Sat 12:30–11:30pm; Sun noon–9pm. Metro: Pedro de Valdivia.

Inexpensive

Bar Liguria ★★★ *Moments* CHILEAN BISTRO   This bistro/bar is one of my favorites in Santiago. Bar Liguria is vibrant, warm, and the "in" spot in Providencia for actors, writers, businesspeople, and just about everyone else who comes to soak up the kitschy, bohemian atmosphere. The Bar Liguria at Luis Thayer Ojeda Street has a large and lofty upstairs dining room that allows energy to simply radiate throughout the place, but I like the lively atmosphere at the Manuel Montt location better. The Liguria serves ample portions of emblematic Chilean dishes (and a few Italian dishes), as well as hefty sandwiches and salads that are reasonably priced. In the evening, the Bar Liguria is absolutely packed, and you might have to wait 10 to 15 minutes for a table; however, the bar makes a great hangout in the meantime.

Luis Thayer Ojeda 019: (✆) 2/231-1393. Av. Providencia 1373: (✆) 2/235-7914. Reservations not accepted. Main courses $6–$10 (£3.10–£5.10). AE, DC, MC, V. Mon–Sat noon–1am (till 3am Fri–Sat). Metro: Los Leones (Ojeda branch), and Manuel Montt (Providencia branch).

LAS CONDES (EL BOSQUE NORTE)/VITACURA

The street El Bosque has it all: Chilean, French, seafood, steakhouses, fast-food courts, and more. For American fare, there's a **T.G.I. Friday's** with the usual fattening menu at Goyenechea 3275 ((✆) **2/234-4468;** Sun–Thurs noon–1:30am, Fri–Sat noon–2:30am). The best place for breakfast and lunch is **Cafe Melba,** Don Carlos 2898 ((✆) **2/232-4546;** Mon–Fri 8am–3pm, Sat–Sun 8:30am–3:30pm). You'll need a cab to reach restaurants in Vitacura, but they're well worth seeking out.

Expensive

Agua ★★★ FUSION   Sleek and minimalist, Agua was a pioneer in fashionable dining among Santiago's well-to-do, who clambered for reservations in what was then *the* place to see and be seen. Aqua still bustles with beautiful people, and although its founding chef has since moved on, Agua continues as the apex of culinary innovation and creativity that focuses around top Chilean products such as Magellanic lamb, king crab, shellfish, tuna from Easter Island, and more. The food is divine, and a sample menu could include grouper with a fava bean puree or a lobster risotto with scallops and chives; or you can order their tasting menu and choose four dishes from their main menu that are served in smaller portions, with dessert for $22 (£11) per person. Service is attentive and fast.

Nueva Costanera 3467. (✆) 2/263-0008. www.aguarestaurant.cl. Reservations recommended. Main courses $12–$19 (£6.15–£9.75). AE, DC, MC, V. Mon–Fri 12:30–3pm and 7:30pm–midnight; Sat 8:30pm–midnight.

Cuerovaca ★★★ STEAKHOUSE   Santiago's top steakhouse focuses on providing carnivores with the finest cuts of meat available in Santiago, including *wagyu,* the Japanese-origin Kobe beef, lamb from the Falklands Island, and locally produced Angus and Hereford beef. If you're not a beef eater, there are seafood dishes that specialize in Easter Island imports and locally produced salmon. Cuerovaca strives to educate diners and build a "culture" around the appreciation of fine beef, and they'll happily provide you with background information about your cut. The ambience is urban-contemporary, with flagstone walls, wood, and glass, and they feature an outstanding wine list. Note that accompaniments and salads are an additional cost to prices listed below.

El Mañío 1659. ℂ **2/206-3911**. www.cuerovaca.cl. Reservations recommended. Beef cuts $13–$16 (£6.65–£8.20); Kobe Beef cuts average $48 (£25); seafood courses $11–$17 (£5.65–£8.70). AE, DC, MC, V. Daily 1–4pm and 8–11:30pm.

Europeo ✸✸✸ CENTRAL EUROPEAN   Another darling of local food critics, this restaurant is named for the food it serves: central European–based cuisine expertly prepared by the restaurant's Swiss-born and -trained chef. In a word, the food is heavenly, and the offer of a more upscale main dining area and a more economical adjoining bistro makes the Europeo suitable for any budget. Delectables include foie gras sautéed in a reduction of white wine, steak tartare on rye, "strudel" of lobster and spinach on vanilla-infused bisque, and savory Austrian-style desserts. The bistro, **La Brasserie**, offers a less formal ambience and a menu that is not as elaborate as the restaurant's, but it's of excellent quality nonetheless.

Alonso de Córdova 2417. ℂ **2/208-3603**. Reservations recommended. Main courses $17–$25 (£8.70–£13) Europeo; $8–$13 (£4.10–£6.65) La Brasserie. AE, DC, MC, V. Mon–Fri 1–3pm and 8–10:30pm; Sat 8–11pm.

Moderate

Akarana ✸✸ *Finds* FUSION   I can't think of a more delightful place in Las Condes to dine alfresco than on this restaurant's wraparound patio, and Akarana's contemporary, all-white interiors are chic, fresh, and airy. Fusing Asian cuisine with New Zealand specialties, the chef here creates a wonderful feast for the palate, from grilled fresh tuna with chile and lime buerre blanc to good ol' fish and chips. This is an excellent place to enjoy well-prepared afternoon cocktails and a plate of appetizers, listening to frequent live music.

Reyes Lavalle 3310. ℂ **2/231-9667**. Reservations recommended. Main courses $6–$10 (£3.10–£5.10). AE, DC, MC, V. Daily noon–midnight.

Inexpensive

Tiramisu ✸✸ PIZZA & SALADS   This is a popular lunch spot during the weekdays, so come early or make a reservation. Tiramisu serves thin-crust pizzas (which are large enough for two when accompanied by a salad) baked in a stone oven and served in a delightful wood-and-checkered-tablecloth atmosphere. With dozens and dozens of combinations from traditional tomato and basil to arugula with shaved Parmesan and artichokes, you'll have a hard time choosing. There are fresh, delicious salads, too, and desserts that of course include tiramisu. The dining area is mostly outdoor covered seating.

Av. Isidora Goyenechea 3141. ℂ **2/335-5135**. www.tiramisu.cl. Pizzas $8–$12 (£4.10–£6.15); salads $6–$12 (£3.10–£6.15). AE, DC, MC, V. Daily 1–4pm and 7pm–midnight. Metro: El Golf.

SANTIAGO AFTER DARK

There are plenty of theaters, nightclubs, and bars to keep your evenings busy in Santiago. Like Buenos Aires, Santiago adheres to a vampire's schedule, dining as late as 10pm, arriving at a nightclub past midnight, and diving into bed just before the sun rises. It can take a little getting used to, and there are many early-hour nighttime attractions if you can't bear late nights. Several newspapers publish daily listings of movies, theater, and live music as well as Friday weekend-guide supplements such as *El Mercurio*'s "Wiken."

THE PERFORMING ARTS

Santiago is known for its theater, from large-scale productions to one-person monologues at cafes. The following are some of the more well-established theaters in Santiago.

I recommend two theaters in Bellavista that offer contemporary productions and come-dies in an intimate setting: **Teatro Bellavista,** Dardignac 0110 (© 2/735-2395; Metro: Salvador), and **Teatro San Ginés,** Mallinkrodt 76 (© 2/738-2159; www.teatro sangines.cl; Metro: Salvador). As the name implies, the nearby **Teatro La Comedia,** Merced 349 (© 2/639-1523; Metro: Baquedano), hosts comedy, but it is better known for cutting-edge productions. The cultural center **Estación Mapocho,** at the Plaza de la Cultura s/n (© 2/787-0000; Metro Cal y Canto), hosts a large variety of theater acts, often concurrently. The new **Centro Mori** (© 2/777-6246; www.centromori.cl) at Constitución 183, hosts well-respected, avant-garde theater acts that change weekly and, occasionally, live music.

But let's be realistic. If you do not speak Spanish, even the city's hit production of the moment is going to be a waste of your time and money. Stick to something more accessible such as a symphony, ballet, or opera at the city's gorgeous, historic **Teatro Municipal,** located downtown at Agustinas 749 (© 2/463-1000; www.municipal.cl; Metro: Universidad de Chile). The National Chilean Ballet and invited guests hold productions from April to December, with contemporary and classic productions such as *The Nutcracker.* There are musical events and special productions throughout the year; the best way to find out what's on is to check the theater's website. You can even **reserve and buy tickets** on the site, and select a seat from a diagram and find out which seats have only a partial view. Tickets are also sold over the phone Monday through Friday from 10am to 6pm, or bought in person at the theater itself Monday through Friday from 10am to 7pm and Saturday and Sunday from 10am to 2pm. Tickets are sold beginning 1 month before the starting date.

Visiting orchestras, the Fundación Beethoven, and contemporary acts play at the **Teatro Oriente** at Av. Pedro de Valdivia 099 (© 2/334-2234); buy tickets at the theater or from Ticketmaster. **Teatro Universidad de Chile** at Av. Providencia 043 (© 2/634-5295; http://teatro.uchile.cl) hosts ballet and symphony productions, both national and international, throughout the year. You may buy tickets at the theater near Plaza Italia or by phone. **Ticketmaster** sells tickets for nearly every act in Santi-ago, at CineHoyts cinemas, Falabella department stores, or by calling © **2/690-2000** from 10am to 7pm daily.

THE BAR & CLUB SCENE

Crowd-pulling national and international megabands typically play in the **Estado Nacional,** the **Espacio Riesco,** or the **Estación Mapocho.** Espacio Riesco is on the road to the airport, about a 15-minute drive from Las Condes, and with no public transportation available you'll need a taxi. Both Espacio Riesco and Estación Mapocho are infamous for their tinny sound system. You'll find listings for concerts in the daily newspaper or the *El Mercurio*'s website, **www.emol.com,** under "Tiempo Libre."

If you're looking for something mellower, **Bellavista** is a good bet for jazz, bolero, and folk music that is often performed Thursday through Saturday at venues such as **La Casa en el Aire** at Antonia López de Bello 0125 (© 2/735-6680; www.lacasa enelaire.cl), with a cozy, candlelit ambience. Across the street at Antonia López de Bello 0126 is **El Perseguidor** (© 2/777-6763; www.elperseguidor.cl), a happening jazz club with nightly performances starting around 11pm.

There are dozens of smaller music venues spread across the city, but the one that attracts the best bands and has the most variety is **La Batuta,** Jorge Washington 52 (© 2/274-7096; www.batuta.cl), located in the Ñuñoa neighborhood, about a 10- to 15-minute taxi ride from downtown and Providencia. The atmosphere is underground, but the crowd profile depends on who's playing. The **Club de Jazz,** José Pedro Alessandri 85 (© **2/326-5065;** www.clubdejazz.cl), has been jamming since 1943, and it's one of the city's more traditional night spots. Louis Armstrong once played here, and the club continues to pull in talented acts from around Latin America and the world. Live music happens on Thursday, Friday, and Saturday beginning at 11pm.

In **Providencia,** the wildly popular **Bar Liguria** (with two locations, Luis Thayer Ojeda 019 [© **2/231-1393**] and Av. Providencia 1373 [© **2/235-7914**]), is without a doubt the best nightspot for visitors of any age. The Ligurias are open until 2am on weeknights, until 5am on weekends, and closed Sunday, and they serve food practically until closing time. The newest chic watering hole is **Bar Yellow,** General Flores 47 (© **2/946-5063**), a hole-in-the-wall where they shake up the city's best martinis, and cocktails made from imported liquor—but they're not cheap. Bellavista, long the hot spot for nightclubs mobbed by teens and university students, is now drawing in a more refined (and older) crowd with cosmopolitan bars, many of which are restaurants by day. **Santo Remedio,** Roman Díaz 152, provides one of the funkier atmospheres in Santiago, and it is the only bar open on Sunday nights (except for hotel bars).

In Bellavista, **Etniko** (p. 388) is a standby for a lively, sophisticated crowd, DJ music, a full bar, and an airy atrium that's ideal on a summer evening. Across the street at Constitución 187 is the new **Ozono** (© 2/735-3816), a bar/restaurant within the old adobe walls of an antique *casona* that has all-white interiors, chill out music, and outdoor seating. Around the corner, at Antonio López Bello 0135, is **Off the Record** (© 2/777-7710), a bohemian pub/bar that attracts literary types and has interiors that hearken back to the early 1900s; the walls here are adorned with photos of famous Chilean artists, past and present.

Santiago's club scene caters to an 18- to 35-year-old crowd, and it all gets going pretty late, from midnight to 6am, on average. If you like electronica, you might check out "fiestas" publicized in the weekend entertainment sections of newspapers that list 1-night-only raves and live music, or, in Bellavista, try **La Feria** at Constitución 275, in an old theater, open Thursday through Saturday. **Blondie,** Alameda 2879 (© **2/681-7793;** www.blondie.cl), is a goth/'80s revival/electronic dance club, depending on the night. I recommend **Galpón 9** (no phone) for occasional live bands, a dance floor and bar, and music that ranges from hip-hop to pop to electronica. It's near the Pablo Neruda museum in Bellavista at Chucre Manzur 9; doors open at 11pm from Thursday to Saturday.

5 Around Santiago & the Central Valley

Santiaguinos and travelers agree that the best thing about Santiago is its proximity to a wealth of attractions such as beaches, nature preserves, hot springs, wineries, ski resorts, and more. These destinations are an alleviating escape when Santiago is smoggy; and all excursions are within 1 to 2 hours' drive from the city. Using Santiago as a base, it's possible to visit a few destinations listed in this chapter for the day, although I recommend spending a night or two at destinations such as Viña el Mar or Valparaíso. If you are an independent traveler and can afford a rental vehicle, get one; however you won't need one for ski resorts unless only visiting for the day (resorts are all-inclusive with no town to navigate). Organize a shuttle instead. You may consider renting a vehicle at the Santiago airport, drive to the coast or wine country, return the vehicle and taxi into Santiago, or vice versa. Chile's national coach system is better than that of the U.S.

The following section proposes ideas for 1-day and multiple-day adventures outside of Santiago. If you'd like a tour operator to plan a trip for you with a bilingual guide, transportation, and local know-how, try **Santiago Adventures** (© 2/244-2750 in Santiago, or 802/904-6798 in the U.S.; www.santiagoadventures.com).

VIÑA DEL MAR & VALPARAISO

These popular coastal destinations are less than a 1½-hour drive from the capital. Viña del Mar is largest and best-known beach resort town, founded in 1874 as a weekend retreat for wealthy Santiaguinos and located 120km (74 miles) northwest of Santiago. Viña is made of manicured lawns, exuberant gardens, a bustling little downtown, and a waterfront lined with towering apartment buildings, restaurants, hotels, nightclubs, and a casino. Some refer to the town as Chile's Riviera, but most simply call it Viña—you'll call it chaos if you come during the high season between December and late February, when thousands of visitors arrive for summer vacation. There is, however, a heightened sense of excitement during these months with so much activity happening in the area.

Viña is home to plenty of fine beaches, but the beach to see and be seen at is in Reñaca, about 6km north of Viña (see "Exploring Viña del Mar," below).

Just 15 minutes north of Viña is one of Chile's most captivating cities, Valparaíso. The historical importance of this city paired with its vibrant *porteño* culture make Valparaíso a far more interesting destination to visit and to spend the night, especially now that there are several boutique hotels and many outstanding restaurants. The jumble of multicolored clapboard homes and weathered Victorian mansions that cling to sheer cliffs and other unusual spaces provide endless photo opportunities. You could spend days exploring the maze of narrow passageways and sinuous streets that snake their way down ravines and around hillsides. The city has a bohemian flair so lacking in overdeveloped coastal towns, but it is a little rough on the edges with so many abandoned waterfront buildings and decrepit homes.

ESSENTIALS
Getting There
BY BUS   Both **Tur Bus** (© 600/660-6600; www.turbus.cl) and **Pullman** (© 600/320-3200; www.pullman.cl) offer service to Viña and Valparaíso, leaving every 15 minutes from the Terminal Alameda (Metro: Universidad de Santiago). The fare averages $4.25 (£2.20) one-way and takes about 1½ hours depending on traffic. Purchase a round-trip ticket on weekends and holidays if you can. Taxis are available at both bus stations and are a good idea at night.

BY CAR   To get to Viña del Mar and Valparaíso from Santiago, take Avenida Alameda (Bernardo O'Higgins) west until it changes into Ruta Nacional 68. There are two tollbooths that charge between 1,200 and 3,000 pesos ($2.40–$6/£1.25–£3.10) on Ruta 68. Santiago's new "Costanera" tunnel is the speediest and easiest way to get out of the city; ask someone at your hotel to explain how to access the hard-to-find entrances tunnels, or check the map at **www.costaneranorte.cl**. Street parking is plentiful; in Valparaíso there is a central parking garage on Calle Errázuriz, across from the Plaza Sotomayor and near the visitor center.

Getting Around
Walking is really the only way to see Valparaíso. Viña, too, can be managed by foot, and there is a pleasant beachfront promenade for a stroll. The easiest way to travel between both towns is by **taxi** (about $18/£9.25 one-way) or aboard the **Metrotren**

(also known as the "Merval"; ⓒ **32/238-1500;** www.merval.cl), an interurban train that leaves every 5 to 10 minutes from 7:30am to 10pm during weekdays, and every 15 to 20 minutes from 9:30am to 9pm on Saturdays, Sundays, and holidays. To ride the train, you must first make a one-time purchase: a rechargeable card for $1.50 (75p) that you then charge with enough money to cover the cost of your trip ($1.40/70p one-way). If you're with friends or family, you need only purchase one card for your group.

Visitor Information

The **Oficina de Turismo de Viña** is located on Plaza Vergara, next to the post office near avenidas Libertad and Arlegui (ⓒ **800/800-830,** toll-free in Chile; www. visitevinadelmar.cl). Summer hours are weekdays from 9am to 9pm (closed 2–3pm); off-season hours are weekdays from 10am to 7pm (closed 2–3pm); Saturday and Sunday from 10am to 7pm all year. A helpful staff (a few speak basic English) can provide visitors with accommodations information, with maps, events details, and accommodations information, including private cabin rentals.

FAST FACTS: VIÑA DEL MAR   Most major **banks** can be found on Avenida Arlegui, open Monday through Friday from 9am to 2pm only; all have 24-hour ATMs (RedBancs), as do pharmacies and gas stations. *Casas de cambio* (money-exchange houses) are open in the summer Monday through Friday from 9am to 2pm and 3 to 8pm, Saturday from 9am to 2pm; in the winter, Monday through Saturday from 9am to 2pm and 4 to 7pm, Saturday from 9am to 2pm. Several *cambios* can be found along Avenida Arlegui.

If you need to reach the **police** in an emergency, dial ⓒ **133.** For **fire,** dial ⓒ **132.** To call an **ambulance,** dial ⓒ **131.** For **medical attention,** go to **Hospital Gustavo Fricke** on calles Alvarez and Simón Bolívar (ⓒ **32/675067,** or 32/652328 for emergencies).

EXPLORING VIÑA DEL MAR

BEACHES   The **Playa Caleta Abarca** beach is located in a protected bay near the entrance to Viña del Mar, next to the oft-photographed "flower clock" and the Cerro Castillo—it is not the city's finest beach. Northeast and fronting the rows of terraced high-rise apartment buildings, you'll find **Playa Acapulco, Playa Mirasol,** and **Playa Las Salinas** (the latter is near the naval base). These beaches all see throngs of vacationers and families in the summer. The *in* spot for beaches is just north of Viña at **Reñaca**—it's close enough to take a taxi (about $4–$7/£2.05–£3.60 one-way), or grab a bus numbered 1, 10, or 111 at Avenida Libertad and Avenida 15 Norte.

Casino Municipal 🌟🌟   Built in 1930, the Casino Municipal was the most luxurious building in its day and is worth a visit even if you're not a gambler. The interior has been remodeled over time, but the facade has withstood the caprices of many a developer and is still as handsome as the day it opened. Semiformal attire (that is, no T-shirts, jeans, or sneakers) is required to enter the gaming room. Minimum bets of 5,000 pesos ($10/£5.10) will deter budget travelers, but there are slot machines and video poker. The casino also holds temporary art exhibits on the second floor, and there are three bars.

Plaza Colombia between Av. San Martín and Av. Perú. ⓒ **32/250-0600.** www.hoteldelmar.cl. Hours vary, but generally in winter, game room Mon–Thurs noon–4am, Fri–Sun 24 hr.; in summer, daily 24 hr.

Museo de Arqueología e Historia Francisco Fonck 🌟🌟 *Kids*   The natural history display at the Museo Fonck spans the entire second floor, but what really warrants a visit here is the museum's 1,400-piece collection of Rapa Nui (Easter Island) indigenous art and archaeological artifacts, including one of the only six Moai sculptures found outside the island. The display is more complete than the archaeological museum on Easter Island itself. Also on display are art and archaeological remnants of all cultures in Chile, and the size of the museum is just right to not grow tiresome—you'll need about 45 minutes here. There is also an on-site store selling jewelry, Easter Island art replicas, woolen goods, and more.

Av. 4 Norte 784. ℭ 32/268-6753. www.museofonck.cl. Admission $3 (£1.55) adults, $1 (50p) children. Tues–Fri 10am–6pm; Sat, Sun, and holidays 10am–2pm (Oct–Mar Sat 10am–6pm).

Museo Palacio Rioja ⊙⊙⊙   This enormous 1906 Belle Epoque stone mansion has been preserved in the architectural and decorative style of one of Viña's elite families in the early-20th-century elite. Built by Spaniard Fernando Rioja, a banker, and originally spanning 4 blocks, the palace took opulence to a new level, with a stone facade featuring Corinthian columns and a split double staircase. Interiors are made of oak and stone, with enough salons to fit a family of 10. Although a fraction of what it once was, the palm-fringed garden surrounding the house is idyllic for a quick stroll. Though much is self-explanatory, there are, unfortunately, no tours in English.

Quillota 214. ℭ 32/248-3664. Admission 75¢ (38p) adults, 35¢ (17p) children. Tues–Sun 10am–1:30pm and 3–5:30pm.

Quinta Vergara Park/Museum of Fine Art ⊙⊙   A compact but absolutely lovely park, the Quinta Vergara pays homage to the future with its spaceship-like music amphitheater, and to the past, with its converted 1910 Venetian-style palace, the former home of historical heavyweights the Alvarez/Vergara family, now converted into a fine arts museum. Every February, this park fills with music lovers who come for the yearly Festival of Song; the rest of the year the park is an idyllic spot for a quiet stroll. The park, which features many exotic, imported plants from Europe and Asia, was once the residential grounds of Portuguese shipping magnate Francisco Alvarez and his wife, Dolores; their old mansion now houses their collection of baroque European paintings, as well as oil paintings of Chilean VIPs during the 19th and early 20th century.

Near Plaza Parroquia. Park: Free admission. Daily 7am–6pm (until 7pm in summer). Museum: ℭ 32/225-2481. Admission $1 (50p) adults, 50¢ (25p) children. Tues–Sun 10am–2pm and 3–6pm.

EXPLORING VALPARAISO

Cementerio 1, 2 & De Disidentes ⊙⊙   Featuring fascinating, baroque antique mausoleums, this museum offers stunning views and a walk through the past. Focus your visit on the Cemeterio de Disidentes; this is where the tombs of British and European immigrants lie, having been shunned from the principal cemeteries for not being Catholic. This cemetery is by far more intriguing than the other two for its matter-of-fact gravestones spelling out often dramatic endings for (usually very young) adventurers who arrived during the 19th century. It's a short, but hearty, walk up Ecuador Street to get here.

Between Av. Ecuador and Cumming (Cerro Panteón). No phone. Free admission. Daily; general hours 10am–5pm.

La Sebastiana ⊙⊙⊙   La Sebastiana is one of poet Pablo Neruda's three quirky homes that have been converted into museums honoring the distinguished Nobel laureate's work and life. Neruda is Chile's most beloved poet, and its most famous literary export. Even if you haven't familiarized yourself with Neruda's work, this museum is worth visiting to explore this eccentric home and view the whimsical knickknacks he relished collecting while traveling. There are self-guiding information sheets that explain the significance of important documents and items on display, and visitors are allowed to wander freely at their own pace—something you can't do at Neruda's other museums. The walk from Plaza Victoria is a hike, so you might want to take a taxi. From Plaza Ecuador, there's a bus, Verde "D," or the *colectivo* No. 39.

Calle Ferrari 692 (Cerro Bellavista). (C) **32/225-6606.** www.lasebastiana-neruda.cl. Admission $5 (£2.55) adults, $1.75 (90p) students. Mar–Dec Tues–Sun 10am–6pm; Jan–Feb Tues–Sun 10:30am–6:50pm.

Museo Naval y Marítimo ✿✿   This museum merits a visit even if you do not particularly fancy naval and maritime-related artifacts and memorabilia. The museum is smartly designed and divided into four salons: the War of Independence, the War against the Peru–Bolivia Confederation, the War against Spain, and the War of the Pacific. Each salon holds antique documents, medals, uniforms, and war trophies. Of special note is the Arturo Prat room, with artifacts salvaged from the *Esmeralda*, a wooden ship that sank while valiantly defending Valparaíso during the War of the Pacific.

Paseo 21 de Mayo, Cerro Artillería. (C) **32/228-3749.** Admission $1 (50p) adults, 40¢ (20p) children under 12. Tues–Sun 10am–5:30pm.

WALKING TOURS OF VALPARAISO

The Fundación Valparaíso has done an exceptional job of mapping out the new Bicentennial Heritage Trail, a looping 30km (19-mile) walking tour divided into 15 thematic stages. I urge visitors to pick up a copy of the trail guide to supplement the walking tour described below; the guide can be found at the Gato Tuerto bookstore, located at Héctor Calvo 205 (Espíritu Santo Funicular), or other bookstores (if you are cruising, you may find the book at the Baron's Pier shopping gallery). Each stage takes approximately 90 minutes to 3 hours to walk, and the guide provides historical and architectural information, literary gossip, and fun anecdotes about the city. To help you navigate, the Fundación has placed arrows on the street at various stages of the trail. For visitors with limited time in the city, the walking tour outlined below will take you to the city's finest viewpoints and top attractions.

With a city map in hand, head toward Plaza Sotomayor, Valparaíso's civic center until 1980. Here, you'll encounter the **Monument to the Heroes of Iquique,** under which the remains of Prat, Condell, and Serrano, heroes of the War of the Pacific, are buried. To the left of the plaza, next to the Palacio de Justicia, ride the Ascensor Peral (ca. 1902) for 30¢ (15p) to the top of Cerro Alegre, and there you'll find the **Paseo Yugoslavo**—a terrace walkway built by Pascual Baburizza in 1929, whose **Palacio Baburizza** houses the Fine Arts Museum; delayed plans for renovations have stalled the re-opening of the museum. The walkway curves to the right around a tiny plaza; follow it until you reach Calle Alvaro Besa. Take the shortcut down **Pasaje Bavestrello,** a cement stairway at the left. Continue until you reach Calle Urriola, which you'll cross, and then walk up to another stairway, Pasaje Gálvez. At Calle Papudo, climb the stairway and turn left into **Paseo Gervasoni,** lined with stately, 19th-century mansions. This street looks out onto the port of Valparaíso. Here, you'll also find the **Museo de Casa Lukas,** an exhibition of illustrations made by Renzo Pecchenino, who dedicated his career to sketching Valparaíso's eccentric characters, open Tuesday through Sunday from 11am to 8pm; admission is 70¢. From here, descend via Ascensor Concepción or continue around Gervasoni until you reach Papudo. At Paseo Atkinson, you'll find another pedestrian walkway, bordered by antique English homes. Continue down the pedestrian stairway until you reach Calle Esmeralda, and

Valparaíso

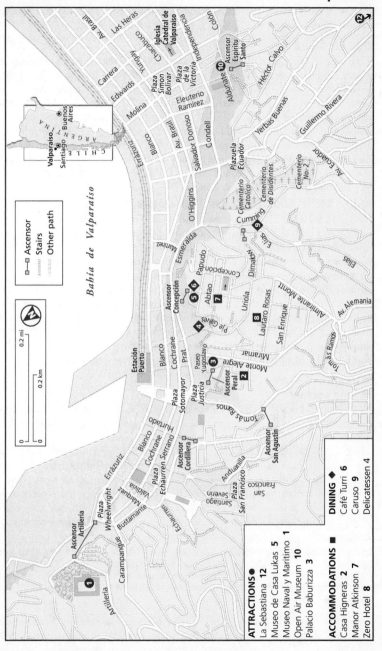

Bahía de Valparaíso

Ascensor
Stairs
Other path

0.2 mi
0.2 km

ATTRACTIONS ●
La Sebastiana **12**
Museo de Casa Lukas **5**
Museo Naval y Marítimo **1**
Open Air Museum **10**
Palacio Baburizza **3**

ACCOMMODATIONS ■
Casa Higueras **2**
Manor Atkinson **7**
Zero Hotel **8**

DINING ◆
Café Turri **6**
Caruso **9**
Delicatessen **4**

the end of the walk. You can also descend by doubling back and riding the Ascensor Concepción to Calle Prat.

OTHER SHORT WALKS

THE PORT NEIGHBORHOOD   Begin at the **Aduana (Customs House),** the grand, colonial American–style building built in 1854 and located at the north of town at Plaza Wheelwright at the end of Cochrane and Calle Carampangue. To the right, you'll find the **Ascensor Artillería,** built in 1893; it costs 20¢ (10p). The wobbly contraption is a delight, and it takes visitors to the most panoramic pedestrian walkway in Valparaíso, **Paseo 21 de Mayo.** This lovely promenade has a lookout gazebo from which it is possible to take in the town's bustling port activity. Follow the walkway until you reach the **Museo Naval y Marítimo** (see "Exploring Valparaíso," above). To return, double back and descend via the *ascensor,* or head down the walkway and take a left at Calle Carampangue.

PLAZA VICTORIA/MUSEO A CIELO ABIERTO/LA SEBASTIANA (PABLO NERUDA'S HOUSE)   In the late 1880s, Plaza Victoria was the elegant center of society, as is evident by the grand trees, trickling fountain, and sculptures imported from Lima that recall that era's heyday. From the plaza, head south on Calle Molina to Alduante for the **Open Air Museum,** which features more than 20 murals painted on cement-retainer and building walls along winding streets. The project features murals conceived by well-known Chilean painters and carried out by students. Begin at the steep stairway at Calle Alduante and turn left at Pasaje Guimera, and left again at the balcony walkway that leads to **Ascensor Espíritu Santo.** (You can ride the funicular up and backtrack this route, walking down.) Continue along Calle Rudolph until you reach Calle Ferrari. Head down Ferrari all the way to Edwards and Colón. The Open Air Museum neighborhood has improved but is still grubby.

WHERE TO STAY
In Viña del Mar

Hotel del Mar 🤍🤍🤍   This is Viña's first five-star hotel, opened in 2003 as part of the city's casino and overlooking the sea. Architects carefully adapted the style of the hotel to match the handsome, eggshell-colored casino, and the results are quite lovely. The central location near restaurants and fronting the beach is the best of any hotel in town. Guest rooms are contemporary and very spacious; most come with balconies that offer some of the best sea views in the area. The Salute Health Center and its infinity pool deserve special mention for their panoramic views, too. After a rough beginning, the hotel staff has streamlined its service and guests can now expect prompt, friendly assistance with whatever needs they may have. The hotel's restaurants are some of the best in the area, and rooms include free entrance to the casino.

Av. San Martín 199. ℭ **32/250-0800.** Fax 32/250-0801. www.hoteldelmar.cl. 60 units. $279 (£143) double Sun–Thurs and $319 (£164) Fri–Sat; $429 (£220) suite Sun–Thurs and $515 (£264) Fri–Sat. AE, DC, MC, V. Valet parking. **Amenities:** 4 restaurants; bar; indoor pool; fitness center and spa; children's game room; business center; 24-hr. room service; babysitting; laundry service; solarium; art gallery; cabaret shows. *In room:* A/C, plasma TV/DVD w/pay-per-view movies, dataport, hair dryer, safe, CD player.

Hotel Monterilla 🤍🤍 *Finds*   This delightful, family-run boutique hotel, located near the beach and casino, is an excellent value and one of the best-kept secrets in Viña del Mar. Cheerful service and a central location are definite draws, but the hotel's contemporary decor is what really makes the Monterilla special. Chromatic furniture contrasted against white carpet, and walls adorned with colorful postmodern art provide crisp, eye-catching surroundings, and though the guest rooms are not huge, they're fresh and comfortable. There is one apartment with a kitchenette for four guests, but some doubles are on the small side. Centrally located yet quiet, the Monterrilla offers frequent promotions for parents with kids, and they have a special "Cruise Tourist" promotion that includes transportation from the Seaport in Valparaíso and from the hotel to the Santiago airport.

2 Norte 65, Plaza México, Viña del Mar. ℂ 32/297-6950. Fax 32/268-3576. www.monterilla.cl. 20 units. $125 (£64) double; $173 (£89) suite. AE, DC, MC, V. **Amenities:** Cafeteria; bar; office services; laundry service. *In room:* Cable TV, Wi-Fi, minibar, hair dryer, safe.

Miramar Sheraton ★★★
Viña's newest hotel opened its doors in 2006 for visitors seeking luxury, sweeping ocean views, a state-of-the-art spa and fitness center, and an endless range of high-end services. The hotel hugs the shore and is located across from Viña's famous flower clock, about a 10-minute walk to beachfront restaurants. The Sheraton glitters in white-and-glass minimalism, yet the hotel's sleek packaging and voluminous public spaces accented with little or no furniture creates an air of emptiness. This is not a place where you will experience personalized service; rather, it is difficult to shake the feeling that anyone knows you're there. The Sheraton's guest rooms are gorgeous and plush: every detail, from the silky cotton sheets to the marble inlaid bathrooms, is impeccable. All guest rooms come with ocean views, with small terraces. If you're a spa lover or are seeking pool time, this is your place. Call or check their website for off-season discounts and special promotions.

Av. Marina 15. ℂ 32/238-8600. www.starwoodhotels.com/sheraton. 142 units. $185–$245 (£95–£126) double. AE, DC, MC, V. Valet parking. **Amenities:** 2 restaurants; bar; indoor and outdoor pools; state-of-the-art fitness center and spa; business center; salon; 24-hr. room service; babysitting; laundry service; jewelry store; gift shop. *In room:* Plasma TV, minibar, hair dryer, iron, safe.

Offenbacher-hof Residencial ★ *Moments*
Housed in a 100-year-old Victorian perched high atop Cerro Castillo, the Offenbacher has sweeping views of the city and the hills beyond, and a splendid glass-enclosed patio. It is by far one of the more interesting places to lodge, and its location on this historic hill puts you near some of the city's oldest homes—a delightful location, but guests must either grab a taxi to reach the beach, or hoof it. The mix-and-match decor is on the funky side, as if they purchased everything at a flea market, but it's hard to balk considering the panoramic views. Superior rooms are worth the extra $10 (£5.10) for better views and substantially more space.

Balmaceda 102, Cerro Castillo, Viña del Mar. ℂ 32/621483. Fax 32/662432. www.offenbacher-hof.cl. 15 units. $51–$61 (£26–£31) standard double; $61–$71 (£31–£36) superior double. AE, DC, MC, V. **Amenities:** Cafe; bar; gym; whirlpool; sauna; tours and airport transfers; laundry service; solarium. *In room:* Cable TV, Wi-Fi.

In Valparaíso
Valparaíso is the epicenter of stylish boutique lodging, whereas Viña is known more for full-scale hotels and resorts with all the bells and whistles and beach access. You'll still spot a few *hostales* whose pretty, flower-boxed facades belie awful conditions within, but even these establishments are being bought up by hoteliers who see the potential in Valparaíso becoming the next hot tourism destination rather than just a character-rich—but down-at-the-heels—city suited only for a day visit.

Casa Higueras ★★★ *Moments*
If you've got the bucks and are looking for a luxurious and intimate hideaway, look no farther than this brand-new boutique hotel. A top Chilean interior designer took a more masculine, 1930s-era approach with the renovation

of this former mansion, using lots of dark wood flooring and paneling, and minimal, but well-placed, designer furniture—a crystal chandelier here, a velvet pin-tuck couch there. The guest rooms have panoramic windows and amenities such as rich linens and plasma TV screens, and outside, the three-story hotel descends over a rectangular pool that is attractively landscaped into the hillside. There is also a minispa for unwinding after a day tromping up and down Valparaíso's hills. If you bore of your balcony, and it's hard to imagine you would, you can kick back on their rooftop terrace or the hotel restaurant's patio.

Higueras 133, Cerro Concepción. (C) **32/249-7900** (Valparaíso); 2/657-3950 (Santiago). www.hotelcasahigueras.cl. 20 units. $195–$238 (£100–£122) double; $265–$322 (£136–£165) suite. AE, DC, MC, V. **Amenities:** Restaurant; outdoor pool; whirlpool; sauna; limited room service; massage; laundry service; Internet. *In room:* Plasma TV/DVD player, Wi-Fi, minibar, hair dryer, safe.

Hotel Manoir Atkinson *ʁʁ Value*

For all-around value you can't beat this charming little B&B, located in the heart of Cerro Concepción and run by an immensely friendly staff (the owner is a French Canadian and very helpful with day-tour planning). Like other hotels in the city, the Atkinson is also within an old home, so all bedrooms are unique and sized differently, yet very cozy, with a country decor and small bathrooms. The rooftop terrace is especially noteworthy, however only the "attic" rooms 5 and 6 have direct access; there are two other terraces to offer plenty of areas to lounge and soak up the city's atmosphere.

Paseo Atkinson 165, Cerro Concepción. (C) **32/235-1313.** www.hotelatkinson.cl. 7 units. $150 (£77) double, $165 (£85) double with terrace and bay view; $195 (£100) suite with terrace and bay view. AE, DC, MC, V. **Amenities:** Cafeteria; 24-hr. room service; laundry. *In room:* TV, Wi-Fi, safe, hair dryer.

Zero Hotel *ʁʁʁ Finds*

Relatively indistinguishable from its residential neighbors due to its tiny sign and soft lilac facade, this is another of Valparaíso's top lodging options—a boutique hotel that effectively blends a contemporary, whimsical decor with lovingly refurbished antique ceilings, wall panels, and parquet floors. The house overlooks a twisting road and, beyond that, wide views of the Valparaíso port, with outdoor terraces and a light and airy dining and lounge area. The location is ideal, close to restaurants. The bathrooms, like the Casa Higueras, feature fluffy robes, high-end amenities, and Egyptian cotton sheets. Rooms that face the hillside are considerably cheaper than rooms with a port view, so if you're not planning to spend a lot of time in your room, the views from the terrace will suffice.

Lautaro Rosas 343, Valparaíso. (C) **32/211-3114.** www.zerohotel.com. 9 units. $170–$265 (£87–£136) double. AE, DC, MC, V. **Amenities:** Cafe; on-call massage. *In room:* TV, Wi-Fi, hair dryer.

WHERE TO DINE
In Viña del Mar

There are dozens of restaurants lining Avenida San Martín, including fast-food joints such as Pizza Hut and McDonald's; and downtown Viña, along Avenida Valparaiso and around the plaza, visitors will find cheap eateries and sandwich shops. For afternoon tea, try **The Tea Pot,** 5 Norte 475 ((C) **32/268-7671;** Mon–Fri 10am–2pm and 4:30–9pm, Sat 10am–9pm), which offers more than 60 kinds of tea and delicious pastries. Along the beach there are several wood-and-glass concessions that serve sandwiches, drinks, coffee, and pastries. For nighttime cocktails and appetizers, try the slick **Barlovento** (2 Norte 195; (C) **32/297-7472**), a bar/restaurant with a second-floor lounge popular with young professionals.

EXPENSIVE

Savinya ★★★ INTERNATIONAL   Savinya is part of the Hotel del Mar and known for its outstanding haute cuisine. It's Viña's most refined, and expensive, restaurant, and the place to go if you're looking to blow your budget on a special meal. Still, when compared to restaurants of the same caliber in the U.S., the prices at Savinya could be considered quite reasonable. The menu changes seasonally, but what doesn't change is the chef's impeccable technique and presentation of each dish, blending uncommon flavors and textures that work surprisingly well together, with a list of complementary palate-pleasing wines. On my last visit, I enjoyed an appetizer of king crab, pistachio, and sweet pea, served with quail eggs and black caviar; an entree of creamy asparagus-and-scallop risotto; and a dessert of green apple sorbet with a muscatel sauce. Attentive, agreeable service comes with the price, as does an elegant-chic ambience and gigantic picture windows that offer a gorgeous view overlooking the ocean.

Av. Perú and Los Héroes. ✆ 32/250-0800. www.hoteldelmar.com. Reservations recommended for dinner. Main courses $13–$24 (£6.65–£12). AE, DC, MC, V. Daily 12:30–3:30pm and 8pm–12:30am.

MODERATE

Cap Ducal SEAFOOD   This Viña del Mar institution is notable for one reason only: an intimate, candlelit dining experience with a view of the sparkling coastline and the crashing surf. The restaurant is designed to resemble a ship moored against the cliff, and it has been a fixture in the Viña dining scene since 1936. However, the ambience outshines the food, which is not bad but does lack creativity. The focus here is Chilean cuisine and international-style seafood.

Av. Marina 51. ✆ 32/262-6655. Main dishes $9.50–$14 (£4.90–£7.15). AE, DC, MC, V. Daily 1pm–midnight.

Divino Pecado ★★ ITALIAN   Cozy and centrally located, this chef-owned restaurant boasts delicious fresh pastas and other Italian dishes, as well as sharp service. For an aperitif, order a pisco sour—this restaurant is known for its delicious Peruvian variety. The menu features a build-your-own pasta section so that diners may invent their own concoction, or pick a pasta dish from their list of specialties, of which the standout is by far the "black" raviolis made with calamari ink and stuffed with curried shrimp. Divino Pecado specializes in "boutique" fish, that is, specialty fish such as sole, the delicate *mero* (grouper), and tuna, and they offer meats such as filet mignon.

Av. San Martín 180 (in front of casino). ✆ 32/297-5790. divinopecado@terra.cl. Reservations recommended. Main courses $11–$16 (£5.65–£8.20). AE, DC, MC, V. Daily 12:30–3:30pm and 8–11pm (Sat–Sun until 1am).

El Gaucho ★ STEAKHOUSE/ARGENTINE   Carnivores will find a home here at El Gaucho, which serves succulent cuts of just about any kind of meat, served sizzling off their huge indoor *parrilla* (grill). The Argentine-style "interiors" appetizers include blood sausage, sweetbreads, and crispy intestines. If that doesn't make your mouth water, try starting with grilled provolone cheese with oregano. Entrees include beef loin, ribs, chicken, sausages, and other grilled items and salads. Wood floors and brick walls create a warm, comfortable ambience.

Av. San Martín 435. ✆ 32/269-3502. Main courses $8–$14 (£4.10–£7.15). AE, DC, MC, V. Daily 12:30–3:30pm and 7:30–11pm (Fri–Sat until 1am).

Enjoy del Mar ★★ INTERNATIONAL   The best alfresco dining venue in Viña is on Enjoy del Mar's open-air deck, with the sea breeze in your face and a cold glass of chardonnay in your hand. The restaurant is part of the Hotel del Mar, but it is located across the street on the beach. The main courses strive for gourmet caliber, but never quite achieves that; instead, the best bet here is their barbecue, which includes a choice of steak, chicken, or ribs, and includes soup, a salad bar, wine, or beer and dessert, for a very reasonable $15 (£7.70) per person. There are also sandwiches, burgers, and an ice cream parlor. The restaurant is always open, from the early morning until the wee hours, and they host live music on weekends.

Av. Peru 100. ℂ **32/268-7755**. Main courses $5–$10 (£2.55–£5.15). AE, DC, MC, V. Daily 9am—1am (Thurs–Sat until 3 or 4am).

In Valparaíso
MODERATE

Café Turri 𝖌𝖌 *Moments* FRENCH/CHILEAN   Valparaíso's emblematic restaurant has—at last!—changed ownership, and the nasty waiters, fluorescent lights, and awful food are thankfully a thing of the past. This restaurant has always reigned as the city's best spot for alfresco dining, and it's well located at the top of the La Concepción funicular and close to other points of interest. The new owners (a French/Chilean pair) have preserved the restaurant's lovely antique interiors, but they've given them a contemporary update. They've also hired a cheery waitstaff. That said, while the food is night-and-day better than before, it still isn't as good as places like Pasta e Vino. The French-influenced fare includes duck confit, steak tartare, grilled fish and meats, salads, and such appetizers as grilled Camembert cheese. For a primo table, book at least a day ahead on weekends.

Calle Templeman 147 (Cerro Concepción; take the Concepción lift). ℂ **32/236-5307**. www.cafeturri.cl. Reservations recommended for outdoor seating. Main courses $11–$15 (£5.65–£7.70). AE, DC, MC, V. Daily 10am–midnight, but closed Mon Apr–Nov.

Caruso 𝖌 *Finds* SEAFOOD   A fun little restaurant, Caruso is located on the newly gentrifying hill Cerro Cárcel. The folksy restaurant, with whitewashed walls, local art, and wooden tables, specializes in seafood, especially rockfish such as *vieja* and *tomollo*, delicious varieties caught by local fishermen with harpoons. Their menu changes daily, and sometimes throughout a single day depending on what's fresh and available. Dishes boast hints of Peruvian-style cooking; my favorite dish here is the king crab in phyllo pastry with a chardonnay sauce and spinach. The relaxed ambience of Caruso captures the city's eclectic rhythm, but note that service here is slower than Monday, so don't come if you're in a hurry.

Av. Cumming 201, Cerro Carcel. ℂ **32/259-4039**. caruso@vtr.net. Reservations recommended. Main courses $8.50–$12 (£4.35–£6.15). AE, DC, MC, V. Lunch Tues–Sun 1–4pm; dinner Thurs–Sat 8:30pm–midnight.

Delicatessen 𝖌 *Finds* FUSION   Fresh, homemade, honest products (nothing comes from a can or jar) are the focus of this family-run restaurant, located in a blink-and-you-miss-it glass storefront along sloping Urriola Street. Delicatessen operates without much fanfare, and its popularity has grown by word of mouth. The young chef is talented at blending flavors from the Mediterranean to the Pacific Rim, creating food that is "fusion" without being "confusion." Their menu changes monthly and is scrawled out on a giant chalkboard. For a light meal, try their tapas and a bottle of wine from an excellent but pricey list.

Urriola 383. ℂ **07/698-7873**. urriola.383@gmail.com. Reservations recommended on weekends. Main courses $11–$15 (£5.65–£7.70). No credit cards. Mon–Tues and Thurs 10am–11pm; Fri–Sat 10am–midnight; Sun 10am–6pm.

Pasta e Vino 𝖌𝖌𝖌 CONTEMPORARY ITALIAN   The day Pasta e Vino opened its doors to the public, it became immediately clear what Valparaíso had been missing all these years: a warm, intimate ambience, fabulous cuisine, and owner-attended service. Pasta e Vino virtually launched the culinary metamorphosis in Valparaíso, and it remains the best restaurant in this city—the reason why you'll need to make reservations days in advance. The last time I was here, we ordered ginger-lime clams, squid risotto, plump salmon ravioli, a fresh green salad, and a crisp chardonnay from their outstanding wine list. The ambience is exposed brick walls and sophisticated chic, but wooden tables and a lively atmosphere keeps the restaurant down-to-earth.

Templeman 352. ℂ **32/249-6187.** pastaevino@hotmail.com. Reservations required. Main courses $9–$15 (£4.60–£7.70). AE, DC, MC, V. Wed–Sat 8pm–midnight; Sun 1–5pm.

VALPARAISO AFTER DARK

Most restaurants and bars do not adhere to a set closing hour, but instead close "when the candles burn down." Try **El Cinzano** at Aníbal Pinto 1882 (ℂ **32/221-3043**), which spotlights tango crooners in a wonderful, early-20th-century ambience. **La Columbina** (ℂ **32/223-6254**) is frequented by the 30-and-up crowd for its comfortable ambience, live jazz, and bolero music. **La Piedra Feliz,** Errázuriz 1054 (ℂ **32/225-6788**) is a trendy bar inside the converted storehouse of an old shipping company, has a subterranean lounge with DJs (open Thurs–Sat) and two salons with tango and salsa lessons available. Twenty- and thirty-somethings sweat to electronic music at the ultracool **Mundo Pagano,** Blanco 236 (ℂ **32/223-1118;** www.mundopagano.cl), which has nightly dance parties and occasionally live music. On Cerro Concepcion, a trendy hole-in-the-wall is the bar **Gremio** (Pasaje Gálvez 173; ℂ **32/222-8394**).

CAJON DE MAIPO

Cajón de Maipo is a quick city escape that puts visitors in the middle of a rugged, alpine setting of towering peaks and freshly scented forest slopes along the Río Maipo. A highlight in this area is **El Morado National Park** (see below), but it is certainly not a requisite destination. Cajón de Maipo offers a wide array of outdoor activities, such as rafting, horseback riding, hiking, climbing, and more, but it also offers a chance to linger over a good lunch or picnic, stroll around the area, and maybe even lay your head down for the night in one of the cabañas that line the valley. Take the Metro Line 4 toward Puente Alto and get off at the Las Mercedes station, for a *taxis colectivo,* which leaves every 10 minutes from 7am to 8pm and costs $2.50 (£1.30) per person. Regular taxis (with the yellow roof) from the Mercedes Metro station can run anywhere from $15 to $20 (£7.70–£10) depending on your destination in the Cajón. Always negotiate a price with the driver beforehand. By car, the easiest way from Las Condes or Providencia is to take Avenida Vespucio Sur and head south until the avenue turns into a highway. Exit at Las Torres and continue straight along the lateral road and make your first left, heading under the freeway. After turning left, get in the right lane and veer right immediately onto Avenida La Florida. Continue along this road for 12km (7½ miles) until you see the road fork at Puente Alto; head left at the sign pointing toward San José de Maipo. If you are downtown, follow Vicuña Mackenna street until you hit Departamental, and head left (east) until you run into Avenida La Florida. Take a map and count on snarling weekend traffic.

EXPLORING THE AREA & STAYING ACTIVE

EL MORADO NATIONAL PARK This 3,000-hectare (7,410-acre) park is just 90km (56 miles) from Santiago, yet the dramatic, high-alpine landscape makes visitors here feel as if they are hundreds of miles away from the city. A great spot to take in all this beauty is the Tyrolean mountain lodge **Refugio Lo Valdés** (ℂ **9/220-8525;**

www.refugiolovaldes.com), a rustic "shelter" that serves a delicious, fixed-price lunch and dinner, where you can eat out on the deck while gazing at the snowcapped peaks. The owners of the Refugio also plan outdoor activities such as day hiking or overnight climbing trips; horseback riding, visits to the hot springs and nature tours. There are clean, bunk-bed–style accommodations (there is one double room for couples), and a cozy dining area warmed by a huge woodstove. Rates are $27 (£14) per adult, $20 (£10) children 6 to 12, and $10 (£5.10) kids 1 to 5; breakfast is included.

The Conaf park ranger hut is at **Baños Morales.** The park is open daily October through April from 8:30am to 6pm and costs $3 (£1.55) to enter. There is an outstanding 8km (5-mile) easy-intermediate trail that borders an alpine lake and ends at a glacier, offering a profile view of the El Morado mountain (about 6 hr. round-trip). There are natural hot springs at **Termas de Colina,** in the form of clay pools descending a slope. The expansive alpine setting adds a sense of grandeur to the experience. It takes time to get here due to the condition of the road; continue past Lo Valdés for 12km (7½ miles).

RAFTING   Santiago is one of the only metropolitan cities in the world that offers Class III and IV rafting little more than half an hour from downtown. The season runs from September to April, but the river really gets going from November to February. Two reliable companies offer half-day rafting excursions: **Cascada de las Animas** (© 2/861-1303; www.cascadadelasanimas.cl) arranges rafting trips from its tourism complex (see "Where to Stay & Dine in Cajón de Maipo," below) in San Alfonso, but it's best to reserve beforehand. Another highly respected outfitter is **Altué Expediciones,** in Santiago, Encomenderos 83 (© 2/232-1103; www.altue.com). Altué is cheaper at $25 (£13) per person (minimum of four), yet Cascada has hotel pickup and drop-off, and includes lunch for $80 (£41) per person (minimum of four).

HORSEBACK RIDING   Visitors to El Morado can rent horses with a guide at Baños Morales or Termas de Colina for about $6 to $15 (£3.10–£7.70) per person, depending on group size and duration. Cascada Expediciones has horseback riding through its own private chunk of the Andes and El Morado park, as does Altué Expediciones. Horseback rides are suitable for families.

WHERE TO STAY & DINE IN CAJON DE MAIPO

Cascada de las Animas 𝄢𝄢 is a tourism center that's run by long-time residents who own a tremendous amount of acreage outside San Alfonso, part of which is used for excursions and 80 campground and picnic sites scattered about a lovely, wooded hillside (Camino al Volcán 31087; © 2/861-1303; www.cascadadelasanimas.cl; $85/£44 cabaña for two). The complex includes nine rustic yet enchanting log cabins with fully equipped kitchens and wood-burning stoves, and the tiny **Hostal La Casa Grande** in San Alfonso, 4 blocks from the entrance to their complex, a brand-new hostel housed in a renovated 1930s home and surrounded by greenery. Cascada offers a swimming pool, kayaking, rafting, and horseback-riding excursions, and meditation sessions and a women's spiritual retreat. There is a full-service restaurant that looks out over the river, with excruciatingly slow service.

The gorgeous new **Hotel Altiplanico San Alfonso** at Camino al Volcán 29955 (© 2/861-2078; www.altiplanico.com) is the valley's upscale option, with shingled exteriors, an artsy decor, and flagstone floors; it also has a swimming pool, horseback riding, and wine trips to the Maipo Valley. Rates include lodging, meals, and tours and cost $250 (£128) per person based on double occupancy.

Trattoria Calypso 😋😋 serves fresh, homemade pasta and, Saturday and Sunday only, stone oven–baked pizzas (Camino el Volcán 9831; ℂ **2/871-1498;** Thurs–Sat 12:30–10pm, Sun 12:30–6pm). Everything is made using organic and local farm ingredients, and there's outdoor seating. If you don't eat at **Casa Bosque** 😋, stop here anyway to admire the fabulously outlandish architecture: polished, raw tree trunks left in their natural shapes form zany door frames, ceiling beams, and pillars. Casa Bosque is a parrilla serving barbecued meats paired with fresh salads and other accompaniments. Good food, great atmosphere, but service is slow and inattentive (Camino el Volcán 16829; ℂ **2/871-1570;** Mon–Thurs 12:30–6pm, Fri–Sat 12:30pm–midnight). **La Petite France** 😋 serves French bistro classics and Chilean and international dishes, as well as incredible pastries (Camino el Volcán 16096; ℂ **2/861-1967;** Tues–Sun noon–midnight). This is a good place to enjoy outdoor seating and afternoon tea.

SKIING & SNOWBOARDING THE ANDES

It's no longer just a summer getaway for skiing fanatics searching for the endless winter; these days it seems everyone in the know is heading south for a summer ski vacation. Skiers have discovered that the Andean terrain is world class, with easy groomers to spine-tingling steeps, and with so few people on the slopes here, powder lasts for days, not hours. There are few lift lines, and the ambience is relaxed and conducive to making friends and waking up late. For families, the kids are on vacation, and most resorts offer reduced rates or free stays for kids under 12.

Resorts centered on the Farallones area, such as Valle Nevado, La Parva, and El Colorado, can be reached in a 1- to 2-hour drive from Santiago or the airport. The all-inclusive and venerable Portillo is a little over 2 hours from Santiago, Termas de Chillán is a short flight and a 1-hour transfer shuttle away, or a 5-hour train ride, offering tree skiing, a casino and an extensive spa.

GETTING TO THE RESORTS   You do not need to rent a vehicle if you are planning to spend the night at any of the resorts listed in this chapter. Portillo organizes transfers through its own company; **Ski Total** (ℂ **2/246-0156;** www.skitotal.cl) has transfer shuttles to Valle Nevado, El Colorado, and La Parva for $15 (£7.70) round-trip per person, and $16 (£8.20) round-trip per person to Valle Nevado. The shuttles leave at 8:30am from their offices at Av. Apoquindo 4900, no. 42 (in the Omnium shopping mall in Las Condes—there's no Metro station nearby, so take a taxi), and no reservation for these shuttles is required. Round-trip transportation with hotel pickup costs $26 (£13) per person and requires a reservation made 24 hours in advance; pickup time for this service is 8am.

Ski Portillo 😋😋😋 *(Kids)*   Internationally famous, Portillo is South America's oldest resort and one of the more singular ski destinations in the world. The resort is set high in the Andes on the shore of Lake Inca, and unlike most ski resorts, there is no town at Portillo, just one sunflower-yellow lodge and two more economical annexes. Although open to the public for day skiing, Portillo really operates as a weeklong, package-driven resort that includes lodging, ski tickets, all meals, and use of its plentiful amenities. The ski area is smaller than Valle Nevado and Termas de Chillán; however, Portillo offers steeper terrain and fewer crowds. Portillo is billed as a "boutique resort" with a maximum of 450 people, giving visitors the sensation of skiing in their own private resort.

Intermediate skiers are strongly urged to take advantage of Portillo's top-rated ski school and use the week as a "training camp." Rooms are on the small side but entirely comfortable; the best rooms are on the sixth floor. The Octagon annex has shared rooms with four bunks and a private bathroom; the Inca annex is for backpackers and has tiny, shared rooms with a common bathroom. Dining takes place in the hotel's main restaurant, the cafeteria, or their mountainside restaurant. On certain nights, the party can really ignite with live music in the hotel bar, a thumping nightclub, and an off-site *cantina*.

There are 13 lifts, including five chairs, five T-bars, and three "slingshot" lifts that leave skiers at the top of vertiginous chutes. The terrain is 43% beginner and intermediate, 57% advanced and expert.

Hotel Portillo's 7-day packages include lodging, lift tickets, four meals per day, and use of all facilities. Per person rates are as follows: double with lake view $1,550 to $2,890 (£795–£1,482); suites $2,000 to $3,650 (£1,026–£1,872); family apartments (minimum four people) $1,200 to $2,150 (£615–£1,102). Children under 4 stay free in parent's room; kids 4 to 11 are half price; and kids 12 to 17 are charged about 25% less than the adult rate. The **Octagon Lodge** includes the same amenities as above for $890 to $1,390 (£456–£713). The **Inca Lodge** charges $590 to $700 (£303–£359); meals for guests of the Inca Lodge are taken in the cafeteria.

Renato Sánchez 4270, Santiago. ⓒ **800/829-5325** in the U.S., 800/514-2579 in Canada, or 2/263-0606. Fax 2/263-0595. www.skiportillo.com. Lift tickets $33 (£17) adults, $25 (£13) children under 13. AE, DC, MC, V. **Amenities:** Restaurant; cafeteria; bar; nightclub; theater; outdoor heated pool; fitness center; full-court gymnasium; sauna; child-care center; game room; salon; massage; laundry; ski tuning and repair; ski rental; cybercafe.

Valle Nevado 🌟🌟 *Kids*   Valle Nevado sits high above Santiago, near El Colorado and La Parva resorts, and it is the only resort in this "Three Valleys" area that offers a full-service tourism infrastructure. The resort complex is not a town, but there are clothing, gear, and souvenir shops, a variety of excellent restaurants, and a full-service spa, making Valle a good destination for nonskiing guests accompanying their family or friends. The French-designed resort is Chile's answer to Les Arcs, with three hotels and two condominium buildings that straddle a ridge line. The terrain is large enough to entertain skiers for days, and they can purchase an interconnect ticket and traverse over to La Parva and El Colorado. The steeper runs are at Portillo, yet Valle is larger and the runs longer. Of all the resorts in Chile, Valle is the most snowboard-friendly, offering a terrain park and monster half-pipe, and the resort hosts the Nokia Snowboarding World Cup every year. Many Santiaguinos visit Valle Nevado on weekends, and traffic up the hill can back up for hours if there has been a recent snowfall. Saturdays and Sundays bring long lift lines and crowded slopes. The terrain is 15% expert, 30% advanced, 40% intermediate, and 15% beginner.

Valle Nevado offers all-inclusive packages that include lodging, ski tickets, breakfast, and dinner, which can be taken in any one of the resort's restaurants. Prices are per person, double occupancy, and the range reflects low to high season. The five-star **Hotel Valle Nevado** (elegant, though closer to a four-star) is, per night, $195 to $330 (£100–£169) for a standard double, and $327 to $503 (£168–£258) for a suite. During their holiday season, from July 13 to July 26, they sell weeks only for $2,470 (£1,267) per person, double occupancy.

The midrange **Hotel Puerta del Sol,** which is popular with families, is $160 to $251 (£82–£129) a night for a double, and $193 to $295 (£99–£151) a night for a suite. Holiday periods run 7 nights from $1,970 to $2,365 (£1,010–£1,213).

Hotel Tres Puntas has rooms with either two twins or four-bed bunks which are great values for their private bathrooms. The hotel is popular with younger guests and families; rates are $120 to $194 (£62–£99) per night, with holiday weeks costing $1,820 (£933) per person, double occupancy.

Office at Av. Vitacura 5250, #304, Santiago. ℭ **2/477-7700.** Fax 2/477-7736. www.vallenevado.com. Lift tickets $29–$38 (£15–£19) adults, $19–$25 (£9.75–£13) children under 13. AE, DC, MC, V. **Amenities:** Nightclub; cinema; outdoor heated pool; full-service spa w/fitness gym; full-court gymnasium; whirlpool; massage and sauna; child-care center; game room; room service; laundry. For the public, there's a bank; high-end boutiques; and a minimarket. *In room:* TV; safe; minibar.

La Parva 𝕎𝕎   La Parva caters to Santiago's well-heeled skiers and snowboarders, many of whom own condos or chalets here. Apart from a condominium complex with independent units, there are few services for the ordinary tourist. La Parva offers good off-piste skiing conditions and the steepest inbounds terrain of the resorts in the area (however, an interconnect ticket means skiers can traverse to La Parva from Valle Nevado). The resort's terrain breaks down into 15% expert, 30% advanced, 40% intermediate, and 15% beginner. They offer 4 chairs and 10 surface lift runs, such as T-bars. Dining options here include **La Marmita de Pericles** for fondue, **El Piuquén Pub** for après ski and nightlife, and the **St. Tropez** for Italian food and breakfasts. There is also a dance club, with a happy hour from 10pm to midnight.

Condominium lodging is the only option at La Parva, and during the high season in July they must be rented for 7 nights from Friday to Friday (call for shorter, last-minute stays). Standard condos for five to six people are $1,600 to $2,600 (£821–£1,333); and superior apartments, for seven to eight people, are $2,600 to $3,400 (£1,333–£1,744). Maid service is an additional $20 (£10) per day.

Av. Isidora Goyenechea 2939, #303, Santiago. ℭ **2/431-0420** (in Santiago), or 2/220-9530 (direct). Fax 2/431-0458. www.laparva.cl. Lift tickets low to high season: $32–$37 (£16–£19) adults, $20–$23 (£10–£12) children 5–12 and seniors, $6.50 (£3.35) children under 5.

El Colorado/Farallones 𝕎   Farallones is a collection of chalets and mom-and-pop shops sprawled across a ridge a little lower than the ski area El Colorado. Of the three resorts, El Colorado is the blue-collar brother, an older, more economical option that sees more Chileans than foreigners and is popular with beginning skiers, nonskiers who come to throw snowballs and take part in tubing, and so on. There is an ample variety of terrain and fewer skiers and snowboarders on the slopes than the neighboring resorts, but the lift system is dated. If you're looking for cheaper lodging at the Three Valleys area, this is where you'll find it. The 1,000-hectare (2,470-acre) resort has 5 chairlifts and 17 surface lifts, such as T-bars. There's a bit of off-piste skiing, and there are 22 runs: 4 expert, 3 advanced, 4 intermediate, and 11 beginner. El Colorado is also snowboard-friendly, and they have a snow park and half-pipe. The El Colorado Apart-Hotel is modern and clean, with two- and three-bedroom units with kitchenettes for $198 to $336 (£101–£172) per person, double occupancy, including meals.

Apoquindo 4900, no. 47–48 (Edificio Omnium). ℭ **2/246-3344.** Fax 2/206-4078. www.elcolorado.cl. Lift tickets low to high season: $27–$37 (£14–£19) adults, $17–$22 (£8.70–£11) children 5–12, $9 (£4.60) seniors and children under 5. Ski rental available.

Ski Arpa 𝕎𝕎 *Moments*   Ski Arpa is Chile's only Sno-Cat operation, offering outstanding off-piste powder skiing and snowboarding, tremendous views and more vertical for a much lower price than heliskiing. Ski Arpa covers 4,000 hectares (10,000 acres) of terrain located close to the town of Los Andes, fairly close to Portillo. The road to Ski Arpa is not paved and 4×4 vehicles are almost always necessary. There are two Sno-Cats that take skiers up about 3,500m (11,480 ft.) to an awesome, direct view of the 6,962m (22,835-ft.) peak Aconcagua, the highest in the Western Hemisphere. Ski Arpa now arranges packages that include lodging in a 19th-century hacienda (the lovingly restored Casa St. Regis) and visits to top local wineries and hot springs, providing foreigners with a more "authentic" Chilean experience than available at any of Chile's resorts—a great place for 2 days of skiing before or after heading to Portillo or Valle Nevado. Santiago Adventures runs Ski Arpa's central reservations, and they can arrange transfers, ski rentals, and tours to other regions.

Campos de Ahumada s/n. (C) **802/904-6798** (in the U.S.); 2/415-0667 (Santiago). Fax 2/234-9783. www.skiarpa.com. Prices approximately $100 (£51) for 4 runs; $200 (£103) a day including transportation from Santiago, lodging, and meals.

THE CENTRAL VALLEY & CHILLAN

Just outside the city limits of Santiago, the scenery opens into a patchwork of poplar-lined agricultural fields and grapevines, and tiny towns hearken back to a quieter, colonial era where it is common to see weathered adobe homes, horse-driven carts, and dirt roads. This is Chile's breadbasket, a region that boasts a mild, Mediterranean climate, fertile soil, and plenty of irrigation thanks to the Andes, and testament of this natural bounty can be seen at the myriad of roadside stands hawking fresh fruit and vegetables and unbelievably cheap prices. Beyond the central valley is one of Chile's largest and most deluxe ski and summer resorts, Termas de Chillán.

The wine touring area with the most developed infrastructure is **Colchagua,** centered on the town of Santa Cruz, about a 2-hour drive from Santiago. Chile's best museum is here, the **Museo de Colchagua** ★★★ ((C) 72/821050; www.museo colchagua.cl; daily 10am–6pm; $6/£3.10). The diverse collection here includes pre-Colombian archeological artifacts, Spanish conquest–era helmets and artillery, immigrant household items, carriages, collections of *huaso* and indigenous arts and clothing, farm machinery, and more. There is so much to see here you'll want to plan on spending 1 to 2 hours.

The way to see the valley is by contacting the **Ruta del Vino,** Plaza de Armas 298, Santa Cruz ((C) **72/823199;** www.colchaguavalley.cl), which offers half-day and full-day tours to some of Chile's most important wineries, such as **Viña Montes, Viu Manent, Casa Silva, Emiliana Orgánica,** and **Casa Lapostolle's Clos Apalta.** Reservations are required.

Clos Apalta ★★★ *(Moments*   The Colchagua Valley's most luxurious and exclusive lodging option is one of the most special places to stay in Chile. Clos Apalta has four *casitas* or small individual units, nestled in on a hillside near their winery, and a guesthouse, which is more or less the main body of the winery area itself and offers less privacy. The guest rooms are elegantly appointed and modern in decor, with lots of dark wood, white and ecru-colored fabrics, freshly cut flowers, plush bathrooms, and, in the case of the *casitas,* with wooden decks that afford truly magnificent, wide-open views of the Apalta Valley.

Hijuela Villa Eloisa, Camino San Fernando a Pichilemu, Km 36. (C) 72/321803. www.closapalta.cl. $800 (£410) for 2, all-inclusive. AE, MC, V. **Amenities:** Gourmet restaurant; outdoor pool; wine tours; massage. *In room:* Wi-Fi.

Hotel Santa Cruz Plaza ★★   This hotel has turned the Colchagua Valley into a destination not unlike Napa Valley. The hotel sits on the main plaza, yet is relatively inconspicuous with its mellow mustard wash–and–ironwork window terraces. The guest rooms and bathrooms are not large, but they offer enough space for comfort and are decorated in a terra cotta–colored, country style featuring antiques and decorations found throughout the Santa Cruz area. Their buffet breakfast is terrific, and the Wine Route office is next-door, making it easy to plan excursions. The hotel's **Restaurante Los Varietales** is excellent, and the best restaurant within Santa Cruz proper.

Plaza de Armas 286, Santa Cruz. ⓒ/fax 72/821010. www.hotelsantacruzplaza.cl. 41 doubles, 3 suites. $200 (£103) double; $250–$325 (£128–£167) suite. Rates include breakfast. AE, DC, MC, V. **Amenities:** Restaurant; outdoor pool; sauna; babysitting; laundry service. In room: A/C, TV.

A VISIT TO CHILE'S OLDEST HOTEL

Hacienda Los Lingues 🌟🌟🌟 *Moments*   About 125km (78 miles) south of Santiago and nestled among poplar-lined country fields and rolling hills is the Hacienda Los Lingues, one of the oldest and best-preserved haciendas in Chile that is now run as a splendid, full-service hotel. There certainly are more luxurious, newer lodging options around, but nothing comes close to this hotel's character, charm, and sumptuous natural surroundings. A visit here is like taking a step back in time to colonial Chile. The estate has remained in the same family for 400 years, though most of the buildings were built around 250 years ago. From the ruby-red French salon to the formal sitting room, every room is accented with crystal chandeliers, Oriental rugs, and antique furniture, and is brimming with decorative pieces, family photos, collector's items, and fascinating odds and ends that you could spend hours observing and admiring. The guest rooms are decorated individually, and come with fresh flowers and buckets of champagne. A bountiful breakfast is served to you in bed.

Reservations in Santiago: Av. Providencia 1100, no. 205. ⓒ **2/431-0510.** Fax 2/431-0501. www.loslingues.com. 19 units, 2 suites. $100 (£51) double May–Aug; $150 (£76) double Sept–Oct; $190 (£97) double Nov–Apr. AE, DC, MC, V. **Amenities:** Outdoor pool; 2 clay tennis courts; game room; room service.

CHILLAN & TERMAS DE CHILLAN RESORT

Chillán is a midsize city located 406km (252 miles) south of Santiago, and it is the gateway to the popular **Termas de Chillán,** one of South America's largest and most complete ski and summer resorts. A tidy city of 145,000, with five spruce plazas and hodgepodge, tasteless architecture, bustling streets, and street dogs, Chillán looks like any other Chilean city in the Central Valley. There is really only one reason to stop here, the **Feria de Chillán** 🌟🌟🌟, one of the largest and most colorful markets in Chile. The Feria is located between Maipón, Arturo Prat, 5 de Abril, and Isabel Riquelme streets; across Maipón Street is the food market, with everything from pickled vegetables to dried fruit to Chillán's famous sausages. The Feria is open every day.

Essentials

GETTING THERE   By Air   Chillán is served by the **Aeropuerto Carriel Sur** in Concepción, about an hour away. There are direct flights here from Santiago several times daily from **LAN** and **Sky** airlines. If you've made hotel reservations at Termas de Chillán, their transfer service will pick you up and take you directly there. If not, you must take a taxi to the bus terminal, where buses for Chillán leave every 20 minutes.

By Bus   Línea Sur and **TurBus** offer daily service from most major cities, including Santiago. The trip from Santiago takes about 5 to 6 hours and costs $13 (£6.65) one-way. The bus terminal in Chillán is located at Av. O'Higgins 010, and from there you can grab a bus for the Termas.

By Train   EFE (Terrasur) offers a highly recommended 5-hour train trip from Santiago, leaving from the Estación Central, and arriving in Chillán at the station at Calle Brasil (ⓒ **2/585-5000;** www.efe.cl). The cost is $17 to $53 (£8.70–£27) per person.

Tips **Get Your Funds in Order Before You Arrive**

There are no ATMs or gas stations in Termas de Chillán, so do your banking beforehand and fill up at the last Copec on the road from Chillán to Termas de Chillán.

TERMAS DE CHILLAN

Termas de Chillán ★★ *(Kids)*   About 80km (50 miles) from the city is Termas de Chillán, a full-season resort that is principally known for skiing, but offers great hiking, biking, and horseback riding opportunities in the summer. The resort is nestled in a forested valley under the shadow of the 3,212m (10,535-ft.) Chillán Volcano. The resort has 28 runs, 4 chair lifts, and 5 T-bars, as well as heliskiing, dog sledding, an international ski school, equipment rental, and restaurants. Many of the lifts are old and slow-going; Termas is notoriously anti-snowboard, and they will not allow snowboarders on certain poma lifts. Nevertheless, the off-piste terrain is excellent for snowboarding and skiing.

Termas is known for its spa facilities and outdoor hot springs, produced by the natural geothermal fissures in the area. The spa offers hydrotherapy, aromatherapy, mud baths, and massages.

There are two hotels at the base of the lifts: the five-star **Gran Hotel Termas de Chillán,** with 120 rooms, and the three-star **Hotel Shangri-La,** with 48 rooms; there is also one hotel in Las Trancas, the **Hotel Pirmahuida** (transportation available to and from the resort). Rates include breakfast and dinner, ski tickets, and spa facilities. But here's the major caveat: the ski resort's concession was open to bidders at the time of publication, and therefore rates are not available. Contact the resort or see their website for 2008 prices.

San Pío X 2460, #508 (Santiago). ✆ 42/434200 (in Chillán) or 2/233-1313 (in Santiago). www.termaschillan.cl. Average lift tickets $35 (£18) adults, $25 (£13) children. AE, DC, MC, V. **Amenities:** Restaurant; bar; squash court; gym; state-of-the-art spa; child-care center; game room; salon; room service; laundry. *In room:* TV, Wi-Fi, hair dryer, safe.

---

6 The Desert North

SAN PEDRO DE ATACAMA

Quaint, unhurried, and built of adobe brick, San Pedro de Atacama sits in the driest desert in the world 1,674km (1,039 miles) north of Santiago, a region replete with bizarre land formations including giant sand dunes, jagged canyons, salt pillars, boiling geysers, and a smoking volcano. Better to call it a moonscape than a landscape. For adventure seekers, a wealth of activities is available to participate in, including hiking, mountain biking, and horseback riding—or you can just sightsee with a tour van. This region was the principal center of the Atacamanian Indian culture, and relics such as Tulor, an ancient village estimated to have been built in 800 B.C., still survive. There's also a superb archaeology museum that boasts hundreds of artifacts that have been well preserved by the desert's arid climate. This is one of the top stargazing areas in the world; once you leave the village and are enveloped by a thick blanket of twinkling lights, you'd be forgiven for feeling that the galaxy was not so far, far away after all. The town has fomented somewhat of a bohemian ambience, but with the variety of activities and lodging options, the region appeals to just about everyone. To visit the major sites here, you'll need 3 or 4 days, a few more to see everything including

The Desert North

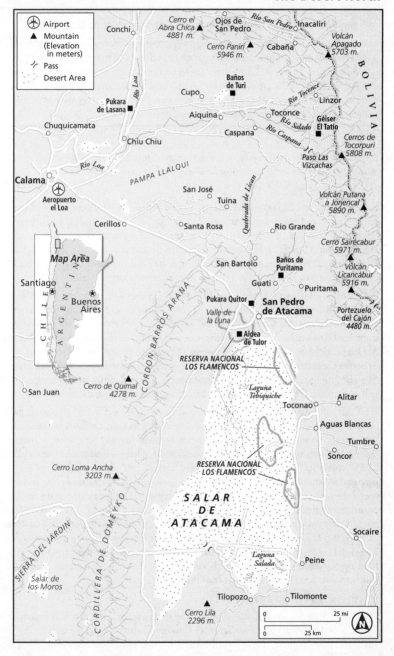

Airport
▲ **Mountain** (Elevation in meters)
/ **Pass**
: **Desert Area**

Conchi

Cerro el Abra Chica 4881 m. ▲
Ojos de San Pedro ○
Río San Pedro
Inacaliri

Cerro Paniri 5946 m. ▲
Cabaña ○
Volcán Apagado 5703 m. ▲

B O L I V I A

Baños de Turi ■
Cupo ○
Río Toconce
Linzor ○

Pukara de Lasana ■
Aiquina ○
Toconce ○
Río Salado
Géiser El Tatío

Chuquicamata
Chiu Chiu ○
Caspana ○
Río Caspana
Cerros de Tocorpuri 5808 m. ▲

Río Loa

Calama
PAMPA LLALQUI
Paso Las Vizcachas

Aeropuerto el Loa
San José ○
Volcán Putana a Jorjencal 5890 m. ▲

Cerillos ○
Tuina ○
Santa Rosa ○
Río Grande ○

Quebrada de Lican

Cerro Sairecabur 5971 m. ▲

Map Area
Santiago ☆
CHILE
ARGENTINA
Buenos Aires ☆

San Bartolo ○
Baños de Puritama ●
Guati ○
Puritama ○
Volcán Licancábur 5916 m. ▲

Pukara Quitor ■
San Pedro de Atacama
Portezuelo del Cajón 4480 m.

Valle de la Luna

San Juan ○
Cerro de Quimal 4278 m. ▲
Aldea de Tulor ▲

CORDÓN BARROS ARANA

RESERVA NACIONAL LOS FLAMENCOS

Laguna Tebiquiche
Toconao ○
Alitar ○

Aguas Blancas ○
Tumbre ○
Soncor ○

Cerro Loma Ancha 3203 m. ▲

RESERVA NACIONAL LOS FLAMENCOS

S A L A R
D E
A T A C A M A

Socaire ○

SIERRA DEL JARDIN

Salar de los Moros

CORDILLERA DE DOMEYKO

Laguna Salada
Peine ○

Tilopozo ○
Tilomonte ○

Cerro Lila 2296 m. ▲

| 0 | | 25 mi |
| 0 | | 25 km |

N

Tips **Important Info to Know Before Arriving in San Pedro**

The altitude may slow you down at first, though few visitors are gravely affected by it. Don't undertake any grand expeditions to extreme altitudes during your first 2 days in San Pedro. The town has a small medical clinic, but no hospital. Don't drink tap water here, as the local supply contains trace amounts of arsenic. Bring a flashlight, too; the streets off the main drag are not lit and even a 2-block walk can be difficult to navigate.

---

the outlying villages or the Chuquicamata mine. Outside of the May to July season, rooms can book up as far as 6 months ahead of time, so plan ahead.

GETTING THERE

Calama, a city of 120,000, is the gateway to San Pedro. The city depends on the mining industry, and like most boomtowns, it is ugly and hodge-podge, and reports of petty crime have soared here. Most travelers spend the night only to see the Chuquicamata Copper Mine. The Indian ruins, **Pukará de Lasana,** and the colonial village, **Chiu Chiu,** are also close to Calama, although they can be visited on the way back to Calama from San Pedro via the Tatío Geysers on a very long day trip.

BY PLANE   Calama's **Aeropuerto El Loa** (© **55/361956**) is served by **LAN Airlines** © **600/526-2000;** www.lan.com), **Sky Airlines** (© **600/600-2828;** www. skyairline.cl), and **Air Comet** (© **800/710-3000**). LAN has up to five daily flights from Santiago on weekdays and three on weekends; Sky has two daily flights and Aerolíneas del Sur has one Sunday through Friday. To get to San Pedro de Atacama, **Transfer Licancabur** (© **55/334194**) offers transfer services from 7am to 7:30pm for $16 (£8.20) and, for a minimum of four people, for $20 (£10) after 7:30pm. A taxi will cost about $70 (£36)—be sure to fix a price before leaving the airport.

BY CAR   Rental cars are available at the Calama airport. A word of caution, however, if you choose to rent. This is a vast desert and most areas are fairly isolated; roadside service is available from rental agencies, but without any services or phones on most roads, you will have to flag someone down for help—if someone comes along, that is. If you stay to main routes you should have no problem, but outside of that, be prepared for the worst, and bring extra water, food, and warm clothes in case you must spend the night on the road. A 4×4 is unnecessary unless you plan an expedition along poorly maintained roads. The airport has rental kiosks for **Avis** (© **600/601-9966** or 55/363325; www.avischile.cl), **Budget** (© **2/362-3200;** www.budget.cl), and **Hertz** (© **2/420-5222** or 55/341380; www.hertz.cl). Rates include insurance. **Alamo** (© **2/ 225-3061;** www.alamochile.com) is the cheapest, but you may want to check with a local agency when you arrive at the airport for deals. *Tip:* Fill the tank in Calama. The sole pump in San Pedro charges at least 30% more.

VISITOR INFORMATION

Sernatur operates a small visitor center at the plaza on the corner of Antofagasta and Toconao (no phone). Hours are Saturday through Thursday from 9:30am to 1:30pm and 3 to 7pm. The best site for information is **www.sanpedroatacama.com**; it's information is listed in English and Spanish.

ATTRACTIONS NEAR CALAMA

CHUQUICAMATA COPPER MINE   Ghost towns dot the northern desert from Chile's nitrate-mining days, but the copper-mining industry is alive and well, as is evident by Calama's **Chuquicamata mine.** This is the largest open-pit mine in the world at 4km (2½ miles) across and more than half a kilometer deep—everything at its bottom looks Lilliputian. The mine is owned by Codelco and yields more than 600,000 tons of copper per year, or 25% of Chile's export income. Few man-made wonders in the world provoke the visual awe of Chuquicamata; however, the tour will not appeal to travelers who have no interest of the inner workings of Chile's industrialization, or those with little time.

Tours run every weekday, except holidays, from 2 to 3pm; you must present yourself at the Chuquicamata office at the mine (Av. Tocopilla and José Miguel Carrera) at 1:30pm. For reservations, call ✆ **55/322122** or 55/345345, or e-mail visitas@codelco.cl. To get to the office, take an all-yellow *colectivo* taxi signed CALAMA CHUQUI from the corner of Ramirez and Aboroa in the plaza, or hire a regular taxi for about $7 (£3.60) one-way. The mine tour is free, but donations to a foundation for underprivileged kids are encouraged. For safety reasons, wear trousers, long-sleeved shirts, and closed shoes.

COLONIAL VILLAGES & PUKARAS   Travelers interested in archeology and seeking an excursion with little physical exertion will enjoy the attractions listed below.

Chiu Chiu 𝕲 was founded by the Spanish in the early 17th century as part of an extensive trading route that included Brazil. This speck of a village is known for the **Iglesia San Francisco** 𝕲, the most picturesque church in the north. The whitewashed adobe walls of this weather-beaten structure are 120cm (47-in.) thick, and its doors are made of cedar and bordered with cactus, displaying a singular, Atacamanian style.

But it is more fascinating to explore the ruins of the National Monument **Pukará de Lasana** 𝕲𝕲, a 12th-century Atacama Indian fort influenced by the Incas, abandoned after the Spanish occupation and restored in 1951. You'll want to spend at least a half-hour wandering the labyrinthine streets that wind around the remains of 110 two- to five-story buildings.

North of Chiu Chiu is the engaging village of **Caspana,** surrounded by a fertile valley cultivated in a terraced formation like a sunken amphitheater. The village is characterized by its rock-wall and thatched-roof architecture. In the center, a tiny museum is dedicated to the culture of the area and there's an artisan shop selling textiles made from alpaca. Caspana also boasts a colonial-era church, the **Iglesia de San Lucas,** built in 1641 of stone, cactus, and mortar and covered in adobe.

Near Caspana is another National Monument, the **Pukará de Turi** 𝕲𝕲, the largest fortified city of the Atacama culture, built in the 12th century, and widely believed to be an Inca administrative center. The size of these ruins, with their circular towers and wide streets, is impressive, and you'll need about a half-hour to soak it all in.

EXPLORING SAN PEDRO

Museo Arqueológico Padre le Paige 𝕲𝕲   This museum near the plaza displays one of South America's most fascinating collections of pre-Columbian artifacts, gathered by Padre le Paige, a Belgian missionary. The Atacama Desert is so arid that most artifacts are notably well preserved, including hundreds of ceramics, textiles, tablets used for the inhalation of hallucinogens, tools, and more, all displayed according to time period. The museum's famous mummies and deformed craniums have been taken out in respect for the indigenous community, which was, for many, the high-light of a visit here, so plan on just 30 minutes to see everything.

Toconao and Padre Le Paige. ℂ **55/851002.** Admission $3 (£1.55) adults, $1.50 (75p) children. Jan–Feb daily 10am–1pm and 3–7pm; rest of the year Mon–Fri 9am–noon and 2–6pm, Sat–Sun 10am–noon and 2–6pm.

WHAT TO SEE & DO

OUTDOOR ACTIVITIES Excursions in the area either fall into preplanned trips (all-inclusive hotels), pre-planned tours (made ahead of time with your travel agent), or locally owned operations. If you can afford it, I strongly recommend hiring a private guide. A private guide will take you on uncommon tours, such as backcountry roads to high-altitude salt lakes, and can adapt to your whims. For traditional tours (Valle de la Luna, the Salar de Atacama, Tatio Geysers, and archaeological tours), the following are tried and true: **Desert Adventure,** corner of Tocopilla and Caracoles (ℂ/fax **55/851067;** www.desertadventure.cl); **Cosmo Andino Expediciones,** Caracoles s/n (ℂ **55/851069**); or **Atacama Connection,** Caracoles and Toconao (ℂ/fax **55/851421;** www.atacama connection.com). For traditional tours with a wildlife theme, try **Natura Expeditions,** Domingo Atienza 388 (ℂ **55/851825**). For mountain biking and sandboarding, try **Southamericanadventure,** Caracoles 317 (ℂ **55/851373**). Average prices are: Valle de la Luna, $10 (£5.10); Tatio Geysers, $40 (£21); Salt Flat and altiplanic lakes, $45 (£23).

The Atacama Desert is the apex of **stargazing** in the world, due to a lack of moisture in the air, low light pollution, and the high altitude. **Celestial Explorations** gives amateur astronomers an opportunity to view the galaxy's most stunning constellations that are only visible in the Southern Hemisphere. The 2½-hour tour leaves nightly except for evenings around a full moon and costs $12 (£6.15), which includes transportation, use of powerful telescopes and an easy-to-understand interpretation of the stars by a trilingual astronomer (Caracoles 166; ℂ **55/851935;** www.spaceobs.com).

Marvel at the clear night skies with **Celestial Explorations,** Caracoles 166 (ℂ **55/ 851935;** www.spaceobs.com), which gives amateur astronomers an opportunity to view constellations visible only in the Southern Hemisphere. The 3-hour tour leaves nightly except for evenings around a full moon and costs $20 (£10), which includes transportation, use of powerful telescopes, and an easy-to-understand interpretation of the stars by a trilingual astronomer.

The **Atacama Salt Flat** ✦✦, a gigantic mineralized lake that is covered in many parts by a weird, putty-colored crust, is also home to a **flamingo reserve.** There's also an interpretive center (no phone); it's open September through May daily from 8:30am to 8pm, and June through August daily from 8:30am to 7pm. A local favorite here is **Laguna Sejar** ✦, 19km (12 miles) from San Pedro. This emerald lagoon is encircled by white salt encrustations that resemble and feel like coral reef—so bring flip-flops. Sejar affords a remarkable swimming experience, floating in water so saline it renders you virtually unsinkable.

A highlight in the Atacama Desert is the **Geysers del Tatio** ✦✦✦; this excursion is not the easiest, as tours leave at 4 or 5am (the geysers are most active around 6–8am). These are the highest geysers in the world, and it is a marvelous spectacle to watch thick plumes of steam blow from holes in such a windswept, arid land. Interspersed between the geysers, bubbling pools encrusted with colorful minerals splash and splutter—but exercise extreme caution when walking near thin crust; careless visitors burn themselves frequently. I strongly recommend travelers not drive here—even habitual drivers to the geysers can get lost in the dark morning. If you insist, buy a map in San Pedro, or download a detailed map from **www.turistel.cl**, and get an experienced driver to run you through details of the route, or hire a day guide. If you take a day tour, make certain it stops at **Baños de Puritama** 𝕲𝕲, a hot springs oasis composed of rock pools that descend down a gorge, about 60km (37 miles) from the geysers (or 28km/17 miles from San Pedro, heading out on the road that borders the cemetery). Hotel Explora (see "Where to Stay in San Pedro," below) runs the hot springs and charges a steep $20 (£10) to enter, but it is worth it. You may want to tote a snack and a bottle of wine to enjoy while there. Changing rooms and bathrooms are available.

Two interesting archaeological sites are near town: the 12th-century, pre-Inca defensive fort **Pukará de Quitor** 𝕲𝕲 and the **Aldea de Tulor** 𝕲𝕲, the Atacama's oldest pueblo (dating from 800 B.C.). The Quitor is about 3km (2 miles) from San Pedro; to get there, walk, bike, or drive west up Calle Tocopilla and continue along the river until you see Quitor at your left. The Aldea de Tulor is a 9km (5½-mile) bike ride or drive southwest of San Pedro.

Sports Activities

BIKING The Atacama region offers excellent terrain for mountain-bike riding, including the Quebrada del Diablo (Devil's Gorge) and Valle de la Muerte (Death Valley); however, it is also enjoyable to ride across the flat desert to visit sites such as Tulor. Bike rental shops can be found along Caracoles, and they all are the same in terms of quality and charge about $9 (£4.60) per day.

HORSEBACK RIDING Horseback riding is a quiet, relaxing way to experience the Atacama and view Indian ruins that are inaccessible by bike. If you are adept at galloping, fulfill your Lawrence of Arabia fantasies and race across a sand dune. **Rancho Cactus,** Toconao 568 (𝄞 **55/851506;** www.rancho-cactus.cl), and **La Herradura,** Tocopilla s/n (𝄞 **55/851087;** laherraduraatacama@hotmail.com), offer short and full-day rides to a variety of destinations for an average of $7 (£3.60) per hour.

SANDBOARDING Sandboarding is the sand-dune version of snowboarding. Several places in San Pedro rent boards, and the place to head is Valle de la Muerte. It's best to go by bike or car. The more similar the bindings on your board to snowboard bindings, the easier it will be to keep your balance. Also, take the more tapered, slightly longer boards instead of those short, wheelless skateboards some places offer. No ski lifts here—don't forget to take water and sunblock on this excursion, as you'll spend lots of time climbing back up the steep dunes in the heat.

VOLCANO ASCENTS Climbing one of the four volcanoes in the area requires total altitude acclimatization and good physical condition. It is a heart-pounding hike up, but if you can hack it, the sweeping views and the experience in itself are exhilarating. The most popular ascent is up the active Volcano Láscar to 5,400m (17,712 ft.), about a 4-hour climb, and leaves San Pedro before sun-up. However, recent activity means this climb may not be available. Volcano Lincancabúr is also popular, but it requires an overnight stay at a rustic *refugio* just across the border and a Bolivian guide. Many tour companies offer these excursions; among the best is **Azimut 360,** Caracoles s/n (𝄞 **2/235-1519;** www.azimut.cl).

WHERE TO STAY IN SAN PEDRO

Hotel Altiplánico 𝕲𝕲 This hotel recently expanded and landscaped its grounds. The hotel sits just outside of town, on the road to the Pukará de Quitor, and is a 10-minute walk to town. Like that of its predecessors, the striking architecture stays true to the style of the zone: river rock patios, adobe walls, peaked straw roofs, and tree trunks left in their spindly, natural state. It is quite an attractive hotel and a lower-cost option than Explora (see above), and it is located on a spacious property with open views. Rooms are very comfortable, and the pool a delight, but what really makes the Altiplánico special is its friendly, helpful service. This is a good hotel for a group, as it has a barbecue area near the pool for private parties.

Domingo Atienza 282, San Pedro de Atacama. © **55/851212**. Fax 55/851238. 23 units. $140 (£72) double. AE, DC, MC, V. **Amenities:** Cafeteria; bar; large outdoor pool; bicycles; room service; laundry service. *In room:* No phone.

Hotel Awasi ⭐⭐⭐   The Awasi was the travel magazine darling of 2007, garnering awards from publications such as *Condé Nast Traveller* as the best new hotel in Latin America. It is luxury at its finest, with elegantly designed guest rooms centered on an open-air common area featuring a bar, restaurant, and pool. As boutique hotels go, the Awasi is small and its seems impossible not to meet your fellow travelers while there— with just eight suites, this is definitely a hotel for those seeking intimacy. The stylish decor uses high-quality materials and features top amenities. And, like Hotel Explora, this is one hotel that plans journeys that escape the crowds for a more personalized, "adventurous" experience. Guest rooms are referred to as cottages, with lots of space. The Awasi has all-inclusive packages and single night prices (which include transfers and breakfast) that are substantially cheaper than Explora.

Tocopilla 4, San Pedro de Atacama. © **55/851460** (local), or 888/880-3219 in the U.S. www.awasi.com. 8 units. All-inclusive rates, double occupancy, per person: 2 nights $900 (£462); 4 nights $1,610 (£826); single night double occupancy $390 (£200). AE, DC, MC, V. **Amenities:** Restaurant; bar; outdoor pool; excursions; massage; laundry service; horseback riding. *In room:* Hair dryer.

Hotel Explora ⭐⭐⭐ *(Moments)*   The Hotel Explora was the first luxury lodging hotel to open in San Pedro, but now there are a few other properties that are equal in quality, if not better. Explora is an all-inclusive hotel with an outstanding on-site restaurant, and this coupled with a 3-block, dusty walk to San Pedro, means guests often spend little time in town. Like its counterpart in Patagonia, the Explora in Atacama is elegant yet unpretentious. The exteriors are plain, but the lounge and guest rooms are decorated with local art and painted in quiet, pastel tones. The lounge, with soaring ceilings, is enormous, stretching the length of the building and scattered with plush, multicolored couches for sinking into and cooling off with a pisco sour. Guest rooms have ultracomfortable beds with crisp linens and fluffy down comforters; each bathroom comes with a Jacuzzi tub. Slatted boardwalks lead guests around the property to a sybaritic, adobe-walled massage salon, a stargazing platform (with state-of-the-art telescopes), a barbecue *quincho,* and four irrigation-style pools.

Explora's excursions seek to introduce guests to the unknown, those off-the-beaten places where few others go. If a destination is popular, Explora guides show guests the other side, or encompass the destination into part of a more thorough expedition. Packages include lodging, all excursions, meals, airport transfers, and an open bar. Check their website for information about new add-on trips to Bolivia and Argentina.

Domingo Atienza s/n, San Pedro de Atacama (main office: Américo Vespucio Sur 80, Piso 5, Santiago). © **55/851110** (local), or 866/750-6699 in the U.S. and 2/206-6060 in Santiago (reservations). Fax 2/228-4655; toll-free fax 800/858-0855 (U.S.), 800/275-1129 (Canada). www.explora.com. 52 units. All-inclusive rates, double occupancy, per person: 3 nights $1,642 (£842); 4 nights $2,190 (£1,123). Reduced rates available for children and teens. AE, DC, MC, V. **Amenities:** Restaurant; bar; 4 outdoor pools; sauna; mountain bikes; massage; babysitting; laundry service; TV room; horseback riding. *In room:* Hair dryer, safe.

Hotel Kimal ⭐⭐ *(Finds)*   The Hotel Kimal is one of my favorites in San Pedro. It doesn't have the same prestige as Explora, but it offers a little slice of tranquillity for the traveler. The location is central, the guest rooms are handsome, and the beds are heavenly soft. The rooms are softly lit by skylights and are fringed outside by pimiento trees and stone walkways, and most rooms have a little seating area outside. The restaurant is principally outdoors, and its proximity to the circular pool makes it a refreshing place to sit on a hot day. Consult their website for adventure-travel and relaxation-oriented packages.

Domingo Atienza 452 (at Caracoles), San Pedro de Atacama. *C* 55/851152. Fax 55/851030. www.kimal.cl. 19 units. $134 (£69) single; $154 (£79) double. AE, DC, MC, V. **Amenities:** Restaurant; bar; outdoor pool; Jacuzzi; room service; laundry service; Internet; fax. *In room:* Minibar.

Hotel Tambillo *✿* The Tambillo is the best option in this price range. The 15 units here are lined along both sides of a narrow, attractive pathway inlaid with stone. Units have arched windows and doors, and no decoration other than a light, but it's not unappealing—on the contrary, the atmosphere is fresh and clean. There's also a large restaurant and a tiny sheltered patio. It's a 4-block walk to the main street.

Gustavo (Padre) Le Paige 159, San Pedro de Atacama. *C*/fax **55/851078.** www.hoteltambillo.cl. 15 units. $60 (£31) double. No credit cards. **Amenities:** Cafeteria. *In room:* No phone.

WHERE TO DINE IN SAN PEDRO

Many restaurants fill up after 9pm so arrive early or consider making a reservation if the restaurant accepts them. Competition has drawn waiters onto the street to harangue for business; check out each restaurant's fixed-price menu, as it is often an excellent value. If you're looking for a quick, light lunch of empanadas or pizza, try **Petro Pizza** at Toconao 447 (*C* **09/2916347;** pizzas $1–$4/50p–£2.05); for dessert lovers, **Las Delicias de Carmen,** Gustavo (Padre) Le Paige 370 (*C* **9/089-5673**), offers apple and lemon pie, walnut tarts, strudel, and several kinds of cakes made to order or to try there at the restaurant. **Café Tierra** at Caracoles 271 (*C* **55/851585;** daily 9am–10:30pm) has vegetarian, whole-meal empanadas made from scratch while you wait, as well as sandwiches and breakfast. For a splurge, dine at the **Hotel Explora** (see above), which serves incontestably the best fusion cuisine in northern Chile. Reservations must be made 24 hours in advance.

Adobe *✿✿* CONTEMPORARY CHILEAN   One of the best choices for dining, but it must be said that the service and quality of food has fallen over the past few years. Expect grilled steaks or chicken paired with fries or rice, and a few pastas; it's the kind of place you go after a huge workout for a platter of food. What sets the mood here is the blazing bonfire, around which diners sit at wooden tables under a semi-enclosed thatched roof. Live music often takes place here, and though the Adobe serves dinner until 11:30pm only, the restaurant converts into a bar serving light snacks thereafter.

Caracoles 211. *C* **55/851132.** www.cafeadobe.cl. Main courses $7–$10 (£3.60–£5.10). AE, DC, MC, V. Daily 8am–1am.

Encanto *✿* CHILEAN   Encanto is the newest eatery on the scene, with a menu that highlights local Atacaman dishes and products such as *sopa de gigote,* or poor-man's stew, and dishes with the local grain *quinoa.* The ambience is fresh and clean, with molded adobe booths and soft light. Outside, an outdoor seating area with a fire pit makes for a pleasant place to dine. It's a good choice if you'd like to taste a few local items, and solid wine list, too.

Caracoles 195. *C* **55/851939.** Reservations not accepted. Main courses $6–$10 (£3.10–£5.10). No credit cards. Daily 9am–1am.

La Casona ✶✶ CHILEAN   La Casona is restaurant/bar housed in an old colonial building with soaring ceilings. Candlelit, wooden tables adorned with a few sprigs of flowers, and a crackling fireplace set a quieter ambience. There's also daytime outdoor seating, a pub, and an outdoor bar in the back warmed by a blazing fire, and though it isn't the hot spot it once was with locals, it can get lively at night nevertheless. La Casona serves predominately Chilean specialties, in a slightly updated style, and delicious breakfasts. Don't miss their new wine shop with an outstanding selection; it is really the only place to buy a decent bottle of wine in town.

Caracoles 195. © **55/851004.** Reservations accepted. Main courses $6–$10 (£3.10–£5.10). AE, DC, MC, V. Daily 8am–11pm.

Restaurant Blanco ✶✶ CHILEAN/INTERNATIONAL   Restaurant Blanco is a newcomer to the San Pedro restaurant scene brought to you by the owners of Adobe and La Estaka. True to its name, the atmosphere is almost entirely white and minimalist, a simple backdrop for its hallmark cuisine. You shouldn't miss its fresh Easter Island tuna with pepper sauce, but consider trying the vanilla beef and sample its impressive wine list.

Caracoles 195. © **55/851939.** www.blancorestaurant.cl. Main courses $11–$13 (£5.65–£6.65). AE, DC, MC, V. Daily 7–11pm.

7 The Chilean Lake District ✶✶✶

The region south of the Río Biobío to Puerto Montt is collectively known as the Lake District, a fairy-tale land of emerald forests, snowcapped volcanoes, frothing waterfalls, and hundreds of lakes and lagoons that give the region its name. It is one of the most popular destinations in Chile, not only for its beauty, but for the diverse outdoor activities available and a well-organized tourism infrastructure that allows travelers to pack in a lot of action and yet rest comfortably and well fed in the evening.

Summers are usually balmy, but the rest of the year this region is very wet and impermeable clothing is essential, especially if planning on being outdoors. *Tip:* For a map of Chile's lake district, please refer to the Lake District map on p. 139.

EXPLORING THE REGION

The Lake District is composed of the **Región de la Araucania,** which includes the city **Temuco** and the resort area **Pucón,** and the **Región de los Lagos,** home to the port cities **Valdivia** and **Puerto Montt, Puerto Varas,** and **Frutillar,** and the island **Chiloé.** There's plenty more to see and do outside these principal destinations, including hot springs, boat rides, adventure sports, and miles of bumpy dirt roads that make for picturesque drives through enchanting landscapes. Towns such as Puerto Varas and Pucón are excellent bases from which to take part in all of these activities. Most visitors will find they need 3 to 4 days to explore each destination, more if planning to backpack, fish, or really get out and see everything. You may consider crossing into the equally beautiful Argentine Lake District, which can be done by vehicle from Pucón or by boat from Puerto Varas.

TEMUCO

Temuco is the third-largest city in Chile, and its airport serves as the gateway to Pucón except for January and February when LAN Airlines offers direct service to Pucón. Temuco is home to a regional highlight, the **Mercado Municipal** ✶✶, a vibrant, crafts-filled market. If you've already done your souvenir shopping in Pucón (and there's a lot on offer there), skip Temuco. For information about getting to Temuco, see "Getting There" under "Pucón," below.

The Mercado can be found at Portales and Aldunate and is open Monday through Saturday from 8am to 8pm, Sunday and holidays from 8:30am to 3pm; from April to September, the market closes at 6pm Monday through Saturday. Rows of stalls sell everything from high-quality woven ponchos, knitwear, textiles, woodwork, hats, and silver Mapuche jewelry, to assorted arts and crafts.

PUCON ✯✯✯

789km (489 miles) S of Santiago, 25km (16 miles) E of Temuco

Nationally and internationally known as the **"Adventure Capital of Chile,"** Pucón offers every outdoor activity imaginable: fly-fishing, rafting the Río Trancura, hiking Huerquehue and Villarrica national parks, and skiing the slopes of Volcán Villarrica— or even climbing to its bubbling crater. Yet there's also an abundance of low-key activities, such as hot-spring spas and scenic drives through landscapes that seem to have been the inspiration for every fairy tale written. You could just hang out on the beach and sun yourself, as hundreds do during the summer. Pucón is almost entirely dependent on tourism, and during the summer season, particularly December 15 to the end of February, as well as Easter week, the town teems with throngs of tourists. Hotel and business owners take advantage of this and jack up their prices, sometimes doubling their rates.

ESSENTIALS
Getting There
BY PLANE   Visitors normally fly into Temuco's **Manquehue Airport** and then arrange transportation for the 1- to 1½-hour ride into Villarrica or Pucón. Most hotels will arrange transportation for you, although it's usually at an additional cost. **Transfer & Turismo de la Araucanía** (© **45/339-900**), a minivan service at the airport, will take a maximum of 10 guests (minimum of 4) to Pucón for $45 (£23). Pucón's airport is now operational and equipped to handle jets, but for the time being, only two flights a week (on Fri and Sun) touch down here from Santiago, and only during the highest season, from mid-December to late February. Additional service is expected as demand continues to increase; for fares and up-to-the-minute schedule information, contact **LAN** at (© **600/526-2000;** www.lan.com) and **Sky Airline** (© **600/600-2828;** www.skyairline.cl).

BY CAR   From the Pan-American Highway south of Temuco, follow the signs for Villarrica onto Ruta 199. The road is well marked and easy to follow. If coming from Valdivia, take Ruta 205 to the Carretera Panamericana Norte (Hwy. 5). Just past Loncoche, continue east, following signs for Villarrica and Pucón.

BY BUS   **Tur Bus** (© **600/660-6600** toll free, or 2/270-7510; www.turbus.cl) offers service to Pucón from destinations such as Santiago, stopping first in Temuco and Villarrica. The trip is about 9 to 11 hours and generally a night journey; the cost is about $28 (£14) for an economy seat and $53 (£27) for an executive seat. **Buses JAC** (in Santiago, Av. Providencia 1072; © **2/235-2484**) has service from Santiago to Pucón every half-hour from its Santiago terminal at Balmaceda and Aldunate (© **45/231330**).

VISITOR INFORMATION   The local tourism board has an office at the corner of Brasil and Caupolicán streets; it's open daily from 9am to 8pm December through

March and from 10am to 6:30pm the rest of the year (© **45/441671**). The staff does not speak English very well.

OUTDOOR ACTIVITIES

With so many outdoor adventures available here, it's no wonder there's a surplus of outfitters eager to meet the demand. When choosing an outfitter in Pucón, remember that you get what you pay for, and be wary of those that treat you like just another nameless tourist. You want an experience to be memorable for the fun you've had, not for the mishaps and accidents. Most outfitters include insurance in the cost of a trip, but verify what their policy covers.

For more things to see and do in this area, see "Hot Springs Outside of Pucón" and "Natural Attractions Outside of Pucón," later.

TOUR OPERATORS   **Politur,** O'Higgins 635 (© **45/441373;** www.politur.com), is a well-respected tour company that offers fishing expeditions, Mapuche-themed tours, and sightseeing trips around the Seven Lakes area, in addition to volcano ascents. They're slightly more expensive than other agencies but are worth it. **Aguaventura,** Palguín 336 (© **45/444246;** www.aguaventura.com), is run by a dynamic French group, and their main focus is snowboarding in the winter with a shop that sells and rents boards, boots, and clothing; they also do volcano ascents with ski/snowboard descents, and rafting and kayaking, and they offer a half-day canyoneering and rappelling excursion. **Sol y Nieve,** O'Higgins and Lincoyán (© **45/463860;** www.chile-travel.com/solnieve.htm), has been on the scene for quite a while, offering rafting and volcano ascents as well as fishing, airport transfers, and excursions in other destinations around Chile; however, there have been some complaints recently of lackluster service. **Trancura,** O'Higgins 211-C (© **45/498575;** www.trancura.com), sells cheap trips to the masses, and they are best known for their rafting excursions, which they've been doing forever. Beyond that, I do not recommend any other trips with this company because of their yearly roster of inexperienced guides hired on the cheap. They do have ski and bike rentals, however, with low prices.

BIKING   Several outfitters on the main street, O'Higgins, rent bicycles by the hour and provide trail information and guided tours. Bicycle rentals run an average of $8 (£4.10) for a half-day. You can also just pedal around town, or take a pleasant, easy ride around the wooded peninsula. **Miropucón,** Fresia 415, Local 6 (© **45/444874;** contacto@miropucon.cl), offers 3- and 4-hour medium-difficulty bike tours to the Ojos de Caburgua.

CANOPY TOURS 🌟🌟   The newest available adventure for thrill-seekers, a canopy tour is much like a "flying fox," a swing through the treetops suspended by a cable and secured by a harness. Anybody can do this, and it is a great half-day adventure. Book your trip at **Spirit Exploraciones,** Palguin 323 (© **45/442481;** www.spiritexplora.com).

CLIMBING THE VOLCANO 🌟🌟🌟   An ascent of Volcán Villarrica is perhaps the most thrilling excursion available here—there's nothing like peering into this percolating, fuming crater—but you've got to be in decent shape to tackle it. The excursion begins early in the morning, and the long climb requires crampons and ice axes. Note that the descent has traditionally been a combination of walking and sliding on your behind in the snow, but so many have done this that the naturally formed "luge" run is now enormous, slippery, and fast, and people have been hurting themselves on it lately—so be cautious. Volcán Villarrica is perpetually on the verge of exploding, and sometimes trips are called off until the rumbling quiets down. Tour companies that offer this climb are **Politur** and **Sol y Nieve** (see above). The average cost is $140 to $250 (£72–£128), depending on group size, and includes transfers, entrance fee, insurance, equipment, and guides, but not lunch.

FISHING 🎣 You can pick up your fishing license at the visitor center at Caupolicán and Brasil. Guided fishing expeditions typically go to the Trancura River or the Liucura River. See a list of outfitters above for information, or try **Off Limits,** O'Higgins 560 (© **45/441210** or 9/949-2481).

FOUR TRACK TOURS   These guided tours on four-wheel motorcycles are for people who either can't or don't want to walk through nature, and they are available in any kind of weather. Tours lead riders through native forests and, on clear days, to points with impressive volcano views. Only one company offers this excursion (about $12/£6.15 per hr.): **Ronco Track,** O'Higgins 615 (© **45/441801;** roncotrack@hotmail. com).

GOLFING 🎣 Pucón's private 18-hole **Península de Pucón** golf course is open to the playing public. For information, call © **45/443965,** ext 409. The cost is $42 (£22) for 18 holes. This is really the only way to get onto the private—and exclusive— peninsula that juts into the lake, by the way.

HIKING 🎣🎣 The two national parks, Villarrica and Huerquehue, and the Cañi nature reserve offer hiking trails that run from easy to difficult. An average excursion with an outfitter to Huerquehue, including transportation and a guided hike, costs about $22 (£11) per person. By far the best short-haul day hikes in the area are at Huerquehue and the Cañi nature reserve.

HORSEBACK RIDING 🎣 Half- and full-day horseback rides are offered throughout the area, including in the Villarrica National Park and the Liucura Valley. The **Centro de Turismo Huepil** (© **9/643-2673**) offers day and multiday horseback rides, including camping or a stay at the Termas de Huife, from a small ranch about a half-hour from Pucón; you'll need to make a reservation beforehand. All-inclusive multiple-day trips cost about $100 (£51) per person, per day. Beginning riders are given an introductory course in the corral before setting out. Contact a tour agency for day rides in Villarrica Park, which go for about $60 (£31) for a full day. Tour agencies will also organize rides that leave from the **Rancho de Caballos** (© **45/441575**), near the Palguín thermal baths. If you're driving, the Rancho is at 30km (19 miles) on the Ruta International toward Argentina.

RAFTING 🎣 Rafting season runs from September to April, although some areas might be safe to descend only from December to March. The two classic descents in the area are the 14km (8¾-mile) Trancura Alto, rated at Class III to IV, and the somewhat gentler Trancura Bajo, rated at Class II to III. Both trips are very popular and can get crowded in the summer. The rafting outfitter **Trancura** (see above) also offers an excursion rafting the more technical Maichin River, which includes a barbecue lunch. **Sol y Nieve** also offers rafting. The 3-hour rafting trip on the Trancura Alto costs an average of $37 (£19); the 3-hour Trancura Bajo costs an average of $24 (£12).

SKIING   The **Centro Esquí Villarrica** gives skiers the opportunity to schuss down a smoking volcano—not something you can do every day. There's a sizable amount of terrain here, and it's all open-field skiing, but, regrettably, the owners rarely open more than two of the five chairs, due to nothing else but laziness. You'll need to take a chair lift to the main lodge, which means that nonskiers, too, can enjoy the lovely views from the lodge's outdoor deck. There's a restaurant, child-care center, and store. The Centro has a ski school and ski equipment rental; there are slightly cheaper rentals from **Aguaventura, Sol y Nieve,** and **Trancura,** among other businesses along O'Higgins. Lift ticket prices vary but average about $36 (£18). Most tour companies offer transport to and from the resort. For more information, contact one of the tour operators above.

WHERE TO STAY

Pucón is chock-full of lodging options, the majority of which are *cabañas,* self-service cabins for visitors who desire more independence. Reservations are essential if visiting during the high season from December to the end of February; prices during this period nearly double at some hotels, so price-conscious travelers would be wise to visit outside these dates. Rates below show high and low season rates. Private parking or ample street parking is available and free for all hotels. Please note that the Hotel del Lago, the town's 5-star hotel, burned to the ground in 2007, and the owners plan to rebuild and open again in 2009.

For inexpensive lodging, these hostels are pleasant and more "adult" than "youth": **¡école!** ⭐ at General Urrutia 592 (ℂ/fax **45/441675;** www.ecole.cl) has small but clean shared and private rooms, with beds blanketed with goose-down comforters for $32 to $48 (£16–£25) for a double; they also have a restaurant (p. 424) with excellent breakfasts. The showers are so-so, but the price is nice. **Refugio Peninsula Bed & Breakfast** ⭐ at Clemente Holazpfel 11 (ℂ **45/443398;** www.refugiopeninsula.cl) is a hostel with a central location near the beach and restaurants, shared rooms with private bathrooms ($24/£12 per person), and two doubles for $56 (£29) per night.

Hotel Antumalal ⭐⭐⭐ *(Finds)*   The minute you arrive here, you know you've come upon something special. Perhaps it is the Antumalal's Bauhaus design and the lush gardens that reach down to a private beach, or perhaps it's the sumptuous view of the sunset on Lake Villarrica seen nightly through the hotel's picture windows or from its wisteria-roofed deck. Either way, this is simply one of the most lovely and unique hotels in Chile. Low slung and literally built into a rocky slope, the Antumalal was designed to blend with its natural environment. The lounge features walls made of glass and slabs of araucaria wood, goat skin rugs, tree-trunk lamps, and couches built of iron and white rope. It's retro-chic, and the friendly, personal attention provided by the staff heightens a sense of intimacy with your surroundings. The rooms are all the same size, and they are very comfortable, with panoramic windows that look out onto the same gorgeous view, as well as honey-wood walls, a fireplace, and a big, comfortable bed. The hotel's restaurant serves some of the best cuisine in Pucón.

Camino Pucón-Villarrica, Km 2. ℂ **45/441011.** Fax 45/441013. www.antumalal.com. 16 units. $224 (£115) double. Rates include full breakfast. AE, DC, MC, V. **Amenities:** Exquisite restaurant; bar; kidney-shaped outdoor pool; tennis court; room service; massage; laundry service. *In room:* Hair dryer, safe.

Hotel Huincahue ⭐⭐ *(Finds)*   If you like to be in the center of town, steps from all the shops and restaurants, in a quiet and sophisticated setting, then this is your best bet. This newer hotel sits right on the main plaza and has an elegant homey feel to it. From the cozy lobby lounge with a fireplace and adjoining library to the peaceful pool in the lovely garden, this place feels more like a private mansion than a hotel. Rooms have pleasant beige carpets, and wrought iron–and-wood furniture, and a few have spectacular views of the volcano (room no. 202 is best). Second-floor rooms have small balconies. The marble bathrooms are large and many have windows as well. On busy weekends, some rooms are loud due to partygoers in the plaza.

Pedro de Valdivia 375. ©/fax **45/443540** or 442728. www.hotelhuincahue.cl. 20 units. $163–$178 (£84–£91) double. Rates include continental breakfast. AE, MC, V. **Amenities:** Restaurant; bar; lovely outdoor pool; room service; massage; babysitting; laundry service. *In room:* TV.

Monte Verde Hotel & Cabañas &&& *Kids*   Built in 2003 and tastefully designed using nearly every kind of wood available in the area (including recycled alerce), this six-room hotel is located about 6km (3¾ miles) from Villarrica, meaning you'll need a taxi or rental car to get here. The hotel and *cabañas* are perched on a hill to afford views of the volcano and the lake. The distance from town means no summer crowds from December to February. All rooms are decorated differently; four have king-size beds and all but one have private balconies with lake views. The bathrooms are decorated with old-fashioned sinks and bathtubs obtained from a turn-of-the-20th-century hotel in Villarrica. Attentive service and a complimentary bottle of red wine upon arrival are welcoming touches. There is also a cozy lounge with wood-burning fireplace and board games; during the high season, there are kayaks and boats available for guest use at the beach below and an outdoor pool, whirlpool, and hot tub.

Camino Villarrica-Pucón Km 18. © **45/441351.** Fax 45/443132. www.monteverdepucon.cl. 6 units, 14 *cabañas*. $67–$110 (£34–£56) double; $85–$190 (£43–£97) *cabaña*. Rates include buffet breakfast. AE, DC, MC, V. **Amenities:** Lounge; room service. *In room:* Kitchenette, TV.

Villarrica Park Lake Hotel &&   Luxurious and expansive, this property strives to be the best in southern Chile. It has only 70 rooms, but it feels like a big corporate hotel, with its large lobby and aloof but polite staff. Extra-wide doors made of local wood lead into comfortable and spacious modern rooms, all with sliding French doors that open up onto a balcony with a view of the lake. The marble bathrooms come with tub/shower combinations and heated towel racks. The spa has an exquisite selection of facials and body-work offerings. This is an excellent base for travelers who prefer large, full-service hotels, although you'd be well advised to book way in advance, as it occasionally fills up with corporate retreat groups for days at a time. Always request promotional rates when making your reservations.

Camino Pucón–Villarrica Km 13. © **45/450000.** Fax 45/450202. www.villarricaparklakehotel.cl. 70 units. $320 (£164) double; from $400 (£205) suite. AE, DC, MC, V. **Amenities:** Restaurant; bar; lounge; heated indoor pool; health club and spa; limited watersports equipment; concierge; business center; salon; room service; massage; laundry service; dry cleaning. *In room:* TV, fax, high-speed Internet, minibar, hair dryer, iron, safe.

Cabañas

Cabañas are independent cabins that come with a kitchen or kitchenette. Travelers spending a few days or more, or who have children or wish to cook occasionally, will find *cabañas* a tempting option. Here are a few of the best. **Cabañas Ruca Malal** & at O'Higgins 770 (©/fax **45/442297;** www.rucamalal.cl) are custom-made, cozy cabins within walking distance to shops and restaurants, and they have an outdoor pool and sauna. **Almoni del Lago Resort** && has a superb location on the lapping shore of Lake Villarrica (Camino Villarrica-Pucón, Km 19; © **45/442304;** www.almoni.cl; $43–$92/£22–£47 *cabaña* for two). The *cabañas* are a 5-minute drive from town and come with an outdoor pool, tennis courts, and barbecues.

WHERE TO DINE

Patagonia, Fresia 223 (© **45/443165**), or **Patagonia Plaza,** Pedro de Valdivia 333 (© **45/444715**), are good spots for a hot chocolate and a piece of cake on a rainy day or an ice cream in the summer. **Café de la "P,"** Lincoyán 395 (© **45/442018;** www. cafedelap.com), has a menu with sandwiches, cakes, coffee drinks, and cocktails. It's a nice place to unwind with a drink in the evening and is open until 4am in the summer.

Antumalal ☆☆ *Moments* INTERNATIONAL   The Hotel Antumalal's restaurant serves some of the most flavorful cuisine in Pucón, with creative dishes that are well prepared and seasoned with herbs from an extensive garden. In fact, most of the vegetables used here are local and organic; the milk comes from the family's own dairy farm. Try a thinly sliced beef carpaccio followed by chicken stuffed with smoked salmon, grilled local trout, or any one of the pastas. There's a good selection of wine and an ultracool cocktail lounge for an after-dinner drink (but it's tiny and not a "happening" spot). It's worth a visit for the view of Lake Villarrica alone.

Camino Pucón–Villarrica, Km 2. © **45/441011.** Fax 45/441013. Reservations recommended. Main courses $9–$11 (£4.60–£5.65). AE, DC, MC, V. Daily noon–4pm and 8–10pm.

¡école! VEGETARIAN ☆ *Value*   This is a predominantly vegetarian restaurant serving calzones, quiche, pizza, burritos, chop suey, and more. Sandwiches come on homemade bread, and breakfast is very good and inexpensive, featuring American breakfast as well as Mexican and Chilean. There are also fresh salads, and a lovely outdoor patio where you can dine under the grapevine in good weather. The service is slow and disorganized, and they usually offer a shorter menu during the winter.

General Urrutia 592. ©/fax **45/441675.** Main courses $6–$8 (£3.10–£4.10). MC, V. Daily 8am–11pm.

La Maga ☆☆ URUGUAYAN STEAKHOUSE   La Maga is undoubtedly the best parrilla (steakhouse) in town. The restaurant originated in the beach town of Punta del Este, Uruguay, and the food is excellent, especially the meat, chicken, and fish grilled on the giant barbecue on the patio. Order a bottle of wine and a large fresh salad and people-watch through large picture windows overlooking the street. Try the grilled salmon with capers if you're in the mood for fish. But, really, the best cuts here are the beef filets, known as *lomos,* served with mushrooms, Roquefort, or pepper sauce. The *bife de chorizo* (sirloin) is thick and tender. For dessert, the flan here stands out.

Fresia 125. © **45/444277.** Main courses $7–$10 (£3.60–£6.10). AE, MC, V. Daily noon–4pm and 7pm–midnight.

Viva Perú! ☆ *Kids* PERUVIAN   This Peruvian restaurant is a favorite hangout for locals, offering warm, personalized service and tasty cuisine. For solo travelers, there is bar seating, and there is a patio with a volcano view. The restaurant specializes in ceviche and seafood *picoteos* (appetizer platters), which are excellent accompaniment to a frosty pisco sour. Daily fixed-price lunch specials include a mixed salad, entree (steamed or grilled fish, pork loin, or chicken), and coffee for about $8 (£4.10). The restaurant offers one of the few kids' menus in the area. Try the sugary-sweet *suspiro limeño,* a creamy Peruvian traditional dessert.

Lincoyan 372. ©/fax **45/444025.** Main courses $9–$12 (£4.60–£6.15). AE, DC, MC, V. Daily noon–2am.

PUCON AFTER DARK

At press time, Pucón's **casino** has been rebuilt following a fire that gutted the Hotel del Lago and Casino; the new casino is at the same location at Miguel Ansorena 121. For bars, **El Bosque,** 524 O'Higgins (©/fax **45/444025**), is a popular local hangout open from 6pm until around 3am Tuesday through Sunday; it has Internet and a good fusion cuisine menu. **Mamas & Tapas** at O'Higgins 597 (©/fax **45/449002**) has long been one of the most popular bars in Pucón. It gets packed in the summer and has excellent music, even with DJs during peak season.

HOT SPRINGS OUTSIDE OF PUCON

All the volcanic activity in the region means there are plenty of *baños termales,* or hot springs, that range from rustic rock pools to full-service spas with massage and saunas. The two spas below are my favorites.

Termas de Huife 🐾   Nestled in a narrow valley on the shore of the Liucura River, Huife operates as a full-service health spa for day visitors, and there are attractive cabins for overnight stays. The complex features two large, soothing outdoor thermal pools and a cold-water pool, as well as private thermal bathtubs, individual whirlpools, and massage salons. There are two- and four-person cabañas with wood-burning stoves and Japanese-style, sunken showers and baths that run thermal water—but the price is expensive for Chilean cabin lodging. Because these *termas* are closer to Pucón, they receive many visitors during the summer.

Road to Huife, 33km (20 miles) east of Pucón. ©/fax **45/441222.** www.termashuife.cl. 10 units. $188–$240 (£96–£123) double. Day-use fee $9 (£4.60) adults, children 10 and under free. AE, DC, MC, V. Thermal baths daily 9am–8pm year-round. **Amenities:** Restaurant; cafeteria; 3 outdoor pools; exercise room; Jacuzzi; sauna; game room; massage. *In room:* TV, minibar, safe.

Termas Geométricas 🐾🐾🐾 *Finds*   I can't stop raving about these hot springs. They are a 40-minute drive from Pucón (near Coñaripe), but if you have the time, put these *termas* on your itinerary because they are the best in Chile. Designed by the architect of the Explora hotels, there are more than a dozen pools built of handsome gray slate tiles in a lush, jungle-draped ravine, each one linked by a winding, terra cotta–colored boardwalk. The style is minimalist and decidedly Japanese, with touches such as sinks with stream-fed taps, and changing rooms with grass roofs—utterly relaxing and enjoyable day or night, winter or summer. A small restaurant serves coffee and snacks; picnic lunches are allowed during the winter only, and alcohol is prohibited. It's not cheap ($20/£10 to enter), but it's money well spent. Check their website for a map, or ask any tour company to take you here.

12km (7½ miles) from Coñaripe on the road to Palguín. © **2/214-1214** or 9/442-5420. Fax 2/214-1147. www.termas geometricas.cl. $20 (£10) adults, $10 (£5.10) children under 15. Rate includes towel. No credit cards. Thermal baths daily 10am–10pm summer, 11am–8pm rest of year. **Amenities:** Cafe.

NATURAL ATTRACTIONS OUTSIDE OF PUCON
PARQUE NACIONAL HUERQUEHUE

Parque Nacional Huerquehue boasts the best short-haul hike in the area, the **Sendero Los Lagos.** This 12,500-hectare (30,875-acre) park opens as a steeply walled amphitheater draped in matted greenery and crowned by a forest of lanky araucaria trees. There are a handful of lakes here; the first you come upon is Lago Tinquilco, upon whose shore sits a tiny, ramshackle village built by German colonists in the early 1900s.

GETTING THERE & BASICS   The park is 35km (22 miles) from Pucón. JAC buses have daily service to the park (several times per day depending on season), and most tour companies offer minivan transportation. If you're driving your own car, head out of Pucón on O'Higgins toward Lago Caburga until you see the sign for Huerquehue that branches off to the right. From here it's a rutted, dirt road that can be difficult to manage when muddy. Conaf charges $5 (£2.55) for adults and $1 (50p) for kids to enter, and is open daily from 8:30am to 6pm.

VALDIVIA ★★

839km (520 miles) S of Santiago

Valdivia is a university town on the edge of a river delta, about a 20-minute drive from the coast. It has more charm than Temuco or Puerto Montt, yet Valdivia receives mixed reviews from visitors. I personally enjoy this historic town and find that there is quite a bit to do and see in 1 day. Parts of Valdivia are indeed ugly, with a mess of architectural styles—yet many lovely, old German immigrant homes line the waterfront, and a lively market where visitors can watch fishmongers peddle their catch of the day while pelicans, cormorants, and gigantic sea lions beg for scraps. There are also trips around the delta. If you are in Pucón for several days, consider a quick visit here or an overnight stay.

Valdivia has suffered attacks, floods, fires, and the disastrous earthquake (the strongest ever recorded) and tsunami of 1960 that nearly drowned the city under 3m (10 ft.) of water. During World War II, Valdivia's German colonists were blacklisted, ruining the economy. So if Valdivia looks a little weary—well, it's understandable. There are tours here to visit the tiny towns and ancient forts at the mouth of the bay that protected the city from seafaring intruders.

ESSENTIALS
Getting There

BY PLANE   Valdivia's **Aeródromo Pichoy** (© 63/272295), is about 32km (20 miles) northeast of the city. **LAN Express** (© 600/526-2000; www.lan.com) has two daily flights from Santiago, one daily flight to Concepción, two weekly flights to Temuco, and one weekly flight to Puerto Montt. A **taxi** to town costs about $18 (£9.25), or you can catch a ride on one of **Transfer Valdivia's** (© 63/225533) minibuses for $5 (£2.55).

BY BUS   The bus terminal (© 63/212212) is at Anwandter and Muñoz, and nearly every bus company passes through here; there are multiple daily trips from Pucón and Santiago. The average cost for a ticket from Santiago to Valdivia is $36 (£18); from Pucón to Valdivia, it is $4 (£2.05).

BY CAR   From the Pan-American Highway, take Ruta 205 and follow the signs for Valdivia. A car is not really necessary in Valdivia, as most attractions can be reached by boat, foot, or taxi. It's about a 2-hour drive from Pucón, 1½ hours from Temuco, and 3 hours from Puerto Montt.

SPECIAL EVENTS

The city hosts a grand yearly event, the **Verano en Valdivia,** with several weeks of festivities that begin in January, culminating with the **Noche Valdiviana** on the third Saturday in February. On this evening, hundreds of floating candles and festively decorated boats fill the Valdivia River, and there is a fireworks display. Valdivia is packed during this time and hotel reservations are essential.

WHAT TO SEE & DO

Elisabeth Lajtonyi at **Outdoors Chile** (© 63/287833; www.outdoors-chile.com) can plan your Valdivia itinerary, including hotels, transfers, and personalized sightseeing tours.

BOAT TRIPS   Valdivia's myriad waterways make for an enjoyable way to explore the region, and there are a variety of destinations and boating options that leave from the pier Muelle Schuster at the waterfront, including yachts, catamarans, and an antique steamer. Tours are in full swing during the summer, and although there's limited service during the off-season, it is possible for a group to hire a launch for a private trip. The most interesting journeys sail through the **Carlos Anwanter Nature Sanctuary** to the **San Luis de Alba de Cruces Fort** and to **Isla Mancera** and **Corral** to visit other 17th-century historic forts; both tours run about 5 to 6 hours round-trip and usually include meals.

Embarcaciones Bahía (© 63/348727; sergiosalgado60@yahoo.es) operates throughout the year with quick trips around Isla Teja ($6/£3.10 per person; children under 10 ride free), and tours to Isla Mancera and Corral can be arranged during the off-season with a negotiated price or when there are enough passengers. Other trips to Isla Mancera and Corral are offered by **Orión III** (©/fax **63/247896;** hetours@telsur.cl), which also includes a stop at the Isla Huapi Natural Park (also a Convention Center; www.islahuapi.cl); the price is $28 (£14) for adults, $15 (£7.70) for children ages 3 to 12. Prices include the trip, lunch on Isla Huapi, and afternoon tea on board. By far the most luxurious is the **Catamarán Marqués de Mancera** (© **63/249191;** www.marquesdemancera.cl), which offers Isla Mancera and Corral tours, with lunch and snacks included, and evening dinner cruises (only specially organized for large groups); both cost from $20 (£10) per person.

OTHER ATTRACTIONS

The bustling **Mercado Fluvial** 🎭🎭 at Muelle Schuster (Av. Prat at Maipú) is the principal attraction in Valdivia; kids especially love to see the array of fish spread out by fishmongers and watch lanky pelicans and enormous sea lions bark for handouts.

A block up from the waterfront, turn right on Yungay and head south until the street changes into **General Lagos** at San Carlos, where you'll find stately, historic homes built by German immigrants between 1840 and 1930. At General Lagos 733 is the **Centro Cultural El Austral** 🎭, commonly known as the Casa Hoffman for the Thater-Hoffman family, who occupied the home from 1870 until 1980. It's open Tuesday through Sunday from 10am to 1pm and 4 to 7pm; admission is free (© **63/213658**). The first floor of this handsome building has been furnished to re-create the interior as it would have looked during the 19th century. At the junction of General Lagos and Yerbas Buenas, you'll find the **Torreón Los Canelos,** a 1781 defensive tower built to protect the southern end of the city—but if you're strapped for time, forget it.

Across the bridge in the neighborhood known as Isla Teja, visitors will find the splendid history museum, the **Museo Histórico y Antropológico Mauricio van de Maele** 🎭🎭 (© **63/212872;** Mon–Sun 10am–1pm and 2–8pm Dec 15–Mar 15, Tues–Sun 10am–1pm and 2–6pm the rest of the year; admission $2/£1 adults, 50¢/25p children under 13). To get there, cross the Pedro de Valdivia bridge, walk up a block, turn left, and continue for half a block. The museum is housed in the grand family home of Karl Anwanter, brewery owner and vociferous supporter and leader of German immigrants. The museum is a collection of antiques, photos, letters, everyday objects, and more culled from local well-to-do families, historical figures, Mapuche Indians, and Spanish conquistadors. Next door is the **Museo de Arte Moderno** 🎭 (© **63/221968;** www.macvaldivia.uach.cl), one of Chile's most important modern art museums, with rotating displays. Leaving the museum, turn right and continue north on Los Laureles until you reach the **Universidad Austral de Chile.** Once inside the campus, the road veers right; follow it and the signs to the **Jardín Botánico** 🎭🎭, a lovely botanical garden created in 1957.

WHERE TO STAY

Airesbuenos International Hostel ⭐ *Value* This beautiful house is a historical monument in Valdivia and dates back to 1890. The young and friendly owner, Lionel Brossi, has meticulously restored the entire house and oversees the day-to-day operation of the hostel. Special touches can be found everywhere, which is rare when it comes to budget accommodations. A vintage staircase leads to 11 rooms of varying sizes, all with beautiful (and original) hardwood floors. Some of the rooms have bunk beds for backpackers; the bathroom in the hallway is clean and spacious. The five rooms with private bathrooms are pleasant and bright; the front room even has a balcony with river views. The hotel is located about a 15-minute walk from the market and most restaurants. A common kitchen is available for cooking, and there's a book exchange.

General Lagos 1036, Valdivia. ©/fax 63/206304. www.airesbuenos.cl. 11 units. $15 (£7.70) per person in a shared room; $40 (£21) double with private bathroom; all rates include breakfast. AE, DC, MC, V. **Amenities:** Lounge; Internet.

Hotel Naguilán ⭐ *Moments* About a 20-minute walk from the edge of downtown, the Hotel Naguilán boasts a pretty riverfront location and attractive accommodations. The hotel is housed in a converted 1890 shipbuilding edifice. All rooms face the Río Valdivia and the evening sunset; from here it's possible to watch waterfowl and colorful tugs and fishing skiffs motor by. The rooms are divided into 15 newer (superior) units in a detached building and 17 (standard) units in an older wing with a more dated decor. The newer terrace units sit directly on the riverbank and feature contemporary floral design in rich colors, classic furniture, ample bathrooms, and a terrace patio. The hotel has a private dock for guests to board excursion boats, and the hotel restaurant, serving international cuisine, has picture windows with a view of the river.

General Lagos 1927, Valdivia. © 63/212851. Fax 63/219130. www.hotelnaguilan.com. 32 units. $94 (£48) standard double (older units); $109 (£56) double (newer units); from $144 (£74) suite. AE, DC, MC, V. **Amenities:** Restaurant; bar; outdoor pool; game room; concierge; room service; laundry service. *In room:* TV, minibar.

Puerta del Sur ⭐ *Overrated* *Kids* This quiet resort just across the bridge on Isla Teja offers all the amenities a guest would expect from a full-service hotel, but its drab decor and mediocre service don't quite live up to expectations. However, it does boast a gem of a location on the shore of the Nature Sanctuary. It's about a 7-minute walk to downtown, but you'll feel miles away. All rooms come with views of the river and are fairly comfortable; double superiors are roomy, as are the sparkling bathrooms. The suites have giant, triangular picture windows, but are not much larger than double superiors.

Outside, a path winds past the pool and whirlpool to a private dock where guests can be picked up for boat tours or launch one of the hotel's canoes. There are also bikes available for guests at no extra charge.

Los Lingues 950, Isla Teja, Valdivia. © 63/224500 or 2/633-5101 for reservations (in Santiago). Fax 63/211046. www.hotelpuertadelsur.com. 40 units. $150 (£77) double, breakfast included; from $250 (£128) suite. AE, DC, MC, V. **Amenities:** Restaurant; bar; large outdoor pool; tennis court; Jacuzzi; sauna; game room; room service; babysitting; laundry service. *In room:* TV.

WHERE TO DINE

For an inexpensive meal, the **Municipal Market** at the waterfront at Yungay and Libertad has several simple restaurants with fresh seafood and Chilean specialties. Valdivia's two traditional cafes, Café Haussman and Entre Lagos, are excellent spots for lunch. **Café Haussman,** O'Higgins 394 (© **63/202219;** Mon–Sat 8am–9pm), is a tiny, old-fashioned diner that serves *crudos* (steak tartare), beer on tap, and sandwiches amid local color. **Entre Lagos,** Pérez Rosales 640 (© **63/212039;** daily 9am–10pm), is famous in Chile for its chocolate and marzipan, and now it serves equally delicious crepes, juicy sandwiches, heavenly cakes, and cappuccinos.

La Calesa ⭐ *Finds* PERUVIAN/INTERNATIONAL   Owned and operated by a Peruvian family, the cozy La Calesa features spicy cuisine served in the old Casa Kaheni, a gorgeous, 19th-century home with high ceilings, wood floors, and antique furnishings. The menu features Peruvian fare along with several international dishes. Standouts include grilled beef tenderloin in a cilantro sauce; *ají de gallina,* a spicy chicken and garlic stew with rice; or any of the nightly specials. The pisco sours are very good, as is the wine selection.

Yungay 735. © **63/225437.** Dinner reservations recommended. Main courses $8–$12 (£4.10–£6.15). Mon–Fri noon–4pm and 8pm–midnight; Sat 8pm–midnight.

New Orleans INTERNATIONAL   This is Valdivia's most popular restaurant, tucked away on a side street a few streets in from the river, and it seems to always be busy. There's a pleasant, if crowded, patio and a charming dining room with more spacious seating. The food here is consistently good and fresh and the menu changes often. Main courses often include pastas, grilled salmon or tuna, chicken, and steak. This is a loud, boisterous place, often filled with families with children early in the evening. Later, the atmosphere is more publike.

Esmeralda 682. © **63/218771.** Dinner reservations recommended. Main courses $9–$13 (£4.60–£6.65). AE, DC, MC, V. Mon–Fri noon–4pm and 7pm–midnight; Sat 5pm–midnight.

FRUTILLAR ⭐⭐
58km (36 miles) S of Osorno, 46km (29 miles) N of Puerto Montt

Frutillar offers a rich example of the architecture popular with German immigrants to the Lago Llanquihue area, and it is situated to take advantage of the dynamite view of the Osorno and Calbuco volcanoes. The town is smaller and quieter than Puerto Varas, and is farther away from the national park, but all tour operators can plan excursions around the area from here (see "Outdoor Activities" under "Puerto Varas," below). Frutillar is divided into the rather scrappy "high" area, which you'll drive straight through, and the "low" area along the lakeshore, where visitors will find a good supply of attractive hotels and bed-and-breakfasts.

ESSENTIALS
GETTING THERE   For general information, see "Puerto Varas," below. For local bus service, frequent, inexpensive buses leave from the bus terminal in Puerto Montt; from Puerto Varas, take one of the small buses labeled FRUTILLAR that leave from the corner of Walker Martínez and San Bernardo.

By Taxi   Taxis will take you to Frutillar for around $18 to $25 (£9.25–£13), depending on whether you're coming from Puerto Varas, Puerto Montt, or the airport. Agree on a price with your driver before leaving.

By Car   From Puerto Montt or Puerto Varas, head north on the Panamericana Highway and look for signs for Frutillar. Remember to continue down to Frutillar "Bajo" (along the lakeshore) instead of getting off at Frutillar "Alto."

VISITOR INFORMATION   The **Oficina de Información Turística** is located along the coast at Costanera Philippi (© **65/421080**); it's open January through March daily from 8:30am to 1pm and 2 to 9pm. The **Oficina de Turismo Municipal** is open year-round and can be found at Av. Bernardo Philippi 753 (✆ **65/421685;** daily 8am–1pm and 2–5:30pm).

EXPLORING FRUTILLAR

The two most-visited attractions in town are the **Museo de la Colonización Alemana de Frutillar** ★★ and the **Reserva Forestal Edmundo Winkler.** The museum (✆ **65/421142**) is located where Arturo Prat dead-ends at Calle Vicente Pérez Rosales. Admission is $2.50 (£1.30) adults, 85¢ (45p) children 12 and under; it's open April to November, Monday through Sunday from 10am to 1pm and 2 to 6pm, and December to March, from 10am to 1pm and 3 to 8pm. It features a collection of 19th-century antiques, clothing, and artifacts gathered from various German immigrant families in the area. It's quite interesting if you have 30 minutes to spare.

The Reserva is run by the University of Chile and features a trail winding through native forest, giving visitors an idea of what the region looked like before immigrants went timber-crazy and chopped down a sizable percentage of trees in this region. It's open year-round, daily from 10am to 7pm; admission costs $1.80 (90p) for adults and 80¢ for kids. To get there, you'll have to walk 1km (a half-mile) up to the park from the entrance at Calle Caupolican at the northern end of Avenida Philippi.

WHERE TO STAY

Private parking or ample street parking is available and free for all hotels. Hotels can arrange excursions in the area, or can put you in contact with a tour operator who does.

Hotel Ayacara ★★ *Finds* The Ayacara is a top choice in Frutillar, housed in a superbly renovated, 1910 antique home on the coast of Lago Llanquihue. The interior of the hotel is made of light wood and this, coupled with large, plentiful windows, translates into bright accommodations. The rooms come with comfy beds, crisp linens, wood headboards, country furnishings, and antiques brought from Santiago and Chiloé. The Capitán room is the largest and has the best view. An attractive dining area serves dinner during the summer, and there's a small, ground-level outdoor deck and a TV/video lounge. The staff can arrange excursions around the area; fly-fishing excursions are their specialty.

Av. Philippi 1215, Frutillar. ✆/fax **65/421550.** www.hotelayacara.cl. 8 units. $90–$105 (£46–£54) double; $100–$130 (£51–£67) Capitán double. Rates include breakfast. AE, DC, MC, V. **Amenities:** Restaurant; bar; tour desk. *In room:* TV.

Hotel & Cabañas Centinela ★★ *Moments* This hotel is located near Puerto Octay (a very small town next to Frutillar), at the tip of a peninsula, at the end of a tree-lined dirt road. The Centinela is a hidden gem with its own private beach, and it's a destination in itself considering that town is a long walk away. Originally built in 1914 as a bordello, it has long since been turned into a homey lodge with 12 rooms and 18 cabins. Rooms have thick Berber carpets, down comforters, and antique furnishings. The bathrooms vary in size, and are simple and clean. The downstairs living room has a beautiful fireplace. The restaurant serves excellent Chilean cuisine cooked by a well-known chef. This place exudes charm, not luxury; there's no spa but there's a rustic wood-fired hot tub. Six of the cabins sit right on the water's edge; request numbers 21 to 26 for the best views. The hotel's friendly staff can arrange fly-fishing expeditions and regional tours.

Península de Centinela, Km 5, Puerto Octay. ✆/fax **64/391326.** www.hotelcentinela.cl. 30 units. $115–$135 (£59–£69) double; from $110 (£56) *cabaña* for 4 people; $140 (£72) *cabaña* for 6 people. Rates include full breakfast. AE, DC, MC, V. **Amenities:** Restaurant; lounge; Jacuzzi; limited watersports equipment rental. *In room:* Fridge (in *cabañas* only).

WHERE TO DINE

You'll find better restaurants in Puerto Varas, and that town's proximity makes it feasible to plan on dining there. Otherwise, the traditional **Club Alemán** &, San Martín 22 (✆ **65/421249;** daily noon–4pm and 8pm–midnight), serves Chilean and German specialties. For smoked meats, game, and standard Chilean fare, try **El Ciervo,** San Martín 64 (✆ **65/420185;** daily noon–10pm).

PUERTO VARAS &&&

20km (12 miles) N of Puerto Montt; 996km (618 miles) S of Santiago

Puerto Varas is one of Chile's most charming villages, located on the shore of Lago Llanquihue. Like Pucón, it is an adventure travel hub, and it is also the gateway to the **Parque Nacional Vicente Pérez Rosales** (see "Parque Nacional Vicente Pérez Rosales & the Lake Crossing to Argentina," below). Unlike its neighbor Puerto Montt, 20 minutes away, it is a spruce little town, with wood-shingled homes, a rose-encircled plaza, a handsomely designed casino, and an excellent tourism infrastructure that provides all the necessary services for visitors without seeming touristy. It can get crowded during the summer months, but not as busy as Pucón; seemingly because of its distance from Santiago. The city was built by the sweat and tenacity of German immigrants, and later it became a port for goods being shipped from the Lago Llanquihue area to Puerto Montt (mostly timber). Today most of the area's middle- and uppermiddle-class residents call Puerto Varas home and commute to Puerto Montt and other surrounding places for work.

ESSENTIALS

BY PLANE **El Tepual** airport (✆ **65/294161**) is almost equidistant from Puerto Montt and Puerto Varas; it's about 25km (16 miles) from the airport to Puerto Varas. A taxi from the airport costs between $15 and $22 (£7.70–£11), or you can arrange a transfer with **ETM,** by either calling ahead or approaching their booth at the airport (✆ **32/294294**). They charge $20 (£10) for a car for a maximum of three people. Because there are fewer flights here, there normally are a few people waiting for a transfer, so the price can drop if there are others. **LAN Express** serves the El Tepual airport with nine daily flights from Santiago. **Sky Airline** (✆ **600/600-2828;** www.skyairline.cl) also has one daily flight to the El Tepual airport, and **Aerolíneas del Sur** (✆ **800/710-3000**) has two flights. Ask your hotel about a transfer shuttle, as many include one in their price.

BY BUS The following buses offer service to and from major cities in southern Chile, including Santiago: **Buses Cruz del Sur,** San Francisco 1317 and Walker Martínez 239 (✆ **65/236969** or 65/231925); and **Buses Tas Choapa,** Walker Martínez 320 (✆ **65/233831**). Buses **Tas Choapa** and the Argentine company **Andesmar,** Walker Martinez 320 (✆ **65/233831;** www.andesmar.com.ar), have service to Bariloche, Argentina (Tas Choapa Thurs–Sun; Andesmar on Mon, Wed, and Fri). **Bus Norte,** Walker Martínez 239 (✆ **65/236969**), has daily service to Bariloche.

BY CAR Puerto Varas is just 20km (12 miles) north of Puerto Montt and 88km (55 miles) south of Osorno via the Panamericana. There are two exits leading to Puerto Varas, and both deposit you downtown. To get to Frutillar, you need to get back on the Panamericana, go north, and take the exit for that town. There is about a 70¢ (35p) toll to enter the off-ramp, and another toll for about $1 (50p) to enter Puerto Montt.

GETTING AROUND   BY BUS   Buses Cruz del Sur offers transportation to Chiloé and nearly 20 daily trips to Puerto Montt, leaving from an office in Puerto Varas, at Walker Martínez 239 (© **65/236969** or 65/231925). There are also cheap minibuses that leave frequently from the corner of Del Salvador and San Pedro across from the pet shop, leaving you at the bus terminal in Puerto Montt. You'll also find minibuses at San Bernardo and Walker Martínez that go to Ensenada, Petrohué, and Lago Todos los Santos every day at 9:15 and 11am, 2 and 4pm. **Andina del Sud,** Del Salvador 72 (© **65/232811;** fax 65/232511; www.andinadelsud.com), has daily trips to this area as well.

BY CAR   Renting a car is perhaps the most enjoyable way (but also the most expensive) to see the surrounding area. Try **Adriazola Turismo Expediciones,** Santa Rosa 340 (© **65/233477;** adriazolaflyfishing@yahoo.com); **Hunter Rent a Car,** San José 130 (© **9/920-6888;** www.lstravel.com); **Jardinsa,** Mirador 135 (©/fax **65/235050;** www.jardinsa.cl); or **Travel Sur** at San José 261 (© **65/236000;** www.travelsur.com).

VISITOR INFORMATION   The **Casa del Turista** tourism office can be found at the pier on the shore (© **65/237956;** www.puertovaras.org) and is open daily from December to March from 9am to 10pm, and the rest of the year daily from 9am to 1:30pm and 3 to 7pm.

A WALK AROUND TOWN

Puerto Varas is compact enough to explore by foot, which is really the best way to view the wood-shingled homes built by German immigrants from 1910 until the mid-1930s. Eight of these homes have been declared national monuments, yet there are dozens more clustered mostly around the old train tracks reached by walking west on Del Salvador (heading away from downtown).

Take a quick tour by walking up San Francisco from Del Salvador and turning right on María Brunn, to view the neo-Romantic **Iglesia del Sagrado Corazón de Jesús,** built between 1915 and 1918 and modeled after the Marienkirche in the Black Forest. Continue along María Brunn and turn right on Purísima, where you'll encounter the **Gasthof Haus** (1930), the **Casa Yunge** (1932), the **Casa Horn** (1925), and finally **Casa Kaschel** at Del Salvador. More homes are concentrated near Dr. Giesseler and San Ignacio streets, reached by heading left on Del Salvador. Follow the road that borders the train tracks north and then east until it ends; then turn right and then left on Klenner, and follow it to Turismo Street to view the town's grandest historical home, **Casa Kuschel** (1910), now owned by American ecologist/philanthropist Doug Tompkins. A pleasant, easy walk (or short drive) extends up a dirt road from Casa Kuschel to **Parque Phillippi,** a lookout point with a sweeping view of Puerto Varas, the lake, and Mt. Osorno. Pick up a map at the visitor center.

OUTDOOR ACTIVITIES

TOUR OPERATORS & OUTFITTERS   Tour companies and outfitters have changed ownership over the past few years, but, thankfully, these companies have matured and I can now recommend several with a clear conscience. **Aquamotion Expediciones,** San Pedro 422 (© **65/232747;** fax 65/235938; www.aquamotion.cl), is a professional, competent operation with a bilingual staff that can organize trekking, rafting the Petrohué, horseback riding, canyoneering, photo safaris, journeys to Chiloé, and much more. They also custom-plan excursions and offer packages that include accommodations; and they are better than their competition, CTS, across the street. **Tranco Expediciones,** San Pedro 422 (©/fax **65/311311**), and Aquamotion

Expediciones both offer ascents of Volcano Osorno, for about $180 (£92) for two, which includes gear, lunch, and transportation. They also offer an alternative photography-oriented walk on the volcano for $73 (£37) per person.

For city tours and sightseeing tours around the Lake District, including trips to Frutillar, Puyehue, and Chiloé, try **Andina del Sud,** Del Salvador 72 (© **65/232811;** fax 65/232511; www.andinadelsud.com). Andina del Sud is the company that provides boat excursions on Lago Todos los Santos and the Chilean leg of the lake crossing to Argentina (for information, see "Parque Nacional Vicente Pérez Rosales & the Lake Crossing to Argentina," below).

For trips to Bariloche via road, contact **LS Travel,** San José 130, Puerto Varas (© **65/232424;** www.lstravel.com).

BOATING   From December to February, visitors may rent kayaks and canoes near the pier at the beach.

FISHING   Fly-fishing is one of the region's top outdoor activities, principally along the shores of Río Puelo, Río Maullín, and Río Petrohué. The most exclusive fishing expeditions are offered to guests at the Yan Kee Way Lodge (see "Where to Stay," below). There's also **Gray's Fly-Fishing Supplies,** which has two shops, at San José 192 and San Francisco 447 (© **65/310734;** www.grayfly.com). Gray's is a central hub for information, gear, and fishing licenses, and they can arrange day trips for river and lake fishing. Another good option for day trips is **Adriazola Fly Fishing,** Santa Rosa 340 (© **65/233477;** www.adriazolaflyfishing.com). The owner, Adrian, will custom-arrange any fly-fishing and trolling day tour with a bilingual guide. Both outfitters charge around $130 (£67) for a half-day and $300 (£154) for a full day (for two guests, including transportation, boat, lunch, wine, and fishing guides).

The exclusive, full-service **Río Puelo Lodge** (© **2/229-8533** in Santiago; fax 2/201-8042; www.riopuelolodge.cl) caters to fly-fishermen and hunters, but also offers horseback riding, boat rides, water-skiing, and more. The stately wood-and-stone lodge is tucked well into the backcountry on the shore of Lago Tagua Tagua, and it caters mainly to groups of guys who come to have fun in the backcountry. Packages average around $350 (£179) per person per day, including meals, open bar, guide, boats, horseback riding, trekking, and heated pool. Ask about discounts for groups.

HORSEBACK RIDING   **Campo Aventura,** San Bernardo 318, Puerto Varas (© **65/ 232910;** www.campo-aventura.com), offers year-round horseback riding leaving from a camp in Valle Cochamó, south of the national park. Campo Aventura has day and multiday trips, and Aquamotion also has day trips within the national park. Horseback riding through a forested area is a good rainy-day activity—just throw on a waterproof jacket and pants and let the horse walk through the mud for you.

KAYAKING   **Ko'Kayak,** a small outfit run by French kayak enthusiasts, is the best choice for kayaking both for the day and for multiday kayak/camping trips. They have a base in Ensenada at Km 40, but make a reservation at their main office at San José 320 (© **65/511648** or 9/310-5672; www.kokayak.com).

RAFTING   Few rivers in the world provide rafters with such stunning scenery as the Río Petrohué, whose frothy green waters begin at Lago Todos los Santos and end at the Reloncaví Estuary. Rafters are treated to towering views of the volcanoes Osorno and Puntiagudo. The river is Class III and suitable for nearly everyone, but there are a few rapids to negotiate with sudden bursts of heavy paddling, so timid travelers might consult with their tour agency before signing up. For rafting, go to **AlSur Expediciones,** Del Salvador 100 (© **65/232300;** www.alsurexpeditions.com).

WHERE TO STAY
Colonos del Sur ★★   The Colonos del Sur is a favorite among travelers to Puerto Varas and one of the nicer hotels in town. The hotel has the best panoramic views, cheery interiors, and an outdoor pool, and there is a lounge with sweeping views of town. You can't miss the hotel: a red-and-white building perched high on the hills just above downtown, with the giant sign HOTEL affixed to the roof. The corner rooms offer the best views so try to get one. At the Gran, the common areas are large and plentiful, and the interiors have an old-fashioned country decor. Doubles with a lake view are slightly larger, for the same price; others face the casino and are not much of a value. The large suites have wraparound windows and sparkling bathrooms.

Gran Hotel: Del Salvador 24, Puerto Varas. © 65/233369, or for reservations 65/233039. Fax 65/233394. www.colonosdelsur.cl. 60 units. $85–$110 (£44–£56) double; from $160 (£82) suite. AE, DC, MC, V. **Amenities:** Restaurant; lounge; bar; small indoor pool; sauna; room service; laundry service; dry cleaning. In room: TV, minibar, safe. Hotel Colonos de Sur Express: Estación 505. © 65/235555. Same website. $60 (£31) double. AE, DC, MC, V. **Amenities:** Restaurant; bar; outdoor pool; laundry. In room: TV.

The Guest House ★★ (Finds   Owned and operated by an American, this bed-and-breakfast is a more intimate lodging option, located in a quiet residential area about a 4-block walk from the plaza. The hotel is in a converted 1926 mansion, and like most bed-and-breakfast inns, the experience here is much like staying at a friend's home, with a comfy living area decorated with art that has been collected, not store bought, and a dining area with one long family-style table and a spacious kitchen (visitors have the opportunity to help out with the cooking, if they dine in). The rooms are not huge, but they have high ceilings, comfortable beds, and a simple, clean decor.

O'Higgins 608, Puerto Varas. © 65/231521. Fax 65/232240. www.vicki-johnson.com/guesthouse. 10 units. $70 (£36) double standard. Rates include continental breakfast. AE, MC, V. **Amenities:** Room service; laundry.

Hotel Bellavista ★★ (Value   Another waterfront hotel with gorgeous views, the Bellavista recently renovated all of its guest rooms, giving it the edge on its competitors. The hardwood floors here aren't as cozy as the carpeted rooms found in other hotels; however, the fresh linens and handsome earth-toned decor is quite sophisticated, and their restaurant and bar is an inviting place to while away an hour with a coffee and admire the view of the volcano. A cozy fireside lounge also makes for a cozy retreat. Four larger guest rooms face a forested cliff and would be ideal for those seeking a quiet room. The two-storied duplex apartments for five to six people, with panoramic views, for $143 (£73) a night are the best value.

Av. Vicente Pérez Rosales 60, Puerto Varas. © 65/232011. Fax 65/232013. www.hotelbellavista.cl. 50 units. $120 (£62) double. Rates include buffet breakfast. AE, DC, MC, V. **Amenities:** Restaurant; bar; lounge; sauna; laundry service. In room: TV, minibar, hair dryer, safe.

WHERE TO DINE
Puerto Varas has many good restaurants, but service generally moves at a snail's pace, so have patience. For a casual meal, try **Pim's** (San Francisco 712; © **65/233998**), a country/western-style pub with burgers, sandwiches, American-style appetizers such as buffalo wings, and salads. It is popular with locals and the nighttime ambience is very lively.

Another good spot for a drink at night is the **Barómetro** (San Pedro 418; © **65/236371**), with a wood-hewn bar and tree-trunk tables, a cozy atmosphere, and snacks.

Café Dane's ⚘ *Value* CHILEAN CAFE   It's often hard to get a table during the lunch hour in this popular local restaurant. Dane's serves inexpensive, hearty food in good-size portions, plus mouthwatering desserts. The interior is simple and unassuming, and much of the food is standard Chilean fare, all of it good or very good. The fried empanadas, especially shellfish, deserve special mention. Dane's serves a daily set menu for $6 (£3.10) Monday through Saturday and $9 (£4.60) on Sunday, as well as a special dish, or *plato del día*, for $3.50 (£1.80). It's less busy before 1pm or after 3pm. You can also buy food to go from the front counter.

Del Salvador 441. ℂ 65/232371. Main courses $3.50–$8 (£1.80–£4.10); sandwiches $2–$5.50 (£$1–£2.80). No credit cards. Daily 7:45am–1am.

Club de Yates ⚘⚘ SEAFOOD   Like its counterpart in Puerto Montt, this brand-new restaurant juts over the water, affording excellent views of Volcano Osorno and giving the sensation of being on a ship. The food here is better than the Puerto Montt branch, although there are better restaurants in town in terms of food quality. Club de Yates specializes in seafood, and the lengthy menu offers just about every kind of fish or shellfish cooked every way: grilled, sautéed, or fried, with sauces and your choice of a side dish. There are also good appetizers such as Parmesan razor clams and occasionally *locos,* or abalone, and they serve enough meat dishes to satisfy those who aren't in the mood for seafood. The dining area is semiformal, with high ceilings and an airy atmosphere. The Club de Yates closes occasionally for private lunches for cruise-ship passengers.

Santa Rosa 161. ℂ 65/232000. www.clubdeyates.cl/puertovaras.asp. Main courses $7–$13 (£3.60–£6.65). AE, DC, MC, V. Daily noon–4pm and 8pm–midnight.

La Cucina d'Alessandro ⚘⚘ PIZZA/PASTA   The authentic, fresh pastas and thin-crust pizzas at this restaurant are made by an Italian family who immigrated to Puerto Varas only a few years ago, bringing with them Italian gastronomy know-how. The pizzas are what really shine here, and their special two-for-one pizza offer from 4 to 8pm every day makes this restaurant a good value. It has a cozy atmosphere and is housed in a typical, shingled home across from the beach. There are a few wooden tables that are large enough for groups of six to eight diners. It's a 15-minute walk from downtown. Apart from pasta and pizza, La Cucina has good seafood dishes and is open all day. It's a tiny restaurant, so make reservations for dinner and come early for lunch.

Av. Costanera. ℂ 65/310583. Main courses $5–$9 (£2.55–£4.60). No credit cards. Daily noon–midnight.

Mediterráneo ⚘ *Moments* INTERNATIONAL   Boasting an excellent location right on the Costanera, this new restaurant has a glass-enclosed terrace with water views. The cheerful orange tablecloths add to its bright ambience, as does the pleasant waitstaff. Mediterráneo is known for its imaginative dishes (think Chilean-Mediterranean fusion) that change weekly. The owners use mostly local produce, including spices bought from the Mapuche natives. Here, you'll find big fresh salads mixing such ingredients as endives, Swiss cheese, anchovies, olives, and local mushrooms. For the main course, the venison here is excellent, served with a tasty zucchini gratin. For dessert, try one of the yummy fruit sorbets.

Santa Rosa 068, corner of Portales. ℂ 65/237268. AE, DC, MC, V. Main courses $4–$25 (£2.05–£13). Apr–Nov daily noon–3:30pm and 7:30–11pm; Dec–Mar daily 10am–2am.

PARQUE NACIONAL VICENTE PEREZ ROSALES & THE LAKE CROSSING TO ARGENTINA ★★

About 65km (40 miles) from Puerto Varas is Chile's oldest national park, Vicente Pérez Rosales, founded in 1926. It covers an area of 251,000 hectares (620,000 acres), incorporating the park's centerpiece, Lake Todos los Santos, and the Saltos de Petrohué cascades and three volcanoes: Osorno, Tronador, and Puntiagudo. The park is open daily from December to February 8:30am to 8pm, March to November 8:30am to 6:30pm; admission to the Saltos de Petrohué is $3.30 (£1.70) adults and $2.50 (£1.30) kids. Conaf's **information center** (© 65/486115) can be found toward the end of the dirt road.

By far the most popular excursions here are boat rides across the absinthe-colored waters of **Lago Todos los Santos,** and there are several options. **Turismo Peulla** (© 65/236150;** www.turismopeulla.cl) offers trips departing from Puerto Montt or Puerto Varas to Peulla on the far side of the lake.

From Petrohué, you can book a day trip to the Margarita island in the middle of the lake or cross to Peulla, a 1¾-hour crossing that departs daily at 10:30am October through April and in July; the rest of the year, the ship doesn't cross on Sundays.

Travelers may then return or continue on to Bariloche with the Argentine company **Cruce de Lagos** (© 65/236150; www.crucedelagos.cl). **Andina del Sud** (the owner of Turismo Peulla) has a ticket office at the pier and an office in Puerto Varas, at Del Salvador 72 (© 65/232811; $140–$170/£72–£87). This is a very popular and very touristy journey; though the trip to Bariloche offers rugged, panoramic views, the trip is not worth the money on stormy days. And too much of the cattle herd mentality exists here as tourist-weary guides shuttle passengers in and out quickly, over 50,000 per season. The ferry portions of this journey are broken up by short bus rides from one body of water to the other.

There are relatively few hiking trails here. A short, touristy trail to the **Saltos de Petrohué** (admission $3/£1.55) takes visitors along a walkway built above Río Petrohué to admire the foaming, inky-green water crash through lava channels formed after the 1850 eruption of Volcán Osorno. One of my favorite treks here is a 1-night/2-day trek to the **Termas del Callao** thermal baths, the trail head of which is accessible only by boat. You can hire one of the boats at the dock (six-person maximum for $50/£26), or arrange a trip with **Expediciones Petrohué** (see "Outdoor Activities," above) for an all-inclusive package. A rustic cabin is at the hot springs; check with Expediciones for availability. If you're into backpacking, pick up a copy of the JLM map "Ruta de los Jesuitas" for a description of longer trails in the park.

Volcán Osorno Ski Resort ★ (© 65/233445; www.volcanosorno.com) on the western slope of the volcano, with two basic chair lifts and a T-bar, is a small resort on the volcano of the same name. It has just 600 hectares (1,482 acres) of terrain, but there are sweeping views and runs apt for every level. This is not a ski resort that travelers head to Chile specifically for, such as Valle Nevado or Portillo; it's more of a novelty for those in the area during the mid-June to early October season. The snow can be armor piercing, as this side of the lake receives a lot of wind, and all the terrain is above tree level. Lift prices run $30 (£15) for a full day, $20 (£10) for a half-day, and $16 (£8.20) for students.

WHERE TO STAY NEAR THE PARK

Private parking and ample street parking are available and free for all hotels.

Hotel Natura ★★ *Finds*   Built in 2005 on the fringe of the forest and the floodplain near Peulla, the building is less of a lodge than its name suggests; in fact, it's more of a traditional grand wood-and-stone style you see in hotels much, much older. Rooms are chic and large; the matrimonial suit features a king-size bed, chimney, flatscreen TV, and a Jacuzzi, along with a balcony. The hotel also has a two-room family apartment, and 23 doubles with king-size beds. Irrespective of its traditional looks, it offers plenty of modern outdoor activities: canopying 15m (49 ft.) in the air over an 800m (½-mile) span, riding, and fly fishing. You can zoom down nearby rivers like the Río Negro on a jet boat, and wind down with one of the 85 wines on the restaurant's list.

Lago Todos los Santos. ✆ 65/560483. www.hotelnatura.cl. 45 units. $163–$190 (£84–£97) double. AE, MC, DC, V. **Amenities:** Restaurant; bar; gym; sauna; watersports equipment; game room; massage; laundry service; Internet; Wi-Fi. *In room:* TV, high-speed Internet, hair dryer, safe.

Hotel Petrohué ★★   The brand-new Hotel Petrohué (built to replace the old lodge that had burned to the ground in 2002) is recommended because it puts travelers right where the outdoor action is, without having to commute from Puerto Varas every day to the park—and the hotel has a excursion outfitter with a range of daily activities. It sits perched above the shore of the Todos los Santos Lake and is surrounded by thick rainforest, a gorgeous location even on an overcast day. The hotel looks like a large Alpine chalet and is a tad austere given the absence of homey touches such as artwork or plants, but the contemporary design of its interiors (stone, heavy wood beams, fresh white couches) is attractive, and the rooms are comfortable, with crisp linens and panoramic windows. The hotel also has four cabins with kitchenettes and maid service.

Petrohué s/n Ruta 225, Km 64, Parque Nacional. ✆ 65/212025. www.hotelpetrohue.cl. 13 units, 4 *cabañas.* $179 (£92) double; $189 (£97) double with half-board; $169 (£87) *cabaña* for 2; $230 (£118) *cabaña* for 8. AE, MC, V. **Amenities:** Restaurant; bar; lounge; outdoor pool; outdoor excursions; room service; laundry service. *In room:* Kitchenette in *cabañas.*

Yan Kee Way Lodge ★★★ *Finds*   The name "Yan Kee Way" is a play on words, a gringo's pronunciation of Llanquihue, and coincidentally it's owned and managed by an American, who could not have chosen a more picture-perfect site: nestled in a thick forest of *arrayán* trees on the shore of Lago Llanquihue, and facing an astounding view of Volcano Osorno directly in front of the lodge.

The Yan Kee Way Lodge offers the best fly-fishing opportunities in the area, taking an eight-person maximum fishing per day via inflatable boats, horseback, or walk-and-wade to places other operations can't access due to transportation limitations. The lodge also offers a Sport Adventure all-inclusive package including rafting, mountain biking, hiking, horseback riding, and wine-tasting sessions. The hotel complex has independent units in standard rooms, two-story bungalows, and apartments, the latter of which are spacious and good for a family or group of friends. Blending with the surroundings, each elegant building here is painted in tones of terra cotta and forest green, with contemporary decor such as ebony leather couches, and furniture and art imported from Mexico and Argentina. Service is attentive and friendly, and the owner strives to provide the very best, including an extensive wine cellar with rare wines, a wine-tasting cave, and the region's finest restaurant, Latitude 42.

At the end of the day, many guests unwind in the spa or in the two wood-fired hot tubs that face the lake and the volcano.

Road to Ensenada east of Puerto Varas, Km 42. ✆ 65/212030. Fax 65/212031. www.southernchilexp.com. 18 units. $175 (£90) single; $250 (£138) double; $318 (£163) per person per day all-inclusive sport adventure package, which includes all meals and house wines with dinner and 20 activities from which to choose. AE, DC, MC, V. **Amenities:**

Restaurant; bar; lounge; exercise room; spa; Jacuzzi; sauna; watersports equipment; room service; massage; laundry service; free Internet. *In room:* Fridge, hair dryer, safe.

PUERTO MONTT

1,016km (630 miles) S of Santiago; 20km (12 miles) S of Puerto Varas

This port town of roughly 110,000 residents is the central hub for travelers headed to lagos Llanquihue and Todos los Santos, Chiloé, and the parks Alerce Andino and Pumalín. It is also a major docking zone for dozens of large cruise companies circumnavigating the southern cone of South America and several ferry companies with southern destinations to Laguna San Rafael National Park and Puerto Natales in Patagonia.

The town presents a convenient stopover point for travelers, but it is an ugly place when compared to Puerto Varas or Frutillar, due to its mishmash of office buildings and its scrappy industrial port. There is an extensive outdoor market here that sells Chilean handicrafts, clothing, and other tourist souvenirs.

ESSENTIALS
GETTING THERE

BY PLANE   Puerto Montt's **El Tepual** airport (© **65/294159**) is currently served by airlines **LAN Express** (© **600/526-2000;** www.lan.com) and **Sky** (© **600/ 600-2828;** www.skyairline.cl), with multiple daily flights to Santiago, Punta Arenas, Balmaceda (Coyhaique), and Temuco. **Aero Taxi,** Antonio Varas 70 (©/fax **65/ 252523**), has two daily flights to Chaitén, and the cost is $115 (£59) round-trip. This is a deal because the ferry to Chaitén takes 10 hours. An **ETM bus** from the airport to the city's downtown bus terminal costs $1.50 (75p); a taxi costs $9 (£4.60). Agree on the fare before getting into the cab. There are several **car-rental agencies** at the airport, including Hertz and Avis.

BY BUS   Puerto Montt's main terminal is at the waterfront (Diego Portales s/n), a 10- to 15-minute walk from downtown, or there are taxis to transport you. Regular bus service to and from most major cities, including Santiago, is provided by **Cruz del Sur** (© **65/254731**), **Tur Bus** (© **65/253329**), **Tas Choapa** (© **65/254828**), and **Bus Norte** (© **65/252783**).

BY CAR   The Pan-American Highway ends at Puerto Montt.

GETTING AROUND   By Foot   The city center is small enough to be seen on foot. The crafts market and fish market in Angelmó are a 20-minute walk from the center, or you can take a cab.

By Bus   Buses Cruz del Sur (© **65/254731**) leaves for Puerto Varas 19 times daily from the bus terminal, and so do the independent white shuttle buses to the left of the coaches; look for the sign in the window that says PUERTO VARAS. Cruz del Sur also serves Chiloé, including Castro and Ancud, with 25 trips per day. **TransChiloé** (© **65/254934**) goes to Chiloé seven times per day from the terminal.

VISITOR INFORMATION   The municipality has a small **tourist office** in the plaza at the corner of Antonio Varas and San Martín (© **65/261823**); it's open December through March daily from 9am to 9pm, and April through November Monday through Friday from 9am to 1pm and 2:30 to 7pm, Saturday and Sunday from 9am to 1pm. A largely unhelpful tourism kiosk is located in the main plaza (© **65/261808;** turismomontt@puertomonttchile.cl).

FAST FACTS   For currency exchange, try **Trans Afex,** Av. Diego Portales 516; **Cambios Inter,** Paseo Talca 84 (© **64/343683**); **La Moneda de Oro,** in the bus terminal, Office #37; and **Eureka Tour,** Guillermo Gallardo 65. **Hospital de la Seguridad** is at Panamericana 400 (© **65/257333**). Get online at **Arroba Cibercafé,** Guillermo Gallardo 218 #A, or **New Ciber,** San Martín 230. Cybercafes come and go, but most are on Urmenta Street. Internet service costs about $2 (£1) per hour, but many hotels have access for guests.

TOUR OPERATORS & TRAVEL AGENCIES   **Ace Lagos Andinos,** Antonio Varas 445 (© **65/257686** or 9/707-9445), offers just about everything you could want, including tours to Vicente Pérez National Park, the Termas de Puyehue, and Chiloé; sightseeing tours around the circumference of Lago Llanquihue; 2-night treks around Volcán Osorno with an overnight in a family home; and more.

   Andina del Sud, Antonio Varas 437 (© **65/257797;** www.andinadelsud.cl), is the tour agency with the monopoly on Lago Todos los Santos for the lake crossing to Bariloche; they also offer city tours and sightseeing journeys, and transportation service to attractions.

ATTRACTIONS IN PUERTO MONTT

Museo Juan Pablo II 🎯   This museum contains a medley of artifacts culled from this region, including historical photos and objects made by local Mapuche and Chilote Indians, as well as an interpretive exhibit of the Monte Verde archaeological dig that found bones estimated to be 12,000 years old. The museum is a good place to kill time or stop by if in the area; if not, forget it.

Av. Diego Portales 991. © **65/344457**. Admission $1 (50p). Mon–Fri 9am–7pm; Sat–Sun 10am–6pm.

SHOPPING

Puerto Montt is a great place to pick up souvenirs. On Avenida Angelmó, from the bus terminal to the fish market, is the **Feria Artesanal de Angelmó** (daily 9am–7pm; until 9pm Dec–Feb), with dozens of stalls and specialty shops that peddle knitwear, ponchos, handicrafts, jewelry, regional foods, and more from areas around the Lake District, including Chiloé. It's about a 20-minute walk from the plaza, or you can take a taxi.

WHERE TO STAY

Private parking and ample street parking are available and free for all hotels.

Hotel Club Presidente 🎯   This well-tailored hotel's classic, nautical-themed design appeals equally to executives and tourists, and handy kitchenettes give guests a little extra freedom. Located on the waterfront, in a central location close to shops, the Presidente is on busy Avenida Portales, but double-paned windows keep noise to a minimum. All rooms have either queen-size or king-size beds. The doubles are spacious, but the superiors are much larger and worth the extra $5 (£2.55); they also have ocean views. Most come with a small loveseat and a table and chairs. The rooms are decorated with creams and terra cotta, striped curtains, and nubby bedspreads. A breakfast buffet is served daily in the comfortable restaurant/bar on the eighth floor.

Av. Diego Portales 664, Puerto Montt. © **65/251666**. Fax 65/251669. www.presidente.cl. 50 units. $103–$124 (£53–£64). Rates include buffet breakfast. AE, DC, MC, V. **Amenities:** Restaurant; bar; small heated pool; sauna; business center; laundry service. *In room:* TV, kitchenette, safe.

Hotel Gran Pacífico 🎯🎯   Opened in late 2001, the Gran Pacífico is the city's only luxurious hotel, and its imposing 10-story structure towers over the waterfront. The Art

Deco lobby is sleek and modern with lots of wood and marble. The rooms follow the same motif and are spacious, modern, and bright. They have wood headboards, off-yellow wallpaper, and large-screen TVs. Those overlooking the water have breathtaking views (request an upper-level oceanview floor when you check in). The marble bathrooms are a tad small, but the size of the room makes up for it. For such a high caliber hotel, the staff is not too efficient nor do they speak much English, so be patient.

Urmeneta 719, Puerto Montt. © **65/482100.** Fax 65/292979. www.hotelgranpacifico.cl. 48 units. $93–$117 (£48–£60) double. AE, DC, MC, V. **Amenities:** Restaurant; bar; lounge; exercise room; sauna; business center; room service; laundry service. *In room:* TV, minibar, safe.

WHERE TO DINE

Puerto Montt is Chile's **seafood capital,** offering the widest variety of shellfish and fish found anywhere in the country. It'd be a crime if you left here without sampling at least a few delicacies. And where better to see, smell, and taste these fruits of the sea than the **Fish Market of Angelmó,** located at the end of Avenida Angelmó where the artisan market terminates; it's open daily from 10am to 8pm. Like most fish markets, it's a little grungy, but a colorful stop nevertheless, and several restaurant stalls offer the freshest local specialties around.

Club de Yates ⊛ SEAFOOD   The light-blue Club de Yates looks like a traditional seafood restaurant that sits out over the water like a pier. Inside, though, the atmosphere is white tablecloths, candlesticks, and sharp waiters in bow ties; it's one of the more elegant dining areas in town. This is a good place to come if you're looking for typical Chilean seafood dishes, such as razor clams broiled with Parmesan, or sea bass margarita, a creamy shellfish sauce. It has a great waterfront view and is located about 1km (½ mile) from the plaza toward Pelluco.

Av. Juan Soler Manfredini 200. © **65/82810.** Main courses $20–$25 (£10–£13). AE, DC, MC, V. Daily noon–4pm and 7:30pm–midnight.

Pazos CHILEAN   This is the place to come if you're interested in sampling *curanto* but don't have time to make it to Chiloé. *Curanto* is that island's specialty, a mixture of mussels, clams, sausage, chicken, pork, beef, and a gooey pancake steamed in a large pot and served with a cup of broth. Pazos also serves a variety of other seafood items, such as sea urchin omelets and the shellfish cornucopia, *sopa marina.* The restaurant is on the waterfront in Pelluco, in a 90-year-old home. It's very popular with summer visitors to Puerto Montt.

Av. General Juan Soler Manfredini s/n, Balneario Pelluco. © **65/252552.** Main courses $8–$12 (£4.10–£6.15). AE, DC, MC, V. Daily 12:15–3pm and 8:15–10pm.

8 Patagonia ⭐⭐⭐

Few places in the world have captivated the imagination of explorers and travelers like Patagonia and Tierra del Fuego. The region's harsh, wind-whipped climate and its geological curiosities have produced some of the most beautiful natural attractions in the world: the granite towers of Torres del Paine and Los Glaciares national parks, the Southern and Northern ice fields with their colossal glaciers, the flat pampa broken by multicolored sedimentary bluffs, and the emerald fiords and turquoise lakes. In the end, this is what compels most travelers to plan a trip down here, but Patagonia's seduction also lies in the "remote"—the very notion of traveling to "the end of the world."

Argentine Patagonia

For coverage of destinations on the Argentine side of Patagonia and Tierra del Fuego, see chapter 4. For a complete map of Patagonia, please refer to p. 153 in chapter 4.

EXPLORING THE REGION

For the region's tremendous size, Patagonia and Tierra del Fuego are surprisingly easy to travel, especially now that most destinations have opened airports. Travelers can plan a circuit that loops through, for example, Ushuaia, Punta Arenas, Torres del Paine, and then El Calafate and El Chaltén. If you're planning a trip to Chile or Argentina, you'll really want to include a visit to this region if possible—there's so much to see and do here, you'd be missing out if you went home without setting foot in this magical territory. Prices jump and crowds swell from early November to late March, and some businesses open during this time frame only. The busiest months are January and February, but these summer months are not necessarily the best months to visit Patagonia, as calmer weather prevails from mid-October to late November, and from mid-March to late April.

PUNTA ARENAS

Punta Arenas is the capital of the Magellanic and Antarctic Región XII, and it is Patagonia's most important city, with a population of 110,000. Upon arrival, it seems unbelievable that Punta Arenas is able to prosper as well as it does in such a forsaken location on the gusty shore of the Strait of Magellan, but its streets hum with activity and its airport and seaports bustle with traffic passing through the strait or in transit to Antarctica. Citizens from Punta Arenas consider themselves somewhat of an independent republic due to their isolation from the rest of Chile, and they are an indefatigable bunch who brace themselves every summer against the gales that blow through this town like a hurricane.

Punta Arenas's history, extreme climate, and position overlooking the renowned Strait of Magellan make for a fascinating place to explore. There's enough to do here to fill a day, and you'll want to plan on spending 1 night here, even if your plans are to head directly to Torres del Paine.

ESSENTIALS
Getting There

BY PLANE Punta Arenas's **Aeropuerto Presidente Ibáñez** is 20km (12 miles) north of town and, depending on the season, it's serviced with up to 10 flights per day from Santiago. **LAN Express,** Lautaro Navarro 999 (© **600/526-2000** or 61/241100; www.lan.com), has the most flights per day; they also have a Saturday flight from Balmaceda. **Sky Airline,** Roca 935 (© **600/600-2828;** www.skyairline.cl), has two flights per day. **Air Comet** © **600/625-0000;** www.aircometchile.cl), formerly known as **Aerolineas del Sur,** with two flights from Santiago per day.

LAN Express has a daily flight to Ushuaia, as does the regional **Aerovías DAP,** O'Higgins 891 (© **61/223340;** www.aeroviasdap.cl), with flights to and from Ushuaia every

Cruising from Punta Arenas to Ushuaia, Argentina

Cruceros Australis operates an unforgettable journey between Punta Arenas and Ushuaia aboard its *Mare Australis* and *Via Australis* ships. This cruise takes passengers through remote coves and spectacular channels and fjords in Tierra del Fuego and then heads into the Beagle Channel, stopping in Puerto Williams on Isla Navarino, and later Ushuaia, Argentina. The trip aboard the *Via Australis* lasts 3 nights, 4 days, and the *Mare Australis* has an additional stop at Cape Horn, extending the journey to 4 nights, 5 days.

What is unique about this cruise is the intimacy of a smaller ship and its solitary route that takes passengers to places in Tierra del Fuego that few have a chance to see. Passengers are shuttled to shore via zodiacs (motorized inflatable boats) for two daily excursions that can include visits to glaciers or a sea elephant rookery, walks to view elaborate beaver dams, or horseback rides. There are several excellent bilingual guides who give daily talks about the region's flora, fauna, history, and geology. Service is excellent, and the food is quite good. The accommodations are comfortable, ranging from suites to simple cabins. All-inclusive, per person prices (excluding cocktails) range from $990 to $2,040 (£508–£1,046) depending on cabin, program, and season. The cruises operate from September to April only. For reservations or information, contact their U.S. offices in Miami at 4014 Chase Ave., Ste. 202 (© **877/678-3772**; fax 305/534-9276); or in Santiago at Av. El Bosque Norte 0440 (© **2/442-3110**; fax 2/203-5173); or visit **www.australis.com**.

Tuesday and Friday from November to March; it also has daily service to Porvenir and the only air service to Puerto Williams, and Puerto Natales to Calafate (Nov–Mar only Mon–Fri). From November to March, DAP offers an unforgettable adventure to Cape Horn, with an overland flight and option to stay in Puerto Williams; the cost is $300 (£154).

To get to Punta Arenas from the airport, hire a taxi for about $8 (£4.10) or take one of the transfer services there (which can also arrange to take you back to the airport; their booths are at the baggage claim area). **Buses Transfer Austral** (© **61/229673**) has door-to-door service for $5 (£2.55) per person; **Buses Pacheco** (© **61/225527**; www.buses pacheco.com) has service to its station at Colón 900 for $2.50 (£1.30). Some transfers to Puerto Natales for $14 (£7.20) are on hand to meet flights during daylight hours.

BY BUS From Puerto Natales: **Bus Sur** at José Menéndez 565 (© **61/244464**) has four daily trips; **Buses Fernández** at Armando Sanhueza 745 (© **61/221429**) has seven daily trips; **Buses Transfer Austral** at Pedro Montt 966 (© **61/229613**) has two daily trips; and **Buses Pacheco** at Av. Colón 900 (© **61/242174**; www.busespacheco.com) has three daily trips. The cost is about $5 (£2.55) and the trip takes 3 hours.

To and from Ushuaia, Argentina: **Buses Tecni Austral** (Lautaro Navarro 975; © **61/222078**) and **Buses Ghisoni** (Lautaro Navarro 971; © **61/223205**) leave Punta Arenas Tuesday, Thursday, Saturday, and Sunday and return from Ushuaia on Monday, Wednesday, and Saturday. **Buses Pacheco** at Av. Colón 900 (© **61/242174**) has direct service to Ushuaia on Thursday and Sunday and returns of Friday and Monday

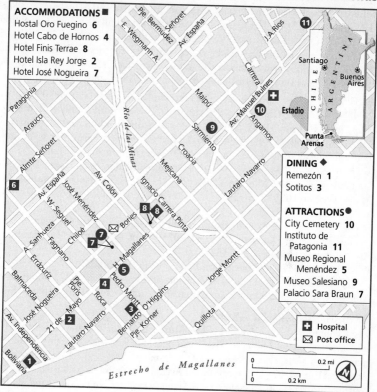

Punta Arenas

ACCOMMODATIONS ■
Hostal Oro Fuegino **6**
Hotel Cabo de Hornos **4**
Hotel Finis Terrae **8**
Hotel Isla Rey Jorge **2**
Hotel José Nogueira **7**

DINING ◆
Remezón **1**
Sotitos **3**

ATTRACTIONS ●
City Cemetery **10**
Instituto de Patagonia **11**
Museo Regional Menéndez **5**
Museo Salesiano **9**
Palacio Sara Braun **7**

✚ Hospital
✉ Post office

for $33 (£17); they also have service to Ushuaia with a stop first in Río Grande for the same price, leaving Monday, Wednesday, and Friday and returning on Tuesday, Thursday, and Saturday. Buses cross through Porvenir or Punta Delgada. The direct trip to Ushuaia takes about 12 hours.

BY CAR Ruta 9 is a paved road between Punta Arenas and Puerto Natales. Strong winds often require that you exercise extreme caution when driving this route. To get to Tierra del Fuego, there are two options: Cross by ferry from Punta Arenas to Porvenir, or drive east on Ruta 255 to Ruta 277 and Punta Delgada for the ferry crossing there.

CAR RENTAL Options include **Hertz** at O'Higgins 987 (© 61/248742; www. hertz.com), **Lubac** at Magallanes 970 (© 61/242023), **Budget** at O'Higgins 964 (© 61/202720; www.budget.cl), **Emsa** at Roca 1044 (© 61/241182), and **Rus Rent a Car** at Av. Colón 839 (© 61/221529).

Visitor Information

There's an excellent **Oficina de Turismo** (© 61/200610) inside a glass gazebo in the Plaza de Armas. The staff is helpful, and they sell a wide range of historical and anthropological literature and postcards. The office is open from December to March

Monday through Friday from 8am to 8pm, Saturday from 9am to 6:30pm, and Sunday from 9am to 2pm. The rest of the year, it is open Monday through Friday from 8am to 7pm only, and Saturday from 9am to 6:30pm (except May–Sept, when it closes on Sat and at 5pm on weekdays). **Sernatur**'s office at Hernándo de Magallanes 960 (© **61/225385;** www.sernatur.cl), on the other hand, is harried and inattentive; it's open Monday through Friday from 8:15am to 12:45pm and 2:30 to 7pm.

FAST FACTS Exchange money at **La Hermandad,** Lautaro Navarro 1099 (© 61/248090); **Cambios Gasic,** Roca 915, no. 8 (© 61/242396); **Cambio de Moneda Stop,** José Nogueira 1168 (© 61/223334); or **Scott Cambios,** corner of Avenida Colón and Magallanes (© 61/244464). Casas de cambio are open Monday through Friday from 9am to 1pm and 3 to 7pm, and Saturday from 9am to 1pm.

For banks with 24-hour ATMs, go to **Banco Santander,** Magallanes 997 (© 61/201020); **Banco de Chile,** Roca 864 (© 61/735433); or **Banco Edwards,** Plaza Muñoz Gamero 1055 (© 61/241175). Banks are open Monday through Friday from 9am to 2pm.

For medical attention, go to **Hospital de las FF.AA. Cirujano Guzmán,** Avenida Manuel Bulnes and Guillermos (© **61/207500**), or the **Clínica Magallanes,** Av. Manuel Bulnes 1448 (© **61/211527**).

For Internet access, try **Telefónica,** Bories 798 (© **61/248230**).

The central **post office** is at José Menéndez and Bories (© **61/222210**); hours are Monday through Friday from 9am to 6pm and Saturday from 9am to 1pm.

EXPLORING PUNTA ARENAS

Begin your tour of Punta Arenas in **Plaza Muñoz Gamero,** in whose center you'll find a bronze sculpture of Ferdinand Magellan, donated by José Menéndez on the 400-year anniversary of Magellan's discovery of the Strait of Magellan. From the plaza on Avenida 21 de Mayo, head north toward Avenida Colón for a look at the newly renovated Teatro Municipal, designed by the French architect Numa Mayer and modeled after the magnificent Teatro Colón in Buenos Aires. Head down to the waterfront and turn south toward the pier to watch the shipping action. At the pier is a 1913 clock imported from Germany that has complete meteorological instrumentation, hands showing the moon's phases, and a zodiac calendar.

City Cemetery ✹✹ They say you can't really understand a culture until you see where they bury their dead, and in the case of the cemetery of Punta Arenas, this edict certainly rings true. Inside this necropolis, opened in 1894, lies a veritable miniature city, with avenues that connect the magnificent tombs of the region's founding families, settlers, and civic workers, and a rather solemn tomb where lie the remains of the last Selk'nam Indians of Tierra del Fuego. The Alice in Wonderland bell-shaped cypress trees that line the tombs make for a surreal atmosphere. The cemetery is about a 15-minute walk from the plaza.

Av. Manuel Bulnes and Angamos. No phone. Free admission. Oct–Mar daily 7:30am–8pm; Apr–Sept daily 8am–6:30pm.

Instituto de Patagonia/Museo del Recuerdo ✹ The Instituto de Patagonia is an engaging exhibit of colonial artifacts called the Museum of Remembrances. Antique machinery and horse-drawn carts are displayed around the lawn and encircled by several colonial buildings that have been lifted and transported here from ranches around the area. One cabin shows visitors what home life was like for a ranch hand, another has been set up to resemble a typical dry goods store, another is a garage with a 1908 Peugeot, and another, a carpenter's workshop. There's a library on the premises with a collection of books and maps on display and for sale. To get into the colonial buildings, you'll need to ask someone in the museum's office to unlock them for you. The museum is about 4km (2½ miles) out of town, so you'll need to take a taxi. The Zona Franca (a duty-free shopping center) is just down the street, so you could tie in a visit to the two.

Av. Manuel Bulnes 01890. ⓒ 61/217173. Admission 70¢ (35p). Mon–Fri 8:30am–noon and 2:30–6pm; Sat 8:30am–noon; erratic hours and closing policies Sun; call ahead.

Museo Salesiano Maggiorino Borgatello ★★   This mesmerizing museum offers an insight into the Magellanic region's history, anthropology, ecology, and industrial history. That said, the lobby-level floor is packed with a fusty collection of stuffed and mounted birds and mammals that at turns feels almost macabre, considering that many have lost their shape; nevertheless, it allows you to fully appreciate the tremendous size of the condor and the puma. Several rooms in the museum display Indian hunting tools, ritual garments, jewelry, an Alacalufe bark canoe, and colonial and ranching implements, as well as the religious artifacts from the Catholic missionaries who played such a controversial role in the native Indians' lives. Perhaps some of the most interesting items on view here are the black-and-white photos of the early missionary Alberto d'Agostini, who took most of the only photos available of the native people who have since disappeared from this region. There's a display of the petroleum industry that will appeal only to anyone interested in that subject.

Av. Manuel Bulnes and Maipú. ⓒ 61/221001. Admission $2.25 (£1.15). Tues–Sun 10am–12:30pm and 3–6pm.

Museo Regional Braun Menéndez ★★ (Moments   This museum is testament to the staggering wealth produced by the region's large-scale, colonial-era sheep and cattle *estancias* (ranches). The museum is the former residence of the Braun Menéndez family, who believed that any far-flung, isolated locale could be tolerated if one were to "live splendidly and remain in constant contact with the outside world." The Museo Regional Braun Menéndez is the former residence of Mauricio Braun and Josefina Menéndez, a marriage that united the two largest fortunes in the Magellanic region.

The home is a national monument and has been preserved in its original state. European craftsmen were imported to craft marble fireplaces and hand-paint walls to resemble marble and leather. The interior fixtures and furniture include gold and crystal chandeliers, tapestries from Belgium, stained-glass cupolas, English and French furniture, hand-carved desks, and more. There is also a small ethnographic exhibit. Plan on 45 minutes to an hour to view the museum.

Museo Regional Braun Menéndez: Magallanes 949. ⓒ 61/244216. Admission $2 (£1) adults, $1 (50p) students and seniors over 60; Sun and holidays free. Oct–Apr Mon–Sat 10:30am–5pm, Sun 10:30am–2pm; May–Oct daily 10:30am–2pm.

SHOPPING

Punta Arenas is home to a duty-free shopping center called the **Zona Franca,** with several blocks of shops hawking supposedly cheaper electronics, imported foodstuffs, sporting goods, perfumes, clothing, booze, cigarettes, and more. The savings here are negligible, except for alcohol purchases, and the selection isn't what you'd hope for, although there certainly is a lot on offer. The Zona Franca is located on Avenida Manuel Bulnes, just outside town. It's open Monday through Saturday from 10am to 12:30pm and 3 to 8pm, and is closed Sunday and holidays.

For regional crafts, try the good selection available at **Chile Típico,** Carrera Pinto 1015 (© **61/225827**). Both have knitwear, carved-wood items, lapis lazuli, and more. For high-end, artsy-craftsy household items such as picture frames, candles, throws, curtains, and the like, try **Almacén Antaño,** Colón 100 (no phone).

EXCURSIONS OUTSIDE PUNTA ARENAS
Tour Operators

Many tour operators run conventional city tours and trips to the penguin colonies, as well as short visits and trekking excursions to Torres del Paine National Park; however, I recommend one of the outfitters listed under tour operators in the Torres del Paine section for multiday excursions there. A city tour here provides the historical background to this region and undoubtedly enriches a visitor's understanding of the hardship the immigrants and Native Indians faced during the past century.

Turismo Yamana, Errázuriz 932 (© **61/710567;** www.yamana.cl), offers kayak trips on and around the Strait of Magellan and Tierra del Fuego with a support boat (about $3,245/£1,664 per person for an all-inclusive 8 days, two persons; $2,934/£1,505 per person for three people). The company also offers multiday trips to Lago Blanco in Tierra del Fuego for trekking, horseback riding, and fishing.

Turismo Comapa, Magallanes 990 (© **61/200200;** www.comapa.com) is the leader for conventional tours such as city tours and visits to the penguin colonies; a trip to Isla Magdalena costs $42 (£22); a city tour costs $44 (£23) and up. City tours last approximately 3 hours. **Turismo Viento Sur,** 585 Fagnano (© **61/226930;** www.vientosur.com), is another respected company offering excursions that include a trip to the little-known Pali Aike National Park. Viento Sur also has half-day and full-day kayaking trips with qualified guides.

Penguin Colonies at Seno Otway & Isla Magdalena

One of the highlights of a visit to Punta Arenas is a trip to the **penguin colonies** at Seno Otway and Isla Magdalena. Both colonies allow visitors to get surprisingly close to the amusing Magellanic penguins at their nesting sites, whisking out sprays of sand or poking their heads out of their burrows. But, this only happens during their natural nesting cycle from October to March—and even by early March they've all pretty much packed up and headed north. November to February provides the most active viewing. Isla Magdalena is the best colony to view the penguins (with an estimated 150,000, as compared to 3,000 at Seno Otway). But, the trip involves a ferry ride and will take up more of your time.

Seno Otway ★★ is accessible by road about 65km (40 miles) from Punta Arenas. A volunteer study group developed the site but now that the founder has passed away the site is run by the founder's family, who clearly care more about making a profit than carrying on the foundation's work. The tickets now cost a whopping $10 (£5.10; kids under 12 are free), and because they have rerouted the road through private land, the owners of the land charge $2 (£1) per adult in a vehicle—yes, it will feel like a bribe. Tours are offered in four languages, and there is an overpriced cafe here, too. Seno Otway is open from October 15 to March 31 from 8am to 8pm. The best time to visit is between 9 and 10am and 5 and 7pm, when the majority of activity takes place (the crowds of visitors are thinner during the morning shift; © **61/224454**). Take Ruta 9 toward Puerto Natales, and then turn left at the sign for Seno Otway—if you reach the police checkpoint you've gone too far.

The penguins at **Isla Magdalena** ✯✯✯ are more timid than those at Seno Otway, but the sight of so many of these birds bustling to and fro is decidedly more impressive. To get here, you need to take a ferry, which makes for a pleasant half-day afternoon excursion. **Turismo Comapa,** Av. Magallanes 990 (✆ **61/200200;** www.comapa.com), puts this tour together. Its boat, the *Barcaza Melinka,* departs from the pier at 3:30pm and returns at 8:30pm on Tuesday, Thursday, and Saturday from December to February ($28/£14 for adults, $13/£ 6.65 children under 12).

Estancia Lolita ✯✯ is a wildlife refuge and zoo for Patagonian fauna and the best place to view rarely seen species, 42km (16 miles) north of Punta Arenas. Josefina, a tame, rambunctious culpeo fox who loves to play with visitors, is one of the most charming living souls you'll meet in Patagonia. Guanacos, pumas, and other wild cats, and parrots and other endemic birds are among the denizens of the *estancia,* which has over 30 species in all (✆ **61/233057;** www.faunapatagonica.com; adults $5/£2.50, children $3/£1.50).

SKIING IN THE AREA

Punta Arenas has a tiny ski resort that operates from mid-June to mid-September: the **Centro de Esquí Cerro Mirador,** situated at the border of the Reserva Nacional Magallanes. The resort is mostly notable for its view of the Strait of Magellan, Tierra del Fuego, and—on a clear day—Dawson Island. During the summer, they often run their only chair lift to carry you to the top of the peak, or you can hike the hill yourself. The resort has 1 lift, 10 runs, ski rental, and a cafeteria. Ski lift tickets cost about $18 (£9.25); a ski rental package is $24 (£12). The resort (✆ **61/241479**) is very close to town; to get here, take a taxi.

WHERE TO STAY

In general, lodging in Punta Arenas is somewhat expensive for the caliber of accommodations available. Price range reflects low to high season (high season is Oct 15–Apr 15). Hotels are usually willing to negotiate a price; always ask for promotional rates when calling a hotel, and check the hotel's website (when available) for Internet-only discounted rates.

Hotel Cabo de Hornos ✯✯   Punta Arenas's top contemporary hotel, it's most conveniently located on the northeast corner of the plaza. Its pinkish, seven-story form vaguely reminds me of the chateau in Quebec City. The Cabo de Hornos sports an impressive, elegant gray stone-clad reception and lounge area, very nicely decorated in a mixture of modern and rustic, though the armrests of the cow-skin chairs at the bar are getting a little frayed. A separate room has a massive fireplace. The adjacent restaurant's chef is currently one of the most fashionable in town. The rooms don't quite match the wow factor of the ground floor, being just a little on the small size, but they are of decent quality and well suited for business travelers. The higher you get, the better the view.

Plaza Muñoz Gamero 1039, Punta Arenas. ✆ **61/715000.** www.hoteles-australis.com. 111 units. $100–$200 (£52–£103) double. AE, DC, MC, V. **Amenities:** Restaurant; lounge; room service; laundry service. *In room:* TV, high-speed Internet, safe.

Hotel Finis Terrae ✯✯   This hotel is very popular with foreigners, especially Americans. The well-lit accommodations and the hotel lobby are quite comfy; rooms have king-size beds in double rooms, and a softly hued decor in peach and beige. And although Richard Gere stayed here in 2002 (he chose the spacious fifth-floor suite with a whirlpool tub and minibar); the rooms are by no means luxurious. The singles here are tiny, so be sure to ask for a larger double for the single price, which they will likely agree to, especially during slower months. The hotel's highlight is its panoramic penthouse restaurant that serves the best breakfast in Punta Arenas.

Av. Colón 766, Punta Arenas. ✆ **61/228200.** Fax 61/248124. www.hotelfinisterrae.com. 64 units. $185 (£95) double. Rates include buffet breakfast. AE, DC, MC, V. **Amenities:** Restaurant; lounge; room service; laundry service. *In room:* TV, minibar, safe.

Hotel José Nogueira ★★★ *(Moments* Undoubtedly the best hotel in town, the José Nogueira is housed in a converted neoclassical mansion once owned by the widow of one of Punta Arenas's wealthiest entrepreneurs; a wing of the building is still run as a museum. The mansion was built between 1894 and 1905 on a prominent corner across from the plaza, with materials imported entirely from Europe. The José Nogueira is appealing for its historical value, but also offers classic luxury. The rooms here are not as large as you would expect, but high ceilings accented by floor-to-ceiling curtains compensate for that. All are tastefully decorated, either in rich burgundy and navy blue–striped wallpaper or rose and cream combinations, Oriental rugs, and lithographs of local fauna; the marble bathrooms are sparkling white.

Bories 959, Punta Arenas. ✆ **61/248840.** Fax 61/248832. www.hotelnogueira.com. 25 units, 3 suites. $119–$190 (£61–£97) double. Rates include buffet breakfast. AE, DC, MC, V. **Amenities:** Restaurant; bar; room service; laundry service. *In room:* TV, minibar.

Hostal Oro Fueguino ★ *(Value* This hostel is a favorite with backpackers and budget travelers for its clean, comfortable rooms and friendly service. The interiors here are painted vibrant colors and decorated with folk art, and there are rooms for doubles, triples, and quadruples—all with private bathrooms. Their plant-filled, colorful dining room and lounge are cozy spots to relax. The hostel is a 5-block walk up from the plaza; look for the bright yellow-and-aqua exterior.

Fagnano 356, Punta Arenas. ✆ **61/249401.** www.orofueguino.cl. 12 units. $75 (£38) double with private bathroom. Rates include continental breakfast. AE, DC, MC, V. **Amenities:** Lounge; laundry. *In room:* TV.

WHERE TO DINE

Remezón ★★★ *(Finds* CONTEMPORARY REGIONAL One of the best restaurants in the region, Remezón breaks from the traditional mold with a warm, intimate dining area decorated with a jumble of art and slightly kitsch items that are as personal as the chef's daily changing menu. The food is, in a word, divine: not too pretentious but always prepared with fresh, regional vegetables, seafood, and meats seasoned to delicious perfection. The menu features five appetizers and as many main dishes handwritten on a chalkboard; on slow nights the chef will approach your table and explain each item to diners before they order. Sample dishes include broiled Parmesan scallops; calamari, zucchini and avocado salad; goose marinated in pisco and lemon; and crepes stuffed with king crab and cream. There are also exotic items such as guanaco and ñandú. The gracious owners love good cooking, and it shows. Remezón is about a 4-block walk from the plaza. Don't miss their calafate-berry piscos.

Av. 21 de Mayo 1469. ✆ **61/241029.** Main courses $8–$13 (£4.10–£6.65). AE, DC, MC, V. Daily noon–3pm and 7:15pm–midnight. Closed Mon Apr–Sept.

Sotitos ★ CHILEAN Don't be fooled by the plain green front with the weathered sign: Sotitos has handsome semiformal interiors with brick walls and white-linen tablecloths. If you're looking for traditional Chilean cuisine, this is your restaurant.

Sotitos offers everything and more than most Chilean restaurants, including steak and seafood, local baked lamb, Valencia shellfish rice (which must be ordered ahead of time), pastas, and fresh salads. The key is that everything is of high quality, regardless of how simple the dish. The service here is attentive but not overbearing. On Friday, Saturday, and Sunday they fire up their *parrilla* (grill) for barbecued meats.

O'Higgins 1138. ℂ **61/221061.** Main courses $12–$20 (£6.15–£10). AE, DC, MC, V. Mon–Sat 11:30am–3pm and 7–11:45pm.

PUNTA ARENAS AFTER DARK

The city has a handful of good bars and pubs, the most popular of which is **Santino** at Colón 657 (ℂ **61/220511**), especially suitable for large groups; or try the more intimate ambience of the **La Taberna** (ℂ **61/248840**) cellar bar, below the Hotel José Nogueira at the corner of Bories and Sequel across from the plaza; appetizers are available. Another popular spot is the **Pub 1900** (ℂ **61/242759**), at the corner of Avenida Colón and Bories. The **Cabo de Hornos Hotel** (ℂ **61/242134**), on the plaza, has a chic yet more somber bar. The **Cine Estrella,** at Mejicana 777 (ℂ **61/225630**), is the only cinema in town; call or check newspaper listings for what's playing.

PUERTO NATALES

Puerto Natales is a rambling town of 15,000, spread along the sloping coast of the Señoret Canal between the Ultima Esperanza Sound and the Almirante Montt Gulf. This is the jump-off point for trips to Torres del Paine, and most visitors find themselves spending at least 1 night here. The town itself is nothing more than a small center and rows and rows of weather-beaten tin and wooden houses, but it has a frontier-town appeal, and it boasts a stunning location with grand views out onto a grassy peninsula and the glacier-capped peaks of the national parks Bernardo O'Higgins and Torres del Paine in the distance. Along the Costanera, elegant black-necked swans drift along the rocky shore. From May to September, the town virtually goes into hibernation, but come October, the town's streets begin to fill with travelers decked out in parkas and hiking boots on their way to the park.

ESSENTIALS
Getting There & Getting Around
BY PLANE   The tiny Puerto Natales airport (no phone) has only one scheduled flight per day, and that is the nine-passenger propeller plane from El Calafate. Contact **Aerovías DAP,** in Punta Arenas, at O'Higgins 891 (ℂ **61/223340;** www.aerovias dap.cl), for information and reservations on charter flights, which can include Río Gallegos on the Atlantic Coast. A taxi from Puerto Natales to the airport costs $2 (£1) and is only a 5-minute drive. Windy days may affect flight schedules.

BY BUS   Puerto Natales is the hub for bus service to Torres del Paine National Park and El Calafate, Argentina. For information about bus service to and from Torres del Paine, see "Parque Nacional Torres del Paine," later in this chapter. There are frequent daily trips between Punta Arenas and Puerto Natales. In Puerto Natales, each bus company leaves from its own office.

To and from Punta Arenas   Buses Fernández, at Ramirez and Esmeralda streets (ℂ **61/411111**), has seven daily trips; **Bus Sur,** Baquedano 558 (ℂ **61/242174**), has three daily trips; **Buses Pacheco,** Baquedano 500 (ℂ **61/414513**), has three daily trips (and the most comfortable buses); and **Transfer Austral,** Baquedano 414 (ℂ **61/412616**), has two daily trips. The trip takes about 3 hours and the cost is about $6 to

$8 (£3.10–£4.10) one-way. Reserve early during the busy season, as tickets sell out fast. Round-trip fares to Punta Arenas are a little cheaper.

To El Calafate, Argentina Options include **Buses Zaahj,** Arturo Prat 236 (© **61/412260;** www.turismozaahj.co.cl); **Bus Sur,** Baquedano 558 (© **61/411859;** www.bus-sur.cl), which leaves at 9am Monday, Wednesday, and Friday, and returns at 8am Tuesday, Thursday, and Saturday; and **Cootra,** Baquedano 244 (© **61/412785**), which leaves at 6:30am daily. The cost is $30 (£15) one-way. The trip takes 5 to 6 hours, depending on the traffic at the border crossing. Note that most of this voyage is on dirt roads. Avoid **Calafate Travel,** which is prone to breakdowns.

BY CAR Ruta 9 is a paved road that heads north from Punta Arenas. The drive is 254km (158 miles) and takes about 2½ to 3 hours. If you're heading in from El Calafate, Argentina, you have your choice of two international borders: Cerro Castillo (otherwise known as Control Fronterizo Río Don Guillermo) or Río Turbio (otherwise known as Controles Fronterizos Dorotea y Laurita Casas Viejas). Both are the same in terms of road quality, but Río Turbio is busier, with Chileans heading to Argentina for cheaper goods. Both are open 24 hours from September to May, and daily from 8am to 11pm the rest of the year. Gas is much cheaper in Argentina, so fill up there.

Car rentals in Puerto Natales are offered by **Motorcars,** Encalada 330, no. 2 (© **61/413593**); **EMSA** (an Avis representative), Av. Manuel Bulnes 632 (© **61/410775**); and **Trans Patagonia,** Blanco Encalada 330 (© **61/413593;** www.transpatagonia.cl), among several others.

BY BOAT **Navimag** runs a popular 3-night ferry trip between Puerto Natales and Puerto Montt, cruising through the southern fjords of Chile. This journey passes through breathtaking (though repetitive) scenery, and it makes for an interesting way to leave from or head to Chile's Lake District. Navimag leaves every Thursday evening; its offices are at Manuel Bulnes 533 (© **61/414300;** www.navimag.com).

Visitor Information

Sernatur operates a well-stocked office on the Costanera at Pedro Montt and Philippi (© **61/412125;** www.sernatur.cl); it's open October through March Monday through Friday from 8:30am to 8pm, Saturday and Sunday from 9:30am to 1pm and 2:30 to 6:30pm; April through September, it's open Monday through Friday from 8:30am to 1pm and 2:30 to 6:30pm, closed holidays. Better yet is the **Municipal Tourism office,** tucked in a corner of the historical museum at Bulnes 285 (© **61/411263**), with a wealth of information on lodgings, restaurants, and day trips; the staff here is far more helpful than at Sernatur.

SAILING TO PARQUE NACIONAL BERNARDO O'HIGGINS ✪

This national park, tremendous in its size, is largely unreachable except by boat tours to the glaciers Balmaceda and Serrano, tours that involve kayaking (for kayaking trips, see the information on Bigfoot Expeditions under "Tour Operators & Adventure Travel Outfitters," below), and the new Skorpios journey to the grand Pio XI glacier (see below). A low-key, traditional day trip takes travelers to the Serrano and Balmaceda glaciers, with a stop at the Monte Balmaceda Hostel and a short walk along the glacier and its iceberg-studded bay. The best option is to take this journey on your first day and continue on with a zodiac ride to Torres del Paine, or vice versa (see "Getting There & Away" under "Parque Nacional Torres del Paine," below), as the round-trip journey can be monotonous.

Turismo 21 de Mayo, Eberhard 560 (℅ **61/411978;** www.turismo21demayo.cl) has a cutter and a yacht, and leaves daily November through March and every Sunday from April to October (other days are dependent on demand). The trip leaves at 8:30am and returns at 5:30pm.

The cruise company **Skorpios,** Augusto Leguia Norte 118 (℅ **2/231-1030** www. skorpios.cl), has an all-inclusive 6-day journey from Puerto Natales to Pio XI Glacier, the largest glacier in the Southern Hemisphere. The size of the Pio XI dwarfs other glaciers that descend from the Southern Ice Field, such as Glacier Grey in Torres del Paine, and thereby provide a truly awesome experience. This journey is recommended for travelers who are not very physically active and who wish to take a low-key, yet special journey to an out-of-the-way destination few get the chance to see.

TOUR OPERATORS & ADVENTURE TRAVEL OUTFITTERS

The many tour operators in Puerto Natales can be divided into two groups: conventional sightseeing day tours to Torres del Paine, Perito Moreno Glacier in Argentina's Los Glaciares National Park, the Cueva de Milodon, the Nordenskjöld Trail, and the icebergs at Lago Grey; and adventure travel outfitters that arrange multiday, all-inclusive excursions, including trekking the W or the Circuit and climbing in Torres del Paine, kayaking the Río Serrano in Parque Nacional Bernardo O'Higgins, and taking horseback trips. Keep in mind that it's very easy to arrange your own trekking journey in Torres del Paine; the bonus with these outfitters is that they carry the tents (which they'll set up) and food (which they'll cook). They also will pick you up from the airport and provide guided information about the flora and fauna of the park.

CONVENTIONAL DAY TOURS These tours are for people with a limited amount of time in the area. Tours typically leave at 7:30am, return around 7:30pm, and cost about $30 (£15) per person, not including lunch or park entrance fees. For day tours, try **Turismo Mily,** Blanco Encalada 266 (℅ **61/411262**), or **Viaterra,** Bulnes 632 (℅ **61/410775;** www.viaterra.cl); Viaterra has transfers from Punta Arenas directly to the park on a charter basis. Probably the most interesting way to see the Cueva de Milodon is with **Estancia Travel** (℅ **61/412221;** www.estanciatravel.com), which offers a horseback-riding trip there for $108 (£55) per person, including transfers, equipment, a bilingual guide, lunch, and a horse you'll feel comfortable with.

ADVENTURE TRAVEL Apart from the local guiding outfitters here in Puerto Natales, several American and Chilean companies offer well-planned trekking excursions in Torres del Paine, specifically **Mountain-Travel Sobek** and **Cascada Expediciones.** Mountain-Travel has multiday trekking journeys around Torres del Paine; Cascada operates from their base at Hostería los Torres, where they have dome-shape cabins for lodging before or after a trekking journey.

Most of the following operators offer custom packages. **Indómita,** Bories 206 (℅ **61/414525;** info@indomitapatagonia.com), is one of the most respected local outfitters for climbing, mountaineering, and kayaking; they also own the concession for the unforgettable ice walk across Glacier Grey (described later in this chapter). One of their most popular trips is a 3-day kayak descent of the River Serrano, with a paddle around Serrano Glacier. Partner **Antares,** Barros Arana 111 (℅ **61/414611,** or ℅ 415/703-9955 for their U.S. office; www.antarespatagonia.com), focuses on the "softer" (meaning less strenuous and/or technical) side of adventure travel, with a variety of multiday trekking journeys through the park that can include horseback riding, kayaking, and sailing. **Chile Nativo Expeditions,** Eberhard 230 (℅ **61/411835;**

www.chilenativo.com), offers high-end trekking, bird-watching, and horseback-riding adventures outside of the more "touristy" areas. **Onas,** Blanco Encalada and Eberhard (©/fax **61/614300;** www.onaspatagonia.com), has a half-day zodiac trip down the Río Serrano.

WHERE TO STAY

Many homes large enough to rent out a few rooms have hung an HOSPEDAJE sign above their door—these simple, inexpensive accommodations can be found every-where, and quality is about the same. The high season in Puerto Natales runs from October to April, and the price range shown reflects this. For all hotels, parking is either free, or street parking is plentiful.

For inexpensive lodging, try **Casa Cecilia** ✸ at Tomás Roger 60 (©/fax **61/ 411797;** redcecilia@entelchile.net), which has a kitchen, clean rooms, a tour desk, and equipment rental; a double room costs $21 to $35 (£11–£18), less for a shared bathroom. Another popular *hostal* is **Concepto Indigo** at Ladrilleros 105 (© **61/ 413609;** www.conceptoindigo.com), which has rooms that are noteworthy only for their direct view of the sound. A double here costs $46 (£24).

At press time, a new upscale hotel called the **Hotel Altiplanico** (©**55/851212;** www.altiplanico.cl) was on the verge of opening for the 2006 season. Architects designed the hotel, located 3km (2 miles) outside of town, to appear as if it were built into the hillside, using grass-thatched roofs and a sloping edifice. There are 22 attrac-tive rooms, a restaurant, bar, and sweeping views of the Ultima Esperanza Sound. Call or e-mail for more information.

Concepto Indigo ✸✸✸ *(Moments* The Concepto Indigo was always hip, but it has undergone a total transformation from backpackers' haunt to reopen as Puerto Natales' sole boutique hotel in late 2006, offering the finest views of the glaciers across the sound. Rooms are in the multistory, red-and-black cube that overshadows the shingled former hostel, now a restaurant on the ground floor and a lounge on the top floor where you can check your e-mail on iMacs. The hotel's top-level spa features heated whirlpools that overlook the sound. The airy, midsize rooms have comfy beds and good views and finishings. Concepto Indigo just slightly edges out Remota as the best place in town and will be preferred by more independent travelers.

Ladrilleros 105, Puerto Natales. © 61/413609. www.indigopatagonia.com. 29 units. $210 (£108). AE, DC, MC, V. **Amenities:** Restaurant; bar; sauna; travel and tour services; massage; Internet; Wi-Fi. *In room:* Hair dryer.

Hotel Remota ✸✸✸ *(Moments* Black and a bit forbidding from the outside and topped by chimneys reminiscent of huge metal candy canes, the interiors of Remota couldn't be more different. Huge floor-to-ceiling windows flood the white walls and columns with light amid a generous lounge and dining areas. Yellow cushions and huge fireplaces add to the coziness, while a collection of archaeological finds from around the country draw your eye. Rooftops, here too, are covered in grass, and a look around here will show you a gorgeous panorama across the bay. Myriad details such as irregular angles of columns, native woods, and wooden structures similar to sheep corrals quote Patagonian heritage. Rooms also feature native woods, its boards even retaining shreds of bark, along with stone floors and white ceilings. Among its many superlative elements, I was most impressed by its indoor pool, a beautiful black mar-ble rectangle reflecting the sky and landscape from the outside.

Huerto 279, 1.5km (less than a mile) north of Puerto Natales. © 61/414040. www.remota.cl. 77 units. 3-night package $1,160 (£595) per person double; $1,680 (£862) single. Rates include excursions, meals, spa, and transfers. AE, DC, MC, V. **Amenities:** Dining area; bar; indoor pool; bicycles; massage; Wi-Fi. *In room:* Hair dryer, safe.

Weskar Patagonian Lodge ★★   If you're idea of the Patagonia experience is more rustic than hip, look no farther than this hillside lodge above the waterfront, a 10-minute walk from town. Cozy and made of native lenga wood and stone, it has gabled oriels and fine views across the water and of the town itself. Though the brand-new hotel's style gives it a look suggesting it was built decades ago, the good-size rooms are modern in decor, with wooden headboards and colorful wool bed covers on white linens. The dining area's tables are placed marvelously to take advantage of the views.

Ruta 9 norte, Km 1, Puerto Natales. © 61/414168. www.weskar.cl. 17 units. $90–$127 (£46–£65) double. AE, DC, MC, V. **Amenities:** Restaurant; bar; excursions available; laundry service; Internet.

WHERE TO DINE

El Living ★★ *Finds* CAFE/VEGETARIAN   If you're looking for a friendly, comfortable place to kick back and spend the evening, then look no further. At El Living, run by a British expatriate couple who have lived in the area for more than a decade, you can lounge on a comfortable sofa with a pisco sour or have an excellent vegetarian dinner at one of their handmade wooden dining tables. The menu is simple and inexpensive but fresh and delicious. The Sweet and Sour Red Salad is a perfect mix of beetroot, red cabbage, kidney beans, and onion; the veggie burger is delicious and served on a whole-wheat baguette. This is one of the only places in Chile that serves a peanut-butter-and-jelly sandwich. There's also French toast with fried bananas, and a variety of cakes baked daily. A full bar and wine list round out this excellent place.

Arturo Prat 156. © 61/411140. Main courses $6–$9 (£3.10–£4.60). No credit cards. Daily 11am–midnight.

Hotel CostAustralis ★★ *Moments* INTERNATIONAL   Recently expanded, this is the only restaurant approximating fine dining in Puerto Natales, with tasty cuisine and a wonderful ambience. The sunset views from the picture windows in combination with your candlelit table make for a sumptuous environment. The chef tries hard to maintain the regional angle in the menu. A good example is the lamb and potato stew typical of this region but not easy to find in restaurants. Salmon and conger eel are usually the fresh catches of the day. Other specialties include wild hare marinated in red wine and herbs, and pork loin with mustard and whiskey. Top off your dinner with the apricots and peaches stewed in syrup and served with cream of wheat, or minty pears poached in wine with chocolate ice cream.

Pedro Montt 262. © 61/412000. Main courses $10–$13 (£5.10–£6.65). AE, DC, MC, V. Daily noon–3pm and 7:30–11pm.

Pez Glacier ★ SEAFOOD   The Hotel Indigo's restaurant sports dynamite views and a fresh, contemporary ambience, with an upstairs bar specializing in a variety of pisco sours (very good). The menu leans more toward seafood prepared in a creative fashion, which is welcome given that most restaurants in town serve the same fried fish and potatoes combo. Their ceviche is especially good, as is any fresh catch of the day (the menu changes frequently). An excellent wine list and attentive service round out the experience here. During high season, make a reservation.

Ladrilleros 105, Puerto Natales. © 61/413609. www.indigopatagonia.com. Main courses $7–$12 (£3.60–£6.15). Reservations recommended during high season. AE, DC, MC, V.

PARQUE NACIONAL TORRES DEL PAINE ✦✦✦

This is Chile's prized jewel, a national park so magnificent that few in the world can claim a rank in its class. The park is made of granite peaks and towers that soar from sea level to upward of 2,800m (9,184 ft.); golden pampas and steppes that are home to guanacos and more than 100 species of colorful birds, such as parakeets and flamingos; electric-blue icebergs that cleave from glaciers descending from the Southern Ice Field; and thick, virgin beech forest. The park is not something you visit; it is something you experience.

Although it sits next to the Andes, **Parque Nacional Torres del Paine** is a separate geologic formation created roughly 3 million years ago when bubbling magma pushed its way up, taking a thick sedimentary layer with it. Glaciation and severe climate weathered away the softer rock, leaving the spectacular Paine Massif whose prominent features are the *Cuernos* (which means "horns") and the one-of-a-kind Torres—three salmon-colored, spherical granite towers. *Paine* is the Tehuelche Indian word for "blue," and it brings to mind the varying shades found in the lakes that surround this massif—among them the milky, turquoise waters of lakes Nordenskjold and Pehoé.

This park is a backpacker's dream, but just as many visitors find pleasure staying in lodges here and taking day hikes and horseback rides—even those with a short amount of time here are blown away by a 1-day visit.

Lamentably, a careless backpacker in February 2005 ignited a forest fire that burned nearly 15,000 hectares (37,050 acres) around the Laguna Amarga and Laguna Azul areas of Torres del Paine. Although the park's major highlights (such as the Towers, Horns, and the Glacier Grey region) were left unscathed, the blackened landscape at the Laguna Amarga entrance are a bleak welcome for visitors to the park.

For more information, check out the website **www.torresdelpaine.com**.

WHEN TO GO & WHAT TO BRING

This is not the easiest of national parks to visit. The climate in the park can be abominable, with wind speeds that can peak at 161kmph (100 mph) and rain and snow even in the middle of summer. The period in which your chances are highest of avoiding wind and rain are early October to early November and mid-March to late April, but keep in mind that the only thing predictable here is the unpredictability of the weather. Spring is a beautiful time for budding flowers and birds; during the fall, the beech forests turn striking shades of crimson, orange, and yellow. The winter is very cold, with relatively few snowstorms and no wind—but short days. Summer is ironically the worst time to come, especially late December to mid-February, when the wind blows at full fury and crowds descend upon the park. When the wind blows it can make even a short walk a rather scary and often frustrating experience—just try to go with it and revel in the excitement of the extreme environment that makes Patagonia what it is.

It is imperative that you bring the right gear (especially waterproof hiking boots if you plan to do any trekking), including weatherproof outerwear, and warm layers, even in the summer. The ozone problem is acute here, so you'll need sunscreen, sunglasses, and a hat.

GETTING THERE & AWAY

Many travelers are unaware of the enormous amount of time it takes to get to Torres del Paine. There are no direct transportation services from the airport in Punta Arenas to the park, except with package tours and hotels that have their own vehicles, or by chartering an auto or van (try **Viaterra** at (C) **61/410775;** www.viaterra.cl). If you're relying on bus transportation (as most do), it's only logical that you will need to spend the night in Punta Arenas or Puerto Natales.

BY BUS   Several companies offer daily service from October to April. During the low season, only **Bus Sur** offers service to the park. Buses to Torres del Paine enter through the Laguna Amarga ranger station, stop at the Pudeto catamaran dock, and terminate at the park administration center. If you're going directly to the Torres trail head at Hostería Las Torres, minivan transfers waiting at the Laguna Amarga station charge $3 (£1.55) one-way. The return times given below are when the bus leaves from the park administration center; the bus will pass through the Laguna Amarga station about 45 minutes later.

Bus Sur, Baquedano 668 ((C) **61/614220**), leaves daily at 7:30am and 2:30pm; **Fortaleza Aventura,** Arturo Prat 234 ((C) **61/410595**), leaves at 7am and 2pm, returning at 2 and 6pm; **Turismo María José,** Av. Manuel Bulnes 386 ((C) **61/414312**), leaves at 7:30am, returning at 2pm; and **Andescape,** Eberhard 599 ((C) **61/412592**), leaves at 7am, returning at 5pm (and there's a second departure at 2pm, returning at 10pm). The cost is around $14 (£7.20) one-way.

BY CAR   A brand-new road linking Puerto Natales with Torres del Paine opened in 2007, and not only does it shave more than an hour off the trip to the park, it is also one of the most visually stunning drives in Chile. Head toward the park from Puerto Natales and turn left at the sign for the Milodon Cave; the road continues from here and enters near the administration center, about 80km (50 miles). The old road is 140km from Puerto Natales (87 miles) and is best for backpackers interested in beginning their trek in the park with the Towers hike. When entering, follow the road toward the Laguna Amarga entrance.

CROSSING LAGO PEHOE BY CATAMARAN   Day hikes to the Glacier Grey trail and backpackers taking the W or Circuit trails will need to cross Lake Pehoé at some point aboard a catamaran, about a 45-minute ride. The cost is $16 (£8.20) one-way. Buses from Puerto Natales are timed to drop off and pick up passengers in conjunction with the catamaran (Dec–Mar 15 leaving Pudeto at 9:30am, noon, and 6pm, and from Pehoé 10am, 12:30, and 6:30pm; in Nov and Mar 16–30 from Pudeto at noon and 6pm, and Pehoé at 12:30 and 6pm; in Oct and Apr, from Pudeto at noon, from Pehoé at 12:30pm; closed May–Sept but may expand service—check with Conaf). Hikers walking the entire round-trip Glacier Grey trail can do so only from December to March 15 by taking the 9:30am boat and returning at 6:30pm.

GETTING TO OR FROM THE PARK BY BOAT   Few are aware that they can leave or arrive by boat to or from Puerto Natales through the Ultima Esperanza Sound and up the Río Serrano. Visitors ride a zodiac inflatable boat along the Río Serrano and past the glaciers Tyndall and Geike, terminating at the Serrano Glacier. Here you disembark for a walk up to the ice, and then board another boat for a 3½-hour ride to Puerto Natales. The trip costs $85 (£44) depending on the season. **Onas** is the company to call ((C)/fax **61/614300;** www.onaspatagonia.com).

Active travelers will be interested in following the same Río Serrano route but by **kayak,** about a 3-day journey. This trip is suitable for travelers on their way back to Puerto Natales, to take advantage of the river's downward current; at night, travelers camp out on shore. Check with **Antares** ((C) **61/414611;** www.antarespatagonia.com) on Barros Arana 111 in Puerto Natales.

WHERE TO STAY & DINE IN TORRES DEL PAINE
Hotels & *Hosterías*

Hostería Lago Grey ★★ This spruce little white *hostería* (small hotel) is tucked within a beech forest, looking out onto the beach at Lago Grey and the astounding blue icebergs that drift to its shore. It's colder on this side of the park, but the view is better here than at the Hostería las Torres, and Lago Grey has a transfer van and guides for excursions to all reaches of the park. The 30 rooms are spread out from the newly expanded dining and lounge area, and there is a spacious outdoor deck. The high-season price suggests more luxurious rooms, but they are cozy even though the walls are a tad thin. There are many trails that branch out from the hotel—both easy and difficult—and the boat ride to Glacier Grey leaves from this hotel. The transfer van will pick you up from anywhere in the park.

Office in Punta Arenas, Lautaro Navarro 1061. © 61/229512. www.lagogrey.cl. 30 units. Oct–Apr $250 (£128) double; May–Sept $95 (£49) double. Rates include buffet breakfast. AE, DC, MC, V. **Amenities:** Restaurant; lounge. *In room:* Hair dryer, safe.

Hostería Las Torres ★ *(Kids* This *hostería* sits at the trail head to the Torres on an *estancia* that still operates as a working cattle ranch. The complex includes a ranch-style hotel, a large campground, and a hostel, meaning there's a lot of traffic coming in and out daily. The main hotel has recently expanded and now has a large conference center and ethnohistorical display, more lounge room, a larger restaurant, and two bars. The *hostería* is a decent value for its standard rooms, but their superior rooms are nothing special for the price and are relatively identical to standard rooms. Las Torres recently inaugurated a small spa, with mud therapy, massage, and sauna. The *hostería* now offers packages that include guided tours, meals, and transportation, much like Explora, and off-season tours to little-explored areas—however, they are very pricey and the views and lodging facilities are a far cry from Explora. Try spending 2 nights here and 2 nights at Hostería Grey, thereby avoiding the steep price of an excursion there. The hotel has a delicious daily buffet dinner for $30 (£15) per person, not including drinks.

Office in Punta Arenas, Magallanes 960. ©/fax 61/710050. www.lastorres.com. 56 units. A 3-night/4-day package including meals, excursions, and airport transfers costs $1,270–$1,420 (£651–£728) double occupancy. AE, DC, MC, V. **Amenities:** Restaurant; lounge; tour desk; room service; laundry service; horseback riding.

Hotel Explora Salto Chico ★★★ *(Moments* Explora in Patagonia has garnered more fame than any other hotel in Chile, and deservedly so. Few hotels in the world offer as stunning a view as does Explora, perched above the milky, turquoise waters of Lago Pehoé and facing the dramatic granite amphitheater of the Cuernos formation. It is terribly expensive, but worth the splurge if you can afford it. Explora's style is relaxed elegance: softly curving, blond-wood walls built entirely from native deciduous beech are a soothing ambience in which to relax after a long hike. A band of picture windows wraps around the full front of the building, and there are large windows in each room. The furniture was handcrafted using local wood, and the smart guest rooms are accented with Spanish-made checkered linens, handsome slate-tiled bathrooms, powerful showers, and warming racks for drying gear. Explora recently expanded to include 20 new guest rooms, meaning it is easier now to get a reservation than before, but the hotel has, in the process, lost a bit of intimacy.

Explora is all-inclusive, with 4- and 8-night packages that cover airport transfers, meals, open bar, and excursions. Every evening, 5 of the 20 full-time guides meet with guests to discuss the following day's excursions, which range from easy to difficult. There are about 15 daily excursions, including horseback riding and photo safaris. Note that the first-day arrival to the hotel is around 6pm, time for a short hike only, and the last day is spent heading to the Punta Arenas airport. Americans make up more than 50% of the guests, who typically leave thrilled with their visit. Check out Explora's new Travesías, add-on journeys to Chaltén and the Fitz Roy National Park and Calafate, both in Argentina.

In Santiago, Américo Vespucio Sur 80, 5th floor. ℂ 866/750-6699 in the U.S. or 2/206-6060 in Santiago. Fax 2/228-4655. www.explora.com. 51 units. Packages per person, double occupancy; 4 nights/3 days from $3,510 (£1,800); 8 nights/6 days from $5,515 (£2,828). Rates include all meals, transportation, gear, and guides. AE, DC, MC, V. **Amenities:** Restaurant; bar; lounge; large indoor pool; outdoor Jacuzzi; sauna; massage.

Refugios & Albergues

Five cabinlike lodging units and one hostel, all with shared accommodation, are distributed along the park's Circuit and W trails, and they are moderately priced sleeping options for backpackers who are not interested in pitching a tent. Although most have bedding or sleeping bags for an expensive rental price, your best bet is to bring your own. The price, at $35 (£18) on average per night (about $63/£32 for room and full board), may seem steep; still, it is a far cry cheaper than many shared accommodations in national parks in the U.S. All come with hot showers, a cafe, and a common area for hiding out from bad weather. Meals served here are simply prepared but hearty, or alternatively, guests can bring their own food and cook for themselves. Each *refugio* has rooms with two to six bunks, which you'll have to share with strangers when they're full. During the high season, consider booking weeks in advance; although many visitors have reported luck when calling just a few days beforehand (due to cancellations). All agencies in Puerto Natales and Punta Arenas book reservations and issue vouchers, but the best bet is to call or e-mail (shown below). There is a scrappy *refugio* near the park administration center, with two rows of sleeping berths that I do not recommend except in an emergency situation! This *refugio* is on a first-come, first-served basis.

The first three *refugios* are owned and operated by **Fantástico Sur,** a division of the Hostería las Torres. They can be booked by contacting ℂ/fax **61/710050** or albergue@lastorres.com.

- **Albergue Las Torres.** This *albergue* (lodge) is the largest and most full-service *refugio* in the park; it sits near the Hostería Las Torres. You may dine in the hotel or eat simple fare in the *refugio* itself. Horseback rides can be taken from here.
- **Refugio Los Cuernos.** This may be the park's loveliest *refugio,* located at the base of the Cuernos. The wood structure (which miraculously holds up to some of the strongest winds in the park) has two walls of windows that look out onto Lago Nordenskjöld.

The first two *refugios* below can be reserved at ℂ/fax **61/412877;** andescape@terra.cl. The Lodge Paine Grande can be booked at ℂ **61/412742;** contact@verticepatagonia.cl.

- **Refugio Grey.** Tucked in a forest on the shore of Lago Grey, this log-cabin *refugio* is a 10-minute walk to the lookout point for the glacier. It's a cold but refreshing setting, and it has a cozy fireside seating area. Spend a day here and take a walking tour on the glacier (see "Excursions around Glacier Grey," below).
- **Refugio Dickson.** This is one of the loneliest *refugios,* due to its location well on the other side of the park (part of the Circuit trail). There are a lot of mosquitoes

in the summer, but you can't beat the rugged location on a grassy glacial moraine, facing Dickson Glacier.

• **Lodge Paine Grande.** This hostel-like "lodge" replaces the old *refugio* Pehoé, at the busiest intersection in the park. It is the hub for several of the trail heads to the park administration center, Glacier Grey, and French Valley, as well as the docking site for the catamaran. Utilitarian in style, the hostel has 60 beds, two lounges, and a cafeteria that can serve 120 people. Day walks to Glacier Grey and French Valley can be taken from here.

TRAILS IN TORRES DEL PAINE

Torres del Paine has something for everyone, from easy, well-trammeled trails to remote walks through rough wilderness. If you have only a few days, stick to the major highlights. If you have a week or more, consider a backpacking trip around the Circuit or a walk to the Valle de Silencio beyond the Towers, or for easier excursions, a horseback ride to Mt. Donoso or a bird-watching trip to Valley Pingo (for bird-watching tours, try **Fantástico Sur,** © **61/247194;** www.fantasticosur.com). Pick up a **JLM Torres del Paine map** or download a map from the website **www.torresdelpaine.com** to begin planning your itinerary.

DAY HIKES & TRIPS

The **Torres (Towers)** trail to view the granite formations that give the park its name is a classic hike, but certainly not the easiest. The 6-hour, moderate-to-difficult hike leaves from the Hostería Las Torres. The **Valle Francés (French Valley)** trail takes hikers into a granite amphitheater and past Paine Grande mountain and its hanging glacier. The trail is moderate and can be reached from Refugio Los Cuernos or the Lodge Paine Grande (at Pehoé). The trail to the face of **Glacier Grey** is a moderate to difficult trail that takes about 3½ hours one-way. From the *refugio* just before the lookout point, day hikers may catch the catamaran to Hostería Grey (see "Excursions around Glacier Grey," below) rather than walk back along the same trail.

The easiest walk in the park is also one of the most dramatic for the gigantic blue icebergs that rest along the shore of **Lago Grey.**

EXCURSIONS AROUND GLACIER GREY

Glacier Grey has receded substantially over the past few years, and now the best way to get an up-close view is aboard the **Hostería Grey catamaran,** a half-day excursion that takes passengers to the glacier's blue walls and around floating icebergs. The round-trip journey leaves from the shore of Lake Grey; however, it is possible to take the early catamaran across Lake Pehoé, walk the approximately 4 hours to the Refugio Grey, and then return by the Lake Grey catamaran. You'll need to arrange vehicle transportation through your hotel; otherwise the Hostería leaves you at the administration center to catch a bus. The trip leaves a little after 8am and 2:30pm, and reservations are essential; contact the Hostería at © **61/229512** (www.lagogrey.cl).

8

Colombia

by Jisel Perilla

If there's a country poised to be the next big ecotourism destination, it's Colombia. With an area equal to that of Spain, France, and Portugal combined, Colombia has coastlines on the Atlantic and Pacific oceans, thick Amazon jungle, immense flat lands evoking the American planes, scorching deserts, and snow-capped mountain peaks. All that plus 45 million residents mean that Colombia is second only to Brazil in ecological and human diversity among South American countries.

Once considered the most dangerous country in the world, Colombia, having implemented security improvements over the last half-decade, is slowly emerging from the internecine bloodshed of the 1980s and 1990s. Indeed, it's entering an era of peace never before experienced by the country's younger generations. The homicide rates in many Colombian cities, once among the highest in the world, have fallen to levels similar to those of U.S. cities such as Milwaukee and Philadelphia. Since President Alvaro Uribe took office in 2002, political kidnappings have decreased by over 70% and a strong military and police presence have made land transportation reasonably safe again.

Thanks to this improving security situation, Colombia is a country ripe for discovery by foreign tourists. Though politically one nation, it is made up of three distinct regions, each with its own customs and traditions. The Atlantic and Pacific coasts, inhabited mostly by descendents of African slaves, are culturally linked to the Caribbean, and rich in musical tradition and spectacular tropical scenery. The central and most densely populated portion of the country, crowned by the Andes Mountains, has managed to grow and prosper despite its unforgiving terrain. Dotted by most of Colombia's largest cities, it is the economic engine of the country. The eastern portion of Colombia is sparsely inhabited by tough, hard-working farmers and traditional indigenous tribes; it's a land of vast planes, thick jungle, unmatched natural beauty, and, unfortunately, high levels of guerilla activity and cocaine production.

Like most of the developing world, Colombia is a country of contradictions. Hip yuppies dress to the nines and sip cocktails at über-upscale bars while the poorest Colombians can barely afford life's necessities. Cosmopolitan cities offer luxury condos, theater, international cuisine, and all the amenities of the modern world while many small *pueblos* seem stuck in the last century, stunted by high unemployment and old-fashioned attitudes. Despite all its woes—economic, social, and political—Colombia remains a fascinating country to visit. *Tip:* For a map of suggested itineraries in Colombia, please refer to the "Itineraries in Bolivia, Brazil, Colombia, Ecuador & Peru" map on p. 222.

El Conflicto Armado: Who's Fighting Whom

Although security conditions have improved dramatically since conservative hard-liner Alvaro Uribe took office in 2002, Colombia can still be an unpredictable place, with flare-ups between guerilla and paramilitary factions. To understand the conflict, it's important to know the players. On the leftist, guerilla side is the **FARC** (Revolutionary Armed Forces of Colombia), the country's largest guerilla army with about 12,000 members. The **ELN** (National Liberation Army) consists of about 5,000 people and is in on-and-off-again demobilization talks. The **M-19** was another deadly, mostly urban guerilla movement that demobilized in the late 1980s. On the far right are the **paramilitaries,** originally formed to combat the guerillas but now major players in the drug trade. **Las Aguilas Negras** are a relatively new group, composed mostly of so-called demobilized paramilitaries.

To make sense of all the acronyms and ideology, not to mention the corruption, consider reading one of the following books, all of which provide excellent background: *Killing Peace* (Information Network of the Americas, 2002) by Gary Leech; *Walking Ghosts: Murder and Guerrilla Politics in Colombia* (Taylor & Francis, 2005) by Steven Dudley; and *More Terrible Than Death: Violence, Drugs, and America's War in Colombia* (Perseus Publishing, 2004) by Robin Kirk.

Although the modern Colombian conflict didn't technically start until 1964 when the FARC was founded, Colombia has had a bloody past almost as long as the country's history. The violence, always rooted in politics, pitted the Liberals against the Conservatives, resulting in both the Thousand Days War, from 1899–1902, and, later on, La Violencia of the 1940s and '50s. Combined, these conflicts took the lives of almost half a million Colombians. After the relative peace of the 1960s and '70s, violence flared up again during the '80s and '90s, mostly owing to the increased involvement of the guerillas and paramilitaries in the drug trade, as well as to Pablo Escobar, who had a hand in frequent bombings, assassinations, and campaigns of terror.

1 The Regions in Brief

Colombia is a country with much to offer the adventurous tourist. Whether you want to enjoy the sophisticated city atmosphere of Bogotá, swim in the clear Caribbean waters of San Andrés or Providencia, or live the cowboy life in the Eje Cafetero, Colombia has what you're looking for.

BOGOTA　Situated at more than 2,400m (8,000 ft.), and bordered by the Andes to the east, Bogotá is the third-highest capital in the world. Its nearly eight million residents make it Colombia's largest city by far, and one that has some of South America's best museums, universities, and restaurants. Bogotá is quickly taking on an international character as more and more multinationals invest in and set up headquarters there.

ANTIOQUIA & THE EJE CAFETERO　This is Colombia's cowboy country, not to mention one of its wealthiest regions, blessed with magnificent mountain scenery,

Unlike most Latin American movements, the FARC, paramilitaries, and other nongovernment armed forces have little backing among Colombia's poor, especially as these armed groups become more involved with narco-trafficking, effectively disregarding their stated ideology. In fact, fighting for control of the lucrative cocaine trade appears to be the top priority for guerilla and paramilitary groups nowadays.

As a foreigner and a tourist, you are unlikely to face threats from any illegal groups, but it's still wise to avoid rural areas, city slums, and other "red zones"—so declared by the government depending on recent guerilla and paramilitary violence. Your best bet is to **stick to cities and heavily patrolled and visited destinations** such as the Eje Cafetero, the department of Boyacá, and most of the Atlantic coast. Unless for some reason you'll be traveling to guerilla- or paramilitary-controlled areas (where you absolutely don't want to talk about the conflict), you're fine to discuss the FARC, paramilitaries, or much-loved President Uribe with taxi drivers, waiters, receptionists, and other Colombians; everyone here seems to have an opinion, and this is a good way to interact with and learn about the locals and their country.

Keep tabs on the ever-changing situation by reading *El Tiempo* (www.eltiempo.com), Colombia's most important and popular newspaper, and by frequently checking the U.S Department of State website regarding travel warnings (http://travel.state.gov/travel). You may also want to keep tabs on the growing tensions between President Alvaro Uribe and Venezuelan President Hugo Chávez, as this might result in further violence along the Colombia–Venezuela border. Although all this information may sound a bit ominous and discouraging, the bottom line is, unless you veer off the beaten path, you shouldn't face any problems.

coffee-terraced slopes, and old-world small towns. But Antioquia and the Eje Cafetero aren't all country: Armenia, Manizales, and Pereira are thriving cities with a coffee-based economy and Medellín, Colombia's second largest metropolis, is one of Latin America's most progressive and innovative cities.

SAN ANDRES, PROVIDENCIA & THE ATLANTIC COAST Some of the safest and most accessible travel experiences in the country are found here. San Andrés, long popular with Colombian tourists, boasts beautiful white-sand beaches and sprawling, all inclusive resorts, while less developed Providencia is famous for its Caribbean-English architecture and scuba diving. Cartagena, the pride and joy of Colombia, has the most impressive Old City in the Americas, dating all the way back to the 16th century. Its many plazas and restaurants come alive at night and its colonial architecture is unmatched anywhere on the western hemisphere.

THE SOUTHWEST & PACIFIC COAST Though still considered dangerous, this region has some accessible areas. Cali, the salsa-music capital of Colombia, claims to have the most beautiful women in Colombia, and its nightlife is unrivaled anywhere in Colombia. Popayán, second only to Cartagena in terms of colonial architecture, is a beautiful, white-washed city with an active student and cafe life. The Pacific coast and El Chocó, inhabited almost exclusively by African descendants, is one of the wettest regions in the world, known for its dense jungles and unnavigable rivers. Unfortunately, much of this region is controlled by leftist guerillas or right-wing paramilitaries, but some intrepid travelers have visited the coast's pristine, virgin beaches. Nariño and its capital, Pasto, in many ways are culturally closer to Ecuador and Peru, and offer some of the highest peaks and best markets in the country. *Warning:* I recommend that travelers avoid this region. If, however, you're intent on going, try to fly to your destination and be sure to check security conditions first. Resources include the U.S. Department of State website (www.travel.state.gov), Colombian newspapers such as *El Tiempo* (www.eltiempo.com), and Colombians themselves.

THE EASTERN PLANES & THE AMAZON JUNGLE Most of Colombia is composed of sparsely inhabited planes and jungle. Los Llanos, as they are known in Colombia, are physically similar to the American Midwest, and inhabitants have a definitively independent, relentless spirit. The eastern planes have recently become safer as the Colombian armed forces battle guerilla and paramilitaries to reclaim the land, but I don't recommend venturing into this region on your own.

The Amazon covers 33% of Colombia, but only 1% of the country's population—mostly indigenous tribes—lives there. Except for Leticia and its surroundings, this area is inaccessible. *Warning:* The dense jungle make this region perfect for coca production as well as paramilitary and guerilla activity; do not venture here unless you're taking a direct flight to Leticia.

2 The Best of Colombia in 2 Weeks

Two weeks in Colombia should provide you with a good feel for the country and give you enough time to see some of the major sights and cities. Keep in mind that road conditions can be unpredictable, so it's best to fly between the far-flung destinations.

Days ❶–❸: Bogotá

Spend your first day in Colombia exploring **La Candelaria** and the historic center. Have breakfast at La Puerta Falsa, Colombia's longest-running business and restaurant. Stop at the **Museo del Oro** (p. 479) at Santander Square, and visit the **Museo Botero** (p. 478) for an overview of Colombia's most famous artist. Recharge your energy by having lunch at any of La Candelaria's quaint eateries, popular with college students. In the afternoon, head to **Plaza de Bolívar** to feed the pigeons and be awed by

Bogotá's eclectic architecture. Stay at the amazing Casa Medina or Hotel de la Opera and eat at one of the many gourmet restaurants in Bogotá's "gourmet district." On Day 2, if you're around on a weekend or holiday, hop on the Turistren, the only remaining steam engine in Colombia. If you're not around on the weekend, visit a few more of Bogotá's 50-plus museums—culture buffs should go to the **Museo de Trajes Regionales** (p. 479) while those interested in Colombian history will enjoy the **Quinta de Bolívar** (p. 479). Also explore some of the city's most popular parks, such as Parque La 93. Dedicate Day 3 to shopping. If you're looking for handicrafts and cheap clothing, shop to your heart's content at **San Victorino Square.** If you're looking for posh designer clothing, leather goods, or jewelry, head to one of the upscale malls in the city's northern districts.

Days ❹–❺: Villa de Leyva

Take a 4-hour bus to the perfectly preserved town of Villa de Leyva, and spend Day 4 exploring the cobblestone streets and handicraft shops. Stay at the Hotel del Molio, a 450-year-old former mill. On Day 5, learn a bit about the Colombian independence movement by visiting the **Museo de Antonio Nariño** (p. 491) and see one of Colombia's most complete collections of religious art at **El Museo de Arte Religioso.** Spend the evening people-watching in the main plaza from one of the many open-air cafes bordering the plaza. Alternatively, book a tour with one of the numerous companies offering adventure and nature activities around Villa de Leyva. Go rock climbing, visit a vineyard, hike in a nearby desert, or explore one of the many waterfalls around town.

Days ❻–❼: Medellín & Antioquia

Fly into Medellín and spend Day 6 exploring the city center. Hop on a Turibus to visit the **Catedral Metropolitana** (p. 496) and other major sites. In early afternoon, take the free cable car up to the *comunas* for great views of Medellín. For dinner, dine at one of the many classy restaurants around **Parque Lleras** before heading to Vía de Las Palmas for a night of dancing. For a change of pace, on Day 7, book a tour of the surrounding Antioquian countryside with **Aviatur** (p. 464).

Days ❽–❿: The Eje Cafetero

Book a farm-stay in the **Eje Cafetero** (p. 500). On Day 8, let yourself relax in the Thermal Waters of Santa Rosa before heading to your colonial-style farm deep in the coffee-growing region. The next day, learn about the coffee-growing process at the Parque Nacional del Café. Spend Day 10 swimming, exploring the verdant countryside, and taking pictures of the breathtaking scenery.

Days ⓫–⓮: The Atlantic Coast

Fly from Pereira, Armenia, or Manizales into the magical city of **Cartagena.** On Day 11, spend the morning sunbathing and swimming in the warm Caribbean waters. In the afternoon, book a *chiva* tour of the city for a brief history and overview of the city's major sights. At night, head to the **Club de Pesca** (p. 511) for a romantic seafood dinner overlooking Cartagena's yacht basin. Stay at the historic **Santa Clara Hotel** (Sofitel Santa Clara, p. 509) in San Diego Square. On Day 12, head to the Old City to explore its many plazas, museums, and shops. Have lunch in Santo Domingo Square. In the evening, book a spot on the Rumba Chiva, a typical Colombia party bus, or, if you're feeling a bit more romantic, take your special someone on a carriage stroll through the Old Town. Spend the next day in **Las Islas del Rosario.** Visit the Aquario de San Martín, and go snorkeling and swimming in the bright green waters of Isla de Baru, 45 hours from Cartagena. If you still have energy left, head to Mr. Babilla, in Getsemaní, or Tu Candela, in La Plaza de Los Coches, for a night of fun and dancing. On day 14, depart Cartagena, flying either directly home from there or connecting in Bogotá.

3 Planning Your Trip to Colombia

VISITOR INFORMATION

Because Colombia's tourism infrastructure is extremely underdeveloped, traveling here can be a bit tricky, especially if you don't speak Spanish. Except for Cartagena and some parts of the Atlantic Coast, many sections of Colombia have seen only a trickle

Staying Safe

Colombia isn't the place to wonder off the beaten path, not even in cities. Stick to neighborhoods you know are safe.

- **Never** resist an attempted robbery—Colombian criminals can be armed and unpredictable.
- **Always** call a cab at night, especially if you have been drinking or are traveling alone. If your level of Spanish is low or you are a woman traveling alone, I advise you to always call a cab to avoid being taken on a long and expensive ride. Always make sure the cab door is locked to avoid an armed assailant hopping in at a stop light.
- **Don't** accept any drinks, drugs, or cigarettes from a stranger or someone you've just met; they could be laced with an odorless drug that makes you lose your will while you are robbed. Also, it's best not to pick up any papers or cash that someone walking ahead of you drops, as this can also be the same kind of trick. This is especially important for women. These types of crimes are rare but not unheard of.

of foreign visitors in the last few decades. Although tourists are generally treated formally and with polite curiosity, don't expect to find an overwhelming amount of tourist information. Remember that a visit to Colombia requires patience and a sense of humor. One of the best ways to prepare for your trip to Colombia is on the Internet, where you will find plenty of useful information, especially from fellow travelers. The following websites contain useful information about Colombia.

- **www.iexplore.com/dmap/Colombia/Travel+and+Trips**: Dedicated to adventure travel, this site provides valuable country, etiquette, and excursion information.
- **poorbuthappy.com/colombia**: A great traveler-created site where you can find information, ask questions, and do research. Especially good for the younger, backpacker crowd.
- **www.roadjunky.com/guide/298/colombia-travel-guide-online**: An okay country guide with basic information.
- **www.colombiaemb.org**: Colombia's embassy in Washington. A good place to start exploring the country.

IN COLOMBIA

The Ministerio de Comercio, Industria y Turismo is Colombia's National Tourism Ministry. The main office is located at Calle 28 no. 13A–15 (© **1/606-7676** or 419-9450), but don't expect them to be very helpful or speak much English. In fact, good luck even getting into the building. But if you read Spanish, you may want to check out their website (www.mincomercio.gov.co/eContent/home.asp).

Colombia's most popular tourism agency, **Aviatur** (© **1/286-5555** or 234-7333; http://site.aviatur.com/portal.htm), will book tours all over Colombia, usually including transportation, lodging, and most meals. The main office in Bogotá is located at Ave. 19 no. 4–62. There are offices throughout Bogotá and all large Colombian cities as well.

Tourism companies frequently come and go, so if you're looking for eco-adventure tours and travel, your best bet is the local tourism office, which can give you information on local tours and tourism agencies, or your hotel, which should also be able to guide you.

ENTRY REQUIREMENTS

A valid passport is required to visit Colombia. Visas are not required if you are a citizen of the United States, the United Kingdom, Canada, Australia, New Zealand, South Africa, France, Germany, or Switzerland. You will automatically be granted permission to stay in the country for 60 days upon entering Colombia. If you plan to spend more than 60 days in the country, you will have to get permission from the Colombian Security Department (DAS) office in any departmental capital, though most tourists do so in Bogotá. To receive this 30- to 60-day extension, you will need to deposit COL$60,400 (US$30/£15) to Bancafé (account #056-99020-3, code 103), and then present your passport, your plane ticket (showing date of departure), four color passport pictures (3cm×4cm), two photocopies of your passport picture page, two copies of your passport entry stamp page, two copies of the Bancafé deposit slip, and two copies of your plane ticket. The process usually takes 1 to 2 hours, but you will be given the extension on the spot. You can repeat the process until you've been in the country 180 days. The **Bogotá DAS office,** at Calle 100 no. 11B–27, Edificio Platino (© 1/601-7200), is open Monday through Thursday 7:30am to 4pm and Friday 7:30am to 3pm. If you stay in Colombia more than 60 days without a visa extension, you can be fined US$60 to US$1,600 (£30–£800).

COLOMBIAN EMBASSY LOCATIONS

In the U.S.: 2118 Leroy Place NW, Washington, DC 20008 (© **202/387-8338;** www.colombiaemb.org)

In Canada: 360 Albert St. Ste 1002, Piso 10 K1R 7X7, Ottawa, ON (© **613/230-3760;** embajada@embajadacolombia.ca)

In the U.K.: 3 Hans Crescent, London, SW1X OLN (© **020/7589-9177;** fax 020/7581-1829; www.colombianembassy.co.uk)

In Australia: 101 Northbourne Ave., Turner, ACT 2601 (© **02/6257-2027;** fax 02/6257-1448)

Telephone Dialing at a Glance

Colombia's phone system features a standardized system of seven-digit local numbers with one or two digit area codes.

- **To place a call from your home country to Colombia,** dial the international access code (011 in the U.S and Canada, 011 in Australia, 0170 in New Zealand, and 00 in the U.K.), the country code (57), the one- or two-digit Colombian city code (Bogotá 1, Medellín 4, Cartagena 5, Pereira 61, Armenia 67, Manizales 69), plus the seven-digit local number.
- **To place a local call within Colombia,** dial the one- or two-digit city code followed by the seven-digit local number. To call within a city, you only need to dial the seven-digit number.

CUSTOMS

Upon entering Colombia, you will be asked to complete a Customs form detailing your personal effects. There is a regularly updated limit on cash and goods you may take out of the country. Because of strict drug-trafficking laws, *do not* try to take more money out of Colombia than you claim—at a minimum, this could result in heavy questioning. For more information regarding this limit, call © **1/546-2200** or 457-8270. When leaving the country, you must pay an airport departure tax of about COL\$114,520 (US\$57/£29), though this tax is often included in your airline ticket.

MONEY

The **Colombian peso** is the official currency. Money is denominated in notes of 1,000, 2,000, 5,000, 10,000, 20,000, and 50,000, and coins of 20, 50, 100, 200, and 500 pesos. At press time, the exchange rate was about **COL\$2,000 to US\$1** and about **COL\$4,000 to £1.** These rates can fluctuate somewhat, so it's important to check the latest exchange rate at **www.xe.com/ucc**.

CURRENCY EXCHANGE   Unlike in other Latin-American countries, the U.S. dollar is not widely accepted in Colombia. You can convert your currency in upscale hotels, at *casas de cambio* (money-exchange houses), at most banks, and at the airport. It's not recommended to bring traveler's checks to Colombia. They can be exchanged at some banks and used at high-end hotels, but usually they aren't accepted elsewhere. Make sure your bank or issuer has a representative in Colombia before purchasing traveler's checks.

ATMs   Cash machines are easy to find in urban areas and most medium-to-large towns, though they are almost impossible to come across in rural areas. Withdrawing money from ATMs is preferable to exchanging money in banks, which charge a some-times hefty transaction fee. ATMs also give you the most up-to-date rate of exchange. Thefts at ATMs have been reported, however, so if you are taking out large sums of money, be sure not to put all your cash in one place (spread the bills among your pockets). *Warning:* If you are having trouble with an ATM, do not accept help from anyone, even if he or she seems friendly and honest. This is the easiest way to wipe out your bank account.

CREDIT CARDS   Credit cards, particularly Visa and MasterCard, are generally accepted in midrange and upscale shops, as well as at upscale restaurants and hotels around the country. In rural areas and small towns, you are unlikely to find establishments that accept credit cards. When booking tours, you're likely to get a better deal when using cash.

WHEN TO GO

PEAK SEASON   In the Andean Region, the dry season falls between December and March and July and August. Christmas is a particularly festive time in Colombia, though prices often rise and hotel rooms fill up quickly in Cartagena and the Atlantic Coast, as well as in other popular tourist destinations. During the Christmas holiday, Easter, and summer vacation, you'll have to book hotels in advance and be prepared to pay a bit extra. If possible, avoid Colombia in October and November, as these are the rainiest months, and flooding and poor road conditions are common.

CLIMATE   Because of its proximity to the Equator, Colombia's temperature varies according to altitude rather than season. In high altitudes, days are cool and nights can dip near the freezing mark. In lowlands, expect a tropical, humid climate with little difference between daytime and nighttime temperatures. As a general guide, the average temperature in Bogotá is 14°C (57°F), in Cartagena 31°C (87°F), and in Medellín 24°C (75°F). See "Peak Season," above, for information on the rainiest months.

PUBLIC HOLIDAYS Colombia has more public holidays than any other nation except Brazil. Usually, if a holiday falls on a Saturday or Sunday, it is celebrated the following Monday. Public Holidays are New Year's Day (Jan 1); Epiphany (Jan 6); St. Joseph's Day (Mar 19); Maundy Thursday and Good Friday (Mar/Apr); Labor Day (May 1); Ascension (May); Corpus Christi (May/June); Sacred Heart (June); Day of St. Peter and St. Paul (June 29); Independence Day (Aug 7); Assumption (Aug 15); Discovery of America (Oct 12); All Saints' Day (Nov 1); Independence of Cartagena (Nov 11); Immaculate Conception (Dec 8); and Christmas (Dec 25).

HEALTH CONCERNS

In major cities, you'll have little cause for worry. Water is generally fine to drink, though cautious travelers may want to stick to bottled water. The problem you're most likely to encounter is **traveler's diarrhea,** from inexpensive food. Use common sense—avoid eating unpeeled fruits and vegetables from street vendors, wash your hands frequently, and when trying a new fruit or vegetable, don't overdo it. Remember to wear sunscreen at all times, even in cool cities like Bogotá. You're closer to the sun, and you don't want to let **sunburn** ruin your vacation. In major cities, health care is adequate and professional, as long as you stick to private clinics. Public clinics tend to have long lines and are usually understaffed and underfunded.

If you are visiting the Andean region, **altitude sickness** is a possibility. Though it generally goes away after 2 to 5 days, it may be helpful to bring along Tylenol, Advil, or another over-the-counter painkiller. Symptoms include headache, shortness of breath, fatigue, nausea, and sleepiness. Try to take it easy the first day or two to avoid worsening your condition. You might experience altitude sickness in Bogotá or Tunja, or when hiking in the high Andes.

Though no vaccines are required to enter Colombia, it's a good idea to consider getting vaccinations for hepatitis A and B; typhoid; and yellow fever if you will be visiting the Atlantic or Pacific Coast, the Amazon region, or any other tropical region. (As a general rule, the more rural your location in the country's tropical regions, the higher your risk of contracting diseases such as **malaria, yellow fever,** or **cholera**). **Dengue fever** is another concern in the tropics, though unfortunately there is no preventative vaccine. You should also consider taking malaria pills if you will be visiting any of the above regions.

GETTING THERE
BY PLANE

Planes arrive at **El Dorado International Airport** (© 1/413-9053; airport code: BOG), located about 13km (8 miles) from the city center. El Dorado handles most international arrivals and you'll likely fly into Bogotá. There is a departure tax of $59 (£30) upon exiting the country, though all or at least part of this is usually included in your ticket.

FROM THE U.S. There are direct flights from New York, Atlanta, and Miami. **Avianca** (© 800/284-2622; www.avianca.com) has several daily flights to Bogotá, as well as one direct daily flight to Medellín and Cartagena. **American Airlines** (© 800/ 433-7300; www.american.com) has three daily flights from Miami to Bogotá, two daily flights to Medellín. From JFK in New York, **Delta** (© 800/221-1212; www. delta.com) and Avianca each have one daily direct flight to Bogotá. From Atlanta, Delta and Avianca each offer one daily flight to Bogotá. **Continental** (© 800/944-0219; www.continental.com), **Copa** (© 800/550-7700; www.copaair.com), and **Taca** (© 800/535-8780; www.taca.com) also offer service to Bogotá, though you'll have to connect.

FROM CANADA **Air Canada** (© 888/247-2262; www.aircanada.ca) offers a direct flight between Toronto and Bogotá several times a week. Otherwise, you'll have to connect in the U.S. using one of the carriers listed above, which might actually turn out to be a cheaper option.

FROM EUROPE & THE U.K. From Paris, **Air France** (© 0870/142-4343; www.airfrance.co.uk) offers one daily direct flight to Bogotá. **Iberia** (© 0845/601-2854; www.iberia.com) flies direct to Bogotá from Madrid. Avianca, American, Continental, and Air France have flights from Madrid to Bogotá, connecting through Paris or in the U.S.; London, Rome, and Frankfurt offer similar options with one connection.

FROM AUSTRALIA & NEW ZEALAND You'll be connecting in the U.S, and possibly Central or South America as well. Your best bet from Australia is on American Airlines, connecting in Los Angeles en route to Bogotá. From New Zealand, some of your better options are **LAN** (© 800/221-572; www.lan.com/index-en-un.html) and **Air New Zealand** (© 0800/737-000; www.airnz.co.nz), though be prepared for at least two stops.

BY BUS
Although you can technically enter Colombia via Venezuela to the east and Ecuador to the south, this is not your safest option. It's much safer than it was a few years ago, but flying is not only much more secure, it's quicker and definitely more comfortable. If you insist on traveling by bus, be sure to make your journey during the daytime, and keep an eye on worsening Colombia-Venezuela relations if you're crossing in from Venezuela. You'll probably have to transfer buses at the border.

BY BOAT
Unless you're going directly to Cartagena, you probably won't be arriving by boat. That said, Cartagena is now becoming a popular stop for Caribbean Cruise liners and private yacht owners.

GETTING AROUND
BY PLANE
Flying is the fastest way to get around Colombia. Precipitous two-lane winding roads can make road travel long, tiring, and a bit nauseating. Distances by plane are usually short (between 30 min. and 1 hr.), though prices are relatively steep. Except to pay about COL$150,000 to COL$500,000 (US$75–US$250/£38–£125) for a 30- to 60-minute flight between major cities. Colombian airline prices are generally fixed and unlikely to vary much between airline carriers. **Avianca/SAM** (© 018000/123-434; www.avianca.com) is Colombia's largest and most extensive carrier, covering both domestic and international routes. That said, service is often inefficient and customer service is poor. **Aerorepública** (© 018000/917-766; www.aerorepublica.com.co) covers much of the same territory as Avianca. **AIRES** (© 018000/524-737; www. aires.com.co) services smaller cities and towns, and **SATENA** (© 01900/331-7100;

www.satena.com) flies to difficult locations such as the Amazon, the Pacific coast, and dozens of other small towns and villages.

Tip: It's important to note that if you will be using an international (non-Colombian) credit card to purchase your airline ticket online, you will need to book your flight at least 3 days in advance, or through a non-Colombian search engine such as Expedia. Another choice if you are short on time is to buy your tickets at the airport, where you won't have any problems using your credit card.

BY BUS

Since President Uribe took office in 2002, road travel in Colombia has improved dramatically. Most routes between major cities and towns are safe, though southwest Colombia can still be dangerous. As a woman traveling alone, I take buses throughout Colombia without incident, but every traveler's comfort level is different. It's a good idea to check security conditions before you board a long-distance night bus, especially if you'll be traveling through high-risk area. You can find a bus to almost any city or town in the country from the Bogotá bus terminal, Terminal de Buses. Bus routes from Medellín, Cali, and Barranquilla also cover much of the country. Road conditions are generally good, but it's important to remember that these are two-lane mountain roads, so if there is a back-up or accident, you're stuck in place for at least a couple of hours. Also during the wet season—particularly October and November—the rain can cause mudslides and unpredictable road conditions.

Unless you're taking a route with irregular departures, it's unnecessary to book in advance, the exception being if you are traveling during Christmas or a Puente weekend (3-day holiday weekend) during which you might want to consider purchasing your ticket a day or two in advance. Bus travel isn't as cheap as in nearby Ecuador or Peru; expect to pay about COL$10,000 (US$5/£2.50) per 100km, but buses are generally comfortable. *Tip:* Stick to large buses, since small *colectivos* are bumpy and uncomfortable. And avoid taking *corrientes,* which seem to stop every couple of meters. No matter what class of bus, be prepared for onboard entertainment of *vallenato* and *ranchera* tunes, as well as ultraviolet movies, at whatever volume your driver chooses.

BY CAR

Renting a car in Colombia is a bad idea. Car accidents are one of the top causes of death in Colombia. In urban areas, Colombians tend to be aggressive and careless behind the wheel, often neither following street signs or traffic lights nor giving pedestrians the right of way. On rural roads and mountain passes, winding roads and near head-on collisions with trucks, as well as the occasional livestock crossing, can be intimidating at best. Public transportation options are safer, cheaper, and much less likely to be stopped by guerillas or paramilitaries than a fancy family-size car. Some upscale hotels offer a chauffeur/car service, which can be rented by the hour or by the day, but don't expect any great deals. If, after hearing all this, you are still determined to drive in Colombia, expect to pay at least COL$102,250 (US$51/£26) a day. Make sure you and the car are insured, and be aware that gas doesn't come cheap in Colombia—we're talking COL$7,158 (US$3.60/£1.80) a gallon. Some companies that rent cars in Colombia are: **Avis** (www.avis.com), **Hertz** (www.hertz.com), and **Budget** (www.budget.com).

TIPS ON DINING

You won't be hungry in Colombia. Though every region has its own specialties, you're never far from a plate of beans, beef, plantains, and rice. Food is good, hearty, and generally cheap, if not particularly varied. For gourmands, major cities such as Bogotá, Medellín, and Cartagena also offer a huge range of upscale, gourmet, and international options. Some typical dishes to look for on your menu include *ajiaco* (chicken soup with potatoes, avocado, corn, and capers); *bandeja paisa* (rice, avocado, salad); *chicharrón* (minced meat, egg, plantain, and yuca); *sancocho* (plantain, yuca, potato, and beef, chicken, or fish soup); *lechona* (stuffed baked pig); *arepa* (flat corn bread often topped with cheese or butter); and *tamales* (corn dough, chicken, and vegetables cooked and served in plantain leaves).

Tinto, black coffee, is Colombia's most popular beverage and can be enjoyed at anytime, just about anywhere. Other popular drinks are beer, *aguardiente* (the licorice-flavored national liquor), hot chocolate, and soda products. Bottled water (or bagged) water can usually be found at most stores and street stands. Thanks to its tropical climate and fertile soil, Colombia has countless exotic fruit juices such as *guanábana* (soursop), *lulo, maracuyá* (passion fruit), and *tomate de árbol* (tree tomato). Wine is not particularly popular in Colombia, and Colombian wines on the whole leave a lot to be desired. However, upscale restaurants and grocery stores generally offer high-quality Argentine and Chilean varieties.

TIPS ON SHOPPING

Handicrafts are relatively cheap and easy to find in Colombia, though the deals aren't as good as you get in Ecuador, Bolivia, and Peru. In urban areas, you're likely to find the best bargains in city centers; handicraft stores in upscale shopping malls charge at least double the price, though you're generally guaranteed quality. In small towns and rural areas, you can expect to find more authentic and regional crafts at fair prices. At markets and such, you may be able to bargain somewhat, though don't expect a price to drop more than a couple of thousand pesos.

Aside from handicrafts, Colombians are serious about clothing. Bogotá, Cartagena, and Cali are a shopaholic's dream come true. At shopping centers and boutiques in more upscale areas, clothing is generally high quality albeit a bit expensive (prices are comparable to stores in the States such as the Limited and Banana Republic). In the most upscale city zones and shopping centers, you'll be greeted by the likes of Armani, Tommy Hilfiger, and other designers. Shoes and leather handbags, as well as gold and emerald jewelry, are popular buys and can be purchased at decent prices; it's best to ask around to find the spots with the best bargains.

FAST FACTS: Colombia

American Express American Express offices are located in Bogotá at Calle 85, no. 20–32 (✆ 1/593-4949).

Business Hours Business hours vary significantly between urban and rural areas. In urban areas, businesses and banks are generally open between 8am and noon and then again between 2 and 6pm. In Bogotá, banks are supposedly open all day between 8am and 4pm. Stores are generally open between 9am to 5pm, while department stores and large supermarkets generally stay open until around 9pm. In the countryside, businesses and stores are generally open fewer hours and don't necessarily stick to their posted schedules. Also, many businesses close down or reduce their hours on Sundays and holidays.

Electricity Electric outlets accept U.S.-type plugs. Electricity in Colombia runs at 110 volts, so transformers are not necessary for tourists from the U.S. If you are planning to use anything with a three-prong plug, bring an adapter, as some establishments only have two-prong outlets.

Embassies In Bogotá: **United States:** Calle 22, Bis. 47–51 (✆ **1/315-0811**); **Canada:** Carrera 7 no. 115–33, Piso 14 (✆ **1/657-9800**); **Australia** (consulate): Carrera 18 no. 90–38 (✆ **1/636-5247** or 530-1047); **United Kingdom:** Carrera 9 no. 76–49, Piso 9 (✆ **1/326-8300** or 317-6423 for visa information).

Emergencies In Bogotá, the police emergency number is **112**. Another emergency number that works throughout the country is **123**. Other good emergency numbers to know: the Security Police (DAS; ✆ **153/0180-0091-9622**); the Tourist Police (✆ **1/337-4413** or 243-1175); and the police station in Bogotá (✆ **156**).

Hospitals Some of the best hospitals in Bogotá are **Clínica Marly,** Calle 50, no. 9–67 (✆ **1/570-4424,** 572-5011, or 343-6600); **Fundación Santa Fe,** Calle 119, no. 9–02 (✆ **1/629-0766** or 629-0477); and **Clínica El Bosque,** Calle 134, no. 12–55 (✆ **1/274-0577,** 274-5445, or 649-9300).

Internet Access You're never far from a cybercafe in Bogotá and other major urban centers. Small towns will also generally have at least one Internet cafe. In rural areas, Internet access is hard to come by. Connections are generally fast and cheap. Expect to pay about COL$1,500 to COL$2,500 (US75¢–$1.50/38p–75p) per hour.

Liquor Laws The legal drinking age in Colombia is 18, though laws are lenient. In urban areas such as Bogotá, Medellín, Cartagena, and Cali, you may be asked to show ID to get into upscale bars and clubs. There are no laws against drinking in public, so if you are low on funds, feel free to open up a bottle of *aguardiente* in the nearby park or plaza.

Maps Maps of Colombia and Bogotá can usually be found in tourist offices, though it's not uncommon for the tourist office to run out of maps. In Bogotá, you can also find high-quality maps in a La Pan Americana (www.panamericana editorial.com/almacenes) and most hotels.

Newspapers & Magazines National and local newspapers and magazines can be found in all cities and most towns. In Bogotá, look for *El Tiempo* and *El Espectador;* in **Medellín** look for *El Mundo* and *El Colombiano;* and in Cartagena, you'll find *El Universal. Semana* is the most popular weekly magazine. Unfortunately, there are few, if any, English-language publications in Colombia.

Post Offices & Mail The postal system in Colombia is relatively efficient in large cities, though the same can't be said for rural area. Servientrega, DHL, FedEx, and DePrisa are available in Colombia for local and international shipping services, as is Avianca Airlines. While mail within Colombia is cheap, sending items abroad is extremely expensive.

Restrooms Bathroom quality varies. Expensive hotels, restaurants, and shops generally have clean facilities and toilet paper. As long as you're polite, restaurant, hotel, and store owners won't mind if you use their facilities. It's a good idea to bring your own toilet paper and hand-sanitizer wherever you go, as budget establishments rarely have these items.

Safety Colombia is still far from being among the safest countries in the world. Much of the rural countryside is still tightly controlled by armed groups and is thus inaccessible to tourists. Travelers are advised to stick to well-touristed areas and keep up to date with the ever-changing political situation to avoid problems. But if you take adequate precautions, you're more likely to have a run-in with common street thieves than with guerilla or paramilitary factions.

That being said, theft is a major problem in Colombia, particularly in cities. Never accept anything (cigarettes, drinks, papers, food, and the like) from strangers, as it could be laced with Burundanga, an odorless, colorless chemical that makes you lose your will, while the thief and his accomplice take you around the city, maxing out your debit card at every ATM in sight. At night, always call a taxi (instead of hailing one on the street), as this crime has been known to occur in taxis.

Many travelers who come to Colombia do so because of the wide-variety of drugs available. While you will probably see many locals smoking marijuana, getting high off of inhalants, and even smoking crack on the streets, I strongly advise against buying or doing drugs in Colombia. You can easily be set up by the "seller," who then turns you in to the "police," who then extorts significant sums of money from you.

If someone approaches you claiming to be a police officer and asks for your documents, go to the nearest police station; never give your money or documents to someone claiming to be an undercover officer.

Women traveling alone may want to dress modestly to avoid unwanted attention from men. Colombia is still very much a "macho" country, and many men will think that a woman traveling alone, particularly one dressed provocatively, is fair game. As an extra precaution, women should call for a taxi rather than hailing it on the street; rapes by taxi drivers have been reported. (Though I have to admit, as a woman traveling alone, I have hailed taxis on the street throughout the country and always without incident.)

Most tourists travel through Colombia without any threats to their safety. To minimize your risk of being robbed, don't use flashy clothes or jewelry, stay away from city centers at night, and keep your guard up, just like you would anywhere else.

Smoking Colombians smoke less than Europeans but more than Americans. Most restaurants, hotels, shopping centers, bars, clubs and other establishments have a no-smoking policy or a separate smoker's section. Make sure to ask if smoking is allowed before lighting up.

Taxes There is a 10% tax on hotel rooms, and a 16% tax on food.

Telephone & Fax The best place to make calls and send faxes is in Internet cafes. Public phones are confusing (with instructions in Spanish). There are many vendors on the street offering minutes to cellphones and landlines for COL$200 to COL$400 (US10¢–US20¢/5p–10p) per minute.

Time Zone All of Colombia is 5 hours behind Greenwich mean time. Colombia does not observe daylight saving time.

Tipping In midrange and expensive restaurants, there is usually a 10% tip included in the bill. It's not common to tip in budget restaurants or in taxis, so there's no need to do so unless you're feeling generous.

Water City water is usually safe to drink, but in nonurban areas it's best to stick to bottled water.

4 Bogotá

At first sight, Bogotá may not impress you. The constant rain, chilliness, and ominous pine-forest mountains make London seem downright sunny. But give Bogotá time and you will discover a sophisticated city of sky scrapers, glitzy upscale shopping centers, restaurants to satisfy even the most discerning palettes, and a nightlife that will leave you needing a vacation from your vacation. Colombia's capital, and by far the country's largest city, Bogotá is a sprawling metropolis, home to eclectic, experimental architecture, a large bohemian university crowd, a lively cafe scene, and dozens of attractive city parks. It is a city bursting with energy and culture.

But it's not all good news. Bogotá is, more than anything, a city of contrasts. Class differences are still very much apparent, with the wealthy, modern northern section a world apart from the sprawling slums, poverty, and high crime rates of the southern part of the city. Though security has improved dramatically in the last few years, the city center can still be dangerous at night, so you're better off not wearing expensive-looking jewelry and clothing when visiting these areas. However, Bogotá is one of Latin America's safer cities and it's unlikely you'll encounter any serious problems.

ESSENTIALS
GETTING THERE
BY PLANE   Planes arrive at **El Dorado International Airport** (© 1/413-9053), located about 13km (8 miles) from the city center. You can get to the city center by taxi or bus. Buses are parked next to the El Dorado Terminal and are marked "Aeropuerto"—the last one each day leaves at 8pm. They drop you off at the city center, from which you will probably have to take a taxi to your hotel. If you have a lot of luggage and don't feel ready to deal with Colombian mass transit, you're best bet is to take a taxi, which costs between COL$18,000 to COL$25,000 (US$9–US$13/£4.50–£6.25) from the airport, depending on where you need to be dropped off. Make sure to obtain a computer-printed slip at the airport exit before getting into your taxi. This slip indicates how much your route will cost and prevents visitors from being ripped off by dishonest taxi drivers. You give this slip to the driver and pay upon arrival at your destination. Do not accept rides from solicitors at the airport exit; these drivers are not associated with the airport and you don't want to be the one to test their honesty. Getting to the city center or northern Bogotá from the airport should take about 20 to 45 minutes, depending on traffic.

BY BUS   Buses arriving in Bogotá drop you off in the main bus terminal, **Terminal de Buses,** or at **El Portal del Norte,** depending on the bus company and where you are arriving from. Virtually every city and town has a bus service to Bogotá.

Bogotá

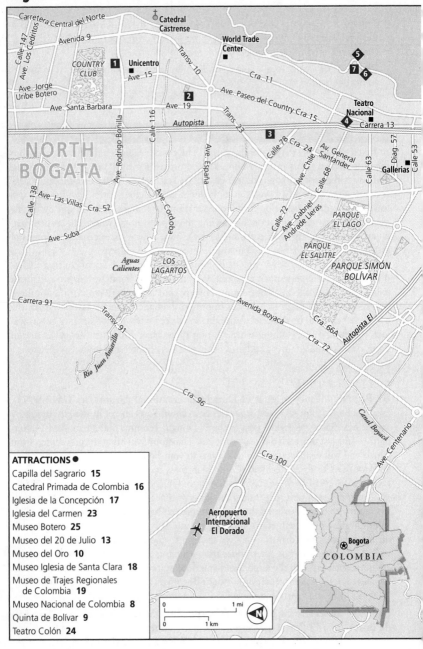

Catedral Castrense

World Trade Center

Unicentro

COUNTRY CLUB

Carretera Central del Norte

Avenida 9

Calle 147

Ave. Los Cedritos

Ave. Jorge Uribe Botero

Ave. Santa Barbara

Ave. 15

Ave. 19

Transv. 10

Cra. 11

Ave. Paseo del Country Cra. 15

Trans. 23

Autopista

Calle 116

Calle 118

Calle 138

Ave. Rodrigo Bonilla

Ave. Las Villas — Cra. 52

Ave. Suba

Ave. Cordoba

Ave. España

NORTH BOGATA

Aguas Calientes

LOS LAGARTOS

Carrera 91

Transv. 91

Río Juan Amarillo

Cra. 96

Cra. 100

Teatro Nacional

Carrera 13

Calle 78 Cra. 24

Ave. General Santander

Ave. Chile

Calle 68

Calle 63

Diag. 57

Calle 53

Gallerias

Calle 72

Ave. Gabriel Andrade Lleras

PARQUE EL LAGO

PARQUE EL SALITRE

PARQUE SIMÓN BOLÍVAR

Avenida Boyacá

Cra. 66A

Cra. 72

Autopista El

Canal Boyacá

Ave. Centenario

Aeropuerto Internacional El Dorado

ATTRACTIONS ●

Capilla del Sagrario **15**
Catedral Primada de Colombia **16**
Iglesia de la Concepción **17**
Iglesia del Carmen **23**
Museo Botero **25**
Museo del 20 de Julio **13**
Museo del Oro **10**
Museo Iglesia de Santa Clara **18**
Museo de Trajes Regionales de Colombia **19**
Museo Nacional de Colombia **8**
Quinta de Bolívar **9**
Teatro Colón **24**

Bogotá

COLOMBIA

0 — 1 mi
0 — 1 km

N

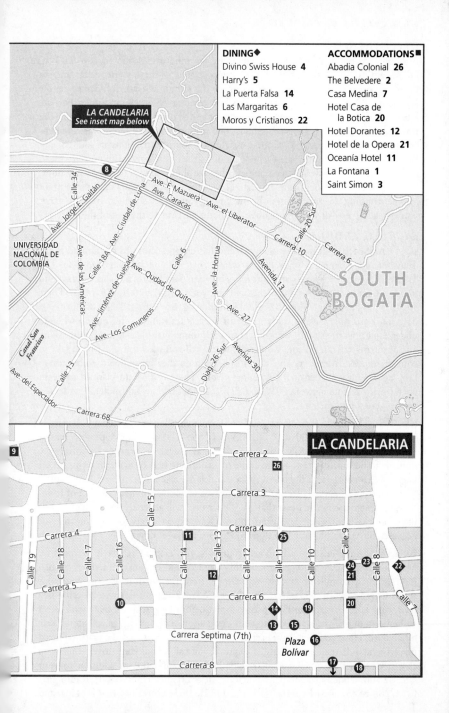

DINING◆

Divino Swiss House **4**
Harry's **5**
La Puerta Falsa **14**
Las Margaritas **6**
Moros y Cristianos **22**

ACCOMMODATIONS■

Abadia Colonial **26**
The Belvedere **2**
Casa Medina **7**
Hotel Casa de
  la Botica **20**
Hotel Dorantes **12**
Hotel de la Opera **21**
Oceanía Hotel **11**
La Fontana **1**
Saint Simon **3**

LA CANDELARIA
See inset map below

UNIVERSIDAD
NACIONAL DE
COLOMBIA

SOUTH
BOGATA

Canal San
Francisco

LA CANDELARIA

Plaza
Bolívar

ORIENTATION

Although Bogotá is a massive, sprawling city covering over 1,555 sq. km (600 sq. miles), almost all tourist attractions are concentrated in the historic center and La Candelaria. Excellent transportation connects La Candelaria and El Centro to the northern section, where most of the city's best restaurants, hotels, and nightspots are located. Laid out in a grid, Bogotá can more or less be divided into three sections: **the north,** home to the city's top restaurants, hotels, shopping, and nightspots; **the center** (including La Candelaria), around which most tourist attractions are located; and **the south,** the poorest and least-visited section of the city. *Carreras* run north to south and *calles* run east to west. Streets and avenues are almost always referred to by number rather than by proper name. La Carrera Séptima is likely Bogotá's most important avenue, running the entire length of the city. If you're ever confused about whether you're heading east or west, remember the mountains are on the east of the city.

GETTING AROUND

BY TRANSMILENIO   One of the fastest and cheapest ways to get around is the Transmilenio, Bogotá's 7-year-old bus system that runs on its own road lane. The Transmilenio runs weekdays and Saturdays between 5am and 11pm and Sundays and holidays 6am to 10pm. A single ticket will cost you COL$1,400 (US70¢/35p). There are 882 buses covering 84km (52 miles) and moving, on average, 1,250,000 people a day. You'll probably have to study the maps at each Transmilenio for quite a while to understand how the system works. If you speak some Spanish, you're best off asking one of the many Transmilenio workers, who can tell you what line and bus to take to your destination. Robberies are known to happen on the Transmilenio, so be sure to keep an eye on your personal belongings. *Note:* There is a Metro planned to begin operating in Bogotá between 2010 and 2016, but for now the Transmilenio is the best way to get around the city.

BY BUS   Hundreds, if not thousands, of buses service Bogotá. You'll pay a flat fare— usually about COL$1,100 to COL$1,300 (US55¢–US65¢/28p–33p)—no matter how far you're traveling. Get off and on buses as quickly as possible, as drivers are unlikely to be courteous enough to come to a complete stop or make sure you get off safely. When going from the north to La Candelaria, take buses marked "Germania." Don't take buses marked "La Candelaria," which will leave you in a bad part of town. When going to the north, buses that say "Unicentro" will generally drop you off a couple of blocks from where you want to go. Don't expect a bus to stop for you just because you're standing at a bus stop; you'll have to flag it down.

BY TAXI   Another smart way to get around the city, taxis are relatively inexpensive. Many foreigners choose to get around this way to avoid Bogotá's sometimes confusing bus and Transmilenio system. You can get from the north to the city center for about COL$8,000 to COL$14,000 (US$4–US$7/£2–£3.50). It's wise to call a taxi from your hotel or restaurant, especially at night. Your biggest risk is that a taxi driver will take an out-of-the-way route to your destination and thus charge you an unfairly inflated fee. However, there have been cases of robbery, assault, and even rape reported involving taxi drivers, particularly at night. If you call a taxi, your driver is likely to charge COL$1,000 to COL$2,000 (US50¢–US$1/25p–50p) in addition to your fare. Recommended taxi companies include **Auto Taxi** (✆ 1/366-6666), **Radio Taxi** (✆ 1/288-8888), **Taxi Express** (✆ 1/411-1111), **Taxis Libres** (✆ 1/311-1111), and **Taxi Ya** (✆ 1/411-1112).

BY CAR   Driving in Bogotá is not for the faint of heart. Almost 50,000 Colombians a year are killed in traffic-related accidents, meaning your chances of being hurt or even killed in a car accident are far greater than your risk of being kidnapped or killed by guerillas or narco-traffickers. Be prepared for honking cars weaving in and out of traffic, reckless drivers, and many near collisions. Pedestrians often cross despite the presence of oncoming traffic, and vendors and beggars often congregate around traffic lights. If, after hearing this, you are still convinced you want to drive in Bogotá, you will need to present an international driver's license when renting your vehicle. See "Getting Around," "By Car," above.

ON FOOT   La Candelaria and El Centro can be easily explored on foot. Usaquen, La Zona Rosa, and Parque de la 93 are other easy neighborhoods to explore on foot, though you'll have to get to these places by taxi, Transmilenio, or bus. Because Bogotá is essentially a grid, it's relatively easy to get from place to place on foot.

VISITOR INFORMATION

Tourist information in Bogotá is mediocre at best. Most of Bogotá's tourists are Colombians, so any brochures you manage to get will probably be in Spanish. The most helpful and informative tourist office is the **Instituto Distrital de Turismo y Cultura** (℗ 1/327-4916; www.culturayturismo.gov.co), at Carrera 8 no. 9–83, right across from Plaza Bolívar. Unfortunately, they are often out of maps and brochures. The office is supposedly open daily between 8am and 6pm, but hours can be reduced, especially on Sunday. Other tourist offices can be found at **El Dorado Airport** (at both the national and international decks), **the main bus station** (Transversal 66 no. 35–11, Local Module 5–27), and the **International Center** (Carrera 13 no. 26–52). The bilingual *Bogotá Turística* is a decent city guide sold at Panamericana shops throughout the city. Your hotel should also be able to offer some information, maps, and a few pointers.

WHAT TO SEE & DO
NEIGHBORHOODS TO EXPLORE

LA CANDELARIA   Bogotá's semirestored colonial quarter is home to most of the city's tourist attractions. It was here that wealthy Spaniards founded the city. The sector has a definitively intellectual feel, being home to half a dozen universities, several museums, galleries, cafes, the famous Teatro Colón, and La Biblioteca Luis Angel Arango, once considered the most important library in the country. La Candelaria, with its many pedestrian-only stone-cobbled streets is the perfect place to spend the morning or afternoon exploring, enjoying a leisurely lunch, taking in the colonial architecture and atmosphere, or visiting a museum or two. Most tourist and cultural attractions are between Calle 7 and Avenida Jiménez, and Circunvalar and Carrera 8. This sector has a long history with writers, artists, and journalists, and you'll probably spend most of your sightseeing time here.

PLAZA DE BOLIVAR   Just South of La Candelaria, this is a great place to people-watch and admire examples of Bogotano architecture. Unfortunately, you have to keep an eye out for the thousands of pigeons that make the plaza their home. See p. 479.

DOWNTOWN   This is a chaotic, noisy, and vibrant area—not the kind of place you want to end up lost at night, but you should be all right during the day. Some of the city's best bargain shopping can be found here, particularly around Plaza San

Vitorino, though you may feel a bit overwhelmed by the sheer number of shops and the somewhat seedy atmosphere.

USAQUEN   Like Candelaria, Usaquén is one of Bogotá's most picturesque neighborhoods. Home to a pleasant plaza, colonial-style church, and many restaurants and bars, Usaquén is also famous for its proximity to the Hacienda Santa Bárbara, a beautiful courtyard mall of upscale stores and boutiques that was once the home of a wealthy family. Usaquén really comes alive at night when the lively university and post-university crowd fills its restaurants and bars. This residential sector feels like a quaint small town and, in fact, it didn't become part of the city until 1954.

LA ZONA ROSA   Located between carreras 11 and 15 and calles 79 and 85, near the upscale Andino mall, La Zona Rosa is Bogotá's most exclusive nightlife center. Home to many clubs, bars, and restaurants, La Zona Rosa is where you'll drop COL$10,000 to COL$30,000 (US$5–US$15/£2.25–£7.50) for a cocktail or COL$100,000 (US$50/£25) for a bottle of *aguardiente,* if you want to party with Bogotá's rich and fabulous. **La Zona T,** a cobblestone pedestrian walkway makes for a pleasant night-time stroll. Just a few steps away, on Calle del Sol, you can window shop at the stores of famous Colombian designers.

PARQUE 93   Located between calles 93A and 93B and carreras 11A and 13, Parque 93 is another exclusive area, popular with the city's worldly and elite. It's home to many international and gourmet restaurants as well as to several clubs, bars, and cafes; the park itself often hosts musical events and is beautifully decorated at Christmas time. During the day, families bring their children to the pleasant green park for ice cream and fresh air, and at night the area comes alive with music and energy.

AVENIDA CHILE   Also known as Calle 72, Avenida Chile occupies the city's former northernmost point. It was once home to Bogotá's wealthiest families, where they built their European-style mansions in the beginning of the 20th century. Over the years, the area has become a bustling, vibrant commercial area with dozens of skyscrapers and some of the city's top hotels. This is the city's most sophisticated cosmopolitan area.

LA ZONA G   Also known as the "Gourmet Zone," La Zona G is adjacent to the Centro Financiero and is home to the city's best restaurants. If you're looking for world-class dining, this is the place to come.

MUSEUMS

There are over 50 museums in Bogotá. Below are some of the highlights.

Museo Botero 🏵🏵   The Botero museum, which opened its doors in 2000, is housed in a restored colonial mansion. Fernando Botero, one of the world's most renowned painters is famous for his voluptuous, over-the-top, Renaissance-inspired portraits. Love him or hate him, Botero is among Colombia's most famous exports, and you'll see his works all over Colombia. With over 120 sculptures, drawings, and paintings by the master himself, the permanent exhibition here, donated by Botero to the Banco de La República, is the largest permanent Botero exhibition in the world. The museum also houses over 80 works by other Colombian artists as well as European masters such as Matisse, Renoir, and Picasso.

Calle 11 no. 4–21/93. ✆ **1/343-1212,** 343-1223, or 336-0200. Free admission. Mon–Sat 9am–7pm, Sun and holidays 10am–5pm. Transmilenio: Avenida Jiménez.

Museo del 20 de Julio   Located on the northeast corner of Plaza Bolívar, the Museo del 20 de Julio, also known as La Casa del Florero (The House of the Vase), dates back to the late 16th century. It was here that a dispute over a vase, between Spaniard José González Llorente and Colombians Antonio and Francisco Morales, led to the War of Independence. The museum's 10 rooms, which feature Independence memorabilia, are a fine example of early Colombian colonial architecture.

Calle 11 no. 6–94. ✆ 1/282-6647. www.mincultura.gov.co/museo/museo20julio.htm. Admission COL$3,000 (US$1.50/ 75p). Tues–Fri 9am–4:30pm, Sat and Sun 10am–3:30pm. Transmilenio: Avenida Jiménez or Museo del Oro.

Museo del Oro ✹✹✹   This is the pride and joy of Bogotá. It's home to one of the world's most impressive collections of its kind: more than 34,000 pieces of gold and 20,000 other pre-Columbian relics. The museum makes a great base from which to learn a bit about the pre-Columbian cultures that inhabited Colombia and South America before the Spanish Conquest. Be prepared to be wowed by the top-floor, 8,000-piece "gold room." English-language tours are available at 11am and 3pm. If you can't make one of the guided tours, there are also English-language audio guides available—just ask at the front desk.

Corner of Calle 16 and Carrera 6. ✆ 1/343-2222 or 343-1424. www.banrep.gov.co/museo. Admission COL$2,600 (US$1.30/65p). Tues–Sat 9am–6pm, Sun 10am–4pm. Transmilenio: Museo de Oro.

Museo de Trajes Regionales de Colombia   This is one of my favorite Bogotá museums. It was originally the home of Simón Bolívar's lover, Manuelita Sáenz, and was turned into a museum in 1972. Small but interesting, the museum provides examples of indigenous and regional clothing dating back from pre-Columbian to modern times.

Calle 10 no. 6–20. ✆ 1/282-6531. www.uamerica.edu.co/museo/museo.html. Admission COL$2,000 (US$1/50p). Mon–Fri 9:30am–4:30pm, Sat 10am–4pm, closed Sun except last Sun of every month (free). Transmilenio: Tercer Milenio or Avenida Jiménez.

Museo Nacional de Colombia   Founded on June 28, 1823, this is Colombia's oldest and longest-functioning museum, providing a good overview of Colombian culture and history. It is currently home to over 20,000 historical and archeological items, dating from 10,000 B.C. to the modern era. Most impressive is the pre-Columbian exhibit of tools, handicrafts, and jewelry produced by Colombian indigenous communities before the Spanish conquest. You'll also find a modern-art collection here, as well as a pleasant cafe.

Carrera 7 no. 28–66. ✆ 1/334-8366. www.museonacional.gov.co. Admission COL$3,000 (US$1.50/75p). Tues–Sat 10am–6pm, Sun 10am–5pm. Transmilenio: Avenida Jiménez.

Quinta de Bolívar   This house was donated by the government of Nueva Granada to Simón Bolívar, in 1820, in gratitude for his quest for independence. The house was acquired and turned into a museum by the Colombian government in 1922. It was recently restored to its original state, when Bolívar and his lover, Manuelita Saenz, lived in the house. Many of El Libertador's personal belongings can be found here.

Calle 20 no. 2–91. ✆ 1/284-6819 or 336-6419. www.quintadebolivar.gov.co. Admission COL$3,000 (US$1.45/75p). Tues–Sat 9am–5pm, Sun 10am–4pm. Transmilenio: Calle 22 or Calle 19.

OTHER ATTRACTIONS

Created in 1539 by Bogotá's founder, Gonzalo Jiménez de Quesada, the **Plaza de Bolívar** has changed substantially over the last 5 centuries but has remained the sentimental center of Bogotá. The square was remodeled to its current appearance in 1960 as a tribute to 150 years of Independence. Plaza de Bolívar provides a good insight into the eclectic architectural styles of Bogotá: Here you'll find the colonial-style Museo del 20 de Julio (see above), the 19th-century Catedral Primal, which evokes the Renaissance churches of Europe, the neoclassical Capitolio, and the palace-like Casa de Nariño. On the northern side, the Palacio de Justicia is an abrupt, monumental building with a tragic history: It has been burned down twice, first by a mob in 1948, and then by M-19 guerillas in 1985. The statue of Simón Bolívar in the middle of the square was the first public monument in Bogotá.

The majestic **Teatro Colón** (Calle 10 no. 5–32; © **1/284-7420;** www.teatro colon.gov.co; Transmilenio: Museo del Oro), in the heart of La Candelaria, took its present form in 1886–95 under the direction of Italian architect Pietro Cantini. Check out the fresco-covered foyer; the wooden, beautifully engraved boxes; and the opulent chandelier marking the center of the theater. With a five-level, 938-person capacity, the theater is home to Bogotá's symphony orchestra and is still used for Bogotá's most important concerts, plays, ballets, and operas. For tickets, call © **1/ 341-0475.** There are individual or group-guided visits from Tuesday to Saturday between 10am to 5pm and Sunday from 1 to 5pm. Admission is COL$4,500 (US$2.25/£1.13), COL$8,000 (US$4.40/£2.20) for character/costume tour.

At an altitude of 10,000 feet, the **Cerro de Monserrate** 🌟🌟 offers spectacular views of Bogotá. It's also home to two excellent restaurants, the elegant **Restaurante San Isidro** 🌟🌟, serving perhaps Bogotá's best French cuisine, and **Casa Santa Clara,** a beautiful wooden building transported piece by piece from its original location in the Usaquén neighborhood. You'll also find decent souvenir shops here, as well as the Santuario de Monserrate, with its 17th-century figure of a fallen Christ, which attracts hundreds of pilgrims every weekend. You can see them climbing the slopes of Monserrate to pay their homage to the Fallen Christ. The top of Monserrate can be reached by cable car or funicular, beginning at Carrera 2E no. 21–48, Paseo Bolívar, Estación del Funicular (© **1/284-5700**). Cable car and funicular cost COL$11,800 (US$5.90/ £2.95), COL$15,000 (US$7.50/£3.75) after 5:30pm. Cable car service is every 20 minutes Monday to Saturday noon to midnight; the funicular runs Monday through Saturday 7am to 11:40pm, Sundays and holidays 5:30am to 5:30pm.

CHURCHES

Church-lovers are in for a real treat in Bogotá. The city's colonial origin means that there are some excellent, fully preserved churches in La Candelaria and El Centro Histórico. Though Bogotá's many churches may be staid on the outside, their insides are often opulent examples of colonial religious art. Below is a list of some of the best churches. Except where noted, admission is free (though donations are accepted).

Capilla Del Sagrario   Built between 1600 and 1700, and restored after the 1827 earthquake, the Capilla Del Sagrario is an excellent example of colonial architecture with Mannerist, Moorish, and even indigenous influences.

Carrera 7 in front of Plaza de Bolívar. © **1/341-1954.** Mon–Fri 7:30am–12:30pm and 3–5:30pm; Sun 4:30–5:30pm. Closed holidays. Transmilenio: Avenida Jiménez.

Catedral Primada de Colombia   Finished in 1823, this cathedral stands in the same spot as the first church of Bogotá, which was finished in 1539. Inside, there are paintings and carvings dating from the 17th and 18th centuries, the tomb of Gonzalo Jiménez de Quesada (the founder of Bogotá), and one of the largest organs in all of Latin America.

Carrera 7 no. 10–11. © **1/341-1954.** www.catedral.org.co. Mon–Sat 8:30am–1pm; Sun 8:30am–2pm.

Bogotá Turistren

The Tren Turístico de la Sabana, as it's officially known, is Colombia's only remaining steam train and is a great way to see Bogotá's picturesque (if cloud-covered) countryside. The train departs from La Estación de la Sabana at 8:30am on Saturdays, Sundays, and holidays, or you can hop on board at the Usaquén train station at 9:20am. Passengers are dropped off at 4:30pm (Usaquén) and 5:30pm (Sabana). The train ride is popular with families, and on board you'll enjoy an authentic "papayera" band playing *vallenatos*, as well as an Andean band playing typical music from the Cundinamarca region. There's also a small on-board restaurant serving up typical Colombian fare such as hot chocolate accompanied by fresh cheese, tamales, and *aguapanela*, a sugar-cane-based hot beverage. You have the choice of disembarking at the salt mines of Zipaquira, where, for an extra fee, you can visit the famous, one-of-a-kind underground salt cathedral; or you can get off at Cajica, a typical Cundinamarca pueblo, with a pleasant plaza, cute stores, and tasty pastries. For more information about the Bogotá Turistren, visit **www.turistren.com.co**.

Note: To purchase tickets, go to the **Sabana station** (Calle 13 no. 18–24; ✆ 1/375-0557) or the **Usaquén station** (Transversal 10 no. 110–8; ✆ 1/629-7407 or 629-7408). Tickets cost COL$28,000 (US$14/£7) for adults, and COL$17,000 (US$8.50/£4.25) children and seniors over 60.

Museo Iglesia de Santa Clara   The single nave here is decorated entirely with painted motifs, and the monastery is considered the most architecturally rich in the country. The Museo Iglesia, built from 1629–74, is one of the best examples of colonial church architecture in Bogotá.

Carrera 8 no. 8–91. ✆ 1/341-1009. Admission COL$2,000 (US$1/50p), COL$1,000 (US50¢/25p) for guided tour. Tues–Fri 9am–4:30pm; Sat–Sun 10am–3:30pm. Transmilenio: Avenida Jiménez.

Iglesia de la Concepción   Once occupied by the nuns of the conception, this historic church is one of the oldest in Bogotá. Construction began in 1583, and the church is another good example of colonial and Moorish architecture.

Calle 10 no. 9–50. ✆ 1/284-6084. Mon–Sat 7am–6:45pm; Sun and holidays 7am–1pm.

Iglesia del Carmen   Built in 1938, my favorite church in the city looks like something out of a Candy Land game. The Iglesia also serves as a prestigious private school—you're best bet is to visit Sunday morning.

Carrera 5 no. 8–36. No phone. Transmilenio: Museo del Oro.

Iglesia de San Francisco   This church once belonged to the Franciscans and was rebuilt after the 1785 earthquake. Check out its beautiful (and very gold) high altar, yet another excellent example of 17th-century church architecture.

Carrera 7 and Avenida Jiménez. ✆ 1/341-2357. Mon–Fri 6am–7:45pm; Sat–Sun 6:30am–12:30pm and 4–7:45pm. Transmilenio: Avenida Jiménez.

SPECTATOR SPORTS & OUTDOOR ACTIVITIES

BIKING   Bogotá is a biker's city, offering almost 300km (186 miles) of bike trails. On Sundays and holidays, the city hosts **Ciclovía,** an event where many roads are closed to automobiles and opened to bikers, walkers, and joggers; thousands of Bogotanos take to the streets between 7am and 2pm.

BULLFIGHTING   Bullfighting season is in January and February at La Plaza de Los Toros Santa María. There are also a number of smaller events held here throughout the year. For information about bullfighting, contact the **Corporación Taurina de Bogotá** (Calle 70A no. 6–24; © 1/334-1628) or **La Plaza de Toros** (Carrera 6 no. 26–50; © 1/334-1482).

FUTBOL **(SOCCER)**   As in most of Latin America, soccer is popular in Bogotá. There are two local teams: **Los Millonarios** (Carrera 9 no.70–09; © 1/347-7080) and **Santa Fe** (Calle 64A no. 38–08; © 1/544-6670), both of which you can contact for tickets. Games take place at **El Estadio Nemesio Camacho El Campín** (Carrera 30 no. 57–60; © 1/315-8726).

TREKKING & ROCK CLIMBING   Several trekking and adventure groups function in and around Bogotá. Try **Caminantes del Retorno** (contact Carlos Avellaneda at © 1/285-5232 or 245-0518; www.caminantesdelretorno.com), **Clorofila Urbana** (© 1/616-8711; www.clorofilaurbana.org), or **Colombia Ecoturística** (contact Arly Sarmiento at © 1/286-3369). For rock climbing, your best bet is **Roca Solida** (Av. 19 no. 133–23; © 1/600-7480; www.suesca.com) or **Rock Climbing** (Carrera 13A no. 35–66; © 1/245-7284).

SHOPPING

Shopping options in Bogotá are plentiful and varied. In the city center, look for bargains and handicrafts. In the north, you'll find upscale shopping malls and boutiques. Colombia is well-known for its shoes, purses, emeralds, and gold. Good deals can be found on these items, but save your bargaining for El Centro; prices are fixed in more upscale northern Bogotá.

It almost seems as if there are more shops than people in Bogotá. The main shopping areas are in Usaquén, La Zona Rosa, Carrera 15, Avenida de Chile, Carrera 13, Calle 53, and the Chapinero neighborhood. Some popular shopping centers are the American-style **Atlantis Plaza** (Calle 81 no. 13–05), **Centro Commercial Andino** (Carrera 11 no. 83–71), **Unicentro** (Av. 15 no. 123–30), and **Hacienda Santa Bárabara** (Carrera 7 no. 115–60), which was once the property of a wealthy Bogotá family. The latter is a unique shopping center that has both a modern and colonial part built around a beautiful courtyard. Inside, you'll find high-quality boutique and jewelry stores.

For budget shopping, try **San Andresito,** at Carrera 38 and Calle 12, where you can find more or less anything you're looking for. The shopping centers and stores around **San Victorino Square** (Carrera 10 and Calle 10) in the core of the city are also very cheap, with a great assortment of clothing, handicrafts, and even electronics. However, the area can be a bit seedy, so try not to make your tourist status too obvious. *Tip:* Bargain hard around San Victorino, especially if it's obvious that you're not Colombian; otherwise you'll end up paying far too much.

ANTIQUES

A couple of good antiques stores are **Anticuarios Gilberto F. Hernández,** Calle 79B no. 7–48 (© 1/249-0041), in the Zona T neighborhood, and **Almacén de Antigüedades Leonardo F,** at Carrera 4 no. 12–34 (© 1/334-8312), in Candelaria.

EMERALDS

Most shops selling emeralds are located around Carrera 6 between calles 12 and 13, the Centro Internacional.

HANDICRAFTS

Try Carrera 15, between calles 74 and 77, the Centro Internacional (International Center), the Centro Histórico (Historic Center) and La Plaza de los Artesanos, located on Calle 63 at Carrera 50. Many handicrafts shops are found around La Candelaria and El Centro. **Artesanías de Colombia S.A.** has several locations throughout Bogotá, including at Carrera 11 no. 84–12 (© **1/218-0672**). There are decent **flea markets** in Santander Square in the city center (daily 9am–6pm at Calle 24 and Carrera 7) and in Usaquén, on Saturday and Sunday, in the parking lot at Carrera 5 and Calle 119. My favorite spot for handicrafts is **Maku** ⊕, at Av. 19 no. 106–30 (© **1/ 620 8573**), in the Santa Bárbara neighborhood. While the prices are a bit higher at Maku than at stores in the city center, no one will hassle you, and goods are of decent quality.

LEATHER GOODS

For discount deals, head to the Restrepo neighborhood. Quality leather goods can also be found in upscale shopping centers. Good leather stores include **Mario Hernández,** which has several locations, including at Unicentro (© **1/213-0165**) and Carrera 68D no. 13–74 (© **1/292-6266**). Another good option is **Julia Rodríguez,** at Calle 81 no. 9–25 (© **1/249-5229**).

WHERE TO STAY

Most budget establishments are located in **La Candelaria** and **El Centro,** near the majority of the city's attractions. La Candelaria is relatively safe and a good place to stay if your budget is rock bottom and you want to save time and money on getting around. However, everything seems to close down when the sun sets and the nightlife that does exist here tends to be slightly bohemian and student-centered. You're best to avoid accommodations in El Centro, as this area can be loud and unpleasant at night. If you're intent on staying here, though, the **Tequendama Intercontinental** (Carrera 10 no. 26–21; © **1/382-2900** or 382-2929) or the **Santa Monica** (Carrera 3 no. 24–11; © **1/336-8080**) are a couple of good higher-end options.

Note: Colombian hotels use the New Year's holiday as an excuse to raise their rates by up to 10%.

IN LA CANDELARIA
Expensive

Hotel Casa de La Botica ⊕⊕ (Finds   This absolutely charming boutique hotel is in a 400-year-old house whose history stretches back to Colombia's independence. It's the place where Colombia's bill of rights was penned. The hotel's 10 rooms are organized around a beautiful, plant-filled courtyard with a working fountain and several tables where visitors can relax and enjoy the warm, colonial ambience. It's definitely worth paying the extra COL$50,000 (US$25/£13) for one of the hotel's five duplex-style two-level suites, two of which have their own chimneys (which come in handy during chilly Bogotá nights). All rooms have a sitting, work, and dining area, with windows facing the gardens that surround the hotel. The hotel has three restaurants: La Pastelería Francesa, which offers tasty desserts, pastries, and coffee; El Oreatrio, featuring an international menu; and Alina, a fine Italian restaurant. The hotel's flawless blue exterior, attractive entryway, helpful staff, and proximity to Plaza de Bolívar make this one of the top lodging options in la Candelaria.

Calle 9 no. 6–45. © 1/281-0811 or 342-1108. www.hotelcasadelabotica.com. 10 units (12-suite addition planned for late 2008). COL$200,000 (US$100/£50) double, COL$250,000 (US$125/£63) suite. COL$50,000 (US$25/£13) for 3rd person. Rates include breakfast. AE, DC, MC, V. Valet parking. **Amenities:** 3 restaurants; terraces, balconies, and patios; Internet. *In room:* TV, minibar. Transmilenio: Plaza Bolívar.

Hotel de La Opera ★★★   The top spot to stay in La Candelaria, De La Opera is on a lovely cobblestone street adjacent to the Teatro Colón. Enjoy live-music shows on Friday and Saturday nights, as well as complimentary use of the pool, Jacuzzi, and sauna. The hotel is two restored colonial homes, and the results are impressive. The restorations give the buildings their original, colonial glory. All guest rooms are decorated Italian style. The spacious, beautifully decorated suites are well worth a splurge. The terrace restaurant, El Mirador, offers great views of La Candelaria, as do most of the hotel's rooms.

Calle 10 no. 5–72. © 1/336-2066. www.hotelopera.com.co. COL$258,000–$319,000 (US$129–$US160/£65–£80) double, from COL$375,000 (US$188/£94) suite. Rates include continental breakfast. AE, DC, MC, V. **Amenities:** Pool; spa; Jacuzzi; terrace; Wi-Fi in public areas. *In room:* TV, Wi-Fi, minibar, hair dryer. Transmilenio: Museo del Oro.

Moderate
Abadia Colonial   Another good choice in La Candelaria, the Abadia Colonial has 12 rooms organized around three small courtyards and a pleasant dining area. The hotel is well maintained and spotless, with a fully-restored Spanish-style exterior complete with wooden balcony. The simple but elegant guest rooms are comfortable, spacious, and tactfully decorated. Located right in the heart of La Candelaria, the hotel is close to the Museo Botero and dozens of cafes and restaurants.

Calle 11 no. 2–32. © 1/341-1884. www.abadiacolonial.com. 12 units. COL$150,000 (US$75/£38) double. Rates include breakfast. AE, DC, MC, V. **Amenities:** Restaurant. *In room:* TV, minibar, hair dryer. Transmilenio: Museo del Oro or Las Aguas.

Inexpensive
Hotel Dorantes   A little renovating wouldn't hurt the Hotel Dorantes. Housed in what used to be the home of a wealthy family, the building has functioned as a hotel for the last 45 years or so and has the look of faded grandeur with its green iron-clad balconies and brick exterior. The three-level hotel has 30 rooms, all varying in size from tiny to large, some with good views of La Candelaria. All rooms have cable TV, rustic but clean bathrooms (with hot water), and old wooden furniture. Though not particularly attractive, rooms are clean and comfortable. As an added bonus, there is a lovely sitting area on the second floor.

Calle 13 no. 5–07. © 1/341-5365. 30 units. COL$50,000 (US$25/£13). AE, DC, MC, V. **Amenities:** Internet point; second-floor sitting area. *In room:* TV. Transmilenio: Museo del Oro.

Oceanía Hotel   This hotel, popular with grad students, Italians, Spaniards, and Argentines, is a decent enough place to stay. Rooms at the Oceanía are clean, and most have a small desk, old furniture, and old-fashioned bathrooms. Some rooms have views over La Candelaria while others have views of an unattractive courtyard—so ask to see your room first if possible. Downstairs, you'll find an attractive dining area with a large statue of Jesus overlooking the buffet table and a pleasant sitting area with Victorian-style furniture. New management took over in 2006, and a TV room and Internet access is planned for the future. The hotel offers continental breakfast for COL$4,000 (US$2/£1), and a buffet lunch for COL$6,000 (US$3/£1.50).

Calle 14 no. 4–48. © 1/342-0560. Fax 1/342-1879. 40 units. COL$50,000 (US$25/£13) double, COL$65,000 (US$33/£16) triple. No credit cards. **Amenities:** Restaurant. *In room:* TV.

IN NORTH BOGOTA

Ever since multinationals started moving in by the droves a few years ago, four- and five-star hotels in Bogotá are often booked at full capacity, and despite the seemingly endless selection of high-end lodging, finding a hotel in the northern part of town is no easy feat. I suggest booking at least 15 to 30 days in advance and calling a few days before arrival to confirm your reservation; guests have sometimes shown up only to discover the hotel is overbooked and they've been moved to another nearby hotel. *Tip:* Hotels in north Bogotá are business oriented, so they often drop their rates (by as much as half) on weekends—be sure to ask about special deals.

Aside from the hotels listed below, **The Charleston** (Carrera 13 no. 85–46; © 1/257-1100) is a pleasant, modern, business-oriented choice in La Zona T. In the Centro Financiero, the **Rosales Plaza** (Calle 71A no. 5–47; © 1/321-5917) is a smart, bright hotel, and **Hoteles América** (Calle 6 no. 8–23; © 1/249-4618), which has an excellent location near the Centro Financiero and La Zona G, is currently being remodeled in order to obtain a four-star rating.

Very Expensive

Casa Medina ⭐⭐   There are five-star hotels, and then there are five-star hotels. The Hotel Casa Medina is a gem located in the heart of the Centro Financiero and in close proximity to Bogotá's most exclusive dining scene. If you can afford it, this is the place to stay in Bogotá. Built in 1945 by the wealthy Don Santiago Medina, the hotel has 58 immaculately decorated rooms with classic furniture and all the modern amenities such as Wi-Fi access and a flatscreen TV. The building itself was declared a national monument in 1985 for its unique Spanish- and French-inspired architectural style. Gorgeous wood furnishings, wrought-iron railings, classical paintings, and antique furniture close the deal. Suites really turn on the charm with their own Jacuzzis and chimneys. The fifth-floor presidential suite is absolutely spectacular and feels more like a penthouse than like a hotel room. All rooms are slightly different, but all have spacious marble bathrooms, a comfortable work area, and double-paned windows to keep out noise. Every floor has elegant sitting areas and balconies, and guests can enjoy a cup of coffee in any of the many terraces and courtyards that make the hotel feel more like a fantasy country-residence than an executive-style hotel. The reception staff is fluent in English, and the hotel even offers a chauffeur/car service which can be rented by the hour or day. In this home away from home, you can dine in style in the intimate, atmospheric restaurant or on the beautiful rooftop terrace, where you'll enjoy a range of tasty international cuisine.

Carrera 7 no. 70A–22. © 1/217-0288. www.hoteles-charleston.com. 58 units. Superiors from COL$620,000 (US$310/£155), grand suites from COL$810,000 (US$405/£203). AE, DC, MC, V. **Amenities:** Restaurant; spa; terrace; business center; secretarial services; small gym; chauffeur service. *In room:* Flatscreen TV, minibar, hair dryer, CD player. Transmilenio: Calle 72 (about 3- to 4-block walk).

Expensive

La Fontana   Located just across the street from Unicentro, La Fontana is an elegant hotel popular with Brazilian, Argentine, and American businesspeople. There are a variety of room types, ranging from comfortable standard rooms (though the bathrooms are a bit snug) to the grandiose Special Suites. As an added bonus, prices on the standards, Juniors, and junior suites are cut in half on Fridays, Saturdays, and

Sundays, making this hotel a great deal on weekends. La Fontana has a beautiful plant-filled courtyard where musical spectacles featuring salsa, tango, Chilean and Andean music, and much more are held free on Sundays. If you stay here over the weekend, be sure not to miss the well-known Cremesse, La Fontana's Sunday artisan fair, where you'll find decently priced jewelry, clothing, and artwork. The reception staff speaks English and is generally helpful. La Fontana's impressive international restaurant, **El Cigarro,** is headed by Luis Ferrero, considered one of the top chefs in Colombia. If you plan to stay in Bogotá for an extended period of time, La Fontana also offers apartments.

Av. 127 no. 15A–10. © 1/615-4400 (274-7868 for reservations). Fax 1/216-0449. www.hotelesestelar.com. 201 hotel units and 97 long-term apartment units. COL$450,000 (US$225/£113) double ($115 on weekends), from COL$500,000 (US$250/£125) suite. Rates include breakfast. AE, DC, MC, V. **Amenities:** 2 restaurants; bar; gym; concierge; room service; laundry service. *In room:* TV, Wi-Fi access in suites, minibar, hair dryer. Transmilenio: 127.

Moderate

The Belvedere   The recently remodeled Hotel Belvedere is well situated close to excellent restaurants and entertainment options, and walking distance to Parque de La 93. Rooms are standard with minibar, satellite TV, blackout curtains, work table, and comfortable bathrooms. The hotel is a good deal in comparison to its competition in the same sector. Located 4 blocks from the Transmilenio, the hotel is popular with national and international corporations, but is also well suited for tourists and families. There's an attractive terrace where patrons can relax and dine, and the small but tasty restaurant serves both typical and international fare. The staff is professional and communicates well in English.

Carrera 17A no.100–16. © 1/257-7700. Fax 1/610-2468. www.ghlhoteles.com. 39 units. COL$200,000 (US$100/£50) double, COL$210,000 (US$105/£53) suite. Rates include breakfast (subject to change). AE, DC, MC, V. **Amenities:** Restaurant; bar; terrace; Wi-Fi. *In room:* Satellite TV, minibar, hair dryer. Transmilenio: 100 (a few blocks away).

Saint Simon   This small European-style hotel in the heart of the Zona T is a good choice in northern Bogotá. The lobby is elegant and the reception staff is bilingual. The hotel's small size allows for personal attention and has many repeat customers. There is a tiny but pleasant dining area and rooms are fresh and comfortable. The hotel is popular with Colombian businesspeople and international solo tourists. There is a small but complete business center, and Wi-Fi is available for an extra fee. All rooms have a work area and small but comfortable bathrooms, and some have views of La Zona T and the mountains. Room size and layout vary, so ask to see a room before booking. As an added bonus, there is a small artisan fair in the plaza across from the hotel, where you can buy Colombian-style mochilas, handicrafts, and clothing.

Carrera 14 no. 81–34. © 1/621-8188. Fax: 1/618-4279. http://saintsimonbogota.com/espanol.htm. 48 units, including 12 suites. AE, DC, MC, V. **Amenities:** Restaurant; conference center; business center; laundry service; Wi-Fi (for an extra fee). *In room:* TV, minibar, hair dryer, fridge. Transmilenio: Los Héroes or Calle 76.

WHERE TO DINE

Bogotá is experiencing a culinary renaissance of sorts, with international and gourmet restaurants springing up all over the place, though there are still plenty of traditional (and cheap) joints where you can grab an *almojabana* (fried cheese-bread) or an empanada. Most exotic, innovative, and upscale restaurants are found in northern Bogotá, while hole-in-the wall eateries and set-menu spots are scattered throughout the center and La Candelaria.

Tipping is generally restricted to high-end restaurants and is sometimes included in your bill. If not, leave about 10%. Tipping isn't expected in budget restaurants. High-end restaurants generally take credit cards, but budget places are unlikely to accept anything but cash.

In addition to the places listed below, here are a few other good restaurant options: **Leo Cocina y Cava** ★★★, at Calle 27B no. 6–75 (© **1/286-7091**), is considered the top Caribbean-inspired restaurant in Bogotá. It's open Monday to Saturday noon to 4pm and 7:30pm to midnight. For the best Italian food in town, head to **Di Lucca,** an intimate, two-story house next to the Zona T located at Calle 13 no. 85–32 (© **1/ 256-3019**). It's open Monday to Saturday 11am to midnight and Sunday noon to 10pm. For high-end Chinese food, head to **Zhangs,** in the Usaquén neighborhood, located at Calle 119 no. 7–08 (© **1/213-3979**). It's open daily noon to midnight.

EXPENSIVE

Divino Swiss House SWISS   Divino Swiss House is one of those places where every detail seems right on, from the antique furniture, to the stained-glass panels, to the tasty Swiss regional specialties. Situated in the Quinta Camacho neighborhood near the New International Center (Centro Financiero), the restaurant is housed in a 1935 Swiss-style house once home to a wealthy Italian family who left behind recently-restored frescoes and paintings. The restaurant offers both casual and formal dining. The well-lit courtyard is perfect for a casual lunch, and the cozy upstairs area is rented out for graduations, birthdays, and other events. Owned by Swiss ex-pat Harry Light-ner, Divino Swiss House offers the largest fondue menu in Bogotá, as well as typical Swiss wines and chocolates. And in case you want to take a little something with you, there's Swiss chocolate for sale as well as do-it-yourself fondue sets. All dishes are Swiss-inspired, some with a Colombian twist. Try the hearty trout with almonds, a true Swiss tradition, or the famous *sombrero tiroles,* which can be shared among up to five people. On Sunday, the restaurant offers a popular brunch where you pay by height— COL$200 (US10¢/5p) per centimeter. Harry's wife, Yvonne, runs Divino Restaurant in the old Bavaria building, near the city center, open weekdays noon to 4pm.

Calle 70 no. 11–29. © **1/313-0595**. Main courses COL$12,000–COL$18,000 (US$6–US$9/£3–£4.50). AE, MC, V. Daily noon–11pm.

Harry's PARRILLA/STEAK   In 2005, brothers (and chefs) Jorge and Harry Sasson debuted this popular steakhouse in the heart of the Zona G, and it's been a hit ever since. With its extensive wine list and posh ambience, Harry's has become one of the hippest places in Bogotá to grab lunch, dinner, or an after-work cocktail. The steaks are excellent, as is the service, and the glass ceiling and windows let in plenty of nat-ural light, creating an attractive, pleasant dining space. Diners can take their meals on the outside patio or in the upstairs dining area for a bit more privacy. Note that din-ers are allowed to bring their own wine and liquor, which can be stored in upstairs lockers and consumed on a subsequent visit. An added bonus: The restaurant will accept dollars if you're hard-up for Colombian pesos.

Calle 70 no. 5–27. © **1/321-3940**. Reservations recommended. Main courses COL$26,000–$80,000 (US$13– US$40/£6.50–£20). AE, MC, V, DC. Mon–Sat noon–midnight, Sun noon–5pm. Closed holidays.

MODERATE

Las Margaritas ★★ *(Finds)* COLOMBIAN   At more than a century old, Las Mar-garitas has got to be doing something right. Friendly and bilingual owner and chef Julio Rios will be more than happy to tell you the restaurant's history and success over the last hundred-odd years. There's nothing pretentious or fancy about Las Margaritas, but it has a rustic charm that keeps customers coming back. Located in the historic Chapinero neighborhood, once home to Bogotá's cream of the crop, Las Margaritas offers more than a dining experience; it's also gives guests a glimpse of Bogotá and Chapinero history and culture. The walls are decorated with news articles depicting the history of the neighborhood and offering praise for Las Margaritas, as well as with black-and-white pictures of turn-of-the-20th-century Bogotá. Start with a serving of empanadas with lemon and (spicy) aji, popularly considered the best empanadas in Bogotá (in fact, so popular that they account for 40% of the restaurant's earnings). Continue with *lengua en salsa* (tongue in sauce) served with salad, rice, and potatoes. If you can't stand the thought of eating tongue, try the roast beef or the *ajiaco*, a typical Bogotá chicken, corn, potato, and avocado soup. For dessert, ask for the *postre de natas*, a mouth-watering and artery-clogging pudding of sorts. To finish off, try a fruit-flavored herb water.

Calle 62 no. 7–77. (Ⓒ) **1/249-9468** or 217-0781. Main courses COL$14,000–$24,000 (US$7–US$12/£3.50–£6). AE, DC, MC, V. Sat–Sun noon–4pm, Tues–Fri 8am–6pm.

Moros y Cristianos CUBAN   Run by Havana native Ana Marti Moya, Moros and Cristianos gets its name from the popular Cuban white-rice and black-bean dish. The restaurant has been open in La Candelaria since 2003 and is a popular lunchtime place with businesspeople. Informal and laid back, the restaurant is well regarded for its tasty Cuban cuisine. The *plato cubano*, consisting of black-bean soup, shredded beef, rice, yuca, *plátano*, stuffed beef, and salad, is a filling, hearty choice, as is the *enchilada marinero*, a popular fish dish. For travelers on a budget, the *plato del día* comes with an appetizer, entree, dessert, and drink for only COL$9,000 (US$4.50/£2.25). There is also an excellent selection of Cuban cocktails such as mojitos and *cuba libres*. The last Friday of every month, there's live Cuban music. Be sure to arrive early to grab a table—this place is popular with business folks on their lunch break.

Calle 7 no. 5–66. (Ⓒ) **1/342-7401.** Reservations not accepted. Main courses COL$12,000–COL$30,000 (US$6–$US15/£3–£7.50); set menu COL$9,000 (US$4.50/£2.25). MC, V. Daily noon–4pm (until 10pm Thurs–Fri).

INEXPENSIVE

La Puerta Falsa (Finds COLOMBIAN   It may be unassuming, but La Puerta Falsa is as authentic as it gets in Bogotá. The quaint two-story eatery is housed in a 400-year-old building and is the best place to enjoy an old-fashioned Santa Fe tamale. Other popular choices are *salchichas* (sausages), eggs with bread, *agua panela* with *queso fresco* and an assortment of typical Colombian pastries and desserts. In 2007, the restaurant was named the best place to eat traditional Bogotano fare in the city. Bogotá's oldest functioning restaurant, the family business has been passed down from generation to generation since 1816, preserving the consistency and quality of the food. The restaurant is popular with businesspeople and can fill up quickly around lunch time. Its location, between La Candelaria and Plaza Bolívar, makes it a convenient breakfast or lunch choice. As an interesting side note, the restaurant got its name because of its location next to the Catedral Primadia. In the early 1800s, churches often had a *puerta falsa*, or false door, which became a reference point for meetings. Businessmen would tell one another to meet in front of the *puerta palsa*, and soon enough, the restaurant came to be known by that name.

Calle 11 no. 6–50. No phone. Reservations not accepted. Main courses COL$2,000–COL$4,000 (US$1–US$2/50p–£1). No credit cards. Mon–Sat 7am–11pm.

Un Tinto, Por Favor

Colombia is one of the world's largest exporters of coffee, and its capital city makes New York's cafe scene look meager. Bogotanos love to take a break from their work day to enjoy a good cup of steaming coffee or hot chocolate, preferably with *queso fresco* or an *almojabana* (fried cheese-bread). For one-of-a-kind cafes, head to La Candelaria, where the large student population drives the thriving cafe scene. **Café Del Sol** (Calle 14 no. 3–60; ✆ **315/335-8576**; daily 8am–8:30pm) has a laid-back, collegial atmosphere and plays mostly chill-out '60s and '70s Spanish music. Enjoy reading the many patron-written poems tacked on the wall while sipping a decent cup of cappuccino or *tinto*. For a truly unique experience, head to **Café de La Estación** ★★ (Calle 14 no. 5–14; ✆ **1/562-4080**; Mon–Fri 7am–10pm, Sat 9am–8pm), a 120-year-old train car where everything but the wood floor is original. The wooden green windowpane, plaid curtain fringes, and many black-and-white pictures of turn-of-the-century Bogotá and Cartagena make you'll feel as if you've stepped back in time. (Though, unfortunately, one side of the cafe has views of an unattractive and definitively modern parking lot.) Café de La Estación is popular with businesspeople looking for an afternoon snack. Try the Chantilly hot chocolate or one of the delicious cheese platters while listening to tangos and old-time Colombian music. **El Duende Café Arte** (Carrera 3 no. 10–49; ✆ **1/281-8946**; Mon–Thurs noon–11pm, Fri–Sat noon–midnight) is rumored to be haunted by a ghost and offers an impressive variety of coffee drinks and light fare; there are musical acts on Friday nights. Finally, to sample the Starbucks of Colombia, head to **Juan Valdez,** which serves up a wide variety of gourmet coffees and cappuccinos. My favorites locations are in the Museo Botero (p. 478) and the Zona G (Calle 70 no. 6–80; ✆ **1/217-7501**).

BOGOTA AFTER DARK

Even though Bogotanos aren't known for their dancing abilities, they do enjoy an enviable night life. There's an active bar and club scene in Usaquén, La Candelaria, La Zona Rosa, and Parque de la 93. Most bars and clubs get going around 11pm and close around 3am. In large clubs, you'll be expected to buy a bottle of liquor if you want to sit at a table; if you just want a shot or two, sit at the bar. Bogotanos dress up to go out, so make sure to look your best.

Andrés Carne De Res ★★★ (✆ **1/863-7880**; www.andrescarnederes.com), at Calle 3 no. 11A–56 (no Transmilenio access), in Chia, is considered the king of Bogotá nightlife by most Bogotanos (even though it's technically located in the municipality of Chia). It's the kind of place where young and old come to dance the night away. The club doubles as a restaurant serving up excellent steaks and is decorated completely with second-hand items. The sprawling establishment plays mostly crossover music, and by the end of the night, everyone is on their feet—don't be surprised if you find yourself table-dancing after several shots of *aguardiente.* Partying doesn't come cheap at Andrés Carne de Res, though: Expect to spend COL$100,000 to COL\$200,000 (US\$50–US\$100/£25–£50), not including the long taxi ride back to Bogotá. Cover is COL\$10,000 (US\$5/£2.50).

Punto G (© 1/616-7046), at Calle 94 no. 11–46, is another popular crossover club. It resembles a hotel reception hall and is popular with the over-30 crowd. There's live music Wednesday through Saturday (featuring reggae, rock en español, salsa, and traditional Colombian beats) as well as a decent food selection. A night of partying at Punto G will also cost you: The average cocktail goes for COL\$20,000 (US\$10/£5), and a bottle of *aguardiente* costs about COL\$90,000 (US\$45/£23). Cover is COL\$16,000 (US\$8/£4) Thursday through Saturday.

For something more akin to an Irish pub, try **The Bogotá Beer Company,** which is popular with the post-university yuppie crowd. It plays '80s and '90s rock beats and serves several varieties of beer produced in a nearby Bogotá beer distillery. All four locations are popular with Bogotanos: Carrera 12 no. 83–33 (© 1/603-071); Carrera 11A no. 93–94 (© 1/621-9914); Av. 19 no. 120–76 (© 1/215-5150); Carrera 6 no. 119–24 (© 1/620-8454); and Calle 85 no.13–06 (© 1/256-6950).

A SIDE TRIP FROM BOGOTA: VILLA DE LEYVA ★★★

The perfectly preserved colonial town of Villa de Leyva (pop. 12,000) was named a national heritage site by the Colombian government in 1954, and ever since, it has become a popular weekend hangout for Bogotanos looking for a break from hectic city life. The cobblestone streets, Spanish-style villas, and small-town pace give the town a charming, lost-in-time feel. Villa de Leyva and the surrounding countryside are among the safest places in Colombia to wonder off the beaten track and do a bit of exploring—and with multiple waterfalls, a nearby desert, adventure-sport opportunities, and even a couple of vineyards, there's plenty of exploring to do.

Even though the town's main sights can easily be explored in 1 day, most visitors end up staying at least 2 to 3 days, drawn in by to the town's irresistible charm.

ESSENTIALS

GETTING THERE   **Libertadores** (© 1/423-3600) offers two direct daily buses from the Bogotá bus station to Villa de Leyva, at 4:30am and 2:20pm. Trip time is about 4 hours. Several other bus companies also offer direct routes, especially on weekends and holidays, but they often stop for passengers along the way, making for a long ride. If you can't make one of these two routes, take one of the buses to Tunja, which depart every 5 minutes or so, and from Tunja you can catch a 45-minute *colectivo* to Villa de Leyva. (At the Tunja station, head upstairs, and then outside and board any of the large vans labeled Villa de Leyva.) In all, getting to Villa de Leyva should cost between COL\$16,000 and COL\$17,500 (US\$8–US\$8.75/£4–£4.38). Take a taxi to the Bogotá terminal module 3, or head to the Portal del Norte, as buses headed for Boyacá and Villa de Leyva pick up passengers there, too. All buses and *colectivos* will drop you off 3 blocks from the main plaza in Villa de Leyva, walking distance from most hotels. If you have a lot of luggage, you may want to consider taking a short COL \$4,000 (US\$2/£1) taxi ride, especially if you're staying in one of the many farms or inns around town.

VISITOR INFORMATION   The Villa de Leyva **tourist office** is located right off the main plaza at Carrera 9 no. 13–04 (© 8/732-0232; www.villadeleyva.net) and is open daily from 8am to 5pm. If you plan to be in town for at least a couple of days, you might want to invest in the English/French *Villa de Leyva Tourist Guide,* available for COL\$12,000 (US\$6/£3) at the tourist office and in some hotels.

WHAT TO SEE & DO IN VILLA DE LEYVA

Villa de Leyva's main attraction is its large **cobblestone plaza** ✦✦✦, supposedly the largest town plaza in Colombia. There are also a number of decent museums and sites in town worth seeing.

Located on the main plaza, the **Iglesia Parroquial De Villa de Leyva** was constructed in 1604, and it's here that independence hero Antonio Nariño lived from 1823–46. Also located on the main plaza is the **Casa Museo Del Maestro Luis Alberto Acuña,** dedicated to the life and eclectic works of the eponymous artist; it's open daily 9am to 6pm. (If the museum appears closed, simply knock and someone will let you in.) Admission is COL$2,000 (US$1/50p) adults, COL$1,500 (US75¢/ 35p) children.

In the **Casa Museo de Antonio Nariño** (Carrera 9 no. 10–21; ✆ **8/732-0342;** Thurs–Tues 8am–noon and 2–6pm; COL$3,000/US$1.50/£1.50), you'll find documents and items belonging to Antonio Nariño. The house was built in 1600, and the independence hero spent a few years here prior to his death.

The **Museo de Arte Religioso** (Plazoleta del Carmen; ✆ **8/732-0214;** Sat–Sun and holidays 10am–1pm and 2–5pm; COL$2,000/US$1/50p) houses one of the country's best collections of religious art (17th–20th c.). At press time it was closed for renovation.

If you're in town on Saturday, be sure not to miss the **Saturday market,** when peasants from Villa de Leyva's rural sector come to town to sell their fruits and vegetables. The market is located 3 blocks from the main plaza, walking toward the Hotel Duruelo (see below).

In addition to the sights listed below, there are many tour companies offering walking tours and day-trips into the Boyacá countryside. **Colombian Highlands,** Carrera 9 no. 11–02 (✆ **8/732-1379** or 311/308-3739; www.Colombianhighlands.com), is run by bilingual biologist Oscar Gilede and offers many eco- and adventure tours that can be done by car or horse. He also runs the clean Renacer Guesthouse, a pleasant hostel about 1km (a half mile) from town. **Terra Touring** (Calle 13 no. 7–63; ✆ **8/ 732-0241**) provides tours in Spanish, French, and English. **Guías y Travesías** (Calle 11 no. 8A–50; ✆ **8/732-0742**) also provides excellent, relatively inexpensive day tours, as does **Aventourese** (✆ **311/877-4338**).

If you're looking for horseback-riding opportunities, contact **Hacienda Flamingo** (✆ **310/480-539;** ask for Rafael Orejuela or Patricia Delgado), **Criadero El Olivo** (✆ **315/324-9832;** elolivo@sinva.com.co), or **Yeguada Alcazaba Del Viento** (✆ **310/ 223-3955;** alcazabadelviento@hotmail.com). They all rent out horses by the hour or day.

WHERE TO STAY

There are about 150 lodging options in Villa de Leyva. Unless you're going to be in town in December, January, or during a holiday weekend, it should be pretty easy to find a hotel room, though since Colombia seems to have more holidays than any other country, it's best to book in advance. It's imperative that you make advance reservations if you'll be here during the Astronomical Festival in the beginning of February, Holy week in March or April, Villa de Leyva's anniversary on June 12, the Gastronomical Fair in July, the National Kite Festival in August, the National Tree Festival in September, or the Festival of Lights in December. Most hotels and *posadas* here are charming, colonial-style places, so it's hard to make a bad hotel choice, but below are some of my favorites.

The **Hospedería Duruelo,** Carrera 3 no. 12–88 (✆ **098/732-0222;** reservas@ duruelo.com.co), is the poshest (and most expensive) place to stay in town, and it's easy to see why. The sprawling, 86-room Spanish-style residence is surrounded by beautiful, well-kept gardens and offers a gorgeous three-tiered pool, full spa service, and spectacular views of Villa de Leyva and the surrounding countryside. Guest rooms are standard, if not particularly impressive, though a splurge on one of the "Especial" rooms will get you a great view of the orange thatched roofs, unspoiled nature, and impressive mountains of Villa de Leyva. If you can't afford to stay at the Hospedería Duruelo but still want to be pampered like the rich and famous, the hotel offers day-use plans, which allow for use of the pool, bar, Jacuzzi, gym, sauna, and Turkish baths for COL$45,000 (US$23/£11) with lunch, COL$25,000 (US$13/£6.50) without lunch. In high season, a standard double will cost you COL$258,909 (US$129/£65). The hotel is a short but uphill walk from the main plaza.

For a truly unique lodging experience, head to the **Hostería Molino La Mesopotamia,** Calle del Silencio (ask for directions; ✆ **8/732-0235**), a more-than-4-centuries-old residence that once served as the town's grain mill. The mill was built in 1568, 4 years before Villa de Leyva itself was founded, and for the last 45 years, it's been a hotel. Its many natural springs, on-site gardens, and natural pool, as well as the colonial-style rooms, make this possibly the most charming place to stay in town. The atmospheric restaurant serves mostly Colombian cuisine made from products grown in and around Villa de Leyva, and the cozy little bar makes you feel as if you've stepped back into medieval Spain. In high season, a double will cost you COL $150,000 (US$75/£35). The hotel is an easy 4-block walk from the main square. Note, however, that you shouldn't expect five-star comfort here, something the ambience helps make up for.

If your budget is low, but you don't want to sacrifice ambience, check out **La Posada de Tejada,** Calle 14 no. 8–16 (✆ **8/732-0322**). Owned and run by the friendly Carlos Hernández, this 300-year-old house was the childhood home of early 19th-century Colombian playwright Luis Vargas Tejada, and only became a hotel in 2007. There's no TV, restaurant, or bar, but the large in-garden weeping willow and the neat courtyard make this one of the most peaceful places to stay in Villa de Leyva. Rooms are simple but elegant, with attractive high ceilings and antique furnishings. The six rooms accommodate two to eight people, so the hotel is great for families and groups. Best of all, the Posada is located only 2 blocks from the main plaza. In high season, expect to pay about COL$40,000 (US$20/£10) per person.

WHERE TO DINE

For a small town, Villa de Leyva has a decent selection of dining options. Monday through Thursday, hours can be limited and many restaurants close down. When possible, call in advance to check hours. For breakfast in town, head to **La Tienda de Teresa,** Carrera 10 no. 13–72, where you can have *arepas* with almost anything you can imagine—cheese, chicken, beans, and even hamburger. If you're here later in the day, try one of their great desserts, starting at COL$1,000 (US50¢/25p). You can even leave your mark by signing the wall, as many visitors have.

Almazara, Carrera 10 no. 11–55 (✆ **310/687-7070**), half a block from the main plaza, is a recently opened restaurant specializing in Spanish food and wine—including some locally produced varieties—is popular with foreigners. On Saturdays, there are wine talks at 6pm, and there is often wine tasting on Sundays. Sometimes, owner Oscar Cely Perilla takes groups to a nearby winery-vineyard. The *tortilla española* and the tapas are particularly tasty, and the locally produced wines are surprisingly decent. Almazara is open 11am to 11pm, weekends and holidays only.

A beautiful little restaurant, **Rincón del Bauchue,** at Carrera 9 no 15A–05 (© **8/732-0884**), specializes in typical Boyacá dishes including *mazamorra chiquita* (well-cooked corn, often in a milky broth), *cuchuco de trigo con espinosa* (wheat/potato vegetable soup), and *cocido boyacense* (a sort of sampler platter that includes soup, potato, beef or pork, and rice). Rincón del Bauchue has its own mini–green house, a ceramics workshop, several dining rooms—including an outdoor eating area—and even offers guest rooms during high season.

Finally, for dessert, head to **La Galleta** ✿, Calle 13 no. 7–03 (© **8/732-1213**), considered the best dessert spot in town. Try the *miloja,* a typical Colombian dessert made with a cookie base, cream, and *arequipe.* This cozy little coffee-dessert shop plays jazz and blues and is open from noon to 7pm on Monday to Friday and 9am to 9pm on Saturday, Sunday, and holidays.

5 Medellín

233km (145 miles) NW of Bogotá; 473km (294 miles) SE of Cartagena

Talk about a makeover. Fifteen years ago, few foreigners would have considered visiting Medellín. Once among the most dangerous cities anywhere, with a murder rate of 435 per 100,000 residents, all-too-frequent bombings, and deadly gang-wars, Medellín was known as the murder and violence capital of the world. But thanks to improvements in infrastructure and community planning, a new emphasis on education, an increased police presence (not to mention the death of drug lord Pablo Escobar), Medellín is now considered a relatively safe large city with a homicide rate less than that of both Washington, D.C., and New Orleans. Medellín is now one of Colombia's wealthiest cities, and a model of excellent urban planning.

A pleasant city with springlike weather year-round (daytime highs of 24°C–29°C/75°F–85°F) and a decent number of tourist and cultural sites, Medellín also makes a great base from which to explore the surrounding countryside and El Eje Cafetero.

GETTING THERE

BY PLANE   You will most likely be arriving in Medellín's international airport, **José María Córdova** (© **4/601-212;** airport code: MDE), which lies about 45 minutes east of the city. Some smaller domestic flights land at **Olaya Herrera National Airport.** Several airlines provide service from the United States to Medellín, including **Avianca, Copa, Delta,** and **American Airlines** (see "Planning Your Trip to Colombia," earlier in this chapter, for contact information). Another option is to connect in Bogotá and take a flight to Medellín. Colombian airlines offer several dozen flights a day from Bogotá and about a dozen each from Cali, Cartagena, as well as a few flights from smaller cities. To get from the José María Córdova airport to Medellín proper, you can take a taxi for COL$45,000 to COL$55,000 (US$23–US$28/£12–£14), or you can take a COL$5,000 (US$2.50/£1.25) minibus, which will drop you off in the city center, the last stop being the Hotel Nutibara (see below). From the city center, you can take a much cheaper taxi to your hotel. Green minibuses are located at the exit of the airport and labeled Medellín. If you arrive after 8pm, you'll have to take a taxi.

BY BUS   You can get to Medellín from most major cities and large towns, but if you can afford to fly, it's worth the investment, as the journey can be long. Unlike most other Colombian cities, Medellín has two bus terminals, **El Terminal del Norte** and **El Terminal del Sur,** so check to see which end of town your hotel is closest to before booking your bus trip. *Tip:* If you will be staying in El Poblado, try to arrive at El Terminal de Sur.

GETTING AROUND

Most of Medellín's tourist attractions are within walking distance of the city center, but there is also a great Metro system (the only one in Colombia) covering 26km (16 miles) east to west and 6km (3¾ miles) north to south. Metro tickets cost COL$1,300 (US65¢/33p) no matter where you go. There is even a free cable car system that moves about 27,000 people a day from the city center to the poorer *comunas* on the surrounding mountainsides. Taxis in Medellín are cheap, efficient, and generally safe to hail on the street during the day; at night you're best bet is to call a cab. A couple of taxi options include **Empresa de Taxis Super S.A.** (© 4/513-9700) and **CityTaxi** (© 4/444-0002).

VISITOR INFORMATION

Getting to Medellín's Tourism office feels a bit like entering a maximum-security prison. It's located in the **Palacio de Exposiciones,** at Calle 51 no. 55–80 (© 4/232-4022), and you'll have to ring many bells and walk through many doors to find the office. As a bonus, though, it seems few tourists venture this way, so the office often gives away maps and activity guides (including a guide that's in English and Spanish). The office is supposedly open between 7:30am and 12:30pm and again between 1:30 and 5:30pm. There are also tourism offices located at **José María Córdoba airport** (© 4/562-2885) and **Olaya Herrera airport** (© 4/285-1048).

The best way to see the city is to take the **Turibus** (© 4/285-1978), which will drop you off at the city's major attractions as well as give you information about Medellín. Ask if there is a bilingual guide available. You can catch the Turibus at Parque Del Poblado. Tickets are COL$12,000 (US$6/£3) for adults, COL$6,000 (US$3/£1.50) for children.

To visit **El Circuito de Oriente** ☆☆, a 1-day trip covering several towns and sites in the Antioquian countryside, contact **Las Buseticas,** Carrera 43A no. 34–95 (© 4/262-7444; www.lasbuseticas.com). The bigger your party, the better the prices. There are other bus and car companies that offer day tours of the Circuito de Oriente; for more information, contact or visit the **Aviatur** office in Parque de Bolívar, at Carrera 49 no. 55–25, Edificio El Parque (© 4/576-5000 or 4/576-5002; www.aviatur.com).

FAST FACTS You can change money at most banks, upscale hotels (though the rate is poor), and both of Medellín's airports. There are ATMs scattered throughout the city, in malls, bus terminals, and in all EXITO stores. It's a bad idea to use ATMs in the city center, as robberies aren't uncommon. Although Medellín is much safer than it was in the past couple of decades, you still want to take basic precautions. Don't carry large amounts of cash, and disperse it on your person, especially in the city center, which can be a bit seedy. *Tip:* Try to withdraw money in the safer **Poblado** or **Laureles neighborhoods.**

If you have an emergency or need medical attention, try **Hospital San Vicente de Paul** (Calle 64 and Carrera 51D; © 4/514-6600), **Clínica Medellín** (Calle 7 no. 39–290, in Poblado; © 4/511-6044), or **Clínica de las Américas** (Diagonal 75B no. 2A–80; © 4/342-1010). Always head to private hospitals for the best care, especially

Medellín

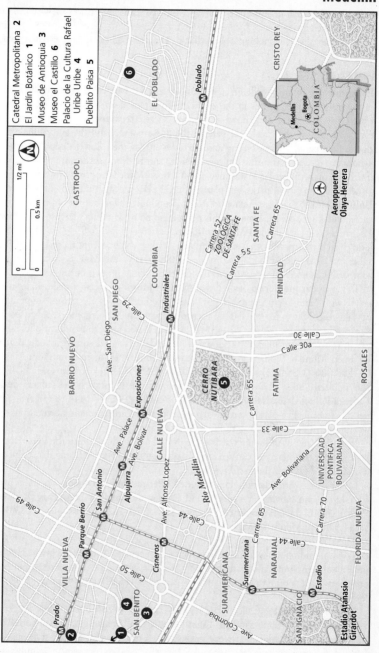

Catedral Metropolitana **2**
El Jardín Botánico **1**
Museo de Antioquia **3**
Museo el Castillo **6**
Palacio de la Cultura Rafael
Uribe Uribe **4**
Pueblito Paisa **5**

CRISTO REY

EL POBLADO

Poblado Ⓜ

COLOMBIA

Bogotá
Medellín
COLOMBIA

Aeroppuerto
Olaya Herrera

CASTROPOL

1/2 mi

0.5 km

SAN DIEGO

Ave. San Diego

Calle 29

COLOMBIA

Industriales Ⓜ

Carrera 52
ZOOLÓGICA
DE SANTA FE

SANTA FE

Carrera 55

Carrera 65

TRINIDAD

BARRIO NUEVO

Exposiciones Ⓜ

Ave. Palace

Calle 30
Calle 30a

CERRO
NUTIBARA
Ⓢ

ROSALES

FATIMA

Carrera 65

Calle 33

VILLA NUEVA

Parque Berrío Ⓜ

San Antonio Ⓜ

Alpujarra Ave. Bolívar

CALLE NUEVA

Ave. Alfonso Lopez

Río Medellín

Calle 44

UNIVERSIDAD
PONTIFICA
BOLIVARIANA

Ave. Bolivariana

Carrera 70

FLORIDA NUEVA

Calle 49

Prado

Cisneros Ⓜ

Calle 50

SAN BENITO

Ⓐ

Ⓖ

SURAMERICANA

Carrera 65

NARANJAL

Calle 44

Ave. Colombia

Suramericana Ⓜ

Estadio Ⓜ

SAN IGNACIO

Estadio Atanasio
Girardot

495

if you have no cash or insurance card on you. There are pharmacies on nearly every corner of the city center.

To contact the metropolitan police, dial ② **112,** for medical and other emergencies dial ② **123.**

WHAT TO SEE & DO

If possible, try to visit Medellín in August, during **La Festival de Flores** ✦✦✦, one of the most unique festivals in the world, when the *campesinos* from Antioquia come to the city to display their flowers. The weeklong celebrations feature a number of events, including the classic car parade; the horse parade; and the grand finale, the flower float parade, where young and old alike display their flower designs in a 3- or 4-hour parade, also featuring dancers, singers, and performers. Be sure to book your hotel and plane ticket far in advance if you'll be in Medellín during this time.

Medellín is a city of parks and plazas. A great place to begin exploring is at **Parque Bolívar** (Metro: Prado), which admittedly is a popular hang-out for old men, prostitutes, and drug-addicts. Even so, this plaza is home to Medellín's largest church, the Romanesque-style **Catedral Metropolitana,** Carrera 48 no. 56–81 (② **4/513-2269**). The church was made with over 1.2 million bricks, which, according to legend, were solidified with bulls' blood. The inside of the massive cathedral is rather dim and somber. The church closes at night, but generally remains open during the day.

To get to **Parque Berrio,** walk down **Avenida Junín**—a pleasant pedestrian promenade with many picturesque balcony-level restaurants and some decent shopping— or take the Metro to the Parque Berrio stop. From here, go to the **Museo de Antioquia,** Carrera 52 no. 52–43 (② **4/251-3636;** www.museodeantioquia.org), which features over 90 artworks donated by Medellín's native son, Fernando Botero. It's open Monday 9:30am to 5pm, Friday to Sunday 10am to 4pm; admission is COL$8,000 (US$4/£2) adults, COL$3,000 (US$1.50/75p) students with college ID; children under 12 are free. On the other side of the plaza is the **Palacio de La Cultura Rafael Uribe Uribe,** Carrera 51 no. 52–03 (② **4/251-1444**), a rather strange neoclassical cakelike-palace-turned–art-museum that features rotating exhibitions and workshops. It's open Monday to Friday 8am to 5pm.

If the Museo de Antioquia wasn't enough Botero for you, head to the **Plazoleta de las Esculturas,** where you can see (and be photographed with) his singular sculptures of *Adam and Eve* and the *Reclining Venus.*

Other parks worth checking out include **El Parque de Los Deseos,** a popular place for couples and movies on weekends; **El Parque de Los Pies Descalzos (Barefoot Park);** and **El Jardín Botánico,** Carrera 52 no. 73–182 (admission COL$3,000/ US$1.50/75p; Metro: Universidad).

The slightly cheesy but free **Pueblito Paisa,** Calle 30 no. 55–64 (② **4/235-8370;** daily 6am–midnight), is a miniature replica of a typical Antioquian town. It offers decent souvenir and handicraft shopping as well as an excellent Paisa restaurant and great views overlooking Medellín. Take a taxi here—ideally on a weekday, when it's less busy.

Museo El Castillo, Calle 9 Sur no. 32–296 (② **4/266-0900;** Mon–Fri 9am– 11:30am and 2–5:30pm, Sat 9am–11am), located in El Poblado, is a mock-gothic castle boasting international artwork, expensive furniture and French-style gardens (though the gardens have seen better days) in what used to be a wealthy family's residence. Unfortunately, the staff members here seem as if they'd rather spend the day talking to each other rather than helping tourists. The easiest way to get to El Pueblito Paisa and the Museo El Castillo is by taxi.

If you're interested in riding Medellín's cable-car system, take the Metro to the Acevedo Station, from which you can board the cable car. You get great views of the city as you ascend—especially of the expansive *comunas*—and from the top, you'll have a great view of the Valle de Aburra, in which Medellín's center was constructed. *Tip:* Avoid the cable-car system between the 4-to-6:30pm rush hour. If you don't want to get off at the top, you can stay in the cable car, which will take you directly back to the Acevedo Metro Station. The *comunas* are relatively safe these days, but you should still exercise caution, especially if you're taking photographs.

SHOPPING

Like most of Colombia, Medellín is a shopper's city. It's one of the largest textile producers in the country, and a fine place to go clothes shopping—in the city center, you will find inexpensive clothing and shoes. Although Medellín isn't particularly known for handicrafts, there are a couple of decent stores around Plaza de Bolívar and on Avenida Junín. For extremely cheap (and possibly contraband) electronics, clothing, and home goods, head to **El Hueco,** Glorieta de San Juan and Avenida del Ferrocarril (© **4/512-7273**), but be sure to keep your guard up. For more traditional shopping, head to **Centro Comercial Vizcaya,** Calle 9 no. 30–382 (© **4/276-5194**); **Centro Comercial Oviedo,** Carrera 43A no. 6 Sur 15, off Avenida el Poblado (© **4/321-6116**); or the ultra-upscale **Parque Comercial El Tesoro,** Carrera 25A 1ASur–45 (© **4/321-1010**). Your taxi driver will be familiar with any of these malls.

WHERE TO STAY

In general, upscale options are located in El Poblado, where you will be close to La Zona Rosa with its many restaurants and bars, as well as to Vía de las Palmas, Medellín's glitzy party row. There are also a number of midrange establishments around Carrera 70, near Medellín's stadium and with quick Metro access. There are dozens of great budget options in the city center, though it's important to note that this area is dodgier than Laureles or El Poblado, especially at night. Though the area isn't particularly *un*safe, it is home to most of the city's prostitutes, homeless, and drug-addicts— not the kind of place where you can enjoy a quiet evening stroll. In addition to the hotels listed below, you might try the **Dann Carlton Medellín,** Carrera 43A no. 7–50 (© **4/444-5151;** www.danncarlton.com), considered the best hotel in Colombia and offering 200 rooms, 16 suites, and a rotating top-floor bar with excellent views of Medellín.

EXPENSIVE

Intercontinental *Kids*   The sprawling 249-room Intercontinental is a good, modern lodging option, close to some of Medellín's best restaurants and nightspots. Part of the large, international Intercontinental chain, the hotel offers 12 meeting rooms, including one with capacity for 2,300 people, considered the largest dancehall in the city. Guest rooms are modern, airy, and comfortable. The Intercontinental is a sport enthusiast's dream come true: There's a great pool, a gym, a spa, tennis courts, a full mini–golf course, and even a bullring that doubles as a volleyball court. If you're really in the mood for a splurge—and we're talking COL$1,350,000 (US$675/£338)—you can stay in the Presidential Suite, considered the best hotel suite in all of Colombia and separated into four luxury rooms as well as a conference room. Although the Intercontinental caters to a mostly business crowd, it's one of the only hotels in this section of town—or in most of Medellín, for that matter—that makes a decent family hotel.

Calle 16 no. 28–51, Las Palmas. © **4/315-4443.** Fax 4/415-4404. www.intercontinental.com/Medellin. 249 units. Standard doubles from COL$277,200 (US$139/£69), suites from $346,500 (US$173/£87). Rates include breakfast. AE, DC, MC, V. No Metro access. **Amenities:** 2 bars; pool; spa; sauna; business center; 16 conference rooms; gift shop; 24-hr. room service; babysitting; laundry. *In room:* Cable TV, Wi-Fi, minibar, hair dryer, alarm.

Park 10 Hotel 𝒢𝒢 A beautiful boutique hotel just 3 blocks from Parque Lleras, the Park 10 offers 55 suites with top-notch modern amenities—some even come with an en-suite Jacuzzi. The English-style hotel has a spectacular outdoor terrace, charming gardens, and fresh, spacious guest rooms, all with views of El Poblado. All rooms feature marble bathrooms, orthopedic mattresses, and stained-glass bathroom doors. For COL$60,000 (US$30/£15) more you might as well splurge on the two-level grand suite and indulge your taste for luxury. The hotel's policy against social events and its location in a residential neighborhood guarantee a quiet, good night's sleep. And if you're feeling a little out of breath, the small upstairs gym offers an oxygen bar as well as exercise equipment. As an added bonus, the hotel's restaurant, **La Fragata,** is considered one of the best seafood restaurants in the country.

Carrera 36B no. 11–12, El Poblado. © **4/310-6060** or 312-7875. www.hotelpark10.com.co. 55 units. COL$280,000 (US$140/£70) standard suites, COL$340,000 (US$170/£85) grand suites. Rates include breakfast. AE, DC, MC, V. Free parking. Metro: 15-min. walk to El Poblado station. **Amenities:** Gym; spa; travel agency; free Wi-Fi in common areas; shopping gallery; 24-hr. room service; laundry; parking; 4 conference rooms. *In room:* Cable TV, Wi-Fi (for an extra fee), minibar, hair dryer, security box.

MODERATE

Hotel Florida The executive-style 50-room Hotel Florida is conveniently located a few blocks from the Metro, shopping centers, bars, clubs, and, in case you're in the mood to exercise, Medellín's stadium, *"el estadio."* There's nothing particularly memorable about Hotel Florida, but it's a good deal in this price category, and located in a safe neighborhood. The 8-year-old hotel is a bit dark, but junior suites are spacious and have excellent lighting. The hotel is divided into two four-story towers, one with an elevator and one without—if you have a lot of luggage, you probably want to head to the tower with the elevator.

Carrera 70 no. 44B–38. © **4/260-0644** or 4/260-4900. 50 units. Doubles from COL$118,320 (US$59/£30), junior suites from COL$245,000 (US$123/£61). Discount rates on weekends. Rates include breakfast. AE, DC, MC, V. Free parking. Metro: Estadio. **Amenities:** Restaurant; business center; travel agency; laundry; free Wi-Fi. *In room:* A/C, cable TV, hair dryer, minibar, safe.

Hotel Nutibara Though it may not be the grand hotel it was in days past, Medellín's first hotel is still a decent midrange option. Centrally located 1 block from Parque Berrio, the Nutibara is walking distance from most of the city's main attractions. It was once the most modern and luxurious hotel in town, and while that's no longer true, it does still exude a certain charm. Rooms are standard, many with good views of Parque Berrio and the Palacio de Cultura, and there's an attractive open-air pool and bar area on the fifth floor. **La Orquídea,** the hotel's restaurant, serves up tasty Paisa cuisine. Common areas and lobbies can be a bit dim, but the service is good, reception staff speaks English, and rooms are comfortable.

Plazuela Nutibara Calle 52A no. 50–46. © **4/511-5111.** www.hotelnutibara.com. 137 units. Doubles from COL$120,000 ($60/£30). Rates include breakfast. AE, DC, MC, V. Free parking. Metro: Parque Berrio. **Amenities:** Restaurant; lobby bar; dance club; pool; gym; sauna; steam room; 11 conference rooms; shopping arcade; salon; massage service; laundry service; Internet. *In room:* A/C, cable TV, room service, minibar, hair dryer, safety deposit boxes.

INEXPENSIVE

The Black Sheep Hostel   Hidden in the leafy Patio Bonito neighborhood and just a short walk from the Metro and trendy Parque Lleras, this is one of the best hostels in Colombia. The Black Sheep is an excellent choice for solo travelers, and caters to the under-30 crowd. There's computer access, wireless Internet, a fully equipped kitchen, a barbecue area, two TV rooms, and—most Colombian of all—a hammock-filled balcony. Opened in 2005 by New Zealand ex-patriot Kelvin Smith, the hostel has a laid-back, backpacker atmosphere and a bilingual daytime staff of informative, friendly university students. An added bonus you're unlikely to find in other budget options: extra-long beds to accommodate tall foreigners. The hostel has one single, four doubles, and six dorm rooms with four, six, and eight beds. Rooms are spacious and comfortable, most featuring en-suite bathrooms. The only downside is that the hostel isn't quite as clean as it could be. In high season (around Christmas/New Year as well as during the Flower Festival in July/Aug), it's hard to get a single or a double unless you stick around for a couple of days, but dorm beds can usually be booked on the spot. There is a minimum 5-day stay during La Feria de las Flores.

Transversal 5A no. 45–133, Poblado. ✆ 4/311-1589 or 4/311-1379. www.blacksheepMedellin.com. 11 units. COL$32,000 (US$16/£8) double or single, COL$16,000 (US$8/£4) dorm bed. Metro: El Poblado. **Amenities:** TV lounge; tourist information; laundry service; Wi-Fi, Internet access; security lockers.

WHERE TO DINE

If you love *arepas* and beans, you're in luck. Food in Medellín is carb-based and filling, and you're never far from the famous *bandeja paisa,* a typical Antioquian plate featuring soup, rice, beans, avocado, salad, sausage, plantain, shredded beef, eggs, *arepa,* and *chicharrón* (pork rinds), which you can get for as little as COL$5,000 (US$2.50/£1.25). You can find plenty of small restaurants offering *almuerzos corrientes,* or set-price lunches, usually between COL$3,000 and COL$8,000 (US$1.50–$4/75p–£2). If you're looking for something a little more refined, head to La Calle de La Buena Mesa, Parque Lleras, or Vía de Las Palmas, where you'll find international and gourmet fare, a more exclusive atmosphere, and sometimes overpriced dishes.

For inexpensive eateries in El Poblado (where most Medellín tourists stay) check out Carrera 43B at Calle 8, right off Parque del Poblado. Try **Flor de Candela, Yulio's Restaurante, Menú Casero** (for typical fare), or **Picolo** (for Italian and pizza).

EXPENSIVE

Hato Viejo ✿ PAISA   Located in a beautifully decorated Spanish-style hacienda, Hato Viejo is a great place to soak in the cowboy spirit that characterizes the people of Antioquia. Waiters dressed in typical 18th-century Paisa attire provide attentive service and will be glad to share their version of the history of Colombia if you ask. (Just make sure you have a couple of free hours.) A typical Spanish courtyard and dozens of hanging flowers give the restaurant an intimate, elegant feel despite its 250-person capacity. For a crash-course introduction to the Paisa diet, try the Plato Montanero, a typical Antioquian dish featuring ground beef, rice, avocado, *chicharrón,* sausage, egg, salad, beans, and fried *plátano.* Unless you're ravenous, ask for the *media porción* (half-portion). The hearty vegetable-beef *campesino* soup or the various Argentine-style steaks are also popular choices. Though typical dishes are the most popular among the mostly American, European, and South American tourist clientele, there's also a variety of fish dishes and a decent salad bar. For more privacy, ask for a table on one of the many balconies overlooking El Poblado. Set in the upscale district of Las

El Eje Cafetero ★★★

In a country of spectacular landscapes, El Eje Cafetero offers perhaps the most stunning scenery in Colombia. This verdant paradise, where orchids grow wild and coffee plants cover nearly every mountain slope, is quickly becoming one of Colombia's best vacation spots. Here you can learn all about the coffee-making process in El Parque Nacional del Café, stay in a traditional farmhouse (blue pillars for Conservatives, red for Liberals), or simply lay back in a hammock, listening to the sounds of birds chirping and not much else.

This region was once a guerilla stronghold, but military action over the last few years has made the coffee-growing region safe again, and tourists are coming back in droves. The best and cheapest way to see the region is to book a tour through **Aviatur** (p. 464; note that the Aviatur office in Medellín is on Plaza de Bolívar) or another tourist agency. These tours can be booked in any major city, but because you'll be driving, you probably want to take off from Medellín, Cali, or Bogotá to minimize driving time. Three- to four-day tours cost between $175 and $300 (£88–£150) per person and include entrance into El Parque Nacional del Café, Panaca, Los Termales de Santa Rosa, lodging, two delicious traditional meals a day, car, and driver. There are lovely farmhouses in the departments of Risaralda, Caldas, and Quindio.

If you insist on checking out the area on your own, consider staying at one of my favorite farmhouses, **Villa María** (for reservations, contact Red de Turismo del Eje Cafetero; ✆ **6/334-9883**; www.turiscolombia.com/villamaria.html). Unlike many so-called coffee farms that have abandoned the coffee-growing process, Villa María is still an active coffee and plantain farm. If you come between August and November or in March and April, you can even

Palmas, Hato Viejo seems worlds away from the noise and congestion of the city center, although there is also a Hato Viejo in the city center.

Calle 16 no. 28–60, Vía de Las Palmas. ✆ **4/268-5412.** Dinner reservations recommended for parties of 4 or more. Main courses COL$16,000–COL$50,000 (US$8–US$25/£4–£13). MC, DC, V. Daily noon–11pm (will sometimes stay open until midnight if business is good). No Metro access.

San Carbón GRILL/STEAKHOUSE   My favorite Medellín grill and steakhouse, San Carbón has a covered terrace, a wine display, a chic bar, high ceilings, and an open-air kitchen, all of which make this a very pleasant and atmospheric place to enjoy the energy of Parque Lleras. Like almost all restaurants around Parque Lleras, San Carbón functions as a bar at night, popular with the city's young and hip. Here, the steak and lobster are good, as are the Argentine and Chilean red wines. Call ahead and ask about live music.

Calle 9A no. 37A–13, Parque Lleras. ✆ **4/268-5570.** Main courses COL$23,000–COL$40,000 (US12–US$20/£5.75–£8.90–£10). Daily noon–2am, though times vary depending on the crowd. AE, DC, MC, V. Metro: El Poblado.

MODERATE

Ave María INTERNATIONAL   An atmospheric and warm place with a bamboo ceiling and brick interior, Ave María is popular with Europeans and Americans, and see the coffee pickers in action and watch the coffee drying process. Located just 16km (10 miles) from Pereira, this farm feels a hundred years removed from the modern world.

Where you stay in the Eje Cafetero has a lot to do with what you'd like to do. If you are interested in high Andes trekking—and you'll need to be in top shape and willing to face rain and snow—your best bet is the outskirts of **Manizales** because of its proximity to the Sierra Nevada Mountains. If you are interested in visiting El Parque Nacional del Café (the national coffee park) and Panaca, a farm-animal park showcasing different types of cattle, goats, oxen, and horses as well as an impressive acrobatic horse show, head to the farms and outskirts around **Armenia.** The Eje Cafetero's most beautiful parks are said to be around Armenia as well. Finally, if you want to be near the thermal waters of Santa Rosa or San Vicente, Parque Ucumari, and Santuario Otun Quimbaya, you should stay in the farm country around **Pereira.** All of these details can be arranged through Aviatur.

Warning: Machismo is more prevalent in Manizales, Armenia, and Pereira than in other Colombian cities, so women may feel uncomfortable traveling alone in the Eje Cafetero. Men in Colombia would never make advances at a woman traveling with a man, but if no man is available, at least travel with a friend or two to ease the discomfort. Robbery and assault is also on the rise in Pereira, so I recommend you don't walk in the city after dark. In fact, you're better off heading straight to the farm and spending as little time as possible in any of these cities, as they are a bit seedy and there aren't any must-see sights.

is known for its international fare. Try the house specialty, *los lomitos Ave María* (beef tenderloin), or one of the other beef specialties. The restaurant, which overlooks Parque Lleras, also functions as a bar at night. It's a great place to enjoy a bottle of good wine, sit back, and take in the action of Parque Lleras on a Friday or Saturday, when it seems the cream of the crop of Medellín society comes to see and be seen. If you're low on funds, check out the special menu from noon to 6pm offering more economical options. Tuesday through Saturday, there's live music. At press time, the owner was planning a changeover to Mexican food.

Carrera 38 no. 9A–13. ⓒ **4/311-5623.** Main courses COL$12,000–COL$40,000 (US$6–US$20/£3–£10). AE DC, MC, V. Mon–Wed noon–midnight, Thurs–Sun noon–2am. Live music Tues–Sat after 8pm. Metro: El Poblado.

Basílica SUSHI/GRILL   Another good choice in Parque Lleras, Basilica offers an eclectic menu featuring sushi, Peruvian, and international fare. Though it might seem that every restaurant in Medellín is trying its hand at sushi, it's actually pretty good here. It's a great place to eat if everyone in your party wants something different. The metallic bars, high ceilings, and rustic dark-wood tables give the place a modern, urban feel. Try the tasty, if a bit small, *ceviche mixto,* or one of the many steak and beef plates the restaurant is well known for. The restaurant offers an excellent wine and cocktail list, and also functions as a bar at night.

Carrera 38 no. 8A–42. (4/311-7366 or 4/311-8527. Main courses COL$13,000–COL$30,000 (US$6.50–$15/ £3.25–£7.50). AE, DC, MC, V. Daily noon–11pm (later on Fri–Sat). Metro: El Poblado.

INEXPENSIVE

Marantial del Mar SEAFOOD   This is my favorite place to eat in the city center. Among the loud, sometimes dingy hole-in-the wall establishments offering *almuerzo corriente* that characterize Medellín's city center, Marantial del Mar is a peaceful respite located in the courtyard of the Villa Nueva shopping center, just 2 blocks from Parque de Bolívar. The beautiful building housing the shopping center used to serve as a cloister, and tables are arranged around a working fountain. The hanging flowers and balconies overlooking the courtyard add a touch of charm and make you forget you're in Medellín's noisy, chaotic core. The restaurant is popular with business folks who work in the area and specializes in seafood, but also offers typical fare. For a good deal, ask for the COL$6,000 (US$3/£1.50) *menú del día,* which generally includes soup, fruit juice, rice, beans, avocado, plantains, and some sort of meat. If the restaurant fills up, try **Los Monitos,** just opposite Maratial del Mar, which offers typical and international fare.

Calle 57 no. 49–44 (Villa Nueva shopping center). (4/251-0365. Reservations not accepted. Main courses COL$6,000–COL$20,000 (US$3–US$10/£1.50–£5). No credit cards. Daily 8am–5pm. Metro: Prado.

MEDELLIN AFTER DARK

Years under the sway of drug cartels left their mark on Medellín, particularly on **Vía de Las Palmas,** Medellín's colorful, Las Vegas–style "party row." Medellinenses love to get their party on, and the city's beautiful women are famous throughout the country (as are their surgically enhanced breasts). Medellín's best dance clubs are located on Vía de Las Palmas, popular with the area's famous as well as with foreigners. **La 70** is another popular party area featuring smaller, less-glamorous clubs and bars. If you're not much of a dancer but enjoy downing a drink or two, head to **Parque Lleras** in La Zona Rosa, one of the most exclusive spots in town and a great place to people-watch. And if you're headed anywhere in La Zona Rosa or La Vía de Las Palmas, make sure you go with a well-stocked wallet. Note, too, that most restaurants in La Zona Rosa turn into bars around 9 or 10pm.

I don't recommend partying in the bars and cantinas in the city center, as these can be a bit seedy and foreigners are likely to be targets. If you're headed to Vía de Las Palmas, be sure to dress appropriately: no flip-flops, sneakers, or ripped jeans. Medellín is one of the few places in Colombia that abides by the "must be 18 to party" rule; if you look young, bring a copy of your passport.

No trip to Medellín is complete without a visit to **Mangos,** Carrera 42 no. 67A–151 ((**4/277-6123**), Medellín's best-known nightspot (although it's technically located in the neighboring municipality of Itagüí). Mango's claims to be the largest dance club in Latin America; whether or not this is true, its crazy, over-the-top atmosphere, complete with costumed servers and frequent shows, are the reason why everyone flocks to Mango's. There is a strange American Old West theme (think lots of cowboy hats) as well as an "anything flies" attitude here—the kind of place to expect the unexpected. On weekends, the club stays open until 5am and there's usually a cover of about COL$20,000 (US$10/£5).

Palmitas, Carrera 38 no. 26–41, Km 2 ((**4/232-7199**), another glitzy crossover dance club, is located on Vía de Las Palmas and often puts on salsa, merengue, and even belly-dancing shows. Popular with foreigners out for a night of dancing and drinking, the club also doubles as a restaurant serving up international and traditional food, not to mention great views of Medellín. The cover charge varies here. Palmitas is open daily 11:30am to 3:30am (dance club opens at 8pm).

If you're a drinker but not a dancer, head to the Scottish-style and English-owned **Pub Escocia,** in Parque Lleras (© **4/311-5607**). The bar is open 10am to midnight (until 2am on weekends). Though it functions mostly as a nightspot, the bar also offers a decent food selection featuring international and British-inspired plates. And if you haven't quite taken a liking to Colombian beers, the pub offers a variety of European and Irish beers. In fact, Pub Escocia claims to have the largest selection of beer and whiskey in the country.

6 Cartagena & the Atlantic Coast

473km (294 miles) NW of Medellín; 658km (409 miles) NW of Bogotá

Cartagena, a UNESCO World Heritage Site, is the Venice of Colombia, with one of the most impressive old towns in the Western Hemisphere. With just the right mix of sun, sand, and colonial charm, it's likely to be the highlight of your trip. Cartagena's tourism infrastructure is more developed than anywhere else in the country, so unlike most Colombian destinations, it's a pretty easy place to travel. A walk through Cartagena's inner walled city feels a bit like stepping onto the set of a 16th-century *telenovela*, complete with cobblestone streets and grandiose balconies overflowing with flowers.

Whether you come to Cartagena to splurge on its many fine hotels and restaurants, to explore its 500 years of history, or to sunbathe on its popular beaches, you'll discover an enchanting place you're unlikely to forget. As Colombia's top honeymoon destination, the city is full of romance, five-star hotels, and excellent dining options.

Note: One of the unpleasant effects of Cartagena's distinction as the tourism capital of Colombia is the presence of persistent beach vendors and Old Town serenaders who can't seem to take "no" for an answer. And saying you don't speak Spanish won't help—these guys seem to speak any language, as long as they're selling you something. The best way to avoid unwanted solicitations or serenades is to say no firmly and definitely avoid eye contact. If you make eye contact, resign yourself to buying a necklace or two or accepting a serenade.

ESSENTIALS
GETTING THERE

BY PLANE Cartagena's **Rafael Núñez Airport** (© **5/666-6610;** airport code: CTG) is located about 3km (about 2 miles) from the historic Old Town. The airport is serviced by national carriers **Avianca** and **Aerorepública** as well as by international carriers **Copa, Mexicana,** and **American Airlines** (see "Getting There," under "Planning Your Trip to Colombia," earlier in this chapter, for contact information). There is a minimum COL$8,000 (US$4/£2) airport tariff for a taxi, though if you don't have too much luggage, you can ask to be dropped off at Avenida 4 and Calle 70 for half the price. You can also take a local bus to the city, but your best bet is to go by taxi.

BY BUS Buses arrive to the **Terminal de Buses,** on the eastern end of the city. From there, you're best off taking a taxi to your hotel. Remember that unless you're coming from somewhere else on the Atlantic coast, a bus trip to Cartagena is exceptionally long (13 hr. from Medellín, 20 hr. from the Eje Cafetero, and 20 hr. from Bogotá), so I recommend that you splurge on a plane ticket.

GETTING AROUND

You'll probably be spending most of your time in the small historic **Old Town,** where most tourist sites are located, or at the city's beaches. The modern part of the city has a Miami-style resort feel and consists of **Bocagrande, El Laguito,** and **Castillo Grande.** This is where you'll find modern high-rises, all inclusive resorts, many of the city's top-notch hotels, and some of Cartagena's better beaches. The outer walled city consists of the **Getsemaní** neighborhood, a poorer, less-glamorous version of the inner walled city. The exclusive neighborhood of **Manga,** about a 5-minute taxi ride from the Old Town, is home to Cartagena's yacht club.

ON FOOT This is the best way to explore the picturesque inner walled Old Town. You can stop and take in Cartagena's imposing churches, people-watch in its many plazas, and enjoy a bit of shopping.

BY TAXI It's safe to hail taxis off the street in Cartagena. However, there is often a difference between what you should pay and what you will pay. Taxi drivers here are used to tourists and won't hesitate to rip you off, albeit usually by COL$1,000 to $2,000 (US50¢–US$1/25p–50p). As a general guide, a taxi from the airport to the Old Town should cost about COL$8,000 (US$4/£2), while a taxi to Bocagrande, Castillogrande, and El Laguito should cost COL$4,000 (US$2/£1). Before getting in your taxi, it's a good idea to ask how much the ride will cost to avoid unpleasant surprises at the end.

VISITOR INFORMATION

The city's best tourist office is located in **La Plaza de La Aduana** (Casa del Marqués del Premio Real; puntodeinformacion@turismocartagenadeindias.com; Mon–Sat 7am–7pm, Sun 9am–5pm) east of the Torre de Reloj. Here you can get a brochure (in both Spanish and imperfect English) with a map and descriptions of Cartagena's major sights. The office can also provide information about tours and excursions, and offers several interactive computers with information about Cartagena and Las Islas del Rosario. You'll also find small tourism offices at Plaza San Pedro Claver, Plaza de los Coches, and Centro de Convenciones de Cartagena. These offices are open Monday through Saturday 9am to 1pm and 4 to 8pm, Sunday 9am to 5pm. There is also tourist information at Rafael Núñez International Airport. Additionally, hotels, whether luxury or budget, are also an excellent source of information.

FAST FACTS Call the police at 🕐 **112.** The national emergency number, **123,** also works in Cartagena. For a medical emergency, head to **Hospital Bocagrande,** Calle 5 and Carrera 6 (🕐 **5/665-5270**), or **Clínica A.M.I.S.A Centro Médico,** Carrera 30 no. 30–29.

If you need to exchange money, head to one of several national banks to the right of **La Torre del Reloj,** immediately before you enter the Old Town (the side opposite the convention center). ATMs are abundant throughout Cartagena.

WHAT TO SEE & DO

Cartagena, especially the inner walled Old Town, offers a wealth of colonial architectural gems and churches. There are also several excellent museums and 400-year-old plazas that can't be missed. In fact, if it weren't for the motorcycles and taxis that whiz through the historic center, you'd think you were in a fantasy 16th-century Spanish town.

Much of the charm of Cartagena lies in strolling through its colonial streets, dining in one of its romantic, top-notch restaurants, and people-watching in one of its many

Cartagena

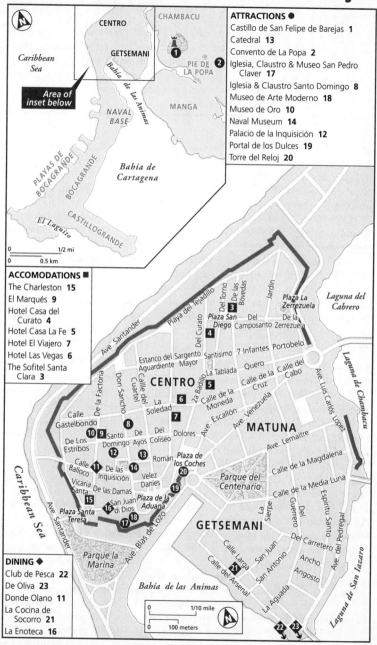

CENTRO

CHAMBACU

GETSEMANI

Caribbean Sea

Bahía de las Animas

PIE DE LA POPA

Area of inset below

NAVAL BASE

MANGA

Bahía de Cartagena

PLAYAS DE BOCAGRANDE

BOCAGRANDE

CASTILLOGRANDE

El Laguito

0   1/2 mi
0   0.5 km

Laguna del Cabrero

Laguna de Chambacu

CENTRO

MATUNA

GETSEMANI

Plaza La Zerrezuela
Plaza San Diego
Del Torno
De las Bóvedas
Jardín
Playa del Tejadillo
Del Curato
Del Camposanto
De la Zerrezuela
Ave. Santander
Estanco del Sargento Aguardiente Mayor
Santisimo
7 Infantes
Portobelo
2a Badillo
La Tablada
Quero
Calle de la Cruz
Calle del Cabo
Ave. Luis Carlos López
Don Sancho
Calle del Cuartel
La Soledad
Calle de la Moneda
Ave. Escallón
Ave. Venezuela
Calle Gastelbondo
De Santo Domingo
De Ayos
Del Coliseo
Dolores
Ave. Lernaitre
Calle de la Magdalena
De Los Estribos
Calle Balloco
De las Inquisición
Román
Velez Danies
Plaza de los Coches
Parque del Centenario
Calle de la Media Luna
Espíritu Santo
Vicaria Santa
De las Damas
San Juan di Dios
Plaza de la Aduana
Plaza Santa Teresa
Ave. Santander
Ave. Blas de Lozo
La Sierpe
Del Guerrero
Del Carretero
Ave. del Pedregal

Caribbean Sea

Parque la Marina

GETSEMANI

Calle Larga
San Juan
San Antonio
Ancho
Angosto
Calle del Arsenal
La Aguada
Bahía de las Animas

Laguna de San Iazaro

0   1/10 mile
0   100 meters

A Wild Ride on the *Chiva*

A *chiva* ⚑ is a colorful bus made entirely of wood. *Chivas* have become a folk-loric symbol of Colombia and are often decorated with festive designs, historical scenes, and even biblical imagery. In the past, *chivas* were used as a mode of transportation, but nowadays they're mostly used for city tours or as a nighttime bar on wheels. Riding a *chiva* is a must-do on a visit to Colombia; you'll see Colombians behaving their wildest.

plazas. Because some of the city's sites, such as the **Castillo de San Felipe de Barejas** and the **Convento de la Popa,** are a bit of a walk from the Old Town, you may want to take a *chiva* or carriage tour to get acquainted with the city. Your hotel will be able to provide (and even book) *chiva* and carriage tours, or you can inquire at the tourism office (see above). Daytime *chivas* should cost between COL$25,000 and COL$35,000 (US$13–US$17/£6.50–8.50), while a horse-drawn carriage tour should cost COL$35,000 to $45,000 (US$17–US$23/£8.50–£12) depending on the length of your trip.

For a uniquely Colombian experience, try the *rumba chivas,* which depart at 8pm (they usually pick you up from your hotel), cost around COL$25,000 (US$13/£6.25), and will give you an oversight of Cartagena at night. In addition, you'll get an unlimited amount of national liquor (*aguardiente,* rum, and the like), a taste of typical Cartagena fried treats (yuca, plaintain, *arepa*), and a demonstration of traditional Colombian folkloric dances. You'll be dropped off at a beachside nightclub around 10:30pm, where you can choose to stay or go back to your hotel at around midnight.

THE HISTORIC OLD TOWN: THE TOP ATTRACTIONS

In 1987, Cartagena's Old Town was declared a World Heritage Site by UNESCO, and its almost perfectly preserved colonial-era mansions, churches, and ornate balconies are the reason why. Where else in the Western Hemisphere can you sit in 16th-century plazas, walk along the walls of a 300-year-old fortress—one of the most impressive architectural feats of military history—and stay at a colonial-era hotel? Below are some of the city's most noteworthy sites.

Enter the city through the historic **Torre del Reloj,** one of Cartagena's most recognized architectural sites. From there, you'll find yourself in the **Plaza de los Coches,** where you can buy traditional Colombian and Cartagenian candy and sweets at the **Portal de Los Dulces.** Next head down Calle de la Amargura, past **La Plaza de La Aduana** (stop here if you're looking for tourist information), to La Plaza de San Pedro, where you can visit the **Iglesia/Claustro/Museo San Pedro Claver,** constructed in 1580, as well as the **Museo de Arte Moderno,** a decent modern-art museum right off the square. Walk down Calle San Juan de Dios to the Cartagena **Naval Museum,** where you can take in antique naval instruments and objects. Walk past La Plaza de Santa Teresa, up Calle de A. Ricaurte (which becomes Calle Santa Teresa) to Plaza de Bolívar, where you can visit the free **Museo de Oro** as well as the **Palacio de La Inquisición** and **La Biblioteca Bartolomé Calvo,** once Cartagena's most important libraries. Be sure not to miss Cartagena's much photographed **Catedral,** built in 1586, destroyed by English pirate Francis Drake, and recently remodeled and opened to the public. Now walk up Calle Nuestra Señora del Carmen before arriving at the **Plaza de Santo Domingo,** one of Cartagena's most popular and vibrant plazas. Be sure to visit the **Iglesia/Claustro Santo Domingo,** a lovely 450-year-old church. Take a break at Plaza Santo Domingo for a light lunch or snack at one of the plaza's many outdoor cafes, where you can enjoy the beautiful colonial atmosphere.

With your energy restored, head north on Calle de la Iglesia (which becomes Calle de Don Sancocho), past El Teatro de Heredia and La Plaza del Merced and turn right on Calle de la Merced (which becomes Calle Del Estanco del Aguardiente and Calle del Sargento Mayor). Next turn left on Calle Chochera del Hobo, where you'll find **La Plaza de San Diego,** with its many stores, restaurants, and the famous Hotel Santa Clara. A short walk up the Calle de las Bóvedas will take you to **Las Bóvedas,** a former jail, used during the Independence period, converted into 23 souvenir shops.

OTHER TOURIST SIGHTS

La Popa, Cartagena's highest point, is where you'll find the convent of Nuestra Señora de La Candelaria. *Warning:* If you decide not to take a *chiva* tour, be sure to come here by taxi; robberies and attacks have been reported for those who've tried to walk. **El Castillo de San Felipe de Borajas** is another Cartagena must-see, and one of the military wonders of the world. The castle/fort was built (1536–1657) to protect the city from attack. Be sure to check out its dark, underground tunnels and peek through its many look-outs. Note that this site will be included in a *chiva* tour.

Las Islas del Rosario, a Colombian national park popular with tourists, is famous for its coral reefs, crystalline waters, and beautiful beaches. The islands are located about 45km (28 miles) from the city and can only be reached by boat. You can arrange a trip to Las Islas del Rosario through your hotel or by heading to the Muelle Turístico where you can buy tickets directly. Another option is to go through **Tesoro Tours,** Carrera 3 no. 6–153 (© **5/665-4713;** www.tesorotours.com). Boat trips generally cost between COL$35,000 and COL$60,000 (US$18–US$30/£8.75–£15), though you will also have to pay a national park tax of COL$9,400 (US$2.35/£1.20). Your boat will most likely take you to the **Acuario San Martín** on the **Isla San Martín de Pajarales,** where you can enjoy a dolphin show and observe other marine animals. Another choice on Isla San Martín de Pajarales is to go snorkeling. The island has excellent coral reefs, and if you've already seen your share of aquariums and dolphin shows, go for the snorkeling.

After visiting the aquarium, most boats will head to Isla de Barú, where you'll have a typical Cartagena-Caribbean lunch, complete with coconut rice, fried plantains, and a whole fish (eyes and all). Your tour will give you about 3 hours on Baru, where you can go swimming, sunbathe, or explore the island. Beware that beach vendors here are persistent, and the best way to be left alone is to get in the water as fast as possible.

If you don't have time to head to Las Islas del Rosario, visit Cartagena's main beaches—Bocagrande, El Laguito, and Castillo Grande, in the south, and, in the north, La Boquilla and Marbella.

SHOPPING

Prices on clothing, handicrafts, and emeralds tend to be higher in Cartagena than in other parts of the country. There are plenty of attractive boutique shops in the historic center, as well as shopping malls in El Laguito and Bocagrande.

If you are looking for handicrafts, head to Las Bóvedas—former jail cells turned souvenir shops. In the historic center there are also plenty of high-end boutique shops selling Colombian designer clothing, leather goods, and emeralds. For discount shopping, head to Getsemaní, where you can buy cheap clothing, shoes, and just about anything else you can imagine; just don't count on top-notch quality.

For a shopping mall, your best bet is **El Pueblito** (Carrera 2 no. 4, in Bocagrande), **La Matuna** (Carrera 8 no. 40, in El Centro), or **Pierino Gallo** (Calle 1L no. 1–12A, in El Laguito).

Tip: It seems everyone in Cartagena's Old Town wants to sell you emeralds; if you decide to purchase Colombia's favorite stone, do so because you love the look of emeralds, *not* because you think you're getting a good deal. Unless you're an expert, it's hard to know the quality of your purchase.

WHERE TO STAY

Most foreigners choose to stay in the historic Old Town. Midrange and expensive lodging options are found in the inner walled city, while the backpacker crowd heads to Getsemaní, the slightly seedy but much cheaper outer walled city. If you're looking for all-inclusive resorts, head to **Capilla del Mar,** Carrera 1 no. 8–12, Bocagrande (© 5/665-1140; www.capilladelmar.com), or **Americas Global Resort,** Anillo Vial Sector Cielo Mar (© 5/656-7222; www.hotellasamericas.com).

Cartagena is jam-packed in December and January, with tourism slowly tapering off by April. July and August are busy again because of summer break. Throughout the year, there are various events when the city fills up again, notably the Miss Colombia Pageant in November. During these times, it's wise to book your hotel ahead of time. The city can also be pretty busy during mid-October, when students have a week off. You should note that notwithstanding the more exclusive lodging options, Cartagena hotels don't usually have hot water. With the heat and humidity, though, this shouldn't be too much of a problem.

In general, I recommend you avoid Cartagena from mid-October through the end of November, the rainiest season when the city often floods, making it difficult to sightsee or head to the beach. During off season, don't be shy about asking for discounts.

EXPENSIVE

The Charleston   Another charming choice, the Charleston dates back to the 17th century when the building functioned as a convent for the Carmelita nuns. Nowadays the Charleston is one of Cartagena's finest (and most expensive) hotels, featuring 91 brightly decorated rooms. The sixth-floor spa is one of the best in Colombia, where you can get any kind of massage imaginable. Interestingly, one of the conference rooms once served as the Carmelita nuns' chapel. Like the Santa Clara (see below), the hotel consists of two architectural styles: The fully-restored, two-story Colonial section dates back to the 1600s, while the much newer five-story Republican section was added during the hotel's recent restoration.

Carrera 3A no. 31–23, Centro Plaza de Teresa. © 5/664-9494. www.hoteles-charleston.com. 91 units. COL$545,000 (US$273/£136) standard double, COL$600,000–$1,240,000 (US$300–US$620/£150–£310) suites. AE, DC, MC, V. **Amenities:** Restaurant; pool; gym; sauna; laundry; 24-hr. room service; parking; 4 conference rooms. *In room:* A/C, flatscreen TV, Wi-Fi, hair dryer, safe, alarm.

El Marqués   El Marqués is Cartagena's best-known boutique hotel. Its lovely Asian-style gardens, multiple springs, and first-floor pool give the hotel a Zen-like quality. Antique wooden balconies overlook the courtyard, and modern artwork decorates the walls. The hotel has a long history in Cartagena, dating back to the 17th century, and is considered one of Cartagena's best and most-established boutique hotels. But prestige doesn't come cheap: Don't expect to pay less than COL$500,000 (US$250/£125) a night. As an interesting side note, the hotel was home to American writer and painter Sam Green in the 1970s, where he entertained guests such as Greta Garbo and Yoko Ono. El Marqués also serves as a spa and sushi bar that's also open to nonguests.

Calle de Nuestra Señora del Carmen no. 33–41, Centro Santo Domingo. (C) 5/664-4438. www.elmarqueshotelboutique. com. 8 units. COL$680,000 (US$340/£170) double; COL$780,000 ($390/£195) suite w/balcony; COL$980,000 ($490/£245) presidential suite. AE, DC, MC, V. **Amenities:** Restaurant; pool; spa; business center; emergency medical services. *In room:* A/C, cable TV, Wi-Fi, minibar, safe, direct national and international phone calls (for a fee).

The Sofitel Santa Clara ★★★

The Sofitel Santa Clara is widely-considered the top lodging option in Cartagena's historic center, and it's conveniently located in San Diego Square, close to some of Old City's best restaurants. The hotel has a history stretching as far back as 1617, when it served as the convent for the Clarisian nuns. In the late 1990s the building was restored and converted into a hotel, quickly becoming one of Colombia's best. Although the Santa Clara is an executive-style hotel, its amazing spa and rooms—with views of the ocean, the Old City, or the beautiful interior courtyards—make it a great choice for couples wanting a romantic getaway. The 102 Republican-style rooms and 17 colonial-style rooms have a chic "summer home" feel, complete with modern artwork, contemporary furniture, warm summer tones, and large windows providing tons of natural light. There's a great pool area and two excellent restaurants: **San Francisco,** which serves up Italian fare, and **El Refrectorio,** situated in a lovely courtyard that once was the Clarisian nuns' dining area.

Calle del Torno, Plaza San Diego. (C) 5/664-6070. www.hotelsantaclara.com. 119 units. COL$760,000 (US$380/£190) double, COL$1,000,000 (US$500/£250) colonial suite. Additional person (over 12 years old) COL$145,000 (US$73/£36). AE DC, MC, V. Free parking. **Amenities:** 2 restaurants; pool; gym; spa; 24-hr. room service. *In room:* A/C, flatscreen TV, Wi-Fi, minibar, digital safe, work area.

MODERATE

Hotel Casa del Curato

A delightful bed-and-breakfast, Casa del Curato dates back to the 18th century. There is a small, peaceful pool in the first-floor courtyard, and the stone wall interior gives the hotel an enchanted ambience. The Casa del Curato served as a clergy house during the colonial period and was restored as a hotel 3 years ago. The 11 rooms are all uniquely decorated, ranging from typical Caribbean-contemporary all-white walls and sheets to Indian and indigenous-inspired decor—think textured walls, colorful tapestries, and carefully selected ethnic bedspreads. Suites have balconies. If there aren't too many guests, ask to check out a couple of rooms to see which one fits your style. The upstairs terrace offers views of the Hotel Santa Clara and La Popa, and is a good place for an afternoon snack.

Calle del Curato no. 38–89, Centro. (C) 5/664-3648. www.casacurato.com. 11 units. COL$186,000–COL$208,000 (US$93–US$104/£47–£52) double, COL$246,000 (US$123/£62) suite. AE, DC, MC, V. Rates include breakfast. **Amenities:** Pool; free business center; 24-hr. reception; 2 sitting areas. *In room:* A/C, cable TV, Internet access, minibar, safe.

Hotel Casa La Fe *(Finds*

This beautifully restored, English-owned bed-and-breakfast offers 11 cozy rooms, which are simple and minimalist. Dark wood furnishings, pastel colors, and marble bathrooms make this a perfectly charming lodging option in the Old City, and a relatively good deal in this price range. There is an attractive downstairs sitting area, and breakfast is served daily in the lovely courtyard. The tropical vegetation gives the hotel a Caribbean feel. Unlike many of the city's historic buildings, 4-year-old Hotel Casa De La Fe dates back from the Republican rather than the colonial era. Be sure to check out the terrace, where you can cool off in the Jacuzzi-pool area or sunbathe under the hot Caribbean sun.

Calle Segunda de Badillo no. 36–125, Centro. ℰ **5/664-0306**. www.casalafe.com. 11 units. COL$220,000 (US$110/£55) first-floor rooms, COL$264,000 (US$132/66) second-floor rooms. AE, DC, MC, V. Rates include breakfast. **Amenities:** Pool; Jacuzzi. *In room:* A/C, ceiling fan, cable TV, Wi-Fi, minibar, safe.

INEXPENSIVE

In addition to the Hotel Las Vegas and Hotel El Viajero (see below), there are several decent budget choices in the Getsemaní neighborhood, the poorer, less glamorous part of Cartagena's Old Town. Even though this neighborhood isn't particularly picturesque and can get a bit seedy at night, it is popular with backpackers, and foreigners rarely encounter problems here. In addition, hotels in this area are only a 5-minute walk from the inner walled city. Don't expect hot water, however. One good option in Getsemaní is the very lovely **Hostal Baluarte** (ℰ **5/664-2208**), at Calle de la Media Luna no. 10–81. The 24 rooms are small and plain, but each is clean and well kept, and each comes with a TV. A double with air-conditioning costs COL$60,000 (US$30/£15), while rooms with only a fan go for COL$35,000 (US$18/£8.75). Note that prices go up in high season. You might also consider the excellent **Hostal La Casona de Getsemaní** (ℰ **5/664-1301**), at Calle Tripita y Media Carrera 10 no. 31–32. All rooms come with en-suite bathroom and cable TV, and some come with air-conditioning. Expect to pay COL$39,000 (US$20/£9.75) for a double without air-conditioning, COL$53,000 (US$27/£13) with air-conditioning. I prefer the hotels in this area because compared to similarly priced hotels in the inner-walled and modern sections of town, you get more amenities for your money.

Hotel El Viajero   All rooms face an unattractive courtyard, but the good news is that the 20-year-old hotel is undergoing an extensive restoration. Currently, rooms are small and clean and mattresses are a bit hard, and no hot water is available. Guests can use the kitchen facilities, and there is a pleasant dining area in case you feel inspired to try your skills at Cartagenan–Caribbean cooking. There is also a pleasant social area with a TV, stereo, and sofas. The friendly hotel staff can arrange tours in an around Cartagena, as well as provide a map and useful information.

Calle del Provenir no. 35–68 (2nd floor). ℰ **5/664-3289**. 17 units. COL$65,000 (US$33/£16) double. Rates go up 20% in high season. No credit cards. **Amenities:** Kitchen facilities/dining area; laundry; social area. *In room:* A/C, TV.

Hotel Las Vegas   Hotel Las Vegas is one of the cheapest lodging options in El Centro Histórico, so don't expect anything too fancy. All rooms have bathrooms (though some are a bit cramped and old-fashioned, and there's no hot water) and most rooms have air-conditioning. Rooms are clean, simple, and all have TVs. Some rooms have a balcony facing a noisy street, so you may want to ask for an interior-facing room, though these can be a bit dimly lit at night. The three-floor hotel is very basic, but a decent option in this price category considering you're within walking distance from most tourist sites.

Calle San Agustín no. 6–08. ℰ **5/664-5619**. 24 units. COL$50,000 (US$25/£13) double. No credit cards. **Amenities:** Laundry. *In room:* A/C, TV.

WHERE TO DINE

Seafood's the name of the game in Cartagena. In general, food is steeply overpriced in the inner walled city, but you'll find some of Colombia's most atmospheric and romantic restaurants here. In Getsemaní, you'll find many uncharming eateries offering cheap *almuerzo corriente,* while the modern city offers midrange and chain-restaurant options. During high season, it's smart to book ahead at Cartagena's more exclusive establishments, particularly at dinner time; during low season you may be the only diner present.

In addition to the places listed below, **La Vitrola,** Calle Baloco no. 33–201 (© 5/ 660-0711), is one of Cartagena's most traditional restaurants, with nightly live Cuban music. **El Santísimo,** Calle del Santísimo no. 8–19 (© 5/660-1531), specializing in fusion cuisine, is well known for its religious decorations. **San Pedro,** Centro Plaza de San Pedro Claver (© 5/664-5121), also offers fusion cuisine, featuring sushi, Asian, and international dishes—be sure to make reservations here in high season.

EXPENSIVE

Club de Pesca ✦✦✦ CARRIBEAN/SEAFOOD

One of the most exclusive and romantic dining options in town, the Club de Pesca is one of my all-time favorite restaurants. Situated in the 300-year-old Fuerte de San Sabastián Pastellillo, the restaurant overlooks Cartagena's marina with its many international boats and yachts. In fact, this is the only restaurant in town where you can arrive by land or by sea. The elegant setting makes the restaurant perfect for a romantic evening with your significant other and is popular for weddings and marriage proposals. The restaurant offers delicious Caribbean-inspired dishes, all with a contemporary touch. Start with the *langostinos portobello,* prawns marinated in orange and *maracuyá* juice and served with grilled portobello mushrooms. Or try the *jaiba de Las Islas del Rosario,* crab marinated in lemon and liquorish and served between two mini-*arepas.* As your main dish, try *los mariscos a la Cartagenera* (Cartagena-style seafood) for an excellent sampling of different Cartagena dishes, including *ceviche,* shrimp cocktail, Creole-style fish filet, coconut rice, and friend plantains. The restaurant also offers an excellent variety of international wines and, for those feeling particularly decadent, a cigar menu to top off the night. There is live music Thursday to Saturday, featuring mostly Bossa Nova, jazz, and flamenco.

Manga, Fuerte de San Sabastián del Pastelillo. © 5/660-5863. Reservations recommended in high season. www. clubdepesca.com. Main courses COL$25,000–COL$55,000 (US$13–US$28/£6.50–£14). AE, DC, MC, V. Daily noon–midnight.

MODERATE

Donde Olano FRENCH/CREOLE

This intimate, bistro-style French restaurant is an excellent dining option near la Plaza de Santo Domingo. The 10-year-old restaurant boasts classic-style artwork and a warm, cozy ambience. Like most restaurants in Cartagena, the restaurant has a strong seafood influence. Try the *tentación de Zeus,* featuring lobster in white wine–and-cognac sauce, crab, shrimp marinated in sweet-and-sour *maracuyá* sauce, coconut rice, and wok-style vegetables. If you've had it with seafood, go for the *lomito de res creole,* featuring tender beef in tomato and onion sauce and white rice. For dessert, try the *flan de café colombiano,* a unique, coffee-flavored flan.

Calle de Santo Domingo and Inquisión. © 5/664-7099. Reservations recommended in high season. www.donde olano.com. Main courses COL$18,000–COL$45,000 (US$9–US$23/£4.50–£11). Credit cards not accepted. Daily noon–11pm.

La Cocina de Socorro CARIBBEAN/SEAFOOD

One of my favorite restaurants in town, La Cocina de Socorro has a 25-year history in Cartagena. The restaurant's style is somewhere between elegant and typical, with a modern waterfall, year-round Christmas lights, and traditional woven baskets hanging from the ceiling. A popular place for business meetings and tourists alike, La Cocina del Soccorro serves up one of best, most generous, and cheapest ceviche dishes in town, and chef María Nelly del

Socorro specializes in tasty Cartagena-inspired dishes. The restaurant has been visited by the likes of Colombia President Alvaro Uribe and soccer star Carlos Valderrama.

On Calle del Arsenal, near the Cartagena Convention Center in Getsemaní. © 5/660-2044. www.lacocinadesocorro. com. Main courses COL$20,000–COL$35,000 (US$10–US$18/£5–£9). AE, DC, MC, V. Daily noon–11pm (later in high season, sometimes earlier in low season).

La Enoteca ITALIAN This 10-year-old Italian restaurant and pizzeria has a wine cave holding over 7,000 wine varieties from dozens of regions in Italy. Indeed, the restaurant has one of the largest wine selections in Colombia. Aside from the wine cave, there's a casual pizza area and an Italian deli. Ask if you can check out the spectacular Italian-style Garibaldi Salon, reserved for special events such as a presidential visit. The antique furniture, year-round Christmas lights, and regal bar area give the restaurant a definitely European feel. On Friday and Saturday night, there is Caribbean-style live music.

Calle San Juan de Dios no. 3–39. © 5/664-3806. Reservations recommended in high season. Main courses COL$8,000–COL$20,000 (US$4–US$10/£2–£5). Credit cards not accepted. Mon–Sat noon–11:30pm; Sun 4–11:30pm.

INEXPENSIVE

De Oliva ARAB/MEDITERANNEAN This 1-year-old restaurant in the Manga area offers some of the best Arab and Mediterranean food in town. Try the *langostinas al curry* (curried shrimp) or the *combo Arabe* (Arab combo), which consists of almond rice, grape leaves, falafel, stuffed cabbage, and—to put a Latin twist on it—a spinach and tahini empanada. This fresh little restaurant is popular with Colombians of Arab descent and businesspeople on their lunch break. Considering the high quality of food here, De Oliva is one of the best restaurant deals in town.

Av. del Pastelillo no. 24–116. © 5/660-6861. Main courses COL$8,000–20,000 (US$4–US$10/£2–£5). AE, DC, MC, V. Daily noon–3pm and 6–10:30pm.

CARTAGENA AFTER DARK

Half the reason Cartagena is Colombia's top tourist destination is because of its vibrant night life. Cartagena's party scene is well developed with something for everyone—whether you want to sip cocktails on the beach, salsa dance Caribbean-style, or jam to '80s rock. Much of the nightlife is centered on Calle del Arsenal, in the Getsemaní neighborhood, though there are also several party options in the inner walled city.

Mr. Babilla, Calle Arsenal no. 9B–137 (© 5/664-8616; daily 8pm–4am), plays crossover music and is by far Cartagena's most famous nightclub. The eclectic decorations, tasty cocktails, and party-hard atmosphere bring in Colombia's cream of the crop and a large foreign clientele. **La Carbonera,** Av. del Arsenal no. 9A–47 (© 5/664-6237; daily 9pm–4am), another popular nightclub in the Getsemaní neighborhood, plays a little bit of everything.

Café Havana ⚐, Calle Media Luna and Calle del Guerrero (© 315/690-2566; daily 7pm–4am), in the Getsemaní neighborhood, is dedicated to Cuban music. This place also offers decent sandwiches and light fare, and it is one of the more atmospheric places in town. There is often live music and the clientele tends to be mostly foreigners.

9

Ecuador

by Eliot Greenspan

While the Galápagos Islands are the prime draw, there's much more to this small South American nation straddling the Equator. In fact, Ecuador likes to boast that it is really four distinct destinations: the Galápagos Islands, the Amazon basin, the Andean Sierra, and the Pacific coast. From the high peaks and paramo of the Ecuadorian sierra, you can quickly descend and visit the rainforests of the Amazon basin. For those seeking more urban and urbane pleasures, Quito contains both the colonial and modern in a blend that is at once stark and stunning, while Cuenca is compact colonial-era treasure, with the ancient Inca ruins of Ingapirca nearby. Part of the country's attraction lies in its being small enough that you can see the best of everything in a relatively short time.

Most visitors begin their journey in Quito, one of the oldest and best preserved cities in the Americas. Meticulously preserved and restored colonial-era churches, monasteries, and mansions abound along the cobblestone streets of the city's Old Town. Within a couple of hours of Quito, you can climb to the top of the highest active volcano in the world or shop for handicrafts in one of the largest and most colorful markets in South America.

Another option is to start your journey in Guayaquil, Ecuador's most populous city and the de facto gateway for all flights to the Galápagos, as well as to the most popular stretches of the country's Pacific coast. A booming metropolis,

Guayaquil boasts a beautiful riverfront promenade, the Malecón 2000, and a host of excellent hotels, restaurants, shops, clubs, and casinos.

Cuenca is the country's most charming city. Before the Spanish arrived, this was the second-most important city in the Inca empire. And even before that it was settled and developed by the mysterious Cañari (also spelled Kañari) people. Today, the ruins and remnants of all three major colonizing civilizations are on display throughout the small city. Cuenca also boasts several excellent restaurants serving Ecuadorian specialties unique to this region.

Then there's the jungle. Early in the morning, you can watch parrots and macaws gather for breakfast. As you take canoe trips down the river, you might spot an anaconda curled up on the shores, waiting patiently for its prey, or perhaps catch a glimpse of playful fresh-water dolphins frolicking in the river. You can also visit local villages, where people live very much the same way their ancestors did hundreds of years ago.

Finally, there's the Galápagos Islands, where you'll come as close as humanly possible to an astounding array of animals. A visit here is a once-in-a-lifetime experience and is sure to stay with you forever—as it did for Charles Darwin. *Tip:* For a map of suggested itineraries in Ecuador, please refer to the "Itineraries in Bolivia, Brazil, Colombia, Ecuador & Peru" map on p. 222.

1 The Regions in Brief

The Republic of Ecuador sits near the northwestern corner of South America. It's bordered by Colombia to the north, Peru to the south and east, and the Pacific Ocean to the west. The Galápagos Islands, which straddle the Equator, are located about 966km (618 miles) to the west in the Pacific Ocean. The country covers an area of 272,046 sq. km (105,037 sq. miles), making it roughly the same size as Colorado.

QUITO   Situated at some 2,850m (9,300 ft.) above sea level, Quito is the second-highest capital city in the world (after La Paz, Bolivia). Though it's the capital of Ecuador, Quito is actually the second-most populous city in the country (after Guayaquil). Still, Quito is a major transportation hub, and most visitors begin and end their trips to Ecuador here. Fortunately, Quito is one of the more charming cities in South America, and there's plenty here to see and do. Its **Old Town,** with its wonderfully preserved colonial-style buildings, was declared a World Heritage Site by UNESCO in 1978, the first city to ever earn the designation. The **New Town** is a lively cosmopolitan area, with all the modern amenities you would expect to find in a world-class destination.

THE NORTHERN SIERRA   The Equator cuts across Ecuador just north of Quito. This invisible line also forms the border that roughly defines the country's Northern Sierra. **Imbabura Province** is the first province you hit, and one of the country's prime tourism destinations. In Imbabura, you can explore the colorful artisan's market of **Otavalo** and visit the small towns surrounding Otavalo, where you'll find the workshops and homes of many of the artisans who supply this fabulous market. In addition, this region is one of high volcanic mountains and crater lakes. There are great hiking opportunities, especially at such beautiful spots as **Cuicocha Lake** and **Mojanda Lakes.**

THE CENTRAL SIERRA   The Central Sierra covers the area south of Quito. **Cotopaxi National Park** is a little more than an hour south of Quito, and it's one of the most popular attractions on mainland Ecuador. Active travelers can climb to the summit of the highest active volcano in the world, while anybody can marvel at its imposing beauty from the high-altitude paramo park that surrounds and contains it. All around the Central Sierra you will find isolated colonial-era haciendas that have been converted into fabulous boutique hotels, lodges and spas. Most offer a variety of active tour options, with hiking and horseback riding being the mainstay at most of them.

CUENCA & THE SOUTHERN SIERRA   Cuenca is the largest and most interesting city in the Southern Highlands. Like Quito, it was declared a World Heritage Site by UNESCO. Cuenca was the second-most important city in the Inca empire (after Cusco). Nearby, you can explore **Ingapirca,** an archaeological site with both Inca and pre-Inca ruins. Cajas National Park is located only an hour outside of the city.

GUAYAQUIL & THE SOUTHERN COAST   Guayaquil is Ecuador's largest city. Historically a port and industrial city, Guayaquil has been reinventing itself at a dizzying pace. The city's attractive riverside walk, **Malecón 2000** has served as the anchor for a mini-renaissance. Guayaquil boasts several excellent museums, as well as top-notch hotels, restaurants, and bars. To the west of Guayaquil lies the Ruta del Sol (Route of the Sun), a string of beach resorts, small fishing villages, and isolated stretches of sand. At the north end of the Ruta del Sol, sits **Machalilla National Park**

as well as **Isla de la Plata,** which is home to a rich variety of wildlife, and is often called the "Poor Person's Galápagos."

EL ORIENTE The eastern region of Ecuador, known as El Oriente, is a vast area of lowland tropical rain forests and wild jungle rivers. It is considered part of the Amazon basin, as the rivers here all feed and form the great Amazon river just a little farther downstream. The wildlife and bird-watching here are phenomenal, with the chance to see hundreds of bird species, over a dozen monkey species, as well as anaconda, caiman, and fresh-water dolphins For the most part, the indigenous people in this region escaped domination by both the Incas and the Spanish, so they have been able to hold on to their ancient rituals and traditions. Most visitors explore this area by staying at a remote jungle lodge, some of which are surprisingly comfortable.

THE GALÁPAGOS ISLANDS The Galápagos Islands, located about 966km (618 miles) off the coast of Ecuador, are one of nature's most unique outdoor laboratories. The unusual wildlife here helped Charles Darwin formulate his Theory of Natural Selection. Fortunately for modern-day visitors, not much has changed since Darwin's time, and the islands still offer visitors the chance to get up close and personal with a wide variety of unique and endemic species, including giant tortoises, marine iguanas, penguins, sea lions, albatrosses, boobies, and flightless cormorants. The best way to explore the area is on a cruise ship or yacht. You should note, however, that this isn't your typical cruise destination—the trips involve packed days of tours and activities, some of them strenuous. A more relaxing option would be to base yourself at a resort in Santa Cruz (the most populated island in the Galápagos) and take select day-trips to the islands of your choice.

2 The Best of Ecuador in 2 Weeks

If you want to visit the Galápagos, it's tough to see much of the rest of Ecuador in just 1 week. You have two options: You can spend your entire trip in the Galápagos on a 7-day tour, or you can see the highlights of the Galápagos on a 3- or 5-day tour and try to see some of the mainland in the few days you have left.

However, if you have 2 weeks, you'll be able to see much of the best that Ecuador has to offer. You'll be able to visit Quito and the highlands, the lovely colonial city of Cuenca, spend a full week in the enchanting Galápagos Islands, and have just enough time for an overnight in Guayaquil, one of South America's most up-and-coming cities. If you can tack on a few more days, then you'll have enough time to take a 3- or 4-day tour in El Oriente, Ecuador's lush Amazon region.

Days ①–②: Quito

Many international flights arrive in Quito in the late afternoon or early evening, so you'll need to check yourself into a hotel for 2 nights to enjoy 1 full day of sightseeing in the capital. Get to bed as early as possible so you can be rested and out the door early on Day 2. After breakfast at your hotel, spend the morning touring **Old Town.** Visit the magnificent **Iglesia de San Francisco** ✸✸ (p. 534), which

dates back to 1535, and allow yourself a good 45 minutes to get a feel for the city's oldest church and its attached museum.

A few minutes' walk away, **La Compañía de Jesús** ✸✸✸ (p. 536) Jesuit church features an incredibly ornate interior that shows baroque and Moorish influences. Nearby, **Casa Museo María Augusta Urrutia** ✸ (p. 533) is a perfectly preserved 19th-century mansion worthy of at least a 45-minute visit. As the sun warms the cool morning air, take some time to stroll around Old Town, ending up at **La Plaza de la Independencia** (p. 536), which was the city's main square in the 16th century. Break for a cup of coffee at a sunny cafe on or around the plaza—there are plenty to choose from here.

Next, grab a taxi and head to **El Panecillo,** where you'll see the Virgin of Quito (p. 533). It's a 10-minute ride up a steep hill. From here, standing below the immense winged Virgin, you have a sweeping view of Old Town and the rest of the city. Right next to the monument is **PIM's Panecillo** (p. 546), a great place to enjoy local cuisine for lunch while you continue to enjoy the view. Remember to drink lots of bottled water, especially in the early afternoon, when the sun is at its highest and the atmosphere its driest.

After lunch, take a taxi to the **Fundación Guayasamín** ☆☆ (p. 538), named after the country's most famous and influential artist, Oswaldo Guayasamín. Expect to spend at least 1½ hours here and at the nearby **Capilla del Hombre** ☆. At both, you'll find original works by Guayasamín, as well as pieces from his personal collection.

You should be pretty beat by now, so head to **Plaza Foch** (p. 549) in the **Mariscal district** of **New Town** for a late-afternoon or early evening cup of coffee or a cocktail. If the weather is good, grab an outdoor table at one of the restaurants around the plaza. If you're lucky, a jazz band will be playing right in front of you.

For dinner, be sure to have reservations at **Zazu** ☆☆☆ (p. 548), the best and hippest spot in Quito. You can end the meal with dessert or with a drink at their popular little laid-back bar. If you have the energy, pull out all the stops and head back to the Mariscal district's many bars and clubs to see where the night and your whims lead you.

Days ❸–❹: Otavalo & Imbabura Province

After your grueling sightseeing day in Quito, it's time to leave the city behind and unwind in the highlands of the northern Sierra for a couple of days. The roughly 2-hour drive is leisurely and scenic, and should include a stop at the new **Quitsato Mitad del Mundo** (p. 555), where you can have your photo taken with one foot in each of the earth's hemispheres.

I recommend **Hacienda Cusín** ☆☆ (p. 560), a rambling, serene inn set amid 4 hectares (10 acres) of lush gardens, on the outskirts of **Otavalo** ☆☆. In the distance, Volcán Imbabura makes for a breathtaking backdrop. Have lunch on the sun-splashed terrace and perhaps take a siesta afterward. In the afternoon, choose from a variety of activities, including horseback riding in the nearby hills, a Spanish lesson, or a meander in the lovely gardens. A candle-lit dinner is served in the cozy dining room, which makes for a perfect ending to a relaxing day. If you feel like going out for a gourmet dinner, make reservations at and take a taxi to **La Mirage Garden Hotel** ☆☆☆ (p. 560), one of the finer restaurants in Ecuador. The drive takes about 20 minutes.

On Day 4, spend your morning perusing the artisans market at **Otavalo** ☆☆☆ (p. 556), a 15-minute taxi ride away, and shop to your heart's content. Then stop by **Peguche** (p. 558) to visit some of the best weavers in Ecuador, before heading up to **Hacienda Pinsaquí** ☆ (p. 561) for lunch at one of the region's most picturesque and historic old haciendas. If you have the energy after lunch, you can take a taxi up to **Lago Cuicocha** ☆ and hike around the rim of this beautiful volcanic-crater lake, or take a more relaxing boat ride on its waters.

In the evening, you can spend a quiet night at Hacienda Cusín or head back into Otavalo for dinner at **Hotel Ali Shungu** ☆☆ (p. 562), and maybe catch some live music at one of the local *peña* bars. Whatever you choose, be sure to get a good night's rest, because you'll have to wake early in order to drive back to the Quito airport for your flight to Cuenca.

Day ❺: Cuenca ⚜⚜⚜

Your 1-hour flight will bring you to Cuenca, one of Ecuador's most charming colonial cities. If you're seated on the left side of the plane, and if there's a break in the clouds, you'll probably get a great view of Volcán Cotopaxi on the way.

By the time you arrive and settle into your hotel, you should be ready for lunch. I recommend that you head to **El Maíz** ⚜ (p. 573), a lovely indoor-outdoor restaurant serving top-notch Ecuadorian cuisine. After lunch, visit the **Museo del Banco Central** ⚜⚜ (p. 568), just steps away from El Maíz. The museum contains an extensive art and archaeology collection, and is located on the site of a major Cañari and Inca ceremonial center. After touring the museum, be sure to walk around the ruins and their botanical gardens.

From the museum, take a taxi to **Mirador de Turi,** a strategic lookout with a beautiful view of Cuenca and its broad valley. Be sure to combine a visit here with a stop at **Taller E. Vega** ⚜⚜ (p. 570), the gallery and workshop of one of the country's most prominent ceramic artists.

At some point during the day, be sure to sign up for a half-day tour to Ingapirca for the following day. Your hotel desk is probably your best bet. Otherwise, contact **Hualambari Tours** ⚜ (© **07/2848-768;** www.hualambari.com) or **Terra-Diversa** ⚜ (© **07/2823-782;** www.terra diversa.com).

For dinner, you should splurge and head for the best restaurant in town, **Villa Rosa** ⚜⚜⚜ (p. 572), which serves creative takes on classic Ecuadorian dishes in a refined and elegant setting. If you have any energy left, have a nightcap at the **Wunderbar Café** ⚜⚜ (p. 573).

Day ❻: Ingapirca ⚜ & Colonial Cuenca ⚜⚜⚜

You'll probably leave just after breakfast for your trip to **Ingapirca** ⚜ (p. 574), the Machu Picchu of Ecuador. Located about a 2-hour drive north of Cuenca, Ingapirca is the largest and most significant archaeological site left by the Incas in Ecuador. It was built on the ruins of a Cañari settlement, and you will see evidence of their culture and architecture here as well. Your tour will likely include lunch, but you should be back in Cuenca with plenty of time to further explore its colonial core.

Start at the colorful **Flower Market** (p. 568), and continue from there to the main square, **Parque Calderón** (the heart of Cuenca). Be sure to visit the Gothic-Romanesque **Catedral Nueva** ⚜⚜ (p. 567), with its exquisite white-marble floors. Then catch a taxi from the square to the most interesting and best-known factory in the country. **Homero Ortega P. & Hijos** ⚜⚜⚜ (p. 570) makes some of the highest-quality Panama hats in the world. You'll get to see how they do it, as well as shop at slightly discounted prices in their showroom store.

For your last night, I recommend combining dinner and nightlife by heading to **Café Eucalyptus** ⚜⚜ (p. 573), where you can dine on a range of exotic tapas while mingling with the crème de la crème of Cuenca.

Days ❼–⓭: The Galápagos Islands ⚜⚜⚜

Getting to the Galápagos from Cuenca will require an early morning departure with a change of planes in Guayaquil. The flight to Guayaquil is only 30 minutes, and from there to the Galápagos it's exactly 1½ hours. A 7-day cruise on one of the 100 vessels plying the waters of these magical islands is the best way to visit the Galápagos; the typical itinerary includes a visit to two islands a day—one in the morning and one in the afternoon.

Day ⑭: Guayaquil ✦

Since all flights from the Galápagos first land in Guayaquil, spend your last night in Ecuador in this economically vibrant and up-and-coming city, the country's largest. Flights from the Galápagos arrive in the early afternoon, leaving you enough time to check into your hotel and stroll over to the **Malecón 2000** ✦✦ (p. 577). You may want to visit the MAAC, the **Museo Antropológico y de Arte Contemporáneo** ✦✦ (**Museum of Anthropology and Contemporary Art;** p. 579), or take a long walk in the interesting neighborhood of **Cerro Santa**

Ana ✦✦✦ (p. 578). Climb to the top for a sweeping view of the city. For your last evening in Ecuador, head over to **Lo Nuestro** ✦✦ (p. 582), the city's best restaurant.

Day ⑮: Fly Home

It's unlikely you'll have much time during your last morning in Guayaquil, but if you do, head to **Parque Histórico Guayaquil** ✦✦ (p. 579), a small theme-park with a re-creation of old colonial-era homes and haciendas, as well as lovely gardens.

3 Planning Your Trip to Ecuador

VISITOR INFORMATION

The Ecuadorian Ministry of Tourism has limited resources, and there are virtually no government-sponsored tourist offices outside Ecuador. But the Ecuador Tourist Board has two similar websites, **www.vivecuador.com** and **www.purecuador.com**. Both have some basic information, as well as forms to fill out to have a brochure sent to you. I've been told a redesign and improvements are scheduled for the latter site, so keep checking back.

The **Corporación Metropolitana de Turismo (Metropolitan Tourism Corporation;** www.quito.com.ec) hands out excellent city maps of Quito and the entire country at all their desks, which includes those at both the major international airports in Quito and Guayaquil. The most detailed map available is produced by **International Travel Maps** (www.itmb.com), available online from the website listed or from **www.amazon.com**.

For specific travel-related information, your best bet is to contact one of Ecuador's better travel agencies. Here is a list of some of my favorites:

- **Metropolitan Touring** ✦✦, De Las Palmeras Av. N45–74 and De Las Orquídeas, Quito (© 02/2988-200; www.metropolitan-touring.com). This is certainly the largest and arguably best-established of the various full-service Ecuadorian travel agencies. They feature a vast selection of tour options, and their guides and customer service are top notch.
- **Safari Ecuador** ✦✦, Calle Foch E5–39 and Juan León Mera, Quito (© 02/2552-505; www.safari.com.ec), offers various Galápagos cruises, an array of Amazon adventures, Andean camping safaris, and mountain climbing.
- **Surtrek** ✦, Av. Amazonas 897 and Wilson, Quito (© 02/2231-534; www.surtrek.com), is a large in-country tour operator and wholesaler specializing in adventure tours. They offer everything from mountain-bike tours to white-water rafting and can customize combination tours.
- **Zenith Ecuador Travel** ✦, Juan León Mera 453 and Roca #202, Quito (© 593-2/2529-993; www.zenithecuador.com). This excellent Quito-based agency can arrange for some of the least expensive Galápagos cruises and land tours in Ecuador.

Telephone Dialing Info at a Glance

- **To place a call from your home country to Ecuador:** Dial the international access code (011 in the U.S. and Canada, 0011 in Australia, 0170 in New Zealand, 00 in the U.K.), plus the country code (593), plus the Ecuadorian area code (for example, Quito 2, Cuenca 7, Guayaquil 4, the Galápagos 5, Otavalo 6), followed by the 7-digit number. For example, a call from the U.S. to Quito would be 011+593+2+0000+000.

- **To place a call within Ecuador:** If you are calling within the same area code inside Ecuador, you simply dial the 7-digit number. However, you must use area codes if you're calling from one area code to another. Note that for all calls within the country, area codes are preceded by a 0 (for example, Quito 02, Cuenca 07, Guayaquil 04, the Galápagos 05, Otavalo 06).

- **To place a direct international call from Ecuador,** dial the international access code (00), plus the country code of the place you are dialing, plus the area code and the local number.

- **To reach an international operator,** dial © 116 or 117. Major long distance company access codes are as follows: **AT&T** © 1800/225-528; **Bell Canada** © 999-175; **British Telecom** © 999-178; **MCI** © 999-170; **Sprint** © 999-171.

ENTRY REQUIREMENTS

A valid passport is required to enter and depart Ecuador. Visas are not required for citizens of the United States, the United Kingdom, Canada, Australia, New Zealand, South Africa, France, Germany, and Switzerland. Upon entry, you will automatically be granted permission to stay for up to 90 days. Technically, to enter the country you need a passport that is valid for more than 6 months, a return ticket, and proof of how you plan to support yourself while you're in Ecuador, but I've never seen a Customs official ask for the last two requirements. If you plan on spending more than 90 days here, you *will* need to apply for a visa at your local embassy (see "Ecuadorian Embassy Locations," below). Requirements include a passport valid for more than 6 months, a police certificate with criminal record from the state or province in which you currently live, a medical certificate, a return ticket, and two passport-size photographs.

ECUADORIAN EMBASSY LOCATIONS

In the U.S.: 2535 15th St. NW, Washington, DC 20009 (© **202/234-7200;** fax 202/667-3482)

In Canada: 50 O'Connor St., Suite 316, Ottawa, ON K1P 6L2 (© **613/563-8206;** fax 613/235-5776)

In the U.K.: 3 Hans Crescent, Knightsbridge, London, SW1X OLS (© **020/7584-8084;** fax 020/7823-9701)

In Australia: 6 Pindari Crescent, O'Malley, ACT 2606 (© **628/64021;** fax 628/61231)

CUSTOMS

Visitors to Ecuador are legally permitted to bring in up to $1,250 (£625) worth of items for personal use, including cameras, portable typewriters, video cameras and accessories, tape recorders, personal computers, and CD players. You can also bring in up to 2 liters of alcoholic beverages and 200 cigarettes (1 carton).

MONEY

Since 2000, the official unit of currency in Ecuador has been the **U.S. dollar.** You can use American or Ecuadorian coins, both of which come in denominations of 1¢, 5¢, 10¢, 25¢, and 50¢. Otherwise, all the currency is in the paper form of American dollars, in denominations of 1, 5, 10, 20, 50, and 100. It's very hard to make change, especially for any bill over $5, especially in taxis. If you are retrieving money from an ATM, be sure to request a denomination ending in 1 or 5 (most ATMs will dispense money in multiples of $1) so that you won't have to worry about breaking a large bill. If you are stuck with big bills, try to use them in restaurants to make change.

ATMs ATMs are ubiquitous in Ecuador. You'll even find them in remote areas such as the Galápagos. Some of the major banks include **Banco de Guayaquil, Banco del Pichincha,** and **Banco del Pacífico.** Most ATMs accept cards from both the **Cirrus** and **PLUS** networks, but some can't deal with PINs that are more than four digits. Before you go to Ecuador, make sure that your PIN fits the bill. *Tip:* If you're unable to use ATMs for any reason, you can get a cash advance from inside the bank.

TRAVELER'S CHECKS You can't change American Express traveler's checks at the American Express offices in Ecuador. (Yes, I know that sounds strange, but it's true.) These offices only allow you to make a cash advance on your Amex card. If you're traveling with traveler's checks, your best bet is to exchange them at a *casa de cambio* (money-exchange house) or a bank. Most upscale hotels and restaurants will accept traveler's checks. For lost American Express traveler's checks, you must call collect to the United States at ✆ **800/221-7282.**

CREDIT CARDS MasterCard and Visa are accepted most everywhere. American Express and Diners Club are less common, but still widely accepted. To report lost or stolen credit cards, you can try the local numbers listed here, or call collect to the United States. For **American Express,** call ✆ **02/2560-488** in Ecuador, or ✆ 910/333-3211 collect in the U.S.; for **Diners Club,** call ✆ **02/2981-300** in Ecuador, or ✆ 303/799-1504 collect in the U.S., for **MasterCard,** call ✆ **02/2262-770** in Ecuador, or ✆ 314/542-7111 collect in the U.S.; and for **Visa,** call ✆ **02/2459-303** in Ecuador, or ✆ 410/581-9994 collect in the U.S.

WHEN TO GO

PEAK SEASON & CLIMATE The peak seasons for travelers in Ecuador last from mid-June to early September and from late December through early January, because most American and European visitors have vacation time during these months. Cruises in the Galápagos will be booked solid during these times of year. But since Ecuador is hardly Disney World, you'll always be able to find a room (or a berth on a ship), and the country never feels overcrowded. I find that Ecuador is great throughout the year, so whenever you visit, you won't be disappointed.

There are four distinct geographical zones in Ecuador that are all subject to their own weather patterns. In the Galápagos, from June through September, the air and water are chilly and the winds can be a bit rough. From October through May, the air and water temperatures are warmer, but you can expect periodic light rain almost daily. On the coast, the rainy season lasts from December through May; this season is marked by hot weather and humidity. The cooler air temperature from June through September attracts whales and dolphins to the waters off the coast. In Quito and the highlands, the weather is coolest from June through September (the dry season), but it's only a few degrees colder than the rest of the year. Keep in mind that although Quito is practically on the Equator, the temperature can get quite cool because it's at such a high altitude (more than 2,700m/8,856 ft. above sea level); the city has an average high of 67°F (19°C) and an average low of 50°F (10°C). In the jungle area, it rains year-round, but the rain is especially hard from December through April. The temperature in the jungle can reach 80°F to 90°F (27°C–32°C) during the day; it's a bit cooler at night.

PUBLIC HOLIDAYS   Official holidays in Ecuador include New Year's Day (Jan 1), Easter, Labor Day (May 1), Simón Bolívar Day (July 24), National Independence Day (Aug 10), Guayaquil Independence Day (Oct 9), All Souls' Day (Nov 2), Cuenca Independence Day (Nov 3), and Christmas Day (Dec 25). The country also closes down on some nonofficial holidays, including Carnaval (Mon and Tues prior to Ash Wednesday), Battle of Pichincha (May 24), Christmas Eve (Dec 24), and New Year's Eve (Dec 31). Foundation of Quito (Dec 6) is observed as a holiday only in Quito.

HEALTH CONCERNS

COMMON AILMENTS   Travelers to Ecuador should be very careful about contracting **food-borne illnesses.** Always drink bottled water. Never drink beverages with ice unless you are sure that the water for the ice has been previously boiled. Be very careful about eating food purchased from street vendors. Some travelers swear by taking supplements such as super bromelain, which helps aid in the digestion of parasites; consult your doctor to find out whether this is a good option for you. In the event you experience any intestinal woe, staying well-hydrated is the most important step. Be sure to drink plenty of bottled water, as well as some electrolyte enhanced sports drinks, if possible.

If you plan on visiting the highlands of Ecuador—Quito, Otavalo, Baños, and Cuenca—you don't have to worry about **malaria.** There have been reports of malaria in rural areas on the coast and in the jungle area. To prevent malaria, the U.S. Centers for Disease Control and Prevention (CDC) recommends taking the drugs mefloquine, doxycycline, or Malarone; consult your doctor for more information. Your best protection is to ward off bites with a mix of insect repellent and proper clothing.

Of concern in areas of high altitude (the Sierra) is **altitude sickness.** Common symptoms include headaches, nausea, sleeplessness, and a tendency to tire easily. The most common remedies include taking it easy, abstaining from alcohol, and drinking lots of bottled water. To help alleviate these symptoms, you can also take the drug acetazolamide (Diamox); consult your doctor for more information.

The **sun** can also be very dangerous in Ecuador, especially at high altitudes. Be sure to bring plenty of high-powered sunblock and a wide-brimmed hat. It gets cold in Quito, but don't let this fool you into complacency—even when it's cold, the sun can inflict serious damage on your skin. In general, the healthcare system in Ecuador is good enough to take care of mild illnesses. For a list of hospitals in Quito, see "Hospitals" in "Fast Facts: Ecuador," later.

VACCINATIONS   No inoculations or vaccines are required for visitors to Ecuador. The CDC recommends that visitors to Ecuador be vaccinated against hepatitis A.

GETTING THERE
BY PLANE

There are two international airports in Ecuador. All flights into Quito land at the **Aeropuerto Internacional Mariscal Sucre** (© 02/2430-555; www.quitoairport. com; airport code: UIO). Most international flights also touch down in Guayaquil's **José Joaquín de Olmedo International Airport** (© 04/2169-209; airport code: GYE). If you plan to go to the Galápagos immediately after you arrive in Ecuador, it's best to fly into Guayaquil. All international passengers leaving by air from Ecuador must pay a $41 (£20) departure tax. A new, modern, international airport is under construction some 24km (15 miles) east of the current facility. It is not expected to be operational until late 2009.

FROM NORTH AMERICA   **American Airlines** (© 800/433-7300 in the U.S. and Canada, or © 02/2995-000 in Ecuador; www.aa.com) has one daily direct flight from Miami; **Continental Airlines** (© 800/231-0856 in the U.S. and Canada, or © 02/2250-905 in Ecuador; www.continental.com) has one daily direct flight each from Houston and Newark; **Delta** (© 800/241-4141 in the U.S. and Canada, or © 1800/101-060 in Ecuador; www.delta.com) has daily direct flights from Atlanta; and **LAN Chile/LAN Ecuador** (© 866/435-9526 in the U.S. and Canada; or © 1800/526-328 in Ecuador; www.lanchile.com) offers direct service from JFK in New York to Guayaquil and direct service from Miami to Quito; **Taca** (© 800/400-8222 in the U.S. and Canada; or © 1800/008-222 in Ecuador; www.grupotaca.com) has regular service to Ecuador from North America, via El Salvador or Costa Rica; while **Copa Airlines** (© 800/359-2672 in the U.S. and Canada; © 02/2273-082 in Ecuador; www.copaair.com) offers daily flights from both Los Angeles and Miami to Ecuador with a quick stop in Panama City. Presently, there are no direct flights from Canada to Ecuador, so Canadians will have to take a connecting flight via the United States.

FROM THE U.K.   There are no direct flights from the United Kingdom to Ecuador. British travelers can fly to the United States (Atlanta, Miami, Houston, or New York) and then hook up with a direct flight (see "From North America," above). **Iberia** (© 0845/2601-2854; www.iberia.com), **LAN Chile/LAN Ecuador** (see above) both offer daily nonstop service between Madrid and Ecuador; convenient daily connections are available from London and a plethora of other European cities including Dublin, Paris, and Berlin. **KLM** (© 08705/2074-074; www.klmuk.co.uk) offers service from many cities in England to both Guayaquil and Quito via Amsterdam and Bonaire.

FROM AUSTRALIA & NEW ZEALAND   To get to Ecuador from Australia or New Zealand, you'll first have to fly to Los Angeles and then on to Miami or Houston, where you can connect with an American Airlines, Continental, or LAN Chile/LAN Ecuador flight to Ecuador. See "From North America," above, for more information.

BY BUS

It is possible to travel by bus to Ecuador from Peru. From Colombia, the best border crossing is at the northern Ecuadorian town of Tulcán. The closest Colombian town to Tulcán is Ipiales, about 2km (1½ miles) north of the bridge that forms the actual border. Tulcán is approximately 5 hours by bus from Quito.

From Peru, the most popular border crossing is from Tumbes to Huaquillas in Ecuador. As you exit Peru, you will need to disembark from the bus and walk across the border. Peruvian buses don't usually cross into Ecuador, so to continue your journey, you will need to catch an Ecuadorian bus. Huaquillas is around 13 hours by bus from Quito, and 5 hours by bus from Guayaquil.

GETTING AROUND

Because Ecuador is one of the smallest countries in South America, traveling from one end of the country to another is not much of a challenge. The bus routes are comprehensive. However, the roads can be a bit rough, and the buses are often hot and crowded. If you're short on time, I really recommend flying, which is cheap and efficient. If you're traveling only a short distance, however, say from Quito to Otavalo (a little more than 2 hr.) or Riobamba (almost 4 hr.), the bus is your best bet.

BY PLANE   Most of Ecuador's major cities and tourist destinations are serviced by regular and reliable commuter air traffic. In some places, remote destinations can best be reached by charter flights, organized by the lodges themselves.

Aerogal (© 1800/2376-425 toll free nationwide; www.aerogal.com.ec), **Icaro** (© 1800/883-567 toll free nationwide; www.icaro.com.ec), and **Tame** (© 02/2909-900 in Quito, or 04/2310-305 or 04/2310-305 in Guayaquil; www.tame.com.ec), are the main commuter airlines.

With the exception of the Galápagos, which is quite expensive, most flights cost between $50 and $80 (£25–£40) for a one-way fare.

BY BUS   In Ecuador, all roads lead to Quito. From Quito, you can find a bus to every corner of the country. But don't expect to get anywhere quickly. Locals never board buses at the actual bus terminals. Instead, buses leave the station empty, and then drive very slowly through the outskirts of town, picking up passengers along the way. This adds at least an hour onto every bus ride. Still, for relatively short distances, buses are your best and cheapest option. The journeys between Quito and Riobamba, Baños, Otavalo, and Cotopaxi are best served by bus, which leave frequently for these destinations. The road between Cuenca and Guayaquil is also a popular bus route.

BY CAR   I don't recommend renting a car in Ecuador. For the most part, the roads are in bad condition, and since signs are nonexistent, it's very easy to get lost. For short-distance journeys, it's much more economical to take a bus, or even a taxi.

Nevertheless, if you're an adventurous type and you want to see the country from the privacy of your own car, you can certainly rent one. **Avis** (© 02/2440-270; www.avis.com.ec), **Budget** (© 02/3300-979; www.budget-ec.com), **Hertz** (© 1800/227-767 toll-free within Ecuador, or 02/2254-257; www.hertz.com.ec), and **Localiza** (© 02/3303-265; www1.localiza.com.ec) are the main rental-car agencies, with offices at both major international airports. As a national company, Localiza also has numerous office in other cities and tourist destinations around Ecuador.

Because the roads are so poorly maintained, I recommend that you rent a 4×4. All of the agencies listed above rent four-wheel-drive vehicles. While you may never use the four-wheel drive, the added clearance will definitely come in handy. Rates run between $40 and $150 (£20–£75) per day, with unlimited mileage, and insurance, depending upon the type of vehicle you rent.

One very interesting option is to use **Rent 4WD.com** ★ (© 02/2544-719; www.rent-4wd.com), which gets you a large, modern four-wheel-drive vehicle, unlimited

---

Heads Up

When hotels quote prices, they rarely include the hefty tax. Unless otherwise noted, expect to pay an additional 22% in taxes on the prices quoted by hotels and listed throughout this chapter.

---

gas and mileage, and driver, for just $150 (£75) per day. They even cover the driver's lodging expenses.

BY TRAIN   Train service is no longer a viable means of getting around Ecuador. All that remains of a once extensive rail system is a popular tourist train from Riobamba to Alausí that travels along switchbacks known as the Nariz del Diablo (Devil's Nose). However, following a dual fatality, rooftop riding on the train ride has been suspended. The train still runs regularly, but the thrilling and chilling chance to make the trip atop the train is now prohibited. However, **Metropolitan Touring's Chiva Express** ✪ (© **02/2988-200;** www.chivaexpress.com), which also makes this run, still offers open-air rooftop seating for this trip.

TIPS ON ACCOMMODATIONS

You'll find a whole range of accommodations in Ecuador. There are very few truly high-end luxury hotels and resorts. Most are in Quito or Guayaquil, and are geared toward business travelers.

The country's strong suit is in elegant, midrange boutique hotels, many housed in old colonial-era homes or haciendas. The antique furnishings and cozy rooms will make you feel as though you are an Ecuadorian aristocrat living in the 18th century. In fact, throughout the Andean highlands, you will find a string of these lovely converted haciendas, which are among the best and most unique accommodations to be found. Some are in buildings over 200 years old.

On the other end of the spectrum are jungle lodges, usually built in the style typical to the Amazon basin (thatched roofs, bamboo walls, and so on). Accommodations are usually basic; the more expensive ones, such as Kapawi Ecolodge & Reserve (p. 563) and Napo Wildlife Center (p. 564), have private bathrooms, but hot showers are a rarity.

In general, inexpensive accommodations are easy to find. In Quito, you can rent a clean room with private bathroom and television for little more than $20 (£10); in smaller towns, you can find a bed for as little as $10 (£5) a night.

In the Galápagos, most visitors spend their nights sleeping on ships. The general rule is that if you don't pay a lot, you won't get a lot. The least-expensive boats have dorm-style common sleeping rooms and one shower for everyone on board.

One good website and Ecuadorian travel operator, **Exclusive Hotels & Haciendas of Ecuador** (www.exclusivehotelshaciendasecuador.com), functions as a one-stop booking agent for various high-end boutique hotels and haciendas around the country.

TIPS ON DINING

In major cities such as Quito, Cuenca, Guayaquil, and Quito, you'll find tons of Ecuadorian restaurants, as well as an excellent selection of international cuisines. In Quito, there is everything from cutting-edge fusion cuisine to Thai food and sushi. Throughout the country, you'll also be able to find authentic pizza joints, as well as Chinese restaurants, known as *chifas.*

While you're in Ecuador, you should definitely try *comida típica* (typical food). *Ceviche de camarones* (shrimp cooked in a tangy lemon juice and served with onions and cilantro) is one of the most popular dishes in Ecuador—you'll find it on almost every menu. *Ceviche* is often served with a side of salty popcorn, fried corn, and fried plantains. The salt complements the tart lemon flavor. Other local specialties include *seco de chivo* (goat stew in a wine sauce), *empanadas de verde* (turnovers made with fried green bananas and filled with cheese), *tortillas de maíz* (small round corn pastries, served with avocado), and *humitas* (a sweet corn mush mixed with eggs, served in a corn husk). In the highlands area, where it can get very cold, locals often have a soup called *locro de papas* (a creamy potato soup with cheese). In Cuenca, *mote pillo con carne* (huge potato-like pieces of corn, mixed with onions and eggs, served with a fried piece of meat and *tortillas de papa*—the Ecuadorian version of potato pancakes) is one of the more popular local dishes.

Fixed-price lunches *(almuerzo del día)* are also common in smaller restaurants. For about $2.50 to $3 (£1.25–£1.50), you will get soup, a main course, dessert, and fresh juice.

Prices on menus don't include tax or tip. Expect to pay an extra 22% in tax and service charges above the prices listed on menus and in this chapter. Although a 10% tip is typically included in the bill, if the service was particularly good and attentive, you should probably leave a little extra.

TIPS ON SHOPPING

It's impossible to leave Ecuador empty-handed. Local artisan traditions have been thriving here for thousands of years. For any serious shopper, it's essential to take a trip up to the artisan's market in Otavalo, one of the best local handicraft markets in all of South America. Here you'll find an amazing array of hand-woven goods, including alpaca scarves, gloves, sweaters, colorful bags, tapestries, and ceramics. In the neighboring towns, you can buy leather goods and beautifully crafted hand-carved wood products. Keep in mind that Ecuadorians are not hagglers. At the markets, the prices are never fixed, but don't expect to spend hours negotiating. In the first few minutes, you can usually convince the seller to lower the price by a few dollars, but that's it. When vendors say that the price is final, it's usually not going to go any lower.

In Quito, you can find most everything from handcrafted silver jewelry to pre-Columbian masks. The Ecuadorian artists have done an excellent job of using traditional techniques to create products that appeal to modern-day tastes.

Cuenca is the largest producer of Panama hats in the world. These aren't your typical Panama Jack hats—these are stylish beauties worn by the likes of Danny Glover, Julia Roberts, and Queen Elizabeth. Ceramics are also a specialty in Cuenca.

FAST FACTS: Ecuador

American Express There are two American Express travel offices in Ecuador—one in Quito, the other in Guayaquil—both run by **Global Tours** (www.global tour.com.ec). In **Quito**, the office is located on Av. República El Salvador 309 and Calle Suiza (© 02/2265-222). In **Guayaquil**, the office is located in the Edificio Las Cámaras, on Avenida Francisco de Orellana and Alcivar (© 04/2680-450).

Business Hours In general, business hours are Monday to Friday from 9am to 1pm and 2:30 or 3 to 6:30pm. In Quito and Guayaquil, most banks stay open all day from about 9am to 5pm, but some still close in the middle of the day, so it's best to take care of your banking needs early in the morning. Most banks, museums, and stores are open on Saturday from 10am to noon. Everything closes down on Sunday.

Doctors If you need an English-speaking doctor, Quito is your best bet for finding one. Contact your embassy for information on doctors in Quito, or check out the Consular Section of the website of the U.S. Embassy in Quito (www.usembassy.org.ec), which has a list of recommended doctors and specialists. See "Hospitals," below, for hospitals in Quito with English-speaking doctors.

Drug Laws If you're caught possessing, using, or trafficking drugs in Ecuador, expect severe penalties, including long jail sentences and large fines. If you're arrested in Ecuador, you should also prepare yourself for a lengthy delay in prison before your case is tried before a judge. It's not uncommon to detain prisoners without bail.

Electricity The majority of outlets in Ecuador are standard U.S.-style two- and three-prong electric outlets with 110/120V AC (60 Hz) current.

Embassies & Consulates In Quito: **United States,** at the corner of Avenida 12 de Octubre and Avenida Patria, across from the Casa de la Cultura (© 02/2562-890, ext. 480); **Canada,** Av. 6 de Diciembre 2816 and Paul Rivet (© 02/2232-114); and **United Kingdom,** Avenida Naciones Unidas and República de El Salvador, Edificio Citiplaza, 14th floor (© 02/2970-800). There is no Australian Embassy in Ecuador, but there is an **Australian Honorary Consul** in Guayaquil, in the Kennedy Norte neighborhood on Calle San Roque and Avenida Francisco de Orellana (© 04/2680-823).

Emergencies In case of an emergency, call © **911** or © **101** for the police only.

Hospitals **Hospital Vozandes** (Villalengua 267 and 10 de Agosto; © 02/2262-142; www.hospitalvozandes.org) and **Hospital Metropolitano** (Mariana de Jesús and Occidental; © 02/2261-520; www.hospitalmetropolitano.org) are the two most modern and best-equipped hospitals in Quito. Both have 24-hour emergency service and English speaking doctors. For hospitals in other cities, see the "Fast Facts" for each individual city.

Internet Access Internet service is available almost everywhere in Ecuador, including the Galápagos. But don't expect to see anything resembling a computer in the jungle. Connections in major cities cost 80¢ to $1 (40p–50p) per hour. In smaller, more remote towns and the Galápagos, the connection can cost up to $3 to $4 (£1.50–£2) per hour.

Language Spanish is the language most commonly used in business transactions. Indigenous languages such as Quichua are also widely spoken throughout the country. Shuar is common in the Amazon basin. It's best to come to Ecuador with a basic knowledge of Spanish. Outside of the major tourist sights, it's hard to find someone who speaks English.

Liquor Laws The official drinking age in Ecuador is 18. At nightclubs, you often need to show a picture ID for admittance.

Newspapers & Magazines There are several Spanish-language daily papers in Ecuador. The most popular and prominent are *El Mercurio*, *El Universo*, and *El Comercio*.

At the airports in Quito and Guayaquil and at the high-end business hotels, you can find the latest edition of the *Miami Herald* for around 50¢ to $1 (25p–50p). English-language copies of *Time* or *Newsweek* are also available at some newsstands in the most touristy areas of Quito.

Police Throughout Ecuador, you can reach the police by dialing ⓒ **101** in an emergency. The tourist police can also help sort out your problems. In Quito, the number for the tourist police is ⓒ **02/2543-983**.

Post Offices & Mail A post office is called *correo* in Spanish. Most towns have a central *correo*, usually located right on the central park or plaza. In addition, most hotels will post letters and post cards for you. Most post offices in Ecuador are open Monday through Friday from 8am to 12:30pm and 2:30 to 6pm, and Saturday from 8am to 2pm. It costs 90¢ (45p) to mail a letter to the United States or Canada, and $1.10 (55p) to Australia and Europe. From time to time, you can buy stamps at kiosks and newsstands. But it's better to mail your letter and buy your stamps from the post office itself, especially since there are no public mailboxes. However, it is best to send anything of any value via an established international courier service. Most hotels, especially in major cities and tourist destinations, can arrange for express mail pick up. Alternately, you can contact **DHL** (ⓒ **02/2485-100**; www.dhl.com), **FedEx** (ⓒ **02/2909-201**; www.fedex.com); **EMS** (ⓒ **02/2561-962**); or **UPS** (ⓒ **02/3960-000**; www.ups.com). *Beware:* Despite what you may be told, packages sent overnight to U.S. addresses tend to take 3 to 4 days to reach their destination.

Restrooms The condition of public facilities is surprisingly good in Ecuador. In museums, the toilets are relatively clean, but they almost never have toilet paper. If you have an emergency, you can also use the restrooms in hotel lobbies without much of a problem. Note that most buses don't have toilet facilities, and when they stop at rest stops, the facilities are often horrendous—usually smelly squat toilets. It's always useful to have a roll of toilet paper handy.

Safety Pickpocketing is a problem in all large cities. But if you keep an eye on your belongings at all times, you should be fine. Never put anything valuable in your backpack. Also be especially careful on the buses and trolleys. At night, large cities can be dangerous, especially in the touristy areas—take a taxi, even if you're only going a short distance. Because the streets in Quito are often deserted at night, I recommend walking in the middle of them to prevent someone from jumping at you from a hidden doorway. Guayaquil used to hold the award for being the most dangerous city in Ecuador, but in the past few years, the city has cleaned up its act. Cuenca is the safest large city in Ecuador and residents routinely walk around at night, especially on weekends. Report all problems to the tourist police (ⓒ **02/2543-983**).

Telephone & Fax Most mid- to high-end hotels in Ecuador have international direct-dial and long-distance service, and in-house fax transmission. But these calls tend to be quite expensive, especially since hotels often levy a surcharge, even if you're calling a toll-free access number.

The least expensive way to make local phone calls is to go to one of many, many *cabinas telefónicas* offices found in every Ecuadorian town. There, you'll have a private booth where you can make all your calls and pay the attendant after you are done. These offices usually have a host of booths, with separate booths for calling numbers specific to each of the major phone companies in the country, thus reducing your calling cost.

You must pay in cash since they don't accept credit cards. It costs roughly 5¢ to 30¢ (3p–15p) per minute for calls within Ecuador. Costs through these *cabinas telefónicas* average around 40¢ (20p) per minute to the U.S. and 60¢ (30p) to the U.K.

Your best bet for making international calls it to head to any Internet cafe with an international calling option. These cafes have connections to Skype, Net2Phone or some other VoIP service. International calls made this way can range anywhere from 5¢ to $1 (3p–50p) per minute. If you have your own Skype or similar account, you just need to find an Internet cafe that provides a computer with a headset.

For tips on dialing, see "Telephone Dialing Info at a Glance," on p. 519.

Time Zone Mainland Ecuador is on Eastern standard time, 5 hours behind Greenwich mean time (GMT). The Galápagos Islands are on Central standard time, 6 hours behind GMT. Daylight saving time is not observed.

Tipping Restaurants in Ecuador add a 10% service charge to all checks. It's common to add 5% to 10% on top of this. Taxi drivers don't expect tips. Hotel porters are typically tipped 50¢ to $1 (25p–50p) per bag.

Water Always drink bottled water in Ecuador. Most hotels provide bottled water in the bathroom. You can buy bottles of water on practically any street corner. Small bottles cost about 25¢ (13p). The better restaurants use ice made from boiled water, but always ask, to be on the safe side.

4 Quito

Quito, Ecuador's capital, sits on a long, level plateau in a valley between towering Andean peaks. It is a city of striking beauty and stark contrasts. Sebastián de Benalcázar founded Quito in 1534. If he were to walk the streets of Old Town today, he might still feel right at home. Many of the original colonial structures here have been magnificently preserved and restored. Quito was—and still is—a city of grand churches with detailed, hand-carved facades and altars. It is a place where 500-year-old buildings, which have survived earthquakes and volcanic eruptions, open onto medieval-style courtyards, complete with columned archways and stone fountains. In 1978, Quito was declared a UNESCO World Heritage Site, the first city to earn that designation.

But that's only one side of Quito. Quito is a place where you can travel to the past but still enjoy modern-day comforts. The living museum of Old Town nicely complements New Town's modern-art and archaeology museums, cosmopolitan restaurants and hopping clubs. Spend a few days here and you can enjoy the best of both worlds. You can also travel to colorful indigenous markets, a unique cloud forest, or the world's highest active volcano—all within 2 hours of the city.

Remember that at 2,850m (9,300 ft.) above sea level, Quito is one of the highest capital cities in the world, and the air is much thinner here. Many visitors quickly feel the effects of the high altitude. Drink plenty of water and do not overdo it as your body acclimates.

ESSENTIALS
GETTING THERE

For more information on arriving in Quito, see "Getting There" in "Planning Your Trip to Ecuador," earlier in this chapter.

BY PLANE   All flights into Quito land at the **Aeropuerto Internacional Mariscal Sucre** (© 02/2430-555; www.quitoairport.com; airport code: UIO). The airport is about 8km (5 miles) from the heart of the New Town. Right before you exit the international terminal, you'll find several information desks. I recommend ordering and paying for your taxi here, and then taking your receipt to one of the many taxis waiting outside the terminal. Taxis shouldn't cost more than $8 (£4). In fact, most rides to downtown hotels are around $5 (£2.50).

BY BUS   The **Terminal Terrestre de Cumandá** (© 02/2570-529), located on the edge of the Old Town, is the main bus station in Quito. A long line of taxis is usually waiting at the arrivals area. A taxi to the New Town should cost $5 to $6 (£2.50–£3); to the Old Town, the fare should only be $2 (£1). If you don't have a lot of luggage, you can also take the Trole (trolley) into the heart of Quito. From the terminal, you have to walk up a serious set of stairs to the Cumandá Station. To get to both the Old and New Town, be sure to get on the Trole going toward "LA Y."

ORIENTATION

Quito is a long and thin city, set in a long and thin valley. It runs 35km (22 miles) from north to south and just 3 miles (5km) from east to west. If you were to combine the most visited areas, that area would measure only about 1.5km (1 mile). Most of the city's attractions are located in two main areas: the **Old Town** and the **New Town.** The Old Town, at the southern end of the city, is where you'll find most of the historic churches, museums, and colonial architecture. **Plaza de la Independencia** is in the heart of the Old Town. From here, you can walk to all the main attractions. The Old Town can be dangerous at night; it's best to sleep in the **New Town** (also known as the **Mariscal**), which is north of Parque El Ejido. Most of the city's hotels are located here. You'll also find a host of good restaurants, Internet cafes, bars, and nightclubs in this part of town. New Town's main commercial street is **Avenida Amazonas,** where most of the banks and travel agencies are located.

All parts of Quito can be dangerous at night. Avoid dark and deserted areas, and take taxis, even when traveling relatively short distances.

GETTING AROUND

BY TAXI   The streets of Quito are swarming with yellow taxis, and they're my preferred means of transport here. Taxis are cheap, costing only $1 to $3 (50p–£1.50) for a ride within the Old or New Town and $4 to $6 (£2–£3) for longer distances. Drivers are required by law to use a meter, but it's obviously not a strict law because few taxis use them. Try to insist on the meter or negotiate a price with your driver before you take off for your destination. Quito can be dangerous at night, so it's best to take a taxi wherever you go, no matter how short the distance. The staff at most restaurants,

Quito

Hospital
Post office

Quito
ECUADOR

Marin
- -□- - **Trole Stop**

2 El Belén
-□- **Ecovía Stop**

0 ———— 1/2 mi
0 ———— 0.5 km

ACCOMMODATIONS ■
Crossroads Hostal **26**
Hilton Colón Quito **20**
Hostal Fuente de Piedra I **28**
Hotel Café Cultura **21**
Hotel Real Audiencia **7**
Hotel San Francisco de Quito **8**
Hotel Sebastián **29**
JW Marriott Hotel **31**
Mansión del Angel **24**
Patio Andaluz **14**
Plaza Grande **12**

DINING ◆
Café Mosaico **18**
Café Tianguez **3**
Chandani Tandoori **30**
El Níspero **36**
La Cueva del Oso **13**
La Querencia **33**

Las Redes **22**
Le Arcate **23**
Mama Clorinda **27**
Mea Culpa **11**
PIM's Panecillo **1**
The Magic Bean **25**
Zazu **32**

hotels, and bars will be happy to call a cab for you. In case you need to call one your-self, try **Taxi Amigo** (© 02/2222-222) or **Taxi Jotajota** (© 02/2639-639).

BY TROLLEY There are three electric trolley lines that wind their way through Quito, running north-south, and connecting the Old Town with the New Town. In the New Town, the **Trole** runs along Avenida 10 de Agosto, which is a few blocks west of Avenida Amazonas. When it reaches the Old Town, it travels along Avenida Guayaquil. To reach Plaza de la Independencia, be sure to get off at the Plaza Grande stop. The **Ecovía** is much more convenient if you want to start your journey in the New Town; it runs along Avenida 6 de Diciembre, which is one of the major streets. Unfortunately, when it reaches the Old Town, it stops several blocks east of the colonial core, and it's a bit of an uphill hike to the heart of the action. If you want to avoid this hike, trans-fer to the Trole at the Simón Bolívar stop. **Metrobus** is the newest line and it runs along the western edge of town, along Avenida América. All three of these trolley lines cost 25¢ (13p) for a one-way trip. The turnstiles accept only exact change, but fortunately, all stations have change machines. Trolleys run from around 5am until midnight. *Warning:* Pickpockets frequently operate on crowded trolleys and buses, so be careful.

BY BUS Quito has an extensive and very complicated system of city buses. In the New Town, buses run along Avenida Amazonas and Avenida 12 de Octubre. If you're only going a short distance along these streets, it's easy to hop on a bus (just flag it down). However, beware that once you pass Avenida Colón, the buses go off in many convoluted directions. Short rides cost 25¢ (13p), but overall, it's much easier to travel through Quito by taxi

VISITOR INFORMATION

The **Corporación Metropolitana de Turismo** (Metropolitan Tourism Corporation; www.quito.com.ec) runs a few helpful information desks at strategic spots around Quito. You'll find one of their desks at the **Mariscal Sucre airport** (© 02/2300-163), after you clear immigration, and just before you exit customs. This is a good place to pick up an excellent free map of Quito, as well as a host of promotional materials. These folks also have two separate desks in the Old Town, as well as at the Museo Nacional del Banco Central and Teleférico. At their **Old Town office** (© 02/2586-591; Calle Chile and García Moreno, Pasaje Arzobispal) you can sign up for guided walking tours led by city policemen.

The nonprofit **South American Explorers** ★★ (© 02/2225-228; www.saexplorers. org/quito.htm), Jorge Washington 311 and the corner of Leonidas Plaza, is perhaps the best source for visitor information and a great place to meet fellow travelers. The offices are staffed by native English speakers who seem to know everything about Ecuador. Membership costs $50 (£25) a year per person ($80/£40 per couple). As a member, you will have access to trip reports (reviews of hotels, restaurants, and out-fitters throughout Ecuador written by fellow travelers) and a trip counselor. If you aren't a member, the staff can give you basic information that will get you on your way.

The government-sponsored **Ministerio de Turismo** information center on Eloy Alfaro N32-300, Third Floor (at the corner of Carlos Tobar), is woefully inadequate. Do not go out of your way to visit here—you can buy a few maps, but don't expect to find much else. The staff is always too busy to help visitors.

Local travel agencies are excellent sources of information. **Cotopaxi.com** ★★ (© 02/2909-640; www.cotopaxi.com), **Metropolitan Touring** ★★ (© 02/2988-220),

Safari Ecuador ⭐⭐ (© 02/2552-505; www.safari.com.ec), and **Surtrek** ⭐ (© 02/2231-534; www.surtrek.com) are some of the best and most helpful.

FAST FACTS   In case of an **emergency,** call © **911.** You can reach an **ambulance** at © **09/2739-801** or 02/2442-974; for **police assistance** call © **101.** For the **tourist police** call © **02/2543-983;** the headquarters are located at Roca and Reina Victoria. You can reach the **Cruz Roja (Red Cross)** by dialing © **131.**

Hospital Vozandes (© **02/2262-142;** www.hospitalvozandes.org), at Villalengua 267 and 10 de Agosto, and **Hospital Metropolitano** (© **02/2261-520;** www.hospital metropolitano.org), at Mariana de Jesús and Occidental, are the two most modern and best-equipped hospitals in Quito. Both have 24-hour emergency service and English-speaking doctors. **Fybeca** is the largest chain of pharmacies in Ecuador. You can call Fybeca's toll-free line (© **800/2392-322**) 24 hours a day for home delivery. The most centrally located Fybeca is at Avenida 6 de Diciembre and Cordero. **Rey de Reyes** (© **02/2557-357**) is a 24-hour pharmacy located at Jorge Washington 416, near the corner of 6 de Diciembre.

The **main post office** is located in New Town (© **02/2561-218**) at Av. Eloy Alfaro 354 and 9 de Octubre. There's also a convenient post office in Old Town (© **02/2282-175**) on Calle Espejo 935, between Guayaquil and Venezuela. Perhaps the most conveniently located post office is on the ground floor of the Ecuatoriana Building, on the corner of Avenida Cristóbal Colón and Reina Victoria.

WHAT TO SEE & DO
IN OLD TOWN
Casa Museo María Augusta Urrutia ⭐   This museum allows modern-day visitors to envision what it must have been like to live in a 19th-century Spanish-style mansion in Old Town. When you enter the house, you immediately find yourself in a gorgeous courtyard. Not much has been changed since Doña María Augusta Urrutia lived here, so the dramatic entry that you see is probably what the pope and many other world leaders also experienced when visiting this home. (Doña María devoted much of her life to philanthropy with a Catholic bent.) The house is surprisingly modern, with a full bathroom and modern kitchen appliances; but there are also a cold storage room, a wood-burning stove, and the oldest grain masher in Ecuador. The interior is gorgeous, featuring antique European furniture, a bed that belonged to General Sucre, hand-painted wallpaper, stained-glass windows, handcrafted moldings, murals on the walls, and Belgian tiles. There is also a rich collection of Ecuadorian art, much of it by painter Víctor Mideros.

Note: Guided tours are available in English. Just ask for a guide when you enter. Most of the written display information is in both Spanish and English. Allow about 40 minutes to visit the entire house.

García Moreno N2–60, between Sucre and Bolívar. © **02/2580-103.** Admission $2 (£1) adults; $1 (50p) students and seniors; 50¢ (25p) children under 12. Tues–Sat 10am–6pm; Sun 9:30am–5:30pm.

El Panecillo (Virgin Monument) *Moments*   From a distance, the hill that hosts a huge statue of the winged virgin does indeed look like a *panecillo* (small bread roll). Since it's directly south of the city, this hill was an ideal spot to construct the 45m-high (148-ft.) *La Virgen de Quito,* an enlarged copy of Bernardo de Lagarda's *La Virgen de Quito* sculpture that is on display on the main altar in the San Francisco church. The Panecillo stands at about 3,000m (9,840 ft.), so you can also see the sculpture from the center of Quito.

The significance of the Panecillo Hill dates back to Inca times, when it was known as Shungoloma (Hill of the Heart). Before the Spanish arrived, the Incas used this hill as a place to worship the sun. Later, from 1812 to 1815, the Spanish constructed a fortress, to control what was going on down below. These days, most people come up here for the 360-degree views of Quito. *Tip:* For the best vistas, try to get here early in the morning (around 10am), before the clouds settle in around the nearby mountains. On a clear day, you can see Cotopaxi in the distance. This is a relatively quick ride from Old Town, and a taxi should only cost about $3 (£1.50) each way. A half-hour is all you'll need to take in the sights.

El Panecillo, south of Old Town. Admission to enter the grounds $1 (50p); admission to climb to the top of the monument $1 (50p). Mon–Fri 9am–6pm; Sat–Sun 9am–5pm.

Iglesia de San Francisco ★★   San Francisco was the first church built in Quito. Construction began in 1535, just 1 month after the Spanish arrived. (It took more than 100 years to finish.) You'll notice that Plaza San Francisco is distinctly sloped; for several hundred years, it was assumed that it followed the shape of the Earth.

Getting High in Quito

One of the city's most popular attractions is **El Telefériqo** ★, six-person cable cars that transport you up the side of Volcán Pichincha to 4,050m (13,280 ft.). The quick climb over 1,000m (3,280 ft.) takes all of 8 minutes. At the top, you will have a magnificent view of the city and surrounding snow-covered mountain peaks. The air is thin up here, but don't worry: The ambitious and very modern complex includes an oxygen bar to replenish the weary traveler, along with several viewing platforms. You'll also find souvenir stands and shops, and a couple of restaurants and fast-food outlets.

If crowds bother you, avoid visiting here on the weekends (and public holidays), when it's packed to the gills. That said, this attraction is enormously popular with Ecuadorian families and it's a wonderful cultural experience just to be out among the locals. People wait patiently in line just to get a glimpse of their city from an elevated perspective. You can escape the crowds by taking one of the marked paths on a stroll through the shrubby highlands. If you have kids in tow, you might want to return to the base of the mountain where you'll find an amusement park, **Vulqano Park,** complete with roller coasters, all kinds of rides, arcades, and video games.

The cable car operates Monday to Thursday from 10am to 8pm and Friday through Sunday from 9am to 11pm. I strongly suggest you splurge for the Fast Pass ticket that will cut your wait time considerably. The cost for a regular ticket is $4 (£2) for adults and $3 (£1.50) for children; the Fast Pass ticket costs $7 (£3.50) for adults and $5 (£2.50) for children. Admission to Vulqano Park is free and prices for the rides average around 50¢ to $1 (25p–50p).

To get here, take a 15-minute taxi ride from the center of Quito. Tell the driver to take you to El Telefériqo at the Vulqano Park. The taxi ride should cost no more than $8 (£4). For more information, visit **www.teleferiqo.com** or call ✆ 02/3250-076.

> ## ⌒Tips Touring Iglesia de San Francisco
>
> The Iglesia de San Francisco closes at noon, earlier than most of the other churches in Old Town, and it doesn't open again until 3pm. So if you're trying to see everything in Old Town in one morning, be sure to visit San Francisco first. If you can't make it before 11:30am, you can visit Museo Fray Pedro Gocial, the museum connected to the church (see below).

However, a group of archaeologists recently discovered that San Francisco was built over an Inca temple, which is the reason the actual church is much higher than other structures in Quito. As you walk up the stairs from the plaza to the church, you can't help but realize how wide the stairs are. Supposedly, the architects designed the stairs this way so that as you approach the church, you have to keep your eyes on your feet to watch where you're going—in other words, you are forced to bow your head in respect.

Like La Compañía (see below), San Francisco is an important baroque church, but the latter is much larger and, for some reason, feels much more somber. The ceilings have a beautiful Moorish design. In the entryway, as in La Compañía, you will notice images of the sun, which were used to lure indigenous people to the Christian religion. Throughout the church are combinations of indigenous and Catholic symbols. For example, the interior is decorated with angels in the shape of the sun—and the faces of these angels have distinct Indian characteristics.

The baroque altar in the front of the church has three important sculptures: The top is *El Bautismo de Jesús (The Baptism of Jesus);* the bottom is a representation of *Jesús de Gran Poder (Almighty Jesus);* and the middle is probably one of the most important sculptures in Ecuador, the original *La Virgen de Quito (The Virgin of Quito),* designed by Bernardo de Legarda. (*La Virgen de Quito* was the model for the huge winged angel on the Panecillo; see above.)

In 2007, the interior of the church began receiving a major restoration and face-lift. Scaffolding had been erected throughout much of the interior, and much of the overhead artwork was covered up, or under repair. The full restoration may take several years. But there's still plenty to see, making this church worth a visit.

Plaza San Francisco. Free admission. Mon–Sat 7am–noon and 3–5:30pm; Sun 7am–noon.

La Basílica del Voto Nacional   Work on the basilica began in 1883 and is still unfinished. Visitors are permitted inside this concrete marvel, which is modeled on Paris's Notre-Dame. The large central nave of this church feels cold, with so much unfinished concrete, but if you look up you'll see fabulous stained-glass works all around. Be sure to stop into the small side chapel, La Capilla de Sacramento, which features a mosaic tile floor, painted walls, columns, and a beautiful high altar of Mary. Most people, however, come here for the spectacular aerial views of the Old City and to see the *La Virgin de Quito* in the distance. For the best views, you have to pay to take the elevator, or climb the 90m (300 ft.) to the top of the towers. **Note:** The elevators don't always work and the final "ladders" to the top are very narrow and quite steep. As you cross the bridge to enter the towers, look for the carved condors—the stonework is impressive and the condors look as though they are about to fly away. The basilica is also famous for its mystical gargoyles in the form of local Ecuadorian icons such as pumas, monkeys, penguins, tortoises, and condors that guard the outsides of the church. There is a cafe on the third floor—a good place to catch your breath after taking in the breathtaking views.

Carchí 122, at the corner of Calle Venezuela. ② **02/2289-428**. Admission $2 (£1) to visit the top of the towers. Daily 9am–5pm.

La Compañía de Jesús ✿✿✿

This Jesuit church is one of the great baroque masterpieces in South America. All the work took 160 years (1605–1765) to complete. The facade won't fail to impress you—the carvings are unbelievably detailed. Notice the Solomonic columns, which are symbolic of the Catholic doctrine that life's journey starts at the bottom (on Earth), but by following the holy path, it ends at heaven.

Almost every inch of the interior has intricate decorations. When you enter La Compañía, look for the symbols of the sun in both the main door to the church and the ceiling. The sun was a very important Inca symbol, and the Spanish thought that if they decorated the entryway with indigenous symbols, it might encourage local people to join the church. The walls and ceilings of La Compañía are typical of Moorish design—you will only see geometric shapes but no human forms. The building has been under renovation for the past several years, and some of the gold leaf on the ceiling and walls has been restored to its original luster. Natural sunlight and candlelight really bring out an angelic brilliance.

Concerts are sometimes held inside this church, and the acoustics and setting are haunting. If you happen to be in Quito on November 1 (Day of the Dead), you can also visit the catacombs here.

On García Moreno near Sucre. Admission $2 (£1). Mon–Fri 10am–1pm and 2–5pm; Sat 10am–1pm.

La Plaza de la Independencia ✿

Also called La Plaza Grande, this became the main square of Quito in the 16th century. The Spanish were afraid that the Incas might poison their water supply, so the Spanish set up their own protected well here, and this plaza subsequently became the social center of town. It also served as a central market and bullfighting area. Today, Old Town's main square is bordered by the Government Palace on the west, City Hall to the east, the Archbishop's Palace on the north, and the cathedral to the south.

The **Government Palace** ✿ is the most interesting building on the plaza. Don't be intimidated by the chain-link fence in front of the palace; everyone is welcome to walk inside the main area—just tell the guard that you're a curious tourist. Once you walk into the main entry area, you can get a sense of the Spanish/Moorish architecture. If you look straight ahead, you'll see the impressive 1966 mural by Guayasamín, of Orellana discovering the Amazon.

The **City Hall** is probably the least impressive structure on the plaza. It was built in 1952, in the Bauhaus style. The **Archbishop's Palace** was built in 1852; it was formerly the mayor's house. You can now walk inside and see the Andalusian- and Moorish-inspired courtyard; note that the floor of the courtyard is made from the spines of pigs. This area is now an informal crafts market. The **cathedral** dates from the 16th century. Inside is a good collection of art from the Quito School, including works by Caspicara and Manuel Samaniego. You can visit the cathedral Monday through Saturday from 6 to 10am. The square is most beautiful at night, when all the buildings are lit up.

Plaza de la Independencia is bordered by Calle Venezuela to the east, García Moreno to the west, Chile to the north, and Espejo to the south. To get to the plaza from the Trole, get off at the Plaza Grande stop and walk 1 block on either Calle Espejo or Chile.

Museo Fray Pedro Gocial (San Francisco Museum and Convent) This museum, which is attached to the San Francisco church (see above), allows visitors to see the convent as well as the church's choir. Tour guides also will show you some of the pieces of the church's fantastic colonial art collection. I highly recommend a visit to the choir. Here you can see the church's original wood ceiling, as well as a beautiful wood inlaid "lyric box" that was used to hold up the music for the singers in the choir. You will also experience Manuel Chile Caspicara's famous crucifix, which dates back to 1650–70. It is said that Caspicara tied a model to a cross to learn how to realistically represent Christ's facial and body expressions; the glass eyes are piercing.

Plaza San Francisco, Cuenca 477 and Sucre. ⓒ **02/2952-911**. Admission $2 (£1). Mon–Sat 9am–1pm and 2–6pm; Sun 9am–noon. Visits only by guided tour, which leave on an as-needed basis. English-language tours are available.

IN NEW TOWN
Museo Nacional del Banco Central del Ecuador ★★ *(Kids)* This huge and enormously rich museum offers visitors an opportunity to learn about the evolution of Ecuador—its human and natural history, as well as its art. When you see all the artifacts, archaeological finds, and works of art displayed chronologically, you get a profound sense of the country not commonly found in museums that focus on one era or type of exhibit. *Tip:* To see everything in this massive museum, you really need at least 4 hours; I recommend taking a guided tour.

If you visit the museum from beginning to end, you will start at the **Archaeological Gallery.** On display are artifacts dating from 11,000 B.C. Artifacts and dioramas explain the beliefs and lifestyle of a wide range of pre-Columbian and pre-Inca peoples. One of the most striking exhibits here is a Cañari mummy, though the **Golden Court** ★★ is my favorite exhibit. Because many indigenous groups worshipped the sun, they used gold to create masks, chest decorations, and figurines to represent the sun. You can see the influence of the sun and the veneration of women in the work displayed in the **Colonial Art Gallery,** which contains pieces from 1534 to 1820. I find the colonial-era art is displayed better here—with better lighting and explanations—than at the Museo Fray Pedro Gocial (see above).

After independence from Spain, Ecuadorian artists began to eschew religious symbolism. In the **Republican Art Gallery,** you can see this transition. Instead of gory religious art and paintings of the Virgin, for example, you'll find lifelike portraits of Ecuador's independence heroes. One of my favorites is *Retrato de Simón Bolívar (Portrait of Simón Bolívar).*

On an entirely different plane is the **Contemporary Art Gallery.** Here you'll see everything from peaceful landscapes from the early 20th century to Oswaldo Guayasamín's tortured and angry portraits, as well as a wide range of modernist works by prominent Ecuadorian artists such as Pilar Bustos, Camilo Egas, Theo Constante, and Enrique Tabara. In addition to the above galleries, the museum also hosts temporary art exhibits. And in the same building, there is a **Museum of Musical Instruments,** which is a lot of fun if you're traveling with kids.

Av. Patria, between 6 de Diciembre and 12 de Octubre. ⓒ **02/2223-258**. Adults $2 (£1), students 50¢ (25p). Tues–Fri 9am–5pm; Sat–Sun and holidays 10am–4pm. Free multilingual guided tours are available throughout the day, and most of the displays are in both Spanish and English.

NORTH OF NEW TOWN
The two nearby attractions are expected to one day be joined in a relatively massive museum, workshop, and cultural center.

Capilla del Hombre (Chapel of Mankind) ✿ A few blocks from the Fundación Guayasamín (see below), this impressive structure is in many ways the culmination of the work and dreams of Ecuador's great modern artist, Oswaldo Guayasamín. Guayasamín, who died in 1999 at the age of 90, wanted to open the museum on the first day of the new century, but financial problems and construction delays postponed its opening until November 2002. Dedicated to "man's progress through art," the architecturally intriguing chapel houses many of the artist's paintings, murals, and sculptures, as well as parts of the his personal collection of colonial art, archaeological finds, and contemporary art. Incan and indigenous mythological beliefs are incorporated into the design of the building, which is three levels and uses the number 3 for various motifs and architectural elements. The eternal flame in the chapel's altar is dedicated to those who died defending human rights (or the rights of man, which explains the name of the museum). Guayasamín himself is buried here, beneath a tree he planted, which has been renamed El Arbol de la Vida (The Tree of Life). Allot yourself about an hour to view the museum.

Corner of Mariano Calvache and Lorenzo Chávez, Bellavista. ✆ 02/2448-492. Admission $3 (£1.50), or $5 (£2.50) combined with the Fundación Guayasamín. Tues–Sun 10am–5pm.

Fundación Guayasamín ✿✿ This powerful museum displays the works and art collections of Oswaldo Guayasamín, one of Ecuador's most famous artists. The museum has three sections. **El Museo Arqueológico (Archaeology Museum)** houses Guayasamín's collection of pre-Columbian art. The artist once said, "I paint from 3,000 or 5,000 years ago." It's interesting to see both his collection and his inspiration. Keep an eye out for the sitting shamans and tribal chiefs, and the jugs with the intricately carved faces.

Across the courtyard is the **Museo de Arte Moderno (Museum of Modern Art)** ✿, which displays Guayasamín's own work. Most impressive is his art from 1964 to 1984 entitled "La Edad de la Ira" (The Age of Anger), which represents his dismay over violence in the world, and in South America in particular. One of the most dramatic pieces is the three-paneled *Homenaje a Víctor Jara (Tribute to Víctor Jara)*. Jara was a Chilean guitarist and Communist Party supporter who was tortured and killed by General Pinochet's army during the 1973 military junta. Military officers cut off his hands to try to stop his protest songs, but it took a machine gun to silence him. The images of a skeleton playing a guitar have a tremendous impact.

In the **Museo de Arte Colonial,** you can view Guayasamín's incredible collection of colonial art. The majority of the pieces are from the Quito School; they give viewers a good idea of the art created by the first inhabitants of Quito. The collection contains more than 80 crucifixes.

There is also a nice patio (with a great view) and a cafe on the premises. It doesn't take more than an hour to explore the entire museum. Take a taxi here (about $2/£1 from the heart of New Town).

Calle José Bosmediano E 15–68 Bellavista (Batán). ✆ 02/2465-265. Admission $3 (£1.50) or $5 (£2.50) combined with the Capilla del Hombre. Tues–Sun 10am–5pm.

SPORTS & OUTDOOR ACTIVITIES

Quito is a large sprawling city, so it's hard to do anything truly outdoorsy within the city limits. The large, central Parque La Carolina is the best spot for outdoor sports and activities. Your best bet, though, is to travel an hour or two outside the city, where you'll find an abundance of outdoor pursuits. These include hiking, climbing, trekking, white-water rafting, mountain biking, and more.

CLIMBING, HIKING & TREKKING   Quito is right in the heart of the "Avenue of the Volcanoes." Within an hour north or south of the city, hiking and trekking opportunities abound. One of the most exciting and rigorous treks is up the glacier-covered Cotopaxi Volcano (covered later). Other options abound, including nearby high Andean peaks and volcanos, around the popular tourist destinations of Mindo and Otavalo. **Cotopaxi.com** ✸✸ (✆ 02/2909-640; www.cotopaxi.com), **Safari Ecuador** ✸✸ (✆ 02/2552-505; www.safari.com.ec), and **Surtrek** ✸ (✆ 02/2231-534; www.surtrek.com) are all Quito-based operators offering a range of hikes, climbs, and treks ranging from 1-day tours to multiday outings.

JOGGING   The downtown Parque La Carolina is your best bet for jogging. This large, central city park has several jogging paths, and you'll usually find plenty of fellow joggers around. The much smaller Parque El Ejido is another option.

HORSEBACK RIDING   The mountains and rolling paramo outside Quito are perfect for horseback riding. Although 1-day tours are available, I really recommend combining your equestrian adventure with a stay at a restored working hacienda. **Hacienda La Alegría** ✸ (✆ 02/2462-319; www.haciendaalegria.com), **Hacienda Zuleta** ✸ (✆ 02/2228-554; www.zuleta.com), and **San Jorge Eco-Lodge & Biological Reserve** ✸ (✆ 02/2247-549; www.eco-lodgesanjorge.com) are my top choices for horseback-based outings.

MOUNTAIN BIKING   Biking down Cotopaxi from the *refugio* (not the summit) is one of the most popular biking trips in the area. Other routes include biking to Mindo (for bird-watching), Otavalo, or Papallacta Hot Spring. **Safari Ecuador** ✸✸ (✆ 02/2552-505; www.safari.com.ec) and **Surtrek** ✸ (✆ 02/2231-534; www.surtrek.com) both offer a range of road and off-road biking options.

SOCCER   Soccer, or *fútbol,* is the principal spectator sport in Ecuador. Soccer season in Quito lasts March through December. Most important games take place at the **Estadio Olímpico Atahualpa** (✆ 02/2247-510), on 6 de Diciembre and Avenida Naciones Unidas. Game day is usually Saturday or Sunday. General-admission seats cost $2 (£1); the good seats go for $10 to $12 (£5–£6). You can buy tickets at the stadium on the day of the game. To get there, take the Ecovía trolley line to the Estadio stop.

TENNIS   If you're not staying at a hotel with its own courts, the Parque La Carolina open-air public courts are your best bet. They are free of charge and awarded on a first-come, first-served basis. They fill up very fast on weekends and tend to be busy on weekdays as well.

WHITE-WATER RAFTING & KAYAKING   The rivers near Quito are usually most rapid in October, November, and December, but it is possible to go white-water rafting year-round. **Ríos Ecuador** ✸✸ (✆ 02/2904-054; www.riosecuador.com) and **Yacu Amu Rafting** ✸ (✆ 02/2904-054; www.raftingecuador.com) are two of the best outfitters with offices in Quito. You can arrange 1-day tours on the Toachi and Blanco rivers (class III to III+); or the Quijos River (class IV to IV+). Longer rafting trips in the jungle and other rivers are also available.

SHOPPING

As in the rest of the country, the shopping scene in Quito mainly consists of local handicrafts (alpaca sweaters, tapestries, figurines, pottery, hats, and jewelry) made by indigenous Ecuadorian artists. Some of the stuff you'll find is mass-produced or of poor quality. But if you know where to go (see below), there are some great shops, which support local indigenous groups. You'll also find more high-end shops here than in other parts of the country.

MARKETS While nothing in Quito compares to the world-famous market in Otavalo (p. 556), a couple of Quito markets are worth visiting, especially if you can't visit Otavalo. In New Town, the **Mercado Artesanal La Mariscal (Mariscal Artisans Market)** is a tight warren of permanent booths selling all sorts of arts, crafts, and clothing. You should definitely be picky here—there are a lot of mass-produced and mediocre wares for sale. But if you shop carefully, you can find high-quality goods. You can bargain a little, but not too much. Located on Jorge Washington, between Reina Victoria and Juan León Mera, it's open daily from around 10am until 7pm. A similar option is available on weekends all along the north end of **Parque El Ejido.**

A note on store hours: Unless indicated below, all stores are open from 9am to 1:30pm and 3 to 7pm. Most stores close for a siesta from 1:30 to 3pm, and most are closed on Sunday.

Café Libro 🐸🐸 This is my favorite bookstore in Ecuador. They have an extensive collection of books in Spanish and English, with loads of books on natural history and tropical biology, as well as a fabulous collection of Ecuadorian and Latin American literature. Poetry readings, lectures, and concerts are often held here. Leonidas Plaza N23–56. ✆ 02/2234-265. www.cafelibro.com.

Magic Hand Crafts 🐸 With an excellent selection of alpaca sweaters, this is the place to come if you're looking for something of better quality than that sold at the street markets. These folks work directly with weavers and producers, and have some unique designs you won't find elsewhere. Juan León Mera N24–237 and Cordero. ✆ 02/2542-345.

Olga Fisch Folklore 🐸🐸 *Finds* We have Olga Fisch to thank for recognizing and inspiring the creation of high-quality, locally made handicrafts. As an artist, Fisch had a very keen eye, and she worked with indigenous groups to create carpets, figurines, jewelry, and decorative arts based on their traditional understanding of the arts. Everything here is displayed in a gorgeous showroom. This store carries high-end art, crafts, and clothing, and the prices reflect the difference in quality that you'll find between the offerings here and those at the street markets. A nonprofit museum here supports the development of these arts in indigenous communities. I suggest that you visit the museum first to get an idea of the local artisan traditions—it will help you understand what you are looking at in the showroom. In addition to the main shop, Olga Fisch has several other storefronts around Quito, including inside the Quicentro and San Marino malls, as well as at the Hotel Patio Andaluz (p. 543), and inside both the Guayaquil and Quito airports. It's open during siesta. Av. Colón E10–53 and Caamaño. ✆ 02/2541-315. www.olgafisch.com.

Ortega P. & Hijos 🐸🐸🐸 This is the local outlet for renowned Cuenca hat manufacturer Ortega and Sons. If you aren't able to get to Cuenca, or to the other traditional Panama hat–making cities of Montecristi and Jipijapa, this is where you should pick up your *super fino.* If you really wait until the last minute, you can visit their outlet at the airport, but the selection there is reduced, and the prices slightly inflated. Isabel La Católica N24–100 and Madrid. ✆ 02/2526-715. www.homeroortega.com.

Tianguez 🐸🐸 Tianguez showcases products similar to those you'll find at Olga Fisch and Galería Latina, including masks, ceramics, and all sorts of pieces inspired by pre-Columbian artisan traditions. Tianguez means "market" in Quichua, and it's an especially appropriate name because the store is housed in a sprawling, mazelike old market in Old Town under the San Francisco church. It feels like the catacombs in Rome. A not-for-profit organization, Sinchi Sacha, runs Tianguez and supports indigenous and *mestizo* artisan groups. It's open during siesta and on Sunday. Plaza San Francisco. (C) **02/2230-609.** www.sinchisacha.org.

WHERE TO STAY
IN NEW TOWN
Very Expensive
Hilton Colón Quito ★ In 1967, when the Hilton Colón opened it was the only high-end hotel in town. It quickly became a major cultural and business-meeting spot for both locals and visitors alike. While today it faces some stiff competition from both large chains and small boutique hotels, the Hilton is still a good and well-located choice—it's right near Parque El Ejido, Casa de la Cultura, and the business center of the city. It is particularly popular as a quick overnight base for folks heading to or from the Galápagos or other far-flung destinations in the country. The deluxe rooms are on the small side, with compact marble bathrooms to match. The superior rooms are a bit larger and more modern, but the real benefit of these rooms is free use of the business center (which includes a free continental breakfast and Internet access). The junior suites are similar to the superior rooms, except they have breakfast tables and two sinks in the bathroom. Suites have separate sitting areas and both tubs and showers in the bathrooms. Over half the rooms here were remodeled in 2007. The service here is quite good. If you book direct via their website, you should do better than the rack rates listed below.

Av. Amazonas and Patria, Quito. (C) **800/221-2424** in the U.S. and Canada, or 02/2560-666 in Ecuador. Fax 02/ 2563-903. www.hilton.com. 395 units. $189 (£95) double; $219–$239 (£110–£120) executive level; $389–$939 (£195–£470) suite. AE, DC, MC, V. Free parking. **Amenities:** 4 restaurants; bar; lounge; casino; midsize outdoor pool; small health club; Jacuzzi; sauna; concierge; tour desk; free airport shuttle; business center; shopping arcade; salon; 24-hr. room service; in-room massage; babysitting; same-day dry cleaning; laundry service; smoke-free floors; executive/club floor. *In room:* A/C, TV, Wi-Fi for a fee, minibar, hair dryer, safe.

Expensive
JW Marriott Hotel ★★★ Quito's most luxurious large business-class hotel, the JW Marriott features perhaps the best rooms and facilities in town. Service is top-notch, the restaurants are fantastic, and the large pool with its central Jacuzzi island and waterfalls makes you feel as if you've escaped to a tropical resort. You enter each room through a carved wooden door that looks as though it should open onto an old-fashioned den. But instead of a den you'll find a large room with colorful bedspreads, heavy wood furniture, and comfy chairs. Most rooms offer views of either the city or of the volcanoes. (If you can, opt for the volcano view; my least favorite rooms have views of the glass-enclosed lobby.) The large marble bathrooms are wonderful—all have separate tubs and showers. The gym here is large and well-equipped with a regular slate of classes and activities. Executive-level rooms and suites include a buffet breakfast and other perks.

Av. Orellana 1172 and Av. Amazonas, Quito. (C) **800/228-9290** in the U.S. and Canada, or 02/2972-000 in Quito. Fax 02/2972-050. www.marriotthotels.com. 257 units. $129–$159 (£63–£77) deluxe; $149–$189 (£73–£92) executive; $219–$259 (£107–£126) suite. AE, DC, MC, V. Free valet parking. **Amenities:** 3 restaurants; bar; large pool; health club; Jacuzzi; sauna; concierge; tour desk; business center; shopping arcade; salon; 24-hr. room service; massage; babysitting; same-day dry cleaning; laundry service; smoke-free floors; executive/club floors. *In room:* A/C, TV, dataport, minibar, hair dryer, iron, safe.

Moderate

Hotel Café Cultura ★★ *Finds*   In the heart of New Town, the Café Cultura is definitely one of the most unique and interesting hotels in Quito. Formerly the French Cultural Center, this old but beautifully renovated house is now the hippest hotel in the city. It's truly an inner-city retreat, complete with a lush garden with resident hummingbirds and doves. All the rooms have hand-painted designs on the walls and their own personal touches. For example, no. 25 has a tree growing through it; no. 1 has a fireplace, French doors, painted furniture, and a claw-foot tub. My favorite room, though, is no. 2, which has a beautiful sitting nook, with wraparound floor-to-ceiling windows. Several of the rooms have sloped wooden ceilings; most have been renovated in the past few years, and all the windows have been soundproofed. In general, the bathrooms are also excellent; there are some rooms, however, where only a curtain separates the bathroom from the rest of the room. Note that all the rooms are smoke-free.

The charming owner, Laszlo Karolyi, has done a great job of making this hotel feel like a real home. It's also one of the few hotels in the city not to charge the full 22% service fee; it adds only the minimum tax of 12% to your bill—although you should tip the service staff accordingly. There's a lovely restaurant adjacent to the lobby, complete with hardwood floors and flickering candles, and a roaring fireplace.

Robles and Reina Victoria, Quito. ℂ/fax **02/2224-271** or 02/2564-956. www.cafecultura.com. 26 units. $99 (£48) double; $109 (£53) triple and junior suite; $139 (£68) suite. AE, DC, MC, V. Free parking. **Amenities:** Restaurant; lounge; free Wi-Fi; tour desk; free airport pickup if you book online; room service 7am–10pm; laundry service.

Hotel Sebastián ★ *Value*   This well-located business-class hotel offers tidy, well-maintained rooms, excellent service, and good value. All of the rooms feature new carpeting and 29-inch flatscreen televisions. The decor is almost stately, with gold bedspreads and subdued colors on the walls. Free Wi-Fi reaches just about every nook and cranny in the hotel. Rooms on the higher floors have great views, especially those on the south side, from which you can see Volcán Cotopaxi on a clear day. With their own filtering system, this is one of the few hotels in Quito, or in the country for that matter, to offer safe drinking water straight from the tap. The small gym here is surprisingly well equipped.

Diego de Almagro 822 and Luis Cordero, Quito. ℂ/fax **02/2222-300** or 02/2222-400. Fax 02/2222-500. www.hotel sebastian.com. 55 units. $79 (£40) double; $89 (£45) junior suite. AE, DC, MC, V. Free parking. **Amenities:** Restaurant; bar; small gym; tour desk; 24-hr. room service; laundry service; free Wi-Fi. *In room:* TV, hair dryer.

Mansión del Angel ★★ *Finds*   Mansión del Angel feels more like a friend's home than like a hotel. In fact, after you stay here for a few days, you will probably meet the owner, who will indeed become a friend. The staff distributes fresh flowers throughout the hotel daily, so everything smells lovely. The sitting areas on the first floor are full of gorgeous antiques, handmade wood furniture, unique art, crystal chandeliers, and gilded mirrors. All the rooms have brass canopy beds, hand-carved moldings, Oriental carpets, and plush bedspreads. The bathrooms are not especially spacious; none have tubs, but they all have very large showers. The larger rooms, on the top floor, have a separate sitting area. Since the rooms in the back of the hotel don't face the street, they are a bit quieter, although I've never found noise to be a problem, even in the street-side rooms. The breakfast, served on the enclosed rooftop terrace, includes fresh-baked breads, and at night the smell of baking bread permeates the entire hotel. Delicious! A formal English tea is served every afternoon, which is a good way to meet other guests.

Wilson E5–29 and Juan León Mera, Quito. ✆ 800/327-3573 in the U.S., or 02/2557-721. Fax 02/2237-819. www.mansiondelangel.com.ec. 11 units. $65–$127 (£33–£64) double. Rates include full breakfast and tax. MC, V. Parking nearby. **Amenities:** Enclosed rooftop breakfast terrace; afternoon tea; laundry service. *In room:* TV, hair dryer, safe.

Inexpensive
Crossroads Hostal
This centrally located Mariscal hostel is everything a hostel should be: friendly, busy, safe, and funky. There are a shared kitchen and a large living area with a television surrounded by beanbag chairs and a couch. One of the dorm rooms comes with a fireplace. Some of the rooms have wood floors, while others are carpeted. Nos. 16, 17, and 18 are my top choices; they're located in a quiet, newer section out back. Every guest gets a lock box in the office, but it's a bring-your-own-lock affair. This is a great place to meet and hook up with fellow travelers, and to arrange trips and adventure tours around the country. They offer free luggage storage, and you can leave some stuff here while you travel outside Quito.

Foch E5-23 and Juan León Mera, Quito. ✆ 02/2234-735 or 022545-514. www.crossroadshostal.com. 4 dorm rooms and 14 private rooms (9 with private bathroom). $6 (£3) per person in dorm room; $18 (£9) double with shared bathroom; $24 (£12) double with private bathroom. MC, V. Parking nearby. **Amenities:** Restaurant; bar; lounge; free Wi-Fi. *In room:* No phone.

Hostal Fuente de Piedra I *(Finds)*
Not to be confused with the less charming Hostal Fuente de Piedra II, this is a great find on a quiet street close to everything. A serene courtyard with a trickling fountain leads to small, simply furnished rooms with exposed stone in some and large picture windows in others. The bathrooms are clean and good-sized, though none have tubs. There's a small balcony with reading chairs for guests on the second floor and a very cozy restaurant with fireplace on the ground floor. This hotel has been open for over a decade, and the management still tries hard to please their guests. They have a good tour desk, and either manage or have close relationships with other hotels across Ecuador.

Wilson 211 and Tamayo, Quito. ✆ 02/2525-314 or tel/fax 02/2900-323. www.ecuahotel.com. 19 units. $45 (£23) double. Rates include full breakfast and taxes. AE, MC, V. **Amenities:** Restaurant; bar; lounge. *In room:* TV.

IN OLD TOWN
Quito's Old Town is in the midst of a major renaissance. Whereas just a couple of years ago I cautioned visitors against staying in this area, there are now several excellent hotel options in various price ranges, and the security situation has improved greatly. That said, you still need to be careful walking some of the streets around here at night, and taxis definitely should be used after nightfall.

Very Expensive
Patio Andaluz *★★ (Finds)*
This stately boutique hotel is a fabulous option in the center of Quito's colonial core. Rooms are spread around the perimeters of two large central courtyard areas. The first courtyard houses the hotel's restaurant, while the second has a pretty garden bar. In addition, several common areas offer comfortable couches, or tables and chairs. The rooms are all large and elegant, with wood floors, Persian rugs, antique-style furniture and beds, large desks, and flatscreen televisions. Only a handful of units have windows facing the street; most have windows opening onto one of the central courtyards. The suites are all two levels, with a bedroom on one level and a comfortable sitting room on the other. But suites have only one bathroom, and sometimes it's located on the level with the sitting room, so if you like your bathroom just steps away from your bedroom, be sure to request one of these units.

Service here is attentive and professional, although I wouldn't mind if the staff got rid of their colonial-period costumes.

Av. García Moreno N6–52, between Olmedo and Mejía, Quito. ✆ 02/2280-830. Fax 02/2288-690. www.hotel patioandaluz.com. 31 units. $150 (£75) double; $175 (£88) suite. Rates include breakfast buffet. AE, DC, MC, V. **Amenities:** Restaurant; bar; lounge; tour desk; laundry service; smoke-free rooms. *In room:* TV, safe.

Plaza Grande 🎯🎯 *Finds*   Old Town's newest hotel is also its most plush, ambitious, and expensive. Housed in the meticulously restored former home of one of Quito's founding fathers, Juan Díaz de Hidalgo, this stylish boutique hotel is opulent and grand. The all-suite hotel fronts the Plaza de la Independencia (Plaza Grande), and the best rooms have large windows and French doors overlooking the plaza. All rooms are beautifully done and feature such perks as soundproofed windows and doors, 42-inch flatscreen televisions, Jacuzzi tubs in large bathrooms with heated floors, and fine cotton linens and down comforters. The decor is refined, with heavy drapes, plush furnishings, fine fabrics, and tasteful art and tapestries on the walls. The hotel's main restaurant and wine cellar match the high standards set by the rooms, and the small but delightful spa is a great place to pamper yourself. Service is prompt, attentive, and friendly. Because this place is new, their prices are well above those at most other high-end hotels in Quito—in most cases more than two to three times as high as other upscale options. But no other downtown hotel can match the Plaza Grande in terms of intimacy, location, and luxury.

On the Plaza de la Independencia, Av. García Moreno N5–16, and Chile, Quito. ✆ 02/2566-497. Fax 02/2559-203. www.plazagrandequito.com. 15 units. $500–$600 (£250–£300) suite; $2,000 (£1,000) presidential suite. AE, DC, MC, V. Free valet parking. **Amenities:** 2 restaurants; cafe; bar; lounge; small, well-equipped spa; sauna; concierge; tour desk; 24-hr. room service; in-room massage; laundry service. *In room:* A/C, TV, free Wi-Fi, minibar, hair dryer, safe.

Moderate

Hotel Real Audiencia   This Old Town standby offers clean, comfortable rooms at good prices. The decor is quite dated and dour, however. The best rooms are spacious and come with views. No. 2A is a corner suite with a fabulous view of the Santo Domingo Plaza, while no. 301 is a floor higher up, with more panoramic views. In fact, the best feature of this hotel is its top-floor restaurant with wraparound picture windows and a view of Santo Domingo Plaza and El Panecillo. The owners aim to be socially and culturally conscious, with solar panels to heat their water, solid-waste recycling, and educational programs for local youths. You'll get a slight discount and free airport transfers if you book directly online with them.

Bolívar 220, at the corner of Guayaquil, Quito. ✆ 02/2952-711. Fax 02/2580-213. www.realaudiencia.com. 32 units. $45 (£23) double; $55 (£28) suite. Rates include full breakfast and taxes. AE, DC, MC, V. **Amenities:** Restaurant; bar; tour desk; laundry service; free Wi-Fi. *In room:* TV.

Inexpensive

Hotel San Francisco de Quito *Value*   This is my favorite budget option in Old Town. Housed in a 17th-century converted residence, the hotel's rooms are on the second, third, and fourth floors, which rise above a classic central stone courtyard with stone fountain. Rooms vary considerably in size, so try to see a few first if you can. Most have varnished wood floors, although a few are carpeted. No. 32 is the best room in the house. a large suite with fireplace and kitchenette, it's located on the fourth floor and has excellent views in several directions.

Sucre 217, at the corner of Guayaquil, Quito. ✆ 02/2287-758. Fax 02/2951-241. www.sanfranciscodequito.com.ec. 32 units. $38 (£19) double; $42–$48 (£21–£24) suite. Rates include breakfast and taxes. AE, MC, V. **Amenities:** Restaurant; Jacuzzi; steam room; sauna; shopping arcade; laundry service; free Wi-Fi. *In room:* TV.

WHERE TO DINE
IN NEW TOWN

In addition to the places listed below, a host of simple restaurants are geared toward the backpacker crowd. For tasty Indian food, try **Chandani Tandoori** (📞 02/2221-053), on Juan León Mera 1312, between Avenida Colón and Luis Cordero. For pastas and pizzas, head to **Le Arcate** (📞 02/2237-659), on Baquedano 358 and Juan León Mera.

Las Redes ★ SEAFOOD   This place serves the best *ceviche* in Quito. You can order any type of *ceviche,* from clams to octopus to fish or shrimp. The chefs here also do an excellent job with all sorts of seafood. One of the specialties is the *gran mariscada,* an enormous, beautiful platter of assorted sizzling seafood. The *arroz con mariscos* (yellow rice with peppers, onions, mussels, clams, shrimp, calamari, octopus, and crayfish) is also delicious. Even though Las Redes is on one of the busiest streets of Quito, the simple wood tables and fishnets hanging from the ceilings make you feel as though you are at a local seafood joint on the coast.

Av. Amazonas 845 and Veintimilla. 📞 02/2525-691. Main courses $5–$11 (£2.50–£5.50). AE, DC, MC, V. Mon–Sat 11am–11pm.

The Magic Bean *Kids* BREAKFAST/INTERNATIONAL   The Magic Bean is a cozy cafe that would be right at home in any college district in the United States, say, in Santa Cruz, California, or Boulder, Colorado. It's not fancy, but it has a pleasant setting with a couple of small dining rooms and covered outdoor tables. Expect to see plenty of the city's expatriates here, especially at breakfast and lunch. The fare is typical cozy cafe food—pancakes, French toast, sandwiches, bagels, omelets, fresh fruit drinks, salads made with organic lettuce, and freshly brewed coffee. Overall, the food is quite good. Just beware: The pancakes are enormous! More substantial options range from grilled local mountain trout to filet mignon. They do a lot of kabobs here, with everything from steak, chicken, and pork, to mahi-mahi and shrimp grilled on a spear. They even have a children's menu. The Magic Bean unabashedly caters to foreigners, but it's comforting to find a place in Ecuador that reminds you of your favorite little spot at home. If you've got a laptop or PDA, this is a good place to come for a free Wi-Fi hookup. Though it's more popular as a restaurant, the Magic Bean also functions as a hostel.

Mariscal Foch 681 and Juan León Mera. 📞 02/2566-181. www.magicbeanquito.com. Sandwiches $4–$6.50 (£2–£3.25); main courses $4.75–$11 (£2.38–£5.50). AE, DC, MC, V. Daily 7am–10pm.

Mama Clorinda ECUADORIAN   This enormously popular restaurant opened in 2004 and immediately garnered a loyal following—mostly of locals. Simplicity is the theme here; the food, not the atmosphere, is the attraction. The focus is on hearty and traditional recipes from the highlands, including *seco de chivo* (goat stew), *llapingachos* (homemade corn tortillas smothered with cheese), and *guatita* (beef, potato, and peanut stew). All varieties of grilled pork are also available, as well as roasted chicken served with *elote* (corn on the cob) and mashed potatoes. If you are a vegetarian, this is not a good place because even the mashed potatoes are cooked with pork fat (which is the traditional Ecuadorian way to cook them). But if you want a taste of what locals consider a fantastic meal, then this is one of your best bets. Round out your meal with a luscious coconut flan or a fresh-fruit salad.

Reina Victoria 1144 and Calama. 📞 02/2544-362. Main courses $3.50–$6 (£1.75–£3). MC, V. Daily noon–9pm.

IN OLD TOWN

If you do come to Old Town at night, I suggest taking a taxi directly here and then asking the restaurant to call you a taxi for your ride back to your hotel. Strolling on the Plaza de la Independencia (Plaza Grande) after dark is relatively safe, and it's the only place in Old Town where people linger late into the evening—but I don't recommend venturing into any of the side streets at night.

Two of the restaurants listed below, Café Mosaico and PIM's Panecillo, are actually located a little bit outside and above the center of Old Town, but for practical purposes—and for the views they provide of Old Town—they are included here. A taxi to either of these restaurants from Old Town should not cost more than $3 (£1.50).

Expensive

Mea Culpa 🦟 *Moments* INTERNATIONAL   This refined restaurant commands one of the most beautiful settings in Old Town. On the second floor of a building that overlooks the Plaza de la Independencia, also known as the Plaza Grande, Mea Culpa is one of the grandest restaurants in the entire city—so grand, in fact, that they require "business casual" attire. Sneakers and T-shirts are not allowed, although exceptions are sometimes made at lunch. There are two large, formal dining rooms. You'll definitely want to be in the front room, with large windows overlooking the plaza. Be sure to reserve a window table, if at all possible. To start things off, I recommend their house specialty, the frittata Mea Culpa (a crepe stuffed with octopus, shrimp, mussels, and calamari). Main courses include everything from pastas and steaks, to pork tenderloin in a raspberry sauce or an ostrich filet flambéed in brandy and served with a maple-soy-apple reduction. The modest wine list leans heavily on Chilean and Argentine vineyards, but with some interesting and less common selections. Those looking to really splurge can drop a little over $400 (£200) on a Château Latour 1997.

2nd floor of the Palacio Arzobispal, on the Plaza de la Independencia, Venezuela and Chile. ✆ 02/2951-190. Reservations recommended. Main courses $10–$19 (£5–£9.50). AE, DC, MC, V. Mon–Fri 12:30–3:30pm and 7–11pm; Sat 7–11pm.

Moderate

La Cueva del Oso *Finds* ECUADORIAN/INTERNATIONAL   While most of Quito's Old Town harkens back to the colonial era, this cozy spot is a tribute to the Art Deco heyday of the early 1900s. Etched glass, plush high-backed leather booths, high ceilings with ornate stucco designs, and marble floors give this place a sophisticated feel. The menu and food are not nearly as upscale as the decor, but they are dependable. You can get a range of standard Ecuadorian fare and well-grilled steaks and a few Continental classics such as cordon bleu. The bar here is also a good choice if you're looking for a quiet watering hole.

Chile 10–46 and Venezuela. ✆ 02/2583-826. Main courses $5–$14 (£2.50–£7). MC, V. Mon–Sat 12:30pm–12:30am; Sun 12:30–4pm.

PIM's Panecillo *Moments* ECUADORIAN/INTERNATIONAL   You might recognize this spot from a segment of *The Amazing Race: All-Stars*. While rivaling the Café Mosaico (see below) in terms of view, it falls far short of its competition in the realms of ambience and cuisine. Still, you're coming here for the view. Located just off the *Virgen de Quito* monument, atop the Panecillo hill, it has plenty of seating with a view, both in the multilevel main dining room and the heated outdoor areas. The menu is massive and ranges from hamburgers and sandwiches to a wide selection of meat, poultry, and seafood options. You can get a pepper steak or trout in almond sauce.

There's a limited children's menu, which includes chicken nuggets and mini-hamburgers. This is a popular tourist destination, and the place is often filled with tour-bus groups.

Calle Melchor Aymerich, on top of the Panecillo. © 02/3172-595. Reservations recommended. Main courses $6.60–$16 (£3.30–£8). AE, DC, MC, V. Mon–Sat noon–midnight; Sun noon–6pm.

Inexpensive

Café Mosaico ★★★ (Finds) INTERNATIONAL Much more than a cafe and every bit an elite gathering place, Mosaico is perhaps the most spectacular eatery in Ecuador. Set in an old house high up on a hill overlooking Old Town, Mosaico is run by an Ecuadorian-Greek-American family. The view is stunning—the entire city stretched at your feet and the place filled with the crème de la crème of Ecuadorian society. Settle at your beautiful table, inlaid with hand-painted mosaic tiles, and take in the view. Many people come here only for cocktails or dessert and coffee, but the food is surprisingly good. The Greek moussaka is delicious, as is the tender souvlaki. The vegetarian lasagna is divine and there's a good selection of delicious sandwiches. Reservations are not accepted and this place fills up fast; be prepared to wait for a table. The best time to come here is late afternoons during the week, before the after-work crowd arrives. That way you'll score a table fast, get to see the place during the day, and also take in the incredible view as the city lights up after dark. New additions here include free Wi-Fi service and a large telescope for stargazing at night and downtown spying during the day. A taxi here should cost under $5 (£2.50)—tell the driver to take you to Itchimbia.

Manuel Samaniego N8–95 and Antepara, Itchimbia. © 02/2542-871. Reservations not accepted. Main courses $3.50–$8 (£1.75–£4). MC, V. Daily 11am–10:30pm.

Café Tianguez ★ (Value) ECUADORIAN This is the perfect place in which to have a quick meal when you're spending the day in Old Town visiting the sights. Just below the Iglesia de San Francisco, the large outdoor cobblestone patio has a sweeping view of the Plaza de San Francisco. The indoor dining room is very small and it can get quite cozy when it's full because you sit elbow to elbow with your neighbors; but the atmosphere is friendly and convivial and the staff works hard to keep everybody happy. The food here is simple and delicious. Order a *plato típico* and you'll get a sampling of local specialties: empanadas, *humitas,* fried yuca, and fried pork. For something lighter, there's a good selection of large salads and sandwiches and fresh-squeezed fruit juices.

Below the Iglesia San Francisco, Plaza de San Francisco. © 02/2570-233. Main courses $3.80–$6.50 (£1.90–£3.25). AE, DC, MC, V. Mon–Tues 9:30am–6:30pm; Wed–Sat 9:30am–11:30pm; Sun 9:30am–10pm.

NORTH & EAST OF NEW TOWN
Expensive

La Querencia ★ ECUADORIAN La Querencia offers delicious Ecuadorian cooking in a beautiful setting. If you're looking to try Ecuadorian specialties, such as *seco de chivo* (lamb stew) or *ceviche* (marinated fish), but you're a bit apprehensive about venturing into a hole-in-the wall restaurant, La Querencia is for you. Other unique dishes include *papas con cuero* (pork skins with potatoes in a peanut sauce) and *arroz con menestra* (a juicy filet served with rice, lentils, and fried bananas). I recommend starting your meal with *empanadas de verde* and *tortillas de maíz.* This is definitely the best restaurant in Quito for high-quality traditional fare.

Eloy Alfaro 2530 and Catalina Aldaz. © **02/2446-654**. Reservations recommended. Main courses $6.50–$22 (£3.25–£11). AE, DC, MC, V. Mon–Sat 11am–10pm; Sun 11am–6pm.

Zazu ✦✦✦ *Finds* FUSION   The Peruvian-born chef at this chic new restaurant uses fresh, local ingredients whenever possible, and flavor always takes precedence over presentation and shock-value. Start things off with the *ceviche martini,* a relatively traditional *ceviche* of sole served in a martini glass, with a freshly shaken passion-fruit martini poured over it as marinade. Don't miss the white-tuna appetizer, which comes baked in a delicate ginger and Peruvian hot chile broth, with bok choy and scallions. For a main dish, I recommend *langostinos Zazu,* which are first cooked tempura style and then served with a sauce made with six types of chilies and a side salad made from green mangos. The best way to dine here, though, is to go with the chef's nightly tasting menu ($30–$35/£15–£18) and to trust his skills and whims. Quito's hippest crowd gathers at the bar, which serves up a wide range of martinis and mixed drinks, including a couple of very tasty original concoctions.

Mariano Aguilera 331 and La Pradera. © **02/2543-559**. Reservations recommended. Main courses $8–$18 (£4–£9). AE, DC, MC, V. Mon–Fri 12:30–11:30pm; Sat 7–11:30pm.

Moderate

El Níspero ✦✦ *Finds* NEW ECUADORIAN   If you're looking for a high-end restaurant serving updated takes on traditional Ecuadorian cuisine, this is the place to come. The restaurant is housed in a charming old home that has been totally renovated with hardwood floors and blue and yellow walls; a serene, quiet atmosphere prevails throughout. Service is gracious and the food is very good. The focus here is on traditional ingredients and recipes updated with an eclectic twist. The roast pork is served with figs and a mint sauce; the fresh prawns with coconut sauce come with an Ecuadorian nut called *tocte;* pancakes are made from yuca flour; and the *humitas* (a kind of corn mush) are served like a pudding, in a bowl. For dessert, try the *oritas*—small Ecuadorian bananas drizzled with local honey—or the éclairs filled with *naranjilla* cream. If you like ice cream, be sure to ask about the *helado* special of the day—it's delicious.

Valladolid N24–438 and Cordero. © **02/2226-398**. Reservations recommended. Main courses $8–$18 (£4–£9). AE, DC, MC, V. Tues–Sat noon–4pm and 7–11pm; Sun–Mon noon–4pm.

QUITO AFTER DARK

From elegant opera performances to dirt-cheap all-you-can-drink bars, Quito offers a range of nocturnal activities for visitors and locals alike. The Mariscal sector, the hub for partying and dining out, has restaurants, pubs and dance clubs pumping out popular salsa and infectious *reggaetón* beats until daybreak. To find out what's going on in Quito while you're in town, pick up a copy of *Quito Cultura* (www.quitocultura.com), a monthly Spanish-language events guide that includes theater listings, concerts, and general cultural events.

In 2001, the city government issued a new law stating that all bars and clubs must close at midnight Monday to Friday and 2am on Saturday and Sunday. But this is only sporadically enforced, and many clubs have found ways around it, including declaring their events as private parties.

Warning: Remember, at night, Quito can be quite dangerous, especially near the bars and clubs. Take a cab, even if it's only for a few blocks; bartenders can call a taxi for you. If you have a cellphone, dial © **02/2222-222** for a taxi 24 hours a day.

BARS & PUBS   Quito's bar scene is extensive, offering options ranging from British-style beer pubs to sophisticated wine bars, and just about everything in between. The majority of places are situated in the Mariscal district. The newly renovated Plaza Foch is generally targeted toward those in search of classier venues, while the majority of other bars, from funky cafes to laid-back bars, are located in and around the streets Calama, Reina Victoria, and Juan León Mera. With such a variety of bars and pubs in one area, the Mariscal is perfect for a pub crawl, although it can sometimes get a little dodgy after dark, so it's advisable not to go alone.

If you're looking to tap into Quito's happening bar scene, try **Six-Nine-Six** (Calama 454 between Amazonas and Juan León Mera), **Naranjilla Mecánica** ✯✯ (Tamayo and Veintimilla; ✆ 02/2526-468), **Huaina** ✯ (Calama and Reina Victoria; ✆ 02/2526-468), or **Sutra Lounge** (Juan León Mera and Calama; ✆ 02/2509-106).

For a mellower time, try either **Reina Victoria** ✯✯ (Reina Victoria 530 and Roca; ✆ 02/2226-369) or **Turtle's Head** ✯ (La Niña 626 and Juan León Mera; ✆ 02/2565-544), two British-style pubs with beer on tap, as well as pool tables, darts and table soccer.

DANCE CLUBS On weekends, Quiteños get their dance grooves on to everything from salsa and merengue to hip-hop and house. **Club Gia** ✯✯✯ (Jose María Ayora and Villalengua; ✆ 02/2924-094) is perhaps the hottest and most happening club in town, with go-go dancers and a varied musical repertoire including anything from Offspring to Tiesto. Entrance costs $8 to $10 (£4–£5) on most nights, or as much as $15 to $20 (£7.50–£10) for special events. For a slightly less see-and-be-seen option, I like **No Bar** ✯ (Calama 380 and Juan León Mera; ✆ 02/2545-145) and **Macondo** ✯✯ (Calama and Juan León Mera; ✆ 02/2227-563). For those looking to dance salsa, **Seseribó** ✯ (Veintimilla 352 and 12 de Octubre; ✆ 02/2563-598) is *the* place to go.

LIVE MUSIC Some live performances to watch out for are those by the jazz quartet **Plaza Foch** on Monday, Wednesday, and Saturday at Coffee Tree (Plaza Foch and Reina Victoria), and the Latin jazz band **Cabo Frío.** A good place to look for jazz is the restaurant and bar **El Pobre Diablo** (✆ 02/2235-194), in La Floresta on Isabel La Católica E12–06 and Galavis. Other groups to watch out for at various venues are some of Ecuador's most influential bands on the South American rock-and-metal scene: **Pulpo3, Muscaria,** and **Sal y Mileto.** Also worth a mention are the psychedelic pop-electronic group **Can Can** and, for a truly Caribbean flavor, **Héctor Napolitano.**

Blues (República 476; ✆ 02/2223-206) is one of Quito's best and most dependable spots to find live music, particularly rock. Thursday night there's live Cuban music and dancing at **La Bodeguita de Cuba** ✯ (Reina Victoria 1721 and La Pinta; ✆ 02/2542-476).

PERFORMING ARTS The **National Symphony** performs weekly in different venues around town, including some colonial churches; call ✆ 02/2256-5733 for up-to-date information. Every Wednesday at 7:30pm, the **Ballet Andino Humanizarte** (✆ 02/2967-152) performs traditional Andean dances at the Fundación Cultural Humanizarte, on Leonidas Plaza N24–226 and Lizardo García. The **Ballet Folkórico Nacional Jacchigua** ✯ (✆ 02/2952-025; www.jacchiguaesecuador.com) performs traditional dances and songs on Wednesday and Friday nights at 7:30pm at the Teatro Aeropuerto. Tickets cost $12 to $14 (£6–£7) and are often easiest to buy through **Metropolitan Touring** (✆ 02/2988-200; www.metropolitan-touring.com) or through your hotel tour desk or concierge.

The newly restored **Teatro Nacional Sucre** ✯✯ (✆ 02/2572-823; www.teatro sucre.com), in Old Town's Plaza del Teatro Manabí N8–131, between Guayaquil and Flores, first opened its doors in 1867; it's Quito's most popular theater and offers a varied and exciting events program including contemporary theater, ballet, electronic-music performances, and opera. Free concerts and street shows put on by the theater frequently take place just outside, on the Plaza del Teatro. Despite being almost completely destroyed by a fire in 1999, the restored neoclassic **Teatro Bolívar,** at Flores 421 and Junín (© **02/2582-486;** www.teatrobolivar.org), continues to host and produce a range of cultural events including theater, dance, music, and Latin American cinema.

Another important outlet for the performing arts is the **Casa de la Cultura Ecuatoriana** (© **02/2902-272;** www.cce.org.ec). Founded in the 1940s by writer, politician, and diplomat Benjamin Carrión ("If we can't be a military or economic power, we can, instead, be a cultural power fed by our rich traditions"), the Casa offers an extensive repertoire of events including rock concerts, art exhibitions, and performances by the National Symphonic Orchestra.

The recently constructed **Teatro del CCI,** at CCI Iñaquito, Avenida Amazonas and Nacionas Unidas (© **02/2921-308**), which opened its doors in January 2006, is a fine example of a modern theater with the latest technology in sound and lighting, offering up a mix of contemporary dance, theater, and music.

SIDE TRIPS FROM QUITO
COTOPAXI NATIONAL PARK 🐸🐸

At 5,897m (19,348 ft.), Cotopaxi is the world's highest continuously active volcano, and Ecuador's second-highest peak. Your first encounter with the almost perfectly cone-shaped and snow-covered Cotopaxi might be from overhead in a plane; I've been on planes that have flown terrifyingly close to the volcano, where I almost felt I could reach out and touch it. From above, it's hard to determine where the clouds end and where the glaciers begin. The snow glimmers in the sunlight and magically blends with the bright blue sky—and what a sight! On a clear day in Quito, even if you're not airborne, it's easy to see Cotopaxi rising high and mighty above the clouds.

Looking down from a plane at a volcano is one thing, but climbing it, camping on its flanks, riding a horse or mountain bike across the paramo, or hiking around it are much more rewarding. The high Andean paramo here features wild horses and llamas grazing. Below the volcano, the flat plains are peppered with volcanic boulders that give stark evidence of the power and fury of Cotopaxi's relatively recent eruptions. And everywhere you turn there are fantastic views of the snow-covered crater—that is, when it's not shrouded in low cloud cover.

Climbing to the summit is serious business, and not for those in merely average physical condition and with no experience at high altitudes. Nonetheless, every year, thousands of intrepid climbers take out their ice axes, strap on their crampons, and conquer the summit. An embarrassing admission: I've never done it. But according to those in the know, the climb is not terribly technical or difficult. On the other hand, I have met several experienced climbers who have been severely affected by the altitude and were forced to turn back early. Be sure to spend several days in Quito and at higher altitudes acclimating before you attempt to summit Cotopaxi. Even if you're feeling fine at 2,800m (9,184 ft.), remember that the air will feel a whole lot thinner at 5,000m (16,400 ft.), especially if you're exerting a lot of energy. You should also note that the climb typically starts at about 11pm to midnight and you will be going uphill on glaciers for about 8 continuous hours before you reach the top. This way, you reach the crater in the early morning light, before the clouds settle in.

Fortunately for the less adventurous and less fit, you really don't need to climb Cotopaxi to enjoy it. A host of outfitters in Quito, and all the hotels close to the volcano, organize day trips to the national park. Many day trips bring you to the small museum and visitor center, which has a somewhat sad collection of stuffed animals, including an Andean condor, as well as a relief map of the volcano and some explanatory materials. From here, these trips commonly take any number of short-to-midlength hikes around the park, most commonly to the Laguna de Limpiopungo. The museum is located at 4,500m (14,760 ft.) above sea level, and most of the hikes around the park take place at this general altitude—note that even at this altitude, the air is quite thin and it's not uncommon to feel lightheaded.

ORGANIZING A CLIMB TO THE TOP   It's very important to make sure that you're climbing Cotopaxi with an experienced guide and good equipment. The best companies provide one guide for every two climbers. The finest and most experienced outfitters include: **Adventure Planet Ecuador** ✸ (⌀ 02/2871-105; www.adventure planet-ecuador.com), **Cotopaxi.com** ✸✸ (⌀ 02/2909-640; www.cotopaxi.com), and **Safari Ecuador** ✸✸ (⌀ 02/2222-505; www.safari.com.ec). Rates run $125 to $200 (£63–£100) per person for a 2-day/1-night trip to the summit, depending upon the size of your group.

All the above companies also organize longer treks around the park and climbs to the summits of other nearby peaks, including Rumiñahui, Iliniza Norte, and Iliniza Sur, all of which are good practice climbs to tackle before attempting Cotopaxi.

VISITING AS PART OF A DAY TRIP   Just about every tour desk and tour operator in Quito offers a day trip to Cotopaxi. The details may vary some, but most head first to the small museum and then spend anywhere from 1 to 3 hours hiking. In addition, most operators offer options for mountain biking or horseback riding.

The best general tour operators, in my opinion, are **Metropolitan Touring** ✸ (⌀ 02/2988-200; www.metropolitan-touring.com) and **Surtrek** ✸ (⌀ 02/2231-534; www.surtrek.com). Day trips to Cotopaxi run $30 to $50 (£15–£25), depending on size of your group and whether lunch is included. The park entrance fee is rarely included.

Alternatively, you can organize a day trip to Cotopaxi on your own. You can hire a taxi in Quito for about $60 to $80 (£30–£40) round-trip. The ride from Quito to the parking lot takes about 1½ hours. Once you reach the parking lot, you can then hike up to the *refugio* or glacier at your own pace while the taxi waits for you.

If you want to tour the park on a mountain bike, contact **Andes World Bike** (⌀ 02/2352-769; www.ecuadorbikingclimbing.com), **Aries Bike Company** (⌀ 02/ 2906-052; www.ariesbikecompany.com), **Cotopaxi.com** ✸✸ (⌀ 02/2909-640; www.cotopaxi.com), or **Safari Ecuador** ✸✸ (⌀ 02/2552-505; www.safari.com.ec).

For horseback-riding tours of Cotopaxi, I recommend **Andean Paths** (⌀ 09/980-8469; www.andeanpaths.com), **Ilalo Expeditions** (⌀ 09/777-8399; www.ilalo expeditions.com), or **Hacienda La Alegría** ✸✸.

Mountain-bike or horseback excursions to Cotopaxi run around $40 to $75 (£20–£38) depending upon the length of the tour and several other variables such as group size and equipment requirements.

LA MITAD DEL MUNDO (THE MIDDLE OF THE WORLD)

One of the most common souvenir photos taken in Ecuador is that which has a visitor with one foot in either hemisphere, straddling the Equator. **Ciudad La Mitad del**

Mundo (☏ **02/2394-806**) is a tourist complex set up on the site where, in 1736, French explorer and scientist Charles-Marie de la Condamine made his final calculations to determine the precise equatorial line. With modern GPS technology, we now know that De la Condamine was close, but erred by some 180m (600 ft.). I find this tourist trap a bit cheesy and highly recommend you get your photo precise by visiting the new **Quitsato Mitad del Mundo Monument** (☏ **09/9701-133**; www.quitsato. org), which is on the road to Otavalo (p. 555).

The centerpiece of the Ciudad la Mitad del Mundo is a large, trapezoidal monument topped with a large globe. At the top of the monument is a viewing area, reached by an elevator, with great views of the surrounding mountains and countryside. My favorite attraction here is the large scale model of colonial-era Quito, called **Museo del Quito en Miniatura (Quito in Miniature).** This is a great way to get your bearings before touring around the colonial core. On the site, there's also a separate **Museo de Etnografía (Ethnographic Museum),** with displays about Ecuador's various indigenous tribes and peoples, as well as a small **Planetarium.** All around are tourist shops and souvenir stands, snack bars, and restaurants. The entire place was built with a mock-colonial styling, sort of a miniature Epcot version of colonial Quito. Frequent shows of folkloric music and dance are performed. Quiteños flock here on Sunday.

Ciudad La Mitad del Mundo is open Monday to Thursday from 9am to 6pm, and from Friday to Sunday from 9am to 7pm. Admission is $3 (£1.50). Admission to the Ethnographic Museum, Planetarium, and Quito in Miniature is an additional $1.50 (75p) each.

Separate from the main attraction, but just a few hundred yards away, is the **Museo Solar Inti-Ñan (Inti-Ñan Solar Museum;** ☏ **02/2395-122**). This interesting attraction has a series of exhibits and ongoing experiments relating to the geography, astrology, and natural sciences of the region. Try your hand at balancing an egg on its end, and watch how water flows down a drain at the Equator. This place is supposedly right on the Equator, although I haven't yet checked this with a GPS. The museum is open daily from 9:30am to 5pm. Admission is $2 (£1).

GETTING THERE   Located some 23km (14 miles) north of Quito, near San Antonio de Pichincha, Ciudad La Mitad del Mundo is connected to Quito by a well-paved road. Just about every tour agency and hotel desk in Quito offers a half-day tour here. Prices range from $8 to $30 (£4–£15), depending on how exclusive the tour is, how many attractions it takes in, and whether or not lunch or admission fees are included in the price.

A taxi ride here from Quito should run about $12 to $15 (£6–£7.50) each way. Regular buses, marked MITAD DEL MUNDO, leave from the Cotocallao stop of the Metrobus trolley line. The trolley costs 25¢ (13p), and the bus costs an extra 40¢ (20p). Be sure to stay on the bus until you reach the actual monument, its final stop.

OTAVALO MARKET ✿✿✿

Though Saturday is the main market day, most Quito-based operators offer daily excursions to nearby Otavalo, and there's plenty of good shopping in Otavalo any day of the week. There's also a lot to see and do around the town. Most tours last all day, with a stop at the artisans market as well as visits to any number of nearby attractions including Cuicocha Lake, Peguche Waterfall, Mojanda Lakes, and Condor Park. Most tours include lunch at one of the area's historic haciendas.

Guided tours to Otavalo run $25 to $80 (£13–£40) per person. As with the tours to Cotopaxi, the price varies depending on group size, what's included, where you have lunch, length of tour, and other factors. For more information on Otavalo, the Otavalo market, and other attractions in the area, see below.

MINDO & BELLAVISTA CLOUD FOREST RESERVE ★★

Hiking through the forests of Mindo and Bellavista is one of the most exciting and rewarding side trips you can take from Quito. Within 2 hours, you will escape the city and find yourself in a cloud forest—a magical ecosystem where near-constant mist, as opposed to heavy rains, gives nourishment to a dense mix of trees, lichen, and epiphytes. Cloud forests are some of the most biologically diverse places on earth. Over 400 bird species have been recorded in the area, including the golden-headed quetzal, tanager finch and, my personal favorite, Chocó toucan. In addition, you will have the opportunity to hike to remote waterfalls, ride inner tubes on pristine rivers, and marvel at the rich array of orchids, butterflies, bromeliads, and flowers.

While the under-2-hour drive makes this a potential (and popular) day-tour destination, I recommend spending at least a night or two. There are several lovely lodges in this region, with excellent naturalist guides, and a host of tour and activity options. In addition to bird- and wildlife-viewing, tour options include horseback riding, zipline canopy excursions, mountain biking, and visits to local butterfly farms.

Much of the cloud forest around Mindo is protected in the **Bosque Protector Mindo-Nambillo (Mindo-Nambillo Protected Forest),** which is administered by **Amigos de la Naturaleza** (© 02/2765-463). While most of the reserve is closed to the public, there are ample private reserves and publicly accessible trails through Mindo's cloud forests. The Mindo-Nambillo reserve was the source of controversy a few years ago, when the government ran an oil pipeline right through it, despite the objections of tourism and environmental groups. Today, the forest is recuperating and covering up much of the damage caused when the pipeline was pushed through.

Mindo is the more developed of these two cloud-forest destinations, with a host of hotels and lodges. The top hotel here is gorgeous **El Monte** ★ (© 09/3084-675; www.ecuadorcloudforest.com). Accommodations are private, wood-and-thatch cabins set near the banks of the clear-flowing Río Mindo. This place is located a couple of miles south of Mindo, and the final leg of your journey to the lodge is via a handcranked cable car over the river. A new and similar choice is the lovely **Séptimo Paraíso** (© 02/2893-160 or 09/9934-133; www.septimoparaiso.com), which has its own private reserve.

The 720-hectare (1,778-acre) **Bellavista Cloud Forest Reserve** (© 02/2116-232 or 09/9490-891; www.bellavistacloudforest.com) is privately owned and has a variety of accommodations options, from private cabins to dorm rooms in the top of a large geodesic dome. It's not a fancy place, but the views over the forest canopy are dramatic, the food is excellent, and the nature guides will open up your eyes to an entirely different world. Rates run $17 to $44 (£8.50–£22) per person, including three meals, but a host of package options are available, including meals, tours, and transportation.

GETTING THERE   If you're staying at a hotel here, you can usually arrange transportation with your hotel or lodge. Alternatively, a taxi from Quito should run around $40 to $50 (£20–£25). Mindo is serviced by a couple of daily buses from Quito. **Cooperativa Flor de Valle** (© 02/2527-495) has buses leaving Quito's main bus terminal, Terminal Terrestre, at 8am and 3:35pm, and returning at 6:30am and 2pm. On weekends, there are additional buses and a slightly varied schedule. The ride takes around 2½ hours, and the fare is $2.50 (£1.25).

It's a little more complicated to travel to Bellavista on your own: You have to take the bus from Quito to the small town of Nanegalito, where you can arrange for a truck taxi to Bellavista. From Nanegalito, it's about a 45-minute ride to Bellavista. The ride should cost about $15 (£7.50) for the entire vehicle, which can hold up to six passengers. Any bus from Quito to Mindo, Puerto Quito, or San Miguel de los Bancos can drop you off in Nanegalito.

5 Otavalo & Imbabura Province ★★

Otavalo: 95km (59 miles) N of Quito, 515km (319 miles) NE of Guayaquil, 537km (333 miles) N of Cuenca

Otavalo is one of Ecuador's most popular destinations. The locals, known as Otavaleños, have been famous for their masterful craftsmanship for centuries, and the artisans market here is world-renowned. Otavaleños still wear traditional clothing and cling to their heritage. Men wear their long straight black hair in distinctive ponytails, and women wear multistranded, bead necklaces. Saturday is the main market day, when the impressive market spills out over much of this small city. Luckily for travelers with tight schedules, the market has become so popular that it now takes place on the other 6 days of the week, too, albeit on a smaller scale. In addition to shopping at Otavalo's market, you can explore the back roads of the province and visit local studios. Some of the smaller towns specialize in specific crafts: **Cotacachi**, for example, is known for leather work, **Peguche** for its weaving, and **San Antonio de Ibarra** for its age-old woodcarving techniques.

Even nonshoppers will love Otavalo and its surroundings. The town has an almost perfect setting. It's nestled in the Sunrise Valley in the shadow of two protective volcanoes, **Cotacachi** and **Imbabura.** According to local legend, Cotacachi is the area's symbolic mother, and Imbabura is the father standing watch. To feel the inspirational powers of Mother Nature, I recommend spending a few days exploring the area, breathing in the fresh air, gazing at the dark-blue waters of the local crater lakes, and standing in awe of the snow-covered volcanoes. Plus, after you find the perfect alpaca sweater, you can wear it as you stroll around **Cuicocha Lake** or hike in the mountains.

ESSENTIALS
GETTING THERE

Every hotel desk and tour agency in Quito sells day tours to Otavalo and shuttle tickets aboard minivans and buses. The rate runs around $5 to $12 (£2.50–£6) per person each way for just transportation, and around $25 to $45 (£13–£23) for a day tour, including lunch. These shuttles and tours will pick you up at most hotels in Quito. If your hotel desk can't set one up for you, contact **Grayline Ecuador** (© 02/2907-577; www.graylineecuador.com) or **Metropolitan Touring** ★ (© 02/2988-200; www. metropolitan-touring.com).

Alternately, a taxi holding up to four passengers should cost $40 to $50 (£20–£25) from Quito to Otavalo.

Buses leave Quito's main bus terminal, Terminal Terrestre, roughly every 20 minutes between 5am and 10pm. The ride takes 2 to 2½ hours, and the fare is $2.60 (£1.30). Otavalo's main bus terminal, Terminal Terrestre, is located on Quito and Atahualpa, about 8 blocks—or a 15-minute walk—from Plaza de los Ponchos.

GETTING AROUND

It's easy to get around Otavalo and the surrounding area by taxi and local bus. Taxis are plentiful. A ride anywhere in the city of Otavalo itself should cost only $1 (50p).

En Route: Straddling Two Hemispheres

The Pan-American Highway north of Quito passes right through the Equator, close to Km 55. On your left, as you drive toward Otavalo, you'll see a cluster of souvenir stands and a small concrete globe allegedly sitting right on the equatorial line. Avoid the temptation to pull over here, and head a few hundred feet farther to the new **Quitsato Mitad del Mundo Monument** (© 09/9701-133; www.quitsato.org), which is on the right-hand side of the road.

Opened in 2006, this attraction was built and is run by the folks at nearby Hacienda Guachala (discussed later). The centerpiece is a tall spire that works as one of the world's most accurate sundials. Stone inlays mark the cardinal directions, as well as the solstice limits and the exact equatorial line. As far as I know, this is the most precise Mitad del Mundo (Middle of the World) attraction in Ecuador, and if you have a GPS, bring it to check. At noon, the spire casts absolutely no shadow in any direction, and on the equinox, the shadow falls exactly on the equatorial line, which is the same width as the spire. The monument is open daily during daylight hours, and admission is free.

If you're traveling farther afield and looking to explore Imbabura province, taxis can be hired for $5 to $8 (£2.50–£4) per hour. A one-way taxi fare to Cotacachi or San Antonio de Ibarra should cost $5 to $6 (£2.50–£3).

If you need a taxi, call **Taxis El Jordán** (© 06/2920-298), **Taxi Otavalo** (© 06/2920-301), or **Taxilagos** (© 06/2923-203).

Most of the surrounding communities, towns, and cities are connected to Otavalo by **local bus service.** Buses leave Otavalo every 5 minutes or so for Ibarra. Other buses head to Intag, Cayambe, El Quinche, Peguche, and Cotacachi. Your best source of information is to simply head to the bus station on Quito and Atahualpa. Bus rides to nearby towns or villages run 15¢ to 50¢ (8p–25p).

VISITOR INFORMATION

The **Otavalo Chamber of Tourism** (Cámara de Turismo de Otavalo; © 06/2921-994) runs a helpful information office on Calle Sucre and Calle García Moreno. You'll find another, similar office run by the **Municipal Tourism Office** (Oficina Municipal de Turismo; © 06/2921-313) on Avenida Bolívar near Calle Juan Montalvo. Your best bet, though, is your hotel tour desk or a local tour agency. My favorite local agency is **Runa Tupari Native Travel** ★★, located right on Plaza de los Ponchos, between Sucre and Quiroga (© 06/2925-985; www.runatupari.com). They are not-for-profit and work to support rural indigenous communities.

FAST FACTS   If you need to contact the **police,** dial © 101 or 06/2920-101. The main hospital in Otavalo, **Hospital San Luis** (© 06/2920-444), is located on Sucre and Estados Unidos. The **post office** is adjacent to Plaza de los Ponchos, on the corner of Salinas and Sucre; it's on the second floor of a dreadful building that is constantly under construction. Yes, it looks as though the building has been condemned, but it hasn't, so head up the stairway and walk past the miniconstruction site to the post office.

Banks are abundant in Otavalo. There's a **Banco Pichincha** (© 06/2920-214) on Bolívar 614, near García Moreno, and a **Banco del Pacífico** (© 06/2923-300) on the corner of Bolívar and García Moreno. You'll find another branch of Banco Pichincha just north of Plaza de los Ponchos, on Sucre between Quiroga and Quito.

There are plenty of pharmacies around downtown Otavalo. The **Farmacia Otavalo** (© 06/2920-716), at Colón 510 between Sucre and Juan Jaramillo, is very helpful. Pharmacies work on a *turno* system, which means that each pharmacy periodically takes responsibility for being open 24 hours.

It's easy to find an Internet cafe in Otavalo; there are over a half-dozen within 2 blocks of the Plaza de los Ponchos. Fast connections can be found at **Native C@ffee Net** (© 06/2923-540), on Calle Sucre between Colón and Morales. Rates run around 50¢ to $1.50 (25p–75p) per hour.

WHAT TO SEE & DO

Aside from wandering around and shopping the outdoor markets (see below), there are few tourist attractions of note right in the town of Otavalo, although the surrounding towns, villages, and countryside are ripe with opportunities for sightseeing, shopping, and adventure activities.

IN TOWN

If you tire of the hustle, bustle, and commerce of the artisans market on the Plaza de los Ponchos, head for the more peaceful Parque Bolívar. You can grab a bench in the gardens here, or venture into the city's main **Catholic church.** Although very plain from the outside, the church features an ornate gold-leaf and gold-painted altar, as well as a pretty tiled ceiling.

If you want to learn about the process of weaving used by the artisans in and around Otavalo, head to the **Museo de Tejidos El Obraje** (© 06/2920-261), which has exhibits about the local weaving tools and techniques, as well as displays on the daily lives of the Otavaleños. This little museum is located on Calle Sucre 608, near Olmedo. It is open Monday to Saturday from 9am to noon and 3 to 6pm. Admission is $2 (£1). They also offer classes on weaving.

OTAVALO MARKET 🎁🎁🎁 Because there are often several, simultaneous markets taking place, it's probably most accurate to talk about Otavalo's "markets" (not "market"). The artisans market presents some of the best bargains in Ecuador and, just as importantly, some of the best people-watching. On Saturday, almost the entire city becomes one big shopping area, and itinerant vendors set up stalls on every available speck of sidewalk and alleyway. It's not just for tourists, either; Ecuadorians come here from miles away, to peddle and buy high-quality, handmade goods. The Otavaleños are extremely friendly and helpful, and they wear beautiful traditional clothing. Overall, this is one of the most colorful markets in Ecuador, and the handicrafts are of excellent quality.

Some of the best buys available here include handmade alpaca sweaters, soft alpaca scarves, wool fedoras, colorful straw bags, hand-embroidered blouses, musical instruments, ceramics, large woven tapestries.

Though Saturday is market day, there is a relatively complete market every day in Plaza de los Ponchos. Whenever you visit, you'll find the same great crafts on sale here, and the same beautiful people selling them. *Tip:* I find that the Saturday market is a bit overwhelming; in fact, I prefer coming on a weekday, when I don't have to visit millions of stands to be sure that I have found the perfect bag or hat. You might also be able to bargain better on an off-day, since fewer tourists mean less demand, and sellers are often a bit more flexible if they really want to make a sale.

Shoppers should expect to do some bargaining, but I've found that prices will only drop a dollar or two (or 20% at most). Don't worry—the asking price is usually quite low, and everything here is already a bargain.

EXPLORING THE AREA

Many of the textiles and crafts sold in Otavalo's markets are produced in the towns and villages nearby. Outside of Otavalo, you can visit weavers' studios in Peguche, leather shops in Cotacachi, and woodcarving workshops in San Antonio de Ibarra.

Nature lovers should also take note: With snow-covered Volcán Cayambe overhead and green mountains in the distance, Imbabura province is a place of stunning beauty. There are several excellent hiking possibilities in the area, including one from Otavalo to the Peguche waterfall, and a 4-hour hike around Cuicocha, a picturesque crater lake. All the travel agencies and tour desks in Otavalo can arrange hiking, trekking, and horseback-riding excursions to a range of beautiful and off-the-beaten-path spots in the area, as well as guided tours to the towns and artisans workshops all around outlying towns and villages.

Runa Tupari Native Travel ✸✸, located right on Plaza de los Ponchos between Sucre and Quiroga (© **06/2925-985;** www.runatupari.com), and **Dicency Viajes,** on the corner of Sucre and Colón (© **06/2921-217**), are the two best agencies in town. Both offer a wide range of tours, hikes, and adventure activities around the area, including guided tours to all the sites and destinations listed below as well as organized climbs of Mount Cotacachi (4,939m/16,200 ft.).

CUICOCHA LAKE ✸✸   Cuicocha is a sparkling blue crater-lake formed about 3,000 years ago, when the crater of the lake's namesake volcano collapsed during an eruption. The crater was covered with snow, which eventually melted and formed the lake. When the Incas came here, they thought that one of the islands in the middle looked like a *cuy* (guinea pig), hence the name Cuicocha (Guinea Pig Lake). You can take a motorized boat ride out and around the two islands in the middle of the lake, although you can't get off and hike on them. From the boat, along the shores and in the shallows, you will see *totora,* the reed used in this area for making baskets and floor coverings. A 20- to 40-minute boat ride should cost no more than $2 (£1) per person. Be sure to bring a warm sweater—the wind here can be vicious.

I prefer hiking here to riding around on a boat (although you can certainly do both). An 8km (5-mile) trail loops around the rim of the crater, which takes about 4 hours to circle. But even if you walk along it for only 5 or 10 minutes, you'll be able to see Otavalo, Cotacachi, Cayambe, and all the volcanoes of Imbabura province. The setting and views are consistently striking. There's a small visitor center, near the end of the road leading from Quiroga to Cuicocha, which has some basic exhibits on the geography, geology, and local history of the lake, and serves as the administration center for this entrance into the Cotacachi-Cayapas Ecological Reserve, of which Cuicocha is a part. Admission is $1 (50p) to visit the lake, $5 (£2.50) to visit other areas of the reserve. Cuicocha Lake is located about 16km (10 miles) west of the town of Cotacachi. Although a paved road leads almost to the crater's edge, no public transportation is available from Otavalo directly to Cuicocha.

Tip: I recommend taking a guided tour here, since robberies of unaccompanied tourists have been reported. If you're doing it on your own, it's best to hire a taxi in Otavalo for the full trip, or to take a bus from Otavalo to Cotacachi or Quiroga, and then hire a cab. If you hire a cab, be sure to either pay for the wait time, or designate a time for your return ride.

COTACACHI   Cotacachi is a sleepy little pueblo with incredible vistas. From here, you can see snow-covered Volcán Cayambe and the lush green mountains in the distance. But no one comes here for the views, because Cuicocha, about 10 minutes up the road, offers much better views—perhaps the best in all of Imbabura province. People do, however, come here to shop. Cotacachi is famous for the leather stores that line Avenida 10 de Agosto. Offerings range from wallets and purses to shoes and clothing. Equestrian enthusiasts can shop for handmade saddles. The quality varies widely, but if you search hard enough you are bound to find some excellent work and great bargains. Cotacachi is about 15km (9½ miles), or 15 minutes, from Otavalo. You can easily take a public bus from the station in Otavalo, or hire a taxi for about $6 (£3) each way.

PEGUCHE   Peguche is home to some of the best weavers in Ecuador. If you stop in the main square, you can start off by visiting the gallery and workshop of José Cotacachi, a master weaver. Peguche is also famous for its musical instruments. You'll find various shops that specialize in making single-reed flutes and *rondadores* (panpipes), as well as guitars and *charangos* (a mandolin-like instrument with five pairs of strings). Traditionally, the back of a *charango* is made from an armadillo shell. If you visit the town on a guided tour (which I highly recommend), you will explore the back streets of Peguche and visit the homes of some of the town's best weavers while learning about the old-fashioned process of spinning wool.

Just outside the town is **Peguche Waterfall** *𝒦*, a popular spot for tourists and locals alike. Peguche Waterfall is a tall and powerful torrent of water with lush vegetation on either side. Near the foot of the falls you'll find broad grassy areas with picnic tables and bench seating. Paths take you around the area, including one that goes to the top of the falls, with a sturdy wooden bridge taking you directly over the rushing water. The Peguche Waterfall plays an important role each year in the concurrent festivals of Inti Raymi and San Juan de Batista, which coincide with the summer solstice. Locals of both indigenous and Catholic faiths come to the falls for cleansing baths at this time of year. The tiny town is located about 10 minutes by car from Otavalo. A taxi should cost $5 (£2.50) each way, and you can also walk to the falls from town in about 45 minutes. The route is well-worn and popular—just ask one of the locals to point you in the right direction.

MOJANDA LAKES *𝒦*   After Cuicocha Lake, the Mojanda Lakes offer some of the best and most scenic hiking around Otavalo. The extinct volcano Fuya Fuya stands majestically above the three high mountain lakes, creating a beautiful setting. This is a great spot for bird-watching—more than 100 species of birds are found here, including the giant hummingbird and the endangered Andean condor. Mojanda Lakes are located about 30 minutes south of Otavalo. A taxi here costs about $12 (£6) each way.

PARQUE CONDOR (CONDOR PARK) *Kids*   Although you'll find Andean condors on display here, you'll find a whole host of other bird species as well. The emphasis is on raptors, with a variety of local raptor species represented, including various different owls. Several large birds are brought out by trainers and allowed to fly each day at 11:30am and 4:30pm. The park is set on a high hillside with a lovely view over Laguna San Pablo, the Otavalo Valley, and Volcán Imbabura. There's a small restaurant with great views, as well as a children's playground.

Parque Condor (✆ **06/2924-429;** www.parquecondor.com) is located outside Otavalo near El Lechero and Peguche. It is open Tuesday through Sunday from 9:30am to 5pm. Admission is $2 (£1). A taxi ride here should cost no more than $4 (£2) each way.

SAN ANTONIO DE IBARRA   Cedar wood is abundant in Imbabura province. Take a trip to the small town of San Antonio de Ibarra and you can see how local woodcarvers transform this raw wood into high art. The town is full of galleries selling wood figurines in almost every shape and size; all are beautifully hand-painted. Many are religious-themed, although there are plenty of artisans making secular decorative and functional pieces as well. The best stores are on the main street, 25 de Noviembre and along Calle Ramón Teanga.

Tip: I recommend starting your tour of San Antonio de Ibarra near the church known locally as La Capilla del Barrio del Sur. This diminutive blue church is near the top of the beautifully restored section of Calle Ramón Teanga. Catty-corner to the church is **Escultura Cisneros** (✆ **06/2932-354**), the workshop of Saul and Alfonso Cisneros, two of the more prominent local sculptors. From here, walk downhill for several blocks, stopping in at shops as they strike your fancy, before jogging over toward the town's central plaza and the main Avenue 25 de Noviembre. Heading out of town on this avenue, be sure to stop at the **Asociación de Artesanos** (✆ **06/2933-538**). This large space exhibits works by a number of local artisans, and also has a large gallery area that often hosts traveling exhibitions. For a real treat, try calling on **Alcides Montesdeoca** (✆ **06/2932-106**), a renowned maker of large Virgin Mary sculptures used in prominent Holy Week processions around the world. Alcides can usually be found at his home workshop, on Calle Bolívar 5–38.

San Antonio de Ibarra is located 5km (3 miles) south of Ibarra, just off the Pan-American Highway. Any bus from Ibarra to Quito or Otavalo will drop you off at the entrance to San Antonio de Ibarra, although it's 10 blocks or more uphill from here to the center of town, so be sure to hop on one of the similarly frequent direct buses to San Antonio proper. These leave roughly every 20 minutes from Ibarra's Terminal Terrestre throughout the day. The fare is 20¢ (10p). A taxi ride here should not cost over $3 (£3).

OUTDOOR ACTIVITIES

Hiking trails abound here. One of my favorite hikes is the 4-hour trek around Cuicocha Lake. Keep in mind, however, that robberies have been reported in the area, so it's best to do the trail with a guide. You can also hike from Cuicocha to the Mojanda Lakes, up Volcán Cotacachi, or around the Mojanda Lakes and up Mount Fuya Fuya. Both **Dicency Viajes** (✆ **06/2921-217**) and **Runa Tupari Native Travel** ★★ (✆ **06/2925-985;** www.runatupari.com) can provide experienced guides and help organize your hiking excursions. Both of these tour agencies also offer **horseback-riding** trips. One of the most popular is the trail around Cuicocha Lake. A half-day trip costs $40 to $60 (£20–£30) per person.

WHERE TO STAY IN OTAVALO
MODERATE
Hotel Ali Shungu ★ This popular hotel is a definite step up from most of the downtown options. The large two-story building is built in a broad horseshoe around a large garden that attracts hummingbirds and other bird species. Ali Shungu translates as "good heart" in the native Quechua, and the owners are expatriated Americans who have put their hearts into this project and the area. The rooms are simple but comfortable, with firm beds and colorful art and handicrafts hanging from the walls. The two family suites are big, with two bedrooms and spacious living areas; they are located on the second floor and have large, inviting balconies. In addition to the rooms, all public indoor areas here are smoke-free. The most recent addition to the hotel is free Wi-Fi access, which extends to all the common areas and reaches most of

the rooms as well. The **restaurant** here (see below) is one of the best in town, and they have a pretty little sister lodge in the mountains outside of town.

Calle Quito and Calle Migue Egas, Otavalo. ✆ **06/2920-750.** www.alishungu.com. 18 units. $40 (£20) double; $80 (£39) apt. No credit cards. Parking nearby. **Amenities:** Restaurant; bar; tour desk; laundry service; free Wi-Fi. *In room:* No phone.

INEXPENSIVE

Budget hotels and hostels abound in Otavalo; the one listed here is my favorite, but feel free to walk around the small town and check out a few for yourself before deciding.

Samay Inn 🏨 *Finds* This simple, budget hotel, centrally located on Calle Sucre, just a block from the Plaza de Ponchos, is a great choice in Otavalo. The rooms all have wood floors and faux-stucco walls painted with bold primary colors and an aged-wash effect. All come with 53-centimeter (21-in.) flatscreen televisions. A relaxing interior courtyard lounge on the second floor is enclosed by a tall brick wall. Interior brick arches and other design touches give this place more charm and class than you'd expect at this price. Be careful, there are two Samay Inn sites in Otavalo—don't head to the one closer to the bus station.

Calle Sucre 1009 and Calle Colón, Otavalo. ✆ **06/2921-826.** samayinn@hotmail.com. 23 units. $20 (£9.75) double. DC, MC, V. Free parking. **Amenities:** Restaurant; bar; tour desk; laundry service. *In room:* TV.

WHERE TO STAY AROUND OTAVALO
VERY EXPENSIVE

Hacienda Cusín 🏨🏨 *Kids* This 17th-century hacienda is a fabulous choice in the Otavalo area, especially if you're looking for a mix of luxury and history. Cusín sits on over 4 hectares (10 acres) of lush gardens and cobblestone courtyards overflowing with bougainvillea, orchids, and palm trees. Rooms are located in the renovated one-story hacienda and come with antique furnishings and high ceilings. The garden cottages are of somewhat recent construction, but have a wonderfully rustic feel; they're scattered throughout the lush grounds and come with working fireplaces and wood bed and armoires. All units have spacious bathrooms with lovely blue tiles. The friendly staff can help you arrange activities, including the popular overnight horseback-riding trip to Volcán Imbabura. Spanish-language classes are also available. There's a computer with Internet access for guests to use at the reception desk. The restaurant serves a wonderful dinner by candlelight so there's no need to leave the property after dark. A full meal plan here will run you $41 (£21) per day.

San Pablo del Lago, Otavalo. ✆ **06/2918-013.** Fax 06/2918-003. www.haciendacusin.com. 42 units. $105 (£53) double; $120 (£60) garden cottage; $250–$300 (£125–£150) suite. Rates include breakfast; suite rates include dinner as well. AE, DC, MC, V. **Amenities:** Restaurant; bar; tour desk; laundry. *In room:* Wi-Fi, no phone.

La Mirage Garden Hotel & Spa 🏨🏨🏨 If you're looking for luxury, you won't find a better hotel in the highlands than this member of the prestigious Relais & Châteaux. All the rooms are essentially suites, with separate sitting areas and fireplaces. Just about every one of them could be featured in the pages of *House & Garden*. Some rooms have brass canopy beds; others have antique wood frames. Crystal chandeliers brighten the rooms, while plush Oriental carpets decorate the floors. The spacious bathrooms come with extra-large showers. Reina Sofía of Spain stayed in stately no. 114, and I'm sure she must have felt right at home. Room no. 109 overlooks a garden with a handful of colorful peacocks. You will surely be spoiled here: Turndown service consists of lighting the fire in your private fireplace and slipping two hot-water bottles in your bed. The spa here was the first one to open in Ecuador and it's a real classic. Indulge in clay baths and body massages, or treat yourself to a full-body purification performed by a local female shaman. The outdoor gardens are also magnificent, as is the fine-dining restaurant.

At the end of Calle 10 de Agosto, Cotacachi. © **800/327-3573** in the U.S. and Canada, or 06/2915-237. Fax 02/ 2915-065. www.mirage.com.ec. 23 units. $250–$280 (£125–£140) double; $300–$700 (£150–£350) suite. DC, MC, V. Rates include breakfast and dinner. **Amenities:** Restaurant; bar; beautiful indoor pool; tennis court; tiny exercise room; full spa services; room service 7:30am–9pm; laundry service. *In room:* TV, hair dryer, safe.

EXPENSIVE

Hacienda Pinsaquí ⭐ *Moments*   Hacienda Pinsaquí is one of the great historic hotels of Ecuador. Simón Bolívar once stayed here. The over-200-year-old hacienda immediately transports you back in time with its antique floors that have the seasoned scent of old wood. The homey smell of well-worn fireplaces permeates the air. The narrow, old-fashioned hallways are filled with flowers fresh from the outdoor gardens. And the rooms are sumptuous; each one is unique, but all have a touch of old-fashioned country elegance. No. 8 has a magnificent canopy bed and beautiful antique furniture, as well as a separate sitting area where you can gaze out onto the property's wonderfully landscaped gardens. This room also has a sunken Jacuzzi tub set near a large window overlooking the gardens. Those in a newer wing but are built to mimic the colonial-era style. Once you leave the comfort of your cozy room, you can walk around the property's gardens or explore the area by horseback—the hotel offers guided riding tours. Superb meals are served in an elegant dining room.

Pan-American Hwy., Km 5, Otavalo. © **06/2946-116** or 09/9727-652. Fax 06/2946-117. www.haciendapinsaqui. com. 30 units. $108 (£54) double. Rates include tax and breakfast. AE, DC, MC, V. **Amenities:** 2 restaurants; bar; tour desk; mountain bike rentals; room service 7am–10pm; laundry service. *In room:* No phone.

INEXPENSIVE

Hacienda Guachala *Value*   Dating to 1580, this claims to be the oldest hacienda in Ecuador. One of the first structures built here was a little chapel, which is still standing, and features a faded fresco from the mid-1700s. It was here that García Moreno, who lived in the hacienda for 7 years, planted the first eucalyptus trees in Ecuador, many of which still flourish on the grounds. The hacienda then passed on to the family of Neptali Bonifaz, the country's first democratically elected president and founder of the Bank of Ecuador. The hacienda remains in the Bonifaz family.

Rooms here are more rustic than those at most of the other converted haciendas, but then again, the prices are substantially lower. All feature wood floors, high ceilings, and rough wood beds and furnishings. Nos. 1 through 10 are slightly newer in feel and comfort. All but two of the rooms feature working fireplaces. There's a small pool under a greenhouse roof, with tropical fruits and flowers planted around it. The hacienda's large church has been converted into a small museum that contains historic photos from the Bonifaz family and some pre-Inca pottery, including huge Cayambe pots. Horseback tours, specializing in nearby archaeological ruins, are offered. To reach this hotel, take the well-marked turnoff near Km 70 on the Pan-American Highway, and head another 2km (1½ miles) along the road to Cangahua.

Km 70 Pan-American Hwy., on the road to Cangahua, Cayambe. © **02/2363-042** or 09/8146-688. Fax 02/2362-426. www.guachala.com. 36 units. $40 (£20) double. AE, DC, MC, V. Free parking. **Amenities:** Restaurant; small, covered pool; tour desk; laundry service. *In room:* No phone.

WHERE TO DINE

In addition to the places listed below, you can treat yourself to some fine dining, with advance reservations, at the restaurant at **La Mirage** (see above) or **Hacienda Cusín** (see above).

If you're looking for somewhere with a view, I suggest dining at a restaurant overlooking Lago San Pablo, a beautiful little lake considered sacred by the local indigenous populations. The restaurant of the **Hostería Puerto Lago** (✆ **06/2920-920;** Lago San Pablo and Pan-American Highway, Km 5/12, Otavalo) sits right on the lake and serves delicious, fresh grilled trout in addition to the usual Ecuadorian and Continental offerings. Almost every table has a lake view with magnificent Volcán Imbabura in the background.

Hotel Ali Shungu 🎕🎕 ECUADORIAN/INTERNATIONAL   The cozy restaurant of this popular hotel is one of the best in the city. Heavy wooden tables are spread around the large central dining room, which features terra-cotta tile floors and a fireplace. Local and regional art and handicrafts serve as decor, and there's a small bar in one corner. The restaurant uses locally grown organic produce whenever possible. The tomato-basil soup is a house specialty and delicious. For a main dish, I recommend the Indian lamb curry or the spinach cheese pie. For lunch you can get excellent sandwiches on homemade bread, or one of their massive hamburgers. Breakfasts are also superb and worth it if you want a change from traditional Ecuadorian morning fare; this is the only place around where you can get fresh waffles with homemade raspberry syrup.

Calles Quito and Miguel Egas. ✆ **06/2920-750.** Reservations recommended. Sandwiches $4.50–$5 (£2.25–£2.50); main courses $6.50–$7.50 (£3.25–£3.75). No credit cards. Daily 7:30am–8:30pm.

Restaurante Mi Otavalito 🎕 *Finds* ECUADORIAN   This lively and popular place is my favorite option for local cuisine. The menu features a wide range of fish, meat, poultry, and specialty items. I especially like the simple grilled trout. For a real value, order the three-course daily special, which costs around $3.50 (£1.75). Tables are spread throughout several rooms connected by arched brick doorways. Some of the walls feature a mix of wood and woven mat paneling. There's a small brick fireplace in the back. During lunch and dinner most days, local bands play Andean folk music—they're working for tips, so don't be stingy.

Calle Sucre, near Calle Morales. ✆ **06/2920-176.** Reservations recommended on weekends. Main courses $4.50–$5.90 (£2.25–£2.95). No credit cards. Daily 8am–10pm.

6 El Oriente 🎕🎕

Lago Agrio: 259km (161 miles) NE of Quito, 674km (418 miles) NE of Guayaquil, 700km (434 miles) NE of Cuenca

The vast territory of Ecuador that stretches from the eastern slopes of the Andes to the border with Peru is known as El Oriente, which means "the east." This area contains over 25% of the nation's territory and is commonly called the Amazon region (Las Amazonas) because the rivers here—created by melting snow from the Andes—flow into the Amazon. The rainforests of El Oriente have been home to Native Americans for thousands of years. Because of the natural barrier formed by the Andes, the people here have lived in almost complete isolation. Some tribes have only had contact with the "outside world" since the 1970s, when oil was discovered. Since then, development has increased dramatically with the construction of new roads by the oil industry. Various tribes inhabit Ecuador's Amazon basin, including the Shuar, Cofán, Huaorani, and Quichua. Their languages and lifestyle are markedly different from that of Ecuadorians on the opposite side of the Andes. When you take a trip to this region, you'll have the opportunity to meet some of the indigenous people, who will share their land with you and teach you some of their age-old secrets, such as how to farm, fish, hunt, or use medicinal herbs and plants.

Fifty-seven percent of all mammals in Ecuador live in the Amazon basin, and more than 15,000 species of plants exist in Ecuador's rainforest. On a trip here, you'll have the chance to see more than 500 different species of tropical birds, as well as freshwater dolphins, monkeys, sloths, anacondas, boas, turtles, and, if you're extremely lucky, the rare and elusive jaguars.

A healthy eco-tourism business has developed here over the past 15 years. Several excellent jungle lodges were built to blend in with the natural environment. Naturalist guides from these lodges take visitors on all sorts of excursions: walks through the forest to learn about the medicinal properties of the local plants; fishing trips to catch piranhas; early morning bird-watching expeditions to see parrots, macaws, and other tropical species; visits to traditional villages; nighttime canoe rides in search of caimans; and outings where you can paddle downriver in an old-fashioned canoe. Just be sure to bring plenty of mosquito repellent!

ESSENTIALS
GETTING THERE
All the jungle lodges listed below arrange their own transportation. Because many of these lodges are extremely isolated and difficult to find, I strongly encourage you to book your trip in advance. Depending on where you're staying, the journey usually involves a commercial flight to Coca, Lago Agrio, or a private landing strip. From there, your lodge will pick you up and take you the rest of the way in a motorized canoe.

ORIENTATION
El Oriente consists of six different provinces, but it is generally divided up into two general areas: the **northern Oriente** and the **southern Oriente.** The geographic distinctions between northern and southern Oriente are of little consequence to most tourists. All the lodges listed below are found in areas of pristine beauty and biological abundance, and are safe for tourists.

JUNGLE LODGES
Trips to the jungle usually last 4 or 5 days. In general, the 4-day trips leave on Friday and return on Monday. The 5-day trips run from Monday through Friday.

In addition to the lodges listed below, I also recommend **Cuyabeno Lodge** ⭐ (www.neotropicturis.com) and **Sacha Lodge** ⭐ (www.sachalodge.com). For a distinct take on this region, book a berth aboard the riverboat **Manatee Amazon Explorer** ⭐ (www.manateeamazonexplorer.com).

Kapawi Ecolodge & Reserve ⭐⭐⭐ Kapawi is an excellent example of sustainable tourism in action. This lodge has been developed with the cooperation and participation of the local Achuar community, who will become the owners in 2011. In the meantime, the current owners—the company Canodros—pays monthly rent for use of the land and provides business and tourism training to the community.

All the structures here were built using traditional methods and environmentally friendly technology. The 20 cabins, which are set on stilts over a black-water lagoon, are rustic, but extremely comfortable, with polished wood floors, thatched roofs, and bamboo walls. After a day of hiking or canoeing, you can relax in a hammock on your own balcony as you gaze down at the river. The bathrooms are small, but the showers have solar-heated hot water (a rarity in the jungle). The food here is delicious.

In addition to the excellent accommodations, the lodge offers well-organized, fun excursions. Two guides—a local from the Achuar community and an English-speaking naturalist—lead the trips, pointing out wildlife and discussing the area's flora. To get you here, the lodge will arrange a private charter flight on a light propeller plane.

On the Río Pastaza, Pastaza province (mailing address: Urbanización Santa Leonor, Manzana 5, Solar 10, Guayaquil). ℂ 800/613-6026 in the U.S. and Canada, or 04/228-5711 in Ecuador. Fax 04/228-7651. www.kapawi.com. 20 units. 4 days/3 nights $650 (£325) per person; 5 days/4 nights $870 (£435) per person; 8 days/7 nights $1,340 (£670) per person. Round-trip airfare from Quito is an additional $224 (£112) per person. Rates are for double occupancy and include accommodations, all meals, all nonalcoholic beverages, guide services, and daily excursions. Rates do not include a $10 (£5) usage fee, given to the Achuar community, or government taxes. Half-price for children under 12. AE, DC, MC, V. **Amenities:** Restaurant; bar; library; laundry service. *In room:* No phone.

Napo Wildlife Center ★★ *Finds* This is the best-run, and most environmentally and socially conscious, of the Rio Napo lodges. A joint venture with the local Añangu Quichua community, the Napo Wildlife Center is actively involved in conservation efforts. The lodge consists of 10 lakefront bungalows, which are quite large and come with one king-size bed in the main living area and a twin-size bed in a small nook separated by a half-wall. The best feature here is the hammock hung on each bungalow's private balcony overlooking the lake. A favorite of bird-watchers, the Napo Wildlife Center's resident guides are excellent. The lodge is very close to two parrot licks—exposed clay riverbanks—where on sunny days you can find hundreds, if not thousands, of parrots of various species gathering to extract salt and other nutrients from the clay. The sight and sound of a parrot lick is not to be missed. The 36m (120-ft.) observation tower is one of the tallest in the area, and there's another, more convenient observation tower just off the bar area. In all, over 560 bird species have been spotted here so far. No motorized vehicles are allowed near the lodge, which is located inside the Yasuni National Park. This means that from Coca it's a 2-hour motorboat ride on the Río Napo, and then either a 2-hour paddle or a 2km (1.2-mile) hike in to the lodge.

On Añangu Lake, off the Lower Río Napo, Coca (Quito office: Calle de las Magnolias 51 y Los Cristantemos, Cumbaya, Quito). ℂ/fax **02/2897-316** reservation office in Quito, or 09/8349-087 cellphone. www.napowildlifecenter.com. 10 units. 4-day/3-night tour $650 (£325) per person; 5-day/4-night tour $795 (£398) per person. Rates include round-trip transportation from and to Coca, all meals and nonalcoholic beverages, daily tours, and taxes. Rates do not include $10 (£5) entrance fee to Yasuni National Park. AE, DC, MC, V. **Amenities:** Restaurant; bar; laundry service. *In room:* No phone.

7 Cuenca ★★

442km (274 miles) S of Quito, 250km (155 miles) SE of Guayaquil, 254km (157 miles) S of Riobamba

Cuenca is Ecuador's third-largest city, but it feels much more like a charming old-world town—with cobblestone streets and a rich collection of colonial-era churches, plazas, and buildings. Before the Spanish arrived here, Cuenca was the second-largest city in the Incan empire (after Cusco). In fact, when the Incas conquered the area, in the late 1400s, the Cañari had already been living here for centuries. The Incas—not unlike what the Spanish would eventually do—used stones from the Cañari structures to build their palaces. In time, these Incan palaces then became the foundations for the city's colonial-era churches and buildings. The **Museo del Banco Central** sits right next to the **Pumapungo** archaeological site, which was an Inca palace. A few blocks away, the **Todos Los Santos** archaeological site literally symbolizes the three

Cuenca

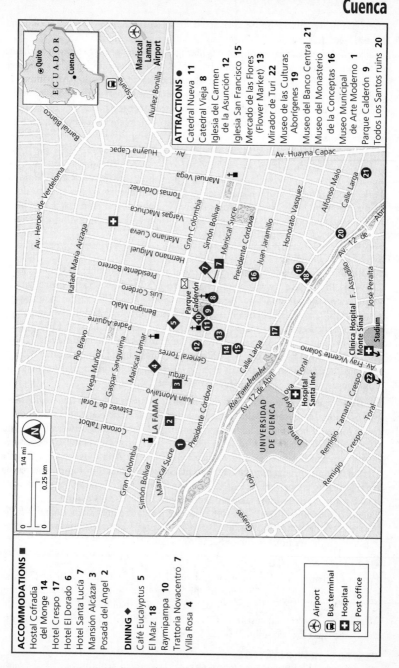

ATTRACTIONS ●
Catedral Nueva **11**
Catedral Vieja **8**
Iglesia del Carmen
 de la Asunción **12**
Iglesia San Francisco **15**
Mercado de las Flores
 (Flower Market) **13**
Mirador de Turi **22**
Museo de las Culturas
 Aborígenes **19**
Museo del Banco Central **21**
Museo del Monasterio
 de la Conceptas **16**
Museo Municipal
 de Arte Moderno **1**
Parque Calderón **9**
Todos Los Santos ruins **20**

ACCOMMODATIONS ■
Hostal Cofradia
 del Monge **14**
Hotel Crespo **17**
Hotel El Dorado **6**
Hotel Santa Lucía **7**
Mansión Alcázar **3**
Posada del Angel **2**

DINING ◆
Café Eucalyptus **5**
El Maíz **18**
Raymipampa **10**
Trattoria Novacentro **7**
Villa Rosa **4**

✈ Airport
🚏 Bus terminal
✚ Hospital
⊠ Post office

layers of history—in one single area, you'll see structures built by Cañari, Incan, and Spanish settlers.

The mysterious Cañari (also spelled Kañari) people were the first known inhabitants of Cuenca, building a city here, around A.D. 500, called Guapondeleg. Their language and customs are largely a mystery, although several nearby villages do have names that end in -*deleg*, a common Cañari suffix. Around 1480 the Cañari were conquered by the Incas, who called the city Tomebamba, which is the current name of one of the rivers that runs through its center. Tomebamba was one of the preferred cities of Incan King Huayna Capac, who spent much time here. But the Incan reign was short-lived—they were vanquished by Pizarro and the Spanish conquistadors in 1534.

Outside Cuenca, there's also plenty to see and do. **Ingapirca,** for example, Ecuador's most impressive Inca ruins, are only 2 hours away; and **Cajas National Park,** which is full of scenic hiking trails and peaceful blue lagoons, is an hour north of the city. If you push yourself, you can visit Cuenca's top sites in just 1 day, but I recommend taking several days to really enjoy the city and its surrounding attractions.

ESSENTIALS
GETTING THERE
BY PLANE **Tame** (© 02/2909-900 central reservation number in Quito, or 07/2889-581 in Cuenca; www.tame.com.ec), **Icaro** (© 1800/883-567 toll-free nationwide; www.icaro.com.ec), and **Aerogal** (© 1800/2376-425 toll-free nationwide; www.aerogal.com.ec) all offer daily flights to Cuenca from both Quito and Guayaquil. One-way tickets cost $45 to $52 (£23–£26) to or from Guayaquil; $55 to $65 (£28–£33) to or from Quito. All planes arrive at the **Aeropuerto Mariscal Lamar** (© 07/2862-203; airport code: CUE), which is located on Avenida España, about 1.6km (1 mile) northeast of downtown. Taxis are always waiting for incoming flights, and a ride from the airport to the center of town costs about $4 (£2).

BY BUS Cuenca is connected to the rest of Ecuador by frequent bus service. Several bus lines leave from Quito's main bus terminal at least every hour, around the clock, for the 9-hour ride. The fare runs around $10 (£5). Buses between Quito and Cuenca stop in Baños and Riobamba along the way. From Guayaquil, a cooperative of five different bus lines takes turns departing from the main bus terminal roughly every half-hour throughout the day. The buses use two different routes, alternating each departure either via Cajas or Cañar. The former route is faster, taking about 4 hours, while the latter route takes around 5 hours. The fare costs around $8 (£4). The Cuenca bus terminal (© 07/2843-888) is on Avenida España, about 1.6km (1 mile) northeast of the center of town, just before the airport. Taxis are always waiting here. A ride from the terminal to the center of town costs about $4 (£2).

GETTING AROUND
Parque Calderón is the commercial and social heart of Cuenca. Most of Cuenca's sights are within walking distance of this main plaza. Still, taxis are abundant in Cuenca. A ride anywhere in town should cost no more than $2 (£1). A ride up to the **Mirador de Turi** should cost from $4 to $5 (£2–£2.50). If you can't flag one down, call **Radio Taxi Patrimonio** (© 07/2853-593).

VISITOR INFORMATION
The main **tourist office** (© 07/2821-035) is located on Mariscal Sucre on the south side of Parque Calderón. The friendly staff can give you maps and help you get your

bearings. But for even better information, you should head to **TerraDiversa** ⚘, on Calle Hermano Miguel, 1½ blocks north of Calle Larga (© **07/2823-782;** www.terra diversa.com); or try **Hualambari Tours** ⚘, Av. Borrero 9–69, next to the post office (© **07/2848-768;** www.hualambari.com). The owners of TerraDiversa are former tour guides who know all of Ecuador like the backs of their hands, while Hualambari is the local representative of Grayline Tours. Both companies can provide a wealth of information and can arrange a wide variety of tours around Cuenca, the region, and the entire country.

FAST FACTS The main **police station** is located on Calle Luis Cordero, near Córdova (© **101**). The main office of the National Police is on Avenida Vallejo and Calle Espejo. You'll find the **post office** on the corner of Borrero and Gran Colombia (© **07/2838-111**). It's open Monday through Friday from 8am to 12:30pm and 2:30 to 6pm, and Saturday from 9am to noon.

Banks and ATMs are abundant in Cuenca and you'll find more than a half-dozen outlets within a block or two of Parque Calderón.

Clínica Hospital Monte Sinai, M. Cordero 6–111 and Avenida Solano (© **07/ 2885-595;** www.hospitalmontesinai.org), is the best hospital in Cuenca. **Fybeca** is a 24-hour pharmacy with several locations, including one at Avenida Huayna Capac 6–15, on the corner of Juan Jaramillo (© **07/2844-501**), and the other on the corner of Gran Colombia and Unidad Nacional (© **07/2839-871**). **Farmacia Los Andes,** at Borrero 7–57 (© **07/2839-029**), is a little closer to the center of town.

Internet cafes are also abundant in Cuenca; two of my favorites are **Hol@net,** located at Borrero 5–90 and Juan Jaramillo (© **07/2843-126**), and **Cuenc@net Café,** on Calle Larga 602 and the corner of Hermano Miguel (© **07/2837-347**). For laundry service, your best and cheapest bet is **La Química Automática,** located at Borrero 7–34, on the corner of Presidente Córdova (© **07/2823-945**).

WHAT TO SEE & DO
PARQUE CALDERON & NEARBY ATTRACTIONS

Parque Calderón is the historical heart of Cuenca and the center of the action. Here you'll find both the Catedral Nueva and the Catedral Vieja. The **Catedral Vieja,** also known as the Iglesia del Sagrario, is the oldest structure in the city. It dates from 1557 and was built over the Inca ruins of Pumapungo. Because cities can't have two cathedrals, once the New Cathedral opened in 1967, the old one went out of business. It was closed to the public when I last visited, although it is scheduled to reopen as a religious art museum sometime in 2008. Construction began on the **Catedral Nueva** ⚘⚘, also known as the Catedral de la Inmaculada Concepción, in 1885, but it wasn't completed for almost another 80 years. It has a mix of styles—Romanesque on the outside with Gothic windows. It is modeled on the Battistero (Baptistery) in Florence. The two massive blue domes are distinctive and visible from various vantage points around the city. The floors are made of white marble imported from Italy, while the stained-glass windows contain a mix of Catholic and indigenous symbols (the sun and the moon, for example). In 1985, when the pope visited this cathedral and saw the Renaissance-style main altar (which is modeled on the one in St. Peter's in Rome), he looked confused and asked, "Am I in Rome?"

Around the corner, on Padre Aguirre and Sucre, is the **Iglesia del Carmen de la Asunción.** The church is not open to the public, but from the outside you should take note of its unique stone entrance and neon-lit altar. The church sits on the delightful and colorful **Mercado de las Flores (Flower Market).** In the early part of the 20th century women weren't allowed to work. To create a diversion for them, the men of the city decided to set up this little market for the use of women only. Nowadays, anyone can wander around the fresh-smelling market. Ecuador is one of the world's largest exporters of flowers, and some beautiful varieties are found here. At the market, you'll find folk remedies for all sorts of illnesses, too. Nearby, on Presidente Córdova and Padre Aguirre, is the **Iglesia y Mercado de San Francisco.**

MUSEUMS & OTHER POINTS OF INTEREST

In addition to the places mentioned below, if you're interested in archaeological finds, stop by the small **Todos Los Santos** (✆ 07/2821-177) archaeological site. Discovered in 1972, the short loop path here takes you through overlapping constructions by the Cañari, Inca, and Spanish cultures. The site is located at the intersection of Calle Large and Avenida Todos Los Santos (a few blocks down from the Museo del Banco Central). When I last visited, the museum had recently been taken over by a university archaeological program, and it wasn't clear if they would begin charging admission. It is currently still free. As you walk the path, you will see the remains of massive Spanish milling stones, alongside an Inca-period wall with four of the style's classic trapezoidal niches, as well as pieces of wall that date to the era of the Cañari. It will only take you about 20 minutes to tour this site.

For a bird's-eye view of Cuenca, take a taxi up to the **Mirador de Turi.** In Quichua, *turi* means twins, and from this sight you can see twin mountains in the distance. A taxi here should cost about $4 to $5 (£2–£2.50) each way. You can—and really should—combine a visit here with a visit to the ceramic gallery **Taller E. Vega** (see below).

Museo del Banco Central ✿✿ (Kids) This massive museum, archaeological site, and botanical gardens is the pride and joy of Cuenca. The museum occupies several floors in a modern building next to the Central Bank building. Exhibits range from rooms filled with colonial and religious artwork, to walk-through re-creations of typical dwellings from the various regions of Ecuador, to an entire numismatic section that chronicles the country's currency from spondylus shells through the now-defunct sucre. The **Tomebamba Hall** ✿ is a highlight. The museum was constructed over the ruins of an Inca palace—Pumapungo—and in this room, you will learn the history of the Incas in Cuenca, as well as see archaeological artifacts found in the area. Afterwards, you can exit and walk behind the museum to see the actual archaeological site, which has a few llamas wandering around it. The complex is set on a high hillside, from which the views are wonderful. In addition to the Inca archaeological excavations, the Museo del Banco Central has recently added some beautiful botanical gardens and a small aviary. This museum complex is huge, and you really need 2 to 3 hours to see it. Groups of more than four people can ask for a free bilingual guide.

Calle Larga and Av. Huayna Capac. ✆ 07/2831-255. Admission $3 (£1.50) adults, $1.50 (75p) children 6–18, children under 6 free. Mon–Fri 9am–6pm; Sat 9am–1pm.

Museo de las Culturas Aborígenes ✿ This amazing private collection includes more than 8,000 Ecuadorian archaeological pieces dating as far back as 500 B.C. Some of the most interesting are the pre-Inca urns that were used to bury the dead in an upright position, and the flutes made from the bones of different animals. The collection ranges far and wide, with works by the Valdivia, Machalilla, Tolita, Yasuni, and Quitis peoples. Near the entrance, there's an excellent gift shop and a pleasant little courtyard cafe and bakery.

Av. 10 de Agosto 4–70 and Rafael Torres Beltrán. © 07/2880-010. Admission $2 (£1). Mon–Fri 8:30am–noon and 1–6pm, Sat 8:30am–12:30pm.

Museo del Monasterio de la Conceptas ⭐

This small museum was a former monastery. The nuns' rooms and common areas of the two-story adobe structure, which dates to the 17th century, are now all wonderfully curated art galleries; the theme is religious art. One of the highlights is an impressive collection of gruesome crucifixes by local artist Gaspar Sangurima. In one of these sculptures, you can see the carved heart through the gaping wounds in Christ's chest. The central courtyard is lushly planted and features a cherimoya tree that bears fruit each fall. Don't miss visiting the back patios, where you'll find the monastery's kitchen, as well as the old indoor cemetery with empty burial crypts.

Calle Hermano Miguel 6–33, between Presidente Córdova and Juan Jaramillo. © 07/2830-625. Admission $2.50 (£1.25), children 8–18 $1.50 (75p). Mon–Fri 9am–5:30pm; Sat–Sun and holidays 10am–1pm.

Museo Municipal de Arte Moderno

Art and sculpture adorn the many rooms and hallways of this old adobe home. It's hard to predict what type of art you'll see when you visit this museum—there are no permanent exhibits. But the museum does display the best of Ecuadorian modern art—previous shows have included works by Guayasamín, Tábara, and Oswaldo Muñoz Mariño. The museum is also famous for hosting the Bienal Internacional de Pintura, a biannual exposition of Ecuadorian and American art. Even if you're not an art-lover, it's nice to come here and relax in the peaceful colonial courtyard.

Calle Sucre 1527 and Coronel Tálbot. © 07/2831-027. Free admission. Mon–Fri 8:30am–1pm and 3–6:30pm; Sat 9am–1pm.

SPORTS & OUTDOOR ACTIVITIES

Cuenca may be Ecuador's third-largest city, but if you venture just a few miles outside the city center, you'll find yourself at one with nature. For the best hiking in the area, head to **Cajas National Park** (see "Side Trips from Cuenca," later in this chapter). **Hualambari Tours** ⭐ (© 07/2848-768; www.hualambari.com) and **TerraDiversa** ⭐ (© 07/2823-782; www.terradiversa.com) both offer horseback-riding and mountain-biking expeditions through the outlying mountains and forests, stopping at small towns along the way. Day trips run $40 to $80 (£20–£40) per person, including lunch, equipment, and transportation. Multiday trips and expeditions can also be arranged.

SHOPPING

Cuenca is a shopper's paradise. Ceramics and Panama hats are the best buys here, but, in general, you can find an excellent selection of folksy handicrafts, as well as some higher-end art and ceramic works.

ARTS & HANDICRAFTS Walk down any street in the center of Cuenca and you are sure to find scads of stores specializing in handmade crafts. **Tejemujeres** ⭐, on Hermano Miguel and Presidente Córdova (© 07/2839-676), sells beautiful hand-crafted sweaters. **Galería de Arte 670,** at Hermano Miguel 6–70 (© 07/2845-631), showcases works of local artists. I also especially like **Arte con Sabor a Café** ⭐ (© 07/2849-828), a gallery and coffee shop with a good rotating selection of local art works and crafts; it's located down by the river, on Paseo 3 de Noviembre 1–48 and Coronel Talbot. In the evenings, this place sometimes has live music.

CERAMICS For hundreds of years, Cuenca has been a center for ceramics. Walk into any museum in the area (see above), and you'll see examples of beautiful pre-Inca jugs and vases. **Artesa** ★★, at the corner of Gran Colombia and Luis Cordero (① 07/2842-647), keeps the tradition alive. This is the best place in the city for hand-painted ceramics.

For a more personalized experience, I recommend visiting **Taller E. Vega** ★★ (① 07/2881-407), located just below the Mirador de Turi. Eduardo Vega is a cerami-cist and one of Ecuador's most famous artists. Monumental ceramic sculptures and murals by Vega can be found around Cuenca, as well as in Quito. A visit to his hill-side workshop and gallery is worthwhile just for the views, but you'll also have a chance to glimpse a bit of his production process, and to buy from his regularly chang-ing collection of decorative and functional works, handicrafts, and wonderful jewelry. Most organized city tours stop here. If you're coming to Taller E. Vega on your own, I recommend calling in advance to be sure it's open.

PANAMA HATS   You may be surprised to know that Panama hats have always been made in Ecuador: For generations, the people on the coast have been using local straw to create finely woven hats. The trade was moved inland, and Cuenca is now the major hub for the production of Panama hats. **Homero Ortega P. & Hijos** ★★★ makes the highest quality Panama hats in the world; patrons include the queen of England. You can visit the factory and learn how the hats are made, and afterwards you can browse in the elegant boutique. The store is located a few minutes outside the center of town, at Av. Gil Ramírez Dávalo 3–86 (① 07/2809-000; www.homeroortega.com). **Som-breros Barranco,** at Calle Larga 10–41, between General Torres and Padre Aguirre (① 07/2831-569); and **K. Dorfzaun** ★, Av. Gil Ramírez Cávalos 4–34 (① 07/2807-563; www.kdorfzaun.com), also sell finely crafted hats. Panama hats in Cuenca vary greatly in price and quality, running from around $10 to $12 (£5–£6) for a basic ver-sion, to around $150 to $250 (£75–£125) for a *super fino.* That *super fino,* though, may cost over $1,000 (£500) in a boutique shop in New York, Los Angeles, or London.

WHERE TO STAY
EXPENSIVE
Hotel El Dorado ★★   The El Dorado is bold and brash, and quite a contrast to the rest of colonial Cuenca. A glass-and-steel staircase leads up to the rooms, and several waterfalls are scattered around the building. The rooms—all spacious and well lit, have a clean and minimalist decor. Some units on the higher floors have good views. I like no. 512, which has a view of the cathedral dome. The presidential suite is a two-room affair with a Jacuzzi tub, glass sinks and elegant bathroom fixtures, a Zen-style water fountain on the writing desk, and a small Buddha sculpture on the bureau. Sev-eral floors have been designated smoke-free, and there's one very well set up room for travelers with disabilities. The entire building has free Wi-Fi access. There's a small spa here, too, which covers the necessary bases, but isn't quite as large or well equipped as I would have expected. On the ground floor is a large, chic restaurant with nothing but full-length walls of glass separating it from the busy sidewalk outside.

Gran Colombia 7–87 and Luis Cordero, Cuenca. ① 07/2831-390. Fax 07/2831-663. www.eldoradohotel.com.ec. 42 units. $100 (£50) double; $125 (£63) junior suite; $160 (£80) presidential suite. Rates include buffet breakfast. AE, DC MC, V. Free parking. **Amenities:** Restaurant; bar; small, well-equipped health club; sauna; steam room; 24-hr. busi-ness center; room service 6am–11pm; massage; babysitting; laundry service; smoke-free rooms. *In room:* TV, free Wi-Fi, minibar, hair dryer, safe.

Mansión Alcázar ★★   This is an elegant oasis in the heart of Cuenca, a meticu-lously renovated 1870s house that once belonged to the president of Ecuador. Behind a large gate you'll enter into a world of old colonial living. A beautifully tiled enclosed courtyard with a fountain leads to plush accommodations on two floors. Out back there's a lovely garden ringed with palm trees and filled with lavender and rose bushes. Each room is unique in size and decor, but they all have one thing in common: Every piece of furniture was made in Cuenca. Elegant antiques and fine objets d'art give the rooms that old colonial feel. The suites have wrought-iron four-poster beds; no. 207 has a mural of angels on its ceiling, but no. 202 is my favorite, with a view over the garden. Bathrooms have Cuencan marble and each one has distinctly hand-painted walls. I think it's worth the splurge for one of the suites, as several of the standard rooms, especially those on the first floor, are quite small. The beautiful dining area overlooks the garden and there are a few tables outside for alfresco dining on warm days.

Calle Bolívar 12–55 and Tarqui, Cuenca. ℂ 800/327-3573 toll-free in the U.S. and Canada, or 07/2823-918 in Ecuador. Fax 07/2823-554. www.mansionalcazar.com. 14 units. $110 (£55) double; $160 (£80) suite. Rates include full breakfast and afternoon tea. AE, DC, MC, V. Free parking. **Amenities:** Restaurant; bar; lounge; room service 7am–10:30pm; laundry service. *In room:* TV, free Wi-Fi, hair dryer, safe.

MODERATE

Hotel Crespo   The building housing this classic Cuenca hotel is more than 140 years old, and built on the steep hillside leading down to the Río Tomebamba. The rambling structure covers some five stories, and there's no elevator, so ask for a room close to the lobby if climbing several flights is a problem for you. The rooms have an old-fashioned charm, with wood paneling, classic green walls, dark furniture, and colorful hand-painted moldings, although some feel a bit dated in their furnishings and decor. The ceilings are charming, too—they are designed to look like antique tin ceilings. The nice bathrooms feature marble tiles, lots of counter space, and a second telephone. The best rooms have views of the river down below. Room no. 408 is my favorite—it has both river and mountain views. Overall, this is a good choice but not nearly as elegant or as intimate as Mansión Alcázar (see above) or the Santa Lucía (see below). These folks will cover your cab fare to and from the airport, if you ask.

Calle Larga 7–93, Cuenca. ℂ 07/2842-571. Fax 07/2839-473. www.hotel-crespo.com. 39 units. $76 (£38) double. Rates include full breakfast. AE, DC MC, V. **Amenities:** Restaurant; bar; tour desk; business center; room service 7am–3pm and 7–10pm; laundry service; free Wi-Fi. *In room:* TV, minibar, hair dryer.

Hotel Santa Lucía ★★★ *Finds*   Several years ago the Hotel Santa Lucía was awarded the prize of "best restoration of a historical building" by the city of Cuenca. What you can expect here is meticulous attention to detail—in both the decor and the service. The owner hails from an old Cuenca family and he will go out of his way to make sure your stay is as exquisite as possible. The large, enclosed courtyard, which contains a 100-year-old magnolia tree and beautiful baby palms, leads to spacious, comfortable accommodations. Rooms, which have the amenities of a large, luxury hotel, include plasma-screen televisions, and the suites have sleeping lofts, hardwood floors, and Persian carpets. Room no. 212 has a view of the cathedral and a small, private balcony overlooking the street. All but four of the spacious bathrooms have tubs, and many feature luxurious multiheaded spa showers. On the second floor, there's a huge private salon with a fireplace for guests to gather around; antiques adorn the hallways and fresh flowers are arranged daily. The entire complex has free Wi-Fi. The airy Trattoria Novacentro (see below), in the courtyard, serves authentic Italian cuisine, while the cozy street-side **Bacchus Café** is very popular for its inexpensive Ecuadorian meals.

Antonio Borrero 8–44 and Sucre, Cuenca. ℂ 07/2828-000. Fax 07/2842-443. www.santaluciahotel.com. 20 units. $83 (£42) double; $110 (£55) suite. Rates include full breakfast and tax. AE, DC, MC, V. Parking nearby. **Amenities:**

2 restaurants; lounge; room service 7am–10:30pm; tour desk; laundry service; dry cleaning. *In room:* TV, free Wi-Fi, minibar, hair dryer, safe.

INEXPENSIVE

In addition to the place listed below, the **Hostal Cofradia del Monge** (✆/fax 07/ 2831-251; cofradiadelmonje@hotmail.com) is an excellent boutique option just across from the Plaza San Francisco.

Posada del Angel *Value*   If you're looking for a bit of colonial charm with artistic touches—all at budget prices—then this is the hotel for you. After an extensive renovation of the 120-year-old large colonial house, the Posada del Angel is a whimsical, airy place. Bright yellow and blue are the themes here. You enter through a large enclosed courtyard, and most of the rooms, which come in all shapes and sizes, are found around the first two floors. All are simply furnished and very clean, and all but three have beautiful hardwood floors. Some rooms have wrought-iron lamps made in Cuenca and attractive wooden armoires. The tiled bathrooms are tiny but sparkling. If you're looking for some privacy, ask for one of the remote rooms located on the third or fourth floors. Free Internet access at a few computers is available for guests in the lobby. Several lounge areas and covered courtyards are spread around the rambling structure.

Bolívar 14–11 and Estévez de Toral, Cuenca. ✆ 07/2840-695. ✆/fax 07/2821-360. www.hostalposadadelangel. com. 17 units. $35–$45 (£18–£23) double. Rates include full breakfast. MC, V. Free parking. **Amenities:** Lounge; laundry service; Internet access. *In room:* TV.

WHERE TO DINE

Cuenca has excellent restaurants, inviting cafes, and wonderful bakeries so you'll eat well here. In addition to the places listed below, there's plenty of street food available all over town. You'll see *cuy* (guinea pig) and whole pigs on spits, or recently roasted, as well as empanadas and *llapingachos,* all for sale by street vendors. While not an option for those with sensitive stomachs, if you've got a sturdy intestinal tract, this is a tasty and inexpensive way to go.

MODERATE

In addition to the places below, I enjoy the fine Italian cuisine served up at **Trattoria Novacentro** 🐒🐒 (✆ 07/2828-000) in a refined and romantic setting inside the Hotel Santa Lucía (see above).

Villa Rosa 🐒🐒🐒 *Finds* ECUADORIAN/INTERNATIONAL   The loveliest restaurant in Cuenca is owned and managed by the friendly Berta Vintimilla. The setting is divine: the enclosed courtyard of an old Cuencan home elegantly restored. Marble floors, crisp white tablecloths, and comfortable wooden chairs give the space a European air, but the creative cuisine has its roots in Ecuador. Mrs. Vintimilla bakes the delicious empanadas herself and the recipes for many of the Ecuadorian specials come from her family. If you're in the mood for something really hearty, try the amazingly good *locro de papas* (potato soup served with a slice of avocado). Main courses include sea bass with crab sauce served with rice and vegetables, tenderloin of beef, jumbo langoustines with fennel, and a variety of daily specials. The service is excellent, the wine list is reasonable, and every ingredient used in the kitchen is of the highest quality. Note that the restaurant is closed on weekends, except for groups of a substantial size who have made prior reservations.

Gran Colombia 12–22 and Tarqui. ✆ 07/2837-944. Reservations recommended. Main courses $5–$14 (£2.50–£7). AE, DC, MC, V. Mon–Fri noon–3pm and 7–10:30pm.

INEXPENSIVE

Café Eucalyptus ★★ *Finds* TAPAS/INTERNATIONAL   This is Cuenca's hippest and most happening restaurant and bar. The city's young and chic flock here to gather for drinks and appetizers. There's seating on two floors—head upstairs if you want to find a somewhat quieter table, or stick to the main floor and bar area to people-watch and mingle. The food here is tapas-style and tapas-sized; most folks order several and share them. Selections are truly international (more than 50 dishes from 20 different countries) and include hot Cuban sandwiches, cheese quesadillas, pad Thai, French bread with tapenade, and stuffed peppers with rice, raisins, and parsley. This is the only place in the city to offer sushi and sashimi, although the rest of their menu is much better. The call liquor and wine lists are quite impressive, and a number of wine choices are available by the glass. Eucalyptus also has the only draft beer in the city, including Llama Negra, which is made in Quito and is a dark stout beer like a Guinness.

Gran Colombia 9–41 and Benigno Malo. ☎ 07/2849-157. Tapas $4.50–$10 (£2.25–£5). AE, DC, MC, V. Sun, Tues–Thurs 11am–midnight; Fri–Sat 11am–1am.

El Maíz ★ ECUADORIAN   Set in a beautifully renovated old house, with a lovely outdoor patio for alfresco dining, this is a great place to come for local cooking. There are actually two outdoor seating areas: a lower patio, with colorful tiles, overlooking a courtyard full of plants, and an upper terrace with a lovely view of the green hills. The indoor dining room features wood floors and red tablecloths. Appetizers include the usual offerings of *humitas,* empanadas, and *locro de papas.* The main courses are terrific and unique. My favorites include the chicken in pumpkinseed and white-wine sauce, beef medallions in a pear sauce, and *hornado cuencano* (roasted pork served with *llapingachos*—mashed potatoes with cheese). Rotating monthly specials are tied to national holidays and celebrations. For dessert, try the *almíbar de babaco* (a compote of a local fruit, tart and sweet).

Calle Larga 1–279 and Calle de los Molinos. ☎ 07/2840-224. Main courses $4.50–$6 (£2.25–£3). MC, V. Mon–Sat noon–9pm.

Raymipampa ★ *Value* ECUADORIAN/CUENCAN   This popular local institution is located right next to the new cathedral. The cozy dining room features a loft area with tables under a low ceiling made of exposed log beams over much of the main dining area. The walls feature imitation baroque bas-reliefs. I like grabbing a table near the front windows, which have a view of Parque Calderón. The menu features a range of meat, poultry, and seafood. You can also get traditional Ecuadorian fare, such as *humitas* and *tamales de maíz.* I like the complete breakfast, which is an excellent deal at $2 (£1), including coffee, fresh juice, two eggs, two fresh-baked croissants, and local cheese. Broken plates and bent silverware have been fashioned into an interesting little sculpture hanging near the entrance.

Benigno Malo 8–59, between Sucre and Bolívar. ☎ 07/2824-169. Reservations not accepted. Main courses $3.50–$6 (£1.75–£3). MC, V. Daily 8:30am–11pm.

CUENCA AFTER DARK

Cuenca used to be a sleepy, provincial city, but in recent years local young people and visiting tourists have turned this into a respectable little party city. For quiet drinking and conversation, **Wunderbar Café** ★★, right off the stairs below Calle Larga and Hermano Miguel, and **El Cafecito,** at Honorato Vásquez 7–36, are both popular spots. Early birds will appreciate the Wunderbar Café's happy hour, which begins at 11am and runs until 7pm. For live music, head to the **San Angel** ★, on Hermano

Miguel at the corner of Presidente Córdova, or **Blanco & Tinto,** on Av. José Peralta 2–132 and Cordero. The 20- and 30-something who's-who of Cuenca gather at **Eucalyptus** ✱✱ (see "Where to Dine," above), which has a popular Ladies' Night every Wednesday and a rowdy salsa night every Saturday. If you're looking to go dancing, **La Fábrica** ✱, on Presidente Córdova and Manuel Vega, is one of the best nightclubs in town, and **La Mesa Salsoteca** ✱, on Gran Colombia between Machuca and Ordóñez, is the best place in town for salsa. Other good spots for mingling with the local crowd include **Tal Cual,** next to the Hotel Crespo (p. 571), and **Tinku** ✱, on Calle Larga at the corner of Alfonso Jerves.

Note: Many venues are only open Wednesday to Saturday. Sunday, Monday, and Tuesday are very quiet nights in Cuenca and hardly anybody ventures out late. Covers are sometimes charged and usually range from $2 to $5 (£1–£2.50), which may include a drink or two.

SIDE TRIPS FROM CUENCA

Hualambari Tours ✱ (© 07/2848-768; www.hualambari.com), **TerraDiversa** ✱ (© 07/2823-782; www.terradiversa.com), and **Metropolitan Touring** (© 07/2837-000; www.metropolitan-touring.com) all offer a wide range of day trips out of Cuenca, including trips to the two attractions listed below.

PARQUE NACIONAL CAJAS (CAJAS NATIONAL PARK) ✱✱

After you've seen the museums and historic sights in Cuenca, it's great to get away from the city and immerse yourself in the area's natural wonders. Cajas is only about 32km (20 miles) west of the city (about a 1-hr. drive), but it feels worlds away. Covering about 29,000 hectares (71,630 acres), the park has 232 lakes. The terrain and ecosystems are varied here, allowing for an impressive variety of flora and fauna. In high-elevation cloud forests, bird species range from the masked trogon and gray-breasted mountain toucan, to the majestic Andean condor. The famed Inca Trail runs right through the park. One of my favorite hikes is up **Tres Cruces,** which offers spectacular views of the area and the opportunity to see the Continental Divide. I also recommend the hike around Laguna Quinoa Pato; the vistas of the lake are impressive, and as you walk on the trails you'll have a good chance of spotting ducks. From the main visitor center, you can explore the flora of the humid mountain-forest climate—mosses, orchids, fungi, and epiphytes are common. *Note:* It can get extremely cold here, so wear warm clothing.

GETTING THERE & VISITING THE PARK   Cajas is huge and much of its wildlife is elusive. I highly recommend exploring the park with a guide. Both Hualambari and TerraDiversa (see above) have excellent naturalist guides. If you want to go on your own, head to the main terminal in Cuenca and catch any Guayaquil-bound bus that takes the route via Molleturo and Cajas. These buses leave roughly every hour throughout the day. Ask to be dropped off at La Toreadora. Return buses run on a similar schedule and are easy to catch from the main road outside the visitor center. Admission to the park is $10 (£5) for adults, $5 (£2.50) for children under 12. If you have any questions, call the park office (© 07/2829-853).

INGAPIRCA ✱

Ingapirca is the largest pre-Columbian architectural complex in Ecuador. However, anyone familiar with the massive ruins of Machu Picchu or of the Mesoamerican Maya will find this site small and simple by comparison. The Incas arrived here around 1470. Before then, the Cañari people had inhabited the area. It's believed that both the Cañari and Incas used Ingapirca as a religious site. When the Incas conquered the area, they ordered all Cañari men to move to Cuzco. In the meantime, Inca men took up residence with Cañari women, as a means of imposing Inca beliefs on the local culture. In the end, Ingapirca, shows a mix of Cañari and Inca influences. For example, many of the structures here are round or oval-shaped, which is very atypical of the Incas. In fact, Ingapirca is home to the only oval-shaped sacred Inca palace in the world.

Ingapirca means "the wall of the Inca," and you can see some fine examples of the famed Inca masonry here. The highlight of the site is **El Adoratorio/Castillo,** an elliptical structure which is believed to be a temple to the sun. Nearby are the **Aposentos,** rooms made with tight stonework, thought to have been used by the high priests. Most of the remains from the Cañari culture have been found at **Pilaloma,** at the south end of the site (near where you first enter). Pilaloma means "small hill," and some archaeologists surmise that this was a sacred spot, especially because it is the highest point in the area. Eleven bodies (mostly of women) have been found here—perhaps the circle of stones was some sort of tomb. On a hill behind the entrance, near the parking area, is a small museum with a relief map of the site and a collection of artifacts and relics found here.

This site is administered and run by the local community. Llamas graze among the archaeological ruins. If you're lucky enough to visit before or after the large tour buses arrive, you'll find the place has a very peaceful vibe to it.

GETTING THERE   The site (☎ 07/2215-115) is open daily from 8am to 6pm; admission is $6 (£3). It's best to visit Ingapirca with an experienced guide because most of the resident guides here do not speak English, and all the explanations inside the museum are in Spanish only. A full-day trip to Ingapirca out of Cuenca, including transportation, lunch, and guided tour of the ruins, but not the admission fee, should cost $30 to $45 (£15–£23). If you want to go to Ingapirca on your own, catch a bus from the main bus terminal in Cuenca. **Cooperativa Cañar** (☎ 07/2844-033) operates buses that stop at the site; they depart at 9am and 1pm, and the 2-hour ride costs $3 (£1.50) each way. The return buses leave Ingapirca at 1 and 4pm.

8 Guayaquil

250km (155 miles) NW of Cuenca; 420km (260 miles) SW of Quito; 966km (618 miles) east of the Galápagos

Guayaquil is Ecuador's most populous and vibrant city. Still, most visitors to Ecuador only look upon Guayaquil as a necessary overnight stop on the way to the Galápagos Islands. But that is changing, and the city continues to reinvent itself at a dizzying pace. At the helm since 2000, Mayor Jaime Nebot has instituted a far-reaching urban renewal project that has already had impressive results. The **Malecón 2000,** the city's main riverfront promenade, and **Cerro Santa Ana (Santa Ana Hill)** are emblematic of Nebot's plan. Whereas crime was once rampant and problematic, Guayaquil is now a relatively safe and tourist-friendly city. Perhaps the city's greatest challenge facing visitors is the sometimes oppressive heat and humidity. Nevertheless, if you avoid the midday heat, you'll find the early mornings, late afternoons, and evenings all very agreeable for taking in the city's pleasures.

Although Guayaquil was founded in 1537, it lacks the colonial architecture that you find in Quito and Cuenca. A devastating fire ravaged the city in 1896, almost completely leveling it. Virtually no buildings escaped the blaze, and today the city has a more modern and contemporary feel than any other major city in Ecuador.

ESSENTIALS
GETTING THERE
BY PLANE All international and national flights arrive at the new **José Joaquín de Olmedo International Airport** (© **04/2169-209;** airport code: GYE), which is located about 10 minutes north of downtown Guayaquil, just next door to the now-defunct Simón Bolívar International Airport. Many international flights to Quito first touch down in Guayaquil, and outgoing international flights often similarly stop in Guayaquil to pick up and discharge passengers. *Tip:* Feel free to break out your laptop or PDA—the new airport provides free wireless connections throughout the terminal.

Tame (© **02/2909-900** in Quito, or 04/2310-305 in Guayaquil; www.tame.com.ec), **Icaro** (© **1800/883-567** toll-free; www.icaro.com.ec), and **Aerogal** (© **1800/2376-425** toll-free; www.aerogal.com.ec) all offer daily flights between Guayaquil and both Quito and Cuenca. One-way tickets range from $55 to $66 (£28–£33) to or from Quito, and from $45 to $52 (£23–£26) to or from Cuenca.

As you exit the Customs area in the international arrivals area, there is a desk with friendly staff who will arrange a taxi for you. You pay at the desk and receive a voucher, which you then present to a driver, who will be waiting for you once you exit the terminal. A taxi to the downtown area should cost no more than $8 (£4).

BY BUS The bus station, **Terminal Terrestre** (© **04/2140-166**), is a few minutes north of the airport. From Quito, buses leave the main terminal (Terminal Terrestre) at least every half-hour for Guayaquil; the 8-hour ride costs $10 (£5). Buses from Cuenca leave on a very frequent schedule as well; the 5-hour bus ride costs $8 (£4).

GETTING AROUND
Guayaquil is a compact city, and it's easy to walk most places around the downtown and Malecón 2000. However, a fair amount of the hotels, shopping centers, and restaurants are located outside of the downtown area. In Guayaquil, taxis are the cheapest and most efficient way to get around. It's easy to find them on any street corner. If you can't flag one down, call **Cooperativa de Taxis Bucaram** (© **04/2403-592**), **Cooperativa de Taxis Centro Cívico** (© **04/2450-145**), or **Cooperativa de Taxis Paraíso** (© **04/2201-877**). Rides within the center of the city cost only $2 to $4 (£1–£2).

VISITOR INFORMATION
The Ministry of Tourism runs a **tourist information office** (© **04/2568-764**) on Pedro Icaza 203, between Pedro Carbo and Panamá, on the sixth floor. The office is open Monday through Friday from 8:30am to 5pm, and provides a city map as well as other useful information on tours and attractions. The city itself maintains an excellent website, crammed with information, at **www.visitaguayaquil.com**.

FAST FACTS In an **emergency**, dial © **911.** To dial the **police** call © **101,** and for the **Cruz Roja (Red Cross)** © **131.**

Most banks in Guayaquil are clustered around the intersection of Pedro Icaza and General Córdova; you'll find branches of **Banco del Pichincha** and **Banco de Guayaquil** here. You'll also find ATMs all over the city and in all the modern malls and shopping centers. The local **American Express** office is run by **Global Tours**

ACCOMMODATIONS■
Hampton Inn **4**
Hotel Oro Verde Guayaquil **12**
UniPark Hotel **3**

DINING◆
El Vigia **9**
La Canoa **2**
Resaca **7**

ATTRACTIONS●
Cementerio General **10**
Cerro Santa Ana **9**
Malecón 2000 **6**
Museo Antropológico y
    de Arte Contemporáneo **8**
Museo Arqueológico
    del Banco del Pacífico **5**
Parque Centenario **11**
Parque Seminario **1**

(℃ **04/2680-450**) in the Edificio Las Cámaras, on Avenida Francisco de Orellana and Alcívar. The main **post office** is located on Clemente Ballén and Pedro Carbo.

The best hospital in Guayaquil is the **Hospital Clínica Kennedy** (℃ **04/2286-963**), located north of the city in the Mall Policentro on Avenida del Periodista; the hospital runs a 24-hour pharmacy. There are scores of other pharmacies around town. The chain **Pharmacy's** (℃ **1800/9090-909**) has various outlets, is open 24 hours, and offers delivery.

There are scores of Internet cafes in Guayaquil. Rates run around 50¢ to $1.50 (25p–75p) per hour. Many city hotels also provide reasonably priced or complimentary Internet connections.

WHAT TO SEE & DO

If you're short on time, it's still possible to get a feel for Guayaquil rather quickly, since the important attractions are quite close together (see "If You're Short on Time," below, for more information).

The **Malecón 2000 (Dos Mil)** ⟅⟅ is the shining star of the new and improved Guayaquil. It's impressive to enter the Malecón 2000 from Avenida 9 de Octubre, where you are greeted by a 1937 statue of the independence heroes Simón Bolívar and San Martín shaking hands. On either side of the statue, you can climb up lookout

If You're Short on Time

Many visitors find themselves with only a few hours in Guayaquil as they connect to or from the Galápagos. If you fall into that category, don't despair: You can still get a good feel for the city in just a few hours.

Grab a cab (or walk, if you're close) from your hotel to the Malecón 2000. The Malecón area is ideally enjoyed on foot, so prepare yourself for a good 3.2km (2-mile) hike and bring protection from the sun. It's best to begin at the southern end, the corner of the Malecón and Avenida Olmedo. Here you can browse the shops selling local artifacts, and the boardwalk is breezy and airy on this end. As you walk north, you'll find many food shops (and more people). Take a break halfway; most of the food stalls here sell freshly squeezed juice that makes an excellent pick-me-up; small bottles of water are also readily available and there are impressively clean public restrooms here, too. At the end of the Malecón, just past the MAAC (see below), you'll find **Las Peñas** neighborhood—a narrow street filled with art galleries and funky shops. After you walk around Las Peñas, climb to the top of **Cerro Santa Ana** 𝕲𝕲 (see below) to get a fantastic view of the entire city, the river, and the surrounding countryside. You'll find many places to eat and drink on the stairs leading up to the top. This is one of the city's safest areas, with specially trained tourist police patrolling the stairs day and night.

towers, which afford great views of the city and the river. Walk south and you'll hit the Moorish Clock Tower, Glorious Aurora's Obelisk, a McDonald's, a mini-mall, and tons of inexpensive food stalls. As you head in this direction, look across the street: You'll see the impressive neoclassical Palacio Municipal. If you walk north from the Bolívar-Martín statue, you'll come across a lively playground and an exercise course.

On the western end of Avenida 9 de Octubre is a separate, newer riverside promenade, along the narrow Estero Salado (Salt Water Estuary), known appropriately as the **Malecón del Estero Salado** 𝕲. Like its more extravagant brethren, the Malecón here is a pleasant riverside pedestrian walkway sprinkled with little parks and plazas, benches for resting, and a few restaurants, shops, and food stands.

In addition to the Malecón 2000, Malecón Salado, and attractions listed below, you can visit a few parks and an interesting cemetery. **Parque Seminario** 𝕲 dates from 1880 and is adjacent to the city's principal church, a neo-Gothic cathedral whose most recent and primary construction dates from 1948. Parque Seminario is also called "Iguana Park" because a healthy population of these prehistoric-looking reptiles inhabit its trees and grounds. Much larger, **Parque Centenario** is in the middle of the city, bisected by Avenida 9 de Octubre. This park is a very popular lunchtime spot for downtown workers and is a pleasant place to relax and people-watch.

One good way to get a feel for the city is to hop on one of the red double-decker tourist buses run by **Guayaquil Vision** (© 04/2885-800; www.guayaquilvision. com). These folks offer several options, including a 1½-hour loop around and through the city, passing its most important landmarks, as well as a 3-hour Gran Guayaquil tour, which makes three stops for visits at Las Peñas neighborhood, Parque Seminario, and the handicraft market. Fares run around $5 (£2.50) for adults, $3 (£1.50) for children, students, and seniors, for the basic loop trip; and $15 (£7.50) adults, $12 (£6) children, students, and seniors for the Gran Guayaquil tour.

Museo Antropológico y de Arte Contemporáneo (Museum of Anthropology and Contemporary Art) ★★

Commanding a spectacular location on the tip of the Malecón, this large and impressive museum is known locally as the MAAC. It focuses on the archaeological finds from around Ecuador (including some relatively recent discoveries from the coastal regions). However, one wing is dedicated to a large collection of Ecuadorian contemporary art, as well as to a smattering of international artists. Constantly changing temporary exhibits focus on local contemporary artists—usually accompanied by short films about those artists, which are quite interesting and worth your while. There are also a library, a bookstore, and a pleasant cafe. It will take you about 2 hours to visit the museum, though plan to spend a little longer if you are interested in the archaeological finds and the films about the artists.

Malecón Simón Bolívar and Calle Loja. ℂ 04/2327-402. Admission $3 (£1.50) adults, $1 (50p) children. Tues–Sat 10am–5:30pm; Sun 10am–4pm.

Museo Arqueológico del Banco del Pacífico ★

This museum runs a close second to the MAAC as my favorite museum in Guayaquil. The museum is small, but it does a good job of showing what life must have been like in the coastal areas of Ecuador thousands of years before Europeans arrived there. You will learn about food, clothing, tools, music, and the use of hallucinogenic drugs in pre-Columbian cultures. The most interesting artifacts come from the Chorrera Period (1000–300 B.C.). Keep an eye out for the double-chambered whistling bottle and the descriptive figurines from this period.

Calle Pedro Icaza 113 and Calle Pichincha. ℂ 04/2566-010. Free admission. Mon–Fri 9am–6pm; Sat–Sun 11am–1pm.

Parque Histórico Guayaquil ★★ (Moments)

This historical theme park is a great place to spend an afternoon and learn more about southern Ecuador. Here, you can walk in a large "forest" filled with regional flora (including endangered plants and trees) and through rows of different banana plants, some endemic to Ecuador (remember that Ecuador is the world's largest banana exporter). A traditional country house replicates how rural farmers lived and what farming utensils they used. In the courtyard of a beautiful old hacienda, plays, staged twice daily, depict life on a farm in the 19th century. The boardwalk here is dubbed Malecón 1900 and gives you a glimpse into how the city looked some 100 years ago. An old-fashioned bakery and cafe serves traditional dishes in a lovely outdoor setting. An old trolley completes the picture. I recommend coming here on a weekday if possible; weekends are very crowded—this theme park has become extremely popular with Ecuadorian families.

Vía Samborondón, between av. Esmeraldas and Central. ℂ 04/2833-807. www.parquehistorico.com. Tues–Sat $3 (£1.50) adults; $1.50 (75p) children under 12; Sun and public holidays $4.50 (£2.25) adults, $3 (£1.50) children. Tues–Sun and holidays 9am–4:30pm.

SHOPPING

The **Mercado Artesanal** (ℂ 04/2306-266), on Baquerizo Moreno, between calles Loja and Juan Montalvo, is the best place to buy local handicrafts. You'll find over 280 stalls and shops run by area businesspeople as well as by the artisans themselves. Everything from tagua nut—also called vegetable ivory—carvings to Otavaleño textiles to Panama hats and ceramics is available.

As a throbbing metropolis, Guayaquil is full of modern shopping malls that include the **San Marino Mall** (© 04/2083-178), **Mall del Sur** (© 04/2085-000), and **Mall del Sol** (© 04/2690-100). Each has scores of shops, a couple of department stores, a food court and independent restaurants, and a multiplex cinema. The **Malecón 2000** shopping center is one of the town's newest and most frequented by visitors. It's located on the Malecón near Calle Junín.

WHERE TO STAY
VERY EXPENSIVE

If there's no space at the hotels below, the **Hampton Inn** ⭑ (© 1800/4267-866; www.hampton.com.ec), **Four Points Sheraton** ⭑⭑ (© 04/2691-888; www.sheraton. com), and **Hotel Oro Verde Guayaquil** ⭑(© 04/2327-999; fax 04/2329-350; www.ororverdehotels.com) are all good options.

Hilton Colón Guayaquil ⭑⭑⭑   This hotel is housed in a modern high-rise and has a welcoming ambience. The Hilton has become an institution in Guayaquil—its restaurants, banquet halls, and bars are frequented by the crème de la crème of local society. The rooms are large with big windows—some rooms offer views of planes taking off and landing at the nearby airport. The suites and executive doubles have new plasma-screen televisions. The corner suites are the most desirable—each has a lovely balcony with a great view. The marble bathrooms are huge and sparkling. The beautiful outdoor pool has a swim-up bar and a snack bar for alfresco dining. The coffee shop serves excellent Ecuadorian specials at reasonable prices; and the Portofino restaurant is the best and most elegant Italian eatery in Guayaquil. Several airline offices, including LAN Chile, TACA, and KLM, are located in the shopping arcade adjacent to the hotel lobby, as is a little sushi bar. *Tip:* The Hilton Colón is located close to the airport, which makes it an ideal place for people trying to catch an early flight to the Galápagos.

Av. Francisco de Orellana, Guayaquil. © 800/445-8667 in the U.S., or 04/2689-000 in Ecuador. Fax 04/2689-149. www.guayaquil.hilton.com. 294 units. $160–$359 (£80–£180) double; $260–$459 (£130–£230) suite. AE, DC, MC, V. Free parking. Free airport shuttle (reserve in advance). **Amenities:** 4 restaurants; 2 bars; beautiful large pool; exercise room; Jacuzzi; sauna; concierge; business center; shopping arcade; salon; 24-hr. room service; massage; babysitting; laundry service; same-day dry cleaning; smoke-free floors; executive/club floors. *In room:* A/C, TV, dataport, Wi-Fi, minibar, coffeemaker, hair dryer, safe.

EXPENSIVE

UniPark Hotel ⭑ *Value*   This large, luxury hotel is located right downtown and connected to the UniPark mall, across from Parque Seminario and the cathedral and just 3 blocks from the Malecón. The rooms are everything you would want and expect in this category. The hotel lacks the pool and extensive facilities of the Hilton Colón and Grand Hotel Guayaquil, but thanks to the local glut of rooms and competition, they've made up for this by dropping their rates substantially. The UniPark has several restaurants, including a sushi bar, and there are scores more in the adjacent mall.

Calle Clemente Ballén 406 and Calle Chimborazo, Guayaquil. © 04/2327-100. Fax 04/2328-352. www.unipark hotel.com. 139 units. $80–$90 (£40–£45) double. Rates include breakfast buffet and free airport shuttle. AE, DC, MC, V. Free parking. **Amenities:** 3 restaurants; 2 bars; small gym; sauna; concierge; business center; 24-hr. room service; massage; laundry service; smoke-free rooms; free Wi-Fi. *In room:* A/C, TV, dataport, minibar, hair dryer, safe.

MODERATE

Apart Hotel Kennedy ⭑ *Value*   Catering to business travelers, the Kennedy is located catercorner to the much fancier Hilton Colón. Rooms are cool, sleek, and spacious. The large suites have separate sitting rooms and kitchenettes, which come in handy if you're here for several days. The decor aims to be elegant, but comes across as a bit kitschy. Still, this is a great value. The entire hotel features free wireless Internet for guests. *Tip:* The rates I list below are their "corporate" rates, which are substantially lower than their rack rates. That said, all you have to do is say you work for any company—heck, make one up—and they are usually more than happy to apply the corporate rate.

Calles Nahum Isaías and Vicente Norero, Kennedy Norte, Guayaquil. © 04/2681-111. Fax 04/2681-060. www.hotel kennedy.com.ec. 49 units. $70 (£35) double; $85 (£43) suite. Rates include buffet breakfast. AE, DC, MC, V. Free parking. **Amenities:** Restaurant; bar; business center; salon; room service 7am–10pm; laundry service; free Wi-Fi. *In room:* A/C, TV, minifridge, hair dryer, safe.

INEXPENSIVE

There are plenty of run-down and seedy budget hotels in Guayaquil, but I really can't recommend any of them. Given the heat and humidity, I think it's worth the splurge for someplace with air-conditioning and a sense of style. If you're looking for a budget hotel, try **Tangara Guest House** (©/fax **04/2282-828** or 04/2282-829; www. tangara-ecuador.com) or the **Iguanazu Hostal** (© **04/2201-143** or 09/9867-968; www. iguanazuhostel.com).

WHERE TO DINE

In addition to the places listed below, **El Vigia** (© **04/2300-218**) is a simple restaurant, but it's my favorite spot on the Cerro Santa Ana, while **Resaca** (© **04/2631-068**) is my top choice right on the Malecón 2000.

EXPENSIVE

La Trattoria da Enrico ★★ *Finds* ITALIAN   It's worth a meal here just to marvel at the fish tanks embedded in the ceiling. However, the Mediterranean-tinged trattoria-style cuisine is also very good. Start with some grilled octopus or a mixed antipasti. There's a wide range of pasta dishes, and the gnocchi here are light and tender. Sure, you can get a steak pizzaiola or veal Marsala, but I recommend sticking with the seafood options, which are extensive. A group can share the mixed seafood platter, which has a little bit of almost everything, from prawns and langoustines to fish and calamari. This place has an excellent wine list. The floral tablecloths are a bit schmaltzy, as is the roving trio of violins and guitar, but they do add to the charm of this local favorite.

Calle Bálsamos 504, between Ebanos and Las Monjas. © 04/2387-079. Reservations recommended. Main courses $6–$24 (£3–£12). MC, V. Daily 12:30–11:30pm.

MODERATE

La Parrilla del Ñato ★ ECUADORIAN/STEAKHOUSE   This local minichain serves up excellent grilled meats in a lively setting. Portions are legendarily large, and easily shared. The dining room is also large and often as "loud" as the large neon signs out front. Still, the food is excellent. I'd stick to the simply grilled meats and seafood, though if you're feeling adventurous you can order a dove breast. I don't know where they get their doves, but they're big. The *brocheta mixta* is a massive shish kebab with a couple of whole sausages and large cuts of meat interspersed with grilled onions and peppers. Avoid the pastas and pizzas, which are not the strong suit here. Other outlets around town can be found in Barrio Kennedy on Avenida Francisco de Orellana and Nahim Isaías (© **04/2682-338**), and at Km 2.5 on the road to Samborondón (© **04/2834-326**).

An Alternative to the Galápagos

If you don't have the time or the money for a trip to the Galápagos Islands, you might consider visiting **Machalilla National Park**. At the park's main attraction, **Isla de la Plata** ⟨⟨⟨, which sits 37km (23 miles) off the coast, you will have the chance to see albatrosses; blue-footed, masked, and red-footed boobies; frigate birds; and sea lions, all of which also live in the Galápagos. There are also some colorful snorkeling spots here. From June through September, it's common to see whales as you make your way out to the island. But be careful—some of the boats are small and light, and the sea can be rough. If you're prone to seasickness, be sure to take some medication before you board the boat.

Isla de la Plata is the best-known attraction in Machalilla, but if you have a few days, you can also explore some archaeological sites (this area of the coast was home to a thriving pre-Columbian civilization) and hike along Los Frailes, a 3-hour trail that will reward you with breathtaking views of the coast.

All the tour agencies and hotels in town offer trips out to Isla de la Plata for around $25 to $30 (£13–£15) including a guided hike, lunch, and snorkeling gear, plus an additional $15 (£7.50) national park fee.

Most visitors to Machalilla base themselves in Puerto López, a tiny little coastal town. Manta is the closest city with regular air and bus connections to Quito, although it's also quite common to visit Puerto López out of Guayaquil.

Av. Estrada 1219 and Laureles. © 04/2387-098. Main courses $5.80–$14 (£2.90–£7). AE, DC, MC, V. Daily noon–midnight.

Lo Nuestro ⟨⟨ ECUADORIAN   The best Ecuadorian restaurant in the city, located 10 minutes from downtown (a taxi will cost about $4/£2), is a small, elegant eatery whose walls are filled with historical photos of Guayaquil. Ask what the fresh fish is: Seafood reigns supreme here. *Ceviches* make for the best appetizers. The grilled sea bass with crab sauce is my favorite main course. There are myriad daily specials, but traditional favorites include homemade empanadas, *seco de chivo* (goat stew), and shrimp served several different ways. Everything is of the highest quality—and meticulously prepared. This is the kind of place where you enjoy a 3-hour meal and where the waiters wheel over a liquor tray to offer you an after-dinner drink. Don't come here if you're pressed for time!

Av. Estrada 903 and Higueras. © 04/2386-398. Reservations recommended. Main courses $6–$14 (£3–£7). MC, V. Mon–Thurs noon–3:30pm and 7pm–midnight; Fri–Sun noon–midnight.

INEXPENSIVE

La Canoa ⟨ ECUADORIAN   You'll have a hard time believing that La Canoa is attached to a hotel (the Continental). During lunchtime, it's one of the most happening places in town. Locals come here for the inexpensive but very satisfying Ecuadorian food. Recommended dishes include *seco de chivo, humitas, ceviche,* grilled chicken, and delicious milkshakes. There's also a large selection of soups, salads, and sandwiches. A great place to take a break if you're seeing the sights of Guayaquil, La Canoa is close to most of the museums and only a few blocks from the Malecón 2000. Before noon, you can choose from a large selection of breakfast specialties.

In Hotel Continental, Chile 510 and 10 de Agosto. ✆ 04/2329-270. Main courses: $3.50–$9 (£1.75–£4.50). AE, DC, MC, V. Daily 24 hr.

GUAYAQUIL AFTER DARK

Guayaquil has made great strides in reducing crime and beefing up security in recent years, and its nightlife has benefited greatly. Bars, cafes, and restaurants are sprouting like mushrooms around the **Zona Rosa** and **Cerro Santa Ana** (both located toward the end of the Malecón). This is the best area to experience the city's nightlife. Have a taxi drop you off by the MAAC, on the tip of the Malecón, at **La Proa Bar.** This modern club, with its long bar and large outdoor patio, is a good spot for a drink; patrons tend to be young and trendy—things don't get going here until after 10 or 11pm—and occasionally there are live bands. For more mellow options, you can stroll up the Cerro Santa Ana, where you'll find a plethora of bars and pubs flanking the steps leading to the top of the hill. Around the corner from the steps, in Las Peñas, is the boho standout **La Paleta.**

For dancing and more lively clubs, try the Zona Rosa, a several-square-block area bordered by the Malecón to the east and Avenida Rocafuerte to the west, and by Calle Juan Montalvo to the north and Calle Manuel Luzarraga to the south. You'll find a score of bars here, and it's a relatively safe area to bar-hop. I like **Heineken Bar Music** ⭐, Rocafuerte and Padre Aguirre, which has atmospheric brick walls and often features live music.

Locals like to head to the handful of clubs and discos found in the neighborhood Kennedy Norte, at the **Mall Kennedy.** These clubs attract a broad mix of Guayaquil's young and restless. There's plenty to choose from, but if you want an all-out party, try **Ibiza Evolution.**

If you're in the mood for some gambling, there are large modern casinos at both the **Sheraton Four Points** and **Hilton Colón.**

9 The Galápagos Islands ⭐⭐⭐

966km (618 miles) W of continental Ecuador

The Galápagos Islands offer some of the best wildlife viewing in the world, not only because the animals themselves are beautiful and interesting but because they are virtually fearless of humans. Through a quirk of evolution, large predators failed to evolve here, meaning, for example, that the famous blue-footed booby will perform its awkwardly elegant two-step mating dance right under your nose, oblivious to your camera. Sea lions will do figure eights to show off their swimming prowess as you snorkel among them. The local penguins are, admittedly, a bit aloof, but even they aren't above using a snorkeler as a human shield as they attempt to sneak up on schools of fish. In the Galápagos, you don't have to get downwind and peer through the bushes to glimpse the wildlife; you do, however, have to be careful not to step on sea lions sleeping on the beach as you position yourself to take a photo.

The islands' geographic isolation, over 960km (600 miles) off the continental coast, has led to the evolution of numerous endemic species here. This, combined with the animals' fearlessness of humans, played a key role in Charles Darwin's development of the theory of natural selection. The wildlife here, which so beguiled Charles Darwin, is no less astonishing now than it was when he visited. However, both the fragile ecosystems and wildlife are facing threats from overdevelopment, overfishing, and the increasing number of visiting tourists and introduced species. In 2007, UNESCO, which has declared the islands a World Heritage Site, announced that they were in serious danger of destruction. Although few formal measures have yet been adopted, the Ecuadorian government has vowed to take special steps to ensure that tourism and overall development on the Galápagos Islands is undertaken in a manner that will ensure the archipelago's survival and sustainability as an ecological wonder.

The best way to see the islands is to book a package tour out of Quito or Guayaquil. Most packages will include airfare and a berth on a local cruise ship, or a planned land-based itinerary. The ships that tour the islands vary widely in size and quality. My advice: Spend as much money as you can afford. But no matter what you can pay, you won't be disappointed.

The Galápagos Islands were formed over 5 million years ago by volcanic eruptions. These (and the ongoing formation and development of the islands) occur primarily over a relatively localized hot spot. However, due to continental drift, the islands are slowly but steadily migrating eastward. Today, the most active islands are Fernandina and Isabela, the westernmost islands, although several others have ongoing volcanic activity.

ESSENTIALS
GETTING THERE

With rare exceptions, travelers come by plane to the Galápagos Islands. **Tame** (© **02/ 2909-900;** www.tame.com.ec) and **Aerogal** (© **1-800/2376-425;** www.aerogal. com.ec) now offer daily flights to both **Baltra Airport,** right off Santa Cruz island, and **Puerto Baquerizo Moreno,** on San Cristóbal island. Note, however, that there are sometimes last-minute changes to flight schedules owing to inclement weather. During the low season (mid-Sept through mid-Dec and mid-Jan through mid-June), flights from the mainland cost around $350 (£175) round-trip. In the high season, they cost just below $400 (£200).

Upon arrival you must pay a $100 (£50) fee to the **National Park** (www. Galapagospark.org), which is good for the duration of your stay. This fee must be paid in cash, so be sure to plan ahead and have it ready. Children under 12 pay $50 (£25).

If you booked a boat tour before you arrived, the airfare and ticket booking should already be included. You can usually expect someone to pick you up at the airport and escort you through the logistics of arriving in the Galápagos and finding the way to your ship. If you plan to base your touring out of a hotel on land, or if you're looking for a last-minute berth on a boat, the place to head is Puerto Ayora, on Santa Cruz, which is accessed from the Baltra airport. I don't recommend using San Cristóbal, as there is far less tourist infrastructure here, although there are a handful of tour operators and hotels in the island's main city, Puerto Baquerizo Moreno.

All flights from the mainland originate in Quito and stop in Guayaquil. If you plan on flying to the Galápagos the day after you arrive in Ecuador, I recommend spending the night in Guayaquil. Most flights to the Galápagos leave Quito early in the morning and then stop for more than an hour to pick up passengers in Guayaquil. You'll have a much more relaxed morning, and gain precious sleep time, if you board the plane there.

GETTING AROUND

The Galápagos archipelago consists of 13 big islands, 6 small islands, and more than 40 islets. **Santa Cruz** is the most populated island; its main town, Puerto Ayora, is the

major city in the Galápagos. From here, you can arrange last-minute tours around the islands, day trips, and scuba-diving excursions. Santa Cruz is also home to the Darwin Research Station, where you can see giant land tortoises. **San Cristóbal** is the second-most populated island. Several tour boats begin their journeys from the its port, Puerto Baquerizo Moreno. While serving as the official capital of Galápagos province, the town of Puerto Baquerizo Moreno is small. Moreover, there's not much to see on this island. **Isabela** is the largest island, but only the third-most populated. In general, most visitors only stop here on a guided tour.

To enjoy the best of what the Galápagos have to offer, I recommend exploring the islands by boat. However, if you're very prone to seasickness or uncomfortable sleeping on a boat, you can take a host of day trips out of Puerto Ayora.

Flights between the islands aren't frequent, but the local Galápagos airline **EME-TEBE** (© 05/2526-177; emetebe@ecu.net.ec) offers service on tiny propeller planes between Santa Cruz, San Cristóbal, and Isabela islands. Fares are $100 to $120 (£50–£60) for each flight segment.

VISITOR INFORMATION

There are only two substantial towns in the Galápagos Islands, **Puerto Ayora** on Santa Cruz island, and **Puerto Baquerizo Moreno** on San Cristóbal island. Both towns

Tips   Organizing a Last-Minute Trip to the Galápagos

There's no way around it—trips to the Galápagos are expensive. But if you book a cruise at the last minute, you can sometimes save off the regular rates. Unfortunately, it's not easy to find a last-minute price, and you run the risk of not finding space. During the high season (June–Sept and late Dec to early Jan), you shouldn't even waste your time looking for one. Even during the low season, you shouldn't expect to come to Ecuador and immediately find a boat that's leaving the next day. In some cases, you may have to wait a week or more before you find an opening. The following info will help you plan a last-minute trip to the Galápagos.

WEBSITE

TOPPSA ⊛, also known as Travel Opportunities South America (www.toppsa. com), manages a website that specializes in offering last-minute trips throughout Ecuador (including to the Galápagos). If you plan to travel to Ecuador within the next 60 days, it's worth a look to see whether special offers are available.

TRAVEL AGENCIES IN QUITO

Note: **Galasam,** on Avenida Amazonas and Cordero, specializes in wildly inexpensive last-minute trips to the Galápagos. But I have heard complaints about the level of service and the inefficiency on its ships. The prices are low, but so is the quality.

- **Ecoventura** ⊛ operates five ships and yachts in the Galápagos. Through the website (www.ecoventura.com), they sometimes offers last-minute deals at reduced rates. If there are no special discounts on the website, stop in or call their local offices in Ecuador. In Quito, they have an office at Almagro N31–80, Edificio Venecia (✆ 02/2907-396); and in Guayaquil they have an office on Av. Central 300A, Ciudadela Miraflores (✆ 04/2207-177). At both offices, you can try to book a last-minute berth at last-minute prices.

- **Zenith Ecuador Travel** ⊛, Juan León Mera 452 and Roca (✆ 02/2529-993; www.zenithecuador.com), has access to information about 100 boats that ply the waters around the Galápagos Islands. Give the staff your dates and your requirements, and they'll talk to their contacts and try to find you a special last-minute deal. Ask to speak to the owner, Mr. Marcos Endara, and tell him you are a Frommer's reader.

have banks, Internet cafes, a post office, pharmacies, and basic health clinics that serve as local hospitals.

In Puerto Ayora, there's a **tourist information office** (✆ 05/2526-613; turismo@santacruz.gov.ec) on Avenida Charles Darwin, close to the corner of Charles Binford. It is open Monday through Friday from 8am to noon and 2 to 5:30pm. *Note:* The Galápagos Islands are 6 hours behind GMT, 1 hour earlier than mainland Ecuador.

EXPLORING THE GALAPAGOS
WHEN TO GO

There's never a bad time to visit the Galápagos. The peak season lasts from mid-June through early September and from mid-December through mid-January. It's almost impossible to find a last-minute deal at these times. The national park limits the number of visitors to each island and coordinates each ship's itinerary, so the Galápagos will never feel like Disney World. But if you visit in the summer, you are less likely to feel a sense of solitude and isolation. Below is a brief summary of the seasons to help you decide what time of year is best for you:

DECEMBER THROUGH MAY   During these months, the water and the air are warmer, but this is the rainy season. It drizzles almost daily for a short period of time. Ironically, this is also the sunniest time of year. The end of December through the beginning of January is still the high season, so expect more crowds than during the rest of the year.

Because the water is warmer at this time, swimming and snorkeling are more enticing. On the flip side, there aren't as many fish to see as there are later in the year. This is the breeding season for land birds, so it's a good time to watch some unusual mating rituals. If you're into turtles, this is when you want to be here; you can watch sea turtles nesting on the beach, and March through May, you can often see land tortoises searching for mates around the lowland areas of the islands. Sea lions also mate in the rainy season—it's entertaining to watch as the males fight for the females. Around March and April, you'll see the adorable newborn pups crawling around the islands.

In February, March, and April, as the rains dissipate, flowers start to blossom and the islands are awash in bright colors. Another benefit of traveling to the Galápagos at this time of year: The ocean is much calmer, so you'll have less chance of getting seasick.

JUNE THROUGH NOVEMBER   June through November, the Humboldt Current makes its way up to the Galápagos from the southern end of South America. The current brings cold water and cold weather, but it also brings water rich in nutrients

---

⌒Tips Bring Your Own Gear & Wear Some Rubber

While most of the ships and boats and all of the dive shops in the Galápagos can provide snorkeling and diving gear, you might consider bringing your own. If nothing else, bring your own mask. A good, properly fitting mask is the single most important factor in predicting the success of a dive or snorkeling outing. Faces come in all sizes and shapes, and I really recommend finding a mask that gives you a perfect fit. If you plan on going out snorkeling or diving more than a few times, the investment will more than pay for itself. Fins are a lesser concern—most operators should have fins to fit your feet.

Even during the dry season, the waters of the Galápagos are much cooler than you'd expect this close to the Equator. Most scuba companies dive with full 6mm wet suits year-round. Even if you are snorkeling, a full or "shortie" wet suit will make the experience much more enjoyable, especially from June to November, when the Humboldt Current makes the water significantly colder. I highly recommend that you find out in advance if your ship or tour operator can provide or rent you a wet suit. If not, consider buying one.

and plankton, which attracts fish and birds. During this season there always seem to be clouds in the air, but it rarely rains. It's also quite windy, and the seas tend to be rougher.

Experienced divers claim that this is the best time of year to visit the Galápagos. Unfortunately, to see the wide variety of underwater marine life, you have to brave the cold water. Because there are more fish in the sea at this time of year, there are also more seabirds searching for these fish. Albatrosses arrive on Española in June and stay until December. Penguins also like the cold water and the abundance of fish, so you're more likely to see them here during this season. On Genovesa, the elusive owls mate in June and July, and you have the best chance of spotting one during this time. Blue-footed boobies also mate now, so it won't be difficult to witness their beautiful mating ritual known as the "sky point."

THE ISLANDS IN BRIEF

Every island in the Galápagos has its own allure. The more time you have, the richer your experience will be, but even if you have only a few days, with proper planning you'll come home with a lifetime of memories. When you're choosing a tour operator, you should always examine the itinerary. Note that 7-day trips often make frequent stops at Santa Cruz or San Cristóbal to collect and drop off passengers. The best trips head out to far-flung places, such as Genovesa, Española, and Fernandina, and spend only 1 day docked in Puerto Ayora, on Santa Cruz. To help you decide which trip might be best for you, here's a list of what each island has to offer.

Santa Cruz You will most likely begin and end your trip to the Galápagos on Santa Cruz. If you plan to arrange your trip on your own, you should use Santa Cruz as your base. The main city here, **Puerto Ayora,** is a bustling and attractive little burg, with a variety of small hotels, restaurants, gift shops, and tour operators. If you're looking for a luxury getaway, this island offers the only such choices, with both the Royal Palm Hotel (p. 593) and Finch Bay Hotel (p. 593). This island is also home to the **Charles Darwin Research Station,** where you can observe tortoises first-hand. Tours of the island include stops at **Los Gemelos (The Twins),** two sinkholes that stand side by side. As you walk around Los Gemelos, you will have a good chance of spotting the beautiful vermilion flycatcher. Some companies will take you to a farm in the highlands, where you can see tortoises in the wild. Most trips make a stop at the lava tubes, where you can wander though underground tunnels created by the movement of hot lava. On the north side of the island is **Cerro** **Dragon,** which is a great place to see the unique Galápagos land iguana.

Bartolomé Bartolomé (or Bartholomew) is famous for its dramatic vistas and barren volcanic landscape. The most common anchorage here is near the oddly shaped **Pinnacle Rock.** From here, you can climb 372 steps of a wooden walkway to reach the top of an extinct volcano. The vigorous but technically easy climb is a lesson in volcano geography, with cooled-off lava flows and parasitic spatter cones clearly visible along the route to the main cone. On the way up, you will certainly see lava cactuses and lava lizards. The panoramic view from the lookout up top is beautiful, with Pinnacle Rock below you. Be sure to ask your guide to pick out a few of the lava rocks to show how light they are. This island has one of the larger colonies of Galápagos penguins, and many snorkelers have spotted penguins off this island.

San Cristóbal Most boats only stop on San Cristóbal to pick up and drop off passengers. The island's principal town, **Puerto Baquerizo Moreno,** features a pretty, and recently remodeled, Malecón, or seafront promenade, with a string of restaurants, cafes, and gift shops. The main attraction on the island is the **Centro de Interpretación (Interpretive Center),** a small, museum with exhibits on the natural, human, and geological history of the island. If you spend any time on San Cristóbal, you will probably stop at **El Lobería,** a beach with sea lions, red crabs, and colorful lava gulls. It's also worth visiting **La Galapaguera de Cerro Colorado,** a natural giant-tortoise reserve. If you sail into or out of Puerto Baquerizo Moreno, you will pass through **Kicker Rock**—a unique rock formation set about 1.5km (1 mile) offshore. Take note of San Cristóbal's fishing and commuter craft; many are ringed with strands of barbed wire to keep off sea lions. Boats without the barbed wire almost always have one or two of these large sea mammals lounging around on the aft deck or sunning on the prow.

Santiago Also called **James Island,** Santiago was a major base where early buccaneers and pirates stocked up on fresh water and food. Santiago is also a case study in the potential destruction caused by introduced species. Supposedly a couple of pairs of feral goats, left here as a future source of food by buccaneers in the 18th century, reproduced to the point where they numbered over 100,000. Recent efforts have greatly reduced the size of the herds of wild goats, but they are still wreaking havoc on certain native species, including giant tortoises. Most of the sea lions in the Galápagos are California sea lions. But on Santiago island, you will have the chance to see the only endemic species of sea lion in the Galápagos, which is incorrectly called the **Galápagos fur seal.** After

you see the fur seal, you will have an opportunity to take advantage of the excellent snorkeling here. The island is also full of coastal birds such as great blue herons, lava herons, oystercatchers, and yellow-crowned night herons.

Española May through December, albatrosses settle down here to mate and take care of their young. In May and June, if you arrive early in the morning, you can witness the beak-cracking mating ritual of the albatross. Later in the season (Sept–Dec), you can see the little chicks. There must be some sort of avian aphrodisiac on this island because this is also a great place to see blue-footed boobies doing their mating dance, where the male extends his wings and lifts his beak at his prospective mate. If the female likes what she sees, she mimics her suitor.

Fernandina This is the westernmost island in the archipelago, and one of the best for wildlife encounters. The largest colony of marine iguanas live here. These cold-blooded animals hug and cuddle with each other to warm up after swimming. Flightless cormorants also inhabit the island; even though these birds can't fly (they are the only flightless cormorants in the world), they still dry their wings in the sun, just like their flying ancestors used to do millions of years ago. At something around 1 million years of age, Fernandina is the youngest of the Galápagos Islands, and one of the most volcanically active. Major eruptions here were recorded as recently as 1995.

Isabela Just to the east of Fernandina, this is the largest island in the Galápagos, formed by the volcanic activity and eventual joining of six different volcanoes—five of which are still active. Darwin's Lake provides an excellent backdrop for dramatic photos of the sea. The island is home to several different species of the giant Galápagos land tortoise, although you might not be able to see them in the wild. You should, however, be able to spot the land iguanas here, and you can take a long hike to a scenic point, from which you can see for miles. Isabela is particularly prized by bird-watchers; owing to its size, the island has a high species count. One of the common species here is the flamingo, found in its namesake **Pozo de los Flamingos (Flamingo Pond),** close to the main town of Puerto Villamil. Among the main attractions on Isabela is **El Muro de Lágrimas (The Wall of Tears),** a stone wall that was used as a torture mechanism for prisoners kept in a penal colony here during the mid-20th century. In town, you can also see graffiti that dates all the way back to 1836.

Rábida ⍟ Rábida, also known as **Jervis Island,** has a beautiful red-sand beach that is almost always heavily populated with sea lions. If you get too close to a female or child, the local bull male will probably make his presence known. Just behind the beach is a small salt-water lagoon that is a good place to see flamingos. A small loop trail leads to the top of a hill, with some good views of the island's coastline. In my opinion, the waters off Rábida offer the best snorkeling in the islands. I recently found myself swimming simultaneously with sea lions and penguins here. Unfortunately, I arrived too late in the day, and the marine iguanas weren't interested in joining us; otherwise I would have scored a wonderful trifecta.

Genovesa (Tower) ⍟ Home to **Darwin Bay** and the popular hiking trail known as **"Prince Philip's Steps,"** Genovesa is located on the far northeastern end of the archipelago. It's a long, often rough sail here, and only the longer tours include a visit to Genovesa. Almost every Galápagos tourist brochure has a picture of a frigate bird puffing up its red neck in an attempt to attract females; on Genovesa you'll have ample opportunities to see these birds in action. This island is also home to the largest colony of red-footed boobies on the archipelago. On another side of the island, you can see masked boobies and storm petrels. If you're lucky, you might spot the elusive short-eared owl—since these guys don't have predators, they are the only owls in the world that are diurnal. Genovese is also home to both sea lions and the endemic Galápagos fur seal.

Floreana ⍟ This small island, the first to be inhabited, is rich in lore and intrigue. Today, some 100 people live on Floreana, which is seldom visited by tourists. If you do come here, be sure to stop at **Post Office Bay,** where a barrel full of letters and postcards sits on the beach. It's a tradition begun by early whalers: If you see a letter or card addressed to someone in your town or country, you are supposed to carry it and post it from home. In exchange, feel free to leave a letter or postcard of your own for someone else to return the favor.

CHOOSING A BOAT TOUR

Hundreds of companies offer trips through the Galápagos, and trying to sift through all the tourist brochures is a daunting task. First and foremost, let me warn you that you tend to get what you pay for here. There are four classes of boats: economic, tourist-class, first-class, and luxury. The **economic boats** have shared dormitories and bathrooms, inexperienced (and non-English-speaking) guides, and mediocre food. On

> **Tips Scuba-Diving Trips**
>
> The waters surrounding the Galápagos offer some of **the best diving in the world** ★★★. If you want to dive here, you have two options: Book a tour on a dedicated dive boat—and dive every day—or take a nondiving cruise and then spend a couple of extra days in Puerto Ayora and arrange diving excursions from there. Two of the best diving outfitters in Puerto Ayora are **SCUBA Iguana** ★ (© 05/2526-497; www.scubaiguana.com), located at the Hotel Galápagos on Avenida Charles Darwin, right below the Darwin Research Station; and **Sub-Aqua** (© 05/2526-633; www.Galapagos-sub-aqua.com), on Avenida Charles Darwin and Avenida 12 de Febrero.

a **tourist-class boat** you may have your own private quarters, but expect them to be cramped. You probably won't have air-conditioning or hot water, and your guide might not have a good command of the English language. **First-class ships** have excellent guides, small but private cabins with hot water and air-conditioning, and passable food. The main difference between first-class and **luxury** service is the food; some luxury boats also have swimming pools or Jacuzzis, but the cabins are not necessarily much bigger.

Another word of caution: Don't expect your cruise in the Galápagos to be a typical pleasure cruise; the boats are used mainly for lodging and transportation purposes. During the day, small dinghies, known as *pangas,* will transport you to the actual islands. Once you're on land, the excursions often involve long, uphill hikes. The Galápagos are not a place for relaxing—expect to participate in strenuous activities. The larger ships, while very pleasant, accommodating, and efficient, definitely have a slight cattle-car feel. If you're looking for a more intimate experience, you'll want to book one of the smaller yachts.

Trips to the Galápagos venture out to the high seas, and the waters can be rough. Be sure to bring Dramamine or another antiseasickness medication with you. Candied ginger also helps settle small stomach upsets and is an alternative to medication. If you know that you are prone to sea sickness, you'll definitely want to book on one of the larger ships, which are much more stable and comfortable.

Recommended Boats & Operators

Galacruises Expeditions (©/fax 02/2509-007 in Ecuador; www.galacruises.com) runs four ships of their own and can book passage on a wide range of other boats and ships. Their boats range from tourist-class monohulls to modern luxury catamaran yachts. They do full-service tours around Ecuador and the region.

KLEIN Tours ★ (© 888/50-KLEIN in the U.S., or 02/2267-000 in Ecuador. www.kleintours.com) is one of the oldest companies operating boats in the Galápagos, and their experience shows. The company maintains three ships: the 20-passenger MY *Coral,* the 26-passenger MY *Coral II,* and the 110-passenger MV *Galápagos Legend.* The guides are excellent and knowledgeable. The *Legend* has large cabins, a swimming pool, massage service, a 24-hour coffee bar, and a jogging track. I prefer the intimate feel of the smaller boats, but on the *Legend,* you won't be lacking for any personal comforts.

Linblad Expeditions ★★ (© 800/397-3348 in the U.S. and Canada; www.expeditions.com) is another luxury-oriented tour agency with decades of experience in the Galápagos, and a particular commitment to protecting the environment and raising environmental awareness. The company operates two small, luxurious cruise ships here, the MV *Islander* and the MV *Polaris*. Various tour extensions around Ecuador are available, as is a Machu Picchu combination tour.

Metropolitan Touring ⭐⭐ (© 02/2988-200 in Ecuador; www.metropolitan-touring.com) runs three luxury ships (MV *Santa Cruz*, MV *La Pinta*, and MV *Isabela II*) and one luxury hotel (Finch Bay Hotel), and is one of the largest and most professional tour agencies in Ecuador. Consider booking with them especially if you want to mix and match time on shore with time on a ship, or if you want to design a package that includes a Galápagos excursion as well as trips to other destinations in Ecuador.

The **MV *Galápagos Explorer II*** ⭐⭐ (© 305/662-2965; www.Galápagosexplorer.com), a 100-passenger luxury cruise ship, offers all the amenities you could ever want: swimming pool, Jacuzzi, bars, first-class cruise food, research center, nightly naturalist lectures, library, game room, and even a medical center. Most important, you don't have to cram yourself into a tiny little cabin. All the accommodations are suites, with small sitting areas, a minibar, and a TV/VCR. Still, what you gain in comfort you sacrifice in intimacy. When you're exploring the islands with 100 other people, the islands lose some of their mystique. It's all a matter of taste. If you like big cruise ships, you'll love the *Galápagos Explorer II*. But if you want to linger on the islands and not feel herded around, you'll be better off on a smaller ship.

Overseas Adventure Travel ⭐ (© 800/493-6824 in the U.S. and Canada; www.oattravel.com) offers good-value itineraries, often combining a Galápagos cruise with time in Ecuador's Amazon or a side trip to Machu Picchu. Tours are limited to 16 people and are guided by experienced naturalists.

SS *Mary Anne* ⭐⭐ (Finds (© 02/3237-186; www.angermeyercruises.com) is the most unique vessel touring the Galápagos. Launched in 1997, the Mary Anne is a true three-masted square-rigged barkentine. Over 60m (200 ft.) long, including her bowsprit, she carries over 93 sq. m (1,000 sq. ft.) of sail, and a maximum of 16 passengers. That's a lot of ship for very few passengers. When all her sails are set, she's an impressive sight. The air-conditioned cabins aren't quite as large and luxurious as those on the more modern-luxury cruise ships listed above, but the Mary Anne's food is good, and what you sacrifice in creature comforts you more than make up for in character and ambience.

Surtrek ⭐ (© 02/2231-534; www.surtrek.com) is one of the better Quito-based general tour-and-adventure tour operators. And their Galápagos connections and experience are top-notch. They can book a wide range of cruises and mixed itineraries, and are often good at finding last-minute bargain berths on ships.

Quasar Náutica ⭐⭐⭐ (© 800/247-2925 in the U.S. and Canada or 02/2446-996 in Ecuador; www.quasarnautica.com) operate five luxury ships in the Galápagos, most of which are small and intimate. Their largest ship, the MV *Evolution*, is a beautiful small cruise ship with 16 double staterooms.

PUERTO AYORA

Puerto Ayora, the largest town in the Galápagos, is a good place to base yourself if you're traveling on your own. The **Moonrise Travel Agency,** Av. Charles Darwin 00160, near the corner of Charles Binford (© 05/2526-402; www.Galápagosmoonrise.com), will be your best source of information. The staff is friendly and they can help you arrange a last-minute cruise of the Galápagos and independent tours around the islands.

WHERE TO STAY

In addition to the luxury hotels listed below, the **Hotel Silberstein** (© 05/2526-277 at the hotel, or 02/2269-626 for reservations in Quito; www.hotelsilberstein.com) and **Red Mangrove Adventure Inn** (© 05/2527-011; www.redmangrove.com) are two excellent choices in downtown Puerto Ayora. Budget travelers should try the **Hotel Sol y Mar** (© 05/2526-139 or 05/2526-281).

Finch Bay Hotel ★★ *Moments*   The only beachfront hotel in Santa Cruz is a 5-minute boat ride from Puerto Ayora. Secluded and serene among the mangroves with a magnificent pool and private beach, the Finch Bay has over 30 species of resident birds, including red-footed boobies. Rooms are tastefully decorated with yellow walls and attractive wooden blinds; bathrooms are large and have spacious showers with good water pressure (rare in the islands). The hotel prides itself on being environmentally friendly, with solar power and a conservation program. There's a Zen garden where yoga is offered in the mornings; bikes, kayaks, and snorkeling equipment are available for guests, too. The excellent restaurant serves three meals a day with an emphasis on healthy, organic ingredients; vegetarian offerings are also available. None of the rooms have TVs, but a lounge offers satellite TV, and there's a computer with free Internet access for guests. When making your reservation, be sure to inquire about the all-inclusive packages, which include transfers from the airport, all meals, and daily tours on the hotel's fast, private yacht, the *Sea Finch*.

Punta Estrada, Isla Santa Cruz. © 877/534-8584 in the U.S. and Canada, or 05/2526-297 at the hotel. Fax 02/3341-439. www.finchbayhotel.com. 21 units. $281 (£141) double. Rates include breakfast buffet. AE, DC, MC, V. **Amenities:** Restaurant; 2 bars; lounge; large outdoor pool; Jacuzzi; watersports equipment; bike rental; tour desk; limited room service; laundry service; smoke-free rooms. *In room:* A/C, dataport, safe.

Royal Palm Hotel ★★★ *Finds*   This exclusive resort sits on 200 lush hillside hectares (500 acres), a 20-minute drive from Puerto Ayora. The Royal Palm attracts a healthy dose of celebrities seeking the privacy and personalized service offered here. There are 10 beautiful villas scattered on the hillside, four veranda studios, and three spectacular suites. The villas each have separate living/dining areas; bedrooms with king-size beds; and a huge bathrooms with large showers, dressing areas, and separate rooms with Jacuzzi tubs. Windows face the serene countryside and the ocean at the bottom of the hill. The three suites are all different from one another—the two-bedroom, two-bathroom Imperial comes with its own Jacuzzi hidden in a private garden, while the Royal has a four-poster bed and an indoor sauna. The studios are the simplest (and least expensive) units but have charming patios with hammocks and spacious bathrooms with Jacuzzi tubs. Service is exquisite, friendly, and not at all stuffy. Note that the hotel is more than a half-hour from the port.

Vía Baltra, Km 18, Isla Santa Cruz. © 05/2527-409. Fax 05/2527-408. www.royalpalmGalapagos.com. 17 units. $345 (£173) studio; $475–$575 (£238–£288) suite; $575 (£288) villa for 2; $825 (£413) Imperial Suite. Rates include American breakfast. AE, DC, MC, V. **Amenities:** Restaurant; bar; beautiful outdoor swimming pool; 2 outdoor tennis courts; exercise room; sauna; concierge; large business center; 24-hr. room service; massage; laundry service; same-day dry cleaning. *In room:* A/C, TV/DVD, dataport, minibar, hair dryer, safe.

WHERE TO DINE

The restaurants at the **Royal Palm Hotel** and **Finch Bay Hotel** (see above) are both excellent. In both cases, reservations are essential, and the food will be quite a bit more expensive than anything else you'll find around town. Another interesting option is the hip **Red Sushi** (© 05/2527-011) at the Red Mangrove Adventure Inn.

La Garrapata Restaurante ★★ ECUADORIAN   This place is where the expats eat—and all the foreign guides who work on the ships. There's a great selection of fresh juices and sandwiches. The open-air dining room features low wooden chairs and round tables with linen tablecloths. But there's nothing formal about either the vibe or service here. Main courses include a wide range of seafood and meat options, as well as some pastas. There's usually a *menú del día* (menu of the day) with soup, main course, and dessert for less than $5 (£2.50). They even have a pretty good wine list. On weekends, sometimes there's live music.

Av. Charles Darwin and Charles Binford, Puerto Ayora. © 05/2526-264. Main courses $4–$15 (£2–£7.50). AE, DC, MC, V. Mon–Sat 9am–4pm and 6:30–10pm.

PUERTO AYORA AFTER DARK

Puerto Ayora has a surprisingly lively, albeit limited, nightlife and bar scene. **Bongo Bar** ★★, the most happening place, is located on a rooftop above and behind La Panga. Bongo Bar opens at 4pm, but usually doesn't get busy until after 8pm. Across the street, the **Limón Café** is popular early in the evening, and you can check e-mail from several computers. Limón Café often gets the crowds up and dancing, but if you're looking for the best dance club in town, head to **La Panga.** For live music, try **La Taberna del Duende,** which is popular with locals and is located inland from the main tourist strip on Calle Juan León Mera and San Cristóbal.

10

Paraguay

by Charlie O'Malley

Paraguay has been ignored for too long. This little-known country is tucked away in the tropical belly of South America, landlocked and dwarfed by its more famous neighbors. Most travelers take its anonymity as a cue to skip it and continue on to more exotic places. If you do decide to go, however you will find a humid, strikingly green enclave of rural plains and muddy rivers, bordered by pristine jungles and dotted with lichen-stained towns and cities.

Paraguay is a country that stands for paradox. The indigenous Guarani people play sentimental European songs on giant harps. Huge Ciudad del Este shopping malls stand next to thundering, tropical waterfalls. Unpaved roads lead to a multibillion-dollar dam called Itaipú. Asunción's squalor is punctuated by architectural jewels, while German Mennonite colonies scratch out a good living on the inhospitable Chaco. In the south, majestic Jesuit ruins in Encarnación hint at a lost Utopia.

Paraguay's history is brutal and sad. Everywhere you go you will find references to the 19th century War of the Triple Alliance, a lonely, ill-advised conflict against the combined might of Brazil, Argentina, and Uruguay that almost wiped out Paraguay's male population. Paraguay's isolation was compounded by a 20th century marked by military coups and long dictatorships. It is only recently that the country has opened up. It is a destination for those who want the new and colorful and can tolerate the occasional discomfort. Its greatest assets are unexplored national parks with excellent wildlife, bird-watching and unlimited potential for eco-tourism.

1 The Regions in Brief

The south of the country is where everybody lives and thus is the best developed. The capital **Asunción** is the only major city in Paraguay and thus is its political and economic center. To the east and south of the capital are flat agricultural plains with sleepy colonial towns and the occasional lake or river resort. It is not unusual to hear the indigenous language Guarani being spoken. The eastern border town of **Ciudad del Este** is a tax-free haven originally built to administer the nearby **Itaipú** hydroelectric dam. On the southern border with Argentina there is the modern town of **Encarnación,** famous for its nearby Jesuit ruins. The river Paraguay leads you north of Asunción to the town of **Concepción.** Indeed many people take the boat to visit there. Beyond is the Brazilian Pantanal or northwest the **Gran Chaco,** a vast territory of scrubland, savannah, and thorn forest. The border road to Bolivia has only recently been paved, and much of the area still requires 4×4 transport to explore. It is here that Mennonite communities chose to settle, and the area is famous for bird-watching.

2 Suggested Paraguay Itineraries

Paraguay has so much to see and do that 1 week is not enough if you really want to get into the wilderness. That said, below is a 1-week itinerary designed as if treating Paraguay as a stepping stone between Argentina and Brazil. A second week gives you the opportunity to dwell a little longer and enjoy the Jesuit ruins of Encarnación and the country's untouched natural parks (see the box "Waterfalls & Jaguars" at the end of this chapter). *Tip:* For a map of suggested itineraries in Paraguay, please refer to the "Itineraries in Argentina, Chile, Paraguay & Uruguay" map on p. 78.

Days ❶–❸: Arrive in Asunción

Fly into Paraguay's riverside capital, stay in the central **Crowne Plaza** (see p. 604) and explore the city by foot and taxi, seeing firsthand the strong tribal heritage in the city's museums. Day 2 can be enjoyed in the leafy upscale suburb of **Villa Mora** and the nearby **Jardin Botanico.** On the third day take the rural tour called *Circuito de Oro* visiting the charming **Iglesia San Buenaventura** and the resort town of **San Bernardino** on Lago Ypacaraí or, if you have jungle fever, visit the pristine rain forest at **Ybycui National Park.**

Day ❹–❺: Ciudad del Este

You might love it or hate it, but you'll certainly enjoy telling the folks back home of your time in the "Supermarket of South America." Revel in the gritty commercialism of the world's third-biggest tax-free zone by visiting its tacky stores and slick shopping malls.

Day ❺–❼: Itaipú and the Border

But it is not all crass consumerism. There is also the engineering blockbuster **Itaipú** and spectacular **Monday Falls.** Then cross the massive **Friendship Bridge** and onto the famous **Iguazú Falls** in Brazil and Argentina. If you do decide to stay in Paraguay, spend it in tropical splendor at the gorgeous **Las Ventanas** hotel (see p. 609).

3 Planning Your Trip to Paraguay

VISITOR INFORMATION

The tourism ministry, known as **Secretaría Nacional de Turismo,** has an informative website in Spanish at **www.senatur.gov.py.** For up-to-date news and information in English, go to **www.paraguayglobal.com,** or for cultural and historical background, head to **www.paraguay.com.**

ENTRY REQUIREMENTS & CUSTOMS

Citizens of the United States, Canada, and Australia need a visa to enter Paraguay. This must be obtained before your trip and costs $65 (£33).

PARAGUAYAN EMBASSY LOCATIONS

In the U.S.: 2400 Massachusetts Ave. NW, Washington, DC 20008 (© **202/483-6960;** fax 202/234-4508; www.embaparusa.gov.py)

In Canada: 151 Slater St., Suite 401, Ottawa, K1P 5H3 (© **613/567-1283;** fax 613/567-1679; www.embassyofparaguay.ca)

In the U.K.: 344 Kensington High St., Third Floor, London W14 8NS (© **207/610-4180**)

Telephone Dialing Info at a Glance

The national telephone company is called Copaco. Telephone centers are ubiquitous in every town and cards for phone boxes can be bought at most corner stores. Use **Hablemas phone cards** when making international calls.

- **To place a call from your home country to Paraguay,** dial the international access code (011 in the U.S., 0011 in Australia, 0170 in New Zealand, 00 in the U.K.) plus the country code (595), plus the city or region area code (for example, Asunción is 21) followed by the number. For example, a call from the United States to Asunción would be 011-595-21-XXX-XXX.
- **To place a domestic long-distance call within Paraguay,** dial a 0 before the area code, and then the local number.
- **To place a direct international call from Paraguay,** dial the international access code (00), plus the country code of the place you are dialing, plus the area code and the number. To make an international collect call, dial 0012. Calls cost 39¢ per minute to the U.S. and 60¢ per minute to Europe.
- **To reach an International Long Distance Operator,** dial ℂ 000-410 for **AT&T,** ℂ 000-412 for **MCI,** or ℂ 000-417 for **Sprint.**

MONEY

Paraguay's currency is called the Guaraní and is designated with a crossed G. Guaranís are available in 1,000, 5,000, 10,000, 50,000, and 100,000 notes; coins come in 50, 100, and 500 guaranís. It is difficult to change this currency outside Paraguay, though you may have some luck in Buenos Aires and Montevideo. All prices in this chapter are quoted in U.S. dollars, with British pound equivalents. *Note:* Dirty or torn U.S. dollars are difficult to change, though they can be replaced by better ones at some banks. The exchange rate was $1 to 5,020 guaranís at press time.

Traveler's checks are accepted by most banks in Asunción but charge up to 5.5% commission. Currency-exchange houses may insist on seeing your purchase receipt before accepting. The most widely accepted **credit cards** are Visa and MasterCard; you'll have less luck with American Express and Diners Club. To report a lost or stolen credit card, call the following numbers: **American Express,** ℂ 0411/008-0071; **MasterCard,** ℂ 636/722-7111 (collect call to the U.S.); and **Visa,** ℂ 0411/940-7915.

ATMS   ATMs on the Cirrus and Visa/PLUS networks are widely available in Asunción and other large towns.

WHEN TO GO

PEAK SEASON & CLIMATE   With its subtropical climate, Paraguay is best to visit from May to September though the weather can be very changeable. The rainy season is from October to April when it rains 1 in 3 days, though it is not unknown to rain throughout the year. January is the hottest month, with average temperatures of 82°F, and July is the coolest month, at 64°F. Temperatures can drop as low as 40°F (5°C) in winter but rarely dip below freezing. It never snows.

PUBLIC HOLIDAYS   National holidays include New Year's Day (Jan 1) and February 3. March 1 is the Memorial Day for former president Francisco Solana López,

Easter is celebrated on Holy Thursday and Good Friday, and Labor Day on May 1, May 14, and May 15. Corpus Christi is a national holiday as are the 12th and 23rd of June. The Battle of Acosta Ñu is celebrated on Child's Day, August 15th. Other holidays are August 25, September 29, October 12, November 1, December 8, and of course Christmas Day (Dec 25). On these holidays, all government offices are closed, but some museums remain open.

HEALTH CONCERNS

Mosquitoes are prevalent, and therefore Dengue fever and Malaria are endemic, especially in the east around Itaipú. The locally made repellent Repel and mosquito coils can keep the bugs at bay. Avoid tap water and salads, as dysentery is not unknown, and typhoid and tuberculoses are risks as well. Hookworm is common, and STDs are on the rise. Goiter and leprosy are also common ailments, but are unlikely to present a risk to travelers. Check the CDC's website at **www.cdc.gov** for the latest information before your trip. Healthcare in Paraguay is like anywhere else in South America; good for the rich, terrible for the poor. So be sure you're insured.

GETTING THERE & GETTING AROUND

BY PLANE   International flights land at **Silvio Pettirossi Airport** (© 0261/645-600), 15km (11 miles) northeast of the city. An airport tax of $25 (£13) is levied when leaving the country. A taxi to downtown costs about $16 (£8); to Villa Mora it's $10 (£5). Paraguay's national carrier is **TAM Mercosur,** Oliva y Ayolas (© 021/465-600; www.tam.com.py), serving domestic and international destinations. There are no direct flights from Europe or North America. TAM flies via Sao Paulo to New York, Paris, Milan, and Miami. There are three daily flights to Buenos Aires and one a day to Cochabamba (Bolivia), Montevideo, Rio de Janeiro, Santa Cruz (Bolivia), and Santiago in Chile. **Gol** (www.voegol.com.br) has regular flights to Buenos Aires and Brazil. **United Airlines,** Mcal López 310 (© 021/213-019; www.united.com), has offices in Asunción that can organize onward flights from Brazil.

BY BUS & BOAT   See "Asunción," below.

BY CAR   A car is essential to visit many of the less accessible national parks but be prepared for many annoying police stops between cities and the occasional solicitation of a bribe. **National Car Rental,** Yegros 501 (© 021/492-157) offers small cars and SUVs. **Avis,** Eligio Ayala 695 (© 021/446-233; www.avis-int.com.) has an office in the airport, as does **American Rent a Car** (© 0991/761-632). Cars for the day start at $32 (£16). For roadside emergencies or general information on driving in Paraguay, contact the **Touring y Automóvil Club Paraguayo,** 25 de Mayo y Brasil (© 021/210-550; www.tacpy.com.py). A reliable tow-truck service is **Allianza** (© 0971/262-529).

FAST FACTS: Paraguay

American Express In Asunción, American Express is located at InterExpress, Yegros 690 y Herrera (© 021/490-111; iexpress@interexpress.com.py). **Banespa,** Independencia Nacional y Moreno (© 021/448-698), changes traveler's checks but require a purchase receipt. Money exchange houses are located on Palma and Estrella, but beware that their rates go up when banks are closed. **Parapiti Cambios,** Palma 449 (© 021/490-032) will change traveler's checks for a small fee.

Business Hours In general, businesses stay open weekdays from 8am to 6:30 or 7pm, with a 2-hour break for lunch around noon. Retail outlets keep similar hours and are usually open a half-day on Saturday as well. Banks are open weekdays from 8:30am to 1:30pm.

Electricity Electricity in Paraguay runs on 220 volts, so bring a transformer and adapter along with any electrical appliances. Note that most laptops operate on both 110 and 220 volts. Some luxury hotels may supply transformers and adapters. Plugs have two pins.

Embassies & Consulates In Asunción: The **U.S. Consulate**, Av. Mcal López 1776 (𝄞 021/213-715; http://asuncion.usembassy.gov), is open Monday to Thursday from 7:30am to 5:30pm and Friday 7:30am to 11:30am. The **U.K. Consulate**, Eulogio Estigarribia 4846 (𝄞 021/663-536), is open Monday to Friday 8am to 1pm and 3 to 7pm; and the **Canada Consulate**, Prof. Ramirez 3, Office 102 (𝄞 021/227-207), is open Monday to Thursday 8am to 4pm and Friday 8am to noon.

Emergencies The general emergency number is 𝄞 911; fire department 𝄞 711. For medical emergencies, call 𝄞 **204-800**.

Internet Access Cybercafes are commonly found around Asunción and other Paraguayan cities. Many hotel business centers have Internet access, as do the guest rooms in high-end hotels.

Post Offices/Mail Post offices are generally open Monday through Friday from 8am to 6pm and Saturday from 8am to 1pm. You can buy stamps there or in mailing centers in shopping malls. The main post office is situated on Benjamin Constant and El Paraguayo Independiente (𝄞 021/498-112).

Safety Paraguay is a relatively safe country, but it is prudent to keep your eyes open and valuables hidden, especially in Ciudad del Este. Downtown Asunción is badly lit at night but there are usually plenty of policemen.

Taxes Value-added tax is called IVA in Spanish. The standard rate in Paraguay is 10%.

Telephones See "Telephone Dialing Info at a Glance," above.

Time Zone Paraguay is 3 hours behind Greenwich mean time (GMT) and 4 hours behind when the country observes (never certain to happen) daylight saving time (should be Mar 1–Oct 31).

Tipping A 10% to 15% tip is common in restaurants. For taxis, round up to the nearest 1,000 guaraní. Tips for porters and guides are discretionary.

Water It is strongly advised to drink bottled water.

4 Asunción

Stand at the corner of Asunción's Plaza Independencia and Palacio Legislativo and you'll see urban South America in all its grisly glory. The peeling pink colonial palace is besieged on one side by a filthy ramshackle slum that tumbles down to the muddy shore of the Rio Paraguay. A stubbly football pitch lies in the distance and a stained cathedral sits on the other plaza corner, surrounded by potholed streets and vigilant policemen. Dirty buses rumble between whitewashed curbs and a hodge-podge of decaying pastel-colored mansions stand squeezed between squalid concrete bunkers.

Asunción is glorious in the sun and miserable in the rain. Like most South American cities, the downtown area is poor, polluted and neglected yet alive with vendors, food stalls, and chaotic traffic. Here you'll find some interesting museums and monuments, and the shade they offer is a cool respite from the sweltering heat. The northeast of the city becomes decidedly tidier but characterless, with long avenues of car dealerships and shopping malls leading to upscale and leafy Villa Morra. Here you'll find some beautiful suburban streets and parks.

With a population of 1.2 million people, Asunción has the feel of a provincial city. Founded in 1557, the Spanish had big plans to make it the gateway to Peru. The vast, impenetrable Chaco soon stopped this idea in its tracks and the city lost its dominance to Buenos Aires and Salta. Thoughtless urban planning saw the destruction of many fine buildings and what remains gives a sense of long-faded glory. Nevertheless, it is the political, economic, and cultural center of Paraguay, with most of the country's population living there or nearby. Those same people are very friendly and welcoming, unfamiliar with tourists and anxious that you enjoy your stay.

ESSENTIALS
GETTING THERE
BY PLANE   To get to Asunción by plane, see "Getting There & Getting Around," above.

BY BOAT   A ferry operates every 30 minutes from Itá Enramada to the Argentine side at Puerto Pilcomayo. Otherwise the only river route is to Concepción in the north. The *Cacique II* operates sailings to Concepción every Wednesday. The journey takes 27 to 30 hours. Another boat, called the *Guaraní*, sails every Friday morning. Times are flexible. It costs about $20 (£10) for first-class, but be prepared for anything but first-class. Bring plenty of drinking water and toilet paper. For something more upscale, try **Crucero Paraguay,** Nuestra Señora de la Asunción 1102 (✆ **021/447-710;** www.cruceroparaguay.info). They conduct luxury 3-day cruises on the Rio Paraguay. The city port is behind the customs office at the end of Calle Montevideo.

BY BUS   Terminal, República Argentina y Fernando de La Mora (✆ **021/552-154** or 021/551-737), is Asunción's long-distance bus terminal and is 20 minutes south of the city center. It connects the capital with cities in Brazil, Argentina, Uruguay, and Bolivia. Buses take about 18 hours to Buenos Aires and 20 hours to Montevideo. **Nuestra Señora de la Asunción** (✆ **021/551-667;** www.nsa.com.py) is one of the main companies. Another is **Chevalier Paraguaya,** Mcal Estigarriba 767 (✆ **021/493-375**). Beware that local buses crossing the border will not wait for you to go through formalities. You must wait for the next one. **Pluma** (✆ **021/445-024**) operates a service to the Brazilian side of Iguazú (5–7 hr.) and Sao Paolo (20 hr.), as does **RYSA,** Eligio and Antequera, Asunción (✆ **021/444-244;** www.rysa.com.py).

ORIENTATION
Asunción is settled on a bluff above the Rio Paraguay, though the river is hardly noticeable as you stroll around the central plazas. The city basically has two centers. One is the busy, polluted downtown with government buildings and grand plazas such as the Plaza de los Heroes. The other is leafy Villa Morra to the east and north,

Asunción

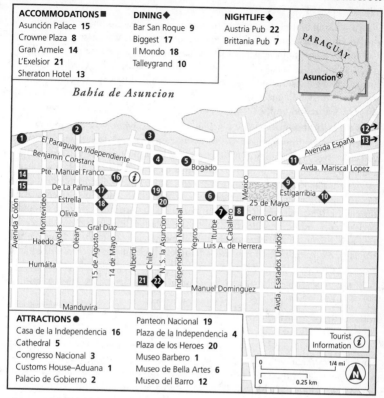

ACCOMMODATIONS ■
Asunción Palace **15**
Crowne Plaza **8**
Gran Armele **14**
L'Exelsior **21**
Sheraton Hotel **13**

DINING ◆
Bar San Roque **9**
Biggest **17**
Il Mondo **18**
Talleygrand **10**

NIGHTLIFE ◆
Austria Pub **22**
Brittania Pub **7**

PARAGUAY

Asuncion ✱

Bahía de Asuncion

El Paraguayo Independiente
Benjamin Constant
Pte. Manuel Franco
De La Palma
Estrella
Olivia
Gral Diaz
Haedo
Humáita
Manduvira

Avenida Colón
Montevideo
Ayolas
Oleary
15 de Agosto
14 de Mayo
Alberdi
Chile
N. S. la Asuncion
Independencia Nacional
Yegros
Iturbe
Caballero
México
Avda. Esatados Unidos

Bogado
Avenida España
Avda. Mariscal Lopez
Estigarribia
25 de Mayo
Cerro Corá
Luis A. de Herrera
Manuel Dominguez

ATTRACTIONS ●
Casa de la Independencia **16**
Cathedral **5**
Congresso Nacional **3**
Customs House–Aduana **1**
Palacio de Gobierno **2**
Panteon Nacional **19**
Plaza de la Independencia **4**
Plaza de los Heroes **20**
Museo Barbero **1**
Museo de Bella Artes **6**
Museo del Barro **12**

Tourist
Information ⓘ

0   1/4 mi
0   0.25 km

which is easier on the eye but very spread out and not suitable for exploring thoroughly on foot. Here you'll find the relaxing parkland of Jardín Botánico.

GETTING AROUND

The downtown is relatively easy to walk around, though some streets toward the south have a steep incline. You will require patience crossing at junctions, however, as there are no pedestrian crossings and drivers are oblivious to those on foot. Villa Morra is best explored by taxi, with many congregating around Plaza de Los Heroes. A ride should not cost more than $10 (£5), but beware there is a 15% surcharge on Saturday, Sunday, and holidays. Old, noisy buses crisscross the city and cost 50¢ (25p). They can be slow in rush hour. Numbers 28 and 31 leave for the terminal from Calle Cerro Corá. To get to Villa Mora, catch any bus going east on España.

VISITOR INFORMATION

Paraguay's **Secretaria Nacional de Turismo** is on Palma 468 (📞 **021/450-965;** www.senatur.gov.py). It is open daily from 7am to 7pm. There's also a branch at the Airport. **Itra Travel,** Av. Venezuela 663 (📞 **021/200-020;** www.itra.com.py), provides good-quality tours of the surrounding area and farther afield to Itaipu and the Jesuit ruins near Encarnación. Another reliable operator is **Vips Tour,** México 782 (📞 **021/441-199;** www.vipstour.com.py).

WHAT TO SEE & DO

Take a walking tour of the city center, starting at the customs house, locally known as the **Aduana,** at Av. Colon and Paraguayo Independiente. Walk east to the **Palacio de Gobierno,** a beautiful Versailles-style palace. It was once decreed that if anybody so much as looked at this building they would be shot on sight. Gladly, this rule no longer applies and now the soldiers in front will only shoo you away, except on Sunday when the building is open to the public. Continue east onto **Plaza Independencia.** The **Cathedral** on the far corner is entered from the side street Bogado.

Casa de la Independencia ✩✩ This quaint, low, white-washed building appears somewhat incongruous amidst the dirty, modern chaos of downtown Asunción. As you enter, two mannequins in full colonial regalia come alive and you realize they are actually two real men. Indeed this museum is very much the real deal. It was here the idea of an independent Paraguay was first formed and the conspirators held clandestine meetings. Alongside is a preserved alleyway where the plotters sneaked in and out through stables and eventually left to march on the Spanish Governor's house and declare independence. Inside you'll find the desk where the declaration was signed as well as a mixture of domestic and historical memorabilia from the era, such as giant-size fans, old cannons, and marvelous Jesuit carvings. All are nicely arranged around a central courtyard. Ask for Maria, the English-speaking guide.

14 de Mayo y Pres Franco. ✆ 021/493 918. www.casadelaindependencia.org.py. Free admission. Tues–Fri 7am–noon and 2:30pm to 6:30pm; Sat–Sun 8am–noon.

Museo de Arte Indigena and Museo del Barro Located 5 blocks from the Sheraton in leafy suburbia, Museo del Barro is one of the more stylish and presentable museums in Asunción, though unfortunately has limited opening hours. Here you'll find excellent indigenous art and handicrafts ranging from ceramic pots and figurines to wooden masks, crochet covers, and upholstered bags. Some of the most interesting exhibits are large urns with climbing children as handles and marvelous clay figurines with big hips and small heads. There is a gift store, book store, and an exhibition room displaying contemporary artists, including the charming, innocent religious art of Mabel Anconda.

Grabadores del Cabichuí, Isla de Francia. Admission $2.50 (£1.25), free on Fri. ✆ 021/607-996. www.museodelbarro.com. Thurs–Sat 3:30–8pm.

Museo Dr Andrés Barbero ✩✩✩ This is the best-stocked museum I came across, with an amazing collection of indigenous objects, including tobacco-stained smoking pipes, brightly colored feather headdresses, giant bows and arrows, carved canoes, and fishing nets. Many of the exhibits were found buried with their Guaraní owners in ceramic funeral urns that also included food supplies and the tools of their trade, thus ensuring a successful reincarnation. Here you'll see clay bottles decorated with the maker's fingerprints and forbidding wooden masks with rattles and whistles. There is also a side corridor of sequenced photos displaying ancient initiation ceremonies. It's very much worth the visit and is located 10 blocks west of downtown. Ring the bell to gain entrance.

España y Mompox. ✆ 021/441-696. Free admission. Mon–Fri 7–11am; Mon, Wed, and Fri 3–5pm; Tues–Sun noon–6pm.

Museo Nacional de Bellas Artes This old, drafty building seems to have more pots catching leaks than actual exhibits. The bottom floor is a bare exhibition room, while up the dank marble stairs you'll find some faded colonial paintings, some nice miniatures, and a variety of busts and statues. The colorful Jesuit wood relief is about the best thing here. Located in the downtown area, it is worth a 5-minute visit to escape the rain.

Iturbe y Mcal Estigarribo. ✆ **021/447-716.** Free admission. Tues–Fri 7am–7pm; Sat 7am–noon.

Pantéon Nacional de los Heroes   Located on the historic Plaza de los Heroes and inspired by Les Invalids in Paris, this monument contains the remains of Mariscal López and the unknown child soldier. It is a grand central dome over a round pit with flag-draped coffins and caskets below. Around it are various plaques and tributes with some nice stained-glass windows. Outside, it is in dire need of renovation, with peeling paint and decapitated statues.

Plaza de los Heroes. Palma y Chile. No telephone. Free admission. Daily 6am–6pm.

OTHER ATTRACTIONS

You can catch some of Paraguay's former railway glory at the **Railway Museum,** Eligio Ayala and Mexico streets (✆ **021/447-848**), open daily 8am to 5pm. If the griminess of the city center gets overwhelming, go northwest on Av. Ortigas, 6km (3¾ miles) to the pastoral 250 hectare (618 acres) park **Jardin Botánico,** Av. Ortigas and Primer Presidente (✆ **021/281-389**). It's open from 7am to 6pm Monday to Friday, Saturday from 7am to 5pm, and Sundays and holidays from 9am to 1pm. It also contains two natural history and indigenous museums. Admission into the park is 20¢ (10p). One kilometer (about a half mile) south of the park is the beautiful and historical church **Santísima Trinidad,** Avenida Santísimo Sacramento and Santísima Trinidad. For something more somber, visit the burned-out shell of **Ycuá Bolaños Supermarket,** Santísima Trinidad and Estigarribia, the scene of a tragic fire in 2004 that killed 700 people. It is now a memorial site.

SHOPPING

For consumer goods, go to Ciudad del Este. In Asunción you can come across some quality handicrafts, especially *Ñanduti* lace from the town of Itauguá. *Aó poí* is another famous product, a type of fine unbleached cotton. It and other textiles are made in the nearby town of Villarica. *Palo Santo* are small items made from Paraguayan wood. You can find some of these items in the markets listed below or at roadside stores on the *Circuito de Oro* tour. A good quality store is **IPA,** Antequerra 241 (✆ **021/498-343;** www.artesania.gov.py). The products are certified and come straight from their creators. For textiles, check out **Taller Fábrica,** Mariscal Estigarribia 2174 (✆ **021/204-081**). For art, go to **Arte Latinoamericano,** Santa Rosa 586 (✆ **021/615-508**). If you like air-conditioned shopping, there are plenty of upscale shopping malls, especially in the Villa Morra area. **Shopping del Sol,** Avenida Aviadores de Chaco and DF de Gonzalez (✆ **021/611-780;** www.shoppingdelsol.com.py), is the biggest in the country and located opposite the Sheraton. Close by is glitzy **Paseo Carmelitas,** Avenida España and Malutin (www.paseocarmelitas.com.py).

MARKETS

For handicrafts, go to Plaza de los Heroes. The biggest and liveliest market is **Mercado Cuatro,** Avenida Dr. Francia and Pettirossi. There they sell everything from food to clothes. On Saturday, Plaza de la Independencia has a morning market with handicrafts and souvenirs, and there is a small passageway with stalls selling similar items on Colon and Presidente Franco.

WHERE TO STAY

For a place with little tourism, the quality of accommodation is surprisingly high. Most of the high-end hotels have business clientele and competition is fierce, so be sure to bargain. The more moderate hotels can vary greatly in quality, so thoroughly check the rooms before accepting. Watch out for noisy air-conditioners, as you can have a very uncomfortable night if the machine in the corner is making hissing or dripping sounds. Most hotels are in the claustrophobic center, but more and more are appearing in leafy Villa Morra. There are no youth hostels.

EXPENSIVE

Crowne Plaza *(Finds* ★ A slick, modern hotel, the Crowne Plaza is on a busy, if somewhat seedy, street in the downtown area (you could say this about all the streets in the city center). However, once you get past the revolving doors and into the expansive lobby with a fountain and zebra skin armchairs, the dirty, bustling city seems miles away. To the right is an all-glass facade that leads to a pleasant courtyard with a garden and chairs—a popular barbecue area on Sundays. A rust-colored partition separates the restaurant and leads to a small, modern bar with red leather seating and high stools. The corridors are windowed on one side and thus have lots of light. The standard rooms are a good size with queen-size beds and a well-stocked, reasonably priced minibar. The bathrooms are immaculate.

Cero Cora 939, Asunción. ©/fax 021/452-682. www.crowneasuncion.com.py. 74 units. $95–$115 (£48–£58) double; from $125 (£68) suite. Rates include buffet breakfast. AE, DC, MC, V. Free parking. **Amenities:** Restaurant; bar; indoor pool; deluxe health club w/fitness center, sauna, and massage; concierge; car rental; salon; room service; babysitting; laundry service; dry cleaning; executive-level floors. *In room:* A/C, TV, dataport, minibar, coffeemaker, hair dryer, iron, safe.

The Excelsior Hotel If there is one thing this old-fashioned hotel does not lack, it's space. Its dark, massive lobby of old-style wood paneling, chandeliers, and gold-gilded furniture seems to go on forever, incorporating a bar with the most ornate coffeemaker I've ever seen. Dotted throughout are busts and hunting paintings. The pride of the place is a somewhat tacky waterfall with plants. It is best to avoid the cheaper rooms, as they are on the noisy events floor. Go instead for the midrange rooms, which must be the biggest in Asunción—half a tennis court in size. If you don't mind clunky phones and deep pile carpets (there are some rooms with tiles), it is not a bad hotel and is centrally located in front of a small shopping mall. There is, however, a little too much brown in the décor, and the flowery bedspreads and lace curtains need updating. The bathrooms are immaculate, and guests are welcomed with a complimentary Caipirinha. Check as sometimes the rates include an airport pickup. Every night there's a traditional song and dance show, and the second restaurant is an upscale Italian eatery.

Chile 980. © 021/495-632. Fax 021/496-748. www.excelsior.com.py. 116 units. $99–$110 (£50–£55) double; from $132 (£66) suite. AE, DC, MC, V. **Amenities:** 2 restaurants; 1 bar; concierge; room service; laundry service; dry cleaning. *In room:* A/C, TV, minibar, hair dryer, safe.

Sheraton Asunción ★★ The Sheraton Asunción is a 10-storey cream-colored building with an interior of bright wood paneling and frosted glass. It is undoubtedly one of the best hotels in Asunción, with a modern, stylish ambience and very courteous staff, many of whom speak English. The lobby is smallish, with a light-filled atrium that illuminates a curved mezzanine and an open-plan restaurant-cum-breakfast room of pine floors and black leather seating. The corridors are bright with windows at either end. The walls are decorated with abstract prints. Rooms are a good size with a profusion of pneumatic pillows and wardrobes. Standard rooms do not come with a coffeemaker, and an iron and board must be requested. The hotel's best asset is a fabulous rooftop restaurant right beside the pool, perfect for a cool beer in the early evening while watching the sunset. The hotel is 8km (5 miles) from the city center in upscale Villa Mora, in front of Paraguay's largest shopping mall and near some of Asunción's best restaurants. It is also convenient for the airport.

Aviadores del Chaco 2066. ✆ **021/617-7000.** Fax 021/617-7001. www.sheraton.com. 100 units. $215 (£108) double; from $255 (£128) suite. AE, DC, MC, V. Rates include gourmet breakfast. **Amenities:** 2 restaurants; bar; rooftop pool; small fitness center and sauna; business center; room service; babysitting; laundry service; dry cleaning. *In room:* A/C, TV, minibar, hair dryer.

INEXPENSIVE

Asunción Palace *Value*   The oldest hotel in Asunción is a cream-colored colonial building, three stories high and close to the river. It might lack the five-star sheen and luxury of other places, but it makes up for it with a very central location, helpful staff, and an interesting history. It once belonged to President López's brother and was used as a hospital during the War of the Triple Alliance. Two balconies run around the entire building, offering good views of the city. The rooms are somewhat bare, but there is lots of space in the midpriced range. The bathrooms are more modern, with powerful showers. Some rooms have private balconies and others are dormitory style with corresponding price. The landings are a little glum, and the steel elevator is from another era. Yet this is a great value hotel, run with efficiency by two sisters, Graciela and Alicia. The continental breakfast includes delicious homemade cakes.

Colon 415. ✆ **021/492-151.** www.geocities.com/aphotel. 27 units. From $50 (£25) double. Rates include buffet breakfast. AE, DC, MC, V. Free parking. **Amenities:** Coffee shop; room service. *In room:* A/C, TV, minibar, hair dryer.

Gran Armele   Location-wise you could not do better. The Gran Armele is not far from the customs house and Palacio Gobierno, and it has great views of the city and river. It is, however, in sore need of some renovations; the decor is very dated. Rooms are good size, with clean and adequate bathrooms. It's a good value option.

Palma y Colon. ✆ **021/444-686.** Fax 021/445903. www.hotelarmele.com.py. 56 units. From $63 (£37) double. Rates include buffet breakfast. AE, DC, MC, V. **Amenities:** Restaurant; bar; heated indoor pool; fitness center; sauna; business center; room service; laundry service; dry cleaning. *In room:* A/C, TV, minibar, safe.

WHERE TO DINE

Asunción has plenty of street stalls and corner bars selling empanadas and *chipas* (a type of cheese bread made from yuca flour or cornflower). More upmarket restaurants offer the delicious river fish, surubi, in countless varieties. The downtown area does not have a great quantity of gourmet style eateries. Instead, many are located in the Villa Morra district. *Parrillas* (grill houses) are plentiful, though the meat can vary in quality.

MODERATE

Bar San Roque PARAGUAYAN/GERMAN   This restaurant has an old-world feel, with its long low counter bar with wood paneling, matching olive green windows and ceiling fans, and black and white tiled floor. It is popular with locals and has an easy, laid-back feel. The menu is meat-based, with a variety of homemade pastas. There's a German connection, thus a good collection of beers and Liebfraumilch on the wine list. It's a good downtown choice.

Eligio Ayala 792. ✆ **021/446-015.** Main courses $5–$8 (£2.50–£4). No credit cards. Daily 11:45am–3:30pm and 7:30pm–midnight.

Mburicao INTERNATIONAL   On a quiet residential street in Villa Mora, Mburicao is where Asunción's great and good come to dine. The large open dining area is attractive if a little uninteresting and lacking character. That said, the food is great—it is here I tried the best asparagus soup ever—it comes with a mound of shredded carrot and onion and a sprinkling of parmesan cheese. The surubi is crisp and succulent and presented on a bed of broad beans and tomatoes. Other items include tilapia in escargot sauce and filet steak with fresh mushroom and baby potatoes. My only complaint is the limited dessert menu, with only one dessert—a lonely strawberry cake with chocolate and custard. Recommended on the Chilean/Argentine wine list is the Ruca Malen Kinien.

Profesor Gonzalez Riobo 737. ℂ 021/660-048. Main courses $10–$15 (£5–£7.50). AE, DC, MC, V. Mon–Thurs noon–2:30pm and 8–11:30pm; Fri–Sat noon–2:30pm and 8–1:30pm.

Il Mondo INTERNATIONAL   This is a good, high-end restaurant in the downtown area. The decor is Romanesque with a touch of the Far East. Toga-like drapes hang from windows and walls, while a large urn sits on a grand central table surrounded by four templelike pillars. All is overlooked by a large wooden Buddha on the back wall. The menu is a 20-page extravaganza of seafood, river food, Far East stir fries, and meat (of course). I tried the pasta, which was excellent and came mixed with bacon, baby tomatoes, and a variety of nuts. The service was spot on, and the staff, though non-English speaking, were very friendly. Il Mondo is part of the Granaderos Hotel.

15 de Agosto y Estrella. ℂ 021/497-921. Main courses $8–$12 (£4–£6). AE, DC, MC, V. Daily noon–4pm and 7pm–1am.

Talleygrand FRENCH   The attractive, solid-white building of adobe walls and thick wooden beams gives assurance in a downtown area sorely lacking in good restaurants. The food is a mixture of French and Spanish, with a Paraguayan twist. This includes eight variations of the ubiquitous surubi, one of which is *surubi a la bonne* (surubi, done in white wine and mustard). The *festival de pasta* is a pasta party for two, with six types of sauce to choose from. There is rabbit with mushroom sauce, and good old-fashioned sirloin served with fried cassava. Out back is a small bar with a waiting area of embroidered curtains and cushions. The waiters are tall, dark, and very serious, but it's a popular place, with relaxing jazz in the background.

Mcal Estigarribia 441. ℂ 021/441-163. Main courses $8–$10 (£4–£5). MC, V. Daily noon–4pm and 8pm–1am.

INEXPENSIVE

Biggest (Value ⭐ JAPANESE   Its name might lack the definite article but this corner diner lives up to its description with good size portions of burgers, fries and pizza. Its location means it's perfect for a midmorning coffee stop in a city that lacks coffee shops. Two matronly waitresses run the place with friendly efficiency.

Estrella and 15 de Agosto. ℂ 021/455-411. Main courses $3–$5 (£1.50–£2.50). No credit cards. Daily 11am–midnight.

ASUNCIÓN AFTER DARK

Don't let the dark streets turn you off. There is a party going on somewhere if you look hard enough. There are plenty of bars dotted all around the city, especially a few blocks east of Plaza Uruguaya. You'll also find some down-at-the-heel karaoke bars around Palma and Colon. The **Britannia Pub,** Cerro Cora 851 (ℂ 021/901-2850), is a British-style bar popular with locals and expats. In existence for 18 years, it is still going strong, with good crowds drinking beer from huge tankards whatever night of the week (except Mon). Another favorite is **Austria Pub,** Austria 1783 y Vienna (℡ **021/604-662**), situated upstairs in a small shopping mall called Excelsior in the downtown area. For something trendier and more upscale, you have to go to Villa Morra and its various glitzy shopping malls. **Kamastro,** Paseo Carmelitas, Avenida España and Senador Long (℡ **021/615-041**), is an interesting art-house bar with psychedelic guitars and naked body prints on the walls. Close by, you'll find **Kilkenny Irish Pub,** Malutin and Avenida España (℡ **021/672-768;** www.kilkenny.com.py). Across the road, in a smaller mall, is **Hooters,** Avenida España and Romulo Feliciangeli (℡ **021/665-215**), a foreign-owned bar boasting cold beers and tasty chicken wings. Some of the best nightclubs are situated on the city outskirts. **Faces,** Mcal López 2585 (℡ **021/672-768**), and **Coyote,** Sucre 1655 (℡ **021/662-816;** www. coyote.com.py), are the biggest and best known.

A SIDE TRIP TO SAN BERNARDINO
54km (34 miles) SE of Asunción

San Bernardino is a small resort town on the eastern shore of Lago Ypacarai. A trip there makes for an interesting day tour known as *Circuito de Oro.* You leave Asunción via Ave. Mariscal López, a busy highway passing *Gone With the Wind*–style diplomatic mansions. Twelve kilometers (8 miles) away is the bustling satellite town of **San Lorenzo** with its gray neo-gothic cathedral. On the open road, you will pass handicraft stores selling a variety of ceramics and basketware, much of it tacky. In the humble town of Yaguaron, be sure to visit **Iglesia San Buenaventura,** one of the most beautiful churches in Paraguay. Built in 1755, it is a small white-faced chapel with spectacular doors carved by indigenous artists. The inner pillars are brightly tinted with red, yellow, and green vegetable inks. The ceiling has 60 tiny individual portraits of the local craftsmen who worked on the church (their signatures) and the altar is a gold painted spectacle with incredible detail. The church is open every day from 6am to 4pm, closing at midday from 11am to 1:30pm. It's open mornings only on Saturdays. The caretaker, Antolin Aleman, will also show you a small museum nearby. Be sure to leave a small donation, as the church is proudly cared for by the local community with little or no help from the authorities.

Back on the road, you'll notice the flatlands become gentle slopes with the occasional rocky cliff. You pass lemon groves, roadside stalls and the occasional wandering farm fowl. Make sure to stop at **Fruteria Paraguan.** This large restaurant sells delicious, syrupy fruit salads. Nearby, in **Pararetá** and **Chololó,** are several beauty spots with small waterfalls and bathing areas popular in the summer. The town of **Pirebebuy** has another interesting colonial church and is infamous for a strong local brew called *caña.* The town was the site of a major battle in the War of the Triple Alliance. Here you are truly in the rural hinterland, with stray cattle and road venders selling bottles of dark honey. Next you arrive at **Caacupé,** the Lourdes of Paraguay. It is a major pilgrimage center, which attracts thousands on the December 8 each year for fireworks, night processions, and amazingly agile dancers balancing pyramids of bottles on their heads. Finally, you reach **Ypacarai Lake** and the pleasant "beach" town of **San Bernardino.** In the summer, its bars, cafes, and shore are bustling with people enjoying the waterside atmosphere. Enjoy a late lunch at **Los Alpes** restaurant and hotel, Ruta Gral. Moringo, Km 46.5 (℡ **512/232-399;** losalpeshotel@hotmail.com). It has a pretty flower-covered veranda and fountain with resident parrots. The restaurant does buffet-style lunches amid tropical decor. The direct route back to Asunción is 54km (35 miles), and the entire day should not take more than 7 hours.

5 Ciudad del Este

327km (209 miles) E of Asunción

Prepare yourself for a city quite unlike any other; a dirty, sweltering warren of frenetic buying and selling, set beside a muddy river upon which thousands cross like ants carrying TVs, computers, even kitchen sinks! Here the currency is either dollars or Brazilian reals, and the nationalities are a melting pot of Taiwanese, Korean, Indian, Syrian, and Lebanese. Ciudad del Este gets a bad rap as South America's capital of contraband and piracy, where you can buy anything from AK47s to bales of marijuana to even babies (so one foreboding Argentine told me). The truth is somewhere in between. What I found was a modern frontier town (indeed three frontiers), choked with billboards and vendors. Shoppers and porters hurriedly dodge money-changers and dealers as motorcyclists weave between stalled cars and buses, all on a frantic break for the border. Stores vary from rickety stalls to giant, luxury malls selling the real and the unreal. Ciudad del Este's existence began with the building of the impressive Itaipú dam and continues with the unchecked flood of Brazilian and Argentine bargain hunters. (It is linked to Brazil through a 500m/1,640 ft. rusting hulk called the "Friendship Bridge.") Ciudad del Este is the third-largest tax-free zone in the world and provides 60% of Paraguay's GDP. It has some good hotels and is close to Iguazú Falls and its smaller counterpart Monday Falls.

ESSENTIALS

GETTING THERE

BY PLANE   Aeropuerto Guarani is 30km (19 miles) west of town (no phone). **TAM,** Curupayty 195 (© **064/420-843**), operates a daily service between Sao Paolo and Asunción

BY BUS   The **Terminal,** Chaco Boreal and Capitan del Puerto (© **061/510-421**) is on southern outskirts of city beside a large soccer stadium. There are buses connecting in Asunción (4½ hours) and Encarnación (3 hours). Local buses leave for Foz de Iguaçu every 15 minutes. **Nuestra Señora de la Asunción** (© **061/510-095;** www.nsa.com.py) operates a reliable service, as does **RYSA** (© **061/500-458;** www.rysa.com.py).

ORIENTATION

All the action takes place around the Microcentro and to the east towards **Puente de la Amistad,** the Friendship Bridge. It is often best to go everywhere on foot, as traffic is often at a standstill.

BORDER CROSSING

The 500m-long (320 ft.) "Friendship Bridge" can be at times very informal, indeed overly friendly—watch out for pickpockets. Rush hour can be incredibly slow and it is often quicker to walk it than to take a bus or taxi. Wednesdays and Saturdays are the busiest days—always be mindful of your belongings. Pedestrians from Brazil walk on the northern side with goods-laden consumers exiting on the other side. If you are a U.S. or Canadian citizen (see "Entry Requirements & Customs," p. 596) you might be tempted to risk crossing without a visa, but be warned. If you're caught, it can mean the temporary confiscation of your passport until you pay a "fine." Local buses do not stop at the customs offices which are at either end of the bridge. You'll find a somewhat shabby but friendly and helpful **tourist office** in the Paraguayan customs building.

WHAT TO SEE & DO

Itaupú Dam   The pride of Paraguay is one of the biggest hydroelectric projects in the world and actually produces 18 times more electricity than Paraguay needs (the remainder is sold to Brazil and Argentina). Although it has proved an economic boon to the area, it has an ambiguous past; its $25 billion price tag plunged all three border countries into debt and had a devastating effect on the surrounding environment. The submerged Sete Quedas falls were actually larger and more impressive than Iguazu. It has also proved a magnet for mosquitoes, boosting the risk of malaria in the area. Nevertheless, it is an engineering masterpiece, impressive in its size, volume, and ugliness. There are two types of tours. One is free via bus, where you cross the dam but see very little of the facility, and another costs $15 (£7.50), but is more technical and you get to disembark. This is recommended as you get to see the 1km-long (about a half mile) machine room. Tours also include a rather technical 30-minute film. On Fridays and Saturdays at 7pm, there is a nighttime illumination and fireworks display. The dam is 20km (12 miles) north of the city, near the town of Hernadarias. ***Don't forget to bring your passport!***

Visitor Center, Hernadarias. ℰ **61/599-8989**. Free admission. Mon–Sat tours start at 8:30 and 10:30am, and 3:30pm. Evening tour Fri and Sat at 7pm.

Flora and Fauna Itaipú Binacional   As a sop to the huge environmental damage caused by the dam, the builders were obliged to spend some money on remedial work such as relocation of wildlife and reforestation. One result is an interesting zoo with displaced jaguars and other animals. Here you will also find two well-organized natural history and archaeological museums. It is located 2km (1¼ miles) from the Itaipú Visitors Center on the road back to Ciudad del Este.

Hernadarias. ℰ **061/599 8040**. Free admission. Mon–Sun 7:30am–1pm and 2–5pm.

Salto Monday   Anywhere else, this waterfall would be the star attraction, but when it's so close to the magnificence of Iguazu, Salto Monday's 80m-high (362 ft.) cascade takes on the role of a younger, neglected brother. Nearby you'll find a popular beach resort and nature reserve called Tati Yupi. The falls are located 10km (6 miles) south of the city, in the town of Puerto President Franco.

Puerto President Franco. ℰ **061/550-042**. Admission 50¢ (25p). Mon–Sun 7am–4pm.

SHOPPING

Ciudad del Este isn't called the shopping center of South America for nothing. It's regarded as the cheapest place for electronic goods on the continent. Its shops and malls are plentiful and vary greatly in quality. The center is a maze of stores and stalls selling all types of cheap and tacky goods. Be careful of counterfeit products, near–name brands, and short-changing. Always haggle. If you get anything wrapped, make sure it is what you bought. Some of the malls are more secure and certainly cleaner such as **Mona Lisa,** Carlos A. Lopez 654 (ℰ **061/513-622;** www.monalisa.com.py), which specializes in luxury goods. **Casa China,** Avenida San Blas 206 (ℰ **561/500-335;** www.casachina.net) sells everything from flowerpots to motorbike helmets.

WHERE TO STAY

Ciudad del Este goes dead after 5pm when the shopping frenzy ends and everybody crosses back over the border to Brazil. At night, the city has a dangerous reputation, which is not entirely unfounded, so be careful of where you choose to stay. The best hotels are situated outside the downtown area. **Las Ventanas,** Avenida Maria de los Angeles and Luis Bordon, Paraná Country Club (ℰ **061/574-500;** www.lasventanas.

Waterfalls & Jaguars

Paraguay has great potential regarding ecotourism. It has 11 national parks and seven reserves offering diverse habitats. However, poor management and little infrastructure mean you really must make an effort to get there. Just be prepared to get your feet wet and your clothes dirty when you do so. For permits and information concerning all of Paraguay's parks, go to **Direccion de Parques Nacionales y Vida Silvestre**, Franco and Ayolas, Asunción (© **021/445-970**). Below are some of the best parks.

- **Parque Nacional Ybycui** is 5,000 hectares (12,350 acres) of rare rainforest, steep woodland, and idyllic waterfalls. It is the country's most accessible park and is famous for its partridges and multitudes of butterflies. It is only 120km (77 miles) south of Asunción and therefore can be crowded on weekends and holidays. On weekdays, its campsites and forest trails are deserted.
- **Parque Nacional Cerro Corrá** was the site of Mariscal López's last stand against his triple alliance enemies and is now a 22,000 hectare (54,340 acre) reserve of tropical forest and savannah grasslands. There are also caves, petroglyphs, and a small museum and information center. The town is 35km (22 miles) from the town of Pedro Juan Caballero, near the Brazilian border.
- **Parque Nacional Defensores del Chaco** is a 780,000 hectare (1.9 million acre) enclave of spectacular bird life, including six-foot storks called jabiru. Jaguar and puma can be found lurking in the dense thorn forest. The park is 830km (531 miles) from Asunción and accessible only by 4×4. Permits are necessary and obtained in Asunción. It is highly recommended that you go with a guide.

com.py), is the newest and trendiest, with comfortable rooms and spacious balconies. Another excellent choice is the colonial **Casa Blanca,** Calle Botero Norte 69, Paraná Country Club (© **061/572-121**; www.casablancahotel.net) situated along the Paraná river. It is in an idyllic, tranquil setting and rooms come with balcony overlooking a beautiful pool. Make sure you get a room in the original building. A good city option is the **Panorama Inn,** Pampliega and Ayola (© **061/500-110**; www.hotelpanorama inn.com.py). It is not five-star but is clean and modern, with the all-essential pool. Another decent downtown hotel is **Hotel Austria,** E.R. Fernandez 165 (© **061/504-213**; www.hotelaustriarestaurante.com).

WHERE TO DINE

You'll find lots of cheap eateries on Garcia Street and in the market place. For something more upscale and European, try the restaurant at **Hotel Austria,** E.R. Fernandez 165 (© **061/504-213**). An excellent Brazillian-style churrascaria (grill house) is **Patussi Grill,** Avenida Monsignor Cedzich and Alejo Garcia (© **061/502-293**). **Belsit,** Avenida Boqueron (no phone), is an excellent Italian restaurant, located away from the city center and close to El Lago de La Republica. For something completely different, try **New Tokyo,** Pampliega (© **061/514-379**), which, as the name implies, provides authentic Japanese food.

11

Peru

by Neil E. Schlecht

When Francisco Pizarro, the Spanish conquistador, and his fortune-hunting cronies descended on Peru in 1528, they found the vast riches they were searching for, as well as an unexpectedly sophisticated culture. The Spaniards soon overpowered the awed and politically weakened Inca empire, but they didn't discover the Incas' greatest secret: the imperial city of Machu Picchu, hidden high in the Andes. Machu Picchu is acclaimed as the pinnacle achievement of the continent's pre-Columbian societies, yet it is only one of the exhilarating discoveries that await visitors to Peru.

Peru has a habit of turning virtually every visitor into an amateur archaeologist. Ruins fire the imagination and outstanding museum collections weave an intricate tale of complex cultures through ceramics, spectacular textiles, and remarkably preserved mummies. You can see the Lord of Sipán in all the glory of the jewels and rituals that accompanied his burial, as well as the frozen corpse of Juanita the Ice Maiden, an Inca princess sacrificed on a mountain ridge more than 500 years ago.

Peru has few peers when it comes to physical beauty and diversity. Its landscapes will delight anyone with an appreciation for the outdoors: the rugged, cloud-ringed Andes; the brilliant azure water of Lake Titicaca, the world's highest navigable body of water; great canyons graced by giant condors; and a teeming Amazon jungle that possesses one of the world's richest repositories of plant and animal life. Peru is fast becoming South America's top destination for mountain climbing, river rafting, bird-watching, river cruises, and rainforest treks. Urban Peru is a mix of laid-back and elegant colonial towns, a chaotic and cosmopolitan capital, and the surprisingly lively Cusco, a grand 16th-century city on Incan foundations that rocks to the beat of global backpackers.

Peru's history of suffering—political mayhem and corruption, surprise attacks from homegrown Maoist "Shining Path" terrorists, cocaine trafficking, and violent street crime—is well documented. In the late 1980s and early 1990s, Peruvians fled the capital and the countryside, and understandably, few travelers were brave enough to plan vacations in Peru. With the 2001 election of Alejandro Toledo, the nation's first president of native Indian origin, many Peruvians were hopeful that the country had finally turned a corner. Although the economy has grown at a rate of 7% to 8% annually for the past 6 years and Peru is safer and superficially more stable than before, widespread poverty, frequent strikes, and continued unease are still prevalent. One disgraced ex-president, Alberto Fujimori, returned from exile in Japan only to be jailed in Peru, while another, Alan García, surprisingly reappeared after his own exile abroad to capture the 2006 presidential election. Still, Peru is more welcoming than ever. Too many unfortunate years of corrupt politicians, lawlessness, and economic disarray clouded—but never succeeded in eclipsing—the resilient beauty of this fascinating Andean nation.

1 The Regions in Brief

Peru, which lies just below the Equator, is the third-largest country in South America, covering an area of nearly 1.3 million sq. km (500,000 sq. miles). Peru shares borders with Ecuador and Colombia to the north, Brazil and Bolivia to the east, and Chile to the south. Peruvians are fond of telling visitors that their country is in fact three countries (or at least three distinct geological components) in one: coast, *sierra* (highlands), and *selva* (jungle). Though Lima lies on the coast, the bold Andes mountain range and Amazon rainforest, which makes up nearly two-thirds of Peru, dominate the country. Its considerable size, natural barriers, and a lack of efficient transportation options make Peru a somewhat difficult and time-consuming place in which to get around.

LIMA & THE CENTRAL COAST The Pacific coastal region is a narrow strip that runs from one end of the country to the other (a distance of some 2,254km/1,400 miles) and is almost entirely desert. Lima lies about halfway down the coast. To the south in one of the driest areas on earth are **Pisco, Ica,** and **Nazca,** cradle of several of Peru's most important ancient civilizations, as well as the famously mysterious **Nazca Lines** and the **Ballestas Islands,** promoted locally as "Peru's Galápagos" for their diverse indigenous fauna. In August 2007, a massive earthquake, which registered 7.9 on the Richter scale, devastated much of Pisco and Ica, killing more than 500 people and leaving nearly 100,000 homeless. The region will take years to rebuild, a factor travelers should keep in mind if they intend to travel to the area.

SOUTH CENTRAL PERU The dramatic Andes mountains of the south, the focus of most first-time visitors to Peru, contain the country's most famous sights, including the former Inca capital of **Cusco** and scenic highland villages that run the length of the beautiful **Sacred Valley.** The valley is dotted with singularly impressive Inca ruins, of which **Machu Picchu** (and the **Inca Trail** leading to it) is undoubtedly the star.

SOUTHERN PERU Massive **Lake Titicaca,** shared with Bolivia, is the largest freshwater lake in South America and the world's highest navigable body of water. **Puno,** at the edge of Lake Titicaca, is a rough-and-tumble town that hosts some of Peru's liveliest festivals. The elegant colonial city of **Arequipa** is gorgeously situated at the base of three snowcapped volcanoes, and nearby is **Colca Canyon,** twice as deep as the Grand Canyon and perhaps the best place in South America to view the regal Andean condor.

NORTH CENTRAL HIGHLANDS The mountain ranges north of Lima are among the highest in Peru. Within **Huascarán National Park,** the Cordillera Blanca stretches for 200km (124 miles) and contains a dozen peaks over 5,000m (16,400 ft.) high. The region is a favorite of trekkers and outdoor adventure travelers. The main jumping-off point for these activities is the town of **Huaraz.** In valleys east of the capital is **Chavín de Huantar,** one of Peru's oldest archaeological sites.

NORTH COAST & NORTHERN HIGHLANDS Peru's north is much less visited than the south, even though it possesses some of the country's most outstanding archaeological sights. **Trujillo, Chiclayo,** and particularly **Cajamarca,** a lovely small city in the highlands, are the main colonial towns of interest. Near Trujillo and Chiclayo are

Off the Beaten Path

Northern Peru is vastly underappreciated; in fact, most of the region is virtually unknown to foreigners who travel to Peru. The few travelers who get to know the north are mainly those with a specific interest in ancient Peruvian cultures or hikers and adventurous travelers looking to get out into the country, beyond the reach of the majority of gringos who trod well-beaten paths in the Andes and southern Peru. If you make it to this part of Peru, you may be in for the not-unwelcome treat of being one of the few.

You wouldn't know it from the paucity of foreign visitors, but the northern coastal desert of Peru holds some of the country's greatest archaeological treasures: **Chan Chan,** the great adobe city of the Chimú civilization; 1,500-year-old Moche temples; and the royal tomb that brought the great Lord of Sipán to the world's attention in 1987—Peru's very own King Tut. Northern beaches draw surfers to some of the best waves off South America, and nestled in the *sierra* is one of the country's most charming and beautiful mountain towns, **Cajamarca,** a mini-Cusco of the north.

Where gringos of a particular ilk and style of outdoor performance gear do make it in significant numbers is the **Cordillera Blanca,** home to some of the most beautiful peaks in South America and some of the finest trekking on the continent. Huaraz is the primary base for excursions into the valleys and mountain ranges of the northern Andes. For years, the destination has been favored principally by sports and adventure travelers, especially hardcore hikers, but the range of activities is opening up and appealing more and more to average travelers who also want a taste of Peru's great outdoors.

AeroCondor (© 01/514-6000; www.aerocondor.com.pe) and **LC Busre** (© 01/619-1300; www.lcbusre.com.pe) fly daily to Trujillo and Cajamarca from Lima; **StarPerú** (© 01/705-9000) flies daily from Lima to Chiclayo (Starerú also flies to Truillo). Agencies offering standard city and archaeological tours in Trujillo include **Guía Tours,** Jr. Independencia 580 (© 044/245-170); **Chacón Tours,** Av. España 106 (© 044/255-212); and **Trujillo Tours,** Diego de Almagro 301 (© 044/233-091). In Chiclayo, **Indiana Tours,** Colón 556, (© 074/222-991) offers a full range of northern archaeological tours.

Traveling by bus from Lima, or from other points along the north coast or the northern Andes, is the only way to get to Huaraz. For the 7- to 8-hour journey from Lima, major companies offering daily service are **CIVA** (© 01/332-5236), **Cruz del Sur** (© 01/424-6158), and **Móvil Tours** (© 044/722-555 in Huaraz). For mountaineering and trekking information, consult the respected **Casa de Guías de Huaraz,** Parque Ginebra 28 (© 044/721-811).

Chan Chan, Túcume, and **Sipán,** extraordinary adobe cities, pyramids, and royal tombs and treasures that vastly predate the Incas.

THE AMAZON BASIN & THE JUNGLE   Though about 60% of Peru is Amazon rainforest, only about 5% of the country's human inhabitants reside there. For the visitor, there are two primary jungle destinations. The northern jungle, of which **Iquitos**

is the principal gateway, is the most explored and has the most facilities. Much less trafficked and more controlled is the Madre de Dios department (one of the administrative districts into which Peru is divided) in the south, which contains **Manu National Park** (and its Biosphere Reserve), **Puerto Maldonado,** and **Tambopata.**

2 The Best of Peru in 2 Weeks

This itinerary will allow you to experience the greatest attractions of southern Peru, from its historic colonial cities to its natural wonders. First on everyone's list, of course, are the lively ancient Inca capital of Cusco and that empire's legendary lost city, Machu Picchu. But in a short amount of time, you can also delve into the dense Amazonian jungle; Lake Titicaca, the world's highest navigable body of water; and one of the world's deepest canyons, Cañón del Colca. Plenty of people linger, particularly in Cusco and the Sacred Valley of the Incas (especially if they want to hike the Inca Trail to Machu Picchu), or don't have a full 2 weeks for travel in Peru. In that case, it's probably best to concentrate on a particular region so that you don't lose too much time traveling. Of course, if your primary interest is wildlife viewing in the great Amazon, you'll want to plan everything around a 4- to 7-day jungle expedition deep into Tambopata National Reserve, Manu Biosphere Reserve, or the jungle around Iquitos in northern Peru. *Tip:* For a map of suggested itineraries in Peru, please refer to the Itineraries in Bolivia, Brazil, Colombia, and Peru map on p. 222.

Day ❶: Arrive in Lima 🖈

All international flights go into the chaotic capital, Lima, and even though most people are headed elsewhere, you may be obligated to spend at least a day in Lima. Make the most of it by touring the colonial quarter, or perhaps by visiting one of the country's great museums, such as the **Museo Arqueológico Rafael Larco Herrera** or **Museo de la Nación,** and hitting either a great *cevichería* or a cutting-edge *novo andino* restaurant. See p. 636. Then get out of Lima on the way to Peru's greatest attractions. (If you're able to get an overnight flight that puts you into Lima early in the morning, you may want to consider flying immediately to Cusco.)

Days ❷–❸: On to Cusco and the Sacred Valley 🖈🖈

The typical thing to do is hit Cusco running, but since the city's altitude, more than 3,600m (11,000 ft.), is daunting to most travelers, a great alternative is to head directly to the serene and beautiful

(as well as lower-altitude) **Valle Sagrado de los Incas** (Sacred Valley of the Incas). Besides great Inca ruins in **Pisac** and **Ollantaytambo,** you'll find excellent crafts markets, a wealth of outdoor activities such as trekking and white-water rafting, small rural villages, and a burgeoning roster of comfortable rustic lodgings. Relax, eat and sleep well, and get ready for Machu Picchu. See p. 678.

Day ❹: The Stuff of Legend: Machu Picchu 🖈🖈🖈

Take the morning train from Ollantaytambo to Aguas Calientes, which sits down below camouflaged **Machu Picchu,** South America's number-one attraction. Spend the day exploring the ruins (hiking up to **Huayna Picchu** if you're in shape) and then spend the night either next to the ruins (if you've got deep pockets) or back down in Aguas Calientes (which is actually more fun). Hit the thermal baths and the bars to share stories with those who've hiked the Inca Trail.

Days ❺–❻: Back to Cusco ✶✶✶

Now that you've acclimatized to the Andes mountains and seen some of the greatest legacies of the Incas, head back by train to the old Inca capital, Cusco. Stroll around the hilly San Blas neighborhood, site of art galleries and shops, check out streets with foundations of Inca stone, and visit the **Cathedral, Plaza de Armas,** and stunning **Qoricancha-Temple of the Sun.** If you didn't catch an archaeology museum in Lima, or even if you did, check out the beautifully designed **Museo de Arte Precolombino.** Enjoy some of the lively cafes, bars, and restaurants of Cusco. If you have time, catch a cab (or walk up to) the fantastic ruins, **Sacsayhuamán,** overlooking the city. See p. 658.

Days ❼–❾: Into the Jungle ✶✶✶

Take an early morning, half-hour flight from Cusco to **Puerto Maldonado,** the gateway to the southern Peruvian Amazon jungle of **Tambopata National Reserve.** See p. 690. Board a boat on the way to a 3-day, 2-night adventure at a jungle lodge (either within 1 hour of Puerto Maldonado, or 4–5 hours along the Río Tambopata; if you're pressed for time, you can also do a 2-day, 1-night trip to one of the lodges along the Río Madre de Dios). On the third day, head back to Puerto and then catch a flight to Cusco. Spend the night in Cusco.

Day ❿: South to Lake Titicaca

From Cusco, take the extraordinarily scenic train to **Puno** and **Lake Titicaca** (or, if you want to visit some of the Inca ruins en route, take one of the premium tour bus services that make a day of the journey). See p. 693. Spend the night in Puno and rest up (and get accustomed to the even higher altitude) for tomorrow's boat trip out on the lake.

Day ⓫: Lake Titicaca and Isla Taquile ✶✶✶

While an overnight trip that allows you to spend a night with a family either on Isla Taquile or Amantaní is the best way to experience the people and customs of Titicaca, you can also do a 1-day trip that allows you to visit the **Uros floating islands** and the fascinating culture of **Isla Taquile.** See p. 698.

Day ⓬: Arequipa ✶✶

Catch an early morning flight from Juliaca (the nearest airport, an hour from Puno) to Arequipa, the elegant southern city known as "La Ciudad Blanca" for its beautiful colonial buildings made of *sillar,* or white volcanic stone. Stay close to the gorgeous **Plaza de Armas** and spend the afternoon at the wondrous **Monasterio de Santa Catalina,** one of the finest examples of colonial religious architecture in the Americas. See p. 705.

Days ⓭–⓮: Colca Valley ✶✶

If you're short on time, spend another day in Arequipa, shopping for alpaca garments and enjoying some of the finest cuisine in Peru. If you have an extra day, though, don't miss an overnight journey to **Colca Valley,** the site of **Colca Canyon** (twice as deep as the Grand Canyon) and the best spot in South America to observe giant Andean condors, which soar overhead at **Cruz del Condor.** See p. 714. Spend your first night at a rustic hotel in Colca, and then head back to Arequipa.

Day ⓯: Morning in Arequipa, then back to Lima ✶

If you were able to squeeze out the extra day, do a little shopping before flying to Lima, where you'll catch your flight back home.

3 Planning Your Trip to Peru

VISITOR INFORMATION

Peru doesn't maintain national tourism offices abroad, so your best official source of information before you go is the **PromPerú** (Commission for the Promotion of Peru) website at **www.peru.org.pe**. Peruvian embassies and consulates usually offer some brochures and other information on traveling to Peru, but it's probably best not to expect too much. Additional websites of interest include:

- **www.peru.info**: The website for PromPerú, the tourism promotion bureau of the Peruvian government
- **www.peruvianembassy.us**: The official website for the Peruvian Embassy in Washington, D.C.
- **www.perurail.com**: Peru Rail's official site with routes and services
- **www.saexplorers.org**: The South American Explorers Club website, especially good for trekking and adventure travel
- **www.traficoperu.com/english**: An online travel agency with information on flights, hotels, and special deals

IN PERU

Visitor information is not handled by a single, centralized government agency across Peru. PromPerú works alongside Mitinci (Ministry of Industry, Tourism & International Business Negotiation) and several private entities. The result is that tourism information is confusingly dispersed among sometimes poorly equipped small municipal offices and is often limited to regional or local information. Occasionally, private travel agencies are more adept at dispensing information, though their goal is, of course, to hawk their services.

PromPerú operates a 24-hour information booth (© **01/574-8000**) in the international terminal of Lima's Jorge Chávez International Airport. The **Tourist Protection Bureau (Indecopi)** operates a 24-hour traveler's assistance line that handles complaints and questions about consumer rights; call © **01/224-7888** in Lima, or 0800/42-579 (toll-free) in other cities. The Tourist Protection Bureau's Lima office is at La Prosa 138, San Borja (© **01/224-8600**); for local branch numbers, see "Fast Facts" in the individual city sections in this chapter.

ENTRY REQUIREMENTS

Citizens of the United States, Canada, Great Britain, South Africa, New Zealand, and Australia require valid passports to enter Peru as tourists. Citizens of any of these countries conducting business or enrolled in formal educational programs in Peru also require visas.

Tourist (or landing) cards, distributed on arriving international flights or at border crossings, are good for stays of up to 90 days. Keep a copy of the tourist card for presentation upon departure from Peru. (If you lose it, you'll have to pay a $4/£2 fine.) A maximum of three extensions of 30 days each, for a total of 180 days, is allowed.

PERUVIAN EMBASSY LOCATIONS

In the U.S.: 1700 Massachusetts Ave. NW, Washington, DC 20036 (© **202/833-9860;** www.peruvianembassy.us)

In Canada: 130 Albert St., Suite 1901, Ottawa, Ontario K1P 5G4 (© **613/238-1777;** www.embassyofperu.ca)

Telephone Dialing Info at a Glance

- **To place a call from your home country to Peru,** dial the international access code (011 in the U.S. and Canada, 0011 in Australia, 0170 in New Zealand, 00 in the U.K.), plus the country code (51), plus the Peruvian area code, followed by the number. For example, a call from the United States to Lima would be 011+51+1+000+0000.

- **To place a local call within Peru,** you do *not* need to dial the city area code (for example, 01 for Lima); dial only the number. To place a long-distance call within Peru, dial 0 plus the city code and the number. For information, dial © 103.

- **To place a direct international call from Peru,** dial the international access code (00), plus the country code of the place you are dialing, plus the area code and the local number.

- **To reach an international operator,** dial © 108. Major long-distance company access codes are as follows: **AT&T** © 0800/50-888; **MCI** © 0800/50-010; **Sprint** © 0800/50-020.

In the U.K.: 52 Sloane St., London SW1X 9SP (© **020/7235-1917;** www.peru embassy-uk.com)

In Australia: 40 Brisbane Avenue, Level 2, Barton, **ACT 2606** (© **02/6273-7351;** www.embaperu.org.au)

In New Zealand: Cigna House, 40 Mercer St., Level 8, Wellington (© **04/499-8087;** www.embassyofperu.org.nz)

CUSTOMS

You are allowed to bring 3 liters of alcohol and 400 cigarettes or 50 cigars into Peru duty-free. New items for personal use, including camera equipment and sports gear such as mountain bikes and kayaks, are allowed. Travelers may bring in up to $300 (£150) in varied gifts, as long as no individual item exceeds $100 (£50). To avoid the possibility of having to fill out forms or pay a bond, it's best not to draw attention to expensive, new-looking items that officials might believe you are intent on reselling. (In other words, take new items out of their original boxes.)

Exports of protected plant and endangered animal species—live or dead—are strictly prohibited by Peruvian law and should not be purchased. This includes headpieces and necklaces made with macaw feathers, and even common "rain sticks," unless authorized by the Natural Resources Institute (INRENA). Vendors in jungle cities and airports sell live animals and birds, as well as handicrafts made from insects, feathers, or other natural products. Travelers have been detained and arrested by the Ecology Police in Lima for carrying such items.

It is also illegal to take pre-Columbian archaeological items, antiques, and artifacts from precolonial civilizations (including ceramics and textiles), and colonial-era art out of Peru. Reproductions of many such items are available, but even their export may cause difficulties at Customs or with overly cautious international courier services if you attempt to send them home. To be safe, look for the word REPRODUCCION or an artist's name stamped on reproduction ceramics, and keep business cards and receipts from shops where you have purchased these items. Particularly fine items may require documentation from Peru's National Institute of Culture (INC) verifying that the object is a reproduction and may be exported. You may be able to obtain a certificate of authorization from the (only occasionally staffed) **INC kiosk** at Lima's Jorge Chávez International Airport or the **INC office** in Lima at the National Museum Building, Sixth Floor, Av. Javier Prado Este 2465, San Borja (© **01/476-9900**).

MONEY

Peru's official currency is the **nuevo sol** (S/), divided into 100 centavos. Coins are issued in denominations of 5, 10, 20, and 50 centavos, and bank notes of S/10, 20, 50, 100, and 200. The U.S. dollar is the second currency; many hotels post their rates in dollars, and plenty of shops, taxi drivers, restaurants, and hotels across Peru accept U.S. dollars for payment. It is often difficult to pay with large bank notes (in either soles or dollars). Try to carry denominations of 50 and lower in both. Throughout this chapter, we give prices of hotels and tours in U.S. dollars as this is how they are typically listed within Peru.

Counterfeit bank notes and even coins are common, and merchants and consumers across Peru vigorously check the authenticity of money before accepting payment or change. (The simplest way: Hold the banknote up to the light to see the watermark.) Many people also refuse to accept bank notes that are not in good condition (including those with small tears, those that have been written on, and even those that are simply well worn) and visitors are wise to do the same when receiving change to avoid problems with other payments. Do not accept bills with tears (no matter how small), and refuse taped bills.

Here's an idea of what things cost in Peru: a short taxi ride, $1 to $2 (50p–£1); a double room at a budget hotel, $20 to $30 (£10–£15); a double room at a moderate hotel, $40 to $80 (£20–£40); a double room at an expensive hotel, $90 to $150 (£45–£75); coffee or bottle of water, $1 (50p); a movie, $3 (£1.50); lunch, $5 to $15 (£2.50–£7.50); dinner, $10 to $30 (£5–£15).

CURRENCY EXCHANGE & RATES At press time, the rate of exchange had dipped to approximately S/3 to the U.S. dollar (from a high of about 3.50). Rates are consistent across the country. If you pay in dollars, you will likely receive change in soles, so be aware of the correct exchange rate. Currencies other than U.S. dollars receive very poor exchange rates. Money can be exchanged at banks; with money changers (legal in Peru), often wearing colored smocks with "$" insignias, on the street; and at rarer *casas de cambio* (money-exchange houses). Money changers offer current rates of exchange, but you are advised to count your money carefully (you can simplify this by exchanging easily calculable amounts, such as $10 or $100 [£5 or £50]) and make sure you have not received any counterfeit bills.

ATMs Peru is still largely a cash society, though in larger tourist destinations you can expect to use credit cards at hotels and some restaurants. In villages and small towns, it may be impossible to cash traveler's checks or use credit cards. Make sure you have cash (in both soles and U.S. dollars) on hand. ATMs, which are the best way of getting cash in Peru, are found in most towns and cities, though certainly not on every street corner. Screen instructions are in English as well as Spanish. Some bank ATMs dispense money only to those who hold accounts there, and lines can be frustratingly long. Peruvian banks include Banco de Crédito, Banco Wiese, Interbank, Banco Central de

Reserva, Banco de Comercio, and Banco Continental. Look for the symbols of major international networks, **PLUS** (☎ 800/843-7587) and **Cirrus** (☎ 800/424-7787). Your personal identification number (PIN) should contain four digits for most ATMs.

TRAVELER'S CHECKS Traveler's checks in Peru are exchanged at fewer places and at a considerably lower rate (often 2%) than cash. If you use traveler's checks, **American Express** is the brand most easily exchanged. Replacing traveler's checks outside of Lima can be very problematic, if not impossible. Keep a record of check numbers and the original bill of sale in a safe place. To report lost or stolen traveler's checks, call American Express at ☎ **01/330-4484.**

CREDIT CARDS Many establishments accept the major international credit cards, including **Visa, MasterCard, Diners Club,** and **American Express.** Visa is the most widely accepted card in Peru. However, some shops and restaurants charge the consumer an additional 10% for paying with a credit card; ask about this practice before you pay. (Offering to pay in cash rather than with a credit card can usually get you a 5%–10% discount.) When using a credit card, be careful to check the amount you are being charged. In rural areas and small towns, cash is essential for payment. At the very least, you should carry a supply of dollars in these areas.

To report lost or stolen credit cards, call Visa (collect) at ☎ **410/581-9994;** MasterCard at ☎ **800/307-7309;** American Express at ☎ **0800/51-531** or collect at **801/945-9450;** and Diners Club at ☎ **01/221-2050.**

WHEN TO GO

PEAK SEASON Peru's high season for travel coincides with the driest months: May through September, with the greatest number of visitors in July and August. May, September, and early October are particularly fine months to visit much of the country. Airlines and hotels also consider mid-December through mid-January to be peak season given the amount of holiday travel.

From June through September in the *sierra,* days are clear and often spectacularly sunny, with nights chilly or downright cold, especially at high elevations. For trekking in the mountains, including the Inca Trail, these are by far the best months. This is also the best time of the year to visit the Amazon basin: Mosquitoes are fewer, and many animals stay close to the rivers (although some people prefer to travel in the jungle during the wet season, when higher water levels allow more river penetration). Note that Peruvians travel in huge numbers around July 28, the national independence day, and finding accommodations in popular destinations can be difficult.

CLIMATE Generally speaking, May through October is the dry season, and November through April is the rainy season. The wettest months are January through April; in mountain areas, roads and trek paths may become impassable. Peru's climate, though, is markedly different among its three vastly different regions. The coast is predominantly arid and mild, the Andean region is temperate to cold, and the eastern lowlands are tropically warm and humid.

PUBLIC HOLIDAYS National public holidays in Peru include New Year's Day (Jan 1); Día de los Reyes (Jan 6); Maundy Thursday and Good Friday; Labor Day (May 1); Fiestas Patrias (Independence; July 28–29); Battle of Angamos (Oct 8); All Saints' Day (Nov 1); Feast of the Immaculate Conception (Dec 8); Christmas Eve (Dec 24); and Christmas (Dec 25).

HEALTH CONCERNS

COMMON AILMENTS   As a tropical South American country, Peru presents certain health risks, but major concerns are limited to those traveling outside urban areas and to the Amazon jungle. The most common ailments for visitors to Peru are common **traveler's diarrhea** and altitude sickness, or **acute mountain sickness (AMS),** called *soroche* locally. Cusco sits at an elevation of about 3,400m (11,150 ft.), Lake Titicaca, 3,800m (12,500 ft.). At these heights, shortness of breath and heart pounding are normal, given the paucity of oxygen. Some people may experience headaches, loss of appetite, extreme fatigue, and nausea. Most symptoms develop during the first day at high altitude, though occasionally travelers have delayed reactions. The best advice is to rest on your first day in the highlands and eat frugally. Drink plenty of liquids, including the local remedy *mate de coca,* or coca-leaf tea (perfectly legal), and avoid alcohol. Give yourself at least a day or two to acclimatize before launching into strenuous activities. Many hotels in Cusco offer oxygen for those severely affected with headaches and shortness of breath. If symptoms persist or become more severe, seek medical attention. People with heart or lung problems and persons with sickle cell anemia may develop serious health complications at high altitudes; consult your doctor before visiting Peru.

VACCINATIONS   Though no vaccinations are required of travelers to Peru, it's wise to take certain precautions, especially if you are planning to travel to jungle regions. A yellow fever vaccine is strongly recommended for trips to the Amazon. The Pan American Health Organization reported an outbreak in 2004, resulting in 52 total cases of yellow fever in Peru. Slightly more than half of those cases were fatal, though just two of those occurred in departments covered in this chapter, Loreto and Madre de Dios. Previously, a 2001 outbreak resulted in 13 deaths from yellow fever cases. The Centers for Disease Control and Prevention (CDC) warn that there is a risk of malaria and yellow fever in all departments except Arequipa, Moquegua, Puno, and Tacna, though Lima and the highland tourist areas (Cusco, Machu Picchu, and Lake Titicaca) are not at risk; consult your doctor about malaria prophylaxes and other preventative treatments.

The CDC also recommends hepatitis A or immune globulin (IG), hepatitis B, typhoid, and booster doses for tetanus-diphtheria and measles, though you may wish to weigh your potential exposure before getting all of these. For additional information on travel to tropical South America, see the CDC website at **wwwn.cdc.gov/travel/regionTropicalSouthAmerica.aspx** as well as the World Health Organization's website, **www.who.int**.

HEALTH PRECAUTIONS   Other recommendations for safe and healthy travel in Peru: Drink only bottled or boiled water (and plenty of it, both at high altitudes and in hot and humid areas); eat only thoroughly cooked or boiled food or fruits and vegetables you have peeled yourself; avoid eating food from street vendors; bring insect repellent containing DEET (diethylmethyltoluamide) if you are traveling to the jungle; and avoid swimming in fresh water.

It is also advisable to get a thorough check-up and take out health insurance before your trip, and to bring along sufficient supplies of any required medicines.

GETTING THERE
BY PLANE

All flights from North America and Europe arrive at Lima's **Jorge Chávez International Airport** (© 01/517-3502; www.lap.com.pe). International flights to Iquitos in the northern Amazon region may be resumed at some point in the near future.

The airport tax on domestic flights is $6 (£3); on international flights, it's $30 (£15). The tax must be paid in cash before boarding.

FROM NORTH AMERICA   From the United States, there are direct flights to Lima from Miami, New York, Newark, Houston, Dallas, and Atlanta. The major carriers are **American** (✆ 800/433-7300; www.aa.com), **Continental** (✆ 800/231-0856; www.continental.com), and **LAN** (✆ 866/435-9526; www.lan.com).

From Canada, **American, Continental,** and **United** all fly to Peru, making stops at their hubs in the United States first. **Air Canada** (✆ 888/247-2262; www.air canada.ca) makes connections with other carriers at U.S. stops, usually Miami. **LAN** partners with other carriers to the United States, making stops in New York, Miami, or Los Angeles on the way to Lima.

FROM THE U.K.   There are no direct flights to Lima from London or any other part of the United Kingdom or Ireland; getting to Peru involves a layover in either another part of Europe or the United States. **American Airlines** (✆ 207/365-0777 in London, or 0845/778-9789) and **Continental** (✆ 0845/607 6760) fly through their U.S. hubs (Dallas, Houston, and Miami) on the way to Lima. European carriers make stops in continental Europe; they include **Iberia** (✆ 870/609-0500; www. iberia.com), **KLM** (✆ 08705/074-074; www.klm.com), and **Lufthansa** (✆ 0845/ 7737-747; www.lufthansa.com).

FROM AUSTRALIA & NEW ZEALAND   You can fly to Buenos Aires on **Aerolíneas Argentinas** (✆ 612/9234-9000 in Australia or 649/379-3675 in New Zealand; www.aerolineas.com.au) and then connect to Lima, or you can go through Los Angeles or Buenos Aires on **Qantas** (✆ 13-13-13 in Australia or 800/808-767 in New Zealand; www.qantas.com) or **Air New Zealand** (✆ 0800/737-000; www. airnz.co.nz). **LAN** (✆ 300/361-400 in Australia and 649/977-2233 in New Zealand; www.lanperu.com) also makes stops in Los Angeles on the way to Lima.

BY BUS

You can travel overland to Peru through Ecuador, Bolivia, or Chile. Though the journey isn't short, Lima can be reached from major neighboring cities. If you're traveling from Quito or Guayaquil, you'll pass through the major northern coastal cities on the way to Lima. From Bolivia, there is frequent service from La Paz and Copacabana to Puno and then on to Cusco. From Chile, most travel from Arica to Tacna, making connections either to Arequipa or Lima.

GETTING AROUND

Because of its size and natural barriers, including difficult mountain terrain, long stretches of desert coast, and extensive rainforest, Peru is not easy to get around. Train service is limited, and many trips can take several days by land. Many visitors with limited time fly everywhere they can. Travel overland, though very inexpensive, can be extremely time-consuming if not altogether uncomfortable. However, for certain routes, intercity buses are your only real option.

BY PLANE

Flying to major destinations within Peru is the only practical way around the country if you wish to see several places in a couple of weeks or less. Some places in the jungle can only be reached by airplane. Flying to major destinations, such as Lima, Cusco, Arequipa, Puerto Maldonado, and Iquitos, is relatively simple and relatively inexpensive; one-way flights to most destinations cost between $69 and $120 (£35–£60).

Puno (and Lake Titicaca), however, requires passengers to fly first to Juliaca before continuing by land the rest of the way (1 hr.)—a reality that prompts many to take a direct train or bus from Cusco to Puno.

Peru's domestic carriers include **AeroCondor** (℃ 01/514-6000; www.aerocondor. com.pe), **LAN Peru** (℃ 01/213-8200; www.lan.com), **Taca Peru** (℃ 01/213-7000; www.grupotaca.com), **LC Busre** (01/619-1300; www.lcbusre.com.pe), and **StarPerú** (℃ 01/705-9000; www.starperu.com). LAN Peru flies to most major destinations in Peru. TANS flies to Cusco, Iquitos, and Pucallpa. AeroCondor flies to Cajamarca and Trujillo. Flight schedules and fares are apt to change frequently and without notice. Flights should be booked several days in advance, especially in high season, and it's very important to reconfirm airline tickets in advance (for local flights, reconfirm 48 hrs. in advance; for international flights, 72 hrs.). You should also make sure you get to the airport at least 45 minutes before your flight to avoid being bumped. In addition, every flight, whether domestic or international, requires payment of an airport tax before boarding.

BY TRAIN

Peru's national railway network was privatized in 1999. The four tourist or passenger train routes operated by Peru Rail, owned by **Orient Express** (℃ 01/444-5020; www. perurail.com), are all very popular and offer scenic journeys. One is the **Cusco–Lake Titicaca Route** (two classes of service: first class $143/£71 one-way and tourist $22/£11). By far, the most popular train routes in Peru are the **Cusco–Machu Picchu** and **Sacred Valley–Machu Picchu** routes, which link Cusco and the Sacred Valley, traveling from the old Inca capital to Ollantaytambo and the world-famous ruins of Machu Picchu. From Cusco to Machu Picchu, there are three classes of service: the new luxury Hiram Bingham, $588 (£294) round-trip; Vistadome, $71 (£35) one-way; and Backpacker, $48 (£24) one-way. From Cusco to Ollantaytambo, prices are Vistadome, $43 to $60 (£21–£30) one-way, and Backpacker, $31 to $43 (£15–£21) one-way. Two antique coaches running the **Puno (Lake Titicaca)–Arequipa** route in southern Peru are available by charter only.

The **Ferrocarril Central Andino** (℃ 01/226-6363; www.ferrocarrilcentral.com.pe), from Lima to Huancayo in the Central Highlands, is again operating after long periods of inactivity over the years. The incredibly scenic, 12-hour passenger train, which crosses 58 bridges and passes through 69 tunnels, runs once a month between July and November ($54 to $87 [£27–£43] round-trip). Trains leave Lima from the **Estación Central de Desamparados.** Check for online updates before you arrive in Peru.

Luggage theft has long been a problem on Peruvian trains; if possible, purchase a premium-class ticket that limits access to ticketed passengers. For additional information, call **Peru Rail** at ℃ 01/444-5020 in Lima and 084/238-722 in Cusco, or visit **www.perurail.com**.

BY BUS

Buses are the cheapest and most popular form of transportation in Peru. A complex network of private bus companies crisscrosses Peru, with a number of competing lines covering the most popular routes. Many companies operate their own bus stations, and their locations, dispersed across many cities, can be endlessly frustrating to travelers. Theft of luggage is an issue on many buses, and passengers should keep a watchful eye on their carry-on items and pay close attention when bags are unloaded. Only a few long-distance buses have luxury buses comparable in comfort to European models (bathrooms, reclining seats, movies). These premium-class ("Royal" or "Imperial") buses cost up to twice as much as regular buses, though for many travelers the additional comfort and services are worth the difference in cost (which remains inexpensive). For many short distances (such as Cusco to Pisac), *colectivos* (smaller buses without assigned seats) are the fastest and cheapest option.

Ormeño (© **01/472-1710**; www.grupo-ormeno.com.pe) and **Cruz del Sur** (© **01/ 311-5050**; www.cruzdelsur.com.pe) are the top two bus companies with the best reputations for long-distance journeys and the most extensive coverage of Peru. **Civa** (© **01/418-1111**; www.civa.com.pe) and **Oltursa** (© **01/225-4499**; www.oltursa. com.pe) are also reputable companies with service to most parts of the country, though their buses are generally a notch down from Ormeño and Cruz del Sur. Given the mercurial and extremely confusing nature of bus companies, terminals, and destinations, it's always best to approach a local tourism information office or travel agency (most of which sell long-distance bus tickets) with a destination in mind and let them direct you to the terminal for the best service.

BY CAR

Getting around Peru by means of a rental car isn't the easiest or cheapest option for most travelers. Distances are long, roads are often not in very good condition, Peruvian drivers are aggressive, and accident rates are very high; the U.S. Department of State also warns against driving in Peru at night or alone on rural roads. A 4×4 vehicle would be the best option in many places, but trucks and jeeps are exceedingly expensive for most travelers. However, if you want maximum flexibility and independence in a particular region (say, to get around the Sacred Valley outside of Cusco, or to visit Colca Canyon beyond Arequipa) and have several people to share the cost, a rental car could be a decent option. By no means plan to rent a car in Lima and head off for the major sights across the country; you'll spend all your time in the car. It is much more feasible to fly or take a bus to a given destination and rent a car there.

The major international rental agencies are found at Lima's airport and around the city, and a handful of international and local companies operate in other cities, such as Cusco and Arequipa. Agencies in Lima include **Avis** (© 01/434-1111 or 01/434-1034; www.avis.com), **Budget** (© 01/442-8703; www.budget.com), **Dollar** (© 01/ 444-3050), **Hertz** (© 01/447-2129; www.hertz.com), **Inka's Rent A Car** (© 01/447-2129), and **Paz Rent A Car** (© 01/436-3941). An economy-size vehicle costs about $50 to $70 (£25–£35) a day. To rent a car, you'll need to be at least 25 years old and have a valid driver's license and passport. Deposit by credit card is usually required. For mechanical assistance, contact the **Touring y Automóvil Club del Peru (Touring Club of Peru)** at © 01/221-3225 in Lima, or 084/224-561 in Cusco.

TIPS ON ACCOMMODATIONS

A wide range of accommodations exists in Peru, including world-class luxury hotels, affordable small hotels in colonial houses, rustic rainforest lodges, and inexpensive budget inns. Midrange options have expanded in recent years, but the large majority of accommodations still court budget travelers and backpackers. Accommodations go by many names in Peru: "Hotel" generally refers to comfortable hotels with a range of services, but *hostal* is used for a wide variety of smaller hotels, inns, and pensions. At the lower end are mostly *hospedajes, pensiones,* and *residenciales.* However, these terms are often poor indicators of an establishment's quality or services. Luxury hotels are rare outside of Lima and Cusco; budget accommodations are plentiful, and many of them are quite good for the price.

Advance reservations are strongly recommended during high season (June–Oct) and at times of national holidays and important festivals. This is especially true of hotels in the middle and upper categories in popular places such as Cusco and Machu Picchu. Many hotels quote their rates in U.S. dollars. If you pay in cash, the price will be converted into soles at the going rate. Note that at most budget and many midrange hotels, credit cards are not accepted. Most published rates can be negotiated and travelers can often get greatly reduced rates outside of peak season simply by asking.

Hotel taxes and service charges are an issue that has caused some confusion in recent years. Most upper-level hotels add a 19% general sales tax (IGV) and a 10% service charge to the bill. However, foreigners who can demonstrate they live outside of Peru are not charged the 19% tax (although they are responsible for the 10% service charge). In practice, hotels sometimes mistakenly or purposely include the IGV on everyone's bill; presentation of a passport is sufficient to have the tax deducted from your tab. Many hotels—usually those at the midlevel and lower ranges—simplify matters by including the tax in their rates; at these establishments, you cannot expect to have the tax removed from your charges. At high-end hotels, be sure to review your bill and ask for an explanation of additional taxes and charges. Prices in this chapter do not include taxes and service charges unless otherwise noted.

Safety is an issue at many hotels, especially at the lower end, and extreme care should be taken with regard to personal belongings left in the hotel. Leaving valuables lying around is asking for trouble. Most hotels have safety-deposit boxes (only luxury hotels have room safes). Place your belongings in a carefully sealed envelope. Also, if you arrive in a town without previously arranged accommodations, you should be wary of taxi drivers and others who insist on showing you to a hotel. Occasionally, they will provide excellent tips, but in general, they will merely be taking you to a place where they are confident they can earn a commission. A final precaution worth mentioning is the electric heater found on many shower heads: These can be dangerous, and touching them while they're functioning can prompt an unwelcome electric jolt.

TIPS ON DINING

Peruvian cuisine is among the best and most diverse cuisines found in Latin America, and it's one of the most important contributors to the wave of pan-Latino restaurants gaining popularity in many parts of the world. Peruvian cooking differs significantly by region, and subcategories mirror the country's geographical variety: coastal, highland, and tropical. The common denominator among them is a blend of indigenous and Spanish (or broader European) influences, which has evolved over the past 4 centuries. In addition to Peruvian cooking, visitors will also find plenty of international restaurants, including a particularly Peruvian variation: the *chifa* (Peruvian-influenced Chinese, developed by the large immigrant Chinese population), a mainstay among many non-Chinese Peruvians. *Chifas* are nearly as common as restaurants serving *pollo a la brasa* (spit-roasted chicken), which are everywhere in Peru.

Traditional Peruvian coastal cooking is often referred to as *comida criolla*, and it's found across Peru. Coastal preparations concentrate on seafood and shellfish, as might be expected. The star dish is *ceviche*, a classic preparation of raw fish and shellfish marinated in lime or lemon juice and hot chile peppers, served with raw onion, sweet potato, and toasted corn. Coastal favorites also include *escabeche* (a tasty fish concoction served with peppers, eggs, olives, onions, and prawns), scallops *(conchitas)*, and sea bass *(corvina)*. Land-based favorites are *cabrito* (roast kid) and *ají de gallina* (a tangy creamed chicken and chile dish).

Highlanders favor a more substantial style of cooking. Meat, served with rice and potatoes, is a mainstay of the diet, as is trout *(trucha)*. *Lomo saltado,* strips of beef mixed with onions, tomatoes, peppers, and french-fried potatoes and served with rice, seems to be on every menu. *Rocoto relleno,* a hot bell pepper stuffed with vegetables and meat; *papa rellena,* a potato stuffed with veggies and then fried; and *papa a la huancaína,* boiled potatoes served with a cheese sauce and garnished with hard-boiled eggs and a lettuce leaf, are just as common (but are occasionally extremely spicy). *Cuy* (guinea pig) is considered a delicacy in many parts of Peru; it comes roasted or fried, with head and feet upturned on the plate.

In the Amazon jungle regions, most people fish for their food, and their diets consist almost entirely of fish such as river trout and *paiche* (a huge river fish). Restaurants feature both of these, with accompaniments such as *yuca* (a root), *palmitos* (palm hearts) and *chonta* (palm-heart salad), bananas and plantains, and rice *tamales* known as *juanes.* Common menu items, such as chicken and game, are complemented by exotic fare: caiman, wild boar, turtle, monkey, and piranha.

Drinking is less of an event in Peru. Peruvian wines and beers can't compare with superior examples found elsewhere on the continent (though the selection of imported wines from Chile, Argentina, and Spain is improving, and top restaurants have good selections, though they're largely limited to those three wine-producing nations). One indigenous drink stands out: pisco, a powerful white-grape brandy. The pisco sour (a cocktail mixed with pisco, egg whites, lemon juice, sugar, and bitters) is Peru's margarita: tasty, refreshing, and ubiquitous. New-wave twists on pisco sours, such as maracuya (passion fruit) sours, are popping up all over the country. Pisco is increasingly used to make local versions of standard cocktails from other lands (such as the caipirpisco, a Peruvian twist on a Brazilian classic). Peruvians everywhere drink *chicha,* a tangy fermented brew made from maize and inherited from the Incas. Often served warm in huge glasses, it is unlikely to please the palates of most foreign visitors, though it's certainly worth a try if you come upon a small, informal place with the *chicha* flag flying (literally—it means something akin to "fresh *chicha* available inside") in a rural village. The potent *chicha* is not to be confused with another drink popular in Peru: *chicha morada,* a nonalcoholic refreshment made from blue corn.

Restaurants range from the rustic and incredibly inexpensive to polished places with impeccable service and international menus. Set three-course menus (*menú económico* or *menú ejecutivo*) can sometimes be had for as little as $2 (£1). In general, you should ask about the preparation of many Peruvian dishes, as many are quite spicy. Informal eateries serving Peruvian cooking are frequently called *picanterías* and *chicherías.* Fancy restaurants may add service charges of 10% and an additional tax of up to 19%, as well as a *cubierto,* or cover charge, which is basically a small fee for bread and the privilege of sitting at a table. Less expensive restaurants usually charge either a 5% tax or no additional tax or service charge. At restaurants, tips normally range from 5 to 10%, whether or not a service charge is levied.

TIPS ON SHOPPING

Peru is one of the top shopping destinations in Latin America, with some of the finest and best-priced crafts anywhere. Its long traditions of textile weaving and colorful markets have produced a dazzling display of alpaca wool sweaters, blankets, ponchos, shawls, scarves, typical Peruvian hats, and other woven items. Peru's ancient indigenous civilizations were some of the world's greatest potters, and reproductions of Moche, Nazca, Paracas, and other ceramics are available.

Lima and Cusco have the lion's share of tourist-oriented shops and markets, but other places may be just as good for shopping. Locals in Puno and Taquile Island on Lake Titicaca produce spectacular textiles, and Arequipa is perhaps the best place in Peru to purchase very fine, extremely soft baby alpaca items. The Shipibo tribe of the northern Amazon produces excellent textiles and ceramics. You'll also see items in the jungle made from endangered species, including alligator skins and turtle shells, but purchasing these items is illegal.

There are scores of *artesanía* shops in many tourist centers, and prices may not be any higher than what you'd find at markets. At both stores and in open markets, bargaining—gentle, good-natured haggling over prices—is accepted and even expected. However, when it gets down to ridiculously small amounts of money, it's best to recognize that you are already getting a great deal on probably handmade goods (not to mention that a couple of soles here or there is likely to matter little to you and greatly to the seller) and relinquish the fight.

FAST FACTS: Peru

Addresses "Jr." doesn't mean "junior"; it is a designation meaning *jirón,* or street, just as "Av." (sometimes "Avda.") is an abbreviation for *avenida,* or avenue. Perhaps the most confusing element in street addresses is "s/n," which frequently appears in place of a number after the name of the street. The designation "s/n" means *sin número,* or no number.

American Express There's an office in Lima at Jr. de la Unión 630 (℃ **01/428-9779**); it's open Monday through Friday from 9am to 5pm. There are other offices at Av. Larco 747–753, Miraflores, Lima (℃ **01/444-4239**), and Av. Paseo de la Republica 3220, San Isidro, Lima (℃ **01/441-2769**). Both offices are housed with Viajes Falabella travel agencies. They will replace stolen or lost travelers' checks and sell American Express checks with an Amex card, but they do not cash their own checks.

Business Hours Most stores are open Monday through Friday from 9 or 10am to 12:30pm and from 3 to 5 or 8pm; banks are generally open Monday through Friday from 9:30am to 4pm, though some stay open until 6pm. In major cities, most banks are also open Saturday from 9:30am to 12:30pm.

Doctors & Hospitals Medical care is of a generally high standard in Lima and adequate in other major cities, where you are likely to find English-speaking doctors. Medical care is of a lesser standard in rural areas and small villages, and it's much less likely that you'll find an English-speaking physician in these locales. Many physicians and hospitals require immediate cash payment for health services, and they do not accept U.S. medical insurance (even if your policy applies overseas). That said, costs are reasonable, as compared to those in the U.S. You should check with your insurance company to see if your policy provides for overseas medical evacuation.

It's best to get vaccinations and obtain malaria pills before arriving in Peru, but if you decide at the last minute to go to the jungle and need to get a vaccine in the country, you may go to the following **Oficinas de Vacunación in Lima:** Av. del Ejército 1756, San Isidro (① **01/264-6889**); Jorge Chávez International Airport, Second Floor; or the **International Vaccination Center,** Dos de Mayo National Hospital, Avenida Grau, Block 13 (① **01/517-1845**). You can also get a yellow fever shot at the airport in Puerto Maldonado before traveling to the Amazon jungle.

Drug Laws Cocaine and other illegal substances are perhaps not as ubiquitous in Peru as one might think, though in Lima and Cusco, they are commonly offered to foreigners. This is especially dangerous; many would-be dealers also operate as police informants, and some are said to be undercover narcotics officers. Penalties for possession and use of or trafficking in illegal drugs in Peru are strict; convicted offenders can expect long jail sentences and substantial fines. Peruvian police routinely detain drug smugglers at Lima's international airport and land border crossings. Since 1995, more than 40 U.S. citizens have been convicted of narcotics trafficking in Peru. If arrested on drug charges, you will face protracted pretrial detention in poor prison conditions.

Electricity All outlets are 220 volts, 60 cycles AC (except in Arequipa, which operates on 50 cycles), with two-prong outlets that accept both flat and round prongs. Some large hotels also have 110-volt outlets.

Embassies & Consulates In Lima: **United States,** Av. La Encalada, Block 17, Monterrico (① 01/434-3000); **Australia,** Victor A. Belaúnde 147/Vía Principal 155, Building 3, Office 1301, San Isidro (① 01/222-8281); **Canada,** Libertad 130, Miraflores (① 01/444-4015); **United Kingdom** and **New Zealand,** Av. Jose Larco 1301, Floor 22, Miraflores (① 01/617-3000).

Emergencies In case of an emergency, call the 24-hour **traveler's hot line** (① **01/574-8000**) or the **tourist police,** or POLTUR (① **01/460-1060** in Lima, or 01/460-0965). The general **police** emergency number is ① **105.** The **INDECOPI** 24-hour hot line can also assist in contacting police to report a crime (① **01/224-7888** in Lima, 01/224-8600, or toll-free 0800/42579 from any private phone).

Guides Officially licensed guides are available at many archaeological sites and other places of interest to foreigners. They can be contracted directly (often for a tip), though you should verify their ability to speak English if you do not understand Spanish well. Establish a price beforehand. Many cities are battling a scourge of unlicensed and unscrupulous guides who provide inferior services or, worse, cheat visitors. As a general rule, do not accept unsolicited offers to arrange excursions, transportation, and hotel accommodations. For a full day's guide, tip $5 to $10 (£2.50–£5).

Internet Access Public Internet booths, or *cabinas,* have proliferated throughout Peru, in major cities such as Lima, Cusco, and Arequipa as well as small towns. Most cities have several to choose from, but few are of the cybercafe variety. Most are simple cubicles with terminals; occasionally, printers are available. The average cost for 1 hour is less than $1 (50p). Many *cabinas* now feature software to make very inexpensive international phone calls via the Internet.

Maps Good topographical maps are available from the **Instituto Geográfico Nacional (IGN),** located at Av. Aramburú 1190, San Isidro, Lima (① **01/475-9960**).

Hiking maps are available from the **South American Explorers Club**, Piura 135, Miraflores, Lima (*©* **01/445-3306**) and Choquechaca 188, Apto. 4, Cusco (*©* **084/245-484**).

Language Spanish is the official language of Peru. The Amerindian languages Quechua and Aymara are spoken primarily in the highlands. English is not widely spoken but is understood by those affiliated with the tourist industry in major cities and tourist destinations. Learning a few key phrases of Spanish will help immensely.

Newspapers & Magazines If you read Spanish, *El Comercio* and *La República* are two of the best daily newspapers. Look for *Rumbos,* a glossy Peruvian travel magazine in English and Spanish with excellent photography. In Lima, you will find copies (although rarely same-day publications) of the *International Herald Tribune* and the *Miami Herald* as well as *Time, Newsweek,* and other special-interest publications. Top-flight hotels sometimes offer free daily fax summations of the *New York Times* to their guests. Outside of Lima, international newspapers and magazines are hard to come by.

Police Peru has special tourist police forces (Policía Nacional de Turismo) in all major tourist destinations, such as Lima, Cusco, Arequipa, and Puno, as well as a dozen other cities. You are more likely to get a satisfactory response, not to mention someone who speaks some English, from the tourist police, who are distinguished by their white shirts. See "Emergencies" above and "Fast Facts" in individual city sections for contact information.

Post Offices/Mail Peru's postal service is reasonably efficient, especially now that it is managed by a private company (Serpost S.A.). Post offices are generally open Monday through Saturday from 8am to 8pm; some are also open Sunday from 9am to 1pm. Letters and postcards to North America take between 10 days and 2 weeks to arrive and cost S/5.50 ($1.75/90p); to Europe, S/6 ($2/£1). If you are purchasing lots of textiles and other handicrafts, you can send packages home from post offices, but it's not inexpensive—more than $100 (£50) for 10 kilograms (22 lb.), similar to what it costs to use DHL, where you're likely to have an easier time communicating. UPS is found in several cities, but its courier services cost nearly three times as much as DHL.

Restrooms Public toilets are rarely available, except in railway stations, restaurants, and theaters. Peruvian men tend to urinate outside in full view; don't emulate them. Use the bathroom in a bar, cafe, or restaurant. Public restrooms are labeled WC (water closet), *damas* (ladies), and *caballeros* or *hombres* (men). Toilet paper is not always provided, and when it is, establishments ask patrons to throw it in the wastebasket rather than the toilet to avoid clogging.

Safety Peru has not earned a great reputation for safety among travelers, although the situation is improving. Simple theft and pickpocketing remain fairly common; assaults and robbery are rare. Most thieves look for moments when travelers, laden with bags and struggling with maps, are distracted.

Although most visitors travel freely throughout Peru without incident, warnings must be heeded. In downtown Lima and the city's residential and hotel areas, the risk of street crime remains high. Carjackings, assaults, and armed robberies are not unheard of; occasional armed attacks at ATMs occur. However, in most heavily touristed places in Peru, a heightened police presence is notice-able. Use ATMs during the day, with other people present.

Street crime is prevalent in Cusco, Arequipa, and Puno, and pickpockets are known to patrol public markets. In Cusco, "strangle" muggings (in which vic-tims are choked unconscious and then relieved of all belongings) were reported in years past, particularly on streets leading off the Plaza de Armas, the San Blas neighborhood, and near the train station. This form of violent assault seems to have subsided, but you should still not walk alone late at night on deserted streets.

In major cities, taxis hailed on the street can lead to assaults. (I highly recom-mend using telephone-dispatched radio taxis, especially at night.) Ask your hotel or restaurant to call a cab, or call one from the list of recommended taxi companies in the individual city sections below.

Travelers should exercise extreme caution on public city transportation, where pickpockets are rife, and on long-distance buses and trains (especially at night), where thieves employ any number of strategies to relieve passengers of their bags. You need to be supremely vigilant, even to the extreme of locking backpacks and suitcases to luggage racks. Be extremely careful in all train and bus stations.

In general, do not wear expensive jewelry; keep expensive camera equip-ment out of view as much as possible; use a money belt worn inside your pants or shirt to safeguard cash, credit cards, and passport. Wear your daypack on your chest rather than your back when walking in crowded areas. The time to be most careful is when you have most of your belongings on your person—such as when you're in transit from airport or train or bus station to your hotel. At airports, it's best to spend a little more for official airport taxis; if in doubt, request the driver's official ID. Don't venture beyond airport grounds for a street taxi. Have your hotel call a taxi for your trip to the airport or bus station.

Large-scale terrorist activities of the local insurgency groups Sendero Lumi-noso (Shining Path) and MRTA (Tupac Amaru Revolutionary Movement)—which together waged a 2-decade guerrilla war against the Peruvian state, killing more than 30,000 people—were effectively stamped out in the early 1990s. However, in recent years there have been growing concerns about a pos-sible resurgence of those groups (especially after a car bomb outside the U.S. embassy in Lima in 2002). In December 2005, a state of emergency was declared in six central Amazon provinces after Shining Path guerrillas killed eight police-men in the remote Huanaco region—upping the total to 19 police and military officers assassinated in 2005 and again raising the specter of renewed violence across Peru. Though it is a situation worth watching, to date the most populous (and traveled) regions of the country have not been affected, and neither group is currently active in any of the areas covered in this book.

Taxes A general sales tax (IGV) is added automatically to most consumer bills (19%). In some upmarket hotels or restaurants, service charges of 10% are often added. At all airports, passengers must pay a $30 (£15) departure tax for international flights, $6 (£3) for domestic flights.

Telephone & Fax Peru's telephone system has been much improved since it was privatized and acquired by Spain's Telefónica in the mid-1990s. (There are now several additional players in the market, including BellSouth.) It's relatively simple to make local and long-distance domestic and international calls from pay phones, which accept coins and phone cards *(tarjetas telefónicas)*. Most phone booths display country and city codes and contain instructions in English and Spanish.

You can also make international calls from Telefónica offices and hotels, though surcharges levied at the latter can be extraordinarily expensive. An inexpensive way to make international calls is through Internet software such as Skype or Net2Phone, which more and more Internet booths in Peru are featuring. Rates are as low as 20¢ (10p) per minute to the United States. Reception, however, can be spotty.

Fax services are available at many hotels, but they are expensive, especially for international numbers ($3/£1.50 per page and up).

Time Zone All of Peru is 5 hours behind GMT (Greenwich mean time). Peru does not observe daylight saving time.

Tipping Most people leave about a 10% tip for the waitstaff in restaurants. In nicer restaurants that add a 10% service charge (which your waiter is unlikely ever to see), many patrons tip an additional 5% or 10% for good service. Taxi drivers are not usually tipped unless they provide some additional service. Bilingual tour guides should be tipped $1 to $2 (50p–£1) per person for a short visit, $5 (£2.50) per person or more for a full day. If you have a private guide, tip about $10 (£5).

Water Do not drink tap water, even in major hotels. Visitors should drink only bottled water, which is widely available. Try to avoid drinks with ice. *Agua con gas* is carbonated; *agua sin gas* is still.

4 Lima

Lima was the richest and most important city in the Americas in the 17th century and was considered the most beautiful colonial settlement in the region. Today, the capital of Peru is a sprawling, chaotic, and mostly unlovely metropolis, and many visitors dart through it rather quickly or bypass it altogether. Peru's blistering poverty is more apparent here than perhaps anywhere else: Depressing shantytowns called *pueblos jóvenes* lacerate the outer rings of the city, and the despair of a large segment of the largely migrant and mestizo population contrasts uncomfortably with the ritzy apartment and office buildings in the residential suburbs. If that's not enough, for most of the year an unrelenting gray cloud called the *garúa* hangs heavy overhead, obscuring the coastline and dulling the city's appearance. The sun comes out in Lima only from December to April; the rest of the time, Lima makes London look like Lisbon.

With a population of more than eight million—about one-third of Peru's total population—and as the seat of the national government and headquarters of most industry, Lima thoroughly dominates Peru's political and commercial life. Lima demands some effort to sift beneath the soot and uncover the city's rewards, especially when such extraordinary treasures hover over the horizon in the Andes and the Amazon jungle. So

Downtown Lima

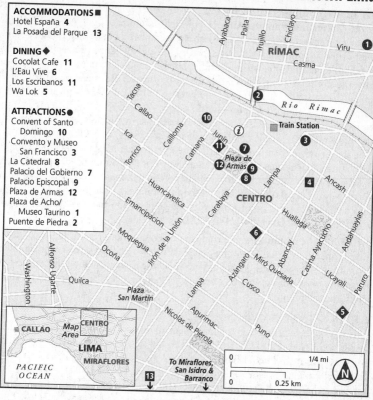

ACCOMMODATIONS ■
Hotel España **4**
La Posada del Parque **13**

DINING ◆
Cocolat Cafe **11**
L'Eau Vive **6**
Los Escribanos **11**
Wa Lok **5**

ATTRACTIONS ●
Convent of Santo
  Domingo **10**
Convento y Museo
  San Francisco **3**
La Catedral **8**
Palacio del Gobierno **7**
Palacio Episcopal **9**
Plaza de Armas **12**
Plaza de Acho/
  Museo Taurino **1**
Puente de Piedra **2**

why come to Lima except to beeline it to Cusco or elsewhere? If you skip Lima altogether, you'll miss a vital part of what is Peru today. Lima has calmed down since its days as a cauldron of chaos in the 1980s and 1990s. The country's finest museums are here, as are its fanciest and most creative restaurants and its most vibrant nightlife. Many of the classic colonial buildings in the old Lima Centro are being refurbished. But the city still feels schizophrenic; outer suburbs such as Barranco are relatively gentle oases, worlds removed from the congestion and grime of the rest of the city.

Even if you have only a day or two for Lima, the city's art and archaeology museums serve as perfect introductions to the rich history and culture you'll encounter elsewhere in the country. If you also squeeze in a tour of colonial Lima, dine at a great *criollo* restaurant or *cevichería*, soak up some energetic nightlife, and browse the country's best shops, you may just come away from Lima pleasantly surprised, even if not exactly enamored of the city.

ESSENTIALS
GETTING THERE
Lima is the gateway for most international arrivals to Peru; see "Getting There" in "Planning Your Trip to Peru," earlier in this chapter, for more detailed information.

BY PLANE   All overseas flights from North America and Europe arrive at Lima's **Jorge Chávez International Airport.** For flight information, call © **01/511-6055.**

To get from the airport to Lima—either downtown, about 16km (10 miles) southwest of the airport, or to Miraflores, San Isidro, and Barranco (the major residential neighborhoods and sites of most tourist hotels), about 45 minutes away—you can take a taxi or private bus. **Taxis** inside the security area at the international arrivals terminal charge around $12 (£6) to Miraflores and $10 (£5) to downtown Lima (Lima Centro). The **Urbanito Airport shuttle** service (© **99/573-238**) delivers passengers to the doors of their hotels. Stop by its desk in the international terminal; buses to downtown ($6/£3) and Miraflores and San Isidro ($8/£4) leave every half-hour or so. The shuttle stops by the hotel of each passenger; at peak hours, if there are many fellow passengers, this may not be the fastest way from the airport. Unless you're alone, it's also probably not the cheapest. Call a day ahead to arrange a pickup for your return to the airport (© **01/814-6932**). Private limousine taxis (*taxis ejecutivos* or *remises*) also have desks in the airport; their fares range from $35 to $50 (£17–£25) round-trip. One is **MitsuTaxi** (© **01/349-7722**).

BY BUS   The multitude of bus companies serving various regions of the country all have terminals in Lima. Many are located downtown, though several companies have their bases in the suburbs. Most bus terminals have nasty reputations for thievery and general unpleasantness; your best bet is to grab your things and hop into an airport shuttle or cab pronto.

ORIENTATION

The city beyond central Lima **(Lima Centro)** is a warren of ill-defined neighborhoods; most visitors are likely to set foot into only a couple of them. Several of Lima's top museums are in **Pueblo Libre,** a couple of miles southwest of Lima Centro, while **San Borja,** a couple of miles directly south of Lima Centro, holds two of the finest art and archaeology collections in all of Peru. **San Isidro** and **Miraflores,** the most exclusive residential and commercial neighborhoods, and also where most tourist hotels are located, are farther south toward the coast. **Barranco,** a former seaside village now known primarily for its nightlife, is several miles farther out along the ocean, as is **Chorrillos,** a residential neighborhood known primarily for its Pantanos de Villa, or swamps that are rich with flora and fauna.

GETTING AROUND

Navigating Lima is a complicated and time-consuming task, made difficult by the city's sprawling character (many of the best hotels and restaurants are far from downtown, spread among three or more residential neighborhoods), heavy traffic and pollution, and a chaotic network of confusing and crowded *colectivos* and unregulated taxis.

BY TAXI   Taxis hailed on the street are a reasonable and relatively quick way to get around in Lima. However, taxis are wholly unregulated by the government and do not use meters: All anyone has to do to become a taxi driver is get his hands on a vehicle—of any size and condition, though most are the tiny Daewoo "Ticos"—and plunk a cheap TAXI sticker inside the windshield. He is then free to charge whatever he thinks he can get—with no meters, no laws, and nobody to answer to besides the free market. I counsel visitors to be a bit wary taking taxis in Lima, though I personally have never had problems greater than a dispute over a fare. (If you're not fluent in Spanish, and even if you are but you have an obviously non-Peruvian appearance, be prepared to negotiate fares.) If the issue of getting into quasi-official cabs makes you nervous, by all means call a registered company from your hotel or restaurant—especially at night (even though the fare can be twice as much).

Registered, reputable taxi companies—the safest option—include **Taxi Amigo** (© **01/349-0177**), **Taxi Móvil** (© **01/422-6890**), or **Taxi Seguro** (© **01/275-2020**). Whether you call or hail a taxi, you'll need to establish a price beforehand—be prepared to bargain. Most fares range from $2 to $5 (£1–£2.50).

BY BUS   Local buses are of two types: *micros* (large buses) and *combis* (minibuses or vans). They're both quite crowded, with a reputation for pickpockets, and can be hailed at any place along the street without regard to bus stops. Routes are more or less identified by signs with street names placed in the windshield, making many trips confusing for those unfamiliar with Lima. Some do nothing more than race up and down long avenues. (For example: TODO AREQUIPA means it travels the length of Av. Arequipa.) For assistance, ask a local for help; most Limeños know the incredibly complex bus system surprisingly well. Because they make so many stops, trips from the outer suburbs to downtown can be quite slow. Most *micros* and *combis* cost S/1.50 or S/2 (50¢–70¢/25p–35p); it's slightly more after midnight and on Sunday and holidays. When you wish to get off, shout *"Baja"* (getting off) or *"Esquina"* (at the corner).

BY FOOT   Lima can be navigated by foot only a neighborhood at a time. (And even then, congestion and pollution strongly discourage much walking.) Lima Centro and Barranco are best seen by foot, and though large, Miraflores is also walkable. Between neighborhoods, however, a taxi is essential.

VISITOR INFORMATION

A 24-hour tourist information booth, **iperu** (© **01/574-8000**), operates in the international terminal at the Jorge Chávez International Airport. The **Oficina de Información Turística** in Lima Centro is well located a block off the Plaza de Armas at Pasaje Los Escribanos 145 (© **01/427-6080**); it's open Monday through Friday from 9am to 6pm, Saturday and Sunday from 10am to 5pm. The most helpful iperu office is in Miraflores, at the **Larcomar** shopping mall, Módulo 14, Av. Malecón de la Reserva 610 (© **01/445-9400**); it's open Monday through Friday from 8am to 5pm. One of the best private agencies for arrangements and city tours as well as general information is **Fertur Peru,** Jr. Junín 211 and Azángaro 105, within the Hotel España (© **01/427-1958**). Also well worth a visit, especially for members, is the Lima office of the **South American Explorers Club,** Piura 135, Miraflores (© **01/445-3306;** www.saexplorers.org).

FAST FACTS   Peruvian and international **banks** with currency-exchange bureaus and ATMs are plentiful throughout central Lima and especially in the outer neighborhoods, such as Miraflores, San Isidro, and Barranco, which are full of shopping centers, hotels, and restaurants. Money changers, almost always wearing colored smocks (sometimes with obvious "$" insignias), patrol the main streets off Parque Central in Miraflores and Lima Centro with calculators and dollars in hand.

English-speaking medical personnel and 24-hour emergency service are available at the following hospitals and clinics in Lima: **Clínica Anglo-Americana,** Alfredo Salazar, 3rd block, San Isidro (© 01/221-3656); **Clínica San Borja,** Guardia Civil 337, San Borja (© 01/475-4000); and **Maison de Sante,** Calle Miguel Adgouin 208–222, near the Palacio de Justicia (© 01/428-3000, or emergency 01/427-2941). For an ambulance, call **Alerta Médica** (© 01/470-5000) or **San Cristóbal** (© 01/440-0200).

The **Policía Nacional de Turismo (National Tourism Police)** has an English-speaking staff and is specifically trained to handle needs of foreign visitors. The 24-hour tourist police line is ℭ **01/574-8000.** The main office in Lima is next to the Museo de la Nación at Av. Javier Prado Este 2465, Fifth Floor, San Borja (ℭ 01/225-8698 or 01/476-9879).

Internet *cabinas* are everywhere in Lima. Rates are S/1.50 to S/2.50 (50¢–85¢/ 25p–40p) per hour, and most are open daily from 9am to 10pm or later. Lima's main **post office (Central de Correos)** is located on the Plaza de Armas, Camaná 195 (ℭ **01/427-0370).** The Miraflores branch is on Petit Thouars 5201 (ℭ **01/445-0697),** the San Isidro branch, Calle Las Palmeras 205 (ℭ **01/422-0981).** A **DHL/ Western Union** office is located at Nicolás de Piérola 808 (ℭ **01/424-5820).** The principal **Telefónica** office, where you can make long-distance and international calls, is on Plaza San Martín (Carabaya 937) in Lima Centro.

WHAT TO SEE & DO

Many visitors to Lima are merely on their way to other places in Peru. But, since everything goes through the capital, most people take advantage of layovers to see what distinguishes Lima: its colonial old quarter, once the finest in the Americas, and several of the finest museums in Peru, all of which serve as magnificent introductions to Peruvian history and culture.

Much of the historic center has suffered from sad neglect; the municipal government is committed to restoring the aesthetic value, but with limited funds it faces a daunting task. Today, central Lima has a noticeable police presence and is considerably safer than it was just a few years ago. A full day in Lima Centro should suffice; depending on your interests, you could spend anywhere from a day to a week traipsing through Lima's many museum collections, many of which are dispersed in otherwise unremarkable neighborhoods. Few people, however, spend more than a couple of days in the capital.

LIMA CENTRO: COLONIAL LIMA

Lima's grand **Plaza de Armas** ℛ (also called the Plaza Mayor), the original center of the city and site where Francisco Pizarro founded the city in 1535, is essentially a modern reconstruction. The disastrous 1746 earthquake that initiated the city's decline leveled most of the 16th- and 17th-century buildings in the old center. The oldest surviving element of the square is the central bronze fountain, which dates from 1651. Today the square, while perhaps not the most beautiful or languid in South America, is still rather distinguished beneath a surface level of grime and bustle (and it has been named a UNESCO World Heritage Site). On the north side of the square is the early-20th-century **Palacio del Gobierno (Presidential Palace),** where a changing of the guard takes place daily at noon. The **Municipalidad de Lima (City Hall)** is on the west side of the plaza. Across the square is the **Catedral** (cathedral), rebuilt after the earthquake, and the **Palacio Episcopal (Archbishop's Palace),** distinguished by an extraordinary wooden balcony next to it.

A block north of the Plaza de Armas, behind the Presidential Palace, is the Río Rímac and a 17th-century Roman-style bridge, the **Puente de Piedra** (literally, "stone bridge"). It leads to the once-fashionable **Rímac** district, today considerably less chic—some would say downright dangerous—though it is the location of a few of Lima's best *peñas,* or live *criollo* music clubs. The **Plaza de Acho** bullring, once the largest in the world, and decent **Museo Taurino** (bullfighting museum) are near the river at Hualgayoc 332 (© **01/482-3360**). The ring is in full swing during the Fiestas Patrias (national holidays) at the end of July; the regular season runs from October to December.

Five blocks southwest of Plaza de Armas is Lima Centro's other grand square, **Plaza de San Martín.** This stately square with handsome gardens, inaugurated in 1921, was recently renovated. At its center is a large monument to the South American liberator José de San Martín.

Lima's **Barrio Chino,** the largest Chinese community in South America (200,000 plus), is visited by most folks to get a taste of the Peruvian twist on traditional Chinese cooking at the neighborhood's *chifas.* The official boundary of Chinatown is the large gate, Portada China, on Jirón Ucayali.

Convento y Museo de San Francisco ★★

Probably the most spectacular of Lima's colonial-era churches, the Convent of St. Francis is a strikingly restored 17th-century complex that survived the massive earthquake in 1746. The facade is a favorite of thousands of pigeons, which rest on rows of ridges that rise up the towers—so much so that from a distance it looks like black spots, adding an unexpectedly funky flavor to this baroque church. Cloisters and interiors are lined with beautiful *azulejos* (glazed ceramic tiles) from Seville; carved *mudéjar* (Moorish-style) ceilings are overhead. The mandatory guided tour takes visitors past the cloisters to a fine museum of religious art, with beautifully carved saints and a series of portraits of the apostles by the studio of Francisco Zurbarán, the famed Spanish painter. For many, though, the most fascinating component of the visit is the descent into the catacombs, which were dug beginning in 1546 as a burial ground for priests and others. (As many as 75,000 bodies were interred here before the main cemetery was built.) Also of great interest are the church, outfitted with an impressive neoclassical altar, and a fantastic 17th-century library, which was the second-most important of its time in the Americas (after one in Quito) and holds 20,000 books (many date from the earliest years after Lima's foundation). A breathtaking carved Moorish ceiling over a staircase is a reconstruction of the original from 1625.

Ancash s/n (Plaza de San Francisco). © **01/426-7377.** Admission S/5 ($1.65/85p) adults, S/2.50 (80¢/40p) students. Guides available in English and Spanish. Daily 9am–6pm.

La Catedral ★

Lima's baroque cathedral, an enlargement of an earlier one from 1555, was completed in 1625. It suffered damage in earthquakes in 1687 and was decimated by the big one in 1746. The present building, though again damaged by tremors in 1940, is an 18th-century reconstruction of the early plans. Twin yellow towers sandwich an elaborate stone facade. Inside are several notable Churrigueresque altars and carved wooden choir stalls, but the cathedral is best known for the chapel where Francisco Pizarro lies. The founder of Lima and killer of Inca chieftain Atahualpa was himself assassinated in the Plaza de Armas in 1541, but his remains weren't brought to the cathedral until 1985. (They were discovered in a crypt in 1977.) Look closely at the mosaic on the far wall of the chapel; it depicts his coat of arms, Atahualpa reaching into his coffer to cough up a ransom in the hopes of attaining his release, and other symbols of Pizarro's life. The cathedral also houses a small **Museo de Arte Religioso,** which has a few fabulous painted glass mirrors from Cusco, a collection of unsigned paintings, and a seated sculpture of Jesus, with his chin resting pensively on his hand—it's as bloody a figure of Christ as you're likely to see.

Plaza de Armas. © **01/427-5980.** Admission to cathedral and museum S/10 ($3.35/£1.70) adults, S/5 ($1.70/85p) students. Guides available in English and Spanish (tips accepted). Mon–Sat 10am–5pm.

THE TOP MUSEUMS

Museo Arqueológico Rafael Larco Herrera ⊛⊛　Founded in 1926, this is the largest private collection of pre-Columbian art in the world. It concentrates on the Moche dynasty, with an estimated 45,000 pieces—including incredibly fine textiles, jewelry, and stonework from several other ancient cultures—all housed in an 18th-century colonial building. Rafael Larco Hoyle, the author of the seminal study *Los Mochicas,* is considered the founder of Peruvian archaeology; he named the museum after his father. The Moche (A.D. 200–700), who lived along the northern coast in the large area near present-day Trujillo and Cajamarca, are credited with achieving one of greatest artistic expressions of ancient Peru. The pottery gives clues to all elements of their society: diseases, curing practices, architecture, transportation, dance, agriculture, music, and religion. The Moche are also celebrated in the modern world for their erotic ceramics. The Sala Erótica is separated from the general collection, like the porn section in a video store. The Moche depicted sex in realistic, humorous, moralistic, and religious—but above all, explicit—terms. If you're traveling with kids, expect giggles or questions about the ancient Peruvians' mighty phalluses.

Av. Bolívar 1515, Pueblo Libre. ℂ 01/461-1312. http://museolarco.perucultural.org.pe. Admission S/25 ($8.30/£4.15) adults, S/15 ($5/£2.50) students. Private guides available in English and Spanish (tip basis, minimum S/10/$3.35/£1.70). Daily 9am–6pm. Take a taxi or the "Todo Brasil" *colectivo* to Av. Brasil and then another to Av. Bolívar. If you're coming from the Museo Nacional de Arqueología, Antropología e Historia del Perú (below), walk along the blue path.

Museo de la Nación ⊛⊛ *Kids*　Peru's ancient history is exceedingly complicated. Peru's pre-Columbian civilizations were among the most sophisticated of their time; when Egypt was building pyramids, Peruvians were constructing great cities. Lima's National Museum, the city's biggest and one of the most important in Peru, guides visitors through the highlights of overlapping and conquering cultures and their achievements, seen not only in architecture (including scale models of most major ruins in Peru) but also highly advanced ceramics and textiles. The exhibits, spread over three rambling floors, are ordered chronologically—very helpful for getting a grip on these many cultures dispersed across Peru. In case you aren't able to make it to the archaeology-rich north of Peru, pay special attention to the facsimile of the Lord of Sipán discovery, one of the most important in the world in recent years. Explanations accompanying the exhibits are usually in both Spanish and English. Allow 2 to 3 hours to see it all.

Av. Javier Prado Este 2465, San Borja. ℂ 01/476-9878. Admission S/6 ($2/£1) adults, S/3 ($1/50p) seniors, S/1 (35¢/15p) students. Guides in several languages can be contracted. Tues–Sun 9am–6pm. You can get here by *colectivo* along Av. Prado from Av. Arequipa, but it is much simpler to take a taxi from Lima Centro or Miraflores/San Isidro.

Museo Nacional de Arqueología, Antropología e Historia del Perú ⊛　With such a mouthful of an official name, you might expect the National Museum of Archaeology, Anthropology, and History to be the Peruvian equivalent of New York's Met. It's not, but it's a worthwhile and enjoyable museum that covers Peruvian civilization from prehistoric times to the colonial and republican periods. There are ceramics, carved stone figures and obelisks, metalwork and jewelry, lovely textiles, and mummies in the fetal position wrapped in burial blankets. There's also a selection of erotic ceramics from the Moche culture, but not nearly as extensive as that of the Rafael Larco Herrera museum (above). Individual rooms are dedicated to the Nazca, Paracas, and Moche and Chimú cultures. Toward the end of the exhibit, which wanders around the central courtyard of the handsome 19th-century Quinta de los Libertadores mansion

Overrated All That Glitters Isn't Necessarily Gold

The privately held **Museo de Oro del Perú (Gold Museum)**, Av. Alonso de Molina 1100, Monterrico (© 01/345-1292), for decades, was the most visited museum in Peru. But that was before the National Institute of Culture and the Tourism Protection Bureau declared just about everything in the museum—some 7,000 or more pieces—to be fake. The massive collection, mainly consisting of supposed pre-Columbian gold, was assembled by one man, Miguel Mujica Gallo—who, perhaps fortunately, died just days before the investigation into his collection was launched. Although the museum was expensive and poorly organized, all that glittering gold—augmented by hundreds (if not thousands) of ceremonial objects, tapestries, masks, ancient weapons, clothing, several mummies, and military weaponry and uniforms from medieval Europe to ancient Japan—certainly caught many a visitor's eye over the years. Though the museum contends that everything on display is authentic, it's pretty difficult to recommend visiting a collection with such a fraudulent history; a taxi is the most direct and timesaving way to get here. It's open daily from 11am to 7pm; admission costs S/30 ($10/£5) for adults, S/15 ($5/£2.50) for students.

(once lived in by South American independence heroes San Martín and Bolívar), is a large-scale model of Machu Picchu. Basic descriptions throughout the museum are mostly in Spanish, though some are also in English. Allow about an hour for your visit.

From the museum, you can follow a walking path along a painted blue line to the Rafael Larco Herrera museum. It's about 1.5km (1 mile), or 20 minutes, straight into traffic on Antonio de Sucre (make sure you turn at the Metro supermarket on Leguia Melendes).

Plaza Bolívar s/n, Pueblo Libre. © 01/463-5070. http://museonacional.perucultural.org.pe. Admission S/11 ($3.65/£1.85) adults, S/3 ($1/50p) students. Private guides available in English and Spanish (tip basis, minimum S/10 [$3.35/£1.70]). Tues–Sat 9am–5pm; Sun 10am–4pm. Take a taxi here, or take the "Todo Brasil" *colectivo* to Av. Vivanco and then take a 15-min. walk.

SHOPPING

Lima has the greatest variety of shopping in Peru, from tony boutiques to artisan and antiques shops. In Lima, you can find handicrafts from across Peru; prices are not usually much higher and the selection may be even better than in the regions where the items are made. One exception is alpaca goods, which are better purchased in the areas around Cusco, Puno, and Arequipa, both in terms of price and selection. Miraflores is where most shoppers congregate, though there are also several outlets in Lima Centro and elsewhere in the city.

LIMA CENTRO   The best spot for handicrafts from around Peru is the **Santo Domingo** *artesanía* **arcades** across the street from the Santo Domingo convent on Conde de Superunda and Camaná. Lima Centro's crowded **Mercado Central** is south of the Plaza Mayor, at the edge of Chinatown (at the corner of Ayacucho and Ucayali). The **Feria Artesanal** on Avenida de la Marina in Pueblo Libre has a wide variety of handicrafts of varying quality but at lower prices than most tourist-oriented shops in Lima Centro or Miraflores. Haggling is a good idea.

SUBURBS Miraflores houses the lion's share of Lima's well-stocked shops overflowing in handicrafts from around Peru, including weavings, ceramics, and silver. Several of the largest malls are here, and several dozen large souvenir and handicrafts shops are clustered on and around Avenida Ricardo Palma (look for **Artesanías Miraflores,** no. 205) and Avenida Petit Thouars (try **Artesanía Expo Inti,** no. 5495). Other handicraft shops in Miraflores include **Agua y Tierra,** Diez Canseco 298 (© 01/445-6980), and **Silvania Prints,** Diez Canseco 378 (© 01/242-0667). Alpaca sweaters and other items can be had at **Alpaca 111,** Av. Larco 671 (© 01/447-1623); **Alpaca Perú,** Diez Canseco 315 (© 01/241-4175); **Mon Repos,** Tarata 288 (© 01/445-9740); and **All Alpaca,** Av. Schell 375 (© 01/427-4704). Look for silver jewelry and antiques along Avenida La Paz. *Platerías* and *joyerías* (silver and jewelry shops) worth a visit are **Ilaria,** Av. Larco 1325 (© 01/444-2347), and **El Tupo,** La Paz 553 (© 01/444-1511). Antiques shops include **El Almacén de Arte,** Francia 339 (© 01/445-6264), and **Porta 735,** Porta 735 (© 01/447-6158).

For fine *retablos* (gradines) and artisanship typical of Ayacucho (which produces some of Peru's most notable pieces), visit the **Museo-Galería Popular de Ayacucho,** Av. Pedro de Osma 116 (© **01/247-0599**), in Barranco. The finest upscale purveyor of crafts and home furnishings from across Peru is **Dédalo,** Saenz Peña 295 (© **01/477-0562**), which also has a cafe and patio out back, in Barranco. There are small handicrafts markets, open late to catch bar and post-dinner crowds, in the main squares in both Miraflores and Barranco.

WHERE TO STAY

Lima Centro has its share of hotels and budget inns, but most people head out to Miraflores, San Isidro, and, to a lesser extent, Barranco. These barrios have little in the way of sights but are more convenient for nightlife and shopping and probably safer, if not necessarily much quieter, than Lima Centro.

LIMA CENTRO
Inexpensive

Hotel España 🎯 *Value*   Near the Convento de San Francisco and just 4 blocks from Plaza de Armas, this extremely popular budget hostel has a funky flair and communal atmosphere. If you're looking to hook up with backpackers from around the globe and set off to explore Peru, you can't do better than Hotel España. It occupies a rambling colonial building bursting with paintings, ceramics, faux Roman busts, plants, and even the occasional mummy and skull. A maze of rooms, most with shared bathrooms, are up a winding staircase. The rooms themselves are simple, with concrete floors but brightly colored walls; they're well kept, but with cheesy bedspreads. The leafy rooftop garden terrace, with views of San Francisco, is a good place to hang out and trade travel tales. Some complain that security is a little lax, so lock your stuff in the lockers. Hot water goes to the early bird. The place can be noisy, but that's part of its charm.

Azángaro 105, Lima. ©/fax 01/428-5546. www.hotelespanaperu.com. 30 units, 6 with private bathroom. $9 (£4.50) double without bathroom, $14 (£7) with bathroom. No credit cards. **Amenities:** Cafe; tour desk; laundry service. *In room:* No phone.

Posada del Parque 🎯 *Value*   Monica Moreno runs this safe, great-value, and delightful guesthouse, which occupies a lovely 1920s casona on what has to be one of the most peaceful streets—it's a long cul-de-sac lined with gardens and other stately

Miraflores map. Scale: 0–1/4 mi, 0–0.25 km. North arrow. *(i)* Information

Inset map: CALLAO, CENTRO, LIMA, MIRAFLORES, PACIFIC OCEAN, Map Area, Bartolome

Streets: Gonzales Prada, Crl. Inclán, Pershing, Av. Arequipa, Narciso de la Colina, R. Paima, Manuel Bonilla, Esperanza, Cantuarias, Diez Canseco, Schell, Paseo de la República, Mariano Odicio, 2 de Mayo, José Pardo, Bellavista, PARQUE CENTRAL, Av. José Larco, Av. La Paz, Weberbauer, PARQUE REDUCTO, Berlin, Grau, Gerdes, F. Reccavaren, PARQUE KENNEDY, Diagonal, Av. Benavides, Colón, San Martín, Alcanfores, Grimaldo del Solar, Av. La Paz, Bolognesi, Porta, 28 de Julio, Rainoso, Plaza Bolognesi, Tripoli, Venecia, Malecón los Francescos

DINING ◆
Astrid y Gastón **7**
Café Suisse (La Tiendecita Blanca) **5**
Cebichería La Mar **2**
La Trattoria di Mambrino **6**
Las Brujas de Cachiche **4**

ACCOMMODATIONS ■
Casa Andina Classic-Miraflores San Antonio **10**
Hotel Antigua Miraflores **3**
Inkawasi Guest House **1**
Miraflores Park Hotel **11**
San Antonio Abad **9**
Sonesta Posada del Inca Miraflores **8**

homes—near the center of Lima. Her house, in the Santa Beatriz district, is stuffed with Peruvian popular art and offers unusual amenities at an economic rate, such as Internet access, satellite TV, and beer and homemade pizzas upon request. Monica is more than willing to help travelers with all their needs. The rooms are spacious and impeccable, with excellent bathrooms and hot water. The owner also has a one-bedroom suite (Suite del Parque) nearby, which is perfect for longer stays.

Parque Hernán Velarde 60 (off Av. Petit Thouars, Santa Beatriz), Lima. © **01/433-2412.** Fax 01/332-6927. www.inca country.com.pe. 9 units. $33 (£16) double (rates include taxes). No parking. **Amenities:** Communal TV room, Internet access. *In room:* No phone.

MIRAFLORES
Very Expensive
Miraflores Park Hotel ⭐⭐⭐ The exceedingly elegant Miraflores Park Hotel bathes business executives and upscale tourists in unsurpassed luxury. It hugs the malecón, the avenue flush with parks that traces the Lima coastline. From the cozy, library-like lobby and handsome restaurant to the tastefully appointed, plush rooms (including marble and granite bathrooms most New Yorkers would give their left arms to live in), the hotel is a distinguished address. All rooms are suites with comfortable king-size beds and sitting areas. Many rooms have ocean views—at least on the few

days of the year when one can see the coast in Lima. Special promotional rates are often available online.

Av. Malecón de la Reserva, 1035 Miraflores, Lima. © 01/242-3000. Fax 01/242-3393. www.mira-park.com. 81 units. $400 (£200) deluxe double; from $465 (£232) suite. AE, DC, MC, V. **Amenities:** Restaurant; cafe; bar; small outdoor rooftop pool; squash court; exercise room; sauna; concierge; extensive business center and executive services; salon; room service; laundry service. *In room:* A/C, TV/VCR, fax, dataport, minibar, hair dryer.

Expensive

Sonesta Posada del Inca Miraflores ✦ The Miraflores branch of a chain with
a handful of hotels across Peru, this small modern hotel has an excellent location and is efficient and professionally run. Centrally located just 2 blocks from Parque Central (Parque Kennedy), it's within easy walking distance of Miraflores's many nightclubs, restaurants, and shops. The well-appointed rooms aren't huge, but they come with comfortable beds, good-size bathrooms, and an ocher-and-deep-green color scheme with plaid bedspreads.

Alcanfores 329, Miraflores, Lima. © 800/SONESTA or 01/241-7688. Fax 01/447-8199. www.sonesta.com/miraflores. 28 units. $95 (£47) double; $115 (£57) suite. Rates include taxes, service charge, and breakfast buffet. AE, DC, MC, V. Free parking. **Amenities:** 24-hr. cafe and bar; fitness center (half-block from hotel); concierge; business center; room service; babysitting; laundry service; nonsmoking rooms. *In room:* A/C, TV, minibar, hair dryer on request, safe.

Moderate

Casa Andina Classic Miraflores San Antonio ✦ (Value) Well located and well exe-
cuted, like all Casa Andina properties, this midsize hotel—surprisingly enough, the only one the Peruvian chain has in the capital—has ample bedrooms that are cheerfully decorated, with brightly striped bedspreads and sunburnt-yellow walls. Marble bathrooms are large, and the breakfast buffet is a winner. Casa Andina is perfect for the traveler who seeks comfort, good value, and no unpleasant surprises. A second Casa Andina Classic is located nearby, at Av. Petit Thouars 5444.

Av. 28 de Julio 1088, Miraflores, Lima. © 01/241-4050. Fax 01/241-4051. www.casa-andina.com. 49 units. $79 (£40) double. Rates include breakfast buffet. AE, DC, MC, V. **Amenities:** Concierge; business center; room service; babysitting; laundry service; nonsmoking rooms. *In room:* A/C, TV, minibar, hair dryer on request, safe.

Hotel Antigua Miraflores ✦ (Finds) This charming early-20th-century mansion,
full of authentic Peruvian touches and color, calls itself "a hidden treasure in the heart of Miraflores." As many return visitors know, that's not just hype. The hotel is owned and operated by a North American who's a long-time Lima resident. The house is elegant and tasteful, lined with colonial Peruvian art and built around a leafy courtyard. The staff is exceptionally helpful and friendly. Rooms range from huge suites with large Jacuzzis and kitchenettes to comfortable double rooms with handcrafted furniture and good-quality beds. Most bathrooms are quite luxurious, with colonial tiles, brass fixtures, and bathtubs. The public rooms look more like an art gallery than a hotel lobby (the paintings are for sale).

Av. Grau 350, Miraflores, Lima. © 01/241-6116. Fax 01/241-6115. http://peru-hotels-inns.com. 35 units. $85–$99 (£42–£49) double; $125 (£62) suite. Rates include taxes and a nice selection of breakfasts. AE, DC, MC, V. Free parking. **Amenities:** Restaurant; bar; small gym; Jacuzzi; tour desk; room service; laundry service. *In room:* A/C, TV, minibar, hair dryer.

San Antonio Abad (Value) Named for a saint, this clean and very friendly neighbor-
hood hotel aims high. Its goal is to be welcoming and comfortable, and it succeeds. The colonial building, near the commercial center of Miraflores and several parks, has a garden terrace, fireplace, and sitting room. The rooms, which are simply decorated

but ample, have private bathrooms. Because of street noise, ever present in Lima, you might ask for a room with an interior courtyard view.

Av. Ramón Ribeyro 301, Miraflores, Lima. © 01/447-6766. Fax 01/446-4208. www.hotelsanantonioabad.com. 24 units. $55 (£27) double; $120 (£60) suite. Rates include taxes and breakfast buffet. AE, DC, MC, V. Free parking. **Amenities:** Restaurant; bar; room service; laundry service. *In room:* A/C, TV, minibar, hair dryer on request, safe.

Inexpensive

Inkawasi Guest House (Value (Kids   Designed to appeal to backpackers, this pleasant bed-and-breakfast is a step up from most Peruvian hostels. It features an airy and comfortable homelike atmosphere in a secure part of Miraflores, just a few blocks from supermarkets, shops, restaurants, banks, and cinemas. There are two fully equipped kitchens available to guests, an interior patio and garden, and a roof garden and barbecue area. All rooms have private bathrooms, and suites have queen-size beds, desks, kitchenettes with microwaves, and cable TV. The inn is especially family-friendly; kids can enjoy a play area with toys and children's videos.

Alfredo Salazar 345, Miraflores, Lima. ©/fax 01/422-7724. 10 units. $10 (£5) per person, or $25–$35 (£12–£17) double; $45 (£22) suite. Rates include taxes and continental breakfast. Use of kitchen $2 (£1) a day; extra bed $5 (£2.50); children's bed $2 (£1). **Amenities:** Laundry service. *In room:* TV, kitchenette in suites, minibar, no phone.

SAN ISIDRO
Expensive

Sonesta Lima Hotel El Olivar (★★ (Value   The Sonesta chain's top-of-the-line property, aimed squarely at visiting business travelers, is named for the historic Olive Grove Park, which it faces. This seven-story hotel is well located for its clientele, in a peaceful section of the San Isidro business district of the city. The rooms, a step up from the more rustic decor in the chain's Posada del Inca, are quite large, with boldly colored fabrics and beige marble bathrooms. Service is friendly and efficient, and the amenities outdo those of most hotels in the city. The recently revamped restaurant is winning accolades in the Peruvian press and is an excellent spot for lunch or dinner.

Pancho Fierro 194, San Isidro, Lima. © 800/SONESTA or 01/712-6000. Fax 01/712-6099. www.sonesta.com/lima. 134 units. $195–$230 (£98–£165) double; $265–$400 (£133–£200) suite. Rates include breakfast buffet. Children under 8 stay free in parent's room. AE, DC, MC, V. Free parking. **Amenities:** 2 restaurants; cafe; cocktail lounge; bar; fitness center w/rooftop outdoor pool; Jacuzzi; sauna; concierge; business and conference center; salon; massage; babysitting; 24-hr. laundry service; nonsmoking rooms. *In room:* A/C, TV/VCR w/pay movies, minibar, hair dryer, safe.

WHERE TO DINE

Lima offers the most cosmopolitan dining in Peru, with restaurants for all budgets serving a wide range of cuisines. Sometimes, there are entire streets and neighborhoods specializing in a single type of food: In Lima Centro, you can visit the *chifas* of Chinatown, and in Miraflores, a pedestrian street off Parque Central, La Calle de las Pizzas, is lined with scores of look-alike pizzerias and quasi-Italian restaurants. Lima is the top spot in the country to sample the dish it is perhaps best known for: *ceviche.*

LIMA CENTRO
Moderate

L'Eau Vive FRENCH/PERUVIAN   If you're feeling helpless and obscenely rich in this impoverished country, you'll do a tiny bit of good by eating here. The restaurant, run by a French order of nuns, donates its proceeds to charity. In a colonial palace 2 blocks from the Plaza de Armas, it features several large dining rooms with high ceilings. If you come for the cheap lunch set menu, though, you'll have to sit in the simpler front rooms. The "a la carte" dining rooms are considerably more elegant. Though

---

> **Tips** **Peruvian** *Chifas*
>
> Chinatown (Barrio Chino), southeast of the Plaza de Armas and next to the Mercado Central (beyond the Chinese arch on Jr. Ucayali, a pedestrian mall that is lined with scores of *chifas*), is a good place to sample the Peruvian take on Chinese food. These *chifas*, inexpensive restaurants with similar menus, are everywhere in the small but dense neighborhood. Among those worth visiting (generally open daily 9am–10pm or later) are **Wa Lok** ⟨⟩, Jr. Paruro 864 (ⓒ 01/ 427-2750), probably the best known (and most expensive) in the neighborhood; and **Salón China**, Jr. Ucayali 727 (ⓒ 01/428-8350), which serves a good lunch buffet for S/30 ($8.55/£4.30).

---

the lunch menu is a deal, you get a pious show free with dinner: The nuns sing "Ave María" promptly at 9:30pm. The French menu includes items such as prawn bisque and grilled meats; it also incorporates some international dishes from around the globe—chiefly the many countries from which the order's nuns hail. The restaurant's heyday was clearly a few years ago, and some travelers have complained that the food and service weren't up to snuff, but this is still an old favorite you can feel good about.

Ucayali 370. ⓒ 01/427-5612. Reservations recommended on weekend evenings. Main courses S/9–S/43 ($3–$14/ £1.50–£7); set lunch menus S/9–S/14 ($3–$4/£1.50–£2). AE, MC, V. Mon–Sat 12:30–3pm and 7:30–9:30pm.

Los Escribanos PERUVIAN   On one of Lima Centro's more appealing streets, a tiny pedestrian passageway near the Plaza de Armas, this unassumingly elegant two-story restaurant has an attractive terrace with outdoor tables. Popular with local businessmen and travelers who trickle out of the tourism information office next door, it offers particularly good deals at lunch (with bargain *platos únicos* and a fixed-price menu that's served until 9pm). The evening menu lists plenty of *criollo* and seafood plates from the Peruvian coast, including gourmet dishes with pre-Columbian influences. At lunch, though, most people sit down to more standard fare such as grilled trout and fettuccine Alfredo, served with a salad and beverage.

Pasaje Nicolás de Ribera El Viejo (Los Escribanos) 137–141. ⓒ 01/427-9102. Reservations recommended on weekend evenings. Main courses S/10–S/28 ($3–$9/£1.50–£4.50); menú del día S/25 ($8/£4). MC, V. Mon–Thurs 9am–9pm; Fri–Sat 9am–midnight.

Inexpensive
Cocolat Café BISTRO   A good and quick spot for lunch or dinner, this simple little bistro rests on the popular pedestrian passageway near the Plaza de Armas. It serves sandwiches, salads, and sides such as empanadas. The midday menu is a good deal; it's just $4 (£2) for an appetizer and main course, or under $6 (£3) for a full "chef's menu." It's also a good spot for breakfast. Whenever you visit, you'll want to top off your meal with a great selection of homemade chocolates and good coffee, and you might just want to linger for a while on the sidewalk terrace.

Pasaje Nicolás de Ribera El Viejo (Los Escribanos) 121. ⓒ 01/427-4471. Reservations not accepted. Main courses S/7–S/12 ($2–$4/£1–£2); menú del día S/14–S/20 ($5–$7/£2.50–£3.50). No credit cards. Mon–Sat 8am–6:30pm.

MIRAFLORES & SAN ISIDRO
Very Expensive
Astrid y Gastón ⟨⟩⟨⟩⟨⟩ PERUVIAN/INTERNATIONAL   Hidden discreetly behind a nonchalant facade (though one of an antique colonial house), on a busy side

street leading to Parque Central, is this warm and chic modern colonial dining room and cozy bar. It continues to be my favorite restaurant in Peru. Gastón Acurio is the celebrity chef of the moment, with a burgeoning empire of fine-dining restaurants not only in Lima but a handful of other cities on the continent (and coming soon to the U.S.). His signature restaurant in the capital has high white peaked ceilings and orange walls decorated with colorful modern art. In back is an open kitchen where one of the owners, Gastón, can be seen cooking with his staff, and a secluded wine-salon dining room. The place is sophisticated and hip but low-key, a description that could fit most of its clients, who all seem to be regulars. The menu might be called *criollo*-Mediterranean: Peruvian with a light touch. Try spicy roasted kid or the excellent fish called *noble robado*, served in miso sauce with crunchy oysters. The list of desserts—the work of Astrid (the other half of the husband-wife team), is nearly as long as the main course menu, and they are spectacular.

Cantuarias 175, Miraflores. ⓒ **01/444-1496.** Reservations recommended. Main courses S/34–S/79 ($11–$26/£5.50–£13). AE, DC, MC, V. Mon–Sat 12:30–3:30pm and 7:30pm–midnight.

Cebichería La Mar ⭐⭐⭐ CEVICHERIA/SEAFOOD The restaurant everyone in Lima seems to be lining up to get in—no reservations are accepted, so get there early or sneak in late in the afternoon—is this upscale *cevichería,* courtesy of hot chef Gastón Acurio. Fashionable, stylishly designed, and moderately priced, it represents the best of traditional Limeño cooking, but with an edge. Some *ceviche* purists will insist that you don't need to go to a hip, expensive spot for *ceviche,* and while it's true that most authentic *ceviche* spots are no-frills neighborhood joints, there's nothing wrong with jazzing up the formula in my book. The airy, plant-filled space has a chic, modern touch, with an angular, poured concrete facade, bamboo roof, turquoise chairs, and cement floors. The fish—choose from several types of a couple dozen types of *ceviche,* as well as rice-based seafood dishes and whole fish—is always fresh and carefully prepared. Although La Mar is only open for lunch, it features a cool cocktail bar with great pisco-based drinks, such as the "Cholopolitan," that would surely be a hit late into the night were it to stay open. But owing to *cevichería* tradition, it's strictly a daytime affair. For now.

Av. La Mar 770, Miraflores. ⓒ **01/421-3365.** Reservations not accepted. Main courses S/24–S/36 ($8–$12/£4–£6). AE, DC, MC, V. Mon–Fri noon–5pm; Sat–Sun 11:30am–5:30pm.

Las Brujas de Cachiche ⭐⭐ PERUVIAN/CRIOLLO The Witches of Cachiche celebrates 2,000 years of local culture with a menu that's a tour of the "magical" cuisines of pre-Columbian Peru. The chef even uses ancient recipes and ingredients. The extensive menu includes classic Peruvian dishes, such as *ají de gallina* (creamed chicken with chiles), but concentrates on fresh fish and shellfish and fine cuts of meat with interesting twists and unusual accompaniments. Brujas de Cachiche sole, for instance, comes with Asian and *criollo* spices, plus peas and bell peppers sautéed in soybean sauce. Most of the excellent desserts continue the indigenous theme, such as *mazamorra morada* (purple corn pudding and dried fruit). The restaurant, in a sprawling old house with several warmly decorated dining rooms, is popular both night and day with well-heeled Limeños, expat businesspeople, foreign government officials, and tourists; it's exclusive and it's expensive, but it's worth the splurge. A lunch buffet is served Tuesday through Friday and Sunday from 11am to 4pm.

Jr. Bolognesi 460, Miraflores. ⓒ **01/447-1883.** Reservations recommended. Main courses S/30–S/62 ($10–$21/£5–£10); lunch buffet S/120 ($40/£20), including 2 glasses of wine. AE, DC, MC, V. Mon 1pm–midnight; Tues–Sat 11am–midnight; Sun noon–5pm.

Moderate

Café Suisse (La Tiendecita Blanca) SWISS/INTERNATIONAL   This classic old-style cafe, a Lima institution founded in 1937, is decorated with cool enamel doors and staffed by waitresses in folkloric red-and-white dresses. It's best known for its exquisite gourmet food shop, but the Little White Store is also a good little restaurant, perfect for lunch and even breakfast. Choose from fresh-baked quiches, empanadas (stuffed savory pastries), and sandwiches, or go Swiss with a fondue for two. There's a daily lunch *menú de la casa* for $10 (£5). Of course, if you spot that long counter bursting with homemade desserts, you may be unable to resist spoiling your meal.

Av. Larco 111, Miraflores. ✆ 01/445-9797. Reservations not accepted. Main courses S/20–S/34 ($7–$11/£3.50–£5.50). AE, DC, MC, V. Daily 8am–10pm.

La Trattoria di Mambrino ITALIAN   One of Lima's most popular and enduring Italian eateries is this attractive bistro, owned by an Italian gentleman who makes the rounds most evenings. Decorated in warm Roman tones, the restaurant is often packed with families and young couples. La Trattoria bakes its own delicious rustic bread; with a bit of olive oil, it's an appetizer in itself. Among the many excellent homemade pastas are several stuffed versions, such as the anglotti with rabbit, pork, and beef. There are daily specials such as ragout of rabbit over pappardelle and stuffed peppers with prawns. Pizzas, from the wood-burning oven, and large fresh salads round out the menu.

Manuel Bonilla 106, Miraflores. ✆ 01/446-7002. Reservations recommended. Main courses S/20–S/60 ($7–$20/£3.50–£10). AE, DC, MC, V. Daily 1–3:15pm and 8–11:15pm.

Segundo Muelle *(Value)* SEAFOOD/CEVICHE   At the top of most people's lists of favorite Peruvian dishes is *ceviche,* and you won't have trouble finding a *cevichería* anywhere along the coast. This informal, lunch-only place in San Isidro, popular with local office workers, is one of the most reasonable options in Lima for excellent fresh fish and *ceviche* plates without any fuss. If you're new to *ceviche,* you can't go wrong with the *mixto* (white fish, octopus, prawns, snails, scallops, and squid). There is a long list of other fish dishes, including sole, salmon, and varied rice and seafood plates. Top off your meal with *chicha morada,* a sweet and delicious purple corn beverage made with pineapple and lemon. Kids' plates are available for S/12 ($4/£2). There's a second branch in San Isidro at Av. Conquistadores 490 (✆ **01/421-1206**).

Av. Canaval y Moreyra 605 (at the corner of Pablo Carriquirry), San Isidro. ✆ 01/224-3007. www.segundomuelle. com. Reservations not accepted. Main courses S/18–S/30 ($6–$10/£3–£5). MC, V. Daily noon–5pm.

BARRANCO

Expensive

Manos Morenas *(Finds)* PERUVIAN/CRIOLLO   In a beautiful, early 1900s house on a quiet, leafy street in Barranco, this is one of the coolest restaurants in Lima. The name makes reference to the country's small but culturally potent Afro-Peruvian population and its traditions, influences crucial to both the menu and the lively, costumed music and dance shows that the restaurant has become famous for. The main dining room is very appealing, with handsome wooden chairs and tables, and art for sale on the elegant yellow walls. A nice bar greets you at the entrance in case you have to wait for a table. The kitchen, staffed by women dressed like the restaurant's logo of a black woman in a head wrap, creates excellent versions of Peruvian standards such as *lomo saltado* (beef strips with onions, tomatoes, peppers, and french-fried potatoes, served with rice) and *piqueos* (assorted appetizers). *Corvina Manos Morenas* is sea bass served with mashed potatoes, spinach, prawns, and a béchamel sauce. The restaurant charges a substantial cover for the live shows.

Av. Pedro de Osma 409, Barranco. © 01/467-0421. Reservations recommended. Main courses S/21–S/48 ($7–$16/ £3.50–£8). Live show cover Tues–Sat S/40 ($13/£6.50). AE, DC, MC, V. Mon–Sat 12:30–4pm and 7pm–1am.

Moderate

Antica Trattoria ⊛ (Value) ITALIAN

This is a charming and laid-back Italian restaurant that perfectly suits the surrounding Barranco barrio. It has a number of small, separate dining rooms decorated with a rustic and minimalist masculinity: stucco walls, dark wood-beamed ceilings, country-style wood tables, and simple, solid chairs. The house specialty is gourmet pizza from the wood-fired ovens, but the menu has several tempting ideas to lure you away from pizza, such as homemade pasta and *osso buco* or delicious *lomo fino a la tagliata*, buried under a mound of arugula. The relaxed environment makes this a great date place, as well as the perfect spot for dinner before hitting one of Barranco's live music or dance clubs.

San Martín 201, Barranco. © 01/247-5752. Reservations recommended. Main courses S/19–S/39 ($6–$13/£3– £6.50). AE, DC, MC, V. Daily noon–midnight.

LIMA AFTER DARK

As its largest city, Lima certainly has Peru's most varied nightlife scene. The best after-dark scenes are in Miraflores and particularly Barranco. Bars open in the early evening around 8pm, but dance clubs and live-music clubs generally don't get started until 10pm or later. Many are open very late, until 3 or 4am.

PEÑAS You should check out at least one *peña*, a *criollo*-music club that quite often inspires rousing participation. **Caballero de Fina Estampa** ⊛, Av. del Ejército 800, Miraflores (© 01/441-0552), is one of the most chic, with a large colonial salon and balconies. **De Rompe y Raja** ⊛, Manuel Segura 127, Barranco (© 01/247-3099), is a favorite of locals. Look for the popular Matices Negros (an Afro-Peruvian dance trio). **Las Guitarras,** Manuel Segura 295, Barranco (© 01/479-1874), is a cool spot where locals go to play an active part in their *peña*. It's open Friday and Saturday only. **Brisas del Titicaca** ⊛, Jr. Wukulski 168 at the first block of Avenida Brasil, Lima Centro (© 01/332-1901; www.brisasdeltiticaca.com), is a cultural institution with *noches folklóricas* Thursday through Saturday and some of the best shows in Lima.

THE BAR & CLUB SCENE **Freiheit,** Lima 471, Miraflores (© 01/247-4630), is a warmly decorated bar in the style of a German tavern. The dance floor is separate from the bar area. There's a drink minimum on weekends. **O'Murphy's Irish Pub,** Shell 627, Miraflores (© 01/242-1212), is a longtime favorite drinking hole. Expect a pool table, darts, Guinness on tap, and Brits and Irish hoisting it. **Son de Cuba,** Bulevar San Ramón 277, Miraflores (© 01/445-1444), is on the pedestrian street called "Little Italy" by locals, but the club focuses on the rhythms and drinks of the Caribbean from Tuesday through Sunday. **Mochileros,** Av. Pedro de Osma 135, Barranco (© 01/477-4506), is a cool pub that hops with young people who spill out into the courtyard.

My vote for best live music club in Lima is **La Noche** ⊛⊛, Bolognesi 307, Barranco (© 01/247-2186; www.lanoche.com.pe); despite its prosaic name, this sprawling multilevel club feels like a swank treehouse, with a great stage and sound system and good bands every night of the week that run the gamut (though are frequently jazz), plus a hip mixed Limeño and international crowd. The Monday night jam sessions are particularly good and have no cover charge; otherwise, covers range from S/8 to S/15

($3–$5/£1.50–£2.50). There's now a new branch of La Noche in Lima Centro, at the corner of Quilca and Camaná, near Plaza San Martín (📞 **01/423-0299**). **El Ekeko,** Av. Grau 266, Barranco (📞 **01/247-3148**), is a two-level place with live music Wednesday through Saturday; most acts fall within the Latin category, often Cuban. Covers range from S/12 to S/20 ($4–$7/£2–£3.50). **La Estación de Barranco** ★, Pedro de Osma 112 (📞 **01/247-0344**), is another nice place, with live music Tuesday through Saturday and a slightly more mature crowd. **Satchmo,** Av. La Paz 538, Miraflores (📞 **01/444-4957**), is a classy joint with a variable roster of live bands; it's a good date spot. Covers are S/20 to S/45 ($7–$15/£3.50–£7.50). Another very good jazz club, down a pedestrian-only walkway, is **Jazz Zone,** La Paz 646 (📞 **01/241-8139;** www.jazzzoneperu.com). It features a diverse program of live music, including Afro-Peruvian, Monday through Saturday.

Many of Lima's dance clubs are predominantly young and wild affairs. Check out **Deja-Vu Trattoria & Bar,** Av. Grau 294, Barranco (📞 **01/247-3742**), whose decor is based on TV commercials. The music trips from techno to trance; it's a dance fest Monday through Saturday. **Kitsch,** Bolognesi 743, Barranco (📞 **01/247-3325**), is one of Lima's hottest bars—literally, as it sometimes turns into a sweatbox—with over-the-top decor (flowery wallpaper and a fish tank in the floor) and recorded tunes that range from 1970s and 1980s pop to Latin and techno.

AN EXCURSION FROM LIMA: THE NAZCA LINES ★★

The unique Nazca Lines remain one of the great enigmas of the South American continent. The San José desert, bisected by the great Pan-American Highway that runs the length of Peru, is spectacularly marked by 70 giant plant and animal line drawings, as well as a warren of mysterious geometric lines, carved into the barren surface. Throughout the Nazca Valley, an area of nearly 1,000 sq. km (386 sq. miles), there are at least 10,000 lines and 300 different figures. Most are found alongside a 50km (30-mile) stretch of the Pan-American Highway. Some of the biggest and best-known figures are about 21km (13 miles) north of the town of Nazca. Most experts believe they were constructed by the Nazca (pre-Inca) culture between 300 B.C. and A.D. 700, though predecessor and successor cultures—the Paracas and Huari—may have also contributed to the desert canvas. The lines were discovered in the 1920s when commercial airlines began flights over the Peruvian desert. From the sky, they appeared to be some sort of primitive landing strips.

As enigmatic as they are, the Nazca Lines are not some sort of desert-sands Rorschach inkblot; the figures are real and easily identifiable from the air. With the naked eye from the window of an airplane, you'll spot the outlines of a parrot, hummingbird, spider, condor, dog, whale, monkey with a tail wound like a top, giant spirals, huge trapezoids, and, perhaps oddest of all, a cartoonish anthropomorphic figure with its hand raised to the sky that has come to be known as the "Astronaut." Some figures are as much as 300m (1,000 ft.) long, while some lines are 30m (100 ft.) wide and stretch more than 9km (5½ miles).

Questions have long confounded observers. Who constructed these huge figures and lines and why? Apparently, the Nazca people, over many generations, removed hard stones turned dark by the sun to "draw" the lines in the fine, lighter colored sand. The incredibly dry desert conditions preserved the lines and figures for more than 1,000 years. Why the lines were constructed is more difficult to answer, especially considering that the authors were unable to see their work in its entirety without any sort of aerial perspective. A scientist who dedicated her life to study of the lines was a German mathematician, María Reiche. She concluded that the lines formed a giant astronomi-cal calendar, crucial to calculating planting and harvest times. According to this theory, the Nazca were able to predict the arrival of rains, a valuable commodity in such bar-ren territory. Other theories, though, abound. Nazca is a seismic zone, with 300 fault lines beneath the surface and hundreds of subterranean canals; an American scientist, David Johnson, proposed that the trapezoids held clues to subterranean water sources. Some suggest that the lines not only led to water sources, but that they were pilgrim-age routes, part of the Nazca's ritual worship of water. Notions of extraterrestrials and the Nazca's ability to fly over the lines have been dismissed by most serious observers.

By far the most convenient—although certainly not the cheapest—way to see the lines is as part of a 1-day round-trip package from Lima with **AeroCondor,** Jr. Juan de Arona 781, San Isidro (© **01/614-6014;** www.aerocondor.com.pe). The full-day package includes a flight over the Nazca Lines, lunch, and a short sightseeing tour of Ica; it costs $350 (£175) per person, with a minimum of two people. **AeroIca,** Diez Canseco 480B, Miraflores (© **01/445-0859** or 034/522-434; www.aeroica.net/icahomeing.html), offers similar packages for $299–$339 (£150–£170) per person. **Aeroparacas,** Av. Santa Fe 274 (© **01/271-6941;** www.aeroparacas.com), offers package deals originating in Nazca that include a night's accommodations, a flight over the Nazca Lines, and a tour to Chauchilla for $69 (£35) per person. Unfortu-nately, there are no independent flights from Lima to Nazca (or from any other city to Nazca), so you'll have to get there by bus—an 8-hour ride.

Overflights organized in Nazca run $50 to $79 (£25–£40) per person (those origi-nating in Ica run about $150–$180/£75–£90). The small aircraft seats between three and five passengers; if you're prone to airsickness, you should note that these flights take some stomach-turning dips and dives. (Only 10 min. into one recent flight, the four French travelers onboard with me were all tossing their *petits déjeuners* into the white plastic bags that had been thoughtfully provided.)

5 Cusco ★★★

1,153km (715 miles) SE of Lima

As the storied capital of the Inca dynasty and the gateway to Machu Picchu, Cusco is one of the undisputed highlights of South America. Paved with stone streets and build-ing foundations laid by the Incas more than 5 centuries ago, the town is far from a mere history lesson; it is also remarkably dynamic, enlivened by throngs of travelers who have transformed the center around the Plaza de Armas into a mecca for South American adventurers. Cusco is one of those rare places that seems able to preserve its unique char-acter and enduring appeal despite its prominence on the international tourism radar.

Cusco looks and feels like the very definition of an Andean capital. It's a fascinating blend of pre-Columbian and colonial history and contemporary mestizo culture. Cusco's highlights include Inca ruins and colonial-era baroque and Renaissance churches and mansions. The heart of the historic center has suffered relatively few modern intru-sions, and despite the staggering number of souvenir shops, travel agencies, hotels, and restaurants overflowing with visitors soaking up the flavor, it doesn't take an impossibly fertile imagination to conjure the magnificent capital of the 16th century.

Today, Cusco thrives as one of the most vibrant expressions of Amerindian and mestizo culture anywhere in the Americas. Every June, the city is packed during Inti Raymi, the celebration of the winter solstice and the sun god, a deeply religious festi-val that is also a magical display of pre-Columbian music and dance. Thousands trek out to Paucartambo for the riveting Virgen del Carmen festival in mid-July. Other traditional arts also flourish. Cusco is the handicrafts center of Peru, and its streets teem with merchants and their extraordinary textiles, many hand-woven using the exact techniques of their ancestors.

Spectacularly cradled by the southeastern Andes Mountains, Cusco sits at a daunting altitude of 3,400m (11,150 ft.). The air is noticeably thinner here than in almost any other city in South America, and the city, best explored on foot, demands arduous hiking up precipitous stone steps, leaving even the fittest of travelers gasping for breath. It takes a couple of days to get acclimatized before moving on from Cusco to explore the mountain villages of the Inca's Sacred Valley, the Amazon basin, and, of course, Machu Picchu, but many visitors find Cusco so seductive that they either delay plans to explore the surrounding region, or add a few days to their trip to allow more time in the city. Increasingly, travelers are basing themselves in one of the lower-altitude villages of the Sacred Valley, but there is so much to see and do in Cusco that an overnight stay is pretty much required of anyone who hasn't previously spent time in the area. The charms of Cusco become quickly addictive, and many travelers linger in the old Inca capital, even forsaking other travel plans in Peru.

ESSENTIALS
GETTING THERE

BY PLANE   Most visitors to Cusco arrive by plane from Lima (a 1-hr. flight). In high season, LAN Perú, Taca, and other carriers' flights arrive by the dozens from Lima as well as Arequipa, Puerto Maldonado, and La Paz at **Aeropuerto Internacional Velasco Astete** (© **084/222-611**). See "Getting Around" in "Planning Your Trip to Peru," earlier in this chapter, for more flight information. Flights are occasionally delayed by poor weather.

Transportation from the airport to downtown Cusco, about 20 minutes away, is by taxi or private hotel car. Taxis are plentiful and inexpensive. (A less convenient *combi*, or small bus, passes outside the airport parking lot and goes to Plaza San Francisco; unless you have almost no baggage and your hotel is right on that square, it's not worth the few soles you'll save to take a *combi*.) Most hotels, even less expensive hostels, are happy to arrange airport pickup. If you take a taxi, note that the fare is likely to drop precipitously if you merely refuse the first offer you get (likely to be S/15–S/20 or $5–$7/£2.50–£3.50). Taxi fare to Cusco is generally S/10 ($3.35/£1.70) from the airport to the center. If you have arranged for your hotel to pick you up, be certain that you are dealing with someone authorized by the hotel and who possesses your exact arrival information.

BY BUS   Buses to Cusco arrive from Lima, Arequipa, Puno/Juliaca, and Puerto Maldonado in the Amazon basin. From Lima to Cusco is 26 hours by land; from Puno, 7 hours; and from Arequipa, 12 hours. There is no central bus terminal in Cusco. Buses arrive at either a terminal on Avenida Pachacutec or (more commonly) at the newer **Terminal Terrestre,** Av. Vellejos Santoni, Cdra. 2, Santiago (© **084/224-471;** several miles from the city center on the way to the airport). Buses to and from the Sacred Valley (Urubamba buses, which go through either Pisac or Chinchero) use small, makeshift terminals on Calle Puputi s/n, Cdra. 2 and Av, Grau s/n, Cdra 1.

BY TRAIN   There are two main Perurail train stations in Cusco. Trains from Puno and Arequipa arrive at **Estación de Huanchaq** (also spelled "Wanchac"), Av. Pachacútec s/n (© **084/238-722** or 084/221-992; www.perurail.com), at the southeast end of

Cusco

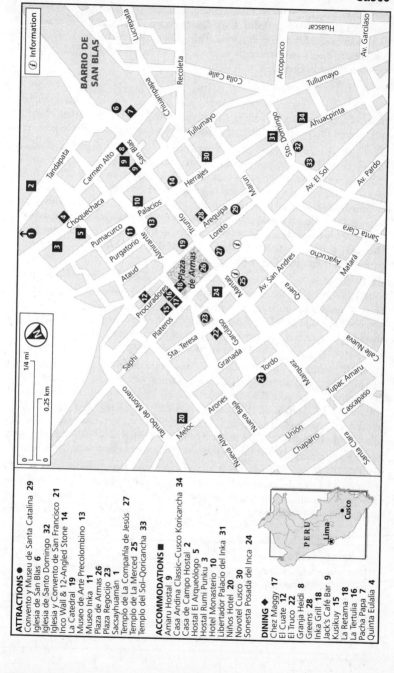

Avenida El Sol. Trains from Ollantaytambo, Machu Picchu, and the Amazon jungle arrive at **Estación de San Pedro,** Calle Cascaparo s/n (© **084/221-352** or 084/221-313), southwest of the Plaza de Armas. Thieves operate in and around both stations, but visitors should be particularly cautious at San Pedro station, which is near the crowded Mercado Central.

GETTING AROUND

Getting around Cusco is straightforward and relatively simple, especially since so many of the city sights are within walking distance of the Plaza de Armas in the historic center. You will mostly depend on leg power and inexpensive taxis to get around.

BY TAXI   Unlike in Lima, taxis are regulated in Cusco and charge standard rates (although they do not have meters). Taxis are inexpensive (S/2–S/3 or 70¢–$1/ 35p–50p for any trip within the historic core during the day, S/3–S/6 or $1–$2/ 50p–£1 at night) and are a good way to get around, especially at night. Hailing a cab in Cusco is considerably less daunting than in Lima, but you may still wish to call a registered taxi when traveling from your hotel to train or bus stations, going to the airport, and when returning to your hotel late at night. Licensed taxi companies include **Okarina** (© **084/247-080**) and **Aló Cusco** (© **084/222-222**). Taxis can be hired for return trips to nearby ruins or for half- or full days.

BY BUS   Most buses—called variously *colectivos, micros,* and *combis*—cost S/1.50 (50¢/25p) or slightly more after midnight, on Sundays, and on holidays. You aren't likely to need buses often, or ever, within the city, though the *colectivos* that run up and down Avenida El Sol are also a useful option for some hotels, travel agencies, and shopping markets (taxis are much easier and not much more expensive). A bus departs from Plaza San Francisco to the airport, but it isn't very convenient.

BY CAR   Renting a car in the Cusco region—more than likely to visit the beautiful Sacred Valley mountain villages—is a more practical idea than in most parts of Peru. Rental agencies include **Avis,** Av. El Sol 808 (© **084/248-800**), and **Localiza,** Av. Industrial J-3, Urbanización Huancaro (© **084/233-131**). Rates range from $50 (£25) per day for a standard four-door to $75 (£37) per day for a Jeep Cherokee 4×4. Check also with **4×4 Cusco,** Urb. San Borja, Huanchaq (© **084/227-730**), which has pickups and even Toyota Land Cruisers, though renters need to be at least 28 years old.

BY FOOT   Most of Cusco is best navigated by foot, though because of the city's 3,400m (11,150 ft.) elevation and steep climbs, walking is demanding. Allow extra time to get around and carry a bottle of water. You can walk to the major ruins just beyond the city—Sacsayhuamán and Q'enko—but you should be fit to do so.

A Safety Note

Over the years, Cusco has earned a reputation for being rather unsafe for foreign visitors, especially at night when violent muggings have been known to occur on empty streets. While I have never had a problem in the city in more than 20 years, it's advisable to take some precautions. Do not walk alone late at night; have restaurant or bar staff call a taxi to transfer you to your hotel. Please refer to "Safety" in "Fast Facts: Peru" on p. 628 for more details.

Tips   Altitude Acclimatization

You'll need to take it easy for the first few hours or even couple of days in Cusco—which sits at an altitude of just over 3,400m (11,150 ft.)—to adjust to the elevation. Pounding headaches and shortness of breath are the most common ailments, though some travelers are afflicted with nausea. Drink lots of water, avoid heavy meals, and do as the locals do: Drink *mate de coca,* or coca-leaf tea. (Don't worry, you won't get high or arrested, but you will adjust a little more smoothly to the thin air.) If that doesn't cure you, ask whether your hotel has an oxygen tank you can use for a few moments of assisted breathing. If you're really suffering, look for an over-the-counter medication in the pharmacy called "Sorojchi Pills." And if that doesn't do the trick, it may be time to seek medical assistance; see "Fast Facts," below. Those who think they may have an especially hard time with the altitude might consider staying the first couple of nights in the slightly lower Sacred Valley (near Urubamba, Yanahuara, or Ollantaytambo).

VISITOR INFORMATION

As the top tourist destination in Peru, Cusco is well equipped with information outlets. There's a branch of the **Oficina de Información Turística** (© 084/380-145) at the Velasco Astete Airport in the arrivals terminal; it's open daily from 6:30am to 12:30pm. The principal **Oficina de Información Turística** is located on Mantas 117-A, a block from the Plaza de Armas (© 084/222-032). It's open Monday through Saturday from 7am to 7pm and Sunday from 7am to noon. It's very helpful and efficient, and it sells the essential *boleto turístico* (tourist ticket; see "Cusco's *Boleto Turístico*" on p. 653). However, the new **iperu office,** Av. El Sol 103, Of. 102 (© 084/252-974), is better stocked with information and has been more helpful on recent visits; it's open daily from 8:30am to 7:30pm. Another information office is located in the **Terminal Terrestre de Huanchaq** train station, Av. Pachacútec s/n (© 084/238-722); it's open Monday through Saturday from 8am to 6:30pm.

FAST FACTS   Most Peruvian and international **banks** with money-exchange bureaus and ATMs are located along Avenida El Sol. There are also a couple located at entrances to stores and restaurants on the Plaza de Armas and at the Huanchaq train station. Money changers, usually wearing colored smocks, patrol the main streets off the Plaza de Armas.

In a **police emergency,** call © 105. The **National Tourist Police** are located at Saphy, 510 (© 084/249-654). You can also try the **iperu/Tourist Protection Bureau,** Portal Carrizos 250, Plaza de Armas (© 084/252-974). If you have a medical emergency, contact **Tourist Medical Assistance** at Heladeros 157 (© 084/260-101). English-speaking medical personnel are available at the following hospitals and clinics: **Hospital Essalud,** Av. Anselmo Alvarez s/n (© 084/237-341); **Clínica Pardo,** Av. de la Cultura 710 (© 084/624-186); **Hospital Antonio Loren,** Plazoleta Belén s/n (© 084/226-511); **Hospital Regional,** Av. de la Cultura s/n (© 084/223-691); and **Clínica Paredes,** Lechugal 405 (© 084/225-265).

Internet *cabinas* are everywhere in the old section of Cusco, and many permit cheap overseas Internet-based (Web2Phone) calls for as little as S/1 (35¢/15p) per minute. Rates are generally S/1.50 (50¢/25p) per hour. Most keep very late hours,

Cusco = Cuzco = Q'osqo

Spanish and English spellings derived from the Quechua language are a little haphazard in Cusco, especially since there's been a linguistic movement to try to recuperate and value indigenous culture. For example, you may see *Inca* written *Inka; Cusco* written *Cuzco, Qosqo,* or *Q'osqo; Qoricancha* as *Coricancha* or *Koricancha; Wanchac* as *Huanchac* or *Huanchaq; Sacsayhuamán* as *Sacsaywaman;* and *Qenko* as *Kenko, Q'enko,* or *Qenqo.*

opening at 9am and staying open until 11pm or midnight. Cusco's main **post office,** Av. El Sol 800 (© 084/224-212), is open Monday through Saturday from 7:30am to 7:30pm and Sunday from 7:30am to 2pm. A **DHL/Western Union** office is located at Av. El Sol 627-A (© 084/244-167). The principal **Telefónica del Perú** office, for long-distance and international calls, is at Av. El Sol 382 (© 084/241-114).

WHAT TO SEE & DO

The stately and lively **Plaza de Armas** 𝓻𝓻, lined by arcades and carved wooden balconies and framed by the Andes, is the focal point of Cusco. Next to Machu Picchu, it is one of the most familiar sights in Peru. You will cross it, relax on the benches in its center, and pass under the porticoes that line it with shops, restaurants, travel agencies, and bars innumerable times during your stay in Cusco. The plaza—which was twice its present size in Inca days—has two of Cusco's foremost churches and the remains of original Inca walls on the northwest side of the square, thought to be the foundation of the Inca Pachacutec's palace.

The Incas designed their capital in the shape of a puma, with the head at the north end, at Sacsayhuamán (even its zigzagged walls are said to have represented the animal's teeth). This is difficult to appreciate today; even though much of the original layout of the city remains, it has been engulfed by growth. Still, most of Cusco can be seen on foot, certainly the best way to appreciate this historic mountain town.

Many principal sights within the historic quarter of Cusco and beyond the city are included in the *boleto turístico* (see box, below), but a few very worthwhile places of interest, including the Templo del Qoricancha (Temple of the Sun), are not.

AROUND THE PLAZA DE ARMAS

Convento y Museo de Santa Catalina 𝓻𝓻   A small convent located a couple of blocks west of the Plaza de Armas, Santa Catalina was built between 1601 and 1610 on top of the Acllawasi, where the Inca sequestered his chosen Virgins of the Sun. The convent contains a museum of colonial and religious art. The collection includes an excellent collection of Cusqueña School paintings, featuring some of the greatest works of Amerindian art—a combination of indigenous and typically Spanish styles—in Cusco. The interior of the monastery is quite beautiful, with painted arches and an interesting chapel with baroque frescoes of Inca vegetation. Other items of interest include very macabre statues of Jesus and an extraordinary trunk that, when opened, displays the life of Christ in 3-D figurines (it was employed by the Catholic Church's traveling salesmen, used to convert the natives in far-flung regions of Peru). The main altar of the convent church is tucked behind steel bars.

Santa Catalina Angosta s/n. © 084/223-245. Admission included in *boleto turístico.* Daily 8:30am–5:30pm.

(*Value*) Cusco's *Boleto Turístico*

Cusco's municipal tourism (Calle Mantas 117-A) office sells a tourist pass, or *boleto turístico,* that is virtually essential for visiting the city and surrounding areas. It is your admission to 16 of the most important places of interest in and around Cusco, including some of the major draws in the Sacred Valley. Though it has doubled in price in the last few years, the *boleto* is still a good value, and you cannot get into some churches and museums without it. The full ticket costs S/70 ($23/£11) for adults and S/35 ($12/£6) for students with ID and children; it's valid for 10 days and is available at the tourism office at Mantas 117-A (✆ **084/263-176**), which is open Monday through Friday from 8am to 6:30pm and Saturday from 8am to 2pm. The *boleto* allows admission to the following sights: Convento y Museo de Santa Catalina, Museo Municipal de Arte Contemporáneo, Museo Histórico Regional, Museo de Sitio Qoricancha, Museo de Arte Popular, Centro Qosqo de Arte Nativo de Danzas Folklóricas, Monumento Pachacuteq, Museo Palacio Municipal, as well as the Inca ruins of Sacsayhuamán, Q'enko, Puka-pukara, Tambomachay, Pikillacta, and Tipón, and the Valle Sagrado attractions of Pisac, Ollantaytambo, and Chinchero. La Catedral, the cathedral on the Plaza de Armas, was formerly included in the *boleto* but now charges separate admission. Other principal attractions not covered by the *boleto* include the Templo Qoricancha, Museo Inca, and Iglesia de San Blas.

Not all of these attractions are indispensable, and you probably won't end up checking off absolutely everything on your color photo–coded *boleto,* but it remains the best admission ticket in Cusco. (You can also buy a partial ticket for S/40, or $13 [£6.50], that covers either attractions in the city, or ruins outside of Cusco.) Make sure you carry the ticket with you when you're planning to make visits (especially on day trips outside the city), as guards will demand to see it so that they can punch a hole alongside the corresponding picture. Students must also carry their International Student Identification Card (ISIC), as guards often demand to see that ID to prove that they didn't fraudulently obtain a student *boleto* and thus cheat the city out of 10 bucks.

In addition to the main Tourist Office, the *boleto* can be purchased at: OFEC, Av. El Sol 103, office 106 (Galerías Turísticas; ✆ **084/227-037,** from 8am–6pm Mon–Sat); and Casa Garcilaso, at the corner of Garcilaso y Heladeros s/n (✆ **084/226-919**).

La Catedral ✦✦   Built on the site of the palace of the Inca Viracocha, Cusco's cathedral is a beautiful religious and artistic monument that dominates the Plaza de Armas. Completed in 1669 in the Renaissance style, the cathedral possesses some 400 canvases of the distinguished Cusqueña School, painted from the 16th to 18th centuries. There are also amazing woodcarvings, including the spectacular cedar choir stalls. The main altar—which weighs more than 882 pounds and is fashioned from silver mined in Potosí, Bolivia—features the patron saints of Cusco. To the right of the altar is a particularly Peruvian painting of the Last Supper, with the apostles drinking *chicha* (fermented maize beer) and eating *cuy* (guinea pig). The **Capilla del Triunfo** (the first Christian church in Cusco) is next door, to the right of the main church. It holds a painting by Alonso Cortés de Monroy of the devastating earthquake of 1650 and an altar adorned by the locally famous "El Negrito" (El Señor de los Temblores, or Lord of the Earthquakes), a brown-skinned figure of Christ on the cross that was paraded around the city by frightened residents during the 1650 earthquake (which, miracle or not, ceased shortly thereafter).

The entrance to the cathedral and ticket office, where you can purchase the *boleto turístico*, is actually at the entrance to the **Capilla de la Sagrada Familia,** to the left of the main door and steps.

Plaza de Armas (north side). Admission not included in *boleto turístico;* S/16 ($5/£2.50) adults, S/5 ($1.65/85p) students and children. Mon–Sat 10–11:30am and 2pm–5:30pm.

Museo Inka ⊛   Housed in the impressive Admirals Palace, this museum contains artifacts designed to trace Peruvian history from pre-Inca civilizations and Inca culture, including the impact of the conquest and colonial times on the culture. On view are ceramics, textiles, jewelry, mummies, architectural models, and an interesting collection (reputed to be the world's largest) of Inca drinking vessels *(qeros)* carved out of wood, many meticulously painted. The museum is a good introduction to Inca culture, and there are explanations in English. The palace itself is one of Cusco's finest colonial mansions, with a superbly ornate portal indicating the importance of its owner; the house was built on top of yet another Inca palace at the beginning of the 17th century. In the courtyard is a studio of women weaving traditional textiles.

Cuesta del Almirante 103 (corner of Ataúd and Tucumán). ⓒ 084/237-380. Admission not included in *boleto turístico;* S/10 ($3.35/£1.70) adults, S/5 ($1.65/85p) students. Mon–Sat 9am–5pm.

Templo de la Compañía de Jesús ⊛   Cater-cornered to the cathedral is this Jesuit church, which rivals the cathedral in grandeur and prominence on the square (an intentional move by the Jesuits, and one that had Church diplomats running back and forth to the Vatican). Begun in the late 16th century, it was almost entirely demolished by the quake of 1650, rebuilt, and finally finished 18 years later. Like the cathedral, it was also built on the site of the Inca Huayna Capac (said to be the most beautiful of all the Inca rulers' palaces). Inside, it's rather gloomy, but the gilded altar is stunning, especially when illuminated. The church possesses several important works of art, including a picture of St. Ignatius de Loyola by the local painter Marcos Zapata, and the Cristo de Burgos crucifixion by the main altar. Also of note are the paintings to either side of the entrance, which depict the marriages of St. Ignatius's nephews; one is the very symbol of Peru's mestizo character, as the granddaughter of Manco Inca wed the man who captured the last Inca, Tupac Amaru, leader of an Indian uprising.

Plaza de Armas (southeast side). Admission not included in *boleto turístico;* S/10 ($3.35/£1.70) adults, S/5 ($1.65/85p) students. Mon–Sat 11am–noon and 3–4pm.

SOUTH & EAST OF THE PLAZA DE ARMAS

Barrio de San Blas ⊛⊛   Cusco's most atmospheric and picturesque neighborhood, San Blas, a short but increasingly steep walk from the Plaza de Armas, is lined with artists' studios and artisans' workshops, and stuffed with tourist haunts—many of the best bars and restaurants and a surfeit of hostels. It's a great area to wander around—many streets are pedestrian-only—though you should exercise caution with your belongings, especially at night. The neighborhood also affords some of the most

The Magic of Inca Stones: A Walking Tour ★★

The ancient streets of Cusco are lined by dramatic Inca walls, mammoth granite blocks so exquisitely carved that they fit together, without mortar, like jigsaw puzzle pieces. The Spaniards razed many Inca constructions but built others right on top of the original foundations. (Even hell-bent on destruction, they recognized the value of good engineering.) Colonial architecture has, in many cases, not stood up nearly as well as the Incas' bold structures, designed to withstand the immensity of seismic shifts common in this part of Peru.

Apart from the main attractions detailed in this section, a brief walking tour will take you past some of the finest Inca constructions that remain in the city. East of the Plaza de Armas, **Calle Loreto** is one of the best-known Inca thoroughfares. The massive wall on the left-hand side, composed of meticulously cut rectangular stones, was once part of the Acllahuasi, or the "House of the Chosen Maidens," the Inca's Virgins of the Sun. This is the oldest surviving Inca wall in Cusco, and one of the most distinguished. Northeast of the Plaza de Armas, off Calle Palacio, is **Hatunrumiyoc,** a cobbled street lined with impressive walls of polygonal stones. Past the Archbishop's Palace on the right side is the famed **12-angled stone** (now appropriated as the symbol of Cuzqueña beer and appearing on its labels), magnificently fitted into the wall. Originally, this wall belonged to the palace of the Inca Roca. Although this large stone is impressively cut, the Incas almost routinely fitted many-cornered stones (with as many as 32, as seen at Machu Picchu, or even 44 angles) into structures. From Hatunrumiyoc, make your first right down another pedestrian alleyway, Inca Roca; about halfway down on the right side is a series of stones said to form the shape of a **puma,** including head, large paws, and tail. It's not all that obvious, so if you see someone else studying the wall, ask him or her to point out the figure. Other streets with notable Inca foundations are Herrajes, Pasaje Arequipa, and Santa Catalina Angosta. Only a couple of genuine Inca **portals** remain; one is at Choquechaca 339 and another at Romeritos 402, near Qoricancha.

Not every impressive stone wall in Cusco is Inca in origin, however. Many are transitional period (postconquest) constructions, performed by local masons under the service of Spanish bosses. Peter Frost's *Exploring Cusco* (available in local bookstores) has a good explanation of what to look for in distinguishing an original from what amounts to a copy.

spectacular panoramic vistas in the city. In the small plaza at the top and to the right of Cuesta San Blas is the little white **Iglesia de San Blas** ★★, said to be the oldest parish church in Cusco (admission apart from *boleto turístico;* S/6, or $1.70/85p). Though a simple adobe structure, it contains a marvelously carved, Churrigueresque cedar pulpit. It's carved from a single tree trunk; some have gone as far as proclaiming it the finest example of woodcarving in the world. The pulpit comes with an odd story, and it's difficult to determine whether it's fact or folklore: It is said that the carpenter who created it was rewarded by having his skull placed within his masterwork (at the top, beneath the feet of St. Paul) upon death. Also worth a look is the baroque gold-leaf main altar.

Museo de Arte Precolombino (MAP) ✦✦   A spectacular new addition to the Cusco cultural landscape is this archaeological museum run by and featuring part of the vast collection of pre-Columbian works, an outpost of the terrific Rafael Larco Herrera Museum in Lima. Housed in an erstwhile Inca ceremonial court and later mansion—now handsomely restored—of the Conquistador Alonso Díaz are 450 pieces (about 1% of the pieces in storage at the museum in Lima), dating from 1250 B.C. to A.D. 1532. Beautifully illuminated halls carefully exhibit gold and precious metal handicrafts, jewelry, and other artifacts depicting the rich traditions from the Nazca, Moche, Huari, Chimú, Chancay, and Inca cultures. The museum—which is open late and boasts one of the city's finest restaurants, in a contemporary glass box in the courtyard—is especially worthwhile for anyone unable to visit the major archaeological museums in Lima or any of the premier sites in northern Peru.

Plaza de las Nazarenas s/n, San Blas. © 084/237-380. Admission S/16 ($5.35/£2.70) adults, S/8 ($2.65/£1.30) students. Daily 9am–10pm.

Templo del Sol–Qoricancha (Temple of the Sun) & Iglesia de Santo Domingo ✦✦✦   Qoricancha and Santo Domingo together form perhaps the most vivid illustration in Cusco of Andean culture's collision with Western Europe. Like the Great Mosque in Córdoba, Spain—where Christians dared to build a massive church within the perfect Muslim shrine—the temple of one culture sits atop and encloses the other. The extraordinarily crafted Temple of the Sun was the most sumptuous temple in the Inca Empire and the apogee of the Inca's naturalistic belief system. Some 4,000 of the highest-ranking priests and their attendants were housed here. Dedicated to worship of the sun, it was apparently a glittering palace straight out of El Dorado legend: Qoricancha means "golden courtyard" in Quechua, and in addition to hundreds of gold panels lining its walls, there were life-size gold figures, solid gold altars, and a huge golden sun disc. The sun disc reflected the sun and bathed the temple in light. During the summer solstice, the sun still shines directly into a niche where only the Inca chieftain was permitted to sit. Other temples and shrines existed for the worship of lesser natural gods: the Moon, Venus, Thunder, Lightning, and the Rainbow. Qoricancha was the main astronomical observatory for the Incas.

After the Spaniards ransacked the temple and emptied it of gold, the exquisite polished stone walls were employed as the foundations of the Convent of Santo Domingo, constructed in the 17th century. The baroque church pales next to the fine masonry of the Incas—and that's to say nothing about the original glory of the Sun Temple. Today all that remains is Inca stonework. Thankfully, a large section of the cloister has been removed, revealing four original chambers of the temple, all smoothly tapered examples of Inca trapezoidal architecture. Stand on the small platform in the first chamber and see the perfect symmetry of openings in the stone chambers. A series of Inca stones displayed reveals the fascinating concept of male and female blocks and how they fit together. The 6m (20-ft.) curved wall beneath the west end of the church, visible from the street, remains undamaged by repeated earthquakes and is perhaps the greatest example of Inca stonework. The curvature and fit of the massive stones is astounding.

After the Spaniards had taken Cusco, Juan Pizarro was given the eviscerated Temple of the Sun. He died soon after, though, at the battle at Sacsayhuamán, and he left the temple to the Dominicans, in whose hands it remains.

Plazoleta Santo Domingo. (C) **084/222-071.** Admission not included in *boleto turístico;* S/6 ($2/£1) adults, S/3 ($1/50p) students. Mon–Sat 8:30am–5:30pm; Sun 2–5pm.

SOUTHWEST OF THE PLAZA DE ARMAS

Iglesia y Convento de San Francisco   This large and austere 17th-century convent church extends the length of the plaza of the same name. It is best known for its collection of colonial artwork, including paintings by Marcos Zapata and Diego Quispe Tito, both of considerable local renown. A monumental canvas (12×9m/ 39×30 ft.) that details the genealogy of the Franciscan family (almost 700 individuals) is by Juan Espinoza de los Monteros. The Franciscans also decorated the convent with ceiling frescos and a number of displays of skulls and bones.

Plaza de San Francisco s/n. (C) **084/221-361.** Admission S/3 ($1/50p) adults, S/2 (65¢/30p) students. Mon–Sat 9am–4pm.

Templo de La Merced 🏛   Erected in 1536 and rebuilt after the great earthquake in the 17th century, La Merced ranks just below the cathedral and La Compañía in importance. It has a beautiful facade and lovely cloisters with a mural depicting the life of the Merced Order's founder. The sacristy contains a small museum of religious art, including a fantastic solid gold monstrance swathed in precious stones. In the vaults of the church are the remains of two famous conquistadors, Diego de Almagro and Gonzalo Pizarro.

Calle Mantas s/n. (C) **084/231-821.** Admission S/5 ($1.65/85p) adults. Mon–Sat 8:30am–noon and 2–5pm.

INCA RUINS NEAR CUSCO

The best way to see the following set of Inca ruins just outside of Cusco is on a half-day tour. The hardy may want to approach it as an athletic archaeological expedition: If you've got 15km (9 miles) of walking and climbing at high altitude in you, it's a beautiful trek. Otherwise, you can walk to Sacsayhuamán and nearby Q'enko (the climb from the Plaza de Armas is strenuous and takes 30–45 min.) and take a *colectivo* or taxi to the other sites. Alternatively, you can take a Pisac/Urubamba minibus (leaving from the bus station at Calle Intiqhawarina, off Av. Tullumayo, or at Huáscar 128) and tell the driver you want to get off at the ruins farthest from Cusco, Tambomachay, and work your way back on foot. Some even make the rounds by horseback. (You can easily and cheaply contract a horse at Sacsayhuamán, but know that you'll walk to all the sites alongside a guide.) Visitors with less time in Cusco or interest in taxing themselves may wish to join a guided tour, probably the most popular and the easiest way of seeing the ruins. Virtually any of the scads of travel agencies and tour operators in the old center of Cusco offer them. Well-rated traditional agencies with a variety of city programs include **Milla Turismo,** Portal Comercio 195, Plaza de Armas ((C) **084/234-181;** www.millaturismo.com); **SAS Travel,** Portal Panes 167, Plaza de Armas ((C) **084/255-205;** www.sastravelperu.com); and **Top Vacations,** Portal Confituria 265, Plaza de Armas ((C) **084/263-278**).

Admission to the following sites is by *boleto turístico,* and they are all open daily from 7am to 6pm. Official and unofficial guides hover around the ruins; negotiate a price or decide on a proper tip. There are other Inca ruins on the outskirts of Cusco, a couple of which even appear on the *boleto,* but the ones discussed below are the most interesting.

These sites are generally safe, but at certain times of day—usually dawn and dusk before and after tour groups' visits—several ruins are said to be favored by thieves. It's best to be alert and, if possible, go accompanied.

SACSAYHUAMAN ✮✮✮   The greatest and nearest to Cusco of the ruins, Sacsayhuamán reveals some of the Incas' most extraordinary architecture and monumental stonework. Usually referred to as a garrison or fortress—it was constructed with forbidding, castlelike walls—it was probably a religious temple (though most experts also believe it had military significance). The festival Inti Raymi (June 24) is celebrated here annually, and it's a great spectacle.

The ruins cover a huge area, but they constitute perhaps one-quarter of the original complex. Surviving today are the astounding outer walls, constructed in a zigzag formation of three tiers. Many of the base stones employed are almost unimaginably massive; some are twice as tall as a 1.8m (6-ft.) man, and one is said to weigh 300 tons. Like all Inca constructions, the stones fit together perfectly without the aid of mortar. After victory here, the Spaniards made off with the more manageable blocks to build houses and other structures in Cusco. It's easy to see how hard it would have been to attack these ramparts; with 22 distinct zigzags, the design would automatically expose the flanks of an opponent.

Above the walls are the circular foundations of three towers—used for storage of provisions and water—that once stood here. The complex suffered such extensive destruction that little is known about the actual purpose Sacsayhuamán served. What is known is that it was the site of one of the bloodiest battles between the Spaniards and native Cusqueños. More than 2 years after the Spaniards initially marched on Cusco and installed a puppet government, the anointed Inca (Manco Inca) led a seditious campaign that took back Sacsayhuamán and nearly defeated the Spanish in a siege of the Inca capital. Juan Pizarro and his vastly outnumbered but superior armed forces stormed Sacsayhuamán in a horrific battle in 1536 that left thousands dead. Legend speaks of their remains as carrion for giant condors in the open fields here.

A flat, grassy esplanade separates the defense walls from a small hill where you'll find the "Inca's Throne" and large rocks with well-worn grooves, used by children (and, almost as frequently, adults) as slides. Nearby is a series of claustrophobia-inducing tunnels (pass through them if you dare).

Night visits to the ruins are now permitted from 8 to 10pm. Under a full moon in the huge star-lit Andean sky, Sacsayhuamán is so breathtaking that you'll instantly grasp the Incas' worship of the natural world, in which both the sun and moon were considered deities. If you go at night, take a flashlight and a few friends; security is a little lax, and assaults on foreigners have occurred.

If you're walking, it's a steep 2km (1¼-mile) walk from the center of Cusco. There are a couple of paths. Head northwest from the Plaza de Armas. You can take Palacio (behind the cathedral) until you reach stairs and signs to the ruins, or at the end of Suecia, climb either Huaynapata or Resbalosa (the name means "slippery") until you

---

Can't Leave Well Enough Alone

The Peruvian authorities are notorious for messing with ruins, trying to rebuild them rather than letting them be what they are: ruins. You'll notice at Sacsayhuamán and other Inca sites that unnecessary and misleading restoration has been undertaken. The grotesque result is that small gaps where original stones are missing have been filled in with obviously new and misplaced garden rocks—a disgrace to the perfection pursued and achieved by Inca masons.

come to a curve and the old Inca road. Past the San Cristóbal church at the top, beyond a plaza with fruit-juice stands, are the ruins.

Q'ENKO ✿   The road from Sacsayhuamán leads past fields—where Cusqueños play soccer and have cookouts on weekends—to the temple and amphitheater of Q'enko (*ken-koh*); it's a distance of about 1km (a half mile). A large limestone outcrop was hollowed out by the Incas, and in the void they constructed a cavelike altar. (Some have claimed the smooth stone table inside was used for animal sacrifices.) You can also climb on the rock and see the many channels cut into the rock, where it is thought that either *chicha* or, more salaciously, sacrificial blood coursed during ceremonies.

PUCA PUCARA   A small fortress (the name means "red fort") just off the main Cusco-Pisac road, this may have been some sort of storage facility or lodging. It is probably the least impressive of the sites, but it has nice views of the surrounding countryside.

TAMBOMACHAY ✿   About 8km (5 miles) from Cusco on the way to Pisac (and a short, signposted walk off the main road) is this site, known as Los Baños del Inca (Inca Baths). Water still flows across a system of aqueducts and canals in the small complex of terraces and a pool, but these were not baths as we know them—they were most likely a place of water ceremonies and worship.

SHOPPING

Cusco is Peru's acknowledged center of handicraft production, especially of hand-woven textiles, and its premier shopping destination. Many Cusqueño artisans still employ ancient weaving techniques, and they produce some of the finest textiles in South America. From tiny one-person shops to large markets with dozens of stalls, there are few better places to shop than Cusco for excellent-value Andean handicrafts. Items to look for include alpaca wool sweaters, shawls, gloves, hats, scarves, blankets, and ponchos; antique blankets and textiles, beautiful but pricey; woodcarvings, especially nicely carved picture frames; fine ceramics and jewelry; and Cusqueña School reproduction paintings.

The barrio of **San Blas,** the streets right around the **Plaza de Armas** (particularly calles Plateros and Triunfo), and **Plaza Regocijo** are the best and most convenient haunts for shopping outings. You won't have to look hard for whatever it is that interests you, but a bit of price comparison is always helpful. If merchants think you've just arrived in Peru and don't know the real value of items, your price is guaranteed to be higher. Although bargaining is acceptable and almost expected, merchants in the center of Cusco are confident of a steady stream of buyers, and as a consequence are often less willing to negotiate than their counterparts in markets and more remote places in Peru. Most visitors will find prices delightfully affordable, though, and haggling beyond what you know is a fair price when the disparity of wealth is so great is generally viewed as bad form.

For a general selection of *artesanía,* **Galería Latina,** Calle San Agustín 427 (© **084/ 246-588**), has a wide range of top-end antique blankets, rugs, alpaca wool clothing, ceramics, jewelry, and handicrafts from the Amazon jungle in a large shop near the Hotel Libertador. About a block away from the Plaza de Armas on Plateros and also at Triunfo 393, you'll find good-size markets of crafts stalls. **Centro Artesanal Cusco,** at the end of Avenida El Sol, across from the large painted waterfall fountain and Hotel Savoy, is the largest indoor market of handicrafts stalls in Cusco, and many goods are slightly cheaper here than they are closer to the plaza. Especially noteworthy is the

Centro de Textiles Tradicionales del Cusco ✦✦, Av. El Sol 603 (☎ **084/228-117;** www.textilescusco.org), an organization dedicated to fair-trade practices. It ensures that 70% of the sale price of the very fine textiles on display goes directly to the six communities and individual artisans it works with. On-site is an ongoing demonstration of weaving and a very good, informative textiles museum. Prices are a bit higher than what you may find in generic shops around town, though the textiles are also higher quality, and much more of your money will go to the women who work for days on individual pieces.

San Blas is swimming with art galleries, artisan workshops, and ceramics shops. You'll stumble upon many small shops dealing in reproduction Cusqueña School religious paintings and many workshops where you can watch artisans in action. Several of the best ceramics outlets are also here. Check out **Artesanías Mendivil,** Plazoleta San Blas 619 (☎ **084/233-247**), known for saint figures with elongated necks; the **Juan Garboza taller** (studio), Tandapata 676/Plazoleta San Blas (☎ **084/248-039**), which specializes in pre-Inca style ceramics; and **Artesanías Olave,** Triunfo 342 (☎ **084/252-935**), a high-quality crafts shop.

Several shops feature wool or alpaca *chompas,* or jackets, with Andean designs (often lifted directly from old blankets and weavings). For other upscale alpaca fashions—mostly sweaters and shawls—try **Alpaca 3,** Calle Ruinas 472 (☎ **084/226-101**); **Alpaca 111,** Herladeros 202 (☎ **084/243-233**); or **Royal Alpaca,** Santa Teresa 387 (☎ **084/252-346**). **Werner & Ana,** a Dutch-Peruvian design couple, sell stylish clothing in fine natural fabrics such as alpaca. They have a shop on Plaza San Francisco 295-A, at Calle Garcilaso (☎ **084/231-076**).

For jewelry, **Ilaria** deals in fine silver and unique Andean-style pieces and has two branches in Cusco: one at Hotel Monasterio, Calle Palacios 136 (☎ **084/221-192**), and another at Portal Carrizos 258, Plaza de Armas (☎ **084/246-253**). The contemporary jewelry designer **Carlos Chaquiras,** Triunfo 375 (☎ **084/227-470**), is an excellent craftsman; many of his pieces feature pre-Columbian designs. Lots of shops have hand-carved woodwork and frames, but the best spot for handmade baroque frames (perfect for your Cusqueña School reproduction or religious shrine) is **La Casa del Altar,** Mesa Redonda Lote A (☎ **084/244-712**), not far from the Plaza de Armas. In addition to frames, they make *retablos* and altars.

Cusco's famous, frenzied **Mercado Central** (near the San Pedro rail station) is shopping of a much different kind—almost more a top visitor's attraction than a shopping destination. Its array of products for sale—mostly produce, food, and household items—is dazzling, and even if you don't come to shop, this rich tapestry of modern and yet highly traditional Cusco still shouldn't be missed. Don't take valuables (or even your camera), though, and be on guard, as it is frequented by pickpockets on the lookout for tourists.

WHERE TO STAY

In recent years, the number of lodgings has really blossomed in Cusco, now numbering in the hundreds. Still, advance reservations in high season (June–Sept) in Cusco are essential, especially around the Inti Raymi and Fiestas Patrias festivals at the ends of June and July, respectively. Outside of high season, look for bargains, as hotel rates come down considerably. Most of the city's most desirable accommodations are very central, within walking distance of the Plaza de Armas. The San Blas neighborhood is also within walking distance, though many hotels and hostels in that district involve very steep climbs up the hillside. (The upside is that guests are rewarded with some of

---

> **Tips** **No Sleeping In**
>
> Most Cusco hotels have annoyingly early checkout times—often 9 or 9:30am—
> due to the deluge of early morning flight arrivals to the city. At least in high
> season, hotels are very serious about your need to rise and shine, but you can
> always store your bags until later.

---

the finest views in the city.) Many hotels and inns will arrange free airport transfers if
you communicate your arrival information to them in advance. Hot water is an issue
at many hotels, even those that swear they offer 24-hour hot showers.

Several of the hostels below are cozy, family-run places, but travelers looking for
even greater contact with a Peruvian family might want to check out the very inexpensive inns belonging to the **Asociación de Casas Familiares (Family Home
Association),** which operates a website (www.cusco.net/familyhouse) with listings of
guesthouses with one or more rooms available for short- or long-term stays.

NEAR THE PLAZA DE ARMAS
Very Expensive

Hotel Monasterio ✦✦✦   Peru's most extraordinary place to stay, this beautiful
hotel occupies the San Antonio Abad monastery, constructed in 1592 on the foundations of an Inca palace. The Monasterio—converted into a hotel in 1995—exudes
grace and luxury. While checking in, you relax in a lovely hall while sipping coca tea.
(Altitude-challenged guests can also immediately hook up to an oxygen tank.) As
much a museum as a hotel, it has its own opulent, gilded chapel and 18th-century
Cusqueña School art collection. The hotel makes fine use of two courtyards with stone
arches; one is set up for lunch—about as beautiful a setting as there is to be found in
Cusco. Rooms are impeccably decorated in both colonial and modern styles; the
accommodations off the first courtyard are more traditionally designed and authentic-
feeling. For a special treat, consider one of the two-story suites. The Tupay Restaurant
is housed in the original vaulted refectory of the monastery; early risers, many on their
way to Machu Picchu, enjoy a terrific buffet breakfast serenaded by Gregorian chants.
There are travelers who prefer the Libertador (see below) and have had reservations
about the service at the Monasterio, but for me, the historic quarters and splendid
grounds at the latter take the prize. If you're suffering from altitude sickness, the
Monasterio is the only hotel in the world that can pipe oxygen into your room (for an
additional $30 [£15] per day).

Calle Palacios 136 (Plazoleta Nazarenas), Cusco. ✆ **084/241-777.** Fax 084/246-983. http://monasterio.orient-express.
com. 122 units. $470 (£235) deluxe double; $560–$1,240 (£280–£620) suite. Rates include buffet breakfast. AE, DC,
MC, V. **Amenities:** 2 restaurants; cafe; bar; concierge; room service; laundry service. *In room:* A/C, TV/VCR, minibar,
hair dryer, safe.

Libertador Palacio del Inka ✦✦   One of Cusco's top two hotels, the Libertador,
could just as easily be called the Conquistador. Directly across from the Inca Temple
of the Sun and built on the foundations of the Aclla Huyasi, where the Inca chief kept
maidens, this elegant traditional hotel occupies a historic house once inhabited by
Francisco Pizarro. The handsome art- and antiques-filled hotel is built around a dramatic colonial courtyard marked by perfect arches, terra-cotta tiles, and a Spanish-
style fountain; the swank lobby has a massive pyramidal skylight and exposed Inca

walls. Guest rooms are spacious and refined; furnishings have rustic colonial touches, and the marble bathrooms are large and well equipped. Many rooms have small terraces. But the Libertador perhaps most distinguishes itself with attentive and very professional service. The fine but pricey restaurant, Inti Raymi, named for Cusco's important winter solstice festival, is built around the edges of the courtyard and features a nightly dance and music show.

Calle San Agustín 400 (Plazoleta Santo Domingo 259), Cusco. ℂ **084/231-961.** Fax 01/233-152. www.summit hotels.com. 254 units. $205 (£102) deluxe double; $405 (£202) suite. Rates include taxes. AE, DC, MC, V. **Amenities:** Restaurant; coffee shop; fitness center; sauna; concierge; business center and executive services; salon; room service; laundry service. *In room:* A/C, TV/VCR, fax and dataport in some units, minibar, hair dryer, safe.

Expensive

Novotel Cusco 🕸 One of Cusco's newer upmarket hotels, a member of the French Novotel chain, is built around the guts of a 16th-century colonial building with a handsome courtyard, but the majority of rooms are in new sections. Opened in 2001, the hotel is modern and dependable, with good services and amenities, though in most regards, it's a notch below the city's two top-flight luxury hotels. Rooms are well equipped and brightly colored, but are otherwise standard accommodations. The hotel, a short distance from the Plaza de Armas, features a nice garden-side restaurant serving French fare, and a warm bar with a fireplace.

Palacio San Agustín 239 (corner of Pasaje Santa Mónica), Cusco. ℂ **084/881-030.** Fax 084/228-855. www.novotel. com. 99 units. $125–$185 (£62–£92) double. Rate includes taxes and breakfast. AE, DC, MC, V. **Amenities:** Restaurant/cafe; sauna; concierge; business facilities; salon; room service; babysitting; laundry service. *In room:* AC, TV, minibar, hair dryer.

Moderate

Casa Andina Classic-Cusco Koricancha 🕸 *Value* Similar in concept to the Sonesta Posadas del Inca, this very professionally run, midprice hotel is one of three—soon to be four—belonging to this upstart Peruvian hotel chain. Visitors to Casa Andina know what to expect: excellent service and clean, ample rooms that are colorfully decorated. The hotel on San Agustín, 3 blocks from the main square, is built around a restful colonial courtyard and is in a somewhat quieter neighborhood, while the other two, smaller locations are virtually on top of the Plaza de Armas. All boast the same prices and same features (though the Cusco Catedral hotel has an Inca wall within the hotel). Look for the new, upscale "Private Collection" Casa Andina in an historic house near Quoricancha, sometime in late 2006.

San Agustín 371, Cusco. ℂ **084/252-633** or 01/446-8848 for reservations in Lima. Fax 084/222-908. www.casa-andina.com. 57 units. $99 (£49) double. Rates include taxes and breakfast buffet. AE, DC, MC, V. **Amenities:** Concierge; business facilities; babysitting; laundry service. *In room:* TV, minibar, hair dryer on request, safe.

Hostal El Arqueólogo *Kids* It takes a little bit of effort to uncover this hostel, named for the profession responsible for discovering so much of Peru's pre-Columbian past and owned by a Frenchman who's a longtime Cusco resident. Down a stone alleyway and tucked behind the unprepossessing facade of a late-19th-century house, it certainly doesn't jump out at you, but once inside, you'll find a lovely, sunny garden—with ample space for kids to play—and rooms that run along a corridor overlooking the patio. Rooms are simply furnished but comfortable and cozy. That said, prices have risen steadily, and the hostel is now overpriced, but promotional deals may be available online. The French restaurant, La Vie en Rose, is fairly upscale and surprisingly good for an inn of this size.

Pumacurco 408, Cusco. ℂ **084/232-569**. Fax 084/235-126. www.hotelarqueologo.com. 20 units. $59–$69 (£29–£34) double; $79–$89 (£39–£44) suite. Rates include taxes and breakfast buffet. MC, V. **Amenities:** Restaurant; travel agency; small business center w/Internet; room service; laundry service. *In room:* TV, hair dryer, no phone.

Sonesta Posada del Inca   Like the rest of the hotels belonging to this small and very well-run Peruvian group, the Posada del Inca is cozy, cheery, and a good value. It's sandwiched between the Plaza de Armas and Plaza Regocijo—about as centrally located as you can be in Cusco, without too much of the additional all-night noise of being right on the plaza. Rooms aren't large, but they are comfortable, and the homey lounge has a fireplace. Deals are often available, including one with the possibility of staying 1 night at this hotel and another night at the chain's lovely place in the Urubamba valley (in Yucay) for a slightly discounted rate.

Portal Espinar 108, Cusco. ℂ **084/227-061**. Fax 084/248-484. www.sonesta.com. 23 units. $100–$125 (£50–£63) double. Rates include taxes and breakfast buffet. AE, DC, MC, V. **Amenities:** Cafe/restaurant; concierge; business facilities; room service; babysitting; laundry service. *In room:* TV, minibar, hair dryer.

Inexpensive

Hostal Rumi Punku ✸ *Finds*   A glance at the name or address of this idiosyncratic family-owned hostel will give you an indication of its strong connection to Cusco's Inca roots. The massive portal to the street is a fascinating original Inca construction of perfectly cut stones, once part of a sacred Inca temple. (The door is one of only three belonging to private houses in Cusco, and elderly residents of the city used to do the sign of the cross upon passing it.) Inside is a charming, flower-filled colonial courtyard with a cute little chapel and gardens along a large Inca wall. The clean bedrooms are ample, with hardwood floors and Norwegian thermal blankets. The top-floor dining room, where breakfast is served, has excellent panoramic views of Cusco's rooftops. The hostel is on the way up to Sacsayhuamán, but only a short walk from the Plaza de Armas. Rumi Punku, by the way, means "door of stone" in Quechua. In 2006, the inn added a sauna and Jacuzzi.

Choquechaca 339, Cusco. ℂ **084/221-102**. Fax 084/242-741. www.rumipunku.com. 30 units. $40–$60 (£20–£30) per person. Rates include taxes and continental breakfast. MC, V. **Amenities:** Restaurant; laundry service. *In room:* No phone.

Niños Hotel ✸✸✸ *Kids* *Value*   The Dutch owner of the charming "Children's Hotel" says she has a story to tell, and it's an inspirational one. Jolanda van den Berg, in just 7 years in Peru, has mounted a small empire of goodwill through the Foundation Niños Unidos Peruanos: She adopted 12 Peruvian street children; constructed an extremely warm and inviting (not to mention great-value) hotel in the old section of Cusco that puts all its profits toward care for needy children; constructed a learning center and restaurant for 125 such kids; and created a second center with athletic facilities and additional medical attention for another 125 disadvantaged youth of Cusco.

The good news for travelers is that, should they be lucky enough to get a room here (reserve about 6 months in advance for high season, though especially in off season you're likely to score a reservation only days in advance), they won't have to suffer for their financial contribution to such an important cause. The main hotel, in a restored colonial house just 10 minutes from the Plaza de Armas, is one of the finest, cleanest, and most comfortable small inns in Peru. The large rooms—named for the couple's adopted children—are very nearly minimalist chic, with hardwood floors and quality beds, and they ring a lovely sunny courtyard, where breakfast is served. The ambitious Niños project has now added a second hotel, also of the same character in a historic building, and, incredibly, two more families (totaling 15 girls and another 2 boys). On the same street as the second hotel are four terrific apartments for longer stays, ideal for small families, in the first of the children's learning and day-care facilities.

Meloq 442, Cusco. © **084/231-424.** www.ninoshotel.com. 20 units. $40 (£20) double with private bathroom; $36 (£18) double with shared bathroom. Apartments (minimum 2-week stay) $350 (£175) per month double occupancy. Rates include taxes. No credit cards. **Amenities:** Restaurant/cafe; laundry service. *In room:* No phone.

SAN BLAS & BEYOND
Moderate
Casa de Campo Hostal *Finds*   Lodged in the hills of the traditional neighborhood of San Blas, Casa de Campo means "country house," and the air up here, high above Cusco, has the freshness of country air. An organic complex, its chalet-style rooms appear to have sprouted one from the other. An exceptionally friendly and comfortable place, it's nonetheless not for everyone, especially not those who are tired of climbing the steps of Inca ruins. The climb up to the hotel is taxing enough, but once inside the gate, guests must use their remaining reserves to amble up several more flights of stone steps. Once there, though, they're rewarded with nice gardens and several terraces with unparalleled sweeping views of the city and surrounding mountains, as well as a cozy lounge with a large fireplace. Rooms are rather small, but they have good firm beds and are rustically decorated, with exposed wood beams and thick wool blankets. One special room has a fireplace (for the same price as a regular room); another is like a cottage towering above the city. The staff will build a fire in the bar on request and arrange a free city tour in Cusco.

Tandapata 296, San Blas, Cusco. © **084/243-069.** Fax 084/244-404. www.hotelcasadecampo.com. 25 units. $55 (£27) double. Rates include taxes, breakfast buffet, and airport pickup. AE, MC, V. **Amenities:** Restaurant; laundry service. *In room:* No phone in some units.

Inexpensive
Amaru Hostal *Value*   Popular with legions of backpackers, this hostel, in a pretty colonial-republican house in the midst of the San Blas artist studios and shops, has a lovely balconied patio, with a very nice garden area (which tends to attract sunbathers) and good views of Cusco. Rooms are very comfortable, attractively decorated, and a good value. Several have colonial-style furnishings and lots of natural light. (Ask to see several rooms if you can.) This is a very friendly and relaxed place.

Cuesta San Blas 541, San Blas, Cusco. ©/fax **084/225-933.** www.cusco.net/amaru. 16 units. $35–$40 (£17–£20) double with bathroom; $18 (£9) double with shared bathroom. Rates include taxes, continental breakfast, and airport pickup. No credit cards. **Amenities:** Coffee shop; laundry service. *In room:* No phone.

WHERE TO DINE
Visitors to Cusco have a huge array of restaurants and cafes at their disposal; eateries have sprouted up even faster than hostels and bars, and most are clustered around the main drags leading from Plaza de Armas. The large majority of them are economical, informal places favored by backpackers and adventure travelers—some offer midday three-course menus for as little as S/6 or S/7 ($2/£1)—though there are now a greater number of upscale dining options than ever before, which for many travelers tend to be excellent values. Calle Procuradores, which leads off the Plaza de Armas across from the Compañía de Jesús church, is sometimes referred to as "Gringo Alley," but it could just as easily be called "Restaurant Row" for the cheap eateries that line both sides of the narrow passageway. Many are pizzerias, and Cusco has become known for its wood-fired, crispy-crusted pizzas.

Few restaurants in Cusco accept credit cards; many of those that do, especially the cheaper places, will charge a 10% surcharge to use plastic, so you're better off carrying cash (either soles or dollars). Top-flight restaurants often charge both a 10% service charge and 18% sales tax.

EXPENSIVE

El Truco *๙* PERUVIAN   In a 17th-century *casona* that operated as a mint for the Spanish vice-regency and later as a gambling house, this restaurant combines good Peruvian cooking and *platos típicos* with a loud and lively *peña* show each night (8:30–10:30pm). The restaurant, virtually an institution now that it's been around for 40 years, has an attractive colonial interior and offers a daily lunch buffet of Peruvian specialties. At night, it's a la carte only. Dishes include pork *tamales,* roasted pork, roasted lamb, and stuffed *rocoto* peppers. The lively music and dance show, along with consistently good food, make El Truco very popular with upscale tour groups.

Plaza Regocijo 261. *✆* **084/235-295.** Reservations recommended. Main courses S/19–S/40 ($6–$13/£3–£6.50); daily lunch buffet S/35 ($12/£6). AE, DC, MC, V. Mon–Sat noon–11pm.

Inka Grill *๙๙* PERUVIAN/NOVO ANDINO   A large and attractive modern two-level place right on the Plaza de Armas, the distinguished Inka Grill serves what might be called *novo andino* fare and is one of Cusco's best dining experiences. Start with a bowl of yummy *camote* (sweet potato) chips and green salsa. The best dishes are Peruvian standards such as sautéed alpaca tenderloin served over *quinoa* (a grain) and *ají de gallina* (shredded chicken with nuts, cheese, and chile peppers), and desserts such as coca-leaf crème brûlée. The extensive menu also features a wide range of international dishes, including pizza, pasta, and risotto.

Portal de Panes 115. *✆* **084/262-992.** Reservations recommended. Main courses S/24–S/55 ($8–$18/£4–£9). AE, DC, MC, V. Mon–Sat 8am–midnight.

La Retama *๙* PERUVIAN/INTERNATIONAL   Overlooking the Plaza de Armas from a huge second-floor space, La Retama is one of Cusco's most enduring favorites. The views and nightly folklore shows bring in the tour groups, but the food is good enough to warrant a visit even by those who fear long tables with group leaders and interpreters. The menu focuses on classic Peruvian dishes, such as pink trout and king fish from Lake Titicaca, *seco de cordero* (lamb), *anticucho de lomo* (beef brochette), *cuy,* and trout *ceviche.* International dishes include chicken curry and trout Florentine. The restaurant's walls are lined with the art and handicrafts of Peru, and there's also a gift shop. Folklore shows begin nightly at 8pm.

Portal de Panes 123, 2nd floor. *✆* **084/226-372.** Reservations required. Main courses S/18–S/39 ($6–$13/£3–£6.50). AE, DC, MC, V. Mon–Sat noon–midnight.

MODERATE

Greens *๙๙* *(Value)* INTERNATIONAL/NOVO ANDINO   Having moved from its home in the bohemian heart of San Blas, Greens has gone upscale, on the second floor in an old building just off the Plaza de Armas. It remains one of Cusco's most stylish and intimate restaurants, though it is more sedate and less funky than its previous incarnation. The romantic space has just a handful of tables with candlelight and a soundtrack of laid-back dance beats. The creative organic and vegetarian menu features delicious salads, steaks, homemade pastas, and curries.

Santa Catalina Angosta 135. *✆* **084/243-579.** Reservations recommended. Main courses S/27–S/40 ($9–$13/£4.50–£6.50). No credit cards. Daily 11am–11pm.

Cusco's *Quintas*

When the day warms up under a huge blue sky in Cusco, you'll want to be outside. Cusco doesn't have many sidewalk cafes, but it does have a trio of *quintas*, traditional open-air restaurants that are most popular with locals on weekends. These are places to get large portions of good-quality Peruvian cooking at pretty reasonable prices. Among the dishes they all offer are *tamales, cuy chactado* (fried guinea pig) with potatoes, *chicharrón* (deep-fried pork, usually served with mint, onions, and corn), alpaca steak, *lechón* (suckling pig), and *costillas* (ribs). You can also get classics such as *rocoto relleno* (stuffed hot peppers) and *papa rellena* (potatoes stuffed with meat or vegetables). Vegetarian options include *sopa de quinoa* (grain soup), fried yuca, and *torta de papa* (potato omelet). *Quintas* are open only for lunch (noon–5 or 6pm), and most people make a visit their main meal of the day. Main courses cost between S/15 and S/45 ($5–$15/£2.50–£7.50).

Quinta Eulalia ⓖ, Choquechaca 384 (🕾 **084/224-951**), is Cusco's oldest *quinta* (open since 1941). From a lovely colonial courtyard, there are views of the San Cristóbal district to the surrounding hills from the upper eating area. It's a great place on a sunny day, and the Andean specialties are reasonably priced. **Pacha Papa,** Plazoleta San Blas 120 (🕾 **084/241-318**), is in a beautiful courtyard across from the small church in San Blas. In addition to Andean dishes, you'll find sandwiches. The house specialty, *cuy,* must be ordered 1 day in advance. Alpaca steak is served in several varieties, including alpaca goulash and alpaca kabob.

Kusikuy ⓖ ⓕⁱⁿᵈˢ ANDEAN/INTERNATIONAL If you've resisted trying the Andean specialty that makes most foreigners recoil or at least raise an eyebrow, this could be the place to get adventurous. The restaurant's name in Quechua means "happy little guinea pig," so *cuy al horno* is, of course, the house dish. The rest of the menu focuses on other typical Peruvian dishes and adds stuff for gringos, such as pasta and basic chicken and meat dishes. It also serves a good-value lunch menu. The cozy and good-looking loftlike space, in a new location on a hilly street above the Plaza de Armas, is warmly decorated with hardwood tables, and a mix of antiques and musical instruments from the Amazon. With pillows and couches, it is also a cool, relaxed spot for a drink.

Suecia 339. 🕾 **084/262-870**. Reservations not accepted. Main courses S/12–S/38 ($4–$13/£2–£6.50). MC, V. Mon–Sat 8am–midnight.

INEXPENSIVE

Chez Maggy ITALIAN/PERUVIAN This bustling little joint, which has been around for over 25 years and spawned a couple of branches in other parts of Peru, has a bit of everything, from trout and alpaca to homemade pasta to Mexican food, but most people jam their way in for the freshly baked pizza. Made in a traditional wood-burning brick oven, it's some of the best in Cusco. Chez Maggy is usually packed in the evenings, and there's often live *andina* music when roaming street musicians pop in to entertain diners. The restaurant is a long corridor with shared bench tables full of gringos—a good way to meet other travelers, since you'll be jockeying for elbow space with them. A second location is on Procuradores, better known as Gringo Alley. If you want a pizza on the terrace of your hostel, Chez Maggy will deliver for free.

Plateros 339. ⓒ 084/234-861. Reservations not accepted. Main courses S/12–S/30 ($4–$10/£2–£5). MC, V. Daily 6–11pm.

El Cuate 🌟 MEXICAN   I'm usually very wary about trying out Mexican restaurants while traveling in countries other than Mexico because they almost always serve a crummy imitation of Tex-Mex. But this animated hole-in-the-wall on Gringo Alley is Cusco's first Mexican restaurant, and it dishes out pretty authentic Mexican food for scores of backpacker types. El Cuate's success has spawned several imitators who've felt compelled to add Mexican dishes to their Peruvian and Italian menus. But if you're sure you want Mexican, this is still the place to come. It has a number of bargain menus offering six courses for S/25 ($7.15/£3.55) or S/15 ($4.30/£2.15), or five items for just S/10 ($2.90/£1.45), offered at lunch and dinner, and dishes such as *enchiladas suizas* (cheese enchiladas), Mexican soup, tacos, and burritos. With long bench tables, often shared, it's a jovial place.

Procuradores 386. ⓒ 084/227-003. Reservations not accepted. Main courses S/10–S/25 ($3–$8/£1.50–£4). MC. Daily 11am–midnight.

Granja Heidi 🌟 *Finds*   HEALTHFOOD/VEGETARIAN   A healthy new addition to the Cusco dining scene is this cute upstairs place in San Blas serving great breakfasts and very good-value fixed-price menu meals. With a high ceiling and the airy, sun-filled look of an art studio, it's perfect for the neighborhood. Run by a German woman who also has a farm of the same name outside of Cusco, the restaurant features fresh ingredients and products, such as yogurt, cheese, and quiches, that taste like they came straight from the farm. The daily menu offers vegetarian and nonvegetarian choices, and might start with pumpkin soup, followed by lamb or a veggie stir-fry, fruit salad, and tea. Don't pass on dessert or you'll miss excellent home-baked cakes, such as the cheesecake or the irresistible Nelson Mandela chocolate cake.

Cuesta San Blas 525. ⓒ 084/233-759. Reservations not accepted. Main courses S/7–S/24 ($2–$8/£1–£4); daily menu S/10 ($3/£1.50). No credit cards. Daily 8am–9:30pm.

Jack's Café Bar 🌟🌟 CAFE/INTERNATIONAL   One of the most popular gringo hangouts in Cusco, owned by the guy who runs a thriving Irish pub in town, this isn't just a spot to have a drink and check out some American and British magazines. It serves very fresh, very good meals throughout the day, and features enough variety that you wouldn't be the first to eat here several times during your stay. For breakfast, try scrumptious fluffy pancakes; at lunch, sample towering salads or creative gourmet sandwiches. Finish with a dinner of "really hot green chicken curry" or a red wine, beef and mushroom casserole. There are plenty of items for vegetarians, smoothies, wine and beer, as well as great coffee drinks and hot chocolate (for those cool Andean nights). And it's a friendly place to linger and meet folks, to boot.

Choquechaca 509 (corner Cuesta San Blas). ⓒ 084/806-960. Reservations not accepted. Main courses S/9–S/24 ($3–$8/£1.50–£4). No credit cards. Daily 7am–10pm.

La Tertulia *Value* BREAKFAST/CAFE FARE   A classic Cusco spot for breakfast or other light meals, this little restaurant is a gringo hangout *par excellence*. The name means "discussion," which is fitting because people gather here to read newspapers and foreign magazines, and to exchange books and advice on hiking the Inca Trail and other far-flung adventures across South America. Many come to fuel up as early as

6:30am before setting out on one of those trips, and the superb breakfast buffet does the trick. It's all-you-can-eat eggs, fruit salads, granola, amazing homemade whole-meal bread, French toast, *tamales,* fresh juices, and coffee—truly the breakfast of champions and an excellent value. The breakfast menu also features 16 types of crepes. There is a fixed-price lunch deal and a nice salad bar, as well as pizza, sandwiches, and fondue. If you feel bad about stuffing yourself at breakfast, you can feel good about the fact that La Tertulia donates S/1 of each buffet to a Peruvian orphanage.

Procuradores 44, 2nd floor. ⓒ 084/241-422. Reservations not accepted. Main courses S/9–S/20 ($3–$7/£1.50–£3.50); buffet breakfast S/12 ($4/£2). MC, V. Daily 6:30am–3pm and 5–11pm.

CUSCO AFTER DARK

Most first-time visitors to Cusco, discovering an Andean city with such a gentle, per-vasive Amerindian influence and colonial feel, are surprised to find that it has such a rollicking nightlife. It's not as diverse as Lima's, true, but if you like your nights full of predominantly young and rowdy patrons in the latest trekking gear, Cusco's your kind of place. I have heard countless young backpackers from countries across the world exclaim, in universal MTV lingo and with pisco sour in hand, "Cusco rocks!" Perhaps the best part is that, even though the city is inundated with foreigners many months of the year, it isn't just gringoland in the bars. Locals (and Peruvians from other cities, principally Lima, and other South Americans) tend to make up a pretty healthy per-centage of the clientele. Clubs are in close range of each other—in the streets just off the Plaza de Armas and to a lesser extent in San Blas—and virtually everyone seems to adopt a pub-crawl attitude, bopping from one bar or dance club to the next, often reconvening with friends in the plaza before picking up a "free drink ticket" and free admission card from any of the many girls on the square handing them out and mov-ing on to the next club. It's rare that you'll have to pay a cover charge in Cusco.

For those who are saving their energy, there are less rowdy options, such as Andean music in restaurants, more sedate bars, and English-language movies every night of the week.

BARS & PUBS   Bars are often very crowded with gringos hoisting cheap drinks and trading information on the Inca Trail or latest jungle or rafting expedition. They're generally open from 11am or noon until 1 or 2am. Most have elongated or frequent happy hours with half-price drinks, making it absurdly cheap to tie one on. **Cross Keys** ⓡ, Portal Confiturias 233, Plaza de Armas, Second Floor (no phone), is one of the oldest pubs in town, owned by the English honorary consul and owner of Manu Expeditions. It's especially popular with Brits who can play darts or catch up on Euro-pean soccer on satellite. **Los Perros** ⓡⓡ, Tecsicocha 436 (ⓒ 084/226-625), is one of the coolest bars in Cusco, a funky lounge with sofas, good food, and drinks (includ-ing hot wine), as well as live jazz on Sunday and Monday nights. **Norton Rat's Tav-ern,** Loreto 115, Plaza de Armas (ⓒ 084/246-204), is American-owned and sometimes it can feel like you're in Ohio, hanging with bikers—there's pool and lots of sports on the tube. **Paddy Flaherty's,** Triunfo 124, Plaza de Armas (ⓒ 084/246-903), is a cozy, relaxed, and often crowded Irish bar. **Rosie O'Grady's,** Santa Catalina Ancha 360, around the corner from the Plaza de Armas (ⓒ 084/247-935), sports fancier digs in which to down your (canned) Guinness.

LIVE MUSIC   Live music starts around 11pm in most clubs. By far the best place in Cusco for nightly live music is **Ukukus** ⓡⓡ, Plateros 316, Second Floor (ⓒ 084/227-867). The range of acts extends from bar rock to Afro-Peruvian, and the crowd

> ## *Tips* Raw Fish: A Cure for What Ails You
>
> If you hang out so much and so late in Cusco that you wind up with a wicked hangover, adopt the tried-and-true Andean method of reviving yourself. For once, the solution is not coca leaf tea—it's *ceviche* that seems to do the trick. Something about raw fish marinated in lime juice and chilies delivers a nice slap in the face. When I lived in Ecuador (a country that fights with Peru not only over national boundaries, but also for credit for having invented *ceviche*), late Sunday mornings at the *cevichería* were part of the weekly routine for pale-faced folks hiding behind sunglasses.

jams the dance floor. Often the mix is half gringo, half Peruvian. It's open late nightly (until 4 or 5am), and there's pizza and 24-hour Internet. Pick up a pass for free entrance so you don't get stuck paying a cover. **Kamikase,** Plaza Regocijo 274, second floor (© **084/233-865**), is a two-level bar and a live music area with tables and funky decor. Music ranges from "rock en español" to reggae. **Rosie O'Grady's** (see "Bars & Pubs," above) also has live music on weekends (usually Peruvian, jazz, and blues).

DANCE CLUBS   A young crowd of both backpackers and Peruvians is lured to the dance clubs by the free-drink cards handed out on the Plaza de Armas. Popular and often full and sweaty, **Mama América,** at the corner of Calle Triunfo and Santa Catalina Angosta, just off the Plaza de Armas (Portal Belén 115, Second Floor; © **084/241-979**), spins a good international dance mix of Latin, reggae, rock, and techno, as does its spin-off, **Mama Africa** (Portal Harinas 191; © **084/241-979**). Both are decent downscale spots for cheap drinks. **Eko,** Plateros 334, Second Floor (no phone), is the hottest dance club. It throbs with a variety of rock and techno; for those who need a break, there's a cool and laid-back lounge out back. With two bars and a fleet of what seems like dozens of young girls enticing visitors with free-drink cards, **Bar Xcess,** Portal de Carnes 298 (© **084/240-901**), swarms with one of Cusco's youngest crowds.

TRADITIONAL PERUVIAN MUSIC   You can catch Peruvian bands with a beat at Ukukus and Rosie O'Grady's (see "Live Music," above), but for a traditional folk music–and-dance show, you'll need to check out one of the restaurants featuring nightly entertainment. In addition to **El Truco** (p. 665) and **La Retama** (p. 665), **Tunupa,** Portal de Confitura 233, Plaza de Armas (© **084/252-936**), has a pretty good traditional music and dance show.

MOVIES   Probably the best selection of films, mostly American, shows at **The Film Movies & Lounge,** Procuradores 389, Second Floor (© **084/962-589**); it has a nice little bar and serves food. Other screens showing movies, usually daily, can be found at **Ukuku's,** Plateros 316 (© **084/242-951**), and **Andes Grill,** Portal de Panes, Plaza de Armas (© **084/243-422**).

6 The Sacred Valley of the Incas

The Urubamba Valley, better known as the Valle Sagrado de los Incas, or Sacred Valley of the Incas, is a relaxed and picturesque stretch of villages and ancient ruins spread across a broad plain and the gentle mountain slopes northwest of Cusco. Through the valley rolls the revered Río Urubamba, a pivotal religious feature of the Incas' cosmology. With the river as its source, the fertile valley was a major center of agricultural

Tips **Boleto Turístico in the Valle Sagrado**

The Cusco *boleto turístico* (tourist pass) is pretty much essential for visiting the Sacred Valley, in particular the ruins of Pisac and Ollantaytambo, as well as the market and town of Chinchero. You can purchase it in any of those places if you haven't already bought it in Cusco before traveling to the Valley. See p. 653 for more information.

production for the Incas, who grew native Andean crops such as white corn, coca, and potatoes, and it continues to function as the region's breadbasket today. Along with Cusco and Machu Picchu, the Valle Sagrado ranks as one of the highlights of Peru—if you're visiting either of the former, it would be a shame not to spend at least a couple of days in the valley. The magnificent ruins found from Pisac to Ollantaytambo and beyond are testaments to the region's immense ceremonial importance. The Incas built several of the empire's greatest estates, temples, and royal palaces between the sacred centers of Cusco and Machu Picchu. Today, the rural villages of the Sacred Valley remain starkly, charmingly traditional. Quechua-speaking residents work the fields and harvest salt with methods unchanged since the days of the Incas, and market days—although now conducted to attract the tourist trade as well as intervillage commerce—remain important rituals.

If you have the time, a good way to explore the valley is to advance town by town toward Machu Picchu or vice versa, starting out from Machu Picchu and returning piecemeal towards Cusco. Seeing the valley's highlights on a daylong guided bus tour is certainly doable, but it can't compare to a leisurely pace that allows you an overnight stay and the chance to soak up the area's immense history, relaxed character, stunning scenery, and, in the dry season, equally gorgeous springlike weather. Not only that, the valley is about 500m (1,640 ft.) lower than Cusco, making it much more agreeable for those potentially afflicted with altitude-related health problems. More and more visitors are now spending several days in the valley, choosing to base themselves at least initially in Pisac, Urubamba, or Ollantaytambo rather than the capital of the department, Cusco.

ESSENTIALS
GETTING THERE & AROUND
BY GUIDED TOUR   Nearly every Cusco travel agency offers a 1-day Sacred Valley tour for as little as $20 (£10) per person, and most provide English-speaking guides. The tours tend to coincide with market days (Tues, Thurs, and Sun) and generally include Pisac, Ollantaytambo, and Chinchero. It's not enough time to explore the ruins, though a quickie tour gives at least a taste of the Valley's charms.

BY TRAIN   The only spots in the Sacred Valley you can reach by train are Urubamba and Ollantaytambo, roughly midway on the Cusco–Machu Picchu route. All trains traveling from Cusco to Machu Picchu stop at Ollantaytambo. Passengers traveling just from Ollantaytambo to Machu Picchu, or the reverse, take either the **Vistadome** ($43–$60/£21–£30 one-way) or **Backpacker** ($31–$43/£15–£21 one-way) train.

Trains depart Cusco from **Estación San Pedro**, Calle Cascaparo s/n (© **084/221-352** or 084/221-313), and arrive in Ollantaytambo about 2 hours later. The train station in Ollantaytambo is a long 15-minute walk from the main square. Besides the

Inca Trail, the train is the only option for traveling from Ollantaytambo to Machu Picchu. For reservations, call © **084/238-722.**

BY BUS Local buses (often small *combis* or *colectivos*) are the easiest and cheapest way to get around the Sacred Valley. They are often full of color if not comfort. (Tall people forced to stand will not find them much fun, however.) Buses to and from the Sacred Valley use terminals on Calle Huáscar and Calle Intiqhawarina, off Tullumayo, in Cusco. They leave regularly throughout the day, departing when full. Fares are S/3 ($1/50p). The trip to Pisac takes about an hour; for Urubamba, just over 2 hours from Cusco, you can go via Pisac or via Chinchero. To travel to Ollantaytambo, you'll need to change buses at the terminal in Urubamba. The train is a simpler option if you don't plan on intermediate stops in the valley. Shared private cars *(autos)* to Urubamba leave from Calle Pavitos 567, with four passengers per car (they're generally station wagons with room for luggage in back and take just 50 min.) for just S/6 ($2/£1) per person.

In **Pisac,** buses leave for Cusco and other parts of the valley from the main street just across the river (about 3 blocks west of the main square). In **Urubamba,** buses for Cusco and Chinchero leave from the Terminal Terrestre about 1km (a half mile) from town on the main road to Ollantaytambo (just beyond and across from the Incaland Hotel). *Combis* for other points in the valley and shared *autos* for Cusco depart from the intersection of the main road at Avenida Castilla. In **Ollantaytambo,** buses for Cusco depart from Avenida Estación, the main street leading away from the rail terminal.

BY TAXI You can easily hire a taxi for a daylong tour of the Sacred Valley or any of the valley towns; expect to pay about S/70 ($20/£10). While a taxi to Pisac on your own may cost S/35 ($10/£5), it is often possible to go by joining other travelers in a private car for as little as S/5 ($1/50p) per person. Private taxis from Ollantaytambo or Urubamba to Cusco generally charge about S/70 ($23/£11).

VISITOR INFORMATION

You're best off getting information on the Sacred Valley before leaving Cusco at the helpful main Tourist Information Office (see "Visitor Information," earlier in this chapter). Cusco's **South American Explorers Club,** Choquechaca 188, Apto. 4 (© **084/245-484;** www.saexplorers.org), is also an excellent source of information, particularly on the Inca Trail and other treks, mountaineering, and white-water rafting in the valley. Inquire there about current conditions and updated transportation alternatives. In the valley itself, you may be able to scare up some limited assistance in Urubamba (Av. Cabo Conchatupa s/n), Ollantaytambo (the CATCCO museum, off Principal), and Yucay (office of Turismo Participativo, Plaza Manco II 103; © **084/ 201-099**). In Aguas Calientes (at the foot of Machu Picchu), there's an **iperu** office at Av. Pachacútec, Cdra. 1 s/n, Of. 4, in the INC building (© **084/211-104**). Beyond that, the best sources of local information are hotels.

FAST FACTS You can exchange dollars—in cash—with small shops in Pisac or Ollantaytambo; in Urubamba, there are ATMs on either side of the main road to Yucay, and there's an ATM on the Plaza de Armas in Pisac.

In a medical emergency, contact **Centro de Salud,** Av. Cabo Conchatupa s/n, Urubamba (© **084/201-334**), or **Hospital del Instituto Peruano de Seguridad Social,** Avenida 9 de Noviembre, Urubamba (© **084/201-032**). For the police, contact **Policía Nacional,** Calle Palacio s/n, Urubamba (© **084/201-092**).

Urubamba has the best Internet *cabinas* in the region, with a good supply of machines and fast connections. **Academia Internet Urubamba,** begun with the help

Extreme Sacred Valley

The Sacred Valley region is one of the best in South America for white-water rafting, mountain biking, trekking, hang gliding, and paragliding. River runs are extremely popular, and justifiably so: Peru has some of the world's wildest rivers. The most popular activity is, of course, hiking the Inca Trail to Machu Picchu, but there are plenty of other adventure opportunities. Many tour operators in Cusco organize adventure trips. Participants range from novices to hard-core adventure junkies; no experience is required for many trips, but make sure you sign up for a program appropriate for your level of interest and ability. Extreme sports being what they are, thoroughly check out potential agencies and speak directly to the guides, if possible. Hunting for bargains in this category is not advisable; quality equipment and good English-speaking guides are fundamental for safety considerations.

WHITE-WATER RAFTING There are some terrific Andean river runs near Cusco, ranging from mild class II to moderate and world-class IV and V. Recommended agencies include **Amazonas Explorer** ★★ (② 084/236-826 or 084/225-284; www.amazonas-explorer.com); **Apumayo Expediciones** (② 084/246-018; www.apumayo.com); **Eric Adventures** ★, Plateros 324 (② 866/978-4630 in U.S. and Canada, or 084/228-475; www.ericadventures.com); **Instinct Travel** (② 084/233-451; www.instinct-travel.com); **Loreto Tours,** Procuradores 50 (② 084/233-451); and **Mayuc,** Portal Confiturías 211 (② 084/242-824; www.mayuc.com).

TREKKING In addition to the groups that organize Inca Trail hikes (see "Hiking the Inca Trail" on p. 684), the following agencies handle a wide variety of trekking excursions: **Apu Expeditions,** Casilla Postal 24 (② 084/957-483); **Aventours,** Av. Pardo 545, Of. 6 (② 084/224-050; www.aventours.com); **Manu Expeditions,** Urbanizacion Magisterio, Segunda Etapa G-5 (② 084/226-671; www.manuexpeditions.com); **Mayuc,** Portal Confiturías 211 (② 084/242-824; www.mayuc.com); and U.S.-based **Peruvian Andean Treks,** Av. Pardo 705 (② 800/683-8148 or 617/924-1974; www.andeantreks.com). **Peru Discovery** (see "Mountain Biking," below) also organizes excellent trekking expeditions. **Peru Uhupi** (② 084/201-568; www.peru.uhupi.com), run by Chalo, the owner of cool, eco-styled lodge Las Chullpas, leads small-group treks into the Urubamba range.

MOUNTAIN BIKING Mountain biking is really just beginning to catch on, and tour operators are rapidly expanding their services and equipment. **Peru Discovery,** Triunfo (Sunturwasi) 392, Of. 113 (② 054/247-007; www.perudiscovery.com), is the top specialist, with a half-dozen bike trips that include hard-core excursions. **Ecomontana** (www.ecomontana.info), run by Omar Zarzar, rents mountain bikes and leads tours throughout the Sacred Valley. **Amazonas Explorer, Apumayo Expediciones, Eric Adventures, Instinct Travel** (see "White-Water Rafting," above), and **Manu Ecological Adventures** (② 084/261-640; www.manuadventures.com) offer 1- to 5-day organized mountain-biking excursions ranging from easy to rigorous.

of an American exchange student, is 2 blocks northeast of the Plaza de Armas, on the corner of Jirón Belén and Jirón Grau. The **post office** in Pisac is on the corner of Comercio and Intihuatana, in Ollantaytambo and Urubamba on their respective Plazas de Armas.

PISAC 🏵🏵

The pretty Andean village of Pisac lies at the eastern end of the valley, 32km (20 miles) from Cusco. Though the town seems to be prized principally for its Sunday artisan market, Pisac should be more widely recognized for its splendid Inca ruins, which rival Machu Picchu. Perched high on a cliff is the largest fortress complex built by the Incas. The commanding distant views from atop the mountain, over a luxuriously long valley of green patchwork fields, are breathtaking.

Pisac's famed **market** draws hundreds of visitors on Sunday mornings in high season, when it is without doubt one of the liveliest in Peru. (There are slightly less popular markets on Tues and Thurs as well.) Hundreds of stalls crowd the central square and spill down side streets. Sellers come from many villages, many of them remote places high in the Andes, and wear the dress typical of their village. Dignitaries from the local villages usually lead processions after Mass (said in Quechua), dressed in their versions of Sunday finery. The goods for sale at the market—sweaters, ponchos, rugs—are familiar to anyone who's spent at least a day in Cusco, but prices are occasionally lower on selected goods such as ceramics. The market begins at around 9am and lasts until midafternoon.

The Pisac **ruins** 🏵🏵 are some of the finest in the entire valley. The best but most time-consuming way to see the ruins is to climb the hillside, where you'll encounter an extraordinary path and slice of local life. Trudging along steep mountain paths is still the way most Quechua descendants from remote villages get around these parts; many people you see at the Pisac market will have walked a couple of hours or more to get there. To reach the site on foot (about 5km/3 miles, or about 90 min.), you'll need to be pretty fit and/or willing to take it very slowly. Begin the ascent at the back of the main square, to the left of the church. The path bends to the right through agricultural terraces. There appear to be several competing paths; all of them lead up the mountain to the ruins. When you come to a section that rises straight up, choose the extremely steep stairs to the right (the path to the left is overgrown and poorly defined). If an arduous trek is more than you've bargained for, you can also hire a taxi in Pisac (easier on market days) to take you around the back way (about S/15, or $5/£2.50). If you arrive by car or *colectivo* rather than by your own power, the ruins will be laid out the opposite of the way they are described below. The ruins are open daily from 7am to 5:30pm; admission is by *boleto turístico* (see "Cusco's *Boleto Turístico*" on p. 653).

From a semicircular terrace and fortified section at the top, called the **Quorihuayrachina,** the views south and west are spectacular. The Pisac nucleus was both a fortress and ceremonial center, and its delicately cut stones are some of the best found at any Inca site. The most important component of the complex is the **Templo del Sol (Temple of the Sun),** one of the Incas' most impressive examples of masonry, found on the upper section of the ruins. There you'll find the **Intiwatana,** the so-called "hitching post of the sun," which looks to be a sundial but, in fact, is an instrument that helped the Incas determine the arrival of important growing seasons. Nearby (just paces to the west) are another temple, thought to be the Temple of the Moon, and a ritual bathing complex, fed by canals. Continuing north from this section, as you pass along the eastern edge of the cliff, you'll arrive at a tunnel, which leads to a summit lookout at 3,400m (11,150 ft.).

WHERE TO STAY Paz y Luz ⋆⋆, Carretera Pisac Ruinas s/n (☏ **084/203-204;** www.pazyluzperu.com), about a 20-minute walk from the village along a road up to the Inca ruins, is a cool B&B and healing center run by a woman from New York, Diane Dunn. Rooms ($40/£20 double including breakfast) are in comfortable bungalows with splendid views of the Pisac ruins and surrounding valley. Andean healing workshops and sacred-plant ceremonies are a good part of the attraction for guests interested in the Sacred Valley's spiritual offerings. The small, pleasant, and central **Hotel Pisaq** ⋆, Plaza Constitución 333 (☏ **084/203-062;** www.hotelpisaq.com), right on the main square, is a great place to stay in town. The cozy little inn, run by a Peruvian-American couple, has a stone-heated sauna and an attractive courtyard, as well as a good restaurant serving wood-fired pizzas; the nicely decorated double rooms with private bathrooms cost $35 (£17).

WHERE TO DINE A genial and inexpensive spot for any meal, from breakfast to hearty lunches and vegetarian options, is **Ulrike's Café** ⋆, Plaza de Armas 828 (☏ **084/203-195**). A relaxed cafe on the main square run by a German expat, Ulrike's can be counted on for a great-value lunch menu, homemade lasagna, omelets, salads, and great desserts (like Ulrike's famous strudel) and coffee. For very good trout dishes from the river, check out **Restaurant Valle Sagrado,** Amazonas 116 (☏ **084/436-915**). Another good bet is the excellent **bakery** using traditional, wood-fired colonial ovens, on the corner of the main square next to Hotel Pisaq, and on Mariscal Castilla 372, a short walk from the plaza. The bakery serves excellent empanadas and breads; it is especially popular on market days.

URUBAMBA & ENVIRONS

Centrally located Urubamba (77km/48 miles northwest of Cusco) is the busiest of the Sacred Valley towns. Although the town itself doesn't have much more than magnificent mountain scenery and a popular main square to offer visitors, several of the best hotels in the region are located just south near Yucay, about 3km (1¾ miles) down the road, and north toward Ollantaytambo. Yucay is an attractive colonial village backed by a sophisticated system of agricultural terraces and irrigation canals. The area is a fine base from which to explore the Sacred Valley region.

The main square of Urubamba, the Plaza de Armas, is handsomely framed by a twin-towered colonial church and *pisonay* trees. Dozens of *mototaxis,* a funky form of local transportation not seen in other places in the valley, buzz around the plaza in search of passengers. Worth visiting in town is the beautiful home and workshop of **Pablo Seminario** ⋆, Calle Berriozábal 111 (☏ **084/201-002**), a ceramicist whose whimsical work features pre-Columbian motifs and is sold throughout Peru. The grounds are a minizoo, with llamas, parrots, nocturnal monkeys, falcons, rabbits, and more. Seminario now has shops in the Sonesta Posada del Inca hotel in Yucay as well as Cusco.

About 6km (3½ miles) down the main road toward Ollantaytambo is the amazing sight of the **Salineras de Maras** ⋆⋆, thousands of individual ancient salt pans that form unique terraces in a hillside. The mines, small pools thickly coated with crystallized salt like dirty snow, have existed in the same spot since Inca days and are still operable. Families pass them down like deeds and continue the backbreaking and poorly remunerated tradition of salt extraction (crystallizing salt from subterranean spring water). To get to the salt pans, take a taxi to a point near the village of Tarabamba. (You can either have the taxi wait for you or hail a *combi* on the main road when you return.) From there, it's a lovely 45-minute walk along a footpath next to the river. There are no signs; cross the footbridge and bend right along the far side of the river and up through the mountains toward the salt pans. As you begin the gentle climb up the mountain, stick to the right to avoid the cliff-hugging, inches-wide trail that forks to the left. Another great walking route to the salt pans, more taxing but even more spectacular, is along a path from the town of Maras (90 minutes) or from the Inca agricultural site Moray (3 hours).

WHERE TO STAY   One of the best hotels in the region is the handsome, ranch-style **Sonesta Posada del Inca** ✿✿, Plaza Manco II de Yucay 123, Yucay (🕾 **084/ 201-107;** fax 084/201-345; www.sonesta.com). Originally a monastery in the late 1600s (with a picturesque chapel to prove it) and then a hacienda, it is now a colonial villagelike complex with great character, great mountain views, and relaxed comfort. It recently added a nice spa with massages, yoga, a sauna, an outdoor Jacuzzi, and other treatments. Double rooms cost $125 (£62).

A funky place to stay is **Las Chullpas** ✿ (🕾 **084/201-568;** www.chullpas.uhupi. com), an "ecological guest house" that is more like something you'd find in the Amazon cloud forest rather than the Sacred Valley. Run by a young Chilean and his German expat wife (a midwife who works with campesina women from the countryside), the nine rooms are connected huts that have the feel of tree forts, but with an abundance of style, including comfortable beds and hand-painted tiles in the bathrooms. Profits from the huge suite go toward Leonie's midwifery practice. Chalo prepares excellent organic and vegetarian meals in the cozy, fireplace-warmed dining room. Rates with breakfast are S/60 ($20/£10) per person; the suite runs $60 (£30) per night. In Huicho, 2km (1¼ miles) west of Urubamba, **Sol y Luna Lodge & Spa** ✿✿ (🕾 **084/201-620;** fax 084/ 201-084; www.hotelsolyluna.com) is a French- and Swiss-owned cluster of 28 invitingly decorated, circular bungalow-style rooms (including four family bungalows) with private terraces, surrounded by beautifully landscaped gardens and gorgeous mountain views. The hotel has a nice (if small) pool, as well as a restaurant and pub, fancy new spa, and adventure club offering all sorts of outdoor activities (horseback riding, mountain biking, trekking, paragliding) in the region. Opened in 2000 and continually expanding, Sol y Luna is one of the nicest spots in the valley. Doubles cost $154 (£77).

Two new hotels by Peruvian chains in the hamlet of Yanahuara, on the way to Ollantaytambo, are among terrific new options in the burgeoning Sacred Valley. **Casa Andina Private Collection** ✿✿, Yanahuaara (🕾 **084/976-550;** fax 01/445-4775; www.casa-andina.com) is one of the group's few upscale offerings, a large (85-room), mountain-chalet-type hotel in a beautiful setting with large and handsomely decorated rooms with excellent views of the countryside. The hotel features an excellent, full-service spa, a good restaurant, and even a planetarium, making it popular with groups of diverse size. Two-story suites with balconies are especially alluring. Rates are $125 (£62) for doubles, $180 (£90) for suites. The **Libertador Valle Sagrado Lodge** ✿✿, Yanahuaara, sector Pucará (🕾 **084/251-526;** www.vallesagradolodge.com), is up a long dirt road from Casa Andina and is a smaller, more intimate offering, built like a small colonial village with fountains and gardens and fantastic mountain and valley views. Doubles—which are spacious, warmly decorated, and nicely distributed among the grounds—run $110 (£55). Given its small size (just 16 rooms), it only hosts individuals and very small groups.

WHERE TO DINE   Many guests dine at their hotels, and the major ones above (Casa Andina, Libertador, and Sonesta) all have very good restaurants. The best restaurant in Urubamba is **El Huacatay** ★★, Jr. Arica 620 (© 084/201-790), open Monday through Saturday from 2 to 10pm. Sit on the garden terrace or in the small, elegant dining room and enjoy local specialties such as alpaca lasagna. The fine restaurant of Sol y Luna (see above), **Killa Wasi** ★, is open for lunch and dinner (and serving a buffet lunch on Valley market days). A longtime local favorite is **La Casa de la Abuela,** Bolívar 272 (© 084/622-975), a charming, warm house a couple of blocks from the Plaza de Armas. Specializing in wood-fired pizza, pasta, and tasty home-cooked Peruvian dishes (such as delicious trout), the restaurant has several dining rooms and an inviting living room/bar area. After a couple of years of spotty activity, the restaurant is again operating at full speed, if without the enthusiasm of past years (it's best to have your hotel call ahead to inquire).

   The Muse Too, Plaza de Armas (at the corner of Comercio and Grau; © 084/201-280), the cutely named sister establishment of the Cusco bar/restaurant **The Muse,** is a funky two-story pub/restaurant that features tasty soups, sandwiches, and cocktails. At night, it is more music pub than restaurant. Out on the main road going toward Yucay, **Quinta Los Geranios,** Av. Cabo Conchatupa s/n (© 084/201-093), is a good open-air restaurant, set around a garden. It gets hit midday with tour buses but still manages to concoct fine versions of Peruvian standards such as *rocoto relleno* (stuffed hot peppers) and a number of indigenous soups. The three-course lunch menu is a good value.

OLLANTAYTAMBO ★★★

A tongue twister of a town—the last settlement in the Valley before Agua Calientes and Machu Picchu—this historic and lovely little place 97km (60 miles) northwest of Cusco is affectionately called Ollanta (oh-*yan*-tah) by locals. Plenty of outsiders who can't pronounce it fall in love with the town, too. The scenery around Ollantaytambo is some of the most stunning in the region. The snowcapped mountains that embrace the town frame a much narrower valley here than at Urubamba or Pisac, and both sides of the gorge are lined with Inca stone *andenes,* or agricultural terraces. Most extraordinary are the precipitous terraced ruins of a massive temple-fortress built by the Inca Pachacutec. Below the ruins, Ollantaytambo's old town is a splendid Inca grid of streets lined with adobe brick walls, blooming bougainvillea, and perfect canals, still carrying rushing water down from the mountains. Though Ollanta has exploded in popularity in just the last few years, except for the couple of hours a day when tour buses deposit large groups at the foot of the fortress (where a handicrafts market habitually breaks out to welcome them) and tourists overrun the main square, the town remains pretty quiet, a traditional and thoroughly charming Valle Sagrado village.

   The Inca elite adopted Ollantaytambo, building irrigation systems and a crowning temple designed for worship and astronomical observation. The **temple ruins** ★★ represent one of the Incas' most formidable feats of architecture—and are perhaps second only to Machu Picchu in their grandeur and harmony with the surrounding landscape. Rising above the valley and an ancient square (Plaza Mañaraki) are dozens of rows of stunningly steep stone terraces carved into the hillside. They appear both forbidding and admirably perfect. The Incas were able to successfully defend the site against the Spanish in 1537, protecting Manco Inca after his retreat here from defeat at Sacsayhuamán. The complex, in all probability, was more a temple than a citadel to the Incas. The upper section—reached after you've climbed 200 steps—contains typically masterful masonry of the kind that adorned great Inca temples. A massive and supremely elegant doorjamb—site of many a photo—indicates the principal entry to the temple; next to it is the **Temple of Ten Niches.** On the next level are six huge pink granite blocks, amazingly cut, polished, and fitted together, which appear to be parts of rooms never completed. This **Temple of the Sun** is one of the great stone masonry achievements of the Incas. On the stones, you can still make out faint, ancient symbolic markings in relief. Across the valley is the quarry that provided the stones for the structure; a great ramp descending from the hilltop ruins was the means by which the Incas transported the massive stones from several kilometers away. The ruins are open daily from 7am to 5:30pm; admission is by *boleto turístico* (see "Cusco's *Boleto Turístico*" on p. 653). To see the ruins in peace before the tour buses arrive, get there before 11am. Early morning is best of all, when the sun rises over mountains to the east and then quickly bathes the entire valley in light.

A footpath winds up the hill behind an outer wall of the ruins to a clearing and wall with niches that have led some to believe prisoners were tied up here—a theory that is unfounded. Regardless of the purpose, the views south over the Urubamba Valley and of the snowcapped peak of Verónica are outstanding. At the bottom of the terraces, next to the Patacancha River, are the **Baños de la Ñusta (Princess Baths),** a place of ceremonial bathing. Wedged into the mountains facing the baths are granaries built by the Incas. Locals like to point out the face of the Inca carved into the cliff high above the valley. (If you can't make it out, ask the guard at the entrance to the ruins for a little help.)

Ollantaytambo's outstanding **Old Town** 🎨🎨, below (or south of) the ruins and across the River Patacancha, is the finest extant example of the Incas' masterful urban planning. Many original residential *canchas,* or blocks, each inhabited by several families during the 15th century, are still present; each *cancha* had a single entrance opening onto a main courtyard. The finest streets of this stone village are directly behind the main square. Get a good glimpse of community life within a *cancha* by peeking in at Calle del Medio (Calle Chautik'ikllu), where a couple of neighboring houses have their ancestors' skulls displayed as shrines on the walls of their living quarters. The entire village retains a solid Amerindian air, unperturbed by the crowds of gringos who wander through, snapping photos of children and old women. It's a traditional place, largely populated by locals in colorful native dress and women who pace up and down the streets or through fields absentmindedly spinning the ancient spools used in making hand-woven textiles.

On the edge of the old town, 2 blocks northwest of the Plaza Mayor, is an enjoyable and well presented but not indispensable **Museo CATCCO** (Centro Andino de Tecnología y Cultural de las Comunidades de Ollantaytambo; ✆ **084/223-627**), an ethnographic and history museum. It's open Tuesday through Sunday from 10am to 1pm and 2 to 4pm; admission is S/5 ($1.45/75p).

WHERE TO STAY   El Albergue 🎨🎨, located next to the railway station platform in Ollantaytambo (✆/fax **084/204-014;** www.rumbosperu.com/elalbergue), is the best choice in town; it's an attractive and homey hostel owned by an American long-time resident of Ollantaytambo. With large, comfortable, and nicely—if austerely—furnished rooms, great gardens, a wood-fired sauna, three Labrador retrievers roaming the grounds, and a spot right next to the train to Machu Picchu, it's often full, even though prices have climbed steadily over the years. Rooms with shared bathrooms cost $62 (£31). Wendy Weeks, the owner, has added a simple but comfortable budget option with shared bathrooms in the old town, **Hostal Matacuy,** Calle del Costado (www.matacuy.com), where rates are just $5 (£2.50) per person. On the road from the train station to town, **Hotel Pakaritampu,** Av. Ferrocarril s/n, Ollantaytambo (© 084/204-020; fax 084/204-105; www.pakaritampu.com), is surprisingly upscale for unassuming Ollantaytambo. Rooms are tasteful, with sturdy, comfortable furnishings, and there's a nice restaurant/bar. Double rooms cost $109 (£54). Sandwiched between the main square of the village and the CATCCO museum, **Hostal Sauce,** Calle Ventiderio 248, Ollantaytambo (© 084/204-044; fax 084/204-048; www. hostalsauce.com.pe), is a modern and comfortable building with a smattering of very clean, nicely equipped rooms, which cost $89 (£45). Some rooms have superb views of the ruins. Budget travelers gravitate toward **Hostal La Ñusta,** Carretera Ocobamba (© 084/204-032), a clean and friendly place with good views from the balcony but small and plain rooms. Doubles with shared bathrooms are $20 (£10).

WHERE TO DINE   **Kusicoyllor,** Plaza Araccama s/n (© 084/204-103), is a cool cafe/bar right next to ruins, so you might expect it to be a tad touristy and overpriced, which it is—but it's still nice. It serves standard Peruvian and predominantly Italian dishes and offers a fixed-price menu ($7/£3.50). Breakfast is especially good, making it a fine stop after an early morning tour of the ruins. **Tunupa Restaurant & Pizzeria,** Av. Beniterio s/n (no phone), is an inexpensive family-run terrace joint between the main plaza and the ruins, and it has a very agreeable open-air atmosphere. It serves breakfast, lunch, and dinner, and has a surprisingly wide-ranging menu and great views of the ruins. Other cheap restaurants, principally pizzerias, such as **Bar Ollantay,** ring the main square in the Old Town. **Ganso,** Calle del Costado (no phone), is the swankest place in town for a drink.

MACHU PICCHU ✶✶✶

The stunning site of Machu Picchu, the fabled "lost city of the Incas," is South America's greatest attraction. The Incas hid Machu Picchu so high in the clouds that the empire-raiding Spaniards never found it. It is no longer lost, of course, and you can now zip there by high-speed train as well as by a more traditional 2- or 4-day trek, but Machu Picchu retains its great sense of mystery and magic. No longer overgrown with brush, as it was when it was discovered—with the aid of a local farmer who knew of its existence—by the Yale historian Hiram Bingham in 1911, it still cannot be seen from below. The majestic setting that the Incas chose for it remains unchanged. When the early morning sun rises over the peaks and methodically illuminates the ruins' granite stones row by row, Machu Picchu leaves visitors as awestruck as ever.

The great majority of visitors to Machu Picchu still do it as a day trip from Cusco, but many people feel that a few hurried hours to the ruins at peak hours, amidst throngs of people following guided tours, simply do not suffice. By staying at least 1 night, either at the one upscale hotel just outside the grounds of Machu Picchu or down below in the town of Aguas Calientes (also called Machu Picchu Pueblo), you can remain at the ruins later in the afternoon after most of the tour groups have gone home, or get there for sunrise—a dramatic, unforgettable sight. Aguas Calientes is a tiny tourist trade town where weary backpackers rest up and celebrate their treks along the Inca Trail over cheap eats and cheaper beers. There are some additional good hikes in the area, but most people head back to Cusco after a couple of days in the area.

GETTING TO MACHU PICCHU

BY TRAIN   The 112km (69-mile) train ride from Cusco to Machu Picchu is a truly spectacular journey. It zigzags up Huayna Picchu and then through lush valleys hugging

Machu Picchu

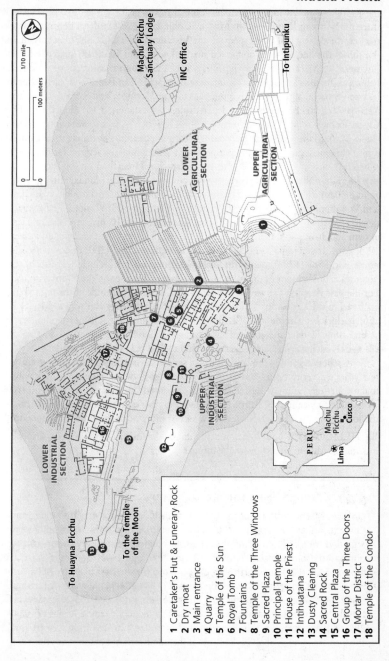

Machu Picchu Sanctuary Lodge

INC office

To Intipunku

LOWER AGRICULTURAL SECTION

UPPER AGRICULTURAL SECTION

LOWER INDUSTRIAL SECTION

UPPER INDUSTRIAL SECTION

To Huayna Picchu

To the Temple of the Moon

1/10 mile

100 meters

1 Caretaker's Hut & Funerary Rock
2 Dry moat
3 Main entrance
4 Quarry
5 Temple of the Sun
6 Royal Tomb
7 Fountains
8 Temple of the Three Windows
9 Sacred Plaza
10 Principal Temple
11 House of the Priest
12 Intihuatana
13 Dusty Clearing
14 Sacred Rock
15 Central Plaza
16 Group of the Three Doors
17 Mortar District
18 Temple of the Condor

PERU

Machu Picchu
Cusco

Lima

the Río Urubamba, with views of snowcapped Andes peaks in the distance. There are three tourist trains from Cusco to Machu Picchu, taking just under 4 hours: the **Back-packer,** the slowest and least expensive; the **Vistadome,** the faster first-class service; and the top-of-the-line, newly inaugurated luxury line **Hiram Bingham** (named after the discoverer of Machu Picchu). The first two of these tourist trains, all of which now belong to Orient-Express, depart from Cusco's **Estación San Pedro** on Calle Cascaparo; it's open Monday through Friday from 5am to 3pm, Saturday and Sunday from 5am to 12:30pm. Hiram Bingham trains depart from Poroy station, a 15-minute drive from Cusco, 6 days a week in high season (Apr–Oct) and 4 days a week in low season (Nov–Mar). Make your train reservations as early as possible. The online reservation system is extremely rudimentary, requiring one to send a booking request for the selected itinerary. Once in Cusco, one has to go to **Estación Huanchaq** on Av. Pachacutec to pay (in cash, dollars) for tickets reserved in advance. It's open Monday through Friday from 8:30am to 5:30pm, Saturday and Sunday from 8:30am to 12:30pm. Backpacker and Vistadome class trains, though, depart from Estacion de San Pedro. The Backpacker departs Cusco at 7am and arrives in Aguas Calientes at 10:10am; the Vistadome leaves at 6am and arrives at 9:40am; and the Hiram Bingham starts out at 9am and arrives at 12:30pm. Fares are $48 (£24) one-way for Backpacker, $60 (£30) one-way for Vistadome, and $588 (£294) round-trip for Hiram Bingham (which includes brunch, afternoon tea, a guided tour of the ruins, and cocktails and dinner on the return trip). *Note:* For the best views on the way to Machu Picchu, sit on the left side of the train. Travelers based in the Urubamba Valley can go by the **Sacred Valley Railway** to Machu Picchu. Backpacker Shuttle and Vistadome service originates in Ollantaytambo, leaving several times a day; the journey takes under 2 hours. The trip costs $31 to $43 (£15–£21) each way in Backpacker class, $43 to $60 (£21–£30) in Vistadome.

Train schedules and names and classes of service have changed frequently in the past few years, so verify hours and fares before you go (www.perurail.com). It's wise to make your reservation at least a day (or more) in advance, especially in high season; Vistadome service from Ollantaytambo requires reservations 10 days in advance. For the luxury service, reservations several weeks or more in advance are recommended.

BY HELICOPTER All helicopter flights to Machu Picchu have been suspended indefinitely, due to environmental concerns.

(Tips) **Package Visits to Machu Picchu**

One-day Machu Picchu tour packages that include a round-trip train ride from Cusco to Aguas Calientes (Machu Picchu Pueblo), a bus to the ruins, admission, a guided tour, and sometimes lunch at Machu Picchu Sanctuary Lodge, can be purchased from travel agencies in Cusco. Package deals generally start at around $130 (£65); it's worth shopping around for the best deal. Try **Milla Turismo,** Portal Comercio 195, Plaza de Armas (© 084/234-181; www.millaturismo. com); **SAS Travel,** Portal Panes 167, Plaza de Armas (© 084/255-205; www.sas travelperu.com); **Top Vacations,** Portal Confituria 265, Plaza de Armas (© 084/ 263-278); or any of the tour agencies that organize Inca Trail treks (see "Hiking the Inca Trail" on p. 684). Packages that include overnight accommodations can also be arranged.

BY BUS You can't travel from Cusco to Machu Picchu by bus, but if you walk the Inca Trail or ascend the slope to the ruins from the town of Aguas Calientes, you can take one of the frequent buses that depart from the railroad tracks. The buses wend their way up the mountain, performing exaggerated switchbacks for 15 minutes before suddenly depositing passengers at the entrance to the ruins. The cost is $12 (£6) round-trip. There's no need to reserve; just purchase your ticket at the little booth in front of the line of buses. Buses begin running at 6:30am and come down all day, with the last one descending at dusk. Some people choose to purchase a one-way ticket ($6/£3) up and walk down (30–45 min.) to Aguas Calientes.

BY FOOT The celebrated **Inca Trail (Camino del Inca)** is almost as famous as the ruins themselves, and the trek is rightly viewed as an attraction in itself. See "Hiking the Inca Trail" on p. 684 for more details.

EXPLORING MACHU PICCHU

Since its initial exploration by American archaeologists from 1911 to 1915, Machu Picchu has resonated far beyond the status of a mere archaeological site. Reputed to be the legendary "lost city of the Incas," it is deeply steeped in mystery and folklore. The ruins of the complex—the only significant Inca site to escape the ravenous appetites of the conquistadors in the 16th century—rank as the top attraction in Peru, arguably the greatest in South America, and for my money, one of the world's most stunning sights. Countless glossy photographs of the ruins, gently positioned like a saddle between two massive peaks swathed in cottony clouds, can't do it justice.

Invisible from the Urubamba Valley below, Machu Picchu lay dormant for more than 4 centuries, nestled nearly 2,400m (7,872 ft.) above sea level under thick jungle and known only to a handful of Amerindian peasants. Never mentioned in the Spanish chronicles, it was seemingly lost in the collective memory of the Incas and their descendants. Its unearthing raised more questions than it answered, and experts still argue over its purpose. Was it a citadel? An agricultural site? An astronomical observatory? A ceremonial city or sacred retreat for the Inca emperor? Or some combination of all of these? Adding to the mystery, this complex city of exceedingly fine architecture and masonry was constructed, inhabited, and abandoned all in less than a century—a flash in the 4,000-year history of Andean Peru. It was very probably abandoned even before the arrival of the Spanish, perhaps a result of the Incas' civil war. Or perhaps it was drought that drove the Incas elsewhere.

Yale historian Hiram Bingham had thought Machu Picchu to be the lost city of Vilcabamba, the last refuge of the rebellious Manco Inca. Machu Picchu is not that lost city, which exists deeper in the jungle, at Espíritu Pampa. Most believe that the Inca Pachacutec, who founded the Inca Empire, had Machu Picchu built sometime in the mid-1400s. It appears that the complex was both a ceremonial and agricultural center. Never looted by the Spanish, many of its architectural features remain in excellent condition—even if they do little to advance our understanding of the exact nature of Machu Picchu.

One thing is certain: Machu Picchu is one of the world's great examples of landscape art. The Incas revered nature, worshipping celestial bodies and more earthly streams and stones. The spectacular setting of Machu Picchu reveals just how much they reveled in their environment. Steep terraces, gardens, granite and limestone temples, staircases, and aqueducts seem to be carved directly out of the hillside. Forms echo the very shape of the surrounding mountains, and windows and instruments appear to have been constructed to track the sun during the June and December solstices. Machu Picchu lies

300m (1,000 ft.) lower than Cusco, but you'd imagine the exact opposite, so nestled are the ruins among mountaintops and clouds.

Appreciating Machu Picchu for its aesthetic qualities is no slight to its significance. The Incas obviously chose the site for the power of its natural beauty. They, like we, must have been in awe of the snowcapped peaks to the east; the rugged panorama of towering, forested mountains and the sacred cliff of Putukusi to the west; and the city sitting gracefully like a proud saddle between two huge peaks. It remains one of the most thrilling sights in the world. At daybreak, when the sun's rays creep over the jagged silhouette, sometimes turning the distant snow peaks fiery orange and then slowly casting brilliant light on the ruins building by building and row by row, it's enough to move some observers to tears and others to squeals of delight.

Visiting the Ruins

From May to September, as many as 2,500 visitors a day (the maximum allowed) visit the ruins. The place is large enough to escape most tour group bottlenecks, though people fearful of the crush should plan to arrive as early as possible in the morning, especially to see the sun rise, and/or stay past 3pm. Perhaps the worst time to visit is from July 28 to August 10, when Peruvian national holidays bring untold numbers of school groups and families to Machu Picchu.

The ruins are open from dawn to dusk; the first visitors, usually those staying at the hotel next door or arriving from the Inca Trail, enter at 6am. Everyone is ushered out by 6pm. Tickets no longer can be purchased at the entrance; they must be purchased (take your passport) at the **Machu Picchu Cultural Center** in Aguas Calientes, Av. Pachacutec, s/n (✆ **084/211-196**), near the main plaza. They may also be purchased at the **Instituto Nacional de Cultural** (INC) offices in Cusco, Calle San Bernardo, several blocks from the Plaza de Armas. The entrance fee has doubled to S/120 ($40/£20; half-price with an ISIC card). Some speculate that the fee will increase again by as much as 100% in 2008. Tickets are valid for 3 days from date of purchase, but are good for a single day's entrance only. You will be given a map of the ruins, which gives the names of the individual sections, but no detailed explanations. The numbers indicated in brackets below follow our own map on p. 679. For a detailed guide of the ruins and their history, Peter Frost's *Exploring Cusco,* available in Cusco bookstores, is quite excellent.

English-speaking guides can be independently arranged on-site. Most charge around $20 to $30 (£10–£15) for a private 2-hour tour. You can also join a tour group for about $5 (£2.50) per person.

Inside the Ruins

After passing through the ticket booth, you can either head left and straight up the hill, or down to the right. The path up to the left takes you to the spot above the ruins, near the **Caretaker's Hut** and **Funerary Rock** [1], which affords the classic postcard overview of Machu Picchu. If you arrive early enough for sunrise (6:30–7:30am), by all means go here first. The hut overlooks rows and rows of steep agricultural terraces. From this vantage point, you can see clearly the full layout of Machu Picchu, which had clearly defined agricultural and urban zones; a long **dry moat** [2] separates the two sectors. A population of perhaps 1,000 lived here at the high point of Machu Picchu.

Head down into the main section of the ruins, past a series of burial grounds and dwellings and the **main entrance to the city** [3]. A section of stones, likely a **quarry** [4], sits atop a clearing with occasionally great views of the snowcapped peaks (Cordillera Vilcabamba) to the southwest.

Tips **Come Prepared**

Take a bottle of water in a knapsack to Machu Picchu (not to mention a good sun hat and sunscreen), no matter how long you plan to stay. It gets very warm, the sun is incredibly strong at this elevation, and there's nowhere to go for refreshment (and few places to find shade) besides the hotel at the entrance.

Down a steep series of stairs is one of the most famous Inca constructions, the **Temple of the Sun** [5] (also called the Torreón). The rounded, tapering tower has extraordinary stonework, the finest in Machu Picchu; its large stones fit together seamlessly. From the ledge above the temple, you can appreciate the window perfectly aligned for the June winter solstice, when the sun's rays come streaming through at dawn and illuminate the stone at the center of the temple. The temple is cordoned off, and entry is not permitted. Below the temple, a cave carved from the rock, is a section traditionally called the **Royal Tomb** [6], even though no human remains have been found there. Inside is a meticulously carved altar and series of niches that produce intricate morning shadows. To the north, just down the stairs that divide this section from a series of dwellings called the **Royal Sector,** is a still-functioning canal and series of interconnected **fountains** [7]. The main fountain is distinguished both by its size and excellent stonework.

Back up the stairs to the high section of the ruins (north of the quarry) is the main ceremonial area. The **Temple of the Three Windows** [8], each a trapezoid extraordinarily cut with views of the Andes in the distance across the Urubamba gorge, is likely to be one of your lasting images of Machu Picchu. It fronts one side of the **Sacred Plaza** [9]. To the left, if you're facing the Temple of the Three Windows, is the **Principal Temple** [10], which has masterful stonework in its three high walls. Directly opposite is the **House of the Priest** [11]. Just behind the Principal Temple is a small cell, termed the **Sacristy** and renowned for its exquisite masonry. It's a good place to examine how amazingly these many-angled stones (one to the left of the doorjamb has 32 distinct angles) were fitted together by Inca stonemasons.

Up a short flight of stairs is the **Intihuatana** [12], popularly called the "hitching post of the sun." It looks to be a ritualistic carved rock or sort of sundial, and its shape echoes that of the sacred peak Huayna Picchu beyond the ruins. The stone almost certainly functioned as an astronomical and agricultural calendar. It appears to be powerfully connected to mountains in all directions. The Incas built similar monuments elsewhere across the empire, but most were destroyed by the Spanish (who surely thought them to be instruments of pagan worship). The one at Machu Picchu survived in perfect form until 2001, when authorities allowed the filming of a Cuzqueña beer commercial here and the crew sneaked in a 1,000-pound crane, which fell over and chipped off the top section of the Intihuatana. All to sell more beer!

Follow a trail down through terraces and past a small plaza to a **dusty clearing** [13] with covered stone benches on either side. Fronting the square is the massive sculpted **Sacred Rock** [14], whose shape mimics that of Putukusi, the sacred peak that looms due east across the valley. This area likely served as a communal area for meetings and perhaps performances.

To the left of the Sacred Rock, down a path, is the gateway to **Huayna Picchu,** the huge outcrop that serves as a dramatic backdrop to Machu Picchu. Though it looks forbidding, it can be climbed by anyone in reasonable shape. Note, however, that only 400 people per day are permitted to make the climb; if you are keen on ascending Huyana Picchu for the views and exercise, arrive early. The steep path up takes most visitors about an hour or more, though some (including me) have ascended the peak in less than 25 minutes. Guards at a small booth require visitors to sign in and out; the path is open from 7am to 1pm and the first group of 200 must exit by 10am. The views from the very top, of Machu Picchu below and the panorama of forested mountains, are breathtaking. The climb is highly recommended for all energetic sorts, but young children are not allowed. (I've seen octogenarians climb the path at an enviable clip.) In wet weather, you may want to reconsider, as the stone steps can get very slippery and dangerous.

Returning back down the same path (frighteningly steep at a couple points) is a turnoff to the **Temple of the Moon,** usually visited only by Machu Picchu completists. Cleaved into the rock at a point midway down the peak, it almost surely was not a lunar observatory, but it is a strangely forlorn and mysterious place of caverns and niches and enigmatic portals. It has some terrific stonework. The path takes about an hour round-trip from the detour.

Continuing back into the complex, enter the lower section of the ruins, separated from the spiritually oriented upper section by a **Central Plaza** [15]. The lower section was more prosaic in function (it was mostly residential and industrial). Eventually, you'll come to a series of cells and quarters, called the **Group of the Three Doors** [16] and the **Mortar District** or Industrial Sector [17]. By far the most interesting part of this lower section is the **Temple of the Condor** [18]. Said to be a carving of a giant condor, the rock above symbolizes the great bird's wings. You can actually crawl through the cave at the base of the rock.

HIKING THE INCA TRAIL ★★★

The Incas conceived of both Machu Picchu and the great trail leading to it in grand artistic and spiritual terms. Hiking the Inca Trail—the ancient royal highway—is hands-down the most authentic and scenic way to visit Machu Picchu and get a clear grasp of the Incas' overarching architectural concept and supreme regard for nature. As impressive as Machu Picchu itself, the trail traverses a 325-sq.-km (125-sq.-mile) national park designated the Machu Picchu Historical Sanctuary. The zone is replete with extraordinary natural and man-made sights: Inca ruins, exotic vegetation and animals, and dazzling vistas.

Visitors have two options when hiking to Machu Picchu: either along an arduous 4-day, 3-night path, or as part of a more recently opened 2-day, 1-night trail. You can hire porters to haul your packs or suck it up and do it the hard way, but **you must go as part of an organized group arranged by an officially sanctioned tour agency** (see "Inca Trail Regulations," below). Independent trekking (without an official guide) on the Inca Trail has been prohibited since June 2001. However, a couple or small number of people can organize their own group if they are willing to pay higher prices for the luxury of not having to join an ad-hoc group. The classic 4-day route is along hand-hewn stone stairs and through sumptuous mountain scenery, amazing forest, and dozens of Inca ruins. The zone is inhabited by rare orchids, 300-plus species of birds, and even the indigenous spectacled bear. The trek begins at Qorihuayrachina, more easily described as Km 88 of the railway to Aguas Calientes. The 43km (27-mile) route passes three steep mountain passes, including the dreaded "Dead Woman's

Pass," to a maximum altitude of 4,200m (13,776 ft.). Virtually all groups enter the ruins of Machu Picchu at sunrise on the fourth day.

Others choose to take the 2-day trek, a reasonable alternative if time or fitness are lacking. This trail begins closer to Machu Picchu, at Km 104, and circumvents much of the finest mountain scenery and ruins. Groups spend the night near the ruins of Wiñay Wayna before arriving at Machu Picchu for sunrise on the second day. More and more people of all ages and athletic abilities are tackling the Inca Trail; the Peruvian government, in addition to adopting more stringent regulations governing its use, also placed flush toilets in campsites in 2003 in an attempt to make the trail cleaner and more user-friendly.

Either way you go, it is advisable to give yourself a couple of days in Cusco or the Sacred Valley to acclimatize to the high elevation. Cold- and wet-weather technical gear, a solid backpack, and comfortable, sturdy hiking boots are musts (also needed: a sleeping bag, flashlight, and sunblock). Above all, respect the ancient trail and its environment. Whatever you pack in, you must also pack out. You must also choose your dates extremely carefully. The dry season (June–Sept) is the most crowded time on the trail but excellent in terms of weather. Shoulder seasons can be best of all, even with the threat of a bit of rain; May is perhaps the best of these, with good weather and low numbers of trekkers. Other months—especially December through March—are simply too wet for all but the hardest-core trail vets. The entire trail is now closed for maintenance and conservation during the entire month of February—which was one of the rainiest and least appealing months for trekking to Machu Picchu anyway. For the most popular months (May–Sept), early booking (at least 3 months in advance) is essential.

The Peruvian government has sought to limit numbers of trekkers (now capped at 500 per day, including tourists and trek staff) on the Inca Trail but also to maximize revenue from one of its foremost attractions. Thus, the cost of hiking the trail has steadily climbed: It now costs at least three times what it did just a few years ago. Standard-class treks, the most common and economical service, cost start at about $350 and $330 (£175 and £165) per person, including entrance fees ($73/£37 adults and $36/£18 students) and return by tourist train. Independent trekkers generally join a mixed group of travelers; groups tend to be between 12 and 16 people with guaranteed daily departures. The cost includes a bus transfer to Km 88 to begin the trek, an English-speaking guide, tents, mattresses, three daily meals, and porters who carry all common equipment. Tips for porters or guides are extra. Personal porters, to carry your personal items, can be hired for about $50 (£25) for the 4 days. Premium-class services generally operate smaller group sizes (a maximum of 10 trekkers), and you often get an upgrade on the return train. Prices for premium group treks, organized for private groups, range from $450 to as much as $1,000 (£225–£500) per person.

Prices vary for trail packages based on services and the quality and experience of the agency. In general, you get what you pay for. Rock-bottom prices will probably get you a guide who speaks little English, food that is barely edible, camping equipment on its last legs, and a large, rowdy group. Especially important is the ability of an agency to guarantee departure even if its desired target number of travelers is not filled. Never purchase Inca Trail (or, for that matter, any tour) packages from anyone other than officially licensed agencies, and be careful to make payments (and get official receipts) at the physical offices of the agencies. If you have questions about whether an agency is legitimate or is authorized to sell Inca Trail packages, ask for assistance at the main tourism information office in Cusco.

Inca Trail Regulations

For decades, individuals trekked the Inca Trail on their own, but hundreds of thousands of visitors—as many as 75,000 a year—left behind so much detritus that not only was the experience compromised for most future trekkers, but also the very environment was placed at risk. The Peruvian government has finally instituted changes and restrictions designed to lessen the human impact on the trail and on Machu Picchu itself. In the first couple of years, regulations were poorly enforced, but the government recently announced its intentions to fully and strictly enforce them.

All trekkers are now required to go accompanied by a guide and group. Since 2000, entrance fees for both the trail and the ruins have quadrupled ($73/£37 adults, $37/£18 students); the overall number of trekkers permitted on the trail was significantly reduced, to 200 per day; only professionally qualified and licensed guides are allowed to lead groups on the Inca Trail; the maximum loads porters can carry has been limited to 20 kilograms (44 lb.); tourists are no longer permitted to travel on the local train from Aguas Calientes to Machu Picchu (or vice versa); and all companies must pay porters the minimum wage (about $15/£7.50 per day).

These changes have cut the number of trekkers on the trail in half and have made advance reservations essential in high season. Guarantee your space on the trail by making a reservation at least 1 week in advance of your trip in low season (but several months or more in advance for June–Sept; reservations can be made as much as a year in advance). Travelers willing to wing it *might* still find available spots 4 or 5 days before embarking on the trail, perhaps even at discounted rates, but waiting is a huge risk if you're really counting on doing the Inca Trail.

At least 140 tour operators have been granted government licenses to sell and operate Inca Trail treks. Recommended agencies (all based in Cusco) for organizing treks along the Inca Trail include **Andean Life,** Plateros 372 (© 084/249-491; www. andeanlife.com); **Big Foot Tours,** Triunfo 392-2nd level (© 084/238-568; www.big footcusco.com); **Explorandes,** Av. Garcilaso 316-A (© 084/238-830; www.explorandes. com); **Q'Ente,** Garcilaso 210 (© 084/222-535; www.qente.com); **SAS Adventure Travel,** Portal Panes 167, Plaza de Armas (© 084/255-205; www.sastravelperu.com); **Top Vacations,** Portal de Panes 143/Plaza de Armas (© 084/263-278); and **United Mice,** Plateros 351 (© 084/221-139; www.unitedmice.com).

To guarantee a spot with an agency (which must request a trek permit for each trekker) it is imperative that you make a reservation and pay for your entrance fee at least 15 days in advance (several months in advance if you plan to go during the peak months of May–Sept). Reservations can be made as much as a year in advance. Gone are the days when trekkers could simply show up in Cusco and organize a trek on the fly. Changing dates once you make a reservation is difficult if not impossible. If spots remain on agency rosters, they are offered on a first-come, first-served basis.

WHERE TO STAY IN AGUAS CALIENTES

The **Machu Picchu Sanctuary Lodge** ⚜ is a newly transformed, extraordinarily expensive luxury lodge next to the ruins (℃ **084/246-419;** www.orient-express.com). Rooms are not especially large, but they have a good deal of Peruvian character, and one-third of them have views of the ruins. Clearly, you are paying for the unique proposition of staying right next to Machu Picchu. Rooms cost a staggering $795 to $1,085 (£398–£543) for a double, $1,320 (£660) for a suite (though rates include three meals a day); even at those prices, you must reserve 3 months in advance during high season (May–Sept). You must also hold a reservation in Cusco at the Hotel Monasterio. Easily the best place to stay if you can't get into the Machu Picchu Sanctuary Lodge (or are understandably scared off by its prices and restrictions) is the **Machu Picchu Pueblo Hotel** ⚜⚜, Avenida Imperio de los Incas (℃ **800/442-5042,** or 084/211-122 for reservations; www.inkaterra.com). This rustic 15-year-old hotel, a compound of Spanish-colonial bungalows, has real flavor, though it too has gotten very expensive. It is craftily set into lush gardens, and it offers orchid tours, bird-watching, and guided ecological hikes. The large, comfortable rooms (many with fireplaces) start at $569 (£285) for a double, $675 (£338) for a suite.

Quite a notch down in both price and comfort is **Gringo Bill's Hostal,** Colla Raymi 104, Plaza de Armas (℃/fax **084/211-046;** www.gringobills.com), was started by an American expat and has been a backpacker's institution since the early 1980s, though lately it's gone quite a bit upscale. The comfortable and clean rooms have good beds, and many have great views of the Upper Amazon tropical rainforest. Double rooms with private bathrooms cost $75 (£37); suites (at Gringo Bills! No!) range from $105 to $135 (£52–£117). **Hostal Machupicchu,** Av. Imperio de Los Incas s/n (℃ **888/790-5264** toll-free or 084/211-065; fax 084/212-034; www.hostalmachupicchu. com), is one of the best midrange options in Aguas Calientes. Restored and redecorated a few years ago, it has very clean, well-furnished, and airy rooms, some painted in funky colors. Double rooms with shared bathrooms cost $35 (£17). One of the best of the inexpensive hostels along the main drag and railroad tracks, **Hostal Continental,** Av. Imperio de Los Incas 177 (℃ **084/211-034**), is very tidy, and you won't lack for hot water. Rooms aren't large, but the beds are pretty decent for a budget backpacker; $35 (£17) will get you a double with a shared bathroom.

WHERE TO DINE IN AGUAS CALIENTES

Scores of small and friendly restaurants line the only two streets in Aguas Calientes, Avenida Imperio de Los Incas and Avenida Pachacutec. Many are fairly generic, serving decent, cheap *menús* and pizza from wood-fired ovens. If you're just looking for pizza and a cold beer, **El Fogón de las Mestizas** and **Chez Maggy** (on Pachacutec) and **Incawasi, Inti Killa, Pizzería Su Chosa,** and **Pachamama** (all on Av. Imperio de los Incas) are all dependable. Menu hawkers, often the kids of the cook or owner, will try to lure you in with very cheap menu deals. If you're just looking for lunch during visits to the ruins, you have two choices: the overpriced buffet lunch at Machu Picchu Sanctuary Lodge, or a sack lunch. I recommend the latter (pick one up at Gringo Bill's or assemble one from your hotel's buffet breakfast). The best restaurant in town is the friendly **Indio Feliz** ⚜⚜, Calle Lloque Yupanqui 112 (℃ **084/211-090**), serving Peruvian and French cuisine. Other good dining options include **Pueblo Viejo,** Av. Pachacutec s/n (℃ **084/211-193**), a simple and cozy restaurant specializing in grilled meats; **Toto's House,** Av. Imperio de los Incas s/n (℃ **084/211-020**), a large, airy place that sits overlooking the river and serves good Peruvian dishes, barbecue, and pizzas (often to the tune of Altiplano music); and **Restaurant Manu,** Av. Pachacutec 139 (© **084/211-101**), a relaxed and friendly spot featuring lots of international and Peruvian items, including pizza, homemade pasta, baked trout, and grilled chicken.

7 The Southern Amazon: Manu & Tambopata ⭐⭐⭐

Puerto Maldonado: 500km (310 miles) NE of Cusco

Nearly two-thirds of Peru is Amazon rainforest, which thrives with some of the richest biodiversity on the planet. Not surprisingly, jungle ecotourism has exploded in Peru. The Amazonian regions are now more accessible, even though some areas remain very complicated and time-consuming to get to, and there are more lodges and eco-options than ever.

Cusco is the gateway to the southeastern jungle and some of Peru's finest Amazon rainforest expeditions. Two of Peru's top three jungle sites—among the greatest not just in South America, but the world—are found in the southern Amazon. The region's two principal protected areas, the **Manu Biosphere Reserve** (which encompasses the Parque Nacional del Manu, or Manu National Park) and the **Tambopata National Reserve** (Reserva Nacional de Tambopata), differ in terms of remoteness and facilities. Manu, considered to be one of the most pristine jungle regions in the world, is complicated and expensive to visit; travel is possible only with one of eight officially sanctioned agencies. Most expeditions last a minimum of 5 days and involve both overland and air (not to mention extensive river) travel. The jungle frontier city of Puerto Maldonado, the unassuming capital of the region and a half-hour flight from Cusco, is the jumping-off point to explore more accessible Tambopata. Travelers without the time or budget to accommodate Manu often find Tambopata a worthy alternative.

Lodge visits include boat transportation and three meals daily, as well as guided visits and activities (some, such as canopy walks, entail additional fees). For both destinations, airfare from Cusco to Puerto Maldonado or Boca Manu (the gateway to the Manu Biosphere Reserve) is usually extra. Cheaper tours travel overland, stay at lesser lodges (or primarily at campsites), and may travel on riverboats without canopies. Independent travel to Tambopata and two-way overland travel to either are options only for those with a lot of time and patience on their hands. Organizing your trip with a specialized tour operator is highly recommended (and in the case of Manu, required). Most have fixed departure dates throughout the year. Do not purchase any jungle packages from salespeople on the streets of Cusco; their agencies may not be authorized to enter restricted zones, and last-minute "itinerary changes" are likely.

Dry season (May–Oct) is the best time for southern jungle expeditions; during the rainy season, rivers overflow and mosquitoes gobble up everything in sight. But intense heat and humidity are year-round constants in the jungle.

MANU BIOSPHERE RESERVE

Manu is the least accessible and explored jungle in Peru, and about as close as you're likely to come to virgin rainforest anywhere in the world. A UNESCO World Heritage Site and the largest protected area in Peru (and one of the largest in the world), Manu—about half the size of Switzerland—has a surface area of nearly 1.7 million hectares (4 million acres) of varied habitats, including Andes highlands, cloud forests, and lowland tropical rainforests. The Manu Biosphere Reserve comprises three zones: **Manu National Park,** an area of dedicated conservation reserved for scientific study;

Tips   **Wildlife Viewing**

Peru's Amazon jungle regions have some of the greatest recorded biodiversity and species of plants and animals on earth. However, you may be disappointed if you go expecting a daily episode of *Wild Kingdom*. An expedition to the Amazon is not like a safari to the African savanna. Many mammals are extremely difficult to see in the thick jungle vegetation, and though the best tour operators employ guides skilled in ferreting them out, there are no guarantees. Even in the most virgin sections, after devoting several patient days to the exercise, you are unlikely to see a huge number of mammals, especially the rare large species such as tapirs, jaguars, and giant river otters. If you spot a single one of these prized mammals, your jungle expedition can be considered a roaring success. However, in both Manu and Tambopata you are very likely to see a wealth of jungle birds (including the region's famous macaws), several species of monkeys, black caimans, butterflies, and insects.

the **Reserve Zone,** up the River Manu northwest of Boca Manu, is by permit and accompanied by an authorized guide only for ecotourist activities; the Multi-Use or **Cultural Zone,** home to traditional nomadic groups and open to all visitors. The whole of Manu is unparalleled for its wealth of wildlife, which includes more than 1,000 species of birds, 1,200 butterfly species, 15,000 plants, 200 mammal species and 13 species of primates. Bird-watchers thrill at the prospect of glimpsing bird populations that account for 10% of the world's total, more than those found in all of Costa Rica. Other Manu fauna include jaguars, tapirs, spectacled bears, ocelots, and giant otters. Manu is also home to untold quantities of reptiles, amphibians, and insects, as well as dozens of native tribes, some of which have contact with the modern world.

Only a handful of travel agencies in Cusco are authorized to organize excursions to Manu. Getting to Manu is an eco-adventure in itself. Overland access to the Manu Reserve Zone from Cusco is a stunning 2-day journey through 4,000m (13,120-ft.) mountains and cloud forest before descending into lowland rainforest. Because the reserve is so isolated and access is so restricted, Manu visits are rather expensive, ranging from $500 to more than $2,000 (£250–£1,000) per person for a 5- to 8-day trip.

MANU TOUR OPERATORS

Only eight tour companies are permitted to run organized expeditions to Manu (and they are limited to 30 travelers each per week). The best of the firms listed below are closely involved with conservation and local development programs.

- **InkaNatura** ☆☆☆, Calle Ricardo Palma N° J1, Urb Santa Monica, Cusco (© **084/ 25-5255;** www.inkanatura.com). Perhaps the most serious and sophisticated outfit operating ecotourism trips in the Peruvian Amazon, InkaNatura, associated with the Peruvian conservation group PerúVerde and the American organization Tropical Nature, organizes stays at the famed **Manu Wildlife Center.** The lodge, opened in 1996, is located near the world's largest tapir clay lick, as well as the Blanquillo macaw clay lick, and it features 48 km (30 miles) of nature trails and two canopy-viewing platforms. Accommodations are in 22 spacious, private bungalows with tiled bathrooms. Packages at Manu Wildlife Center range from 4 days, 3 nights for $1,170 (£585) to 5 days, 4 nights for $1,270 (£635). InkaNatura also operates several lodges in Tambopata (see below). Outside Peru, trips can be organized through **Tropical Nature Travel,** P.O. Box 5276 Gainesville, FL 32627-5276 (© **877/827-8350** toll-free in the U.S.; www.tropicalnaturetravel.com).

- **Manu Expeditions** ⭐⭐⭐, Urbanización Magisterio, Segunda Etapa G-5, P.O. Box 606, Cusco (© **084/226-671;** www.manuexpeditions.com). One of the pioneering ecotourism operators in southern Peruvian Amazon, Manu Expeditions—run by an ornithologist who is the British Consul in Cusco, has been organizing rainforest tours for more than 2 decades. Tours include stays at the **Manu Wildlife Center,** of which the group is part owner (see above), near the famed macaw clay lick, and a safari camp facility deep at Cocha Salvador within the Manu Biosphere Reserve. The Wildlife Center is considered the best lodge in Peru for birding. The longer tours include initial stays at the **Cock-of-the-Rock Lodge** in cloud forest. First departures of each month include stays at Casa Machiguenga Lodge. Four-, six-, and nine-day tours range from $1,110 to $1,810 (£555–£905) per person.

- **Manu Nature Tours** ⭐⭐⭐, Av. Pardo 1046, Cusco (© **084/252-721;** www.manuperu.com). A highly professional, prize-winning outfit with 20 years' experience in Manu, it operates the well-known and comfortable **Manu Lodge,** situated next to a pristine lake and the only full-service lodge within Manu National Park itself (5-day, 4-night trips, $929–$1,422/£465–£711), and the excellent **Manu Cloud Forest Lodge,** the first of its kind in Peru, overlooking a waterfall (3-day, 2-night trips, $849/£425). Add-on options include mountain biking, rafting, and tree canopy climbs. The company runs Manu Café & Restaurant in Cusco, next to its offices.

- **Pantiacolla** ⭐, Saphy 554 or Plateros 341, Cusco (© **084/238-323;** www.pantiacolla.com). An initiative of a Dutch biologist and Boca Manu-born conservationist, the agency operates the small **Pantiacolla Lodge,** with double rooms in bungalows, on bluffs overlooking the Madre de Dios River at the edge of Manu National Park. The organization also operates a community-based ecotourism project with the Yine Indians of the Manu rainforest, with a lodge that will be entirely turned over to the community in 2011. Pantiacolla is favored by eco-travelers on a budget, offering camping and lodge trips ranging from $990 (£495) for 5 days to $1,064 (£534) for 7 days for Reserve Zone tours.

Other reputable Manu tour companies, which run economical camping-based trips, include **Manu Ecological Adventures,** Plateros 356, Cusco (© **084/261-640;** www.manuadventures.com); and **SAS Travel,** Portal Panes 167, Plaza de Armas, Cusco (© **084/255-205;** www.sastravelperu.com), a well-run and popular all-purpose agency that offers varied programs to both Manu and Tambopata and stays at various lodges.

TAMBOPATA NATIONAL RESERVE

Accessible from Puerto Maldonado, jungle lodges in and around the Tambopata National Reserve—a massive tract of tropical rainforest in the department of Madre de Dios—are located either along the Tambopata or Madre de Dios Rivers. The National Reserve covers 275,000 hectares (nearly 700,000 acres), while the entire area, including the Bahuaja-Sonene National Park, encompasses some 1.5 million hectares (3.7 million acres) of Amazonian jungle. Visits to lodges here are considerably more accessible than those in Manu. Most trips involve flying a half-hour from Cusco and then boarding a boat and traveling by river for 45 minutes to up to 5 hours to reach a jungle lodge. Although man's imprints are more noticeable in the Tambopata region, the area remains one of superb environmental diversity, with a dozen different types of forest. Many environmentalists claim that Tambopata has one of the greatest diversities of wildlife recorded, owing to a location at the confluence of lowland Amazon forest with three other ecosystems. At least 13 endangered species are found in the region, including the jaguar, giant river otter, ocelot, harpy eagle, and giant armadillo. The farther one travels from Puerto Maldonado, the greater the chances of wildlife viewing. The famous **Macaw Clay Lick (Colpa de Guacamayos)** within Tambopata National Reserve is one of the largest natural clay licks in Peru and perhaps the wildlife highlight of the country. Thousands of brilliantly colored macaws and parrots arrive daily at the cliffs to feed on mineral salts.

Flights to Puerto Maldonado from Cusco are about $60 (£30) each way. (Flights are often included in packages.) Packages begin with 2-day, 1-night arrangements, but 3-day, 2-night packages are better. Lodge stays generally allow visitors to see a large variety of trees, plants, and birds, as well as caimans, but few wild mammals apart from monkeys. Rare species such as the jaguar or tapir are infrequently seen, though visitors to Lago Sandoval, an oxbow lake, have the exciting opportunity to see an extended family of resident giant river otters (*lobos de río*). Lodges within an hour or so of Puerto Maldonado are generally cheaper, but because they are located in secondary jungle and are not nearly as remote, they best serve as introductory visits to the Amazon rainforest.

TAMBOPATA LODGES

- **Explorer's Inn** ⚅⚅⚅, the only lodge located within the Tambopata National Reserve, is a comfortable 30-year-old lodge that hosts both ecotourists and scientists. It's a little over 3 hours upriver from Puerto Maldonado along the River Tambopata and is excellent for viewing fauna, including otters, monkeys, and particularly jungle birds. Accommodations are in rustic, thatched-roof bungalows. Trips are arranged through **Peruvian Safaris,** Alcanfores 459, Miraflores, Lima (© 01/447-8888; www.explorersinn.com or www.peruviansafaris.com), at the edge of the Tambopata Reserve Zone, Prices range from $198 (£99) for 2 nights to $450 (£225) for a 4-night Macaw Clay Lick program.

- **Posada Amazonas** ⚅, about 2 hours up the Tambopata River from Puerto Maldonado, is owned jointly with the Infierno indigenous community and is quite good for inexpensive, introductory nature tours. It has an eagle nest site and a canopy observation tower, and two parrot clay licks are within a kilometer of the lodge. The lodge, inaugurated in 1998, features 30 rustic rooms and a wall open to the forest. It is operated by award-winning **Rainforest Expeditions,** Av. Aramburú 166-4B, Miraflores, Lima (© 877/905-3782 toll-free in the U.S., or 01/421-8347; www.perunature.com). This veteran ecotourism company promotes tourism with environmental education, research, and conservation and operates two Tambopata lodges. The prices are $225 to $425 (£112–£212) for 3- to 5-day trips. The 13-room **Tambopata Research Center** ⚅⚅⚅ is more remote (8 hr. upriver from Puerto Maldonado), located just 500m (1,640 ft.) from the jungle's largest and most famous Macaw Clay Lick. Just one of three Peruvian lodges in a protected national nature reserve, it is the best lodge in Tambopata for in-depth tours and viewing wildlife, including several species of monkeys. It's certainly *the* place to see flocks of colorful macaws and parrots. Trips usually entail an overnight at Posada Amazonas before continuing on to the Research Center. Prices are $745 to $945 (£373–£473) for 5- to 7-day trips and can be booked through Rainforest Expeditions.

- **Reserva Amazónica** ⭐⭐, (© **01/610-0404;** toll-free in the U.S. and Canada, © 800/442-5042; www.inkaterra.com). Less than an hour downriver by boat from Puerto Maldonado, this stylish, luxurious lodge is very professionally run and a great, and supremely comfortable, introduction to the Amazon. Operated by owners of the ecofriendly, upscale Machu Picchu Pueblo Hotel, Reserva Amazónica features the plushest private, African-style bungalow accommodations and coolest dining room and lounge, as well as the best food and wine, in the Peruvian jungle. It also offers massages and spa treatments. Though the immediate jungle in and around the lodge doesn't teem with wildlife (except for sonorous russet-backed Oropendula birds that make waking up a treat), the lodge offers a private monkey island of rescued spider, capuchin, and squirrel monkeys and a superb canopy walk, as well as visits to Sandoval Lake. If you're after creature comforts as well as a taste of nature, this is the best option. Rates range from $197 (£99) per night in a standard cabaña to $651 (£325) for 3 nights in a swank Amazonia suite.

- **Sandoval Lake Lodge** ⭐⭐, Calle Ricardo Palma N°1, Urb Santa Monica, Cusco (© **084/25-5255;** www.inkanatura.com). Though relatively near to Puerto Maldonado—getting there involves a 45-minute boat ride downriver along the Madre de Dios, and then a 1-hour walk and a 30-minute paddle across Sandoval Lake— Sandoval is the best option for those hoping to see a good diversity of wildlife and scenery without venturing too deep into the jungle. Located on a bluff overlooking a beautiful oxbow lake ringed by palm trees, the lodge is rustic but comfortable, with two wings of connected rooms open at the ceiling. Wildlife-viewing centers around leisurely paddled catamaran and canoe trips on the lake; most visitors not only see a wealth of aquatic and jungle birds but several species of monkeys, caimans, and the elusive, highly prized community of giant river otters (a family of 10 resides in the lake). Prices range from $235 to $335 (£118–£168) for 3- to 4-day stays. InkaNatura's newest lodge is the remote **Heath River Wildlife Center,** situated another 3 hours downriver near the Bolivian border, within easy reach of a large macaw clay lick and owned and staffed by the indigenous Ese'Eja Sonene people; it is possible to combine a couple of nights at either lodge. Heath River prices range from $595 (£298) for 4 days to $740 (£370) to 6 days. Outside Peru, trips can be organized through **Tropical Nature Travel,** P.O. Box 5276 Gainesville, FL 32627-5276 (© **877/827-8350** toll-free in the U.S. and Canada; www.tropicalnaturetravel.com).

8 Puno & Lake Titicaca

388km (241 miles) S of Cusco

Puno, founded in the late 17th century following the discovery of nearby silver mines, is a ramshackle town that draws numbers of visitors wholly disproportionate to its innate attractions. A mostly unlovely city on a high plateau, it has one thing going for it that no other place on earth can claim: Puno hugs the shores of fabled Lake Titicaca, the world's highest navigable body of water, a sterling expanse of deep blue at 3,830m (12,562 ft.) above sea level. The magnificent lake straddles the border of Peru and Bolivia; many Andean travelers move on from Puno to La Paz, going around, or in some cases over, Titicaca. Before leaving Puno, though, almost everyone hops aboard a boat to visit at least one of several ancient island-dwelling peoples. A 2-day tour takes travelers to the Uros floating islands, where Indian communities consisting of just a few families construct tiny islands out of *totora* reeds; there are two inhabited natural islands, Amantani and Taquile.

Puno has one other thing in its favor. Though dry and often brutally cold, the city is celebrated for its spectacular festivals, veritable explosions of *cultura popular.* The unassuming town, where the people descended from the Aymara from the south and the Quechua from the north, reigns as the capital of Peruvian folklore. Its traditional fiestas, dances, and music—and consequent street partying—are without argument among the most vibrant and uninhibited in Peru. Among those worth planning your trip around are the **Festival de la Virgen de la Candelaria (Candlemas)** ⟨⟨⟨, February 2 to 15; San Juan de Dios, March 8; Fiesta de las Cruces Alasitas, May 8; San Juan, San Pedro, and San Pablo, June 24 to 29; Apóstol Santiago, July 25; and **Puno Week** ⟨⟨, celebrating the birth of the city and the Inca Empire, November 1 to 7. Of these, Candlemas and Puno Week (especially Nov 5) are the most exceptional and attract the greatest number of visitors.

ESSENTIALS
GETTING THERE
BY PLANE   Puno does not have an airport; the nearest is **Aeropuerto Manco Capac** (© 054/322-905) in Juliaca, 45km (28 miles), or about an hour, north of Puno. **LAN Peru** and **TANS** fly daily from Lima and Arequipa to Juliaca. Flights are generally available for $79 to $120 (£40–£60; depending on the season) one-way. LAN Peru flies from Cusco to Juliaca for similar fares. Tourist buses run from the Juliaca airport to Puno, depositing travelers on Jirón Tacna (S/10, or $3.35/£1.70).

BY BUS   Puno has a modern, safe bus station, **Terminal Terrestre**, Jr. (© 051/364-733), Primero de Mayo 703, Barrio Magistral. Road service from Cusco to Puno has greatly improved, and many more tourists now travel by bus, which is faster and cheaper than the train.

The trip between Puno and Arequipa by bus is no longer tortuous; the long-awaited highway between the cities, completed in 2002, has dramatically shortened travel time from 12 to just 5 hours. **Cruz del Sur** (© 051/622-626) and **Ormeño** (© 051/352-321) make the trip for around S/30 ($10/£5).

From Cusco, executive-, imperial-, or royal-class buses make the trip in less than 7 hours (though some services, such as Inka Express, make stop-offs at Inca ruins en route, extending the trip a couple of hours; this is highly recommended if you have the extra time) and range in cost from $20 to $25 (£10–£12). **Imexso** (© 084/240-801), **Inka Express** (© 051/365-654), and **Cruz del Sur** (© 051/622-626) operate buses with videos and English-speaking tour guides. **Ormeño** (© 084/227-501) has daily direct departures between Cusco and Puno (6 hr.).

Given the confusing number of bus companies and services, it's wise to make bus reservations with a travel agent. See "Puno Travel Agencies & Tour Operators" on p. 698.

BY TRAIN   The Titicaca Route journey from Cusco to Puno, along tracks at an altitude of 3,500m (11,500 ft.), is one of the most scenic in Peru. Though it is slower (10 hr. and prone to late arrivals) and has experienced its share of onboard thievery, it is a favorite of travelers in Peru and preferable to the bus if you've got the time and money. *Note:* Keep a careful eye on your bags and, if possible, lock backpacks to the luggage rack. Also keep valuables close to your person.

Take It Easy

Puno's elevation of 3,300m (10,824 ft.) is nearly as high as Cusco, and unless you've already spent time in the Andes, you'll almost certainly need to rest for at least a day to acclimatize. See "Health Concerns" in "Planning Your Trip to Peru," earlier in this chapter, for further information on how to address altitude sickness.

Trains from Cusco to Puno depart from **Estación Huanchaq** (© **084/238-722**), at the end of Avenida Sol. Service to Puno is Monday, Wednesday, and Saturday year-round, departing at 8am and arriving at 6pm. Andean Explorer (first class) costs $143 (£72) one-way in swank coaches and includes lunch in luxurious dining cars; tourist (Backpacker) class, which is comfortable enough but offers no food or drink, is $22 (£11). Only Andean Explorer tickets can be reserved. The Puno train station (© **051/351-041**) is located at Av. La Torre 224.

Train service from Arequipa to Puno is now available by charter only, though hopefully it will be revived sometime in the future; check **www.perurail.com** for the latest information.

GETTING AROUND

Few visitors spend more than a day or two in Puno, and the little getting around that needs to be done in town is either on foot or by taxi. Taxis are inexpensive and plentiful, are easily hailed on the street, and are best used at night and to get back and forth from the hotels out on the banks of Titicaca. Most trips in town cost no more than S/3 ($1/50p). Taxis can also be hired for return trips to nearby ruins or for half- or full days. Visits to Lake Titicaca and its islands, as well as the ruins on the outskirts of town, are best done by organized tour; see "Puno Travel Agencies & Tour Operators" on p. 698.

VISITOR INFORMATION

A small **tourist information office** is located at Pasaje Lima 549 (© **051/365-088**), the pedestrian-only main drag of Puno (at Jr. Deustua, just off the Plaza de Armas), though you're probably better off going to one of the travel agencies that organizes Titicaca and area trips, such as All Ways Travel or Edgar Adventures. See "Puno Travel Agencies & Tour Operators" on p. 698.

For those crossing into Bolivia who need visas or other information, the **Bolivian Consulate** is located at Jr. Arequipa 120 (© **051/351-251**). North Americans and Europeans do not need a visa to enter Bolivia, but the border is a historically problematic one (it was closed for more than a month in 2001 and again in 2005 during the widespread strikes that paralyzed parts of Bolivia), so you may need to check on the status of the crossing before traveling to Bolivia.

FAST FACTS You'll find **banks** and **ATMs** located along Jirón Lima (also called Pasaje Lima), just before the tourist information office. Money changers can generally be found along Jirón Tacna, where most bus stations are located, and the market near the railway and Avenida de los Incas.

For medical attention, go to **Clínica Puno,** Jr. Ramón Castilla 178–180 (© **051/368-835**), or **Hospital Nacional,** Av. El Sol 1022 (© **051/369-696**). The **tourist police** are located at Jr. Deustua 530 (© **051/353-988**).

Pretty fast Internet connections are available at **Qoll@internet,** Jr. Oquendo 340 (Parque Pino), where you can make inexpensive international calls. It's open Monday through Saturday from 8am to midnight and Sunday from 3 to 9pm; rates are S/1.50 (50¢/25p) per hour. Other Internet *cabinas* are located along Pasaje Lima. Puno's main **Serpost post office** (© 051/351-141) is located at Moquegua 269; it's open Monday through Saturday from 8am to 8pm. The **Telefónica del Perú** office is on the corner of Moquegua and Arequipa.

WHAT TO SEE & DO IN PUNO

Puno itself is a rather bleak and unimpressive place if you don't count its enviable geography. The top attractions in Puno are outside the city: Lake Titicaca and the ancient Sillustaini ruins. What there is to see in Puno doesn't delay most visitors more than a half-day or so. However, if you stumble upon one of Puno's famously colorful festivals, you may want to linger.

The large **cathedral,** on the west side of the Plaza de Armas (at the end of Jr. Lima), is the focal point of downtown Puno. The 18th-century baroque church is big, but no great shakes; the elaborate exterior is much more impressive than the spartan, spacious, chilly interior. On the plaza is the 17th-century **La Casa del Corregidor** (© **051/351-921**), Deustua 576, purportedly Puno's oldest house, with an impressive Spanish balcony; it now houses a lovely "cultural" cafe and is the best spot in town for a breather. Nearby, the **Museo Municipal Carlos Dryer,** Conde de Lemos 289, is the town's principal (but small) museum. It has a decent selection of pre-Inca ceramics and textiles, as well as mummies with cranial deformations, but it's not very well illuminated. It's open Monday through Friday from 7:30am to 3:30pm; admission is S/3.50 ($1.35/70p). For a superb view of Lake Titicaca and a vantage point that makes Puno look more attractive than it is, climb the steep hill to **Mirador Kuntur Wasi** and **Huajsapata Park,** about 10 minutes southwest of the main square. On top is a statue of Manco Capac, the first Inca.

Back down below, Jirón (Pasaje) Lima is a pedestrianized mall, chock-full of shops, restaurants and bars, that runs from the Plaza de Armas to **Parque Pino,** a relaxed square populated by locals. Puno's seedy **central market** is 2 blocks east, and it spills across several streets. Although not attractive, it's a realistic look at the underbelly of the Peruvian economy. Beyond the railroad tracks is a **market** targeting tourists with all kinds of alpaca and woolen goods, often much cheaper than those found in Cusco and other cities.

LAKE TITICACA ✶✶✶

South America's largest lake and the world's highest navigable body of water, Lake Titicaca has long been considered a sacred place among indigenous Andean peoples. According to Andean legend, Lake Titicaca—which straddles the modern border between Peru and Bolivia—was the birthplace of civilization. Viracocha, the creator deity, lightened a dark world by having the sun, moon, and stars rise from the lake and occupy their places in the sky. The people who live in and around the lake consider themselves descendants of Mama Qota (Sacred Mother), and they believe that powerful spirits live in the lake's depths.

Lake Titicaca is a dazzling sight, worthy of such mystical associations: Its deep azure waters seemingly extend forever across the Altiplano at more than 3,800m (12,540 ft.). The lake covers more than 8,500 sq. km (5,300 sq. miles); it is 176km (109 miles) long and 50km (31 miles) wide. The sun is extraordinarily intense at this altitude,

Tips **Traveling to Bolivia**

Plenty of travelers continue on to Bolivia, which shares Lake Titicaca with Peru, from Puno; several travel agencies in Puno sell packages and bus tickets. The most common and scenic route is from Puno to La Paz via Yunguyo and Copacabana. The trip to La Paz takes 7 or 8 hours by bus. You can also go by a combination of overland travel and hydrofoil or catamaran, a unique but very time-consuming journey (13 hr.). At the border, visitors get an exit stamp from Peru and a tourist visa (30 days) from Bolivia. Foreigners are commonly tapped for phony departure and entry fees; resist the corrupt attempts. For more information on Bolivia, see chapter 5.

scorching off 600 cubic m (21,000 cubic ft.) of water per second. Daybreak and sunset, as the sun sinks low into the horizon, are particularly stunning to witness.

Lake Titicaca has been inhabited for thousands of years. *Totora* reed boats roamed the lake as early as 2500 B.C. Titicaca's 16 islands—both man-made and natural—are home to several communities of Quechua and Aymara Indians, groups with remarkably different traditions and ways of life. Visiting them, and staying overnight on one of the islands if you can, is one of the highlights of Peru and one of the most unique experiences in South America.

The most convenient way to visit is by an inexpensive and well-run guided tour, arranged by one of several travel agencies in Puno; see "Puno Travel Agencies & Tour Operators" on p. 698. Although it is possible to arrange independent travel, the low cost and easy organization of a group don't encourage it. Even if you go on your own, you'll inevitably fall in with groups, and your experience won't differ radically. You can go on a half-day tour of the **Uros Floating Islands** or a full-day tour that combines **Taquile Island,** but the best way to experience Lake Titicaca's unique indigenous life is to stay at least 1 night on either Taquile or Amantani, preferably in the home of a local family. Those with more time and money to burn may want to explore the singular experience of staying on private **Isla Suasi,** home to little more than a solar-powered hotel and a dozen llamas and vicuñas.

UROS FLOATING ISLANDS (LAS ISLAS FLOTANTES) 🞉

As improbable as it sounds, the Uros Indians of Lake Titicaca live on floating "islands" made by hand from *totora* reeds that grow in abundance in the shallow waters of Lake Titicaca. This unique practice has endured since the time of the Incas, and today, there are some 45 floating islands in the Bay of Puno. The islands first came into contact with the modern world in the mid-1960s, and their inhabitants now live mostly off tourism. To some visitors, this obvious dependency is a little unseemly. Many visitors faced with this strange sight conclude that the impoverished islanders can't possibly still live on the islands, that it must be a show created for their benefit. True, they can seem to be little more than floating souvenir stands; the communities idly await the arrival of tourist boats and then seek to sell them handmade textiles and reed-crafted items while the gringos walk gingerly about the spongy islands—truly a strange sensation—photographing the Uros's houses and children.

But it's not just a show. A couple hundred Titicaca natives continue to live year-round on the islands, even if they venture to Puno for commercial transactions. The largest island, Huacavacani, has homes and a floating Seventh-day Adventist church, a candidate for one of the more bizarre scenes you're likely to find in Peru—or anywhere. Others islands have schools, a post office, a public telephone, and souvenir shops. Only a few islands are set up to receive tourists, though. The vast majority of the Uros people live in continued isolation and peace, away from curious onlookers and camera lenses.

The Uros, who fled to the middle of the lake to escape conflicts with the Collas and Incas, long ago began intermarrying with the Aymara Indians, and many have now converted to Catholicism. Fishermen and birders, the Uros live grouped by family sectors, and entire families live in one-room, tentlike, thatched huts constructed on the shifting reed island that floats beneath. They build modest houses and boats with fanciful animal-head bows out of the reeds and continually replenish the fast-rotting mats that form their fragile islands. Visitors might be surprised, to say the least, to find some huts outfitted with TVs powered by solar panels (donated by the Fujimori administration after a presidential visit to the islands).

Inexpensive tours that go only to the Uros Islands last about 3 hours and include hotel pickup, an English-speaking guide, and motorboat transportation to the islands. Unless you're unusually pressed for time, it's much more enjoyable and informative to visit the Uros as a brief stop en route to the natural islands of Amantani or Taquile.

TAQUILE ISLAND (ISLA TAQUILE) 🎞🎞🎞

Taquile is a fascinating and stunningly beautiful island about 4 hours from Puno. The island is only 1km (a half mile) wide and about 6km (3¾ miles) long. It rises to a high point of 264m (870 ft.), and the hillsides are laced with formidable Inca stone agricultural terraces. The island is a rugged ruddy color, which contrasts spectacularly with the blue lake and sky. Taquile is littered with Inca and pre-Inca stone ruins.

The island is as serene as the views. Taquile has been inhabited for 10,000 years, and life remains starkly traditional; there are no vehicles and no electricity, and islanders (who number slightly more than 1,000) quietly go about their business. Taquile natives allow tourists to stay at private houses (in primitive but not uncomfortable conditions), and there are a number of simple restaurants near the central plaza. Though friendly to outsiders, the Quechua-speaking islanders remain a famously reserved and insular community. Their dress is equally famous—Taquile textiles are some of the finest in Peru. Men wear embroidered, woven red waistbands *(fajas)*, and embroidered, wool stocking caps that indicate marital status: red for married men, red and white for bachelors. Women wear layered skirts and black shawls over their heads. Taquile textiles are much sought-after for their hand-woven quality, but they are considerably more expensive than mass-produced handicrafts in other parts of Peru. There's a cooperative shop on the main plaza, and stalls are set up during festivals. Locals are more reluctant to haggle than artisans in other parts of Peru.

If you are lucky enough to catch a festival on the island, you will be treated to a festive and traditional pageant of color, with picturesque dances and women twirling in circles, revealing as many as 16 layered, multicolored skirts. Easter, Fiesta de Santiago (July 25), August 1 and 2, and New Year's are the best celebrations. Any time on the island, though, is a splendid and unique experience—especially once the day-trippers have departed and you have the island and incomparable views and stars virtually to yourself. Taquile then seems about as far away from modernity and "civilization" as you can travel on this planet.

Access to the island from the boat dock is either by a long path that wends around the island or by an amazing 533-step stone staircase that climbs to the top, passing through two stone arches with astonishing views of the lake. Independent travelers sign in and pay a nominal fee. Those wishing to spend the night can arrange for a family-house stay; expect to rough it a bit without proper showers. Many islanders do not speak Spanish, and English is likely to be met with blank stares.

Most single-day tours of the Uros and Taquile islands depart early in the morning and stop at the islands of Uros for a half-hour en route. For most visitors, a day trip—which allows only 1 or 2 hours on the island and 8 hours of boat time—is too grueling and insufficient to appreciate the beauty and culture of Taquile Island.

AMANTANI ISLAND (ISLA AMANTANI) 🎯🎯

Amantani, a circular island about 4½ hours from Puno (and about 2 hr. from Taquile), is home to a very different but equally fascinating Titicaca community. Also handsomely terraced and home to farmers, fishers, and weavers, in many ways Amantani is even more rustic and unspoiled than Taquile. It is a beautiful place, with a handful of villages composed of about 800 families and ruins clinging to the island's two peaks, Pachatata and Pachamama (Father Earth and Mother Earth). The islanders, who for the most part understand Spanish, are more open and approachable than natives of Taquile.

Amantani is best visited on a tour that allows you to spend the night (visiting the Uros islands en route) and travel the next day to Taquile. Tour groups place groups of four or five travelers with local families for overnight stays. Not only will the family prepare your simple meals, you will be invited to a friendly dance in the village meeting place. Most families dress up their guests in local outfits—women in layered, multicolored, embroidered skirts and blouses, and the men in wool ponchos—for the event. Though the evening is obviously staged for tourists' benefit, it's low-key and charming rather than cheesy. It's a good idea to bring small gifts for your family on Amantani, since they make little from stays and must alternate with other families on the island. Pens, pencils, and batteries all make good gifts. The tour price normally includes accommodations, lunch and an evening meal on the first day, and breakfast the following morning.

SILLUSTANI RUINS 🎯

Just beyond Puno are mysterious pre-Inca ruins called *chullpas* (funeral towers). The finest sit on the windswept Altiplano on a peninsula in Lake Umayo at Sillustani, 32km (20 miles) from Puno. The Colla people—a warrior tribe who spoke Aymara—buried their elite in giant cylindrical tombs, some as tall as 12m (40 ft.). The Collas dominated the Titicaca region before the arrival of the Incas. After burying their dead along with foodstuffs, jewels, and other possessions, they sealed the towers. The stone masonry is exquisite; many archaeologists and historians find them more complex than and superior to Inca engineering. The structures form quite an impression on such a harsh landscape.

The best way to visit Sillustani is by guided tour, usually in the afternoon; see "Puno Travel Agencies & Tour Operators," below. Dress warmly, as the wind gets bitter here.

PUNO TRAVEL AGENCIES & TOUR OPERATORS

Most travel agencies in Puno handle the conventional tours of Lake Titicaca and Sillustani, along with a handful of other ruins programs. Two of the best agencies are All

Ways Travel and Edgar Adventures. **All Ways Travel** ★★, Jr. Deustua 576 (in courtyard of La Casa del Corregidor; ✆ 051/353-979; www.titicacaperu.com) and Jr. Tacna 234 (✆ 051/355-552; awtperu@terra.com.pe), is run by the very friendly and helpful Víctor Pauca and his daughter Eliana (temporarily on leave in Chicago). They offer well thought-out, progressive cultural trips in addition to the standard tours. **Edgar Adventures,** Jr. Lima 328 (✆ 051/353-444; www.edgaradventures.com), is run by a Peruvian husband-and-wife team. Both can arrange bus and air travel as well, including travel to Bolivia. Another agency worth checking out for travel arrangements is **Highland Travel Experts,** Jr. Independenica 273 (✆ 051/964-139; hightravel@latinmail.com). Uros Islands trips cost about $6 (£3) per person; full-day Uros Floating Reed Islands/Taquile Island trips are $10 (£5) per person; 2-day, 1-night Uros, Amantani, and Taquile islands trips are $15 to $25 (£7.50–£12) per person; and 3-hour Sillustani tours are $5 to $7 (£2.50–£3.50) per person.

WHERE TO STAY

Puno has grown rapidly as a tourist destination in the past few years, and its accommodations are no longer geared almost exclusively toward the backpacker crowd. A couple of good midrange options are in town, but if you don't mind relying on taxis to get back and forth, the best options are out on the banks of Lake Titicaca (about a 10-minute cab ride).

EXPENSIVE

Hotel Libertador Lake Titicaca ★ Ensconced in splendid isolation on the shore of a small island 5km (3 miles) from Puno, overlooking the expanse of Lake Titicaca, this hotel, built in the late 1970s, takes full advantage of its privileged—or inconvenient, depending on your perspective—location. Part of the higher end Libertador chain, the hotel's rooms are spacious if a little bland, and about half have panoramic views of the lake. Those views, though, are spectacular. Service is excellent, and the large white-block hotel has soaring ceilings, but it doesn't have as much character as the better-value Sonesta Posada del Inca (see below), which has views that are almost as good. The hotel is linked to the mainland by a causeway, and the only way back and forth to Puno is by taxi (about $3/£1.50 each way).

Isla Esteves s/n, Lake Titicaca. ✆ 054/367-780. Fax 054/367-879. www.libertador.com.pe. 123 units. $170–$195 (£85–£98) deluxe double; $220–$260 (£110–£130) suite. Rates include breakfast buffet. AE, DC, MC, V. **Amenities:** Restaurant; bar; fitness center; sauna; concierge; room service; laundry service. *In room:* A/C, TV, minibar, hair dryer, safe.

Sonesta Posada del Inca ★★ *Kids Value* Like the Libertador, Posada del Inca is perched on the shores of Titicaca, but it fits more sensitively into its enviable surroundings. Opened in 1999, it is imaginatively designed, with warm colors and Peruvian touches, including bright modern art and folk artifacts. Rooms are large and comfortable, and bathrooms are also large and nicely equipped. The restaurant and many rooms look over the lake; other rooms have views of the mountains. The relaxed lobby has a cozy fireplace. Service is friendly, and the staff can arrange visits to Titicaca's islands. Children will enjoy the miniversion of a floating lake community on the grounds by the lake.

Sesquicentenario 610, Sector Huaje, Lake Titicaca. ✆ 051/364-111. Fax 051/363-672. www.sonesta.com. 62 units. $125 (£66) double. Children under 8 stay free in parent's room. Rates include breakfast buffet. AE, DC, MC, V. **Amenities:** Restaurant; cocktail lounge; concierge; business center; room service; laundry service. *In room:* A/C, TV, minibar, hair dryer, safe.

MODERATE

Casa Andina Classic Tikarani (★) (Value)   This Peruvian chain of popular and comfortable midsize hotels, with good service and impeccable rooms, has two locations in downtown Puno; this branch, 5 blocks from the Plaza de Armas, is the larger and quieter of the two. (The other, Casa Andina Puno Plaza, on Jr. Grau 270, is just a short block from the square and one off the main pedestrian drag.) As always, the rooms are good-sized, extremely clean, and well-equipped. Those on the second floor in the interior are quietest. Casa Andina recently added one of their signature upscale hotels, Private Collection Puno, on the banks of Lake Titicaca; it has marvelous lake views and is a relatively good value, at $120 (£60) double.

Jr. Independencia 185. ✆ **051/367-803.** Fax 051/365-333. www.casa-andina.com. 53 units. $65 (£32) double. Rates include breakfast buffet. AE, DC, MC, V. **Amenities:** Concierge; laundry service. *In room:* A/C, TV, minibar, hair dryer, safe.

Hotel Colón Inn (Value)   A small and charming Belgian-owned hotel (but affiliated with Best Western) in the heart of busy Puno, the Colón inhabits a 19th-century republican-era building on a corner. Built around an airy, sky-lit, colonial-style lobby, it has three floors of good-size and comfortably appointed rooms with marble bathrooms and desks. The cozy, top-floor pub is advertised for its panoramic views, but in reality, all you see are the tops of concrete buildings. The two restaurants, Sol Naciente and Pizzeria Europa, are a couple of the better places in Puno for lunch or dinner.

Calle Tacna 290, Puno. ✆/fax **051/351-432.** www.titicaca-peru.com. 21 units. $60 (£30) double. Rate includes taxes and breakfast buffet. AE, DC, MC, V. **Amenities:** 2 restaurants; bar; room service; laundry service. *In room:* TV, minibar, safe.

INEXPENSIVE

Hostal Los Uros   One of the most popular Puno hostels targeting backpackers, Los Uros represents a good value at the low end. The basic rooms are clean, beds are pretty decent, the place is quiet, and if you get chilly, the staff will dole out extra wool blankets. Rooms have either private or shared bathrooms. Your best bet for hot water is in the evening. Breakfast is available at the simple cafeteria.

Jr. Teodoro Valcarcel 135, Puno. ✆ **051/352-141.** Fax 051/367-016. www.losuros.com. 24 units. $15 (£7.50) double with private bathroom; $10 (£5) with shared bathroom. Rates include taxes. No credit cards. **Amenities:** Cafeteria. *In room:* No phone.

WHERE TO DINE

Most of Puno's more attractive restaurants, popular with gringos, are located on the pedestrian-only main drag, Jirón Lima. In addition to those listed below, check out the two restaurants at Hotel Colón Inn (see above).

MODERATE

Apu Salkantay PERUVIAN/INTERNATIONAL   In a new, chic location on the same street, this restaurant, named for a Quechua mountain god, attracts plenty of people for drinks next to the fireplace-stove. But it's also a good place for Peruvian dishes, such as *cuy,* alpaca steak with *quinoa* rice, and alpaca *piqueo* with fries, onions, tomatoes, and peppers; and standard soups, pizza, pasta, and basic fish (king fish and trout). The daily *menú* includes a soft drink, bread, and main course.

Jr. Lima 425. ✆ **051/363-955.** Reservations not accepted. Main courses S/18–S/25 ($6–$8/£3–£4); daily *menú* S/24 ($8/£4). DC, MC, V. Daily 9am–10pm.

Incabar (★) NEW PERUVIAN/INTERNATIONAL   Awfully stylish and downright funky for rough-around-the-edges Puno, this lounge bar/restaurant aims high. The menu is much more creative and flavorful than other places in town (even if dishes don't always succeed), with interesting sauces for lake fish and alpaca steak, curried dishes, and artful presentations. For a recent meal, I had a spinach-and-tomato-cream soup and *atravezados de pollo*—chicken rolls marinated in sesame, ginger, and garlic and served with pineapple, peppers, and rice. Incabar is also a good place to hang out, have a beer or coffee, and write postcards—the back room has comfortable sofas. Breakfast is also served (S/10/$3.35/£1.70). Also check out the owners' new restaurant down the street, Colors Lounge, Lima 342.

Jr. Lima 356. ℭ 051/368-865. Reservations recommended. Main courses S/18–S/28 ($6–$9/£3–£4.50). AE, DC, MC, V. Daily 9am–10pm.

La Casona ✦ PERUVIAN/INTERNATIONAL   Puno's most distinguished restaurant calls itself a "museum-restaurant." In a town such as Puno, with relatively few attractions, that's fair enough. La Casona ("big house") has traditional, rather old-style Spanish charm, with lace tablecloths. The three dining rooms are filled with antiques and large religious canvases, but it retains a decidedly informal appeal. Its specialty is Lake Titicaca fish, such as trout and king fish *(pejerrey)*, served La Casona style, with an everything-but-the-kitchen-sink preparation of rice, avocado, ham, cheese, hot dog, french fries, and mushrooms. Chicken and beef are prepared the same way. If that's a little overwhelming for you, go with the simple trout served with mashed potatoes. In the evening, make a point about asking for the *menú del día,* the fixed-price meal that is offered and is a great deal (essentially half-price) but not advertised. Service can be a little slow, but there's not much to do in Puno anyway.

Jr. Lima 517. ℭ 051/351-108. Reservations recommended. Main courses S/15–S/36 ($5–$12/£2.50–£6); *menú* S/18 ($6/£3). DC, MC, V. Daily 9am–10pm.

INEXPENSIVE
Pizzería El Buho *(Value* PIZZA/ITALIAN   El Buho's new location is bigger and a bit less cozy, but its wood-burning oven/chimney still kicks out some of Puno's best pizzas. It's extremely popular with both gringos and locals. The menu also lists a good number of pastas and handful of soups, but I swear I've never seen anyone have anything other than pizza.

Jr. Lima 371. ℭ 051/363-955. Reservations not accepted. Main courses S/9–S/25 ($3–$8/£1.50–£4). DC, V. Daily 4:30–11pm.

9 Arequipa

1,020km (632 miles) SE of Lima; 521km (323 miles) S of Cusco; 297km (184 miles) SW of Puno

The southern city of Arequipa, the second-largest in Peru, may well be the country's most handsome. Founded in 1540, it retains an elegant historic center constructed almost entirely of *sillar* (a porous, white volcanic stone), which gives the city its distinctive look and nickname *la ciudad blanca,* or the white city. Colonial churches and the sumptuous 16th-century Santa Catalina convent gleam beneath palm trees and a brilliant sun. Ringing the city, in full view, are three delightfully named snowcapped volcanic peaks: El Misti, Chachani, and Pichu Pichu, all of which hover around 6,000m (20,000 ft.).

Arequipa has emerged as a favorite of outdoors enthusiasts who come to climb volcanoes, raft on rivers, trek through the valleys, and above all, head out to Colca Canyon—twice as deep as the Grand Canyon and the best place in South America to see giant condors soar overhead. Suiting its reputation as an outdoor paradise, Arequipa enjoys weather that is Southern California perfect: more than 300 days a year of sunshine, huge blue skies, and low humidity. Arequipa looks very much the part of a desert oasis.

The commercial capital of the south, Arequipa not only looks different, but it also feels dissimilar from the rest of Peru. Arequipeños have earned a reputation as aloof and distrusting of the centralized power in Lima. Relatively wealthy and a place of prominent intellectuals, politicians, and industrialists, Arequipa has a haughty air about it—at least to many Peruvians who hail from less distinguished places.

As beautiful and confident as it is, Arequipa has not escaped disaster. A devastating earthquake (which registered 8.1 on the Richter scale) struck the city and other points farther south in June 2001. Though international reports at the time painted a picture of a city that had caved in on itself, thankfully, that wasn't the case. Poorly constructed housing in some residential districts was destroyed, but the colonial core of the city survived intact. The major damaged structure, the cathedral on the Plaza de Armas, is still undergoing repair, its asymmetry of towers no doubt a serious aesthetic offense in this stately city.

ESSENTIALS
GETTING THERE
BY PLANE **Aeropuerto Rodríquez Ballón** (© 054/443-464 or 054/443-458), Av. Aviación s/n, Zamácola, Cerro Colorado, is about 7km (4 miles) northwest of the city. There are daily flights to and from Lima, Juliaca, and Cusco on **LAN Peru** (© 01/213-8200; www.lan.com) and **Star Peru** (© 01/705-9000; www.starperu.com).

From the airport, transportation is by taxi (about $5/£2.50) or shared *colectivo* service (about $2/£1 per person) to downtown hotels.

BY BUS The main **Terminal Terrestre** (© 054/427-798), Avenida Andrés Avelino Cáceres, at Av. Arturo Ibáñez s/n, is about 4km (2½ miles) south of downtown Arequipa; nearby is a newer station, **Nuevo Terrapuerto** (© 054/348-810), Av. Arturo Ibáñez s/n. Both stations are on Avenida Andrés Cáceres (Parque Industrial). A huge number of bus companies travel in and out of Peru's second city from across the country, and you'll need to ask if leaving Arequipa by bus whether it departs from Terminal or Terrapuerto. From Lima (16 hr.), recommended companies include **Ormeño** (© 01/472-1710), **Cruz del Sur** (© 01/428-2570), **Civa** (© 01/428-5649), and **Oltursa** (© 01/476-9724 or 054/426-566); from Puno and Juliaca (5 hr.), **Civa** (© 054/426-563), **Cruz del Sur** (© 054/216-625), and **Julsa** (© 054/430-843 or 054/331-952); from Cusco (10–12 hr.), **Cruz del Sur** (© 054/221-909); and from Chivay/Colca Canyon (3–4 hr.), **Reyna** (© 054/426-549), and **Cristo Rey** (© 054/213-094).

A Note of Caution
Arequipa's bus and rail stations—as well as the buses and trains themselves—are said to be notorious for attracting thieves (though I've never encountered any difficulties). Travelers are advised to pay very close attention to their belongings, even going so far as to lock them to luggage racks. The route between Arequipa and Puno especially has earned a bad reputation. It's best to opt for more exclusive and safer, as well as more expensive, first-class seats on the more upscale bus companies recommended above.

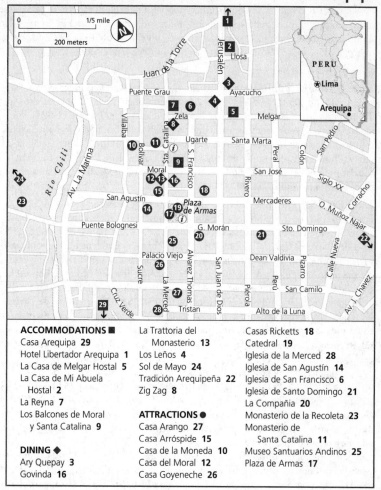

Arequipa

ACCOMMODATIONS ■
Casa Arequipa **29**
Hotel Libertador Arequipa **1**
La Casa de Melgar Hostal **5**
La Casa de Mi Abuela
  Hostal **2**
La Reyna **7**
Los Balcones de Moral
  y Santa Catalina **9**

DINING ◆
Ary Quepay **3**
Govinda **16**

La Trattoria del
  Monasterio **13**
Los Leños **4**
Sol de Mayo **24**
Tradición Arequipeña **22**
Zig Zag **8**

ATTRACTIONS ●
Casa Arango **27**
Casa Arróspide **15**
Casa de la Moneda **10**
Casa del Moral **12**
Casa Goyeneche **26**

Casas Ricketts **18**
Catedral **19**
Iglesia de la Merced **28**
Iglesia de San Agustín **14**
Iglesia de San Francisco **6**
Iglesia de Santo Domingo **21**
La Compañia **20**
Monasterio de la Recoleta **23**
Monasterio de
  Santa Catalina **11**
Museo Santuarios Andinos **25**
Plaza de Armas **17**

BY TRAIN   The Arequipa rail station is at Av. Tacna y Arica 200, 8 blocks south of the city center (© **054/215-640,** or 054/223-600 for reservations), but you're unlikely to use it. Puno-to-Arequipa trains are now available only by private charter for groups; check **www.perurail.com** for the latest information.

GETTING AROUND
Arequipa is compact, and most of its top attractions can easily be seen on foot. Taxis are inexpensive and plentiful, easily hailed on the street, and best used at night. Most trips in town cost no more than S/3 ($1/50p). To call a taxi at night, try **Taxi Seguro** (© **054/450-250**), **Taxi Sur** (© **054/465-656**), **Master Taxi** (© **054/220-505**), or **Ideal Taxi** (© **054/288-888**).

A car isn't necessary in Arequipa unless you wish to explore the countryside, especially Colca and/or Cotahuasi canyons, independently. Try **Lucava Rent-A-Car,** Aeropuerto and Centro Comercial Cayma no. 10 (© **054/663-378**); or **Avis,** Aeropuerto (© **054/443-576**) and Palacio Viejo 214 (© **054/282-519**).

VISITOR INFORMATION

There's a **tourist information booth** at the Aeropuerto Rodríquez Ballón, Calle Moral 316 (© **054/444-564**), open Monday through Friday from 9am to 4pm. There's also an office at Portal de la Municipalidad 112 (© **054/211-021**), on the Plaza de Armas across from the cathedral; it's open daily from 8am to 6pm. The best information office in town is in **Casona de Santa Catalina,** Santa Catalina 210 (across from the Convent; © **054/221-227**); it's open daily from 9am to 9pm. The **tourist police,** Jerusalén 315 at the corner of Ugarte (© **054/201-258**), also give out maps and tourism information.

FAST FACTS You'll find ATMs in the courtyards of the historic Casa Ricketts, San Francisco 108, now the offices of **Banco Continental.** Other banks in the historic center include **Banco Latino** at San Juan de Dios 112 and **Banco de Crédito** at San Juan de Dios and General Morán 101. Money changers can generally be found waving calculators and stacks of dollars on the Plaza de Armas and major streets leading off the main square. There are several *casas de cambio* (money-exchange houses) near the Plaza de Armas, and Global Net ATMs in several shops around the Plaza.

In an emergency, call **Policía Nacional** at © **054/254-020** or **Policía de Turismo,** Jerusalén 315 at the corner of Ugarte, at © **054/201-258.** For medical attention, go to **Clínica Arequipa,** Avenida Bolognesi at Puente Grau (© **054/253-416**), **Hospital Regional,** Av. Daniel Alcides Carrión s/n (© **054/231-818**), or **Hospital General,** Peral/Don Bosco (© **054/231-818**).

Arequipa has plenty of Internet *cabinas.* Two of the cheapest and fastest are **La Red,** Jerusalén 306B (© **054/286-700**), and **TravelNet,** Jerusalén 218 (© **054/205-548**). Another good spot is **Catedral Internet,** Pasaje Catedral 101 (© **054/282-074**), in the small passageway behind the cathedral. Most *cabinas* are open daily from 8am to 10pm, charge S/1.50 (50¢/25p) per hour, and have Net2Phone or other programs allowing very cheap Web-based international phone calls.

The main Serpost **post office** is located at Moral 118 (© **054/215-247**); it's open Monday through Saturday from 8am to 8pm and Sunday from 9am to 1pm. There's a **DHL** office at Santa Catalina 115 (© **054/220-045**). The **Telefónica del Perú** main offices are located at Av. Los Arces 200 B, Cayma district (© **054/252-020**).

WHAT TO SEE & DO
THE TOP ATTRACTIONS

Casa del Moral ⨊ An extraordinary mestizo-baroque mansion, built in 1733 by a Spanish knight and nicely restored with period detail in 1994, Casa del Moral offers one of the best windows onto colonial times in Arequipa. Named for an ancient mulberry tree—the *moral* found in the courtyard—the home is also distinguished by a magnificent stone portal with heraldic emblems carved in *sillar.* Handsome furnishings, carved wooden doors, and Cusco School oil paintings decorate large salons, built around a beautiful courtyard in the largest of the colonial residences in the city. Look for 17th-century maps that depict the borders and shapes of countries quite differently from their usual representations today. A second courtyard, painted cobalt blue, was used as the summer patio. Climb to the rooftop for a great view of Arequipa and the surrounding volcanoes. Visits are by guided tour (at no extra cost).

Calle Moral 318 (at Bolívar). © **054/210-084.** Admission S/5 ($1.65/85p) adults, S/3 ($1/50p) students. Mon–Sat 9am–5pm; Sun 9am–1pm.

Monasterio de la Recoleta ⟨𝔽⟩   Across the Río Chili from the historic center of town, distinguished by its tall brick red-and-white steeple, is the Recoleta convent museum. It's only a 10-minute walk or short cab ride from the Plaza de Armas. Founded in 1648 and rebuilt after earthquakes, the peaceful Franciscan convent contains impressive cloisters with *sillar* columns and lovely gardens; today, just four of the original seven remain. The convent museum comprises several collections. In one room is a collection of pre-Inca culture artifacts, including funereal masks, textiles, and totems; in another are mummies and a series of paintings of the 12 Inca chieftains. At the rear of the convent is a small Amazonian museum, stocked with curious items collected by Franciscan missionaries in the Amazon basin. The missionaries were understandably fascinated by prehistoric-looking fish, crocodiles, and piranhas, and the clothing of indigenous communities. Those souvenirs pose an interesting contrast to the Dominicans' fine library containing some 20,000 volumes, including rare published texts from the 15th century. Guides (tip basis) are available for 1-hour tours in English, Spanish, and French.

Recoleta 117. © **054/270-966.** Admission adults S/5 ($1.65/85p), students S/3 ($1/50p), free for seniors. Mon–Sat 9am–noon and 3–5pm.

Monasterio de Santa Catalina ⟨𝔽𝔽𝔽⟩ ⟨Kids⟩   Arequipa's stellar and serene Convent of Santa Catalina, founded in 1579 under the Dominican order, is the most important and impressive religious monument in Peru. This is not just another church complex; it is more like a small, labyrinthine village, with narrow cobblestone streets, plant-lined passageways, pretty plazas and fountains, chapels, and cloisters. Tall, thick walls, painted sunburned orange, cobalt blue, and brick red, hide dozens of small cells where more than 200 sequestered nuns once lived. Built in 1569, the convent remained a mysterious world unto itself until 1970, when local authorities forced the sisters to install modern infrastructure, a requirement that led to opening the convent for tourism. Today, only a couple of dozen cloistered nuns remain, out of sight of the hundreds of tourists who arrive daily to explore the huge and curious complex.

Santa Catalina feels like a small village in Andalucía, Spain, with its predominantly *mudéjar* (Moorish-Christian) architecture, intense sunlight and shadows, and streets named for Spanish cities. In all, it contains 3 cloisters, 6 streets, 80 housing units, a square, an art gallery, and a cemetery. Though the nuns entered the convent having taken vows of poverty, they lived in relative luxury, having paid a dowry to live the monastic life amid servants (who outnumbered the nuns), well-equipped kitchens, and art collections. Today, the convent has been nicely restored, though it retains a rustic appeal. Visitors are advised to wait for an informative guided tour (in English and other languages, available for a tip), though it's also transfixing just to wander around, especially before the crowds arrive. Of particular note are the Orange Tree Cloister, with mural paintings over the arches; Calle Toledo, a long boulevard with a communal *lavandería* at its end, where the sisters washed their clothes in halved earthenware jugs; the 17th-century kitchen with charred walls; and the rooms belonging to Sor Ana, a 17th-century nun at the convent who was beatified by Pope John Paul II and is on her way to becoming a saint. Visitors can enter the choir room of the church, but it's difficult to get a good look at the main chapel and its marvelous painted cupola. To see the church, slip in during early morning mass (daily at 7:30am); the cloistered nuns remain secluded behind a wooden grille. Allow a couple of hours or more here.

Santa Catalina 301. (©) **054/229-798.** www.santacatalina.org.pe. Admission S/25 ($8/£4). Daily 9am–4pm.

Museo Santuarios Andinos (*Kids*) Now in a new location south of the Plaza de Armas, the Museum of Andean Sanctuaries features a small collection of fascinating exhibits, including mummies and artifacts from the Inca Empire, but it is dominated by one tiny girl: Juanita, the Ice Maiden of Ampato. The victim of a ritualistic sacrifice by Inca priests high on the volcano Mount Ampato and buried in ice at 6,380m (20,926 ft.), "Juanita"—named after the leader of the expedition, Johan Rhinehard—was discovered in almost perfect condition in September 1995 after the eruption of the nearby Sabancay Volcano melted ice on the peak. Juanita had lain buried in the snow for more than 550 years. Only Inca priests were allowed to ascend to such a high point, where the gods were believed to have lived. Juanita, who became famous worldwide through a *National Geographic* report on the find, died from a violent blow to the head; she was 13 at the time of her death. Her remarkable preservation has allowed researchers to gain great insights into Inca culture by analyzing her DNA. Today, she is kept in a glass-walled freezer chamber here, less a mummy than a frozen body, in astoundingly good condition, nearly 600 years old. Displayed nearby and in adjacent rooms are some of the superb doll offerings and burial items found alongside Juanita's corpse and those of three other sacrificial victims also found on the mountain. Guided visits, which begin with a good *National Geographic* film, are mandatory. Allow about an hour for your visit.

La Merced 110. (©) **054/200-345.** Admission S/15 ($5/£2.50) adults, S/5 ($1.65/83p) students, free for seniors. Mon–Sat 9am–6pm; Sun 9am–3pm.

Plaza de Armas (🕏🕏) Arequipa's grand Plaza de Armas, an elegant and symmetrical square of gardens and a central fountain lined by arcaded buildings on three sides, is the focus of the city's urban life. Dominated by the massive, 17th-century neoclassical **Catedral** (🕏), it is perhaps the loveliest main square in Peru, even though its profile suffered considerable damage when the great earthquake of 2001 felled one of the cathedral's two towers and whittled the other to a delicate pedestal. The cathedral, previously devastated by fire and other earthquakes, has now been fully restored to its original grandeur. The cathedral is open Monday to Saturday from 7 to 11:30am and 5 to 7:30pm, Sunday from 7am to 1pm and 5 to 7pm.

La Compañía (🕏🕏), just off the plaza at the corner of Álvarez Thomas and General Morán, opposite the cathedral, is a splendid 17th-century Jesuit church with an elaborate (plateresque) facade carved of *sillar* stone. The magnificent portal, one of the finest in Peru, shows the end date of the church's construction, 1698, more than a century after work began on it. The interior holds a handsome carved cedar main altar, bathed in gold leaf, and two impressive chapels: the Capilla de San Ignacio, which has a remarkable painted cupola, and the Capilla Real, or Royal Chapel. Next door to the church are the stately Jesuit cloisters, of stark *sillar* construction, now housing upscale boutiques (enter on Calle Morán). Climb to the top for good views of the city's rooftops and distant volcanoes. The church is open Monday through Saturday from 9 to 11am and 3 to 6pm.

Tips **Arequipa's Colonial Churches**

Arequipa has a wealth of colonial churches that are well worth a visit if you have the time. They include **Iglesia de San Francisco** (Zela 103), built of *sillar* and brick in the 16th century with an impressive all-silver altar and a beautiful vaulted ceiling; **Iglesia de San Agustín** (at the corner of San Agustín and Sucre), with a superbly stylized baroque facade, an excellent example of 16th- and 17th-century mestizo architecture (it was rebuilt in 1898 after earthquake damage and was restored, with an unfortunate new bell tower, again in October 2005); **Iglesia de Santo Domingo** (at Santo Domingo and Piérola), with a handsome 1734 cloisters, and **Iglesia de La Merced** (La Merced 303).

SHOPPING

Arequipa is one of the best places in Peru to shop for top-quality baby alpaca, vicuña, and woolen goods. Many items are more expensive than the lesser-quality goods sold in other parts of Peru. In Arequipa, though, you'll find nicer designs and export-quality knit sweaters, shawls, blankets, and scarves. Arequipa also has good leather goods and several excellent antiques shops featuring colonial pieces and even older items (remember, though, that these antiques cannot legally be exported from Peru).

Three general areas are particularly good for alpaca items. One is the cloisters next to La Compañía church at General Morán and San Juan de Dios, housing several alpaca boutiques and outlets. Another is Pasaje Catedral, the pedestrian mall just behind the cathedral. A third is Calle Santa Catalina. Shops with fine alpaca items include **Millma's Baby Alpaca,** Pasaje Catedral 177 (© **054/205-134**); **Baby Alpaca Boutique,** Santa Catalina 208 (© **054/206-716**); **Anselmo's Souvenirs,** Pasaje Catedral 119 (no phone); and an outlet store of the chain **Alpaca 111,** Calle Zela 212 (© **054/223-238**).

For antiques, Calle Santa Catalina and nearby streets have several antiques shops. I found lots of items I wished I could have taken home at **Curiosidades,** Zela 207 (© **054/952-986**); **Alvaro Valdivia Montoya**'s two shops at Santa Catalina 204 and Santa Catalina 217 (© **054/229-103**); and **Arte Colonial,** Santa Catalina 312 (© **054/214-887**).

There is a general handicrafts market with dozens of stalls in the old town jail, next door to the Plazuela de San Francisco (between Zela and Puente Grau). For handmade leather goods, stroll along Puente Bolognesi, which leads west from the Plaza de Armas, and you'll find numerous small stores with handbags, shoes, and other items.

A very good bookstore with art books and English-language paperbacks is **Librería El Lector,** San Francisco 221 (© **054/288-677**).

WHERE TO STAY

Arequipa has an ample roster of hotels and hostels at all levels. Several occupy historic houses in the old quarter. The area north of the Plaza de Armas is nicer and less chaotic and commercial than the streets south of the square. If you hop in a taxi from the airport or bus or train station, insist on going to the hotel of your choice; taxi drivers will often claim that a particular hotel is closed in order to take you to one that will pay them a commission.

House Tour: Arequipa's Other Colonial Mansions

Arequipa possesses one of the most attractive and harmonious colonial nuclei in Peru. Several extraordinary seigniorial houses were constructed in white *sillar* stone. They are predominantly flat-roofed single-story structures, a design that has helped them withstand the effects of frequent earthquakes that would have toppled less solid buildings. Most of these houses have attractive interior patios and elaborately carved facades. Best equipped for visitors is the restored **Casa del Moral** (see above), but several others are worth a look, especially if you have an interest in colonial architecture.

Just off the main square, **Casa Ricketts** (also called **Casa Tristán del Pozo**; San Francisco 108), a former seminary and today the offices of Banco Continental, is one of the finest colonial homes in Arequipa. Built in the 1730s, its beautiful portal, perhaps Arequipa's finest expression of colonial civil architecture, has delicate representations of the life of Jesus. Inside are two large, beautiful courtyards with gargoyle drainage pipes. On the other side of the cathedral, **Casa Arróspide** (also called **Casa Iriberry**; at the corner of Santa Catalina 101 at San Agustín), built in the late 18th century, is one of the most distinguished *sillar* mansions in the city. Now the **Cultural Center of San Agustín University** (© 054/204-482), it hosts temporary exhibits of contemporary art and photography; you'll also find an art shop and nice cafe with a terrace and great views over the top of the cathedral. Other colonial houses of interest include **Casa Arango** (Consuelo at La Merced), a squat and eclectic 17th-century home; **Casa Goyeneche** (La Merced 201), now the offices of Banco de Reserva; and **Casa de la Moneda** (Ugarte at Villaba).

About a 15-minute cab ride outside of town, in Huasacache, is the **Mansión del Fundador** (© 054/442-460), one of the most important *sillar* mansions in Arequipa. Said to have been constructed by the founder of Arequipa, Manuel de Carbajal, for his son, it features terrific vaulted ceilings and a large interior patio. The house is open daily from 9am to 5pm; admission is S/10 ($3.35/£1.70).

EXPENSIVE

Hotel Libertador Arequipa ⚘ (Kids)   Arequipa's swankest hotel near the historic center is in this handsome 1940s colonial-style building. In the midst of quiet Selva Alegre, the largest park in Arequipa, the midsize hotel is about a 15-minute walk from the main square. It maintains a colonial theme throughout, with soaring ceilings, historical murals, and dark-wood period furnishings in expansive, elegantly appointed rooms. The rooms, equipped with marble bathrooms, are about as large as you're likely to find. The hotel has a lovely outdoor pool (unheated) among nice gardens and tall palm trees. Families will appreciate the outdoor recreation and game area for children.

Plaza Bolívar, Selva Alegre, Arequipa. © 054/215-110. Fax 054/241-933. www.libertador.com.pe. 88 units. $125–$148 (£63–£74) deluxe double; $185 (£93) suite. Rates include taxes. AE, DC, MC, V. **Amenities:** 2 restaurants; bar; large outdoor pool; fitness center; Jacuzzi; sauna; concierge; room service; laundry service. *In room:* A/C, TV, minibar, safe.

MODERATE

Casa Arequipa ★★★ *Value*   This outstanding inn, akin to a European boutique hotel—something very unusual for Peru—is one of the most luxurious places to stay in the country and boasts bargain prices. In a beautifully restored, pink 1950s mansion in the quiet Vallecito residential district, just a short walk or cab ride from the Plaza de Armas, the inn features elegantly designed guest rooms, with nicely chosen antiques, comfortable beds, and the finest towels and bed linens you'll find in Peru. Photographs of the Andes, taken by the owner (who splits his time between Arequipa and Washington, D.C.), decorate the rooms, and fresh flowers are placed in every room and throughout the house. The excellent bathrooms, several of which have tubs, are of gleaming marble. The breakfast buffet and personal attention are worthy of a five-star hotel.

Av. Lima, Vallecito, Arequipa. © 054/284-219, or 202/332-1942 for reservations in U.S. Fax 054/253-343. www. arequipacasa.com. 88 units. $55–$75 (£28–£38) double. Rates include taxes. AE, DC, MC, V. **Amenities:** Concierge; CD library. *In room:* A/C, TV, CD player.

La Casa de Melgar Hostal ★★ *Value*   A spectacular colonial house made of white *sillar* (volcanic stone), this charming small hotel is one of the nicest and most relaxed in Peru, as well as one of the best values. Just 3 blocks from the Plaza de Armas, the lovingly restored 18th-century mansion—the former residence of the bishop of Arequipa—has massive, thick walls, and three interior courtyards. The decor echoes the rich, brick-red and royal-blue tones of the Santa Catalina Monastery, making it the perfect place to stay if you're a fan of colonial architecture. The ample rooms have good beds. Some rooms—especially those on the ground floor that have high vaulted brick ceilings—exude colonial character; if the hotel isn't full, ask to see these. A new wing of rooms, also in a colonial building, behind a garden and terrace are lovely; some have incredibly high ceilings. The staff is very friendly. Breakfast is served in the little cafe next door in one of the courtyards. Advance reservations are a must in high season, as the inn is justifiably popular.

Melgar 108, Cercado, Arequipa. ©/fax 054/222-459, or 01/446-8343 for reservations. www.lacasademelgar.com. 30 units. $40 (£20) double. Rates include taxes and breakfast. V. **Amenities:** Restaurant/bar; laundry service. *In room:* No phone.

La Casa de Mi Abuela Hostal ★   One of the friendliest and best-run small hotels in Peru, My Grandmother's House is tucked behind a security gate but welcomes everyone with open arms and an easygoing atmosphere. An organic place that has grown from a tiny B&B into a very popular 50-room hotel, it is still family-run. Today, it's a self-contained tourism complex, with a restaurant, live-music *peña* bar, Internet access, book exchange, travel agency, and beautiful gardens with views of El Misti. Some rooms have roof terraces, others balconies. Many rooms are plainly decorated and cramped, but the hostel is still a very good deal given the level of services, facilities, and security. The hostel is about a 10-minute walk (6 blocks) north of the main square. It's often filled, so make advance reservations. They serve nice breakfasts in the garden (extra charge).

Jerusalén 606, Cercado, Arequipa. © 054/241-206. Fax 054/242-761. www.lacasademiabuela.com. 50 units. $44 (£22) double. Rate includes taxes. DC, MC, V. **Amenities:** Restaurant; bar; pool; game room; laundry service. *In room:* TV, minibar, safe.

INEXPENSIVE

La Reyna *Value*   A popular backpacker inn, La Reyna is smack in the middle of the historic center, just a block from the famed Santa Catalina monastery and paces away from plenty of bars and restaurants. The hostel's many rooms feed off a labyrinth of narrow staircases that climb up three floors to a roof terrace, a popular spot to hang out. There are simple, rock-bottom dormitory rooms for zero-budget travelers and a couple of rooftop *casitas* that have private bathrooms and their own terraces with awesome views of the mountains and the monastery below—something akin to backpacker penthouse suites. Room no. 20 is worth reserving if you can. The hostel, though a little haphazardly run, organizes lots of canyon treks and volcano climbing tours, and even offers Spanish classes.

Zela 209, Arequipa. ©/fax **054/286-578**. 20 units. $7 (£3.50) double without bathroom, $10 (£5) double with bathroom; $3.50 (£1.75) per person in shared rooms. Rates include taxes. No credit cards. **Amenities:** Laundry service. *In room:* No phone.

Los Balcones de Moral y Santa Catalina ⭐ (Value)   This inviting small hotel is very comfortable and decently furnished, a nice step up from budget hostels for not much more money. In the heart of the old quarter, it's only a couple of blocks from the Plaza de Armas. Half of the house is colonial (first floor); the other is republican, dating from the 1800s. The house is built around a colonial patio with a sunny terrace. Furnishings are modern, with wallpaper and firm beds. Eleven of the good-size rooms have hardwood floors and large balconies with nice views looking toward the back of the cathedral; the other rooms are carpeted and less desirable (though quieter). All have good, tiled bathrooms.

Moral 217, Arequipa. ©/fax **054/201-291**. losbalconeshotel@hotmail.com. 17 units. $27 (£13) double. Rate includes taxes. MC, V. **Amenities:** Restaurant; laundry service. *In room:* TV.

WHERE TO DINE

Arequipa is one of the finest cities in Peru for gastronomic adventures, and at very reasonable prices. Several restaurants in the historic quarter—the two streets leading north from the Plaza de Armas are the main hub of nighttime activity—specialize in traditional Arequipeña cooking, though two of the best are a short taxi ride beyond downtown.

MODERATE

Ary Quepay ⭐ (Value) PERUVIAN/AREQUIPEÑA   A relaxed and friendly, rustic restaurant with a gardenlike dining room under a bamboo roof and skylights, Ary Quepay, a longtime favorite of both locals and in-the-know visitors, specializes in traditional Peruvian cooking. It's less fancy than a couple of the better-known restaurants specializing in Arequipeña cooking in the city. Starters include *choclo con queso* (corn on the cob with cheese) and stuffed avocado. The main dishes are classic: *rocoto relleno* (stuffed peppers), *adobo* (pork stew with *ají*), and *escabeche de pescado* (spicy fish stew). There are a number of dishes for vegetarians, as well as good breakfasts, juices, and milkshakes. In the evenings, there's often live folkloric music.

Jerusalén 502. © **054/672-922**. Main courses S/12–S/27 ($4–$9/£2–£4.50). DC, MC, V. Daily 8am–10pm.

La Trattoria del Monasterio ⭐⭐ (Value) ITALIAN   Cleaved into the outer *sillar* wall of the splendid Santa Catalina monastery, this chic but unassuming Italian restaurant—a new addition to the Arequipa dining scene—is an excellent spot to linger over an intimate dinner. It's considerably quieter than the hopping restaurant row just 1 block over on San Francisco. Spilling into three elegant, small, whitewashed dining rooms, it specializes in Italian favorites like risottos, lasagnas, ravioli, and *osso buco*. For

cognoscenti, it features both long and short pastas. The menu was prepared by the hot chef of the moment in Peru, Gastón Acurio of Astrid & Gastón, La Mar, and other spots in Lima and up and down South America. You'll also find a good selection of wines, great desserts, and fine, attentive service.

Santa Catalina 309. © **054/204-062.** Main courses S/18–S/36 ($6–$12/£3–£6). AE, DC, MC, V. Mon–Sat noon–3pm and 7–11pm; Sunday noon–4pm.

Sol de Mayo ⭒⭒⭒ (Value) PERUVIAN/AREQUIPEÑA   A 5-minute taxi ride from downtown Yanahuara, the city's nicest residential neighborhood, this longtime stalwart (it's been around more than a century) is the standard-bearer for Arequipeña cooking. A favorite of upscale locals and tourists alike, it is perhaps the most delightful of the city's restaurants. The colonial tables are set around the edges of a breezy, picture-perfect courtyard with thick grass, geraniums, cacti, a small pool and cascading waterfall, and strolling Altiplano musicians. There are also dining rooms inside the brick red–and-yellow *sillar* stone building, but nothing beats eating outdoors here. Peruvian specialties such as *chicharrón de chancho* (fried pork), ostrich, and a lineup of *ceviches* are Sol de Mayo's calling card. Starters include a yummy mixed salad of *choclo* (white corn), tomato, and avocado. The pisco sours are a must to start off your meal. Even for budget-oriented backpackers, this is *the* place in Arequipa to splurge.

Jerusalén 207, Yanahuara. © **054/254-148.** Reservations recommended. Main courses S/15–S/42 ($5–$14/£2.50–£7). AE, DC, MC, V. Daily 11am–10pm.

Tradición Arequipeña ⭒⭒ (Value) PERUVIAN/AREQUIPEÑA   It's a few miles outside of town in the Paucarpata district, so you'll need to grab a taxi to get to this classic open-air restaurant. Elegantly set amid beautiful gardens with stunning views of snowcapped El Misti from the upper deck, it's open only for lunch (although you could also squeeze in an early dinner at 5 or 6pm). Most encouraging is how popular it is among tourists and locals alike. It serves large portions of classic Peruvian and Arequipeña dishes, such as *cuy, adobo,* and *ceviche,* but they're more carefully prepared here than in many other *comida típica* restaurants. A good starter is the combination fried cheese and fried yuca with *picante* sauce and *salsa verde* (green sauce). Meals are very affordable for such a refined place.

Av. Dolores 111, Paucarpata. © **054/426-467.** Reservations recommended on weekends. Main courses S/12–S/39 ($4–$13/£2–£6.50). AE, DC, MC, V. Daily noon–7pm.

Zig Zag ⭒⭒ SWISS/GRILLED MEAT   This is one of my favorite restaurants in Arequipa; it's chic enough to appeal to young people on dates and comfortable enough for families and small tourist groups. Zig Zag occupies a cool two-level, *sillar*-walled space with a fantastic, twisting iron staircase, and it recently expanded into the space next door. The house specialty is stone-grilled meats, including ostrich and alpaca. The owners like to educate their customers about these lean meats as a healthy alternative to other meats. Try the ostrich carpaccio in lemon or ostrich stone-grilled with Swiss-style hash browns. Big-time meat eaters should order the *piedra criolla* (stone-grilled *chorizo,* beef, lamb, pork, hearts, intestines, and gizzards with potatoes and chimichurri sauce); it's a bargain for just S/35 ($10/£5). The two-level restaurant plays hip music and has attentive service. A couple of tables upstairs are perched on a ledge overlooking the attractive Plazuela San Francisco.

Zela 210. © **054/206-020.** Reservations recommended. Main courses S/25–S/40 ($8–$13/£4–£6.50). AE, DC, MC, V. Daily 6pm–midnight.

INEXPENSIVE

Govinda VEGETARIAN/INDIAN   A good all-around vegetarian restaurant, Govinda—part of a chain across Peru, with the original in London—has a pleasant outdoor garden dining area and good value dishes. It serves vegetarian Italian, Asian, and Peruvian items, as well as pizza, pasta, soup, salad, and yogurt dishes—a welcome reprieve from many travelers' overdose of chicken, pork, and alpaca in Peru. The daily fixed-price menus are very cheap, though the self-service buffet is not all-you-can-eat and its lineup of vegetarian dishes isn't the most creative you've ever seen. It's a good place for breakfast, with muesli, brown bread, fruit salad, and juice.

Santa Catalina 120. © **054/285-540.** Reservations not accepted. Main courses S/6–S/18 ($2–$6/£1–£3); *menú* S/6–S/15 ($2–$5/£1–£2.50); buffet S/12 ($4/£2). No credit cards. Daily 7am–9:30pm.

Los Leños PIZZERIA   This is a charming cave of a pizza place, where diners share long wooden tables, and the footprints of many hundreds of travelers carry on in the graffiti that covers every square inch of stone walls up to a vaulted ceiling. The house specialty is pizza from the wood-fired oven; among the many varieties, the Leños house pizza is a standout, with cheese, sausage, bacon, ham, chicken, and mushrooms. Those who've had their fill of pizza can go for other standards, such as lasagna and a slew of other pastas. Los Leños opens early; you can choose from among 20 different "American breakfasts."

Jerusalén 407. © **054/289-179.** Reservations not accepted. Main courses S/6–S/15 ($2–$5/£1–£2.50). No credit cards. Daily 7am–11pm.

AREQUIPA AFTER DARK

Arequipa has a pretty hopping nightlife in the old quarter, with plenty of bars, restaurants, and dance clubs catering both to gringos and locals. Sunday through Wednesday is usually pretty quiet, with things heating up on Thursday night. Virtually every bar in town advertises extended happy hours, with drinks going for as little as 3 for S/10 ($3.35/£1.70). Calles San Francisco and Zela are the hot spots.

Las Quenas, Santa Catalina 302 (© **054/281-115**), is a *peña* bar and restaurant featuring live Andean music Monday through Saturday from 9pm to midnight and special dance performances on Friday and Saturday nights. There's a nominal cover charge of S/5 ($1.65/85p). It's a cozy little place that serves pretty good Peruvian dishes. You can also catch *peña* music at **El Tuturutu,** Portal San Agustín 105 (© **054/201-842**), a restaurant on the main square. Another spot for folkloric music is **La Troica,** Jerusalén 522 (© **054/225-690**), a tourist-oriented restaurant in an old house.

As for pubs and bars, **Siwara,** Santa Catalina 210 (© **054/626-218**), is a great-looking beer tavern that spills into two patios in the building of the Santuarios Andinos museum, across from the Santa Catalina monastery. **Farrens Irish Pub,** Pasaje Catedral 107 (© **054/238-465**), which is very popular with visiting gringos, is a cool two-level joint with good drink specials and a rock and pop soundtrack. Another good spot for a drink is **Montreál Le Café Art,** Ugarte 210 (© **054/931-2796**), which features live music Wednesday through Saturday and has happy hours between 5 and 11pm. **La Casa de Klaus,** Zela 207 (© **054/203-711**), is a simple and brightly lit tavern popular with German, British, and local beer drinkers.

For a little more action, check out **Forum Rock Café,** San Francisco 317 (© **054/202-697**), a huge place that is equal parts restaurant, bar, disco, and concert hall. It sports a rainforest theme, with jungle vegetation and "canopy walkways" everywhere. Live bands (usually rock) take the stage Thursday through Saturday. Just down the street, **Déjà Vu,** San Francisco 319 (© **054/221-904**), has a good bar with a mix of locals and gringos, a lively dance floor, and English-language movies on a big screen every night at 8pm. **Kibosh,** Zela 205 (© **054/626-218**), is a chic, upscale pub with four bars, a dance floor, and live music (ranging from Latin to hard rock) Wednesday through Saturday.

AN EXCURSION FROM AREQUIPA: COLCA VALLEY

The primary day trips and overnight excursions from Arequipa are to Valle del Colca, site of Colca Canyon and **Cruz del Cóndor,** a lookout point where giant South American condors soar overhead; and trekking, rafting, and mountaineering expeditions through the valley. Tour agencies have mushroomed in Arequipa, and most offer very similar city, canyon, countryside *(campiña),* and adventure trips. Going with a tour operator is economical and by far the most convenient option—public transportation is poor and very time-consuming in these parts. Only a handful of tour operators in Arequipa are well run, however, and visitors need to be careful when signing up for guided tours to the canyon and valley. Avoid independent guides who don't have official accreditation. Adventure and sports enthusiasts should contact one of the specialist agencies listed later in this chapter. A minimum of 2 or 3 days is needed to see a significant part of the valley.

COLCA CANYON ✸✸✸

Mario Vargas Llosa, novelist and the most famous Arequipeño, described Colca as "The Valley of Wonders." That is no literary overstatement. Colca, located 165km (102 miles) north of Arequipa, is one of the most scenic regions in Peru, a land of imposing snowcapped volcanoes, artistically terraced agricultural slopes, narrow gorges, arid desert landscapes and vegetation, and remote traditional villages, many visibly scarred by seismic tremors common in southern Peru.

The Río Colca, the origin of the mighty Amazon, cuts through the canyon, which remained largely unexplored until the 1970s, when rafting expeditions descended to the bottom of the gorge. Reaching depths of 3,400m (11,152 ft.)—twice as deep as the Grand Canyon—the Cañón del Colca forms part of a volcanic mountain range more than 100km (62 miles) long. Among the great volcanoes, several of which are still active, are Mount Ampato, where a sacrificed Inca maiden was discovered frozen in 1995, and Mount Coropuna, Peru's second-highest peak at 6,425m (21,200 ft.).

Dispersed across the Colca Valley are 14 colonial-era villages that date from the 16th century, distinguished primarily by their small but often richly decorated churches. Local populations, descendants of the Collaguas and Cabanas, pre-Inca ethnic groups, preserve ancient customs and distinctive traditional dress. Ethnic groups can be distinguished by their hats; some women wear hats with colored ribbons; others have elaborately embroidered and sequined headgear. The valley's meticulous agricultural terracing, even more extensive than the terraces of the Sacred Valley, were first cultivated more than 1,000 years ago. Colca villages are celebrated for their vibrant festivals, as authentic as any in Peru, throughout the year.

Most organized tours of the region are very similar if not identical. The road that leads out of Arequipa and into the valley, bending around the Misti and Chachani volcanoes, is poor, long and unbearably dusty. It passes through the **Salinas and Aguada Blanca Nature Reserve,** where you'll usually have a chance to see vicuñas, llamas, and alpacas grazing from the road. The Altiplano landscape, especially outside the rainy season, is barren and bleak. Most tours stop at volcano and valley lookout points along the way before arriving in Chivay.

The gateway to the region is **Chivay,** the Colca's main town on the edge of the canyon, a little more than 3 hours from Arequipa. This easygoing market town lies at an altitude of 3,600m (11,520 ft.). From here, many organized tours embark on short treks in the valley and visit the wonderfully relaxing hot springs of **La Calera,** about 4km (2½ miles) from Chivay. Evening visits to the hot springs allow visitors to bathe in open-air pools beneath a huge, starry sky; artificial light in the valley is almost non-existent. Charming colonial villages in the valley often visited by tours include Yanque, Coporaque, Maca, and Lari.

Most 2-day tours head out early the following morning for **Cruz del Cóndor,** a lookout point that has become famous throughout Peru; most mornings, it overflows with hundreds of binocular- and camera-toting tourists hoping to get close-up views of the mighty Andean condors. Beginning around 9am, Andean condors—the largest birds in the world, with wingspans of 3.5m (12 ft.)—begin to appear, circling far below in the gorge and gradually gaining altitude with each pass, until they soar silently above the heads of awestruck admirers. Condors are such immense creatures that they cannot lift off from the ground; instead, they take flight from cliff perches. Each morning, the condors glide and climb theatrically before heading out along the river in search of prey. To witness the condors' majestic flight up close is a mesmerizing sight, capable of producing goose bumps in even the most jaded travelers. The condors return late in the afternoon, but fewer people attend the show then.

GETTING THERE   The great majority of travelers to the Colca Valley visit on guided tours, arranged in Arequipa. Conventional travel agencies offer day trips to Cruz del Cóndor, leaving at 3 or 4am, with brief stops at Chivay before returning to Arequipa (about $20/£10 per person)—it's an awful lot to pack into a single day, especially at high altitude. Two-day "pool" (group) tours ($30–$55/£15–£27), with an overnight stay at a hotel—at a choice of backpacker inns and rustic upscale lodges—are much more enjoyable. Private tours to the valley, in chauffer-driven cars with guides, cost $150–$350 (£75–£175) per person. The best all-purpose agencies in Arequipa are **Giardino Tours,** Calle Jerusalén 604-A (© 054/241-206); **Santa Catalina Tours,** Santa Catalina 219 (© 054/216-994); **Colonial Tours,** Santa Catalina 106 (© 054/286-868); and **Illary Tours,** Santa Catalina 205 (© 054/220-844).

The best hotels in Colca Valley are, at the upper end, **Parador del Colca** ★★★ (© 01/242-3425; colca@peruorientexpress.com.pe), an Orient-Express hotel, and **Colca Lodge** (© 054/531-191; www.colca-lodge.com), which has its own thermal bath pools; and at the midrange **Casa Andina Colca** (© 054/531-020; www.casa-andina.com), which has a cool planetarium on-site, and **La Casa de Mamayacchi** (© 054/241-206), owned by Giardino Tours. The inns offered by tour operators at backpacker rates tend to be in the town of Chivay and are very basic, but acceptable. A special note about the new **Inkari Eco Lodge** (© 054/284-292), owned by Santa Catalina Tours: though tacky, it's comfortable and has bargain rates.

Local buses travel from Arequipa to Cabanaconde, near the Cruz del Cóndor, with stops in Chivay. **Reyna,** Terminal Terrestre (© 054/426-549), and **Cristo Rey,** San Juan de Dios 510 (© 054/213-094), make these runs.

OUTDOOR ADVENTURES IN COLCA VALLEY
The countryside around Arequipa is some of the best in Peru for outdoor adventure travel. Trails crisscross the Colca Valley, crossing mountain ridges, agricultural terraces,

and curious rock formations, and passing colonial towns and fields where llamas and vicuñas graze. The most common pursuits are river running, treks through the canyon valleys, and mountain climbing on the volcanoes just beyond the city. Many tour agencies in Arequipa offer 2- and 3-day visits to the Colca and Cotahuasi canyons, as well as longer, more strenuous treks through the valleys. (Some of the most interesting, but most time-consuming and difficult, expeditions combine rafting and trekking.) Your best bet for organizing any of these activities is with one of the tour operators below; several in Arequipa focus solely on eco- and adventure tourism.

Cusipata Viajes y Turismo, Jerusalén 408-A (© 054/203-966), is the local specialist for Chili and Colca rafting and kayaking (including courses), and its guides frequently subcontract out to other agencies in Arequipa. **Ideal Tours** (© 054/244-433) handles Chili and Majes rafting, as well as Colca and other standard tours. **Apumayo Expediciones,** Garcilaso 265 Int. 3, Cusco (© 084/246-018; www.cuscoperu.com/apumayo), is good for long trekking/rafting expeditions to Cotahuasi and Colca, as is **Amazonas Explorer,** Zela 212 (© 054/212-813; www.amazonas-explorer.com), an international company that organizes hardy multisport trips to Cotahuasi and Colca (which can be combined with tours to Cusco, the Inca Trail, and Machu Picchu). **Apu Expediciones,** Portal Comercio 157, Cusco (© 084/652-975), arranges rafting trips to Majes and Colca, among other adventure options.

Colca Trek, Jerusalén 401-B (© 054/224-578), and **Peru Trekking,** Jerusalén 302-B (© 054/223-404), are two other local outfits that offer canyon treks of 3 to 5 days or more and a number of other adventure activities, such as horseback riding, mountain biking, rafting, and climbing.

For mountain climbing, one agency stands out: **Zárate Aventuras,** Santa Catalina 204, no. 3 (© 054/202-461; fax 054/263-107; www.zarateadventures.com), which is run by Carlos Zárate, perhaps the top climbing guide in Arequipa (a title his dad held before him). He can arrange any area climb and has equipment rental and a 24-hour mountain rescue service. Climbing expedition costs (per person) are El Misti, $50 (£25); Chachani, $70 (£35); and Colca Canyon, $75 (£38). They also organize rafting and mountain biking adventures.

10 Iquitos & the Northern Amazon

1,860km (1,153 miles) NE of Lima

Iquitos, the gateway to the northern Amazon, is Peru's largest jungle town and the capital of its largest region, Loreto (which occupies nearly a third of the national territory). Though you must fly to get here—unless you have a full week to kill for hot and uncomfortable river travel—the pockets of jungle down- and upriver from Iquitos are among the most accessible of the Peruvian Amazon basin. Some of the best jungle lodges in the country are located just a few hours by boat from Iquitos. Because the region is the most trafficked and developed of the Peruvian Amazon, costs are lower for most jungle excursions than they are in the more exclusive Manu Biosphere Reserve in southeastern Peru.

Founded by Jesuits in the 1750s, Iquitos lies about 3,220km (2,000 miles) upriver from the mouth of the Amazon River. Its proximity to South America's greatest rainforest and its isolation from the rest of Peru have created a unique tropical atmosphere. In the late 1860s and 1870s, pioneering merchants got rich off the booming rubber trade and built ostentatious mansions along the river. Today, though, those great homes are faded monuments to the city's glory days, and just blocks from the main square lies the fascinating Belén district, where families live in a squalid pile of ramshackle wooden houses on the banks of the river. Some houses are propped up by spindly stilts, while others float, tethered to poles, when the river rises 6m (20 ft.) or more. Belén looks Far Eastern, and Iquitos seemingly has more in common with steamy tropical Asian cities than the highlands of Peru. Like a South American Saigon, the air is waterlogged, and the streets buzz with unrelenting waves of motorcycles and *motocarros* (or rickshaws). Locals speak a languid, mellifluous Spanish unmatched in other parts of the country, and they dress not in alpaca sweaters and shawls, but in flesh-baring tank tops and short skirts.

Iquitos has an intoxicating feel that's likely to detain you for at least a couple of days. But for most visitors, the lure of the Amazon rainforest is the primary attraction. Virgin rainforest, though, is hard to find. To lay eyes on exotic wildlife, such as pink dolphins, caiman, and macaws, you have to get at least 80km (50 miles) away from Iquitos and onto secondary waterways. Options for rainforest excursions include lodge visits, river cruises, and independent guided treks.

ESSENTIALS
GETTING THERE
BY PLANE Iquitos's **Aeropuerto Francisco Secada Vigneta,** Av. Abelardo Quiñones, Km 6 (© **065/260-147**), was not so long ago an international airport; flights from Miami were suspended in 1999. **LAN** (© **01/213-8200;** www.lan.com), **Aerocondor** (© **01/614-6014;** www.aerocondor.com.pe) and **StarPeru** (© **01/705-9000;** www.starperu.com) also fly daily from Lima and other cities in the Loreto department.

The airport is usually chaotic when flights arrive, with dozens of representatives of tour operators competing for your attention. Do not let anyone take your bags, and don't let anyone you don't know hop in a cab with you. To downtown Iquitos, an automobile taxi costs about S/10 ($3.35/£1.70), by *motocarro* (rickshaw) costs S/7 ($2.35/£1.20).

BY BOAT Arriving by boat is an option only for those with the luxury of ample time and patience; it takes about a week when the river is high (and 3–4 days in the dry season) to reach the capital city of Loreto upriver along the Amazon from Pucallpa or Yurimaguas. The Iquitos port, **Puerto Masusa,** is about 3km (2 miles) north of the Plaza de Armas. To travel to Colombia or Brazil by boat, your best bet is by river cruise (p. 721). Cruises to Manaus, Santarém, and Belém in Brazil are offered by Amazon Tours & Cruises (see below). Direct service all the way to Manaus has been suspended.

GETTING AROUND
BY TAXI/*MOTOTAXI* Motorcycle buggies or rickshaws *(motocarros)* are everywhere in Iquitos; if you don't mind the noise and wind in your face (and aren't worried about accidents), it's a great way to get around. In-town fares are S/1.50 (50¢/25p). Regular car taxis are only slightly less ubiquitous; most trips in town cost S/2 (65¢/30p).

BY BUS *Combis* (minivans) and *ómnibuses* (buses) travel principal routes, but are much less comfortable and not much less expensive than more convenient *motocarros*.

BY FOOT Though the city is spread over several square kilometers, the core of downtown Iquitos is compact and easy to get around on foot, and even the waterfront Belén district is easy to walk to. Some hostels and hotels are a distance from the main square, though, requiring the occasional use of inexpensive *motocarros*.

ATTRACTIONS ●
Barrio de Belén
  (market & port) **12**
Casa de Fierro **7**
Iglesia Matriz **5**
Malecón Tarapaca **8**
Museo Amazónico **10**
Plaza de Armas **6**

ACCOMMODATIONS ■
El Dorado Plaza Hotel **4**
Hospedaje La Pascana **1**
Victoria Regia Hotel **11**

DINING ◆
El Nuevo Mesón **2**
Fitzcarraldo **3**
Regal (Casa de Fierro) **7**
Restaurant Gran Maloca **9**

VISITOR INFORMATION

A municipal **tourism information booth** is located in the arrivals terminal at the airport (© **065/260-251**). It maintains a chart of hotels and prices, and the staff is happy to dispense information about the various jungle tour and lodge operators. One of Peru's more helpful tourism information offices is at Napo 226 on the north side of the Plaza de Armas (© **065/236-144**). The English-speaking staff offers free maps and lists of all recommended hotels and tour operators (including photo albums of lodges) and will try to sort through the (often intentionally) confusing sales pitches of jungle-tour companies. The office is open Monday through Saturday from 8am to 8pm, as well as occasional Sunday mornings.

FAST FACTS   Banks and ATMs are located along Putumayo and Próspero, on the south side of the Plaza de Armas. Two banks that exchange traveler's checks and cash are **Banco de Crédito,** Putumayo 201, and **Banco Continental,** Sargento Lores 171. Money changers can usually be found hanging about the Plaza de Armas and along Putumayo and Próspero, but figure the exchange beforehand and count your money carefully.

   If you're planning to cross into Brazil or Colombia, I suggest you make contact with your embassy in Lima or even at home before traveling to Peru. For questions about border-crossing formalities for jungle travel to and from Brazil and Colombia (regulations have been known to change frequently), contact the **Migraciones** office at Malecón Tarapacá 382 (© **065/235-371**).

In a medical emergency, call **Cruz Roja (Red Cross)** at © **065/241-072.** For medical attention, visit **Clínica Ana Stahl,** Av. la Marina 285 (© **065/252-535**); **Essalud,** Av. la Marina 2054 (© **065/250-333**); or **Hospital Regional de Loreto,** Av. 28 de Julio s/n, Punchana (© **065/252-004**). The **tourist police** office is located at Sargento Lores 834 (© **065/242-081**).

There are several **Internet** *cabinas* near the Plaza de Armas, particularly on Próspero and Putumayo. The one next to the entrance to the Casa de Fierro is pretty dependable. Most stay open late, and rates are about S/2 (65¢/30p) per hour. Iquitos's **post office** is located at Arica 402, at the corner of Morona (© **065/223-812**); it's open Monday through Saturday from 8am to 7:30pm. The **Telefónica del Perú** office is at Arica 276.

WHAT TO SEE & DO
IN IQUITOS

The Plaza de Armas, while perhaps not Peru's most distinguished, is marked by an early-20th-century, neo-Gothic **Iglesia Matriz** (parish church) and the **Casa de Fierro.** The walls, ceiling, and balcony of this Gustave Eiffel–designed house (for the 1889 Paris Exhibition) are plastered in rectangular sheets of iron. Said to be the first prefabricated house in the Americas, it was shipped unassembled from Europe and built on-site where it currently stands.

One block away from the plaza, facing the Amazon River, the riverfront promenade known as the **Malecón Tarapacá** was recently enlarged and improved with fountains, benches, and street lamps, making it the focus of Iquitos's urban life. It is lined with several exquisite 19th-century mansions; the most spectacular is probably **Casa Hernández,** no. 302–308. The **Museo Amazónico,** Malecón Tarapacá 386 (© **065/231-072**), has occasionally interesting exhibits of Amazon folklore and tribal art, as well as a curious collection of 76 Indian statues made of fiberglass but fashioned as if they were bronze. It's open Monday through Friday from 8am to 1pm and 3 to 7pm, Saturday from 9am to 1pm; admission is S/3 ($1/50p). Other houses worth checking out are **Casa Fitzcarrald,** Napo 200–212, an adobe house belonging to a famed rubber baron; **Casa Cohen,** Próspero 401–437; **Casa Morey,** Brasil, first block; and the **Logia Unión Amazónica,** Nauta 262.

The waterfront **Barrio de Belén** 🎯, about a 15-minute walk south along the malecón, is Iquitos's most interesting quarter. Known for its sprawling and odiferous open-air market, where you'll find a bounty of strange and wonderful Amazon fish, fauna, and fruit, Belén's residential district is a seedy but endlessly fascinating shanty-town. Houses are constructed above the waters of the Amazon, and when the river is high, the primary mode of transportation is by canoe. You are free to walk around in dry season (or take a locally arranged canoe trip during much of the year), but you should go in a group and only during the day.

JUNGLE LODGES & TOURS

Though the town itself holds a kind of sultry fascination, ecotourism is the primary draw for visitors to Iquitos, and the giant Amazon River system just beyond the city holds a wealth of natural wonders: rustic jungle lodges, canopy walks, and opportunities for bird-watching, piranha fishing, visits to Indian villages, and wildlife-spotting (as well as less-standard activities, such as shaman consultations and *ayahuasca* drug ceremonies). The mighty Amazon reaches widths of about 4km (2½ miles) beyond Iquitos, and the river basin contains some 2,000 species of fish; 4,000 species of birds; native mammals such as anteaters, tapirs, marmosets, and pink dolphins; and 60 species of reptiles, including caiman and anacondas. Your options for exploring the jungle are lodge stays (which include jungle activities such as treks and canoe excursions), river cruises, or more adventurous guided camping treks. Don't expect to spend your time in the jungle checking off a lengthy list of wildlife sightings, though; no matter where you go, your opportunities for viewing more than a couple of these birds, fish, and mammals will be severely limited by their natural shyness and the density of the tropical vegetation. The northern Amazon basin within reach of Iquitos has been explored and popularly exploited far longer than the more remote southern jungle areas of Manu and Tambopata.

For a quick and simple experience, you can stay at a lodge only an hour or two by boat from Iquitos, in secondary jungle. You're likely to see more fauna and have a more authentic experience in primary rainforest, but you'll have to travel up to 4 hours by boat and pay quite a bit more for the privilege. Generally speaking, you'll have to trade comfort for authenticity. A true foray into virgin jungle, far from the heavy footsteps of thousands of guides and visitors, requires at least a week of demanding camping and trekking. Hard-core eco-types may wish to contract private guides to go deep into the *selva* and camp; ask at the tourism information office for a list of licensed, official guides. (They also have a list of blacklisted guides.)

Prices for lodges and tours vary tremendously. Costs are directly related to distance from Iquitos; the farther away, the more expensive they are. For conventional lodges contracted in Iquitos, lodge tours average around $40 to $50 (£20–£25), going up to $150 (£75) or more per person per day for lodges located farthest from the city. Some budget lodges offer bargain rates, as little as $25 to $30 (£12–£15) per day (in most cases, you get what you pay for), and independent guides may charge as little as $15 (£7.50) a day. Costs include transportation, lodging, buffet-style meals, and guided activities. (Beverages are extra.)

Beware: There are many look-alike lodges and tours. Hustlers and con artists abound in Iquitos, and you need to exercise a certain amount of caution before handing over your money for a promised itinerary. The local tourism office (© **065/260-251**) works hard to ferret out guides, tours, and lodges with bad reputations. If you're making a tour decision on the ground in Iquitos, it's a good idea to visit the office first for the most up-to-date information.

Tips Economizing

You can almost certainly get a better deal by going door-to-door to the lodge and tour sales offices in Iquitos and comparing programs and prices than you would by contracting one in Lima or from your home country prior to stepping foot in Peru. However, you risk not getting the tour you want when you want it. For many travelers, the extra hassle and uncertainty may not be worth the dollars saved. Prices quoted on websites and through travel agents may be quite negotiable if you contact operators directly, depending on season and occupancy rates.

Jungle Lodges

Most jungle lodges have either individual thatched-roof bungalows or main buildings with individual rooms; communal dining areas; hammock lounges; covered plank walkways; toilets; and hot- or cold-water sinks and showers. A few lodges have extras such as swimming pools, lookout towers, canopy walkways, and electricity. Guests are taken on guided day- and nighttime excursions, including jungle walks, piranha fishing, and canoe and motorboat trips to spot birds, caimans, and dolphins. Many lodges offer cheesy visits with local Indian tribes, staged for your pleasure, and some host *ayahuasca* rituals (with the privilege of taking a natural hallucinogenic potion prepared by an "authentic" Indian shaman at $15 [£7.50] a shot—the local version of taking peyote with Don Juan).

The following tour operators and lodges have good reputations, though the list is not by any means exhaustive.

- **Explorama** ✦, Av. la Marina 340 (© **800/707-5275** in the U.S. and Canada, or 065/252-530; www.explorama.com). The most established jungle tour company in Iquitos (now into its fifth decade) and owned by an American, Explorama operates three lodges and a campsite, ranging from 40km to 160km (25–100 miles) downriver from Iquitos. Near **Explornapo** (the lodge deepest in the jungle), there's a splendid canopy walkway high above the treetops. Explorama owns the jungle's most luxurious lodge, **Ceiba Tops,** a jungle resort hotel with air-conditioning, pool, and Jacuzzi. Prices range from $210 (£105) for a 2-day, 1-night trip to $820 (£410) for a 5-day, 4-night trip to Explornapo. Web specials are frequently available.

- **Tahuayo Lodge** ✦✦✦, Amazonia Expeditions, 10305 Riverburn Dr., Tampa, FL (© **800/262-9669** in the U.S.; www.perujungle.com). The finest lodge in the northern Amazon, this 11-year-old low-impact eco-property, associated with the Rainforest Conservation Fund, lies on the shores of the River Tahuayo, about 4 hours from Iquitos. *Outside* magazine has touted it as one of the top-10 travel finds in the world. It is the only lodge with access to the Tamshiyacu-Tahuayo Reserve, a splendid area for primate and other wildlife viewing (it counts 500 species of birds). Because of its remoteness, it recommends visits of at least a week; programs are individually tailored. The 15 cabins are open year-round, and the lodge offers an excellent schedule of excursions ranging from the rugged (jungle survival training) to relaxed; most enticing are zip-line canopy ropes for tree-top viewing. An 8-day, 7-night trip is $1,295 (£648) per person.

- **Yarapa River Lodge** ✦✦✦ (© **065/993-1172** or 315/952-6771 in the U.S. and Canada; www.yarapa.com). Associated with Cornell University (which built a field lab for students and faculty here), this attractive, conservation-minded lodge is 186km (110 miles) upriver on the Yarapa River, near the Reserva Nacional Pacaya-Samiria. Surrounded by pristine jungle and oxbow lakes, the handsome lodge features composting, full solar power, and flush toilets with a waste-management system. The lodge is a two-time winner of World Travel Awards' "Best Resort in Peru." A 4-day, 3-night trip (with private bathroom) runs $760 (£380) per person; a 7-day, 6-night trip is $1,190 (£595) per person. Travelers can opt for an overnight in the remote Pacaya-Samiria National Park Reserve, 4 hours away by boat.

CRUISES

Riverboat cruises down the Amazon and along its tributaries don't allow you to see much in the way of fauna or pristine jungle, though you will likely spot lots of birds and dolphins. Cruises are best for people who don't want to rough it too much and like the romance of traveling the Amazon by boat. Many cruises stop off at reserves for jungle walks and visits to local villages.

- **Amazon Tours & Cruises,** Requena 336 (© **800/423-2791** in the U.S. and Canada, or 065/231-611; www.amazontours.net). This American-owned company has been active in the northern Amazon for more than 4 decades. Its midlevel cruises are aboard older, air-conditioned fleets that aren't as nice or as expensive as those of Jungle Expeditions (see below). A 5-night riverboat cruise is $2,195 (£1,098; per person in double room).
- **Jungle Expeditions** ⊕, Av. Quiñones 1980 (© **065/261-583;** www.junglex. com). This company offers luxury river cruises on a fleet of six very elegant, 19th-century style boats, and cruises upriver along the Río Ucayali. Prices range from $1,698 to $2,598 (£849–£1,299) for 7-day expeditions. The company only accepts passengers through their Lima booking office (© **01/241-3232**) or **International Expeditions** (© **800/633-4734;** www.internationalexpeditions.com) in the United States, which offers air-inclusive packages and programs with Cusco and Machu Picchu extensions.

SHOPPING

The most intriguing shopping option in town is the Belén open-air market, though it's likely you'll find more to photograph and smell than actually buy. For local artisans' goods, there aren't many options; try the sparsely populated market downstairs from the malecón. **Centro Artesanal Anaconda,** Malecón Tarapacá-Boulevard, or the larger market, **Mercado Artesanal de San Juan,** with stalls selling hammocks, wood-carvings, and paintings on Avenida Quiñones 4.5km (3 miles), on the way out to the airport (about 3km/2 miles from downtown). Some of the best crafts, including textiles and pottery, come from the Shipibo Indian tribe.

WHERE TO STAY

Iquitos has fewer good hotels than its environs have attractive jungle lodges—which is perhaps logical, since the jungle is the primary attraction here. All but the cheapest will arrange for a free airport transfer if you pass on your arrival information ahead of time.

EXPENSIVE

Hotel El Dorado Plaza ⊕   With a privileged location on the Plaza de Armas, the El Dorado Plaza has filled a gaping hole in the Iquitos hotel scene—the city never before had a bona fide high-end hotel. A modern high-rise, with a soaring lobby, good restaurant, and bar, this is clearly the finest hotel in town. Rooms are large and nicely outfitted, if not quite at the upper-echelon levels found in Lima or Cusco. Guests have a view of either the main square or the pool. The hotel has quickly become popular with foreigners who come to Iquitos for top-of-the-line jungle tours. The staff is very friendly and helpful. Occasionally there are deals for as much as half the rack rate.

Napo 258 (Plaza de Armas), Iquitos. © 065/222-555. Fax 065/224-304. www.eldoradoplazahotel.com. 65 units. $130 (£65) double. Rate includes breakfast buffet. AE, DC, MC, V. **Amenities:** Restaurant; coffee shop; 2 bars; excellent outdoor pool; fitness center; Jacuzzi; sauna; concierge; room service; laundry service. *In room:* A/C, TV, minibar, hair dryer, safe.

MODERATE

Victoria Regia *(Value)*   An extremely comfortable and friendly midsize hotel, the Victoria Regia—named for the lily found throughout the Amazon—is a good choice for both independent travelers and business execs with long-term affairs to attend to in Iquitos. It's a modern block hotel on a busy residential street about 10 minutes from the main square. The rooms are built around an indoor pool and are just a notch below the El Dorado in terms of comfort, although they have air-conditioning that really cranks.

Av. Ricardo Palma 252, Iquitos. (℃)/fax **065/231-983,** or 01/421-9195 for reservations. www.victoriaregiahotel.com. 65 units. $70–$82 (£35–£41) double; $82–$116 (£41–£58) suite. Rates include breakfast buffet. AE, DC, MC, V. **Amenities:** Restaurant/bar; covered pool; small business center; laundry service. *In room:* A/C, TV, minibar, safe.

WHERE TO DINE

The relaxed restaurants in Iquitos are a good place to sample dishes straight out of the Amazon, such as turtle meat soup, *paiche* (a huge fish), heart of palm salad, and *juanes* (rice *tamales* made with chicken or fish). Although protected species are not supposed to appear on menus, they often do. If you venture into the Belén market, you'll see even more exotic foodstuffs, such as monkey and lizard meat.

MODERATE

El Nuevo Mesón PERUVIAN   Open to the passing parade of people, souvenir sellers, and curious locals on the malecón, this lively restaurant is a good place for an introduction to regional specialties and the city itself. If you come on a weekend night, you'll be entertained not only by Altiplano musicians inside, but also by all kinds of locals hovering near the sidewalk tables, some gawking at your meal. (Several kids jostled for the rights to my leftovers; disadvantaged people often hang around outside restaurants hoping for part of a meal.) Service can be a little haphazard, but most dishes are pretty well prepared. Try regional dishes such as the ubiquitous *pescado a la Loretana* (fish filet with yuca, fried bananas, and *chonta*) and freakier fare such as alligator crisps with fried manioc or curried turtle. There's a long list of fish, dominated by *dorado* (a kind of flaky catfish), served a variety of ways (such as "poor boy," with potatoes, salad, bananas, eggs, and rice), as well as steaks and *mariscos* (shellfish).

Malecón Tarapacá 153. (℃) 065/231-837. Reservations recommended for groups. Main courses S/15–S/28 ($5–$9/ £2.50–£4.50). MC, V. Daily noon–midnight.

Fitzcarraldo ⊛ INTERNATIONAL   This popular joint right on the malecón has a diverse menu to appeal to tourists of all stripes and appetites. You can go light, choosing from a number of salads such as *chonta* with avocado and tomato, or opt for a regular dinner including *pescado a la Loretana,* or even turtle in ginger sauce with manioc. There are also excellent pizzas, sandwiches, and hamburgers, as well as large salads. The restaurant is a convivial, lively place in an open-air house with views of the Amazon, good music, sidewalk tables, and underpowered ceiling fans.

Napo 100 (at Malecón Tarapacá). (℃) 065/243-434. Reservations recommended for groups. Main courses S/10–S/38 ($3–$13/£1.50–£6.50). MC, V. Daily noon–midnight.

Regal (Casa de Fierro) INTERNATIONAL/PERUVIAN   In the famed Iron House on the Plaza de Armas, this British pub and hangout is also a reputable restaurant exuding a desultory colonial atmosphere. There are great views from the wraparound iron balcony, with its slowly rotating old-style ceiling fans. It's a good place to try local dishes such as *paiche* (Amazon river fish), which is served any number of ways, or the house specialty, Regal *lomo fino* (beef tenderloin in port-wine sauce), served with salad, Greek rice, a peach stuffed with Russian salad, and french fries. Some find that the food suffers in comparison with the general ambience, so you might opt just to kick back with the expat Brits around the bar for a pint.

Putumayo 182, Plaza de Armas (2nd floor). © 065/222-732. Reservations recommended. Main courses S/16–S/33 ($5–$11/£2.50–£5.50). AE, DC, MC, V. Daily noon–10pm.

Restaurant Gran Maloca *(Value* PERUVIAN/AMAZONIAN   One of Iquitos's most celebrated traditional restaurants, located in a grand, tile-covered (and air-conditioned!) 19th-century house, Gran Maloca serves both *platos de la selva*—jungle dishes—and standard upscale fare. Try Amazon-style venison (with cilantro, coconut, and yuca), tropical alligator, or less risky items such as filet mignon or tenderloin with mushroom risotto. The split personality of the restaurant is present in the decor: The would-be formal trappings and pastel color scheme coexist with a large collection of colorful butterflies adorning the walls. (If you like those, wait until you get a load of the framed Amazonian bugs, tarantulas, and other creepy crawlers in the bathrooms.) Gran Maloca serves a cheap three-course daily lunch special for just S/12 ($3.50/ £1.75).

Sargento Lores 170. © 065/233-126. Reservations recommended. Main courses S/18–S/36 ($6–$12/$3–$6). AE, DC, MC, V. Daily noon–10pm.

IQUITOS AFTER DARK

More locals than gringos usually make it to the coolest spot in Iquitos, **Café-Teatro Amauta,** Nauta 250 (© 065/233-366), a bar with great bohemian flavor, a romantic interior, and sidewalk tables. Calling itself El Rincón de los Artistas (The Artists' Corner), it supports live music of diverse types (Peruvian, Latino, and Amazon sounds) Monday through Saturday from 10pm until 3am. Along the malecón are a couple of lively bars with good views of the river. **Arandú Bar** (© 065/243-434) is particularly hopping, and a good place for a pitcher of sangria. You can also grab a drink at **The Yellow Rose of Texas,** Putumayo 180 (© 065/241-010), a spot owned by the former head of the local tourist office (a Texan). Locals hang out at **Noa-Noa** (© 065/232-902), a rock bar near the Plaza de Armas at Pevas 298.

12

Uruguay

by Charlie O'Malley

Brazil gets most of the glamour and Argentina most of the attention, but tucked between these colossal countries is that rare find in South America—a nation that is clean, safe, and peaceful. The 3.2 million Uruguayans—among the continent's most friendly and welcoming people—are quite happy to let their neighbors steal the limelight, but they will proudly tell you that they have the best beaches, the best meat, the best *fútbol,* the best wine, the best health service, and, perhaps most important, the least corrupt government. Whether you are a day-tripper to unassuming Montevideo or a night owl amid the glitzy bars and clubs of Punta del Este, you might come to think the same. *Tip:* For a map of suggested itineraries in Uruguay, please refer to the "Itineraries in Argentina, Chile, Paraguay & Uruguay" map on p. 78.

1 The Regions in Brief

Uruguay's origins as a country rest firmly in Europe; the indigenous people inhabiting the region were displaced by the colonizing Portuguese and Spaniards in the late 17th and early 18th centuries. You will find the European influence most evident among the historic treasures of **Colonia,** where the Portuguese first entrenched themselves, and amid the rich architecture of **Montevideo,** where the Spaniards landed. Montevideo is the cultural heartland of the country, a place where you will discover the bold accomplishments of Uruguay in music, art, and literature. Among the several internationally accomplished artists are Pedro Figari, who inspired a school of painters; José Enrique Rodó, Uruguay's famed essayist from the early 20th century; and Mauricio Rosencof, the politically active playwright from recent decades. Outside the capital, miles of pastureland and rolling hills draw your attention away from the urban capital to a softer, quieter life. But this rural lifestyle stops at the coast, where world-class resorts centered on **Punta del Este** lure the continent's rich and famous.

2 Suggested Uruguay Itineraries

Most people arrive in Uruguay from Argentina and the itinerary below is designed accordingly. If you're traveling with family, my advice is to go straight to the beach.

Days ❶–❷: Arrive in Colonia ⭐⭐⭐
Popular with day-trippers, **Colonia** deserves your attention and is worth an overnight stay to truly enjoy its old-time, otherworldly pace of life. Stay at the colonial-style Hotel Plaza Mayor, and explore the Barrio Histórico on foot or by scooter.

Day ❸: Montevideo

Stay in the upscale neighborhood of Carrasco at the intimate **Belmont House** (p. 732). From here you can walk the coastal road, La Rambla, to the rundown but historical Old City, stopping off to enjoy the **Port Market.** Dine at the very grand **Arcadia** restaurant (p. 734) atop the Plaza Victoria.

Days ❹–❼: Punta del Este

Pass most of your time on Uruguay's famous beaches and rub shoulders with the glitterati. If sunbathing is not your thing, you'll find plenty of outdoor activities such as horseback riding and watersports.

3 Planning Your Trip to Uruguay

VISITOR INFORMATION

The Internet is an excellent source of information on Uruguay. Try **www.turismo. gub.uy** or **www.uruguaynatural.com** for official visitor information. Additional countrywide tourist information can be found at **www.visit-uruguay.com**.

ENTRY REQUIREMENTS & CUSTOMS

Citizens of the United States, the United Kingdom, Canada, and New Zealand need only a passport to enter Uruguay (for tourist stays of up to 90 days). Australian citizens must get a tourist visa before arrival.

URUGUAYAN EMBASSY LOCATIONS

In the U.S.: 2715 M St. NW, Third Floor, Washington, DC 20007 (✆ **202/331-1313;** fax 202/331-8142; www.embassy.org/uruguay)

Telephone Dialing Info at a Glance

Uruguay's national telephone company is called ANTEL. You can buy a telephone card from any kiosk or ANTEL *telecentro* location. You can also make domestic and international calls from *telecentro* offices—they are located every few blocks in major cities—but be warned that international calls are very expensive, especially during peak hours.

- **To place a call from your home country to Uruguay,** dial the international access code (011 in the U.S., 0011 in Australia, 0170 in New Zealand, 00 in the U.K.) plus the country code (598), plus the city or region area code (for example, Montevideo 2, Punta del Este 42, Colonia del Sacramento 11) followed by the number. For example, a call from the United States to Montevideo would be 011+598+2+000+0000.
- **To place a domestic long-distance call within Uruguay,** dial a 0 before the area code, and then the local number.
- **To place a direct international call from Uruguay,** dial the international access code (00), plus the country code of the place you are dialing, plus the area code and the number.
- **To reach an International Long Distance Operator,** dial ✆ 000-410 for AT&T, ✆ 000-412 for **MCI,** or ✆ 000-417 for **Sprint.**

In Canada: 130 Albert St., Suite 1905, Ottawa, ON K1P 5G4 (© **613/234-2727;** fax 613/233-4670; www.iosphere.net/~uruott)

In the U.K.: 140 Brompton Rd., Second Floor, London SW3 1HY (© **207/589-8835**)

MONEY

The official currency is the **Uruguayan peso** (designated NP$, $U, or simply $); each peso comprises 100 **centavos.** Uruguayan pesos are available in $10, $20, $50, $100, $200, $500, $1,000, and $5,000 notes; coins come in 10, 20, and 50 centavos, and 1 and 2 pesos. The Uruguayan currency devalued by half in July 2002, and the exchange rate as this book went to press was approximately 21 pesos to the U.S. dollar. The value of the peso fluctuates greatly with inflation, so **all prices in this chapter are quoted in U.S. dollars** with British pound equivalents.

Traveler's checks are accepted only at some currency-exchange houses. The most widely accepted **credit cards** are Visa and MasterCard; you'll have less luck with American Express and Diners Club. To report a lost or stolen credit card, call the following numbers: for **American Express,** © **0411/008-0071;** for **MasterCard,** © **636/722-7111** (collect call to the U.S.); and for **Visa,** © **0411/940-7915.**

ATMS   ATMs on the Cirrus network are widely available in Montevideo and Punta del Este. If you travel to Colonia or elsewhere outside these cities, you should bring Uruguayan pesos.

WHEN TO GO

PEAK SEASON & CLIMATE   The best time to visit Uruguay is October through March, when the sun shines and temperatures are mild. (Remember that seasons are reversed from those of the Northern Hemisphere.) Punta del Este overflows with tourists from Argentina in summer; if you're seeking a more relaxed time to visit the beaches of the coast, consider going between October and December. Average temperatures are 62°F (17°C) in spring, 73°F (23°C) in summer, 64°F (18°C) in autumn, and 53°F (12°C) in winter.

PUBLIC HOLIDAYS   National holidays include New Year's Day (Jan 1), Día de los Reyes (Jan 6), Carnaval (the days leading up to Ash Wednesday), Easter, Desembarco de los 33 Orientales (Apr 19), Labor Day (May 1), Batalla de las Piedras (May 18), Natalicio de José Gervasio Artigas (June 19), Jura de la Constitución (July 18), Independence Day (Aug 25), Día de la Raza (Oct 12), Día de los Difuntos (Nov 2), and Christmas (Dec 25).

HEALTH CONCERNS

There are no specific health concerns or vaccination requirements for travel to Uruguay. The **U.S. Centers for Disease Control and Prevention** does recommend that travelers to South America be up-to-date on tetanus-diphtheria and measles vaccines, as well as getting vaccinated for hepatitis A and B and typhoid. Check the CDC's website at **www.cdc.gov** for the latest information before your trip. Health care in Uruguay is adequate to excellent.

GETTING THERE & GETTING AROUND

International flights land at **Carrasco International Airport** (© 02/604-0386), located 19km (12 miles) from downtown Montevideo. A taxi to downtown costs about $30 (£15). Uruguay's national carrier is **Pluna** (© 0800/118-811 or 02/604-4080;

www.pluna.aero), serving domestic and international destinations. **American Airlines** (𝒞 800/433-7300 in the U.S., or 02/916-3929 in Uruguay) offers connecting service from the United States. **Aerolíneas Argentinas** (𝒞 02/901-9466; www.aerolineas.com) connects Buenos Aires and Montevideo; the flight takes 50 minutes. **Varig** (𝒞 800/469-2744; www.varig.com.br) offers flights from the U.K. or Europe. **LAN** (𝒞 866/435-9526; www.lan.com) and Aerolíneas Argentinas connect Australia and New Zealand. A new airport is under construction and due to open in 2010.

Be aware that at press time Argentina and Uruguay were in a diplomatic dispute over the construction of a paper mill that might pollute the Río Uruguay, near the Argentine town of Gualeguaychú. Access to Uruguay, at times, is restricted because of ongoing protests, and extra security is sometimes in place at crossings, airline gates, and the Buquebús terminal. From Montevideo, the easiest way to reach Colonia and Punta del Este is by bus (see "Getting There," under "Essentials," in the Montevideo section below).

FAST FACTS: Uruguay

American Express In Montevideo, **American Express Bank** is located at Rincón 477, 8th Floor (𝒞 02/916-0000). **Turisport Limitada,** Calle San José 930 (𝒞 02/902-0829; fax 02/902-0852), acts as an agent of American Express Travel Services in Uruguay; hours are Monday through Friday from 9am to 5pm.

Business Hours In general, businesses stay open weekdays from 9am to 6:30 or 7pm, with a 2-hour break for lunch around noon. Retail outlets keep similar hours and are usually open a half-day on Saturday as well. Banks are open weekdays from 1 to 5pm.

Electricity Electricity in Uruguay runs on 220 volts, so bring a transformer and adapter along with any electrical appliances. Note that most laptops operate on both 110 and 220 volts. Some luxury hotels may supply transformers and adapters.

Embassies & Consulates In Montevideo: **U.S.,** Lauro Muller 1776 (𝒞 02/418-7777; http://uruguay.usembassy.gov); **U.K.,** Marco Bruto 1073 (𝒞 02/623-3630); and **Canada,** Plaza Independencia 749, Office 102 (𝒞 02/902-2030; www.dfait-maeci.gc.ca/uruguay).

Emergencies The general emergency number is 𝒞 **911.** Outside Montevideo, dial 𝒞 **02-911** to connect with Montevideo Central Emergency Authority. The following numbers also work: police 𝒞 **109;** ambulance 𝒞 **105;** and fire department 𝒞 **104.**

Internet Access Cybercafes are commonly found around Montevideo and other Uruguayan cities. Many hotel business centers have Internet access, as do the guest rooms in high-end hotels.

Post Offices/Mail Post offices are generally open Monday through Friday from 8am to 6pm and Saturday from 8am to 1pm. You can buy stamps there or in mailing centers in shopping malls.

Restrooms It's permissible to use the toilets in restaurants and bars without patronizing the establishment; offer a nice smile on the way in. Nobody should bother you unless they're having a bad day.

Safety Uruguay is one of the world's safest countries, although petty crime in Montevideo has risen in recent years. Outside the capital, cities and beach resorts such as Punta del Este are considered safe. Travelers visiting Uruguay are nevertheless advised to take common-sense precautions.

Taxes Value-added tax is called IVA in Spanish. IVA is 14% for hotels, 23% in restaurants, and 24% for general sales tax; the tax is almost always included in your bill. The departure tax when leaving the country is $25 (£13).

Telephones See "Telephone Dialing Info at a Glance," above.

Time Zone Uruguay is 1 hour ahead of eastern standard time, although the country doesn't observe daylight saving time.

Tipping A 10% to 15% tip is common in restaurants. For taxis, round up to the nearest peso. Tip bellhops 50¢ (25p) per bag.

Water Locals swear that the drinking water in Uruguay is perfectly healthy; in fact, Uruguay was the only country in the Americas (along with the nations of the Caribbean) to escape the cholera pandemic of the early 1990s. If you are concerned, stick with bottled water (*agua mineral sin gas*).

4 Montevideo

A wide, blustery waterfront with a backdrop of gray Soviet-style apartment blocks contrasts with handsome government buildings and crumbling mansions. Karaoke sailor bars stand next to art deco diners, and fishermen tend their catches while elders sip *mate* (a tealike beverage and national obsession) in the city parks, all buffeted by a sea breeze that reveals this city, the southernmost capital on the continent, is in fact surrounded on three sides by water.

Montevideo is often regarded as a downsized Buenos Aires, but it has a discreet charm and useful compactness that its sister city lacks across the wide choppy waters of the Río de la Plata. Its colorful port area betrays its strong maritime past, first as a Spanish fort and then as a major port city. Rich architecture reveals a diverse immigrant population, and though this city may have seen better times, it makes for a relaxing stopover and an interesting destination to linger, stroll, and relax.

ESSENTIALS
GETTING THERE

BY PLANE   To get to Montevideo by plane, see "Getting There & Getting Around," above. A private, unmetered taxi or *remise* (radio taxi) from the airport to downtown costs about $20 (£10) and takes 30 minutes.

BY BOAT OR HYDROFOIL   **Buquebús,** Calle Río Negro 1400 (© **02/916-8801** or 130), operates three to four hydrofoils per day between Montevideo and Buenos Aires; the trip takes about 3 hours and costs about $110 (£55) round-trip. Montevideo's port is just over 1.5km (1 mile) from downtown. Taxis from here to downtown cost about $10 (£5) and take 7 minutes. If you have taken a ferry to Colonia, you can get connecting bus service to Montevideo; the bus terminal is near the port on Manuel de Lobos and Avenida Roosevelt. The trip takes 3 hours and costs $10 (£5). Try **COT** (© **02/409-4949**).

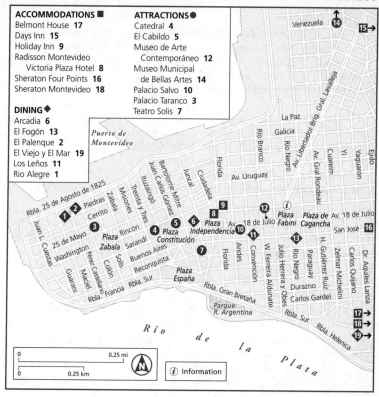

ACCOMMODATIONS ■
Belmont House **17**
Days Inn **15**
Holiday Inn **9**
Radisson Montevideo
  Victoria Plaza Hotel **8**
Sheraton Four Points **16**
Sheraton Montevideo **18**

DINING ◆
Arcadia **6**
El Fogón **13**
El Palenque **2**
El Viejo y El Mar **19**
Los Leños **11**
Rio Alegre **1**

ATTRACTIONS ●
Catedral **4**
El Cabildo **5**
Museo de Arte
  Contemporáneo **12**
Museo Municipal
  de Bellas Artes **14**
Palacio Salvo **10**
Palacio Taranco **3**
Teatro Solis **7**

BY BUS **Terminal Omnibus Tres Cruces,** General Artigas 1825 (© **02/409-7399** or 02/401-8998), is Montevideo's long-distance bus terminal, connecting the capital with cities in Uruguay and throughout South America. Buses to Buenos Aires take about 8 hours. **COT** (© **02/409-4949**) offers the best service to Punta del Este ($46/£23), Maldonado ($53/£27), and Colonia ($68/£34).

ORIENTATION

The Old City begins near the western edge of Montevideo, found on the skinny portion of a peninsula between the Rambla Gran Bretaña and the city's main artery, Avenida 18 de Julio. Look for the Plaza Independencia and the Plaza Constitución to find the center of the district. Many of the city's museums, theaters, and hotels reside in this historic area, although a trip east on Avenida 18 de Julio reveals the more modern Montevideo, with its own share of hotels, markets, and monuments. Along the city's long southern coastline runs the Rambla Gran Bretaña, traveling 21km (13 miles) from the piers of the Old City past Parque Rodó and on to points south and east, passing fish stalls and street performers along the way.

GETTING AROUND

It's easy to navigate around the center of Montevideo on foot or by bus. Safe, convenient buses crisscross Montevideo, making it easy to venture outside the city center, for

Safety Note

Although Montevideo remains very safe by big-city standards, street crime has risen in recent years. Travelers should avoid walking alone, particularly at night, in Ciudad Vieja, Avenida 18 de Julio, Plaza Independencia, and the vicinity around the port. Take a taxi instead.

15 Uruguayan pesos (about 60¢/30p). Taxis are safe and relatively inexpensive, but it can be difficult to hail one during rush hour. I recommend calling **Remises Carrasco** (© **09/440-5473**). To rent a car, try **Thrifty** (© **02/481-8170**). Cars start at $60 (£30). For roadside emergencies or general information on driving in Uruguay, contact the **Automóvil Club de Uruguay,** Av. Libertador 1532 (© **02/902-4792**), or the **Centro Automovilista del Uruguay,** E. V. Haedo 2378 (© **02/408-2091**).

VISITOR INFORMATION

Uruguay's **Ministerio de Turismo** is at Av. Libertador 1409 and Colonia (© **02/908-9105**). It assists travelers with countrywide information and is open daily from 8am to 8pm in winter, and from 8am to 2pm in summer. There's also a branch at Carrasco International Airport and Tres Cruces bus station. The **municipal tourist office,** Explanada Municipal (© **1950**), offers city maps and brochures of tourist activities and is open weekdays 11am to 6pm, weekends 10am to 6pm. It also organizes cultural city tours on weekends. In the event of an emergency, the **Tourist Police** can be reached at (© **0800-8226**), and their office is at Colonia 1021.

FAST FACTS   To exchange money, try **Turisport Limitada** (the local Amex representative), San José 930 (© **02/902-0829**); **Gales Casa Cambiaria,** Av. 18 de Julio 1046 (© **02/902-0229**); or one of the airport exchanges.

For medical attention, go to the **British Hospital,** at Av. Italia 2420 (© **02/487-1020**).

Internet cafes appear and disappear faster than dance clubs, but you won't walk long before coming across one in the city center. Reliable cybercafes include **El Cybercafé,** Calle 25 de Mayo 568; **Arroba del Sur,** Guayabo 1858; and **El Cybercafé Softec,** Santiago de Chile 1286. The average cost is $2 (£1) per hour of usage.

The main **post office** is at Calle Buenos Aires 451 (© **0810/444-CORREO**), open weekdays from 9am to 6pm.

WHAT TO SEE & DO

Catedral ☆   Also known as Iglesia Matriz (parish church), the cathedral was the city's first public building, erected in 1804. It houses the remains of some of Uruguay's most important political, religious, and economic figures, and is distinguished by its domed bell towers.

Calle Sarandí at Ituzaingó. Free admission. Mon–Fri 8am–8pm.

El Cabildo (Town Hall) ☆   Uruguay's constitution was signed in the old town hall, which also served as the city's jailhouse in the 19th century. Now a museum, the Cabildo houses the city's historic archives as well as maps and photos, antiques, costumes, and artwork.

Juan Carlos Gómez 1362. © **02/915-9685**. Free admission. Tues–Sun 2:30–7pm.

Museo de Arte Contemporáneo 🌟   Opened in 1997, this museum is dedicated to contemporary Uruguayan art and exhibits the country's biggest names. To promote cultural exchange across the region, a section of the museum has been set aside for artists who hail from various South American countries. Allow an hour for your visit.

Av. 18 de Julio 965, 2nd floor. 𝒞 02/900-6662. Free admission. Daily noon–8pm.

Museo Municipal de Bellas Artes Juan Manuel Blanes 🌟   The national art history museum displays Uruguayan artistic styles from the beginning of the nation to the present day. Works include oils, engravings, drawings, sculptures, and documents. Among the great Uruguayan artists exhibited are Juan Manuel Blanes, Pedro Figari, Rafael Barradas, José Cúneo, and Carlos González. Plan to spend an hour here.

Av. Millán 4015. 𝒞 02/336-2248. www.montevideo.gub.uy/museoblanes. Free admission. Tues–Sun noon–5:45pm.

Palacio Salvo   Often referred to as the symbol of Montevideo, the Salvo Palace was once the tallest building in South America. Although its 26 stories might not impress you, it remains the city's highest structure.

Plaza Independencia.

Palacio Taranco 🌟   Now the decorative arts museum, the Taranco Palace was built in the early 20th century and represents the trend toward French architecture during that period. The museum displays an assortment of Uruguayan furniture, draperies, clocks, paintings, and other cultural works; they've recently added a small section exhibiting Islamic art, including a collection of ancient Egyptian statuettes. An hour should give you enough time to see it all.

Calle 25 de Mayo 379. 𝒞 02/915-1101. Free admission. Tues–Sat 10am–6pm.

Plaza Independencia 🌟🌟   Originally the site of a Spanish citadel, Independence Square marks the beginning of the Old City and is a good point from which to begin your tour of Montevideo. An enormous statue of General José Gervasio Artigas, father of Uruguay and hero of its independent movement, stands in the center.

Bordered by Av. 18 de Julio, Florida, and Juncal.

Teatro Solís 🌟🌟   Montevideo's main theater and opera house, opened in 1852, underwent an extensive renovation a few years back. It hosts Uruguay's most important cultural events, and it's the site of the **Museo Nacional de Historia Natural (National Museum of Natural History).** While the structure on its outside remains historical, the interior is a thoroughly modern contrast.

Calle Buenos Aires 652. 𝒞 02/916-0908. Free admission. Museum Mon–Fri 2–6pm.

SHOPPING

Shopping in Montevideo is concentrated in a few downtown shops and in three major shopping centers. In Uruguayan stores, expect to find leather goods, jewelry, and local crafts and textiles—including sweaters, cardigan jackets, ponchos, coats, and tapestries made of high-quality wool (Uruguay is the world's largest exporter of wool). International stores carry American and European products. Montevideo's most fashionable mall is the **Punta Carretas Shopping Center,** Calle Ellauri and Solano, located on the site of a former prison next to the new Sheraton hotel. Downtown, the **Montevideo Shopping Center,** Av. Luis Alberto de Herrera 1290, is the city's original mall with more than 180 stores and a 10-screen theater. **Portones de Carrasco,** avenidas

Bolivia and Italia, is another recommended shopping center in the Carrasco neighborhood. **Tres Cruces Shopping Mall** is part of the bus terminal complex, with dozens of shops. It's at Avenida Serra with Acevedo Díaz (© **02/408 8710;** www.trescruces. com.uy). Leather goods at great prices are at **Casa Mario Leather Factory,** Piedras 641 at Bartolomo Mitre (© **02/916-2356;** www.casamarioleather.com).

MARKETS The **Villa Biarritz fair,** at Parque Zorilla de San Martín-Ellauri, takes place Saturday from 9:30am to 3pm and features handicrafts, antiques, books, fruit and vegetable vendors, flowers, and other goodies. The **Mercado del Puerto (Port Market)** ⭐ opens afternoons and weekends at Piedras and Yacaré, letting you sample the flavors of Uruguay, from small *empanadas* to enormous barbecued meats. Saturday is the best day to visit, when cultural activities accompany the market. **Tristán Narvaja,** Avenida 18 de Julio in the Cordón neighborhood, is the city's Sunday flea market (6am–3pm), initiated more than 50 years ago by Italian immigrants. **De la Abundancia/Artesanos** is a combined food and handicrafts market. It takes place Monday through Saturday from 10am to 8pm at San José 1312.

WHERE TO STAY

Montevideo's hotel infrastructure is improving and foreigners no longer pay tax on the rates (unlike the locals). Prices are jacked up during Carnaval time in February and when major conventions come to town, however. Parking is included in the rates of most Uruguay hotels.

EXPENSIVE

Belmont House ⭐⭐ *Finds* A boutique hotel in Montevideo's peaceful Carrasco neighborhood, Belmont House offers its privileged guests intimacy and luxury. Small elegant spaces with carefully chosen antiques and wood furnishings give this hotel the feeling of a wealthy private home. Beautiful guest rooms feature two- or four-poster beds; rich, colorful linens; and marble bathrooms with small details such as towel warmers and deluxe toiletries. Many of the rooms feature balconies overlooking the pretty courtyard and pool, and two of the rooms have Jacuzzis. Gourmands will find an excellent international restaurant, afternoon tea, and a *parrilla* open weekends next to the pool.

Av. Rivera 6512, 11500 Montevideo. © **02/600-0430.** Fax 02/600-8609. www.belmonthouse.com.uy. 28 units. $220 (£110) double; from $255–$360 (£128–£180) suite. Rates include gourmet breakfast. AE, DC, MC, V. Amenities: Restaurant; tearoom; bar; beautiful outdoor pool; discounts for tennis and golf; small fitness center; sauna; business center; babysitting; laundry service; dry cleaning. *In room:* A/C, TV, minibar, hair dryer.

Radisson Montevideo Victoria Plaza Hotel ⭐⭐ The Victoria Plaza has long been one of Montevideo's top hotels. Standing in the heart of the financial district, this European-style hotel makes a good base and there is lots of business and social activity. The tower houses spacious guest rooms and executive suites with classic French-style furnishings and panoramic city or river views. The busy hotel has a large multilingual staff that attends closely to guests' needs. Inquire about weekend spa packages. Plaza Victoria is famous for its casino, with French roulette tables, blackjack, baccarat, slot machines, horse races, and bingo. There are two lobby bars, in addition to the casino bars. **Arcadia** (p. 734), on the 25th floor, is the city's most elegant dining room.

Plaza Independencia 759, 11100 Montevideo. © **02/902-0111.** Fax 02/902-1628. www.radisson.com/montevideouy. 254 units. $160 (£130) double; from $210 (£110) suite. Rates include breakfast at rooftop restaurant. AE, DC, MC, V. **Amenities:** Restaurant; cafe; 2 bars; excellent health club w/skylit indoor pool; fitness center; aerobics classes; Jacuzzi;

sauna; concierge; travel agency; business center w/high-speed Internet access; room service; massage service; laundry service; dry cleaning; executive floors. *In room:* A/C, TV, dataport, minibar, hair dryer, safe.

Sheraton Montevideo 🌟🌟

The Sheraton Montevideo is the city's most luxurious hotel. A walkway connects the hotel to the Punta Carretas Shopping Center, one of the city's best malls. Spacious guest rooms have imported furniture, king-size beds, sleeper chairs, marble bathrooms, 25-inch televisions, and works by Uruguayan artists. Rooms on the top two executive floors feature Jacuzzis and individual sound systems. Hotel service is excellent, particularly for guests with business needs. The main restaurant, Las Carretas, serves Continental cuisine with a Mediterranean flair. Don't miss the dining room's spectacular murals by contemporary Uruguayan artist Carlos Vilaró. Next door, the lobby bar is a popular spot for casual business meetings and afternoon cocktails.

Calle Víctor Soliño 349, 11300 Montevideo. 𝄞 **02/710-2121**. Fax 02/712-1262. www.sheraton.com. 207 units. From $200 (£100) double; from $250 (£125) suite. Rates include buffet breakfast. AE, DC, MC, V. **Amenities:** Restaurant; bar; indoor pool; deluxe health club w/fitness center; sauna; concierge; car-rental desk; business center and secretarial services; room service; massage service; babysitting; laundry service; dry cleaning; executive floors; emergency medical service. *In room:* A/C, TV, dataport, minibar, hair dryer, safe.

MODERATE

Holiday Inn 🌟

This colorful Holiday Inn is actually one of the city's best hotels, popular both with tourists and business travelers. It's in the heart of downtown, next to Montevideo's main square. Bilingual staff members greet you in the marble lobby, which is attached to a good restaurant and bar. Guest rooms have simple, contemporary furnishings typical of an American chain. Because the hotel doubles as a convention center, it can become very busy. On the flip side, rooms are heavily discounted when the hotel is empty; be sure to ask for promotional rates, which can be as low as $50 (£25) per night.

Colonia 823, 11100 Montevideo. 𝄞 **02/902-0001**. Fax 02/902-1242. www.holidayinn.com.uy. 137 units. From $72 (£36) double. Rates include buffet breakfast. AE, DC, MC, V. **Amenities:** Restaurant; bar; heated indoor pool; fitness center; sauna; business center; room service; laundry service; dry cleaning; Wi-Fi in public areas. *In room:* A/C, TV, Internet, minibar, safe.

Sheraton Four Points Montevideo 🌟🌟

The Sheraton Four Points is considered a four-star property, but it falls somewhere between four and five, save for its smaller size. The lobby is stark and modern, with polished black-granite panels over white walls in the soaring atrium. Walkways open on to the atrium on each floor, all connected by a glass elevator. Rooms are on the dark side, with charcoal carpeting, dark woods, and rust-colored bedspreads. The bathrooms are spacious, however, and suite bathrooms have hydromassage bathtubs. All rooms have high-speed Internet access, at a charge of $16 (£8) a day. Wi-Fi access is also available, all at the same price as an in-room connection. The desks make a great work space.

Ejido 1275 at Soriano, across from the Intendencia or City Hall, 11000 Montevideo. 𝄞 **02/901-7000**. Fax 02/903-2247. www.fourpoints.com/montevideo. 135 units, including 18 suites. From $200 (£100) double; from $285 (£143) suite. AE, DC, MC, V. Free parking. **Amenities:** Restaurant; bar; indoor pool; health club w/fitness center; sauna; concierge; business center; 24-hr. room service; babysitting; laundry service; dry cleaning. *In room:* A/C, TV, dataport, minibar, hair dryer, safe.

INEXPENSIVE

Days Inn Obelisco 🄥🄰🄻🄸🄴

The modern Days Inn caters to business travelers looking for good-value accommodations. The hotel is located next to the Tres Cruces bus station and not far from downtown or the airport. Rooms are comfortable and modern, if not overly spacious. Free local calls are permitted.

Acevedo Díaz 1821, 11800 Montevideo. ✆ 02/400-4840. Fax 02/402-0229. www.daysinn.com. 60 units. From $65 (£33) double, $100 (£50) suite. Rates include buffet breakfast. AE, DC, MC, V. Free parking. **Amenities:** Coffee shop; small health club; business center; room service. *In room:* A/C, TV, minibar, hair dryer.

WHERE TO DINE

Restaurants in Montevideo serve steak—just as high quality as Argentine beef—and usually include a number of stews and seafood selections as well. You will find the native barbecue, in which beef and lamb are grilled on the fire, in any of the city's grill restaurants, referred to interchangeably in Spanish as *parrillas* or *parrilladas*. Sales tax on dining in Montevideo is a whopping 23%. As in Argentina, there's usually a table cover charge, called the *cubierto*, as well—usually about 25 pesos ($1.20/60p) per person.

MODERATE

Arcadia ✦✦ *(Moments)* INTERNATIONAL   This elegant restaurant is a quiet paradise and the best restaurant in Montevideo. Tables are nestled in semiprivate nooks with floor-to-ceiling bay windows. The classic dining room is decorated with Italian curtains and crystal chandeliers; each table has a fresh rose and sterling silver place settings. Creative plates such as terrine of pheasant marinated in cognac are followed by grilled rack of lamb glazed with mint and garlic, or duck confit served on a thin strudel pastry with red cabbage.

Plaza Independencia 759. ✆ 02/902-0111. Main courses $30–$40 (£15–£20). AE, DC, MC, V. Daily 7pm–midnight.

El Fogón ✦ URUGUAYAN   This brightly lit *parrillada* and seafood restaurant is popular with Montevideo's late-night crowd. The extensive menu includes calamari, salmon, shrimp, and other fish, as well as generous steak and pasta dishes. Food here is priced well and prepared with care. The express lunch menu comes with steak or chicken, dessert, and a glass of wine.

San José 1080. ✆ 02/900-0900. Main courses $10–$15 (£5–£7.50). AE, DC, MC, V. Daily noon–4pm and 7pm–1am.

El Palenque ✦ SEAFOOD/PARRILLADA   Located in the Mercado del Puerto, this is one of the area's most popular restaurants, crowded with locals and tourists alike. It gets especially crowded when the cruise ships come in. It has been around since 1958. Fish is the highlight, but they also have tapas, pasta, paella, and lots of grilled meat. A specialty is the Paella Exotica, made with rabbit.

Pérez Castellano 1579 (at Rambla 25 de Agosto 400 in the Mercado del Puerto). ✆ 02/917-0190 or 02/915-4704. www.elpalenque.com.uy. Main courses $15–$30 (£7.50–£15). AE, DC, MC, V. Mon–Sat noon–1am; Sun noon–5pm.

El Viejo y el Mar ✦ SEAFOOD   Resembling an old fishing club, El Viejo y el Mar is on the riverfront near the Sheraton. The bar is made from an abandoned boat, while the dining room is decorated with dock lines, sea lamps, and pictures of 19th-century regattas. You'll find every kind of fish and pasta on the menu, and the restaurant is equally popular for evening cocktails. An outdoor patio is open most of the year.

Rambla Gandhi 400. ✆ 02/710-5704. Main courses $15–$30 (£7.50–£15). MC, V. Daily noon–4pm and 8pm–1am.

Los Leños ✦✦ URUGUAYAN   This casual *parrillada* resembles one you'd find in Buenos Aires—except that Los Leños also serves an outstanding range of *mariscos* (seafood), such as the Spanish paella or *lenguado Las Brasas* (a flathead fish) served with prawns, mushrooms, and mashed potatoes. From the *parrilla*, the *filet de lomo* is the best cut—order it with Roquefort, mustard, or black-pepper sauce. The restaurant's fresh produce is displayed in a case near the kitchen.

San José 909. (©) **02/900-2285**. Main courses $15–$30 (£7.50–£15). AE, DC, MC, V. Daily 11:45am–3:30pm and 7:30pm–midnight.

INEXPENSIVE
Río Alegre *(Value* SNACKS   This casual, inventive lunch stop specializes in quick steaks off the grill. Ribs, sausages, and most cuts of beef are cooked on the *parrilla*, made to order. Río Alegre is a local favorite because of its large portions, good quality, and cheap prices.

Calle Pérez Castellano and Piedras, at the Mercado del Puerto, Local 33. (©) **02/915-6504**. Main courses $10–$12 (£5–£6). No credit cards. Daily 11am–3pm.

MONTEVIDEO AFTER DARK
As in Buenos Aires, nightlife in Montevideo means drinks after 10pm and dancing after midnight. For earlier entertainment, ask at your hotel or call the **Teatro Solís,** Calle Buenos Aires 652 (© **02/916-0908**), the city's center for opera, theater, ballets, and symphonies, for performance information. **SODRE,** Av. 18 de Julio 930 (© **02/ 901-2850**), is the city's "Official Radio Service," which hosts classical music concerts from May to November.

Gamblers should head to the **Plaza Victoria Casino,** Plaza Independencia (© **02/ 902-0111**), a fashionable venue with French roulette tables, blackjack, baccarat, slot machines, horse races, and bingo. It opens at 2pm and keeps going through most of the night.

Mariachi, Gabriel Pereira 2964 (© **02/709-1600**), is one of the city's top bars and dance clubs, with live bands or DJ music Wednesday to Sunday after 10pm. **Café Misterio,** Costa Rica 1700 (© **02/600-5999**), is another popular bar. **New York,** Calle Mar Ártico 1227 (© **02/600-0444**), combines a restaurant, bar, and dance club under one roof and attracts a slightly older crowd. Montevideo's best tango clubs are **La Casa de Becho,** Nueva York 1415 (© **02/400-2717;** Fri–Sat after 10:30pm), where composer Gerardo Mattos Rodríguez wrote the famous "La Cumparsita," and **Cuareim,** Zelmar Michelini 1079 (no phone; Wed and Fri–Sat after 9pm), which offers both tango and *candombe,* a lively dance indigenous to the area, with roots in early slave culture. The tourist office can give you schedule information for Montevideo's other tango salons.

5 A Side Trip to Colonia del Sacramento
242km (150 miles) W of Montevideo

The tiny gem of Colonia del Sacramento, declared a World Heritage City by UNESCO, appears untouched by time. Dating from the 17th century, the Old City boasts beautifully preserved colonial artistry down its dusty streets. A leisurely stroll from the Puerta de Campo into the **Barrio Histórico** (Old, or Historic, Neighborhood) leads under flower-laden windowsills to churches dating from the 1680s, past exquisite single-story homes from Colonia's time as a Portuguese settlement and on to local museums detailing the riches of the town's past. The Barrio Histórico contains brilliant examples of colonial wealth and many of Uruguay's oldest structures. Yet while the city resides happily in tradition, a mix of lovely shops, delicious cafes, and thoughtful museums make the town more than a history lesson.

ESSENTIALS
GETTING THERE

The easiest way to reach Colonia from Buenos Aires is by ferry. **FerryLíneas** (© **02/900-6617**) runs a fast boat that arrives in 45 minutes. **Buquebús** (© **02/916-1910**) also offers two classes of service. Prices range from $20 to $45 (£10–£23) each way. A new ferryboat-and-bus combination service opened in 2006 to compete with what had been a monopoly for Buquebús. **Colonia Express** (in Buenos Aires, © **54/11/4313-5100;** in Montevideo, © **02/901-9597;** www.coloniaexpress.com) offers similar prices but a less frequent schedule. Colonia is a good stopping-off point if you're traveling between Buenos Aires and Montevideo. **COT** (© **02/409-4949** in Montevideo) offers **bus service** from Montevideo and from Punta del Este.

VISITOR INFORMATION

The **Oficina de Turismo,** General Flores and Rivera (© **052/27000** or 27300), is open daily from 8am to 8pm. Speak with someone at the tourism office to arrange a guided tour of the town.

WHAT TO SEE & DO
A WALK THROUGH COLONIA'S BARRIO HISTORICO

Concentrate in the **Barrio Histórico (Old Neighborhood),** located on the coast at the far southwestern corner of town. The sights, which are all within a few blocks, can easily be visited on foot in a few hours. Museums and tourist sites are open daily (except Wed) from 11am to 5:45pm. For less than $1 (50p), you can buy a pass at the Portuguese or Municipal museum that will get you into all the sights.

Start your tour at **Plaza Mayor,** the principal square that served as the center of the colonial establishment. To explore Colonia's Portuguese history, cross Calle Manuel Lobo on the southeastern side of the plaza and enter the **Museo Portugués.** Upon exiting the museum, turn left and walk to the **Iglesia Matriz,** among the oldest churches in the country and an excellent example of 17th-century architecture and design.

Next, exit the church and turn left to the **Ruinas Convento San Francisco.** Dating from 1696, the San Francisco convent was once inhabited by Jesuit and Franciscan monks. Continue up Calle San Francisco to the **Casa de Brown,** which houses the **Museo Municipal.** Here you will find an impressive collection of colonial documents and artifacts, a must-see for history buffs.

For those with a more artistic bent, turn left on Calle Misiones de los Tapes and walk 2 blocks to the **Museo del Azulejo,** a unique museum of 19th-century European and Uruguayan tiles housed in a gorgeous 300-year-old country house. Then stroll back into the center of town along Calle de la Playa, enjoying the shops and cafes along the way, until you come to the **Ruinas Casa del Gobernador.** The House of the Viceroy captures something of the glorious past of the city's 17th- and 18th-century magistrates, when the port was used for imports, exports, and smuggling. After exploring the opulent lifestyle of colonial leaders, complete your walk with a visit to the **UNESCO-Colonia** headquarters.

WHERE TO STAY & DINE

Few people stay in Colonia, preferring to make a day trip from Buenos Aires or stop along the way to Montevideo. If you'd rather get a hotel, however, your best bets are the colonial-style **Hotel Plaza Mayor,** Calle del Comercio 111 (© **052/23193**), and

Hotel La Misión, Calle Misiones de los Tapes 171 (© **052/26767**), whose original building dates from 1762. Both hotels charge from $90 (£45) for a double. A small **Sheraton,** Continuación de la Rambla de Las Américas s/n (© **052/29000**), recently opened in the heart of Colonia, offering doubles from $149 (£75); it has a spa and a golf course. The **Four Seasons,** Ruta 21, Km 262, Carmelo (© **0542/9000;** www. fourseasons.com/carmelo) operates a luxury resort in nearby Carmelo, about 45 minutes away. Rooms start at $320 (£160).

For dining, **Mesón de la Plaza,** Vasconcellos 153 (© **052/24807**), serves quality international and Uruguayan food in a colonial setting. **Pulpería de los Faroles,** Calle Misiones de los Tapes 101 (© **052/25399**), in front of Plaza Mayor, specializes in beef and bean dishes and homemade pasta.

6 Punta del Este

140km (87 miles) E of Montevideo

Few resorts in South America rival Punta del Este for glamour. It might be geographically located in Uruguay, but it's where the glitterati and elite of Buenos Aires make their homes for the summer. As Mar del Plata's reputation downscales, this Uruguayan resort area has become the new place to see and be seen.

Punta is actually a reference to several towns on a small peninsula where the Río de la Plata meets the Atlantic Ocean. Together they have over 50km (31 miles) of waterfront. The majority of the city's major hotels are on the calmer river side. As a general rule, the farther you get from the center, the less crowded the beaches. Little of historical value is left anymore except a few buildings, such as the *faro* (lighthouse), churches, schoolhouses, and turn-of-the-20th-century buildings. The port is often jammed with yachts in the summer.

Punta has lost some of its higher-end clients, who have gone elsewhere to look for greater exclusivity. About 10km (6 miles) up from Punta del Este is the small town of La Barra. Many young beachgoers flock here, and it's never quiet in high season.

Farther along Ruta 10 is the very exclusive José Ignacio, a small quiet community that's even more expensive than La Barra. Summer season lasts from October to March, but "the Season," as it is known in the area, is a very specific time; from a few days after Christmas through the first 2 weeks of January, the Punta, La Barra, and José Ignacio swell with movie stars and models.

ESSENTIALS
GETTING THERE
BY PLANE   Punta del Este has its own international airport, **Laguna del Sauce Airport** (© **042/559777**), about 16km (10 miles) from the city center, which has direct flights from Buenos Aires's Jorge Newberry Airport. **Aerolíneas Argentinas** (© **000-4054-86527** in Punta, or 0810/222-86527 in Buenos Aires; www.aerolineas.com.ar) services the airports. **Pluna Airlines** is another carrier (© **042/492050** in Punta, or 11/4342-4420 in Buenos Aires; www.pluna.aero).

BY BUS   The **Terminal de Buses Punta del Este,** Rambla Artigas and Calle Inzaurraga (© **042/489-467**), has buses connecting to Montevideo, Colonia, and other cities throughout Uruguay. **COT** (© **042/486-810,** or 02/409-4949 in Montevideo) offers the best service to Montevideo. The trip takes 1½ to 2 hours and costs about $10 (£5 round-trip.

BY CAR   If you are driving from Montevideo, you can reach Punta in 1½ hours by taking Route 1 east past Atlántida and Piriápolis to the turnoff for Route 93.

GETTING AROUND

If you're staying in Punta del Este itself, the beaches are just a quick walk over either the **Rambla Claudio Williman,** on the Río de la Plata side, or the **Rambla Lorenzo Batlle Pacheco,** on the Atlantic side. Although these two *ramblas* have different names, they are part of the same coastal highway, Ruta 10. The city's main shopping street is **Avenida Gorlero,** lined with stores and cafes. Another shopping street is **El Remanso,** 1 block parallel.

Many people hitchhike—it's not considered dangerous here. It's best to rent a car, though, if you want to do some exploring or head to La Barra or José Ignacio without the threat of being stranded or sleeping on the beach. Car rental can be expensive, however, starting at $90 (£45) a day in high season. **Europcar** has an office at Gorlero and Calle 20 (© **042/495017** and 042/445018; www.europcar.com.uy). **Dollar** is at Gorlero 961 (© **042/443444;** www.dollar.com.uy).

Taxis are hard to come by, especially in high season. Keep the following numbers handy: **Shopping** (© **042/484704**), **Parada 5** (© **042/490302**), and **Aeropuerto** (© **042/559100**). The bus company **COT** (© **042/486810**) runs a service up and down the coastal routes, connecting the various towns in the area. You may have to wait a long time for one to pass by, though. The company **Taller Rego,** Lenzina and Artigas, Parada 2 (© **042/486732**) rents motorcycles and bicycles.

VISITOR INFORMATION

Punta del Este has several tourist information centers. Within the bus station **Terminal Punta Del Este** (© **042/494042**), there is a very small one with a very helpful staff. Overlooking the ocean at Parada 1 near Calle 21, the **Liga de Fomento** has a Tourist Information Center (© **042/446519**). Another city office is at **Plaza Artigas,** on Gorlero between calles 25 and 23 (© **042/446519**). The city's offices are open daily from 10am to 10pm. The government of Uruguay also maintains a tourist information office for the entire country at Gorlero 942 between calles 30 and 29 (© **042/441218**). The national office is open 10am to 7pm every day in the summer, and in winter daily from 10am to 5pm. The city government website (www.maldonado.gub.uy) has a section on tourist information; also visit **www.uruguaynatural.com**. Pick up *Liga News* or *Qué Hacemos Hoy,* two free tourist publications, available throughout the city, with information on events around town.

WHAT TO SEE & DO

The main reason to visit Punta del Este is the beach, but you'll also find a few sights of interest. The symbol of Punta del Este is **La Mano,** a giant concrete hand sculpture rising out of the sands of the Atlantic, opposite the bus station. On the tip of the peninsula, **Puerto Punta del Este** is pleasant for strolling and watching the boats come in. A tranquil change of pace from the beach is the church **Nuestra Señora de la Candelaria,** at the corner of Calle 12 (or Virazon) and Calle 5 (or El Faro), a beautiful sky-blue-and-white Victorian structure. Across the street is the **Meteorological Station,** Calle 5 (or El Faro) and Calle 10 (or Calle Dos de Febrero), a modern lookout tower built over a 100-year-old schoolhouse. Directly across the street is **Faro de Punta del Este,** the city's symbolic lighthouse, dating from 1860, at Calle 5 (or El Faro) and Calle 10 (or Calle Dos de Febrero). **Plaza Artigas,** at Gorlero and Arrecifes, has a daily artist market with souvenirs and crafts. Along Ruta 10, just outside downtown La Barra, is the **Museo del Mar** ✸✸ (℘ **042/771-817**), an interesting museum open daily in summer from 10am to 10:30pm, and in winter daily from 11am to 6pm.

SHOPPING

The majority of shops run along Avenida Gorlero and Calle 20, also known as El Remanso, or the Little Paris. Many stores do not open until the evening. For leather goods, try **Leather Corner,** Calle 31 at Inzaurraga and Gorlero (℘ **042/441901**). **Duo,** Calle 20 at Calle 30 (℘ **042/447709**), is an upscale sportswear store for men and women. **100% Uruguayo,** Gorlero 883 at Calle 28 (℘ **042/446530**), has a large collection of handmade and distinctive locally produced goods; leather is the highlight. **Punta Shopping** is the main mall, (Av. Roosevelt at Parada 7; ℘ **042/489666;** www.puntashopping.com.uy). **Plaza Artigas,** at Gorlero and Arrecifes, has a daily artist market with souvenirs and crafts. The town of La Barra is better known for its art galleries, including the popular **Trench Gallery,** Ruta 10, Km 161, Parada 45 (℘ **042/771597;** www.trenchgallery.com).

WHERE TO STAY

Unless otherwise indicated, prices listed below are for summer peak season and are often half that in the off season. **Semana Santa** (Dec 24–31) is the busiest, most expensive week. Reserve well ahead.

VERY EXPENSIVE

The Awa Hotel ✸✸   This small, well-designed boutique hotel was an instant success when it opened in 2006. The building has clean lines—a sort of 1950s interpretation of Alpine architecture, set on a landscaped hill with soaring pine trees. Rooms are a good size, set in pure radiant white, with African-made, wall-to-wall cotton carpeting in neutral tones. Bathrooms are large and the suites have hydromassage tubs. One of the most amazing things about the hotel is its theater. The hotel is a bit of a walk from the beach, but it's surrounded by several restaurants, and it's close to the Punta Shopping Mall.

Pedragosa Sierra and San Ciro; CP 20100, Punta del Este. ℘ 042/499999. www.awahotel.com. 48 units, including 4 suites and 8 executive corner oversize rooms. In low season from $110 (£55) double; from $210 (£105) suite; high season from $265 (£133) double, from $530 (£265) suite. Rates include buffet breakfast. AE, DC, MC, V. Free on-site parking. **Amenities:** Restaurant; heated outdoor pool; small health club; spa; concierge; business center; room service; massage service; laundry service; dry cleaning; minitheater; Wi-Fi in lobby. *In room:* A/C, TV, Wi-Fi, minibar, hair dryer, safe.

The Conrad Hotel and Casino ✸✸✸   This 14-story complex, a blue streamlined structure, has became the de facto town center and is a hive of activity. Some rooms have a California vibe, with casual decor in terra cottas and neutral tones; others are modern and more severe; and still others have a tropical playfulness to them. All rooms facing the Río de la Plata have balconies, and the suites have balconies enormous enough for entertaining several guests, which is common in the summertime. There are several restaurants in the lobby and other areas of the hotel. The pool and spa complex is a combination of indoor and outdoor spaces, with a view to the Río de la Plata. There is also the children's complex, where you can leave your kids and gain some free time. The 24-hour casino has 450 slot machines and 63 gaming tables; it's definitely worth visiting even if you're not staying here. (During your time in Punta, you'll likely hear "meet me at the Conrad" more than once.)

Parada 4 on Rambla Claudio Williman (between Chivert and Biarritz on Playa Mansa), CP 20100, Punta del Este. ✆ 042/491111. Fax 042/490803. www.conrad.com.uy. 302 units, including 24 suites. In low season from $180 (£90) double; from $400 (£200) suite; high season from $340 (£170) double, from $500 (£250) suite, $7,500 (£3,750) for Conrad suite. Rates can fluctuate drastically within various date ranges. Rates include luxurious buffet breakfast. AE, DC, MC, V. **Amenities:** 5 restaurants; several bars; indoor and outdoor heated pools; large health club; spa; children's center; concierge; business center; shopping arcade; 24-hr. room service; massage service; babysitting; laundry service; dry cleaning; 24-hr. casino; theater and show complex; Wi-Fi in lobby. *In room:* A/C, TV, high-speed Internet access, kitchens in select suites, minibar, hair dryer, safe.

EXPENSIVE

L'Auberge ★★ *(Finds)*   This exclusive boutique hotel lies in the quiet residential neighborhood of Parque de Golf and is 2 blocks from the beach. Formerly an 18th-century water tower, the hotel today houses beautiful guest rooms decorated with antiques and has a dedicated staff committed to warm, personalized service. The colorful gardens and pool will draw you outside, and the staff can help you arrange horseback riding, golf, tennis, or other outdoor sports in the surrounding parks. The sophisticated resort has an elegant European tearoom overlooking the gardens, famous for its homemade waffles. An evening barbecue is offered by the pool.

Barrio Parque del Golf, 20100 Punta del Este. ✆ 042/482-601. Fax 042/483-408. www.laubergehotel.com. 40 units. From $320 (£160) double; from $810 (£405) suite. Rates include continental breakfast. AE, DC, MC, V. **Amenities:** Outdoor pool; golf; tennis court; fitness center; spa; concierge; business center and secretarial services; room service; babysitting; laundry service; dry cleaning. *In room:* TV, minibar, hair dryer, safe.

MODERATE

Best Western La Foret ★ *(Kids)*   La Foret offers spacious guest rooms 1 block from Playa Mansa. The amenities are extensive and the hotel is a nice option for families (children under 12 stay free, and there's a children's playground and babysitting services). There's also a good international restaurant and coffee shop with a multilingual staff.

Calle La Foret, Parada 6, Playa Mansa, 20100 Punta del Este. ✆/fax 042/481-004. www.bestwestern.com. 59 units. From $170 to $250 (£85–£125) double. Rates include buffet breakfast. AE, DC, MC, V. **Amenities:** Restaurant; bar/lounge; pool; Jacuzzi; sauna; concierge; business services; babysitting. *In room:* TV, dataport, minibar, hair dryer, safe.

Days Inn Punta del Este ★★ *(Value)*   This atypical Days Inn sits on the waterfront and offers excellent value for its location. It features simple but modern rooms, many with ocean views. The Conrad Resort & Casino is next door, along with restaurants, cinemas, and excellent beaches. This is the best midrange hotel in Punta.

Rambla Williman, Parada 3, Playa Mansa, 20100 Punta del Este. ✆ 042/484-353. Fax 042/484-683. www.daysinn. com. 38 units. From $115 (£58) double. Rates include buffet breakfast. AE, DC, MC, V. **Amenities:** Bar/lounge; indoor heated and outdoor pool; room service; babysitting; laundry service. *In room:* TV, dataport, minibar, hair dryer, safe.

WHERE TO DINE
EXPENSIVE

El Viejo Marino ★ SEAFOOD/PARRILLA   This charming seafood restaurant and *parrilla* has a strong sailor theme. The smiling friendly waitresses all wear dresses inspired by sailor uniforms. The dark interior mimics a ship, with navy-blue walls, dark woods, rope-back chairs, and old marine equipment scattered about. The menu has interesting combinations, such as sole cooked with Roquefort or mozzarella, several varieties of salmon, and catches of the day, much of it from the Río de la Plata.

Calle 11 at Calle 14. ✆ 042/443565. Main courses $15–$20 (£7.50–£10). AE, MC, V. Daily noon–3pm and 8pm–2am (in summer, if busy, they will remain open between lunch and dinner).

Lo de Tere ☆ INTERNATIONAL   Overlooking the yacht-filled port, this elegant but casual restaurant is a good choice. The menu includes fish, *parrilla*, pasta, and sandwiches named for celebrities (including the hunky beef sandwich called the Brad Pitt).

Rambla de Puerto at Calle 21. © 042/440492. www.lodetere.com. Main courses $8–$30 (£4–£15). AE, DC, MC, V. Daily noon–4pm and 8pm–1 or 2am.

INEXPENSIVE

Los Caracoles ☆ *Value* URUGUAYAN   The town's most recommended *parrillada* also serves excellent seafood, including Spanish-style paella. A good salad bar accompanies the hearty selection of meats and fish, and there are a number of homemade pastas to choose from as well. Packed with 70 tables, the rustic dining room is casual and boisterous.

Calle Gorlero 20. © 042/440-912. Main courses $6.50–$8 (£3.25–£4). AE, DC, MC, V. Summer daily noon–6pm and 8pm–3am; winter daily noon–4pm and 7pm–1am.

PUNTA DEL ESTE AFTER DARK

The **Conrad Resort & Casino,** Parada 4, Playa Mansa (© 042/491-111), is the focal point for evening entertainment in Punta, featuring Las Vegas–style reviews and other music, dance, and magic shows—sometimes around the torch-lit swimming pools. The enormous 24-hour casino has tables playing baccarat, roulette, blackjack, poker, dice, and fortune wheel.

Bars and dance clubs come and go with considerable frequency in Punta, often changing names from one season to the next. The best bar is **Moby Dick,** located at Rambla de la Circunvalación (© 042/441-240), near the yacht harbor. Punta's bronzed Latin bodies then make their way to **Gitane** and **La Plage** (© 042/484-869), two dance clubs next to each other on Rambla Brava, Parada 12. In recent years La Barra 10km (6 miles) to the north has become the main strip for bars and nightclubs that perennially change name and location.

13

Venezuela

by Eliot Greenspan

As Venezuela's outspoken and controversial leader, Hugo Chávez, continues to make headlines, spar with the United States, and lead the country on a path toward socialism, this vast and varied destination remains largely undiscovered and undervisited, which is a shame. From snowcapped Andean peaks to white-sand Caribbean beaches, from the Orinoco River to the skyscrapers of Caracas, there's an astounding range of places to see and things to do. Adventurous types can hike to the foot of Angel Falls, the tallest waterfall on the planet, or fish for piranha and wrangle anaconda on the flooded plains of Los Llanos.

Venezuela is exceptionally rich in biological diversity and pure natural beauty. With 43 national parks and a score of other natural monuments and protected areas, it's a fabulous destination for nature lovers, bird-watchers, and adventure travelers. There's great windsurfing, kite boarding, scuba diving, fishing, mountain biking, mountain climbing, hiking, trekking, and river rafting.

Venezuela has the richest oil reserves in the Western Hemisphere. Thanks to the oil, it is one of the most modern and industrialized countries in Latin America. Still, despite skyrocketing crude oil prices and over 9 years of rule under the populist Chávez, nearly half of the population still lives below the poverty line. Widespread unemployment, underemployment, and crippling poverty spur high levels of crime and violence, especially in Caracas and other urban areas.

Venezuela, the closest South American country to the United States, has frequent and affordable air connections to both the U.S. and Europe, and is thus easily accessible to international tourists. Most of the country is connected by an excellent network of paved roads and a good internal commuter air system. This chapter covers the top tourist destinations—Caracas, Isla de Margarita, Los Llanos, Mérida and Los Andes, Los Roques, and Canaima and Angel Falls—and will guide you to some unforgettable experiences.

1 The Regions in Brief

Venezuela lies between 1° and 12° north latitude and goes from sea level to 5,007m (16,443 ft.)—giving it everything from steamy equatorial jungles to perennially snowcapped mountains. There are dry barren deserts and lush tropical rainforests. More than 90% of the population lives in cities located in the northern part of this country, bordered by the Caribbean Sea, Colombia, Brazil, and Guyana,

Given the wide range of destinations, attractions, and adventures offered in Venezuela, the itinerary you choose will greatly depend on your particular interests and needs. Business travelers in Caracas with a free day or two should head to Los Roques for some fun in the sun, and a chance to go fishing or scuba diving. Adventure travelers should definitely visit Mérida and the Andes. Bird-watchers and nature lovers should not miss Los Llanos. Families looking for an all-inclusive resort vacation with plenty of activities to keep the kids busy should choose Isla de Margarita. And those seeking an adventurous tour through some of South America's most stunning scenery should head to Canaima and Angel Falls.

CARACAS   Caracas is an overcrowded, inhospitable, and famously violent city. The city center occupies a flat valley surrounded by high mountains and hillsides. Urban sprawl has covered most of these hillsides with dense *ranchitos* (shantytowns). A total of some four million inhabitants, or Caraqueños, make up the greater metropolitan area. Despite the widespread poverty and overcrowding, Caracas is one of the more cosmopolitan and architecturally distinctive cities in Latin America, with a vibrant and active population.

THE URBAN BELT   From Maracaibo in the west to Cumaná and Maturín in the east is a more or less linear belt of urban development, much of it based around major petroleum, mining, and agricultural centers, and most of it on or close to the Caribbean coast. Major cities include Maracaibo, Barquisimeto, Valencia, Maracay, and Caracas. An estimated 80% of the country's population lives within this relatively narrow urban belt. In fact, Venezuelans refer to almost all the rest of the country as "the interior."

THE CARIBBEAN COAST & THE ISLANDS   Venezuela has 3,000km (1,860 miles) of coastline and hundreds of coastal islands, most of them uninhabited. The largest of the islands, **Isla de Margarita,** is Venezuela's most popular tourist destination. **Los Roques,** an archipelago of 42 named islands and 200 sand spits, mangrove islands, and tiny cays, is also very popular. The coastal region closest to Caracas, known as **El Litoral,** was devastated in 1999 by massive landslides and flooding, which left an estimated 20,000 dead and many more homeless. While this region has largely recovered, it still shows the effects of the disaster. The coastal areas farther east and west of El Litoral offer scores of relatively undiscovered and undeveloped beaches for the more intrepid and independent travelers. The climate all along the coast and on the Caribbean islands is hot and tropical, and much drier than the rest of the country.

THE ANDES   The great South American mountain chain, the Andes, runs through Venezuela from the Colombian border in a northeasterly direction through the states of Táchira, Mérida, and Trujillo. The mountains here, in three major spines—the Sierra Nevada, Sierra de La Culata, and Sierra de Santo Domingo—rise to more than 5,000m (16,400 ft.). The principal city here is **Mérida,** a picturesque and bustling college town nestled in a narrow valley. However, there are many small mountain towns, as well as some interesting indigenous villages, that are scattered about and worth exploring. This is a prime area for hiking, trekking, and a wide range of adventure sports.

LOS LLANOS   Located on plains that roll on for hundreds of miles south and east of the Andes, **Los Llanos** is an area of flat, mostly open cattle ground, punctuated with some isolated stands of forest. During the latter part of the rainy season (July–Nov), the plains are almost entirely flooded, with only a few raised highways and service roads passable in anything that doesn't float. In the dry season, the land reemerges and wildlife congregates in dense herds and mixed flocks around the ponds and creeks that are left behind. The quantity and variety of wildlife visible at the nature lodges located in Los Llanos are truly phenomenal—anaconda, caiman, capybara, deer, and even wildcats are commonly sighted. This is one of the top spots on the planet for bird-watching.

SOUTHERN VENEZUELA & THE GRAN SABANA Southern Venezuela is a largely uninhabited and wild region of tropical forests and jungle rivers. The region is home to several ancient indigenous tribes, including the Piaroa, Pemón, and Yanomami, who still live an often-nomadic lifestyle based on hunting and gathering. This area is home to vast expanses of forest, including **Canaima National Park,** the largest national park in Venezuela, and the sixth largest in the world, as well as **Angel Falls,** the highest waterfall on the planet, and a series of stunning steep-walled mesas called *tepuis.* Much of this region is also known as the Gran Sabana (Great Plains), as it features large stretches of flat savanna broken up only by these imposing *tepuis.*

THE ORINOCO DELTA The eastern end of Venezuela comprises the largely uninhabited Orinoco Delta. Second in size and import to the Amazon (both as a river and a river basin), the Orinoco Delta is a vast area of shifting rivers, tributaries, mangroves, rainforests, and natural canals. The area is also known as the Delta Amacuro, after a smaller river that empties into the basin and forms part of the border with Guyana. This area is just starting to develop as a destination for naturalists and ecotourists.

2 The Best of Venezuela in 2 Weeks

This itinerary will take you from the turquoise waters and white sands of Venezuela's Caribbean islands to the snowcapped peaks of Los Andes. In between you'll marvel at the amazing biological diversity of Los Llanos and swim at the foot of Angel Falls, the world's tallest waterfall. Some travelers opt to extend their time in any one of the destinations listed below, or have less than 2 weeks budgeted. If so, you'll have to make some tough choices, but you'll want to use this route as a reference point.

Day ❶: Arrive and Head Immediately to Los Roques 🎨🎨

Venezuela's principal airport is right on the Caribbean coast, in **Maiquetia.** Don't even leave the airport. You'll visit Caracas later. Instead, hook up with a local commuter flight to **Los Roques** and settle into your *posada* in time for a sunset cocktail overlooking the sea at **Bora El Mar.** See p. 789.

Day ❷: Commandeer an Island for the Day 🎨🎨🎨

Have your posada arrange for a morning transfer to **your own private cay.** Be sure to bring plenty of water and sunscreen and a shade umbrella, in addition to your packed lunch. Spend the day beachcombing and snorkeling, until the motor launch comes to pick you up in the afternoon. See p. 785.

Day ❸: Head to Canaima 🎨🎨

Fly from Los Roques down to **Canaima** and check in to **Jungle Rudy Campamento** 🎨🎨 (p. 805). You should have time to take an afternoon boat tour of **Canaima Lagoon,** with views of **Hacha, Golondrina,** and **Ucaima Falls.** Be sure also to allow time for a visit to **Makunaima Arte Indígena** 🎨 (p. 804), an excellent gift shop filled with local and regional arts and crafts.

Day ❹: Visit Angel Falls 🎨🎨🎨

This entire day will be devoted to visiting **Angel Falls** 🎨🎨🎨. Be sure to insist on some good quality time at the foot of the falls, for bathing and soaking in the sights. On the return trip you'll probably visit **Sapo Falls.** Be prepared to get wet again on the hike behind and under the waterfall. See p. 804.

Days ⑤—⑥: Spot Anaconda, Caiman & Capybara in Los Llanos 🐾🐾

Take an early morning flight out of Canaima to Ciudad Bolívar or Puerto Ordaz and connect with a subsequent flight or land transfer to **Hato El Cedral** 🐾 (p. 799). You should arrive in time for an afternoon tour. If not, settle into your room and prepare to wake up early for a full day of intense wildlife viewing. In addition to the animals listed above, you'll see scores, or more, of bird species, and probably fish for **piranha.**

Days ⑦—⑩: Get High in Mérida & the Venezuelan Andes

Head from Los Llanos to **Mérida** 🐾🐾 either by land or air, and check in to **Posada Casa Sol** 🐾🐾 (p. 795). Spend your time here taking advantage of the high mountain scenery and numerous tour options. Those who are physically fit and adventurous should definitely take a **canyoning** trip with **Arassari Treks** 🐾🐾 (p. 793). Less extreme travelers can ride **El Teleférico** 🐾🐾 (p. 792) to the top of Pico Espejo, and tour some of the nearby mountain villages.

Days ⑪—⑫: Isla Margarita 🐾

You've earned a little more beach time, so take a commuter flight to **Isla Margarita** and decompress on the beaches of this Caribbean island. Be sure to reserve a table at **Casa Caranta** 🐾🐾🐾 (p. 782) for dinner one night. On the other evening, head to **Guayoyo Café** (p. 783), or do some gambling at the casino at the **Hilton Margarita** (p. 780).

Days ⑬–⑭: Caracas

Return to **Caracas** and take a crash course in this capital city. Visit the **Museo de Arte Contemporáneo de Sofía Imber** ✦✦ and the **Iglesia de San Francisco** ✦✦ (p. 763). Be sure to schedule a trip to **El Hatillo** ✦✦ (p. 771), which will include a shopping excursion to the **Hannsi Centro Artesanal** ✦✦✦ (p. 765). After dinner, be sure to cap everything off with a drink at **360°** ✦✦ (p. 771), taking in the view of the city from the uppermost rooftop bar here.

3 Planning Your Trip to Venezuela

VISITOR INFORMATION

Good tourist information on Venezuela is hard to come by. The country's **Ministry of Tourism** (MINTUR; see "In Venezuela," below) was formed in 2005, to either directly replace or oversee several other rudderless bureaucracies. However, they offer precious little in the way of information or help geared toward individual travelers, and their website is entirely in Spanish. Your best bet is to search the Internet, or deal directly with hotels and tour operators working in Venezuela. The following websites contain useful information pertaining to the country.

- **http://lanic.utexas.edu/la/venezuela**: The University of Texas Latin American Studies Department's database features an extensive list of useful links.
- **http://think-venezuela.net**: Although somewhat clunky and poorly organized, Think Venezuela is still probably the best all-around general tourism site on Venezuela.
- **www.embavenez-us.org**: The website for the embassy of Venezuela in the United States has current information and a small section of links.
- **http://english.eluniversal.com**: The English-language site of one of the country's main daily newspapers, *El Universal*.

IN VENEZUELA

MINTUR (✆ 0212/208-4511; www.mintur.gob.ve) is the national tourism ministry. Its main office, located at the intersection of avenidas Francisco de Miranda and Principal de La Floresta, is open weekdays during business hours. The staff can give you a basic map and some brochures for hotels and attractions; however, they are not really geared to serve as an information source for individual tourists.

For the best tourism information in the country, contact the established tourism agencies, including **Akanan Travel & Adventure** (✆ 0212/715-5433 or 0414/116-0107; www.akanan.com), **Cacao Expeditions** (✆ 0212/977-1234; www.cacaotravel.com), **Lost World Adventures** (✆ 800/999-0558 in the U.S., or 0212/577-0303 in Caracas; www.lostworldadventures.com), and **Natoura Adventure Tours** (✆ 0274/252-4075; www.natoura.com). Most bookstores and many hotel gift shops around the country stock a small selection of maps and useful books (some in English) on Venezuelan history, culture, and tourism.

ENTRY REQUIREMENTS

You need a valid passport to enter Venezuela. Upon arrival, citizens and residents of the United States, Canada, Great Britain, Australia, and New Zealand who enter by air or cruise ship are issued a free general visa valid for 90 days. You can extend your visa for up to 60 days at the Caracas office of the national immigration agency, **Dirección de Identificación y Extranjería** (**DIEX;** ✆ 0800/664-3390 or 212/483-2070;

www.onidex.gov.ve; Avenida Baralt, Edificio 1000, El Silencio, across from Plaza Miranda). In theory, you can apply for two consecutive extensions. The extensions cost between BsF45 and BsF70 ($21–$33/£10–£16), depending on the length of time you apply for. The office is open Monday through Friday from 7:30am to 4:30pm.

If you plan to enter Venezuela by sea or land, it is advisable to try to obtain a visa in advance from your nearest Venezuelan embassy or consulate, although, in practice, this is usually not necessary. When applied for in advance through a Venezuelan embassy or consulate, the visa costs BsF65 ($30/£15). However, you may be charged more depending on the processing fees and policies of your local embassy or consulate. I've heard reports that you may face an arbitrary charge of between BsF5 and BsF21 ($2.35–$9.80/£1.15–£4.80) at some of the crossings along the borders with Colombia and Brazil.

Venezuela requires children under 18 traveling alone, with one parent, or with a third party to present a copy of their birth certificate and written, notarized authorization by the absent parent(s) or legal guardian granting permission to travel alone, with one parent, or with a third party. For more details, contact your embassy or consulate.

VENEZUELAN EMBASSY LOCATIONS

In the U.S.: 1099 30th St. NW, Washington, DC 20007 (© **202/342-2214;** fax 202/342-6820; www.embavenez-us.org)

In Canada: 32 Range Rd., Ottawa, ON KIN 8J4 (© **613/235-5151;** fax 613/235-3205; www.misionvenezuela.org)

In the U.K.: 1 Cromwell Rd., London SW7 2HW (© **020/7584-4206;** fax 020/7589-8887; http://venezuela.embassyhomepage.com)

In Australia & New Zealand: 7 Culgoa Circuit, O'Malley, Canberra, ACT 2606 (© **02/6290-2967;** fax 02/6290-2911; www.venezuela-emb.org.au)

Telephone Dialing Info at a Glance

Venezuela's phone system features a standardized system of seven-digit local numbers, with three-digit area codes. Note that you must add a zero before the three-digit area code when dialing from within Venezuela, but not when dialing to Venezuela from abroad.

- **To place a call from your home country to Venezuela,** dial the international access code (011 in the U.S. and Canada, 0011 in Australia, 0170 in New Zealand, 00 in the U.K.), plus the country code (58), plus the three-digit Venezuelan area code (Caracas 212, Isla de Margarita 295, Mérida 274), plus the seven-digit phone number.
- **To place a local call within Venezuela,** dial the seven-digit local number. To call another area within Venezuela, you must add a 0 before the three-digit area code. If you are calling from a cellphone, or between competing cellphone companies, you must also add the 0 before the three-digit area code. For information, dial © **113;** to place national collect calls, dial © **101.**

CUSTOMS

You may bring into Venezuela all reasonable manner of electronic devices and items for personal use (including cameras, personal stereos, and laptop computers). Officially, you may bring in up to $3,000 (£1,500) worth of miscellaneous merchandise—tobacco, liquor, chocolate, and the like. However, this is only loosely enforced. The guiding rule is to try to not attract the interest of immigration officials. Once their interest is piqued, they could decide to give you a hard time.

MONEY

In January 2008, Venezuela changed its unit of currency from the **bolívar (Bs)** to the **bolívar fuerte (BsF).** The change simply involves chopping three decimal points off of the severely devalued bolívar. So BsF1 is equivalent to the old 1,000 Bs. The former currency was popularly referred to as *bolos,* and it's my guess that the new currency will be called simply *fuertes* to distinguish it. During 2008, for an indefinite period, both currencies will freely circulate until the general public, banks, and businesses have had sufficient time to make the complete change. The new bolívar fuerte comes in paper bills of 2, 5, 10, 20, and BsF50, while there are coins of BsF1, as well as 1, 5, 10, 12.5, 25, and 50 céntimos. There are 100 céntimos (cents) to each BsF. In terms of the old bolívares, paper bills come in denominations of 1,000, 2,000, 5,000, 10,000, 20,000, and 50,000 bolívares. There are coins of 5, 10, 20, 50, 100, and 500 bolívares. There are even coins for céntimos (fractions of a bolívar), but the currency has devalued so much that these are virtually meaningless and increasingly rare. *Tip:* Many taxis, small shops, and restaurants are reluctant (and sometimes unable) to change larger denomination bills, so it's always good to try to keep a few smaller notes and coins on hand.

CURRENCY EXCHANGE & RATES At press time, the official exchange rate was **BsF2.15 to US$1,** and BsF4.37 to £1. However, the black-market exchange rate is radically different from the official rate. At press time, the unofficial exchange rate was approximately BsF4.50 to the dollar and BsF9.15 to the British Pound. The most common place to exchange hard currencies for bolívares at the black-market rate is the Simón Bolívar International airport. While this is technically illegal, and you should be careful about whom you deal with, it is very common. Note that if you are dealing with a Venezuelan-based tour agency, be sure to ask if they would be willing to buy your dollars, euros, or pounds at a more favorable rate. They usually are willing and able to exchange currency for you, and this takes some of the risk out of dealing with an unknown entity at the airport.

Prices in this book are listed at the official exchange rate. Most restaurants, tour agencies, and attractions set their prices in bolívares fuertes. On the other hand, many hotel prices, particularly at the higher-end hotels, as well as tours and car rentals, are quoted in and pegged to the U.S. dollar.

Many banks do not exchange foreign currencies, and those that do often make the process cumbersome and unpleasant. But there are currency exchange offices in most major cities and tourist destinations, as well as 24-hour exchange offices in both the national and international airport terminals at the Simón Bolívar International Airport. While the official money exchange bureaus at the airport and around Caracas exchange at the official rate, you may find money exchange offices *(casas de cambio)* in outlying cities and tourist destinations that give a better rate. All credit card purchases and ATM withdrawals are charged at the official exchange rate.

Note: Exchanging your dollars, euros, or pounds at the black-market rate will more than double your buying power.

ATMs   ATMs are readily available in Caracas and most major cities and tourist destinations. **Cirrus** (*©* **800/424-7787;** www.mastercard.com) and **PLUS** (*©* **800/ 843-7587;** www.visa.com) are the two most popular networks; check the back of your ATM card to see which network your bank belongs to. Use the toll-free numbers to locate ATMs in your destination. It might take a few tries, but you should be able to find one connected to either, or both, of the PLUS and Cirrus systems that will allow you to withdraw bolívares against your home bank account. However, these will be sold to you at the official exchange rate.

TRAVELER'S CHECKS   In an era of almost universally accepted bank and credit cards, traveler's checks are becoming less and less common. Most hotels, restaurants, and shops that cater to foreign tourists will still accept and cash traveler's checks— some will actually change them for you at or near the going black-market exchange rate—but most will only change them at the official exchange rate, and they often exact a surcharge as well. Money-exchange houses will only change traveler's checks at the official rate and usually charge an additional 1% to 5% fee.

To report lost or stolen traveler's checks, see "Credit Cards," below.

CREDIT CARDS   Credit cards are widely accepted at most hotels, restaurants, shops, and attractions in all but the most remote destinations. American Express, MasterCard, and Visa have the greatest coverage, with a far smaller number of establishments accepting Diners Club. It is currently common practice to have to show a passport or photo ID when making a credit card purchase in Venezuela. Remember, credit card purchases are billed at the official exchange rate.

To report lost or stolen credit cards or traveler's checks, call the following numbers: **American Express,** *©* **0212/206-0222** or 0212/206-2796; **Diners Club,** *©* **0500/ 600-2424** or 0212/503-2461; **MasterCard,** *©* **0800/100-2902;** and **Visa,** *©* **0800/ 100-2167** or 0212/285-2510.

WHEN TO GO

PEAK SEASON   November through February, when it's cold and bleak in Europe and North America, is the peak season in Venezuela, but you can enjoy the country any time of year. Venezuelans travel a lot within the country on holidays and during the school break lasting from late July through early September. It is often difficult to find a hotel room or bus or airline seat during these holidays, as well as during Christmas and Easter vacations. April through June is a fabulous time to enjoy great deals, deserted beaches, and glorious solitude in the more popular destinations.

CLIMATE   Venezuela has two distinct seasons: rainy (June–Oct) and dry (Nov–May). The rainy season is locally called *invierno* (winter), while the dry season is called *verano* (summer). However, temperatures vary principally according to altitude. Coastal and lowland areas are hot year-round, and temperatures drop as you rise in altitude.

Set at an altitude of some 1,000m (3,280 ft.), Caracas has an average temperature of 72°F (22°C), with little seasonal variation. Daytime highs can reach around 90°F (32°C) on clear sunny days. Nights get a little cooler, but you'll rarely need more than a light jacket or sweater.

PUBLIC HOLIDAYS   Official public holidays celebrated in Venezuela include New Year's Day (Jan 1); Carnaval (the Mon and Tues before Ash Wednesday); Easter (Thurs and Fri of Holy Week are official holidays); Declaration of Independence (Apr 19); Labor Day (May 1); Battle of Carabobo (June 24); Independence Day (July 5); Birth of Simón Bolívar (July 24); Día de la Raza, or Discovery Day (Oct 12); and Christmas Day (Dec 25).

HEALTH CONCERNS

COMMON AILMENTS   Your chances of contracting any serious tropical disease in Venezuela are slim, especially if you stick to the major tourist destinations. However, malaria, dengue fever, yellow fever, hepatitis, and leptospirosis all exist in Venezuela, so it's a good idea to be careful and consult your doctor before a trip here.

Yellow Fever, while very rare, does exist in some remote areas of Venezuela. A yellow fever vaccine, though not required, is often recommended and is good for 10 years. If you do get a yellow fever vaccine, be sure to carry a copy of the proof of vaccination.

Malaria is found predominantly in the jungle areas of the Amazonas and Bolívar states, as well as in the Orinoco Delta. Malaria prophylaxes are often recommended, but several have side effects and others are of questionable effectiveness. Consult your doctor as to what is currently considered the best preventive treatment for malaria. Be sure to ask whether a recommended drug will cause hypersensitivity to the sun; it would be a shame to travel here for the beaches and then have to hide under an umbrella the entire time. If you are in a malarial area, wear long pants and long sleeves, use insect repellent, and either sleep under a mosquito net or burn mosquito coils (similar to incense but with a pesticide).

Of greater concern may be **dengue fever,** which reached epidemic proportions in 2001 and again in 2003. Dengue fever is similar to malaria and is spread by an aggressive daytime mosquito. This mosquito seems to be most common in lowland urban areas, although dengue cases have been reported throughout the country. Dengue is also known as "bone-break fever" because it is usually accompanied by severe body aches. The first infection with dengue fever will make you very sick but should cause no permanent damage. However, a second infection with a different strain of the dengue virus can lead to internal hemorrhaging and may be life-threatening. Take the same precautions as you would against malaria.

Although **cholera** exists in Venezuela, your chances of contracting cholera while you're here are very slight. Avoid tap water and all unpeeled fruits and vegetables in more remote areas and at any hotels, restaurants, or public facilities that are obviously unsanitary.

The most common health concern for travelers to Venezuela is a touch of **diarrhea.** The best way to protect yourself from diarrhea is to avoid tap water and drinks or ice made from tap water. Those with really tender intestinal tracts should avoid uncooked fruits and vegetables likely to have been washed in tap water, unless you can peel and prepare them yourself.

VACCINATIONS   No specific vaccinations are necessary for travel to Venezuela, although it is recommended that you be up-to-date on your tetanus, typhoid, and yellow-fever vaccines. It is also a good idea to get a vaccination for hepatitis A and B.

HEALTH PRECAUTIONS   Staying healthy on a trip to Venezuela is predominantly a matter of being a little cautious about what you eat and drink, and using common sense. Know your physical limits and don't overexert yourself in the ocean, on hikes, or in athletic activities. Respect the tropical sun and protect yourself from it. Also try to protect yourself from biting insects, using a combination of repellent and light, loose long-sleeved clothing. I recommend buying and drinking bottled water or soft drinks, although the water in Caracas and in most of the major tourist destinations is reputed to be safe to drink.

GETTING THERE
BY PLANE

The **Simón Bolívar International Airport** (☎ **0212/355-2858;** www.aeropuerto-maiquetia.com.ve; airport code CCS) in Maiquetía, 28km (17 miles) north of Caracas, is the gateway to Venezuela and the point of entry for most visitors to the country. There is an departure tax of BsF38 ($18/£8.70) combined with an airport tax of BsF94 ($44/£21). These taxes are often included in the airline ticket price, so be sure to ask before paying twice.

FROM THE U.S.   Miami, which is only 3 hours and 15 minutes away by air, is the principal gateway to Caracas. **American Airlines** (☎ 800/433-7300; www.aa.com) has several daily direct flights between Miami and Caracas, as well as once weekly flights each from Dallas and New York's JFK. **Continental** (☎ 800/231-0856; www.continental.com) has a daily direct flight from Houston; **Delta Airlines** (☎ 800/241-4141; www.delta.com) has a daily flight from Atlanta. Venezuelan airlines **Aeropostal** (☎ 888/912-8466; www.aeropostal.com) and **Santa Bárbara** (☎ 866/213-2457; www.sbairlines.com) both have one daily direct flight from Miami. **Mexicana** (☎ 800/531-7921; www.mexicana.com) and **Grupo Taca** (☎ 800/400-8222; www.grupotaca.com) have flights from Los Angeles connecting through Mexico City, Mexico, and San José, Costa Rica, respectively.

FROM CANADA   **Air Canada** (☎ **888/247-2262;** www.aircanada.com) flies four times weekly between Toronto and Caracas. **American, Continental, Delta,** and **Mexicana** have flights from Montreal, Toronto, and Vancouver to Caracas, connecting through Atlanta, Miami, Los Angeles, or New York.

There are numerous charter flights from Toronto and Montreal to Isla de Margarita, particularly during the winter months. Ask your travel agent, check online, or look in the Sunday travel section of your local newspaper to find them.

FROM EUROPE AND THE U.K.   **American Airlines** offers flights to Caracas, connecting through the U.S. or Puerto Rico. **Air Europa** (www.air-europa.com) from Madrid; **Air France** (www.airfrance.com) from Paris; **Alitalia** (www.alitalia.com) from Rome and Milan; **Iberia** (www.iberia.com) from Madrid; and **Lufthansa** (www.lufthansa.com) from Frankfort, all offer regular service to Venezuela, with connections from London. **Santa Bárbara** (www.sbairlines.com) flies direct from Madrid several times weekly.

FROM AUSTRALIA & NEW ZEALAND   To fly to Venezuela from either Australia or New Zealand, you will almost certainly have to connect via the United States. **Air New Zealand** (☎ **0800/737-000** in New Zealand, or 13-24-76 in Australia; www.airnewzealand.com) and **Qantas** (☎ **13-13-13** in Australia, or 0800/808-767 in New Zealand; www.qantas.com) are the two main carriers. **American Airlines** and **LAN** offer service with connections in Los Angeles and Santiago, Chile, respectively.

BY BUS

Venezuela is serviced by international bus routes via Colombia to the west and Brazil to the south. In general, crossings from Colombia are considered dangerous, due to guerrilla and drug-cartel activity. The only road route between Brazil and Venezuela connects Boa Vista, Brazil, and Santa Elena de Uairén, Venezuela. Two recommended companies are **Bus Ven** (© **0212/953-8441;** www.busven.com) for travel to and from Colombia, and **Expreso Internacional Ormeño** (© **0212/471-7205**) for travel to and from Brazil. The latter company actually runs buses from Caracas all the way to Buenos Aires, Argentina.

BY BOAT

There are ferry services between several Caribbean islands and Isla de Margarita, Venezuela. Routes and schedules vary seasonally and change on short notice. Islands with the most consistent connections include Barbados, St. Vincent, and Trinidad and Tobago.

GETTING AROUND

BY PLANE Because distances are relatively long and land travel time consuming, Venezuela has an excellent network of commuter airlines servicing the entire country and all major tourist destinations. Fares run around BsF150 to BsF500 ($70–$233/ £34–£114) each way, depending on destination, distance, availability, and demand. On any internal flight, you have to pay an airport tax of BsF2 to BsF11 (95¢–$5.15/45p–£2.50), depending on the local airport you are using. For the names and contact information of individual commuter airlines, see "Getting There," in each destination section in this chapter.

BY BUS Regular and inexpensive buses service all of terrestrial Venezuela. Most popular destinations are also serviced by *expreso* (express), *ejecutivo* (executive), and/or *de lujo* (luxury) buses. In most cases, it's worth the few extra dollars for the *expreso, ejecutivo,* or *de lujo* options. Two reputable luxury lines are **Aeroexpresos Ejecutivos** (© **0212/226-2321;** www.aeroexpresos.com.ve) and **Rodovías** (© **0212/577-6622;** www.rodovias.com.ve). There are two principal bus terminals in Caracas, Terminal La Bandera and Terminal del Oriente, although depending on the route, destination, and bus line, you may embark from either of these or a private terminal.

BY CAR I do not recommend a rental car as a means of exploring Venezuela. Many of the top destinations—Los Roques, Canaima, and Angel Falls, for example—are inaccessible by car. (*Note:* The only two destinations included in this chapter where a car would come in handy are Isla de Margarita and Mérida. In both cases, you'd be better off flying to the destination and renting a car there for the duration of your stay.) Venezuelan drivers are aggressive and ignore most common traffic laws and general rules of road safety. Moreover, roads are not well marked, distances between destinations are considerable, and you run the risk of becoming a target for one of many robbery schemes. If you do decide to rent a car, many of the major international agencies operate in Venezuela, with offices in Caracas (often with a branch at the airport) and in most major cities and tourist destinations. Rates run BsF95 to BsF250 ($44–$117/£22–£57) per day.

Your best bet for renting a car, both in terms of rates and reliability, is to choose one of the major international agencies and book in advance from your home country. **Avis** (© **800/331-1084** in the U.S., or 0800/227-7600 in Venezuela; www.avis.com),

Budget (© **800/472-3325** in the U.S., or 0800/283-4381 in Venezuela; www.budget.com.ve), **Dollar** (© **800/800-3665** in the U.S., or 0212/993-2469 in Venezuela; www.dollar.com), **Hertz** (© **800/654-3001** in the U.S., or 0800/800-0000 in Venezuela; www.hertz.com), and **Thrifty** (© **800/847-4389** in the U.S., or 0800/250-8453 in Venezuela, www.thrifty.com) all have offices both in Caracas and at Simón Bolívar International Airport.

One upside of driving around Venezuela is that gas is amazingly cheap, around BsF (5¢/20p) per liter, or BsF3.8 (15¢/90p) per gallon.

BY ORGANIZED TOUR   Considering the current state of affairs, organized tours are a reasonable way to go in Venezuela. The country is still a bit inhospitable and unused to freewheeling independent exploration. The tourism industry here was built top-down, with lots of big hotels and big operations that almost seem to not want to waste their time on independent travelers. In many cases, tour operators and wholesalers are able to get better rates on rooms, tours, and transfers than you'd be able to find on your own. Many of them use the hotels and local tour operators recommended in this book.

Akanan Travel & Adventure 🎔🎔 (© **0212/715-5433** or 0414/116-0107; www.akanan.com) is one of my favorite operators on the ground in Caracas. It offers a wide range of tour options. **Lost World Adventures** 🎔🎔 (© **800/999-0558** in the U.S., or 0212/577-0303 in Caracas; www.lostworldadventures.com) is an excellent operator and a pioneer in Venezuelan travel. It offers a wide range of tour options and can customize a trip to your needs and specifications.

Geodyssey (© **020/7281-7788;** www.geodyssey.co.uk) is a British operator with a good amount of experience in Venezuela. **Journey Latin America** (© **020/8747-3108;** www.journeylatinamerica.co.uk) is a large British operator specializing in Latin American travel, that often has excellent deals on airfare.

TIPS ON ACCOMMODATIONS

You'll find hotel rooms in all price ranges, although in Caracas and on Isla Margarita, the offerings are skewed toward high-end business travelers—and rates tend to be high. There are a dozen or so large, all-inclusive resorts on Isla de Margarita. However, in Merida, Canaima, Los Roques and Los Llanos, you can find delightful small hotels and isolated lodges. While Venezuelan tourism is relatively strong, there are still very few foreign tourists visiting Venezuela. Still, there is a major glut of hotel rooms throughout the country, and competition is often fierce. Few of the large hotels actually charge their published or advertised rack rate. You can get especially good deals in the off season and midweek. It always pays to bargain, especially if you book directly by phone, fax, or the Internet. Finally, you can also save substantially if you pay in cash, especially if you exchange at the black-market rate.

Venezuela has a broad network of *posadas,* small inns, and lodges. If you're looking for a small, intimate hotel experience, your best bets are Mérida and Los Roques, where *posadas* abound.

When booking a room, if you ask for a double *(doble),* you may be given a room with two twin beds. If you want a double or queen-size bed, be specific and ask for a *cama matrimonial.*

TIPS ON DINING

Although both Caracas and Isla de Margarita have a wide range of restaurants serving a gamut of international cuisines, your choices will be much more limited throughout most of the rest of the country. Venezuelan cuisine is neither very distinctive nor noteworthy. Most meals consist of a meat or chicken dish (either fried, grilled, or in a stew), accompanied by some stewed vegetables, rice, and the ubiquitous *arepa,* the traditional cornmeal patty that's a kind of cross between a tortilla and a biscuit. Vegetarians may have a particularly hard time. If you are vegetarian, try to coordinate your meals in advance with hotels and tour agencies.

For those with a sweet tooth, be sure to try a piece of the national cake, *bienmesabe,* a soft sponge cake soaked in a sweet coconut-cream sauce. (Its name literally means "Tastes good to me!") Also be sure to sample some of the fresh fruit drinks, or *batidos.* These are made with whatever ripe tropical fruits are on hand. My favorite *batido* is made of mango, but *parchita,* or passion fruit, runs a close second.

TIPS ON SHOPPING

Outside of the massive malls in Caracas, which have all the standard international designer stores you could ask for, shopping is far from rewarding in Venezuela. Your best bet is to look for and stick to local and indigenous arts and crafts. Masks are particularly attractive and varied. Keep an eye out for the local hammocks, called *chinchorros,* which are an intricate weave of thin strands of rough natural fibers. You'll also find a variety of woven baskets, hats, and handbags, as well as simple ceramic wares. Despite its duty-free status, Isla de Margarita is unlikely to be of much interest for international shoppers. Prices and selection are comparable to what most folks can find at home.

Outside of department stores, hotel gift shops, and malls, you should bargain. In many cases, street merchants and sellers at outdoor markets and souvenir shops can easily be bartered down by 25% to 30%.

FAST FACTS: Venezuela

American Express American Express is represented by the **Quo Vadis** (www.quovadis.com.ve) travel agencies with offices around Caracas and other parts of Venezuela. You'll find the main Quo Vadis office in Caracas at Torre Banca Lara, Avenida Blandin, La Castellana (© **0212/206-5200**); it's open Monday through Friday from 8am to noon and 2 to 4:30pm. For Global Assist, call © **0212/206-0333**. To report a lost card, call © **0212/206-2796,** or call collect 336/393-1111 in the United States.

Business Hours Most businesses open between 8am and 9am, and close between 5 and 6pm. Many businesses and stores close down for an hour or more for a lunch break between noon and 2:30pm. On Saturday, most shops are open and most businesses are closed. On Sunday, only shops in malls and major shopping districts are open. Most banks are open Monday to Friday from 8:30am to 4pm; however, banks and exchange houses in some of the major malls are open during shopping hours, which often include the early evenings and weekends.

Doctors & Dentists Medical and dental care generally ranges from acceptable to high quality in Venezuela. If you need care while in the country, contact your embassy, ask at your hotel, or look in the English-language *Daily Journal* (www.dj.com.ve). In the event of a medical emergency, contact one of the clinics listed under "Fast Facts" in "Caracas," later in this chapter.

Drug Laws Venezuelan drug laws are strict, and punishment, especially for foreigners, is severe. Do not try to smuggle, buy, or use illegal drugs in Venezuela.

Electricity Electric current is 110 volts AC (60 cycles). U.S.-style flat-prong plugs are used. However, three-prong grounded outlets are not universally available. It's helpful to bring a three-to-two prong adapter.

Embassies & Consulates In Caracas: **Canada,** avenidas Francisco de Miranda and Sur, Altamira (© **0212/264-0833** or 0212/600-3000; http://geo.international. gc.ca/latin-america/caracas); **United Kingdom,** Torre La Castellana, Avenida Principal La Castellana, Piso 11 (© **0212/263-8411;** www.britain.org.ve); and the **United States,** calles F and Suapure, Colinas de Valle Arriba (© **0212/975-6411;** http://caracas.usembassy.gov).

Australia and **New Zealand** do not have embassies in Venezuela. The Canadian and U.K. embassies (see above) will assist Australian and Kiwi travelers in most instances, except for the issuing of passports. The nearest Australian Embassy is in Brasília Brazil (© **55/61-3226-3111;** www.dfat.gov.au/geo/ venezuela/index.html); the nearest New Zealand embassy is also in Brasília (© **55/61-3248-9900;** www.nzembassy.com).

Emergencies Venezuela has an integrated emergency network (police, fire, ambulance). To reach it, dial © **171.** You can dial 171 from any pay phone, without using a calling card. Don't expect the operator to speak English.

Internet Access There are Internet cafes all over Venezuela, particularly in tourist destinations. Rates run BsF1 to BsF10 (45¢–$4.65/45p–£2.30) per hour.

Language Spanish is the official language of Venezuela. Although most hotels and tourist destinations have staff and guides with at least some command of English, it is not widely spoken among the general population.

Liquor Laws The official drinking age in Venezuela is 18, although it is rarely enforced.

Police Venezuela has a host of overlapping police departments but no specific tourist police. Depending on the circumstances, you may encounter metropolitan police *(policía metropolitana),* municipal police *(policía municipal),* investigative police *(policía técnica judicial),* the National Guard *(guardia nacional),* or transit police *(policía de tránsito).* Their uniforms and specific responsibilities vary. Corruption and indifference are widespread. Venezuela has an integrated emergency network (police, fire, ambulance). To reach it, just dial © **171.** However, don't expect the operator to speak English.

Post Offices/Mail **Ipostel** (www.ipostel.gov.ve) is the national mail service. It is considered neither swift nor secure for international correspondence. Generally, a letter or postcard takes 10 to 20 days to reach most parts of the United States and Europe. There are branch post offices in most cities and tourist destinations, and some malls even have Ipostel offices. Still, your hotel is usually your best bet for buying stamps and mailing a letter. Feel free to mail home postcards and letters, but avoid using Ipostel for anything of value or importance.

In the event that you need to mail anything of value or personal import, call any of the following international courier services: **DHL** (✆ **0800/225-5345** or 0212/205-6000; www.dhl.com), **FedEx** (✆ **0800/463-3399** or 0212/205-3333; www.fedex.com), or **UPS** (✆ **0212/401-4900**; www.ups.com).

Restrooms There are few readily available public toilets in Venezuela. Your best bet is a restaurant, hotel, or service station. Some of these establishments (particularly service stations and roadside restaurants) will actually charge you a small fee for the use of the facilities. It's always a good idea to carry a small amount of toilet paper with you, especially on the road, as the facilities at many service stations—and at lower-end restaurants and hotels—might not have any.

Safety Venezuela has developed a reputation for its violence and crime, much of it deserved. Caraqueños talk about muggings, car thefts, and burglaries with amazing candidness and regularity. The greatest danger to travelers is theft. If you use common sense and standard precautions, you should have no problems. Keep a tab on your belongings, use hotel safes whenever possible, and don't carry large sums of money with you or wear obviously expensive clothing or jewelry. Stick to the well-worn tourist parts of Caracas and other major cities. Avoid the *ranchitos* (shantytowns) and poorer *barrios*. Take reputable taxis whenever possible and definitely avoid strolling around cities at night. If you have a rental car, always leave it in guarded parking and never leave anything of value inside.

Taxes There is a 15% sales tax on all purchases, including both goods and services.

Telephone & Fax There are public phones all around most cities and major tourist destinations. You'll even find public phones in places as remote as Canaima and Los Roques. Most work with magnetic-strip calling cards that are readily available in stores all over the country. Look for signs or stickers advertising CANTV calling cards. A local call costs just a few pennies per minute. Calls to cellphones or between competing phone companies can be much more expensive. Your hotel is usually your best bet for sending and receiving faxes, although they may charge exorbitant rates for international faxes. For tips on dialing, see "Telephone Dialing Info at a Glance," on p. 747.

Time Zone Venezuela is 4 hours behind Greenwich mean time (GMT) and does not observe daylight saving time. In 2007, President Chávez announced on his weekly television show that Venezuela would be moving its clocks back an extra half-hour, or 4 ½ hours behind GMT. However, when the September 2007 date for the change rolled around, authorities realized that the banking, airline, and government systems were all unprepared for the change, which has been delayed until further notice.

Tipping Most restaurants automatically add a 10% service charge. If you feel the service was particularly good, you should leave an additional 5% to 10%. If they don't add the service charge, tip as you would at home. Similarly, tip the hotel staff as you would at home. Since most taxi drivers do not use meters and are almost always overcharging foreigners, it is not customary to tip them. If you feel you are getting an extremely good deal, or beyond-the-call-of-duty treatment, by all means, tip your driver.

Water Although the water is considered safe to drink in most urban areas, I recommend that visitors stick to bottled water to be on the safe side. Ask for *agua mineral sin gas* (noncarbonated mineral water).

4 Caracas

With a well-deserved reputation for violence and danger, Caracas is a daunting city for many travelers. It is still one of the more cosmopolitan cities in Latin America, with vibrant business, social, and cultural scenes. Architecturally, Caracas is one of the most modern and distinctive cities in Latin America. Concrete and plate glass reign supreme, much of it showing the bold forms and sleek lines of the Art Deco and postmodern architectural currents of the last half of the 20th century. Aficionados will enjoy works of Carlos Raúl Villanueva, a local architect who often integrated into his designs large kinetic sculptures by such renowned figures as Alexander Calder and Jesús Soto.

Caracas, and the international airport in Maiquetía, is the de facto hub for travel to and around Venezuela. If you plan on visiting several destinations in the country, you will be passing through Caracas as part of your itinerary. You can easily get a good feel for the city and its major attractions in a couple of days.

ESSENTIALS
GETTING THERE
The **Simón Bolívar International Airport** (© 0212/355-2858; www.aeropuerto-maiquetia.com.ve; airport code CCS) in Maiquetía, 28km (17 miles) north of Caracas, is the gateway to Venezuela and the point of entry for most visitors to the country. *Note:* The airport is most commonly referred to as the Maiquetía Airport by locals, travel agents, and taxi drivers. For information on arriving by plane, see "Getting There" in "Planning Your Trip to Venezuela," earlier in this chapter.

A taxi from the airport should cost between BsF80 and BsF120 ($37–$56/£18–£27), depending on where in the city you are going. Official fares are slightly higher after 5pm. You will be immediately set upon by both official and informal or "pirate" *(pirata)* taxi drivers as soon as you exit customs. Unless your hotel or tour agency sends a trusted driver, I recommend you use the official airport taxi company **Astrala** (© 0212/860-8138). Even though official rates are posted at several spots around the terminal, you will usually have to negotiate your fare in advance, even with the official cab drivers. While you may be offered a slightly better fare by one of the *pirata* drivers, there have been reports of mistreatment and muggings of tourists by these operators. The downside of the official company, however, is that they use a fleet of Ford Explorers. In fact, it was the high accident and death rates caused by rollovers and tire-tread separations of Ford Explorers in Venezuela that first drew attention to safety problems with this model.

Caracas

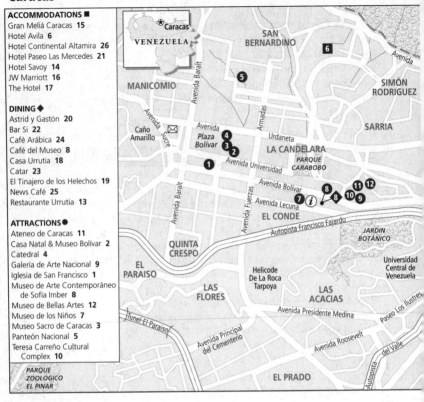

Por puestos (private buses and vans) run between the airport and the Gato Negro Metro station. The fare is BsF4 ($1.85/90p); however, note that you should not use this option at night or if you have much luggage. There are regular free shuttles between the national and international terminals at Maiquetía.

ORIENTATION

Of greatest interest to tourists are the **Capitolio** area around **Plaza Bolívar,** the historic center of Caracas, and **Parque Central,** a modern zone of high-rise office towers and home to several important museums and theaters. The **Sabana Grande** is an open-air pedestrian mall of small shops and street vendors that stretches on for nearly a mile, between the Plaza Venezuela and Plaza Chacaito. However, the Sabana Grande area has become increasingly seedy and dangerous, especially after dark. Today, shoppers and affluent Caraqueños tend to favor modern malls and the more exclusive areas of **Altamira, El Rosal,** and **Las Mercedes.** The latter three zones are the principal upscale residential, business, and shopping districts, respectively—they all have a mix of hotels, restaurants, cafes, shops, and private residences.

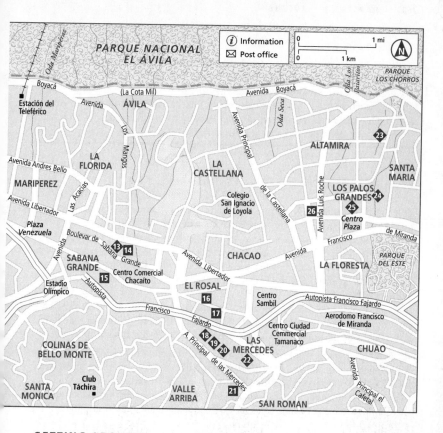

GETTING AROUND

BY METRO   Caracas has a clean, relatively safe, and efficient Metro system (© 0212/
507-4211; www.metrodecaracas.com.ve). The main line of the system crosses the city
from Palo Verde in the east to Propatria in the west.

Ticket prices are BsF0.50 (20¢/10p) for a one-way fare, and BsF0.90 (40¢/20p) for
a two-trip ticket. You can buy a 10-trip ticket for BsF4.50 ($2.10/£1.05). Even if you
buy a one-way fare, keep your ticket handy because you have to pass it through the electronic turnstiles upon entering and again upon exiting at some stations. The Metro
operates daily from 5:30am to 11pm. Although the Metro is generally safe, be wary of
pickpockets and muggings at either very busy or very desolate times and stations.

BY BUS   There are two parallel bus systems in Caracas. The **Metrobús** (© 0212/
507-4211; www.metrodecaracas.com.ve) is a traditional urban bus system that, in
theory, can be used in conjunction with the Metro. More common are the *por
puestos,* private buses or vans running fixed routes servicing most of the metropolitan
area. Fares on both systems are extremely inexpensive, but I don't recommend them
as the transportation of choice because there's little rhyme or reason to the routes and,
in the case of the *por puestos,* no readily available maps or guides. Moreover, crowded
buses are prime haunts of pickpockets and petty thieves.

(*Tips* **Safety First**

It's not just hype: Caracas is one of the most violent and dangerous cities in Latin America. Be very careful about where you walk, what you wear, and with whom you associate. Don't wear fancy jewelry or flash lots of cash, and keep close watch on your personal belongings. Take a well-marked taxi, or one called by your hotel, whenever possible. Be wary of unofficial cabs, or *piratas*. And, finally, don't get too adventurous at night.

BY TAXI Taxis in Caracas generally do not have meters. Most rides within the city limits should cost you BsF10–BsF25 ($4.65–$12/£2.90–£5.70). There are a host of different taxi companies, some of which are based in certain zones, others at specific hotels and malls. In general, taxis based at a hotel or mall will charge more than a typical cab hailed on the street. However, given the current economic environment, the difference is often inconsequential. As a traveler, you will likely be a target for overcharging. Always try to ask hotel staff or other locals what a specific ride should cost and negotiate in advance with the driver. Taxi drivers are legally allowed to charge an additional 20% after 6pm.

If you can't flag a cab in the street, try **Móvil Express** ✪ (© 0212/899-7880; www.movilexpressservice.com), **Taxiven** (© 0212/985-5715), **Taxitour** (© 0800/829-4800; www.taxi-tour.com.ve), or **Taxco** (© 0212/576-8322; www.taxco.com.ve).

BY FOOT Caracas is not particularly amenable to exploration by foot. Street crime is a real problem in all but a few neighborhoods. In fact, almost no place is absolutely safe. The safest neighborhoods to walk around are Las Mercedes, El Rosal, Los Palos Grandes, and Altamira. With care, you should also be fine during the daytime around the Capitolio, Sabana Grande, and Parque Central areas, although their popularity as tourist destinations attracts pickpockets.

VISITOR INFORMATION

MINTUR (© 0212/208-4511; www.mintur.gob.ve) is the national tourism ministry. Its main office, located at the intersection of avenidas Francisco de Miranda and Principal de La Floresta, is open weekdays 9am to 5pm. The staff can give you a basic map and some brochures for hotels and attractions; however, they are not truly geared towards attending to independent travelers.

A good alternative is to head to the offices of **Akanan Travel & Adventure** ✪✪ (© 0212/715-5433 or 0414/116-0107; www.akanan.com; Calle Bolívar, Edificio Grano de Oro, Chacao), one of my favorite operators in Caracas. Not only are they well located, close to the Altamira Metro stop, but they have a welcoming and informative staff, and will usually allow travelers to check e-mail, chat, or make a VoIP call on one of their many computers.

Most bookstores around town and many hotel gift shops stock a small selection of maps to Caracas and the rest of the country. The best bookshops for English-language materials are the **American Book Shop,** Centro Plaza, Nivel Jardín, Avenida Francisco de Miranda, Los Palos Grandes (© 0212/285-8779), and **Read Books,** Calle Paris, Las Mercedes (© 0212/991-5562; www.readbookscafe.com).

FAST FACTS   There are a couple of currency exchange offices, including an **Ital-cambio** branch, at the airport, as well as scores of money-exchange houses around town. Many hotels will change dollars and traveler's checks, although usually at or even slightly below the official exchange rate. Most banks won't change money, but they often have ATMs.

Simón Bolívar, El Libertador

The great hero of Latin American independence, Simón Bolívar, was born in Caracas on July 24, 1783, into a *criolla* family of the city's commercial *cacao* elite. The second of four children, young Simón lost both parents by the time he was 9 years old. Raised by an uncle and sent to private schools in both Venezuela and Europe, Bolívar was well-educated and erudite. In 1802, while in Europe, he met and married María Teresa Rodríguez del Toro, a Spanish aristocrat. However, María Teresa died of yellow fever just a few months later, soon after the couple's return to Venezuela. Despondent, Bolívar sought solace in travel.

His travels following the death of his wife brought him into direct contact with the leaders of and results of both the French and American revolutions. In Europe, he also met famed scientist and explorer Alexander von Humbolt, who further sowed the seeds of Bolívar's revolutionary work. Humbolt allegedly told Bolívar that South America was ripe for freedom but lacked a charismatic leader to lead the struggle.

Upon his return to Venezuela, Bolívar began political opposition to Spanish rule and, soon after that, armed struggle. By 1812, he had taken over the Venezuelan independence movement and spent most of the next 20 years in armed combat. Bolívar mounted a series of impressive long-range campaigns against Spain that are still admired and studied. He ultimately liberated the area comprising modern-day Venezuela, Colombia, Panama, Ecuador, Peru, and Bolivia. However, his dream of a united "Gran Colombia" never took hold, and Bolívar himself fell quickly out of political favor following the defeat of the Spanish.

Bolívar may have set the model for military men seizing and dictating political power throughout Latin America. He was an eloquent and stirring orator. In private, he was also renowned for his saucy tongue and numerous affairs. His most famous lover, Manuela Sáenz, was an Ecuadorian woman who saved him from an assassination attempt. Their story is immortalized in Gabriel García Márquez's *The General in His Labyrinth*.

Bolívar died of tuberculosis on December 17, 1830, in Santa Marta, Colombia, nearly broke and on his way to living in self-imposed exile in Europe. Twelve years later, in 1842, his remains were interred in Caracas. In 1876, they were ceremoniously transferred to the Panteón Nacional. Today, his presence and legacy are omnipresent in Venezuela: The principal public park in every town and city bears his name, as does the country's currency.

Venezuela has an integrated **emergency** network (police, fire, ambulance). To reach it, just dial ☎ **171.** Don't expect the operator to speak English. In the event that you need medical care, consult with your hotel first or head to the **Hospital de Clínicas de Caracas,** Avenida Panteón, San Bernardino (☎ **0212/508-6111);** the **Policlínica Las Mercedes,** Avenida Principal Las Mercedes and Calle Monterrey (☎ **0212/993-2059;** www.policlinicalasmercedes.com); or the **Clínica El Avila,** Avenida San Juan Bosco and 6th Transversal, Altamira (☎ **0212/276-1111;** www.clinicaelavila.com).

Internet cafes are located all over town, and most hotels either have their own Internet cafe or can refer you to the closest option. Rates run BsF1 to BsF5 (45¢–$2.35/20p–£1.15) per hour.

Ipostel is the national mail service. The main **post office,** or *correo,* is located at Avenida Urdaneta and Norte 4 (☎ **0800/476-7835;** www.ipostel.gov.ve), near the Plaza Bolívar, and is open weekdays from 8am to 6pm, closing an hour earlier on weekends. There are quite a few branch post offices around town and in the suburbs, and several of the modern malls have Ipostel offices; many of these have a reduced schedule. Your hotel is usually your best bet for getting stamps and mailing a letter.

You'll find public phones all around Caracas. Most phones work with magnetic-strip calling cards that are readily available in stores and hotels all over the city. You can send and receive faxes and make credit card international calls from the **CANTV Centro Plaza** office (☎ **0212/285-6788;** fax 0212/286-2261; www.cantv.net), on Avenida Francisco Miranda in Los Palos Grandes, 2 blocks east of the Altamira Metro station. However, your best bet is to find one of the many Internet cafes around town that offer calling via Skype or some other VoIP service.

WHAT TO SEE & DO
ATTRACTIONS
Plaza Bolívar & El Capitolio

Pigeons, pedestrians, park benches, and a towering bronze statue of El Libertador on his sturdy steed are the hallmarks of this square city block, which was once the heart of colonial Caracas. Within a 4- or 5-block radius, you will find several important museums and cathedrals, as well as the birthplace of Simón Bolívar, the national Congress (El Capitolio), and the Panteón Nacional, the country's most important mausoleum. This area is relatively safe to explore during the day, but I would definitely avoid it after dark.

Casa Natal & Museo Bolívar   These side-by-side attractions, housed in two old colonial era homes, make up the restored birthplace of Simón Bolívar and a modest museum of memorabilia and historic items related to El Libertador—his life, death, and military and political campaigns. A place of pilgrimage for many Venezuelans, the simple house where Bolívar was born on July 24, 1783, features a series of large oil paintings depicting important historical events, while the museum has exhibits of his clothing, battle gear and writings. Give yourself about an hour to visit both sites.

Av. Universidad and Norte 1. ☎ **0212/541-2563.** Free admission. Tues–Sun 9am–noon and 2:30–5:30pm. Metro: Capitolio.

Catedral ☀   Anchoring the eastern end of Plaza Bolívar, this is the national cathedral. The present-day church was built between 1665 and 1713, after the original building was destroyed in the 1641 earthquake. It's home to the personal Bolívar family chapel and features a painting by Rubens. Adjoining the cathedral is the **Museo**

Sacro de Caracas ★, which has a good collection of religious art and sculpture, as well as colonial-era dress and relics and a delightful little cafe. Of ghoulish interest to many is the restored, yet still dank and dark, ecclesiastical prison once housed here. About half the museum exhibits here are in English.

Plaza Bolívar. Cathedral ✆ **0212/862-4963**; museum ✆ 0212/861-5814. Free admission to cathedral; admission to museum BsF2 (95¢/45p) adults, BsF0.50 (20¢/10p) children. Cathedral daily 7am–1pm and 3–6pm; museum Tues–Sun 10am–5pm. Metro: Capitolio.

Iglesia de San Francisco ★★   Not as large or ornate as the Catedral, this is the church where Bolívar was proclaimed El Libertador in 1813, and the site of his massive funeral in 1842—the year his remains were brought back from Colombia, some 12 years after his actual death. Begun in 1575, the church bears the architectural influences of various periods and styles but retains much of its colonial-era charm. The ornate gilded altars and religious paintings that line both of the long side walls are worthy of stroll through the building.

Av. Universidad and Norte 2. ✆ **0212/484-2442**. Free admission. Mon–Fri 7am–noon and 2–5pm; Sat–Sun 10am–5pm. Metro: Capitolio.

Parque Central & Bellas Artes

Galería de Arte Nacional & Museo de Bellas Artes ★   Making up an area popularly known as the Plaza de los Museos, these side-by-side and loosely connected institutions house a broad collection of Venezuelan art, ranging from the fine arts and modern masters to folk art and crafts, dating from the colonial period to the present. One of the nicer features here is the shady sculpture garden, which borders Parque Los Caobos. The Bellas Artes gift shop has a small, but worthwhile, selection of mostly high-end artworks and indigenous crafts.

Plaza Morelos, beside the Parque Los Caobos, in front of the Caracas Hilton. ✆ **0212/578-1818**. www.gan.org.ve. Free admission. Mon–Fri 9am–5pm; Sat–Sun and holidays 10am–5pm. Metro: Bellas Artes.

Museo de Arte Contemporáneo de Sofía Imber ★★   The 13 rooms here form a minimaze covering several floors of the angular concrete architecture of Parque Central. The permanent collection features a good representation of the conceptual works of Venezuelan star Jesús Soto, as well as a small but high quality collection of singular works by such modern masters as Picasso, Red Grooms, Henry Moore, Joan Miró, and Francis Bacon. The museum regularly hosts traveling exhibits of international stature. The small sculpture garden here is nowhere near as lovely as that found at the nearby Bellas Artes, but the elegant museum cafe is one of the nicer casual dining spots on this side of town.

Parque Central. ✆ **0212/573-8289**. Free admission. Tues–Sun 10am–6pm. Metro: Bellas Artes.

Museo de los Niños (Children's Museum) (Kids)   It's nothing truly spectacular, but this museum is a great place to pass a couple of hours if you've got children with you. A wide range of interactive and participatory exhibits cover the natural sciences, physics, medicine, and more. This place is often quite crowded with school groups during the week and families on weekends.

Av. Bolívar, between the 2 towers of Parque Central. ✆ **0212/575-3022**. Admission BsF10 ($4.65/£2.30) adults, BsF5 ($2.35/£1.14) children. Mon–Fri 9am–6pm; Sat–Sun 9am–5pm. Metro: Bellas Artes.

Safety Advice

Although outwardly inviting, I recommend that you avoid El Calvario Park, which lies on the western end of the Capitolio area. In recent years, it's become a dangerous and unprotected area.

SPORTS & OUTDOOR ACTIVITIES

BASEBALL   Baseball is the number-one sport in Venezuela. Venezuelans follow the sport with devotion and fervor. It's hard to find pickup games, but if you're in town for the season, you might want to catch a game. The local professional season runs October 20 through January 30 every year. As this is the off-season for U.S. Major League Baseball, plenty of Venezuelan and international professional and minor-league players play here to stay in shape. There are a couple of professional teams in Caracas, as well as teams in most major cities around the country. The main Caracas team is Los Leones; another popular team (formerly of Caracas, but currently based out of Valencia) is Los Magallanes. The Leones-Magallanes rivalry is quite heated. You can get tickets to most games rather easily for BsF5 to BsF30 ($2.35–$14/£1.15–£6.85). I'd recommend splurging for the more expensive seats, as they often provide protection from the sun, the rain, and the rowdier crowds. Los Leones play at the Estadio Universitario de Caracas (at the university). Tickets can be purchased in advance by calling © **0212/762-1211,** although you can usually buy tickets the day of the game.

HIKING   The place to go for hiking around Caracas is **Parque Nacional El Avila** ⍟, located on the northern edge of the city and encompassing some 82 hectares (203 acres) of the coastal mountain range separating the city from the Caribbean Sea. There are dozens of trails through the park as well as a well-developed network of restrooms, ranger stations, and campsites. The park and its trails get crowded on weekends. You should be able to reach **Pico El Avila** (2,153m/7,062 ft.) in 2 to 4 hours of semistrenuous hiking, depending on the pace and route you choose. The highest peak here, **Pico Naiguatá,** rises to 2,765m (9,070 ft.). Be prepared for wide ranges in temperatures and the possibility of late afternoon rains on the forested slopes of the park. It's best to hike in groups of at least four persons, as some robberies and muggings have been reported in the park. The most popular access to the park is from the northern end of the Altamira district, at the end of Avenida San Juan Bosco, and from all along Avenida Boyacá. You can take the Metro to the Altamira stop, although it's a steep 10-block walk uphill from both the Metro station and from the San Bernardino area to the entrance to the park. Admission to the park is free.

EL TELEFERICO ⍟   Another, much less strenuous, way to reach Pico El Avila is via the *teleférico.* This cable-car system stretches from the Maripérez station on the northern edge of the city to the top of El Avila mountain. The 3.4km (2-mile) ride to the top takes between 12 and 15 minutes, where you'll find a skating rink, rock-climbing wall, telescopes, simple restaurants, souvenir shops and snack stands, and the dormant 14-story Hotel Humbolt. Plans include the reopening of this landmark hotel, a modern casino, and further development of the peak's recreational facilities. However these plans, which also include the restoration and reopening of the tramway section down to the coastal city of La Guaira, have never gotten off the ground. Nevertheless, the entire operation was taken over by the Venezuelan government in 2007, and things may just change.

When the weather is clear, there are fabulous views over both Caracas and down the coastal mountains to the Caribbean sea. At the summit, you can also hire a taxi to take you to one of the dozen or so restaurants in and near the small mountain village of Galipán. These restaurants range from simple roadside shacks, to fine dining establishments serving everything from Mexican to French cuisine.

The *teleférico* (© **0800/28452**) is open Tuesday through Sunday from 10am to 8pm. The round-trip cost is BsF25 ($12/£5.70) adults, and BsF10 ($4.65/£2.30) children 4 to 12. A light sweater or windbreaker is recommended, as it can get chilly up top. To get here, just ask a taxi to take you to *el terminal Maripérez del teleférico.*

JOGGING   Joggers should definitely head to either **Parque del Este** for more or less flat terrain, or **Parque Nacional El Avila** (see "Hiking," above) for more challenging mountainous terrain.

SHOPPING

Venezuelans—and most visitors—tend to shop at one of the many modern malls that have been built around Caracas over the past 20 years. Of these, the **Centro Comercial Sambil** ✺, Avenida Libertador (Metro: Chacao), is perhaps the most popular. Reputed to be the largest mall in South America, it features everything from a multiplex cinema to gourmet restaurants to a performing arts space to a mini–amusement park. Other prominent malls include the **Centro Comercial Ciudad Tamanaco (CCCT),** Autopista Francisco Fajardo and Calle La Estancia (no Metro); and the **Centro Lido,** Avenida Francisco de Miranda, El Rosal (Metro: Chacaito).

Las Mercedes ✺ is an upscale district of restaurants, shops, nightclubs, and art galleries, which makes it the choice spot for a leisurely afternoon of browsing and buying.

If you're looking for arts and crafts, you can head to the **Mercado Guajiro** ✺, Paseo Las Flores near the western end of Plaza Chacaito, a collection of 30 shops featuring indigenous and other arts and crafts. However, perhaps the best shopping for Venezuelan arts and crafts is to be found in El Hatillo at the **Hannsi Centro Artesanal** ✺✺✺, Calle Bolívar 12 (© **0212/963-7184;** www.hannsi.com.ve). This huge indoor bazaar has everything from indigenous masks to ceramic wares to woven baskets. The selection is broad and covers everything from trinkets to major pieces of fine craftsmanship.

Finds Parque del Este

This large **urban oasis** ✺✺ is a favorite spot for Caraqueños. Joggers, yoga and tai chi enthusiasts, tennis players, and people looking for pickup soccer and basketball games fill this park on most mornings and throughout the weekend. You can take part in any of the aforementioned activities or just stroll the paths, sit on a bench, or visit the tiny zoo. On weekends you can catch one of the shows at the Humbolt Planetarium here. The park is open Tuesday through Sunday from 5am to 5pm, Monday from 5 to 9am. Admission is free. Metro: Parque del Este.

WHERE TO STAY

Hotel rates in Caracas are crazy. Business travelers fill almost every room in the city Monday through Thursday, and hotels slash their rates on weekends. Moreover, the high occupancy and heavy corporate traffic have made rack rates at most Caracas hotels almost meaningless. Few hotels actually charge their published and advertised rack rate. It always pays to ask for a corporate or special rate, and if that fails, try to bargain at all but the truly top-end hotels.

Note: Most of the upscale hotels in Caracas either list their prices in dollars, or peg them to the dollar.

VERY EXPENSIVE

In addition to the hotels listed below, the **Gran Meliá Caracas** ★★ (Av. Casanova and El Recreo, Sabana Grande; ✆ **888/956-3542** in the U.S. and Canada, or 0212/762-8111 in Venezuela; www.solmelia.com), is a top notch luxury hotel in a decidedly sketchy neighborhood.

The Hotel ★★ Billing itself as the only "design" hotel in Caracas, this midsize boutique hotel does offer a refreshing alternative to the large chain options that dominate here in Caracas. The Hotel is certainly chic and modern. Flatscreen LCD and plasma TV screens are everywhere—in the lobby, lounge, restaurant, and even the elevators. Rooms are sleek and stylish, with marble or wood floors, thick down feather bed cushions and comforters, and modern entertainment systems ready for you to plug in your laptop, iPod, or video camera. There's a range of suite categories, all of which come with Jacuzzi tubs, and some of which have private steam showers. The standards are quite acceptable, but lack these perks. All, except the larger suites are on the compact side, especially at these prices. All rooms are nonsmoking.

Calle Mohedano, El Rosal, Caracas. ✆ **0212/951-0268.** Fax 0212/952-6515. www.thehotel.com.ve. 63 units. BsF665 ($309/£152) double; BsF837–BsF2, BsF190 ($389–$1,019/£191–£499) suite. AE, MC, V. Free valet parking. **Amenities:** Restaurant; bar; lounge; small, well-equipped spa and exercise room; concierge; tour desk; 24-hr. business center; small shopping arcade; salon; 24-hr. room service; massage; laundry service/dry cleaning. *In room:* A/C, TV, dataport, free Wi-Fi, minibar, hair dryer, safe.

JW Marriott ★★★ This upscale hotel caters primarily to business travelers, though it works just as well for a casual traveler. The rooms are all very comfortable and spacious, with lush furnishings and decor, and sleek marble bathrooms. There are two towers here, and one contains suites entirely. The regular deluxe rooms all come with separate tubs and showers, although oddly some of the suites only have a tub/shower combo. The large "spa suites" come with a private Jacuzzi tub. Most rooms, particularly those on higher floors, have wonderful views, but the best view to be found is on the 17th-floor bridge connecting the two towers. Service is attentive and accommodating. Dining options include Sur, an excellent *Nuevo Latino* restaurant, as well as a sushi bar.

Av. Venezuela and Calle Mohedano, El Rosal, Caracas. ✆ **888/236-2427** in the U.S. and Canada, or 0212/957-2222 in Venezuela. Fax 0212/957-1111. www.marriott.com. 269 units. BsF621 ($289/£142) double; BsF664–BsF729 ($309–$339/£152–£166) suite. AE, MC, V. Valet parking BsF5 ($2.35/£1.15). **Amenities:** 2 restaurants; bar; coffee shop; outdoor pool; small, well-equipped health club; concierge; tour desk; car-rental desk; 24-hr. business center; small shopping arcade; salon; 24-hr. room service; massage; laundry service/dry cleaning; nonsmoking rooms; executive floors. *In room:* A/C, TV, dataport, minibar, coffeemaker, hair dryer, iron, safe.

EXPENSIVE

In addition to the hotels listed in this section, the **Hotel Paseo Las Mercedes** 🟊, Centro Comercial Paseo Las Mercedes (© **0212/993-6644;** www.hotelpaseolasmercedes. com), is a business-class hotel located in the heart of the fashionable Las Mercedes shopping and dining district.

Hotel Continental Altamira 🟊   This hotel offers a great location, acceptable levels of comfort, and a good array of amenities. The high-rise building is located about a block and a half from the Altamira Metro station and the heart of the area's restaurants and shops. Most of the rooms are quite large and qualify as junior suites, although the bathrooms in most cases are disproportionately small. Maintenance and upkeep have historically been lax, but it was in pretty spiffy shape when I visited in 2007. The nicest feature here is the shady outdoor terrace area surrounding the hotel's surprisingly inviting little pool.

Av. San Juan Bosco, Altamira, Caracas. © **0212/261-0644.** Fax 0212/261-0131. www.hotel-continental.org.ve. 82 units. BsF290–BsF396 ($135–$184/£66–£90) double. AE, MC, V. Free valet parking. **Amenities:** Restaurant; bar; small outdoor pool; tour desk; limited room service; laundry service. *In room:* A/C, TV, safe.

MODERATE

Hotel Avila *(Finds)*   The aged grande dame of Caracas hotels, this place is worth considering. Built by Nelson Rockefeller in 1942, the hotel is a quiet oasis located about 15 minutes from downtown on the flanks of Mount Avila. The lush grounds and flowering gardens are a welcome change from the cold concrete and glass that characterize most of Caracas. The hotel definitely shows its age, and perennially feels as if it could use some major maintenance and upkeep. Yet, it still retains a certain dignity and charm, if not glamour. Most of the rooms are comfortable and spacious, with high ceilings, new carpeting, and rattan furnishings, although most do not have air-conditioning. The suites are a mixed bag: Some are quite nice, while others are less appealing than the standard rooms. The Tower and Executive suites are the best rooms in the house. Meals are served in the poolside dining area and adjacent open-air dining room. A taxi from the hotel to downtown will cost you BsF15 to BsF20 ($7–$9.30/£3.40–£4.55).

Av. Washington, San Bernardino, Caracas. © **0212/555-3000.** Fax 0212/552-3021. www.hotelavila.com.ve. 113 units. BsF180–BsF250 ($84–$117/£41–£57) double; BsF300 ($140/£68) junior suite; BsF330–BsF380 ($154–$177/£75–£87) suite. Rates include breakfast buffet. AE, MC, V. Free parking. **Amenities:** Restaurant; bar; lounge; small oval outdoor pool; 6 lighted tennis courts; small health club; concierge; tour desk; salon; room service; massage; laundry service. *In room:* TV, safe.

INEXPENSIVE

Hotel Savoy *(Value)*   This long-time favorite is probably your best budget choice in Caracas, if you want a relatively safe and tidy room at a reasonable rate. The rooms are well kept and comfortable and come with air-conditioning, cable television, and small refrigerators. Most aren't particularly large, but some have small private balconies. The Savoy is just a block off the main pedestrian mall of Sabana Grande, close to a score of restaurants, and about 4 blocks from the nearest Metro stop. The hotel staff is friendly and helpful. Be careful in this neighborhood after dark.

Av. 2 Las Delicias, Sabana Grande, Caracas. © **0212/762-1971.** Fax 0212/761-7154. www.hotelsavoycaracas. com.ve. 95 units. BsF86–BsF150 ($40–$70/£20–£34) double. AE, MC, V. Free parking. Metro: Chacaito. **Amenities:** Restaurant; room service 7am–11pm; laundry service; free Wi-Fi. *In room:* A/C, TV, fridge.

NEAR THE AIRPORT

Years after *la tragedia de Vargas* (the Vargas tragedy), the coastal area near Venezuela's principal airport is still struggling to get back on its feet. In December 1999, heavy rains caused massive landslides all along El Litoral, killing as many as 20,000 and leaving many, many more homeless. Somehow, the international airport at Maiquetía survived, but almost all of the hotels and towns in the area were wiped out or severely damaged. The towns and cities of Catia La Mar, Maiquetía, La Guaira, Macuto, and Caraballeda were devastated, and the heavy runoff, debris, and detritus have left the beaches here decidedly unappealing.

Nevertheless, there are several options within a 15-minute radius of the airport. It is once again feasible and often recommended to stay near the airport and thus avoid Caracas altogether, a particularly good option if your travel plans are predominantly built around the natural wonders and beautiful beaches found farther afield. In addition to the option listed below, there is also a **Eurobuilding Express Hotel** ★, Avenida La Armada, Urbanización 10 de Marzo, Maiquetía (© **0212/700-0700;** www.hoteleuroexpress.com), located just across from the Simón Bolívar International Airport. This business-class hotel offers little in the way of personality, but they do have a free shuttle to the airport, and if you arrive late and leave early the next morning, it's worth considering. If you're looking for a budget option in the area, try the **Buenavista Inn,** Avenida el Hotel con Calle 4, Playa Grande, Catia La Mar (© **0212/ 352-9136;** www.buenavistainn.com.ve).

EXPENSIVE

Hotel Olé Caribe ★★   This is by far the most comfortable option on the coast near the airport. A comfortable and well-maintained luxury hotel, the Olé Caribe is filling the void left by the closings of the nearby Sheraton and Meliá properties. The rooms are all clean, bright, and well maintained, and feature a handful of amenities to be expected in this class. Most of the rooms have ocean views; those that don't, face the coastal mountains behind the hotel. The Olé Caribe is a bit inland from the sea and there are no worthwhile beaches close by; however, the pool area and surrounding landscaped grounds are tropical and inviting. Located 15 minutes from the airport, this is a top choice of local and international tour operators who are increasingly having their guests bypass Caracas altogether.

Av. Intercomunal, El Playón Macuto. © 0212/620-200. Fax 0212/620-2060. www.hotelolecaribe.com. 122 units. BsF301–BsF357 ($140/£166 double/£69–£81); BsF559 ($260/£127) suite. Rates include buffet breakfast. AE, MC, V. Free parking. **Amenities:** 3 restaurants; 2 bars; large outdoor pool w/unheated Jacuzzi and children's pool; unlit tennis court; squash court; small gym; concierge; tour desk; car-rental desk; business center; salon; 24-hour room service; massage; laundry service; dry cleaning. *In room:* A/C, TV, free Wi-Fi, minibar, hair dryer.

WHERE TO DINE

Caracas has a lively restaurant scene. The local upper and middle classes support a host of fine restaurants and trendy joints. World and fusion cuisines are the rage, along with sushi bars and upscale steakhouses. New places open and close with the frequency and fanfare worthy of New York City. If you're serious about delving into the local restaurant scene, pick up a copy of the latest edition of Miro Popic's *Guía Gastronómica de Caracas* ★★ (www.miropopic.com), a comprehensive, accurate, and bilingual guide to metropolitan restaurants, cafes, and nightspots.

In addition to the places listed below, **Chez Wong,** Plaza La Castellana (© **0212/ 266-5015**), is widely considered the best Chinese restaurant in town, while **Da Guido,** Avenida Francisco Solano, Sabana Grande (© **0212/763-0937**), and **Vizio** ★,

Avenida Luis Rocha, bottom floor of the Casa Rómulo Gallegos, Altamira (© **0212/ 285-5675**), are recommended for Italian cuisine.

On a more popular level, simple *arreperías* and informal *fuentes de soda,* the local equivalent of diners, are ubiquitous. Be sure to stop in to one or two of them for a light meal and a bit of local color. Given the prevalence and popularity of huge modern malls, you can usually count on finding a wide selection of restaurants, as well as an assortment of U.S.-based and -styled fast-food chains, in most of them.

EXPENSIVE

In addition to the places below, you can check out the local branch of famed Peruvian restaurant **Astrid y Gastón** (© **0212/993-1119;** Calle Londres, Las Mercedes), which opened here in 2006. See p. 642.

Bar Si 👙👙 PAN-ASIAN   A change in chefs has added a touch of Peruvian fusion to the menu here, but the broader offerings still include a mix of various Asian classics and its modern offshoots. There's a wide selection of Japanese dishes, including a small sushi bar. You can start things off with some sushi or one of the many *ceviche* choices. For a main dish, I always enjoy the Thai-inspired grouper in a coconut-milk curry with fresh mango, all served in a banana leaf. The low ceilings and low lighting this place an intimate (though sometimes claustrophobic) feel. The bar here is extremely popular on weekends, and sometimes features live music or DJs. The food is expensive, but definitely top-notch.

Calle Madrid, between Veraruz and Caroní, Las Mercedes. © **0212/993-9124.** Reservations recommended. Main courses BsF20–BsF60 ($9.30–$28/£4.55–£14). AE, MC, V. Mon–Wed noon–3pm and 7–11pm; Thurs–Sat noon–3pm and 7pm–midnight; Sun noon–3pm.

Restaurante Urrutia 👙👙 SPANISH   This has been one of the most popular restaurants in Caracas for more than 50 years. As befits a family-run institution, the place has an intimate family feel, with low ceilings and dark-wood beams. Start with a carpaccio of beef or salmon, or a *tapa* of Spanish tortilla (a potato-and-egg omelet). Although everything's delicious, one specialty here is the *piquillo* peppers stuffed with your choice of grouper, squid, or *bacalao* (cod) in a tomato-based Vizcaina sauce. If you make it through the extensive menu with room to spare, try the homemade *membrillo* jam with Manchego cheese for dessert. They have another branch, **Casa Urrutia** (© **0212/993-9526**) in the Las Mercedes district, at Calle Madrid and Calle Monterrey.

Av. Francisco Solano and Los Manguitos, Sabana Grande. © **0212/763-0448.** Reservations recommended. Main courses BsF18–BsF55 ($8.40–$26/£4.10–£13). MC, V. Mon–Sat noon–11pm; Sun noon–5pm.

MODERATE

Catar 👙 INTERNATIONAL   The outgrowth of a popular bakery and deli operation, this casual restaurant serves a wide range of fare, from simple pizzas and panini and ornate organic salads, to full meals. Everything is well-prepared and tasty. For a main dish, I recommend the seared tuna in a soy-ginger sauce. There are two main dining rooms. Both feature walls of glass, and marble-topped tables, and they are both often busy. This place is housed in a small shopping center known as the Cuadro Gastrónomico (Gastronomic Block) and is surrounded by several other good restaurants.

6th Tranversal, between Avs. 3 and 4, Los Palos Grandes. © **0212/285-0649.** Reservations recommended. Main courses BsF22–BsF45 ($10–$21/£5–£10); pizzas BsF22–BsF33 ($10–$15/£5–£7.50). MC, V. Daily 11:30am–11pm.

El Tinajero de los Helechos ⊛ VENEZUELAN There are plenty of reputable steakhouses in Caracas, but this is my favorite—as much for the casual vibe as for the fine meats and side dishes. There's an extensive selection of meat dishes, and nearly as many fish and chicken choices. The classic *pabellón criollo* and *asado negro* are both excellent. If you want something less traditional, try the chateaubriand or medallions of sirloin in a port sauce. A wide range of traditional Venezuelan appetizers and sides are available as well. Four rooms of differing contain indigenous craftworks and plenty of ferns—*helecho* is Spanish for fern—which liven up the decor.

Av. Rio de Janeiro, between Caroní and New York, Las Mercedes. ℂ 0212/993-3581. Reservations recommended. Main courses BsF14–BsF42 ($6.50–$20/£3.20–£9.60). AE, DC, MC, V. Daily 11:30am–midnight.

News Café ⊛⊛ *Finds* INTERNATIONAL This multifaceted joint tries to do it all and does a great job on all counts. Part bookstore, part cafe, part jazz club, and full-time restaurant, it serves breakfast, lunch, and dinner daily. There are several rooms and environments, including an open-air rooftop terrace with heavy marble tables under white canvas umbrellas, a second-floor balcony space, and a vibrant main dining room with cracked-tile mosaic floors. The food is simple and straightforward, with a host of interesting sandwiches served on fresh-baked baguettes, mixed with a selection of salads, crepes, bruschettas, and pastas. More substantial entrees include medallions of beef in a white wine, porcini, and cream sauce, or, my favorite, Salmon al Matteotti, which is served in a champagne-and-almond reduction. There's live music most afternoons for lunch, as well as Thursday through Saturday evenings.

1st Transversal de los Palos Grandes and 1st Av. Quinta d'Casa. ℂ 0212/286-5096. Reservations recommended for dinner. Sandwiches BsF8–BsF18 ($3.70–$8.40/£1.80–£4.10); main courses BsF12–BsF28 ($5.60–$13/£2.75–£6.40). AE, MC, V. Mon–Fri 10am–1am; Sat–Sun 8am–1am.

INEXPENSIVE

El Fogón *Finds* VENEZUELAN Take a table on the second-floor open-air balcony of this popular local joint. Hanging ferns and wind chimes give the place an air of sophistication, but the food is as traditional as it comes. Order an *arepa* to start things off, or try a *cachapa*—a sweet corn pancake folded over your choice of filling. The *asado* here is excellent, and they almost always have *hallacas,* the local equivalent of tamales, cornmeal paste stuffed with chicken, pork, olives, raisins, boiled egg, and other goodies, wrapped in a banana leaf, and boiled or steamed. For dessert, have some fried *churros.*

Calle La Paz, El Hatillo. ℂ 0212/963-1068. Reservations recommended on weekends. Main courses BsF4–BsF14 ($1.85–$6.50/90p–£3.20). No credit cards. Tues–Fri 9am–8pm; Sat–Sun 8am–10pm.

SNACKS & CAFES

For a good view of the passing spectacle of bustling Caracas, you can grab a table at any one of the many covered sidewalk cafes lining the Sabana Grande. In addition to the News Café (see above), another nearby coffeehouse worth checking is the **Café Arábica** ⊛, Avenida Andres Bello between 1st Transversal and Avenida Francisco Miranda (ℂ 0212/285-3469), a trendy joint on the ground floor of the Multicentro Los Palos Grandes mall that roasts its own beans bought from local producers.

If you're hungry for a quick bite and there's a *fuente de soda* handy—the local equivalent of a diner or deli—you should definitely try an *arepa,* the traditional cornmeal patty that usually comes stuffed with meat, cheese, or chicken.

CARACAS AFTER DARK

Caracas is a big, cosmopolitan city, and your nighttime options are many and varied. It's advisable to stick to the more upscale and relatively safe neighborhoods such as Altamira, El Rosal, and Las Mercedes, or one of the popular malls.

In terms of malls, the **Centro Comercial San Ignacio,** has emerged as a popular one-stop shop for young Caraqueños looking to party. However, my favorite bar in Caracas is located atop the Altamira Suites hotel. As its name implies, **360°** ★★ (© **0212/284-1874;** 1st Av. Los Palos Grandes and 1st Tranversal) offers up panoramic views from it's rooftop perch. The bar actually starts out with a large indoor space on the 19th floor, with plush cushions, couches, and even hammocks for seating, and climbs two more stories outdoors with a handful of different open-air patios, bars, and seating areas.

The **Juan Sebastián Bar** ★★, Avenida Venezuela, El Rosal (© **0212/951-5575**), is a popular restaurant and bar—and the most consistent place in the city to catch live jazz. Rockers head to **Greenwich** ★, Avenida San Juan Bosco, Altamira (© **0212/267-1760**), a small place with live bands; or **Little Rock Café,** Avenida 6 between 3rd and 4th Transversal, Altamira (© **0212/267-8337**), a knock-off of the Hard Rock chain that also has live bands on most nights. And there's even an official franchise of the **Hard Rock Café** (© **0212/267-7662**) located in the huge Centro Comercial Sambil. **El Maní Es Así** ★, Avenida Francisco Solano and Calle El Cristo, Sabana Grande (© **0212/763-6671**), is one of the more popular salsa and Latin dance spots. Open every night except Monday from 5pm until around 5am, they charge no cover and always have a live band.

Located just across from the Caracas Hilton, the **Teresa Carreño Cultural Complex** (© **0500/673-7200** or 0212/576-6411) and the **Ateneo de Caracas** (© **0212/573-4799**) are the places to go for live performances. Top-notch popular and classical concerts take place in the Teresa Carreño, while film series and modern theater are often on tap at the Ateneo. The **Trasnocho Cultural** ★, Centro Comercial Paseo Las Mercedes (© **0212/993-1910;** www.trasnochocultural.com), is a popular option with a beautiful theater and a couple of cinemas offering a steady diet of live music, theater, and avant-garde cinema. They also have a hip little bar and cafe. Check the local papers or ask at your hotel for a performance schedule. Ticket prices range from BsF2 to BsF40 (95¢–$19/45p–£9.10).

SIDE TRIPS FROM CARACAS

Caracas-based tour companies offer a host of **tour options,** from guided city tours and adventure activities to longer excursions to destinations such as Los Roques and Angel Falls (see below). Some of the more popular day-tour options from Caracas include mountain-bike or jeep tours through Parque Nacional El Avila. Prices for day tours range from BsF65 to BsF200 ($30–$93/£15–£46) per person. A half-day guided tour to El Hatillo usually runs around BsF60 ($28/£14) per person.

Akanan Travel & Adventure ★★ (© **0212/715-5433** or 0414/116-0107; www.akanan.com) and **Cacao Expeditions** (© **0212/977-1234;** www.cacaotravel.com) are both reputable local operators offering a wide range of single and multiday options.

EL HATILLO ★★   This neocolonial town, located 15km (9 miles) southeast of downtown, is a great place to spend a few leisurely hours and grab a meal. You'll want to spend most of your time strolling around, but be prepared—it's hilly here. Moreover, the narrow streets have even narrower sidewalks, so beware of car traffic. Window-shop the many crafts and artisan jewelry stores and be sure to sample some homemade sweets at one of the many local pastry and candy shops. You'll find a good selection of restaurants, cafes, and bars here. Stop in for a coffee or a light bite at **Croquer,** Calle Bolívar 17 (© **0212/961-4269**). After admiring the memorabilia, try to grab one of the third-floor tables under canvas umbrellas on the terrace. A taxi to El Hatillo should cost around BsF20 ($9.30/£4.55).

LOS ROQUES 🏵🏵   Perhaps the most popular excursions from Caracas are to Los Roques, a gorgeous archipelago of small islands around a calm saltwater lagoon in crystal-clear Caribbean waters. **Aerotuy** (© **0212/212-3110;** www.tuy.com) is by far the most established operator offering trips to Los Roques. The cost for a full-day trip is around BsF660 ($308/£151) per person. Children's rates are roughly half price, and rates are slightly lower during the low season and midweek. For more information, see "Los Roques National Park," later in this chapter.

PARQUE NACIONAL HENRI PITTIER 🏵   Venezuela's first national park, founded in 1937, is named after a Swiss botanist who pioneered efforts to create the country's national park system. The park covers much of the northern state of Aragua, running from the Caribbean Sea almost to the city of Maracay. The park encompasses a wide range of ecosystems, from coastal lowlands to cloud forest to rainforest, with mountains inside the park rising to more than 2,000m (6,560 ft.). The flora and fauna here is extremely rich and diverse, and Henri Pittier is one of the world's prime bird-watching spots, with more than 550 resident and migratory species recorded. The park is the gateway to the tourist towns of Choroní and Puerto Colombia and a string of isolated and beautiful Caribbean beaches. The area can be reached by bus and taxi from Maracay, or as part of a tour from Caracas (see info on tour options above).

CANAIMA & ANGEL FALLS 🏵🏵   You may actually see advertisements for or be offered a day tour to Canaima and Angel Falls. However, given the distance, travel time, and outstanding natural beauty of the area, I highly recommend a longer trip. See "Canaima, Angel Falls & the Río Caura," later in this chapter, for more information.

5 Isla de Margarita 🏵

40km (25 miles) N of Cumaná

Known locally as *"La Perla del Caribe,"* or the Pearl of the Caribbean, Isla de Margarita is Venezuela's most popular tourist destination. Venezuelans come here in droves for weekend and holiday getaways, and to take advantage of the island's status as a duty-free port, while Canadian, European, and Latin American travelers come to enjoy the warm sun, white sands, and turquoise waters of this small Caribbean island. In many ways, the pleasures to be had on Isla de Margarita mirror and compete with those offered in Cancún, Punta Cana, Varadero and other beach destinations around the Caribbean, although on a much smaller scale. And Margarita remains relatively undiscovered and unexplored by Americans. Columbus actually landed here, in 1498, on his third voyage, and named the island La Asunción. However, 1 year later it was rechristened La Margarita.

Margarita is really two islands joined in the middle by a stretch of sand, mangrove, and marsh that make up **La Restinga National Park.** The western side, called the **Peninsula de Macanao,** is largely undeveloped. It's an extremely arid and dry area,

Isla de Margarita

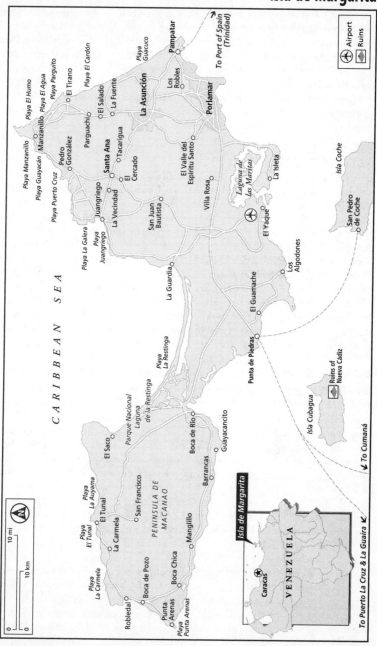

crisscrossed with rugged dirt roads and horse trails, and it's home to the endemic yellow-headed and yellow-shouldered Margaritan parrot. Almost all development is found on the larger, eastern side, which boasts three principal cities—**Porlamar, Pampatar,** and **La Asunción**—and a couple of dozen different beaches and resort areas. The island has two national parks and three nature reserves, as well as several colonial-era forts and churches.

Margarita's climate is hot and tropical, with ample sunshine and very little rainfall year-round. You're most likely to encounter some rain during the months of July and August and between November and January.

ESSENTIALS
GETTING THERE
BY PLANE   Several international airlines and dozens of charter carriers have service to Margarita's **Aeropuerto Internacional del Caribe Santiago Mariño** (© 0295/269-1081; airport code PMV) from major European cities, as well as from Toronto, Montreal, Miami, and New York. Many of these are sold as package tours.

From Caracas, there are a couple of dozen flights to Margarita throughout the day. **Aeropostal** (© 0800/284-6637; www.aeropostal.com), **Aserca** (© 0800/648-8356; www.asercaairlines.com); **Avior** (© 0501/284-67737; www.aviorairlines.com), **Conviasa** (© 0500/266-84272; www.conviasa.aero), and **Laser** (© 0501/527-3700; www.laser.com.ve) all fly between Caracas's Simón Bolívar International Airport and Isla de Margarita. Fares vary radically according to season and day of the week, ranging from BsF150 to BsF300 ($70–$140/£34–£68) each way. Midweek and low-season fares are considerably less expensive. Conversely, seats sell out well in advance and at a premium on weekends and holidays and during the high season. Flight schedules and travel agents refer to the airport as Porlamar, although it is around 20km (13 miles) from the city, on the southern part of the island near the beach of El Yaque.

BY FERRY   Although losing ground to air traffic, ferry service has and continues to be one of Margarita's principal links to the mainland. Visitors, residents, cars, buses, and much of the island's goods and merchandise travel by sea. The main ferry station is at Punta de Piedras on the southern end of the island. The main departure points for ferries to Margarita are Puerto La Cruz and Cumaná on the northern coast of Venezuela several hours east of Caracas. There are numerous public buses throughout the day from Caracas to both Puerto La Cruz and Cumaná. The bus trip runs about 5 hours from Caracas to Puerto La Cruz (fare BsF10–BsF20/$4.65–$9.30/£2.30–£4.55), and 7 to 8 hours to Cumaná (fare BsF12–BsF25/$5.60–$12/£2.75–£5.70). You can also try the **Unión Conductores de La Guira** (© 0212/482-3344), or the **Unión Conductores de Margarita,** Terminal Oriente, Caracas (© 0212/541-0035 or 0295/287-0931). The latter has a direct combined trip that costs around BsF50 ($23/£11) each way.

Basically, there are two types of ferries running from Puerto La Cruz and Cumaná: the older regular ferries, which take between 3 and 4 hours each way, and the newer "express" ferries, which make the crossing in around 2 hours. **Conferry** also has regular express service between La Guaira (just outside Caracas) and Margarita. The crossing takes just under 5 hours to or from La Guaira. Ferry schedules change drastically according to season and demand, and even the set schedules are sometimes somewhat flexible. For current ferry schedules and fares, contact **Conferry** (© 0501/266-33779; www.conferry.com), or **Gran Cacique Express** (© 0800/227-2600 or 0295/239-8339; www.grancacique.com.ve).

It's recommended to try buying tickets in advance on weekends and during high season. Costs range from BsF15 to BsF65 ($7–$30/£3.40–£15) per person, each way, and BsF45 to BsF75 ($21–$35/£10–£17) per car. The cost difference for passengers is tied to the "class" of your ticket and speed of the boat. I recommend you splurge for the higher-class fares on the express ferries, which will get you a seat in an enclosed and air-conditioned lounge deck, and a quicker ride.

GETTING AROUND

Renting a car is not essential, but it does make getting around Margarita easier. **Avis** (© **0295/269-1230;** www.avis.com); **Budget** (© **0295/269-1490;** www.budget. com.ve), **Hertz** (© **0800/800-0000** or 0295/269-1237; www.hertz.com), and **Margarita Rentals** (© **0295/263-2711**) all have offices at the airport. It costs BsF70 to BsF200 ($33–$93/£16–£46) per day to rent a car. Several outfits around the island rent scooters and mopeds for between BsF60 and BsF75 ($28–$35/£14–£17) per day.

Por puesto buses service most of the island. They are a very inexpensive and reliable way to get around, although the going can be slow, as they often stop to pick up and discharge passengers at maddeningly short intervals. Typical service hours are daily from 6am to 8pm. Fares range from BsF.50 to BsF2 (20¢–95¢/10p–45p).

Taxis are also readily available. It will cost you around BsF30 ($14/£6.85) to travel between the airport and Porlamar; BsF10 ($4.65/£2.30) between Porlamar and Pampatar; BsF20 ($9.30/£4.55) between Playa El Agua and either Porlamar or Pampatar; and BsF50 ($23/£11) between Playa El Agua and the airport. If you can't flag one down on the street you can order a cab by calling **Taxis Isla Bella** (© **0295/808-6762**) or **Taxis Unidos** (© **0295/263-2269**).

VISITOR INFORMATION

There is a simple, very basic information desk at the airport in Porlamar. However, you're better off heading to one of the scores of tour agencies to be found around Porlamar and Pampatar and at most major hotels on the island.

FAST FACTS   You'll find a couple of **currency exchange** offices at the airport and a dozen or more money-exchange houses in Porlamar, Pampatar, and around the island. Most major hotels here will change money for you as well, although most will exchange at the official rate, or even slightly below. There are scores of **banks** on Isla de Margarita. They often have ATMs connected to PLUS or Cirrus systems that will advance you bolívares against your home account. You'll find ATMs in both Porlamar and Pampatar, as well as at all the large malls and some of the large resort hotels.

In case of any medical emergency, consult with your hotel first, or head to the **Luis Ortega Hospital** in Porlamar (© **0295/261-6508**).

Internet cafes are located in most malls and major resorts, as well as in Porlamar, in Pampatar, and along Playa El Agua. For regular mail, there are **Ipostel** offices in both Porlamar and Pampatar. Most hotels will also post mail for you.

WHAT TO SEE & DO
ATTRACTIONS
Cities & Towns

Porlamar is the largest city and the commercial hub of the island. Founded in 1536, Porlamar is not particularly attractive. The city center is a chaotic jumble of shops and small department stores. However, these days the majority of shoppers are heading to large, modern malls built on the outskirts of the city. Still, Porlamar has the highest concentration of shops, restaurants, bars, and dance clubs on Margarita.

Pampatar, about 10km (6 miles) northeast of Porlamar, is much more picturesque and calm. Founded in 1535 around the island's most protected deep-water harbor, Pampatar still retains much of its colonial-era flavor and architecture. The main attraction here is the **Castillo de San Carlos Borromeo** ✪, a 17th-century fort that protected the town and harbor from foreign and pirate attacks. The fort's thick stone walls and bronze cannons still watch over the beach, harbor, and Caribbean Sea. The fort is open Monday through Saturday; admission is free. Across from the fort, you'll find the **Iglesia de Santísimo Cristo del Buen Viaje,** a church of great importance to the sailors and fishermen of Margarita. Legend has it that the crucifix here was left as a last resort, when the colonial-era vessel transporting it was unable, after repeated attempts, to leave the harbor. At the eastern end of the harbor are the ruins of the **Fortín de la Caranta,** which offers excellent views of the town and bay.

Located on a hillside, inland from Pampatar, **La Asunción** is the capital of the island and of the entire state of Nueva Esparta. The city's church, **La Catedral de Nuestra Señora de la Asunción** ✪, is said to be the oldest in Venezuela. A few minutes from the center of town is the **Castillo de Santa Rosa,** another of the island's historic and battle-worn forts.

In between Porlamar and Pampatar is the area known as **Los Robles.** Here, you'll find the colonial-era **Iglesia El Pilar de Los Robles,** whose statue of the Virgin Mary is reputed to be of solid gold.

On the road north of La Asunción is the town of **Santa Ana.** In 1816, Simón Bolívar signed the proclamation of the Third Republic in the small church here. It's now best known as the hub for a series of small artisan villages and roadside crafts shops.

Finally, on the northern coast of the island is the popular fishing village and bay of **Juangriego** ✪. This spot is becoming increasingly popular, particularly for **sunsets.** The small **Fortín La Galera** ✪✪✪, on a bluff on the northern end of the bay, is probably the most sought-after spot for sunsets on the island. Arrive early if you want a prime table and viewing spot at one of the small open-air restaurants and bars here.

The Beaches ✪✪

Isla de Margarita is ringed with dozens of white-sand beaches. Some have huge modern resorts and facilities, others are home to a handful of fishermen and locals, and some are entirely undeveloped and deserted. Perhaps the most popular beach on the island is **Playa El Agua,** a long, broad, straight stretch of white sand with moderate surf, backed by palm trees and a broad selection of restaurants and shops. **Playa Parguito** has begun to rival El Agua in terms of popularity. Both of these beaches can get packed on weekends and during peak periods. To the south and north of Playa El Agua, you'll find beaches such as **Manzanillo** ✪, **El Tirano** ✪, **Cardón,** and **Guacuco.** Manzanillo and El Tirano are my favorites, because they are the least developed and often quite deserted. Manzanillo is a great place to watch sunsets. Playas Parguito and El Tirano are the best surf breaks on the island. Close to Porlamar, folks head to **Playa Bella Vista** and **Playa Morena,** although I'm not particularly taken by the vibe or water quality at either.

On the northern coast of Margarita you will find a string of excellent and less-developed beaches, including **Playa Caribe** ✪, **Playa Pedro González,** and **Playa Puerto Viejo.** These are some of my favorite beaches on Margarita, and they are building up fast. Those looking for solitude should head to the still-undeveloped beaches that ring the Macanao Peninsula.

Although one of the least attractive beaches on the island, **Playa Pampatar** is nonetheless quite popular with locals. It is also lined with a string of simple restaurants set on the sand, just a few yards from the sea.

National Parks

LA RESTINGA NATIONAL PARK ✿   This 10,700-hectare (26,429-acre) park encompasses a zone of mangroves, marshland, sandbar, and coral-sand beaches making a natural land bridge between the two islands that today are Isla de Margarita. A visit to the park usually involves a boat tour through the mangroves, followed by some beach time on the 10km (6-mile) stretch of beach that forms the isthmus uniting the two sides of Margarita. You'll find some simple beachside restaurants and souvenir stands here. The bird-watching is excellent in the mangroves, and the park's beach is renowned for its supply of seashells. To reach La Restinga, take a taxi or the Línea La Restinga *por puesto* out of Porlamar. At the park entrance you'll have to pay a BsF1 (45¢/25p) entrance fee and then walk to the nearby pier, where there are scores of boats waiting to take you on a tour. The boats charge BsF15 to BsF35 ($7–$16/ £3.40–£8) per person, depending on the size of your group. The trip through the mangroves usually lasts between 30 minutes and 1 hour, at which point you will be left at the beach. Have the boatman wait, or arrange a firm pickup time and place for your return to the pier.

Islas Coche & Cubagua

The entire state of Nueva Esparta is made up of Isla de Margarita and two much smaller neighboring islands, **Isla Coche** and **Isla Cubagua.** The pearl beds off these two islands were major sources of wealth during the colonial period. Both islands are popular destinations for day cruises, which bring folks to their pristine and nearly deserted beaches. Isla Coche has some development and rolling hills, while Isla Cubagua is mostly barren, flat, and undeveloped. One of the only attractions here are the ruins of Nueva Cádiz. Founded on Isla Cubagua in 1528, this was the first Spanish town formally established in the Americas. However, its heyday was short-lived: An earthquake and tidal wave destroyed the town in 1541.

Day tours by small cruise ships and converted fishing boats are common. The full-day tour usually includes round-trip transportation from your hotel to the marina, continental breakfast, a buffet lunch, an open bar, beach chairs, umbrellas, and organized activities on the island. Prices range from BsF60 to BsF120 ($28–$56/£140–£27) per person. *Be forewarned:* There's a real cattle-car feel to most of these tours.

There's also a daily Conferry vessel leaving at 6am from the Punta de Piedras pier for Isla Coche and returning at 6pm. The cost is BsF3 ($1.40/£70p) per person, BsF15 ($7/£3.40) per car.

OUTDOOR ACTIVITIES

In addition to the activities mentioned below, jet skis and WaveRunners are available at many beaches and resorts around the island, as are parasail flights.

AMUSEMENT PARKS   **Parque El Agua,** Avenida 31 de Julio, El Cardón, on the way to Playa El Agua (℗ **0295/263-0710;** www.parqueelagua.com), is a fairly extensive and well-maintained water park with an assortment of pools, slides, and rides. The park is open daily from 10am to 6pm. Admission is BsF45 ($21/£10) for adults, BsF35 ($16/£8) for children.

Diverland *(Kids*, Isla Aventura near Pampatar (© **0295/267-0571;** www.parque diverland.com), is a combination amusement park and water park, with a wide range of attractions and rides. You'll find typical amusement park rides, such as Ferris wheels and roller coasters, as well as go-karts, a petting zoo, and batting cages. They also have trained dolphin and seal shows, as well as a swim-with-the dolphins program. However, I find both the shows and the swim program rather sad and unfortunate for the animals. It's open from 10am to 11pm daily throughout the high season and most weekends the rest of the year. Operating days and hours are much more limited during the week and low season. Admission is BsF20 ($9.30/£4.55) for adults and BsF10 ($4.65/£2.30) for children for unlimited use of the rides and pools. Some features and exhibits, such as swimming with dolphins, have additional fees.

BIKING The stunning scenery and combination of off-road and paved highway possibilities make Margarita a good place to rent a bike for exploring. Be careful, though: The sun can be brutal, and the distances between towns and beaches can quickly become more daunting than you might expect. The best place for mountain biking is the Macanao Peninsula.

CRUISES & SAILBOAT CHARTERS The most popular day cruises from Margarita are to the islands of Coche, Cubagua, and Los Frailes. Trips cost from BsF60 to BsF180 ($28–$84/£14–£41) per person for a full-day tour with lunch. See "Islas Coche & Cubagua," above, and "Scuba Diving & Snorkeling," below, for more information.

With the constant trade winds and translucent turquoise waters, Margarita is a great place to sail. A host of charter vessels anchor in the Pampatar harbor and other protected anchorages and bays around Margarita. The fleet fluctuates seasonally, but a sailboat is always available for a day cruise or multiday charter. Day tours cost from BsF70 to BsF220 ($33–$103/£16–£50) per person. Rates for all-inclusive multiday charters range from BsF200 to BsF500 ($93–$233/£46–£114) per person per day. Contact **Explore Yachts** (© **0212/2870517** or 0414/287-7554; www.explore-yachts.com), which manages a fleet of vessels.

FISHING The waters off Isla de Margarita are excellent fishing grounds. A day's catch might include any combination of tuna, dorado, marlin, and sailfish. You can hire a guide and a boat for the day, with lunch and beverages, for between BsF800 and BsF2,400 ($373–$1,118/£182–£547), depending on the size of the boat, number of fishermen, and game sought; check with your hotel or call **Explore Yachts** (see above).

GOLF There's only one working 18-hole course on the island. The **Isla Margarita Golf Club** (© **0295/265-7371**) at the Hesperia Isla Margarita is a 70-par links course. The course is fairly flat and open, with few trees, little rough, and very inconsistent groundskeeping. On my last visit in 2007, the course was in terrible shape. This isn't a popular golf destination, so tee times generally aren't required, but it never hurts to make a reservation. Greens fees are free for guests at both Hesperia hotels on the island and BsF86 ($40/£20) for visitors.

HORSEBACK RIDING Whether you fancy a ride on the beach, through the forested hills of the Cerro El Copey, or over the barren desertlike landscape of the Macanao Peninsula, there are great opportunities for horseback riding all over Margarita. Inquire at your hotel, or contact **Cabatucan Ranch** (© **0416/681-9348**), which specialize in tours of the Macanao Peninsula. A 2-hour ride, with transportation to and from your hotel, should run around BsF86 ($40/£20) per person.

JEEP TOURS Small 4×4 jeeps are the ideal transport for a full-day tour taking in a wide range of the sights and scenery of Isla de Margarita. The tours usually include pickup at your hotel, a trip to the top of Cerro El Copey, visits to a couple of churches and forts, a boat ride through La Restinga, stops at several beaches, and lunch and an open bar. The prices range from BsF85 to BsF140 ($40–$65/£20–£32) per person. Contact **Walter's Tours** ★(✆ **0295/274-1265** or 0416/696-2212; www.margaritais landguide.com).

KITESAILING & WINDSURFING Although you can rent a Windsurfer on many of the beaches on Margarita, **Playa El Yaque,** on the southern end of the island near the airport, is the place to be if you are a windsurfer or kitesailer. A handful of small hotels here cater specifically to windsurfers and kitesailers, usually with a wide selection of boards and sails for rent, and lesson options. **El Yaque Paradise** (✆ **0295/ 263-9418;** www.hotelyaqueparadise.com) and **El Yaque Motion** (✆/fax **0295/263-9742;** www.elyaquemotion.com) are both excellent options.

SCUBA DIVING & SNORKELING As this is the Caribbean, count on some good snorkeling and scuba diving on and around Isla de Margarita. Conditions immediately around the island can be a little too rough and murky. Two of the more popular dive sites close to Margarita are **Los Frailes,** a group of small rock islands about 11km (7 miles) offshore that are good for both snorkeling and scuba, and the **Cueva el Bufón,** a small cave near Pampatar thought to be a hiding place for pirate loot that can only be visited with scuba gear. Off **Isla Cubagua,** you can dive the wreck of a sunken ferry, with intact cars still aboard.

Snorkel trips average between BsF85 to BsF140 ($40–$65/£20–£32) per person for a full-day tour with lunch, and scuba tours cost around BsF140 ($65/£32) for a two-tank dive trip. Contact **Atlantis Diving Center** (✆ **0295/249-1325**) or **Ecobuzos** (✆ **0295/262-8255;** www.ecobuzos.com).

SURFING If the swell is right, you can find ridable surf on the island. **Playa Parguito,** just south of Playa El Agua, and **El Tirano,** a little farther south, are the principal breaks on Margarita.

SHOPPING

Venezuelans and visitors alike take advantage of the island's status as a duty-free port, although the fact is the deals and selection are not all that special. The downtown heart of Porlamar is a chaotic jumble of shops and small department stores selling everything from perfume to lingerie to electronics and appliances to liquor and foodstuffs. In 2002, the Puerto de la Mar pier was opened for cruise-ship traffic, allowing cruise passengers to disembark in downtown Porlamar, just blocks from the aforementioned jumble of shops and stores. However, as is the trend across Venezuela, large malls draw shoppers away from the downtown options. The biggest of the bunch is the **Centro Sambil Margarita,** Avenida Jovito Villalba, Pampatar. Other popular malls include the **Centro Comercial Rattan Plaza,** Avenida Jovito Villalba, Los Robles; and **Centro Comercial Jumbo,** Avenida 4 de Mayo.

For better bargains and a more local feel, head to **El Mercado de los Conejeros.** Located on the northwestern outskirts of Porlamar, it's a sort of permanent flea market of food, crafts, and dry-goods stalls. It's open daily from the wee hours of the morning until around 2pm.

At shops and roadside stands around the island, you will come across locally produced jewelry and ceramic wares of varying quality. Among of the nicer and more readily available handicrafts for sale on Margarita are the local hammocks, or *chinchorros*, an intricate weave of thin strands of rough natural fibers. You'll also find woven baskets, hats, and handbags. The town of Santa Ana and the roads that form a triangle between Santa Ana, Pedro González, and Juangriego are prime hunting grounds for crafts shops and galleries.

WHERE TO STAY

Isla de Margarita has hundreds of hotels and thousands of rooms. Visions of a tourist mecca led to the construction of massive resorts in the style of Cancún and the Dominican Republic. The tourists never arrived in large enough numbers, and the current political climate has further affected the industry. There's a glut of rooms, construction has been halted on a number of big projects, and several hotels have folded in recent years. The glut and desperate competition to fill beds is good news for travelers.

In general, all-inclusive packages here are a good bet and can often come quite cheap. Charter packages to Margarita from the United States, Canada, and even Europe, including round-trip airfare, can cost as little as $900/£442 per person for a full week. Another alternative is to book your tour in bolívares through a Venezuelan-based tour agency. Margarita hotels do about 80% of their business with national tourists, competition is steep, and if you exchange money at the black-market rate, you can get a real bargain. Try **Akanan Travel & Adventure** ✸✸ (© **0212/715-5433** or 0414/116-0107; www.akanan.com) or **Cacao Expeditions** (© **0212/977-1234;** www.cacaotravel.com).

The prices listed below are the hotels' published rack rates. These tend to be the highest rate applicable, and as in Caracas, most hotels here sell very few rooms at the actual rack rate. Prices fluctuate radically according to season and demand. If you book direct, feel free to bargain—it may pay off with some deep discounts.

VERY EXPENSIVE

Hilton Margarita ✸✸   This is the luxury hotel on Margarita, although it's geared more toward business travelers than those looking for a beach getaway. Still, it has a more elegant feel than the all-inclusive resorts that cater to the latter. The rooms and facilities are all top notch, and there's a good range of restaurants and shops, both on the grounds and nearby. All the rooms come with a small private balcony and a view to the sea. The end units on the north tower have larger balconies and full-on ocean views. The rooms are large, well-equipped, and consistently maintained. Still, if unadulterated beach time is what you're after, you might want to head elsewhere. The Hilton is located on a relatively unspectacular small stretch of sand, although it is always calm and safe. The hotel does have extensive and delightful pool areas. The casino here is one of the largest and swankiest on the island, and the hotel is a quick taxi ride away from both Porlamar and Pampatar.

Calle Los Uveros, Costa Azul, Isla de Margarita. © **800/HILTONS** in the U.S., or 0295/260-1700. Fax 0295/262-0810. www.hilton.com. 336 units. BsF452–BsF516 ($210–$240/£103–£118) double; BsF516–BsF817 ($240–$380/ £118–£186) suite. AE, DC, MC, V. Free valet parking. **Amenities:** 3 restaurants; 3 bars; 2 outdoor pools connected by a faux-river channel; children's pool; 2 lighted tennis courts; well-equipped exercise room; children's programs; concierge; tour and activities desk; car-rental desk; business center; shopping arcade; salon; room service; in-room massage; laundry service; nonsmoking rooms; Wi-Fi. *In room:* A/C, TV, dataport, minibar, hair dryer, safe.

EXPENSIVE

Hesperia Isla Margarita ⚝ This luxury resort is located on the northern end of the island, near Pedro González. The hotel has the only operational 18-hole golf course on the island, a well-equipped and luxurious spa, and a lovely little section of semiprivate beach. The central lobby is a large hexagonal area heavily draped in ferns and tropical plants that reach up five stories to a skylight. The rooms are large, with dark-wood floors, high ceilings, rattan furnishings, and comfortable bathrooms. A large wall of windows lets in plenty of light. Around 70% of the rooms have an ocean view. The best are those that look out over the pool and golf course to the sea; those with the least impressive views face inland over a mostly barren landscape.

The hotel is about a 30- to 35-minute taxi ride from either Porlamar or the airport, although they do provide a twice-daily shuttle to Porlamar.

Playa Bonita, Pedro González, Isla de Margarita. ✆ **0295/400-7111.** Fax 0295/400-7150. www.hesperia.com. 312 units. BsF516–BsF753 ($240–$350/£118–£172) double; BsF1,075–BsF2,150 ($500–$1,000/£245–£490) suite. Rates are all-inclusive. AE, DC, MC, V. Free self-parking. **Amenities:** 4 restaurants; 3 bars; 2 lounges; large rectangular pool w/children's pool; 18-hole links golf course and pro shop; 2 lighted tennis courts; well-equipped health club and spa; watersports equipment rental; children's programs; concierge; tour and activities desk; car-rental desk; modest business center; shopping arcade; salon; room service; in-room massage; babysitting; laundry service; nonsmoking rooms. *In room:* A/C, TV, minibar, hair dryer, safe.

Laguna Mar ⚝⚝ *Kids* This massive resort has the most extensive and impressive facilities on the island. From the wave pool to the water-slide pool to the private watersports lagoon, the installations here make it a great choice for families with children and anyone looking for constant activity. The rooms are spacious and cool, with plenty of light. Some rooms have private balconies, and the best of the lot have ocean views and balconies. All the bathrooms come with bidets, although some are quite cramped. The hotel is located on a long stretch of beautiful beach, which can get a bit rough at times. Free jitneys circulate constantly to take you around the extensive grounds. With a steady flow of European all-inclusive travelers, Laguna Mar's bars, dance club, and casino stay fairly lively. Most of the meals are served buffet-style. Reserve early if you want to eat at one of the a la carte restaurants. The resort sells a mix of all-inclusive packages and timeshares, and you can often get great deals, either through travel agencies or directly via Internet bookings.

Pampatar, Isla de Margarita. ✆ **0295/400-4033.** Fax 0295/262-1445. www.lagunamar.com.ve. 409 units. BsF345–BsF515 ($161–$240/£79–£117) double; BsF515–BsF752 ($240–$350/£117–£172) suite. Rates are all-inclusive. AE, DC, MC, V. Free self-parking. **Amenities:** 5 restaurants; snack bar; 4 bars; dance club; midsize casino; 6 outdoor pools and several children's pools; 9 lighted tennis courts; exercise room; 3 Jacuzzis; watersports equipment rental; children's programs; babysitting; tour and activities desk; car-rental desk; small business center; shopping arcade; salon; 24-hour room service; laundry service. *In room:* A/C, TV, safe.

MODERATE

In addition to the hotels listed below, there is a growing range of small *posadas*, bed-and-breakfasts, and condo rentals, particularly at the popular beaches. Two of the best are **Casa Caracol** (✆ **0295/416-8439;** www.posadacaracol.com) and **La Bella Luna Inn** (✆ **0295/249-0127;** www.labellaluna.net).

Hesperia Playa Agua *Value* This all-inclusive resort has a bit of a small village feel to it, although it is rather large. Rooms are either in small duplex or triplex bungalows, or one of the hotel's four seven-story towers. All the rooms are clean, comfortable, and contemporary. Rooms in the towers have private balconies, some of which have ocean views. The hotel is located just across the street from the gorgeous central section of Playa El Agua. Buffet meals are served in the large, central dining area; at the beachside **Frailemar** restaurant; or around the main pool. There are nightly entertainment reviews and a variety of organized activities throughout the day. This hotel doesn't have near as many facilities as Laguna Mar or some of the other large all-inclusives, but it does have a great location, plenty to keep you busy, and is much less expensive.

Playa El Agua, Isla de Margarita. © 0295/400-8111. Fax 0295/400-8151. www.hesperia.com. 355 units. BsF258–322. BsF50 ($120–$150/£59–£74) standard double; BsF430–BsF860 ($200–$400/£98–£196) suite. Rates are all-inclusive. AE, DC, MC, V. Free self-parking. **Amenities:** 2 restaurants; 3 bars; 4 outdoor pools; 3 lighted tennis courts; limited watersports-equipment rental; children's programs; tour and activities desk; car-rental desk; laundry service; outdoor nightly entertainment revue and dance club. *In room:* A/C, TV, fridge, safe.

Hotel Costa Linda Beach *(Finds)*   This charming hotel is one of the better options on the island, especially if you want an alternative to the large all-inclusive resorts. The rooms are spacious and cool, with rustic red-tile floors and white stucco walls. Most have high ceilings with exposed wood beams. The best rooms are higher up and have a private balcony with a hammock. Everything is set around the small central pool area, which is planted with lush gardens. The hotel is located about 200m (656 ft.) inland from the central section of Playa El Agua, and they have an arrangement with one of the beach restaurants there that gets you free beach lounges and umbrellas, as well as use of their facilities.

Playa El Agua, Isla de Margarita. © 0295/249-1303. Fax 0295/249-1229. www.hotelcostalinda.com. 40 units. BsF225–BsF285 ($105–133/£51–£65) double. Rates include buffet breakfast. MC, V. Free self-parking. **Amenities:** Restaurant; bar; small outdoor pool; tour desk; laundry service. *In room:* A/C, TV, hair dryer, safe.

WHERE TO DINE

Despite the fact that most visitors to Isla de Margarita stay at all-inclusive resorts, there are a host of restaurants around the island. Many of the beaches have simple restaurants on or close to the sand; they're great options for a lunch of fresh fish, lobster, or *pabellón,* the Venezuelan national dish consisting of shredded beef, rice, beans, and fried plantains.

Tip: Even if you are staying at an all-inclusive resort, I recommend heading out on the town to any of the restaurants recommended below, at least once or twice during your stay.

In addition to the places listed below, **El Rancho de Pablo,** Avenida Raúl Leoni, Porlamar (© 0295/263-1121), and **El Rincón de la Isla,** Boulevard Turistico, Playa El Agua (© 0295/249-0035), are two excellent open-air waterfront restaurants specializing in fresh local seafood, while **Café Mediterráneo,** Calle Campos, Porlamar (© 0295/264-0503); **Il Positano,** Calle Fermín and Calle Tubores, Porlamar (© 0295/264-1110); and **La Scala,** in the Hilton Margarita (© 0295/262-4111), are all recommended options for Italian. Both El Rancho de Pablo and Il Positano have sister restaurants in the Sambil Mall.

Casa Caranta *(★★★)* *(Finds)* FUSION/SEAFOOD   Housed in a beautifully restored colonial-era house in downtown Pampatar, this creative restaurant is a must stop on any visit to Isla Margarita. Italy, Asia, and the Americas are the principal inspirations for the regularly changing menu, which is handwritten on a few large chalkboards and brought to your table. Options range from homemade pasta with shrimp and porcini mushrooms to fresh grouper in a green curry sauce. The excellent wine list is fairly priced. In fact, given the hefty size of the portions, this place is actually a bargain. With live music most nights, the joint really gets going after around 10pm each evening.

Pampatar. ✆ 0295/262-8610. Reservations recommended. Main courses BsF19–BsF42 ($8.85–$20/£4.35–£9.60). MC, V. Daily 7pm–12:30am; closed Sun during the low season.

El Pacífico ✦ VENEZUELAN/SEAFOOD   This is the best of the bunch among the strip of beachside joints lining Playa El Agua. Get a table near the large windows overlooking the sea, or live dangerously and dine at a table under one of the tall coconut palms. Start things off with the *plato de pescado ahumado* (plate of smoked fish) and follow it with the fresh grilled red snapper or *langostinos al parchita* (jumbo shrimp in passion-fruit sauce). The elegant presentation of plates garnished with swirled sauces and parsley flakes contrasts nicely with the plastic lawn furniture and worn tablecloths.

Playa El Agua. ✆ 0295/249-0749. Reservations recommended during high season. Main courses BsF12–BsF32 ($5.60–$15/£2.75–£7.30); lobster BsF30–BsF64 ($14–$30/£6.85–£15). AE, MC, V. Daily 9am–11pm.

ISLA DE MARGARITA AFTER DARK

Given its status as a vacation getaway, Isla de Margarita has plenty of bars and night-clubs. Still, many visitors stick to their all-inclusive resort, which usually features a small collection of bars and a dance club and nightly entertainment revue. Others like to barhop sections of Avenida 4 de Mayo and Avenida Santiago Mariño.

By far the hippest and most happening scene can be found at **Kamy Beach** (✆ 0295/267-1185), located on Playa Varadero, just outside Pampatar. For a similar vibe, you can try **Beach Bar** (✆ 0295/267-2392), on Calle El Cristo in the La Caranta section of Pampatar.

If you're looking for something somewhat familiar, **Señor Frogs** (✆ 0295/262-0451), the popular Mexican chain, has a lively restaurant and bar in the Centro Comercial Costa Azul, near the Hilton, which turns into a raging dance club most evenings after 11pm. While over in the Sambil Mall, there's a local branch of the **Hard Rock Café** (✆ 0295/260-2400).

For a mellower scene, with a lot more atmosphere, I recommend both **Guayoyo Café** ✦ (✆ 0295/262-4514) and **Mykonis Lounge** (✆ 0295/267-1850), two side-by-side joints set on a steep cliff overlooking the ocean in Pampatar.

Casino gaming is an option on Margarita, with modern and well-fitted casinos at the Margarita Hilton, Laguna Mar, and Marina Bay hotels. The casino at the Hilton, by far, is the swankiest and most popular.

SIDE TRIPS FROM ISLA DE MARGARITA

Perhaps the most popular excursions from Margarita are to either **Los Roques** or **Canaima** and **Angel Falls.** By far the most established company making trips to both destinations is **Aerotuy** (✆ 0212/212-3110; www.tuy.com), although there's often a cattle-car feel to their operation, and the price is hefty. The cost for the Los Roques day trip is BsF665 ($310/£152) per person; to Canaima and Angel Falls, the cost is BsF1,375 ($640/£314) per person. The fares for children are roughly half price, and rates are slightly lower during the low season and midweek. See the sections on each destination below for more information.

6 Los Roques National Park ✮✮✮

166km (103 miles) N of Caracas

Few Caribbean island getaways are as remote, romantic, intimate, or idyllic as Los Roques. Hundreds of deserted little islands of soft white sand surrounded by crystal-clear turquoise waters and lively tropical reefs make Los Roques one of the prime vacation destinations in Venezuela. About 42 named islands—only a couple of which are inhabited—and 200-plus sand spits, mangrove islands, and tiny cays surround a 400-sq.-km (156-sq.-mile) central lagoon. The most popular activity here is getting dropped off on an isolated little island in the morning with a beach umbrella, some chaise lounges, and a cooler full of food and drink, and getting picked up again in the late afternoon. You spend your day beachcombing, sunbathing, swimming, and snorkeling. Depending on your point of view, you can imagine yourself shipwrecked on a deserted island or the ruler of some new territory.

Declared a national park in 1972, Los Roques protects vast areas of sea-grass beds, mangroves, and coral reef. The park is an important sea-turtle nesting ground. Of the 92 recorded bird species here, you are likely to see brown- and red-footed boobies, as well as scores of pelicans, gulls, terns, and other assorted shorebirds. There's even a small flock of pink flamingos on one of the isolated cays here. The barrier reefs that protect the archipelago's perimeter make this one of the premier dive spots in the country. Near-constant trade winds from the northeast also make this a great place to sail and windsurf.

ESSENTIALS
GETTING THERE

BY GUIDED TOUR   One of the most popular ways to visit Los Roques is on a day tour from Caracas or Isla de Margarita. These trips are sold by almost every travel agent and tour company in Caracas and are aggressively hawked at the airport. **Aerotuy** ✮ (✆ **0212/212-3110;** www.tuy.com) is by far the most established operator on the archipelago, with a fleet of catamarans anchored at Gran Roque. The tour generally leaves between 6 and 8am, arriving on Gran Roque in less than an hour. Soon after arrival, you'll board one of the catamarans for a sail to one or more of the nearby cays, with one or more stops for beach time and snorkeling, as well as a buffet lunch onboard the vessel. You'll return to Gran Roque in the late afternoon for your flight back to Caracas. The cost is BsF665 ($310/£152) per person. Although there is a cattle-car feel to the operation, organization is tight, and the bilingual guides tend to be helpful, knowledgeable, and cheerful. However, Los Roques is so isolated and enchanting, you'll definitely wish you had spent the night . . . or two.

BY PLANE   There are several daily flights to Los Roques from both Caracas and Isla de Margarita, with extra scheduled and charter flights on weekends and during peak periods. **Aerotuy** (✆ **0212/212-3110;** www.tuy.com), **Blue Star Airline** (✆ **0412/310-1962;** www.bluestar.us), **Sol de América** (✆ **05212/266-9518**), and **Transaven** (✆ **0212/355-1349;** www.transaven.com) all offer regular service to Los Roques. Round-trip airfare from Caracas or Margarita costs from BsF280 to BsF620 ($131–$289/£64–£141). Prices fluctuate a little seasonally, and you can sometimes get good deals midweek or on afternoon flights to Los Roques.

All visitors to Los Roques must pay a BsF38 ($18/£8.65) one-time entrance fee for the national park, good for the duration of your stay.

GETTING AROUND

There are no cars on Gran Roque—just a garbage truck, a water truck, and a handful of golf carts. You can walk from one end of the town of Gran Roque to the other in less than 10 minutes; you can hike to the more distant spots on the island in under an hour.

The only permanent settlement is on the main island of Gran Roque. There are some private vacation homes and fishermen's shacks on some of the other islands, but for all intents and purposes, a visit to Los Roques implies a visit to Gran Roque.

Four crushed-coral-and-sand streets run lengthwise through the town, beginning at the airstrip on the eastern end of the island. The small Plaza Bolívar is just a block or so from the airstrip. The public dock is on the southern side of the island nearly smack-dab in the middle of town.

VISITOR INFORMATION

Los Roques is not particularly geared toward independent travelers. Almost all visitors come as part of an organized tour or an all-inclusive stay at one of the *posadas* (inns) on Gran Roque. Given the isolation and limited number of hotel rooms, you should make firm reservations before arriving, particularly on weekends and during the high season.

Independent travelers can purchase, a la carte, all the typical tours and activities offered on the islands. Inquire at your hotel or at one of the small information/tour desks beside the airstrip.

FAST FACTS There is actually a branch of the **Banesco** (✆ **0237/221-1265**), which has an ATM and will change money. Some hotels and shops are reluctant to change money, and quite a few do not accept credit cards. Many will accept dollars for payment. The local ATM may or may not be able to access funds in your home account, so it's always best to bring a sufficient supply of bolívares for your stay, although if you ask around you should be able to find someone who will change foreign currency at or near the going black-market rate.

If you have a medical emergency, you will have to be air-evacuated on the next scheduled flight or special charter. Local dive shops often have dive masters and instructors schooled in first aid.

An Internet cafe is on the back street near Posada Guaripete. They charge BsF20 ($9.30/£4.55) per hour and can get quite busy, as they are the only game in town. Also, note that there is no Ipostel office on the island—you'll have to mail your postcards and letters from the mainland. A handful of public phones operate on calling cards available at one of the few general stores on Gran Roque.

WHAT TO SEE & DO

Most of the fun to be had here is either on or below the surface of the water. The most popular activity on Los Roques is to take a day trip to one of the nearby uninhabited cays. If your hotel doesn't include excursions to the outer islands and cays, you can hire a *peñero* (small boat) at the main docks for between BsF15 and BsF65 ($7–$30/£3.40–£15) per person, depending on the distance to the cay chosen and the number of people in your party. You should pack a lunch, bring plenty of drinks, and try to secure a beach umbrella for shade. Make sure you firmly arrange a pickup time and place for your return to Gran Roque.

OUTDOOR ACTIVITIES

In addition to the activities discussed below, you should be able to find a Windsurfer, Hobie Cat, or kayak to rent for a few hours or for the day. Ask at your hotel or around town.

HIKING Two volcanic humps mark the western end of Gran Roque and give the archipelago its name. The tallest of these is just 130m (426 ft.) above sea level. There's an active lighthouse on the farthest hump, as well as an abandoned lighthouse on a high hill toward the center of the island. Both make nice little hikes, providing wonderful views of the Caribbean Sea, turquoise lagoon, and surrounding islands.

SNORKELING & DIVING The diving and snorkeling around Los Roques is some of the best in the Caribbean. Barrier reefs surround the archipelago, with sheer walls on the southern and eastern flanks dropping off steeply to depths of as much as 900m (2,952 ft.).

Almost all of the hotels and local operators will include snorkel equipment (or help arrange rental) as part of their day tours to the outlying cays. A knowledgeable guide will be able to point you to many excellent shallow reefs for great snorkeling. *Tip:* Whenever you sign up for a snorkel trip, insist on being taken to a live and active reef. Many of the trips are more geared towards bringing guests to the nearest and most popular cayes, where the reefs may be dead or unspectacular, at best.

Ecobuzos (© 0237/221-1235; www.ecobuzos.com) is the best and most established dive operation on Gran Roque. Rates run around BsF183 ($85/£42) for a full day of diving (two tanks), including a guide and gear. Your hotel will most likely pack you a bag lunch. Ecobuzos also offers package tours and certification courses.

Scuba divers will have to pay a one-time BsF5 ($2.35/£1.15) national park dive fee, in addition to the park's entrance fee paid upon arrival.

FISHING Bonefish *(pez ratón)* is the primary game fish here. They are stalked in the shallow waters and grass flats all over the archipelago. Offshore fishing options include tuna, dorado, marlin, and sailfish.

You can hire a guide and a boat for the day, with lunch and beverages, for between BsF400 and BsF900 ($186–419/£91–£205) for bonefishing, and up to BsF3,225 ($1,500/£735) for offshore fishing, depending on the size of the boat, number of fishermen, and game sought. Most hotels either have their own fishing guides, or will hook you up with one. Alternately, you could look into working with a specialized fishing operation such as **Pez Ratón Fishing Lodge** (© 800/245-1950 in the U.S., or 0414/257-0167; www.pezraton.com).

SAILING A handful of charter vessels anchor in the Gran Roque harbor. With the constant trade winds and flat water, Los Roques is an ideal place to sail. The fleet fluctuates seasonally, but there's always a sailboat available for a day cruise or multiday charter. Rates range from BsF215 to BsF550 ($100–$256/£49–£125) per person per day, all-inclusive, for multiday charters with a minimum of four people. Day tours cost BsF95 to BsF215 ($44–$100/£22–£49) per person. Ask at your hotel, or contact **TTM** (© 0212/978-4092; www.roques.org) or **Explore Yachts** (© 0414/287-7554; www.explore-yachts.com), both of whom manage a fleet of vessels.

WHERE TO STAY

Given its status as a national park, building is extremely regulated and limited on Los Roques. There are some 50 or so *posadas* on Gran Roque, all of which are small, usually between 3 and 10 rooms. A great majority of the *posadas* are owned and managed by Italians, to the point that you might imagine you're in Sardinia. Rooms are at a premium, and the *posadas* fill up fast on weekends and during holiday periods.

Most of the *posadas* on Los Roques are all-inclusive, which means they provide breakfast and dinner at the lodge, as well as a day trip to one of the outlying cays, with a packed lunch. In some cases, alcoholic beverages are included in the price; in others, they cost extra. Many *posadas* offer a 2-day/1-night package, taking advantage of the early flights in and late-afternoon departures out of Gran Roque. With this package, you'll get lunch and a tour on both days.

Note: While somewhat true around the country, prices in Los Roques are almost exclusively pegged to hard currencies, either dollars or euros, with the bolívar fuerte conversion done at black-market rates. For example, if a *posada* charges $100 per day, the price in BsF will be BsF400, which then converts to $186 (£91) at the official exchange rate. The bottom line is that if you use dollars, you pay $100; if, however, you use a credit card, you'll be charged $186.

VERY EXPENSIVE

Macanao Lodge ✮ This has long been considered one of the top lodges on Los Roques, but I'm not sure it's worth the rates charged. The rooms have wood floors, heavy wood doors, and attractive latticework above the windows. All have high ceilings, ceiling fans, two twin beds, and mosquito netting over the beds, although no televisions or phones. Room nos. 8, 9, and 10 have ocean views. It's a pet peeve of mine, but I strongly prefer a real queen- or king-size bed over two twin beds pushed together, which is what you get in most of the rooms here. The large central courtyard, with its seagrape trees and fountains, is the nicest feature here and perhaps the best on the island. There's also a comfortable rooftop terrace for enjoying the sea views and sunsets. The restaurant serves a mix of Italian and Venezuelan cuisine.

Los Roques. ✆ **0237/221-1301.** Fax 0237/221-1040. www.macanaolodge.com. 8 units. BsF800–BsF1,000 ($373–$466/£182–£228) per person per day, all-inclusive. AE, MC, V. **Amenities:** Restaurant; bar, lounge. *In room:* No phone.

Posada Albacora ✮✮ With just three rooms, this intimate Italian-run *posada* has some of the best equipped accommodations on the island, with quiet, modern air-conditioned units and satellite television. One room is a minisuite with the bedroom on a second floor and a living room and bathroom below. While a tad compact, the two standard rooms are plush and inviting, with understated yet tasteful decor and well-equipped bathrooms. Excellent meals are served on the rooftop terrace, and service is quite personable and attentive.

Los Roques. ✆ **0237/221-1305** or 0414/282-6131. posadalbacora@hotmail.com. 3 units. BsF323–BsF452 ($150–$210/£74–£103) per person per night, double occupancy. Rates include meals and nonalcoholic drinks. MC, V. **Amenities:** Restaurant; bar, lounge. *In room:* A/C, TV, minifridge, hair dryer, no phone.

Tips **BYOM**

Although all the dive and snorkel operators will provide equipment, either free of charge or for a small fee, I highly recommend you bring your own mask. A good mask that properly fits your face is your most important piece of equipment and a worthwhile investment. Nothing will ruin a day of snorkeling more than a leaky mask.

EXPENSIVE

In addition to the places listed below, **Posada Cayo Luna** (☎ **0237/221-1272;** www. posadacayoluna.com), **Posada La Cigala** (☎ **0414/236-5721;** www.lacigala.com) and **Posada La Gaviota** (☎ **0414/324-2092;** www.posadalagaviota.com) are other excellent options in this price range.

Posada Acquamarina ☆ This is another small, Italian-run *posada,* but it sets itself apart by offering more amenities than most of the other options around. All the rooms here have air-conditioning, televisions, in-room sound systems, minifridges, and hair dryers. The best rooms are those around the central interior courtyard. Excellent Italian and Venezuelan inspired meals are served family-style on the hotel's rooftop terrace. These folks also have their own airline, Blue Star (see above), as well as a small, rustic three-bedroom *posada* on the tiny Rasqui cay, for those looking for a romantic and isolated getaway.

Los Roques. ☎ **0412/310-1962** or ☎/fax 0212/267-5769. www.posada-acquamarina.com. 9 units. BsF390 ($182/£89) per person per night, double occupancy. Rates include meals and nonalcoholic drinks. MC, V. **Amenities:** Restaurant; bar, lounge. *In room:* A/C, TV, minifridge, hair dryer, no phone.

Posada Acuarela ☆ Artistic touches abound in this popular *posada.* The walls are inlaid with hand-painted tile, bits of colored glass and shell, and whole bottles. Each of the rooms features an original painting or two by the owner, Angelo Belvedere. The nicest room has a small private rooftop terrace up a steep flight of stairs. Meals are served family-style in the common dining room, and Angelo is also an excellent chef. Five of the rooms feature air-conditioning.

Los Roques. ☎ **0237/221-1228** or ☎/fax 0212/952-3370. www.posadaacuarela.com. 11 units. BsF320–BsF420 ($149–$196/£73–£96) per person per night, double occupancy. Rates include meals and nonalcoholic drinks. AE, MC, V. **Amenities:** Restaurant; bar, lounge. *In room:* No phone.

MODERATE

Posada Guaripete This *posada* has a slightly funky feel, but I mean that in a good way. The clean rooms feature Italian tile floors and built-in beds. All have mosquito netting, as well as fans. Hanging shell and driftwood mobiles decorate the building. The rooftop terrace here is partially covered for shade and features a bar. The homemade Italian meals are served family-style in the common lounge and living area.

Los Roques. ☎ **0237/221-1368** or 0414/291-9216. www.posadaguaripete.com. 7 units. BsF230–BsF305 ($107–$142/£52–£70) per person per night, double occupancy. Rates include meals, drinks, and day tour. AE, MC, V. **Amenities:** Restaurant, bar. *In room:* No phone.

INEXPENSIVE

There are few true budget options on Los Roques. You'll find a couple of rather rustic *posadas* around the Plaza Bolívar. **Posada Doña Magalis** (☎ **0414/287-7554;** www.magalis.com) and **Posada Doña Carmen** (☎ **0414/318-4926**) are your best bets in this category. At the far end of town **Posada El Botuto** (☎ **0416/621-0381;** www.posadaelbotuto.com) is another excellent less expensive option on Gran Roque.

You can also camp on Gran Roque and a few of the other cays. You'll need a permit, which is issued free by **Inparques** from its office at the western end of town. A few of the isolated cays are open to campers; ask at Inparques for the current list. *Be forewarned:* The few shops and general stores on Gran Roque have very limited supplies and often run out of even the most basic goods. If you plan on camping, come prepared. If you camp on any other island, you'll have to bring all your own food and water and make firm arrangements in advance to be picked up at a specific time on a specific day. Also, remember it gets very hot here, and many tents only increase the heat.

WHERE TO DINE

As mentioned above, most visitors to Los Roques come as part of a package tour or stay at an all-inclusive *posada*. There are, in fact, very few independent restaurants on Gran Roque. If you're not staying at an all-inclusive *posada,* or if you want to broaden your culinary horizons on the island, stop in at the **Bar & Restaurant Acuarena** ⊛, which is on the water between the airstrip and Plaza Bolívar. You can grab a table on the sand and order up some fresh grilled fish, or just spend the night working through their extensive list of cocktails. They also have good breakfasts and lunches, as well as one of the better gift shops on the island. The restaurant is open daily from 6:30am to 11pm, and even offers up free Wi-Fi. Other options for independent dining include **Bora El Mar** and **Canto de la Ballena.**

Note: Lobster season runs November 1 through April 30. Technically, restaurants should not serve lobster outside of the season. If they do, it is either frozen or illegal.

LOS ROQUES AFTER DARK

There are a couple of small bars around the Plaza Bolívar. Of these, the **Rasquatekey Bar** and **La Chuchera** are the most popular. If you're looking for a mellower vibe, try **Bar & Restaurant Acuarena** or **La Gotera.** For a sunset cocktail, **Bora El Mar, La Gotera,** and the rooftop bar at **Natura Viva** are your best options—but you'll want to arrive early as tables with views are limited. In general, hours of operation for bars are 4pm to midnight, although they are very seasonal—some close during low periods and some will stay open as long as there are customers buying drinks.

7 Mérida, the Andes & Los Llanos ⊛⊛

680km (422 miles) SW of Caracas

Mérida is a picturesque and bustling college town set on a flat plateau, nestled in a narrow valley between two mountain rivers, the Albarregas and Chama. It is flanked by two high Andean ridges, the Sierra Nevada and Sierra La Culata. Mérida's narrow streets and colonial architecture make it a great city to wander at your leisure, while the roaring rivers, towering Andean peaks and rugged mountain terrain make it a prime base for some serious adventure. Thanks to the presence of the Universidad de los Andes (ULA), along with a bustling tourist industry, Mérida has a great assortment of cafes, restaurants, bars, and discos.

Despite the imposing snow-covered peaks that surround it, Mérida enjoys a mild, springlike climate year-round. Days are generally warm, although you'll probably need a light sweater or jacket at night. May through November is the rainy season, with August and September being the wettest months.

ESSENTIALS
GETTING THERE

BY PLANE   There are more than a dozen commuter flights daily to Mérida from Caracas's Simón Bolívar International Airport. The principal airlines serving this route are **Avior** (© 0501/284-67737; www.aviorairlines.com), **Conviasa** (© 0500/266-84272; www.conviasa.aero), and **Santa Bárbara** (© 0800/865-2636 or 0274/262-0381 in Mérida; www.santabarbaraairlines.com). Fares range from BsF140 to BsF260

($65–$121/£32–£59) each way, depending on season and demand. Flight time is 1 hour and 20 minutes.

Mérida's **Alberto Carnevalli Airport** (© 0274/263-0722; airport code MRD) is about 5 minutes southwest of downtown. There are frequent *por puesto* minibuses that pass right in front of the airport and will take you into downtown for BsF1 (45¢/25p). A taxi to the center or will cost around BsF3 ($1.40/70p).

BY BUS   Several bus lines (**Expresos Occidente, Expresos Mérida,** and **Expresos Flamingo**) have daily service between Caracas and Mérida. Many depart between 6:30 and 10pm and drive through the night. The trip takes 10 to 12 hours and costs around BsF45 to BsF55 ($21–$26/£10–£13). Most buses leave from La Bandera Terminal, near La Bandera Metro stop, although Expresos Flamingo has its own terminal near the Parque del Este. The bus station in Mérida is located about 3km (2 miles) southwest of downtown on the Avenida Las Américas and is connected to downtown by regular *por puestos* and inexpensive taxis.

BY CAR   The fastest route to Mérida from Caracas is via Barinas. It's mostly flat to Barinas, after which you rise quickly and dramatically into the Andes, passing through Santo Domingo, Apartaderos, and Mucuchíes. This route takes between 9 and 11 hours. For a more scenic tour through the Andes, you can turn off at Guanare and head up to Trujillo. From Trujillo, the Trans-Andean highway passes through Valera, Timotes, and Paseo El Aguila (Eagle Pass), before heading into Mérida. If you come this way, you can drive to the summit of **Pico Aguila;** at 4,007m (13,143 feet), it's the highest point in Venezuela you can reach in a car.

GETTING AROUND

Mérida is a town of many parks and plazas. The two most important are the **Plaza Bolívar,** which is the de facto center of town, and the **Plaza Las Heroínas** (located about 5 blocks south of Plaza Bolívar), which is the town's tourism hub and site of the tramway's first station.

You can easily walk to most destinations and attractions in downtown Mérida. Taxis are relatively plentiful and inexpensive. Most rides in town will run you BsF3 to BsF6 ($1.40–$2.80/70p–£1.35). There's also a good system of local buses and buses to nearby towns, which is a good way to get around for next to nothing. In 2007, Merida inaugurated a **Trolebus,** fixed-route electric-bus units that are more akin to an urban train or trolley than a bus. The only current route runs on the outskirts of downtown, from a point near the southwestern corner of the airport to Ejido further southwest of the city center. However, a downtown route is scheduled to open sometime in 2008.

Both **Budget** (© 0274/263-1768; www.budget.com.ve) and **Dávila Tours** (© 0274/266-1711) have offices at the airport and rent cars for BsF95 to BsF250 ($44–$117/£22–£57) per day.

VISITOR INFORMATION

Cormetur, the Mérida Tourism Corporation (© 0274/263-4701), has a half-dozen information booths around town, including locations at the airport, bus terminal, and on the Plaza Las Heroínas. Office hours vary slightly according to location, but most are open Monday through Saturday from 8am to 6pm. Their main office is beside the airport on Avenida Urdaneta and Calle 45, but you can get a copy of the map they distribute and their list of hotels and tour operators at any of their branches.

Mérida

DINING ◆
Entrepueblos **19**
Heladería Coromoto **15**
L'Abadia **4**
L'Astilla **2**
La Fonda Vegetariana **16**
La Mama & Sushi **5**
La Trattoria Europa
  da Lino **13**
Mogambo **14**
T'Café **17**

ACCOMMODATIONS ■
Hotel & Spa La Sevillana **18**
Posada Casa Sol **3**
Posada La Montaña **11**
Posada Luz Caraballo **1**

ⓘ Information
✉ Post Office

ATTRACTIONS ●
Basílica Menor de la
  Inmaculada Concepción **10**
Casa de Cultura Juan Félix
  Sánchez **8**
El Teleférico **12**
Museo Arqueológico **9**
Museo de Arte Colonial **6**
Jardín Botánico de Mérida **20**
Museo de Arte Moderno **7**

Before coming to Mérida you could check out **www.andesholidays.com**, which is the English-language sister to the more up-to-date and extensive **www.andes.net**.

FAST FACTS There's an **Italcambio** branch at the airport, and several currency-exchange houses and a host of banks around town, although you are best off asking at your hotel or one of the tour operators around town to find someone who will exchange your dollars or euros at a more favorable rate.

If you need medical attention, ask at your hotel, or head to **Centro Clínico** on Avenida Urdaneta, opposite the airport (© **0274/262-9111**). It has an emergency room and a variety of doctors on staff with offices nearby. Or you can contact the bilingual doctor **Aldo Olivieri** (© **0274/244-0805**).

There are scores of Internet cafes all over town. Rates run between BsF1 and BsF3 (45¢–$1.40/25p–70p). The main **Ipostel** office is on Calle 21 between avenidas 4 and 5; there's also a branch office at the main bus terminal.

Mérida is a great place to brush up on your high school Spanish or take a crash course in the language. **The Iowa Institute,** Avenida 4 and Calle 18 (© **0274/252-6404**; www.iowainstitute.com), runs programs of between 1 week and 6 months. Class sizes are small, and home stays can be arranged. Costs run around BsF290 ($135/£66) per week for classes, BsF323 ($150/£74) per week for room and board with a local family. Alternately, you can try **CEVAM** (© **0274/263-1362;** www. cevam.org), which is tied to the U.S. Embassy in Venezuela and specializes in private lessons.

WHAT TO SEE & DO
ATTRACTIONS

Mérida's principal church, the **Basílica Menor de la Inmaculada Concepción** ✦, took more than 150 years to complete, but the effort paid off in one of the most impressive and eclectic cathedrals in Venezuela. Originally based on the design of the 17th-century cathedral in Toledo, Spain, work was begun in 1803. A couple of earthquakes and several distinct periods of construction have left it a mixed breed, with artistic and architectural touches representing various epochs, including some beautiful stained-glass work and large frescos.

Within a 4-block radius of Plaza Bolívar, you'll find a handful of local museums. The small but interesting **Museo de Arte Moderno (Museum of Modern Art)** ✦, Avenida 2 and Calle 22, is housed within the city's new Cultural Arts Complex, where you can often find out what concerts, exhibits, and performances are happening around town, if none are happening in the complex's own performing arts center. The nearby **Casa de Cultura Juan Félix Sánchez (Juan Félix Sánchez Cultural House;** © **0274/252-6101**), Avenida 3 and Calle 23, has rotating exhibits of local and popular artists. The **Museo Arqueológico** (Museum of Archeology; © **0274/240-2344**), Edificio del Rectorado at the Universidad de los Andes, Avenida 3 and Calle 23, has a small collection of archaeological relics, including tools, ceramics, and jewelry. The highlight here is a reconstructed pre-Columbian grave and a fairly well-preserved headless mummy. Admission is BsF1 ($45¢/25p). The **Museo de Arte Colonial (Museum of Colonial Art;** © **0274/657-2340**), Avenida 4 and Calle 20, has a decent collection of mostly religious art and crafts from the colonial period. Admission is free. Both of the above museums are housed in perfectly preserved old colonial homes, with pretty central courtyards.

Finally, there's the **Jardín Botánico de Mérida (Mérida Botanical Gardens;** © **0274/240-1241;** Avenida Alberto Carnevali) ✦✦, an extensive collection of neotropical flora. The gardens feature an extensive collection of bromeliads, as well as sections dedicated to medicinal plants, orchids, and aquatic species. The gardens are open Monday through Friday from 9am to 5pm. Admission is BsF2 (95¢/45p).

EL TELEFERICO ✦✦

With a final stop on the summit of Pico Espejo at 4,765m (15,629 ft.), the *teleférico* (© **0274/252-5080;** www.telefericodemerida.com) is the world's highest cable-car system. At 13km (7 ¾ miles), it is also the longest. The tramway is actually divided into four stages, beginning at the Plaza Las Heroínas. The entire trip without missing a connection takes about 1 hour each way. At the end of each stage, you can take a brief walk around while awaiting the next car. If you want, you can skip a car and stay longer. Small snack bars are located at each station.

The trip begins with a quick and high crossing over the Río Chama, followed by a steep ascent over lush forests. The montaneforests turn to cloud forest as you gain altitude. The flora changes quickly, and soon you'll see the scrub pines and distinctive velvety-leafed *frailejones* of the paramo. By the final stage, you've left the paramo and are above the tree line over barren mountains, with traces of snow on the highest peaks.

At the top, you'll be greeted by a statue of the Virgen de las Nieves (Virgin of the Snows), and if the clouds permit, a good view of **Pico Bolívar,** the highest mountain in Venezuela.

A health note: Visitors in poor physical shape or with heart conditions should seriously consider stopping at the end of the third stage at Loma Redonda at 4,045m (13,268 ft.). The high altitude and thin oxygen can take their toll.

Typically, the *teleférico* makes outbound trips Wednesday through Sunday from 7am through noon. The last car returning from Pico Espejo usually leaves around 2pm. During peak periods, the hours are sometimes stretched a little, and they often open every day of the week. During the low season, the operation may be shut down during normal working hours. Tickets cost BsF60 ($28/£14) for adults and BsF40 ($19/£9.10) for children. During the high season, tickets can sell out days in advance, so I highly recommend you reserve online, or have your hotel or tour agency get you tickets ahead of time.

OUTDOOR ADVENTURES & TOURS

There are a score of tour agencies and adventure tour companies in and around Mérida. You'll find the greatest congregation of them around the Plaza Las Heroínas. The competition is cutthroat and you can often find good deals by shopping around. However, be careful, as some of them are fly-by-night operations. I highly recommend the companies mentioned below, as their level of service, quality of guides and equipment, and safety standards are consistent and dependable. Whatever tour company you choose, be absolutely sure that you feel confident about the competence of the guides and the quality of the equipment.

Arassari Treks 🏕🏕, Calle 24 no. 8–301, behind the *teleférico* (①/fax **0274/ 252-5879;** www.arassari.com), **Natoura Adventure Tours** 🏕🏕, Calle 31 between Avenida Don Tulio and Avenida 6 (① **0274/252-4075;** www.natoura.com), and **Xtreme Adventours** 🏕, Calle 24 and Avenida 8, (① **0274/252-7241;** www.xatours. com) are the most established and trustworthy tour companies in town. All offer the majority of the outdoor adventure options listed below, and then some. And all of them can help you with onward tours and trips to Los Llanos and most other destinations in Venezuela.

CANYONEERING This is a relatively new adventure sport here, and I highly recommend **Arassari Treks,** which is the pioneering operator in the field. The tour, which consists of a mix of hiking, sliding, and rappelling down a river canyon, is full of thrills and chills. No experience is necessary, but you should be prepared to get very wet. A 6.3m (21-ft.) natural water slide is just one of the highlights. The cost for the full-day tour, with a snack and late lunch at the end (around 4pm), is BsF107 ($50/£24) per person.

CLIMBING & TREKKING At 5,007m (16,423 feet), **Pico Bolívar** is Venezuela's highest peak. Crowned with a statue of its namesake hero, it's the most popular summit for visiting climbers. Although the simplest routes are not technically difficult, the sheer altitude and variable weather conditions make a summit climb here plenty challenging. Only experienced climbers in good shape should attempt it. There are also more challenging routes over steep rock and ice for die-hard climbers. One of the nicest things about climbing Pico Bolívar is that you have the option of riding the *teleférico* down.

Other high Andean summits here include **Pico Humbolt** (4,944m/16,216 ft.), **Pico La Concha** (4,922m/16,144 ft.), **Pico Bonpland** (4,883m/16,016 ft.), and **Pico El Toro** (4,755m/15,596 ft.). Several of these peaks can be combined into a multiday trek. Some require ropes, crampons, and ice-climbing gear. All should be attempted only with a guide, proper conditioning, and proper acclimation.

For those looking for less adrenaline and a touch of culture, multiday treks of the high paramo that visit several small towns and Andean villages can also be arranged. Bird-watchers can also hire specialized guides for day hikes and multiday treks. Although you can see hundreds of species in the area, one of the most sought-after sightings, albeit rare, is that of a giant Andean condor.

Prices for climbing and treks range from BsF85 to BsF150 ($40–$70/£19–£34) per person per day, depending on group size, season, itinerary, and equipment rentals. Porters can be hired for around BsF40 ($19/£9.10) per day.

HORSEBACK RIDING If walking or biking don't strike your fancy, you can saddle up and tour the area on horseback. Prices range from around BsF40 ($19/£9.10) for a half-day tour to between BsF80 and BsF120 ($37–$56/£18–£27) for a full-day tour. Overnight and multiday tours are also available.

MOUNTAIN BIKING The same Andean peaks and paramo that make this such a great area for mountain climbing and trekking also make it a prime area for mountain biking. A variety of options are available, from simple half-day jaunts to multiday adventures. Tours can be designed to suit your skill level, experience, and conditioning. Prices range from BsF85 to BsF120 ($40–$56/£19–£27) per person per day. Rental of a decent bike should cost around BsF20 ($9.30/£4.55) per day.

PARAGLIDING The high mountain walls of the Andes and near-constant thermal wind currents make the Mérida valley perfect for paragliding. You may not see a condor, but you will get a condor's-eye view of things. Experienced paragliders will want to fly solo, but beginners can also enjoy the thrill, strapped into the front of a double harness with an experienced pilot behind them. If conditions are right, air time can exceed 90 minutes. A typical 3-hour tour, with 20 to 40 minutes in the air, will cost BsF100 to BsF150 ($47–$70/£23–£34) per person. Xtreme Adventours (see above) is the place to go for paragliding.

WHITE-WATER RAFTING Rafting here is possible year-round, but the high season for it is May through November. Rafting is conducted down in the lower elevations near Barinas, so a hefty car or van ride is involved, and the trips are generally a minimum of 2 days. The rivers run include the Acequias, the upper and lower Canagua, and the Sinigui, which range in difficulty from Class I to Class V. Arassari is the main rafting operator, and it operates a **lovely lodge** 🏕 on the banks of the Acequias River to make the trips even more enjoyable. Prices run around BsF345 ($161/£79) per person for a 3-day, 2-night adventure.

WHERE TO STAY
MODERATE
Hotel & Spa La Sevillana 🏕🏕 Located up a winding narrow road in the foothills above Mérida, this small spa is a great getaway. The place feels as much like a cozy B&B as a spa. The rooms are all comfortable and well equipped and come with either two twin beds or one king-size bed. Flowering gardens, small ponds, and little waterfalls fill the grounds. There are nice views of the surrounding cloud forest from the

shared verandas of the second-floor rooms, and there's great bird-watching all around. The spa is small but well equipped and offers a wide range of very fairly priced treatment options. There's a comfortable lounge and bar area, with a central stone fireplace and spinet piano. A taxi here from to the airport or downtown will cost around BsF8.60 to BsF15 ($4–$7/£2–£3.50); the ride takes around 20 minutes.

Sector Pedregosa Alta, Mérida. © 0274/266-3227. Fax 0274/266-2810. www.andes.net/lasevillana. 12 units. BsF119 ($55/£27) double. Rates include full breakfast. MC, V (with 8% surcharge). Discounts for cash payment. Free parking. **Amenities:** Restaurant; bar/lounge; small spa w/sauna, Jacuzzi, and hydrotherapy; laundry service. *In room:* TV, dataport, coffeemaker, hair dryer, iron, no phone.

INEXPENSIVE

A backpacker and adventure-tourist hot spot, Mérida has scores of inexpensive *posadas* geared toward backpackers in Mérida. Many are congregated in close proximity to the Plaza Las Heroínas and the tramway start-point. Most charge BsF20 to BsF35 ($9.30–$16/£4.55–£8) per person. I think **Posada La Montaña** (© **0274/252-5977;** www.posadalamontana.com) is the best of this bunch, but it's quite easy to comparison shop and check out a handful before committing.

Posada Casa Sol ★★ *Finds*   This downtown option is the most unique and stylish joint in Mérida. Artistic touches abound. Intricate wood and metal work ranges from random sculptures, spread around the rambling colonial-era building, to the entrance door, which is a work of art in itself. Rooms vary in size, but all are clean, inviting, and well kept, with firm beds, plush down comforters and tasteful decor. Most have high ceilings. My favorite rooms are the second-floor units with small balconies overlooking the central courtyard. Guests enjoy free Internet access. Those with a laptop can connect to the Internet via Ethernet cable or Wi-Fi from any room; the rest must share the hotel's communal desktop. Service is attentive and friendly. The hotel has no formal restaurant, although breakfast is served daily, as well as light snacks and drinks throughout the day.

Av. 4, between calles 15 and 16, Mérida. © 0274/252-4164. www.posadacasasol.com. 17 units. BsF90–BsF105 ($42–$49–£21–£24) double; BsF120 ($56/£27) suite. Rates include full breakfast. MC, V. Parking nearby. **Amenities:** Tour desk; laundry service. *In room:* TV, dataport, free Wi-Fi, safe, no phone.

Posada Luz Caraballo   Located on the charming little Plaza Milla (Sucre) at the northeast end of town, this is another solid budget option with plenty of colonial flavor. The rooms are spread over three floors connected by interior courtyards and verandas. Rooms are simple and clean; a few have mattresses a little too thin and soft for my taste, others have comfortable new beds. If possible, ask for one of the rooms in the "new" wing, or request nos. 30 or 35; the latter two have great views over tile roofs, over the plaza, and onto the Andes. As at Posada La Montaña, you also get a tiny television with cable here. The simple restaurant is popular and inexpensive.

Av. 2, no. 13–80, in front of Plaza Milla, Mérida. © 0274/252-5441. 36 units. BsF100 ($47/£23) double. No credit cards. Limited free parking. **Amenities:** Restaurant; laundry service. *In room:* TV, no phone.

WHERE TO DINE

There are dozens of inexpensive Venezuelan restaurants around town—and almost as many pizza places. Most are pretty good. Walk around and choose one whose menu and ambience strike your fancy. If there's trout on the menu, it's likely to be fresh and local.

Moments Heladería Coromoto

The **Heladería Coromoto** ✦✦ (© **0274/252-3525**), Avenida 3 and Calle 29, in front of the Plaza El Llano, holds the Guinness world record for the most ice-cream flavors. Adventurous souls can sample smoked trout, garlic, beer, avocado, or squid. The eclectic and *long* list takes up two walls in the joint. The count currently exceeds 850 flavors, with roughly 100 choices available on any given day. Open Tuesday through Sunday from 2 to 10pm.

Vegetarians should head to **La Fonda Vegetariana** (© **0274/252-2465**), Calle 29, between avenidas 3 and 4. My favorite pizza joint is **L'Astilla** (© **0274/251-0832**), which fronts the pretty Plaza Milla. For a pizza place that's a bit different—they also serve sushi—try **La Mama & Sushi** (© **0274/263-5455**) on Avenida 3, between Calles 19 and 20. This latter place often has live music on weekends.

Finally, there are a couple of excellent options a bit farther afield. Both **Cabañas Xinia & Peter** ✦✦ (© **0274/283-0214**) and **Casa Solar** ✦ (© **0416/674-5653**) serve up excellent international fare in elegant and intimate settings outside of town.

An interesting culinary note: In Mérida, and throughout much of the Andes region, *arepas* are made with wheat flour instead of the traditional cornmeal.

Entrepueblos ✦✦ *Finds* INTERNATIONAL   This tiny little restaurant serves up some of the most creative and eclectic fare in the region. Generous cuts of meat, chicken, and fresh fish come in a wide range of preparations with sauces based on everything from green peppercorns to prunes. There are daily chalkboard specials and tempting desserts. Six small tables are crowded into the main dining room. However, I prefer the two tables on the front porch, even though they are roadside. This place has a sister restaurant on the road to Jají, which is only open on weekends and during holiday periods.

Av. 2 Bolívar, no. 8-115. La Parroquia. © 0274/271-0483 or 0416/674-1957. Reservations recommended. Main courses 8. BsF60–BsF22 ($4–$10/£1.95–£5). AE, DC, MC, V. Mon and Wed–Sat noon–11pm; Sun noon–6pm.

L'Abadia ✦ *Finds* INTERNATIONAL   Tables and chairs are spread around a host of rooms and several interior and exterior courtyards occupying two floors of this old downtown building. The entire place exudes a sense of rustic elegance, and interesting decorative touches abound. My favorite seats are those on the second-floor covered patio. The menu is broad, and features salads, sandwiches, and pastas, as well as a few more hefty main dishes. You can get a steak or chicken breast with a variety of sauces that range from a creamy Roquefort sauce to an oriental preparation with ginger, soy sauce, and scallions. There are also a few vegetarian options and excellent desserts. The upstairs is home to a popular Internet cafe. These folks have opened a very similar sister restaurant, La Abadía del Angel, on Calle 21 between avenidas 5 and 6 (© **0274/252-8013**).

Avenida 3, between Calles 17 and 18. © 0274/251-0933. Reservations not necessary. Main courses BsF20–BsF33 ($9.30–$15/£4.55–£7.50). MC, V. Mon–Sat 9am–midnight.

La Trattoria Europa da Lino ✦ *Finds* ITALIAN   Delicious pastas and authentic Italian cuisine have defined this cozy place since Lino's family imigrated here in the 1950s. There's a long list of pastas, many, including the gnocchi, tortelli, and

agnolotti, are homemade. I like to start off with the Sicilian *caponatina,* a savory marinade of eggplant, peppers, olives and carrots. If you're hankering for a meat dish, I recommend the rabbit served with radicchio in a white wine and rosemary sauce.
Couples looking to squeeze the most romance possible out of Mérida should grab a
table in the dimly lit brick-walled side room. There's a good selection of Italian and
Chilean wines at fair prices.

Pasaje Ayacucho, no. 25-30, Vía Teleférico, in front of El Seminario. ② 0274/252-9555. Pastas BsF15–BsF19
($7–$8.85/£3.40–£4.35). Main courses BsF19–BsF29 ($8.60–$14/£4.20–£6.60). MC, V. Tues–Fri noon–2:30pm and
7–10pm; Sat–Sun noon–10pm.

Mogambo ⊛ *⍟alue* INTERNATIONAL/CAFE   With old saxophones and photos
of jazz artists on the wall, this simple bistro is at once elegant, comfortable, and lively.
The menu ranges from sandwiches to fajitas to fondue. The *mero en salsa verde,* a fresh
fish filet in a parsley-based green sauce, is excellent. There are good salads and delicious desserts. Live music on weekends makes this a great alternative to the dance
clubs and rowdy bar scene.

Av. 4 and Calle 29. ② 0274/252-5643. Sandwiches BsF6–BsF12 ($2.80–$5.60/£1.35–£2.70). Main courses 8.
BsF60–BsF18 ($4–$8.40/£1.95–£4.10). AE, MC, V. Daily 8–10am and 7–11pm.

MERIDA AFTER DARK

This is both a college town and a popular backpacker and adventure-tourism destination, so you'll find a relatively active nightlife here. In general, the bars get going
around 9pm and shut down around midnight to 2am. Discos get cranking around
10pm and close their doors between 3 and 4am. None of the bars in town charge a
cover; some of the dance clubs will occasionally charge BsF1 to BsF5 ($45¢–$2.35/
25p–£1.14) admittance, but it will usually get you a drink or two.

   La Cucaracha Racing Bar, Alto Prado, and **El Bodegón de Pancho,** Centro Comercial Mamayeya, are both multienvironment establishments and two of the more
popular nightspots in town. **El Hoyo Queque** ⊛ and **Grada's Sports Bar,** Avenida 4
and Calle 19, are two happening bars almost always overflowing with the local college
crowd; they're located straight across the street from each other. For a mellower scene,
try **T'Café** ⊛, on the corner of Avenida 3 and Calle 29, across from Heladería
Coromoto.

SIDE TRIPS FROM MERIDA

Mérida is surrounded by picturesque mountain towns and villages. These can be visited in a rental car or as part of guided tours. Most have quaint little *posadas* for
overnight stays, and some even have pretty nice lodges and hotels.

   Los Nevados ⊛, a tiny, isolated mountain village, is one of the more popular destinations. Trips here are often done in a circuit, with one leg conducted by jeep and
the other by mule and the *teleférico.* **Mucuchies** is best known for its namesake breed
of dog. On the road just outside of Mucuchies, on the way to Barinas and Los Llanos,
is the beautiful little stone church of **San Rafael de Mucuchíes** ⊛, built by Juan Félix
Sánchez. Another stone church, also built by Sánchez, can be seen in **El Tisure.** Other
popular towns include **Tabay, Jají** ⊛, and **Mucutuy.** The trails, lakes, and waterfalls
of the **Mucubají** ⊛⊛ section of the **Sierra Nevada National Park** make a great destination for a day trip.

Isolated Lodges, or *Hatos*

Hato is the local term for a very large expanse of land. It designates a ranch or farm much larger than a *finca* or a hacienda. With the international boom in ecotourism, *hato* has also become the local term for an isolated nature lodge. *Hatos* in Los Llanos range from almost luxurious lodges—with boats for river and lagoon excursions and large, open-air safari-style trucks for land tours—to basic camps with a zinc shelter over a concrete slab where hammocks are hung inside mosquito nets. Tours at the more basic *hatos* are usually conducted by foot or horseback and, occasionally, in boats.

WHERE TO STAY IN THE MOUNTAIN TOWNS AROUND MERIDA

There are several pleasant options for spending a night or two in the mountain towns outside Mérida. One of the nicest is the intimate **Cabañas Xinia & Peter** ⭐⭐, La Mucuy Baja, Tabay (② **0274/283-0214;** www.xiniaypeter.com), a delightful and artistically done retreat about 20 minutes outside Mérida. Close to Jají is the rustic **Hacienda El Carmen** (② **0414/639-2701;** www.haciendaelcarmen.com), a former coffee plantation that retains the ambience of its working past. Located about 60km (37 miles) outside Mérida, **Casa Solar** ⭐, Apartaderos (② **0416/674-5653;** www.casasolar.info), is a small lodge that bears the distinction of being the highest hotel in Venezuela at 3,500m (11,500 ft.).

A SIDE TRIP TO LOS LLANOS ⭐⭐

Located on plains that roll on for hundreds of miles south and east of the Andes, **Los Llanos** is an area of flat, mostly open cattle ground, punctuated with some isolated stands of gallery forest. During the latter part of the rainy season (July–Nov), the plains are almost entirely flooded, with only a few raised highways and service roads passable in anything that doesn't float. In the dry season, the land reemerges and wildlife congregates in dense herds and mixed flocks around the ponds and creeks left behind. Traditionally agricultural land, Los Llanos have also garnered fame as a destination for wildlife lovers and bird-watchers.

The quantity and variety of wildlife visible at the nature lodges located in Los Llanos is phenomenal—anaconda, caiman, capybara, deer, massive flocks of birds, and even wildcats are commonly sighted.

GETTING THERE

Most folks visit Los Llanos as part of a package tour out of either Mérida or Caracas. In this case, your transportation will be taken care of. It is possible to reach the gates, or at the least, nearby towns of most of the *hatos* by bus as well, but since you have to coordinate your arrival time and pickup with the lodge, it is best that you coordinate any independent travel closely with the lodge beforehand.

Note: It's hot in Los Llanos year-round, and in the dry season, the sun can be downright brutal. Definitely bring sunscreen, but also make sure that you've got a wide-brimmed hat. Mosquitoes and other insects can also be plentiful here. Although repellent is recommended, I often prefer using lightweight long-sleeved shirts and pants. Also, be sure to bring glasses or sunglasses on the safari-style tours. When the trucks pick up a bit of velocity, particularly around dusk or on the night tours, you'll find your corneas attracting insects like a semi's windshield.

WHAT TO SEE & DO

Folks come to Los Llanos to **see and photograph wildlife** ✦✦✦. And for that, they are richly rewarded. From pink river dolphins to giant anaconda, this is a wildlife lover's dream come true. Hundreds of bird species are also to be seen, many in massive flocks. Among the highlights are the Jabiru and wood stork; scarlet macaw; numerous species of hawks, herons, and parrots; and large flocks of scarlet ibis. The Hoatzin is one of the more bizarre and louder members of the avian world. Common mammals here include the white-tailed deer, red howler *(araguato)* and capuchin monkeys, giant anteater, gray fox, peccary, and giant river otter. Although difficult to spot (and far from guaranteed), jaguars, pumas, and ocelots are relatively common in Los Llanos. However, you *are* guaranteed to see large families of capybara *(chigüire)*, as well as dozens of spectacled caiman *(baba)*. Tours are conducted year-round, with a much higher percentage of boat tours in the rainy season, of course.

WHERE TO STAY & DINE

In addition to the lodges listed below, many of the tour agencies in Mérida arrange trips to the Llanos. Price wars are waged on the streets of Mérida. However, by opting for the cheapest options you may find yourself in an overcrowded van and sleeping in primitive conditions. That said, 4-day, 3-night tours from Mérida run between BsF500 and BsF900 ($233–$419/£114–£205) per person; the price includes transportation, meals, and a variety of tours. The price range generally reflects the level of luxury you'll find in transportation and accommodations.

Hato El Cedral ✦   There are so many capybara, caiman, and anaconda here that it feels like a zoo. More than 350 species of birds have been recorded. The newer rooms here are quite large, with two double beds and high ceilings. If you ask, they'll even string up a hammock inside for your afternoon *siesta*. The older rooms, which are found around the pool, are somewhat smaller, have only one double and one twin bed, and feature lower ceilings. All the rooms are a bit spartan and could use some decorative touches to spruce things up. Buffet-style meals are served in a common dining room, and there's usually a concert of local *llanero* music after dinner. There are some 140km (87 miles) of roads, a couple of rivers and streams, and some forest trails within this massive *hato,* so you'll have plenty of options for tours and adventures.

⌒Tips Choosing Your *Hato*

Both **Hato Piñero** and **Hato El Cedral** (see above) are well-run nature lodges, with capable and friendly bilingual guides offering a steady stream of wildlife watching tours. At each, you will see enough birds, mammals, and reptiles to keep you pinned to your binoculars and reeling off shots on your camera. However, they are different: In a nutshell, Piñero will give you greater diversity (of species), while El Cedral will give you greater density. Piñero is considered a better spot for spotting jaguar and other wildcats, although their spotting is still extremely rare. You can sometimes spot as many as 100 different species of birds in 1 day at Piñero. On the other hand, the sheer number of capybara at El Cedral—more than 50,000—is mind-boggling. Moreover, El Cedral is perhaps the best spot for spotting anaconda, particularly in the dry season.

Near Mantecal. Mailing address: Av. La Salle, Edificio Pancho, Piso 5, PH, Los Caobos, Caracas. ⓒ 0212/781-8995 or ⓒ/fax 0212/793-6082. www.elcedral.com. 25 units. BsF275–BsF325 ($128–$151/£63–£74) per person double occupancy. Rates include 3 meals, 2 guided tours, and all nonalcoholic beverages. AE, MC, V. **Amenities:** Restaurant; lounge; postage stamp–size outdoor pool; laundry service. *In room:* A/C, no phone.

Hato Piñero ✦ This pioneer nature lodge is the most charming of the *hatos*. A working farm and ranch, Piñero has the feel of a traditional hacienda. Rooms are comfortable but rustic, with cold-water showers, polished concrete floors, and two built-in twin beds. The best features here are the high ceilings, whitewashed walls, and blue-trimmed wooden windows opening up to the outdoors and an interior hallway. Six rooms have air-conditioning. Buffet-style meals are served in a common dining area, and guests congregate in the small lounge and bar. However, the nicest place to hang, when you're not out on a horseback- or safari-style tour, is the large veranda at the entrance to the lodge. You'll also want to check out the library and biological exhibitions at the lodge's own biological research center. Early on, Piñero declared much of its property a biological preserve, and they've maintained a steady stream of invited scientific researchers, student groups, and interns, who have their own residence and basic research facilities.

El Baúl. Mailing address in the U.S.: Poba International N. 156, P.O. Box 521308, Miami, FL 33152-1308. ⓒ 0212/991-8935. Fax 0212/991-6668. www.hatopinero.com. 10 units. BsF323–BsF340 ($150–$158/£74–£76) per person double occupancy. Rates include 3 meals, 2 guided tours, all beverages, and taxes. Transportation by car from Caracas costs BsF389 ($181/£89) round-trip for up to 4 persons. AE, MC, V. **Amenities:** Restaurant; lounge. *In room:* No phone.

8 Canaima, Angel Falls & the Río Caura ✦✦

725km (450 miles) SE of Caracas

Angel Falls is the world's tallest waterfall. It's an imposing sight, and the trip there is definitely an adventure. In addition to Angel Falls and hundreds of other tropical jungle waterfalls, Venezuela's southeastern region, or Gran Sabana, is known for its unique geological formations, or *tepuis*—massive steep-walled and flat-topped mesas that inspired Sir Arthur Conan Doyle's *The Lost World*. A large chunk of this region, more than 3 million hectares (7 million acres), is protected within **Canaima National Park,** the largest national park in Venezuela and the sixth largest in the world.

The small Pemón Indian village and tourist enclave of Canaima is the gateway to Angel Falls and much of this region. Set on the edge of a black-water lagoon ringed with soft, pink-sand beaches; fed by a series of powerful waterfalls; and surrounded by miles of untouched jungle, the word "idyllic" doesn't do this spot justice.

Located south of Ciudad Bolívar, and a fair bit north of Canaima, a trip along the **Río Caura** to **Para Falls** offers many of the same sights and experiences to be had on a trip to Canaima and Angel Falls, with a more undiscovered feel to it, and fewer fellow travelers.

ESSENTIALS

VISITOR INFORMATION & TOURS Almost all visitors to Canaima come as part of a prearranged package that includes meals, accommodations, and tours. These packages can be arranged with either the local lodges listed below or any number of agencies and operators in Caracas or abroad. Given the remote location, lack of roads, and limited accommodations, you should make reservations prior to your arrival. If you decide to visit on your own, there are usually several local tour agencies waiting for incoming flights at informal information desks at the small airport. Independent travelers can quickly shop around and try to arrange the best price and timing for a trip to Angel Falls, as well as local accommodations, which can range from a hammock under a simple roof to one of the nicer lodges mentioned below.

WHEN TO GO   Because Canaima is such a popular destination, it can get quite busy during the high season, particularly from July to August and from November to January. During peak periods, prices can get inflated, and the river, lagoon, and waterfall tours can seem downright crowded.

Although flyovers are conducted year-round, trips to Angel Falls itself are only possible during the rainy season, when the water level is high enough in the rivers to reach its base. The unofficial season for tours to the foot of Angel Falls runs from June through November. October and November are regarded as the best months to visit, since the rains are winding down but the water level remains high. Depending on the river level, trips can sometimes be made as late as December and even January. August and September are definitely the rainiest months to visit, and although the falls are thick and impressive, visibility may be limited. Although there are no organized trips to Angel Falls in the dry season (Jan–May), this is also a good time to take advantage of low-season bargains and the relative desolation of Canaima. The dry season is a good time to visit the region as a beach destination, as the many pink- and white-sand beaches that line the rivers' edges throughout the dry season all but disappear during the rainy season.

GETTING THERE

BY CAR   There are no year-round serviceable roads into Canaima, and even in the dry season the road here is so long and arduous as to be an unviable option for travelers.

BY PLANE   Most visitors to Canaima come on package tours that include air transport. If you decide to book your travel by yourself, be forewarned that flight schedules to and from Canaima change frequently and seasonally. Given the isolation and distance, flights here often sell out well in advance. It's recommended that you book your flights with a confirmed departure out of Canaima, so as to not find yourself waiting standby for several days.

Fun Fact **The *Tepuis***

Formed over millions and millions of years, the sandstone *tepuis* of the Gran Sabana are geological and biological wonders. With vertical edges that plunge for thousands of feet, most are unclimbed and unexplored. The highest, Roraima, at 2,810m (9,217 ft.), towers over the savanna below. Auyántepui, or "Devil's Mountain," is some 700 sq. km (275 sq. miles) in area—roughly the size of Singapore. Given their age and isolation, the *tepuis* host an astounding number of endemic species, both flora and fauna. In some cases, as much as half of all species of flora and fauna on a given *tepui* will be endemic.

(*Fun Fact* **Jimmy Angel**

Angel Falls are named after American bush pilot and gold-seeker Jimmy Angel, who first spotted the falls in 1935. Although earlier anecdotal reports exist about them, and certainly the local Pemón people knew of them, Jimmy Angel gets most of the credit. In 1937, Angel crash-landed his plane on the top of Auyántepui. No one was injured, but the pilot, his wife, and two companions had to hike for 11 days to descend the *tepui* and reach safety. For decades, the silver fuselage of "El Río Coroní" could be seen on the top of Auyántepui. In 1970, it was salvaged by the Venezuelan Air Force. The plane was restored and is currently on display at the airport in Ciudad Bolívar.

There are no direct flights to Canaima from Caracas. To get there you must first fly to Ciudad Bolívar or Puerto Ordaz. **Aeropostal** (© 888/912-8466; www.aeropostal.com), **Aserca** (© 0800/648-8356; www.asercaairlines.com), and **Rutaca** (© 0800/788-2221; www.rutaca.com.ve) all have regular flights to both gateways from Caracas. Fares from Caracas to either city run BsF200 to BsF300 ($93–$140/£46–£68) each way. **Serami** (© 0286/952-0424; www.serami.com) flies to Canaima daily from Puerto Ordaz. **Transmandu** (© 0285/632-1462; www.transmandu.com) flies between Canaima and both Ciudad Bolívar and Puerto Ordaz. Flights between Canaima and Puerto Ordaz or Ciudad Bolívar cost between BsF300 and BsF500 ($140–$233/£68–£114) each way.

If you get to Ciudad Bolívar or Puerto Ordaz on your own, either by air or bus, you can usually find a tour or charter company with a trip heading to Canaima, although the scheduling and costs can vary immensely depending on demand. If you need to overnight in Ciudad Bolívar, be sure to check in to the **Posada Casa Grande** (© 0212/977-1234; www.cacaotravel.com), a gorgeous little hotel in the colonial center of the city.

Aerotuy (© 0212/212-3110; www.tuy.com) runs daily day tours (BsF1,375/$640/£314) to Canaima from Isla de Margarita, including a flyover of Angel Falls and a visit to Salto El Sapo. It also uses this flight to bring people to and from its own remote riverside hotel, **Arekuna Lodge.** The flight leaves Margarita at 8:30am and departs Canaima around 3pm. The hours are subject to change, as it often juggles its itinerary to Canaima and Arekuna. These flights operate as a code share with **Avior** (© 0501/284-67737; www.avioirlines.com), which sells just the flight portion. Note that this route often sells out far, far in advance.

All visitors to Canaima must pay the BsF8 ($3.70/£1.80) park entrance fee. The fee is collected at the airport upon arrival and is good for the duration of your stay.

GETTING AROUND

Besides the few dirt tracks that ring the eastern edge of the lagoon and define the tiny village of Canaima, there are virtually no roads in this region. Transportation is conducted primarily by boat in traditional dugout canoes called *curiaras*. From Canaima, numerous tours are arranged to a half-dozen waterfalls, including Angel Falls, and neighboring indigenous communities. Aside from strolling around the small village of Canaima and walking along the edge of the lagoon or to the lookout over Ucaima Falls, you will be dependent upon your lodge or tour operator for getting around.

FALLS, FALLS & MORE FALLS: WHAT TO SEE & DO IN CANAIMA
ANGEL FALLS ★★★

With an uninterrupted drop of 807m (2,648 ft.) and a total drop of 979m (3,211 ft.), Angel Falls is an impressive sight—and as you are already aware, the tallest waterfall on Earth. The vast majority of tourists who visit Angel Falls get to see it only from the window of their airplane. Almost all flights to Canaima, both commercial and charter, attempt a flyover of the falls. However, given the fact that Angel Falls is located up a steep canyon that is often socked in with clouds (especially in the rainy season), the fly-overs are sometimes either aborted or offer limited views. Moreover, even on a good day, when the plane makes a couple of passes on each side, the view is somewhat distant and fleeting. If for some reason your flight doesn't make the pass in front of Angel Falls, you can arrange for a quick flyover for BsF108 to BsF215 ($50–$100/£25–£49) per person, with a minimum of four persons. Ask at your hotel or check at the airport. **Be aware:** If you choose to purchase a flyover trip to Angel Falls, most operators will *not* refund your money, even if you don't catch the slightest glimpse of the falls.

If you want to really enjoy the splendor of Angel Falls, you'll have to take a trip there in a boat. Almost all the hotels and tour agencies in Canaima offer 1-, 2-, and 3-day tours to Angel Falls. As the route and distance traveled are the same, the only difference is the amount of time you actually spend at the falls—and whether or not you spend a night or two in a hammock at one of the rustic camps, near the base of the falls. Typically the tour begins at 5am with a pickup at your hotel and transfer to the tiny port atop Ucaima Falls. From here, you travel up the Carrao River, with a portage around some particularly rough rapids, to Isla Orquídea or another camp for a breakfast stop. After breakfast, it's back into the boats and on to the narrow Churún River, which snakes up Cañón del Diablo (Devil's Canyon) and over scores of rapids to Isla Ratoncito (Little Mouse Island) at the base of the falls. On average, the upriver journey takes 4 to 5 hours. Keep your eyes peeled and you might see a toucan, cock-of-the-rock, or some howler monkeys. Once at the base, you'll still need to hike for another hour or so uphill through tropical forest to reach the pools at the foot of the falls. The hike is somewhat strenuous and can be slick and muddy, but a swim in the refreshing pool at the foot of the massive falls makes it worth the effort. Back on Isla Ratoncito, you'll have lunch before boarding the boats once again for the trip back to Canaima. With the current, the trip is a bit faster and you should even get to visit Salto El Sapo before being dropped back off at your hotel around sunset.

Multiday tours sometimes leave later in the morning or afternoon, sacrificing a visit to the falls on the first day. However, once there, you get to spend a longer time at the foot of the falls, and/or visit the falls on consecutive days. Moreover, because of positioning, the sunrise and early morning sun directly hits the falls, while in the afternoon they are more backlit, with the sun setting behind Auyántepui.

Day tours from Canaima range from BsF215 to BsF538 ($100–$250/£49–£123) per person. Two-day, one-night tours to Angel Falls can cost between BsF300 and BsF600 ($140–$280/£68–£137). Be careful about trying to save a few dollars: Paying more for a respectable operator will often get you a boat with two working engines (required by law, but not always the case in practice), a more experienced captain (important, given the nature of the rivers), and a better and truly bilingual guide.

OTHER AREA FALLS ✦✦

Several distinct and impressive falls work together to form the Canaima lagoon. All of these are easily visited in organized boat trips out of town. The most popular of these falls is **Salto El Sapo,** which is located on the backside of small Anatoly's Island, on the north end of the lagoon. A visit to Salto El Sapo includes a 15-minute hike across the island, from the foot of Hacha Falls to the base of Salto El Sapo. After a swim in the pool here, you are led along a path that passes behind the falls (be prepared to get wet), then up around the other side, with a visit to the smaller El Sapito Falls, and then (when the water level permits) across the top. Walking behind El Sapo Falls in the rainy season is very impressive. Tours to Salto El Sapo often include lunch, or at the very least a refreshment.

Hacha, Golondrina, and **Ucaima falls** are located in a neat row fronting the lagoon. They can be observed and enjoyed from just about any point along the edge of the lagoon or by dugout canoe. At a 15-minute hike uphill from the small village, you'll find a little lookout built as part of the small hydroelectric plant on the top of Ucaima Falls. It's not Niagara, but it's a pretty good view. A 10-minute drive and then a 15-minute boat ride downstream are the wide and roaring **Yuri Falls.** A visit to Yuri Falls usually includes a short but interesting walk through the forest. All the hotels and tour operators in town offer trips to these waterfalls, in half- and full-day combinations, which often include a little bit of hiking, a little bit of swimming, and lunch and/or refreshments. Prices range from BsF55 to BsF120 ($26–$56/£13–£27) for a half-day tour, and from BsF100 to BsF250 ($47–$117/£23–£57) for a full-day tour.

OUTDOOR ADVENTURES

Few organized adventure sports are regularly practiced in this region. Despite the scores of rivers, with ample rapids and white water, no one yet is offering any rafting or kayaking in the area. Aside from the relatively soft adventures mentioned above, multiday treks around the region, including climbs of Auyántepui and Roraima, are possible. If you're interested in a multiday trek, you can ask one of the local tour operators in Canaima, or try **Akanan Travel & Adventure** ✦✦ (© 0212/715-5433 or 0414/116-0107; www.akanan.com), **Cacao Expeditions** ✦✦ (© 0212/977-1234; www.cacaotravel.com), or **Lost World Adventures** ✦✦ (© 800/999-0558 in the U.S., or 0212/577-0303 in Caracas; www.lostworldadventures.com).

SHOPPING

Several gift shops are located in and around the small village of Canaima. By far, the best of the bunch is **Makunaima Arte Indígena** ✦ (© 0286/621-5415), located just beyond Waku Lodge. This place has a broad and reasonably priced selection of local indigenous crafts, including Pemón blowguns, Yanomami baskets, and Piaroa masks, as well as quality jewelry, ceramics, and woodwork. Another good option—but with a much more limited selection—is the **Kayarinwa Gallery** (no phone), located right in the small village of Canaima. Unless you need toothpaste or some basic goods from their attached general store, avoid the **Canaima Souvenir Shop** (© 0414/884-0940), which has a broad but overpriced selection of crafts.

WHERE TO STAY & DINE

As previously mentioned, most visitors here come on prearranged packages that include transportation, meals, and tours. All the lodges listed below offer packages, but package prices vary greatly depending on whether or not you visit Angel Falls and how long you stay. Per-night rates are listed below, with the various tours as add-ons.

In addition to the places listed below, **Tapuy Lodge** (② 0212/977-1234; www.cacaotravel.com) is a new, comfortable option built right on the lagoon's edge and run by the folks at Cacao Expeditions.

Finally, budget travelers can find several options for hanging a hammock, or sleeping in a rented hammock. Rates run around BsF15 to BsF30 ($7–$14/£3.40–£6.80) per person per night. However, I think the best budget option is to head to the **Campamento Tomás Bernal** (② 0414/854-8234; www.bernaltours.com) across the lagoon on Anatoly Island. There's always a convivial hostel-like vibe at Bernal's, with a mix of hammocks and simple rooms. Their hammock camp up near Angel Falls, has an excellent early morning view. There's usually a representative of Bernal Tours at the airport.

Jungle Rudy Campamento ★★ *Finds*
Located a short boat ride up the Río Carrao above Ucaima Falls, this small and simple nature lodge is a wonderful and romantic retreat. The lodge was founded and built up over a period of decades by the late, legendary Rudy Truffino, and is still run by his family. The rooms are simple, with indigenous artifacts and wildlife photos on the walls. Rooms numbered 11 to 16 are my favorites, although somewhat smaller than some of the others; they feature small private terraces fronting the river. There are well-tended gardens and grounds, and two riverside swimming nooks formed by natural and sculpted rock formations. The hotel has a computer with high-speed Internet access available for guest use, and free Wi-Fi around the main lodge. All the standard tours are offered, including to Salto El Sapo, Yuri Falls, and Angel Falls. Jungle Rudy's camp near the base of the falls is the plushest by far, and the only one where you sleep in a real bed, instead of a hammock.

Canaima (Parque Nacional Canaima, Sector Laguna de Canaima, Gran Sabana, Edificio Bolívar). ②/fax **0286/962-2359** in Canaima, or 0212/693-0618 in Caracas. www.junglerudy.com. 15 units. BsF546 ($254/£125) per person per day. Rates include 3 meals, welcome cocktail, and airport transfers. AE, MC, V. **Amenities:** Restaurant; bar; laundry service; free Wi-Fi. *In room:* No phone.

Waku Lodge ★★
Set right on the banks of the Canaima lagoon, with a fabulous direct view of the Hacha and Ucaima falls, this lodge has the most comfortable and modern rooms in the area. The rooms are all spacious and modern, and feature a front patio with a couple of chairs and a hammock overlooking the grounds and the lagoon. Rooms numbered 11 to 15 actually have views of the waterworks. The restaurant is housed in a large, open-air structure with a thatched roof, and their lounge area features a television with DirecTV hookup. These folks handle a lot of the day-tour traffic, and there can be a bit of a cattle-car feel to the operation at times.

Canaima (Parque Nacional Canaima, Sector Laguna de Canaima, Gran Sabana, Edificio Bolívar). ② **0286/962-0559.** www.wakulodge.com. 15 units. BsF580 ($270/£132) per person per day. Rates include 3 meals, a quick boat tour around the lagoon, and airport transfers. AE, MC, V. **Amenities:** Restaurant; bar; laundry service. *In room:* A/C, free Wi-Fi, no phone.

A SIDE TRIP: RIO CAURA & PARA FALLS ★★★

The Río Caura is a major affluent of the Orinoco River. A trip up the Río Caura is a voyage to a remote and untouched land. All trips here begin in Ciudad Bolívar, a small colonial-era city on the banks of the Orinoco. From Ciudad Bolívar, it's a 4-hour drive to the tiny village of Las Trincheras, on the banks of the Río Caura. After an overnight in or near Las Trincheras, it's time for a 5-hour boat ride up the Caura. Along the way, if you're lucky, you'll see freshwater dolphins, and perhaps fish for *cachamba,* a large and tasty river fish. This is an area of dense primary rainforest, and it is rich in tropical flora and fauna. You'll see (and hear) howler monkeys in the trees and catch sight of scarlet macaws flying overhead. The only civilization you'll pass along the way is the small Yekuana indigenous community of Nichere. At the end of the ride, you'll come to El Playón, another small indigenous community on a large, natural, freshwater beach set at the base of two converging and raging rapids. The beach here is incongruous, with soft white sand that seems as if it were imported from the Caribbean. At El Playón, you'll find accommodations in a series of large, circular, open-air ranchos, with hammocks strung around the circle. The accommodations and shared bathrooms are rustic but clean. Meals are simple and filling. From El Playón, it's a 3- to 4-hour hike to an overlook across from the impressive Para Falls. This is a full-day tour, and somewhat strenuous. The only inhabitants of this region are the Yekuana and, to a lesser extent, Pemón indigenous peoples. Both tribes excel in craftworks, and you'll have ample opportunities to buy ceramic wares, woodcarvings, and woven baskets, both in Nichere and El Playón.

Akanan Travel & Adventure (② **0212/715-5433** or 0414/116-0107; www. akanan.com) and **Cacao Expeditions** (② **0212/977-1234**; www.cacaotravel.com) are the two best operators working the Río Caura. Cacao actually owns and runs the quite comfortable **Cacao Lodge** in Las Trincheras, as well as a wonderful hammock camp, **Yokore Lodge,** on an island a 20-minute ride upstream from Las Trincheras.

Most trips here are 6-day/5-night affairs, with an overnight in Ciudad Bolívar to start things off, followed by an early morning departure for Las Trincheras. The second night is spent either in Las Trincheras or at Yokore Lodge. The next 2 nights are spent at El Playón, and the final night is spent back at Las Trincheras, allowing for an early departure for Ciudad Bolívar or Puerto Ordaz, in time for a connecting flight onward.

Index